THE HISTORY OF
WORLD WAR II

Lt-Colonel E. Bauer

THE HISTORY OF
WORLD WAR II

Lt-Colonel E. Bauer

Consultant editors
Brigadier General James L. Collins Jr.,
Chief of Military History, U.S. Department of the Army
Correlli Barnett,
Fellow of Churchill College, Cambridge

THE MILITARY PRESS

New York

© 1966 Jaspard Polus, Monaco
Revised edition © 1979 Orbis Publishing Ltd.

This 1984 edition published by The Military Press,
distributed by Crown Publishers, Inc.

ISBN: 0-517-426773

h g f e d c b a

Printed in Hungary

Frontispiece: Churchill, Roosevelt
and Stalin, at Yalta
Page 6: the Allied nations tear the
Swastika apart

Contents

Introduction

Lieutenant-Colonel Eddy Bauer's history of World War II is a definitive and classic work: one of the most complete and objective accounts of that great struggle ever to have appeared. Brigadier General James L. Collins, Chief of Military History, U.S. Department of the Army, has described it as follows:

"Truly global in scope, massive in manpower and destruction, rich in heroic deed, and scarred with countless examples of man's inhumanity to man, the Second World War has been written about by historians, playwrights, and novelists. Yet most of these authors suffered from the myopia of being participants in the events described or have looked at the war from the sole viewpoint of one or another of the combatants. Now, a Swiss military historian, Lieutenant-Colonel Eddy Bauer, has clearly and without the bias of involvement set forth, as impartially as any one writer can, the tremendous story of millions of men and women surging in battle across the continents.

"Colonel Bauer, from the depths of his profound study and his understanding of humanity, has produced an extraordinarily well balanced account of the conflict. His story, illuminated by many maps and enlivened with authentic pictures of the times, many in colour and only recently discovered, sharpens and deepens our awareness of the conflict and makes clear the forces driving the strategies, the tactics, and even the individuals of the nations at war. To understand these, free from ideological bias, is to understand better how to avoid a future cataclysm."

Born in 1902 in Switzerland, where he spent most of his life, Eddy Bauer combined a brilliant academic career as Professor of History at Neuchâtel University with that of a successful officer in the Swiss Army. Throughout his life he contributed regularly to newspapers and journals in France and Switzerland; it was, in fact, as a correspondent in the Spanish Civil War that he first investigated modern warfare. This firsthand experience, combined with his academic training, was a vital factor in his appointment as head of the Swiss Second Division's Intelligence Services at the outbreak of World War II. During this time he was able to collect the immense range of detailed information on which he based the military diary that was printed weekly in the Swiss newspaper *Curieux*. After the war he wrote his monumental study of armoured warfare, *La Guerre de blindés;* at the same time he continued to work for Swiss

Intelligence. The climax of his academic career came when he was elected Rector of his University, Neuchâtel. He completed 16 books, and was working on a seventeenth, a *History of Secret Services* when he died in 1972.

It is clear that Lieutenant-Colonel Bauer had an admirable vantage-point from which to write. As a Swiss, he was not encumbered by national prejudices which might affect his judgement; yet as a member of Swiss Intelligence during the war years he gained privileged insight into the progress of events. His academic training enabled him to analyse with clarity and depth the relationship between the various theatres of war and the influence of the individual campaigns; and his judgements on the generals and politicians concerned are impartial and sometimes severe. Yet his training and experience as a journalist ensured that this objectivity and balance in no way affected the flow of the narrative.

Since his death, of course, there have been new discoveries and new revelations. In order to incorporate some of this research, a group of distinguished American scholars, including Martin Blumenson and Henry Shaw, have, under the direction of Brigadier General Collins, amplified those sections of the work dealing with Operation "Torch" and certain of the Pacific campaigns. Contributions on Burma and the final battles of the Italian campaign written by the British historians Brigadier Michael Calvert and Lieutenant-Colonel Alan Shepperd have also been added to the book.

Lastly, the eminent British military historian Correlli Barnett – whose own books have given us fascinating new perspectives on the war – has incorporated the most valuable discoveries which recent research on the subject has produced. For example, Soviet material to which Bauer had no access enables us to describe more precisely the role of the Red Army during the war, and, of course, the secrets of the "Enigma" machine now give us new insights into the decisions and policies of the Allied leaders. In addition, Mr. Barnett has contributed special sections on the Allied conferences at Casablanca, Quebec, Cairo and Teheran, which had such a decisive influence on the course of war itself and the peace which was to follow.

Colonel Bauer's magisterial text, supplemented by the work of leading American and British scholars, offers an unparalleled history of the greatest war mankind has ever known.

CHAPTER 1
The Aftermath of Munich

On November 11, 1918, the Armistice ending World War I came into effect. The "war to end all wars" was over, and the Treaty of Versailles of the following year established a new order in Europe. Three empires – Russia, Germany and Austria-Hungary – had been destroyed, and new states had been created. Yet by 1938, less than 20 years after the Versailles settlement, Europe seemed once again to be on the verge of a general war, because the growing power and ambitions of Adolf Hitler's Germany threatened the stability of the international order.

Nevertheless, it seemed as though there might be grounds for hope. On December 6, 1938, the French and German Foreign Ministers, Georges Bonnet and Joachim von Ribbentrop, had met in Paris and signed a declaration which, following the Munich agreement of the same year, seemed on the face of it to promise an end to the traditional hostility between the two countries.

It was a move which the British Government had encouraged in the tense weeks since Munich. In their joint declaration, France and Germany expressed their conviction that "peaceful and neighbourly relations between Germany and France form one of the essential elements in the consolidation of the European situation, as well as in the general maintenance of peace". Bonnet did not regard this document as an empty "scrap of paper": Article 2 expressed the mutual agreement that no territorial disputes between France and Germany remained, and that both countries "solemnly regarded the existing frontier between their countries as the definitive frontier". Although those provinces were not mentioned by name, Ribbentrop's signature on this freely-contracted agreement prevented Germany from ever again laying a legal claim to Alsace and Lorraine. After the signature of the agreement, Ribbentrop said to Bonnet: "Do not forget that the renunciation of Alsace and Lorraine which I have just made in the name of Germany is a very sensitive point as far as our national self-esteem is concerned."

The French diplomats could also congratulate themselves in that Article 3 expressly stated that France's existing international commitments were not affected. The most important were the Franco-Polish Treaty of 1921 and the Franco-Soviet Pact of 1936. Neither Lukasiewicz, Polish Ambassador to Paris, nor Suritz, the Soviet Ambassador, raised any objections to France's new agreement with Germany. Also in Article 3, France and Germany declared their willingness to "discuss all questions concerning their two countries, and to consult each other whenever one of these questions threatens

"Peace in our time": Chamberlain returns from Munich.

to lead to international difficulties".

So it was that in Paris it almost seemed that Hitler and Ribbentrop really had abandoned their policy of aggression and unilateral expansion which had threatened to set Europe ablaze three times in the last three years.

Events were indeed to prove how futile such hopes were; but in every capital in Europe people still vividly remembered Adolf Hitler's raucous voice announcing from the Berlin Sportpalast on September 26, 1938: "Once the Sudeten problem is settled no territorial problem in Europe will remain. It is the last territorial demand I have to make in Europe. This I guarantee. We want no Czechs at all." Hitler had said the same to British Prime Minister Neville Chamberlain during their meeting at Bad Godesberg on September 22, and Chamberlain had been convinced. He had returned to England to announce: "I think I should add that [Hitler] repeated to me with great earnestness what he had said already at Berchtesgaden, namely, that this was the last of his territorial ambitions in Europe and that he had no wish to include in the Reich people of other races than Germans. In the second place he said, again very earnestly, that he wanted to be friends with England and that if only this Sudeten question could be got out of the way in peace he would gladly resume conversations. It is true he said, 'There is one awkward question, the Colonies . . . but that is not a matter for war.' "

Naturally, in January 1939 neither the French nor the British had at their disposal the vast, incriminating mass of documents which would be laid before the International Military Tribunal at Nuremberg in 1946. But even in January 1939 there were men in high places who were not completely blind to the dangers of the situation, or to the possibility of the Third Reich once again breaking its pledged word and engineering another coup.

Nor did Hitler's Germany stand alone: it was aligned with the Italian Fascist Empire created by Benito Mussolini. Together the two dictatorships formed the "Berlin-Rome Axis", a grandiose concept which Mussolini had outlined in November 1936. He saw the "Axis" as a polarising influence around which the other European countries "may work together".

The Munich agreement had been signed on September 29, 1938. One of its clauses had stipulated that an international guarantee of Czechoslovakia's future security be given by each of the contracting powers. As far as France and Great Britain were concerned, this guarantee was the essential condition for their agreeing to the dissection of Czechoslovakia. It was a substitute for the natural strategic frontiers which the surrender of the Sudetenland to Germany had torn from Czechoslovakia. The same guarantee would be required from Germany and

Italy – on one condition. As Article 1 of the agreement put it, "when the question of the Polish and Hungarian minorities in Czechoslovakia has been settled, Germany and Italy will each give a similar guarantee to Czechoslovakia". Poland had been first to share the spoils. After an ultimatum from Warsaw on September 27, 1938, Czechoslovakia had ceded to Poland the district of Těšín (Teschen) – some 625 square miles with a population of 230,000.

With Poland satisfied, the thorny problem of the Hungarian claims remained. Both sides negotiated at Komárno for a "direct agreement" to put an end to the national and territorial disputes stemming from the Treaty of Trianon in 1920. After four days of discussion – or rather recrimination – neither side had given way. Hungary would willingly have gone to war to settle the problem but Germany and Italy intervened, and the governments of Prague and Budapest submitted to their arbitration.

On November 2, 1938, the Czech and Hungarian Foreign Ministers, František Chvalkovský and Kálmán Kánya, met in the sumptuous Belvedere Palace in Vienna. After both parties had pleaded their respective cases the Axis arbitrators, Ribbentrop and Count Galeazzo Ciano, the Italian Foreign Minister, retired to consider their verdict. After much disagreement they announced their joint decision: "to allot to Hungary those territorial zones which otherwise could well have become the objects of numerous bitter disputes".

The sentence of Vienna did not satisfy Hungary's aspirations to all of Sub-Carpathian Ruthenia, but she still got the districts of Mukačevo, Užhorod, Košice, Lučenec, Levice, and Nové Zámky (in all an area of 7,500 square miles with a population of 775,000). This left Czechoslovakia with only one city on the Danube: Bratislava, capital of Slovakia. All ceded territories, it was announced, must be evacuated by November 10.

This compromise aroused great indignation in Budapest, and Hitler and Mussolini were hard put to it to prevent the Hungarians from using force to secure the provinces which had been denied them. Nor was it any better received in Bratislava, where the Slovak leaders accused the Prague Government of having sold them out in agreeing to the dismemberment of their lands. This completely overshadowed the new measures of autonomy granted to the Slovaks by the Czech Government in Prague – a concession which now officially hyphenated the country as Czecho-Slovakia.

The Slovaks did not know that during the Italo-German arbitration in Vienna the unfortunate Chvalkovský had managed to whisper in Ciano's ear: "I will have to resign tomorrow. No government could survive such a shock." But back in Prague, where a new government with

9

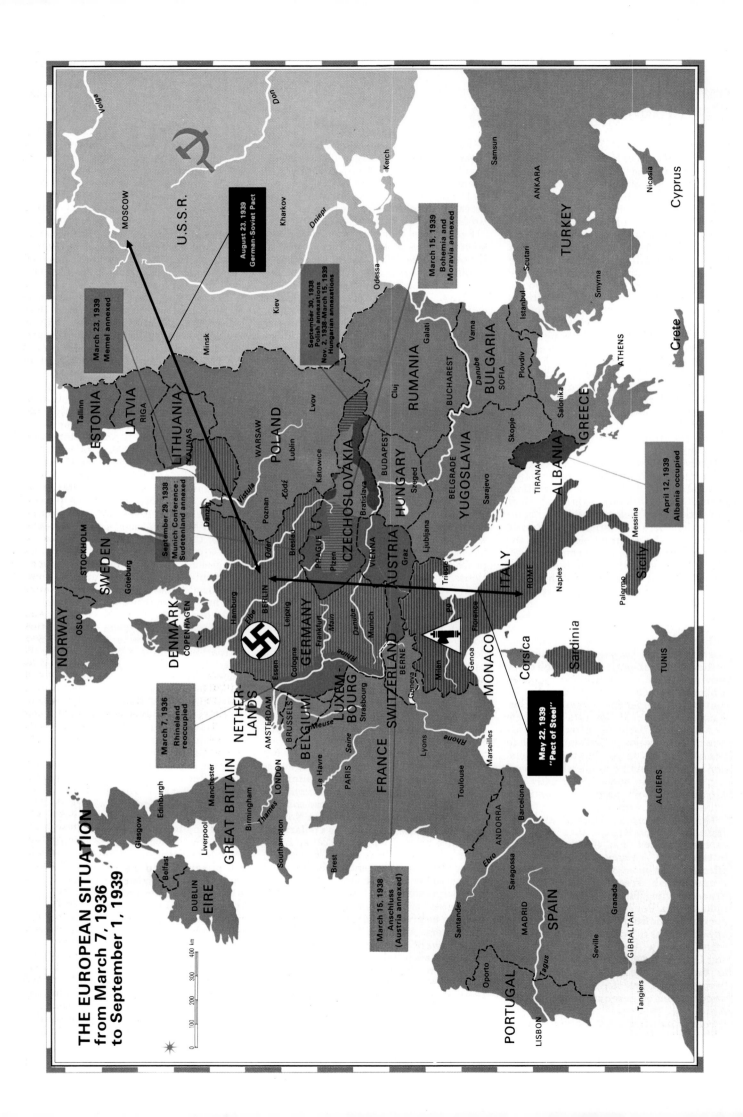

THE EUROPEAN SITUATION
from March 7, 1936
to September 1, 1939

Rudolf Beran as Prime Minister had taken over on October 7, the administration found or thought it had found some measure of compensation in the whole deplorable arrangement.

Having appeased the Polish and Hungarian demands in accordance with the Munich agreement, Czecho-Slovakia was now entitled to ask for the promised guarantees from Italy and Germany. On November 5 Chvalkovský raised the point in a discussion with Dr. Hencke, German *chargé d'affaires* in Prague, only to get the reply: "The question of the guarantee will not arise until the new frontiers have been defined in detail by the commissions."

This had been done by November 20, but when a Czech official raised the point again Hencke had no scruples in replying that "the question of the guarantee had no direct connection with the settlement of the frontiers". This was not Ciano's view. He saw no reason for evading the Czech request, but when he gave his opinion that Germany would acquiesce "readily", it is obvious that Ribbentrop had led his Italian opposite number into a fool's paradise.

After this significant piece of evasion by the Germans, Ribbentrop's visit to Paris in early December to sign the Franco-German declaration gave Georges Bonnet an excellent opportunity to put his oar in. But when the conversation came round to Czecho-Slovakia and the German guarantee, all Ribbentrop gave Bonnet was an ambiguous reply which gave the latter much food for thought. First, he said, Germany was going to see how things

Hermann Göring: Hitler's right hand man and commander of the Luftwaffe.

went. Second, a four-power guarantee would only "encourage" the Prague Government to return to the "errors" of ex-President Eduard Beneš (who had resigned on October 5)–by which he meant relying on support from France, Britain, and the Soviet Union in the event of pressure from Germany.

Despite this rebuff, so lightly wrapped up in diplomatic double-talk, the French Cabinet tried again. Its new spokesman was Ambassador Robert Coulondre, who had just been transferred from Moscow to Berlin. On December 21, 1938, Coulondre carried out his orders to raise the subject of the joint guarantee with German Secretary of State Baron Ernst von Weizsäcker. The latter, however, repeated the evasive gambit: "Czecho-Slovakia is not pressing the point, and the Czech Foreign Minister will not be coming to Berlin until after the holidays. There is no hurry."

This was rather an insidious answer, since if Prague had made no official request for the guarantee to Berlin it was only because the first tentative approaches made by Chvalkovský had met with such an unpromising attitude on the part of Hencke.

Obviously the French Foreign Ministry was not deceived by Weizsäcker's reply. All the evidence now showed that the Munich agreement had not put an end to Hitler's ambitions, despite his solemn protestations to the contrary. All that Munich had done was to give Hitler a springboard for further advances. The suspicions of French Prime Minister Edouard Daladier and Bonnet would have been amply confirmed if they could have seen the Directive of October 21, 1938, in which Hitler had ordered the Wehrmacht to prepare for the final liquidation of "the remainder of Czecho-Slovakia".

Under these conditions, what remained of the Franco-German "joint declaration" of December 6? André François-Poncet, the retiring Ambassador, had returned from a farewell audience with Hitler at Berchtesgaden on October 18. With some apprehension, he wrote: "If these undertakings are kept they will considerably relieve the tension in Europe. But if they are broken, the guilty party will have a heavy moral responsibility to bear."

Across the Atlantic, the American Congress reflected two sentiments, each contradicting the other. One sector of opinion was deeply opposed to the totalitarian, racist dictatorships which had arisen in Europe; the other condemned American involvement in Europe in any shape or form.

This was underlined by the excitement caused by a speech made by William Bullitt, American Ambassador to France, on September 4, 1938. If war should break out in Europe, he said, it would be impossible to say whether or not the United States would become involved. Cautious as it was, this statement caused a furore in the United States, and Roosevelt felt himself obliged to make a public dis-

avowal of Bullitt's words. On September 9, 1939, he reassured the American press. That the United States would side with France and Great Britain against Germany, he declared, was "one hundred per cent" impossible.

What were Britain's feelings in the New Year of 1939?

In describing the Munich agreement to the House of Commons, Neville Chamberlain expressed his belief that an end to surprise military coups had been reached, and that "an era of peace" stretched ahead. The House seemed to have rewarded him with a verdict of 366 Conservative votes against 144 Labour and Liberal votes. But Chamberlain's triumph was far from complete. It was marred by the protest resignation of Duff Cooper, First Lord of the Admiralty. Quite apart from the outspoken lambasting by Winston Churchill–"We have sustained a total and unmitigated defeat"–Chamberlain had to swallow the abstention of 40-odd Members who until Munich had been staunch party supporters.

For all that, Chamberlain's position would remain secure so long as Hitler kept to the terms of the Munich agreement and of the Anglo-German declaration which had followed it. Hitler, however, saw things in a very different light. There existed in Great Britain, he claimed, a clique hostile to peace. If this clique should come to power there would be another world war. For this reason, he announced on October 9, he had decided to extend the fortified zone of the *Westwall* or "Siegfried Line" to include Saarbrücken and Aachen.

Above all, he added: "It would be well for people in Great Britain to start abandoning the superior airs which they have given themselves since the time of Versailles. We will no longer tolerate as we have in the past the interference of British governesses. Enquiries by British politicians concerning Germans within the Reich–*or any peoples dependent upon the Reich*–are misplaced. For our part, we do not concern ourselves with what happens in Britain."

Despite this affront, the German Ambassador in London, Herbert von Dirksen, reported to the Wilhelmstrasse that Chamberlain retained his "complete confidence in the Führer". He followed the same policy of appeasement towards Mussolini. Many politicians in close contact with the Prime Minister felt the same. In particular, Sir Samuel Hoare, the Home Secretary, held that discussions for the limitation of aerial weapons and the "humanising" of war, by the proscription of poison gas and of the bombing of large towns and cities, would be generally welcomed by British public opinion.

The question of the colonies had already been touched upon, but it was obvious that this point would arouse determined opposition from many important quarters. In any case, Chamberlain wondered if this tricky problem really could be tackled now, or "if it would not be better to wait until the German Government has found a satisfactory solution to the urgent problems raised by the cession of the Sudetenland to the Reich and the new pattern of relations between Czecho-Slovakia and her neighbours".

Less than three weeks later, on November 17, Dirksen was writing that Chamberlain was no longer in the least disposed to reopen negotiations with Germany on the lines proposed at Munich. In his report to Ribbentrop on that day, Dirksen suggested two reasons for this.

First, the many invitations for negotiations made in speeches by Chamberlain, Foreign Secretary Lord Halifax, and Hoare had been completely ignored by Berlin. From this the British Cabinet could only conclude that Hitler and Ribbentrop had no interest whatsoever in seeing Anglo-German relations improved.

The second reason was the revulsion caused by a new and vicious pogrom in Germany. On November 7, in Paris, a young Jew named Herschel Grynszpan had assassinated a secretary of the German Legation, Ernst vom Rath, in protest against the deportation to Poland of German Jews. Hideous reprisals were taken against Jews in the Reich. In the "Night of the Broken Glass", which began on the night of November 9–10, the régime had encouraged the most brutal excesses on the part of the German populace. In correct diplomatic language–but with a clarity which left nothing in doubt– Ambassador Dirksen told Ribbentrop of the deep impression which this brutal pogrom had made on every sector of British public opinion. The opponents of appeasement, who had never ceased to condemn the Munich agreement, had been immensely strengthened in their attacks upon Chamberlain's Government, while the supporters of an Anglo-German *rapprochement*–"morally very hard hit"– had been reduced to silence.

Dirksen added: "If this atmosphere persists it will be impossible for Chamberlain to hope for success in his plan of reaching a secure agreement with Germany." Even worse, he added (without actually saying that this was his view), "many well-informed personalities" believed that the Prime Minister was in fact revising his assessment of the future of Anglo-German relations.

Chamberlain had indeed felt affronted by Hitler's speech on October 9. In particular the offensive reference to "British governesses" stuck in Chamberlain's throat. Apart from that, the silence which had greeted his suggestions for co-operation and disarmament had seemed to be a bad omen for the future. Despite this, however, Chamberlain had not yet despaired of his hopes for world peace.

When it came down to it, the Munich settlement had prevented a direct clash between France and Germany in which Great Britain must have been involved as well. Certainly Britain could never remain a passive observer of a defeat of France without endangering her own security, both in north-western Europe

and in the Mediterranean.

Once he was master of the Continent and had disarmed the defeated states, Hitler could reduce his land forces to a level in proportion with the military strength of the Soviet Union. He could then use the industrial potential thus made available to begin a large-scale programme of warship construction which would in time threaten the Royal Navy's numerical lead. This was why Chamberlain and Halifax were somewhat relieved to hear the news, on December 6, that a new "joint declaration", not unlike the one signed by Hitler and Chamberlain in Munich on September 30, had been issued in Paris by Ribbentrop and Bonnet.

War had been averted in north-western Europe, but another flashpoint still glowed in the western Mediterranean. It was intensified by Italy's denunciation of the Laval-Mussolini agreements of 1935 (in which France had agreed not to obstruct Italian colonial expansion), and by the incredible anti-French propaganda campaign launched by the Italian Fascist Government.

The Axis foreign ministers, Ribbentrop of Germany and Ciano of Italy, with the Führer.

On November 30, 1938, Mussolini addressed the Fascist Grand Council. He outlined the majority of Italy's "claims" and, in his personal style, went on to add some more. "I will now describe to you," he told the Council, "the next objectives in the Fascist programme. As Adowa [Italy's defeat in Abyssinia in 1896] has been avenged in Agyssinia, so will we avenge Valona [Italy's expulsion from Albania in 1920]. Albania will become Italian. I cannot and will not tell you when or how. But so it will be. And for our security in this Mediterranean world which surrounds us, we must have Tunisia and Corsica. Our frontier with France must be extended to the Var. I do not aspire to Savoy, for it lies beyond the Alps. But instead I am thinking of the Ticino, for Switzerland has lost her cohesion and, like several other small states, is destined for partition one day.

"All this constitutes our programme. I

cannot give you a definite date for its completion: I am only outlining the objectives ..."

In order to counter these Italian claims and the anti-French press campaign which followed at Mussolini's direct instigation, Edouard Daladier made a whistle-stop tour of Corsica, Tunisia, and the other French territories in North Africa. "We will never," he asserted during his journey, "yield an inch of territory which belongs to us." That word "never" provoked renewed fury from the Fascist propagandists. But worse was to come. At Ajaccio in Corsica, as was the custom, a presentation dagger was given to the French statesman. Daladier jokingly brandished the dagger, made a ferocious face, and transfixed an imaginary foe. The scene was captured by the camera and was published by the Italian press with fearful imprecations. Daladier was threatening Italy with his dagger! He was defying Italy!

War between France and Italy seemed more than likely, for–quite reasonably– France was certainly not going to yield to Italy's ambition of spreading her empire across the whole of North Africa and of turning the western Mediterranean into an Italian lake. But could such a conflict be localised if it broke out? London thought not. It was to be hoped that Hitler would curb Mussolini, but this was no real guarantee that Mussolini would not go to war of his own accord. If it came to a fight, the advantage would definitely lie with France. Yet no one seriously believed that Hitler would allow his sole friend and ally in Europe to be defeated and if Hitler went to Mussolini's aid Britain would have to intervene too.

London was therefore most anxious to pour oil on these troubled waters. On April 16, 1938, a protocol had settled the differences between Italy and Great Britain in the Mediterranean, East Africa, and the Middle East on the basis of the

Munich: Chamberlain confronts Hitler, with Mussolini in the centre.

status quo. Once this agreement was in force, Chamberlain thought he could intervene both in Rome and in Paris. Speaking in the House of Commons on December 14, 1938, he made his attitude to both sides quite clear: "In the view of His Majesty's Government, the undertaking to respect the *status quo* in the Mediterranean, as embodied in the Anglo-Italian Agreement, certainly applies to Tunis."

Such was Britain's attitude in January 1939. Chamberlain had come a long way from the euphoria in which he had returned from Munich, but his honest naïveté still prevented him from expecting the worst from a man who had signed a declaration of Anglo-German friendship.

"A conqueror always likes peace," Clausewitz had written in his notes *On War*; "he would prefer to invade us without meeting resistance." By January 1939 the three great coups of the Third Reich– the reoccupation of the Rhineland, the Austrian *Anschluss*, and the seizure of the Czech Sudetenland–had proved that Adolf Hitler was adept at making realities out of this theory. But the events of the four months after the Munich agreement– October 1938–January 1939–had shown that Hitler was an innovator in another sense. He had invented the modern concept of the "Cold War", the "Phoney Peace", using the troubles and tensions of the world to get what he wanted without fighting wars.

As early as autumn 1937 Hitler could look back on an impressive list of successes. These included the dissolution of the Franco-British-Italian "Stresa Front" (the last alignment of World War I's Allies against Germany), formed in 1935 after Hitler's announcement of German rearmament and the reintroduction of conscription in Germany. Moreover, the Spanish Civil War was increasing the already bitter differences between Fascist Italy and Republican France. But when Hitler considered his next move–the incorporation into the Reich of Austria and Czechoslovakia–he knew that world opinion would be seriously alarmed and

that he was running the risk of a major war.

On November 5, 1937, Hitler called a special conference at the new Chancellery. Those present at this meeting included Field-Marshal Werner von Blomberg, the War Minister; Colonel-General Freiherr Werner von Fritsch, Commander-in-Chief of the Army; General Hermann Göring, Commander-in-Chief of the Luftwaffe; Grand-Admiral Erich Raeder, Commander-in-Chief of the Navy; Baron Konstantin von Neurath, Foreign Minister–and Colonel Friedrich Hossbach, military adjutant to the Führer, whose account of what Hitler had to say at this meeting was to play an important rôle at the Nuremberg Tribunal after the war.

Some historians have questioned both the accuracy and the validity of the "Hossbach Memorandum". Firstly, it must be remembered that the "Hossbach Memorandum" we know today does not exist in its original form, being only a copy of a copy used by the Americans at Nuremberg; and secondly, that it was not Hitler's "last will and testament", but just a long-hand narrative written from memory five days later.

One of the most penetrating accounts of Hitler's intentions during the meeting has been provided by the British historian, A. J. P. Taylor, who has suggested that it was in fact a manoeuvre by Hitler in Germany's domestic affairs. The influential President of the Reichsbank, Hjalmar Schacht, was arguing against increased arms expenditure which Hitler saw as essential for maintaining the momentum of the Nazi movement. Hitler's intention was to isolate Schacht from the conservative chiefs of the Wehrmacht by persuading them that the arms programme must be stepped-up as Germany might find herself at war in the future. And although the service chiefs argued against risking a general war, they accepted Hitler's reasoning for an increase in armament production.

What Hossbach wrote in his Memorandum was not a detailed war blueprint: it was not even remotely justified by the actual course of events. It shows Hitler thinking aloud, putting the possibility of war to the leaders of the Wehrmacht.

Hitler began by explaining that the purpose of the meeting was so important that he thought it best not to bring it before the complete Reich Cabinet. "What he was going to say," noted Hossbach, "was the result of profound deliberation and of his four years in power; he would explain to the gentlemen present his basic ideas on the opportunities and the requirements for the basic growth of our external political situation."

Hitler continued: "The aim of German policy is to secure and protect the racial community [*Volksmasse*] and to enlarge it. It is therefore a question of living space [*Lebensraum*]."

Having established these principles, Hitler went on to describe the economic opportunities offered to a nation of 85 million Germans–a figure including Aus-

A German military band, the ceremonial side of Europe's most efficient army.

trians and Sudeten Germans, with an annual birth-rate put at 560,000. He then outlined Germany's most obvious needs: non-ferrous metals for industrial expansion, and increased food supplies.

Could these serious deficiencies be made good by trade? Hitler thought not, for two reasons: too many countries, former exporters of foodstuffs, had become industrialised since 1918; and the development of Germany's overseas trade (without her former colonies in Africa) would make the Reich dependent upon her two "irreducible enemies"–Great Britain and France.

As a result, Hitler continued: "Only force can solve Germany's problems, and force always has its risks . . . if we deliberately resort to force, having accepted these risks, the next questions are 'When?' and 'How?'."

As far as the timing was concerned, Hitler told his audience that the impressive superiority in weapons and equipment at present enjoyed by the Wehrmacht would dwindle, approaching zero after 1943–45. As a result, if he were still alive, Hitler was "irrevocably determined to settle the problem of Germany's living-space by 1943–45 at the latest".

Two conditions, however, could make it necessary for the Third Reich to act before then: if France's social problems became so acute that the French Army had to be called in and became neutralised in the process; or if France got herself so involved in a war with a third power that she could not respond with sufficient force to a German attack. In any event, Germany must seize the chance to deal with Austria and Czechoslovakia. If secured "with lightning speed", a German success would deter the Societ Union and Poland from any serious ideas of intervening. As for Great Britain, who "in all probability" had written off Czechoslovakia", it was extremely unlikely that she would go to war to restore that country's independence, particularly if she were involved with France in a war against Italy.

The acquisition of Austria and Czechoslovakia would, given the right conditions, provide sufficient extra foodstuffs for five to six million Germans. More important, Germany would experience "a great lightening of politico-military burdens by shortening and strengthening the Reich's frontiers. This would enable troops to be released for service elsewhere. It would also give the Reich 12 new divisions for the army, one division for every million inhabitants" thus incorporated into the Reich.

Blomberg and Fritsch protested at once, reminding Hitler of "the need for Ger-

many to avoid having England and France as enemies". They also doubted that a war with Italy would weaken France sufficiently to prevent her from invading the Rhineland. (It should be remembered that the German Army manoeuvres of September 20–26, 1937, had in fact been planned with the contingency of war with the Soviet Union in mind.) Neurath, in his turn, objected that an Italo-French conflict was more remote than the Führer seemed to think. Hitler, however, rejected all these objections.

Hitler had scant regard for the German High Command. As he later said to Hans Frank, the Governor-General of conquered Poland: "For years these gentlemen in their fancy red-striped breeches have betrayed, forgotten, or sold out the principles of Moltke and Schlieffen. This presumptuous Junker caste is in reality nothing more than a collection of muddleheads, vacillators, and stuffed shirts."

This was borne out by what happened to the three men who protested on November 5, 1937. Blomberg was dismissed in January 1938, ostensibly because of the scandal caused by his marrying a former prostitute. Fritsch fell the same month, on a trumped-up charge of homosexuality (from which he was honourably acquitted by an army court). On February 4, 1938, Hitler assumed the office of Commander-in-Chief of the Armed Forces High Command, or "O.K.W." (for *Oberkommando der Wehrmacht*), which now replaced the War Ministry of Blomberg's day. Colonel-General Wilhelm Keitel (an obsequious, unintelligent, but thoroughly reliable yes-man) became Chief-of-Staff. Göring, who had hoped to replace Blomberg, was promoted to Field-Marshal in compensation, while Colonel-General Walter von Brauchitsch replaced Fritsch. Neurath, too, was dismissed from the Foreign Ministry. His place was taken by the vain, conceited Joachim von Ribbentrop, of whom Mussolini said: "You have only to look at his head to see that he has a small brain."

On March 12, 1938, Hitler was able to carry out his bloodless annexation of Austria. Czechoslovakia proved a harder proposition, with the real danger of intervention from Britain and France. But the Munich agreement gave Hitler all the conditions he would need to complete the liquidation of the Czechoslovak state, once more without having to resort to war.

What, in fact, were Hitler's long-term war plans? When did he think that his land and sea armaments would be sufficient for a general war, once Central Europe had been subdued? "In three or four years" is what Ribbentrop told Ciano on October 28, 1938. But was the German foreign minister trying to deceive Ciano? This is hardly believable. It is far more likely that Ribbentrop failed to foresee that in Paris and in London Germany's blatant violation of the Munich agreement would lead to a full-scale revival of the crisis.

Hitler was thinking on similar lines.

The height of Nazi Party ceremonial: standard-bearers at Nuremberg.

This is shown by the "Z-Plan", the extremely ambitious programme of warship construction submitted by Grand-Admiral Raeder and approved in January 1939. This programme included the building of nine huge battleships and battle-cruisers for an expanded fleet which was intended to be ready for a war by 1948. Hitler agreed to a deadline of 1944–45 for the surface warships and 1943 for the 249 U-boats provided for in the Z-Plan.

Hitler's plan for the dismemberment of Czecho-Slovakia followed the Clausewitzian ideal: he would have liked to invade without meeting resistance from either Paris or London. This was no doubt wishful thinking, but the impression he had received from his meetings with Chamberlain and Daladier at the time of Munich had convinced him that this would be possible. As far as Czecho-Slovakia was concerned, Hitler's mind was already made up. Barely two days after the Munich agreement he had sent a secret message to Keitel at the O.K.W., asking how much time and military strength would be needed to break the resistance of the Czechs. On October 11 Keitel replied that it would take little time and not much effort.

In Czecho-Slovakia, Beneš had resigned as President on October 5, and it was not until November 30 that the Czech National Assembly found a permanent successor in Dr. Emil Hácha. Hencke, German *chargé d'affaires* in Prague, had this to say about Hácha in his report to Ribbentrop on December 2: "Until now, very little has been heard of Dr. Hácha. He has hardly enjoyed anything in the way of popularity. The new President is 66 years old. The strongest argument in his favour is that he is one of the few men in this country about whom it is impossible to say anything but good. His previous career as a judge has been impeccable, and one is struck by his integrity and by his judgement in all aspects of human and judicial affairs. He has never involved himself in politics and knows nothing about it, as he is the first to admit." Hencke added that Hácha had stated "that his country and his people can only survive if, despite all the psychological obstacles, a new relationship based on genuine mutual confidence without compromise" were established with Germany.

Without waiting for the outcome of the Czech Parliamentary elections, the Czech Foreign Minister, Chvalkovský, had been trying to head the foreign policy of his unfortunate country in this direction.

The results were not auspicious. Following the provisions of the Munich agreement, Chvalkovský had been forced to comply with every last territorial demand made by Berlin. As a result, together with the Sudeten Germans some 800,000 Czechs had passed under German rule without the least guarantee of their cultural autonomy. On the other hand, the 478,000-odd Germans who remained behind Czecho-Slovakia's new frontiers had received the privileged status of *Volksdeutsche*, which in many ways shielded them from Czech authority.

On November 19, 1938, two protocols were signed in Berlin by the newly-appointed German Ambassador in Prague, Ritter, for Germany, and by General Husárek for Czecho-Slovakia.

The first protocol contained the agreement of the Prague Government to the building of an *autobahn* (motorway) across Czecho-Slovakia to connect Silesia and Austria, on condition that this new highway (with its obvious strategic importance) should be extra-territorial. As far as its customs and passport authorities were concerned, these should be under German control. The second protocol registered a similar agreement to build a Danube-Oder Canal across Czecho-Slovakia. A link between this new waterway and the Elbe would be considered in due course.

It was now clear that since the Munich agreement the Czech Government had determined to do everything in its power to fulfil the wishes of the Reich. It had renounced the European rôle which Tomáš Masaryk and Beneš had envisaged for Czecho-Slovakia after 1920 for that of a small neutral, placed, like Switzerland, under the guarantee of the major powers. Docility towards Germany was felt in Prague to be the only way of securing the guarantee which had been promised in the Munich agreement.

But Prague was soon undeceived. On November 21 Colonel-General Keitel approved an O.K.W. note which laid down harsh conditions for the status of the Czecho-Slovak Army:

1. No fortifications to be built or planned along the Czech-German frontier;
2. The composition and equipment of the Czech Army (to be reduced in size as much as possible) to be approved by the German Government;
3. Standardisation of all weapons and munitions; the adaptation of Czecho-Slovak industry to suit the needs of German national defence;
4. All Intelligence activity which could be used against Germany to be forbidden, and Czecho-Slovakia to be closed to foreign Intelligence agencies; and
5. Germany to have the right, in peace and war, to transfer troops across Czecho-Slovak territory between Austria and Silesia, by road or railway, without prior notice being given.

Here, in fact, was what Hitler really had in mind for future German-Czecho-Slovak relations: not a balance between a powerful guarantor and a small guaranteed state, in which Germany would be joined by Great Britain, France, and Italy, but a German exclusion of all intervention from without, to reduce Czecho-Slovakia to the status of a German vassal state.

In a visit to Rome between January 11–13, 1939, Chamberlain had tried to pin down the Italians on the guarantee promised to Czecho-Slovakia, but Mussolini and Ciano skirted the issue. Ciano telephoned Ribbentrop that Chamberlain's visit had been a fiasco–"big lemonade". On the 21st, rumours that Germany was planning the final takeover of Czecho-Slovakia brought Chvalkovský hot-foot to Berlin, summoned for an interview with Hitler. The Führer was in a bullying mood, stating that the German guarantee should be matched by the Prague Government with the demobilisation of all but 10,000 to 20,000 Czech soldiers and the acceptance of the O.K.W. requirements. Chvalkovský certainly could not agree to these demands, which not only betrayed the original promise of the guarantee but also amounted to the surrender of Czecho-Slovakia's independence. But he was careful not to give Hitler any excuse for resorting to armed force.

15

Dr. Emil Hácha, the new president of Czecho-Slovakia.

To avoid a complete violation of his own undertakings, Hitler would therefore have to strike from within rather than invade Czecho-Slovakia openly. During the Italo-German arbitration at Vienna in November 1938, Ribbentrop had angered Ciano by refusing to endorse the complete Hungarian claims in Slovakia with regard to Sub-Carpatian Ruthenia. Now Ribbentrop and Hitler, without changing their tune, planned to use Hungary's continued territorial ambitions in the area to force the Slovaks onto the horns of a dilemma and so further German plans towards Czechoslovakia.

This boiled down to giving the Slovaks two blunt alternatives. On the one hand, the autonomous Slovak Government in Bratislava could continue to exist according to the statute granted to it in the previous autumn by the Prague Government, which as far as Berlin was concerned was still motivated by the "spirit of Beneš". In which case the Reich would settle accounts with the Czechs and would have to leave Slovakia to the mercies of Poland and Hungary.

On the other hand, Slovakia could demand immediate independence from Prague. If she did so Germany would offer her all-powerful protection to the new state, and would shield her from the territorial greed of Warsaw and Budapest.

This is what Hitler put to Professor Vojtech Tuka, one of the principal supporters of the growing Slovak separatist movement, on February 12. Listening with Tuka was Franz Karmasin, leader of the German minority in Slovakia and now Slovak Secretary of State. The two men returned to Bratislava and reported Hitler's offer to Monsignor Jozef Tiso, Premier of the autonomous Slovak Government granted by the Czechs on October 6, 1938–and the fateful mechanism engineered by Hitler and Ribbentrop began to move with increasing speed.

On March 9, the negotiations between Prague and Bratislava for further grants of autonomy to Slovakia were stopped in their tracks. Acting within his constitutional prerogative, President Hácha took it upon himself on the following day to dismiss Tiso and two of his ministers, Durčanský and Pružinský, for "separatist activity prejudicial to the unity of the state". At the same time Hácha occupied Bratislava with government troops. Hitler's reaction was to order the preparation of a seven-point ultimatum to the Czech Government on the following day. Next came a meeting with the Slovaks. Hitler received Tiso and Durčanský on the afternoon of March 13 in the presence of Ribbentrop, Keitel, Brauchitsch, Minister of State Meissner, and Secretaries of State Dietrich and Keppler (who had been a German agent in Bratislava).

Hitler began by recounting the list of Czech "deceptions" with which he had met since the Munich agreement. He then told Tiso that, as the situation had become "intolerable" during the last weeks, he had decided to settle Slovakia's position once and for all without further delay. "It was no longer a question of days, but of hours . . . if Slovakia wanted her independence he would support her efforts and

stand surety for her success". He would only intervene from now on if German interests were threatened, which would never be the case east of the Carpathians. Germany, Hitler finished by declaring, had no interest in Slovakia, a country which historically had never formed part of Germany.

Asked for the most recent developments of the situation, Ribbentrop put an edge on Hitler's proposals by stressing that Tiso would only have a few hours in which to make his decision. A dispatch had just reached him, he said, which told of Hungarian troop movements towards the Slovak frontier.

But the Slovak ministers were not told that these troop movements, which were in fact aimed at Sub-Carpathian Ruthenia, had been organised by the Germans. Sent to Budapest on Ribbentrop's orders, Councillor Altenburg had put the idea to Admiral Miklós Horthy, Regent of Hungary, on the morning of March 13. By 1725 hours the same day, Berlin had been informed that it had been received "with enthusiasm". In fact, the lack of training in the Hungarian Army had forced the Hungarian Chief-of-Staff, who had been present at the audience with Horthy, to ask that the operation be postponed until the following week, but Altenburg had promptly retorted that this would be too late. And so Hitler was sent the following schedule by Horthy: Thursday, March 16–"frontier incident"; Saturday, March 18–"military coup".

It was in this explosive atmosphere that on the following day, March 14, the Bratislava Diet yielded to its fears of Hungarian aggression and proclaimed the independence of Slovakia. Hitler was asked "to guarantee the existence of the new state, and to take every measure to assure the protection of its frontiers". Cut off from Prague by Slovakia's secession, Sub-Carpathian Ruthenia considered itself obliged to follow Bratislava's example and its new President, Monsignor Vološín, also asked for Hitler's guarantee. But already six Hungarian brigades were advancing up the valleys towards the peaks of the Carpathians and the Polish frontier. In this situation, Berlin sent a categorical "no" to the Ruthenian President at 1700 hours on March 15, together with the advice to drop any ideas of resistance.

The Republic of Czecho-Slovakia was no more. Slovakia had adopted Hitler's patronage. Sub-Carpathian Ruthenia had been marked down to Hungary. Bohemia and Moravia, the Czech lands, stood alone–and now it fell to President Hácha, despite his chronic heart trouble, to shoulder the agonising burden of the last frightful hours which lay ahead.

At last, the final blow fell on Czecho-Slovakia. At 1100 hours on Wednesday, March 14, Hácha, at his own invitation, and Chvalkovský arrived in Berlin. There they found, gathered around Hitler, Ribbentrop, Meissner, Weizsäcker, Dietrich, and–significantly–Göring and

*German troops enter
Czechoslovakia.*

the German Reich. The Führer accepted this declaration and expressed his intention of taking the Czech people under the protection of the German Reich, and of guaranteeing them an autonomous development of their ethnic life as suited to their character.

In token of which the present document has been signed by both parties."

Rudolf Beran, the Czech Prime Minister, and General Jan Syrový, Minister for National Defence, gave in without being pushed about or given injections. This was certainly not surprising in the case of Beran: to the question of whether or not it would be better to capitulate or to stand up to the Reich with the aid of the Red Army, Beran replied, brandishing his wallet: "Hitler will not take this from me. With Voroshilov I am not so sure . . . That is why I would rather be swallowed by Hitler than saved by Voroshilov."

With this document Hitler had got everything he wanted, and German troops proceeded to occupy the whole of Bohemia and Moravia as effortlessly as though they were on manoeuvres. But photographs of the event clearly show the feelings of humiliation, grief, and anger with which the Czechs greeted their oppressors. They had lost–but now the threat of a general war was imminent.

The Czech Army was disbanded but many of its officers reached the West and took up arms again a few months later, first under the French and then under the British. The Czech Army's equipment, which was abundant and relatively modern, was eagerly taken over by the Wehrmacht – especially the excellent Škoda tanks. Some 336 T-35 and T-38 tanks were used to equip the newly-formed 6th, 7th, and 8th Panzer Divisions during the "Phoney War" of 1939–40, units which would play a key rôle in the German offensives in the summer of 1940.

As might have been expected, the Germans went through the Czech Army archives in minute detail. They found much of importance. In the files of the Czech Military Intelligence department they found a report on the most recent French fortifications in north-east France. Illustrated with sketches, this document had been drawn up by a team of highly-skilled officers who had visited a sector of the Maginot Line a few years before. Its information added considerably to the data gathered by the Germans from their inspection of the Czech fortifications in the Sudetenland which had fallen into their hands after Munich.

In the field of military hardware, the important Škoda works at Pilsen were soon making an important contribution to German military preparations and to the war effort of the Third Reich. Moreover, the Škoda works had been the main source of supply for the weapons of the Rumanian and Yugoslav Armies. The Prague coup would thus prove of considerable help to Berlin in stepping up the pressure on Yugoslavia and Rumania when the time came.

Keitel. Hácha and Chvalkovský were led to a room where they faced Hitler, Ribbentrop, and Göring. On the table lay a document which contained the total abdication of Czecho-Slovakia's sovereignty. "This is no time for negotiation," declared Hitler. "It is time to take note of the irrevocable decisions of the German Government." With that Hitler signed the document and stalked out of the room.

It was 0130 hours. The order had gone out for the German troops to commence the occupation of Bohemia and Moravia at 0630 hours. Five hours in which to yield! All through the night Hácha protested against this brutality and strove desperately to avoid signing his country's death-warrant. He argued that he must obtain the consent of his ministers. A telephone link to Prague was arranged. Meanwhile the German ministers pushed the two men around the table, constantly waving the papers under their noses, thrusting pens into their hands, threatening that in two hours half the city of Prague could be destroyed by 800 bombers which were only waiting for the order to take off. During this long and terrible night, Hácha had to be brought round

several times by doctors standing by in the next room. At about 0345 he lost consciousness entirely and had to be given injections. From this moment his resistance was broken and he signed in desperation, convinced that if he did not he would expose his country to a pitiless bombardment.

Pushed to the final limits of their endurance, the two Czech statesmen had no alternative but to yield. They accepted the conditions laid down in the O.K.W. note of March 11, and put their names to a joint declaration which read as follows:
"Berlin, March 15, 1939.
At their request, the Führer has today received President Hácha and Foreign Minister Chvalkovský in the presence of Reich Foreign Minister von Ribbentrop. At this meeting the grave situation created by the events of recent weeks in the present Czecho-Slovak territory was examined with complete frankness.

"Both sides unanimously expressed the conviction that every effort must be made to preserve calm, order, and peace in this part of Central Europe. The Czecho-Slovak President declared that, in order to pursue this object and to achieve complete pacification, he confidently placed the fate of the Czech people and country in the hands of the Führer and

CHAPTER 2
The Pact of Steel

After Munich, Hitler was planning not only the dismemberment of Czecho-Slovakia but began to consider the expansion of the Fatherland in new areas. Poland had been entered on the agenda.

On October 24, 1938, Ribbentrop was lunching at the Grand Hotel in Berchtesgaden with Józef Lipski, Polish Ambassador to Berlin. Between the dessert and the cheese, Ribbentrop suddenly presented his plan for a "joint solution" to all possible German-Polish differences. Warsaw should consent to the restoration of the Free City of Danzig to the Reich, to the building of an *autobahn* and railway, both extra-territorial, across the famous "Danzig Corridor" in Polish Pomerania, and to joining the Anti-Comintern Pact. In return Berlin would guarantee Poland's economic rights and railway access to Danzig, extend the 1934 German-Polish Non-Aggression Pact, originally scheduled to run for ten years, by 25 years, and guarantee Poland's frontiers.

Ribbentrop was no more liked in Poland than he was in France. According to Count Jan Szembek, Polish Under-Secretary for Foreign Affairs, Lipski considered Ribbentrop "a most disagreeable partner who does not understand the Danzig problem, but merely keeps on repeating that Danzig is a German city. By contrast, Göring has shown that he knows full well that Danzig, if incorporated into the Reich and deprived of its Polish hinterland, would be more or less condemned to perish."

After warning his host that he saw absolutely no chance of the Free City returning to the Reich, Lipski hastened to inform his chief, Polish Foreign Minister Józef Beck, that Ribbentrop had sounded him out on the subject. Beck proved as quick on the uptake as Lipski. Less than a week after Ribbentrop's approach on the 24th, Beck's reply to Lipski left Warsaw. It contained a detailed statement on the subject of Danzig which Lipski was charged with explaining to the leaders of the Reich.

In Beck's opinion, the 1934 agreement with Germany had shown its value during the recent crisis in Europe. As far as Warsaw was concerned, it was not "a tactical and provisional expedient" but an expression of the definite wish of the two nations to remedy a situation which, after centuries of mutual hostility, could profit neither side. Thus it was intended to consolidate the friendly relations which the two former enemies had established.

Beck was certainly not prepared to sacrifice the rights in Danzig given to Poland by the Treaty of Versailles for the sake of German-Polish concord. The importance of Danzig's maritime trade, the expansion of its merchant fleet, and its industrial production made a concession of this nature unacceptable to Poland. In any case the administration of the Free City, instituted in 1919, in no way affected the rights of the German population.

Nevertheless, not wishing to appear intransigent, Beck told Lipski to suggest another solution to Ribbentrop.

This would "substitute a bilateral German-Polish agreement for the pact of 1934. The new agreement would guarantee the continued existence of the Free City of Danzig in such a way that the national and cultural way of life of the German majority would be unimpaired, and that all existing Polish rights would be guaranteed. Despite the complications," Beck concluded in his instructions to Lipski, "the Polish Government is obliged to state that any other solution, and in particular the proposal to incorporate the Free City into the Reich, would inevitably lead to a conflict. Such an eventuality would not only lead to local trouble but could fatally obstruct the course of German-Polish understanding."

All this was logical. But as far as Hitler and Ribbentrop were concerned, the 1934 agreement was exactly what Beck had said it was not: "a tactical and provisional expedient". The future of German-Polish relations mattered far less to them than the gaining of Danzig. However, Lipski took his time in passing on Beck's instructions. Doubtless thinking that there was no harm in letting things ride, he waited until November 19 before calling at the German Foreign Ministry in the Wilhelmstrasse and giving Ribbentrop the gist of his instructions from Warsaw. According to Lipski's report to Beck the same day, Ribbentrop's attitude was "completely friendly", and Ribbentrop had given him to understand that his attitude on October 24 had been taken "on his own initiative". Lipski thought that Hitler had not approved of Ribbentrop's suggestions and that there was no need for his chief in Warsaw to alarm himself.

With certain reservations, Beck adopted Lipski's point of view. He considered that Ribbentrop was a novice diplomat and was very close not only to the Junker class but also to the aggressive German nationalists who followed a tradition of hostility to Poland and of general scorn for the states of eastern Europe. Personal ambition and the desire to score an impressive success had led Ribbentrop, Beck believed, to exceed Hitler's brief. Hitler, however, saw refusal in Poland's attitude. On November 24, he ordered the commanders of Germany's armed forces to set in motion preparations for the occupation of Danzig.

Beck, however, was brought down to earth with a terrific jolt when, visiting Berchtesgaden on January 5, 1939, he listened to Hitler describing how he felt about the Danzig problem. His views were identical to those which Beck had believed had merely been dreamed up by the tactless Ribbentrop in an excess of zeal.

Hitler resumed the claims put forward by Ribbentrop on October 24: Danzig and the *autobahn*-railway link across the Corridor between the Reich and East Prussia. But he did so without any heat at all—no veiled threats or hints of future trouble. In particular, he gave Beck his word that no *fait accompli* would be engineered in Danzig by Germany.

Hitler stated that his attitude towards Poland had not changed in the least since the pact of 1934. "In any circumstances," he continued, "Germany would be greatly interested in the continued existence of a strongly nationalist Polish state because of what might happen in Russia. Whether Russia had a Bolshevik, Tsarist, or any other kind of régime, Germany's attitude towards Russia would always be marked by extreme caution . . . Quite apart from that, the existence of a strong Polish Army lightened Germany's load to a considerable degree. The divisions which Poland kept on her frontier with Russia spared Germany from a similar military burden." But Hitler's assurances did not cause Beck to consent to the required concessions. Still less did they disperse the apprehension which he felt about them. Replying, Beck said that the Danzig problem was extremely difficult and that he would certainly be unable to discuss it without bearing in mind the unanimous wishes of the Polish nation, which he could not and would not contravene.

Returning from Berchtesgaden, Beck had another meeting with Ribbentrop in Munich in which he spoke his mind. He asked Ribbentrop to repeat to Hitler, "that while he had always been optimistic as to the outcome of the discussions which he had had with the German statesmen, this was the first time he had felt at all pessimistic". Ribbentrop's reply was "that Germany did not envisage any violent solution" to the problems under discussion between Germany and Poland. After this first Polish rebuttal, Hitler took the initiative again on January 9: he gave Poland to think that in return for her co-operation *vis-à-vis* Danzig, Germany would help her to realise her nationalistic ambitions.

When Ribbentrop travelled to Warsaw for the fifth anniversary of the German-Polish Non-Aggression Pact (January 26, 1939), both he and Beck held their different viewpoints about Danzig and the proposed extra-territorial routes. What is more, Beck turned down a suggestion from Ribbentrop that Poland should join Germany, Italy, and Japan in their Anti-Comintern Pact. But although there were no signs of any reconciliation of the different interests of Germany and Poland, the tone of the discussions remained courteous.

The implications of the German move into Czecho-Slovakia hit Poland like an earthquake. Admittedly, it gave Poland the common frontier with Hungary which she had wanted for years, and which a few months later would allow many Poles to escape to the West and carry on the fight against Germany from there. But the cynicism with which Hitler had broken his word; his callousness towards the principle of national self-determination, in whose name he had claimed and won the Sudetenland; his open contempt for the Slav peoples – all these provoked general indignation, and as far as the Polish Government was concerned proved that any negotiations on the lines proposed by Berlin would be futile.

Apart from this, the "protection" given to Slovakia by Germany caused much worry to the Polish Government and General Staff. Justified fears that the Wehrmacht would now be able to operate from Slovak territory meant that Poland would have to extend the deployment of her frontier armies along the Carpathians for at least a further 220 miles. Thus the strategic envelopment of Poland was tragically assisted by Slovakia's new rôle.

Given this situation, Ribbentrop's interview with Lipski on March 21 sounded like the first rumble of the storm to Warsaw. Ribbentrop not only resumed the German claims on Danzig and the Corridor: he insisted that the German-Polish agreement

German troops occupy Memel.

could not survive without Poland showing "a clear anti-Soviet attitude. Poland must understand that she has to choose between Germany and Russia." Worse still, two days later Beck read the newspaper announcements that after an ultimatum, Germany had recovered from Lithuania the port and hinterland of Memel, lost at Versailles in 1919. This made the Poles more sensitive than ever as far as Danzig was concerned.

Beck considered the situation to be "so tense" that he called a meeting of his principal ministers on March 24. According to the notes taken by Count Szembek, Beck justified his pessimistic outlook by the fact that "one of the two factors which have always governed the position of our State – Germany – has lost the sense of responsibility shown up to now . . . we know the exact limit of our own interests . . . beyond that limit Poland can only announce a *non possumus*. It is very simple, we shall fight!"

On the other hand, if "the enemy" had "abandoned every moderation in thought and deed", he might change his tune if he found that he was dealing with a state which stuck to its guns – something which

had never yet happened to Nazi Germany. Hitler and his colleagues knew that "[Poland's] political settlement of accounts with Germany will not be like the others".

In Berlin, Ambassador Lipski certainly noted the "marked coolness" with which Ribbentrop greeted him on March 26. According to Beck's instructions, Lipski restated the Polish point of view. Commenting on certain military measures which Warsaw had thought fit to take, Ribbentrop showed "a certain degree of apprehension" and added: "any aggression against Danzig on your part will be regarded as aggression against the Reich." With the peculiar blend of confidence and pessimism which typified him after March 24, Beck thought it advisable to match this last announcement with one of his own. On the 28th he summoned the German Ambassador, Hans von Moltke, and told him that "any attempt by the German Government to change the *status quo* in Danzig will be considered an act of aggression against Poland". Beck toned down the bluntness of this message by denying that Poland wanted to cause trouble in Danzig, and by declaring that he still wanted to know

An easy victory for Italy: one of the four Bersaglieri regiments which invaded Albania coming ashore on April 6, 1939.

what kind of settlement to the Danzig problem could be reached by the two states.

"You want to negotiate at bayonet-point!" exclaimed the German Ambassador.

"That is your own method," replied Beck coldly.

Hitler's takeover of Prague was followed within weeks by Mussolini's takeover of Albania. The German coup on March 15 had angered and humiliated the Duce, and it was Ciano who suggested that Italy's reputation might be restored in Albania. Ciano recorded his thoughts in his diary. "Germany's intervention does not destroy the Czechoslovakia of Versailles but the country set up at Munich and Vienna. What weight can be given in the future to those declarations and promises which concern us more directly? It is useless to deny that all this worries and humiliates the Italian people. It is necessary to give them satisfaction and compensation: Albania. I spoke about it to the Duce, to whom I also expressed my conviction that at this time we shall find neither local obstacles nor serious international complications in the way of our advance. He authorised me to telegraph to Jacomoni [Italian Minister to Albania], asking him to prepare local revolts, and he personally ordered the Navy to hold the second squadron ready at Taranto."

But Mussolini vacillated. He was worried about Yugoslavia: an Italian move against Albania might well encourage a separatist movement by the Croats in Yugoslavia, who, accepting German "protection" as the Slovaks had done, would permit the extension of German influence into the Balkans. It was not until March 23 that Mussolini gave Ciano instructions to go ahead with plans for a surprise move against Albania, which would improve Italy's strategic position considerably.

These plans were enshrined in an "Italo-Albanian agreement" composed of three dry articles, whose tone, Ciano commented, was "far more like a decree than an international pact". It was hardly likely to induce King Zog of Albania to sign it without losing face. Rome replied to King Zog's objections with an ultimatum at noon on April 6, and the following day the spearheads of an Italian expeditionary force, under General Alfredo Guzzoni – of four *Bersaglieri* regiments and a tank battalion – landed at several points on the Albanian coast. Resistance to this underhand attack was feeble and sporadic. On April 8 ex-King Zog and his wife (who had given birth to a son three days before) fled to Greece.

King Victor Emmanuel III formally assumed the Crown of Albania on April 16, adding it to those of Italy and Ethiopia. In his opinion, the game was not worth the candle . . .

While Hitler and Ribbentrop were completing their preparations for breaking their word and swallowing the rest of Czecho-Slovakia, the politicians in Paris and London would have been extremely surprised if anyone had predicted that a general conflict would shortly arise out of Germany's and Poland's failure to reach agreement over Danzig.

In his memoirs, Georges Bonnet describes the astonishment he felt when he discovered the extent to which Beck had kept him in the dark over Poland's discussions with the Third Reich. "Why did Beck keep his opinions from the French Ambassador, his ally?" Bonnet asked Daladier later. "Did he not dare to admit to himself and to others the failure of his policy? Did he wish to keep France in the dark in order to add credibility to the efforts of his propagandists in Paris, who were eventually trying to convince us that France had more to gain than Poland in maintaining the alliance? Or did he really think that he could settle the Danzig Corridor business himself, talking with Germany as an equal?"

When Bonnet wrote his memoirs (1946–47) he did not know of the relevant documents for the period from the German Foreign Office archives. These indicate that Beck did believe that Poland could settle the Danzig problem herself. Beck clung to Hitler's statement that Germany, in view of the menace of Russia, needed the continued existence of a "strongly nationalist Polish state". Be that as it may, there is no denying that Beck's refusal to communicate fully with Britain and France meant that those powers continued to be more preoccupied with the likelihood of war in the Mediterranean than in Poland.

Many historians, writing before 1939, had argued that it was the failure of Great Britain in the years before 1914 to convince Germany that Britain would fight in aid of France, with or without a violation of Belgian territory, which resulted in the outbreak of war in the West. It was this argument which caused both France and Britain – France on January 6, 1939, and Britain on February 6 – to proclaim to the world that in the event of a war they would co-operate. In his speech to the House of Commons, Chamberlain added: "Any threat to the vital interests of France, from wherever it might come, will necessarily provoke the immediate involvement of our country."

So it was that Mussolini, at the moment when he was doubling the strength of the Italian Army in Libya and insulting France with a mud-slinging press campaign, suddenly realised that any Italian attempt to take over Tunis would automatically bring the British Fleet against him.

France and Britain, however, were brought rudely to their senses when Hitler's troops marched into Bohemia and Moravia on March 15. The Prague coup produced an immediate and indignant protest from both countries. In a note dated March 17, France condemned the "flagrant violation of both the letter and the intent" of the Munich agreement, declaring that "the circumstances in which the leaders of the Republic of Czechoslovakia were forced to submit on March 15 have no foundation in right . . ." and concluded: "The Government of the Republic, under these circumstances, does not recognise the validity of the new situation created in Czechoslovakia by the action of the Reich." The British Ambassador in

Berlin, Sir Nevile Henderson, handed over a similar note.

On March 31 the funeral speech of appeasement was pronounced when Neville Chamberlain rose in the House of Commons and announced Britain's guarantee of immediate military aid in the event of any threat to Poland's independence. France had no need to make a similar declaration: her aid had already been pledged in the Franco-Polish military treaty of 1921, which had never lapsed. The result of the Italian takeover of Albania in the following week was two more guarantees on April 13, from France as well as from Britain, to Rumania and Greece.

Chamberlain, then, had pledged his country to fight against the future ambitions of the Axis—but the French were quick to point out that Britain lacked the military wherewithal to do so. Conscription was the stumbling-block. To France it was ludicrous that Britain should rely on her paperweight Regular Army to enforce such solemn guarantees of military aid to foreign powers. In Britain, however, the Labour Opposition took more persuading. After the war the Labour Party in the House of Commons was the first to put the blame for World War II on "Tory mismanagement" in the years before 1939. But it had been the Labour M.P.s who had voted down pleas for British rearmament in the 1930's with vicious attacks on "Tory armaments", and who in early 1939 championed the fight against the reintroduction of conscription in Britain. Yet there was no stopping Chamberlain now: his mind was made up.

The vote for conscription was cast on April 27, and it was passed by 380 votes to 143. It was, of course, far too late for Britain to produce a sizeable and battleworthy conscript army for service in 1939. Yet the symbolic value of the reintroduction of conscription was not lost.

Especially not on Adolf Hitler. He reacted promptly in a speech in the Reichstag on the following day, April 28. American correspondent William Shirer, who witnesses the event, recorded his feelings in his *Berlin Diary:*
"Berlin, April 28.
Hitler in the Reichstag today denounced a couple more treaties . . . loudly applauded by the rubber-stamp 'parliamentarians'. Hitler denounces the naval accord with Britain [signed in June 1935, giving Germany the right to build up a navy of 35% of the strength of the Royal Navy] on the grounds that London's 'encirclement policy' has put it out of force—a flimsy excuse; of course no excuse at all. The second treaty denounced, the 1934 pact with Poland, is more serious, the excuse, incidentally, being the same . . .
"Still much doubt here among the informed whether Hitler has made up his mind to begin a world war for the sake of Danzig. My guess is he hopes to get it by the Munich method."
This, then, was the background to the gradual Italo-German *rapprochement* which culminated, on May 22, 1939, in the signing of the "Pact of Steel".

On November 6, 1937, Italy had joined the Anti-Comintern Pact, which had bound Germany and Japan since November 25 of the previous year. This diplomatic line-up was not, in fact, an alliance in the full sense of the word. It did not even recognise the Soviet Union as a state, but was intended to counter the subversive activity allegedly organised all over the world by the Comintern, from Moscow. This was why Article 1 of the Anti-Comintern Pact stated: "The contracting powers undertake to inform each other of the activity of the International Communist Party, to consult each other on measures of defence and to execute these measures of defence in direct collaboration."

Mussolini had not joined the Pact because of fears for his own Fascist régime in Italy: he wished rather to end the isolation into which his ventures in Ethiopia and in Spain had led Italy. The day after the signing of the Anti-Comintern Pact, Ciano noted in his diary: "After signing the Pact we went to the Duce's residence. I have rarely seen him so happy. The situation of 1935 is no more. Italy has broken through her isolation: she is at the centre of the most formidable military and political system which has ever existed."

Perhaps, wrote Ciano, the common road which the three powers were now treading would even lead them to battle, to the "necessary battle" which must be fought to break the restrictions on the energies and aspirations of young nations. Nevertheless the Anti-Comintern Pact, like the old Triple Alliance of 1882 between Berlin, Rome, and Vienna, was basically nothing more than what Bismarck once called a "treaty of accord".

Had Baron von Neurath, still Reich Foreign Minister at the time, been thinking of a more direct relationship between Germany and Italy? Or had he accepted the advice which his Ambassador in Rome, Ulrich von Hassell, had given him (to the fury of Ciano and Mussolini): not to put any trust in Italy's military and economic strength? There is no way of knowing. In any case, Neurath was replaced in February 1938 by Ribbentrop, one of whose first acts was to dismiss Hassell in disgrace. Hassell's replacement was Hans Georg von Mackensen, a man with far more sympathy towards the totalitarian régimes of the Führer and the Duce.

Ribbentrop's anglophobia caused Ciano to write "Very good!" in his diary when he heard that Ribbentrop had taken over as Reich Foreign Minister. But many different factors prevented the formation of a direct alliance between Germany and Italy until May 1939.

First came the Austrian *Anschluss* in March 1938. Mussolini was not unwilling to see Austria absorbed by the Third Reich, but he and his advisers did have doubts about the reactions which such an annexation would provoke south of the Brenner Pass, among the pro-German population of the region which the Italians call the Alto Adige and the Austrians the South Tyrol. Then, on April 16, 1938, the signature of the Anglo-Italian Protocol, settling the

two countries' differences arising from the war in Abyssinia, made Ciano shelve the idea of an alliance with Germany. And finally there was a personality problem: Ribbentrop. He seemed completely unable to inspire any sympathy or confidence.

When Hitler and Ribbentrop visited Italy between May 3–9, 1938, the "exuberance" of the new Reich Foreign Minister disturbed Ciano greatly. On May 6 Ciano noted: "The Duce says that [Ribbentrop] is one of those Germans who mean only trouble for Germany. He speaks of war—war to the left, war to the right—without naming his enemy or defining his objectives. Sometimes he is all for joining forces with Japan and destroying Russia. At other times he wishes to hurl his thunderbolts against France and England. He has often hinted that he would like to take on the United States. All this makes me treat any ideas of his with the greatest caution."

On May 12, 1938, with Franco-Italian negotiations about the Red Sea and Spain hanging fire, Mussolini told Ciano to sound out Berlin on the possibility of an alliance with Germany in which Japan would also be associated. But the negotiations were postponed on Hitler's request.

Hitler seems to have thought that the conversion of the Anti-Comintern Pact into a triple alliance at that time would have more drawbacks than advantages. In Paris and London, such a move would undermine the positions of Daladier and Chamberlain, both of whom, he knew, favoured peace. As for the United States, the inclusion of Japan in such a combination would discourage the isolationist party and make the American Government more likely to seek a closer relationship with France and Britain. Apart from these reasons the Wehrmacht had much to say on the military implications of an Italian alliance (but this was kept from Mussolini). The German military chiefs were deeply divided as to the worth of the Italian armed forces and how much of a liability they might prove. Grand-Admiral Raeder welcomed the prospect of getting help from Mussolini's navy; Colonel-Generals Keitel and Brauchitsch had many reservations about the fighting value of Italy's land forces.

This resulted in a veritable cross-fire of notes, all of them friendly, but all dilatory. Agreement seemed impossible.

Immediately after the Munich conference, Ribbentrop suggested a triple alliance to Ciano, claiming that this would be "the greatest thing in the world". But Ciano did not share Ribbentrop's facile enthusiasm; he noted coldly: "I think that we will study this very carefully and then put it aside for a while."

Hitler had therefore changed his tune since May. He justified this by referring to two new factors which the Sudetenland crisis had made apparent. Before Munich the position of the French and British Governments had been so secure that even the conclusion of a triple alliance would not have endangered them seriously. Second, on sensing the threat of war the

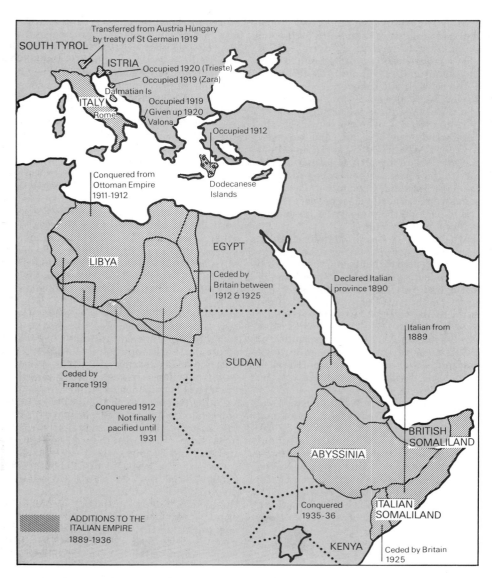

SOUTH TYROL

Transferred from Austria Hungary
by treaty of St Germain 1919

ISTRIA

Occupied 1920 (Trieste)

Occupied 1919 (Zara)

Dalmatian Is

ITALY
Rome

Occupied 1919
Given up 1920
Valona

Occupied 1912

Conquered from
Ottoman Empire
1911-1912

Dodecanese
Islands

EGYPT

LIBYA

Ceded by
Britain between
1912 & 1925

Declared Italian
province 1890

Italian from
1889

Ceded by
France 1919

SUDAN

Conquered 1912
Not finally
pacified until
1931

BRITISH
SOMALILAND

ABYSSINIA

ADDITIONS TO THE
ITALIAN EMPIRE
1889-1936

Conquered
1935-36

ITALIAN
SOMALILAND

KENYA

Ceded by Britain
1925

*The Italian empire in Africa and
the Mediterranean in 1936.*

United States had shown every sign of a desire for isolation. This feeling would only be strengthened if Japan should be involved by treaty in any new conflict provoked by Germany or Italy.

On October 28 Ribbentrop—"vain, shallow, and boastful", as Ciano later described him—visited Mussolini and Ciano and explained that war with the Western democracies must be considered inevitable within the next three or four years. But the Fascist leaders, while listening politely, managed to avoid giving a straight reply. Both Ciano and Mussolini had different—not to say completely opposing—reasons for this. On the evening of the audience Ciano noted: "[Ribbentrop] has war on the brain. He wants war—*his* war. He has no precise plan, or at least he does not say that he has. He does not name his enemy nor define his objectives. Yet he wants war in three or four years. I was as reserved as possible, but I gave him to understand that we have many other problems which need solving, and different conceptions of the organisation and future of international life."

For his part Mussolini assured Ribbentrop that he was keen to conclude such an alliance, but that he felt the time was not yet ripe. It would be necessary beforehand to get the bulk of the Italian population enthusiastic about the scheme. He also added that Nazi Germany's anti-Catholic policies had considerably damaged the goodwill of the Italian people towards Germany. But above everything else the defensive nature of the alliance suggested by Ribbentrop did not satisfy Mussolini. There was absolutely no need, said Mussolini, for an alliance of this nature. "No one would dream of attacking the totalitarian states. We wish, for our part, to change the map of the world. To do that we need to settle objectives and conquests. We Italians already know where we must go."

Ribbentrop agreed heartily with all this, which certainly suited him better than the reserved attitude of Ciano, but the talks halted there for the time being. Two months later, Mussolini revised his attitude again. Returning to Rome for the New Year, he explained to Ciano that the current course of events no longer justified the reservations which he had expressed on October 28 as to when it would be possible to convert the Axis relationship into a military pact.

The similar arrangement which existed (according to Mussolini) between Britain and France, the "bellicose" attitude of the French Government, not to mention the rearmament of the United States, evidently intended to assist the Western democracies—all these made the forming of an alliance capable of withstanding any possible coalition both necessary and urgent. In any case, the current tension between France and Italy had made the idea of an alliance with the Third Reich far more popular in Italy.

The following day Ciano wrote to Ribbentrop in this vein, for Mussolini wanted to sign the treaty in the first ten days of January. But the third member of the projected alliance—Japan—had other ideas. On September 26, 1938, Japan's Prime Minister, Prince Konoye, had dismissed General Ugaki from his post as Foreign Minister. After holding the office himself for several months, Konoye gave the Foreign Ministry to Baron Hiranuma on February 4, 1939. And this change of ministers in Tokyo put the brake on Japan's swing in favour of the Axis.

Baron Hiranuma did not reject out of hand the idea of converting the Anti-Comintern Pact into a military alliance. He had grave reservations, however, as to whether or not Japan should involve herself in the various quarrels of Italy and Germany on the other side of the world. Ambassadors Toshio Shiratori in Rome, and General Hiroshi Oshima in Berlin, both encouraged Hiranuma in his scepticism.

The result was a series of extremely delicate negotiations which took up the first three months of 1939. To cut a long story short, Japan declined to join the proposed alliance because of the Italo-German insistence on excluding France and Britain. But the Japanese formula, directed solely against the Soviet Union, was not attractive to Italy and Germany. Italy felt absolutely no threat to herself from Moscow; nor did Germany, now that details of the chaos caused in the Red Army by Stalin's purges were beginning to reach the West. Neither Germany nor Italy were at all inclined to get involved in a full-scale war over some remote incident in Japanese Manchuria or eastern Siberia.

However, negotiations between Rome and Berlin continued. On April 5–6, the German and Italian Chiefs-of-Staff, Colonel-General Keitel and General Alberto Pariani, met at Innsbruck. Both agreed that war between the totalitarian powers and the Western democracies was inevitable, although it would probably not come for three or four years. But it is noteworthy that while Pariani said nothing to Keitel about Mussolini's plans to attack Albania, Keitel said nothing to Pariani about Hitler's plans to attack Poland.

Here it was already, then: the fatal pattern of "parallel war" which was to bedevil the war efforts of the two Axis powers in the years ahead, with Italy and Germany pursuing their different objectives in the Mediterranean and European theatres.

But the record of the Keitel-Pariani talks reveals another inconsistency which was just as serious for the Axis.

When Keitel expressed the hope that it would be possible to localise the Italo-French conflict which seemed likely to break out at any moment, Pariani replied grandly that if this happened all Italy would ask of her German partner would be supplies of raw materials and weapons. However, three weeks later, on April 29, Mussolini declared himself "extremely annoyed" with the woeful lack of readiness in the Italian Army and Air Force.

Such was Mussolini's anger that Ciano added some comments of his own. "The military make great play with a lot of names. They multiply the number of divisions, but in reality these are so small that they scarcely have more than the strength of regiments. The depôts are short of ammunition. Our artillery is obsolete. Our anti-aircraft and anti-tank guns are totally inadequate. There has been a good deal of bluffing in the military sphere, and even the Duce has been deceived – a tragic bluff. We will not talk about the Air Force. Valle [Air Force Chief-of-Staff and Under-Secretary of State for the Air] states that there are 3,006 first-line aircraft, while the Navy information service says that there are only 982. A gross exaggeration..." Nor were the leaders of Germany's armed forces in ignorance of this lack of Italian preparedness for war.

Returning to the subject on May 2, Ciano did not hesitate to blame Mussolini, writing: "But what is the Duce doing? His attention seems to be directed mostly to matters of drill: there is trouble if the 'present arms' is badly performed, or if an officer does not know how to do the goose-step, but he seems little concerned about the real weaknesses, of which he is certainly very well aware. In spite of my formal charges in connection with the results of the investigations by Cavagnari [Under-Secretary of State and Chief-of-Staff for the Navy] into the efficiency of our Air Force he has done nothing, absolutely nothing; and today in his conversation with Cavagnari he did not mention the matter. Why? Does he fear the truth so much that he is unwilling to listen?"

But Mussolini was not so blind to the facts as Ciano feared. Without abandoning the idea of a military alliance with the Third Reich, he tried to arrange matters so that it would not come into effect as far as Italy was concerned until 1943. This was why, when Ciano was preparing to meet Ribbentrop at Lake Como on May 6, Mussolini had told him to state the following considerations:

"It is my firm belief that the two European Axis powers need a period of peace of at least three years. It will be only after 1943 that a war programme will have a really good chance of success. Italy needs such a period of peace for the following reasons:
1. To complete the military organisation of Libya and Albania, pacify Abyssinia, and to form from the latter an army of 500,000 men;

2. To build and fit out six new battleships;
3. To up-date our medium and heavy artillery;
4. To thwart, by achieving self-sufficiency, the attempts of the colonial democracies to blockade us;
5. To celebrate the 1942 Exhibition, commemorating the 20th anniversary of the Fascist Régime, which will bring in much hard currency;
6. To bring home the Italians working in France – a very serious problem from both the military and moral points of view;
7. To complete the transfer, which has already begun, of many war industries from the Po Valley to southern Italy; and
8. To strengthen the ties not only between our two governments but between our peoples. A reconciliation between the Nazi Party and the German Catholic Church, as well as the Vatican, would be of great value here.

"For all these reasons, although convinced that the outcome is inevitable, Fascist Italy does not want a premature European war. It may be, too, that in three years Japan will have concluded her war in China."

In the end Ciano met Ribbentrop at Milan, not Como. As certain Parisian newspapers had hinted that Ribbentrop would not be well received in the Lombard capital, Mussolini demanded that the last conference before the signing of the alliance must be held there. During the discussions on May 6–7, Ciano was favourably impressed by the "pleasant restraint" which Ribbentrop displayed on this occasion. An agreement was reached on a military alliance between the two Axis powers, and after a telephone call from Mussolini on the evening of the 6th it was decided, after Hitler had given his consent, to announce the alliance to the press.

At this historic meeting, Ribbentrop declared his belief that peace would last for another four or five years. This, he added, would allow Germany to build up her army to full strength and to complete the construction of a fleet of heavy warships and so decrease Allied supremacy at sea.

When Ciano got on to the subject of the German-Polish problem, Ribbentrop refused to be drawn. While remaining ready to take "the very hardest line" if Warsaw chose to try a political offensive, he could affirm that the intentions of the Reich were to let the question alone without making any new offers, but without closing the door on negotiations.

"The programme," noted Ciano, "is not one of taking the initiative: time is on Germany's side. There are signs that people in France and Britain are getting tired of the Polish problem, and it is certain that in a few months not a Frenchman nor an Englishman will march to Poland's aid."

But on April 13, 1939, Hitler had approved *Fall Weiss* ("Case White") – a conditional plan for the military destruction of Poland. As in 1938 Hitler was preparing for an attack if necessary, while hoping that his enemies' nerve would crack and

give him conquest without war.

On May 13 Ciano read the draft of the pact for the first time. "I have never read such a pact," he noted. "It contains some real dynamite."

Ciano was right. In the preamble, the two peoples affirmed their resolution to stand shoulder to shoulder with combined forces "for the realisation [*Verwirklichung*] of their living space and the maintenance of peace". But even more serious was the fact that the reason for the alliance, described in Article 3 of the Pact, contained none of the diplomatic precautions in current use to shield either party from an obligation to aid the other if either of them resorted to unprovoked aggression.

It stated, quite clearly: "If the desires and hopes of one of the contracting powers leads it into war with another power or number of powers, the other contracting power will immediately come to its partner's aid with its full military strength, on land, on sea, and in the air." The Pact, in short, bound Italy to consider every power in the world as a possible enemy – even traditional allies such as Great Britain.

If Ciano raised no objection to Article 3, it could well have been because its wording guaranteed reciprocal aid from Germany in the event of possible Italian ventures against Greece or Tunisia. The obligation for mutual consultation between the two powers, laid down in Articles 1 and 2, must also have appeared to Ciano as sufficient guarantee – one gentleman's pledge to another.

However, Ciano did ask for three amendments to be made to the drafts:
1. The insertion into the preamble of a phrase defining the Brenner Pass as the Italo-German frontier (this clause would then clearly define the Alto Adige or South Tyrol as Italian territory);
2. The replacement of the sabre-rattling word "realisation" of living space with the word "safeguarding" [*Sicherung*];
3. The limitation of the treaty to a period of ten years.

There was no objection to these modifications, and Ciano duly set out for Berlin. When Ribbentrop met Ciano's train on May 21, he repeated to Ciano that no change had been made to the decisions reached in Milan, and he stressed that "Germany's intention is still to assure a period of peace of at least three years".

On the following day, seated at Hitler's right hand, Ciano signed the document which Berlin and Rome flamboyantly entitled the "Pact of Steel". Ciano would have been disenchanted, however, if he could have guessed that within 24 hours Hitler would make a mockery of the Pact by talking of war that very year.

Ciano was warmly congratulated for the signing of the Pact, and King Victor Emmanuel of Italy emerged from his habitual reserve so far as to send him a telegram. Later, in an audience with Ciano, the King told him: "I have not sent a telegram to a minister since 1900. I thought that to break this tradition would prove to you how sincere my feelings are."

Chapter 3
The Final Manoeuvrings

The Pact of Steel was not 48 hours old before Hitler declared his intention of seizing the first available opportunity of settling matters with Poland once and for all. On May 23 he presided over a conference at the New Chancellery in which he addressed the Wehrmacht commanders-in-chief and chiefs-of-staff. It was at this meeting that Hitler directed a vitriolic outburst against Poland to his conservative generals who felt that his ideas were too risky.

Hitler began with a review of the current political situation and how he believed future events should be directed. The agenda had four basic points:
1. An analysis of the current political and military situation in Europe;
2. Objectives for the Wehrmacht, given this situation;
3. The probable consequences for the Wehrmacht because of these objectives;
4. The precautions to be taken to keep all political decisions and military preparations secret, as this was considered an essential condition for success.

Poland was defined as Germany's Public Enemy Number One:

"The political and national unification of the German people is generally completed, with some small exceptions. Further successes can no longer be attained without bloodshed . . .

"The settling of our frontiers is a matter of military importance. The Pole is not a secondary enemy . . .

"Poland will always side with our enemies. Despite a treaty of friendship, it has always been part of Poland's intentions to turn every possible circumstance against us . . .

"Danzig is not the objective of the dispute at all. We must enlarge our living space in the East . . ."

Poland, in fact, had to be destroyed—for "living space", and to avoid the probability of her joining a hostile alliance encircling Germany. The long-term objective was the destruction of France and Great Britain, to free Germany forever from the menace of external blockade.

Like the Hossbach Memorandum of November 5, 1937, Hitler's address of May 23 was not a specific blueprint for war but an exposition of some of his thoughts on German-Polish relations.

By the spring of 1939 the big question was the attitude of Soviet Russia. If it had come to war in 1938, the Czechs would have counted on holding out long enough for help to reach them from the French and from the Russians. When Poland became the object of German ambitions after the Prague coup in March 1939, Moscow's position became more important than ever.

Hitler in full flood in the Reichstag (opposite top). A parade of the Condor Legion, the German force that had fought for Franco (opposite bottom).

At first it seemed that the Soviet Union would back the cause of the Western powers. This was certainly the intention of the Soviet Foreign Commissar, Maxim Litvinov, whose policy was to contain Hitler by collective action. Three days after the Prague coup, on March 18, Litvinov proposed a six-power combination—France, Great Britain, Poland, Soviet Russia, Rumania, and Turkey—to prevent any future aggression on the part of Germany. Chamberlain, however, rejected this suggestion as "premature".

On March 23 Hitler blackmailed Lithuania into surrendering Memel and its hinterland, and Litvinov continued to press for an anti-German coalition. He cannot have been helped by Chamberlain's unilateral guarantee to Poland on March 31, which was easy to interpret as an indication that Britain would prefer an alliance with Poland to one with Soviet Russia. Litvinov made his last bid for an anti-German coalition on April 16, when he received the British Ambassador in Moscow and proposed an Anglo-Franco-Soviet mutual-assistance pact. This, too, was rejected. And on May 3 came the news that Litvinov, who had held the position since 1930, had been replaced by Vyacheslav Molotov. It was a deeply significant move; as Germany's representative in Moscow reported to Berlin: ". . . it seems that his dismissal must be due to a spontaneous decision by Stalin . . . At the last Party Congress Stalin urged caution lest the Soviet Union be dragged into conflicts. Molotov, who is not a Jew, has the reputation of being the 'most intimate friend and closest collaborator' of Stalin. His appointment is obviously intended to provide a guarantee that foreign policy will be conducted strictly on lines laid down by Stalin."

With the Western powers vacillating again, and with this startling shift in the official outlook in Soviet foreign policy, there was every chance that Hitler could achieve a *rapprochement* with the Soviet Union. That he did so was the result not only of his own opportunism but of the co-operation of the Soviet Government itself.

The replacement of Litvinov by Molotov did not cause any immediate reversal of Moscow's attitude. Stalin still wanted to reach agreement with Britain and France—but only on equal terms. It soon became apparent that the prospects of such a coalition were jeopardised by Poland's unwillingness to conclude a mutual defence pact with Soviet Russia. Added to this was Chamberlain's obvious preference for a direct alliance with Poland. In fact, Stalin's position was simple. He had to safeguard Soviet Russia from the consequences of a probable German attack on Poland, but he was not prepared to enter into any agreement with the Western powers without receiving full co-operation from them.

Molotov asked for a representative of the British Government to go to Moscow for talks. But whereas Chamberlain had had no hesitation in flying to Germany in person for meetings with Hitler, he considered it sufficient now to send William Strang, an able official but one virtually unknown outside the British Foreign Office. Strang arrived in Moscow in the middle of June. Not surprisingly, Stalin and Molotov were put out at having to deal with only an official; not surprisingly, either, the talks got nowhere, and on July 23 Molotov proposed that Britain and France send a military mission to Russia.

This duly arrived, but in an extremely leisurely fashion. The mission—with Admiral Sir Reginald Drax representing Britain and General Joseph Doumenc France—travelled by ship to Leningrad and only arrived in Moscow on August 11. Here, again, was an apparent affront. Before their arrival neither representative was well known in Moscow. More than this, Drax had not only been given no powers to negotiate, but also told to "go very slowly with the military negotiations, watching the progress of the political negotiations". The Soviet verdict, in the official *History of the Great Patriotic War*, was severe: "When B. M. Shaposhnikov [Red Army Chief of the General Staff] said that the Soviet Union was ready to make available against the aggressor 120 infantry divisions, 16 cavalry divisions, 5,000 medium and heavy guns, 9,000 to 10,000 tanks, and 5,000 to 5,500 bomber and fighter planes, General Heywood, a member of the British Mission, talked about one mechanised and five infantry divisions. This in itself was enough to suggest a frivolous British attitude to the talks with the Soviet Union."

The Soviet leaders did not hide their displeasure at this apparently casual approach, and Drax was obliged to contact London and request full credentials. But by the time these arrived, on August 21, the Germans had seized their chance.

It seemed unbelievable to Hitler and Ribbentrop that the Western powers would fritter away their chances of bringing the Soviet Union into their camp, but they were swift to seize their opportunity and did not make the same mistakes as Chamberlain and Daladier. Even before the dismissal of Litvinov, there had been discussions on the prospects of improving German-Soviet relations, and these continued throughout May, June, and July with the balance swinging more and more in favour of the Germans. Ribbentrop stressed that there were "no differences" between Berlin and Moscow which could not be solved easily. He expressed his desire to reach first an economic and later a political agreement with the Soviet Union, and stated that he was willing to go to Moscow in person for discussions. Here was an attitude very different from that displayed by Britain and France—

25

Young Danzigers proclaim their pro-Nazi sympathies in a carefully posed alfresco rally.

and Stalin welcomed it eagerly.

By the middle of August the military talks between the Russian and the French and British missions had reached a crux: would Poland permit troops to operate on her territory in the event of war with Germany in which Soviet Russia would side with Poland, Britain, and France? Here everything turned on Beck's deeply-rooted anti-Russian bias. Bonnet urged him to give way on this point, but Beck refused. And on August 20, the day of the Polish refusal, Marshal Edward Rydz-Smigly, the Polish Commander-in-Chief, made the fatal statement which confirmed every Russian suspicion that the Western powers were insincere: "With the Germans we would risk losing our liberty. With the Russians we would lose our soul." It was now too late for France and Britain to conclude an agreement with Russia, but such was Daladier's desire for one that on the next day he sent a telegram to the members of the French mission in Moscow authorising them to sign a military agreement, presumably as the British Ambassador in Warsaw had managed to obtain a preliminary agreement from the Polish Government. There is no proof for this, but in any case Voroshilov replied that the French had no right to conclude an agreement for another sovereign nation. In fact, Polish concurrence was not sought until later.

Soviet Russia had, in fact, taken the easy way out without waiting for Poland's refusal. Churchill's memoirs contain an interesting account of Russia's attitude in 1939, given in Stalin's own words. When Churchill visited Moscow in August 1942, Stalin had explained to him how things had been in 1939. " 'We formed the opinion,' said Stalin, 'that the British and French Governments were not resolved to go to war if Poland were attacked, but that they hoped the diplomatic line-up of Great Britain, France, and Russia would deter Hitler. We were sure it would not.'

" 'How many divisions,' Stalin had asked, 'will France send against Germany on mobilisation?' The answer was, 'About a hundred.' He then asked, 'How many will England send?' The answer was, 'Two, and two later.' 'Ah, two, and two later,' Stalin had repeated. 'Do you know,' he asked, 'how many divisions we shall have to put on the Russian front if we go to war with Germany?' There was a pause. 'More than three hundred.' "

Those who support Stalin's decisions in 1939 have argued that Hitler bullied Stalin into signing the Nazi-Soviet Non-Aggression Pact of August 1939 with a tacit ultimatum, implying that Soviet Russia would be considered an enemy of Germany if events should result in a military showdown with Poland. But there is no evidence of this in Hitler's telegram to Stalin on August 20. Its message is clear: Hitler did not state that the Soviet Union would be involved in Germany's quarrel with Poland –he did not blackmail Stalin at all. In Paragraph 5 of the telegram, Hitler announced that Germany's march on Poland could be provoked at any time: "The tension between Poland and Germany has become intolerable, and Poland's current attitude means that a crisis may arise any day. Faced with such arrogance, Germany

has already decided to safeguard the interests of the Reich with every resource at her disposal."

Hitler's telegram concluded: "In my opinion, it is desirable, in view of the intention of the two states to enter into a new relationship, not to lose any time. For this reason I would like you to talk to my Foreign Minister again on Tuesday, August 22, or at the latest on the 23rd. The Reich Foreign Minister will have full and extraordinary powers to reach agreement on a non-aggression pact."

Where is the threat? There is none. Not even Hitler's conversation with Generals Halder and von Brauchitsch on August 14, faithfully recorded by Halder, reveals any hint of putting pressure on Stalin.

Paradoxical as it may seem, then, Stalin and Molotov did not yield to any pressure from Hitler and Ribbentrop. On the contrary, it was the latter who followed the line laid down by Moscow. As early as May 20, Molotov had told Count Friedrich von der Schulenburg, the German Ambassador in Moscow, that it would be impossible for the Soviet Union to embark on economic negotiations with Germany until some measure of "political understanding" had been reached.

Here, in fact, was the origin of the Non-Aggression Pact of August 23. Stalin did not grant Hitler the benefit of Russia's benevolent neutrality without imposing a final condition. On August 19, Molotov had read to Schulenburg a draft, five-article pact, containing the provision that "the present pact shall be valid only if a special protocol is signed simultaneously covering the points in which the High Contracting Parties are interested in the field of foreign policy. This protocol must be an integral part of the pact."

Hitler granted this request without even discussing it, and no more obstacles remained. Stalin's telegram inviting Ribbentrop to Moscow to sign the pact arrived on the 21st. Albert Speer remembers: "During dinner a note was handed to Hitler. He read it through quickly, stared for a moment, turned red with emotion, and then banged on the table, making the glasses rattle. In a high-pitched voice he exclaimed: 'I've got them! I've got them!'" Ribbentrop flew to Moscow on the 23rd and signed both the Pact and Protocol in an atmosphere of great cordiality. The Pact itself was a conventional statement of non-aggression, but the text of the Protocol, which was revealed only in 1948, shows it for what it was: a cynical agreement between two ruthless exponents of *realpolitik*.

Soviet leaders have stated that the Pact was not in conflict with other treaties already signed by the Soviet Union, but in fact the Russo-Polish Non-Aggression Pact of 1932 stipulated that in the event of one of the parties being attacked by a third party, the other was to remain neutral.

The conditions of the secret Protocol speak for themselves:

"On the occasion of the signature of the Non-Aggression Pact between the German Reich and the Union of Soviet Socialist Republics the undersigned plenipotentiaries of each of the two parties discussed in strictly confidential conversations the question of the boundary of their respective spheres of influence in Eastern Europe. These conversations led to the following conclusions:

1. In the event of a territorial and political rearrangement in the areas belonging to the Baltic States (Finland, Estonia, Latvia, and Lithuania) the northern boundary of Lithuania shall represent the boundary between the spheres of interest of Germany and the U.S.S.R.
2. In the event of territorial and political rearrangement of the areas belonging to the Polish State, the spheres of influence of Germany and the U.S.S.R. shall be bounded approximately by the line of the Narew, Vistula, and San rivers.

   The question of whether the interests of both parties make desirable the maintenance of an independent Polish state and how such a state should be bounded can only be definitely determined in the course of further political developments. In any event both Governments will resolve this question by means of friendly agreement.
3. With regard to South-Eastern Europe attention is called by the Soviet side to its interests in Bessarabia. The German side declares its complete political disinterestedness in these areas.
4. This Protocol shall be treated by both Parties as strictly secret."

Since August 16, there had been an extraordinary contrast between the haste shown by the Germans and the temporising attitude of the Russians. This, combined with the date of the agreement, August 23, supports the argument that Stalin and Molotov were setting the pace in the negotiations. Ribbentrop was in Moscow for only 25 hours, and he signed the Pact within hours of touching down at the airport. In those 25 hours he had also had to squeeze in two hasty meals at the German Embassy and his journeys to and from the Kremlin – not to mention the impromptu celebrations and toast-drinkings after the ceremony and a brief sleep on the night of August 23–24 before his departure at 1325 hours on the 24th. Thus there was little time to discuss last-minute amendments to the draft pact (such as Stalin's inquiry as to whether or not the

Frequently at daggers drawn: Hitler and Keitel confer with Army C.-in-C. Brauchitsch (extreme right) and his chief-of-staff, Halder.

ports of Windau and Libau would fall within the Russian sphere of influence). Ribbentrop must therefore have signed the Pact as it stood. There was, of course, a perfectly good reason why Ribbentrop's hands were tied: Hitler had brought forward the date for the invasion of Poland and fixed it for dawn on the 26th, thus giving Ribbentrop no time to waste.

When Stalin and Molotov agreed to meet Ribbentrop on the 23rd, did they in fact know how compliant he would be because of the time factor? More important, was Hitler trapped into acting more in the interests of the Soviet Union than of Germany?

On September 4–the fourth day after Germany had taken the plunge and attacked Poland–Schulenburg, on Ribbentrop's instructions, asked Molotov:
"1. Would the U.S.S.R. object if, to hasten the destruction of the Polish Army, the Wehrmacht were to conduct operations in the Soviet sphere of influence?
2. Would the U.S.S.R. not consider it desirable to send Russian forces in good time into the zone of influence defined for the U.S.S.R. in Polish territory?"
The following day Molotov sent Ribbentrop his telegrammed reply, via Schulenburg. "We agree with you on the absolute necessity for us to take concrete action. We feel, however, that the moment for this has not yet come. We may be proved wrong, but we feel that excessive haste may prejudice our interests by helping to unite our adversaries. We believe that as operations develop one or both of our two powers may well be momentarily obliged to cross the demarcation line between our respective spheres of influence. But considerations of this nature must not prevent the strict execution of the envisaged plan."

This document suggests that during the discussions on August 23 a plan was adopted by mutual agreement which implied the Soviet Union taking "concrete action" against Poland. All this was in complete contrast with Molotov's statements on the evening of August 22, when he had told the French Ambassador "that the fundamental policy of the U.S.S.R. remains unchanged: to keep the peace and resist aggression. The Soviet Government, as France's representative in Moscow can attest, has already signed several non-aggression pacts, including one with Poland. In agreeing to negotiate with Germany, the U.S.S.R. has no intention of departing from this essentially peaceful attitude."

Such was Soviet Russia's claim, and since then Soviet historians have argued that in dealing with Hitler, Stalin was trying to buy time to reorganise and re-equip his armies. But this argument overlooks the 136 infantry and cavalry divisions, the 5,000 medium and heavy guns, the 9,000 to 10,000 tanks, and the 5,000 to 5,500 aircraft which Voroshilov and Shaposhnikov had described to General Doumenc and Admiral Drax (unless the figures were grossly inflated). In any case, if Russia were so weak, her leaders had brought her to the brink of destruction and defeat with their lack of foresight. On September 1, 1939, a coalition of the Soviet Union, Poland, France, and Britain could have unleashed 270 divisions against Germany's 108.

On June 22, 1941, the German Army totalled 208 divisions, of which 55 were tied down in secondary theatres. But by then the Wehrmacht had received the aid of 50 satellite divisions and brigades, and could therefore throw 203 divisions against the Russian 176.

On August 22, when Stalin had agreed to Ribbentrop's visit to Moscow, Hitler called a meeting, at the Berghof, of the Wehrmacht's senior commanders, to brief them on the current situation, give them their orders, and try to instill in them some of his "savage resolution". Even in these solemn, if not tragic, circumstances there was a comic element: Göring. His appearance on this occasion made a vivid impression on General Erich von Manstein, who recalled it in detail afterwards. "Over a white, open-necked shirt he wore a green, sleeveless leather jerkin with big yellow leather buttons. He wore grey shorts, and long grey stockings strained over his massive calves. Enormous shoes added to the frivolous appearance of his costume. But most splendid of all was a big red and gold belt draped round his belly, from which hung a hunting-knife in a scabbard of red leather ornamented with gold."

At this meeting, notes were taken by Admiral Hermann Böhm, Fleet-Commander, which preserved the essential points made by Hitler in his harangue. Hitler started by describing the key personalities whose attitudes favoured Germany and made it inadvisable for Germany to delay any longer in settling accounts with Poland. First came Hitler himself. "He had united the German people. He possessed a measure of confidence and a weight of authority which any successor would find difficult to match. But at any moment he could be disposed of by an enemy bullet, mental failure, or disease. As far as the solution of the problems of the German people was concerned, his life was a factor of the highest importance."

After Hitler himself, Mussolini. "With Italy treaties did not matter, but personalities. Mussolini assured the maintenance of the alliance; although one had doubts about what he might do, his achievements spoke for themselves. Mussolini was a man without nerves. If proof was wanted, one had only to think of Abyssinia."

Franco, too, was an important man. Admittedly, all Hitler wanted from Spain was a benevolent neutrality, but Hitler judged that Franco alone was strong enough to resist partisan influences from within Spain.

As far as the Reich's enemies were concerned, it was Germany's good fortune that the men holding their reins of power were mediocre vacillators rather than leaders of a stature comparable with Hitler's own. Moreover, France and Britain would find themselves seriously hampered by other factors in bringing any effective help to Poland during the attack which was being prepared and which would soon pour over her borders.

In the Far East, Great Britain was neutralised by Japan. In the Mediterranean, after the conquest of Albania, she was held in check by Italy, as was France. The R.A.F.'s manpower was only a third of the Luftwaffe's. As for the British land forces, the five or six divisions (if that) which Britain could put into the field were a drop in the ocean. From all these points Hitler found himself bound to conclude: "It seems to me impossible that any responsible British statesman dare, under these conditions, accept the risks of open warfare."

Nor was France any better off. The deficiencies of her armaments and the lack of sufficient recruits of military age meant that she would be unable to endure the cost of a long-term war. It was unlikely that France would hurl her army, accustomed as it was to the strategy of defending the Maginot Line, against the strong-points of the Siegfried Line; without any guarantee of success, the French High Command would have to risk 250,000 men in an operation of this nature. Neither Paris nor London, argued Hitler, would dream of invading Germany via neutral territory. "Switzerland would fire at any power who violated her neutrality. Holland would observe a strict neutrality for fear that Japan, should she become involved, would threaten the Dutch colonies in the Far East. Belgium would also remain strictly neutral: in World War I she had the searing experience of acting as the principal battle-ground without gaining any profit whatsoever." All these considerations made up Hitler's thesis that "the probability of the Western powers intervening in the conflict is a small one".

It was true, Hitler continued, that Great Britain and France could counter the invasion of Poland by recalling their ambassadors from Berlin and blockading Germany. But this possibility, which he had already discussed with Generals von Brauchitsch and Halder on August 14, would be countered by the non-aggression pact which was to be signed the following day in Moscow. Germany, in fact, could now prepare for the conflict without having to plan for a two-front war. According to a document produced in evidence at Nuremberg after the war, the authenticity of which has been questioned, Hitler exclaimed: "I have struck from the hands of the West the weapon which Soviet help would have given them. The possibility now exists of inflicting a mortal blow on Poland. Everything now shows that the path is open for the soldier," and he added: "My only fear is that some *schweinehund* will make a proposal for mediation!"

It is clear that Hitler's words were very favourably received by the generals and admirals present. The conclusion of the non-aggression pact seemed a master-stroke, saving Germany from the danger of a war on two fronts which had confronted Kaiser Wilhelm II some 25 years before. None of them doubted that Poland could be defeated in 15 days or three weeks, provided that France and Great Britain did not intervene. In which case, surely the Western democracies would once again resign themselves to a *fait accompli*?

Although Hitler may have been posturing for his generals' benefit, he made the mistake of thinking that his enemies would see things in the same light. From this mistake would come the war, first European and later world-wide, which Hitler believed had been made impossible by the German-Soviet Non-Aggression Pact.

In Paris, the news of the imminent conclusion of the pact, which had come as a great surprise, caused Bonnet, with Daladier's consent, to call a meeting of the Committee of National Defence on August 23. Those present included the Ministers, the Chief-of-Staff for National Defence (General Maurice Gamelin), the C.-in-C., French Navy (Admiral Jean Darlan), the C.-in-C., *Armée de l'Air* or French Air Force (General Joseph Vuillemin), the Army and Air Force Chiefs-of-Staff (Colson and Têtu), and the Secretary-General to the War Office (Jacomet).

Given the new circumstance of the Moscow Pact, for which Poland was partially responsible, it had to be decided whether or not France should revise her relations with her allies in Eastern and South-Eastern Europe. In Daladier's opinion, the need for this decision led to the following questions:

"1. Could France, without intervening, passively accept the removal from the map of Europe of Poland and Rumania, or of one of these powers?

2. What means were at France's disposal to prevent this?

3. What measures should be taken?"

The first question being essentially a military one, it fell to Gamelin to reply, and his view was simple. "Asked what sort of resistance Poland and Rumania would be able to put up, he said that he expected Poland to make an honourable resistance which would tie down the main armies of Germany, preventing them from turning against us until spring, by which time England would be at our side."

When questioned as to Rumania's powers of resistance, Gamelin was not able to be so precise. This would depend on the attitudes which Yugoslavia and Hungary adopted in the event of war. Gamelin insisted, however, on the importance of Italy's continued neutrality, in which he was energetically supported by Admiral Darlan.

Would it be necessary, in fact, for France to agree to another compromise in order to gain the time which might be needed to confront Germany on better terms? The Committee of National Defence said no, and elaborated its reason: "After much discussion, it is clear that if we will be stronger in a few months, Germany will be as well, especially as she will have all the resources of Poland and Rumania at her disposal."

In consequence, France had no choice. "The only solution to be considered is that of keeping our agreements with regard to Poland, despite the fact that they were made before the negotiations with the U.S.S.R." As for France's military readiness, Air Minister Guy La Chambre showed himself wildly optimistic, both about France's large-scale production of modern fighters and about the R.A.F.'s capacity to carry out "massive bombing raids" on North Germany. He was also confident in the French Air Force's ability to co-operate with the ground forces. The Navy was ready, Admiral Darlan declared; this was perfectly true. And so, said Gamelin, was the Army.

Gamelin has often been blamed for making erroneous claims about the French Army's efficiency at the outbreak of war in 1939. This accusation, he stated later, is a misleading interpretation of what he actually said on August 23: he was only stating that the mechanism for mobilisation and troop concentration was ready. And he added: "A modern army is never ready. Neither the French Army nor the German Army was ready in 1914... In 1939 Germany was ready to attack Poland: she was not ready to attack France. In 1940 she was not ready to attack England. On the eve of battle you rarely have all the *matériel* you asked for." What is more, Gamelin emphasised constantly during the meeting that France could put only 120 divisions into the field against Germany's 200.

Should Gamelin carry the blame for having misled the French Government as to the fighting efficiency of the Army? All the documents made available in 1945 show that the Committee of National Defence was not mistaken in its conclusions on August 23, 1939, and that Hitler's chances would have been much greater in 1943 or 1944 than in 1939.

What would Britain's reaction have been if the French Government and its military advisers had reached a different decision? Relations between Paris and London remained excellent–but there can be no doubt that they would not have survived a French suggestion for another Munich. Soviet Russia's ill-judged adherence to the Reich made absolutely no difference to the resolution of the British Government, Parliament, and public.

On August 25 Lord Halifax, British Foreign Secretary, and Count Edward Raczyński, Ambassador Extraordinary and Plenipotentiary of the Polish Republic in London, signed a Mutal Assistance

The flamboyant Göring, whose Luftwaffe would soon dominate Europe's skies.

General Gamelin (centre) with General Kaspryzcki (right), Polish War Minister, at manoeuvres in May 1939.

Pact. Article 1 of this agreement defined the basis of agreement between the two powers: "If one of the contracting Parties finds itself engaged in hostilities with a European power as a result of aggression by that power, the other contracting Party will give immediate help to the Party engaged in hostilities with every source in its power." The possibility of this treaty, which had been decided upon as early as April 1939, had been one of the major stumbling blocks in the negotiations between the Western powers and the Soviet Union during the summer of 1939.

Article 2 covered the eventuality of indirect aggression: Britain undertook to take up arms if Poland were obliged to use force to counter any action which represented an indirect threat to her independence (such as Danzig). But Poland undertook the same obligation if Britain should have to go to war to safeguard the independence or neutrality of another European state, which meant, although they were not named, the Netherlands, Belgium, and Switzerland.

To last for five years, the Anglo-Polish Treaty of Mutual Assistance, according to its concluding Article 8, came into force from the moment of its signature. A secret protocol, not revealed until much later, specified Germany as the major enemy.

In Berlin, the news of unwonted British firmness in this matter made Hitler very uneasy, although Chamberlain, as early as August 22, had written to Hitler informing him in no uncertain terms that Britain would honour her earlier assurance to Poland. Every argu-

ment which Hitler had put to his generals and admirals at the Berghof on the 22nd had been proved wrong. Informed of the treaty on the afternoon of the 25th, Hitler decided to give himself time to think, and at 1930 hours he gave instructions that O.K.W. be telephoned and ordered to call off the attack on Poland and pull back its troops to the German frontier.

"Y"-Day, as the Germans called it, had been fixed for the morning of August 26, and H-Hour for 0030. At 2030 hours on the 25th, the German army group commanders had been told of the counter-order and had immediately passed it on to their subordinates. But all this took time to reach the front line troops. It was possible to halt most of the troops in the centre, but not on the flanks, where certain patrols were already in action on Polish territory. This led to violent incidents on the frontier of East Prussia and also on the Jablonika Pass, an important point in the Carpathians on the Polish-Slovak frontier, where the *Brandenburg* special operations unit, which had been trained to create "incidents", was operating.

While Great Britain had thrown in her lot with Poland, Ciano was trying to prevent Italy from being dragged into war by the terms of the Pact of Steel. The German-Soviet Non-Aggression Pact had come as a total surprise to the Italians, and the intervention of the Western powers seemed certain to Ciano. This would therefore mean a general war, which Hitler and Ribbentrop had assured him in May would not come about until 1943 or 1944 at the earliest. Considering the sorry state of the Italian Army and Air Force, Ciano believed that it would be folly for Italy to go to war with France and Great Britain, especially

as Germany would be concentrating the majority of her forces against Poland.

Mussolini, on whom so much depended, found it impossible to consider affairs with any detachment or assurance. Ciano's daily record in his Diary shows Mussolini at his worst: hesitant, open to any form of influence, constantly deceived by his generals, bitter against everyone, yielding to his contradictory impulses in misinformed outbursts, and generally trying to play a rôle inconsistent with his poor health. He could find no fault in Ciano's argument that Hitler and Ribbentrop had made a mockery of the Pact of Steel; he knew all the faults in the Italian war machine; and he also knew that it would be impossible to put them right quickly without the raw materials needed. But he believed that while neutrality might be fitting for small nations like Belgium or Switzerland it was unworthy for a great imperial power like Fascist Italy. He also felt that to remain neutral would damage his reputation both at home and abroad.

On August 25, however, Ciano and Mussolini reached a compromise, and Mussolini informed Hitler in the evening that "it would be better if I did not take the *initiative* in military operations in view of the *present* situation of Italian war preparations. Our intervention can, however, take place at once if Germany delivers to us immediately the military supplies and raw materials to resist the attack which the French and English would direct against us."

At the moment that French Ambassador Coulondre left Hitler's presence after handing over the solemn warning of the French Government, Italy's Ambassador, Bernardo Attolico, arrived with Mussolini's message that Italy was not ready for war. (It had been Attolico who had told Coulondre on the 25th that Hitler had made the decision for war, and thus enabled the latter to inform his minister of the fact immediately.) Interpreter Schmidt later recalled that "this letter was a bombshell. Hitler was wounded and deeply shaken by the sudden *volte-face*, which he had not expected. With an icy expression he dismissed Mussolini's representative, telling him that there would be a reply very soon. 'The Italians are behaving just as they did in 1914,' he declared once the door had closed. And the corridors of the Chancellery echoed with unfavourable comments on the disloyal Axis partner.

"General Keitel came in hastily. And a few moments later we heard that the go-ahead for the attack on Poland had been countermanded."

On Berlin's request, the Italians devoted August 26 to drawing up a list of their country's needs. Ciano urged the military chiefs to omit nothing, and they did not fail him. "It's enough to kill a bull, if a bull could read," he noted happily. Nor was he exaggerating.

Italy requested 150 batteries of anti-aircraft guns and an unspecified number of other weapons. The raw materials which Germany was asked to send to Italy – to serve the needs of one year of war – totalled 16,529,800 metric tons. Included in the total were coal, oil fuel, metals for munitions, chemicals for explosives, and substantial amounts of rubber and timber for a multitude of other war purposes.

Ciano estimated that this would take up 17,000 train loads. And Mussolini added a footnote of his own to this prodigious bill: "If these deliveries cannot be guaranteed, it is my duty to tell you that the sacrifices for which I would ask the Italian people could all be in vain, and that in pursuing my own affairs I might compromise yours."

Attolico added to the confusion by making a premeditated *gaffe*. Asked how soon Italy would expect the delivery of these supplies, he told Ribbentrop: "Right away. Before hostilities begin." This earned him a disagreeable reply from Ribbentrop, but it was part of Mussolini's desire to get his personal declaration of insolvency counter-signed by Hitler himself.

This was done in a letter dated August 26, which Ribbentrop read over the telephone to Mackensen in Rome the same day. It declared that Hitler would supply the amounts of timber, coal, steel, and potassium carbonate for which Mussolini had asked. But he could offer only 30 anti-aircraft batteries instead of the 150 which had been requested, and none of the other materials. The letter was couched in the most friendly terms. "In these circumstances," it concluded, "I understand your position, Duce, and I ask you to contribute nothing more than active propaganda and appropriate military demonstrations to the action which I have in mind to contain the English and French forces."

The Reich would benefit, more than anything else, from the silence which until the last minute Italy was to maintain with regard to her intention of limiting herself to a policy of "non-belligerence". Hitler hoped that doubts about Italy's position would prevent Britain and France from rapid counter-moves. But this policy amounted to making Italy the lightning-conductor in this diplomatic atmosphere which crackled with electricity – a rôle which, surreptitiously, Italy would refuse to play. And, despite Hitler's hopes to the contrary, all these fluctuations in Italian policy were known in Paris and London.

Hitler had calculated that the news of the Moscow pact would make Chamberlain, with his preference for peace, drop any further idea of going to war. But even before Ribbentrop had got back from Moscow to Berlin, a personal note from the Prime Minister to the Führer arrived at the Berghof – and dispelled all remaining doubts, stating that Britain would give military aid to Poland in the event of German aggression.

If the German leaders in 1939 thought little of France, they gave much more thought to England. "Corporal Hitler" himself, a veteran of the Western Front in World War I, respected the cold tenacity of the British and their willingness to

fight on until final victory was won. He could not shrug off the conclusion of Chamberlain's letter: "It would be a dangerous illusion to think that a war, once begun, could be brought to a rapid end, even if success were won on one of the many fronts to which it would spread."

Hitler's main concern now was to neutralise the British, who, he believed, had persuaded the French to model their attitude on that of London. As Hitler and Ribbentrop saw it, Britain was the prime mover of the Western coalition. Paris, without enthusiasm, certainly, had echoed the bellicose attitude of the British; but Paris would return to a pacifist outlook if the British could be persuaded to do the same. According to the British *Blue Book*, the Germans "were constantly looking for a way to make the Anglo-Polish alliance break up. On August 24, Göring told the Polish Ambassador in Berlin, Lipski, that the hurdle between their two countries was not Danzig but the alliance with Great Britain." On August 25, therefore, Hitler received the British Ambassador in Berlin, Sir Nevile Henderson, and spoke to him along the following lines:

Nothing the Prime Minister could say could cause the least modification to the claims of the Reich on Danzig and the Corridor. If war should result from Mr. Chamberlain's words, however, Germany would be in a much more advantageous position than 1914, for she would not have to fight on two fronts. But was war between Britain and Germany unavoidable? If Britain would consent to stay at peace, Hitler was prepared to guarantee the security of the whole of the British Empire, and would offer co-operation "wherever in the world such co-operation might be necessary". On August 25, also, Hitler received Coulondre again and blamed the break in Franco-German relations on France. On the next day, Daladier sent Hitler a conciliatory letter, but the German Führer had gone too far for conciliation.

Here, then, was a third reason for the postponement of the attack on Poland, after the news of the Anglo-Polish alliance and Attolico's message that Italy's programme must be one of "non-belligerence". Now Hitler knew that he could not open hostilities until he had received the British Government's reply to these, his latest proposals.

The British Ambassador was given the use of a German aircraft to take these proposals in person to London, where he arrived on the morning of August 26. By the evening of the 28th he was back at the New Chancellery with Chamberlain's reply. The offer of German protection for the British Empire had – not surprisingly – failed. "In no case can the British Government, in return for an advantage offered to Great Britain, agree to a settlement which would jeopardise the independence of a State to which it has given its firm guarantee."

Hoping that an "equitable" solution could be reached over the differences

Marshal Edward Rydz-Smigly C.-in-C. and head of state. "A capable soldier but in no way a statesman".

between Germany and Poland, Chamberlain suggested that "the next step should be the opening of direct negotiations between the German and Polish Governments", in respect of which he had already received "certain assurances from the Polish Government". If such negotiations could arrive at a settlement, this would "open the door to world-wide peace"; but failure to do so would put an end to all hopes of an understanding between Great Britain and Germany. What was more, it would precipitate first the two countries and then the whole world into war. This would be a tragedy without parallel in history.

Hitler now knew that there were no hopes of winning over the British, before his military timetable ran out. But he still had a faint chance of localising the conflict. He had the time to convince the German people that he had done everything in his power to avoid bloodshed. He also had to give some satisfaction to the appeals for peace which were flooding in from the World's neutral states.

On August 29, Hitler received Henderson and told him: "In these circumstances, the German Government agrees to accept the British Government's offer of their good services in securing the despatch to Berlin of a Polish Emissary with full powers. They count on the arrival of this Emissary on Wednesday, August 30."

Hitler ignored Henderson's objections that this left far too little time for a Polish envoy to arrive in Berlin for negotiations. But was it really a question of negotiation? Hitler's attitude implied that he was prepared to talk with a one-man surrender deputation – with or without a white flag – who would be ready to sign a document defining Germany's terms for Danzig and the Corridor. In any case, Hitler never dreamed that Warsaw would find his request acceptable. According to Halder, Hitler had set the following timetable on August 29:

"August 30: Polish envoy arrives in Berlin. August 31: Rupture [*zerplatzen*] with Poland.
September 1: Resort to force."

German troops on the Polish frontier.

The interview between Ribbentrop and Henderson at midnight August 30, just before the deadline laid down by Hitler for the arrival of a Polish envoy, was one of the stormiest encounters in the relations between the Western democracies and the Reich, and shows Hitler's completely shameless determination to make the breach at all costs.

Henderson began by stating that it was unreasonable to expect the British Government to arrange for the arrival of a Polish envoy on 24 hours' notice. "The time is up," replied Ribbentrop icily; "Where is the Polish envoy?" Henderson began to lose control. His face reddened and his hands began to shake as he started to read the official British reply to Hitler's request that Britain and Poland should refrain from aggressive troop movements. "What unheard-of impudence!" Ribbentrop interrupted furiously, and, crossing his arms on his chest, added provocatively: "Have you anything else to say?" "That the Germans are committing acts of sabotage in Poland!" "That is an abominable lie!" shouted Ribbentrop in a rage; "All I have to tell you is that the situation is damned serious!" Henderson could take no more. Stabbing a finger at Ribbentrop, he shouted: "*Damned serious*, you say? That is not how responsible statesmen talk!" Ribbentrop leaped out of his chair. "What did you say?" he shouted. Henderson also jumped up, and the two diplomats faced each other like fighting cocks. But their fury passed; they controlled themselves, and sat down again. Ribbentrop pulled out of his pocket a sheet of paper which contained a proposal for the settlement of the Polish problem. He read it carefully, taking his time. Then the blow fell. Henderson asked that he be given the text of this document to pass it on to his government – a perfectly reasonable request. "I could hardly believe my ears," recalled Schmidt, the interpreter, "when Ribbentrop replied with a taut smile: 'No, I cannot give you these proposals.' And he threw the paper on the table, saying: 'In any case, it is too late: the Polish envoy has not come.'"

"I suddenly realised," Schmidt continued, "what sort of game Hitler and Ribbentrop were actually playing. At this moment – midnight, August 30 – it was clear to me that their proposition was nothing but a lure and could never have come to anything. At any price the Poles must not know about it, for they might accept! All I could do was to draw a thick red line across the notes I was taking of Ribbentrop's statements – a line which marked the transition-point when the decision for peace or war was taken."

The following day, at 1830 hours, Ambassador Lipski called on Ribbentrop to inform him that the Poles were favourably considering the British suggestion for direct discussion between Warsaw and Berlin. All Ribbentrop asked him was:

"Do you have full powers to treat with us?"

"No," replied Lipski.

"Then," Ribbentrop concluded, "It is completely useless for us to discuss the matter further." The last effort towards maintaining world peace came from Mussolini at 1200 hours on the next day, when he proposed that France, Great Britain, Germany, Italy, and Poland get together around a conference table. It was too late: Hitler had decided to go to war.

But already, at 1700 hours on the 31st, General Gerd von Rundstedt, commanding Army Group South on the Neisse and who was to lead the main offensive against Poland, had received the signal which would unleash the attack at dawn on the following day: "Y = 1.9.0445".

CHAPTER 4
The Invasion of Poland

The German invasion of Poland was launched after the Polish Ambassador in Berlin refused to see Hitler's proposals for a peaceful solution to the problem of Danzig and the Corridor. But it is obvious that these "proposals" had only been drawn up for the sole purpose of driving a very hard wedge between Poland and her western allies, Britain and France. The German attack went in while Italy was submitting to Paris and London the suggestion for a five-power conference that was to meet on September 5 and "examine the clauses in the Treaty of Versailles which are at the root of the trouble".

In taking the step of launching the invasion, Hitler was caught by his own military timetable. Another 24 hours and he might have repeated his Munich triumph. He gambled that the western powers would not go to war for Poland. He was wrong.

On Friday, September 1, on hearing that the armed forces of the Reich had attacked Poland, Britain and France proclaimed general mobilisation and charged their Ambassadors in Berlin with delivering identical messages to the German Foreign Ministry: Germany must halt her invasion of Poland and withdraw her troops from Polish territory immediately. If she did not, Britain and France would "fulfil their obligations to Poland without hesitation".

The withdrawal of the German troops was seen as the essential preliminary to the five-power conference suggested by Mussolini. But the demand for this withdrawal, reasonable though it was, caused Mussolini to abandon the idea—and in fact it is difficult to see how he could have recommended such a solution to Hitler. Despite Hitler's express wishes, however, Ciano took it upon himself to inform the British and French Ambassadors in Rome that Italy would keep to a policy, if not of neutrality, at least of non-belligerence. In so doing, Ciano acted with prudence, for there were many exiled Italians in Paris and London who urged France and Britain to issue Mussolini with an ultimatum, calling upon him to open Italian territory to the British and French forces, or even to give his word that he would put his fleet at their disposal.

Great Britain declared war on Germany at 1100 hours on Sunday, September 3, on the expiry of her ultimatum presented two hours earlier. At noon, the French Ambassador in Berlin called on Ribbentrop, and on receiving Germany's refusal to suspend operations against Poland, informed the German Foreign Minister that a state of war would exist between France and Germany as from 1700 hours.

The time lag between these two declarations of war resulted from dissension in Paris and London. The British Admiralty pressed for an early opening of hostilities, so that British warships might be able to intercept Germany's merchant shipping while it was still at sea and to prevent her submarines from escaping from the North Sea. On the other hand, the French Army High Command asked for sufficient time to complete the first phases of mobilisation without the threat of German air attack. But Daladier put pressure on the General Staff, and succeeded in getting the declaration of war, originally fixed for 2100 hours on the 4th, brought back to 1700 hours, September 3.

By then the Polish Army had already been in battle for 60 hours and 30 minutes . . .

What were the main strengths and weaknesses of the two sides when World War II began? How, if at all, could the Allies have helped Poland?

The Allies had an enormous naval superiority. Admittedly, the British and French warships were weak in anti-aircraft defence, as the German dive-bombers were to prove during the battle for Norway in 1940. But with 676 ships (built or launched) against 130, the Allies clearly had the upper hand at sea. Their position was strengthened by the fact that the pressing needs of German war production forced Grand-Admiral Raeder to abandon the "Z-Plan" programme of heavy warship construction; even the two German aircraft-carriers—one of which, the *Graf Zeppelin*, had already been launched—could not be completed.

Germany had 57 U-boats, under the command of Commodore Karl Dönitz, 32 of them small boats designed for coastal operations (Types I and II). They could challenge the Allied control of the North Sea but were totally unsuitable for Atlantic commerce-raiding. This, however, was not all: within a few weeks, Dönitz was to learn that his U-boats suffered from glaring technical faults in their torpedoes.

On the other side of the ledger, the Luftwaffe was supreme in the air. On the first day of war, its order of battle totalled some 4,700 aircraft (including 552 three-engined Junkers Ju 52 transports). The anti-aircraft defences of the Reich, and the German mobile A.A. forces in the field, were the best in Europe, totalling over 9,000 guns. Of these, 2,600 were heavy-calibre weapons (8.8-cm and 10.5-cm).

But the Luftwaffe's trump card in the Polish campaign was its nine dive-bomber units flying the Junkers Ju 87 Stuka. (The notorious word "Stuka" is an abbreviation of the German "*Sturzkampfflugzeug*", or dive-bombing aircraft.) These gave the Wehrmacht a reserve of "flying artillery", which could be called in to deliver pinpoint bombing attacks at crucial moments in the offensive. Thoroughly trained in co-operation with the armoured and motorised units of the army, the Stukas gave the latter every opportunity to use their manoeuvrability and speed to the full without getting tied down in set-piece attacks which called for traditional artillery support.

In the Allied camp, the Polish Air Force, totalling 842 aircraft, was weak and obsolescent. France had virtually no modern bombers which could be pitted against the German fighter and A.A. defences. The Royal Air Force totalled 3,600 aircraft, of which a large proportion was totally obsolete; the R.A.F. also had to reserve many aircraft for duties outside Europe.

There were absolutely no plans for co-operation between the French and British air forces except for a mutual agreement not to bomb German territory—for fear of massive reprisals against either of their two nations. In any case, the resources of R.A.F. Bomber Command were so puny that they would have been capable of inflicting only pinpricks on Germany during the autumn of 1939.

There was also no agreement in the Allied High Command, and personal rivalries, normally camouflaged by official courtesy, undermined planning for joint operations. The French journalist "Pertinax" noted one example in 1940: "In the meeting on April 3 General Weygand delivered a long monologue. He wished to create a Balkan front, estimating that the hundred-odd divisions scattered throughout the Balkan states friendly to the Allies could be concentrated under French leadership. While Weygand was reading this memorandum, Daladier muttered and shrugged his shoulders. Gamelin did not say a word, but merely raised his eyes to heaven. All this struck him as dangerous and absurd. Afterwards, in private, he explained: 'Obviously, it would be desirable to make Germany fight on several fronts. But the time for the Western offensive will soon be here . . .' "

As far as the land forces were concerned, the total manpower strengths meant nothing until the differing processes of mobilisation had been completed, by which time it was too late to help Poland.

Thanks to Hitler's retention of the political initiative, the Wehrmacht was better prepared than its opponents to jump off at 0430 hours on September 1. But general mobilisation in Poland had not been proclaimed until 1100 hours the day before, while mobilisation in France, ordered on the first news of the German invasion of Poland, did not get under way until September 2. The result was that Marshal Edward Rydz-Smigly, the Polish Commander-in-Chief, never had all the resources that would have made his plan for concentration work, and that by the time that General Gamelin had completed his own preparations, Poland had already received her death-blow.

Every one of the 53 German first line divisions in the field had modern arms and

Colonel de Gaulle, one of the few proponents of tank warfare in France.

equipment. This was not the case with the 28 French divisions, recruited at the same time, assigned to the North-East Front in France. And in the Polish Army, most of the available weapons were obsolescent, a large part of them dating from the 1920's or even earlier. In the Wehrmacht, the larger formations did have certain weaknesses in their armament, especially in artillery. But in the French Army matters were far worse, particularly in the "Category B" reserve divisions, which had been mobilised with grave deficiencies in every sphere.

The biggest contrast of all was in the motorised and armoured divisions of either side. True, the French Army had seven motorised divisions while the German Army had only four, with a fifth made up of the 23,000 men of the *Waffen-S.S.* (military S.S.). But General Maurice Gamelin's order of battle had nothing to match the six German *Panzer* or armoured divisions. Nor did the two French light mechanised divisions come up to the standard of the four *Leichte Divisionen* of the Wehrmacht.

The French concentrated on forming brigades equipped with modern heavy tanks, ·but as they could not be given adequate air cover, Gamelin refused to group the existing brigades into divisions, although he was in the process of raising armoured divisions from scratch. In the German Army, on the other hand, the Panzer division was merely the basic unit, two of them being combined to make an armoured corps. When the Polish campaign began, Generals Heinz Guderian, Erich Hoeppner, Hermann Hoth, Ewald von Kleist, and Gustav von Wietersheim soon showed their skill in commanding and manoeuvring such corps of armour.

So much for the deficiencies of the French Army in organisation and equipment. Both would bear disastrous fruits in the months to come. But what of its manpower, its morale? Was the French Army lacking in offensive spirit? And do

the operations of 1939 deserve the description given to them by Colonel A. Goutard in his excellent study of the 1940 campaign as "the war of lost opportunities"?

In his memoirs, published in 1963, ex-Prime Minister Paul Reynaud condemned Gamelin's half-hearted strategy, quoting the statements made at Nuremberg after the war by members of the German High Command. General Alfred Jodl's opinion was: "In 1939 catastrophe [the continuation of the war] was not averted because 110 French and British divisions did not attack our 25 divisions in the West." General Keitel, too, was quoted as saying: "We were surprised that France did not attack Germany during the Polish campaign. Any form of attack would have shaken our screen of 25 reserve divisions and could only have encountered feeble resistance."

The figures quoted by Jodl and Keitel are, however, wrong. On September 1, 1939, the German Army Group "C", commanded by Colonel-General Wilhelm Ritter von Leeb, held the front between Basle and Aix-la-Chapelle. It was not made up of 25 divisions but of 34, to which was added two-thirds of the 22nd Airborne Division. The group was also reinforced after the news came in that France and Britain were at war with Germany: the Army High Command (O.K.H., for *Oberkommando des Heeres*) decided to add nine reserve divisions to the Western Front armies. These divisions completed their move by September 10, so that Leeb's strength on the next day totalled $43\frac{2}{3}$ divisions.

Similarly, the French forces facing Leeb were much weaker than Jodl and Keitel claimed at Nuremberg. For a start, there were no British forces at all until the I Corps took up its place in the line, at Lille, on October 3–a full month after Britain's declaration of war. Nor were there anything like 110 Allied divisions on the Western Front.

The decree of mobilisation gave Gamelin 81 infantry (seven of them motorised), three cavalry, and two light mechanised

divisions, excluding the 13 garrison divisions of the Maginot Line. This immediately brings down Jodl's and Keitel's overall figure from 110 to 86 divisions. But even this is misleading, for Gamelin had to cover the Italian and Spanish frontiers as well as the Western Front.

At the time of France's declaration of war, the French Army in the field totalled 30 infantry divisions. Fourteen of these were in North Africa, manning the French "Mareth Line" defences and keeping an eye on Italian concentrations in Libya. Nine others were deployed on the Alpine front. Seven were available for the Western Front, and there were a few battalions of Pyrenean *chasseurs*, mountain troops, screening the Spanish frontier.

The acute shortage of manpower was not helped by the fact that mobilisation and concentration was no faster in 1939 than it had been in 1914. It took three weeks. Not until September 20 were the last units in position. Under these conditions how could Gamelin have launched a rapid attack on the Germans in the West while Polish resistance continued? Adding the manpower of the Maginot Line, Gamelin by now had a total of 57 divisions –52 infantry, three cavalry, and two light mechanised divisions–deployed between Belfort and Maubeuge. Of these, 31 were earmarked for operations in the Saar between September 1 and 12.

Gamelin's army lacked not only the wherewithal to attack: it had also never been intended that the French Army should be prepared for an immediate offensive.

Since June 1932, the fortunes of France and of her army had been supervised by a succession of 19 governments, eight war ministers, and eight ministers of finance. This was bad enough, but the roots of the trouble ran even deeper. In 1925, Paul Painlevé, the War Minister, had laid down that the ideal rôle of the French Army should be "to achieve a rational system of national defence, adequate in times of danger but unsuited to adventures and conquests".

This made the French Army essentially reservist and defensive in character, and also meant that the preparation of the French war machine would be slow.

It is interesting to note that all this was not lost on the Polish High Command, and that Warsaw did everything that it could to mitigate the consequences. After the fall of Warsaw in September 1939, General von Manstein, Chief-of-Staff of the German Army Group "South", had access to the Polish Army archives and unearthed some fascinating material. In the first months of 1938, General Kutrzeba, the Director of the Polish Military Academy, had submitted his views on the defence of the nation to Marshal Rydz-Smigly. Kutrzeba's personal opinion was a sound one: he held that "it will be necessary to wait for help from France; Poland will have to rely on her own forces for six to eight weeks, even if the French react promptly."

The following year the same question was the subject of a 48-hour series of talks between General Gamelin and General Kasprzycki, the Polish War Minister, on May 16–17. A protocol emerged, containing the following points:

"As soon as part of the French forces is available (about the 3rd day after France's general mobilisation), France will launch a series of progressive offensives with limited objectives.

"As soon as the main German attacks come to bear on Poland, France will launch an offensive with the bulk of her forces (not earlier than the 15th day after France's mobilisation)."

General Joseph Georges, commanding the French North-East Front, intervened in the discussion to give "some information on the Siegfried Line and on the artillery that will be needed to attack it". His estimate was that "to attack this line and achieve a breakthrough cannot be contemplated until the 17th day [after mobilisation]".

Gamelin then declared that three-quarters of the French Army could—before any operations were launched on the North-East Front—undertake an offensive between the Rhine and the Moselle on the 15th day after mobilisation. But as far as the actual course of events in the Polish campaign was concerned, this meant the day before Soviet Russia stabbed Poland in the back and attacked from the East . . .

The relevant documents do not show that the Polish War Minister raised any objection to Gamelin's programme. From this one can only conclude that Marshal Rydz-Smigly and the majority of his French colleagues had absolutely no conception of the paralysing effects of dive-bombing attacks or of the imaginative use of armoured forces. (This, to be fair, applied to many German commanders.)

In addition to this paradoxical situation there was the incredible optimism of Gamelin himself. Pierre-Etienne Flandin recalled: "I met Gamelin on August 27. He spoke in the most optimistic terms about the Polish forces. When I pointed out that [the Germans] had expressed their belief that they could crush Poland in three weeks, Gamelin rebuked me for believing Hitler's predictions. 'I know the Polish Army perfectly,' he said. 'Its troops are excellent and its commanders beyond praise. The Poles will hold out and we will lose no time in coming to their aid.' And when I remained sceptical and asked how we could help the Poles, he replied with great conviction: 'The Poles will hold out for at least six months and we will come to their aid via Rumania.' I left the War Ministry, horror-stricken."

Operation "Saar", the plans for which were contained in a French Army Instruction of July 24, 1939, was the first of the limited offensives mentioned by Gamelin. It was directed by General Gaston Prételat, commander of the French 2nd Army Group. The attack went in on September 7, and was a complete fiasco.

German artillerymen spring into action. German artillery outnumbered that of the Poles by more than three to one.

Everything was against the French. For a start, the sector of the frontier between the Rhine and the Moselle selected for the French attack had been defined by the victors of Waterloo in 1815 with the express purpose of making French aggression difficult. Thus in 1939 the Germans held all the high ground. German-held salients also extended into French territory, and these would have to be reduced before the Siegfried Line proper could be assaulted. In addition to this, the Siegfried Line was sufficiently far behind the German front line to compel the French to bring their own artillery (if it was to be within range of the casemates of the Line) within range of German counter-battery fire.

After patrolling operations, Prételat launched his attack on September 7, but it hardly got past its start-lines. A total of 31 divisions had been put at Prételat's disposal, including 14 first-line units, but only nine were used eventually. General Edouard Réquin's 4th Army, with its right flank in the Bitche region and its left on the Saar, managed to capture seven and a half miles of German territory, while its neighbour, General Condé's 3rd Army, pinched out the heavily-wooded Warndt Forest salient.

Commanding the German 1st Army,

A Heinkel He 111 drops a stick of bombs over Warsaw.

General Erwin von Witzleben had 17 divisions to meet this attack, and ten of these had been recruited only recently. But his troops made skilful use of their advantage in terrain, relying heavily on cleverly-sited anti-tank and anti-personnel minefields. The French were unfamiliar with this threat and possessed no mine detectors. Houses booby-trapped with explosives added to the German minefield defences.

What of the Siegfried Line itself, which the French had planned to attack after September 17? General Siegfried Westphal has gone on record as describing the Line as a "gigantic bluff", but it was not. Its defences were sound, and the French artillery could do little damage to them. Major-General Ulrich Liss, head of "Section West" of German Army Intelligence, stated that the French 155-mm shells caused negligible damage. The heavier 220-mm and 280-mm guns were not provided with delayed-action fused shells, which would have enabled the projectiles to penetrate the casemates before exploding. Liss admitted that the

French guns maintained a high and accurate rate of fire, but stated that a large number of the French shells failed to explode as they came from stocks dating back to World War I.

By the 17th day after France's proclamation of general mobilisation, Poland's existence as an independent state was destroyed. There had been no precedent for such a catastrophe since Napoleon's destruction of Prussia at Jena in 1806. It was the result not so much of Poland's military weaknesses at the crucial moment as of the *matériel*, numerical, and strategic superiority of the German Army and of the Luftwaffe, helped by the fatal mistakes of the Polish High Command. Hitler had Poland at his mercy.

Within the frontiers which had been laid down by the Treaty of Versailles, Marshal Rydz-Smigly and his commanders had a difficult problem in planning the defence of Poland against Hitler's rearmed Germany. A glance at the map will show the reason for this. From Suwałki, on the frontier between East Prussia and Lithuania, to the Carpathians south of Przemyśl, the Polish frontier to be defended included the Slovak border

and formed a huge salient with a front line of some 1,250 miles – excluding the defence requirements of Danzig and the Corridor. To defend this vulnerable salient, the Polish High Command had only 45 divisions at its disposal.

When the Germans examined the Polish Army archives after their victory in 1939, they found that the French had given several warnings to their Polish opposite numbers about the dangers of the situation. One of them, prepared by General Weygand between 1931 and 1935, had advised the Poles "to base [their] defences behind the line formed by the Rivers Niemen, Bobr, Narew, Vistula, and San". And Weygand went on to add: "From the operational point of view this concept is the only sound one, for it disposes of every possibility of envelopment and places strong river barriers in the path of German armoured formations. More important, this line is only 420 miles long, instead of the 1,250-mile front from Suwałki to the Carpathian passes."

As early as the German reoccupation of the Rhineland, Gamelin had given Rydz-Smigly the same advice during a visit to Warsaw, and he reiterated the point in his discussions with General Kasprzycki on May 16. The Polish High Command, however, replied to these French suggestions by pointing out that Poland could not continue to fight a prolonged war if she gave up the industrial regions of Upper Silesia and Łódź, and the rich agricultural regions of Kutno, Kielce, and Poznań without firing a shot. For this reason General Kutrzeba, according to the German examination of the Polish archives, proposed to include these regions in the defensive perimeter, but without stationing troops further west than the Warta river or cramming garrison forces into the Danzig Corridor, which would have meant that in the north the Polish troops were stationed where they had to face a two-front war, from German Pomerania and from East Prussia.

Whatever the reasons behind it, this was a rash plan. But when Rydz-Smigly stationed a full fifth of his resources around Poznań and in the Corridor itself it smacked of megalomania – and he did this despite the fact that his Intelligence department had provided him with extremely accurate figures for the forces massing against Poland. Moreover, general mobilisation was not proclaimed in Poland until 1100 hours on August 31, and this meant that on the first day of the German attack the Polish front was held by only 17 infantry divisions, three infantry brigades, and six cavalry brigades. Thirteen Polish divisions mobilised by the time of the German attack were still moving to their concentration areas, while another nine divisions were still mustering in barracks.

To crown everything, the Polish High Command was fatally vulnerable in its communications with the forces in the field. There was no adequate command structure between Rydz-Smigly and his eight army commanders, and the com-

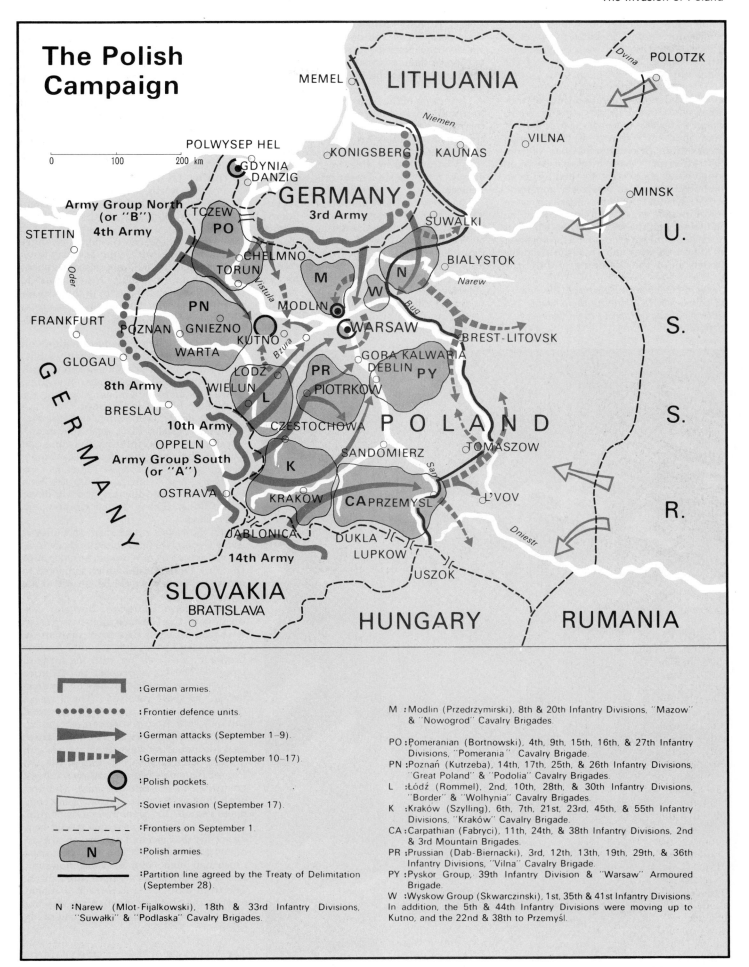

The Polish Campaign

POLWYSEP HEL

0   100   200 km

Army Group North (or "B")
4th Army

3rd Army

Army Group North (or "B")
4th Army

8th Army

10th Army

Army Group South (or "A")

14th Army

:German armies.

:Frontier defence units.

:German attacks (September 1–9).

:German attacks (September 10–17).

:Polish pockets.

:Soviet invasion (September 17).

:Frontiers on September 1.

N :Polish armies.

:Partition line agreed by the Treaty of Delimitation (September 28).

N :Narew (Mlot-Fijalkowski), 18th & 33rd Infantry Divisions, "Suwałki" & "Podlaska" Cavalry Brigades.

M :Modlin (Przedrzymirski), 8th & 20th Infantry Divisions, "Mazow" & "Nowogrod" Cavalry Brigades.

PO :Pomeranian (Bortnowski), 4th, 9th, 15th, 16th, & 27th Infantry Divisions, "Pomerania" Cavalry Brigade.

PN :Poznań (Kutrzeba), 14th, 17th, 25th, & 26th Infantry Divisions, "Great Poland" & "Podolia" Cavalry Brigades.

L :Łódź (Rommel), 2nd, 10th, 28th, & 30th Infantry Divisions, "Border" & "Wolhynia" Cavalry Brigades.

K :Kraków (Szylling), 6th, 7th, 21st, 23rd, 45th, & 55th Infantry Divisions, "Kraków" Cavalry Brigade.

CA :Carpathian (Fabryci), 11th, 24th, & 38th Infantry Divisions, 2nd & 3rd Mountain Brigades.

PR :Prussian (Dab-Biernacki), 3rd, 12th, 13th, 19th, 29th, & 36th Infantry Divisions, "Vilna" Cavalry Brigade.

PY :Pyskor Group, 39th Infantry Division & "Warsaw" Armoured Brigade.

W :Wyskow Group (Skwarczinski), 1st, 35th & 41st Infantry Divisions. In addition, the 5th & 44th Infantry Divisions were moving up to Kutno, and the 22nd & 38th to Przemyśl.

munication network on which he depended for control in battle was cut to ribbons by the Luftwaffe's precision attacks within the first few days of the campaign.

This unbelievable combination of mistakes contributed greatly to the Wehrmacht's success, but nothing can detract from the thoroughness of the German preparation. Brauchitsch's plan of concentration for "Case White" was based on sound concepts of strategy, and had been explained clearly to the lower command levels. Ground and air missions were co-ordinated; every man knew what he had to do; and the result got the most out of the new concept of co-operation between an armoured army and a modern air force. Drawn up at the beginning of July, the

German troops march through Warsaw on October 5, 1939 during the massive victory parade following the defeat of Poland.

O.K.H. Directive stated: "The objective of the operation is the destruction of the Polish armed forces. The political conduct of the war demands that it be fought with crushing, surprise blows to achieve rapid success.

"Intention of the Army High Command: to disrupt, by a rapid invasion of Polish territory, the mobilisation and concentration of the Polish Army, and to destroy the bulk of troops stationed to the west of the Vistula–Narew line by converging attacks from Silesia, Pomerania, and East Prussia."

The armoured and motorised divisions with which Germany attacked Poland totalled 55 divisions, including reserves, on "Y-Day", but by September 18 this figure had risen to 63. The front line divisions were divided into two large army groups with the following strengths and objectives:

1. **East Prussia and Pomerania** – Army Group North (Colonel-General Fedor von Bock).

Left flank: 3rd Army (General Georg von Küchler), with eight infantry divisions, was to assist in the destruction of the Polish forces in the Corridor and drive south towards the Vistula and Warsaw.

Right flank: 4th Army (General Günther Hans von Kluge), with six infantry divisions, two motorised divisions, and one Panzer division, was to attack from Pomerania and destroy the main body of Polish troops defending the Corridor, cutting off the Poznań-Kutno group from the north.

2. **Silesia and Slovakia** – Army Group South (Colonel-General Gerd von Rundstedt).

Left flank: 8th Army (General Johannes Blaskowitz), with four infantry divisions and the S.S. motorised regiment *Leibstandarte Adolf Hitler*, was to engage the Polish forces in the Poznań-Kutno region and keep them from counter-attacking the central army of the group.

Centre: 10th Army (General Walter von Reichenau), with six infantry divisions, two motorised divisions, three light divisions, and two Panzer divisions, was to drive north-east, straight for Wieluń, Łódź, and Warsaw.

Right flank: 14th Army (General Sigmund Wilhelm List), with one mountain division, six infantry divisions, one light division, two Panzer divisions, and the S.S. motorised regiment *Germania*, was to strike across the Carpathians from Slovakia and pin down the Polish forces around Kraków and Przemyśl.

Hitler, however, intervened and altered Army Group North's schedule. By switching its forces east of Warsaw, he made sure that any Polish forces which managed to cross the Vistula would be cut off to the east of the Capital.

For General Guderian, however, the opening of the German offensive started with near disaster. He was in command of XIX Panzer Corps and, a sound armour tactician, was well up with his forward troops. "The corps crossed the frontier simultaneously at 0445 hours on September 1," he later recalled. "There was a thick ground mist at first which prevented the Luftwaffe from giving us any support. I drove forward with the 3rd Panzer Brigade in the first wave [until it came into action]. Contrary to my orders, the 3rd Panzer Brigade's heavy artillery felt itself compelled to fire into the mist. The first shell landed 50 yards in front of my command vehicle, the second 50 yards behind. I was sure that the next one would be a direct hit and ordered my driver to turn about and drive off. The unaccustomed noise had made him nervous, however, and he drove flat-out straight into a ditch. The front axle of the half-track was bent so that the steering mechanism was put out of action. This marked the end of my drive..."

The first stage of the campaign saw the Polish cavalry of the "Pomorze Army"

Łódź Airfield, now in German hands.

(Pomeranian Army), under General Bortnowski, charge the tanks of Guderian's XIX Panzer Corps as they thrust across the Corridor towards the Vistula, which they crossed at Chełmno on September 6, making contact with 3rd Army on the far bank. As late as September 15–18, when the campaign was already lost, the Polish "Sosnkowski Group" (11th and 38th Divisions), marching by night and fighting by day, managed three times to break through the ring which the German 14th Army was trying to close behind it. Fighting their way across the San river, the Sosnkowski divisions managed to capture 20 guns and 180 vehicles from 14th Army.

All this was achieved under non-stop bombing raids by the Luftwaffe. Although the Polish Air Force managed to keep up sporadic air attack up to September 17, the Luftwaffe dominated the air. *Luftflotten* (Air Fleets) I and IV, commanded by Generals Albert Kesselring and Alexander Löhr, concentrated their attacks on communication centres, pockets of resistance, and Polish forces on the move. *Luftflotte* I operated with Bock's Army Group North, *Luftflotte* IV with Rundstedt's Army Group South. Between them, the two air fleets totalled 897 bombers and 219 Stukas.

The advantage of unchallenged air power helped the German 10th Army to win rapid successes in its advance on Warsaw. It is true that on September 8 its 4th Panzer Division failed in its attempt to take Warsaw by surprise, but two days later 10th Army reached the Vistula at Góra Kalwaria and tore the Polish "Łódź Army" to shreds. At the same time the Polish "Prussian Army" had also been cut off, broken up, and destroyed in a battle against heavy odds. Marshal Rydz-Smigly's order for the Polish armies to withdraw eastwards had gone out on September 6, but it was already too late.

This withdrawal led to one of the most dramatic episodes in the Polish campaign. Falling back on Warsaw, the "Pomorze" and "Poznań" Armies were challenged by

the German 8th Army, coming up from Łódź, which tried to bar their retreat. The result was the hard-fought "Battle of the Bzura", which began on September 10. The Polish troops succeeded in capturing bridgeheads across the Bzura river near Łowicz, and drove back the German 30th Infantry Division. Thanks to Hitler's order to switch the advance east of Warsaw, Army Group North was unable to intervene fast enough to cover the flank of Army Group South. But Rundstedt rose to the crisis. While Stukas attacked the Bzura bridgeheads, the motorised and Panzer divisions of 10th Army wheeled north and caught the Polish forces in flank. There was vicious fighting around Łowicz and Sochaczew before the Poles pulled back; but at last, completely cut off and hemmed in about Kutno, General Bortnowski was forced to order the surrender of his 170,000 men on September 19.

While 8th Army closed the inner pincers of the German advance by investing Warsaw and Modlin, the plan imposed by Hitler aimed at a wider sweep to trap the remaining Polish fragments retreating east of the Vistula. This was achieved by a deep Panzer penetration led by Guderian. His XIX Panzer Corps had been transferred across East Prussia after its initial successes in the Corridor, and on September 9 it forced the Narew river upstream of Łomza. Six days later it had driven as far south as Brest Litovsk, and its 3rd Panzer Division, pressing south towards Włodawa, had made contact with advance units of 10th and 14th Armies from Army Group South. 14th Army, which had advanced eastwards as far as L'vov, had swung north-east to complete this link-up.

Until this moment the Soviet Union had observed the letter of the Soviet-Polish Non-Aggression Pact of 1932, which, renewed on May 5, 1934, was intended to run until the end of 1945. But when it became obvious that the destruction of

the Polish Army was imminent, Moscow decided to intervene in order to make sure of the territories (east of the line formed by the Narew, Vistula, and San rivers) conceded to the Soviet Union by the secret protocol attached to the German-Soviet Non-Aggression Pact. At 0300 hours on September 17, Vladimir Potemkin, Deputy Commissar for Foreign Affairs, told Polish Ambassador Grzybowski that "the fact is that the Polish State and its Government have ceased to exist".

"For this reason," ran the note which Potemkin read to Grzybowski, "the treaties concluded between the Soviet Union and Poland have lost their validity. Abandoned to its own fate and deprived of its rulers, Poland has become an area in which could develop all manner of circumstances potentially dangerous to the Soviet Union. This is why, having maintained its neutrality up to now, the Soviet Union cannot remain neutral in the present situation.

"The Soviet Union can no longer remain indifferent to the sufferings of its blood-brothers the Ukrainians and Belorussians, who, inhabitants of Polish territory, are being abandoned to their fate and left defenceless. In consideration of this situation the Soviet Government has ordered the High Command of the Red Army to send its troops across the frontier and to take under their protection the lives and welfare of the populations of the western Ukraine and western Belorussia." The note had been drawn up with the full agreement of Germany, which had undertaken not to conclude an armistice with Poland.

The Polish Ambassador refused to accept this note, but a few hours later large Red Army forces crossed the frontier and pushed motorised and armoured columns westward towards Vilna, Brest-Litovsk, Kovel', and L'vov. Within days their

General Blaskowitz (left) reads out the surrender terms to the Polish delegates (backs to the camera) in his command post outside Warsaw.

spearheads had made contact with Wehrmacht troops in Galicia and along the River Bug.

The intervention of the Red Army ended the last vain hopes of the Polish High Command for prolonging resistance in a last-ditch campaign in eastern Galicia with their backs to the Rumanian frontier. On the morning of September 18, President Mościcki, Colonel Beck, and the remainder of the Polish Government, together with Marshal Rydz-Smigly, fled to Rumania and claimed political asylum. Poland's formal resistance was over.

During this 18-day campaign the German armies had largely over-run the demarcation line agreed between Stalin and Ribbentrop on August 23. This led to a new settlement between Moscow and Berlin: the "German-Soviet Treaty of Delimitation and Friendship", signed on September 28 by Ribbentrop after another journey to Moscow. The agreement, which split Poland in two, was made at Stalin's insistence, as he refused to countenance a German suggestion for the establishment of a Polish state of 15 million inhabitants.

In this partition agreement, Germany accepted the inclusion of Lithuania into the Soviet sphere of influence; in compensation, the parts of the province of Warsaw already conceded in the agreement of August 23, plus the entire province of Lublin, were conceded to Germany. In central Poland the new demarcation line connected the Vistula and Bug rivers; in Galicia it remained on the San river, for

Stalin refused to give up the petroleum wells of Drohobycz and Boryslaw.

Another protocol declared that the Soviet Union would not make any difficulties for citizens of Estonia, Latvia, and Lithuania who might wish to leave the Soviet zone of influence, taking their personal goods with them. In this agreement, Stalin and Hitler renewed the anti-Polish engagements which had bound together the Romanovs and Hohenzollerns in Imperial days. "The undersigned plenipotentiaries, on concluding the German-Soviet Treaty of Delimitation and Friendship, have declared their agreement on the following points:

"The two parties will tolerate in their territories no Polish agitation affecting the territory of the other party. They will suppress in their territories all beginnings of such agitation and inform each other concerning suitable measures for this purpose."

The same day, September 28, Warsaw surrendered after 14 days of heroic resistance. Luftwaffe bombing had set the city flourmills ablaze, and the filtration and pumping stations for the water supply had been more than half destroyed. A humane commander, General Blaskowitz of the German 8th Army allowed the honours of war to Warsaw's defenders, who had been galvanised by their leader, General Rommel, formerly the commander of the "Łódź Army". Among the prisoners-of-war was General Kutrzeba, who had broken out of the Kutno pocket with four divisions. Modlin capitulated a few hours before Warsaw.

The last shots of the campaign were fired in the Półwysep Hel peninsula, north of Danzig, where Admiral Unruh surrendered with 4,500 men on October 2.

When Hitler broadcast to the German people on September 30, he announced the number of Polish prisoners taken as 694,000, compared with German losses of 10,572 killed, 3,400 missing, presumed dead, and 30,322 wounded. These figures support Guderian's comment to Hitler on September 5, when the latter visited Guderian's sector: "Tanks are a life-saving weapon."

From the time of the first successes won by the German Army in Poland, Hitler had made constant visits to the front-line areas to judge the importance of the victories for himself. "On October 5," General von Manstein recalled, "a big military parade was held, which unfortunately ended with a disagreeable incident showing Hitler's bizarre attitude towards his generals. We were accompanying him on his return to the airfield, and we felt that at least we might expect a few words of thanks. A table had been laid at which Hitler and his generals could sample some soup prepared by the field kitchens. But when he saw the white tablecloth and the flower decorations which had been provided in his honour, Hitler turned brusquely aside, tasted two or three mouthfuls of soup, chatted briefly with the soldiers, and got straight into his aeroplane. Apparently he wanted to show his close ties with the people. But I doubt that this gesture was really to the taste of our brave grenadiers, who would have understood perfectly that if the Head of State chose to eat with his generals he would be paying equal homage to the troops. For us, it was an affront which gave us much food for thought."

For its part, the Red Army rounded up some 217,000 prisoners, many of whom were destined to die in Russia in circumstances that will be examined in due course. About 100,000 Poles managed to escape to the West via Rumania and carry on the fight against Germany from France and Britain.

On September 13, General Georges, commanding the French North-East Front, taking Poland's defeat as virtually completed, ordered General Prételat "not to advance beyond the objectives attained, but to strengthen your dispositions in depth and to arrange as soon as possible for replacement divisions to relieve your front-line divisions, in particular the motorised divisions".

So ended Operation "Saar", which had cost the French Army 27 killed, 22 wounded, and 28 missing. General Vuillemin's air force had lost nine fighters and 18 reconnaissance aircraft. Both Gamelin and Georges later justified this decision to halt operations against Germany on the following grounds. Everything suggested that with Poland annihilated, Hitler would turn against the West with his full strength, with the assurance of a superiority of about 100 divisions to 60. Moreover, it was possible that Mussolini, drawn by the ease with which Poland had been conquered, might attack France himself before the Alpine passes were snowed up and rendered impassable.

CHAPTER 5
The Russo-Finnish war

After the German-Soviet Treaty of September 28, 1939, the Soviet Government imposed "mutual defence agreements" upon Estonia, Latvia, and Lithuania. These provide for the garrisoning of Soviet troops on the islands of Dagö and Osel in Estonia, and at Windau and Libau in Latvia.

Moscow then proceeded to make similar demands upon Finland. On October 14, a Finnish delegation in Moscow listened to the following claims, put to them by Stalin, Molotov, and Deputy Foreign Commissar Potemkin:

1. Finland to cede her islands in the Gulf of Finland;
2. Finland to withdraw her frontier in the Karelian Isthmus between the Baltic and Lake Ladoga;
3. An aero-naval base at Hangö at the mouth of the Gulf of Finland to be leased by Finland to the Soviet Union for 30 years;
4. Finland to cede to the Soviet Union her portion of the Rybachiy Peninsula in Lappland; and
5. Conclusion of a mutual assistance treaty, between the Soviet Union and Finland, for the defence of the Gulf of Finland.

In compensation for these sacrifices, Moscow offered Finland an "adjustment" (albeit a considerable one) of the frontier in Karelia.

Faced with these demands, the Finnish Government of President Cajander did not reject the proposals outright. After consultation with Marshal Carl Gustav Mannerheim, Commander-in-Chief of Finland's armed forces, the Finnish Government inclined towards compromise as far as the islands in the gulf and the Karelian frontier were concerned, provided only that the fortified line across the isthmus remained in Finnish hands; but all claims for the base at Hangö and for the frontier adjustments in the Rybachiy Peninsula were rejected.

Deadlock was reached on October 23, when the Russians refused to budge an inch from their proposals of the 14th and the Finns, led by Ministers Paasikivi and Tanner, held equally firmly to their counter-proposals. After a month of fruitless discussion, Molotov announced on November 26 that Finnish artillery had opened fire on Soviet troops, and demanded that the Finnish troops should retire 15 miles from the frontier. The Helsinki Government did not reject the demand: it simply asked that as a condition for such a retirement, Soviet Russia should withdraw her troops the same distance on her side of the frontier. This tipped the scale, and on November 30 the Soviet land, sea, and air forces took the offensive against Finland without any declaration of war.

The Soviet official *History of the Great Patriotic War* contains no information of any use concerning the opening phase of the "Winter War"-no orders of battle, names of generals, or any of the normal statistics usually quoted in abundance by Soviet historians. But on November 30, 1939, it can be estimated that the Red Army deployed against Finland 19 rifle (infantry) divisions and five tank brigades, grouped into the following armies:

1. Karelian Isthmus: 7th Army, with eight divisions, a tank corps, and two independent tank brigades, was to force the defences of the Mannerheim Line, take Viipuri, and push on to Helsinki by the third day of the offensive;
2. East shore of Lake Ladoga: 8th Army, with six divisions, was to assist 7th Army in its frontal attack by drawing off the Finnish defence;
3. Central Finland: 9th Army, with four divisions, was to launch two columns across the "waist" of Finland, the left column making for Oulu and the right for Kemi; and
4. Lappland: 14th Army, with one division, was to take Petsamo and sever northern Finland's communications with Norway.

Because of the growing tension between Finland and the Soviet Union, the Helsinki Government had already proceeded to call up the Finnish reserves; but on the day of the Soviet attack, Marshal Mannerheim had only nine divisions at his disposal:

1. Karelian Isthmus: five divisions (II and III Corps) under the command of Lieutenant-General Hugo Ostermann;
2. East shore of Lake Ladoga: two divisions (IV Corps) under Major-General Hägglund;
3. Central Finland: a screen of nine frontier battalions (V Corps) under Major-General Vilpo Tuompo;
4. Lappland: four independent battalions under Major-General Kurt Wallenius; and
5. In reserve: two incomplete divisions (I Corps) and a cavalry brigade.

Finland's full mobilisation would provide the manpower for 15 divisions, but she faced the initial onslaught with only 120,000 Finnish against 300,000 Soviet troops, well-armed and backed up by 800 aircraft. Finland's air force had about 100 aircraft, and many of these were not battle-worthy.

The Finnish soldiers-used to the forest, efficient hunters, skilled on skis, and natural fighters-soon showed themselves to be master-practioners of the art of irregular warfare. True, their weapons were neither modern nor fully adequate. The Finnish *Suomi* 9-mm submachine gun functioned perfectly in sub-zero conditions, but it was not a weapon ideally suited to forest warfare. Nor were the improvised incendiary grenades known as "Molotov cocktails". The Finnish Army also contained 90,000 female auxiliaries (known as *Lottas*)-a telling commentary on the patriotism of Finland's small population of 3,700,000.

Two circumstances favoured the defenders. First was the terrain. Finland's vast forests gave ample cover and allowed the small detachments in which the Finnish Army operated to launch ambushes on the few roads that penetrated their forests. Second was the winter cold; this froze up the 35,000 lakes which would otherwise have helped the defenders even more, but the abnormal temperatures of the winter of 1939-40 (often 30 or 40 degrees below zero on the Centigrade scale) hit the Russians far harder than the Finns, for the latter were falling back on their own strongpoints and were able to make more effective use of a "scorched earth" policy in so doing.

None of this, however, would have been of value without the admirable resolve of the Finnish nation, which ignored the blandishments of the Communist leader Otto Kuusinen and his "People's Government of the Finnish Democratic Republic", set up at Terijoki behind the Soviet lines. The Finns disowned him virtually to a man; and Kuusinen soon became so great an embarrassment to the Soviet Government, in view of the disastrous failures of the Red Army in the field, that he was quietly abandoned in the early part of 1940.

By the end of 1939 the Red Army had suffered a series of resounding and humiliating defeats.

In the Karelian Isthmus, advancing on a front of 87 miles, the Soviet 7th Army was stopped in its tracks by the Mannerheim Line's pillboxes and anti-tank obstacles. The Soviet 8th Army, advancing in support of the 7th on the far shore of Lake Ladoga, suffered even worse: after its 139th and 75th Divisions reached Tolvajärvi on December 12, they were ambushed and cut to pieces by seven Finnish battalions under Colonel Talvela, in an action which cost the Russians over 5,000 dead.

In central Finland, the Soviet column from 9th Army advancing on Oulu was counter-attacked at Suomussalmi by Colonel Siilasvuo's detachment. On December 11, the Soviet 163rd Division was cut off; on the 28th, the Soviet 44th Division, trying to retreat, was ambushed and destroyed in turn.

Accurate figures of Russian losses are not available, but the Red Army lost about 27,500 dead against a total figure of 2,700 Finnish dead and wounded. The Finns also captured 80 tanks and 70 guns, and rounded up 1,600 prisoners-of-war.

The fact that so few prisoners were taken proves that the Russian soldier knew how to fight and die. This is not the impression given by the Soviet *History of the Great Patriotic War*, which tends to blame the troops. A typical critical passage reads: "In attack the Soviet troops

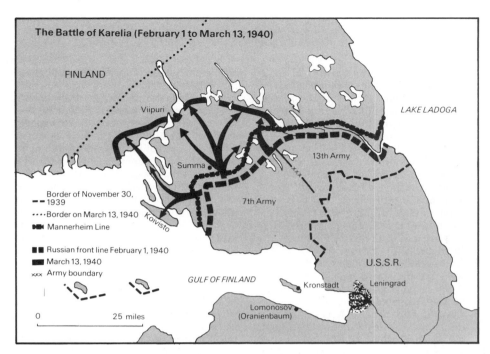

The Battle of Karelia (February 1 to March 13, 1940)

FINLAND

Viipuri

LAKE LADOGA

Summa

13th Army

Border of November 30, 1939
Border on March 13, 1940
Mannerheim Line

7th Army

Koivisto

Russian front line February 1, 1940
March 13, 1940
Army boundary

U.S.S.R.

GULF OF FINLAND

Kronstadt
Leningrad

0   25 miles

Lomonosov
(Oranienbaum)

*The Russian assault which broke
through the Mannerheim Line.
The Finns put up a brave
defence, but inevitably the
weight of Soviet forces carried
the day in February 1940.*

showed certain failures in preparation and command. Some formations had been insufficiently trained in fighting on skis, in sub-zero conditions, and in regions of dense forests and lakes. There was lack of experience in attacking permanent installations and concrete emplacements."

Stalin and Molotov were to a great extent to blame for having made light of the patriotism of the Finnish people, and so were their military advisers for having misjudged the capacity for resistance and the manoeuvrability displayed by the Finnish Army. In addition to this, grave blunders had been made by the Soviet High Command, most notably the suicidal tactic of sending armoured and motorised columns along forest roads where there was no possibility of manoeuvre.

Throughout the campaign, Hitler maintained a malevolent neutrality towards Finland. To the great indignation of Ciano, he forbade the transit across Germany of Italian war material intended for Finland.

In his *Memoirs*, Mannerheim has summed up the cardinal weaknesses in the Red Army's first attack on Finland: "In December, the enemy attacks resembled a badly-directed orchestra with every instrument ignoring the beat. Their artillery deluged us with shells, but its practice was very bad and not at all related to the movement of its own infantry and tank forces. The latter had curious tactics of their own: they would advance, open fire, and fall back before their supporting infantry had had time to make any move. These mistakes cost the Red Army very dear."

Mannerheim's comments on the psychology of the Russian soldier are equally to the point: "The Russian infantryman was brave, tough, and content with little, but he lacked initiative. He was a gregarious fighter, incapable of independent action. In the first battles the Russians would often advance singing across minefields in serried ranks—sometimes even with linked arms—without seeming to be worried by the explosions or the punishing fire of the defenders.

"Moreover, while many of their divisions were made up of men who originally came from wooded areas, they were incapable of moving and fighting successfully in forests. A dearth of compasses added to their difficulties and the forest—the best ally of the Finnish guerrillas—struck terror into the Russians. It was in the forests that the 'white death' prowled: the Finnish partisan in his winter equipment. But the biggest weakness of the Russian soldiers was their inadequate training for ski operations. They tried to make up for this during the first weeks, but proficiency on skis cannot be learned in a few weeks, and certainly not on the battlefield."

Far more serious was the result of Stalin's purge of the Red Army's officer corps in 1937–38, which had killed off most of the Red Army's "brains": the field commanders. Raymond L. Garthoff, in his *Soviet Military Doctrine*, quotes the following figures: three out of five marshals had been purged; 13 out of 15 army generals; 57 out of 85 corps commanders; 110 out of 195 divisional commanders; and 220 out of 406 brigade commanders. This meant that about 403 out of 706 generals had been liquidated. Apart from the fact that their replacements were bound to be loyal adherents of the régime first and foremost, rather than being capable professional soldiers, the Red Army's new officer corps was not prepared for a full-blooded campaign in December 1939. It had had no

time for the new officers to train their units into efficient fighting machines.

It was hardly likely that Stalin would accept these setbacks. Nor could he afford to: in a session of December 12, 1939, the League of Nations had condemned the aggression of the Soviet Union against Finland and had registered its approval of the intervention of its member-states on Finland's behalf. The Supreme Soviet was forced to redress the situation by using resources which it would have preferred to reserve for other eventualities. West of the Urals, the Military Districts of the Volga, of Kiev, of the Caucasus, and of Transcaucasia were now called upon to contribute to a new offensive against Finland.

According to Marshal Mannerheim, no less than 45 divisions were thrown into the second phase of the "Winter War"—about 40% of the land forces stationed in the European provinces of the Soviet Union. In the Karelian Isthmus, the Soviet 7th Army, which had failed to break the Mannerheim Line, was now moved to the Gulf of Finland on the extreme left of the line, to allow the new 13th Army to take its place in the line with its right flank on Lake Ladoga. The Soviet armies on the Finnish front were put under the command of Marshal Semyon Timoshenko and given a new hard-core strength of 24 infantry divisions, with three more in reserve, on the Karelian front—13 more infantry divisions than those which had attacked on November 30. These were backed up by 20 artillery regiments (about 720 guns) and seven armoured brigades (455 tanks). Together with 15 new regiments of the Red Air Force (450 aircraft), these reinforcements gave the Russians a superiority of three to one over the Finns.

Timoshenko's offensive began on February 1, 1940, on the Summa sector, in a temperature of −30 degrees Centigrade. There was a new method in the Soviet attacks, and it was not lost on the Finns. Mannerheim wrote: "The Russians had now learned to co-ordinate their different arms. Their artillery fire was flexible, adapted to the movements of the infantry, and it was directed with great precision from observation balloons and by observers mounted on tanks. As the enemy spared neither his men nor his tanks, his losses were still terrible. Sometimes several regiments would get themselves jammed together in restricted terrain, forming a compact, immobile target for our artillery. Enemy losses were so heavy that on one day we took prisoners from as many as 20 freshly-committed units. One new Russian tactic consisted of using trains of armoured sledges drawn by tanks, with each vehicle—tanks included—loaded with infantrymen. Flame-throwing tanks were also used against us."

The Finnish troops fought desperately to hold Summa with all their customary tenacity, but were gradually forced back. Timoshenko then switched the main weight of his offensive further to the east, and by February 11 had made the first breakthrough of the Mannerheim Line's defences. During the following days repeated Red Army attacks widened the breach, and Mannerheim was forced to order a retreat.

The Finns withdrew in perfect order and the Russians lost contact during the retreat, thanks to determined Finnish counter-attacks. The new line which the Finns took up on February 18 was longer than the previous one, and the Finnish reserves were now stretched very thin. More withdrawals soon became necessary, although the Finns kept up their counter-attacks. But after March 4 a new danger threatened the communications of the Finnish troops in Karelia; on February 24 Soviet troops had seized the island fortress of Koivisto in the Gulf of Finland, and as soon as the ice was thick enough to bear the weight of tanks, Timoshenko ordered the 7th Army to cross to the mainland and take Viipuri. On March 5 Mannerheim reported that long-term resistance would be impossible because of the lack of manpower and ammunition; and on the 8th a Finnish deputation–Ryti, the Prime Minister, Paasikivi, Minister without Portfolio, General Walden, Minister of Defence, and Professor Voionmaa, speaker of the Committee of Foreign Affairs–set out for Moscow to sue for peace.

On March 12 the Russo-Finnish Treaty was signed in Moscow, according to the terms demanded by the Soviet delegation composed of Molotov, General Alexei Zhdanov, and General A. M. Vasilevsky:
1. Finland to cede the Viipuri district;
2. Finland to lease the Hangö Peninsula, at the mouth of the Gulf of Finland, for 30 years;
3. Finland to cede the Salla district;
4. Finland to cede her portion of the Rybachiy Peninsula in Lappland; and
5. Finland to build a railway between Murmansk and Kemijärvi.

The final clause, which would permit the Soviet Union to use railway support for any offensive operations against Sweden, aroused strong protests in Stockholm, but Finland had no choice. Like the other demands, the proposed railway was a *sine qua non*.

Mannerheim's assessment of the treaty's full meaning is a sombre one. "The territory ceded amounted to 16,000 square miles, and its inhabitants formed 12 per cent of the population of the country. Nearly 500,000 people had to abandon the homes and the land which had belonged to their forefathers for generations. These regions had contributed 11 per cent of the country's economic life–in agriculture, industry, and timber.

"The treaty had catastrophic effects on our strategic situation. We lost all the defiles which had allowed us to halt invading armies. The new frontier left Finland naked to any aggressor, and Hangö was a pistol pointed at the heart of the country. The treaty removed our security and any freedom in foreign policy. The only consolation in this calamity was

that the Kremlin had not forced a defensive alliance upon us."

A cease-fire came into being on March 13, 12 hours after the signing of the Treaty of Moscow. In six weeks, the Soviet 7th Army had gained barely 20 miles, while the achievements of the 13th Army were so modest that its commander was disgraced. Although the Finnish Army was exhausted its morale had held firm: only a very few Finnish prisoners had been taken by the Red Army.

Finland had called at least 600,000 men to the colours; of these, 24,934 had been killed and 43,557 wounded. These figures indicate how bitter the fighting had been. But Finland's losses were far lower than those of the Russians. Between Lake Ladoga and the Arctic Ocean, five Red Army divisions had been destroyed and three others decimated in the five months between November 1939 and March 1940. Molotov's announcement to the Supreme Soviet on March 29 that the Soviet Union's losses could be assessed as 48,745 killed and 158,863 wounded must therefore be taken with a pinch of salt. Certainly the losses of the Red Army during February 1940 alone must have been considerable, especially as the medical facilities of the Red Army were very poor and the climate extremely severe.

As far as war material was concerned, the Red Army had lost 1,600 tanks and 872 aircraft to achieve this hard-won triumph.

Soviet Russia's attack on Finland was generally condemned both in Europe and in America. France, Great Britain, Denmark, Norway, Sweden, Belgium, Hungary, Italy, and the United States all expressed their sympathy for Finland in plans to send weapons, ammunition, medicine, and food to Finland, and authorised the despatch of volunteer fighters to join the Finnish troops in their struggle. Sweden alone sent more than 8,000 volunteers, plus 85 anti-tank guns,

112 field guns, 104 anti-aircraft guns, 500 machine guns, and 80,000 rifles–all with ammunition.

Germany, however, supported Soviet Russia. On December 7 Ribbentrop issued a German Foreign Ministry circular defining the official attitude to be taken by the German diplomatic missions on the campaign in Finland: "In your conversations, you should stress the Russian point of view. You are requested to avoid any expression of sympathy for Finland's position."

Ribbentrop went further. As already mentioned, he informed Italy that Germany would not permit the shipment of fighter aircraft intended for Finland across Germany, and Belgium was told that the same applied to a proposed shipment of ammunition. He even imposed a "non re-exporting" undertaking, halting the delivery of certain supplies destined for Sweden and thence Finland. For his part, Hitler, on Grand-Admiral Raeder's suggestion, agreed to a request from Moscow that German ships should supply Soviet submarines operating in the Gulf of Bothnia. This negative attitude of Germany forced the neutral powers favourable to Finland to content themselves with the Norwegian ports and Swedish railway links to deliver their weapons and supplies to Finland.

Denmark, Sweden, and Norway did not apply the verdict of the League of Nations and join forces against the Soviet Union on Finland's behalf. But although the Scandinavian powers refrained from forming a coalition and taking the field, their interests prevented them from acquiescing to the subjection of Finland. Norway feared that the Russians would threaten her base at Kirkenes; Sweden had no wish to see a Soviet fleet based on the Aland

A winter-clad Finnish sniper, a deadly irritant to the ponderous Russian columns.

Islands, aimed strategically at Stockholm. Both were determined to help Finland, but this help stopped short of outright war.

In both Paris and London, the Russo-Finnish War aroused concern about the iron ore export route from northern Scandinavia to Germany. The Swedish mines at Kiruna and Gällivare were the two main sources; the ore was shipped from the Swedish port of Luleå and the Norwegian port of Narvik. From the moment the war began, a determined opponent of Hitler, the Saar iron magnate August Thyssen (who had emigrated from Germany to France) had pointed out to the French and British Governments that Germany imported two-thirds of her iron ore from Scandinavia. Thyssen argued that if the Allies cut the "iron route" Germany would be forced to capitulate soon afterwards.

The First Lord of the Admiralty, Winston Churchill, was immediately taken with the idea. On September 29 he suggested several measures for intercepting German iron-ore freighters sailing for Germany along the "Leads"—the sheltered seaway corridors between Norway's offshore islands and the mainland. But Chamberlain and Halifax rejected the idea: the Leads were in Norwegian territorial waters, and Churchill's suggestion of laying minefields in them, if carried out, would violate Norwegian neutrality. The Soviet Union's attack on Finland at the end of November, however, raised the problem again.

If they were to implement the verdict of the League of Nations and help the Finns against Soviet Russia, the French and British Governments believed that they should persuade the Norwegian Government to allow them to land troops at Narvik, and that they should persuade the Swedish Government to allow them to use the iron-ore railway connecting Narvik, Kiruna, Gällivare, and Luleå, which also went on to cross the Finnish frontier at Tornio.

Churchill has given his own point of view in The Second World War. "I sympathised ardently with the Finns and supported all proposals for their aid; and I welcomed this new and favourable breeze as a means of achieving the major strategic advantage of cutting off the vital iron ore supplies to Germany. If Narvik was to become a kind of Allied base to supply the Finns, it would certainly be easy to prevent the German ships loading ore at the port and sailing safely down the Leads to Germany. Once Norwegian and Swedish protestations were overborne, for whatever reason, the greater measures would include the less."

In France, public and governmental opinion was firmly on the side of the Finns. The cutting of the "iron route" was advocated by Paul Reynaud as a welcome diversion from the stagnation on the Western Front; and it was also supported by the veteran Marshal Franchet d'Esperey, who had conquered the Balkans from the Allied lodgement at Salonika in World War I.

Soon Britain and France had agreed to send a joint expeditionary force to Scandinavia in two echelons. The first would consist of French Alpine troops, two Foreign Legion battalions, and a Polish battalion; the second would consist of two British divisions. The complete force, totalling 57,500 men, was to be placed under British command. On March 12, 1940, after many delays, Admiral Darlan was told by London that "D-Day" had been fixed for the following day.

But it was too late. Sweden and Norway both feared that an Allied landing at Narvik would provoke an immediate German invasion of Scandinavia, for which Germany was far better placed geographically than Britain and France. On March 2–3, Sweden and Norway had given their respective refusals to allow the Allies to make use of their territories, and the Swedish Government put mounting pressure on the Finns to make their peace with Moscow. The very day that the Franco-British preparations for their Scandinavian venture had been completed—March 12—the Treaty of Moscow was signed and the Finnish war was over. The Allies had been deprived at the 11th

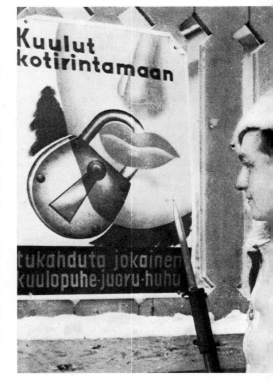

A frozen Russian corpse (opposite top). "Careless Talk Costs Lives"—a Finnish variation (opposite). A Finnish fuel dump burns (above).

hour of their excuse for making their landings at Narvik.

This setback spelled Daladier's downfall. On March 20 he resigned, after a vote which had given his government only 239 supporters with 300 deputies abstaining. He was succeeded as Prime Minister by Paul Reynaud, but the new government had a majority of only one, and even that single vote hung in the balance.

Reynaud set up a small war cabinet. He kept the Foreign Ministry for himself and brought in Daladier to head the Ministry of National Defence. Reynaud's opinion was clear: the Finnish war had not resolved the crucial problem of Germany's shipments of Scandinavian iron ore. Totally won over by August Thyssen's arguments, Reynaud was determined to block the iron route by force.

For once, General Gamelin agreed with his government. On March 16 he wrote a memorandum on how Finland's defeat affected the situation in Scandinavia.

The memorandum also contained the following recommendations to the government: "We should forbid Sweden, under pain of blockade, to sell her ore to Germany. If Sweden agrees, we will have gained our objective. If Germany should invade Sweden we will also have gained our objective, provided that we intervene before the spring thaw. If Sweden refuses, we should intercept Scandinavia's maritime trade, allowing us to negotiate for a commercial agreement which will strengthen our blockade."

In a communication to the British Government on March 25, Reynaud summed up the problem of the iron route: "With regard to Scandinavia, having considered every likely possibility of future developments of the situation of Finland, the French Government believes that it should take steps to control commercial traffic in Norwegian territorial waters to the advantage of the Allies."

Reynaud pleaded his case at a meeting of the Inter-Allied Supreme War Council in Downing Street on March 28, backed by Gamelin and Darlan. But Chamberlain, Halifax, and Churchill asked for the implementation of Operation "Royal Marine", a

plan to float mines down the Rhine from the Strasbourg region—which the French had always opposed. After much discussion the following decisions were reached:

"Scandinavian Theatre

1. To deliver a joint diplomatic note to the Norwegians and Swedes on April 1 or 2, warning them that we will consider ourselves free to intercept the iron ore traffic destined for Germany;

2. To sow minefields at three points along the Norwegian coastal sea lane on April 4 or 5, giving a general warning of our intentions; and

3. To examine the possibility of laying minefields from aircraft along the Swedish coastal route after the spring thaw.

"North-East Theatre

1. To put Operation 'Royal Marine' into operation on April 4 or 5;

2. To use the full moon of April 15 to lay mines from aircraft in German rivers and waterways; and

3. To present these operations as a reprisal for Germany's violation of international maritime law."

The big question now was whether or not troops should be landed to prevent the Norwegians from clearing the minefields from their territorial waters, and what the German reaction would be. Admiral Darlan thought that it was likely to be swift. When Daladier had ordered him to release the shipping concentrated for the expeditionary force intended for Finland, on March 18, Darlan had pointed out that it would take about 15 days to assemble it again should it be needed in a hurry. After the Supreme War Council session, Darlan wrote on March 30: "it would be foolhardy to suppose that the Germans will take no action to counter our intervention in Norwegian waters. Germany has one vital preoccupation in her relations with the Scandinavians: her iron ore imports. Recent reports show that Germany has assembled shipping which could be intended for an expedition either to southern Norway (Stavanger) or to Sweden. It is not unreasonable to imagine that Germany will react to our diplomatic announcements or to our laying of mines—that is, between April 3-6—by invading Scandinavia to open up land communications with the sources of ore. If we do not wish to lose the initiative we must be ready to land forces in Norway—at Narvik in particular—to occupy the iron ore region before the Germans." He wanted a Franco-British expeditionary force to be standing by, ready to land in Norway on April 3.

Darlan's hopes were ruined, however, by a fatal delay. The French asked for a postponement of "Royal Marine"; the British reacted by postponing the mining of the Leads. Churchill went to Paris and worked out a compromise whereby "Royal Marine" should be put off for three months, but the operations in Norway—now given the code-name "Wilfred"—had lost 72 hours. They would begin on the night of April 7-8.

But the Allies had delayed too long. The Germans had beaten them to it.

CHAPTER 6
Denmark and Norway Invaded

In the unequal struggle between the new German Navy and the might of the Royal Navy, Grand-Admiral Raeder had always been acutely aware of the strategic importance of Norway. On October 3, 1939 he had noted the following observations in his diary, intending to put them to Hitler: "We must find out if there is any possibility of obtaining bases in Norway by applying joint pressure with Russia. This would radically improve our strategic situation. The following points must be settled:

(a) What Norwegian ports would make the most suitable bases?

(b) If we cannot obtain these bases without fighting for them, will we be able to overcome Norwegian resistance?

(c) If we take them, can we hold them?

(d) Will the ports need total reorganisation to serve as bases, or will they provide us with ready-made facilities?

(e) How much help will be given to our naval operations by a base in northern Denmark – at Skagen, for example?"

At this stage Raeder was relying on diplomacy rather than armed force to secure the Norwegian bases that would open the North Atlantic to U-boat and surface raider operations.

Norway's military weaknesses – both in her field army and in her coastal defences – were obvious. Raeder had to answer the following questions for himself. What would happen if the British suddenly descended on Bergen, Trondheim, and Narvik? The Norwegians would be completely unable to resist. In which case, the Royal Navy and Air Force would be able to seal off the entire North Sea, from Scapa Flow to Stavanger. Germany would not only be cut off from the Atlantic; she would be threatened even in the Baltic.

On December 11 Alfred Rosenberg, the crackpot philosopher of the Nazi Party, introduced Major Vidkun Quisling to Raeder. Quisling was the head of the Norwegian Fascist Party, the *Nasjonal Samling*. His career had started on the right lines and he had risen to the office of War Minister, but his subsequent embracing of Fascism had then made him a resounding failure in Norwegian politics. Quisling assured Raeder that no British intervention in Norway would be resisted by the Norwegian Government, stressing the ties of friendship between the "Jew" Carl Hambro, President of the *Storting* or Norwegian Parliament, and Sir Leslie Hore Belisha, the British Secretary of State for War. Quisling wished to circumvent these dark designs by means of joint action between the *Nasjonal Samling* and the German Wehrmacht.

Raeder immediately took Quisling to Hitler, but the Führer, occupied with the planning of Germany's spring Western Front offensive, showed little enthusiasm. He listened in virtual silence while Quisling described his projects, and after the interview told Raeder to handle the affair with discretion. Raeder had already warned Hitler of the danger to the Baltic which would arise if the British should establish themselves in Norway.

At first the idea was to establish German supremacy in Norway by "fifth-column" tactics. Quisling would be raised to power by means of a conspiracy and would promptly ask for the armed protection of the Third Reich. But this soon fell through. Quisling's *Nasjonal Samling* supporters numbered barely 10,000. In the meantime the German Legation in Oslo and the various German consulates in Norway were packed with Nazi Party members who would play a key rôle when the German invasion went in.

On January 27, 1940, Hitler ordered a small planning staff to be set up to consider "Case N" (for "North"), and gave the code-name *Weserübung* ("Exercise Weser") to the plan which this staff submitted for his approval.

The situation in Scandinavia became more crucial when Timoshenko opened the second Red Army offensive against Finland on February 1. But on February 16 came the incident which precipitated Hitler's go-ahead order for the invasion of Norway: the British interception of the *Altmark*. This vessel, formerly a supply ship for the *Graf Spee*, had been making for Germany along the Norwegian coast, inside territorial waters, after her return from the Atlantic. She carried 299 British Merchant Navy prisoners battened down below decks, and was armed. The Norwegian authorities who searched her at Bergen claimed that they had found neither prisoners nor armament, and let her proceed. But on Churchill's orders, Captain Philip Vian of the destroyer *Cossack* informed the Norwegian authorities that he was going to stop the *Altmark*, boarded her in Jössing Fjord on the night of the 16th, and sailed back to Britain in triumph with the liberated prisoners.

Here was the clearest possible indication that the Norwegians could do nothing to stop either the British or the Germans from intervening at will in Norwegian coastal waters. Two Führer Directives (February 26 and March 1) laid down the objectives for *Weserübung* and appointed a commander, General Nikolaus von Falkenhorst, to head the operation. German Army High Command objections were overcome: Norway must be dealt with before the Western Front offensive was launched, and Denmark must be taken *en passant* to facilitate the descent on Norway. The forces for *Weserübung* were originally as follows:

1. Two army corps (XXI Corps for Norway and XXXI Corps for Denmark) containing:

   (a) one *Gebirgsdivision* (mountain division) for the Norway attack; and

   (b) seven infantry divisions (the 69th,

163rd, 181st, 196th, and 214th for Norway, and the 170th and 198th for Denmark);

2. An air force corps (X *Fliegerkorps*), commanded by Lieutenant-General Hans Geissler and containing 290 bombers, 40 Stukas, 100 fighters, 70 floatplane and land-based reconnaissance machines, and 500 Ju 52 three-engined transports; and

3. Every serviceable warship in the fleet plus 41 troop, weapons, and fuel transports. Some of the latter merchantmen were under orders to make for their destined Norwegian ports on the eve of "D-Day", sufficiently late to ensure that the regulation search by the Norwegian authorities would have to be put off until the following day.

Weserübung was the first major operation by the Reich Navy, which had five primary groups for the invasion:

1. Narvik Group (ten destroyers, carrying the 139th *Gebirgsjäger* Regiment);

2. Trondheim Group (heavy cruiser *Hipper* and four destroyers, carrying the 138th *Gebirgsjäger* Regiment);

3. Bergen Group (light cruisers *Köln* and *Königsberg*, gunnery-training ship *Bremse*, depôt ship *Karl Peters*, and two torpedo-boats, carrying two battalions of the 69th Division);

4. Kristiansand/Arendal Group (light cruiser *Karlsruhe*, depôt ship *Tsingtau*, and three torpedo-boats, carrying one battalion of the 310th Regiment); and

5. Oslo Group (pocket-battleship *Lützow* [ex-*Deutschland*], heavy cruiser *Blücher*, light cruiser *Emden*, and three torpedo-boats, carrying two battalions of the 163rd Division).

Originally scheduled for March 20, *Weserübung* was put back until April 9. The five naval groups which would land the German spearheads in Norway were to sail before that date in order to arrive simultaneously at their objectives, and would sail between midnight on the 6th and dawn on the 8th.

German preparations on this scale did not pass unnoticed. Excellent information became available on April 4, after Colonel Hans Oster of the *Abwehr* (German Armed Forces Intelligence) had taken Major J. G. Sas, the Dutch Military Attaché, into his confidence. Sas, however, passed the word not only to the French but to the other neutrals – Belgium, Denmark, Sweden, and Norway. If the Norwegian Cabinet had decreed general mobilisation on April 5 or 6, the first German troops on Norwegian soil might well have met with a bloody repulse from fully alerted defences. But the Cabinet did nothing, despite the urgings of the Army Chief-of-Staff.

At 0700 on April 8, the French and British Ministers at Oslo informed the Norwegian Government that three minefields had been laid off the Norwegian coast during the night. By now the movements of the German shipping off the mouth of the Baltic were unmistakable danger-signals. To crown everything, a telephone call from Kristiansand at 1815 on the 8th told Oslo that 122 survivors had been picked up from the German transport *Rio de Janeiro*, which had been torpedoed in the morning by the Polish submarine *Orzel*. They were German soldiers, and they told their rescuers that they were the first wave of troops which the Führer was sending to Norway's aid. But still the Norwegian Cabinet vacillated.

Because of its government's failure to act in time, Norway's resistance to the first German landings was extremely uneven and depended more or less on the initiative of the local commanders.

As they headed for the port of Narvik, Commodore Paul Bonte's German destroyers surprised the elderly coastal defence ships *Eidsvold* and *Norge*. When Commander Askim refused the German demand for surrender, the two Norwegian ships were immediately blown out of the water. Minutes later, Lieutenant-General Eduard Dietl, commanding the 3rd *Gebirgsjäger* Division, led his troops into Narvik and obtained the surrender of the town from Colonel Konrad Sundlo, a Quisling. Part of the 139th *Gebirgsjäger* Regiment occupied the depôt at Elvegardsmoen and captured some of the equipment of the Norwegian 6th Division. Bonte's destroyers had been ordered to withdraw from the Narvik approaches without delay, but the tanker which had been sent to fuel them was intercepted by a Norwegian ship and was forced to scuttle herself–a setback which was to result in the loss of Bonte's entire force.

The Germans occupied Trondheim without any trouble and only suffered light casualties at Bergen–but during the Bergen landings the light cruiser *Königsberg* was crippled by two 210-mm shells from a coastal battery. Unable to put to sea, she was sunk at her moorings by aircraft of the British Fleet Air Arm on April 11. Covering the landings at Kristiansand and Arendal, the light cruiser *Karlsruhe* was torpedoed and sunk by the British submarine *Truant*. Sola airfield and Stavanger itself were quickly taken by German paratroops.

But in Oslo Fjord the force led by Rear-Admiral Oskar Kummetz came under heavy fire from the batteries at Oscarborg and in the Dröbak Narrows. Battered by shells, the heavy cruiser *Blücher* was sunk by two torpedoes launched from shore installations, while the pocket-battleship *Lützow* was badly damaged and forced to turn tail. By great daring, Major-General Erwin Engelbrecht of the 163rd Division managed to occupy half of Oslo, take the arsenal at Horten, and push on to Fornebu airfield where, early on the afternoon of April 9, Ju 52 transports brought in the first German airborne troops.

In Denmark, King Christian X and his Government yielded to Hitler's ultimatum

The Germans land on Norwegian soil (top).

Their French counterparts prepare to embark (below).

and the German XXXI Corps under General Kaupisch occupied the country with ease, apart from a few minor incidents. In Norway, however, the Government of King Haakon VII had rejected the German ultimatum and was determined to put up a fight–but at the moment when general mobilisation was decreed only one Norwegian division (the 6th, in the Harstad-Tromsö region) was not already in action against the invader. To make matters worse, the titular Norwegian Commander-in-Chief was unfit for service and a replacement had to be found. Colonel Otto Ruge was promoted to General and appointed to the position, and quickly brought his energy and capabilities to bear. But he could do virtually nothing. The only thing that could have improved the situation would have been a swift British and French intervention.

Vidkun Quisling and his accomplices played a much smaller rôle in the takeover

of Norway than had been anticipated. But the notoriety of Quisling's "fifth column" was still remembered at the end of the war, when it took much of the blame for the disaster of 1940 off the shoulders of President Nygaardsvold, Foreign Minister Dr. Halvdan Koht, and Minister of Defence Ljungborg, men in fact far more responsible for Norway's unreadiness and subsequent defeat than Quisling.

The Franco-British reaction to this gamble, considering the vast Allied superiority in naval power, was late, weak, and disorganised. On April 5 the British battle-cruiser *Renown* had put to sea with four destroyers to cover the mine-laying operations off Norway. On the evening of the 7th, Admiral Sir Charles Forbes, commanding the Home Fleet, sailed from Scapa Flow. His total force, reinforced by warships from Rosyth, amounted to two battleships, one battle-cruiser, four cruisers, and 21 destroyers,

and headed north-east as fast as the extremely rough sea would allow. This sortie was the result of Intelligence reports of an imminent German operation against Norway which had reached the British Admiralty, and which corroborated observations made in the North Sea by R.A.F. Coastal Command. But the message which had sent Forbes to sea ended with the confusing statement that "all these reports are of doubtful value and may well be only a further move in the war of nerves". It was typical of the Admiralty to compose messages which tried to cover any eventuality–but this one 'meant that Forbes, investigating German intentions towards Norway, was also asked to consider a possible German

The last moments of the Glowworm, *under fire from the* Hipper *(above), and the rescue of the survivors (below).*

break-out into the North Atlantic.

At 0900 on the 8th, the British destroyer *Glowworm*, which had been one of the destroyers escorting *Renown* during the mine-laying operations, ran head-on into the *Hipper* off Trondheim and came under heavy gunfire. Battered and burning, *Glowworm* heroically rammed *Hipper* and before sinking managed to send out a warning that the Germans were at sea. The British Admiralty reacted with a series of precipitate and badly thought-out orders. The aircraft-carrier *Furious* was packed off to sea so quickly that she had no time to embark her fighter group. At Rosyth, the cruisers which had taken on the troops destined for Narvik, Trondheim, Bergen, and Stavanger were ordered to disembark the soldiers and rejoin the Home Fleet at once. Admiral Forbes, who could have entered Trondheim on the heels of the Germans, was told that his

main task must be to intercept the *Scharnhorst* and *Gneisenau*. This, in fact, was what the Germans wanted: *Scharnhorst* and *Gneisenau*, operating as a battle squadron independent of the landing forces in Norway, were the bait which, it was hoped, would keep the Home Fleet away from the Norwegian coast.

. In any event, the situation was all too clear by the evening of April 9: Hitler had not "missed the bus" as Chamberlain had proclaimed. German troops held all the key Norwegian ports, including the vital iron-ore port of Narvik. Prevarication had cost the Allies the campaign.

At the mouth of the Vestfjord which leads to Narvik, Captain B. A. W. Warburton-Lee, commanding the British 2nd Destroyer Flotilla, was quick to take the initiative. At dawn on April 10 he sailed up the fjord and surprised the German destroyers which had taken Narvik the previous day. In the ensuing mêlée both Warburton-Lee and Bonte were killed and both sides lost two destroyers. But three other German destroyers had been damaged, and as they retreated down the fjord the British ships torpedoed and sank the merchantman *Rauenfels*, which had been bringing ammunition for Dietl's troops. On the 13th a destroyer flotilla, led by the battleship *Warspite*, flying the flag of Vice-Admiral W. J. Whitworth, crowned Warburton-Lee's success by destroying the German destroyers which had survived the first battle. It was a day of triumph at London, where Churchill exclaimed: "This confounded corridor has been shut for ever!" The same held true in Paris, where Reynaud announced in the Chamber of Deputies: "The permanent route for shipping Swedish iron ore to Germany has been and will remain cut."

At Narvik things looked black for Dietl's force, cut off from their seaborne ammunition and supplies. There can be no doubt that they would have been unable to resist an immediate Allied landing. Even Hitler wavered: on the 15th he wanted to order Dietl to fall back on Trondheim or, if the worst came to the worst, to accept internment in Sweden. But a courageous intervention by the O.K.W. Operations Bureau caused him to change his mind.

On the morning of the 15th the British 24th Guards Brigade was landed at Harstad on the island of Hinnöy–some 60 miles from Narvik, separated from the port by a sea channel and snow-covered mountains. There was no chance of a rapid pounce on Narvik, and matters were made worse by a disagreement between Admiral of the Fleet Lord Cork and Orrery, commanding the naval units of the expeditionary force, and Major-General P. J. Mackesy, commanding the land forces. Lord Cork pressed for an immediate move against Narvik; Mackesy considered this unsound. In Narvik, Dietl profited by the delay; enlisting 2,600 survivors from Bonte's destroyer flotilla, he formed five "mountain marine" battalions. He had weapons for them, too:

8,000 rifles and 325 machine guns had been found in the Norwegian base and in Elvegardsmoen.

On April 15–16, the 146th Brigade (Major-General A. Carton de Wiart) landed at Namsos and the 148th Brigade (Major-General B. T. C. Paget) landed at Andalsnes. It was hoped that these two forces would take Trondheim by a converging attack and join forces to link up with the Norwegian forces retreating northwards along the Gudbrandsdal and Österdal valleys. But in the meantime General von Falkenhorst had received considerable reinforcements both by air and by sea, despite the Allied submarines operating in the Skagerrak. The 181st Division had reinforced the 2nd *Gebirgsjäger* Division at Trondheim, while the 196th Division had landed at Oslo and was at Falkenhorst's immediate disposal for operations in central Norway.

The British troops in Norway were not equipped for mountain fighting and, to make matters worse, the countermanding of their original sailing orders meant that their formations and equipment were incomplete. The Germans, on the other hand, were a fully-balanced team. This explains why Carton de Wiart's force was checked at Steinkjer and why Paget's force, pushing down the Gudbrandsdal, was halted at Lillehammer and had to make a fighting retreat to Åndalsnes. Neither the landing of the French 5th

German paratroops run to collapse the billowing parachute of a comrade.

Demi-Brigade of *Chasseurs Alpins* at Namsos, nor the arrival of the British 15th Brigade at Åndalsnes, could redress the balance. On April 26 the German 196th Division, the right-hand column of the XXI Corps in the Österdal, joined forces with the German 181st Division south of Trondheim.

Above all else, the Luftwaffe held the mastery of the air. The bombers of X *Fliegerkorps* harried the movements of the Allied troops, attacked their positions, set fire to their depôts (where the wooden sheds burned like torches), and kept up a non-stop offensive against the British and French warships, which suffered from a general inadequacy of A.A. guns in the first place and a perpetual shortage of ammunition in the second.

Under these circumstances, the Inter-Allied Supreme War Council which met in London on April 26 decided to abandon central Norway and concentrate all available forces against Narvik. King Haakon and General Ruge, despite this hard decision, were determined to fight on and took ship for Tromsö, together with the Government and the gold reserves of Norway. Also removed was the stock of heavy water from the Rjukan factory, which the French Government had bought, on the suggestion of Frédéric Joliot-Curie, to make "a high-power bomb".

Just as the Russo-Finnish Treaty of March 12 had led to the downfall of Daladier's government in France, so the

withdrawal from Åndalsnes and Namsos resulted in the fall of Neville Chamberlain's government in London.

In view of the grievous news from Norway, the Liberal and Labour Members of the Opposition brought a motion of censure before the House of Commons. In the session of May 8 it was rejected with a Government majority of 81, but over 30 Conservatives had cast their votes with the Opposition and 60 more had abstained. Chamberlain, it was clear, had lost the moral support of his own party. Moreover, the Labour and Liberal Members refused to serve in any national government under his leadership.

So it was that on May 10, 1940–the very day that Hitler unleashed the Wehrmacht on its offensive against the West–the reins of power were taken up by Winston Churchill, to whom the Opposition parties offered their collaboration in the formation of a national government. There is no doubt that not all of Churchill's decisions as First Lord had been fortunate ones, particularly in the Norwegian campaign to date–the frequent interventions by the British Admiralty, on Churchill's instigations, had had a most confusing effect. But this did not prevent the new Prime Minister from taking to himself the office of Minister of Defence, and inspiring the Government of the United Kingdom and her Empire with his indomitable resolution, aggressiveness, resilience, and breadth of imagination.

The Franco-British evacuation of Namsos and Andalsnes had been completed by

Narvik Bay: Norwegian fishing vessels circle around a sinking German merchant vessel while a warship stands by.

May 3, but the plan to take Narvik remained unaltered. The objective was no longer to save the whole of Norway, but to secure the blocking of the iron route by Narvik's capture. The command of all the land forces earmarked for this mission now went to Lieutenant-General Claude Auchinleck, who had replaced Major-General Mackesy (recalled on Lord Cork's insistence).

Commanded by General Marie Emile Béthouart, the 1st *Chasseur* Light Division disembarked in the Narvik sector between April 28 and May 7. The division included the 27th *Chasseur* Demi-Brigade, the 13th Foreign Legion Demi-Brigade, and the 1st Carpathian *Chasseur* Demi-Brigade (the last made up of escaped Polish troops). But General Dietl was to be reinforced as well: on May 15 a paratroop battalion was dropped to him and a few days later the 137th *Gebirgsjäger* Regiment, which had been given a hurried parachute course, was also dropped over the Narvik perimeter. Auchinleck was also able to use his 24th Brigade in the Mo-Bodo region to block the advance of the 2nd *Gebirgsjäger* Division (Group Feuerstein), which had been moved north from Trondheim to assist Dietl's hard-pressed garrison at Narvik. Thus the battle of Narvik, on paper, finally saw 13 Allied battalions pitted against 10 German battalions.

On May 13, General Béthouart pushed forward the 27th Demi-Brigade from Elvenes, at the end of Gratangerfjord, to join up with the Legion forces landed at Bjerkvik. The Legionnaires had been landed under the covering fire of the battleship *Resolution*, the cruisers *Effingham* and *Aurora*, and five destroyers; this was also the first time in the war that specialised infantry and tank landing-craft, later such an integral element in amphibious operations, saw action.

On May 28, therefore, the 13th Foreign Legion Demi-Brigade, reinforced by the Norwegian 6th Division, finally captured Narvik. They were helped in their attack by the Carpathian *Chasseurs*, who assaulted the German flank. Dietl's force lost ten field guns and 150 machine guns and was forced into a desperate position, with its back to the Swedish frontier and with the French 1st *Chasseur* Division having pushed up the Kiruna iron-ore railway as far as the 10-mile stage. But on June 7 the Germans found that the Allied troops had gone. The Allied forces had taken Narvik only in order to cover their own evacuation of Norway.

The 25,000 men of the Franco-Polish-British Expeditionary Force were landed in Scotland. King Haakon, his Government, and the Norwegian gold reserves were also embarked in the British cruiser *Devonshire* and reached England in safety. It fell to General Ruge, on June 10, to sign the instrument of capitulation for the Norwegian Army. The Norwegian troops and the officers of the reserve were allowed to go home; the same favour was granted to Norwegian professional officers who undertook not to take up arms against the Reich. Upon his refusal to make such an undertaking, General Ruge was imprisoned in Königstein Castle, where his proud bearing made a deep impression upon the representatives of the Swiss Red Cross who visited him there.

During the Norwegian campaign the Wehrmacht had lost 5,636 men killed and missing. Norwegian casualties totalled 1,335, British 1,869, and Franco-Polish 530.

The O.K.W. failed to interfere with the Allied evacuation of Narvik and northern Norway, but Grand-Admiral Raeder had ordered a naval sweep to attack Allied supply-ships around Harstad. The German squadron consisted of *Scharnhorst*, *Gneisenau*, and the heavy cruiser *Hipper*, escorted by four destroyers. But when his force had reached the latitude of Narvik, German Fleet-Commander Vice-Admiral Wilhelm Marschall took it upon himself to ignore his orders and decided to try to destroy the Allied shipping completing the withdrawal from Norway. On the morning of June 8 he surprised and sank a tanker and the transport *Orama*. However, in accordance with international convention, he spared the hospital-ship *Atlantis*, which in turn acknowledged the conventions by declining to send out warning signals about the German raiding force.

Several hours later Marschall scored his greatest success: he surprised the ancient British aircraft-carrier *Glorious*, which was escorted only by two destroyers. Opening fire at 28,000 yards, *Scharnhorst* and *Gneisenau* landed hits with their first salvoes, and set *Glorious* ablaze. The destroyers, *Acasta* and *Ardent*, made a heroic attempt to hold off the German battle-cruisers but were overwhelmed and sunk in turn; but before she sank the *Acasta* launched a torpedo against *Scharnhorst*, which damaged her severely and killed 48 of her crew. British losses in this sad action were extremely high: 1,515 killed or drowned, with only 43 saved.

The crippling of *Scharnhorst* ended the venture. *Hipper* had already been sent off to Trondheim to refuel, and *Scharnhorst* limped after her. Despite his success, Admiral Marschall was severely criticised by Raeder for not sticking to his orders and was replaced as Fleet-Commander by Vice-Admiral Günther Lütjens. *Gneisenau* was detached to operate independently and cover *Scharnhorst's* retreat, but on June 23 she was badly damaged by a torpedo from the British submarine *Clyde*, which put her out of operation for six months.

Such was the final act of the Norwegian campaign. It was, on the face of it, an overwhelming German success. But the German Navy had lost three cruisers and ten destroyers. The two battle-cruisers and three other cruisers were dockyard cases. These losses meant that the German Navy would be able to play little or no part when the time came to prepare the invasion of England, which was to complicate O.K.H. planning severely.

Chapter 7
The military balance in the West

The catastrophe which began for France on May 10, 1940, and ended with France's capitulation on June 25 in the railway carriage in which Marshal Ferdinand Foch had signed the armistice in 1918, has led to the publication of so many works on the subject that a straightforward bibliography alone would fill a chapter of this history. Even so, the picture remains incomplete: many of the principal actors in the tragedy, such as the late General Georges and Edouard Daladier, have not published memoirs which give their side of the story.

In the autumn of 1940, under the Vichy régime in unoccupied France, several authors – civilian and military, more or less informed – tried to take stock of the origins of the disaster and how it came about. In 1941, many generals testified in an official inquiry at Riom intended to expose "those responsible for the defeat". After the Liberation many similar inquests were held. And since then the flood of literature on the subject of the defeat of 1940 has continued unabated.

But despite all the confusion and the opposing points of view, it is still possible to examine the military theory put into practice by the French High Command between the outbreak of war on September 3, 1939, and the German breakthrough in the West at Sedan in May 1940.

There is a widespread belief that this doctrine was summed up by Marshal Pétain's preface to General Chauvineau's book *Is an Invasion Still Possible?*, which was published in the spring of 1939. It has been argued that Pétain's preface stressed the virtues of the continuous front and defensive strategy – but this is an oversimplification. Pétain spoke out against a *premature* offensive, "which would hazard the nation's security on one throw of the dice". His ideal was the "return attack" with its spoiling effects on the enemy – the sort of offensive which Field-Marshal von Manstein recommended to Hitler in the summer of 1943, to check the growing power of the Red Army in the field.

Was Pétain wrong about the offensive potential of tanks used *en masse*, however? Yes and no. He did indeed reject the idea that an independent tank force would be able to transform a campaign by breaking through the enemy's front and operating independently behind it. But he was quite correct when he said that given adequate preparations it was easy to stop a tank attack dead.

Certain incidents, later in the war, were to prove this question justified. In one such, at Kursk in July 1943, the massive German Panzer offensive (1,457 tanks) was stopped dead by the Soviet "anti-tank fronts".

The principle of the "return attack" was favoured not only by Pétain but by the entire French High Command. This was justified by the argument that between September 1939 and May 1940 the French Army did not have sufficient resources to launch a breakthrough offensive in the West. But it meant leaving the initiative to the other side. Certainly, Gamelin envisaged an Allied offensive for 1941, or – better still – 1942. But what if Hitler felt like striking first?

The plain truth was that in 1940 the French Army was insufficiently equipped for the defensive war on which its leaders proposed to rely. It was all very well for Pétain to write of "minefield defences and anti-tank guns" and of their ability to "blast tracked and armoured vehicles to a standstill", but when it was put to the test it was found that the French had only an insignificant number of mines and were woefully deficient in anti-tank weapons. Nor should it be forgotten that the vital bridgeheads which the Germans captured on the Meuse on May 13, 1940, were won not by German tanks but by the infantry units of the Panzer divisions. This speaks volumes for the French infantryman's failings in defensive fighting.

The French High Command never seemed to realise that to remain on the defensive demands even more aggressiveness and flexibility than is required of the attacker. The attacker has the choice of where and when he is going to attack. The defender, on the other hand, may have excellent Intelligence as to the enemy's intentions but he can never be quite sure. When the time comes, he must be ready to sum up the situation at a glance and counter-attack immediately. He must use collision tactics, not lengthy assessments of the situation until it is too late. "One engages, then one sees," as Napoleon put it.

But the basic French military doctrine during the inter-war years would have none of this. It relied on the ideal of the "directed battle", regulated in careful detail by as high a level of command as possible.

Such fatal caution was not, however, totally inexplicable. Among all the French Army chiefs of 1939 there was not one who did not recoil from the memory of the disastrous French offensives of August-September 1914. Governed by Colonel de Grandmaison's ideal of *"l'attaque à l'outrance"* – the all-out attack – the extravagant French offensives in Alsace, the Ardennes, on the Sambre, and on the Marne had cost the nation 110,000 dead and 275,000 wounded. If the French Army had repeated these tactics when it went to war in 1939, it would have been condemned by the French Government, parliament, press, and public opinion.

Without renouncing the idea of the offensive, then, the French military chiefs in 1939, in the light of their experience in World War I, wished to channel and even to dam up the course of the war. This preconceived doctrine demanded that France should have a freedom of action which she had lost from the moment of the reappearance of German troops on the left bank of the Rhine in 1936. All this was made worse by the fact that any plans for the "return attack" were, at best, badly worked-out improvisations.

It was on September 5, 1939, that General Guderian had said to Hitler: "Tanks are a life-saving weapon." The lessons of the Polish campaign make it clear that if the French had organised and commanded their armoured force properly in 1939 they would have been able to overcome the inherent problems in any strategy they chose to apply – provided that the armour could be backed up by a tactical air force trained to co-operate with the tanks on the ground.

On May 7, 1921, General Jean-Baptiste Estienne, the creator of the French armoured force, which he called "assault artillery", delivered a speech at Brussels in the presence of King Albert. In his address he advocated the promotion of armour from a purely tactical to a strategic level.

At the same time, General Paul André Maistre was pleading the case for tracked and motorised artillery which alone would be capable of supporting the advancing tanks with continuous fire. And in 1927 Colonel Doumenc, lecturing at the *Centre des Hautes Etudes Militaires* on a theoretical armoured corps throwing panic into an enemy army, "surprised, bowled over, cut to pieces, defenceless", concluded with an exultant: "There you have it, gentlemen: the shape of things to come!"

Finally, it fell to Lieutenant-Colonel Charles de Gaulle to synthesise these prophetic views and to make them known outside purely military circles, first in politics, with the eloquent support of Paul Reynaud, and later, helped by certain right-wing newspapers, to capture a public audience. One passage in his famous work *The Army of the Future* sums up his message:

"Six divisions of the line completely motorised and 'caterpillared', and partly armoured, will constitute an army suitable for carrying through a campaign. It will be an organism whose front, depth and means of protection and supply will allow it to operate independently."

To say that de Gaulle's ideas were met by a solid barrier of military conservatism would not be entirely true. Some generals believed that the tank's proper rôle was infantry support rather than independent action, while others thought of tanks only as a new weapon for the cavalry arm. Most of them however, were opposed to the idea of a regular army which would attract the best soldiers and lead the public to believe that the country's defence was a matter for a relatively small professional army.

In his book, de Gaulle replied to such criticisms by quoting general views held by prominent men in positions of author-

A German Pzkw IV with a short 7.5-cm gun, one of the few used in France in 1940.

ity; men like Paul Valéry, who said: "We will see the development of operations by picked men acting in teams, scoring overwhelming successes with lightning speed where least expected."

In the French parliament, the idea of such an army aroused suspicious memories of army coups, such as that which had overthrown the government in the days of Napoleon. Moreover, the "repressive and preventative instrument of manoeuvre" envisaged by de Gaulle went against the disarmament programme currently favoured on the left-wing benches. The régime, as the French politician Léon Blum put it, did not want, "at any price", to create an instrument which would lend itself to "strategic enterprises"–in other words, which would give the French Army the ability to take the initiative in offensive or defensive operations.

But even if the High Command, the government, and parliament had accepted the idea of a specialised army, it is hard to see how one could have been brought into existence for the next five years. It would have required the total alteration of the political, economic, and industrial structure of the state, to which virtually no one in France would have consented.

Moreover, the feeble scale of production meant that Gamelin's "Four Year Plan" of September 7, 1936, which was intended to produce two armoured divisions, suffered disastrously. In the original plan

each division was to have six tank battalions equipped with the Char B, but production delays reduced this to four in 1937 and two in 1939. Light tank units were added to make up the strengths of the new formations, but these machines, designed to co-operate with the infantry, were by no means suited for the new rôle envisaged for the large armoured units. Moreover, only one in five of these light tanks had radio, and some of the turret guns had insufficient muzzle velocity for anti-tank fire, although the remainder had modern 37-mm or 47-mm guns able to penetrate any enemy tank.

There is no doubt that the French High Command was to blame for showing so little interest in the possibilities offered to armoured vehicles by the progress of modern technology. The French infantry and cavalry pundits were equally to blame; the tank was regarded only as a useful aid to attacks by foot-soldiers or cavalrymen; others saw in it only a substitute for cavalry in the latter's classic reconnaissance rôle. Neither Gamelin nor his subordinates, however, were responsible for the chronic weaknesses in France's air power in 1940.

As early as 1931 General Estienne, pressing for the creation of an independent tank arm, had grasped the value of close co-operation between tanks and aircraft. "In my opinion the assault artillery is an independent arm, without the least similarity to the infantry, from which it differs as much in peace as in war, whether stationary or on the move,

by its combat methods, by its weapons, and by its organisation."

Three years later, de Gaulle was only envisaging reconnaissance and camouflage missions for the aerial formations which he wished to attach to each of his projected armoured divisions. But the concept–so clearly realised in World War II–of flying artillery clearing the way for the tanks by laying down a carpet of bombs, did not appear once in the first edition of de Gaulle's book. It was true, however, that at the time de Gaulle was writing no aircraft suitable for the task existed, and that no such aircraft appeared until the Spanish Civil War and the "Condor Legion", which Hitler put at the disposal of Franco and which made invaluable experiments in dive-bombing.

As far as the French Air Force was concerned, the rot which set in after 1930 was not the fault of the land forces but of the political authorities and most particularly of the various heads of the French Air Ministry of the time. Without air formations working in close contact, how could heavy armoured units be given long-range missions which at the end of a single day would lead them a great distance behind the enemy line?

General Gamelin certainly had grave doubts on the subject; he believed that tank development should be subordinated to up-dating the French artillery, and the least one can say is that the experience of the 1940 campaign showed that he was not wrong with regard to the latter.

Everything stemmed from the weakness in the air. Without sufficient air cover the French tanks could never hope to match the speedy advances made by the Panzers; on the other hand, they were exposed to the deadly attacks of the Stukas. There was another, more deadly fault: without having gained any practical experience in aircraft-armour co-operation, how could the French have been expected to foresee the power of the combination in a future war? These shortcomings explain all the weaknesses in the French Army's equipment when it came to the defensive campaign of 1940: air cover, anti-aircraft guns, and anti-tank weapons.

Who, then, was to blame? The only conclusion is that there is no way of condemning any single man, general staff, or basic military doctrine; but that the French weaknesses of 1940 were the inevitable result of the pacifist lethargy which overwhelmed the French nation in 1924 and which was confirmed by the anti-war electoral verdicts in 1932 and in 1936.

The partial disarmament imposed on Germany by the Treaty of Versailles compelled the Weimar Republic to destroy the bulk of the war material which had equipped the armies of Kaiser Wilhelm II. It was a grievous sacrifice–but it also meant a clean break with the encumbrances of the past. Under the leadership of General Hans von Seeckt, the small Reichswehr of 100,000 men, all recruited for long-term service and carefully chosen, was from its beginnings the nucleus of a much greater army and a training-ground for future commanders, who would come into their own once Germany recovered her freedom of action.

However, the military restrictions imposed on Germany were not only quantitative but qualitative. Germany was forbidden to possess or to build submarines, military aircraft, armoured vehicles, or tanks. But the ink on the treaty was hardly dry before several German enterprises specialising in armaments were establishing factories and study centres in countries such as Sweden, Holland, and Switzerland. As far as armour was concerned, the German-Soviet treaty of friendship signed at Rapallo in 1922 allowed the Reichswehr to set up a proving-ground at Kazan'. From 1926, German designers and officers who went to Kazan' familiarised themselves with the many technical and tactical problems created by this new form of combat.

Under the circumstances in which Germany and her army found themselves after their defeat, there was a re-examination of the Prussian military doctrines taught by the War Academy and practised by the German High Command. Were these doctrines, originally formulated by Frederick the Great and inherited by Scharnhorst, Gneisenau, Clausewitz, Moltke, and Schlieffen, responsible for the defeats on the Marne, at Verdun, and in 1918? The question resulted in intense intellectual activity on the part of German military theorists, and the conscientious publications of the *Reichsarchiv* (the historical department of the Reichswehr) made an indispensable and extremely fruitful contribution. Above all, it was argued, Germany in World War I had twice brought the Allied coalition to the brink of defeat and had lost far fewer men than her enemies. It was therefore clear that the principle of the preconceived offensive was basically sound and that the tactics used by the Imperial German Army had certainly proved their worth, not only against the Russians but against the British and French as well.

Moreover, Germany's geographical position meant that she could not adopt a strategy based on an initial defensive campaign followed, as soon as the enemy might make a false move, by vigorous counter-offensives. Against powers like Britain and France, who controlled the sealanes of the world, or the Soviet Union with the vastnesses of Siberia at her back, such a strategy would only subject Germany to strangulation by blockade, situated as she was in the centre of Europe. This was why the risk of a war on two fronts which, step by step, had brought about the defeat of Imperial Germany, had been taken.

French military opinion was virtually unanimous in condemning the fundamental principle of the Schlieffen Plan, which had aimed at the total destruction of the French armies in six weeks, as the unbalanced product of a megalomaniac's mind. The Schlieffen Plan, argued the

French, presupposed that General Joseph Joffre and his generals would stay tamely on the defensive, as Napoleon III and Bazaine had done during the Prussian invasion of France in 1870. Hence the German defeat on the Marne on September 9, 1914.

In Germany, on the other hand, scores of authorities had argued that Schlieffen's ideas had been basically sound but that they had been betrayed in the way they had been implemented by the younger Moltke, Schlieffen's successor as Chief of the German General Staff. Moltke had failed to control his strong-headed subordinates not only because of weakness of character, but because he relied on a network of communications unsuited to the changing circumstances of a war of movement.

This was, of course, an over-simplification of the events of 1914. But the main point was that such arguments kept the spirit of the offensive intact, and the Reichswehr was trained accordingly.

Needless to say, the diminutive Reichswehr was incapable of undertaking any strategic offensive itself. But the German Army's rise to the highest proficiency in the art of war could not have come about without the more modest but essential training of the troops which the Reichswehr achieved. The instructors of the Reichswehr deserve full credit: they turned out a fighting man who was tough, full of initiative, a good marksman and a hardy marcher.

Even before the rise of Hitler and regardless of the unhappy Disarmament Conference of 1932, which saw the concerted efforts of Germany, Great Britain, the United States, Italy, and the Soviet Union defeat the French proposals for international control, the Reichswehr had begun to triple the strength permitted it by the Versailles Treaty. Now it could look much further ahead as far as practical

planning was concerned. And now the problem had to be tackled of how the new mechanised arm would be formed, and what status it would have in the German Army's order of battle.

On October 1, 1931, Lieutenant-Colonel Heinz Guderian had been appointed Chief-of-Staff to the Inspectorate of Motorised Troops in the German War Ministry. Under his direction small units with dummy tanks "armed" with wooden guns were formed in Germany. These carried out manoeuvres both with and against infantry and cavalry, discovering for themselves many lessons about the tactical use of tanks.

Moreover, certain episodes in World War I were studied anew for the strategic lessons they might contain. It was clear, claimed Guderian, that although Moltke had beaten Joffre in the Ardennes and initially on the Marne in 1914, he had been unable to transform his advantage into a decisive victory because he lacked the mobility and hitting-power needed to exploit such success fully.

Obviously, if the Germans had had tanks in 1914, Joffre would never have been allowed to turn and fight on the Marne. But when it came to the British and French use of tanks in 1917 and 1918 there was another lesson to learn. Without infantry and artillery, both of them mechanised, in close support, all the tremendous impression made by a tank attack was wasted until the supporting forces could come up to the tanks. This gave the defenders, initially thrown off balance by the tank attack, time to re-form their line.

All these considerations led Guderian to recommend that the armour should be organised in large mechanised units of all arms. Each should have an engineer detachment to enable it to cope with

German motorcycle reconnaissance troops in action.

rough and broken terrain, artificial obstacles, and enemy demolitions without wasting time. Finally Guderian, who had commanded a radio station in the 5th Cavalry Division in 1914, was very well aware that the independence he advocated for his future Panzer divisions depended completely upon the faultless maintenance of radio communications.

While pressing these reforms Guderian found both supporters and opponents. Among the former were Field-Marshal von Blomberg, War Minister of the Third Reich from 1933 to 1938, Colonel-General von Fritsch, Commander-in-Chief of the Army, General von Reichenau, head of military administration, and Guderian's own chief, General Lutz. Foremost among Guderian's opponents was General Ludwig Beck, Chief of the Army General Staff, whose hostility was recorded in Guderian's book *Panzer Leader*: "He disapproved of the plans for an armoured force: he wanted the tanks to be employed primarily as infantry support weapons, and the largest tank unit that he would agree to was the Panzer Brigade. He was not interested in the formation of Panzer Divisions."

Among his equals and his subordinates in the General Staff, however, Beck's intellectual and moral prestige stood so high that his objections might well have won the day had not Adolf Hitler become Reich Chancellor on January 30, 1933.

A few weeks later, after a demonstration of the development of armoured and mechanised forces at Kummersdorf, Hitler repeatedly exclaimed, according to Guderian: "That's what I need! That's what I want to have!"

By March 16, 1935, when Hitler renounced the military clauses of the Treaty of Versailles, German rearmament was already so well advanced that on October 15 of that year the first three German armoured divisions were formed. Promoted Colonel, Guderian was given command of the 2nd Panzer Division stationed at Würzburg, but for all that he had not yet won set and match. On the contrary; written in early 1937, his important book *Achtung! Panzer!* aroused such heavy criticism from certain contributors to the *Militärwissenschaftliche Rundschau* (*Military Science Review*) that he felt obliged to reply with a long article. His arguments in the latter, strangely enough, amounted to a startling forecast of the situations on the Western Front on May 10, 1940.

Nevertheless, the doubts which Guderian's argument aroused resulted in the creation, at the instigation of the cavalry arm, of three "Light Divisions" (*Leichte Divisionen*). These comprised two motorised rifle regiments and a single tank battalion—a total of 80 tanks, compared to the 324 of a Panzer division.

On February 4, 1938, Hitler dismissed Blomberg and Fritsch and assumed the position of Supreme Commander of the Armed Forces. Among those who benefited from this move was Guderian, who had been promoted Major-General on August 1, 1936. Now he was promoted Lieutenant-General and given command of the XVI Corps, which was made up of the first three Panzer divisions. A few months later the 4th, 5th, and 10th Panzer Divisions, and the 4th Light Division, were formed, and at the same time the first Pzkw III and IV tanks began to leave the factories.

On November 20 of the same year, 1938, Guderian was promoted Chief of Mobile Troops with the rank of General of Panzer Troops (equivalent to Lieutenant-General

British troops take over a French fort.

in the British and U.S. Armies). Hitler's personal rôle in the creation and development of this formidable combat weapon is obvious. There can be no denying it was great, if not decisive.

Nevertheless, the success story of the Panzer divisions would have been very different without the close co-operation provided by the German Luftwaffe, and especially by the Junkers Ju 87 Stuka dive-bomber. Stukas could attack enemy troops which were either dug in or on the move with remarkable accuracy, and could be diverted to the most critical sectors of the battlefield as the need arose. But Hitler and Göring were well aware of the danger from enemy air action; hence the creation, under Luftwaffe organisation, of an anti-aircraft arm which, during the defence of the Albert Canal bridges, of Maastricht and of Sedan, accounted for hundreds of Allied aircraft.

When Germany went to war in 1939 she had six Panzer divisions. During the autumn of 1939 four more were formed—the 6th, 7th, 8th, and 9th—partly from the earlier light divisions and partly from Czech armoured vehicles placed at the disposal of the Wehrmacht after the Prague coup. In addition there were four motorised infantry divisions and the equivalent of three motorised divisions of S.S. troops. This amounted to a total of 17 divisions organised into three corps.

Such was the "armoured wedge", the weapon which Hitler, Guderian, and Manstein expected to force the decision on the Western Front.

On September 27, after his return to Berlin, Hitler summoned Generals von Brauchitsch and Halder and told them why, in his opinion, an immediate offen-

French infantry move up towards the Belgian frontier.

sive should be launched in the West.

In his diary, Halder recorded the basic points of Hitler's arguments: "The Führer will try to use the impression created by our victory in Poland to come to an arrangement.

"Should this fail, the fact that time is working for the enemy rather than for us means that we will have to strike in the West, and do so as soon as possible.

1. Belgium's apparent renunciation of her neutrality threatens the Ruhr Valley. This means that we must gain sufficient territory to serve as a wide protective area for our interests.

2. The advantage given us by the enemy's present weakness in anti-tank and anti-aircraft guns will diminish with time. This means that our superiority in tanks and aircraft will progressively disappear.

3. Britain's war effort is only getting under way now, and it will increase. This makes it necessary to plan an offensive in the West between October 20 and 25. Striking across Holland and Belgium, this would:

(a) Gain the Belgian-Dutch coast, which would give us a base for an air offensive against England;

(b) Crush the Allied military forces in the field; and

(c) Gain for ourselves in northern France sufficient territory to extend the system of our air and naval bases."

The "arrangement" proposed to the Western powers by Hitler in his speech to the Reichstag on October 5 was rejected by both France and Great Britain. Neither power was going to accept Hitler's suggestion and accept tamely the partition of Poland, which had been settled by the treaty signed in Moscow on September 28. On October 9, therefore, in his Directive No. 6, Hitler defined the missions which must be undertaken by the Army, the Navy, and the Luftwaffe in this offensive. This decision came as a surprise to the O.K.H., which had not studied any such

project for 20 years. But Hitler over-ruled the objections of Halder and Brauchitsch with a direct order, and on October 19 they presented a preliminary plan of operations entitled *"Fall Gelb"* ("Case Yellow") which was revised in detail and produced again on the 29th.

Using a total of 102 divisions, of which nine were armoured and six motorised, the plan entrusted the offensive to a strong right wing, which was to destroy the Allied forces north of the Somme and gain possession of Dunkirk and Boulogne. With this aim in mind, Bock's Army Group "B" was especially reinforced to 43 divisions and was to attack west of Luxembourg on both sides of Liège.

Bock's right-wing army (6th Army–Reichenau) contained five Panzer divisions; its objective was Ghent. On the left, Kluge's 4th Army would drive on Thuin on the Sambre (nine miles south-west of Charleroi) with four Panzer divisions. This armoured wedge would be covered on the north flank (Antwerp) by Küchler's 18th Army and on the south flank (Givet) by General von Weichs' 2nd Army.

Meanwhile, Rundstedt's Army Group "A" would attack further to the south with 12th Army (List) and 16th Army (General Ernst Busch) on a front connecting Laon, Carignan, and Longwy. Rundstedt's army group had only 22 divisions, all of them infantry. Facing the Maginot Line, from Thionville south along the Rhine to Basle, Leeb's Army Group "C" (1st and 7th Armies) would remain on the defensive with its 18 divisions.

Held in general reserve, under the orders of O.K.H., were 19 divisions, of which two were motorised.

According to the plan of October 29, the neutral territory of Holland would only be violated in the "appendix" of territory around Maastricht, which would be crossed by 6th Army in its westward drive. Queen Wilhelmina's Government would be left to decide whether or not this constituted a *casus belli*. But Göring feared that the Dutch Government would react to this cavalier treatment by allowing the

R.A.F. to use air bases in Holland for a bomber offensive, and for this reason it was decided to extend the offensive to include the invasion of Holland.

At the time, Hitler raised no objection to the plan put before him by O.K.H.; but in Koblenz Lieutenant-General Erich von Manstein, Chief-of-Staff of Army Group "A", regarded the plan with little enthusiasm. On October 31 he wrote: "It is conceivable that we will meet with the initial success hoped for against Belgium and the forces which the Allies will rush to her aid. But initial success does not mean total victory. This can only come from the *complete destruction* of all enemy forces in the field, both in Belgium and north of the Somme. At the same time we must be able to cope with the French counter-offensive which is certain to come from the south or the south-west."

In this first memorandum, which Rundstedt endorsed and forwarded to O.K.H. under his signature, Manstein's criticisms were complemented by a suggestion. "These considerations argue that the *centre of gravity* [Schwerpunkt] *of the entire operation* should be transferred to Army Group 'A''s southern flank . . . Operating south of Liège, it should drive across the Meuse upstream of Namur and push westwards along the Arras-Boulogne axis, in such a way as to cut off along the Somme all the forces which the enemy cares to push forward into Belgium, and not only throw him back to the Somme."

Did Halder and Brauchitsch interpret these suggestions as a desire on Rundstedt's part to obtain a more prestigious rôle for himself in *Fall Gelb*? Whatever the reasons, Manstein's suggestions were not passed on from O.K.H. to O.K.W. (*Oberkommando der Wehrmacht*, or the High Command of the German Armed Forces). Nor were Manstein's memoranda of November 21, November 30, December 6, and December 18, in which he further improved and expanded his basic idea.

Hitler, therefore, was unaware of Manstein's plan when, on November 9, he announced that he considered the armour in the southern wing to be too weak, and on the 15th ordered the transfer to Army Group "A" of Guderian's XIX Panzer Corps – two Panzer divisions, one motorised division, the motorised regiment *Grossdeutschland*, and the S.S. Regiment *Leibstandarte Adolf Hitler*. Guderian's corps was to drive across the wooded terrain of the Ardennes through Arlon, Tintigny, and Florenville and "secure a bridgehead across the Meuse at Sedan which will create favourable conditions for the pursuit of operations if the armoured units of 6th and 4th Armies should fail to break through".

On the 20th, Hitler went even further towards falling in with the Manstein plan when he ordered O.K.H. to make preparations for transferring the main weight of the coming offensive from Bock's army group to that of Rundstedt, "in case the actual enemy dispositions, as they appear now, turn out to offer greater and more rapid successes to [Army Group 'A']". This was no hypothesis. In October, the cryptology team on the general staff of Army Group "C", helped by the top experts from O.K.H., had broken the radio code used by the French High Command. This striking success was not

A German machine gun crew on the Western Front, equipped with the famous MG 34.

revealed to the public until 1959 by General Liss, the former head of O.K.H. Military Intelligence (Section West), and it means that several former judgements on the campaign of May–June 1940 have had to be revised. Liss claims that "the bulk of the radio traffic between the French War Ministry in the Rue St. Dominique with the army groups, the armies, and the authorities of the Interior, North Africa, and Syria, gradually came into our hands. The change of code which was made every four weeks held us up for only a few days."

So it was that the Germans listened in to many secrets of the organisation and armament of their enemies and learned much of inestimable value. While preparing a major offensive based on the use of armour, they were able, for example, to learn that the general supply of the French 25-mm anti-tank gun was being badly delayed. It was extremely foolish of the French to transmit, and thereby leak, so many vital secrets of this nature over the air.

In the Allied camp, the French *Deuxième Bureau* (Secret Service) had been following the German build-up on the frontiers of Holland and Belgium right from the start, and it had arrived at an estimated figure which was very close to the actual total of German divisions in the West.

The *Deuxième Bureau's* opinion was that the Germans would attack as soon as possible with about 100 divisions, of which ten would be armoured, and that they would launch their main offensive across the open terrain of Holland.

Given this Intelligence, the French and the British had a difficult choice.

On the one hand, the Allies could stand fast on their position along the frontier. This is basically what the new Prime Minister, Paul Reynaud, put to the French War Ministry on April 9, 1940. In his memoirs he says: "So it was that having said in the years before war 'If you want to go into Belgium, arm yourselves', I said on April 9, 1940: 'Unless you are armed, do not go into Belgium.' "

Gamelin later denied that Reynaud said any such thing – a controversy that will be examined in due course. But the fact remains that in September 1939 neither the French nor the British felt that they could adopt so supine a strategy. And this opened the way for the second alternative: an advance across the border into Belgium.

The solemn guarantee made to the nation of Belgium by the two Allied governments meant that they were duty bound to come to Belgium's aid and to help her beat off an invasion. But there were other considerations apart from honour.

1. For Great Britain, it was vital that the Belgian coast should be denied to the Germans, for she had bitter memories of the damage done by Belgian-based U-boats between 1915 and 1918. It was also clear that Belgium's potential as an advance base for the Luftwaffe was too great to be tolerated.

2. France felt that trench warfare along her northern frontier would endanger the industrial region behind it. Any stoppage of work in the steelworks of Denain, Valenciennes, or Fives-Lille would have disastrous results on the output of armoured vehicles.

3. By the time the first two corps of the British Expeditionary Force (B.E.F.) had entered the line at Lille on October 12, General Georges still had only 72 Allied divisions to pit against 102 German. If he could add the 30-odd Belgian and Dutch divisions to his strength, he could meet any German offensive on equal terms. If Georges left the Belgians and Dutch to face defeat or capitulation, he would have to hold the French frontier with a force of seven against ten.

This was why General André Laffargue spoke out against Reynaud's arguments in his book *Justice for the Men of 1940:* "Under these conditions, the 'Frontier' solution demanded 36 divisions, of which we had only 32. It also implied that we would not have the benefit of the Belgian

Opposite page: the German army in training. An 8.1-cm mortar crew prepare to fire a smoke bomb (top left); an MG 34 machine gun crew (top right); a 10.5-cm howitzer (bottom).

and Dutch divisions, which over-strained our dispositions and put our line into a state of 'pre-rupture'." By May 10, 1940, many more reinforcements had joined the Allied front, but in October 1939, General Gaston Henri Billotte, commanding the 1st Army Group, had considerably weaker forces at his disposal.

Italy's non-belligerence and the freezing-up of the Alpine passes had enabled Billotte and his general staff to be moved north from their original base at Lyons. General Georges put Billotte in command of the sector of the front between Longuyon and the North Sea, and on October 24 gave him provisional orders "if the C.-in-C. Land Forces (Gamelin) should decide to move into Belgium in order to accept battle on the Escaut".

If this decision were made, the French 2nd, 9th, and 1st Armies, commanded respectively by Generals Charles Huntziger, André Corap, and Georges Blanchard, would remain in position along the French frontier between Longuyon and Maulde-sur-Escaut. Only the B.E.F. (General Lord Gort) and the French XVI Corps (General Fagalde) were to move eastwards into Belgium. The former was to take up position around Tournai, and the latter was to move further downstream on the Escaut, establish a bridgehead at Ghent, and make contact with the Belgian forces as they fell back from the Albert Canal. The day after the alert of November 9, the French 7th Army (General Henri Giraud), in reserve around Rheims, was ordered to join the XVI Corps.

The weakness of the Escaut Line was that it over-stretched the front to be defended, and that the Allied forces on the Escaut would hardly be assisted by the remnants of the Belgian Army falling back from the line of the Albert Canal with the German tanks on their heels. For this reason, the "personal and secret instruction" of October 24 envisaged a much deeper Allied advance into Belgium. General Billotte was ordered to keep his forces in readiness "for the right circumstances and the order of the general commanding the North-East Theatre of Operations, and then, while remaining in position on French soil between Rochonvilliers and Revin, to advance in force to the line Louvain-Wavre-Gembloux-Namur. To the south the front will be secure by the occupation of the Meuse between Givet and Namur; in the north the British forces on the Dyle will be in touch on their left with the Belgian forces defending Antwerp."

This "Dyle Plan", as it became known, gave the Allies a much shorter front to defend and meant that the Belgians would not have to retreat far before joining the relieving armies. The plan required King Léopold III and the Belgian High Command to keep their allies fully informed of their strategic intentions in the event of German aggression. The alert of November 9 led to the first exchange of information between the Belgian and French supreme headquarters, and on the 14th General Georges' converted the pro-

visional Dyle Plan into a definite order.

As soon as the Belgian Goverment appealed to the French, the 9th Army would advance to a line Mezières–Namur with its units deployed west of the Meuse; 1st Army would take up position between Namur and Wavre; and the B.E.F. would hold the line between Wavre and Louvain, where it would establish contact with the Belgian Army. Giraud's 7th Army would be held in reserve west of Antwerp.

The steady rain of late autumn 1939 forced Hitler at the last moment to call off the offensive which he had ordered for November 12. Between then and January 16, 1940, the elements intervened no less than 13 times to postpone *Fall Gelb*–much to the relief of the German generals, who had the gloomiest view of the plan. They remembered the tenacity of the French at Verdun in 1916, against whom many of the German General Staff had fought as captains or majors. But the former corporal of World War I had other ideas, which led to several appalling scenes with Brauchitsch.

On the afternoon of January 10, 1940, Hitler unexpectedly summoned Göring, Brauchitsch, Raeder, and their Chiefs-of-Staff to his office in the New Chancellery, and told them of his decision to open the German offensive in the West at dawn on the 17th–0816 hours.

Hitler believed that the meteorological situation justified this sudden decision. For about ten days after the 12th or 13th, a ridge of high pressure moving in from the east would result in clear, dry weather over the Low Countries, with the temperature falling to 10–15 degrees below zero Centigrade. This would guarantee fine conditions for air operations, and so the opportunity should be taken to attack according to the Directive of October 29, 1939, and its subsequent modification by O.K.W. on November 20.

The main weight of the German offensive would still lie with Army Group "B"–

some 40 divisions, of which seven were armoured, leaving 22 divisions to Army Group "A", two of them armoured and one motorised. O.K.H. would keep in reserve the XIV Motorised Corps (9th Panzer Division and 13th and 20th Motorised Divisions), plus 11 infantry divisions, with the idea of committing them to Army Group "A" should the latter's advance through the Ardennes prove favourable.

But on January 13, instead of the cold front which had been forecast, a warm front crept in from the north-east, resulting in foggy weather, which effectively grounded the Luftwaffe. Hitler was forced to postpone the offensive until the 20th, and on the 16th, given a forecast of further broken weather, he put back the whole operation until spring.

If the offensive had been launched it would have found the Belgians and the Dutch ready, although it was the adverse weather, rather than the fear that the enemy knew his plans, which caused Hitler to postpone the attack. Nevertheless, Belgium and Holland had been well informed as to the development of the German plans ever since the alert of November 1939, thanks to well placed and well informed sources of information.

On December 30 in Rome, Ciano met Princess Marie-José of Piedmont, the wife of the Italian Crown Prince. The Princess expressed her fears that the Germans would launch an offensive across Belgium, her native country; and as Ciano put it in his diary, he told her "that in the light of our latest information it now seems very probable. She will immediately inform King Léopold. We have agreed that when I obtain further information I will inform her through a trusted person."

The Princess must have wasted no time in informing her brother, for on January

The remains of the orders captured from Major Reinberger on January 10, 1940.

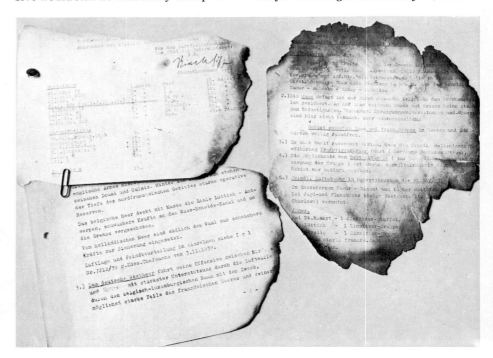

9 General van Overstraeten, Léopold's military adviser, showed his King an appreciation of the situation which Ciano had had passed to Brussels: "The situation is more dangerous than in November, and this time the information that Rome will be displeased will be useless. Only rigorous preparations can avert the storm now." And on the following day Monsignor Micara, Papal Nuncio in Brussels, confirmed this information. This in turn was given a cross-check by a communication from Lieutenant-Colonel Goethals, Belgian Military Attaché in Berlin.

Goethals, it is true, was getting his information second-hand from his Dutch colleague Major Sas, who was in turn dependent for information on Colonel Oster, who worked for Admiral Canaris, chief of the *Abwehr*, the secret service of the Third Reich. A determined enemy of the Nazi régime, Oster believed that it was his duty to oppose Hitler's ventures by passing information to the military representative of any neutral power which might be threatened. "Perhaps I could be called a traitor," he told Sas one day. "But that would not be facing reality. Anyway, I believe I am a better German than those who follow Hitler. My goal, my duty, is to free Germany and the whole world from this scourge."

Even if Brussels and The Hague had remained inactive in the face of this ominous news from Rome, they could not have ignored an incident which occurred on January 10, just inside their border with Germany, proving the scant regard in which Hitler held their neutrality, despite the assurances which Ribbentrop had showered on them in September 1939.

Raymond Cartier has described what happened that day in his book *Hitler and his Generals*. "January 10 was an icy, misty day. At 1130 hours a light aircraft made a crash landing. Two trees ripped off the wings and the engine buried itself in a hedge. From a nearby frontier-post soldiers came running. At first all they saw was one man in a long grey greatcoat, who seemed very agitated. Then, rising behind the hedge, they saw a ribbon of smoke: another man in a greatcoat was burning papers. The soldiers fired into the air and seized the man, stamping out the burning papers.

"Taken to the command post the two men identified themselves: Hoenmans, Major of the Reserve, pilot; Reinberger, Major on the Active List, passenger. They had got lost and had run out of fuel without suspecting that they were over Belgian territory. They demanded to be allowed to telephone their military attaché or their ambassador.

"The command post was heated by a stove. Reinberger, who had seemed to be dozing off, suddenly leaped up, flung open the lid of the stove, and shoved in the papers which the Belgians had left on the table. Captain Rodrigue, the Belgian commander, had just arrived to interrogate the German flyers. He rushed to the stove and, burning his hands, pulled out the papers which had started to burn for the second time.

"Then he turned violently on Reinberger. 'Always the same, the Germans. Treat them correctly and they do the dirty on you!' Instead of replying, Reinberger made a grab at the Belgian officer's revolver, but Rodrigue seized his hands. The German rolled to the floor, then staggered up and banged his head against the wall. 'I'm finished, I'll never be forgiven for what I've done. If I wanted your revolver it was because I wanted to kill myself!' The German pilot, more calm, excused his comrade. 'What do you expect? He is a serving officer. What will become of him?' "

"The veil has been ripped apart", noted General van Overstraeten in his diary the day after the discovery. And in fact the *General Order of Operations: Luftflotte* II, although damaged by fire, set out the Wehrmacht's intentions with unmistakable clarity. The order ran as follows:

"The German Army in the West will take the offensive between the North Sea and the Moselle, with very heavy support from the air forces, across the territory of Belgium and Luxembourg with the effect that . . . as many important units as possible of the French Army and its . . . The forts of Liège and . . . encircled . . . Furthermore, the intention is to occupy Dutch territory with the exception of 'Vesting Holland' ('Fortress Holland') area [shielding Rotterdam, Amsterdam, and the Hague] with a special detachment (X Corps and 1st Panzer Division).

"VIII *Fliegerkorps* must use part of its forces to support a landing by 7th Airborne Division on the day of the attack.

"In direct co-operation with 6th Army (whose main effort will be made to the west of Maastricht) air cover must be provided over the advance of the land forces attacking the defence lines in the Meuse valley, and to destroy the Belgian Army to the west of this region . . . The fighters must win control of the air over the attack zone of 6th Army.

"*Luftflotte* III will launch the bulk of its combat formations against French aerodromes, preventing the French Air Force from intervening in the ground fighting. Afterwards, [*Luftflotte* III] will prevent the advance to the north-east of the French armies in the North . . .

"X *Fliegerkorps*, in liaison with the Navy, will concentrate its attacks on British naval forces . . ."

The *Instructions for 7th Airborne Division* defined the basic mission of this large airborne force. Signed by General Kurt Student, these instructions ordered a landing to be made west of the Meuse, upstream of Namur, in order to prevent the destruction of bridges across the river between Anhée and Dinant, and to establish a bridge-head around Yvoir.

Did the Abwehr experts deceive themselves over the security of this complex plan? General Wenninger, German Military Attaché in Brussels, had certainly failed to deceive the Belgians. He had asked for permission to speak with Reinberger and his request had been granted – but the room provided for the interview was scattered with hidden microphones, and the unfortunate courier was heard to state that after his two attempts to destroy them nothing remained of the papers he had been carrying but "a few fragments of documents no bigger than the palm of one's hand".

In saying so much Reinberger was considerably over-stepping the mark – but his statement confirmed that the papers were not a "plant".

This incident, and the measures subsequently taken by the Belgian and Dutch armies, provoked Hitler's fury.

In his book *The Fall of France, 1940* Colonel Goutard writes: "When he heard of the aeroplane incident Hitler flew into an insane rage. 'I was present,' Keitel declared at Nuremberg, "during the greatest storm I ever saw in my life. The Führer was possessed, foaming at the mouth, pounding the wall with his fists and hurling the lowest insults at the 'incompetents and traitors of the General Staff', whom he threatened with the death penalty. Even Göring came in for a terrible scene, so much so that even on the following day Kesselring found him 'more depressed than I have ever seen him'.

"General Hellmuth Felmy, commanding *Luftflotte* II, was held responsible; he was sacked and replaced by Kesselring."

A special order of the Führer strengthened the already draconian security measures for military secrecy, but in all the projected operation was only amended in two respects:

1. In view of the uncertainty as to the condition of the documents captured by the Belgians, it was decided to cancel the landing to be made by 7th Airborne Division on the right bank of the Meuse, together with the variant intended to expand the bridge-head at Ghent. In addition, apart from the detachment earmarked to capture the Albert Canal bridges and Fort Eben-Emaël, all remaining German airborne forces were to be kept in reserve for landings or parachute drops within the Dutch *Vesting Holland* defence zone.
2. To prevent any further indiscretions all concentration movements before D-Day were to be cancelled, and the existing dispositions adapted so that the army groups would be able to jump off within 24 hours of the order being given – or even sooner. The movement of reserves by road or rail was not to begin until D-Day, all of which would be too rapid for enemy agents to follow.

Such were the points which Hitler developed before the Commanders-in-Chief of the Army, Navy, and Luftwaffe, together with their Chiefs-of-Staff, in a conference on January 20. Basically, all missions and objectives remained unchanged. But Halder noted a "slight difference": should the main weight of the attack be shifted to the south of Liège?

German infantry under bombardment from Allied artillery.

As we already know, the plan which was evolving painfully in Hitler's mind had already been given an almost definitive form by Manstein, Rundstedt's Chief-of-Staff at Army Group "A" H.Q. in Koblenz.

On January 12, with the offensive once again imminent, Manstein sent another memorandum to O.K.H., again with Rundstedt's approval. In this document he restated his doubts about the results which could be gained by the current plan, repeating his former arguments, but this time giving suggestions which he believed would result in the total destruction of the enemy.

Taking account of all that was known of the enemy strength and dispositions, Manstein argued that at best the current O.K.H. plan could only result in sterile and bloody trench warfare from the Somme estuary to the Maginot Line. This meant that the November 20 directive, which aimed at bringing Army Group "A" to the Meuse at Sedan, could only be considered an inadequate palliative. Manstein believed that the revised attack would only make sense if driven home on the left bank of the river. As he saw it, these were the objectives which should be given to Army Group "A":

"While one army on the south of the front acts as a flank guard to the whole operation by taking up an approximate position on the line Carignan-Thionville, it is essential that *another army*, having crossed the Meuse at Sedan, drives to the south-west. This attack will defeat any attempt by the enemy to re-establish himself between the Aisne and the Oise by counter-attacking. Throwing the enemy south of the Aisne might even prevent him from forming a continuous front on the line Thionville-Stenay-Aisne-Somme. This second attack would also assist the redeployment of the northern wing [Army Group "B"] towards the south.

"A *third army*, forcing the line of the Meuse between Dinant and Fumay, will drive towards Saint Quentin to take in flank the enemy forces retreating to the Somme before the advance of the northern wing. Even if this fails, it will clear the way to the Somme for the northern wing.

"Only the execution of this plan will result in a decisive victory over the French Army."

The transfer of the centre of gravity of the attack to the Meuse between Dinant and Sedan implied that Rundstedt's army group should be reinforced with more armoured units and an additional army; but O.K.H. did not reply to Manstein's memorandum of January 12 and refused to forward it to O.K.W. However, the question was soon raised again as a result of two war games. One of these was held at Koblenz on February 7; the other was held on the 14th at Mainz, H.Q. of General List's 12th Army, with Halder present.

Given the known enemy strength in the Ardennes sector, the war game showed that Guderian's XIX Corps could reach the Meuse at Sedan on the fourth day of the attack. What should then be done? Cross the Meuse on the fifth day, was Guderian's opinion. "Absurd," noted Halder in his diary for February 7. O.K.H. would not be able to decide in which direction the offensive should be strengthened until the third day of the attack, which meant that a methodical attack could not be launched across the Meuse until the ninth or even the tenth day.

Several days before, however, Colonel Rudolf Schmundt, who had succeeded Hossbach as Hitler's aide, had been told by the Führer to make an inspection of the front.

On his way to Koblenz on January 30, Schmundt had occasion to hear of the objections which Manstein had been raising about the O.K.H. plan. Manstein's arguments impressed him so much that when he returned to Berlin his principal colleague, Captain Engel, noted: "Schmundt was very excited and told me that he had heard Manstein propose a plan identical to the one which the Führer was constantly proposing to us, but in a much more sophisticated form." Although there is no record of Schmundt's report to Hitler, there is no doubt that he passed on Manstein's idea to Hitler and that the latter received it with delight, as a specialist opinion which justified the prompting of his "intuition".

But this was the last personal intervention made by Manstein. On February 8 he left Koblenz to take command of the XXXVIII Corps, which was being formed at Stettin. To Manstein, this was "indubitable" proof that O.K.H. wanted to "rid themselves of an interloper" who had dared to oppose one of its plans. In *Panzer Leader*, Guderian echoes this opinion. But in fact this transfer—which carried promotion with it—had in fact been envisaged as far back as the preceding autumn; and it was Halder who, on February 26, put Manstein's name at the head of the list of suitable candidates to command the "armoured wedge" on which victory or defeat would depend.

On February 17, after a dinner which he had given in honour of the newly-appointed corps commanders, Hitler led Manstein into his office and invited him to speak freely about what he thought of the coming offensive. Manstein recalled that "with astonishing speed he grasped the points of view which the army group had been defending for months. He gave my ideas his full approval."

Hitler accepted Manstein's plan so completely that on the following day he summoned Brauchitsch and Halder and gave them a summary of what he had heard on the previous evening, omitting nothing but Manstein's name. "One fine day," wrote General von Lossberg, "during a conference at the Chancellery, Brauchitsch and Halder were surprised to see Hitler take a pencil and draw on the map the axis of advance suggested by Manstein in his project to drive towards Abbeville and the sea; and they heard

A Dornier Do 17 with ground crew.

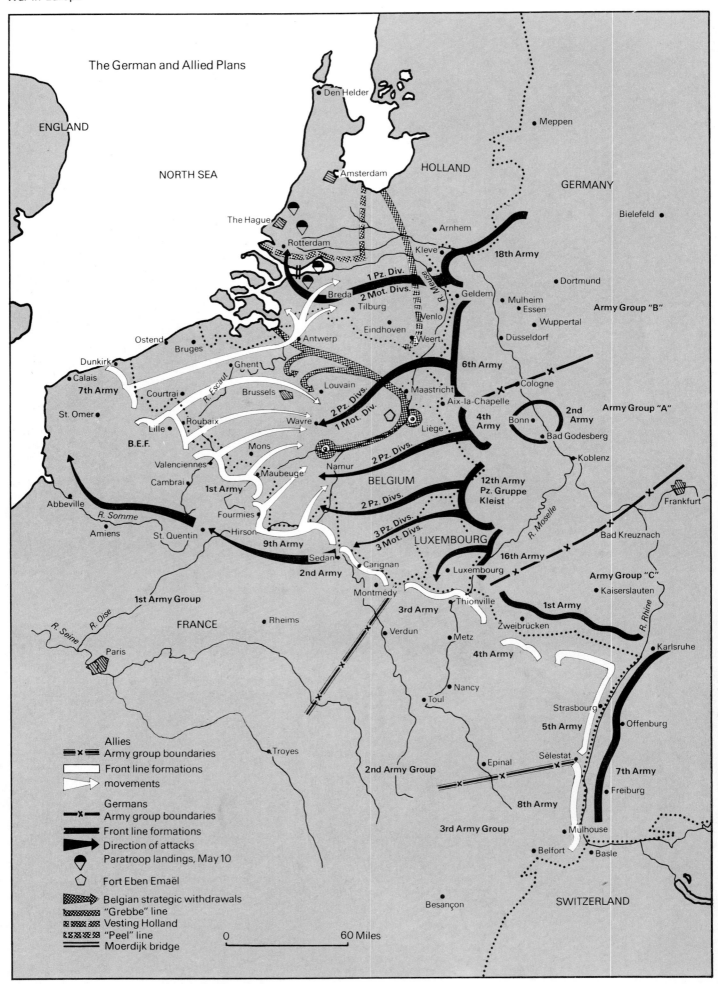

The German and Allied Plans

ENGLAND

NORTH SEA

Den Helder

Amsterdam

The Hague

Rotterdam

HOLLAND

GERMANY

Meppen

Arnhem

Kleve

18th Army

Bielefeld

1 Pz. Div.

2 Mot. Divs.

Breda

Tilburg

Geldern

Venlo

Eindhoven

Weert

Dortmund

Mulheim

Essen

Wuppertal

Dusseldorf

Army Group "B"

Ostend

Bruges

Antwerp

6th Army

Dunkirk

Ghent

Louvain

Maastricht

Aix-la-Chapelle

Cologne

Army Group "A"

Calais

7th Army

Courtrai

R. Escaut

Brussels

2 Pz. Divs.

1 Mot. Div.

Liège

4th Army

Bonn

2nd Army

St. Omer

Roubaix

Wavre

Bad Godesberg

Lille

B.E.F.

Mons

Namur

BELGIUM

2 Pz. Divs.

Koblenz

Valenciennes

Maubeuge

2 Pz. Divs.

12th Army
Pz. Gruppe
Kleist

Frankfurt

Cambrai

1st Army

Fourmies

3 Pz. Divs.

3 Mot. Divs.

R. Moselle

Abbeville

R. Somme

St. Quentin

Hirson

9th Army

Sedan

2nd Army

Carignan

LUXEMBOURG

Luxembourg

16th Army

Bad Kreuznach

Army Group "C"

Amiens

Montmédy

3rd Army

Thionville

Kaiserslauten

1st Army

R. Rhine

1st Army Group

R. Oise

R. Seine

FRANCE

Rheims

Verdun

Metz

Zweibrücken

Karlsruhe

Paris

Nancy

Toul

Strasbourg

4th Army

5th Army

Offenburg

Troyes

2nd Army Group

Epinal

Sélestat

7th Army

Freiburg

8th Army

3rd Army Group

Mulhouse

Belfort

Basle

SWITZERLAND

Besançon

Allies
- Army group boundaries
- Front line formations
- movements

Germans
- Army group boundaries
- Front line formations
- Direction of attacks
- Paratroop landings, May 10
- Fort Eben Emaël
- Belgian strategic withdrawals
- "Grebbe" line
- Vesting Holland
- "Peel" line
- Moerdijk bridge

0   60 Miles

Hitler declare that this direction looked very promising for the main effort! And everyone was astonished by Hitler's strategic brilliance–but it was the justification of Manstein's idea."

Brauchitsch and Halder raised no objections to the change of plan thus thrust upon them. They themselves had arrived at similar conclusions. In fact, the manoeuvre which O.K.W. had just accepted had been strongly recommended by Colonel Heusinger of the O.K.H. Operations Staff for several weeks. Heusinger, in turn, had been encouraging his colleague Schmundt to press for the plan's acceptance.

Events now moved quickly. On February 24 Brauchitsch put his signature to the new version of the *Fall Gelb* concentration plan. Kluge's 4th Army was now transferred from Army Group "B" to Army Group "A", which would also receive Weichs' 2nd Army, once the Meuse had been crossed. The armour was reorganised as *Panzergruppe* Kleist–the armoured wedge or battering ram which was to punch through the Allied front in the Charleville-Sedan area and drive towards the Somme estuary. *Panzergruppe* Kleist contained the following units:

(a) XIX Panzer Corps (Guderian–1st, 2nd, and 10th Panzer Divisions;

(b) XLI Panzer Corps (Reinhardt)–6th and 8th Panzer Divisions;

(c) XIV Motorised Corps (Wietersheim)–2nd, 13th, and 29th Motorised Divisions.

In addition there were the 5th and 7th Panzer Divisions attached to 4th Army, which now came under Rundstedt's command. As a result, Army Group "A" now totalled 45½ divisions–seven of them Panzer divisions and three of them motorised. Bock, whose Army Group "B" had contained 42 divisions according to the original directive of October 29, was reduced to 29 divisions, and he protested

against this severe weakening of his command. Would his two remaining armies be strong enough to carry out their missions–6th Army to force the Albert Canal, keystone of the Belgian defences, and 18th Army to conquer Holland?

O.K.H. rejected the complaints from Army Group "B". However, not all the army commanders shared in the optimism which Guderian and Manstein had managed to instil into Halder and Brauchitsch. Guderian's memoirs contain a significant passage which reveals this.

On March 15 "a conference took place attended by the army and army group commanders of Army Group 'A', accompanied by General von Kleist and myself, in the Reich Chancellery. Hitler was there. Each of us generals outlined what his task was and how he intended to carry it out. I was the last to speak. My task was as follows: on the day ordered I would cross the Luxembourg frontier, drive through southern Belgium towards Sedan, cross the Meuse and establish a bridgehead on the far side so that the infantry corps following behind could get across. I explained briefly that my corps would advance through Luxembourg and southern Belgium in three columns; I reckoned on reaching the Belgian frontier posts in the first day and I hoped to break through them on that same day; on the second day I would advance as far as Neufchâteau; on the third day I would reach Bouillon and cross the Semois; on the fourth day I would arrive at the Meuse; on the fifth day I would cross it. By the evening of the fifth day I hoped to have established a bridgehead on the far bank.

Hitler asked: 'And then what are you going to do?' He was the first person who had thought to ask me this vital question. I replied: 'Unless I receive orders to the contrary, I intend on the next day to continue my advance westwards. The

Erich von Manstein, proposer of the German attack through the Ardennes.

supreme leadership must decide whether my objective is to be Amiens or Paris. In my opinion the correct course is to drive past Amiens to the English Channel.' Hitler nodded and said nothing more. Only General Busch, who commanded the 16th Army on my left, cried out: 'Well, I don't think you'll cross the river in the first place!' Hitler, the tension visible in his face, looked at me to see what I would reply. I said: 'There's no need for you to do so, in any case!' Hitler made no comment."

A patrol of French soldiers haul a light anti-tank gun into position.

CHAPTER 8
Disagreements among the Allies

"One People! One Reich! One Leader!" proclaimed the banners which the Germans hung up in full view of the French troops during the "Phoney War". It was a true enough taunt. Two peoples, two states, and no joint leadership–a telling description of the Franco-British alliance and its policy in the winter of 1939–40.

In London, Prime Minister Chamberlain and Foreign Secretary Lord Halifax were conscientious administrators of their country's affairs, but they were not the men to seize the initiative or try to force a decision. And the removal from the War Office of Hore-Belisha in February 1940 can only be taken as a reflection of the lack of satisfaction which he inspired in the leaders of government and army.

However, on the first day of the war the British Admiralty had signalled to the Fleet: "Winston is back". Churchill's appointment as First Lord of the Admiralty allowed him to join the closed circle of the War Cabinet, in which the basis of British strategy was formed; but even his energy at the head of the Admiralty was given no outlet.

For example, Churchill suggested the conversion of two or three elderly *Revenge*-class battleships for a plan to penetrate the Baltic Sea. With part of their main armament removed to allow for increased bridge armour and more A.A. guns, he believed that these ships would be able to wreak havoc along the Pomeranian coast, as the Russians had done in 1760 during the reign of the Tsarina Elizabeth. (Churchill, however, thinking of the wrong Tsarina, dubbed the plan "Catherine".) But all this conversion work would have taken at least six months, and

The "flying artillery" of the Luftwaffe–the Junkers Ju 87 dive-bomber.

in any case the plan itself aroused heavy criticism from the admirals: in a narrow sea like the Baltic, the battleships' chances of survival would have been slim. They were far more urgently needed for convoy escort duties, considering the threat of the German pocket-battleship raiders.

Another Churchillian brain-child was the plan to sow the Rhine and its tributaries with floating mines, in order to destroy German bridges and river-traffic. The French, however, vetoed the plan, promising though it was. Daladier and his colleagues feared that it would provoke heavy Luftwaffe reprisal raids on French cities, and the French fighter arm and anti-aircraft defences were far too weak to cope with such a menace.

The day after the declaration of war, Daladier had taken over the French Foreign Ministry, from Georges Bonnet, in addition to his post as Minister of National Defence. It is clear that this concentration of power, putting overall responsibility for the diplomatic and strategic direction of the French war effort into the hands of one man, was sound enough in principle; but Daladier was not the right man for the job. Moreover, he soon found himself at daggers drawn with Paul Reynaud, his thrusting Finance Minister. The differences between the two politicians could only have been settled by a ruling from above–and this President Lebrun was constitutionally forbidden to do.

All in all, the political atmosphere in Paris was leaden and depressing.

As far as the Allied armies on the Western Front were concerned, the original "Escaut" (Schelde) manoeuvre of October 24, 1939, had been superseded by the more ambitious and complicated "Dyle Plan".

This was formulated at a conference held at Gamelin's G.H.Q. at la Ferté-sous-Jouarre on November 13.

Gamelin's many critics have condemned this plan as the basic cause of the disaster of May-June 1940. They argue that the actual situation fulfilled none of the conditions needed to meet the German advance on equal terms along such an advanced line as Revin-Namur-Wavre-Louvain-Antwerp. General Blanchard, who had the job of advancing the 1st Army from the French frontier to Gembloux, made much of this argument. He wrote: "It will be impossible to reach our new positions until D+8, and this date is only based on theoretical calculations made by looking at the problem from all sides . . . But before that date we will have no defensive organisation worthy of the name . . . Until the day we actually arrive . . . it will be *impossible* for us to fight. It is therefore absolutely essential that *from the moment the advance begins* we must be completely certain that we will not meet the enemy for at least eight days. Without that assurance we will be running the risk of fighting an improvised battle under the worst possible conditions."

General Billotte, commanding the 1st Army Group, did not share the pessimism of his subordinate. But General Georges, on the eve of the conference at la Ferté-sous-Jouarre, had stated that the elaboration of the Escaut manoeuvre into the Dyle Plan must depend on the fulfilment of certain conditions. And it must be said that these conditions had been only partially met when the German offensive broke on May 10. They included the shape events would take, the ability of the Belgians to resist, and how much time this resistance would gain.

So much for the French. On the British side the High Command was no more enthusiastic. General Sir Edmund Ironside, Chief of the Imperial General Staff, wrote to the British Government as follows: "We understand that the French idea is that, provided the Belgians are still holding out on the Meuse, the French and British armies should occupy the line Givet-Namur, with the British Expeditionary Force operating on the left. We consider it would be unsound to adopt this plan unless plans are concerted with the Belgians for the occupation of this line in sufficient time before the Germans advance . . . Unless the present Belgian attitude alters, and plans can be prepared for early occupation of the Givet-Namur [also called Meuse-Antwerp] line, we are strongly of opinion that the German advance should be met in prepared positions on the French frontier."

From his H.Q. near Arras, Lord Gort tried loyally to command the B.E.F. according to the strategic manoeuvre prescribed by Gamelin. But the British corps commanders–Sir John Dill (I Corps)

and Sir Alan Brooke (II Corps)–both shared Ironside's doubts. Brooke noted in his diary on October 19: "Spent the morning planning for our advance into Belgium in the event of the Germans violating her neutrality. In the afternoon attended two and a half hours G.H.Q. conference at I Corps H.Q. Before the conference Dill and I got hold of Gort and tried to make him realize the serious aspect of the contemplated move, the danger of leaving our present prepared position for one totally unprepared, and the exposure of our flank if Fagalde's 16th Corps does not come up on the left. He will take a very lighthearted view of the situation and is too inclined to underestimate the strength and efficiency of the Germans."

It is clear from this that certain French generals believed that the risks in trying to join hands with the Belgians on the Dyle were prohibitive, and that most of their British colleagues–in the absence of a preliminary agreement with Belgium –also would have preferred to await the clash on the frontier.

On November 17 the Allied Supreme Council adopted the Dyle Plan, which thus became, as a French authority has put it, the "charter" of Franco-British intervention in the Low Countries. According to Daladier, the Western coalition at this date could deploy 44 divisions–20 French, six British, and 18 Belgian–along some 150 miles between Charleville and Antwerp. This would give adequate density to a front which, with a little luck, would link the Allies and Belgians at Louvain.

But did the Dyle Plan stand any chance of success? Hindsight criticism is not good enough here. When the plan was drawn up, the German advance through the Ardennes was only a vague idea at the back of Hitler's mind; and although it had been formulated in much more detail by Manstein, it had been rejected by O.K.H.

Moreover, despite the criticisms quoted above, both Gamelin and the Inter-Allied Supreme War Council had plenty of arguments to put forward in support of the Dyle Plan. It was defended as preferable to the Escaut manoeuvre on the following grounds:
1. It would extend the Franco-British guarantee to Belgium over a greater area of Belgian territory;
2. It would prevent the Germans from gaining U-boat bases at Antwerp, Zeebrugge, and Ostend;
3. It would force the Luftwaffe to operate from more distant bases;
4. It would give much greater security to the industrial region of north-eastern France upon which the French war industries depended; and
5. It would link up the allies with the Belgian Army, should the latter be forced to abandon its position along the Albert Canal.

It is clear that the last of these arrangements played a dominant part–if not the dominant part–in Gamelin's thinking. Belgium's military resources certainly looked strong enough to be worth assisting.

In 1914 King Albert had commanded a Belgian Army of six infantry divisions and one cavalry division. Twenty-five years later his son Léopold had 18, and very soon 22, divisions under arms, all better equipped and better trained than in 1914. Their value, moreover, was doubled by the existence of strong new fortifications and intelligent use of the terrain.

Between the Belgian-German frontier and the Meuse, the routes through the Ardennes had been sowed with minefields, with teams of carefully-trained cyclist patrols awaiting the order to detonate them. Along the Meuse itself, the defences of Namur and Liège had been strengthened to withstand attack from the most dangerous quarters. Better still, the fortified area of Liège, carefully modernised since World War I, was twice as strong because of the construction of new strongpoints as formidable as the biggest emplacements in the Maginot Line itself. On the right bank of the Meuse were Pepinster, Battice, and Neufchateau, while on the left bank stood the key strongpoint of Eben-Emaël, which covered the bridges at Maastricht as well as those crossing the Albert Canal. The Albert Canal itself had been converted into a huge anti-tank ditch, covered from end to end by guns in armoured concrete emplacements.

Remembering the respect in which permanent fortifications were held by the French High Command, there can be no doubt that with Hitler's rise to power, these formidable Belgian defences came to be regarded as a vital factor in the security of north-eastern France, especially after the German reoccupation of the Rhineland. Such were the main arguments in favour of the Dyle Plan, and they cannot be dismissed lightly.

But the Dyle Plan still depended upon two conditions:
1. That the Belgians and the Allies should have sufficient advance warning of the German offensive. This had been available during the alerts of November 1939 and January 1940, thanks to the Oster-Sas-Goethals pipeline. But Hitler's decision to cut down the period between order and execution from four days to 24 hours meant that it was a very different story in May 1940.
2. That General Giraud's 7th Army should not be committed prematurely on the extreme left of the Allied line. In the original plan, 7th Army was to take up a position south-west of Antwerp as the main reserve of 1st Army Group. Among its seven divisions, the 9th and 25th Motorised Divisions and the 1st Light Mechanised Division totalled some 270 armoured vehicles, giving Billotte a respectable counter-attack force, which could be used in support either of the B.E.F. or of the Belgian Army.

However, from November 8, 1939, Gamelin gradually swung to the idea that 7th Army should be put into the line between the Schelde at Antwerp and the Maas. As it seemed at that time that Holland was more directly threatened than Belgium,

The poorly equipped but resilient Belgian Army parades through Brussels.

and as the Belgian main line of defence followed the line of the Albert Canal, there was a danger that Panzer forces striking from Venlo and Roermond could take Breda and cut the Woensdrecht isthmus, key to the Zeeland archipelago. They could then reach Flushing in a single advance. Once established downstream of Antwerp on the right bank of the Schelde, the Germans could cut off the French and British from that port.

Hence the so-called "Breda" manoeuvre, intended to forestall this setback. But despite his normal enthusiasm, Giraud condemned the scheme as impracticable–unless a preliminary agreement could be reached with the Belgians and Dutch, whereby the two latter could release four of their divisions (two infantry and two cavalry) to cover the installation of the 7th Army along a front between Turnhout and 's Hertogenbosch. If this condition could not be met there was every reason to believe that the Germans could be in Breda within 48 hours, surprising the 7th Army while it was still on the move.

A glance at the map shows that Giraud had a good case. There are almost 145 miles between Dunkirk and Breda, the distance of 7th Army's projected advance,

*Lord Gort, the British
C.-in-C., on an inspection
of his troops.*

while to reach Breda from Roermond the Germans had to cover only 85 miles.

Billotte was another energetic general – but he, too, agreed with Giraud's unfavourable comments. And General Georges, joining the discussion in his capacity as Commander-in-Chief in the North-East Front, opposed the Breda manoeuvre on strategic grounds. On December 5 he wrote: "The problem is dominated by the question of the resources at our disposal. It is obvious that our defensive manoeuvre in Belgium and Holland should be conducted with an eye to preventing ourselves from committing the bulk of our resources in this theatre to meet a German move which might be only a diversion. For example, should an attack in force be launched against the centre, on our front between the Meuse and the Moselle, we could well find ourselves deprived of the resources for a counter-attack."

When Georges wrote this the German plan for an "attack in force" between the Meuse and the Moselle had still not yet been accepted by Brauchitsch and Halder. But as a warning hypothesis it was an accurate enough forecast, and Gamelin was as wrong as he could have been to reject it as unlikely.

One point which explains both Gamelin's planning and the doubts felt by his subordinates is the lack of military agreement between the Dutch and the Belgians themselves.

Out of a population equivalent to that of Belgium, Holland had raised an army of only nine divisions, each considerably less well equipped with artillery than its Belgian counterparts, and one light division of cyclist troops. Forced to rely on such restricted resources, the Dutch High Command – even with the deliberate sacrifice of Friesland, could not hope to defend the line between Kampen on the Zuider Zee, Arnhem, Nijmegen, and Roermond. Resistance along this line could only be temporary, with the troops falling back as soon as the German pressure became too

strong. But behind this outpost line two defence lines had been set up, relying on a combination of water barriers and light fortifications.

From Baarn on the south shore of the Zuider Zee to the River Lek, the northern branch of the Dutch Rhine, ran the "Grebbe" Line. Crossing the Waal, or southern branch of the Rhine, and extending up the Maas as far as Grave, ran the "Peel" Line, which ended at Weert on the Belgian frontier. From Weert to Hasselt across the Belgian frontier, however, there was a gap of 25 miles, covered only by light Belgian forces.

Between Den Helder and the mouth of the Maas two Dutch divisions were stationed; seven others were placed between Baarn and Weert, holding a front of 94 miles. General Reynders, the Commander-in-Chief, decided to give battle on the Peel Line with his III Corps, in order to win time for the Allies to intervene. But to do this he was obliged to ask the Belgians to adjust their dispositions, to close the gap between Hasselt and Weert.

When this request was made in the first weeks of 1940, however, the Belgians rejected it. It is hard to blame General van Overstraeten, King Léopold's military adviser, for the reasons he gave. Overstraeten concluded the report for which his King had asked him with the following arguments. "Despite the advantages of covering the widest possible area of national territory, and the hope of hindering a German invasion [between the Albert Canal and Weert] . . . the idea of redeploying substantial Belgian forces for a battle on the Liège-Peel line must be rejected because:

(a) To give battle there would be too complicated a task for our resources;
(b) Our arrival in sufficient time is not certain;
(c) The completion of the link-up with our Dutch neighbours would be hazardous and left solely up to us;
(d) A German breakthrough towards Tilburg and Antwerp from the direction of Kleve would be extremely dangerous to us by making it very costly, if not impossible, to fall back to the Albert Canal; and
(e) A military disaster – envelopment from Dutch Brabant or from the Ardennes – could be the punishment for such a one-sided risk."

With the Belgians taking this attitude, General Reynders (whose strategy had not met with the approval of his government) resigned on February 6 and was replaced by General H. G. Winkelman. Less ambitious than his predecessor, Winkelman thought only in terms of defending the provinces of Holland and Utrecht. With this in mind, the Dutch III Corps was to fall back before the German attack and take up a position on the right bank of the Maas, between Grave and the North Sea, blocking the southern approaches to the *Vesting Holland* perimeter.

When Gamelin heard of this Dutch plan it made no difference at all to his determina-

tion to push 7th Army forward to Breda and Tilburg. He even believed that it would help the Belgians defend the line of the Albert Canal. On March 12, 1940, he therefore insisted to Georges that the 7th Army's move to the lower Schelde be studied once more.

"It is nothing but a gamble . . . if the enemy is only feinting against Belgium, he can manoeuvre elsewhere . . . do not commit our resources to this venture, dismiss the dream." This was how Georges reacted to the Breda project, but his protests were overborne by Gamelin's insistence. On March 20 the decision was taken to go ahead with the "Dyle-Breda" variant, and the objections which Giraud raised on this occasion were also ignored by Gamelin.

Can the Belgians be held responsible in any way for the Allied disaster of May-June 1940?

After the event there were many political and military critics who argued that the scanty co-operation from Belgium was largely responsible for the defeat. But it is not as simple as that.

Since 1936, when French weakness in the face of the German re-occupation of the Rhineland revealed how little reliance could be placed on Belgium's alliance with France, Belgium had adopted a posture of strict neutrality, her defensive dispositions covering the French as well as the German frontier.

The Belgian government believed that to open official conversations with Britain and France about future military co-operation would prejudice Belgian neutrality and invite German aggression. When the British and French made overtures to Brussels in the autumn of 1939 they were, therefore, rejected. However, King Léopold of the Belgians invited Admiral Sir Roger Keyes, an old friend of the Belgian royal family to visit him unofficially. As a result of Keyes' first secret visit on October 12–21 1939, the British were assured that the Belgian army meant to offer its main resistance on the Albert Canal line, but that a steel anti-tank obstacle was being erected on a fall-back position, Wavre-Namur.

Early in November the Dutch and the Belgians learned (correctly) from sources in Berlin and from German troop concentration in the West that a German offensive was imminent. As a result the Belgian Foreign Minister, Paul Henri Spaak, enquired of the French Commander-in-Chief, Maurice Gamelin, what the French would do if his country were invaded. Gamelin answered in general terms that the Allies would not remain static in the French frontier defences but would move up to the aid of the Belgian army. But with the passing of the immediate danger (Hitler postponed the offensive on 7 November because of bad weather), the Belgians grew cool and cautious again. A second visit by Sir Roger Keyes to Brussels on November 12–17, including an interview with Queen Elizabeth of the Belgians, revealed deep Belgian suspicions of French motives.

The Belgians dilemma lay in that they

wanted the Allies to commit themselves in advance to detailed plans to come to the aid of Belgium (and in particular to advance as far as the Albert Canal line), but were unwilling to compromise their neutrality by giving reciprocal information about their own defences and plans, let alone enter into official staff talks – and let alone invite the Allies into Belgium in advance of a German attack.

The "Mechelen Incident" on January 10, 1940 resulted in a deepening of mistrust and misunderstanding between the Allies and the Belgians. In the first place the Belgians refused to give the Allies details of the captured German documents. Secondly, faced with apparently imminent invasion, the Belgians demanded from Britain a guarantee that the independence of Belgium and her empire would be restored after the war – but still without offering to allow the Allied armies to enter Belgium before the German attack actually began. A non-committal British answer served only to annoy the Belgians. Meanwhile Gamelin, the French C.-in-C., had also fallen out with the Belgian authorities. On January 14, French formations were concentrated on the Belgian frontier ready to advance. Next day the French Government sent a note to the Belgian Government urging them to face realities and adding a threat that if the Belgians failed to cooperate now they could not expect the Allies to be so ready to march in some future crisis.

The Belgians rejected this French "ultimatum" – possibly because they had learned from sources in Berlin that the German attack had again been called off. With the approval of King Leopold, General van Overstraeten, the King's chief military adviser, countermanded orders issued by the Belgian Chief-of-Staff, General van den Bergen, to remove barriers on the Franco-Belgian frontier, and issued fresh orders that any foreign troops entering Belgium were to be resisted. Later the King dismissed van den Bergen for demonstrating pro-Allied sympathies, while van Overstraeten informed the French military attaché in Brussels, Colonel Hautcoeur, that a proposed visit by the head of a French military mission was not wanted.

A fresh threat of a German offensive on April 9–11 prompted the Allies again to ask the Belgian Government for permission to enter the country; a request once more refused. The result was that when the German offensive was finally launched on May 10 there was no detailed joint strategy agreed between the Allied and Belgian general staffs: merely a broad understanding that the Belgians would fight as long as possible on the Albert Canal Line in order to cover the Allied approach march and deployment on the Dyle. Since the Belgians similarly refused to sanction formal low-level staff talks or exchanges of information throughout this period, the Allies depended for knowledge about Belgian plans and defences on informal contacts and on information gleaned by Allied officers roving in civilian clothes. This undercover work amassed many useful facts about existing Belgian defences on the Dyle Line, and about the terrain where the British Expeditionary Force was to install itself.

But the failure to agree in advance on full military cooperation and joint plans meant that there was to be fresh friction, confusion and misunderstanding between the Belgians and their would-be rescuers once battle was joined. Moreover the Belgian refusal to allow the Allied armies to enter Belgium and deploy in advance of a German attack exposed those armies to a hazardous approach march under the threat of air attack and to a hasty, last-minute deployment without time to prepare defences.

Shortly before 2200 hours on May 9, 1940, Colonel Oster told the Dutch Military Attaché, Major Sas: "It looks like the real thing this time. The swine has left for the front." In these words Oster confirmed the advance warnings which he had given Sas during the last days of April, concerning the imminence of the attack. Ordered in fact for May 5, it had been put back until May 10 for meteorological reasons.

On May 10, 1940, the land forces of the Wehrmacht totalled 157 divisions or their equivalent – 49 more than on September 1, 1939. Nor had this enormous effort of organisation and equipment been made at the expense of quality. "The attitude of the troops is perfect, their enthusiasm cannot be imagined," declared Colonel Goethals, Belgian Military Attaché in Berlin. On April 5, after a visit to the camp at Konigsbrück, he added: "The troops are ardent and enthusiastic; equipment and turn-out are absolutely perfect. The divisions formed during the winter are as impressive as the former divisions."

Out of these 157 divisions, ten were keeping watch between the Carpathians and the Baltic, seven were still fighting in Norway, one was occupying Denmark, and three were completing their training in Germany. This left 136 divisions for the Western offensive – ten of them armoured and seven motorised – including S.S. units. As far as air power was concerned, the Luftwaffe had retained the lead it had enjoyed in September 1939. The new French Dewoitine 520 and Bloch 151 fighters were too few and too late to make any significant challenge to the mastery of the Messerschmitt Bf 109E. Most of the Spitfires and Hurricanes which formed the mainstay of the R.A.F.'s fighter strength were kept in Britain. And on May 10, 1940, the Luftwaffe had 3,634 front line aircraft of all types, 1,562 of them bombers and 1,016 fighters.

On the ground the Allies fielded nine Dutch, 22 Belgian, ten British, and 94 French divisions – 135 in all, against the 136 German divisions.

In the air the Dutch Air Force was negligible and the Belgian Air Force had only about 50 relatively modern fighters (of these only the Belgian Hurricanes would be able to tackle the Messerschmitts on anything like equal terms). The French Air Force in the North-East theatre had only 418 Morane-Saulnier 406 and Curtiss Hawk 75 fighters and a handful of modern bombers. The R.A.F. had sent 130 fighters and 160 bombers (most of which were obsolescent) and 60 reconnaissance aircraft. So it was that the Allied fighter strength was dwarfed by that of the Luftwaffe, while the Allied bomber units, equally outnumbered, would be totally unable to attack the German columns as effectively as the German Stuka wings would be attacking the Allied forces.

"An army is like a chain," runs an old German military saying; "it is no stronger than its weakest link." And there were far too many weak links in the Allied armies awaiting the German attack in May 1940.

Most serious of all was the extremely low standard of the reserve divisions which had been mobilised. This applied particularly to the Dutch and Belgian forces – in the latter case, despite the energetic attempts of King Léopold to put matters right.

Lord Gort's B.E.F. was totally different. It was an homogeneous force, very well organised; and the British soldier was also well turned out, disciplined, unshakeable under fire, and a good marksman. But on May 10, 1940, there were only ten British divisions in the line – less than one-thirteenth of the total Allied forces.

At this time, as Sir Alan Brooke commented, France had mobilised one man in eight while Britain had mobilised one man in 48. But this tremendous effort had been made at the expense of quality, and many of the 94 divisions which Gamelin deployed in the North-East Theatre were of a very low standard.

Brooke had a front-row seat when he and General Corap, the commander of the French 9th Army, reviewed a typical "Series B" reserve unit. "I can still see those troops now. Seldom have I ever seen anything more slovenly and badly turned out. Men unshaven, horses ungroomed, clothes and saddlery that did not fit, and complete lack of pride in themselves or their units. What shook me most, however, was the look in the men's faces, disgruntled and insubordinate looks, and, although ordered to give 'Eyes Left', hardly a man bothered to do so."

Out of the 67 infantry divisions in the French Army, 20 were "Series A" reserve divisions and 16 "Series B" reserve divisions. And their general state of mind was summed up by Colonel A. Goutard in his *The Battle of France, 1940*: "Three demoralising factors – inactivity, propaganda, drink."

But even stranger than this slip-shod condition of the reserve divisions is the indifference of the senior officers, who showed little concern about this lax state of affairs. The improvement of the situation should have been a matter of the highest urgency, but it was considered more important to use many of these units as a labour force, extending the Maginot Line fortifications. Throughout the winter of 1939–40 only one day per week was given to instruction, training, and marksmanship. And when one remembers that the crucial battle of the 1940 campaign in the West – between Namur and Sedan on May 12–15 – was fought between seven well-trained Panzer divisions and nine French divisions of which four were "Series B" and two "Series A" reserves, the catastrophe on the Meuse is not hard to understand.

It is clear that on May 10, 1940, all was far from well in the Allied camp. It would take Hitler less than a week to win a decisive victory. This was the result of the Germans gaining total surprise as to the direction of their main effort, which enabled O.K.H. to achieve an enormous superiority in numbers and *matériel* at the centre of gravity of their attack.

Between the Zuider Zee and Namur, 26 French and British divisions, of which three were motorised, were faced by the 29 German divisions (three of them Panzer and one airborne) of Army Group "B". Upstream of Namur the French 9th and 2nd Armies totalled 12 infantry divisions (of which nine would bear the brunt of the attack), and four light cavalry divisions. They were faced by seven Panzer divisions

A French colonel reviews a regiment of infantry.

and three motorised divisions, backed by the 20 infantry divisions of 4th Army (Kluge) and 12th Army (List).

Further to the south, the situation was even worse for the Allies. Army Group "C", holding the Siegfried Line, had been reduced to 19 infantry divisions. But Prételat's 2nd Army Group, holding the Maginot Line, had had 27 (not counting fortress troops), until 3rd Army Group, extending southward to Pontarlier on the Swiss frontier, had been given seven of them. As for the strategic reserves on both sides of the Rhine front, the same disproportion existed: 16 on the French side to nine on the German. It is true that Keitel and Brauchitsch, unlike Georges and Gamelin, did not have to worry about attacks via Switzerland or from Italy.

At least 12 of these divisions could have been transferred from the French right flank to the Meuse sector – but every time this was suggested General Prételat put his foot down. At one moment he asked to be relieved of his command, but matters ended with a compromise which meant that no reinforcements were in fact sent to the Meuse.

On March 8, King Léopold got wind of the fact that the Germans had transferred the main weight of their coming offensive from Bock to Rundstedt. Unaware that the "Breda" variant had been definitely adopted by Gamelin, he said to his ministers: "Let us assess the wisdom of

the generalissimo's dispositions: a rash thrust in the direction of Holland would risk getting the Allied north wing crushed against the Zeeland estuaries, while at the same time a German riposte through the Ardennes towards Dinant and St. Quentin could cut off the Allied army group with the hope of hemming it in with its back to the Pas-de-Calais. This would be as disastrous for Belgium as for the Allied cause."

King Léopold went further. On his orders, General van Overstraeten told General Delvoie, Belgian Military Attaché in Paris, to inform Gamelin that: "On the basis of our latest information and the documents captured from the Germans, we are certain that the principal axis of the enemy advance is directed at right angles against the Longwy-Givet front."

General Delvoie duly delivered this message, but he was greeted with much scepticism – not to say lofty disdain. A few days later the theory which he had passed on to Gamelin was restated in a report by Colonel Paillole, head of the German section of French counter-espionage on March 22: "German Intelligence is making urgent inquiries into the state of the major roads along the Sedan-Abbeville axis. Questions include the width of the bridges, the appearance of the banks, the depth of the water-courses, and the state of the roads. The informant is reliable. This points to an attack across Belgium in the direction of the Channel and the North Sea."

Finally, on April 30, the French Military Attaché in Switzerland cabled to Vincennes: "The German Army will attack along the whole front, including the Maginot Line, between May 8–10; the region of Sedan, Belgium, Holland and northern France will be occupied in a week, and France within a month."

Certainly these hints at the nature of the coming offensive did not add up to a precise forecast of the direction of the main German attack. Quite apart from that there is always a considerable time-lag involved when considering Intelligence reports on an enemy's intentions, which gives him the time to change his plans – as Hitler did between January 17 and February 24.

But it is true that the suggestion made by King Léopold on March 8, and emphasised by Colonel Paillole on March 22, should have been accepted as one of the possible moves which the Germans were likely to make; and the possibility of holding a German attack between Namur and Sedan should have been studied. If this had been done, however, the "Breda" manoeuvre would have had to have been scrapped.

In refusing to make this essential revision, Gamelin was flouting a principle laid down by Napoleon: "A commanding general must ask himself several times each day: if the enemy appeared on my front, on my right, or on my left, what would I do? If he finds any trouble his dispositions are wrong, he is off balance, and he must put matters right."

CHAPTER 9
Blitzkrieg in the West

The German airborne assault on the Low Countries was launched at dawn on May 10. It was aimed at the key sectors of the Dutch front, at the Albert Canal bridges, and at Fort Eben-Emaël, and its effect was not limited to significant strategic advantages for Bock's Army Group "B". Because of their sensational nature, these airborne attacks helped to prolong Allied illusions as to where the main weight of the German offensive really lay, though they also achieved important results themselves.

The attack was made by 7th Airborne Division (Student), a Luftwaffe unit, and by 22nd Infantry Division (Sponeck), an army airborne division, with troops and equipment suited to their varying missions. The two divisions had the all-important air support of Kesselring's *Luftflotte* II.

The 22nd Division had to take The Hague and if possible obtain the submission and co-operation of the Dutch Crown. As he was expecting to have to request an audience from Queen Wilhelmina, the divisional commander, General Graf von Sponeck, set out in full-dress uniform. The division's plan was to take the airfields at Valkenburg, Ypenburg, and Ockenburg – to the north, east, and south of The Hague respectively – and close in on the capital from there. But the Dutch I Corps, facing the North Sea, had been alerted in time. A furious battle ensued, in which 22nd Division lost the airfields which had been surprised by the paratroops; Sponeck himself was wounded, and by late evening 1,000 German prisoners were being shipped off to England from the North Sea port of IJmuiden.

The 7th Airborne Division, however, had much better luck. Its troops occupied part of Rotterdam and Waalhaven airport and held their positions in the face of Dutch counter-attacks, thanks to the close support of the aircraft of *Luftflotte* II. At Dordrecht the Germans held both banks of the Maas, although some troops had been dropped in the wrong places. Above all they had taken the Moerdijk bridges across the Maas estuary and so prevented their destruction. The 7th Airborne Division had therefore cleared a corridor which gave the German 18th Army access to the heart of the Dutch *Vesting Holland*. But would 18th Army be able to get to Moerdijk before the spearheads of the French 7th Army?

At dawn on May 10 the Dutch post guarding the bridge at Gennep spotted a patrol of Dutch-uniformed soldiers escorting a handful of German deserters. When the little column reached the bridge it opened fire on the Dutch guards and captured it. The men were all members of the *Brandenburg* Detachment, specially trained for this sort of mission. Similar attempts were made at Nijmegen and Roermond, but they failed. The success at Gennep, however, opened the road to 's Hertogenbosch for the German 18th Army

(Küchler), headed by 9th Panzer Division.

Dutch resistance was uneven. It was tougher on the Grebbe Line (defended by the II and IV Corps) than on the Peel Line, where the III Corps, as mentioned above, had only been intended to slow down the German advance before falling back. The corps' withdrawal, although an orderly one, left the 1st Light Mechanised Division, the vanguard of Giraud's French 7th Army, exposed. Giraud's position had deteriorated even more by the evening of May 11, for the Belgian Army on his right flank was abandoning the Albert Canal and preparing to withdraw to the Antwerp-Louvain line. And by the evening of May 12 the 9th Panzer Division had made contact with the troops of the 7th Airborne Division holding the Moerdijk bridges.

By May 13 the situation along the Dutch front had become so grave that Queen Wilhelmina and her Government had resigned themselves to leaving the country. An appeal to Britain for help had produced no results, and could not have done. France, too, had been asked for help. But it would have been impossible for Giraud to have sent his 60th and 68th Divisions into Zeeland. The Belgian retreat meant that he dare not push his left flank forward to Moerdijk and Dordrecht. In any case, his movements were hampered by the Stuka attacks of VIII *Fliegerkorps*.

On the afternoon of May 14 the notorious "horror raid" on Rotterdam took place. The bombers came at the moment when the Dutch and Germans were parleying for the surrender of the city, and General Rudolf Schmidt, commanding XXXIX Panzer Corps, was not able to make contact with the aircraft of *Luftflotte* II and call off the attack.

Some 25,000 houses were razed, rendering 78,000 homeless. But instead of the figure of 35,000 killed which was announced at the time, today the Dutch claim only 900, and this is the figure which should be accepted.

Considering the situation of the Dutch troops who had been forced back from the Grebbe Line, and determined to spare Utrecht from Rotterdam's fate, General Winkelman made the decision to surrender. His army had lost 2,100 killed and 2,700 wounded. He signed the instrument of capitulation at 0930 hours on May 15, only surrendering the forces under his direct orders, which excepted Zeeland. But Queen Wilhelmina and the Dutch Government continued the struggle in exile, giving the Western Allies the benefit of the Dutch colonies and their resources, a merchant fleet of nearly three million tons, and the well-trained Dutch fleet.

At the moment when General Winkelman ordered the cease-fire, the Belgian Army was preparing to give battle without further retreat, having fallen back to the sector of the Dyle Line agreed in the

earlier discussions between King Léopold and Gamelin. It is true that the Belgian resistance along the Albert Canal had lasted barely 48 hours instead of the four or five days hoped for by the Belgian Government and the Allied High Command; but there was no connection between the surprise attacks which had forced this early withdrawal and the disaster on the Meuse on May 15.

At dawn on May 10 the three regiments of the Belgian 7th Division were holding the line of the Albert Canal with their right flank anchored by the fortified complex of Eben-Emaël, which was armed with two 120-mm guns and 16 75-mm guns in armoured turrets and casemates. While General van Overstraeten was worried about possible sabotage of the demolition planned for the canal bridges, the Belgian dispositions seemed to be reassuring. Eben-Emaël was, after all, the strongest and most modern emplacement of its kind in Europe. One side of the fort rested on the steep banks of the Albert canal and an anti-tank ditch covered the other three.

But no account had been taken of the imaginative flair of Adolf Hitler, who had taken a personal interest in the planning for surprise capture of the Albert Canal bridges, despite the scepticism of O.K.W.

The key factor in this daring enterprise was to be the glider. Paratroops would not have been able to land directly on their objectives with the same precision, and in any case the time needed to re-deploy them would have given the Belgian defenders plenty of warning. For these reasons a special detachment of 42 gliders had been formed under the command of Captain Walter Koch, made up of 424 men (including pilots). For months, the Koch Detachment had undergone rigorous training under conditions of the strictest secrecy – training which included the specialised use of explosives.

On the left bank of the canal, the gliders of the Koch Detachment landed right in the middle of the defences covering the bridges at Veldwezelt and Vroenhoven. Profiting from the confusion caused by the appearance of these unfamiliar aircraft, which had seemed to the Belgians to be ordinary types in difficulties, the Germans cut the cables to the bridge demolition charges as well as the telephone lines, and then threw the explosive charges into the canal. At Canne, however, where the terrain prevented such an accurate landing, the Belgians had time to blow up the bridge, and then inflict heavy losses on the Germans. Meanwhile, 11 gliders had landed on top of Fort Eben-Emaël. Seventy-eight assault pioneers, equipped with two and a half tons of explosives, set about the turrets and casemates of the fort, according to the plans which had been worked out in great detail and rehearsed a hundred times during the previous months. Unlike the Maginot Line, Eben-Emaël was not protected by outer works – and

The Germans advance (above); the B.E.F. retreats towards Dunkirk (opposite top); French and British troops on the Maginot Line (opposite below).

within minutes many of its strong-points had been neutralised by explosive charges thrust into the gun-slits or by hollow-charge blocks applied to their armour.

Deployed along a front of 11¼ miles, the Belgian 7th Division was unable to launch any prompt counter-attacks against the bridgeheads won by the Koch Detachment at Vroenhoven and Veldwezelt. The least activity on the part of the Belgians provoked pitiless Stuka attacks. The Belgians fought back as best they could, but they could not prevent the Germans from bringing in reinforcements as planned. In the morning, machine gun sections were parachuted in; and about noon the advance units of 4th Panzer Divisions made contact. The latter had found the Maastricht bridges destroyed and had crossed the Maas as best they could.

At 0530 hours on May 11 the German pioneers opened a first 16-ton bridge to their traffic, which accelerated the arrival of 4th Panzer Division and XVI Panzer Corps, the spearhead of the German 6th Army (Reichenau). Towards noon, rendered helpless by neutralisation of its guns, the garrison of Fort Eben-Emaël surrendered to the 51st Pioneer Battalion under Lieutenant-Colonel Mikosch; and by the evening the Belgian 7th Division was out of the battle. These events caused King Léopold to issue the withdrawal order already mentioned. The Allies launched repeated air strikes against the Albert Canal bridges, the destruction of which would have cut off the bulk of Reichenau's advance units. But the fighters and anti-aircraft batteries of the Luftwaffe guarded their charges well. On May 11–12, 39 Belgian, French, and British bombers attacked the bridges. Of these, 17 were shot down and 11 were damaged beyond repair – and the Allied bombs caused virtually no damage at all.

The Belgian retreat caused a certain number of incidents of which the most unpleasant centered around the defence of Louvain – a disagreement between the commander of the Belgian 10th Division and Major-General B. L. Montgomery, commanding the British 3rd Division. Despite all this, the withdrawal had been completed by the evening of the 13th; and King Léopold issued the following stirring order of the day: "Our position improves day by day; our ranks are tightening. In the decisive days which lie ahead do not spare yourselves; suffer every sacrifice to halt the invasion. As on the Yser in 1914, the French and British troops are relying on us; the safety and honour of the country demand it."

At 0630 hours on May 10, Captain Beaufre, adjutant to General Doumenc at G.H.Q. Land Forces, Montry, reported to Gamelin at Vincennes. The latter was about to set in motion the complicated Dyle-Breda manoeuvre, swinging the 1st Army Group into the Low Countries – a plan which would involve five armies, 13 corps, 41 divisions: a total of about 600,000 men. Beaufre found Gamelin in an optimistic mood, "pacing up and down the corridors of the barracks, humming audibly with a martial air . . ."

The day before, however, Paul Reynaud had been trying to obtain Gamelin's dismissal in a session of the French Cabinet. Failing because of the opposition of Daladier and his Radical Socialist colleagues, Reynaud had offered his resignation to President Lebrun, but withdrew it when the news of the German offensive broke. Gamelin, although under the shadow of imminent disgrace, faced the new crisis with confidence.

He held to his *War Plan 1940* of February 26, in which he had described how the Allied armies would respond to any German invasion of the Low Countries. "They [the Allies] will be well placed to go over to the counter-offensive, for the enemy will be venturing into open terrain. Only

the battlefield of Luxembourg, Belgium, and southern Holland lends itself to a decisive battle in the country outside the fortified systems and lines of obstacles. If the Germans gain possession of the Albert-Meuse line upstream of Liège, a counter-offensive can be made by turning the Albert Canal from the north and by a thrust between the Ardennes and the Moselle, which would turn the Meuse."

Gamelin was obviously much less defensively-minded than is usually believed. But his projected "thrust between the Ardennes and the Moselle" – a spectre which was indeed to keep Hitler awake at nights – was a pipe-dream. To make it a reality, Gamelin would have had to have at his disposal on May 10 a standing reserve – and this did not exist and was not even being formed.

"There he [Gamelin] was," de Gaulle recalled, "in a setting which recalled a convent, attended by a few officers, working and meditating without mixing in day-to-day duties . . . In his *Thebaïde* [ivory tower] at Vincennes, General Gamelin gave me the impression of a savant, testing the chemical reactions of his strategy in a laboratory."

Far more serious was the multi-channelled chain of command. Gamelin's Vincennes H.Q. had no radio transmitter. Georges, Commander-in-Chief of the North-East Front, was 40 miles away from Vincennes at la Ferté-sous-Jouarre, while yet another key command area was Doumenc's G.H.Q. Land Forces, 22 miles from Vincennes at Montry.

Another snag was that the French army commanders were far from unanimous in their attitude towards Gamelin's plan. When the bad news of the events on the Albert Canal came in on May 11, General René Prioux, whose cavalry corps had the task of covering the arrival of 1st Army in its new sector at Gembloux, told his army commander, General Blanchard that: "because of the weak Belgian resistance and the enemy superiority in the air, the Dyle manoeuvre seems difficult and it would be better to settle for the Escaut manoeuvre."

Blanchard agreed. He passed the message to his army group commander, Billotte, who telephoned Georges a few minutes later: "General Blanchard is pressing for the Escaut solution. I am leaving for 1st Army and will go on to General Prioux to see to the completion of the Dyle manoeuvre, which must be carried out."

In this difference of opinion the impetuous Billotte was in the right. The Dyle-Breda manoeuvre in course of execution could not have been adjusted to fit the Escaut solution, and in any case the rendezvous arranged with the Belgians had to be kept. As for the danger from the air, it was in fact less serious than Generals Prioux and Blanchard imagined – but for reasons which, if those generals had known them, would only have added to their worries. For to give the Ardennes venture its best chance of success, it suited Hitler not to impede the Franco-British advance into the Low Countries.

Although the Belgian retreat to the Antwerp-Louvain line was justified, it had been made earlier than envisaged, which meant that during the Allied advance into Belgium the brunt fell upon General Prioux's cavalry corps for a few days.

The corps consisted of the 2nd and 3rd Light Mechanised Divisions, commanded respectively by Generals Langlois and Bougrain. On the 13th the cavalry corps came to grips with XVI Panzer Corps in the region of Merdorp.

German historians claimed that the armoured units of 3rd Light Mechanised Division, mainly engaged with 4th Panzer Division, showed inferior manoeuvrability; furthermore, Major-General Stever's orders were transmitted more efficiently than those of General Bougrain.

But by the morning of the 15th the French 1st Army, thanks to the delaying actions fought by the cavalry corps, was in position between Namur and Wavre with six divisions in the line and one in reserve. Here it underwent the assault of the German 6th Army, driven home with heavy Stuka attacks. At Gembloux, where Bock had hoped to drive in the French line with the tanks of XVI Panzer Corps, the Germans were held and indeed repulsed by the French IV Corps under General Aymes. At 1630 hours Reichenau called off his troops, planning to resume his advance with a more orthodox, set-piece attack.

Meanwhile, Reichenau's XI Corps had tried to rush Louvain, but the German troops were promptly flung out by a timely counter-attack by the British 3rd Division under General Montgomery. All in all, north of Namur the Allies had the best of May 15. But to the south, at Sedan, matters were altogether different, causing Gort and Blanchard to issue orders for a retreat on the evening of the 15th.

The success of the Dyle manoeuvre depended on the firm holding of the Allied centre by the French 2nd and 9th Armies which, to the west of Longuyon and the south of Namur, blocked the exits from the Ardennes and held the line of the Meuse. All Huntziger's 2nd Army had to do was to hold the positions which it had occupied since September 1939; from Sedan to Givet the same applied to Corap's 9th Army, but his left and centre had to advance from the Rocroi-Fourmies region and take up defensive positions along the Belgian Meuse between Givet and Namur.

A crucial question: had General Billotte been given too much responsibility for one man to carry, dynamic though he was? In the Dyle-Breda manoeuvre he had naturally been more deeply concerned in the intricate manoeuvres of his 7th and 1st Armies than in the static sector of his front (9th and 2nd Armies). And to crown everything, a conference with Daladier, King Léopold, and Gort's Chief-of-Staff, Lieutenant-General H. R. Pownall, at Casteau near Mons on May 12, had charged Billotte with co-ordinating the activities of all Allied armies on Belgian territory. This meant that he had to direct six armies—seven, in fact, if a successful link-up with the Dutch could be achieved.

A German A.A. column (above); and German infantry improvising their own A.A. defences (opposite).

To sum up, Billotte alone was the man who would have to handle the attacks made by the armies of Bock and Rundstedt.

Everything points to the fact that the French troops holding the central "hinge" of the Allied front should have been put under a tighter command, which would have kept them better in hand and compensated for many of their deficiencies.

Without exception, the troops holding the "hinge" were not only mediocre or worse, but also badly equipped and deployed on much too extensive a front. Facing the onslaught of Army Group "A" between Namur and Sedan were seven French divisions spread out along a sector of 85 miles. The current doctrines of defensive warfare demanded at least 12. Moreover, on May 13 only one out of these seven divisions was an active unit: the 5th Motorised Infantry Division on Corap's left flank. The rest were all reserve divisions, as were the 55th and 71st Infantry Divisions of 2nd Army, defending the Sedan sector.

These reserve divisions were appallingly short of anti-tank and anti-aircraft guns. The 55th and 71st Divisions had between them only 21 out of the 104 25-mm anti-tank guns which they should have had, and the 102nd and 61st Divisions of 9th Army were even worse off. As a result of the paucity of the anti-aircraft defences in the Sedan sector, the Stukas could operate virtually

without opposition: 9th Army had only three groups of 75-mm and three batteries of 25-mm A.A. guns, despite the requests of General Corap, who required three times this number.

The ground defences had been neglected during the severe winter and had suffered even more from insufficient supplies of concrete and steel obstacles. In certain sectors of the French Meuse, sandbags had taken the place of proper obstacles. Anti-tank mines, which could have made up for many of these deficiencies, had only been supplied in pitifully small numbers. On the Belgian Meuse, fortifications were virtually non-existent.

On the morning of May 10, Corap and Huntziger sent their cavalry divisions across the Franco-Belgian frontier into the Ardennes, to act as a screen while 9th Army took up its new positions. The 1st and 4th Light Cavalry Divisions, plus the 3rd Brigade of Spahis from 9th Army, managed to reach the Ourthe, but the 2nd and 5th Light Cavalry Divisions from 2nd Army engaged numerous German tanks near Arlon and fell back.

On the 11th, several cavalry engagements confirmed that the Germans were making a major effort in the Ardennes region. The 2nd and 5th Light Cavalry Divisions were thrown back with heavy losses and Corap was obliged to withdraw his cavalry to the left bank of the Meuse. The impression gained from these first skirmishes was confirmed by air observation: "The enemy seems to be preparing

an energetic thrust in the direction of Givet," concluded General d'Astier de la Vigerie, commander-in-chief of the air forces attached to 1st Army Group, in his bulletin at noon on May 11.

Advancing against the four French light cavalry divisions and two cavalry brigades with their 300 tanks and armoured cars were no less than seven Panzer divisions totalling 2,270 armoured vehicles. Given these odds it is hardly surprising that the French cavalry units failed to sustain their delaying action for more than 48 hours, instead of the envisaged four days. But they retreated in good order and blew both bridges across the Meuse after they crossed in the afternoon of May 12.

On the evening of the same day, Major-General Erwin Rommel's 7th Panzer Division reached Houx lock, on the Meuse downstream of Dinant. Urged on by Rommel's enthusiasm, the 7th Motor-cycle Battalion crossed the weir to the left bank and profited from a small gap between the French 5th Motorised Division and the 18th Division to infiltrate, scale the bank, and establish a provisional bridge-head. General Bouffet, commanding the II Corps in Corap's army, was well aware of this weakness in his front, but the battalion which he had sent that afternoon to cover the weir at Houx had completely failed to carry out its orders. Rommel's tiny pocket on the left bank should have been pinched out on the following morning; but under Stuka bombardment the French infantry failed to co-ordinate with the tanks of the 4th Light

Cavalry Division which headed the French counter-attack, and by the evening of the 13th the enterprising Rommel had gained enough ground for his sappers to begin bridging operations across the river.

It will be remembered that 7th Panzer Division, together with the 5th Panzer Division (Hartlieb) following in its tracks, formed Hoth's XV Panzer Corps, which in turn belonged to Kluge's 4th Army. During the night of May 12–13, the French in the sector of 102nd Division observed a heavy column of enemy traffic heading for Monthermé, slightly downstream of the junction of the Meuse and Semois rivers. "It's an onrush, all lit up," reported a French airman—for the Germans were speeding forwards with all lights on.

The 6th and 8th Panzer Divisions (Kempff and Kuntzen), of Reinhardt's XLI Panzer Corps, formed the right-hand column of Kleist's *Panzergruppe*. They attacked at 1600 hours on May 13, only to meet furious resistance from the machine gunners of the 42nd Colonial Demi-Brigade. But all the courage of the latter was no substitute for anti-tank guns. The Pzkw IV tanks and self-propelled guns of the Panzer divisions took up position along the right bank of the Meuse and systematically blasted the French machine gun nests on the opposite bank.

When the latter had been silenced a German battalion crossed the Meuse on inflatable rafts and after bloody fighting took the little town of Monthermé. But they could get no further because of sustained resistance and awkward terrain.

German cavalry in a ruined French town (above). A motorised column of the 4th Panzer Division (below).

This setback at Monthermé was, however, largely eclipsed by the total victory of Guderian and his XIX Panzer Corps in the Sedan sector.

On hearing the alarming reports from the cavalry units, Huntziger had committed his reserve – 71st Division – to assist X Corps. On the morning of the 13th the 71st closed up on the right wing of the 55th Division on the Meuse. Yet the forces released by this move had not reached to their new sector when the Stukas of VIII *Fliegerkorps* launched a series of intensive attacks, pinning down the French troops where they stood.

On May 10 the XIX Panzer Corps – 1st Panzer Division in the lead, 2nd Panzer Division on the right, and 10th Panzer Division on the left – had surged forward at dawn. While crossing the Belgian-Luxembourg frontier some time was lost because of determined resistance from the *Chasseurs Ardennais* of Keyaerts Group and by extensive road demolitions. But by the evening of the 11th Guderian's leading Panzers had broken through to the Semois, having covered 60 miles in 48 hours. Considering the delay suffered by 2nd Panzer Division, Guderian had wanted to postpone a further advance from the 13th to the 14th, but Kleist, wanting to be sure of a close co-ordination between his two corps, would not agree. On the 12th, Guderian closed up his divisions and

agreed with *Luftflotte* III (General Hugo Sperrle) on the measures to be taken to ensure close co-operation between the Luftwaffe and the ground troops.

From noon to 1600 hours the Stukas intensified their attacks, meeting no opposition at all. They concentrated on the artillery positions of 55th Division, while eight concentrations of 10.5-cm and 15-cm guns were pounding a front of 2,700 yards to speed the crossing of Kirchner's 1st Panzer Division. The French emplacements on the left bank of the Meuse were knocked out one by one by high velocity 8.8-cm A.A. guns.

About 1600 hours, when the French guns covering the Meuse had been silenced, the S.S. Motorised Regiment *Grossdeutschland*, sent to help 1st Panzer Division, was

ferried to the left bank in assault boats with outboard engines and on inflatable rafts, and was flung straight into the fray. The resistance of the French 55th Division fluctuated. Some units fought until the Germans broke into their positions; others gave up at the first shot. On the whole, however, the badly-trained reservists who made up the division broke and fled before the German infantry. Worse still, about 1800 hours at Bulson, five miles from Sedan, before any German tanks had crossed the Meuse, panic spread to a French regiment of heavy artillery and to the rear areas like a forest fire. Guns were blown up, telephone lines cut, and terrified troops took to their heels.

Guderian recalled the crossing in the following words: "I was now anxious to take part in the assault across the Meuse by the riflemen. The actual ferrying must be nearly over by now, so I went to St. Menges and from there to Floing, which was the proposed crossing-place of 1st Panzer Division. I went over in the first assault boat. On the far bank of the river I found the efficient and brave commander of the 1st Rifle Regiment, Lieutenant-Colonel Balck, with his staff. He hailed me with the cheerful cry: 'Pleasure-boating on the Meuse is forbidden!' I had in fact coined the phrase myself during the training that we had had for this operation, since the attitude of some of the younger officers had struck me as too light-hearted. I now realised that they had judged the situation correctly."

By midnight, the German penetration south of Sedan was deep enough for Guderian's sappers to open their bridges to XIX Panzer Corps' heavy vehicles. On the right, the forward units of Viel's 2nd Panzer Division had been halted in front of Donchery, while on the left Schaal's 10th Panzer Division had only gained a little ground around Wadelincourt on the left bank of the Meuse. But the French 55th Division had been scattered, leaving 500 dead; the 71st Division was on the brink of destruction and the French had lost 80 guns.

The following day Guderian headed his corps for Abbeville and the Channel, swinging to the west, sending 1st and 2nd Panzer Divisions across the River Bar and the Ardennes Canal. *Grossdeutschland* and 10th Panzer Division guarded the flank of the German penetration around Stonne. On the 14th and even on the 15th, an energetic counter-attack across the rear of 1st and 2nd Panzer Divisions by the 3rd Armoured and 3rd Motorised Divisions of Flavigny's XXI Corps would have had a very good chance of restoring the French front along the Meuse. But nothing was done. Flavigny was content to "contain" the south flank of the pocket. Meanwhile the German flak gunners defended the Sedan bridges with a high degree of skill; 170 bombers, most of them British, were flung against the bridges in near-suicidal missions, and 85 were shot down.

So it was that the 664 tanks of 1st and 2nd Panzer Divisions carved through the right flank of the French 9th Army. Corap tried to block their path by stationing his 3rd Brigade of Spahis and his 53rd Division between the Meuse and Poix-Terron; but the Spahis immolated themselves in a heroic but desperate engagement at La Horgne and the 53rd Division, a typically down-at-heel French reserve unit, went to pieces at the first encounter.

At the same time, further to the north, 8th Panzer Division crossed the Meuse at Nouzonville, midway between Monthermé and Mezières, shouldering aside the French 61st Division. In the sector of the French XI Corps, covering Mariembourg and Philippeville, French resistance wilted on the 14th and collapsed on the 15th, for 5th Panzer Division had followed 7th Panzer across the Meuse, and their combined 654 fighting vehicles had caught the French 22nd and 18th Divisions in the act of installing themselves along an overstretched front of over 23 miles. Neither of these two French divisions was motorised; neither of them had more than 12 battalions apiece in the line on May 12; and both had been counting on at least 48 more hours to complete their redeployment. General Doumenc of G.H.Q. Land Forces, writing of the disorganisation of 9th Army after the German crossing of the Meuse, recalled: "The battlefield retained its air of chaos until evening. These are the impressions of one staff officer: 'On the way, we passed through the swirling smoke of a fuel convoy which had been bombed and was burning beside the road. Further on, an artillery group had been attacked while still on the march. On the roadway and the verges a series of enormous shell craters and many dead horses showed that the attack must have been irresistible.'"

The fate of 1st Armoured Division only made matters worse. Billotte had put this division at the disposal of 9th Army; it had 156 tanks, of which 66 were the formidable Char B type, and prepared to counterattack towards Dinant. But it was surprised while refuelling by the tanks of XV Panzer Corps and virtually wiped out. The technical reason was simple enough: French tanks were laboriously refuelled by tankers, while the Germans used the smaller, handier "Jerricans" for the job. To crown the disastrous events of May 15, 4th North African Infantry Division, going to the help of the French XI Corps, was cut to pieces as well.

In the morning of May 16 the advance units of XIX and XLI Panzer Corps, thrusting forwards from Poix-Terron and from Monthermé, joined hands at Montcornet – deep in the rear of the French XLI Corps. Further to the north the XV Panzer Corps –still subordinated to the German 4th Army–crossed the Franco-Belgian frontier near Fourmies.

In four days of battle *Panzergruppe* Kleist and XV Panzer Corps had destroyed eight divisions of 9th and 2nd Armies and had smashed open a breach of 81 miles in the front held by Billotte's 1st Army Group. And through that breach some

2,200 tanks and armoured cars were streaming towards the Channel. Were the French Government and High Command to blame for relying on a "defensive" front along the Dyle? That has always been the view of Paul Reynaud. But it is true to say that the defeat of this "defensive" army group had come about because it was not defensive enough. How would the story have turned out if, on May 13, the Germans had run into tough, well-prepared French troops waiting for them on the left bank of the Meuse? But to do this the French would have needed enough anti-tank guns to prevent the Panzers on the right bank from knocking out the French fortifications across the river, and enough anti-aircraft guns to break up the precision attacks of the deadly Stukas.

At 0300 hours on May 14, Captain Beaufre accompanied General Doumenc to G.H.Q. "North-East" for a conference with General Georges. With an emotion which 25 years had not dispelled, Beaufre recalled what took place.

"The atmosphere is that of a family keeping vigil over a dead member. Georges rises briskly and comes up to Doumenc. He is terribly pale: 'Our front has been pushed in at Sedan! There have been some failures . . .' He falls into an armchair and a sob stifles him. It was the first man that I had seen weep in this battle. I was to see many others, alas! It made a dreadful impression on me.

"Doumenc, surprised by this greeting, reacts at once. 'General, this is war, and this sort of thing always happens in war!' Then Georges, pale as ever, explains: two second rate divisions have fallen back after a terrible bombing attack. The X Corps has signalled that its position has been overrun and that German tanks arrived in Bulson around midnight. Another sob. All the others in the room stand there, struck silent.

"'Come, General,' says Doumenc, 'all wars have seen collapses like this! Let's look at the map. We'll see what can be done!' He speaks strongly in this encouraging vein and it does me good to hear it.

"Standing before the map, Doumenc sketches a manoeuvre: the gap must be closed, 'plugged' as they used to say in 1918."

Doumenc's optimism was praiseworthy, but he was unaware of two elements of the situation which would ruin his hopes. Nor could he foresee the development of a third element, which would prove equally disastrous.

To start with, during the "collapses" of 1914 and 1918, neither Moltke nor Ludendorff had adequate means with which to keep up the pace of the German pursuit; large cavalry units were far too vulnerable, their endurance was poor, and no cavalry unit had as much fire-power as the infantry anyway. Second, neither Joffre in 1914 nor Pétain and Foch in 1918 had to worry about heavy enemy air attacks in their rear areas, which in 1940 wrought havoc among the troop columns and

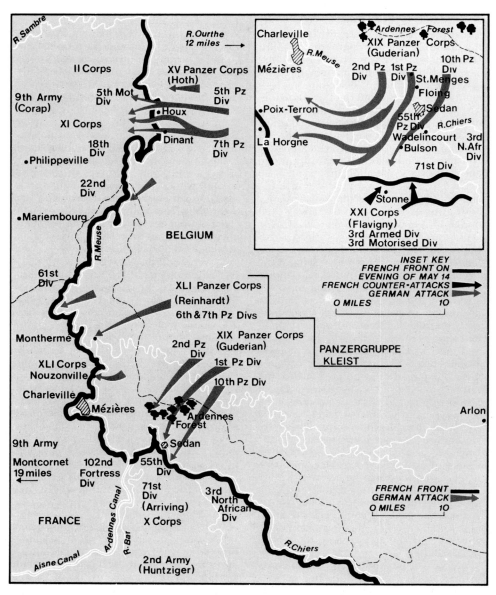

The crossing of the Meuse and (inset) the breakthrough at Sedan.

supply convoys, and the key road and railway junctions.

The third element which Doumenc had not foreseen was the flooding chaos of the refugee "exodus". Jean Vidalenc, who has made a special study of the phenomenon, has estimated that by August 13, 1940, some two and a half million refugees had reached the south, centre, and south-west of France. And this figure does not include the refugees who had found their way home after a brief flight, or who had made for Mayenne or Britanny. The same panic in Belgium also caused bottleneck jams on the roads, and badly disrupted the military operations of May–June 1940.

The whole grim story demonstrates the total failure of French propaganda, which had been entrusted to Jean Giraudoux at the beginning of hostilities. His concept of "psychological warfare" ended by making five million Frenchmen take to their heels.

The overall phenomenon of the civilian exodus put incredible problems in the way of the Allied conduct of military operations, and must be ranked with the other reasons for the Allied defeat. As Vidalenc puts it:

"Columns of refugees now struggled along the roads . . . In the grey light before the dawn, shadows appeared like pale ghosts, their features drawn by their march through the night, through the day before, perhaps through the day before that; the poor went on foot, pushing before them barrows laden with odds and ends. Their feet were raw with blisters; some would stop by the road-side and ease off their shoes. Horse-drawn vehicles, cars piled high with mattresses, suitcases, parcels tied with string, lashed together with straps or held by elastic cords, passed by the tramping pedestrians, their owners wearing the clothes selected as most useful or most valuable when the time came to leave home. The most harrowing sight was the children . . . It was frightful to hear their terrified young voices screaming: 'The planes, mummy, the planes!' and to know that they must already have seen death falling from the skies . . ."

At 0400 hours on May 15 Billotte telephoned Georges and made it clear that 9th Army was "on the brink of catastrophe". Billotte suggested that Giraud, a real leader of men, should take over; he would be able to create the "psychological shock" capable of stiffening 9th Army. Corap, as yet reproached with nothing, should take over 7th Army. By about 1600 hours Giraud, forcing his way along roads choked with refugees, had reached the H.Q. of 9th Army at Vervins–but he brought with him nothing but a solitary aide-de-camp, while he would have liked to hurl the motorised units of his former army against the flank of the Panzer breakthrough.

At 0730 on the 15th Winston Churchill had been jerked from his sleep by the news that Paul Reynaud was calling him by telephone. Churchill picked up the receiver and received Reynaud's message: "We have been defeated . . . the front is broken near Sedan; they are pouring through in great numbers with tanks and armoured cars." In his memoirs Churchill admits that he was unable to recall the precise words used by his French colleague. But he is clear enough about his own reply in which, like General Doumenc, he pointed to historical precedent:

"All experience shows the offensive will come to an end after a while. I remember the 21st of March, 1918. After five or six days they have to halt for supplies, and the opportunity for counter-attack is presented. I learned all this at the time from the lips of Marshal Foch himself."

There was equal astonishment at the French Ministry of National Defence. William Bullitt, the American Ambassador, was in the same room as Daladier when Gamelin telephoned with the news of the breakthrough at Sedan and the Panzer advance. Bullitt was so impressed by what he heard that on the 16th he did not hesitate to cable Washington: "It seems clear that without a miracle like the Battle of the Marne, the French Army will be completely crushed."

This is how Bullitt recalls the scene: "But the telephone rang from Vincennes; the Supreme Commander was calling the Minister. Suddenly Daladier shouted: 'No! That's not possible! You are mistaken!'

"Gamelin had told him that an armoured column had smashed through everything in its path and was at large between Rethel and Laon. Daladier was panting. He found the strength to shout: 'You must attack!' 'Attack? With what?' replied Gamelin. 'I have no more reserves.'

"Daladier's features crumpled more and more. He seemed to be shrinking as I watched.

"The grim conversation ended with the following exchange:

" 'So this means the destruction of the French Army?' 'Yes, this means the destruction of the French Army!' "

Bullitt added that there was already a certain amount of dissension between the French and the British. The latter considered the French attitude "defeatist"; and the analysis of Bullitt's despatch made by the American historian William

L. Langer held that the British were showing reluctance to "risk their own fortunes in the common cause".

None of this was in Churchill's mind when he arrived in Paris on the afternoon of May 16 for a meeting with Reynaud, Daladier, and Gamelin at the Quai d'Orsay. Within five minutes Churchill had been put in the picture and convinced of the gravity of the situation. "I then asked," says Churchill in *The Second World War*, 'Where is the strategic reserve?' and breaking into French, which I used indifferently (in every sense): *'Où est la masse de manoeuvre?'* General Gamelin turned to me and, with a shake of the head and a shrug, said *'Aucune.'*"

Churchill did not know that in Gamelin's "Breda" variant the Supreme Commander had ignored the repeated advice of his subordinates and, for political rather than for strategic reasons, had committed Giraud's 7th Army, which should have formed the *"masse de manoeuvre"*. But this disastrous news did not prevent Churchill from agreeing to send ten more fighter squadrons to join Air-Marshal A. Barratt's force in France, which had already suffered considerable losses.

While these discussions were being held, the archives of the French Foreign Office were being burned by panic-stricken officials in the gardens of the Quai d'Orsay. But as evening drew on the tension eased. Near Rethel, a German colonel strayed into the French lines. He was captured, badly wounded, and was found to be carrying a map on which Arras and Abbeville were marked as the objectives for the Panzer forces, which had been expected to appear before Paris on the following day.

When the first reports of the disaster at Sedan came in, General Georges did what he could to restore continuity to the Allied front. On the eve of the German crossing of the Meuse he had ordered four divisions to head for the threatened sector. The following day, to ease the strain on Billotte, Georges took 2nd Army under his direct orders and diverted General Touchon's 6th Army, originally intended to cover the Swiss frontier, to the Aisne. On May 17 General Frère—not Corap—was given command of 7th Army and ordered to re-establish contact with 9th Army in the region of St. Quentin.

Thus between May 12–17 some 20 divisions were given new orders which would head them towards the breach in the Allied line—a redeployment which necessitated the smooth running of over 500 trains and 30,000 vehicles. But the plan was ruined from the outset by Luftwaffe attacks. During the same period, May 12–17, German bombers cut the French railway network in hundreds of places, isolating the sector exposed to the offensive of *Panzergruppe* Kleist. The roads became clogged with refugees who streamed back from the fighting in every type of vehicle.

This disruption caused a general delay of 24–36 hours before the first troops intended for the sectors of 6th and 7th Armies arrived on the scene. Some units were delayed by constant bombing, while others were forced to set out prematurely. The tracked vehicles of 2nd Armoured Division became pinned down on a stretch of railway 75 miles long between Tergnier and Hirson; the wheeled vehicles of the division, struggling along the roads, became separated from the tanks; and so 2nd Armoured Division was scattered into a shower of small, unco-ordinated detachments, and could not play its part in Georges's "plugging".

Up at the front the Germans made good use of the chaos in the Allied camp. As night fell on May 16, 7th Panzer Division forced the Franco-Belgian frontier near Solre-le-Château. Any commander other than Rommel would have been satisfied with this success, but he drove on through the darkness, surprised Avesnes at midnight, dashed past Landrecies, and arrived before Le Cateau at dawn on the 17th after a breath-taking advance of over 30 miles. He had scattered the surviving units of 18th Division and 1st Armoured Division, sweeping in thousands of prisoners, whom the Germans barely had time to disarm in their haste. Above everything else, Rommel had thrown the rear areas of 9th Army into inextricable confusion.

In his G.H.Q. at Münstereifel, however, Hitler did not share the optimism of his front-line commanders. Halder argued in vain that the Allies were not strong enough to launch a counter-attack towards Sedan, and that the Panzers could be allowed to thrust forwards without any unreasonable risk. Hitler remained paralysed with anxiety, and at noon on the 17th, after a visit to O.K.W. with Brauchitsch, Halder noted: "Apparently little mutual understanding. The Führer insists that he sees the main danger coming from the south. (In fact, I don't see any danger at all!) Therefore, infantry divisions must be brought up as quickly as possible to protect the southern flank; the armour will have to rely on its own resources to enlarge the breakthrough to the northwest."

And a few hours later the same subject arose after an intervention from O.K.W. by telephone: "2100 hours. A rather disagreeable day. The Führer is terribly nervous. Frightened by his own success, he fears to take risks and would prefer to curb our initiative. Reasons for this: his fears for the left flank. Keitel's telephone calls to the army groups and the Führer's personal visit to Army Group 'B' have produced nothing but trouble and doubt." Next morning, the same problem . . .

This friction between O.K.W. and O.K.H. had its repercussions on the battlefield, resulting in order and counter-order. On the night of May 15–16 Guderian received a telephoned order from Kleist to postpone his advance until the supporting infantry had joined up. When Guderian protested vehemently he was authorised

to resume the advance, but only for 48 hours. Despite a brilliant success on May 16, Guderian received a visit from Kleist on the morning of the 17th. Kleist had come to restate this unfortunate halt order to his impetuous subordinate, and he did so in terms which provoked Guderian to offer his resignation.

On Rundstedt's direct orders General List, commander of 12th Army, ended the dispute in the early afternoon. He settled it with a compromise which, made at the moment when every hour counted, saved the campaign from petering out. Guderian, restored to the command of XIX Panzer Corps, would obey Kleist's order to halt, which came from O.K.H. But he was authorised to continue with a "reconnaissance in force" towards the west. Seizing this loophole, Guderian chose to make his "reconnaissance in force" with the entire fighting strength of 1st and 2nd Panzer Divisions, pushing a first bridgehead across the Oise at Moy on the evening of the 17th. By noon on the 19th Guderian's tanks had taken Péronne.

Meanwhile, XVI Panzer Corps (Hoeppner's 3rd and 4th Panzer Divisions) had also been transferred to Rundstedt's Army Group "A" and subordinated to 4th Army. This meant that nine Panzer divisions, followed by six motorised divisions, were now operating on Billotte's right flank and driving across his rear. Billotte's withdrawal to the Escaut Line was being hampered not only by the attacks of Army Group "B" but by Luftwaffe attacks and by the disorganised flood of refugees.

In this total confusion it was hardly surprising that all reinforcements for Giraud's army were sent in vain. Rendered meaningless by the course of events, his orders had either been drawn up for units which no longer existed, or only reached formations which were not yet in their correct position. On May 16 Giraud transferred his H.Q. from Vervins to Wassigny—but the break-up of 2nd Armoured Division after the destruction of 1st Armoured meant that he no longer had enough forces with which to counter-attack, while Rommel was driving towards Landrecies and Guderian's advance towards the Channel was being slowed down only by the untimely and cautious intervention of Kleist.

When Giraud decided to fall back from Wassigny to Le Catelet he found all the roads blocked before him. Abandoning his car for an armoured car, he tried in vain to get through the enemy lines—and at dawn on the 19th became a prisoner of the Germans.

General Doumenc has described how it happened:

"General Giraud had left Wassigny at 1600 hours, taking only two officers with him. After moving to the H.Q. of 9th Division he passed through Busigny only to find that the enemy had armoured cars at every cross-roads on the main road from Cambrai to Le Catelet. By nightfall

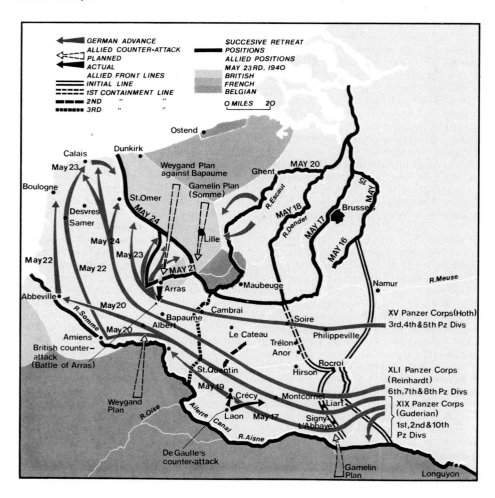

The "Panzer Corridor", the German
armoured thrust to the English Channel,
cutting the Allies in two.

they had got to within seven miles of Le
Catelet; the little group abandoned its
vehicles and after a three-hour march by
the compass had reached Le Catelet, part
of which was burning . . . they ran into a
German outpost and there was an exchange of shots, after which they took
refuge in a wood. The General then
ordered the party to separate. He himself
was slowed down by an old wound and
stopped behind a hedge at the side of the
Cambrai road. Then he saw, coming from
the south, a column of French trucks with
a gun-carrier in the lead, which had by-
passed Le Catelet. He climbed into the
gun-carrier and knocked out the first
German tank which they encountered,
only to run into three more tanks. He then
threw himself into a farmhouse which
seemed isolated."

"Unhappily," runs Giraud's own
account, "this farmhouse was filled with
refugees who probably gave us away to
the first Germans who questioned them.
Within minutes three German tanks surrounded the farmhouse while a large
column drew up on the road. We were
rapidly discovered; I thought it would be
useless to risk the life of the young troops
there, and I ordered them not to fire. It
was 6 o'clock; we were prisoners."

At about 2000 hours on May 20, Spitta's
battalion from Veiel's 2nd Panzer Divi-

sion was the first German unit to reach
the Channel coast near Noyelles. Meanwhile, at Péronne, Corbie, Amiens, and
Abbeville, other formations of XIX Panzer
Corps had outrun the retreating French
7th Army and had established bridgeheads across the Somme.

Thus the "plugging" of the ruptured
Allied front attempted by General Georges
had failed completely. But did it ever have
a chance of success? As Doumenc says,
the breach could have been closed by a
mass redeployment of the five infantry
and three motorised divisions which were
frittered away in vain attempts to assist
9th Army. But to have got this group of
divisions into position (with its right on
St. Quentin and its left on Le Cateau) by
May 16 would have required it to have
been set in motion on May 12, at the very
moment when Rommel's motorcyclists
reached the Meuse.

"This simple statement of dates," comments Doumenc, "shows the impossibility." Certainly, but there can be no
denying that it was fatal to have committed 7th Army in the "Breda" variant
of Gamelin's plan. If 7th Army had been
retained as the mobile reserve for 1st
Army Group, as Georges had originally
recommended, it would probably have
been a very different story. Instead,
Giraud was forced, like General Soubise
after the Battle of Rossbach in the old
song, to go wandering about looking for
his troops, lantern in hand . . .

Napoleon went further. He had said:

"In war, a major disaster always implies a
major culprit."

On May 17 and 19, raids were launched
against the left flank of XIX Panzer Corps
by the French 4th Armoured Division.
These raids made no difference to the outcome of the campaign, but they were
nevertheless an impressive example of
improvisation and resolution. Deficient in
equipment, organisation, and training,
the 4th Armoured was suddenly entrusted
to Colonel Charles de Gaulle. Directly
subordinated to General Georges, it was
ordered to operate to the north-east of
Laon and gain time for 6th Army to take
up its position along the Aisne and the
Ailette.

On May 15 de Gaulle set up his H.Q. at
Bruyères, south of Laon, and on the 17th
he struck towards Montcornet with the
forces at his disposal. Having penetrated
some 21 miles the division was forced to
halt; it was also set upon by Stukas,
against which it was defenceless. By
nightfall de Gaulle had withdrawn half-
way between Montcornet and Laon, having taken 130 prisoners. On May 19,
slightly reinforced but still not up to full
strength, de Gaulle attacked again at
dawn. This time his objective was the
bridges across the Serre and the Marle–la
Fère road, vital to the Panzer forces
advancing westward between the Oise
and Amiens.

On that day, Guderian recalls: "A few
of [de Gaulle's] tanks succeeded in penetrating to within a mile of my advanced
headquarters in Holnon wood. The headquarters had only some 20-mm anti-
aircraft guns for protection, and I passed
a few uncomfortable hours until at last
the threatening visitors moved off in
another direction."

In the early afternoon of the 19th de
Gaulle received Georges' order to break
off. Stuka attacks were still savaging the
French tanks and a German column which
had crossed the Serre by the bridge at
Marle was threatening the flank of 4th
Armoured. In this situation de Gaulle's
forces pulled back behind the Aisne on the
following day without further trouble.

With disaster threatening, Reynaud reshuffled his Cabinet. He yielded the
Foreign Ministry to Daladier and took
over the Ministry of National Defence
himself, naming Georges Mandel as Minister of the Interior. Above all, he recalled
the legendary Marshal Pétain, the hero of
Verdun in World War I, from his Embassy
in Madrid to become a minister and Vice-
President of the Council. This readjust-
ment, announced over the radio by
Reynaud on the evening of the 18th, was
greeted with relief by the Parisian press
and by French public opinion as a whole.

The return of General Weygand from
Syria raised French spirits even more.
The division of responsibility and power
between Gamelin and Georges, aggravated by the decree of January 18 splitting
Supreme Headquarters between Vincennes, Montry, and la Ferté-sous-Jouarre,

had led to nothing but inefficiency, delays, and half measures. On May 19 this reached such a point that Gamelin, venturing into what he called the "battle of Georges", drafted his "Personal and Secret Directive No. 12". This document was familiarly – but not unfairly – called an "umbrella" by Georges. "Without wishing to interfere in the conduct of the battle now being waged, which is in the hands of the Commander-in-Chief of the North-East Front, and approving of all the dispositions made, I consider that, at the present time . . ." began his summing-up of the obvious measures which ought to be taken.

Given the urgency of the situation, Reynaud decided to overrule the objections of Daladier and his Radical-Socialist ministers and entrust the high command to a man who would not be afraid to take risks. Early on May 17 General Maxime Weygand, C.-in-C. Middle East, was ordered to leave Beirut for Paris immediately. Within 48 hours he had arrived in France and at 1430 hours he presented himself in Reynaud's office. After a swift visit to Vincennes and la Ferté-sous-Jouarre Weygand agreed to take over this new command in a spirit of duty and total self-denial.

In 1950 Weygand wrote: "Even today, knowing what I know and what it has cost me, I think that if I had refused the command which I was asked to take over I would have blushed for shame." These words do honour to a man of 73, which was Weygand's age when he assumed, in Beaufre's words, "the burden of command with a daring, a passion, and a fierce will which was a total contrast to the pale, stiff calm of his predecessor . . . Elegant, neat, and poised, direct, kind, but often curt and easily moved to terseness, he gave the impression of intense personal energy, coupled with an astonishing physical stamina."

Here was a far cry from the atmosphere of the Gamelin era, whose headquarters de Gaulle had described as "a sub-

marine without a periscope". On May 21, the new supreme commander, disdaining the threat of the Luftwaffe, set out to join 1st Army Group by air. Landing near Béthune, Weygand proceeded to Ypres where he met King Léopold and General van Overstraeten at about 1430 hours. He promptly disclosed the plan of manoeuvre which he had mulled over during his long flight from Beirut, and which took into account those parts of Gamelin's recent "Personal Directive No. 12" which still made sense.

The deplorable conditions in which Weygand made his journey to Belgium give a good idea of the disorder caused by the overthrow of the armies. Weygand's wanderings in his unguided search for General Billotte included a touching scene which the general later recalled:

"While my aide-de-camp was giving the necessary orders, I went into a little inn near the airfield to order an omelette which would keep us going until evening. The innkeeper's wife was alone except for a little boy. She had heard nothing from her husband, who was at the front. Time and again she would go to the door and watch the stream of people flying from the invasion. She was wondering whether or not to join them, to leave her house and take a chance. While she was preparing our modest meal, I saw a small picture on one of the walls. It was a popular print, widespread in the north, of the signing of the Armistice at Rethondes in 1918. Inside the railway coach the four German plenipotentiaries faced Marshal Foch, who had Lord Wester Wemyss and another British admiral on his right, and on his left his own chief-of-staff: myself. What a strange coincidence! At that moment the woman put the hot omelette on the table and said to me: 'But is that really you there, General?', adding a few words of hope and confidence similar to those which I had heard so often since my return to France, and which I could not wait to justify."

From Arras, still in Allied hands, to the Somme, towards which General Frère's 7th Army was hastening, was a distance

of only 25 miles. An attack from north and south in the direction of Bapaume would execute a pincer movement on the Panzer "corridor" and cut off the German armoured spearhead before the German infantry could join up. But this about-turn by Billotte and the 26 French and British divisions under his orders meant that the Belgian Army must fall back immediately from the Escaut to the Yser. General van Overstraeten, speaking for the Belgian King, objected that such a prolonged retreat would have disastrous consequences on the morale and the discipline of the Belgian troops, who, after the retreat from the Albert Canal, would have to abandon the Antwerp-Louvain line without a fight, and so the King reserved his decision. Weygand was able to speak with Billotte but not with Gort, who was at the front; and he had to leave without having seen Gort. In the evening he embarked at Dunkirk on the torpedo-boat *La Flore*, under a rain of bombs.

Weygand landed at Cherbourg at 0500 hours on the 22nd. At noon he received Reynaud, Churchill, Generals Dill and Ismay, and Air Vice-Marshal Peirse at his H.Q. at Vincennes. By this time Weygand had received the good news that King Léopold had agreed that the Belgian Army should be redeployed in conformity with his plan. Given this situation, Weygand was warmly supported by Churchill when he suggested that:

"1. The Belgian Army should retire to the line of the Yser, and that the country should be flooded;

2. As soon as possible – and certainly by the following day – the British and French should attack towards Bapaume and Cambrai with about eight divisions;

3. As the outcome of this battle was vital to the Allies, and as the British

Troops of a German Panzer column take a rest from their drive to the Channel, while a reconnaissance plane flies above.

The object is achieved: German troops lounge on a Channel beach by a Pzkw III tank.

communications depended on the recovery of Amiens, the Royal Air Force should give maximum support by day and night as long as the battle lasted; and

4. The new French army group heading towards Amiens and forming a front along the Somme should thrust north to effect a junction with the British forces in the region of Bapaume."

This decision to send further air reinforcements to France had not been taken without painful hesitation on the part of Churchill and his Cabinet. Churchill himself explained: "It was vital that our metropolitan fighter air force should not be drawn out of Britain on any account. Our existence turned on this, nevertheless it was necessary to cut to the bone. In the morning, before I started, the Cabinet had given me authority to move four more squadrons of fighters to France. On our return to the Embassy, and after talking it over with Dill, I decided to ask sanction for the dispatch of six more. This would leave us with only the twenty-five fighter squadrons at home, and that was the final limit. It was a rending decision either way. I told General Ismay to telephone to London that the Cabinet should assemble at once to consider an urgent telegram which would be sent over in the course of the next hour or so. Ismay did this in Hindustani, having previously arranged for an Indian Army officer to be standing by in his office."

All this took place on the 16th, and the British dilemma had not changed by the time of the Ypres conference on the 22nd. Air Vice-Marshal Peirse did not hesitate to point out the two main problems of the R.A.F.: the British bombers, particularly the Wellingtons, stood virtually no chance in daylight raids over the battlefield, and the fighters, forced to operate from bases in southern England, could not remain over the battlefield for more than 20 minutes.

After the Ypres conference Weygand drew up his "Operational Order No. 1", detailing the objectives which had been agreed. He believed that the Allies had only one choice: to re-establish a continuous front between 1st Army Group and 3rd Army Group (Besson), which had since May 20 contained the French 6th and 7th Armies. "The German Army," wrote Weygand, "will not be contained or beaten without counter-attacks." He ended by giving the final objective of the planned attack: "The Panzer divisions must be locked in the arena into which they have so boldly rushed. They must not get out."

The following day Weygand ordered 1st and 3rd Army Groups to form a "solid barrier" to prevent the Panzer forces which had "ventured towards the sea" from breaking out to the east. "The Panzer divisions which have ventured so far must find their end there."

But Weygand's plan—logical though it was—never even began to be put into operation. The eight Allied divisions which should have attacked toward Bapaume and Cambrai on the 23rd did not attack on that day, nor on the 24th. This was because General Billotte had been

British prisoners rest on top of a German tank—for them the war is over.

killed in a senseless car accident shortly after the Ypres conference–a severe loss to the Allies, as General Beaufre points out. "So it was that we lost the energetic leadership of the commander-in-chief, a general of great character, whose successor had had his morale worn down by the 12-day battle in Belgium. Moreover, [Billotte] had enjoyed a standing with our British and Belgian allies the loss of which would be cruelly felt."

Gort later claimed that General Blanchard, who took over from Billotte, left the B.E.F. without orders for several days. But Blanchard had had to hand over 1st Army to General Prioux, and Prioux had had to hand over his cavalry corps to General Langlois. Successive delays such as this always mean serious inconveniences. In the situation that existed in the days after the Ypres conference, these inconveniences became catastrophic.

On the south flank of the "Panzer Corridor" the French 7th Army did not cross the Somme and made no attempt to drive on Bapaume. This was not due to any lack of resolution on the part of General Frère: the extension of the battle towards Péronne and then to Amiens and Abbeville forced Frère to spread his forces over too wide a front to allow a concentrated thrust as envisaged by Weygand.

Furthermore, the High Command did not have an uninterrupted communications network connecting it with 1st Army Group. Radio communications existed, but they were decidedly inferior in speed and security to the German system, in which better-organised field interception stations "listened in" to the Allied messages and learned much of value. This deficiency on the Allied side made for further delays and uncertainty.

Given this gloomy state of affairs, Gort's first reaction had been to prepare for the B.E.F.'s retirement to Dunkirk. Loyal to the French, Churchill dissuaded him; and with equal loyalty Gort revised his plans to associate his troops in the southern counter-attack with the French 1st Army. On May 21 the British attacked at Arras with "Frankforce"–two divisions (5th and 50th) and the 74 tanks of 1st Army Tank Brigade. The attack surprised 7th Panzer Division and the S.S. *Totenkopf* Division which were pass-ing south of the town, and was at first successful, taking nearly 400 prisoners. But the well-armoured British tanks were finally driven back by the devastating fire of the German 8.8-cm A.A. guns, which more than made up for the inadequacy of the 3.7-cm anti-tank guns.

On the 21st only part of the French 3rd Light Mechanised Division took part in the British counter-attack. Not until the 24th did the 25th Motorised Division, spearhead of the V Corps (General René Altmayer) advance from Cambrai under successive attacks by waves of 25–40 Stukas. By this time the Panzer forces had handed over the watch on the Somme to the motorised troops of Wietersheim's XIV Corps and had struck out anew towards the north and north-east. Boulogne and Calais were besieged, and 1st Panzer Division established a bridgehead across the Aa Canal, less than 13 miles from Dunkirk. At this stage the British in Arras were 46 miles from Dunkirk.

CHAPTER 10
Dunkirk and the battle of the Somme

When Lord Gort ordered "Frankforce" to retire from Arras on the evening of the 23rd, and then, on the 25th, broke away from the manoeuvre laid down for 1st Army Group, he was not waiting on the course of events. But it was certainly a timely move. If Hitler had not intervened personally on the morning of the 24th and ordered that the Panzers were not to pass the Lens–Béthune–St. Omer–Gravelines line, it is clear that Guderian could have reached Dunkirk and Malo-les-Bains on the evening of the following day.

Hitler's celebrated "halt order" before Dunkirk has been interpreted in many ways, both by German generals and historians of the war. Some have held that Hitler wished to spare the B.E.F. the humiliation of total surrender in order to regain the favour of the British and make them more amenable to a settlement. This is hardly credible. Others have argued that Hitler wanted to give his friend and chosen successor, Hermann Göring, the chance of showing that no troops could

retreat or embark under the bombs of the Luftwaffe. This explanation, however, is even thinner. The fact is that the order which spared nine British divisions and over 110,000 French troops from captivity was sent out to the German 4th Army by telephone, after a visit by Hitler to Rundstedt's H.Q. at Charleville, at 1231 hours on May 24.

According to the war diary of Army Group "A", published by the German historian Hans Adolf Jacobsen, it would appear that Hitler made this decision after a similar suggestion had been made to him by Rundstedt. It is hardly surprising that after the event Rundstedt did not claim the credit for the "halt order".

The reasons given for the "halt order" were the danger involved in committing the Panzer forces in the swampy terrain around Dunkirk and the need to conserve them for Operation "Red", the second phase of the campaign. This decision, made at the top, drew the following bitter comments from Halder on May 25:

"The day began with one of those unfortunate quarrels between Brauchitsch and the Führer, over the closing stages of the battle of encirclement. The battle plan which I suggested requires Army Group 'B', by means of a heavy frontal attack, to force the enemy into an ordered retreat, while Army Group 'A', falling upon an already shaken enemy, cuts its communications and strikes the decisive blow –a job for our tanks. Now the political command has come up with the idea of fighting the decisive battle not on Belgian soil but in northern France. To cover up this political shift, the argument is that the terrain of Flanders, crossed by many water-courses, is unsuitable for a tank battle. As a result, all tanks and motorised

The German attack on the Dunkirk pocket (below). Belgian prisoners are moved back to the rear. Note the horse-drawn German artillery, still a common form of transport in 1940 (opposite).

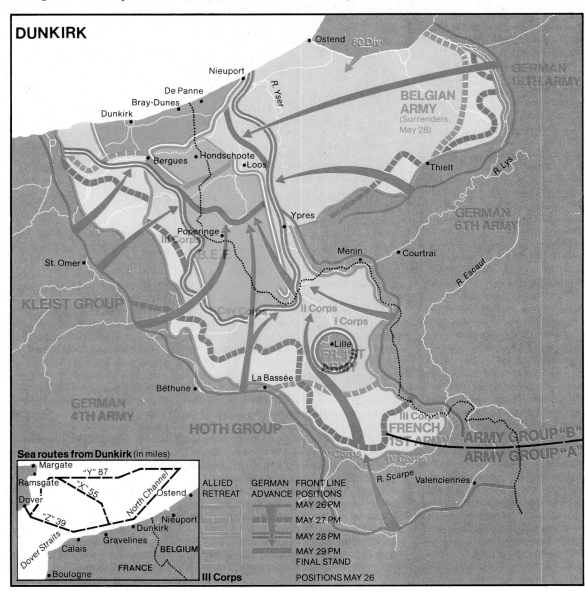

High Command, another segment of Belgian territory had been abandoned without a fight. Nevertheless the Belgians rallied to the call of their King, holding on valiantly along their front, which ran from the Léopold II Canal to the Lys Canal, along the line of the Lys, joining the left flank of the B.E.F. at Menin.

On May 24 the German 6th Army broke through the new position at Courtrai, revealing Reichenau's intention of driving towards Ypres and cutting off the Belgian Army from the B.E.F. The Belgians hit back as best they could; two reserve divisions had entered the line, and the fine showing of the 8th Division and the 2nd *Chasseurs Ardennais* Division limited the effect of the German breakthrough. On the 25th the 12th Division and the 1st *Chasseurs Ardennais* Division, on the Lys Canal and the Lys river respectively, launched timely and vigorous counter-attacks. But the Belgian reserves were rapidly used up, and the British refused to attack the flank of the German column thrusting towards Ypres, but continued their withdrawal to Dunkirk.

On May 26 the Belgian Army was still fighting, but its right was bending under the renewed attacks by Reichenau, and its left was yielding ground before the German 18th Army advancing from the direction of Antwerp. The battle was renewed at dawn on the 27th; and at 1230 hours King Léopold informed Gort that: "The moment is rapidly approaching when our troops will no longer be able to fight. The King will be forced to capitulate to avoid a disaster." Two hours later the King gave General Champon, chief of the French Military Mission, a note which told the same story: "Belgian resistance is reaching the end of its tether. Our front is fraying like a worn-out, breaking rope."

In the centre of the front a breach, 3 to 4 miles wide, was opening in the Thielt area; on the left, the 17th Division was on the point of collapse. From above, the Stukas kept up a non-stop bombardment on the artillery positions and the emptying ammunition dumps. Behind the lines, among a population of 800,000, an equal number of refugees was wandering. At 1700 hours King Léopold overruled the advice of General van Overstraeten (who wanted to wait until the following day) and sent an envoy to the German lines to discuss the Belgian surrender. But the King did not do this without having first informed Colonels Hautcoeur and Haily of the French and British Military Missions. While waiting for the German reply, King Léopold provided for the French 60th Division which had been fighting on the left of the Belgian Army, transporting it in trucks to the Dunkirk sector to be put at the disposal of General Blanchard. In the same spirit he ordered the destruction of the Yser bridges and the blocking of the ports of Ostend and Zeebrugge.

At 2230 hours the Belgian envoy, Major-General Derousseaux, returned to the Belgian G.H.Q. with the message that

troops must be moved quickly to the St. Omer–Béthune line.

"This is a complete reversal of our plan. I wanted to make Army Group 'A' the hammer and Army Group 'B' the anvil of the operation. Now 'B' will be the hammer and 'A' the anvil. But Army Group 'B' is facing a solid front; its progress will be slow and its losses high. Our air force, on which all hopes are pinned, is dependent upon the weather.

"This change means a stepping-up of the tempo which will need more energy than the actual plan of operations. For all that, the battle will be won, by this method or the other . . ."

On the following day, May 26, Hitler cancelled his decision and gave his tanks a free hand, but the time taken to get them on the move again meant that the chance of reaching Dunkirk before the British had been missed.

When Gort made his decision to retreat, he had already found himself obliged to keep close watch on his dwindling stocks of artillery ammunition. It is therefore difficult to find fault with his decision. Post-war memoirs by Gort's subordinates of 1940, such as Alanbrooke and Montgomery, conclude that Gort's decision had only one major fault, that of expecting too much from the French.

The fact remains that the French 1st Army, fighting at the bottom of the Allied pocket, was put in a difficult position by the British withdrawal; the British would have to cover only 47 miles from Arras to Dunkirk, but 1st Army, at Valenciennes, was over 62 miles from the port. When Weygand saw that his planned joint counter-attack, which should have been launched on the 26th, was now impossible, he still hoped that the 1st Army would be able to establish itself in a beach-head at Dunkirk deep enough to save the port from German artillery fire. But by the 26th the situation had deteriorated so badly that Weygand cabled Blanchard: "We (that is to say Reynaud and myself) are fully aware of the situation. You must remain the only judge of what must be done to save what can be saved, above all the honour of the colours of which you are the guardian."

This was not optimistic language–but it took no account of the progressive decline of the Allied situation on the Belgian sector. The Belgian Army had been retreating from the Schelde to the Lys; when Antwerp and Brussels were surrendered on May 17 on the orders of the Belgian

Hitler was demanding unconditional surrender. The Belgian Army, having hidden or destroyed its standards and colours, ceased fire at 0400 hours on May 28. The following day the last Belgian troops surrendered and Belgium's 18-day battle came to an end. In this desperate battle against the invader, the unfortunate King Léopold had rejected the attempts of his ministers to persuade him to leave the battlefield and follow them into exile. King Léopold has been criticised for his conduct in not following the example of Queen Wilhelmina, but it is a false comparison. Under the Belgian constitution he was the Commander-in-Chief of the Belgian Army, a duty which did not apply in Queen Wilhelmina's case. While German propaganda proclaimed to the Allied troops in the Dunkirk pocket: "Your commanders have fled by aircraft. Lay down your arms!", Léopold had announced to his troops: "Whatever happens my fate will be yours." Should he have broken this promise at the very moment when he was being informed of the "defection" of certain units, their morale undermined by the plotting of Flemish agitators in the pay of Hitler?

And how could the Dunkirk evacuation have met with the success it did if the Belgian Army, deprived of the commander in which it had confidence, had laid down its arms on May 26 or 27?

One fact at least is clear, however: the Belgian surrender sealed the fate of the French 1st Army around Lille. Both flanks of the 1st Army were now laid bare, and only 25 miles separated Hoth's *Panzergruppe* at la Bassée from Reichenau's forces at Menin on the French left. On May 28, taking Cassel and the Monts des Flandres, the Germans closed the ring round the French IV and V Corps which were dug in around Lille, Loos, and Haubourdin. These forces put up such an heroic resistance that when they surrendered, General Waeger, commander of the German XXVIII Corps, honoured them with a guard of honour from the 25th Division. General Molinier, the French commander, was allowed to retain his staff car.

General Prioux would not abandon his brave comrades of the IV and V Corps. He hung on at his H.Q. at Steenwerck and was captured there at 1245 hours on the 29th. General de la Laurencie, however, urged his exhausted III Corps north through Poperinge and Hondschoote and saved them from captivity, in a 37-mile night march along the incredibly choked roads. On the morning of the 29th he reported to Admiral Abrial, commanding at Dunkirk, with his 12th and 32nd Divisions and part of the 1st Motorised Division. The survivors of the cavalry corps did useful flank-guard service during this harrowing retreat.

Fagalde's XVI Corps was holding the Dunkirk beach-head with the 60th and 68th Divisions; de la Laurencie's troops came as a welcome reinforcement. Unfortunately, following the strict instructions laid down by the British High Command, they had to abandon most of their heavy weapons and a good deal of ammunition before they were allowed to withdraw into the Dunkirk zone, which caused some recrimination between the Allies. On the same day, May 29, the embarkation of the B.E.F. reached an encouraging figure. On that day 47,310 British troops were evacuated, while on the 27th and 28th the total had been only 25,473. The credit for this success undoubtedly must go to Vice-Admiral Sir Bertram Ramsay, Flag Officer, Dover. Four years later, Ramsay's energy and resourcefulness would be put to far better use than handling the details of an improvised evacuation under constant air bombardment: planning the Allied invasion of France in 1944.

As early as May 20, Churchill had suggested that "as a precautionary measure the Admiralty should assemble a large number of small vessels in readiness to proceed to ports and inlets on the French coast". The War Cabinet agreed, and Ramsay was given the task of putting the scheme into operation. Ramsay took over everything that could float: small passenger ferry-boats from the Channel and the Irish Sea routes; coasters, trawlers, motor yachts and *schuyts* – flat-bottomed Dutch boats which had taken refuge in England.

In all some 850 commercial boats were taken over by the Admiralty, which agreed with some reluctance (in view of the needs of the Atlantic convoys) to detach 39 destroyers as escorts. But Ramsay did not content himself with putting the precious destroyers on purely defensive duties: in the teeth of the German bombers, magnetic mines, and torpedo-boats, he did not hesitate to send in the destroyers to embark troops from the port of Dunkirk and from the beaches of Malo-les-Bains, Bray-Dunes, and De Panne.

Operation "Dynamo", as the evacuation was called, formally went into operation at 1857 hours on May 26. Informed too late of the British intentions, the French were only able to make a comparatively feeble contribution. It was not until the 28th that Rear-Admiral Landriau was put in command of the Pas-de-Calais flotilla, which finally numbered some 300 vessels of every tonnage, including 15 destroyers and torpedo-boats, under the command of Captain Urvoy de Portzamparc.

If the British War Cabinet did take its time to inform the French of its decision to re-embark the B.E.F., Winston Churchill spared no effort to see that Operation "Dynamo" should take off as many French as possible. In his note to the Secretary of State for War on May 29, he wrote: "It is essential that the French should share in such evacuations from Dunkirk as may be possible. Nor must they be dependent only upon their own shipping resources. Arrangements must be concerted at once with the French Missions in this country, or, if necessary, with the French Government, so that no reproaches, or as few as possible, may arise . . ."

On May 30 120,000 men, of which 6,000 were French, were embarked. On the 31st, when Gort received the order to hand over command of the beach-head to Lieutenant-General Alexander, first III Corps and then II Corps – about 150,000 men – had been shipped back to England, together with 15,000 Frenchmen.

From June 1 the defence of the Dunkirk perimeter was taken over by the French XVI Corps. But it should be noted that the British spared no effort, without regard to risk, to spare their French comrades from imprisonment. By the time that Operation "Dynamo" ended on June 4, 113,000 French troops had been shipped to England out of a total of 338,226 Allied troops. That is to say that during the last four days of the evacuation 75,000 British and 98,000 French troops were embarked – and most of them on British ships.

The "miracle of Dunkirk" was only made possible by extremely difficult manoeuvres, one of which has been recalled by Alanbrooke:

"There was little possibility of sleep that night, as the 3rd Division were moving past and I repeatedly went out to see how they were progressing. They were travelling, as we had so frequently practised for our night moves, with lights out and each driver watching the rear of the

A defiant gesture: a British soldier attempts to ward off one of the many enemy air raids.

vehicle in front of him, which had the differential painted white and lit up by a tail-lamp under the vehicle. The 3rd Division through constant practice had become most proficient at this method of movement. However, with the congestion on the roads, road-blocks outside villages, and many other blocks caused by refugees and their carts, the division was frequently brought to a standstill. The whole movement seemed unbearably slow; the hours of darkness were slipping by; should daylight arrive with the road crammed with vehicles the casualties from bombing might well have been disastrous.

"Our own guns were firing from the vicinity of Mount Kemmel, whilst German artillery was answering back, and the division was literally trundling slowly along in the darkness down a pergola of artillery fire, and within some 4,000 yards of a battle-front which had been fluctuating all day somewhat to our disadvantage. It was an eerie sight which I shall never forget. Before dawn came, the last vehicles had disappeared northwards into the darkness, and I lay down for a few hours' disturbed sleep, but kept wondering how the 3rd Division was progressing."

The resistance of the 12th Motorised Division and the 32nd and 68th Divisions was beyond praise; it lasted, contrary to all expectations, until dawn on June 4. General Janssen, commanding the 12th

British soldiers on the way home after their Dunkirk ordeal.

Motorised Division, was at the heart of the fighting and was killed by a bomb; General Fagalde, commanding XVI Corps, was taken prisoner with 40,000 men. Like Vice-Admiral Abrial, "Admiral North", and Rear-Admiral Platon, who embarked under orders at midnight on the 3rd, Fagalde had been the spirit of this battle without hope.

In the narrow sealane of the Straits of Dover, seven French destroyers and torpedo-boats and six British destroyers were sunk by Stukas and by attacks from E-boats (German motor torpedo-boats), together with a quarter of the small boats involved in the operation. In the air the fighters of the R.A.F. gave the Luftwaffe a hard time, greatly helping the embarkation of their comrades on the beaches; at the cost of 106 of their own machines, they accounted for most of the 156 German aircraft shot down during this phase of the campaign.

Despite the undoubted setback represented by the Allied evacuations from Dunkirk, Hitler had scored a crushing victory. For German losses put at 10,252 killed, 42,523 wounded, and 8,467 missing, he announced that 1,212,000 Dutch, Belgian, French, and British prisoners had been taken. In addition, his armies had captured an enormous booty: from the British Army alone, the spoils taken by the Germans amounted to 1,200 field guns, 1,250 anti-aircraft and anti-tank guns, 11,000 machine guns, and 75,000 vehicles. It is not surprising, therefore, that his

letters to Mussolini were flushed with optimism; but setting aside the flamboyant boastfulness, four interesting points are to be found in the letter of May 25 in which Hitler passed judgement on his opponents:

"As for the morale of our enemies, there is this to say:

1. *The Dutch.* They put up a much stronger resistance than we expected. Many of their units fought very bravely. But they had neither appropriate training nor experience of war. For this reason they were usually overcome by German forces which were often numerically very inferior.

2. *The Belgians.* The Belgian soldier, too, has generally fought very bravely. His experience of war was considerably greater than that of the Dutch. At the beginning his tenacity was astounding. This is now decreasing visibly [written some three days before the Belgian surrender] as the Belgian soldier realises that his basic function is to cover the British retreat.

3. *The British.* The British soldier has retained the characteristics which he had in World War I. Very brave and tenacious in defence, unskilful in attack, wretchedly commanded. Weapons and equipment are of the highest order, but the overall organisation is bad.

4. *The French.* Very marked differences appear when it comes to assessing the military capacity of the French. Very bad units rub elbows with excellent units. In the overview, the difference in quality between the active and the reserve divisions is extraordinary. Many active divisions have fought desperately; most of the reserve divisions, however, are far less able to endure the shock which battle inflicts on the morale of troops. For the French, as with the Dutch and Belgians, there is also the fact that they know that they are fighting in vain for objectives which are not in line with their own interests. Their morale is very affected, as they say that throughout or wherever possible the British have looked after their own units and prefer to leave the critical sectors to their allies."

The disastrous course of events in Flanders had forced Weygand to abandon his plan of a joint counter-attack against the "Panzer Corridor". It was even more vital, however, that the bridgeheads won by the Germans on the left bank of the Somme should be destroyed. The outcome of the defensive battle which now had to be fought between Longuyon and Abbeville depended largely upon this.

To this end the French 7th Army and the forces under Altmayer (renamed 10th Army on May 28) were sent into action along the Somme while the retreat to Dunkirk and the evacuation were still in progress.

Upstream of Péronne, the efforts of General Toussaint's 19th Division, ably

*A French victim of
the German advance.*

assisted by the tanks of 2nd Armoured Division under Colonel Perré, restored the French front along the Somme. Between Péronne and Amiens the Germans were also pushed back, but there they managed to hold on to their bridgehead across the river. It was hardly surprising that these counter-attacks were only partially successful. They were made by divisions which were flung into battle one by one and which, given their small numbers, had to cover too wide a front.

The reduction of the Abbeville bridgehead was entrusted to de Gaulle's 4th Armoured Division, hastily re-formed since its raids on May 17 and 19, and reinforced with six infantry battalions. The division attacked on the afternoon of May 28. It struck at the positions held by a regiment of Lieutenant-General Blümm's 57th Division and caused much panic, for the German 3.7-cm anti-tank guns could not pierce the heavy armour of the French tanks. But because it was not promptly exploited, de Gaulle's success was fleeting. During the night of May 28–29, Blümm's force was reinforced by two 8.8-cm flak batteries, and their guns soon demonstrated, as they had done at Arras, their devastating power against tanks.

On May 29–30, the 4th Armoured Division made limited progress but failed to clear the crest of Mont Caubert; by the third day of the battle the division had taken some 500 prisoners, but it had been reduced to a mere 34 tanks. Finally called off on June 3, the counter-attack at Abbeville had achieved little – and on the 5th, Bock's army group attacked along the entire Somme front.

Between the last embarkations from Dunkirk and the unleashing of Operation "Red" – the second and final phase of the Battle of France – there was a pause of little more than a single day.

Although Weygand was bombarded with a constant, bewildering stream of disastrous and disconcerting news, it must be said that he reacted with promptitude and energy throughout. Most of his decisions were sound, and above all there was the powerful, morale-boosting influence which he exerted on his subordinates. In a few days he had restored the spirit of the front-line troops to a remarkable degree. And the evidence for this can be found less on the French side than in the war diaries and memoirs of the Germans.

Weygand had shown his mettle as early as May 24, in a note laying down the measures to be taken against German armour supported by aircraft. On May 26, after his new defence plan had received the unanimous approval of the War Committee presided over by the President of the Republic, he issued the following "General Order of Operations":

"1. The battle on which the fate of the country depends will be fought without any idea of retreat from the positions which we occupy now. All commanders, from army commander to corporal, must be animated by the fierce resolve to stand and fight until death. If commanders set the example their troops will stand; and they will have the right to compel obedience if necessary.

2. To be certain of halting the enemy, constant aggressiveness is essential. If the enemy shows signs of attacking on any sector, we must reply with swift and brutal counter-methods.

   If the enemy succeeds in establishing a bridgehead in our front which he can use for rushing in tanks and then moving on to an armoured attack, it is essential – no matter how insignificant the bridgehead may be – to drive the enemy back to his lines with artillery fire and air strikes, and to counter-attack. Infiltration must be countered with infiltration. If a unit

believes that a neighbouring unit is wavering it must not at any cost fall back but must try to restore the situation. If this is impossible it must dig in and form a 'hedgehog' of resistance. This must apply to all units from divisional right down to company level.

3. The rear areas of the main defence line must be organised, in as great a depth as possible, into a checkerboard of centres of resistance, in particular on the main roads along which the Germans have always moved. Demolition charges must be prepared.

4. Every divisional general must be in constant touch with his colonels, the colonels with their battalion commanders, the battalion commanders with their company commanders, and the captains and lieutenants with their sections and their men.
   Activity – Solidarity – Resolution."

Weygand's note of May 24 had anticipated the methods prescribed by this order. In the face of the "tank-aircraft tandem" attacks of the Blitzkrieg, it amounted to an improvised defensive tactic for which the French lacked sufficient means, but which nevertheless inflicted heavy losses on the victors of this first campaign in France.

Above all, Weygand believed, the Panzers must be cut off, decimated, and annihilated on a prepared battlefield. To do this meant, as he wrote: "substituting for the idea of the line the idea of control of communications", and this must be done by quartering the terrain, establishing the artillery in strongpoints and allocating a third of the artillery for anti-tank use, and by camouflaging all positions against air and ground observation.

A combination of these measures, he thought, would prevent the German infantry from following up as close support for those of their tanks which managed to infiltrate the French positions while the tanks themselves, cut off from the trucks bringing up their fuel and ammunition, would fall victim to the crossfire of the French infantry and artillery. At this critical moment for the attacker, the defenders could send in their infantry to mop up, or to launch more ambitious counter-attacks backed by tanks.

On June 5, 1940, the French lacked sufficient forces to man such a front, as well as the thousands of anti-personnel and anti-tank mines which it required. Apart from these fatal deficiencies, however, the type of front envisaged by Weygand was strikingly similar to the German defences which stopped the British and Americans in the Normandy *bocage* country after D-Day in 1944.

In his book *The Battle of France, 1940,* Colonel Goutard condemned Weygand's plan for being "merely a return to the classical doctrine of a continuous front". But this ignores the fact that the front envisaged by Weygand was far more flexible than previous conceptions of a static defence line, and that without an armoured reserve, any other disposition than the one prescribed by Weygand on May 26 would have laid France wide open to the onrush of the Panzers.

But when Weygand, with his forces diminished by a third, prepared to fight a defensive battle against an intact enemy, did such an armoured reserve exist? In his memoirs, de Gaulle says that it did. On June 1 he proposed the formation of two large armoured units from the 1,200 modern tanks still available for action. Supplied with infantry and artillery complements, he suggested that if the larger group were posted north of Paris and the other south of Rheims they could be used as an adequate mobile reserve. As de Gaulle put it, they would be able to strike at the flank "of any one of the German mechanised corps when, having broken through our front, they would be dislocated in width and extended in depth."

In his reply to General de Gaulle, prepared in 1955, Weygand excused himself for not remembering this suggestion. But he asserted that at the time he had no more than 250 modern tanks at his disposal – not 1,200 – and this bears examination. A contemporary record gives only 86 tanks – Char B and Hotchkiss – to the 3rd Armoured Division, and 50 to the 4th Armoured. The figure for the 2nd Armoured Division on June 5 is not known, but it can hardly have been much higher than that of the other two. The 7th Light Mechanised Division was a recent formation, but even if it was at full strength it would have had only 174 tanks, of which half were Somua S-35's and half Hotchkiss H-35's. Even if the 2nd, 3rd, and 5th Light Cavalry Divisions had survived the disaster, they would have been reduced to skeleton strength.

Weygand's critics have argued that to attempt to defend both Paris and the Maginot Line could only have ended in disaster. This is a facile criticism. As far as Paris was concerned, calculations had been made to determine the effect on the French war effort of the loss of this or that line; and it was clear at the time that having already lost the industrial regions of the north, so vital to the production of tanks, it was essential to defend the line of the Somme and the Aisne.

As for the Maginot Line, it is true that shorter defensive fronts could have been selected, but at best the advantages to be gained by abandoning the Maginot Line could only have been purely military ones. The Rhine basin would have been lost, together with the strongpoints between the Rhine and the Moselle which enabled a front of 220 miles to be defended by a mere 17 divisions, of which ten were "Series B" reserve ones.

The 3rd Army Group had been transferred from the Saone to the Somme. General Garchery had handed over the 8th Army to General Laure, and 8th Army was now attached to 2nd Army Group, with the task of coping with any German attempt to cross the Rhine between Basle and Strasbourg, or to violate neutral Swiss territory. From Sélestat to Bitche stood Bourret's 5th Army, and then,

German motorcycle despatch riders check their positions.

covering the Moselle valley, Condé's 3rd Army. As Weygand had redeployed many of its units to other sectors, 4th Army's strength was reduced to General Hubert's group covering the Saar. In view of the signs which hinted at a possible offensive by the German Army Group "C" on the Saar and across the Rhine at Neuf-Brisach, General Prételat found that his 2nd Army Group had really been reduced to a dangerous level.

Weygand had promoted Huntziger from the command of 2nd Army to that of the new 4th Army Group. The 2nd Army, taken over by General Freydenberg, covered the passes of the Argonne; to the left of 2nd Army, General Réquin's 4th Army held the line of the Aisne between Attigny and Neufchâtel. The 12 divisions of the 4th Army Group had a front of 75 miles to cover; but although the Argonne forest favoured the defenders, the rolling chalk countryside of Champagne was so well adapted to tank warfare that it had been christened the "tankodrome" in French military circles.

Finally, the 150 miles of front between Neufchâtel-sur-Aisne and Abbeville were covered by General Besson's 3rd Army Group. This was made up of three armies: General Touchon's 6th Army on the Aisne; General Frère's 7th Army blocking the approaches to Compiègne and Beauvais; and General Altmayer's 10th Army on the lower Somme. With one division per $8\frac{1}{2}$ miles of front, General Besson's army group presented a very over-stretched network of strongpoints – while the Germans had seven bridgeheads on the left bank of the Somme.

Counting the 16 infantry divisions in army group or supreme command reserve, the seven armoured, mechanised, and cavalry divisions, and the four British and Polish divisions still in France, Weygand had at his disposal a force of 71 divisions. But even to arrive at this unimpressive total he had had to draw upon the reserve armies in the Alps and North Africa, despite the increasing threat from Italy.

As a result of the disastrous opening phase of the campaign, some 25 infantry divisions had been destroyed. Thirteen out of the original 31 active infantry divisions had gone, and six out of the seven motorised divisions. Six out of the original 13 light cavalry, light mechanised, and armoured divisions which Gamelin had deployed on the morning of May 10 had also been removed from the board. Nevertheless, Weygand had managed to form three striking groups out of his surviving armoured units. On June 5, 1940, they were ready for the fight: the first, under General Petiet, around Forges-les-Eaux, the second, under General Audet, in the Beauvais area, and the third, under General Buisson, in the Vouziers area. Weygand, therefore, cannot be accused of having failed to create an armoured reserve, albeit a sadly depleted one.

After Weygand's plan had been accepted by the War Committee on May 25, he had to reject an idea expressed by Reynaud in a note on the 29th; this had required him "to plan for the establishment of a national redoubt around a war port, allowing us to make use of the sealanes and above all to communicate with our allies. This national redoubt should be arranged and supplied, particularly with explosives, to make it *a veritable fortress*. It would consist of the Breton peninsula. The government would remain in the capital and would continue the war by making use of our naval and air forces in North Africa."

Attractive as this idea sounded on paper, the limited resources and the lack of time at the end of May 1940 made it an impossibility. Weygand put it in a nutshell: "The organisation of a 'veritable fortress' would need, after the construction of strongpoints along some 94 miles of front, the diverting of manpower and all kinds of war material, in particular anti-tank and anti-aircraft guns. All these resources were already insufficient to meet the needs of the defence line in process of organisation along the Somme and the Aisne; there could be no question of diverting even a small part of them; for even if it had been possible, there was not enough time."

How much help did France receive from her allies?

In his 2nd Army Group, General Prételat had two divisions of Polish infantry who were soon to put up a magnificent fight under the most desperate conditions. So did the British 51st Division, on the left flank of 10th Army. But the British armoured division, under Major-General R. Evans, serving in the same sector, has been described by one of its officers as "a caricature of an armoured division," not even equipped with "half its official tank strength, no field guns, insufficient anti-tank and anti-aircraft guns, without infantry, without air cover, deprived of most of its auxiliary services, with part of its staff in a vehicle 'armoured' with plywood . . ."

So much for the actual forces in the field. As far as the future of the British cooperation in the Battle of France was concerned, the picture was not good. At a meeting of the Supreme War Council on May 31, Churchill held forth with his customary resolution – but when it came down to details he became reticent and vague. According to the minutes of the meeting, "Mr. Winston Churchill observed that the problem of the invasion of England had changed in appearance, and that yet again he could promise nothing before he knew what could be saved from the North.

"As far as air reinforcements were concerned, he did not have the authorisation of his Government to grant more than had been given."

When Reynaud tried to explain the "vital character" of the battle of the Somme to Churchill, he received the following reply, which Paul Baudouin has preserved: "M. Churchill finally declared that he would think over the French requests and reply to them soon. Perhaps a Canadian division might be ready by June 22; perhaps one of the divisions from Dunkirk.

"Fourteen British divisions were being trained, armed only with rifles and machine

guns. He intended to draw upon the entire forces of the Empire for:
"eight Indian battalions;
"eight battalions from Palestine;
"14,000 Australians;
"the 2nd Canadian Division;
"one brigade from Narvik.
"But he returned to the necessity of guarding Britain . . ."

As far as the British land forces were concerned, post-war studies have indeed established these meagre figures as exact. But how sound were Churchill's motives for insisting that R.A.F. Fighter Command must be kept out of the battle for the Somme?

Churchill's supporters have endorsed the view that Britain would certainly have been invaded in September 1940, if the fighters of the R.A.F. had been sacrificed in the Battle of France. But this viewpoint needs examination. It implies that Churchill was in reality far more pessimistic about the French Army's capacity for resistance than he cared to admit, and that is why he refused to commit the Spitfires and Hurricanes in France. What are the facts? Could the large-scale intervention of British fighters have turned the scale of the Battle of France?

It could be argued that the total sacrifice of R.A.F. Fighter Command in France would have had punishing effects upon the Luftwaffe. The German air fleets might have suffered such heavy losses that they would have been unable to mount any large-scale air offensives against Britain during the autumn and winter of 1940. Moreover, had the 600-odd fighters at the R.A.F.'s disposal entered the fray, they would have been able to count on the aid of the 350–400 French fighters which were surrendered when the armistice was signed.

Against this, it could be claimed that a transfer to France of R.A.F. Fighter Command would have squandered Britain's trump card. For in France the Spitfires and Hurricanes would have been operating without the benefit of radar, a proper logistical backing and the tactical advantage of operating over their own territory, which gave them a considerable endurance advantage over the Germans in the Battle of Britain.

When he presented his battle plan to the War Committee on May 25, Weygand did not conceal the possibility that the time could well come when the French Army, given only these forces and with no hope of reinforcement, would have suffered such heavy losses that it could no longer hold the Germans. He stressed that it was essential "to stand fast on the present Somme-Aisne line and fight to the last there. This line has several weak points, in particular the Crozat Canal and the Ailette. We could be broken there. If this should happen the surviving fragments will dig in. Every part of the army must fight until it drops for the honour of the country."

It was then that President Lebrun made an intervention which Reynaud has des-

R.A.F. crews "scramble" towards their Hurricanes.

cribed as "disastrous", but which was natural enough at the time. What would happen, he asked, if the French armies should be scattered and destroyed? In such a crisis the government would have no liberty of action whatsoever, if proposals of peace came from the Germans. True, the agreements made with Britain on March 28 forbade France from concluding a separate peace; but if "relatively advantageous" conditions were offered by the Reich, they should be examined with care. With Reynaud's agreement, Weygand suggested that Britain should be sounded out on every question which would result from the total destruction of the French armies.

After the surrender of Belgium, Weygand once again raised the subject with Reynaud. Listing the reinforcements which France should request from Britain, he added: "It also seems necessary that the British Government be made aware of the fact that a time might come when France would find herself, against her will, unable to continue a military struggle to protect her soil."

It was this possibility which made Reynaud suggest the formation of a "Breton Redoubt". But as we have seen, it would have been impossible for Weygand to withdraw from the line the 12 or so divisions which this would entail. In any case, on June 5 Reynaud made yet another change in his cabinet. Baudouin replaced Daladier as Foreign Minister, Bouthillier replaced Lamoureux as Finance Minister – and Charles de Gaulle, promoted temporary brigadier-general, became Under-Secretary for War.

CHAPTER 11
The destruction of France

Facing Weygand's 71 divisions, the German commander of Operation "Red" had massed 143 divisions – seven more than on May 10. Three of them had come from the German-Soviet frontier zone, thanks to the benevolent attitude of Stalin and Molotov since the Norwegian campaign. Three others had been diverted from the *Ersatzheer* or training army. And the single infantry division which had been occupying Denmark was also transferred to France. For the coming battle, Hitler and the O.K.W. staff installed themselves in the Belgian village of Brûly-de-Pesche, not far from the O.K.H. headquarters at Chimay.

The French 3rd Army Group was about to be attacked by a new and formidable German concentration under Bock. As the woods and steep gradients of the Chemindes-Dames were unfavourable for armour, the new mass Panzer assault with its usual air support was to be made on the plain of Picardy: Kleist's *Panzergruppe* striking from Péronne and Amiens, and XV Panzer Corps debouching from Longpré, where Rommel's 7th Panzer Division held the railway-bridge. The battle was to rage for 48 hours without the French showing any signs of breaking. In fact, on the evening of June 5 Colonel-General von Bock noted in his war diary: "The French are defending themselves stubbornly."

Certainly, the new tactics which the French were using would not keep the Panzers at bay for long. "For the moment," wrote Hans-Adolf Jacobsen, "[the French tactics] had the following advantage: around Amiens and Péronne, our armoured divisions were able to push their tanks into the gaps between the enemy strongpoints, but our infantry, caught by the flanking fire from the villages, could not follow up. For this reason it was not possible to commit our motorised divisions on the first day."

Strauss' 9th Army, on the Laon sector, also scored mediocre successes on the first day. At Army Group "B" H.Q., the first impression was that this would be a long, hard fight. At Ablaincourt, Captain Jungenfeld, commanding a tank battalion of the 4th Panzer Division, had nine tanks knocked out within minutes. Shortly afterwards his battalion suffered new losses and by noon had only penetrated some 6¼ miles into the French positions. Jungenfeld described the situation in the following words: "In front of us, every village and wood – one might even say every clump of trees – is literally stuffed with guns and defences; even small artillery detachments can put us under direct fire. Behind us is the glare of a vicious battle where one fights not only for each village, but for each house. We are not therefore surprised to find ourselves under fire from all quarters, and one could say: 'Nobody knows which is the front and which is the rear.' "

And resistance like this was being put up by the French 19th Division, covering seven miles of front and faced by two German corps. On June 6, Bock noted in his diary: "A serious day, rich in crises. It seems that we are in trouble." But at the moment when, "with a heavy heart", he was about to order XIV Motorised Corps to break off the action at Amiens to reinforce the attack of XVI Panzer Corps, he heard of the successes of his 9th and 4th Armies.

On the left of the German front, 9th Army had thrust across the Chemin-des-Dames and had reached the Aisne at Soissons. Better still, on the German right, XV Panzer Corps had broken through the French 10th Army, and Rommel's 7th Panzer Division surged forward to Formerie and Forges-les-Eaux on June 7, scattering the 17th Light Division.

This situation forced General Besson to order General Frère to pull back 7th Army into alignment with 6th Army on its right and 10th Army on its left. But this withdrawal amounted to the total sacrifice of the divisions which had defended the line of the Somme so valiantly, and certainly resulted in the loss of most of their heavy weapons. The 7th Panzer Division, exploiting its successes on the 7th, thrust towards Elbeuf, where the Seine bridges were destroyed at the approach of his first tanks, then swung north-west to reach the Channel at Fécamp. This move trapped General Ihler's IX Corps (which included the French 31st and 40th Divisions and part of the British 51st Division, which had been transferred from the Maginot Line) plus the survivors of 2nd and 5th Light Cavalry Divisions, trapped with their backs to the sea. On June 12, 46,000 French and British troops surrendered at St. Valery-en-Caux, while 3,300 succeeded in breaking through the German ring.

On June 9, Rundstedt's Army Group "A" entered the battle with a crushing superiority in men and machines. Its attack was aimed at General Réquin's 4th Army, holding the Aisne between Neufchâtel and Attigny, and the French VII Corps, linking the right of 6th Army with the left of the 2nd. Seven French infantry divisions were assaulted by double their own numbers: the infantry divisions of the German 12th and 2nd Armies.

Despite this unequal struggle the French fought superbly. The German XVII Corps, on the left of List's 12th Army, was held on the Ardennes Canal by General Aublet's 36th Division. In the Voncq region alone, the German 26th Division lost nearly 600 killed and wounded and over 400 prisoners. On the Aisne, the German XXIII Corps received similar treatment at the hands of General de Lattre de Tassigny's 14th Division. Counter-attacked with skill and energy, the Germans lost the bridgeheads which they had won of the left bank of the river, together with about 1,000 prisoners. General Schubert, commanding XXIII

Corps, wrote in his diary: "The attack ran up against an enemy whose morale was unshaken and who, in a well-arranged position, stood up to our preparatory artillery bombardment with minimal losses . . .

"The bearing and tactical skill of the enemy were totally different to those of the earlier battles. The units of the 14th Division let the German infantry approach to within point-blank range in order to make certain of them . . .

"In many places the French marksmen posted in trees kept up their fire until they had exhausted their last cartridge, without heeding the advance of the German forces . . . The morale of the French 14th Division was extraordinary. The French went out to look for their wounded, when their comrades had no chance of evacuating them, and cared for them. They left provisions with the wounded who could not be taken along when they fell back on the night of June 10–11 . . .

"The 14th Division fought on June 9 and 10 in a manner which recalls the attitude of the best French troops of 1914–18 at Verdun."

The forces on List's right wing, together with the German 2nd Army, had better luck. Neither the French 10th Division, around Rethel, nor the 2nd Division, near Château-Porcien, succeeded in driving the Germans back to the north bank of the Aisne. List was therefore able to pass Guderian's *Panzergruppe* across the river, and on the dawn of the 10th XXXIX Panzer Corps struck out for the south. On the afternoon of the same day it was counter-attacked in flank by General Buisson's armoured group, and the heavy Chars B1 *bis* inflicted "sadly heavy casualties". But this was not to last. The collapse of the VII Corps on the left flank of 4th Army opened an enormous breach in the French front, and the Panzers streamed through this. On the evening of June 12 – when Guderian reached Châlons-sur-Marne – General Réquin received a telephone call from General Touchon of the 6th Army and heard him say: "I ought to cover you. It's absolutely impossible. My right-wing corps [VII Corps] has collapsed. Between Montmirail and Sézanne, there's a merry-go-round of tanks. I've nothing with which to fend it off."

In fact this was Kleist's *Panzergruppe*, advancing from Péronne and Amiens. It was fanning out towards the south, sending its XVI Panzer Corps towards Lyons and its XIV Motorised Corps towards Creusot-St. Etienne.

After the battle on the Somme the battle for Champagne was lost, and it was lost in conditions which wrecked Weygand's hopes for a withdrawal to the lower Seine, the northern region of Paris, and the Marne. By June 11 he had only 27 divisions or their equivalent with which to carry on the fight between the western end of the Maginot Line at Longuyon and the Seine estuary – a front of some 280 miles.

For this reason, Weygand ordered Georges, at 1315 hours on June 12, to execute the order which he had drawn up on the previous day for a withdrawal to the line Geneva–Dôle–Avallon–Cosne (on the Loire)–Tours–Argentan–Caen–mouth of the Orne. Quite apart from the lateness of this decision, this new front was much longer than the previous one – and in one week the number of divisions available had fallen from 71 to about 45 . . .

The arrival of the Germans before Paris triggered off another civilian mass exodus. The following eye-witness account contrasts strongly with other terrifying descriptions of the flight from the capital:

"At the risk of scandalising certain readers I must say that the departure of the Parisians appeared to me like a vast picnic-party. The queue of traffic which our car joined at the *Barrière d'Italie* contained vehicles of every description – delivery vans, touring cars, heavy lorries, and even antique horse-drawn cabs. Big lorries contained whole families, who were passing round sausage and wine. Every time the queue stopped – about every 100 yards – people would scatter to the roadside and go into houses, returning with a hunk of bread or a bottle of water. The hot sun blazed down on the happy crowd – a paid holiday."

On June 10, 1940, on Mussolini's orders, Ciano gave the French and British Ambassadors their passports, and Italy went to war.

During the last three months of 1939 the consequences of the German-Soviet Pact – the partition of Poland, the hideous cruelties inflicted on the Poles by the Nazis, and

Germany's connivance at the Soviet assault upon Finland – had resulted in a marked cooling of relations between the Axis partners. In fact, at the end of December 1939, Ciano had not hesitated to reveal (via the Princess of Piedmont) what he knew of Germany's military intentions towards Belgium. Nor did Fascist Italy refuse to sell certain war *matériel* to the Western democracies.

In Italy's swing from non-belligerence to intervention in the war, the effects of the Allied blockade played their part. In February 1940, when Paris and London announced their intention of seizing all shipments of German coal intended for use in Italian industries in mid-Channel, this caused great irritation in Rome; but this move, justified or not, made little direct impression on Mussolini's intentions. His mind was already made up.

To a large extent Mussolini's desire for war can be explained by the fascination which Hitler exercised over him. But much more important was his yearning for grandeur: grandeur for Italy in the eyes of other nations (particularly the Third Reich); grandeur for the Fascist Party in the eyes of Italian public opinion; grandeur for himself in the eyes of the Party.

Mussolini's determination to go to war was revealed on March 31 to the King-Emperor, to Marshals Badoglio and Graziani, Ciano, Balbo, and the navy and air force chiefs-of-staff. "Italy," he began, "cannot remain neutral for the whole of the war without abandoning her rôle, without demeaning herself and reducing herself to the level of a tenfold Switzerland."

On April 2 Mussolini repeated this argu-

ment to Ciano. A neutral Italy, the Duce declared, "would lose prestige among the nations of the world for a century as a Great Power and for all eternity as a Fascist régime". But he was not going to rush into the fray. Reminding Ciano of an Italian folk story on March 16, two days before his meeting with Hitler at the Brenner Pass, he had said: "I shall do as Bertoldo did. He accepted the death sentence on condition that he choose the tree on which he was to be hanged. Needless to say, he never found that tree. I shall agree to enter the war, but reserve for myself the choice of the moment. I alone shall be the judge, and a great deal will depend upon how the war goes."

When he returned from his meeting with Hitler, Mussolini had not greatly changed his point of view. The Italian and German General Staffs had reached agreement on the possible intervention of an Italian army in Alsace, code-named Operation *"Bär"* ("Bear"), which would be directed by Leeb. A force of 20 to 30 Italian divisions would cross the Rhine in the tracks of the German 7th Army and would attack towards Belfort with the Langres plateau as its final objective. However, urged on by Marshal Badoglio, Mussolini fretted at the idea of playing second fiddle to his German ally.

On the German side, O.K.H. calculated that the Italian forces could not reach the Rhine bridgehead at Neuf-Brisach until 12 weeks after mobilisation. Whether the offensive succeeded or failed, the Italians woul arrive too late.

Once again, therefore, it was a question of "parallel war", as Mussolini said in his

German sappers rebuilding a bridge.

note of March 31: each Axis power would strive for its own particular objectives. As far as Italy was concerned, Mussolini's note defined the various rôles which the Italian armed forces would play in each theatre on the declaration of war:

"1. *West.* Defensive on the Western Alps. No initiative. *Vigilance.* Initiative to be taken only in the event – unlikely as I see it – of a total French collapse under the German attack. Corsica could perhaps be occupied but this might not be worth the effort. However, its air bases must be neutralised.

2. *Yugoslavia.* Careful vigilance.

3. *Libya.* Defensive on the Egyptian as well as the Tunisian front. The idea of an offensive against Egypt must be set aside since the constitution of the Weygand army.

4. *Aegean:* Defensive.

5. *Abyssinia:* Offensive to shield Eritrea, and operations against Gedaref and Kassala [Sudan]. Offensive against Djibouti. Defensive and possible counter-offensive on the Kenyan front.

6. *Air.* Offensive or defensive according to the different fronts and enemy initiative.

7. *Sea.* General offensive in the Mediterranean and beyond."

Considering that the Duke of Aosta, Viceroy of Abyssinia, declared that the offensive operations laid down for him (in Abyssinia) could not be carried out, it must be said that this was a very modest programme in view of Mussolini's imperialist intentions. Above all there was absolutely no mention of Malta, and the conquest of that vital strategic island should have been one of the main objectives of the Italian land, sea, and air forces.

Modest as it was, events would prove that this programme was asking too much of the defensive, let alone the offensive, capacities of the armed forces raised by the Fascist régime. On May 9, 1940, Mussolini, commenting on Italy's military preparations, described them as "satisfactory, but not ideal". This was a decided understatement. A breakdown of the 73 Italian divisions mobilised on June 10 shows the following: complete – 19; usable but not complete (100 per cent of their equipment but only 75 per cent of their personnel) – 34; and at a low state of efficiency (50 per cent of their vehicles, horses, and mules, and 60 per cent of their personnel) – 20.

But this was not the full story, for these percentages only refer to the Italian military system which, to produce a higher number of divisions, had resulted in understrength units. This meant that an Italian infantry division only had two infantry regiments and three artillery detachments, while in most armies of the time an infantry division had three infantry regiments and four or five artillery detachments. To cope with tanks, an Italian infantry division only had eight anti-tank guns; a German division had 75, a French division 52, and a Swiss division 36.

On June 10, 1940 the Italian fleet consisted of two modernised battleships, 19 modern cruisers, 126 destroyers and torpedo-boats and 117 submarines. Four other battleships were completing their final trials before joining the fleet. It was an imposing force on paper, but the Italian Navy had two serious problems. First, stocks of fuel oil were low; they were sufficient only for nine months of war operations and there was no guarantee that they could be replenished. Second, Mussolini, when the question had been put to him, had dismissed aircraft-carriers as useless. He believed that in the strategic confines of the Mediterranean land-based aircraft were quite adequate for maritime operations, flying from bases in Sardinia, Sicily, Libya, and the Dodecanese. When this theory was put to the test, General Pricolo's air crews were found to be perfectly incapable of scouting for, defending, or supporting the fleet when it put to sea. Like Grand-Admiral Raeder, Admiral Domenico Cavagnari lacked the support of a trained naval air arm which could work efficiently with the fleet.

Finally, stocks of strategic war *matériel* were low, as was reported on May 13 by General Umberto Favagrossa, Minister of War Production. If hostilities broke out this worrying situation would be given no chance of improvement. Nickel was one of the biggest problems; Italian stocks were absurdly low – and nickel is a vital metal in the production of land, sea, and air weapons, and also of aircraft engines. It seemed unlikely that the industrial potential of Fascist Italy, given the Allied blockade, would be unable to restore the many deficiencies in the armed forces.

When the Pact of Steel had been signed,

After six weeks of campaigning the German troops were exhausted.

Mussolini had told his German ally that a period of at least three years would be needed to put Italian armaments to rights. He was still well aware of this when, on May 29, 1940, he inaugurated *Comando Supremo* – the Italian War High Command – in a solemn session. Even today Ciano's record of the event retains a tragicomic element: "Today at eleven at the Palazzo Venezia the High Command was born! Rarely have I seen Mussolini so happy. He has realised his dream: that of becoming the military leader of his country at war."

The event seemed to blind Mussolini to the continuing existence of Italy's military deficiencies and to refute, one by one, the critics who had urged him not to unite the cause of the country, the monarchy, and the régime with that of the Third Reich, which, this faction hoped, would be beaten as soon as the Wehrmacht ventured out from behind the Siegfried Line. During the Phoney War Mussolini had chafed at the almost unanimous state of Italian public opinion. But after the Norwegian campaign began on April 9, each new German victory restored his confidence and enabled him to reduce his opponents to silence: his own Minister of Foreign Affairs, General Carboni (head of Military Intelligence), Marshal Badoglio, the House of Savoy, and even the Vatican.

As the unavoidable defeat of France would precede that of Britain, Mussolini believed that a few weeks of hostilities would not encroach too severely upon Italy's military capital, all the more so because his war plan of March 31 seemed

to have lowered the cost of intervention as far as possible. Having sounded the kill by this modest assessment, he would be in at the death.

Considering Germany's mastery over Europe, Mussolini believed that it would be much better to present himself to the Germans as a tardy ally than as an inveterate neutral. Nor was he unaware that out of the Führer's 80 million subjects he had only one true friend: Adolf Hitler. All in all, on June 10, 1940, Italian intervention would probably mean less danger for Italy than non-belligerence. For if Mussolini were to remain neutral, would Hitler continue to turn a deaf ear to the claims of the seven million German-speaking former Austrians in the Alto Adige, or to refrain from looking towards Trieste as an access point to the Adriatic?

One thing was certain: Mussolini may have had the dream of his life come true, but he was certainly not fully capable, as far as his health was concerned, of assuming the rôle of the military leader of a great nation at war. Ciano's diary shows him alternately exultant and depressed, hesitant and precipitate – the probable effects of the venereal disease which he had contracted in Lausanne before 1914, compounded by the first symptoms of a vicious stomach ulcer.

In the evening of June 10, on hearing the news that the Germans were crossing the Seine at Andelys and Vernon, President Lebrun and Reynaud's Cabinet left Paris and headed for Tours. Following the example given in 1914 by his predecessor, Myron T. Herrick, U.S. Ambassador

William Bullitt stayed on in Paris. There is a case for the arguments of de Gaulle and the American historian Langer that Bullitt was wrong to do so, for his voice would have carried much weight both in the last French government talks at Bordeaux and in the final inter-Allied discussions. For their part, Generals Weygand and Georges withdrew to Briare with their staffs.

On the 9th, after issuing a vibrant appeal for continued resistance to his troops, Weygand had drawn up a note for the French Government. In it he warned, without yet abandoning hope of stabilising the situation, that the "decisive breakthrough" could come at any moment. He ended: "If this should happen our armies will fight on until they are exhausted, to the last round, but their dispersion will only be a matter of time."

At about 1000 hours on June 10, having listened to the opening paragraphs of Doumenc's report, Weygand sent a note detailing the ever-worsening situation to Reynaud, who had returned to his idea of a "Breton Redoubt" in a directly-argued appeal. Although the word "armistice" had not yet been pronounced, the basic differences between the French Government and High Command were deepening.

The solution to the conflict could have been the replacement of the septuagenerian General Weygand. Reynaud wanted this, and he had sounded out General Huntziger via de Gaulle, his Under-Secretary for War. According to de Gaulle, Huntziger

The Panzers advance south.

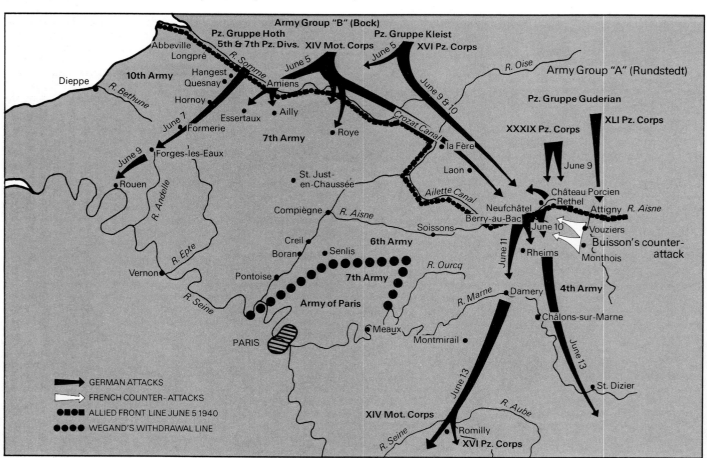

would have agreed readily if the proposition had been put to him. Henri Massis, however, who was serving at the time in the 4th Army Group, takes the opposite view; and considering the personal friendship between Huntziger and Massis his opinion is probably nearer the mark. The affair went no further, Reynaud deciding to leave things as they were; and this is why (if we replace with "armistice" the word "peace", which he uses incorrectly) de Gaulle was right when he wrote that in taking this decision Reynaud was following "the idea of taking the road of war with a supreme commander who wanted to take the road of peace".

In the meeting of the Supreme War Council held at Briare on the evening of June 11 and on the morning of the 12th, Churchill brought the entire French delegation, including Reynaud, round against him. Resolute and optimistic as to the final outcome of the war, but remote from the actual conflict, he gave a definite "no" to the French request for immediate air aid. In *The Second World War*, Churchill states ingenuously that Reynaud should have been ashamed to support, "even tacitly", Weygand's demand for the last British fighter squadrons.

No less than 20–25 British divisions would be fighting beside the French by the following spring; but in the meantime the only British troops in France were the 52nd Division, which had just crossed the Channel, and the 1st Canadian Division, which was disembarking at Brest. A third division would follow on about June 20. At the time of the Briare conference, what more could Churchill offer? It is clear that the R.A.F., entering the fray above the land battles which were developing on the lower Somme and in Champagne, would have been unable to redress the balance, while the French Air Force, left to its own resources, had been largely destroyed as a fighting force. In addition to this, one particular suggestion by Churchill aroused the unanimous opposition of the French leaders: "Will not the mass of Paris and its suburbs present an obstacle dividing and delaying the enemy as in 1914, or like Madrid?"

Quite apart from the fact that Churchill did not apply this argument in the case of the Channel Islands but had them evacuated on the signing of the armistice, his suggestion that Paris be defended was an empty one because neither O.K.H. nor Hitler intended to fight a costly battle for Paris, although this was not known at the French High Command. The French divisions which had been earmarked for the defence of Paris therefore remained inactive, a complete loss to the defence which Weygand was trying to improvise on the Loire.

Churchill's subsequent suggestion that guerrilla warfare should be resorted to "if the period of co-ordinated war ends" and "to prolong the resistance until the United States come in" was also rejected by the French.

The day of June 12, when the debate on these grave matters continued, began with a comical incident which might have influenced Churchill's good humour in the morning discussions. According to Benoist-Méchin: "All was calm at the Château du Muguet where Churchill passed the night. Two officers on Weygand's staff were having their breakfast in the dining room (converted into a conference room the day before). Suddenly the door of the room was flung open. In the doorway there appeared a strange sight, a sort of Japanese demon swathed in an ample red silk kimono held in with a white silk belt, a bulky figure with disordered hair who bellowed angrily: *'Uh ay ma bain?'*"

It was Churchill, finding that the service in the château left much to be desired. The French officers were paralysed by the apparition and took several moments to recover themselves; but, as the British liaison officer, General Spears, noted: "The Prime Minister, as usual, got his way, and efforts were made to satisfy him." When Spears arrived at Muguet he found Churchill dressing in his room. "He was in a very bad humour."

At Briare on June 12, Weygand repeated that he hoped to hold on with British help. But on the afternoon of the same day he declared in the French Council: "I will continue to resist, if the Council orders me to do so. But as of this moment I have to make this clear: the ending of hostilities must be considered soon."

On the 13th, driving through the shattered French armies on the lower Somme and in Champagne, the Panzers fanned out in their southward advance: Hoth's group headed for Normandy; Kleist, using the bridges at Nogent and Romilly-sur-Seine, made for the Massif Central and Burgundy; and Guderian swung east, heading for the flank and rear areas of Prételat's 2nd Army Group.

At this point, from the Siegfried Line, Leeb unleashed Operation "Tiger", sending seven division from General von Witzleben's 1st Army against the French Saar Detachment under General Hubert. The latter consisted only of General Echard's 52nd Division and General Duch's 1st Polish Division; but despite the fire of 229 artillery batteries and an entire Luftwaffe *Fliegerkorps*, the Germans made no notable progress on the 14th. During the night, however, General Hubert had to retreat in accordance with the order intended to realign 2nd Army Group along the Geneva–Dôle front.

This movement favoured the attack of General Dollmann's German 7th Army which, launching Operation "Bear", crossed the Rhine at Markolsheim and Neuf-Brisach at dawn on the 15th. The XXVII Corps under General Brandt succeeded in gaining only $1\frac{1}{4}$ miles on the left bank of the Rhine that day, despite the fact that he was faced merely by fortress troops; but further bridging operations by the German sappers allowed 7th Army to expand into the plain of Alsace and to swing towards Mulhouse for a link-up with *Panzergruppe* Guderian.

Although he complains in his memoirs of having been given contradictory orders, Guderian had lived up to the nickname of "Swift Heinz" which his troops had given him. On the evening of the 12th he had been at Châlons-sur-Marne. By noon on the 14th he had reached St. Dizier, which fell to the 1st Panzer Division, urged on by Guderian towards Langres. Langres fell on the 15th, after an advance of 66 miles, and the division pressed on towards Besançon. On June 17 – his 51st birthday – Guderian joined his 29th Motorised Division (which had been advancing on the right of 1st Panzer Division) at Pontarlier on the Swiss frontier. When the news of this exploit came in, Hitler thought that a mistake had been made and that Guderian meant Pontailler-sur-Saône, 50 miles back.

This astonishing raid by XXXIX Panzer Corps indicates clearly enough that after St. Dizier the Germans found no further organised resistance to their advance, apart from some improvised shellfire at the entrances to towns. The same applied to XLI Panzer Corps. Having taken Verdun and Bar-le-Duc on June 15, XLI Corps found itself, 48 hours later, in the region of Vesoul-Port-sur-Saône and Bourbonne-les-Bains. On June 17 an O.K.H. order subordinated *Panzergruppe* Guderian and the 16th Army on its left to Army Group "C". Without losing a moment, the impetuous Guderian swung his Panzer corps through 90 degrees and gave them the following new objectives: XXXIX Panzer Corps – from Pontarlier and Besançon towards Belfort; and XLI Panzer Corps – from Vesoul and Bourbonne-les-Bains towards Epinal and Charmes.

As the 29th Motorised Division was approaching the Swiss frontier, XVI Panzer Corps on the left of *Panzergruppe* Kleist was entering the suburbs of Dijon. The day before, in a battle near Saulieu and Semur-en-Auxois, XVI Panzer Corps had smashed the last resistance put up by the remnants of the French 3rd Armoured Division and by Major-General Maczek's Polish 10th Armoured Brigade, which was fighting its first engagement. As soon as the armistice negotiations began Maczek marched his brigade across France from east to west and embarked it for England. In 1944 he and his compatriots would return to France to take part in fierce fighting during the battle for Normandy.

The southward flood of the Panzer advance cut off the line of retreat of all French forces east of the Argonne – 2nd Army Group and the 2nd Army on its left – between Longuyon and Vouziers. General Prételat, who had preceded his troops to their new sector, found himself cut off from them, and General Condé, commander of 3rd Army, took command of this last bastion of resistance. But before it became clear whether he would break out of the encirclement or fight and die where he stood, a wide gap, some 50 miles across, opened between the Swiss frontier and the Massif du Morvan, clearing the road to Grenoble, Toulon, and Marseilles for the invader.

Similar catastrophe had enveloped the

The victorious Germans parade past the Arc de Triomphe.

opposite end of the front. On June 16, having reduced the pocket at St. Valery-en-Caux, XV Panzer Corps crossed the Seine with Rommel in the van. In front of XV Panzer Corps was 4th Army, whose XXXVIII Corps, led by Manstein, had just reached la Ferté-Vidame, 49 miles south of the bridgehead which he had won. Weygand tried to form a new 10th Army from the survivors of the Somme battle and troops evacuated from Dunkirk, but these forces were mere debris, thrown piecemeal into the fray as soon as they disembarked and lacking all their heavy weapons.

On June 14 the leading troops of the German 18th Army entered Paris, declared an open city and evacuated the day before on the orders of General Héring. His forces, designated the "Army of Paris" had recently been formed between the right of 6th Army and the left of the 7th, both of them now falling back to the Loire.

In these conditions – made worse by the refugee exodus and German air attacks – discussions continued between the Allied governments and within Reynaud's Cabinet. It was no longer a question of continuing the fight or of defending metropolitan France: the question now was how to bring about an end of hostilities in conditions which would prove the least damaging for the permanent interests of defeated France.

The debate was still conducted according to the terms of the reciprocal undertakings exchanged by France and Britain in London on March 28, on the occasion of Reynaud's first visit, as President, to London. These undertakings pledged the two powers not to conclude any peace treaty or armistice convention without the agreement of the other party. And at Tours on June 13 Churchill gave his formal refusal to release France from the undertaking which she had given.

Certain Frenchmen claimed after the event that as the agreement of March 28 had not been ratified by the French parliament it could not be considered as official. This, surely, is a technical quibble; it was certainly not cited by anyone at the time. But there are no grounds for claiming – as did Reynaud, Georges Mandel, César

Campinchi, Jules Jeanneney, Edouard Herriot and others, both at Tours and at Bordeaux – that armistice negotiations blackened the national honour of France. The expression "When matters are impossible, nothing is binding" is not only common sense but a principle of right which is always valid.

In July 1945 the former President of the Republic, Lebrun, was examined as a witness in the trial of Marshal Pétain. His reply to M. Isorni, one of the defence advocates, was unambiguous: "From the moment when one of the two countries which signed a convention like that of March 28 retains part of its forces for its own defence, instead of risking it in the common battle – as the British Empire did – it can always keep a paper to recall us to the obligations written on it. But it no longer has the moral authority to say: I will not release you from your obligations."

It is perfectly true that in mid-June 1940 the Hurricanes and Spitfires of the R.A.F., which until then had played only a sporadic part in the battle, represented the main defence of the British Empire; more than that, considering the lack of military preparation of the United States, R.A.F. Fighter Command was in fact the champion of the entire free world, including defeated nations and neutrals. But this does not change the fact that the circumstances of 1940 speak strongly in favour of Lebrun's later argument.

In its appalling situation, with no hope of help from Britain, the French Government therefore had the right to claim its freedom of decision. But this does not necessarily imply that Reynaud's successor made the best decision in preferring an armistice to capitulation.

Given this tragic alternative, opinions were divided at the time and remain so today. Hundreds of books have been written on the fall of Reynaud, his replacement by Marshal Pétain, the conclusion of the armistice, and the establishment of the Vichy régime.

A fair analysis can only be made by considering the facts which influenced the key personalities at the time in making their

decisions, or the conjectures which could have influenced their reading of the situation. It is misleading, therefore, to refer to documents later discovered in the German archives, which the victors examined after the German surrender in May 1945, in judging the events of June 1940.

While trying to get Weygand to open negotiations with the Germans for the capitulation of the armies entrusted to him, Reynaud wanted to keep the alliance with Britain intact and continue hostilities against Germany. If it crossed to Algiers, his Government would have been able to use the entire French Navy, what could be saved of the Army and Air Force, and the human and material resources of the French Empire. But the counterpart of this plan meant the total surrender of the army – captivity for every man wearing French uniform. And when the Armistice was signed, the Germans announced that they had taken 1,450,000 prisoners. Moreover, Reynaud and his supporters consented to the total occupation of France, not only by the German victors but also by the Italians, who had been unable to make good their claims by force. Finally installed at Toulon, Marseilles, and Port Vendres, the Axis powers would have been able to carry the war to North Africa.

General Noguès, French C.-in-C. in North Africa, had already been required to send a large proportion of his troops and most of his modern weapons to reinforce the armies in France. On May 20 he had had under his orders 11 infantry divisions, a light division, and two cavalry brigades; a month later he was reduced to eight divisions – three of them territorial – with considerable patrolling and policing duties.

In Libya, Marshal Italo Balbo had mobilised 14 divisions, of which nine were concentrated west of Tripoli. In the west, across the Moroccan frontier, French Intelligence had identified no less than five Spanish divisions, stationed between Ceuta and Larache. How would Spain react if there were no armistice and Hitler decided to carry the war into North Africa? At the very least it seemed that General Franco, who had just occupied Tangier in defiance of international statute, might well open Spain to the passage of the Wehrmacht.

Could the French have reinforced North Africa with troops withdrawn from metropolitan France? This had been thought of, but too late. Nor was this surprising, for according to Navy calculations it would have taken a fortnight to collect sufficient tonnage to transport several hundreds of thousands of men and their equipment. This means that if the project were to have been possible a decision would have had to have been taken around June 1.

On that date it would have been impossible for the French Government to have made the deliberate decision to abandon the whole of France before the crucial battle had been fought – the battle on whose outcome Weygand was far from pessimistic.

In any case, the Germans would have been hard on the heels of the retiring French; and considering the enormous breach which opened on the French right flank, there is every reason to believe that the French defenders of the Loire would have been cut off from the Mediterranean.

The day before the armistice came into being XVI Panzer Corps, which had reached Valence, was ordered by O.K.H. to prepare for an advance against Toulon and Marseilles. At the same time Guderian was ordered to regroup his *Panzergruppe* near Montluçon and head for Toulouse, Bordeaux, and the Atlantic coast. Pétain and Weygand were without a shadow of doubt unaware of these orders when they made their decision in favour of an armistice, but a simple look at the map told them that a new encircling move by the Germans could be started at any moment.

The French and Royal Navies could have

Pétain, a national hero, the man all France now looked to.

intercepted any attempts to land Axis troops on the central sector of the Algerian coast; but the bitter experience of Norway had shown that sea power was of no avail in narrow waters without supremacy in the air. It would have been possible for the Spaniards, reinforced by the Germans, to have attacked Morocco across the Strait of Gibraltar, while the Italians, with the aid of the Luftwaffe, attacked Tunis across the Sicilian Channel. As for the numerous French aircraft which landed in Algeria during the last days of the campaign, the question of their supply and replacement only raised new problems.

Faced with all these difficulties, General Noguès ended by rallying, with a heavy heart, to the idea of an armistice. He lamented that American aid had not been requested but at this stage this was more symbolic than real, for Roosevelt's policy had sadly disarmed the United States.

All this reasoning can be criticised on the grounds that Hitler in fact had no intentions of the kind. This is true, but in war one very rarely has the enemy's plans before one, and every possible enemy move must be considered. And the possibility of Hitler choosing to exploit his victory on the far shore of the Mediterranean could not be taken lightly at the time. This was made clear when, on June 19, the Germans asked the beaten French for the use of certain air bases in North Africa and for the authority to set up meteorological bases there. The fact that the request was dropped when the Vichy Government refused to make any concessions of this kind does not make it any the less significant.

Such were the pros and cons of the choice of policy which Reynaud recommended to his colleagues. But he did not fight for it to the bitter end. It seems clear that he had offered his resignation to President Lebrun before the majority of his colleagues had opposed his plans, knowing (none better) that at this crucial moment there was no alternative but an armistice.

First and foremost among the advantages of the latter solution was the fact that a government would be preserved in France at the moment when, invaded, her communications were cut by German air raids and the demolitions of retreating troops, and when 15 per cent of her population consisted of homeless refugees. The appalling fate of Poland, administered by *Reichkommissare* selected for their Nazi Party fanaticism, had become known to the world by 1940. For France in 1940, it seemed better to spare the population a similar fate, despite the rigours of a military occupation which, it was hoped, would apply to as small a part of the country as possible.

Moreover, an armistice would leave France with an army. Certainly, nobody who supported an armistice believed that the victors would leave the French Army the military necessities to resume the struggle with any chance of success. But the example of the German Army after Versailles spoke for itself. If even a part French Army survived, it could also serve as the basis of future hopes. Meanwhile the

Army would demobilise itself, concealing as much war material from the German commissions of inquiry as it could, and retaining the documentation which would make a future remobilisation possible. In addition, in their habitual secrecy, the Intelligence sections of the Army, Navy, and Air Force, together with the counter-espionage department, would continue to function.

It was clear that Germany and Italy would not agree to any arrangement which, suspending hostilities in metropolitan France, would not also apply to the fleet and to the Empire. For this reason Weygand, on June 13, had proposed that the fleet be sent to Britain to prevent it falling into enemy hands. This solution had met with the approval of both Churchill and Roosevelt. But how could the French fleet have quitted Toulon, Bizerta, and Mers el Kébir without exposing North Africa, Corsica, and possibly even Provence to Italian naval attacks, and perhaps even landings? This suggestion, too, was rejected by the French Council of Ministers.

Despite all this, even though neutralised, the French Empire and its fleet remained trump cards of the French régime set up after the armistice. If Hitler and Mussolini tried to go too far, they could be made to understand that if they were obdurate the Empire and the fleet would go over to the Allies. This naturally worked the other way: Hitler and Mussolini could make it equally clear that the existence of unoccupied France could depend on the submission of the Empire and the fleet.

When Marshal Pétain replaced Reynaud late on June 16, he estimated that the supporters of an armistice would be outnumbered by those who wanted to continue the war, which meant that the army would eventually have to surrender. But Weygand believed that the honour of the army which he still commanded must prevent him from sending envoys to ask for terms. He had violently rejected similar propositions which Reynaud had made to him, even when the latter had offered to absolve him from responsibility by giving him written orders.

If the choice of an armistice proved to be the less disastrous alternative, one good reason was that General de Gaulle had joined the "dissidents", as they were known during the summer of 1940. Among those who heard de Gaulle's appeal on June 17 – "France has lost a battle! But France has not lost the war!" – were Hitler and Mussolini. German and Italian diplomatic documents prove how attentive they were to every manifestation of "Free France", and this restrained them in the two separate armistice negotiations at Rethondes and the Villa Incisa. Future months would prove this; as Hitler complained to Mussolini in January 1941, without de Gaulle and his Free French, the "Weygand blackmail" would have been much more difficult, if not impossible.

In the meantime, the Axis still had to be persuaded to agree to French rearmament in North Africa.

CHAPTER 12
France Surrenders

In the event of France agreeing to a separate armistice, despite the Anglo-French agreement of March 28, what would be the attitude of Britain and her Government–in other words, of Churchill?

When he left the Château du Muguet on June 12, Churchill had taken the Commander-in-Chief of the French Navy aside and had said to him privately, according to Churchill's own account in *The Second World War*: "Darlan, you must never let them get the French Fleet."

Was Churchill already anticipating that France would ignore his urgings that she continue resistance? To say this is so is not reading too much into his words; later, writing on the same subject to President Roosevelt, Churchill mentioned the possibility that the conditions of the Italo-French armistice might be so mild that France, in order to retain Alsace and Lorraine, would seriously consider handing over her fleet to Germany and Italy.

What would this mean? In capital ships alone–the epitome of naval power in 1940 – the Axis strength would be raised to 15 battleships and battle-cruisers (seven of them French), against the Royal Navy's 14. If the two German pocket-battleships were included in the reckoning, the Axis combined battle fleet would be 17 strong. Darlan, however, as Churchill recounts, "promised solemnly that he would never do so". He was quite sincere in this: on May 28 he had written to Vice-Admiral Le Luc: "Should military events result in an armistice in which the conditions would be dictated by the Germans, and should one of those conditions mean the surrender of the fleet, *I have no intention of carrying out that order.*"

If matters were to come to such a pass, Darlan suggested several courses of action, depending on whether or not Italy had entered the war and thus had a say in the armistice. But whatever the outcome, he wrote, "all warships and aircraft, all auxiliary and supply ships capable of putting to sea, are to make for the nearest British port they can reach."

On June 13, Churchill and Lord Beaverbrook met Reynaud at Tours. The latter's Council of Ministers was not present, but met at Cangé after Reynaud's departure. This is how the afternoon began, in Benoist-Méchin's words:

"After lunch M. Baudouin accompanied Mr. Churchill and the British ministers to the Prefecture. There, instead of being driven to Cangé, they were shown into a small room on the first floor that served as the Prefect's office. M. Mandel, the Minister of the Interior, had taken it over for the time being and was on the point of beginning lunch. Churchill records in his memoirs:

" 'His luncheon, an attractive chicken, was uneaten on the tray before him. He was a ray of sunshine. He had a telephone in each hand, through which he was constantly giving orders and decisions.'

"M. Reynaud then arrived, followed a few minutes later by General Spears. Churchill took Spears aside and asked him what was going on. Spears swiftly brought him up to date with the situation. Baudouin, he said, was now 'doing his damnedest to persuade Reynaud to throw up the sponge'. Churchill replied that he had gathered as much: Baudouin had ruined an already inadequate meal by seasoning it with an outpouring of oily defeatism.

"It was now 3.30 pm. The conference was about to begin. Having finished his lunch, M. Mandel left the room, carrying his tray, and Reynaud replaced him at the desk.

"The British ministers and Baudouin sat in a semi-circle in front of him, in this little room in which one of the most important meetings of these 60 days was about to be enacted."

The accounts which we have of the attitudes taken by both parties in this their last meeting before 1945 are contradictory. Churchill's statement to the House of Commons claimed that he definitely turned down Reynaud's plea that France should be released from her engagement of March 28. But was this refusal really so categorical? There are grounds for doubt, for Reynaud, testifying before the Commission of Inquiry between 1947 and 1950, claimed that such authorisation would have been granted to him without his having to ask for it, but that it would have been arranged that he would be able to retract it. To that effect he might have used General de Gaulle, sent to London that evening, as a go-between.

When the French Council of Ministers met at Cangé after the Anglo-French conference at Tours, the mood was sombre: "In such an atmosphere the meeting of the Council opened," wrote Reynaud in his memoirs. "Chautemps was the spokesman of his colleagues ... to whom I gave ... the news that Churchill was not coming ...

"Here is how Georges Monnet in his deposition has retraced for the Committee of Inquiry the incident when Weygand attempted to teach the Government a lesson:

" 'Campinchi was amongst the Ministers who declared most bluntly, in opposition to Weygand, their opinion that we should not lay down our arms or ask for an armistice. It was, therefore, he whom Weygand took to task by asking him: "But, M. Minister, if I had been a politician, if I had been in the Government, I would not have left Paris. I would have acted like the Roman Senators at the time when the Gauls invaded Rome. In my curule chair, I should have awaited the invader. But there has been only one occasion on which the geese have saved the Capitol!'

"Louis Rollin remembers that: 'The President of the Republic, who looked disconcerted by this attitude, was near Weygand. He clapped him on the arm in friendly fashion and said: 'But look now, General, if you follow your argument to its logical conclusion. The Government is taken prisoner, but do you really think that that would do the country any good? How can a captive Government discuss either an armistice or a continuation of the war? It is no longer master of its own will ... Come now, think it over ...'

"The General maintained his position," Reynaud continues. "He was obdurate in his opposition to the policy which I had advocated the day before, that of liberating France with the aid of the Anglo-Saxon world.

"But after finishing his exposition Weygand left the room abruptly on the grounds that one of the Ministers – it was Mandel – had smiled."

Reynaud left the next day for Bordeaux, where the French Government was planning to base itself. His memoirs contain some details of the unhappy journey:

"At 10 o'clock in the morning on the 14th I got into my car in the Cour Renaissance of the Château de Chissay, which was to be bombed only an hour later – proof that the enemy was well informed. But for once those gentlemen were late.

"I drove towards Bordeaux, my car escorted by army motorcyclists. Every mile which carried me away from Paris, now occupied by the enemy, was agony for me. Never has a French head of government been in a situation like mine. 'The Germans are at Noyon,' Clemenceau had said. They had not been in Paris. The English had jeered at Charles VII as 'the King of Bourges'. But now, perhaps, Bourges too would fall in a few days. The entire country could soon be carved up by the tracks of the Panzer divisions.

"On the way we were stopped by a closed level crossing. Some refugees cheered me. One of them said to a gendarme: 'For once we can see a minister and wish him all the best; don't stop us.' A woman came up to me and said: 'I come from Paris. My husband's been called up. So what if Paris has been taken. Hang on! We're all with you.'

"I arrived at the Bordeaux prefecture at about 2000 hours. I walked across the courtyard, bareheaded. Many generals and politicians saluted me in silence.

"I was visited by de Gaulle who asked me where he would find me again and I replied, as he says in his memoirs, 'In Algiers'. He set off for London to organise the shipping for the retreat to North Africa."

On the 16th, there was a meeting of the Council of Ministers which began in the morning and finished only in the evening. Benoist-Méchin recalls:

"M. Reynaud began by reading out

President Roosevelt's reply to his appeal of June 14. M. Lebrun records that the words of the President's telegram had 'a profoundly depressing effect on the Council'.

"M. Chautemps then asked the Premier to inform his colleagues of the result of the representations that the previous night's meeting had instructed him to make to the British Government.

" 'Nothing is settled yet,' M. Reynaud answered defiantly. 'I am still waiting for Mr. Churchill's answer to the questions I put to him last evening through Sir Ronald Campbell. But what I *can* tell you is that the British Cabinet has never ratified its leader's conciliatory statements . . .'

"At this, Marshal Pétain rose to his feet.

" 'I can no longer remain in the government,' he said. 'Our armies are disintegrating more and more as time goes by. The inevitable solution has been put off all too long. I have no wish to be associated with this delay, for which the whole of France is paying.'

"These words brought utter dismay to the meeting. Everyone sensed that in these tragic hours the French were turning more and more to the Marshal. If he resigned, the Government would fall. As he made to leave the room President Lebrun burst out: 'Oh no! You are not going to do *that* to us now!'

The majority of the ministers present begged the Marshal to remain in office and continue to 'afford the government the benefit of his prestige'. The Marshal gave in but refused to sit down again."

At about 1400 hours on the 16th the British Ambassador, Sir Ronald Campbell, accompanied by General Spears, entered President Lebrun's office at Bordeaux.

From left to right: Churchill, Dill, Campbell, Attlee and Reynaud at one of the last meetings of May 1940.

They brought with them a telegram defining the conditions under which the British Government would consent to France entering into negotiations for an armistice with the common enemy:

"June 16, 1940, 12.35 pm.

Our agreement forbidding separate negotiations, whether for armistice or peace, was made with the French Republic, and not with any particular French Administration or statesman. It therefore involves the honour of France. Nevertheless, *provided, but only provided, that the French Fleet is sailed forthwith for British harbours pending negotiations*, His Majesty's Government give their full consent to an enquiry by the French Government to ascertain the terms of an armistice for France. His Majesty's Government, being resolved to continue the war, wholly exclude themselves from all part in the above-mentioned inquiry concerning an armistice."

Reynaud, according to Spears, burst out:

"What a very silly thing to do, to ask that the French Fleet should go to British harbours when it is in fact at this very moment protecting Algeria and the Western Mediterranean. And you ask us to do this at the very moment you are inviting us to go to North Africa: *non, vraiment, c'est trop bête!*"

Spears recalls that Reynaud continued: "This suggestion means offering all French North African harbours to the Italian Fleet as targets . . . It is really too silly. For one thing, the French Fleet is relieving the British in the Mediterranean. To send

ours away would place a fresh strain on yours."

At 1510 another message was sent out from London to be passed onto the French Government by Sir Ronald Campbell, redefining the above terms. The British Government – naturally enough – asked to be kept informed of the progress of negotiations if France should ask for an armistice. Equally naturally, the British asked for the evacuation of all Polish, Czech and Belgian troops fighting with the French Army. Campbell carried out his instructions, with the result that over 24,300 Poles and nearly 5,000 Czechs were embarked for England.

Spears was in the room when a telephone call came through for Reynaud. It was General de Gaulle in London, who proceeded to dictate, word by word, the text of a "Declaration of Franco-British Union". This document was the result of discussions between French Ambassador Corbin, Jean Monnet and René Pleven, members of the Economic Mission in London, and the British leaders. It read as follows:

"At this most fateful moment in the history of the modern world the Governments of the United Kingdom and the French Republic make this declaration of indissoluble union and unyielding resolution in their common defence of justice and freedom against subjugation to a system which reduces mankind to a life of robots and slaves.

"The two Governments declare that France and Great Britain shall no longer be two nations, but one Franco-British Union.

"The constitution of the Union will provide for joint organs of defence, foreign, financial, and economic policies.

"Every citizen of France will enjoy immediately citizenship of Great Britain; every British subject will become a citizen of France.

"Both countries will share responsibility for the repair of the devastation of war, wherever it occurs in their territories, and the resources of both shall be equally, and as one, applied to that purpose.

"During the war there shall be a single War Cabinet, and all the forces of Britain and France, whether on land, sea, or in the air, will be placed under its direction. It will govern from wherever best it can. The two Parliaments will be formally associated. The nations of the British Empire are already forming new armies. France will keep her available forces in the field, on the sea, and in the air. The Union appeals to the United States to fortify the economic resources of the Allies, and to bring her powerful material aid to the common cause.

"The Union will concentrate its whole energy against the power of the enemy, no matter where the battle may be.

"And so we shall conquer."

Reynaud heard of the proposed Union by telephone. Spears records that:

". . . the telephone rang. Reynaud took up the receiver. The next moment his eyebrows went up so far they became indistinguishable from his neatly brushed hair. 'One moment,' he said, 'I must take

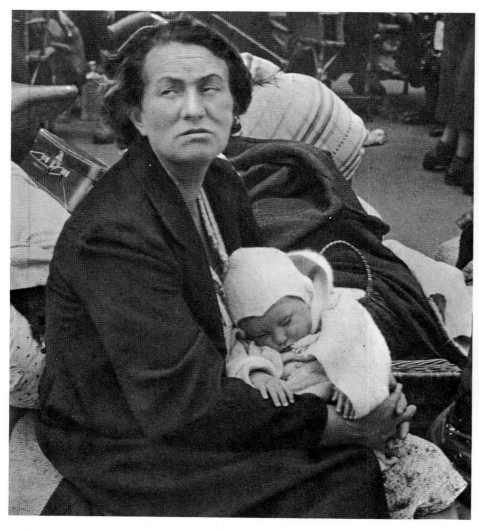

*A French mother clutches her child,
victim of the Blitzkrieg.*

it down,' and grasping a sheet of foolscap on the slippery table, he began to write, using a short gold pencil with an enormous lead. He repeated each word as he wrote it, and listening I became transfixed with amazement. Reynaud was taking down in French, from de Gaulle's dictation in London, the text of the Declaration of Union proposed by the British Government. On he wrote in a frightful scrawl, getting more excited as the message unfolded. The paper skidded on the smooth surface of the table. I held it. As each sheet was covered I handed him a fresh one. His pencil gave out; I handed him mine.

"Finally he stopped and said into the telephone: 'Does he agree to this? Did Churchill give you this personally?' There was a moment's pause and now he was speaking in English. It was evident that de Gaulle had handed the receiver to Churchill, who was assuring him that the document was a decision of the Cabinet. If there were alterations, they would be merely verbal.

"Reynaud put the receiver down. He was transfigured with joy, and my old friendship for him surged out in a wave of appreciation at his response, for he was happy with a great happiness in the belief that France would now remain in the war.

This was his thought as it was ours, and in those first moments this was all that mattered. The sense of the generosity of the offer was overwhelming, the sincerity of the gesture completely convincing."

In his memoirs, Churchill does not hide the fact that his first reaction to the draft of the Declaration of Union was unfavourable, but that he yielded to the wave of enthusiasm which swept the members of his War Cabinet. Nevertheless, this "immense design whose implications and consequences were not in any way thought out," would, he hoped, have the advantage "of giving M. Reynaud some new fact of a vivid and stimulating nature with which to carry a majority of his Cabinet into the move to Africa and the continuance of the war".

In this he was wrong. Reynaud, certainly, remained enthusiastic about the project which Churchill had recommended to him via de Gaulle, but he still had to convince his ministers. In the meantime the two statesmen agreed to meet at Concarneau on the following day. To the approval of General Spears, who had disapproved violently of the British concessions to the French point of view, Sir Ronald Campbell recovered the two telegrams which conflicted with the new instructions received from his Government.

The French Council of Ministers met

again at 1700 hours in the Prefecture of the Gironde. But despite two addresses from Reynaud, the projected Franco-British Union was greeted far more unfavourably than it had been by Churchill the day before.

The majority of the French ministers gave an icy reception to the new plan. Was Reynaud, under the excuse that they had been cancelled, deliberately avoiding mention of the import, and even the existence, of the two telegrams which the British Ambassador had recently brought to his knowledge? Most of the ministers regarded the plan, quite simply, as a will o' the wisp, but not all of them favoured the alternative solution of an armistice concluded in defiance of the British. In fact, the proposals from London could well have led to a French counter-proposal.

But it never came. When the session was suspended Reynaud handed his resignation to President Lebrun and named Pétain as his successor. Reynaud could still hear the old Marshal declaring to the Council on June 13 that if the Government left France, he would consider it desertion, and that he himself would refuse to leave metropolitan France. He would stay with the French people to share in their miseries. "The armistice," he had concluded, "is, as I see it, the only guarantee of the survival of eternal France."

Whether or not Pétain was right, it is quite clear that Reynaud was well aware in advance of the programme which would be adopted by his successor, and that despite his own convictions he did not hesitate to step down in Pétain's favour.

The news of Reynaud's resignation reached Churchill as he was embarking on a special train for Southampton, where a destroyer was waiting to take him to Concarneau. De Gaulle heard of Reynaud's resignation in favour of Pétain as he landed at Bordeaux airport. He did not hesitate a moment about what he must do.

On the night that Reynaud's Government fell, June 16–17, the British merchantman *Broompark* sailed from the small port of Bassens (Gironde). She had just embarked 26 containers containing the 410 pounds of "heavy water" which Frederic Joliot-Curie had earlier removed from Norway with the help of Jacques Allier of French Military Intelligence. The physicists Hans-Heinrich Halban and Lew Kowarski accompanied this precious cargo. They were under orders signed by Bichelonne, principal secretary to Armaments Minister Raoul Dautry, to write a report of the research carried out by the Collège de France, but to keep it absolutely secret. With them sailed Lord Suffolk and Berkshire, scientific liaison officer to the French Government. The groundwork and experiments carried out by Joliot-Curie (with the aim of producing an explosion as a result of atomic fission) were to be a vital link in the chain of events which led to Hiroshima.

While Pétain was waiting for his call to supreme office, he had the time to compile

*French refugees. Some 15 per
cent of the population was to
suffer this plight.*

a list of the men from whom he would form
his Government. Paul Baudouin was
named as Foreign Minister, Yves Bouthillier as Finance Minister, and Camille
Chautemps as Vice-President. Weygand
was named as Chief of National Defence;
General Colson as C.-in-C. Army, General
Pujo as C.-in-C. Air Force, while Darlan
retained the supreme command of the
Navy. Pierre Laval was offered the post of
Minister of Justice, but he turned this
down: he wished to be Foreign Minister.
Pétain, however, was unwilling to give
Laval this post as he wanted to avoid any
move which might be thought provocative
by the British who distrusted Laval.

Pétain's Government was formed at
2330 hours on June 16. It included a Marshal of France, three generals, an admiral,
seven deputies, one senator, and five high-
ranking civil servants, and wasted no
time in carrying out its immediate programme, the conclusion of an armistice.
At 0100 hours on the 17th, Baudouin asked
the Spanish Ambassador to send, via
Madrid, a request to the German Government for negotiations. As morning came
it was realised that a similar approach
must be made to Italy, and the Papal
Nuncio was contacted for this task.

Some hours later the French radio was
broadcasting to every home the poignant
message of Marshal Pétain, announcing
that the enemy had been asked to enter
into discussions on how hostilities might
be ended. It was a noble and dignified
address, but its effect upon the fighting
troops was as unfortunate as on the civilian
population and the local authorities.

A few days before, Chautemps had suggested that the enemy should be sounded
out by undercover means. It was a naïve
idea; the German propagandists would
only have trumpeted the news to the
world. Still more, they would have used
every method at their disposal, especially
pamphlets, to incite the French to stop
fighting there and then.

Until the conditions of an armistice
could be agreed between the French, the
Germans, and the Italians, the fighting
went on – along the Alps, in the Vosges, in
the Maginot Line, on the Loire and in
western France, bringing in more trophies
for Hitler and more setbacks for Mussolini.
For the sake of clarity we will follow the
surrender talks at Rethondes and the
Villa Incisa, and only then attempt to
unravel the operations of this sixth and
final week of the Battle of France.

Meanwhile, however, there occurred an
event which was to prove just as important
as the policy of Marshal Pétain. From the
aerodrome at Bordeaux-Mérignac an aircraft took off for England, carrying
General de Gaulle, Reynaud's former
Under-Secretary of State for War. There
are several descriptions of the event, all

romanticised to some extent; but this is
de Gaulle's own version:

"Late in the evening I went to the hotel
where Sir Ronald Campbell, the British
Ambassador, was residing, and informed
him of my intention to leave for London.
General Spears, who came and joined in
the conversation, declared that he would
accompany me. I sent word to Reynaud. He
made over to me 100,000 francs, on the
secret funds. I begged M. de Margerie to
send at once to my wife and children, who
were at Carentec, the necessary passports
for reaching England, which they could
do by the last boat to leave Brest. On June
17th, at nine in the morning, I flew off
with General Spears and Lieutenant de
Courcel, in the British aeroplane which
had brought me the evening before. There
was nothing romantic or difficult about
the departure."

Passed on without delay by Madrid, the
French Government's request for armis-
tice discussions soon reached the Germans.
Hitler hastened to meet his Italian ally at
Munich: the Axis leaders would have to
be in full agreement between themselves

A few of the many French prisoners.

A German 10.5-cm gun during street fighting in May 1940.

if they were to prevent the defeated French from playing off one against the other.

The Italo-German conference in Munich began at the *Führerbau* in the afternoon of June 18. On the German side were Hitler, Ribbentrop, and Keitel; Mussolini brought with him Ciano and General Roatta, Deputy Chief of the Italian General Staff. Paul Schmidt, Hitler's interpreter, was present, but his memoirs include only a few lines about these discussions. However, the transcript taken by General Roatta has survived. Two years later Ciano gave it to General Carboni, then commanding the "Friuli" Division at Livorno, saying: "Look, this is the bill of sale for the bear's skin. You can use it one day when writing the history of the war."

As the armistice conditions laid down by Hitler on June 18 were on the whole identical to those signed by the French delegation on the 22nd, they can be examined in due course. But the programme drawn up by the Italians during their journey can, according to Carboni's version, be summarised in eight extremely ambitious sections:

1. Immediate demobilisation of the French Army;
2. Immediate surrender of all the Army's weapons, of all warships, and of all aircraft;
3. Occupation of all French territory between the Alps and the Rhône, with bridgeheads on the right bank of the Rhône at Lyons, Valence, and Avignon, and the occupation of Corsica;
4. Occupation of Tunisia and of French Somaliland. Occupation of the naval bases of Algiers, Mers el Kébir and Casablanca. Beirut to become a neutral port, and Italy to have the right to occupy it;
5. Italy to have the right to occupy any part of metropolitan France or her Empire considered necessary for the conduct of operations, the maintenance of peace, or the establishment of order;
6. France to be forbidden to make any demolitions or to evacuate any railway material from the zone marked down for Italian occupation;
7. Denunciation of the Franco-British alliance. Removal of all British forces in metropolitan France and the Empire;
8. Disarmament and disbandment of all Polish, Belgian, and other foreign forces in France.

When Hitler first heard this programme, he approved of the Italian claims to occupy French territory. Joining hands in the region of Geneva, the Axis partners would hold the railway axis of Dijon-Modane, through Ambérieu and Culoz, and would completely encircle Switzerland. However, the immediate handing-over of the French fleet to the Italians seemed, to Hitler, to raise certain problems.

As he saw it, all the evidence suggested that the French would refuse to surrender their fleet. If this were demanded of them, rather than scuttle the fleet they might well prefer to see it pass into British hands, which would be a disaster for the Axis. It would be better to demand a controlled neutralisation of the French fleet, either in French or neutral ports (Spanish for preference), leaving the French with the hope that they might recover it once peace was signed. Mussolini agreed to this.

As to the rest, Mussolini believed that Hitler wanted to spare the German people from another winter of war, and was anxious not to provoke American intervention. On a question put by Ciano to Ribbentrop Hitler had commented: "You must not aim so high; you must be moderate. I hope you have no designs on Croatia and other items of the sort."

Singular moderation, one might think – but it would not prevent Hitler from demanding the annexation of Alsace, Lorraine, and the Briey basin. Moreover, Belgium would have to make several frontier rectifications in favour of the Reich, and Norway would have to submit to the permanent occupation of her main ports, as part of Germany's consolidation of her war gains so far. In Africa, the annexation of the Congo would link together all the former German colonies whose return Hitler would demand. Finally, Spain would receive a protectorate over Morocco with the exception of the ports on the Atlantic, which would go to Germany.

Mussolini had no objections to make to this programme. His own claims comprised the Department of the Maritime Alps, Corsica, Algeria, Tunisia, and French Somaliland. Once Britain had been beaten, British-occupied Egypt plus the Anglo-Egyptian Sudan, and British Somaliland would fall to Italy. Gibraltar would be returned to Spain, but both sides of the Strait of Gibraltar would be declared neutral territory.

But would Britain be beaten? Hitler, as Mussolini noted, had only hinted at a direct cross-Channel attack, and even this hint was extremely vague and totally hypothetical. Was Hitler thinking of playing Charlemagne without giving any more thought to Italy's interests? Ciano

Hitler greets Rudolf Hess at the Armistice ceremony on June 22, 1940.

noted, with a certain amount of uneasiness, the considerate feelings which the majestic edifice of the British Empire inspired in Hitler.

As far as plans for the immediate future were concerned, Keitel assured Roatta, the German Army would not slow down its pursuit; it would strike with its armoured columns at the rear of the French forces defending the Alps at the moment when they were under attack from in front by the Italian thrusts across the Little St. Bernard, the Col de la Madeleine, and along the coast. It was also agreed that the final Franco-German armistice would not come into force until the *Comando Supremo* declared that its requirements had been met. But the two negotiations would remain separate – a fact which was unlikely to be of much advantage to the Italians.

At 1430 hours on June 20 the French deputation left Bordeaux. General Huntziger presided; the former Ambassador to Poland, Léon Noël, was attached as political adviser; Vice-Admiral Le Luc and General Bergeret represented the Navy and the Air Force respectively. The deputation was basically an exploratory one; it was to find out what the German terms were and try to improve on them, but to sign nothing without an express order from the French Government. To the question of what should be done if the Germans made the surrender of the French fleet a *sine qua non* for the granting of an armistice, Admiral Darlan, Noël states, "replied categorically that orders had been given that if this demand were made, whatever the Government's decision, our warships would not fall into the hands of the Germans".

At 1530 hours on the following day General von Tippelskirch, head of the Führer's G.H.Q. staff, led the French delegates into Marshal Foch's railway carriage, which the Germans had moved to the clearing at Rethondes. There they found, standing at the Nazi salute, Hitler, Ribbentrop, Hess, Göring, Keitel, and Raeder. When everyone had taken his place, Hitler gestured to Keitel to proceed. In a thundering voice, Keitel read out a preamble in which lies were masked by a few chivalrous phrases; then, "with a brusque gesture, Hitler handed each of the French delegates a copy of the armistice terms and left the carriage without having said a word. "There was nothing imposing," recalled Noël, "in either his attitude or his gesture: huddled, tired-looking, sullen, wearing a cap too big for him surrounded by a maroon velvet band; his traits, his hands, were vulgar and expressionless."

No discussion worthy of the name followed Hitler's exit, for at the first attempt at modification made by Huntziger, Keitel exclaimed that his task was to comment on the articles of the convention prepared by the Führer, not to discuss them. But on Noël's calm insistence Keitel agreed to put the French deputation in telephone communication with the Government at Bordeaux.

The French and German delegates met twice. With only a few exceptions, the Germans refused to consider any modification to the text of the 24 articles, which were to be accepted as they stood. After a vehement protest by General Bergeret, Keitel, after obtaining Göring's approval, agreed to spare the French from having to hand over their military aircraft as laid down in Article 6. The aircraft would merely be disarmed and put in safe-keeping under German control.

But Article 8 was crucial. It dealt with the French fleet, and its terms are worth quoting in full:

"Article 8. The French battle fleet – apart from the portion which is to be left at the disposition of the French Government for safeguarding France's interests in her colonial Empire – will be collected in ports which have still to be determined, to be decommissioned and disarmed under the control of Germany or Italy respectively.

"The designation of these ports will be made according to the peacetime home ports of the ships. The German Government solemnly declares to the French Government that it has no intention during the war of making effective use of the French warships stationed in ports under German control, with the exception of ships needed for coastal patrolling and minesweeping.

"Moreover, the German Government declares, solemnly and formally, that it has no intention of making further claims on the French battle fleet after the conclusion of peace. With the exception of that part of the French fleet still to be

The Armistice is signed in Foch's railway coach at Rethondes.

determined which will be entrusted with the security of France's interests in her colonial Empire, all warships outside French territorial waters are to be recalled to France."

In the face of these requirements Huntziger countered by pointing out the risk that the French warships forced to return to the German-occupied ports of Cherbourg, Brest, and Lorient could well be bombed and destroyed by the R.A.F. He proposed instead that their decommissioning and disarmament should be carried out in North African naval bases. In fact, Huntziger was trying to prevent the most powerful units in the French battle fleet – *Dunkerque* and *Strasbourg* at Mers el Kébir, *Jean Bart* at Casablanca, and *Richelieu* at Dakar – from being put at the mercy of the Germans.

Obviously, Keitel was not taken in by this. But although he refused emphatically to make the least modification to the basic provisions of Article 8, he nevertheless pointed out to Huntziger that the German text – which would be definitive – did not use the word *müssen* ("must"), which implied a binding imperative, but *sollen* ("should"), a more vague expression of an obligation in principle. This would make possible a solution nearer to the wishes of the Bordeaux Government.

But at 1834 hours on June 22 (German time) the French deputation was given a brutal ultimatum. If Huntziger did not sign the document in front of him within one hour, the order would be given for him to be sent back behind the firing-line and the war would continue. With the dagger at his throat, Huntziger signed.

Next morning the French delegates left Paris for Rome, aboard three aircraft put at their disposal by the Luftwaffe.

At Bordeaux, naturally, the Government still had no way of knowing that Mussolini had finally been converted to Hitler's point of view concerning the neutralisation of the French fleet. Because of this, Darlan, with Pétain's approval, sent the following telegram to Admirals Esteval, Duplat, and Gensoul at 1810 of June 22:

"Should a Franco-German armistice be concluded it cannot be put into force until a Franco-Italian armistice has been signed, giving us the chance of exerting pressure.

"In the event of the Italian terms proving unacceptable, I propose to commit the fleet to a short-range action against military targets and weak sectors along the Italian coastline: 3rd Squadron [Duplat, at Toulon] – the Gulf of Genoa as far as Livorno and Elba; Striking Force [Gensoul, at Oran and Algiers] – Naples, Gaeta; and Sicily and Sardinia . . . for all available vessels under the orders of the Admiral, South [Esteva, commanding the navy in the western Mediterranean]."

If this course of action proved necessary, Darlan proposed to assume the personal sea-going command of the forces engaged in this extremely hazardous operation.

But Darlan's fears as to the attitude of the Italians were proved groundless as soon as the two sides met. Mussolini was not present, and Ciano, Marshal Badoglio, General Roatta, and Admiral Cavagnari took a conciliatory line.

The Duce, probably because of Hitler's intervention, was now making very different claims to those which he had put forward at Munich. He was now limiting his extent of occupation of French territory to the zone which his armies would have conquered in all theatres of operations by the time of the cease-fire. France would be required to demilitarise a further 30-mile zone beyond this limit for the duration of the armistice. Varying levels of demilitarisation would be imposed along the Tunisian and Algerian frontiers with Libya, as well as in Somaliland.

The naval bases at Toulon, Ajaccio, Bizerta, and Mers el Kébir were also to be demilitarised. As far as the French fleet was concerned, Article 12 of the Italian list of terms echoed the requirements made by the Germans at Rethondes; but Marshal Badoglio showed himself to be much more conciliatory than his German colleague about the question of the home ports of the fleet. Moreover, he refrained from making any claims at all on French aircraft. He even so far as to suppress the article which would have required the French Government to hand over all Italian political exiles to the Fascist authorities. On this point, therefore, Huntziger was more satisfied with the discussions at the Villa Incisa than he had been at Rethondes, faced with the brutal intransigence of Keitel.

By the late afternoon of June 24 agreement had, in principle, been reached by the two sides. But then Mussolini called Badoglio by telephone, and what he had to say should have returned the discussion to its starting-point: Mussolini wished

the French to be required to give up to the Italian Army a zone of occupation which would link them up with the Germans at Bellegarde on the Rhône. In so doing, Mussolini was deferring to a suggestion by Hitler, who, forgetting his advice for moderation, had returned to the idea of establishing an Axis barrier between Switzerland and unoccupied France.

Badoglio, however, replied that it was too late and that the discussions were over; and with yet another typical piece of vacillation Mussolini yielded to his subordinate with no further argument. At 1935 hours the Franco-Italian armistice was signed, with the suspension of hostilities between France, Italy, and Germany set for 0035 hours on Tuesday, June 25.

We left the French 2nd Army Group cut off from its commander, General Prételat, and in great danger of being surrounded while carrying out the retreat which Prételat had ordered on June 14. On the 19th this finally happened. The 1st Panzer Division, advancing from Belfort, met the advance-guards of the German 7th Army, rushed from Mulhouse by forced marches, at Montreux-le-Vieux. Trapped in the Vosges by this link-up were some 400,000 French troops of 8th, 5th, 3rd, and 2nd Armies.

During their meeting at Munich, Hitler told Mussolini that this last phase of the campaign would see some bloody fighting; but French ammunition stocks were dwindling rapidly and General Condé, who had taken command in the pocket, was forced to surrender on the evening of June 22.

When he heard of this decision, General Duch, commanding the Polish 1st Division, ordered his men to disperse and make for Britain, individually or in small groups. Many got through, while others went underground and formed useful Intelligence centres behind the German lines.

During its drive on Montbéliard and Belfort, XXXIX Panzer Corps made an improvised attack on the French XLV Corps, which had been ordered to clear a passage through to Besançon. On the 17th, the 67th Division of XLV Corps – a Category "B" reserve division – had been scattered near Baumes-les-Dames. This left the Polish 2nd Division (General Prugar-Kettling) and the 2nd Brigade of Spahis (Colonel de Torcy) cut off in the bend of the Doubs river. After a fierce and gallant stand on the Plateau de Maîche, these troops were forced to cross the frontier and seek internment in Switzerland. General Daille, commanding the corps, was among the last to leave the soil of France.

The XVI Panzer Corps did not halt at Dijon, but drove onwards down the Saône valley. This threatened the rear of the French Army of the Alps, which was preparing to meet an Italian attack in greatly superior numbers between Menton and Mont Blanc. The French commander, General Olry, ordered the bridges at Lyons to be destroyed – but he was reckoning without Edouard Herriot. On June 16, in his capacity as President of the Chamber, Herriot had told Pétain that France would

be disgraced by a separate peace; a few hours later, in his other capacity as Mayor of Lyons, he was ordering the removal of the demolition-charges which the French sappers had prepared at Lyons.

"Gruppe List", which had recently been formed by O.K.H. to reinforce XVI Panzer Corps, had taken Chambéry and Grenoble and crossed the Saône and Rhône bridges without difficulty. The French Army of the Alps would have been stabbed in the back but for the coolness and skill of General Olry. He swiftly improvised the "Cartier Detachment": 13 battalions, with 20 47-mm and 65-mm guns brought from the Toulon arsenal and which were found extremely useful in the anti-tank rôle. Olry emptied the supply dumps in the Arc, Isère, and Romanche valleys, while Cartier tackled the Germans with all the efficiency of a skilled tactician and a resolute commander. By dawn on the 25th Hoeppner's Panzers had been held on the Aix-les-Bains–Voiron–Romans line; on the right bank of the Rhône, they had taken Annonay and had reached St. Etienne.

In the centre of the German front, the 2nd Army had crossed the Loire at Nevers and la Charité; In the latter town a patrol from 9th Panzer Division discovered the entire archives of the French High Command on a train abandoned in the station. This gave Hitler information about the military discussions with Turkey, Greece, and Yugoslavia held by Weygand when he was commanding in the Middle East. According to General Liss, head of "Section West" of the Abwehr, these archives also revealed "an interesting military convention with a neutral Power", which can be identified as Switzerland from a note in Halder's diary dated July 21.

Between Gien and Saumur the wreckage of the French 3rd Army Group tried desperately to hold the Germans along the Loire, in the face of heavy tactical bombing attacks. At Saumur, 2,300 cadets of the Cavalry School under Colonel Michon held off the German 1st Cavalry Division for 48 hours. But on the 19th the Germans crossed the river and by the 23rd General Besson's three armies had been reduced to a strength of no more than 65,000 men still under arms.

In the west the Panzer onrush was so swift that the hope of organising a "Breton Redoubt" for French troops saved at Dunkirk and a new B.E.F. under General Brooke was soon dispelled. From his first contact with French Supreme Headquarters, Brooke had been convinced that if Britain persisted she would lose three divisions with absolutely no benefit to anyone. On June 13–14, this led to acrimonious telephone conversations with General Sir John Dill, Chief of the Imperial General Staff (C.I.G.S.), and with Churchill, both of whom wanted to keep British troops in action on the continent because of the alliance with France.

But Brooke's persistence in withdrawing the British forces won the day, even before Pétain had announced his determination to stop the fighting. Between June 15 and June 20 nearly 145,000 British troops succeeded in embarking; the first of them left from Cherbourg (52nd Division), the 1st Canadian Division from Brest, and the last forces from Bayonne and St. Jean-de-Luz.

It was not before time. On June 18 Rommel's 7th Panzer Division took Cherbourg; the following day 5th Panzer Division occupied Brest, and the 11th Motorised Brigade took Nantes and St. Nazaire. In the latter port, the energy and brilliant seamanship of Captain Ronarch snatched the battleship *Jean Bart* from under the Germans' nose at the last minute, although she was still uncompleted and extremely hard to manoeuvre, with only a few inches of water beneath her keel.

During the evacuation of the French Channel and Atlantic naval bases, all warships and supply ships incapable of putting to sea were ruthlessly scuttled. This was the fate of the destroyer *Cyclone*, five submarines and two tankers, to name only the larger craft. Two battleships (*Courbet* and *Paris*), four destroyers, six torpedo-boats, seven submarines, and 13 gunboats took refuge in British ports. The order which set this evacuation in motion was cancelled after the request for an armistice was made, but the warships leaving other ports also threatened by the Germans were ordered to make for Africa: *Richelieu* anchored at Dakar and *Jean Bart* at Casablanca. It is therefore hard to understand why Churchill wrote in *The Second World War:* "No more French warships moved beyond the reach of the swiftly approaching German power." This remark was made with regard to June 18, the day that *Jean Bart* left St. Nazaire under the bombs of the Stukas. No more French warships followed because there were no more left to do so.

From June 18 onwards the German advance in the west and south-west was a runaway victory. As had been done in the case of Lyons, the Bordeaux Government declared every town with over 20,000 inhabitants an "open town". But many smaller places, crammed with refugees, claimed similar status and hoisted the white flag behind the backs of troops who were still trying to slow the German advance. By the time of the cease-fire, XV Panzer Corps, spearhead of the 18th Army, had pushed south as far as the Marennes – Saintes – Cognac – Angoulême line.

In the north-east of France, the retreat ordered by General Prételat had left the defence of the Maginot Line to the fortress troops. Although completely surrounded and attacked from all sides, these forces continued to fight back. Around the Saar valley a small number of emplacements surrendered after their cupolas had been knocked out by direct hits from 3.7-cm anti-tank and 8.8-cm A.A. guns. But the big forts on the Lauter and between Longuyon and Faulquemont, with their guns mounted in armoured turrets, repulsed every assault despite the fire of 28-cm railway guns and 1,100-lb bombs dropped by Stukas. The deep emplacements were proof against the most severe bombardment, but not against outflanking by tanks and infantry.

On June 25, the Germans and the 220,000 Frenchmen holding the Maginot Line ceased fire; but the French garrisons did not march out until written orders reached them from Weygand. In exchange for their surrender and captivity the Germans withdrew to the demarcation-line agreed at Rethondes. So it was that St. Etienne, Clermont Ferrand, and Lyons were left free for another two years and four months.

In the midst of this disaster, without precedent in the history of France, there was a gleam of honourable success: General Olry's brilliant defence of the Alpine front.

On June 17 Mussolini, completely forgetting the "strict defensive" which he had prescribed for the Prince of Piedmont's army group, suddenly ordered the Prince to take the offensive without delay between Mont Blanc and the Mediterranean. In vain Badoglio argued that this ill-advised reversal of strategy was not only dishonourable but would need 25 days of preparation. He was severely rebuked by the Duce.

The Prince's forces consisted of two armies:

1. Mont Blanc–Monte Viso: 4th Army (General Alfredo Guzzoni) would attack with the *Alpini* Corps and the I and IV Corps, comprising three *Alpini* detachments and nine infantry divisions; and

2. Monte Viso–Ventimiglia: 1st Army (General Pietro Pintor) would attack with the II, III, and XV Corps, comprising 13 infantry divisions.

Behind these front-line forces of 188 infantry battalions and 2,949 guns were the eight mobile divisions of General Mario Vercellino's "Po" Army. The task of these motorised units was to exploit the breaches made by the infantry. The five divisions of the Duke of Bergamo's 7th Army would serve as a general reserve.

Moutiers-en-Tarentaise was named as the first objective for 4th Army; Nice, and finally Marseilles, for 1st Army.

Across the Alps, General Olry found his forces reduced to the bare minimum with which to meet the Italian attack.

On the French left flank was General Beynet's XIV Corps, facing the Italian 4th Army with its 66th and 64th Divisions, (Generals Boucher and St. Vincent), and the fortified sectors in Savoy and Dauphiné (Colonel de la Baume and General Cyvoct).

On the right flank was General Montagne's XV Corps, consisting of General de St. Julien's 65th Division and General Magnien's troops in the fortified sector of the Maritime Alps.

This added up to a total of 185,000 French troops to meet the attack of 450,000 Italians. On the northern sector, between Mont Blanc and the Col de Larche, the terrain favoured the defenders. Further to the south the Franco-Italian frontier

The battle of France, May–June 1940.

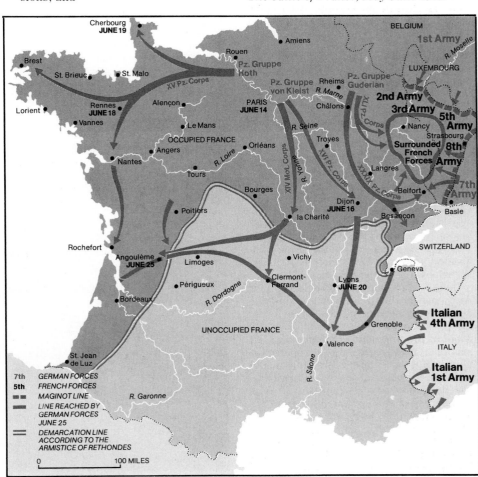

veered away from the mountain peaks in favour of the Italians, but the French had countered this disadvantage by building powerful fortifications. On the night of June 10-11 General Olry had made play with his demolitions network, and had acquired another advantage for his defending troops.

The Prince of Piedmont opened his offensive in bad weather, in the Maritime Alps sector, on June 20; it was to be extended to the whole front on the following day. By the time of the armistice on the 25th the Italians had managed to advance as far as the French defences in a few places; but despite Mussolini's lying and bombastic claims, Italian troops had managed to break through none of them.

At the Little St. Bernard, the *Alpini* Corps pushed down the first few bends in the road leading to Bourg-St. Maurice, but could not take the ruined redoubt which formed part of the French advanced position. In the Maurienne valley the Italian I Corps, scaling the lower passes with a splendid, sporting bravado, did manage to get a few battalions into the Arc valley and to occupy the villages of Lanslebourg and Termignon. But the two French 75-mm guns in the Turra emplacement prevented the Italians from using the road from the Mont Cenis Pass; and Ciano noted in his diary that the Italians' position would have become impossible if the armistice had not intervened and allowed them to be supplied.

On the Col de Mont Genèvre, the Italian IV Corps had no better luck. After three days of effort its "Assietta" Division had taken the old Chenaillet redoubt – defended by 19 men with two machine guns. Mussolini, in a communiqué, described the place as one of the key positions in "the Maginot system of the Alps". But to reach Briançon, the fort at Janus would have to be neutralised – and the most that the artillery of the Duce could do was to plough off a few slivers of steel from the fort's cupolas. Meanwhile the French artillery scored a magnificent success: 101 shells fired by four 280-mm mortars kept ready for the task smashed six of the eight 149-mm gun turrets of the Italian fort at Chaberton, commanding the precipitous approaches to Briançon. Even so, high praise is due to the Italian gunners; knowing the weakness of their protecting armour, they stayed at their posts amid the explosions of the French shells.

In the Maritime Alps the Italian 1st Army had pushed a mile or two into the advanced positions of the French XV Corps and had overrun two-thirds of Menton, flinging whole companies against sections, and regiments against companies. But as General Montagne loyally wrote in his book on the defence of Nice, the defenders met the superior Italian numbers with well-prepared fire from 472 guns, of which half were 155-mm or heavier.

Under this tremendous deluge of fire, the "Cosseria", "Modena", and "Livorno" Divisions of XV Corps, ordered by Musso-lini to "press home the attack regardless of losses", were brought to a halt by the French defence. The Italian armour never saw action. From their small defence post at Pont-St. Louis, 2nd Lieutenant Gros and his nine men kept the Corniche road blocked until the moment of the cease-fire, when a French order came through to reopen the road.

By holding off the two Italian armies and Hoeppner's XVI Panzer Corps, the French Army of the Alps fulfilled its mission brilliantly. Amid all the misery of the fall of France, Olry's army showed that its morale was unaffected. It kept south-eastern France safe from Axis occupation – and better still, it did so at an extremely low cost: 37 killed, 42 wounded, and 150 missing. According to the figures published by the historical branch of the Italian Army in 1949, the Prince of Piedmont's armies suffered considerably more: 631 killed, 2,631 wounded, and 616 missing. Most of the latter were among the dead, for when the armistice came into force all Italian prisoners were released. These totalled 3,878 officers, N.C.O.s, and other ranks. In addition there were 2,151 severe frost-bite cases.

But above all Mussolini's attack on south-eastern France threw a blinding spotlight on the weaknesses of Italy's land forces in 1940. This was not due so much to lack of courage among the troops, but to the failures of the Fascist régime which had proved itself unable to organise, equip, and lead its men properly.

All this led to considerable friction between the Italian Army and the Fascist Party.

The Battle of France was over. On the French side, the spirit of duty and sacrifice shown by some was not enough to compensate for the weaknesses of others. The French had lost 92,000 killed, about 250,000 wounded, and not less than 1,450,000 prisoners. The latter fell into two categories: those who were sent to the rear without escort after being overrun by the Panzers' lightning advances, and those who were captured because of their obedience to orders which forced them to hold their position until their means of defence were exhausted.

France suffered far more heavily than her allies in this battle. The Dutch lost 2,890 killed and 6,889 wounded; the Belgians lost 7,500 killed and 15,850 wounded; and the British lost 3,457 killed and 15,850 wounded, the latter being evacuated to England.

What were the German losses? On June 25, 1940, after the armistice, O.K.W. reckoned on a total of 27,074 killed, 111,034 wounded, and 18,384 missing – most of the "missing" being killed, as their armistices had obliged the Dutch, the Belgians, and the French to release the prisoners they had taken.

There is, however, another slant to these figures. Between May 10 and June 3, the German Army's casualty list amounted to 61,200 officers, N.C.O.s and other ranks – 2,448 men per day. With another total of some 95,300 killed, wounded, and missing between June 4 and June 25, this daily loss went up to 4,332. Effectively, it was more than doubled, since after June 18 (except in eastern France) there was no more organised resistance. If these figures are divided by the number of Allied divisions which fought in May-June 1940 we get the following result: for the first phase of the campaign – May 10 to June 3 – each of the 135 Allied divisions accounted for 450 Germans killed or wounded; in the second phase, after Weygand had taken over, 67 French and four Allied divisions caused three times these casualties: 1,343.

Naturally, only limited deductions can be made from statistics. But in the light of these particular figures there are certainly grounds for asking this question: what would have happened if the methods of command and battle tactics instituted by Weygand had been in force when the campaign began?

A French Alpine soldier on watch on the Franco-Italian border.

CHAPTER 13
The Battle of Britain

The defeat of France, sealed by the signing of the armistices at Rethondes and the Villa Incisa, made no difference to the determination of the British nation and its Coalition Government to pursue the war to its end. Few in Britain–with the exception of men such as the veteran statesman David Lloyd George–had thought of anything but continued resistance and final victory: they saw no reason to doubt that Nazi Germany and Fascist Italy could eventually be crushed. And the discreet attempts made by the Swedish Government to negotiate a solution to the European conflict were suppressed at birth in London.

This fierce spirit of resistance, of fighting back, and of final victory was incarnated on May 10, 1940 by the genial, picturesque, and indomitable person of Winston Churchill. But was the Prime Minister, who was also the Minister of Defence, the universal man of war which he believed himself to be?

Churchill was indeed a man of war, if the main quality of such a man is his capacity to withstand hard blows without allowing himself to be diverted from his objective. If the second necessary quality is that of concentrating his will on a principal aim and of allocating his resources in the correct proportions, doubts must be raised in Churchill's case. On the other hand, the remarkable adaptability displayed by this writer-historian to all the problems of military technology must be stressed. Churchill gave his full support, among other things, to radar development and to the perfection of asdic submarine detection. Many other inventions benefited from his far-sighted imagination, despite others' bureaucratic scepticism.

Added to these talents was Churchill's remarkable skill at swaying men's opinions, which enabled him to win the hearts of the B.B.C. listening public and Members of Parliament alike. His abounding energy gave him to wide-ranging (if sometimes blundering) activity, and he possessed that hint of eccentricity which tends to appeal to the Anglo-Saxon mind. Embracing the whole were deep-rooted moral and religious convictions, extending to an unshakable belief in the providential superiority of the British nation. For the security of the latter, Churchill considered all means not only justified, but also morally desirable. Kipling summed it up: "My country, right or wrong".

To help fill out the portrait, let us look to a typical passage in the Brooke diaries, describing a conference on May 27, 1941, when Brooke was C.-in-C., Home Forces:

"P.M. in great form and on the whole a very successful meeting. It is surprising how he maintains a light-hearted exterior in spite of the vast burden he is bearing. He is quite the most wonderful man I have ever met, and is a source of never-ending interest, studying him and getting to realise that occasionally such human beings make their appearance on this earth–human beings who stand out head and shoulders above all others."

And again, on August 6, 1942, when Brooke refused to exchange his post as Chief of the Imperial General Staff for that of C.-in-C., Middle East, which Churchill was offering him:

"I could not put the real reasons to Winston . . . Whether I exercised any control or not, I knew by now the dangers to guard against. I had discovered the perils of his impetuous nature. I was now familiar with his method of suddenly arriving at some decision as it were by intuition without any kind of logical examination of the problem. I had, after many failures, discovered the best methods of approaching him. I knew that it would take at least six months for any successor, taking over from me, to become as familiar with him and his ways. During these six months anything might happen."

But on June 31, 1940, the future Field-Marshal Lord Alanbrooke was only a corps commander in the British Home Forces. And already the brain tumour which was to kill Admiral of the Fleet Sir Dudley Pound, the First Sea Lord, was beginning to make its presence felt. The result was that Churchill's impetuosity was allowed to prevail, hurling the Royal Navy not against the Germans but against Britain's recent ally.

Hitler and Mussolini had made solemn guarantees as to the future status of the French fleet, but Churchill had every reason to believe that these guarantees were not worth the paper on which they were written. However, unless the warships were ordered to return to France, any attempt by the Germans or Italians to seize them by force seemed bound to fail–as long as they remained at their anchorages of June 25. Obviously, everything would change if the French Atlantic Squadron–composed of modern capital ships–were to return to Brest in compliance with Article 8 of the Franco-German armistice terms.

Darlan's orders concerning the action to be taken by the French warships outside occupied France were issued on June 20, 22, and 24. They were completely unequivocal; they all told the same story; and the order of June 24 is typical:

"I refer to the clauses of the armistice which have been telegraphed *en clair*. I am taking advantage of the last coded messages which I can send to make my thoughts on the subject quite clear:

1. Demobilised warships must remain French, under the French flag, with French crews, and in French ports, either at home or in the colonies;

2. Secret sabotage precautions must be taken so that if the enemy or any other power seizes a warship by force, it will be unable to use it;

3. If the armistice commission charged with interpreting the terms comes to any decision other than that expressed in (1.), the warships, without further orders, will be withdrawn from the enemy's reach–either sailed to the United States or scuttled if there is no alternative. In no case are they to be left intact for the enemy; and

4. Any warships which take refuge with foreign powers must not be used in operations against Germany or Italy without the order of the commander-in-chief."

President Roosevelt had charged Anthony Biddle, his Ambassador in Bordeaux, with taking a very firm line (not to say a threatening one) with the new French Government. The American diplomat carried out his orders on June 18 and duly reported to the White House: "[Baudouin] took pains to assure me in the name of the Government and in the most solemn manner, that the French fleet would never be handed over to the enemy . . . 'There is no question of this.' . . . Baudouin added, however, that he could not guarantee that the French fleet would join the British fleet; it could be sent to other waters, or it could be sunk."

As it is hardly likely that Roosevelt would not have passed the substance of this message to Churchill as soon as he could, the only conclusion is that the British war leaders could have been in no possible doubt that the French Government was prepared to scuttle the fleet rather than put it at the disposal of the enemies of Britain.

But the road to hell is paved with good intentions, and the British were wise to ask themselves what would happen if *Dunkerque*, *Strasbourg*, *Richelieu*, and *Jean Bart* returned to their bases in France. As we have seen, both Keitel and Badoglio showed themselves prepared to forego a literal interpretation of the armistice text: in Turin, on June 29, the Italians agreed without demur that the French fleet should be decommissioned in Toulon and in North Africa; at Wiesbaden on the following day, the Germans, though superficially more unyielding, again showed themselves to be more accommodating, for they merely forbade Vice-Admiral Gensoul's squadron to leave the Mediterranean, fearing that once it reached the Atlantic it would head for Plymouth and the British rather than Brest.

But Churchill's decision had been made a fortnight previously. On June 17 he ordered the establishment of Force H, based on Gibraltar and centred around the battle-cruiser *Hood* and the aircraft-carrier *Ark Royal*, with the task of watching the French fleet. A few days later he reinforced the squadron with the old battleships *Valiant* and *Resolution*, and put the whole under the command of Vice-Admiral Sir James Somerville. Also on

June 17, Admiral Sir Andrew Cunningham, commanding the British Mediterranean Fleet, was told that should France conclude a separate peace, the French fleet was to be seized or sunk. The fact that the French warships which had taken refuge in England—beyond the reach of the enemy—were to suffer the same treatment, shows that the question of the French home ports played only a secondary rôle in the British plan.

Here was the origin of Mers el Kébir. When the orders came through to proceed with Operation "Catapult", Sir Dudley North, C.-in-C., North Atlantic, was horrified and Somerville astonished. Nevertheless, they had no choice but to carry out their orders. On July 3 at 0700 hours, an officer from Force H handed Admiral Gensoul's aide-de-camp the British ultimatum. Gensoul has been criticised for not acting upon the clause in his orders which authorised him to sail his squadron to Martinique, but this is unfair. With the reduced crews manning his ships there was a real danger that they might have been stopped and captured in the attempt.

At 1656 hours on the 13th, the vessels of Force H opened fire on the four French warships in Mers el Kébir. The French ships were reluctant to return the British fire and could only clear the harbour entrance one by one. *Strasbourg* reached the open sea at 1710, but *Dunkerque*, hit by a 15-inch salvo, was forced to anchor at the end of the bay. The elderly battleship *Bretagne* was hit in her after magazines and capsized with the loss of 977 of her crew, *Provence* ran aground, and the big destroyer *Mogador* was hit badly. Somerville ceased firing at 1732 hours and gave chase to the *Strasbourg*, but the latter escaped.

The next day, July 6, torpedo-bombers from the *Ark Royal* attacked. They did not manage to sink the *Dunkerque*, but an explosion aboard a lighter laden with depth-charges killed another 150 men of her crew. This raised the French losses over the two days to 1,297.

What were the reactions of the French Government to the British attack at Mers el Kébir? "Between 1500 and 1600 hours on July 3," wrote Weygand, "I was urgently summoned to the Hotel du Parc. I met M. Baudouin and we went to Marshal Pétain's office, where Admiral Darlan told us what was happening. We heard that a large British naval force was cruising off Mers el Kébir, and that Admiral Somerville had given Admiral Gensoul an ultimatum to weigh anchor and join the British fleet or to scuttle his ships. This ultimatum had been rejected and the British ships had opened fire on our warships in the Mers el Kébir anchorage, which were unable to manoeuvre or to defend themselve adequately. The French fleet replied. The unequal battle continued. We found ourselves confronted with a *fait accompli* whose consequences we could only guess at."

Weygand continued: "Much later, after my return from Germany, I discovered that at the moment when we met with Darlan the engagement had not yet begun and that the British ultimatum contained a third proposition, that of withdrawing our fleet to Martinique until hostilities ended. This proposition might have made possible an arrangement which would have avoided the need for this bloody event. But Darlan, who always kept very secretive on every question concerning the fleet—and, I think, insufficiently informed by Admiral Gensoul—served us with a *fait accompli . . .*"

French battleships Provence *and* Bretagne *at Mers el Kébir, July 3, 1940.*

At Alexandria, the good sense of Admirals Cunningham and Godfroy, and the high esteem in which they held each other, succeeded in sparing Force X, which the French had put at the disposal of the British in the eastern Mediterranean, from a similar tragedy. Cunningham, turning a deaf ear to his orders from London, did not try to force a decision by the end of July 3; and Godfroy fought down the bitterness which the news of the bombardment at Mers el Kébir caused him. Rather like smugglers, each acting against his Government, the two admirals came to the following agreement on July 4:

1. Force X (the battleship *Lorraine*, the cruisers *Duquesne*, *Tourville*, *Suffren*, *Duguay Trouin* and five torpedo-boats) would be demobilised in Alexandria harbour and would land their fuel stocks, immobilising the ships; and
2. The French squadron would hand over breech-blocks from its guns and the detonators of its torpedoes to the French Consulate at Alexandria.

At Dakar on July 8 a torpedo plane from the aircraft-carrier *Hermes* attacked the battleship *Richelieu* and put its two starboard propellers out of action. A similar operation was to have been made against the French squadron in the Antilles (the aircraft-carrier *Béarn*, and the cruisers *Jeanne d'Arc* and *Emile Bertin*) but it was called off because of American intervention.

The French warships in British ports were overwhelmed at dawn on July 3; their crews were disembarked and interned. Churchill went so far as to write, in *The Second World War:* "The whole transaction showed how easily the Germans could have taken possession of any French warships lying in ports which they controlled"—as if the question of the French naval bases was not on the point of being settled, and as if the French sailors in Portsmouth and Plymouth would have taken the same precautions against the British as they would have done against the Germans.

To put it bluntly, Churchill wanted to strike a mighty blow at low cost to galvanise British national—and international opinion. As he wrote in *The Second World War:* "Here was this Britain which so many had counted down and out, which strangers had supposed to be quivering on the brink of surrender to the mighty power arrayed against her, striking ruthlessly at her dearest friends of yesterday and securing for a while to herself the undisputed command of the sea. It was made plain that the British War Cabinet feared nothing and would stop at nothing. This was true."

We have no way of knowing if, when Churchill wrote this after the war, he had consulted Ciano's diary. On July 4 Ciano had noted: "For the moment it proves that

the fighting spirit of His Britannic Majesty's fleet is quite alive, and still has the aggressive ruthlessness of the captains and pirates of the seventeenth century."

But Ciano did not write what would have happened if the British had attacked Taranto and the Italian warships anchored there . . .

Certainly Operation "Catapult" bore bitter fruit. It caused deep and long-standing resentment in the French Navy, which, no less than its commander-in-chief, had always been sympathetic towards Britain, its former ally. The fear of a repeated British attempt of the same kind caused the French fleet to withdraw to Toulon, where it scuttled itself on November 27, 1942, in obedience to the order of June 24, 1940. The latter had not been circulated at the time of Operation "Catapult".

General de Gaulle was also profoundly affected by the drama of Mers el Kébir. "In spite of the pain and anger into which I and my companions were plunged by the tragedy of Mers el Kébir, by the behaviour of the British and by the way they gloried in it, I considered that the saving of France ranked above everything, even above the fate of her ships, and that our

duty was still to go on with the fight.

"I expressed myself frankly about this on July 8th, in a broadcast. The British Government, on the advice of its Minister of Information, Mr. Duff Cooper, was clever enough, and elegant enough, to let me use the B.B.C. microphone for the purpose, however disagreeable for the British the terms of my statement may have been.

"But it was a terrible blow at our hopes. It showed at once in the recruitment of volunteers. Many of those, military or civilian, who were preparing to join us, turned on their heels then. In addition, the attitude adopted towards us by the authorities in the French Empire and by the naval and military elements guarding it, changed for the most part from hesitation to opposition. Vichy, of course, did not fail to exploit the event to the utmost. The consequences were destined to be grave as regards the rallying of the African territories."

And in 1962, discussing the subject with Anthony Heckstall-Smith, Admiral of the Fleet Sir John H. D. Cunningham commented: "Appallingly shameful; appallingly stupid."

As in the days of Philip of Spain, Louis XIV, and Napoleon, Britain's chances of resisting an invasion from the Continent depended on retaining control of the Channel and the North Sea.

For an attack on Britain in 1940, Hitler was considerably weaker than Napoleon had been in 1805. The heavy naval losses suffered in the Norwegian campaign had reduced the German fleet to the strength of one pocket-battleship, four cruisers, and a dozen destroyers. But the enormous superiority of the British Home Fleet, based on Scapa Flow, was countered by the numerical strength of the Luftwaffe, plus the danger represented by U-boats and torpedo-boats. This triple threat would have made Home Fleet operations in the Narrow Seas far too hazardous, and the Admiralty, in the light of the experience of Dunkirk, was unwilling to risk the fleet further south than the Wash.

Thus the Channel and the southern approaches to the North Sea became a sort of naval no-man's-land. In the skies above these waters victory or defeat for the Luftwaffe would decide whether or not Germany risked an invasion attempt.

Would a defeat for the R.A.F. have permitted the Wehrmacht to land—as envisaged by the O.K.H. Directive of July 27, 1940—on the coasts of Kent, Sussex, the Isle of Wight, and Dorset? At the time of the French armistice at Rethondes on June 22, the British Army in Britain totalled some 26 divisions, of which 12 had been formed recently and were not yet fully trained or equipped. The 13–14 divisions which had seen action in France had lost most of their artillery and anti-tank weapons, and had brought back only 25 out of their 600 tanks. Nor had the

General Sir Alan Brooke inspects a gun emplacement on the south coast.

troops been assigned equal sectors of the south coast to defend. Around Brighton, Montgomery's 3rd Division had some 30 miles of coastline to watch; between western Sussex and Wales, Sir Alan Brooke's Southern Command consisted of a corps staff and a mere three divisions, of which two were Territorial.

On June 26, Brooke wrote gloomily: "The main impression I had was that the Command had a long way to go to be put on a war footing . . . The more I see of conditions at home, the more bewildered I am as to what has been going on in this country since the war started. It is now ten months, and yet the shortage of trained men and equipment is appalling . . . There are masses of men in uniform, but they are mostly untrained: why, I cannot think after ten months of war. The ghastly part of it is that I feel certain that we can only have a few more weeks before the *boche* attacks."

This was hardly an exaggeration. On July 19 General Ironside, C.-in-C., Home Forces, had been relieved of his post. Although he was promoted to field-marshal and given a seat in the House of Lords, this was still seen as a disgrace, since it was only two months since he had been replaced as Chief of the Imperial General Staff by General Sir John Dill. But was Ironside alone responsible for the weaknesses of the British Army? In his memoirs, Eden says not. He refers to the "surprising bitterness" with which Dill criticised Hore-Belisha, former Secretary of State

for War. "He had done damage to the army that could not be repaired in years, Dill said, commanders had come to look over their shoulders."

Passing Southern Command to General Auchinleck, who had done so well at Narvik, Brooke took over from Ironside and threw himself into intense and timely activity as commander of the Home Forces. Making lavish use of aircraft transport, he was everywhere, countermanding the strict defensive prescribed to all sectors and releasing mobile reserves for counterattacks. But this was not enough: he also had to order that the areas in which such counter-attacks might have to be made were cleared for action, by demolishing the concrete obstacles which had studded village streets since May.

Brooke's responsibilities were far greater than the resources at his disposal. In the diary which he kept for his wife, he occasionally gave vent to the anguish which the immediate future caused him. On September 15 he wrote:

"Still no move on the part of the Germans. Everything remains keyed up for an early invasion, and the air war goes on unabated. This coming week must remain a critical one, and it is hard to see how Hitler can retrace his steps and stop the invasion. The suspense of waiting is very trying, especially when one is familiar with the weaknesses of one's defences. Our exposed coast line is just twice the length of the front that we and the French were holding in France with about eighty divisions and the Maginot Line. Here we have twenty-two divisions of which only about half can be looked upon as in any way fit for any form of mobile operations. Thank God the spirit is now good and the defeatist opinions expressed after Dunkirk are no longer prevalent. But I wish I could have six months more to finish equipping and training the forces under my command. A responsibility such as that of the defence of this country under existing conditions is one that weighs on one like a ton of bricks, and it is hard at times to retain the hopeful and confident exterior which is so essential to retain the confidence of those under one and to guard against their having any doubts as regards final success."

The organisation responsible for the defence of the island was not likely to soothe Brooke's worries. If the Germans had tried an invasion they would have encountered no inter-service high command capable of co-ordinating the efforts of the British Army, Navy, and Air Force. The First Sea Lord had no less than six "commanders-in-chief" under his orders, while the Chief of the Air Staff had three. And Brooke had no authority to give orders to any of them.

"This system," he wrote after the war, "presented grave dangers. If a landing had taken place I fear that Churchill, as Minister of Defence, would have tried to

A British freighter sinks after an attack by Stukas in the Channel early during the Battle of Britain.

co-ordinate the activity of the different commands himself. This would have been a perilous mistake, for with his impulsive nature he would have tended to take decisions according to his intuition and not from a logical perspective."

It was no less urgent to replace the *matériel* lost at Dunkirk as soon as possible, to raise the divisions still training to battle-worthiness, and to arm the Home Guard, which in August 1940 contained one million volunteers. To this end, guns were taken from military museums and war memorials; the Drury Lane Theatre contributed a dozen rusty old rifles; shotguns and ammunition were commandeered; and even cutlasses from the navy of Nelson's day were distributed to the local defence volunteers.

Meanwhile, the arms factories were accelerating their production all the time. On June 8 there were 72 infantry and cruiser tanks in Britain; this rose to 200 by August, and there were 438 by September 29. The production rate was expected to rise to 12–15 per week for infantry tanks and nine per week for cruiser tanks. But these tanks, although brand new, were—as Rommel was to prove in Libya–already obsolescent for modern armoured warfare.

Britain took over from France the military contracts which the latter had signed with the United States and which had not been completed by the time of the armistice. But, most important of all, Roosevelt agreed to provide Britain with 500,000 rifles and 900 75-mm guns, each supplied with 1,000 shells. By the "cash and carry" principle still in force, the British Merchant Navy was responsible for bringing these precious cargoes home, and this was done with no losses to U-boat attacks. Churchill commented that certain generals turned up their noses at these 900 guns, which dated from the end of World War I. But the British were desperately short of artillery: on June 8 there were only 420 field guns and 163 heavy guns, with 200 and 150 rounds per gun respectively. And during the second phase of the Battle of France the 75-mm gun had proved its worth as a tank-killer. On June 8 the British Home Forces had only 54 2-pounder (40-mm) guns which could be used against tanks.

By September 17 Brooke had the following resources for the defence of Great Britain and Northern Ireland: 29 divisions and eight independent brigades, six of which were armoured. These forces included two Canadian divisions, the 1st and 2nd, of which only the 1st Division had suffered at all (one man killed and five missing) during its recent excursion to France. This little army, faced with invasion, was outnumbered by an estimated four to one–and on top of that it was still not ideally deployed.

During the winter of 1939–40, not wishing to be caught unprepared by a sudden demand from Hitler, Grand-Admiral Raeder had ordered his staff to make a study of the many problems which would have to be settled if he were ordered to transport the German Army across the Channel.

On May 21, 1940, at the moment when the Panzers were driving onwards from Abbeville towards Boulogne and Calais, Raeder told Hitler of the conclusions reached by these studies. But the information fell upon preoccupied ears. As late as June 20 Raeder had still received no reaction from Hitler on the subject: when he made his report and asked for instructions, all he got from the Führer were some vague suggestions for a scheme to transport Jews to Madagascar.

Hitler's indifference to Raeder's invasion suggestions on May 21 was not surprising: his attention was focussed on the battle in hand. He was apprehensive that the temerity of his generals would allow the French to stage a new "Miracle of the Marne", recovering as they had done in 1914. Later, on the eve of the arrival of the French armistice delegates at Rethondes, Hitler's dilatory attitude towards Raeder was the result of his uncertainty about the best road to take now that France had been crushed. At Munich on the 18th, Ciano had seen Hitler as an actor preparing to play the part of Charlemagne, "the gambler who has made a big scoop and would like to get up from the table risking nothing more", and wondering if there were any real advantage in overthrowing the awesome mass of the British Empire. Would Churchill see sense? Would he fall? Either of the two would make an invasion of England unnecessary.

From June 25 to July 5 Hitler remained with a small group of consultants aboard his special train *Tannenberg* at Kniebis, near Freudenstadt in the Black Forest, waiting for the situation to become clarified one way or the other. On July 2 a landing in England was certainly the object of an order—but it was only a hypothetical case, together with several others, and no preparations were to be made yet.

It was on July 16, in Berlin, that Hitler signed his famous Directive No. 16—*Seelöwe* (Operation "Sea Lion"). But the preamble to this document shows that even at this date the invasion was not regarded as inevitable. It stated: "Since England, in spite of her apparently hopeless military situation, shows no sign of coming to terms, I have decided to prepare a landing operation against England, and if necessary to carry it out.

"The aim of this operation is to eliminate the British homeland as a base for the further prosecution of the war against Germany, and, if necessary, to occupy it completely."

This was not, therefore, Hitler's final word. But a month had passed since the fall of Paul Reynaud's government and France's request for an armistice, and those 30 days had not been wasted by the British aircraft industry, ably stimulated by Lord Beaverbrook. Allowing for two more months of preparations and preliminary moves, and an invasion would not be possible until September 16—on the eve of the period of boisterous early autumn weather which would make the Channel impassable to light landing craft.

From the Reichstag on July 19 Hitler addressed an ultimatum, dressed up as an offer of peace, to Winston Churchill. Churchill was recommended, in all conscience, to make the British people see reason, for he, Hitler, could see no reason for the struggle to continue. He would not be responsible for any further shedding of blood. London made no reply to this insolent harangue; and Hitler was forced to go ahead with the build-up for "Sea Lion".

With the cliffs of Kent visible across the Channel, Göring (far right) and Luftwaffe officers await Eagle Day.

On July 27 Brauchitsch–recently promoted to Field-Marshal, together with 12 other Army and Luftwaffe generals–submitted a preliminary invasion plan to O.K.W. With 41 divisions, six of them armoured and three motorised, plus the Luftwaffe's 7th Parachute Division and the 22nd Airborne Division, the plan read as follows:

On D-Day (set at shortly after August 25) Rundstedt's Army Group "A" would cross the Channel with two armies:

Right flank: 16th Army (Busch), concentrated between Ostend and the Somme, would land between Ramsgate and Hastings; and

Left flank: 9th Army (Strauss), concentrated between the Somme and the Orne, would land between Brighton and Littlehampton, with a detachment on the Isle of Wight.

The Gravesend–Reigate–Portsmouth line was designated as the first objective for Rundstedt's army group.

Simultaneously, or after a short delay, depending on circumstances, Bock's Army Group "B" would launch Reichenau's 6th Army from the Cherbourg Peninsula against the Dorset coast. Landing between Weymouth and Lyme Regis it would strike towards Bristol, pushing a detachment across Devon.

At this moment the 9th Army would break the British defences along the North Downs, cross the Thames at Reading, and encircle London from the west. The second objective for Rundstedt and Bock was to be the line connecting Maldon on the North Sea with Gloucester on the Severn.

As the man responsible for the land forces during the assault crossing, and for their supply during the campaign, Raeder denounced the whole ambitious scheme as impracticable. Even by requisitioning every available vessel from the inland waterways and the fishing fleets–which would have serious results on war production and civilian food supplies–he would not be able to assure the landing of a first wave of 13 divisions, even if their numbers were considerably reduced.

The Navy also condemned the idea of a landing on the wide front envisaged by Brauchitsch, stating that adequate protection could not be guaranteed and recommending a crossing in the Pas-de-Calais sector. But Brauchitsch and Halder in turn refused to consider feeding troops into the narrow Ramsgate-Folkestone sector suggested by Raeder and his chief-of-staff, Admiral Schniewind.

The result was a compromise. The 6th Army venture from Cherbourg was dropped completely, and O.K.H. agreed to concentrate its right flank between Ramsgate and Folkestone. But the plan for 9th Army remained unchanged, and Rundstedt would still have a sufficiently wide front for his break-out. This adjustment lowered the invasion force to 27 divisions, nine of them in the first wave, each of which would land 6,700 men on D-Day, now set for September 21. A feint landing against the Norfolk coast was also planned, to draw off the British reserves from immediately behind the landing beaches.

As there was no German battle fleet to give heavy gunfire support, and as the Luftwaffe would be unable to provide total coverage for the assault, it was decided to give the landing troops the benefit of tank fire-power. To do this, some 128 Pzkw III and IV tanks were converted to allow them to be landed offshore and descend to the sea bed, a depth of 25–30 feet below the surface. Because of the extra 0.8 atmospheres pressure created at this depth, careful waterproofing was needed: the turret ring of each tank was sealed with an inflatable tube; and the crew and the engine got their air supply via a long, flexible snorkel tube supported on the surface, while a special valve coped with the exhaust problem. Special landing-craft with hinged ramps, and their bottoms reinforced with concrete to bear the weight of the tanks, would carry the tanks to their launch points off the British coast.

Experiments carried out by Reinhardt's XLI Panzer Corps off the island of Sylt in the North Sea proved that these submarine tanks were perfectly capable of carrying out this task. Finally, long-range artillery support was provided by coastal batteries which could reach the British coast between Ramsgate and Dungeness: four batteries between Sangatte and the north of Boulogne, with four 28-cm, three 30.5-cm, four 38-cm, and three 40.6-cm guns, with ranges of between 28 and 37 miles.

Above all, the Royal Navy and the R.A.F. had to be prevented from attacking the sealanes which the 16th and 9th Armies would use. These extended eastward to Rotterdam and westward to le Havre. In view of the enfeebled state of the German Navy, this task fell squarely on the Luftwaffe. The latter would have to replace naval firepower on D-Day with massive Stuka attacks to neutralise the British coastal defences. But the whole operation depended on the preliminary removal from the board of the R.A.F. as a fighting force, and especially its fighter formations.

Hitler was well aware of this: his Directive No. 17 of August 1 ordered the intensification of naval and air operations against England. The first paragraph read:

"Using all possible means, the German air forces will smash the British air forces

The legendary Spitfire in flight.

in as brief a period of time as possible. Its attacks will be directed in the first instance against formations in flight, their ground facilities, and their supply centres, then against the British aircraft industry, including factories producing anti-aircraft guns."

When this had been done, the Luftwaffe was to turn against Britain's ports, crushing those on which the country depended for its supplies, but sparing the south coast ports which would be needed for supplying the invasion after the first landings. Finally there was to be no "terror-bombing" of open cities without the express order of the Führer: the whole weight of the Luftwaffe was to be used only on Britain's military potential.

Was the Battle of Britain lost before it began? Or did Hitler and Göring fail to make a thorough and methodical use of their advantages?

On August 13, 1940 – *Adlertag*, the "Day of the Eagle" – the losses of the Battle of France had not yet been recouped by the Luftwaffe. (The French Air Force alone had caused the loss of 778 German aircraft.) To tackle England, the Luftwaffe was deployed in three air fleets:

Norway and Denmark: *Luftflotte* V (Stumpff);

Belgium and Holland: *Luftflotte* II (Kesselring); and

Northern France: *Luftflotte* III (Sperrle). On August 13 the Luftwaffe deployed 2,422 aircraft against Britain: 969 level bombers, 336 Stuka dive-bombers, 869 Bf 109 single-engined fighters and 268 twin-engined Bf 110 "destroyer" fighters.

The British, however, had come a long way since the days of the "Phoney War". Fighter production – 157 in January 1940, 325 in May, 446 in June, and 496 in July – was no longer a serious worry. The supply of trained pilots was far more serious. On July 13 Fighter Command, led by Air Chief-Marshal Sir Hugh Dowding, had only 1,341 trained pilots; it would have to draw heavily upon the pilots of Coastal Command and the Fleet Air Arm, as well as forming four Polish and one Czech squadron in a few weeks.

This meant, on the surface, that this decisive battle would pit 1,137 German fighters against 620 R.A.F. Hurricanes and Spitfires – but the comparison is not as simple as that. The Messerschmitt Bf 110 twin-engined "destroyer" fighter – "Göring's folly" – was too slow and too sluggish to hold its own against the British fighters. On the other hand the Messerschmitt Bf 109E single-seat fighter was faster than the Hawker Hurricane Mk. I and about as fast as the Supermarine Spitfire Mks. I and II, although the latter machine had only begun to appear with the front-line squadrons of R.A.F. Fighter Command. The Bf 109 could climb faster than the British fighters; the British fighters were more manoeuvrable, and their batteries of eight machine guns gave them a bigger, though lighter, cone of fire than the German fighters.

Two paramount elements favoured the R.A.F. First was the defence radar network extending from the Shetland Islands to Land's End at the western extremity of

Camera gun sequences of (clockwise from top left) He 111's, an Me 110, a Ju 88 and another He 111.

Cornwall. Radar information enabled the British commanders to get their fighters off in sufficient time to avoid attack on the ground and then, directed over the radio, to intercept the enemy.

Second came the fact that Fighter Command was operating largely over British soil and could recover most of its shot-down pilots. German aircraft shot down over Britain almost always meant the loss of their crews as well as their machines. On August 15, for example, the R.A.F. destroyed 70 German fighters and bombers. Some 28 Spitfires and Hurricanes were shot down that day, but half their pilots eventually rejoined their squadrons.

For some 25 years the accepted idea has been that the German air offensive reached its peak on Sunday, September 15; during a series of German attacks on London, the British defence claimed to have shot down 185 German aircraft, a total lowered to 56 by the official post-war figures. In fact, although the British came close to defeat on the 15th they had already won, as much because of the mistakes of the German high command as the courage of the R.A.F. fighter pilots. The Luftwaffe's offensive had begun badly: in five days of operations between August 13 and August 17, the Germans lost 255 aircraft to the R.A.F.'s 184. As a result Göring withdrew *Luftflotte* V and the Stuka formations from the battle – *Luftflotte* V because it was badly placed to make worthwhile attacks on targets in northern England, and the Stukas because they were too vulnerable.

However, as long as the Luftwaffe kept up its attacks on the Fighter Command bases in southern England it was close to winning set and match. Many British aircraft were destroyed on the ground, and their essential runways riddled with bomb craters. Far more serious, however, was the fact that the operations centres, unfortunately sited on the airfields themselves and insufficiently protected against bombs, suffered heavy damage, which caused additional difficulties in co-ordinating the formations in the air.

During this phase – August 24 to September 6 – the scales tilted heavily in favour of the Luftwaffe, which lost 378 aircraft as opposed to 262 British planes shot down or destroyed on the ground. On paper this suggests that the R.A.F. still had an advantage of 45 per cent – but in fact these figures were far more favourable to the Luftwaffe than might be imagined, because the German losses were shared between the fighters and the bombers. On the British side the brunt fell on Fighter Command, now reduced to under 1,000 pilots, constantly in action and desperately in need of rest.

With casualties of 15 to 20 pilots killed and wounded every day, Fighter Command was nearing its last gasp when suddenly the whole picture changed.

Late in the evening of August 24, a German bomber formation accidentally bombed some non-military targets in London. Churchill's immediate response was to order a reprisal raid on Berlin. The following night, 81 twin-engined bombers took off for the German capital, but only 29 reached Berlin; the others got lost on the way. This modest raid cost the British eight men killed and 28 wounded – but this time it was Hitler's turn to lose control. Forgetting that he had formerly regarded "terror bombing" as a dangerous distraction from the main effort, he immediately ordered that London be given the same treatment as Warsaw and Rotterdam. On September 7 the first heavy "Blitz" raid broke on London, with some 330 tons of bombs being dropped.

The bombing of London was to continue now for 57 long days – but it meant that Hitler and Göring had abandoned the principal objective of the directive of August 1. The Luftwaffe was unable to smother London with terror raids without relaxing the grinding pressure which it had been inflicting on the British fighters. Fighter Command recovered rapidly: between September 7 and September 30 the British gained the upper hand over the Luftwaffe, destroying some 380 aircraft for a loss of 178 of their own.

By October 31 the Luftwaffe had lost 1,733 fighters and bombers to the R.A.F.'s 1,379 fighters – but the R.A.F. had lost only 414 pilots killed (of whom 44 were Allied, mainly Poles). Churchill, therefore, was not exaggerating when he proclaimed the R.A.F.'s victory in the House of Commons with the immortal sentence: "Never in the

field of human conflict has so much been owed by so many to so few." The same praise was repeated when he wrote *The Second World War* after 1945. But at the time he was far less satisfied with the results obtained. The brilliant C.-in-C., Fighter Command, Air Chief-Marshal Sir Hugh Dowding, and the commander of Fighter Command's No. 11 Group, Air Vice-Marshal Keith Park, the real brains behind the victory, were deprived of their commands within weeks and relegated to secondary posts. The ostensible reason was that there had been far too many faults in the field of radio communications and that the battle had been fought too much on the defensive, using "penny-packet" tactics.

Across the Channel the final preparations for Operation "Sea Lion" were being pushed ahead at an uneven pace. On shore, the troops of 16th and 9th Armies were concentrated around their embarkation points. At sea, however, the mine-laying and mine-sweeping programme intended to secure the invasion lanes from British attacks had suffered badly from attacks by Coastal Command – and Göring had failed to smash the R.A.F. Against the German invasion fleet – 2,500 transports, barges, tugs, lighters, and light craft massed in the invasion ports between Rotterdam and Le Havre – R.A.F. Bomber Command was intensifying its attacks. True, the losses of the invasion fleet were under ten per cent, but they still had to be replaced.

On September 11 Hitler announced his intention of beginning the count-down for "Sea Lion" on the 14th, which would place the landing at dawn on Tuesday, September 24. But on the 14th he decided to take three more days to decide whether or not to give the final order.

In 1940, September 27 was the last day in which the tides were favourable for such a venture. From then on into October, the high seas and strong winds which could be expected in the Channel would be too much for the inland craft to risk the crossing; they would have stood a good chance of foundering. On the 17th, Hitler ordered "Sea Lion" to be postponed. Two days later he gave the order for the invasion fleet to be dispersed in order to protect it from British bombing, but in such a way that it could be readily reassembled as soon as he needed it.

But the real implications ran far deeper. On October 12, while the ravages of the German Blitz were being extended across England, Keitel issued the following order from O.K.W.:

"The Führer has decided that until next spring the preparations for *Seelöwe* are to be continued with the sole intention of maintaining political and military pressure on Britain . . .

"Should the projected landing be resumed in spring or early summer, orders will be given for new preparations. In the meantime, it is necessary to shape conditions in the military sphere to suit a final invasion."

This order of October 12 reflects all the conditional uncertainty expressed in the "Sea Lion" Directive, No. 16, of July 16. Why did Hitler abandon the invasion? Was it because of the defeat which the inconstancy and presumption of Göring had brought upon the German air arm?

Certainly he had accepted that the whole idea of a landing in England had to be re-thought. On January 11, 1941, developing the subject during a visit by Ciano, Hitler compared himself with a marksman, only one cartridge in his gun, who wanted to make quite sure that he would hit the mark. But was he telling Ciano the whole truth? Or rather – having signed the "Barbarossa" Directive, No. 21, for the invasion of Soviet Russia three weeks before – was he disguising his real intentions for 1941?

To answer these questions we must examine Hitler's changing attitudes between his supervision of *Fall Gelb* in late 1939 and early 1940 and his postponement of "Sea Lion" in September 1940.

From the end of October 1939 until the end of June 1940, Hitler had been deeply involved in the planning for the invasion of France, in consultation with O.K.H. This was not all wrong: without Hitler's supervision, Manstein's suggestions would certainly have been suppressed and the outcome of the campaign would probably have been quite different. It also shows Hitler's strong desire to live up to his title of "Leader" by assuming total responsibility for the conduct of the war, and to impose his wishes on everyone.

None of this shows through between the signing of the armistice at Rethondes and the suspension of "Sea Lion". Obviously, this was a far more difficult operation for Hitler to dictate: an amphibious invasion without precedent in history. But his repeated retreats to Kniebis and Berchtesgaden, broken by a fortnight's stay in Berlin, show a certain uncertainty on Hitler's part as to the political and military decisions to be taken to assure the perpetual supremacy of the Third Reich.

No document has survived which allows us to unravel the thread of his solitary meditations. But on July 29, 1940, he spoke out.

On the afternoon of that day Jodl, head of the O.K.W. Operations Staff, returned from a visit to Hitler in the Obersalzberg. Aboard his special train *Atlas*, which served him as a mobile command post, he summoned his deputy, Colonel Warlimont, and representatives from the three services: Lieutenant-Colonel von Lossberg, Lieutenant-Commander Junge, and Luftwaffe Major von Falkenstein. Under cover of the strictest secrecy, Jodl revealed the message which, like Moses, he had brought down from the mountain.

The Führer intended to launch an armed invasion of the Soviet Union in the following spring. As this news was received with shocked dismay by his listeners, Jodl followed with this argument:

"The elimination of the Bolshevik menace which constantly weighs on Germany renders this clash of arms inevitable. For

Dornier Do 17M bombers, known as "Flying Pencils", during a daylight raid over north London.

An He 111 bomber flies over the Silvertown area of London. Docks, railways and the river are visible.

this reason the best solution is to introduce it into the course of the present war."

Here was a singular argument, to say the least. But how had Hitler arrived at this fatal decision? Here again, documents are of little help. On June 19 at Munich, as we know from Ciano's diary, Hitler made absolutely no mention of his intention to attack Russia, although Moscow had finally put an end to the independence of Estonia, Latvia, and Lithuania a few days before.

Shortly after the armistice at Rethondes, Molotov summoned the Rumanian Ambassador to the Kremlin and gave him a 48-hour ultimatum to cede Bessarabia – a former province of Tsarist Russia – to the Soviet Union. The Rumanian Government appealed to Germany, but all it received from the Wilhelmstrasse was the advice to accede to Moscow's wishes.

The ensuing Soviet-Rumanian treaty not only restored to Soviet Russia Bessarabia – a territory which the Tsars had ruled since 1812 in defiance of the nationalist principle – but the Bukovina as well. The latter, on the north side of the Carpathians, had once been a province of the Austrian Empire, and the Kremlin had no historical claim whatsoever to it.

Was it the latter demand which precipitated Hitler's decision, being as it was a demonstration of insatiable Soviet imperialism which even a blind man could appreciate? In pushing westward the Soviet-Rumanian frontier from the Dniestr to the Prut, Soviet Russia had advanced 125 miles further to the southwest, putting its bombers within a 30-minute flight of the petroleum wells and

refineries at Ploiesti – and Hitler's obsession with war economy, and liquid fuel in particular, is well known.

All the same, following former Rumanian Foreign Minister Grigore Gafencu and his captivating book *The Origins of the War in the East*, one is bound even today to return to the view that it was the failure of "Sea Lion" which provoked this total change of direction. Just as Napoleon, abandoning the idea of reducing Britain by a direct attack, recoiled eastwards and set off on the road through Ulm, Austerlitz, Tilsit, and Moscow to Waterloo, so Hitler sought in the destruction of the Soviet Union the means of compensation for his helplessness on the Straits of Dover.

It is possible that as early as the end of June 1940 Hitler had been considering the idea of an attack on Russia, but that he shelved it as his attention became more and more focussed on the technical problems of "Sea Lion". He could hardly send the Wehrmacht across the Channel to knock out Britain, the last combatant left, while husbanding all his resources for a trial of strength with Stalin.

Hence Hitler's uncertainties in the summer of 1940. With one eye on London and the other on Moscow, hoping until the beginning of September for an arrangement with the British which would free his armies for an assault on the east, he directed the battle on too loose a rein, and left far too much to Göring. The idea of adopting night bombing instead of a direct attack in order to bring Britain to her knees was totally unreal, considering the losses suffered by the Luftwaffe. Even allowing for new aircraft construction, the Luftwaffe's strength now consisted of:

898 level bombers instead of 969;
375 dive-bombers instead of 346;
730 Bf 109 fighters instead of 869; and
174 Bf 110 fighters instead of 260.

But it is unfair to dwell at length exclusively upon the short-sightedness of Hitler and Göring; for at this period their illusions were shared by every expert on strategic air power. When 36 British Wellington bombers dropped 36 tons of bombs on Turin, London announced that the Fiat factories had ceased to exist . . .

Although it was incapable of doing any serious damage to Britain's war production, the Luftwaffe's Blitz sowed fire and destruction across England and claimed over 40,000 victims, including 16,000 civilian dead. So it was that on Hitler's initiative the war was embarked on the course which between December 1940 and February 1945 would ravage Europe, from the fire raids on London to the destruction of Dresden.

By autumn 1940 all neutral powers and the occupied countries knew that the Anglo-German struggle had not ended, and that this fight to the death would not be resumed until spring. What would happen then? On July 15 Weygand had said to Colonel P. A. Bourget, who had followed him from Beirut to Bordeaux; "although British victory is still not certain, neither is that of Germany". If Weygand was talking in this fashion only 20 days after the signing of the armistice, it is easy to imagine the tremendous encouragement given three months later to the early resistance networks forming in France, Belgium, and Holland by the postponement of "Sea Lion". Now the defeat of May-June 1940 had been proved to be provisional; Hell had become Purgatory; cruel sufferings lay ahead, but they would not last for ever . . .

CHAPTER 14

The war at sea begins

Hitler approached the war at sea with caution. On September 3 the German U-boats were ordered to confine their operations strictly to the limits laid down by the London Convention of 1936 in their attacks against British merchant shipping, and were not to attack passenger liners or French shipping. Hitler did not want to launch an all-out effort against the Western Allies at sea – but above all he wanted to avoid incidents like the sinking of the *Lusitania* in May 1915, which had helped bring the United States into World War I.

On September 24 the restrictions on attacking French shipping were lifted, and on the 27th a free hand was also given to the pocket-battleships *Graf Spee* and *Deutschland*, which had sailed for their "waiting areas" in the North Atlantic several days before the opening of hostilities.

This first phase of the war at sea – September–December 1939 – closed with the Allies slightly on top. The U-boats had scored a total of 114 Allied and neutral merchantmen sunk, with an aggregate tonnage of 421,156. Most of these ships, however, had been isolated sailings, as France and Great Britain had decided to reintroduce the highly successful convoy system which had beaten the U-boats in World War I. By the end of the year, only four ships sailing in convoys had been lost to U-boats. Another fact which favoured the Allies was that the magnetic pistols which detonated the German torpedoes were grossly inefficient and remained so for months. When they did not detonate prematurely – which happened on September 17, saving the British aircraft-carrier *Ark Royal* – they often failed to detonate at all on reaching the target.

Hence the typically disgusted message from Lieutenant-Commander Zahn of *U-56* on October 30. "1000 hours: *Rodney*, *Nelson*, *Hood* [two battleships and a battle-cruiser in company – a submariner's dream target] and ten destroyers in Square 3492, steering 240. Three torpedoes launched. Detonators failed." The U-boat crew had heard the clang of three hits on *Nelson*'s hull. (Despite the claim made by Dönitz in his memoirs, First Lord of the Admiralty Winston Churchill was not on board.)

The Royal Navy's struggle against the U-boats was greatly assisted by the "Asdic" equipment. This was developed at the end of World War I by a committee of Allied scientists; hence the name "Asdic" – Allied Submarine Detection Investigation Committee (the device was known to the U.S. Navy as "Sonar"). Asdic was an ultra-sonic detector which could pick up echoes (from impulses sent out by the apparatus) reflected by submarines – but it needed skilful use, and in the opening months of the war it did not achieve the miracles expected of it. Never-

theless, by December 31, 1939, nine U-boats had been sunk. Six of these were ocean going, and the German U-boat arm had had only 25 ocean-going U-boats at the outbreak of war on September 1.

The pocket-battleships, despite the enormous range given them by their diesel engines, also failed to live up to their expectations. *Deutschland* had left Wilhelmshaven on August 24 for her first North Atlantic war cruise. By the time she was recalled to German waters on November 1, she had sunk only two merchantmen of 7,000 gross tons. On her arrival at her new base, the former Polish port of Gdynia (which Hitler had renamed Gotenhafen), *Deutschland* was rechristened, in deference to Hitler's obsession that no warship named after the Fatherland should be risked at sea. So *Deutschland* became *Lützow*, the former German heavy cruiser of that name having been handed over to the Soviet Union.

In the South Atlantic, the *Graf Spee* was off Pernambuco (Brazil) when on September 27 her commander, Captain Hans Langsdorff, received the order to commence operations against Allied merchant shipping. *Graf Spee*'s war cruise lasted 77 days, taking her at one time eastwards into the Indian Ocean and sending to the bottom nine merchantmen totalling 50,000 tons. Dawn on December 13 found *Graf Spee* heading for the shipping focus of the River Plate area for a last foray before returning to Germany. Instead, *Graf Spee*'s lookouts sighted Commodore H. H. Harwood's South Atlantic cruiser squadron, which immediately prepared to give battle.

The German warship had six 11-inch guns and eight 5.9-inch guns. In weight of shell her armament completely outclassed the British force, the cruisers *Exeter*, *Ajax*, and *Achilles*, which between them only had six 8-inch guns (*Exeter*) and sixteen 6-inch guns (*Ajax* and *Achilles*). Moreover, *Graf Spee*'s heavier armour rendered her safe against anything but direct hits from *Exeter*'s 8-inch guns. Also, she had radar to give the enemy's range, where the British ships did not. Harwood, however, had already laid his plans for immediate action by day or night and he went straight into action, detaching *Exeter* to engage alone while he headed *Ajax* and *Achilles* to take the pocket-battleship in flank.

It took time for *Ajax* and *Achilles* to get into position – time enough for Langsdorff to concentrate the fire of his heavy guns on *Exeter* and make a floating wreck of her. All *Exeter*'s guns were knocked out; she was holed and flooding; but until the last possible minute her captain struggled to keep her in action, launching torpedoes, until *Exeter* was forced to drop out of the battle, trailing a dense pall of smoke, at about 0715 hours.

Ajax and *Achilles* continued the fight, trying to get close enough to do damage

with their light guns, but soon *Ajax*, Harwood's flagship, came under *Graf Spee*'s 11-inch shellfire. Over half of *Ajax*'s guns were knocked out, and by now she had used up three-quarters of her ammunition. *Graf Spee*, however, seemed undamaged, and so *Ajax* and *Achilles* broke off the action at 0740 hours and retired out of range.

Captain Langsdorff had the game in his hands, but he could not see this. A humane and thoughtful commander, he was shaken by the losses to his crew: 36 killed and 59 wounded. The lighter British shells had caused no vital damage, but had inflicted enough superficial destruction to convince Langsdorff that *Graf Spee* could not tackle the wintry North Atlantic and the hazardous passage of the Denmark Strait. This was why he decided to run for Montevideo to seek time to make repairs.

The Uruguayan authorities, however, urged by the British, granted Langsdorff only 72 hours' stay in Montevideo. This was in accordance with international law, for Uruguay was a neutral power; but it left Langsdorff with the choice of having his ship and his crew interned for the duration of the war, or putting to sea with his repairs far from completed. Moreover, he had accepted the many rumours in Montevideo (both natural and propaganda-inspired) that the British battle-cruiser *Renown* and the aircraft-carrier *Ark Royal* would be waiting for him when he came out. On December 17 he saw to it that *Graf Spee* was scuttled and sunk in the approaches to Montevideo harbour. Langsdorff could not bear to survive the loss of his ship and shot himself on December 20.

The threat to the convoy routes caused by the appearance of the pocket-battleships in the Atlantic resulted in the setting-up of separate naval groups to hunt the raiders down. This in turn deepened the collaboration between the British and French navies. The French battle-cruisers *Dunkerque* and *Strasbourg* and three French 10,000-ton cruisers joined these "hunting groups", as they were known; and in the Indian Ocean the French cruiser *Suffren* was helping to guard the convoys bringing the first Australian troops to Egypt. On the British Admiralty's request, the dockyard workers in France were speeding up the completion of the new battleships *Richelieu* and *Jean Bart*, because of setbacks which were likely to delay the commissioning of their British counterparts, *King George V* and *Prince of Wales*.

As First Lord of the Admiralty, Churchill was keenly aware of the value of the Franco-British co-operation at sea. On the state of the French Navy he wrote: "the powerful fleet of France, which by the remarkable capacity and long administration of Admiral Darlan had been brought to the highest strength and degree of efficiency ever attained by the French Navy since the days of the Monarchy."

Another deadly weapon turned against the Anglo-French sea-lanes by Admiral Raeder was the magnetic mine. For the first months of the war at sea these mines did much damage and were a most serious worry to the Allies. Dropped from aircraft or laid by U-boat, the magnetic mine was detonated by the metallic mass of a ship passing over it. Such a submarine explosion from directly underneath usually resulted in the total destruction of the ship. Between November and December 1939, 59 Allied and neutral ships totalling 203,513 tons were sunk by magnetic mines.

But on the night of November 22–23 a German aircraft dropped a magnetic mine off Shoeburyness in the Thames Estuary. This landed on a mud-flat and was discovered at low tide. Commander J. G. D. Ouvry gallantly undertook to defuse the mine. It was a heroic piece of work: Ouvry went about his task, connected to the shore by a throat microphone into which he calmly described what he was about to do next. This was standard practice: if an accident or miscalculation had blown him to eternity, the next man to attempt to disarm a similar mine would at least know what not to attempt.

Ouvry succeeded, and the magnetic mine gave up its secrets. Once these were known, ships began to be "degaussed" as

Right: The Graf Spee *settles in the water after she had been scuttled. Below: The cruise and final battle of the* Graf Spee *in 1939.*

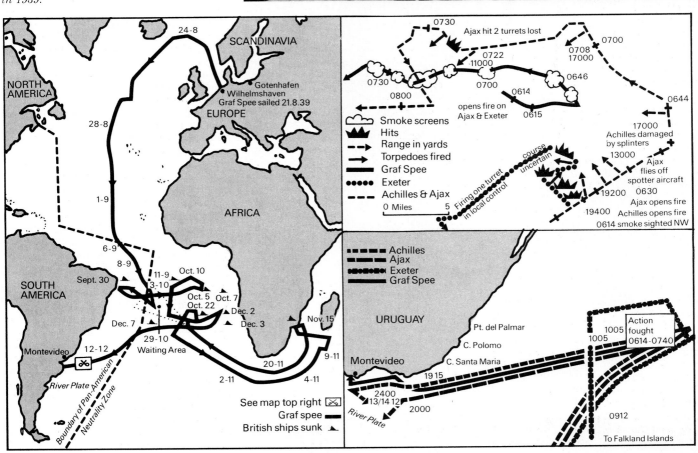

a protective measure. Degaussing involved running a cable around the ship and passing an electric current throught it, which neutralised the ship's magnetic field. Degaussing operations on Allied ships had been largely completed by March 1940.

At the outbreak of war on September 3, Great Britain and France depended for their imports on a combined merchant fleet of 24 million tons. By the end of the year their total losses were well within the safety limit—and the magnetic mine had just been beaten. The Allied losses, moreover, were compensated for to a considerable degree by the amount of German merchant shipping captured or sunk: 75,000 tons.

The numerical odds were too far against the German Navy for there to be any thought of a deliberate engagement with the Allied fleets. Raeder could only wage a guerrilla war—but his U-boats and mine-layers did succeed in drawing blood at

Left: Punch *on the sinking of the* Athenia. *Below: A coastal U-boat.*

the Royal Navy's expense.

Two weeks after Britain had gone to war, on September 17, *U-29* (Lieutenant-Commander Otto Schuhart) sank the first Allied warship to be lost to enemy action in World War II: the elderly aircraft-carrier *Courageous* of 22,500 tons, which was lost with 519 of her crew.

Worse was to come. On the night of October 13–14, under a brilliant display of Northern Lights, Lieutenant-Commander Günther Prien took *U-47* through the maze of channels and currents girdling the stronghold of the British Home Fleet: the vast anchorage of Scapa Flow in the Orkneys, hitherto considered impenetrable to submarines. Prien found that the dog-leg channel in Holm Sound was more weakly defended than the others. He fired three torpedoes at the battleship *Royal Oak* (29,500 tons), which capsized and sank in 13 minutes, taking with her Rear-Admiral H. F. C. Blagrove and 832 crew.

The loss of this veteran warship of World War I made little or no difference to the Allies' superiority at sea, but the moral effect was enormous, both in Germany and Great Britain. Prien and his crew were welcomed as heroes in Berlin, and Prien himself was decorated with the Knight's Cross by Hitler. In London, there were wild rumours that the U-boat could only have got into Scapa Flow by treason, and for a while suspicion centred on a Swiss watchmaker in Kirkwall, largest town in the Orkneys. Not until the war was over was it proved for certain that the Scapa Flow feat had been carefully planned from Luftwaffe aerial reconnaissance photographs.

By mid-November the numerous French and British warships in the Atlantic, hunting what they believed to be two pocket-battleships, led Raeder to order a battle squadron to sail for the North Atlantic on November 21. It was hoped that a demonstration of force in the waters between Scotland and Iceland would draw off some Allied warships from the South Atlantic, easing the problems of *Graf Spee* (still at large). On November 23, the battle-cruisers *Scharnhorst* and *Gneisenau* surprised and obliterated the puny armed merchantman *Rawalpindi* west of the Faeroes.

Admiral Sir Charles Forbes, commanding the Home Fleet, was unable to put to sea and intercept these new raiders. On September 9, he had had to shift his base from Scapa Flow until the defences there—anti-aircraft as well as anti-submarine—had been put to rights. The new anchorages (at Loch Ewe on Scotland's west coast and at Rosyth in the Firth of Forth) were too far to the south to allow sufficient time to intercept German raiders in latitudes so far to the north. The Germans soon got wind of the Home Fleet's change of base and laid magnetic mines in the approaches to Loch Ewe; on December 4, one of them did so much damage to the battleship *Nelson* that she was out of action for several months.

Despite these setbacks, however, the Royal Navy, with the invaluable help of

Above: The magnetic mine defused by Commander Ouvry on November 23, 1939.

its French ally had, by the end of 1939, apparently achieved its double mission: to safeguard the sea-lanes of the Western Allies, and to cut those belonging to the common enemy. But this satisfactory situation was illusory. The German U-boat fleet was receiving new units at an alarming rate, and in any event was certainly not operating at full stretch. Despite the rapid elimination of *Graf Spee*, there was absolutely no guarantee that the Allies could prevent further surface raiders from reaching the Atlantic. And the problem of Germany's inshore supply-routes—those which ran through the territorial waters of Europe's neutral powers—had yet to be tackled.

In the first three months of 1940 the course of the war at sea caused the French and the British little concern. The handful of U-boats at the disposal of Admiral Dönitz had scored only mediocre success against the Allied convoys, which had been organised at the outbreak of the war. Including neutral vessels, only 108 merchantmen totalling 343,610 tons were sunk by U-boats between January 1 and March 31, 1940, and the building capacity of the British shipyards alone was estimated at 200,000 tons per month. In the same period, no less than eight U-boats were sunk by Allied naval escorts, though one was subsequently salved. It was therefore not surprising that at the beginning of April the French and British Admiralties had no worries about the immediate future.

Looking further ahead, the French and the British were well aware that U-boat activity would increase, thanks to the construction capacity of the shipyards of the Baltic and the North Sea. But at the same time the war programmes of the two Western powers were also beginning to bear fruit, and the strength of the convoy

"Degaussing" a warship.

escorts was growing in parallel with increased U-boat production. Admiral of the Fleet Sir Dudley Pound and Admiral Darlan believed that they had the situation well in hand.

Already the dangerous effects of the magnetic mine, which was impervious to traditional mine-sweeping techniques, had been overcome. But in November 1939 the magnetic mine had come as a very disagreeable shock; in that month alone 27 ships – 120,958 tons in all – had been sunk by mines. Once the secret of the magnetic mine had been pierced, however, the French and the British began intense "degaussing" work on their ships. The results of this counter-move were soon apparent. In March 1940 losses to mines

had fallen to 14 ships totalling 35,501 tons.

In the South Atlantic the Battle of the River Plate on December 13, 1939, had put a stop to the modest exploits of the pocket-battleship *Graf Spee*, which by that date had sunk 50,081 tons of shipping. The month before, on November 15, *Graf Spee*'s sister ship *Deutschland* had dropped anchor in Gotenhafen (formerly Gdynia) after a ten-week war cruise in the North Atlantic which had brought her little gain: only two victims, a total of 7,000 tons. Since then no German surface raider had broken out through the Royal Navy's blockade line which stretched between Iceland and the Orkney Islands.

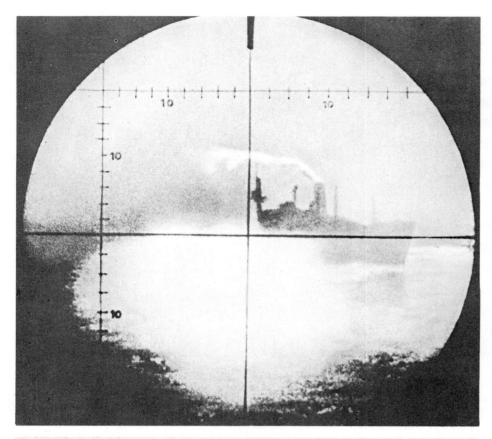

On March 4, 1940, at the moment when he was preparing to send eight U-boats into the North Atlantic and six to the North Sea, Admiral Dönitz was ordered to refrain temporarily from any new operations. It was necessary for the U-boats to participate in *Weserübung*, the invasion of Scandinavia. Their task was to destroy Allied warships which tried to attack the German convoys heading for Norway, while also attacking and destroying the troopships which the Allies, once they had recovered from their initial surprise, were certain to send to the support of the Norwegians in the Trondheim and Narvik regions.

No less than 31 U-boats were involved in this new mission, which meant that during April–May 1940 Germany's submarine commerce-raiding was virtually suspended. According to the figures in *The War at Sea*, the British official history, total Allied and neutral mercantile losses during the Norwegian campaign amounted to only 20 ships totalling little more than 88,000 tons – the lowest losses to U-boats since the outbreak of hostilities.

This was a considerable setback for the German Navy and it was not compensated for by almost total failure in Norwegian waters. There were plenty of tempting targets for the U-boats; their crews were not lacking in courage or training. But their torpedoes, despite reports made during the previous autumn and official promises, were still chronically unreliable.

In reviewing the logs of the U-boats in action between April 11 and 19, Admiral Dönitz was presented with the following depressing account of the failures recorded by his boats:

"April 11:

"Launched torpedoes at two destroyers at 10 in the evening. Result not observed. [*U-25*].

"At 1230 hours, launched three torpedoes at the *Cumberland*. Miss: explosion at the end of the run. At 2115 hours, launched three torpedoes at a *York*-class cruiser. Premature explosions. Depth 23 feet; Zone 4. [*U-48*].

"April 10, 2250 hours: Two failures: an explosion after 330 yards, another after 30 seconds, 110 yards short of a big destroyer. [*U-51*].

"April 15:

"On the 14th, fired without success at the *Warspite* and two destroyers. [*U-48*]. Launched two torpedoes at a transport. Failures. [*U-65*].

"April 18:

"Two premature explosions between Iceland and the Shetlands. [*U-37*].

"April 19:

"Launched two torpedoes at the *Warspite*, at 980 yards. Depth 26 feet, zone 4. A premature explosion and a terminated run. [*U-47*].

"Fired at the cruiser *Emerald*, at the mouth of Vaagsfjord. Premature explosion after 22 seconds. [*U-65*]."

Top: The U-boat's view of her victim at the moment of impact. Left: A torpedoed coaster sinks stern-first.

On April 16 Commander Günther Prien in *U-47*, the "hero of Scapa Flow", was on patrol in the Byddenfjord when he surprised a convoy at anchor – a solid wall of shipping. He fired eight torpedoes, all of which failed. On returning from his cruise he told his superiors "that it was useless to send him to fight with a dummy rifle".

In 1940 the magnetic detonator used in the German torpedo had not come up to expectations. It was not a unique problem: the British suffered from the same trouble in 1941 and the Americans in 1942. The percussion detonator was also found to be useless as the torpedoes ran some 10 feet below the depth for which they had been designed, with the result that they often passed harmlessly beneath the keel of the target.

According to Dönitz, the defective German torpedoes spared an entire British squadron – the battleship *Warspite*, seven cruisers, seven destroyers and five transports. What was worse, the premature explosions of the torpedoes gave away the presence of the U-boats and resulted in violent counter-attacks. Six U-boats were sunk in the North Sea between April 10 and May 31.

In June 1940 the German victory in Norway allowed Dönitz to resume U-boat commerce raiding in the Atlantic. A rapid score of 58 ships sunk (284,113 tons in all) beat the best U-boat record over the last three months. Moreover, from airfields in Holland, Belgium, and northern France, the Luftwaffe was much better placed to attack British shipping in the Channel, either by direct attack or by mine-laying operations, which between them inflicted losses of 44 ships (191,269 tons). The total losses – caused by all forms of Axis attack by sea and air – were about 140 merchant ships (585,496 tons) sunk by the end of June.

The intervention of Italy and the French surrender reversed the entire naval strategic situation in favour of Germany. To challenge the Italians in the Western Mediterranean, formerly the responsibility of Admiral Darlan and the French fleet, now fell to the British Force H, ordinarily composed of one aircraft-carrier and one or two battleships or battle-cruisers, based on Gibraltar. The entire British naval strength in the Mediterranean between Gibraltar and Alexandria amounted to one-third of the capital ships in service with the Royal Navy.

With the exception of the warships which fled for British ports at the time of the French capitulation, about 60 French destroyers and torpedo-boats had been removed from the board and would no longer be able to assist in convoy escort duties as the German submarine offensive took shape again. Despite the attacks of the Luftwaffe, the British shipyards were producing an enormous number of destroyers and corvettes designed specifically for anti-U-boat warfare, but it would be some time before they entered service.

Above all else, the Third Reich had just acquired an enormous strategic advantage for its Navy, which would permit the most varied selection of strategic combinations. At the end of 1914 Colonel-General von Falkenhayn – had he not been halted on the Yser and in front of Ypres – would have been satisfied to provide the Imperial German Navy with the ports of Dunkirk, Calais, and Boulogne. By the end of June 1940 Grand-Admiral Raeder could dispose of every Atlantic port between Tromsö and St. Jean-de-Luz.

It was true that the ports between Rotterdam and Cherbourg were too close to the British air bases to be of service to more than the most lightweight German naval forces. But in this sector the Luftwaffe could stand in for the German Navy. During July 1940 the German bombers sank four destroyers and 18 small merchantmen. German air attacks became so serious that the coal suppliers of Cardiff were told to ship their consignments for the London region via Scotland.

In his work on the story of German naval strategy in the two world wars, Vice-Admiral Kurt Assmann wrote significantly of the situation of the German Navy after the conquest of Norway and the French surrender:

"At this time the situation was the reverse of that of 1914. Then we had been in possession of a navy which could tackle the British Grand Fleet on its own terms, but which had no strategic advantage with regard to its bases. Now we had this strategic advantage, but we had no fleet strong enough to exploit it.

"Moreover, in this new situation, because of the circumstances of World War II we were threatened from the sky, for our bases lay within range of the British air forces, which had not been the case in 1914. From this point of view the British had a distinct advantage over us. The Home Fleet anchorages in northern Scotland were over twice as far away from the German air bases – even those in Norway – than the new German bases in France were from the airfields of the Royal Air Force."

Despite the naval situation created by the German invasion of Norway and the conquest of France, however, Britain's position was not as bad as is often imagined.

The principal convoy routes used in the early stages of the war.

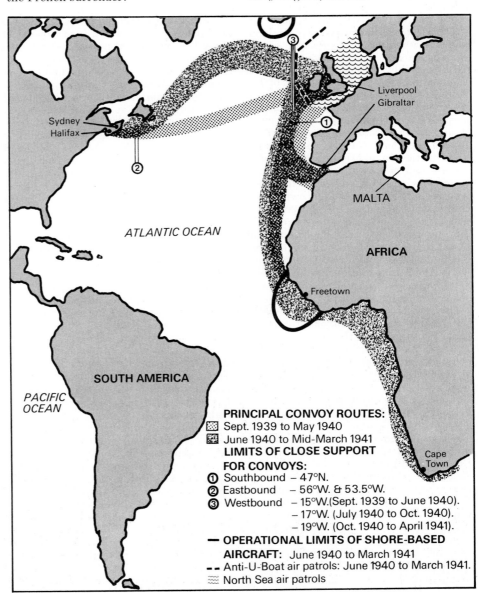

ATLANTIC OCEAN

PACIFIC OCEAN

SOUTH AMERICA

AFRICA

MALTA

Liverpool
Gibraltar

Sydney
Halifax

Freetown

Cape Town

PRINCIPAL CONVOY ROUTES:
▨ Sept. 1939 to May 1940
▨ June 1940 to Mid-March 1941
LIMITS OF CLOSE SUPPORT FOR CONVOYS:
① Southbound – 47°N.
② Eastbound – 56°W. & 53.5°W.
③ Westbound – 15°W.(Sept. 1939 to June 1940).
    – 17°W. (July 1940 to Oct. 1940).
    – 19°W. (Oct. 1940 to April 1941).
— **OPERATIONAL LIMITS OF SHORE-BASED AIRCRAFT:** June 1940 to March 1941
-- Anti-U-Boat air patrols: June 1940 to March 1941.
≈ North Sea air patrols

A U-boat crewman in rough weather.

After the German invasion of Denmark, Britain had proceeded to occupy the former Danish territories of the Faeroe Islands and Iceland on May 10, 1940. Shortly afterwards the British Admiralty set up a naval base at Hvalfjord on the western coast of Iceland, just to the north of Reykjavik. Although it was now unable to blockade the northern exit to the North Sea by controlling the waters between Scapa Flow and Stavanger, the Royal Navy still held the North Atlantic approaches along the line Orkneys–Shetlands–Faeroes–Iceland–Greenland.

The invasion of Norway and of Holland, and the installation in Britain of the Norwegian and Dutch Governments in exile headed by King Haakon and Queen Wilhelmina, put at the disposal of the British all the Norwegian and Dutch merchantmen which the Germans had not surprised in their home ports. This came to about one-third of the strength of the British Merchant Navy at the outbreak of hostilities. In addition, there were the officers and men of the Norwegian and Dutch Navies, like their Polish comrades, whether aboard ships of their own which they had managed to save from disaster or aboard destroyers, escorts, or even submarines which the British High Command put at their disposal. Finally, at the time of the armistice and for some time afterwards, the British took over all the French merchantmen they could get, in port or at sea.

Given these reinforcements, it was with some 28 or even 30 million tons of shipping that Britain faced the Battle of the Atlantic, instead of the 21 million which she had had in September 1939. Another advantage came from the fact that Britain was now released, as a result of the German victory, from the obligation to help supply her French ally.

The installation of the German Air Force and Navy in the French bases on the Channel and the Atlantic led the British Admiralty to route the North American convoys further to the north. Convoys for Freetown, the first or last stage on the Cape of Good Hope route, were sent further to the west. Ships sailing to or from Liverpool now took the North Channel between Ireland and Scotland instead of St. George's Channel, the latter being judged too dangerous. But these detours meant that a convoy steaming at 10 knots would take 15 days to reach Britain from New York, while a convoy steaming at $7\frac{1}{2}$ knots would take 19 days to make the passage from Freetown.

During the first phase of the Battle of the Atlantic the defence of the Western Approaches against U-boat and Luftwaffe attacks had been entrusted to Admiral Sir M. Dunbar-Nasmith, V.C., C.-in-C. Western Approaches, with his H.Q. at Plymouth. Soon afterwards, however, the Western Approaches H.Q. – on which the successful outcome of the war depended – was transferred to Liverpool, and was taken over by Admiral Sir Percy Noble on February 17, 1941.

Across the Channel Admiral Dönitz, high priest of the German U-boat theory and strategy, was not long in seizing the considerable (if not decisive) advantages which the German victories of May–June 1940 had given him.

As the passage of the Channel was closed to them, the U-boats had to reach their hunting-grounds in the North Atlantic by making the long and dangerous northward voyage around the Orkneys, and this limited their operational period considerably. But if they could be based on the French Atlantic ports they would be spared an out-and-return voyage of over 1,000 miles, which would permit them to remain at large for an extra week.

The armistice with France had not yet come into force when Dönitz made his first tour of the western ports, and decided to install himself at Lorient. On July 7, *U-30* became the first German submarine to use the port, taking on fuel and new torpedoes there. From August 3 teams of workers and specialists arrived from Germany to overhaul the port installations and make all the necessary alterations which would be needed by U-boats returning from the high seas. At the same time plans were drawn up for enormous pens in which U-boats would be protected from Allied bombs by 23 feet of concrete. Instead of concentrating on fruitless attempts to knock out the German shipyards, as it did in 1941 and 1942, the R.A.F. would have been better advised to try to destroy the huge U-boat pens before they were completed .

At the end of August 1940, Dönitz finally left his H.Q. at Wilhelmshaven and moved to Kernével, on the outskirts of Lorient. Together with his normal staff, Dönitz brought with him a large team of specialists of all kinds, with sophisticated electronic equipment.

There were radio direction-finding experts, trained to pinpoint the briefest signal sent out by Allied convoys; and decoding experts, who deciphered (without much trouble, it would appear) signals sent from mid-ocean, as well as instructions from the British Western Approaches command. With this kind of information, Dönitz's H.Q. could use powerful radio transmitters to pass information to the U-boats on patrol and direct them to their targets.

What high-quality radio communication had done for the Germans on land, permitting them to campaign with mass tank formations, was about to transform the German U-boat arm. From the H.Q. at Kernével, Dönitz could send out orders and deploy his U-boats not as isolated warships but as hunting packs.

The group attack was the great German innovation in submarine tactics; it had not been used in World War I. The Germans called it *Rudeltaktik* or "pack tactics". To the British the U-boat concentrations were "wolf packs".

Another innovation was that instead of attacking by day from a submerged position, the U-boats now began to attack at night and on the surface. It was not as risky as it sounds: in the darkness, the low silhouette of a U-boat was hard to spot from the higher vantage point of a ship's deck, and movement on the surface was not picked up by the asdic detectors aboard the escorts. An improved percussion detonator, hastily developed, meant that German torpedoes now functioned better than before. The British had been sure that asdic was the answer to the U-boat menace; now they had to think again.

Although Dönitz, as Captain Roskill points out in *The War at Sea*, had revealed these new tactics in a book published just before the war in 1939, the British were surprised by the new turn in the submarine offensive and reacted sluggishly. These are the overall figures of British, Allied, and neutral tonnage sunk by U-boats in the second half of 1940:

July – 38 ships (195,825 tons);
August – 56 ships (267,618 tons);
September – 59 ships (295,335 tons);
October – 63 ships (352,407 tons);
November – 32 ships (146,613 tons);
December – 37 ships (212,590 tons);
Total – 285 ships (1,470,388 tons).

These successes were all the more remarkable in that they were obtained with quite small forces. On September 1, 1940, the German submarine arm had 57 U-boats, exactly the same number as at the outbreak of hostilities 12 months previously which showed that German U-boat construction had managed to compensate for the number of U-boats sunk: 28 in all. Because of the need for training, of the long trial periods before new U-boats were fit for operations, and the time taken up by U-boats in transit, there were never more than eight or nine U-boats operating simultaneously in the waters to the northwest of Ireland. But even more than with R.A.F. Fighter Command, quality counted for more than quantity.

Under picked commanders who had been selected during the numerous peacetime U-boat exercises – leaders such as Prien, Schepke, Kretschmer, Endrass, Frauenheim, and Oehrn – by October 1940 Dönitz's force had reached a level of proficiency which it was never to recover in World War II: 920 tons of shipping per U-boat sunk every day. The blockade of the British Isles, decreed on August 17, 1940, was no empty German boast.

A typical example is the tragic story of

Convoys S.C.7 (34 merchantmen) and H.X.79 (49 ships), one sailing from Sydney, and the other from Halifax, Nova Scotia. In four nights – October 16–20 – six U-boats, attacking on the surface, sank 32 cargo-ships and tankers and damaged four others. The log-book of *U-99*, commanded by top-scoring U-boat ace Otto Kretschmer, tells a vivid story:

"October 18. 2330 hours. Now I attack the head of the right-hand column. Fire bow torpedo at a large freighter. As the ship turns towards us, the torpedo passes ahead of her and hits an even larger ship after a run of 1,740 metres. This ship of 7,000 tons is hit abreast the foremast and the bow quickly sinks below the surface, as two holds are apparently flooded.

"2355 hours. Fire bow torpedo at a large freighter of 6,000 tons at a range of 750 metres. Hit abreast foremast. Immediately after the torpedo explosion there is another explosion, with a high column of flame from bow to bridge. Smoke rises 200 metres. Bow apparently shattered. Ship continues to burn with green flames.

"October 19. 0015 hours. Three destroyers approach the ship and search area in line abreast. I make off at full speed to the south-east, but soon regain contact with the convoy. Torpedoes from other submarines are constantly heard exploding. The destroyers do not know how to help and occupy themselves by constantly firing starshells which are of little effect in the bright moonlight. I now start attacking the convoy from astern.

"0138 hours. Fire bow torpedo at a deeply-laden freighter of about 6,000 tons. Distance 945 metres. Hit abreast foremast. The ship sinks with the explosion.

"0155 hours. Fire bow torpedo at the next ship, of about 7,000 tons. Distance 975 metres. Hit abreast foremast. It sinks in under 40 seconds."

In the period when each of Britain's leaders went to bed wondering if they would be awoken by the news of a German invasion, the number of escorts which could be spared for the convoys remained very small. Incapable of refuelling at sea, they could not venture beyond Longitude 15 West from British ports, while the destroyers escorting east-bound convoys, based on Halifax, could not pass Longitude 35.

Until the new Icelandic base at Hvalfjord was completed there could be no question of filling the "Atlantic gap", as it was called, with the Coastal Command aircraft under Air Chief-Marshal Sir Frederick Bowhill. Coastal Command could put only 226 aircraft a day into the air in September 1940, and reinforcements arrived only in dribs and drabs as top priority was being given to Bomber Command, for an air offensive which was to prove futile in 1941.

The British were not helped by the personal intervention of Churchill, both as First Lord of the Admiralty during the "Phoney War" and afterwards as Prime Minister. Captain Donald Macintyre (a prominent U-boat hunter who had the honour of capturing Otto Kretschmer in March 1941) pulls no punches in his book *The Battle of the Atlantic*, quoting a plea for more offensive tactics which Churchill sent to Sir Dudley Pound at the end of 1939:

"Nothing can be more important in the anti-submarine war than to try to obtain an independent flotilla which could work like a cavalry division on the approaches, without worrying about the traffic or the U-boat sinkings, but could search large areas over a wide front. In this way these areas would become untenable to U-boats."

"A basic error," comments Macintyre,

The destroyer Eskimo, *on escort duty in the North Atlantic, passes near a geyser of water thrown up by an exploding depth charge.*

"which is to recur again and again in strategic thought on the Battle of the Atlantic, is here revealed. At nearly all stages of the Battle, the U-boat proved itself almost immune to surface or airborne search, except in the vicinity of convoys where, the area to be searched being greatly reduced, the submarine could either be kept submerged and so prevented from working its way in to the attack or, if surfaced in order to do so, could be detected and attacked."

The mistake, Macintyre stresses, was to detach escorts which were already too thin on the ground "to hunt U-boats reported perhaps 100 miles or more from the convoys. Search for a mouse reported in a ten-acre field had as much chance of success as these 'offensive' moves."

It was around the convoys themselves that the defenders had the best chance of making contact with U-boats, neutralising them by forcing them to dive, and then attacking and destroying them. So it was that the defensive tactics which Churchill deplored were in fact the best offensive methods possible.

Despite this fact, Britain's naval resources would remain over-stretched until the anti-submarine vessels ordered in the 1939 and 1940 programmes entered service. For this reason, Churchill turned to President Roosevelt, asking as early as May 15, 1940, for the cession of 40 or 50 American destroyers which had been built at the end of World War I. This request was repeated on July 11, as no reply had been received from the White House or the State Department.

It was obvious that any such concession would be in complete breach of the international conventions governing the relations of neutral states with belligerent ones. Although the majority of American public opinion was sympathetic to Britain and applauded her determination to fight on, it was also concerned about the reprisals which such a gesture might provoke from Hitler and Mussolini. In military circles there was also much apprehension that the "great arsenal of the democracies" might find herself involved in war before her production was fully prepared. Such was the level to which Roosevelt's "New Deal" policy had lowered the defensive capacity of the country.

Blending firmness with an admirable sense of compromise, Roosevelt replied to Churchill's request with a counter-proposal which would add to the military security of the United States. In exchange for 50 old destroyers, Great Britain would permit the U.S.A. to set up and occupy bases in Guiana, the Antilles, Bermuda, the Bahamas, and, with the agreement of Canada, in Newfoundland, for a period of 99 years. London accepted these conditions with good grace; as Roskill points out in *The War at Sea*, they placed the defence of these scattered British possessions in the hands of American forces.

However, friction rapidly arose when Roosevelt sought to base the entire transaction on a formal declaration by the British Government that the British fleet would be sailed to America if it could not be maintained in home waters. Although time was vital, Churchill tried to quash this request. It was not that he wished to make the Royal Navy a bargaining-point in case of an invasion, as some authorities have alleged, but that he was displeased that there should be any doubt at all about

the matter. However, as Roosevelt continued to press the point, Churchill made Britain's attitude perfectly clear in the following letter, which he sent on August 31:

"You ask, Mr. President, whether my statement in Parliament on June 4, 1940, about Great Britain never surrendering or scuttling her Fleet 'represents the settled policy of His Majesty's Government'. It certainly does. I must however observe that these hypothetical contingencies seem more likely to concern the German Fleet, or what is left of it, than our own."

It seems clear that Roosevelt, without impugning the good faith or the resolution of the British, was wondering whether Britain's known weaknesses in armaments would result in her suffering the fate of Norway, Holland, Belgium, and France. If this were to happen it would be better if the Home Fleet left Scapa Flow before the Panzers arrived in the far north of Scotland . . .

Seven of the 50 American destroyers were sent to the Canadian Navy; two were manned by Norwegian crews. But even before they entered service, after having been fitted with asdic, the situation improved for the British. The R.A.F. had detected that the concentrations of barges in the invasion ports were being dispersed; and this permitted the Admiralty to divert to the Western Approaches command many destroyers which had hitherto been earmarked for operations against a German invasion fleet in the Narrow Seas.

A good example of how the struggle between the destroyers and the U-boats now began to turn in Britain's favour dates from March 15, 1941: the destruction of ace U-boat commander Joachim Schepke and his *U-100*, described by

E. Romat in his *Atlantic Submarine War:*

"Badly damaged, *U-100* sank to the enormous depth of 750 feet. Schepke had no other alternative than to surface. The two hunters grouped themselves so as to recover contact. *Vanoc*'s radar operator reported a contact to starboard, and almost simultaneously her look-outs spotted a U-boat on the surface 540 yards away. With a violent helm alteration the destroyer wheeled round to starboard, bearing down on the U-boat. Schepke was in bad trouble: his diesel engines had failed and he was running on his electric motors; he could not make his intended torpedo attack against the destroyer, as he lacked the time and speed to reposition his U-boat.

"The threatening bow drove closer and closer. Schepke yelled to his crew to abandon ship. Every man rushed onto the bridge, putting on his lifebelt. At 1318 hours *Vanoc*'s bow rammed *U-100* almost at right angles to the conning-tower, slicing through the pressure hull and crushing Schepke to a pulp against the base of the periscope standards."

Britain would have had much more trouble in fighting the menace of the German maritime blockade if Hitler and Göring had not reduced the German Navy to the lowly status of Cinderella of the German armed forces.

When war broke out it had been decided to abandon the whole "Z-Plan" and concentrate naval construction on the completion of the battleships *Bismarck* and *Tirpitz*, the heavy cruisers *Prinz Eugen* and *Seydlitz*, the aircraft-carrier *Graf Zeppelin*, and above all the output of U-boats which, in about a year, were to enter service at the rate of 29 a month.

Two veteran American four-stacker destroyers arrive in Britain.

Minesweepers from Holland operating off the British coast.

According to German Navy calculations, the whole revised programme would not absorb more than five per cent of German steel production.

But when Hitler gave this order in October 1939 he left its execution to Göring, chief of armaments production, labour, and raw materials. But in his other capacity as head of the Luftwaffe Göring was unassailable, and the Navy got only the crumbs which fell from his table. By March 1940 Grand-Admiral Raeder had to accept a drop of monthly U-boat production from 29 to 25. But worse was to come. He had hoped that the land victories of the Wehrmacht would result in large industrial gains for the Navy; but nothing came of these hopes, for with the preparation first of Operation "Sea Lion" and then of "Barbarossa" his plans were ruined again.

As a result, the monthly U-boat production fell to two during the first half of 1940 and struggled up to six during the second. In 1941 it grew from six to 13, and in 1942 from 13 to 20 – but this last figure marked the limit, because of the fatal effects which the failure of the invasion of Russia had on German industry. Roskill was certainly right when he stated: "The slowness with which the Germans expanded their U-boat construction was to have the most fortunate consequences for Britain."

The influence which Göring exerted on Hitler had equally damaging effects on the success of the U-boat offensive. "Everything that flies is my concern," was his boast. As a result, compared with the systems in use in Britain, the United States, and Japan, the German Navy was denied the fleet air arm which it should have had, and was dependent upon the good humour of Göring for the collaboration (always improvised, at best) of the German air forces. As in Italy, this system of an "autonomous air arm" failed as soon as it was applied to the realities of modern naval warfare.

A case in point was the tragic accident of February 22, 1940, when two German destroyers were lost in the North Sea: *Leberecht Maass* under Stuka bombardment, and *Max Schultz*, which only escaped the bombs of the Stukas by heading into a minefield, with fatal results.

The transfer of the U-boats to the French coasts seemed to offer brilliant opportunities to the Luftwaffe; by flying permanent patrols in the skies over the Western Approaches German aircraft could have kept in contact with the Allied convoys, alerted the "wolf packs", and directed them to their targets. But the essential peacetime training for this rôle was lacking, and pilots were often nearly 100 miles in error in the reports which they made to Kernéval. Moreover, the codes which they used did not allow them to communicate with the operational U-boats directly.

Raeder and Dönitz tried in vain to give Hitler a better understanding of the problem. One can only sympathise with Dönitz when he declared to Hitler, one day in 1943: "The historians will describe World War II in different ways, according to their nationality. On one point, however, they will be unanimous. In the 20th Century – that of the aeroplane – the German Navy fought without airborne information and without its own air force, as if the aeroplane did not exist. And they will be unable to explain it."

We should remember Hitler's own description of the three branches of the Wehrmacht: "I have a National Socialist Air Force, a reactionary Army, and a Christian Navy!" Given this frame of mind it was hardly surprising that Göring's opinions tended to prevail over those of the admirals.

The German surface ships, too, played an important part in the campaign against Britain's sealanes. At the end of October 1940 the pocket-battleship *Admiral Scheer* broke out into the Atlantic and began a commerce-raiding cruise which took her to the Indian Ocean. On March 30, 1941, having returned via the Denmark Strait between Greenland and Iceland, she returned safely to the Baltic.

Even more spectacular were the successes of the disguised merchant raiders in service with the German Navy. They were fast merchant ships equipped with multiple camouflage devices, which enabled them to pass themselves off as Soviet ships in Norwegian waters, Spanish in the central Atlantic, and Dutch or Japanese in the Pacific. Carefully concealed, their armament normally consisted of six 5·9-inch guns, four torpedo-tubes, and a sea-plane, plus around 100 mines, which these dangerous raiders sowed off the Cape of Good Hope and Australian and New Zealand ports.

Between March 31 and December 3, 1940, six of these disguised merchant raiders sailed from German ports. Among them, *Komet* reached the Pacific via the North-East Passage, helped on her way by Soviet pilots and ice-breakers. Before she was sunk by the cruiser *Cornwall* on May 8, 1941, the *Pinguin* wrought havoc among Allied factory-ships and whale-catchers in the Antarctic. *Atlantis* was the most successful of them all. She passed the Denmark Strait at the beginning of April 1940, cruised right round the world, and on November 22, 1941, after 622 days at sea, was sunk in the South Atlantic by the cruiser *Devonshire*. The other four raiders all returned to western European ports and to Germany, as did some of their prizes.

Compared with the successes of the U-boats, the success of the German surface raiders in the second half of 1940 (62 ships sunk, and slightly less than 400,000 tons all told) appears somewhat modest. But their exploits had important strategic results. The British Admiralty made the decision to give battleship support to the convoys and from then on two or three battleships of the Home Fleet were always tied down on convoy escort duties.

On June 11, 1940, the first Italian submarine left La Spezia for the Atlantic and passed through the Strait of Gibraltar without trouble. It was eventually followed by 26 others, which the signing of the French armistice permitted to be based on Bordeaux. Thus was set up the *Comando Sommergibili Atlantici* or *Betasom*, under the command of Admiral Parona.

Unlike the German U-boats, the Italian submarines were much older both in design and construction. They lent themselves only badly to the "wolf-pack" tactics practised with such success by Dönitz's ships. Less manoeuvrable than their German opposite numbers, they suffered much more heavily in the storms of the North Atlantic.

The Italian submarines therefore tended to operate singly in more clement latitudes. But because the principal convoy routes led across the North Atlantic, the Italian contribution to the campaign against the Allied sealanes was modest.

CHAPTER 15
The Italian offensive in the Mediterranean

Fascist Italy had entered World War II at what seemed to her leaders to be her hour of destiny. But the total and unforeseen collapse of the Allied armed forces resulted in crippling problems for Ciano and Mussolini.

What was Hitler planning next? At the time of the conference at Munich on June 19, Ciano got the impression that Hitler did not wish to risk losing his winnings. If he maintained his current attitude, would he hesitate to sacrifice the international claims of Fascist Italy on the altar of a German-British agreement, to restore the racial solidarity, so to speak, of the Teutonic race? The Italian régime believed that a premature peace settlement would hardly suit Italy's interests, as was proved by the fact that the French-Italian armistice had yielded Mussolini nothing more than Menton and two or three Alpine villages.

But although the Fascist leaders were not eager to see a rapid end to hostilities, they certainly did not want to associate their German allies in any military ventures upon which Italy might embark in pursuit of her claims in the Balkans and the Mediterranean. This would only have meant offering Hitler a share of the spoils, and as the past history of the Axis had revealed that Germany always desired at least 50 per cent of the cake it is not hard to understand the Italian doubts.

Hitler's contempt for weaker members of the Fascist Party – men like "that swine", as he called Minister of Justice Count Dino Grandi – extended to King Victor Emmanuel III and the House of Savoy, the Pope and the Vatican, and to the entire aristocracy and bourgeoisie of the country. If, as he believed, "traitors" abounded in the most secret councils of his friend Mussolini, there was all the more reason to reveal only the sketchiest hints of his projects to the Duce, and even then to do it as late as possible.

In his distrustful attitude towards Italy Hitler found no opposition from his generals. Quite the contrary: all of them had fought in World War I and remembered what they called Italy's "defection" from the alliance of the Central Powers to the Allied *Entente* in May 1915. Nor were these professional soldiers in the least impressed by Mussolini's martial swaggering. They strongly suspected that although Fascist Italy's military structure looked impressive, it was built of plaster rather than marble.

As we have seen, the Germany Army High Command had opposed the suggestion to employ an Italian army in Alsace during the last stage of the Battle of France. While armistice negotiations were still in progress, a suggestion from General Mario Roatta, Deputy Chief-of-Staff of the Italian Army, caused great indignation in his colleague Halder, who noted in his diary on June 24: "The Italians are halted before the French fortifications and are

getting nowhere. But in the armistice negotiations they still want to secure an occupied zone of French territory which will be as big as they can get. To this end they have proposed sending to List's front a certain number of Italian battalions to be flown in by air, either by way of Munich or direct to Lyons, and to have them occupy the areas to which Italy wants to extend her right of occupation. All this is nothing more or less than a piece of the most vulgar deception. I have stated that I refused to be associated with the whole business."

Marshal Badoglio, however, also refused to put his name to this sordid project, drawing from Halder the complimentary statement: "According to all appearances, he is the only real soldier among this whole delegation of negotiators."

There can be no doubt that the forthright opinions expressed in Halder's diary were shared by every general close to Hitler and capable of influencing the Führer's decisions.

With all this political and psychological friction there could be no question of the two Axis partners co-ordinating their efforts with a common objective in view, as Britain and the United States would do after Pearl Harbor. Still less was there any chance of creating an Axis counterpart to the Allied Combined Chiefs-of-Staff in Washington, where, although discussions were often acrimonious, the final decisions reached were religiously carried out.

Rome and Berlin therefore followed a system of "parallel war", but with astonishing mutual concealment and even double-dealing. Both General Efisio Marras, for all his title of "Italian Liaison General at O.K.W.", and his opposite number attached to the *Comando Supremo*, General von Rintelen, were scantily, badly, and tardily informed of the intentions of the two dictator-warlords.

The Germans were understandably incensed when, on October 28, 1940, they found that Mussolini had concealed his intention to invade Greece until the last moment. "Shocking and stupid!" exclaimed Keitel, when he heard the news of the first Italian defeats on the Albanian front. Certainly Keitel had a point, for all the harshness of its expression. But what did Keitel say when Hitler made his decision to make a total reversal of his policy and invade Soviet Russia, without informing Mussolini?

Germany's anger about Mussolini's Greek campaign is well attested. "In November I went to Innsbruck to meet the German Chief-of-Staff, Marshal Keitel," wrote Badoglio. "He immediately pointed out that we had launched an offensive against Greece without having made the least notification to the German Command. The Führer was adamant that the situation in the Balkans must not be dis-

turbed. Germany was receiving important supplies from those countries, which she now seemed in danger of losing. 'If I had known,' said Keitel, 'I would soon have come to Rome to halt this campaign.'

"I had to tell him the truth, that I had been ordered by Mussolini to say nothing to Germany. He had in fact given me this order, and when I commented that an alliance put certain obligations on us, Mussolini replied furiously: 'Did they ask us anything before attacking Norway? Did they ask our opinion when they wanted to start the offensive in the West? They have acted precisely as if we did not exist. I'll pay them back in their own coin.'"

One would certainly have expected an operation aiming at the conquest of Greece, and above all of the Greek archipelago, to have been on the agenda of Mediterranean strategy at the Brenner Pass conference on October 4, 1940. No operation of the scale of Operation "Barbarossa", the invasion of Russia, was mentioned – a venture which could have been only prejudicial to Italy's interests in the immediate future.

In attacking the Soviet Union, Hitler proposed to deprive Britain of the last ally which she could win on the Continent. But the relaxation of the pressure of the combined forces of the Wehrmacht on Britain could mean only that the joint enemy of the Axis would be able to recover a certain freedom of action.

Such was the system of "parallel war" which Mussolini congratulated himself upon having established against the wishes of his ally and friend. He was confirmed in his euphoria by another factor: when Churchill ignored Hitler's "peace offer" at the end of June 1940, it meant that the war would continue. And as Mussolini said to Badoglio on September 22: "I am happy that the war will not end quickly, for that would be to our total disadvantage. A rapid peace would be a setback for us."

But again the Duce was forgetting the enormous deficiencies in armaments with which Fascist Italy had gone to war, and the impossibility of making them good in a prolonged war because of Italy's lack of adequate raw materials. It was only a few months since the plain facts had been put before him and he had said to his Chief of the General Staff: "This time I will declare war, but I will not wage it. This way I will get big results for using little effort."

On assuming supreme command, however, Mussolini was soon to give the most obvious proof of his lack of military talent. Before his contemporaries, Benito Mussolini, with his strutting stance, jutting chin, hand on hip or thumb hooked in belt, certainly acted the part of a dynamic and resolute commander. Even today, he is represented by the conformist and ill-informed historical viewpoint as a despot

An Italian bomb bursts near a British freighter in convoy to Malta.

who imposed his inexorable will upon the Italian people, after deep and inhuman meditation. But eye-witness accounts and documents show his weathercock nature, his inability to make a decision and stick to it, his lack of method, his ignorance of the basic problems of organisation and command. No Napoleon, in fact.

An important source is the diary of General Quirino Armellini, Badoglio's main colleague at *Comando Supremo*. Despite the fact that Armellini was opposed to the Fascist régime, the notes which he took between May 11, 1940 and January 26, 1941 – when he was disgraced – are not totally malevolent and tell an eloquent story.

The Alpine offensive had not yet begun when he wrote, on June 21: "The longer I stay at this post, the more I see of the disorder, lack of preparation, and muddle in every sphere, which seriously delays or completely prevents the functioning of the High Command; the more I believe that military necessities are being completely overlooked; and the more I am convinced that everything has yet to be done, or must be done again."

On August 15 he was more bitter still. "What once seemed an interesting prospect today disgusts me! We continue in the greatest disorder and complete chaos. In *Comando Supremo*, everyone commands. The last man to speak is always right. Strategic conceptions are regularly reversed with an astonishing lack of logic.

"Someone will say: 15 days from now we must be ready to march against Yugoslavia; or, in eight days we will attack Greece from Albania – as easily as saying, let's have a cup of coffee. The Duce hasn't the least idea of the differences between preparing for war on flat terrain or in mountains, in summer or in winter. Still less does he worry about the fact that we lack weapons, ammunition, equipment, animals, raw materials."

Armellini's laments are typical of many,

and all would be disastrously confirmed on the battlefield. But when blaming Mussolini and the Fascist régime, how much of the military chaos can be laid at the door of Marshal Badoglio, and, in more general terms, of the Italian Army? In 1946, Badoglio stated that his resignation "would not have resolved the situation", for Mussolini would never have gone back on his pact with Hitler; and Badoglio added: "By retaining my position, I could at least prevent some disastrous move from being made; for this was all that could have been expected from Mussolini, who was completely lacking in any military knowledge."

Badoglio had not invented this explanation to defend himself. On August 15, 1940, he had said to Armellini: "Although it may be a small thing, perhaps I can do more with him than someone else. We must carry on, saving what can be saved, and trying to avoid sudden moves which could lead to more serious consequences."

Writing on St. Helena after Waterloo, Napoleon had thought very differently. "A commander-in-chief cannot take as an excuse for his mistakes in warfare an order given by his minister or his sovereign, when the person giving the order is absent from the field of operations and is imperfectly aware or wholly unaware of the latest state of affairs.

"It follows that any commander-in-chief who undertakes to carry out a plan which he considers defective is at fault; he must put forward his reasons, insist on the plan being changed and finally tender his resignation rather than be the instrument of his army's downfall."

No sooner, however, had Italy entered the war than setbacks assailed her in all theatres of operations.

The air and sea offensive ordered by Mussolini never got off the ground. What was worse, by June 29 the Italian Navy had lost ten out of the 117 submarines with which it had entered the war, sunk in the

Red Sea and the Mediterranean. There was a very good reason for the losses (4 boats) of Italian submarine flotilla based on Massawa in the Red Sea: far too often, when submerged, the accumulator batteries of the submarines gave off poisonous fumes which rendered the crew unconscious.

In Libya, as mentioned above, Marshal Balbo had been ordered to remain on the defensive. If the reports of *Comando Supremo*'s military Intelligence can be taken as correct this was a somewhat odd decision, for 14 centrally-based Italian divisions were opposed by only eight French and five British divisions. But the situation was complicated by an exaggerated interpretation of Allied strength made by the *Servizio Informazioni Militari*. This did not dissuade Mussolini from going to war, but it did paint the strategic picture in excessively pessimistic colours.

On June 10, 1940, the French C.-in-C., North Africa, General Noguès, did have eight divisions under his command; but apart from the fact that three of them were not operational, they were deployed between the Libyan frontier and Spanish Morocco. The *Servizio* on the other hand, reported the French divisions as being massed between Bizerta and the Mareth Line, ready for an invasion of Libya.

General Sir Archibald Wavell, the British Commander-in-Chief, Middle East, had a total strength of five divisions (about 100,000 men), but of these only 36,000 were in Egypt. They were formed into two incomplete divisions: Major-General M. O'Moore Creagh's 7th Armoured Division and Major-General P. Neame's (from August Major-General N. M. Beresford-Peirse's) 4th Indian Division.

In Libya, the Italian forces were disposed as follows:

West: 5th Army (General Italo Gariboldi), consisting of X, XX, and XXIII Corps, with six infantry divisions and two Black Shirt divisions;

East: 10th Army (General Francesco Berti) consisting of XXI and XXII Corps, with three infantry divisions, one Black Shirt division, and one Libyan native division.

A fourth division (the 2nd Libyan Division) was moving up from Tripoli to Benghazi.

All in all, there were in Italian North Africa slightly over 236,000 officers, N.C.O.'s and other ranks, 1,811 guns, 339 light tanks, 8,039 trucks and 151 first line aircraft. The Italian air strength was comparatively weak, but even so was far stronger than that of the British.

The armistice with France was a bitter disappointment to Marshal Balbo. He had hoped that the occupation of Tunisia would put the port of Bizerta at his disposal, allowing him to draw on the material and military supplies in the province. Instead of this, he had to content himself with the demilitarisation of the Mareth Line.

The Italians were kept off balance for another reason: the British 7th Armoured Division did not imitate the action of the Italian 10th Army and remain on the defensive. Instead, it launched daily armoured and motorised raids across the Libyan frontier, which led the Italians to believe that their weapons were inferior. On June 20 Balbo wrote to Badoglio: "Our light tanks, already old and armed only with machine guns, are completely outclassed. The machine guns of the British armoured cars pepper them with bullets which pierce their armour easily. We have no armoured cars. Our anti-tank defences are largely a matter of make-do; our modern weapons lack adequate ammunition. Thus the conflict has taken on the character of steel against flesh, which only too easily explains certain episodes which are luckily of little importance."

There was nothing surprising about the failure of the Italian L-3-33/5 3-ton light tank in Libya, for the "sardine-can", as Franco's men had dubbed it, had cut a sorry figure as early as the Spanish Civil War. One is, however, surprised to read that on June 25 Badoglio announced to Balbo that 70 "magnificent" M-11 tanks were on their way to Libya. In fact this 11-ton tank could be knocked out by any gun with a calibre larger than 20-mm. The standard British anti-tank gun was the 2-pounder (40-mm), and no one in Italy could have been unaware of the fact.

On June 28, on hearing the news that French North Africa would remain loyal to the Government of Marshal Pétain, *Comando Supremo* ordered Balbo to invade Egypt with his total force, even if this meant "cannibalising" the 5th Army. But Balbo never got the order. On the same day he was shot down over Tobruk by his own gunners during the confusion of an alert.

Marshal Rodolfo Graziani, Army Chief-of-Staff, took over Balbo's command and mission, and D-Day was fixed for July 15, 1940.

In the post which he had just left, Graziani had constantly urged Balbo to take the initiative; but as soon as he arrived in Libya he too began to raise the same arguments against an advance which his predecessor had used. His task was not an easy one. There was only one supply-route across the desert between the Libyan frontier and Alexandria, on which were the British bases of Sidi Barrani and Marsa Matrûh. Graziani was not prepared to advance until he had received sufficient trucks and water tankers to supply his transport and the needs of the troops. Moreover, considering the heat of the African summer, he would have preferred to delay the conquest of Egypt until October.

But Mussolini would not hear of this. He wanted to launch the offensive on the same day as the first Germans landed in England. This led to painful scenes between Graziani and *Comando Supremo*, a visit by Graziani to Rome, and, on August 19, a peremptory telegram from Mussolini which concluded: "Marshal Graziani, as I have already told you since our last discussion, time is working against us. The loss of Egypt will be the *coup de grâce* for Great Britain, while the conquest of that rich country, necessary for our communications with Ethiopia, will be the great reward for which Italy is waiting. That you will procure it, I am certain."

Nevertheless, 10th Army's offensive did not get under way until September 13. Four divisions and an armoured group crossed the frontier, commanded by General Annibale Bergonzoli, C.-in-C. XXIII Corps. Difficult terrain, temperatures at times over 50 degrees Centigrade, sand storms, and anti-tank mines slowed the Italian advance to a bare 12½ miles per day. In the afternoon of September 16 the "23rd of March" Black Shirt Division occupied Sidi Barrani. This advance had cost the Italians 120 dead and 410 wounded; the British 7th Armoured Division, which had been ordered to fall back before the advance, had lost 50 men.

In taking Sidi Barrani, Graziani had covered 60 of the 315 miles between the Libyan frontier at Sollum and Alexandria, and was 75 miles from his next objective, Mersa Matrûh. But before moving on Matrûh Graziani was determined to halt until the damage done by the retreating British had been repaired; until the *Via Balbia*, the main road which ran across Libya along the coast, had been extended to Sidi Barrani, where the road to Alexandria began; to set up a fresh-water pipeline; and to stock Sidi Barrani with provisions, ammunition, and fuel. Graziani, a veteran colonial general, was entirely correct in taking all these precautions, for Wavell was hoping to see the Italian forces over-extend themselves by a premature dash on Matrûh.

Mussolini was disappointed by the pause in the offensive. But he consoled himself by reflecting that although the Italians had not passed Sidi Barrani, the Germans had not crossed the Channel.

Mussolini had nobody but himself to blame for the sluggishness and delays of Graziani. If Mussolini had not kept the greater part of the resources which had been released by the Franco-Italian armistice in Italy, things might have turned out very differently during the invasion of Egypt. But at the beginning of July he had decided to smash Yugoslavia, that "creation of Versailles" which had to disappear like the others.

As a result three armies, totalling some 37 divisions, were concentrated in north-eastern Italy. But Hitler was anxious that peace should not be disturbed in this corner of the Continent. On August 17 Ribbentrop, via Ambassador Dino Alfieri, informed Ciano of the Führer's opposition to any venture against Yugoslavia or Greece. Mussolini had to yield, but what was he to do with the armies which were now left without a mission? For reasons of economy, 600,000 soldiers were demobilised and sent home, to be remobilised a few weeks later.

In the summer of 1940, as far as circumstances permitted, the maritime honours went to the Royal Navy, which more than lived up to its aggressive tradition.

Is it fair to blame the Italian admirals for their lack of offensive spirit? They were certainly kept on a far shorter rein by the Italian High Command in Rome – *Supermarina* – than were their opponents. But one reason for *Supermarina*'s reticence was the early realisation that the Italian Air Force was not to be relied upon, whether for reconnaissance missions or for combat.

This was shown clearly during the action off Cape Spartivento on the Calabrian coast on July 9, 1940. The Italian fleet, under Admiral Campioni, was returning to base after having escorted an important convoy carrying troops and material to Benghazi. The British Mediterranean Fleet, under Admiral Cunningham, was also at sea; it was well informed about the movements of the Italian fleet, by aircraft operating from Malta and from the aircraft-carrier *Eagle*; and Cunningham planned to intercept the Italians during their return to Taranto.

Cunningham did not succeed, but the battleship *Warspite* managed to hit the Italian battleship *Giulio Cesare* at a range of 26,000 yards. Campioni broke away under the cover of a smoke screen, and Cunningham, having closed to within 25 miles of the Italian coast, also withdrew. On this occasion the Italian Air Force showed all its weaknesses; no dive-bombing or torpedo attacks were made during the encounter, and only one of the 1,000 bombs dropped scored a hit – on the cruiser *Gloucester*.

This inaccuracy did have its good side: it spared the Italian fleet from heavy losses, when Campioni's ships were enthusiastically bombed by the Savoia-Marchetti 79's of the Italian Air Force. On July 13 Ciano noted in his diary: "The real controversy in the matter of naval

An Italian damage control party checks the fires caused on the Cesare *after her clash with the* Warspite.

armament is not between us and the British, but between our Air Force and our Navy."

Nevertheless, Mussolini announced with a straight face that within three days half the British naval potential in the Mediterranean had been eliminated. On July 19 there was another encounter in the Antikithera Channel off the north-west coast of Crete. The Italian light cruisers *Bartolomeo Colleoni* and *Bande Nere*, which were heading for Leros in the Dodecanese, fell in with the Australian light cruiser *Sydney* and five destroyers. Hit in her engine-rooms, the *Colleoni* was immobilised and sunk by torpedoes, while the *Bande Nere* escaped. This was a clear indication of combat weaknesses of these light warships, in which protection had been sacrificed for the sake of speed.

In early August, however, the naval balance in the Mediterranean appeared to shift heavily in Italy's favour. The battleships *Littorio*, *Vittorio Veneto*, *Caio Duilio*, and *Andrea Doria* joined the Italian fleet. The first two were powerful, modern warships displacing over 41,000 tons, with a main armament of nine 15-inch guns and a top speed of 28 knots. The others were battleships which had been launched in 1913 and completely overhauled in the late 1930's. The two *Doria*-class battleships were each armed with ten 12.6-inch guns and could make 26 knots.

From its central position this formidable battle fleet outnumbered the combined squadrons of Admirals Somerville and Cunningham by six capital ships to five, the British squadrons being separated at opposite ends of the Mediterranean. The British still had a slight advantage in fire-power, but none of the battleships in the Mediterranean Fleet was faster than 24 knots. After the affair off Calabria, the British Admiralty sent to the eastern Mediterranean the battleship *Valiant* (fresh from a refit), the anti-aircraft cruisers *Calcutta* and *Coventry*, and, most important of all, the new aircraft-carrier *Illustrious*, which carried 34 aircraft, of which 12 were Fulmar fighters. With this reinforcement Cunningham's battle fleet could defend itself adequately against the Italian bombers. *Illustrious* and *Valiant* had the additional advantage of being equipped with radar.

Thus the Royal Navy had reacted promptly and skilfully: these new rein-forcements anchored at Alexandria on September 5.

During the operation the veteran air-craft-carrier *Argus*, having steamed to the south of Sardinia, flew off 12 Hurricanes to strengthen the threadbare defences of Malta. It is surprising to note that after the neutralisation of Bizerta with the signing of the armistice, the Italians had made no attempt to take Malta. The defences of the "island fortress" were piti-fully weak: there were only 68 light and heavy A.A. guns instead of the 156 guns which had been envisaged in a pre-war pro-gramme, and the one radar set on the island functioned only sporadically. When Italy entered the war on June 10 Malta's air defences consisted of five Swordfish torpedo-bombers and four Sea Gladiators; one of the latter was soon damaged beyond repair, and the remaining three were christened "Faith", "Hope", and "Charity". These were later joined by nine Swordfish and nine Hurricanes.

Admiral Cunningham had protested against the running-down of Malta's defences which the British Government and the Imperial General Staff had counte-nanced, but his complaints had not been taken up. London had decided that in the event of a war with Italy the Middle East theatre would be supplied by the sea route round the Cape of Good Hope. But in view of the timidity of *Comando Supremo* and the weaknesses of the Italian Air Force it was decided to restore to Malta the offensive rôle which had seemed impos-sible because of the menace of the bomber.

But to do this it would be necessary to proceed by very careful and easy stages while the defences of the island remained as weak as they were. Cunningham saw this very clearly. He wrote at the time: "If we are to avoid a serious threat to Malta itself, it appears necessary that in any given period the scale of attack drawn down should not be disproportionate to the state of the defences it has been possible to install. It is only logical therefore to expect the full weight of Italian attack if our light forces work effectively."

In the long run, the offensive action of the light surface forces and the bombers which would be based on Malta would depend on the parallel development of Malta's defences (fighters, anti-aircraft guns, and radar). This was obvious; it was confirmed by experience. But it did not appeal to Churchill, who reproached Cunningham on September 9 for not being sufficiently offensively minded.

Meanwhile, a local conflict with no direct connection with the war between the major powers was about to become a matter of great importance. Soon it would impinge upon the joint interests of Ger-many and Italy – with fateful results.

We have already mentioned that neither the Hungarian Regent, Admiral Horthy, the various governments at Budapest, or Hungarian national opinion had accepted the territorial restrictions imposed upon Hungary by the Treaty of Trianon in 1920. After Munich, Hungary had obtained sub-stantial frontier rectifications at the expense of Czechoslovakia; later, in March 1939, the Prague coup had enabled her to occupy and annex Sub-Carpathian Ruthenia. But Hungary had other claims to make, against both Yugoslavia and Rumania.

For many years the region of Transyl-vania had been a source of discord between Rumania and Hungary. With the defeat of Austria-Hungary in 1918, Hun-gary had been forced to cede Transyl-vania to Rumania, the latter country being one of the victorious Allies. It was a fair enough decision, considering that the majority of the population was Rumanian and that it had endured harsh treatment while under Hungarian rule. But along the bend of the Carpathians there was a compact bloc of Magyars, known as Szeklers or Sicules. There were around two million of them, and they were cut off from their fellow Magyars on the Danu-bian plain. When they became Rumanian citizens, they had no reason to be pleased with their change of nationality.

After the crushing of France, the Hungar-ian Government once again raised the question of Transylvania. But although King Carol II of Rumania and his Prime Minister, Gigurtu, were prepared to con-sider certain concessions, no complete agreement between the rival countries seemed possible. They would have gone to war but for the intervention of Hitler, who, as we have seen, feared the conse-quences of any outbreak of trouble in the Balkans, and Mussolini, who always tended to favour the cause of the Hun-garians. Rumania and Hungary submitted to Axis arbitration, which was presided over by Ciano and Ribbentrop in the Belvedere Palace in Vienna. On August 30, 1940, the Axis verdict was delivered.

Under the terms of the Axis arbitration, Rumania would retain the western part of Transylvania. Hungary recovered the region of the Szeklers, but in order to extend her 1920 frontier to the Moldavian Carpathians she was also granted territory occupied by some three million Rumanians, plus the important towns of Cluj and Oradea, which for the next four years were known by the Magyar names of Kolozsvar and Nagyvarad.

This high-handed partition of Transylvania still did not satisfy the Hungarian claims in full. On the other hand, coming as it did two months after the loss of Bessarabia and the Bukovina to Soviet Russia, it sparked off deep feelings of resentment among the Rumanians. On September 4 General Ion Antonescu seized power, forced King Carol to abdicate in favour of his son Prince Michael, and, taking the title of "Conducator", set up a dictatorship.

As Italy, of the two Axis partners, had always supported Hungary's cause, it was not surprising that both King Carol and Antonescu had thought it advisable to seek German patronage. Hitler was extremely anxious not to be cut off from the output of the Rumanian oil wells at Ploiești, and to safeguard them from possible Allied attempts at sabotage. As a result, he welcomed eagerly the request made to him by a Rumanian military mission which visited him on September 2. And on October 7, Lieutenant-General Hansen and his staff, together with the first elements of the 13th Motorised Division, arrived in Bucharest.

This move, coming as it did after the guarantee of territorial integrity which had been given to Rumania after the Vienna arbitration, could only be interpreted as a clear-cut anti-Soviet move by Hitler. Stalin and Molotov, however, showed no outward reaction. But the effect on Mussolini was totally different.

On October 12 Ciano visited Mussolini in the Palazzo Venezia. He found the Duce "indignant", claiming that the occupation of Rumania by German troops had had a very bad impression on Italian public opinion. He had made his decision. "Hitler always faces me with a *fait accompli*. This time I am going to pay him back in his own coin. He will find out from the papers that I have occupied Greece. In this way the equilibrium will be re-established."

No other decision of Mussolini's could have been more welcome to Ciano, who had always pressed for imperialist Italian policies in the eastern Mediterranean. Nevertheless he thought it necessary to ask if Mussolini had discussed the matter with Marshal Badoglio. "Not yet," he replied, "but I shall send in my resignation as an Italian if anyone objects to our fighting the Greeks."

On the 15th Badoglio and Roatta, appalled, heard of Mussolini's decision. Three weeks before, acting on his orders, they had demobilised 600,000 men. Now he was asking them to attack Greece within 12 days, D-Day being set as dawn on October 26.

Without objecting to the operation in principle, Badoglio undertook to attack with 20 Italian divisions on condition that the Bulgarians would undertake to tie down six to eight Greek divisions. But General Sebastiano Visconti-Prasca, commanding in Albania, only had eight Italian divisions under his orders. It would therefore be necessary to remobilise 12 more divisions, send them across the Adriatic, and set up the necessary depôts and reserves for them on the spot. Considering the inadequacies of the Albanian ports of Valona and Durazzo, all this needed at least three months.

Mussolini could not accept these arguments: everything suggested that such a delay would allow Hitler to interpose a new veto. Ciano, Jacomoni (Lieutenant-General of Albania), and Visconti-Prasca all supported the idea. During the discussions on October 15 at the Palazzo Venezia they destroyed the objections of Badoglio and Roatta; and they were backed by Admiral Cavagnari and General Pricolo, respectively Under-Secretary of State and Chief-of-Staff of the Navy, and Chief-of-Staff of the Air Force.

As Ciano saw it, the political situation was favourable. Neither Turkey nor Yugoslavia would support Greece, their ally in the Balkan Pact, and Bulgaria's attitude would be favourable to Italy. But above all, the political situation in Athens gave cause for reasonable optimism. Only the Court and the plutocracy remained hostile to Fascist Italy, and a well-organised system of bribery was laying the groundwork for a change of régime.

For his part, Jacomoni claimed that the entire population of Albania was anxious to settle accounts with Greece, its hereditary enemy. "One can even state," he declared proudly, "that the enthusiasm is so great that it [the Albanian people] has recently given signs of disillusionment that the war has not already begun." Asked to present his plan of operations,

The last moments of the Italian cruiser Bartolomeo Colleoni, *caught by the Australian cruiser* Sydney. *She was immobilised by the* Sydney *and then torpedoed on July 19, 1940.*

Visconti-Prasca declared that he foresaw no difficulty in opening the campaign with his current forces in Albania. Leaving a covering force on the Pindus Mountains on the eastern sector, he undertook to conquer Epirus in 10 to 15 days, throwing 70,000 Italians against 30,000 Greeks. Then, reinforced from Italy and from the Ionian Islands through the captured port of Préveza, he would march on Athens, whose fall would end the campaign before the close of the year.

Faced with these arguments, particularly the political explanations of Ciano and Jacomoni, Badoglio gave way. He contented himself with saying that the Peloponnese and Crete should be included as objectives, for otherwise the British would move in. He has been blamed—correctly – for the exaggerated military promises which he made. But at the time he had no idea of the extent to which the claims of Ciano and Jacomoni were totally mistaken.

Nevertheless, Mussolini granted his generals a deadline extension of two days; and he impressed on all parties that the whole affair was to be kept a strict secret from the Germans.

While the preliminary studies for an invasion of Soviet Russia were still under way, Hitler, on the urging of Grand-Admiral Raeder and the suspension of Operation "Sea Lion", was showing signs of interest in a strategic project which could have lessened the weakening effects of the "parallel war" and allowed the Axis partners to co-operate more directly in their fight against the common enemy. This was Operation "Felix", aimed at the conquest of Gibraltar.

If the Wehrmacht could establish itself on the Strait of Gibraltar it could close the Mediterranean to the Royal Navy and give the Italian fleet access to the Atlantic. It would also enable the Axis to put French North Africa, where Weygand had just installed himself, under pressure similar to that already being imposed on Unoccupied France. It would no longer be possible for Vichy France to fend off Hitler's demands by pleading the possible defection of Morocco, Algeria, and Tunisia.

Such an operation would require the co-operation of Spain. When it seemed likely that Hitler was about to invade Britain, the Spanish Government had raised the question of Spain's claims to Oran and the French zone of the Moroccan protectorate. In mid-September Serrano Suñer, Spanish Minister of the Interior and Franco's brother-in-law, met Hitler and Ribbentrop for a series of talks. According to his account, which, it is true, was written after the war, he was disappointed – not to say shaken – by the German reaction to these overtures.

Ciano's diary confirms Suñer's version. On October 1 it records "Serrano's colourful invectives against the Germans for their absolute lack of tact in dealing with Spain. Serrano is right." Hitler and Ribbentrop wanted the Atlantic coast of Morocco for Germany, plus an air and naval base in the Canary Isles. Moreover, they were still uncertain about the economic aid which Germany could send to Spain, for the moment she entered the war Spain would instantly be cut off from her important imports of cereals and fuel, and would then become dependent on Germany.

On October 4 the same question was raised at the Brenner Pass conference between Hitler, Mussolini, Ribbentrop, and Ciano. At the same time the eventual dispatch of a German armoured detachment to North Africa was discussed. But Mussolini, who was still waiting from day to day for Graziani to resume his offensive in Egypt, cold-shouldered the idea. In his opinion, Panzer troops should only be sent to North Africa after the third phase of the operation: when the Italian 10th Army moved east from Mersa Matrûh on Alexandria and Cairo. There can be no doubt, however, that he hoped to be able to avoid German help.

If the Italians had taken Cairo by October 22, Franco could well have acted very differently. As it was, on that day he met Hitler at Hendaye on the Spanish frontier. Franco believed that the war would in fact be a long one and that without firm guarantees of corn and fuel supplies it would only impose further bitter sacrifices on the Spanish people.

As Hitler continued to speak in general terms, affirming that Britain was already beaten, Franco turned down the invitation to enter the war on the day that the

Ribbentrop talks to Rumanian leaders Manoïlescu and Gafencu.

Wehrmacht attacked Gibraltar, provisionally set for January 10, 1941.

Interpreter Paul Schmidt was an eye-witness at this discussion. "To put it bluntly, I was most interested to hear Franco's reply to Hitler's declaration that from the jumping-off point of Gibraltar, Africa could be rid of the British by armoured troops." This was quite possible along the fringe of the great desert, said Franco, "but central Africa is protected against any large-scale land offensive by the desert belt, which defends it as the sea defends an island. I have fought a great deal in Africa and I am certain of it."

Schmidt's account continues: "Even Hitler's hopes of eventually conquering Britain might turn out to be hollow. Franco thought it possible that the British Isles could be conquered. But if this happened the British Government and fleet would carry on the struggle from Canada, with American aid.

"While Franco talked on in a calm, monotonous, sing-song voice like an Arabic muezzin, Hitler began to grow more and more restless. The discussion was clearly fraying his nerves. At one stage he even got up and said that further discussion would be useless, but he soon sat down and continued his attempt to change Franco's mind. Franco declared that he was prepared to conclude a treaty but, in view of the supplies of food and armaments Hitler was prepared to offer from the moment Spain went to war, that the offer was only a hollow sham."

Franco was using the technique which can loosely be described as "yes, but", and it was not at all to the liking of Hitler. Ribbentrop, too, was receiving the same treatment from Serrano Suñer, who had only lately become the Spanish Minister of Foreign Affairs. Ribbentrop's latest proposal had not been well received by Suñer: "Spain will receive territories from the French colonial empire, for which France can be compensated in equal measure by territories from the

British colonial empire."

This was very different to what had been said to Suñer during his visit to Berlin; but Ribbentrop, too, was infuriated by the caution of the Spaniards. Schmidt, who flew to Montoire with Ribbentrop, has described him as "fuming with rage", and spending the journey in invective against "that ungrateful rogue" Franco and "that Jesuit" Suñer.

If Hitler's meeting with Franco at Hendaye was a definite setback for German policies, his meeting with Pétain at Montoire did nothing to compensate for it. Hitler wanted to induce the Vichy French Government to go to war with Britain. Pétain, however, left Hitler in no doubt as to his refusal to allow France to be drawn into a war with her former ally, even on the pretext of reconquering the colonies which had gone over to de Gaulle.

Once again, Schmidt has provided an account of the Montoire meeting.

"As darkness fell on October 24, 1940, it was difficult at first to tell the victor from the vanquished in the feeble lights on the platform of the little station. Standing very straight, despite his great age, in his plain uniform, Pétain put out his hand to the dictator with an almost royal gesture, while fixing him with a quizzical, icy, and penetrating glance. I knew how he felt about Hitler, Göring, and other prominent National Socialists. To most Germans he himself stood for all the military virtues of France, and this was very clear in Hitler's attitude when they met. He was no longer the triumphal victor shown by certain photographs of 1940. Nor was he a corporal intimidated in the presence of a marshal, as certain French publications have since claimed. He behaved without haughtiness and without harshness.

"With a gesture, Hitler invited the Marshal to enter his railway car. I myself was seated before Pétain and was admirably placed to observe him throughout

the talk. His complexion, which had seemed pale to me on the platform, became faintly pink. No emotion or interior tension could be seen behind his mask of impassivity. Ribbentrop, a mute and almost tolerated witness, together with Laval, who was wearing his inevitable white tie, assisted the conversation.

"Pétain listened in silence. Not once did he offer a single friendly word for Hitler or for Germany.

"His attitude conveyed a vaguely haughty impression, rising above the situation of France in this autumn of 1940."

But Hitler had hardly left Montoire when a message from the German Ambassador in Rome threw him into the deepest consternation: his ally was on the brink of invading Greece. In the hope of staving off this dangerous venture, he went straight to Italy instead of returning to Berlin. At 1000 hours on October 28, he was greeted at the station in Florence by Mussolini, all smiles, who announced: "Führer, we are on the march! At dawn this morning our Italian troops victoriously crossed the Albanian-Greek frontier!"

Koritsa, Taranto, and Sidi Barrani were three decisive defeats for Italian arms which severely darkened the prospects of the Axis. They gave the suppressed peoples of Western Europe their first glimmer of hope since June 25, 1940. From the moment the attack began, Mussolini and Ciano watched while the political assumptions on which the war with Greece had been founded began to collapse. They already knew that King Boris of Bulgaria would stay on the sidelines until events had run their course. They had grossly underestimated the patriotism of the Greek nation, which closed its ranks under the feeble Italian bombing raids when it heard that King George II and the Prime Minister, General Joannis Metaxas, had indignantly rejected the Italian ultimatum and had immediately decreed general mobilisation.

The fact was that Italy was violently unpopular in Greece. Quite apart from the historical legacy of the Venetian rule in Crete, the Morea, and the Ionian Islands, the Fascist methods brought to bear on the people of Rhodes and the Dodecanese by Count Cesare de Vecchi had resulted in the unanimous hostility of all sectors of Greek opinion against Mussolini, his régime, and his country.

General mobilisation gave the Greek commander, General Alexandros Papagos, 15 infantry divisions, four infantry brigades, and a cavalry division, formed into five army corps. On paper the Greek divisions were definitely inferior to the Italian divisions, but this disparity was largely balanced by the chronic difficulties of the terrain and of communications, which favoured the defenders.

In the Italian plan the initial assault would be carried out by four divisions attacking in Epirus, with another two

divisions covering the main attack by advancing against the Morova massif. Visconti-Prasca planned a breakthrough which would surprise Papagos before he could concentrate his forces. But the weather was on the side of the Greeks: the Italians crossed the frontier in torrential rain which converted every brook into a torrent and every road into a sea of clinging mud. In these conditions the demolitions carried out by the Greeks added still further to the slowing-up of the Italian advance.

Nevertheless, Visconti-Prasca's left-hand column, formed by the "Julia" Alpine Division, broke through the advanced Greek positions, then their main position, pushed up the Aóos valley and took the village of Vovoússa on November 2. Here the division found itself at the foot of the important Métzovon pass, crossed by the Lárisa–Yanina road, having covered some 25 miles of mountain terrain under an icy rain. On the following day a Greek counter-attack down from the heights forced the Italians into a retreat that was as hasty as it was disastrous.

In the centre, the 23rd "Ferrana" Infantry Division and the 131st "Centauro" Armoured Division, which had Yanina as their first objective, were held up by the Greek forward positions and completely halted by their main position, largely as a result of the action fought by the Greek 8th Division, acting as covering force.

In the coastal sector, the "Siena" Division was luckier. It took Filiates, crossed the raging River Thíamis, and reached Paramithia with the intention

Greek soldiers: they possessed a fighting spirit second to none.

of encircling the Greek position at Yanina. At sea, appalling conditions forced *Comando Supremo* to abandon its projected amphibious operation against Corfu, while bad weather prevented the Italian Air Force from bringing its superiority to bear.

The Italians had lost all the advantage of surprise: the Italian bombers were not able to slow down the mobilisation and concentration of the Greek forces; and all the weaknesses of the plan adopted on the recommendation of Visconti-Prasca were now obvious. By November 12 General Papagos had at the front over 100 infantry battalions fighting in terrain to which they were accustomed, compared with less than 50 Italian battalions.

Visconti-Prasca was dismissed on November 9 and was replaced by General Ubaldo Soddu, Under-Secretary of State for War and Deputy Chief-of-Staff of the Army. He now found two armies under his command: on the right, General Carlo Gelosa's 11th Army, and on the left General Mario Vercellino's 9th Army. But until the remobilised divisions could be shipped across the Adriatic these units were armies only in name.

On the Greek side, General Papagos did not content himself with the success of his defensive strategy; in this war, with 45 million Italians attacking seven million Greeks, a "wait and see" policy would have been tantamount to an admission of defeat. Papagos determined to exploit the errors committed by the Italians and to counter-attack before the enormous numerical and material superiority of the Italian Army could be brought into play. On November 14 the Greek Army went over to the offensive along the entire front from Lake Prespa to the Ionian sea.

On the Greek right, V Corps under General Tzolakoglou, fielding at first three and finally five divisions, broke through at Mount Morova and after eight days' fighting had destroyed the Italian 9th Army at Koritsa, taking 2,000 prisoners, 80 field guns, 55 anti-tank guns and 300 machine guns from the "Tridentina" Mountain Division and the "Arezzo", "Parma", and "Piemonte" Infantry Divisions. This brilliant success was exploited further to the north, and on December 4 the Greek III Corps occupied Pogradec on Lake Ohrida.

On November 21 the II Corps under General Papadopoulos also crossed the Albanian frontier, despite the formidable obstacle of the Grámmos massif, and took Ersekë and Leskovik. This gave the Greek High Command an excellent front between the Koritsa plateau and the valley of the Aóos. On December 5, a gallant action gave the II Corps Përmet, 23 miles inside Albania. On the left, the I Corps under General Kosmas crossed the Thíamis on the heels of the retreating 11th Army. Pushing down the Dhrin valley, the Greek advance guards were greeted enthusiastically by the population of Argyrokastron – which says much for the deep Albanian feelings of loyalty towards Italy which Jacomoni had described to Mussolini. Two days before, the left-flank division under General Kosmas had taken Sarandë, formerly Santi Quaranta, which the Italian Fascist régime had rechristened Porto Edda.

After December 5 the Greek offensive began to peter out. The Greek Army's lack of tanks and its poverty in anti-tank weapons forced it to shun the plains and valleys in its attacks, and so the excellent Greek infantrymen concentrated on the mountain heights for their operations. But by the beginning of December temperatures in the mountains were falling as low as 15 and even 20 degrees Centigrade below zero, and these were rendered even more unbearable by severe snowstorms.

Lacking tanks, lacking even sufficient transport vehicles, the Greeks now began to experience the sufferings of their enemy. The British had no material which they could spare for their new allies. On the other hand, no less than eight Italian divisions had been shipped to Albania between October 28 and the end of December. Far too often, however, the demands of the front led General Soddu to use up his reinforcements piecemeal to plug local breakthroughs. But quite apart from this, the supply of Italian reinforcements was badly organised.

However, the comparatively rapid supply of Italian reinforcements only raised fresh problems with regard to their supplies. On December 4 the Quarter-master-General, Scuero, described the depôt and magazine supplies as almost completely exhausted.

No one could deny the victor's laurels to the Greek soldier. But under conditions like these one can only say that the Italian soldier had earned the martyr's crown a thousand times over.

Meanwhile, the British Mediterranean Fleet had struck as deadly a blow as the Greek Army. From the moment when the aircraft-carrier *Illustrious* joined his command, Cunningham detected a certain lack of offensive spirit in the Italian squadron based on Taranto. This led to the preparation of a British torpedo-bombing attack: Operation "Judgement".

The first idea of Rear-Admiral Lyster, commanding the British carrier force in the Mediterranean, had been to attack on the night of October 21, the anniversary of Trafalgar; but an accident aboard *Illustrious* forced him to postpone "Judgement" until November 11, when the phase of the moon would next favour the venture. Then he had to operate without the aircraft-carrier *Eagle*, which transferred some of her Swordfish aircraft to *Illustrious*, however. Despite all this, Cunningham put to sea on November 6 to co-operate with a sortie by Force H, which was escorting the battleship *Barham* on its journey to the eastern Mediterranean.

On the evening of November 11 an air reconnaissance from Malta carried out by Martin Marylands and Short Sunderlands established that all six of the Italian battleships were in port. Having steamed to within 190 miles of Taranto, Lyster flew off his 21 Swordfish in two waves. Eleven of them were fitted with torpedoes and the other ten with bombs and flares.

Several circumstances favoured the attackers. A few days before, a heavy storm had driven down several balloons

An Italian mountain soldier on the Greek front.

A Swordfish releases its torpedo.
By 1941 the Swordfish was obsolete,
any successes owing much to the
courage of the crews.

from the barrage protecting the Taranto anchorage. The anti-torpedo nets surrounding the warships only extended 26 feet down while the British torpedoes, set to detonate either on contact or by magnetic proximity, ran at 30 feet. Finally, when the alert was sounded, the Italians did not activate the harbour smokescreens, in order not to impair the fire of the anti-aircraft guns. Nevertheless, the Fleet Air Arm crews needed all their dash and gallantry to penetrate the fire of the 21 100-mm batteries and the 200 light A.A. guns, quite apart from the guns aboard the warships, mark their targets, and drop their torpedoes accurately.

Eleven torpedoes were launched, and six scored hits: three on the *Littorio*, two on the *Duilio*, and one on the *Cavour*. The last Swordfish returned to *Illustrious* at about 0300 hours. The British lost only two aircraft. In reply, the Italian land batteries alone had fired some 8,500 shells. Of the aircraft crews, one was killed and three others were taken prisoner. *Littorio*

and *Duilio* were out of action for the next six months and needed considerable repairs. The older *Cavour* was raised, towed from Taranto to Trieste, and abandoned there. Until the summer of 1941 *Supermarina*'s battle fleet was reduced to three battleships, which permitted Admiral Cunningham to release the elderly British battleships *Ramillies* and *Malaya* for much-needed escort duties on the Atlantic convoy routes.

This series of disasters caused near chaos in the Italian High Command. Refusing to put the blame where it belonged – on his own vanity – Mussolini decided to make a scapegoat of Marshal Badoglio. But as the Commander-in-Chief of the Italian Armed Forces could hardly level a public indictment against his own Chief of General Staff, Mussolini opened his campaign against Badoglio with a vicious editorial aimed at the Marshal by Roberto Farinacci, editor of the official paper *Regime Fascista*. Badoglio demanded a public retraction of this allegation that he was not only incompetent but had also betrayed Mussolini's trust by ignorance or deliberate treachery. When he was refused all satisfaction, Badoglio resigned on November 26.

General Ugo Cavallero stepped into his place. Apart from the torrent of defamation poured on his character in Ciano's diary, it must be said that Cavallero was a much-discussed figure among his fellow generals, and that a period of involvement in the arms industry had not added to his prestige. Admiral Cavagnari was dismissed as head of *Supermarina* and Under-Secretary of State for the Navy and was replaced by Admiral Arturo Riccardi, a fact which publicly branded the former as the man responsible for the Taranto fiasco. Finally, de Vecchi resigned and was replaced by General Ettore Bastico as Governor of the Aegean.

Although Hitler was infuriated by the disasters which his friend and ally had brought down on himself, the interests of the Reich nevertheless made it essential for the Wehrmacht to retrieve the situation. On November 18, at the Berghof, Hitler made himself clear to Ciano: he had only sent German troops into Rumania to safeguard the Ploieşti oil wells from Soviet machinations, and now they would be within range of R.A.F. bombers if the British set up air bases in Greece. He therefore proposed to invade Greece via Bulgaria, and set the provisional date at around March 15.

But this new plan of Hitler's meant that Mussolini must reverse his entire policy towards Yugoslavia. Instead of the aggressive attitude which Mussolini had always kept up, it was now essential to bring Yugoslavia into the Axis. Ciano, however, had reservations about the political decisions which governed Hitler's military intervention in the Balkans. It was clear to him that from now on Italy would not be waging a war aimed at her own interests, and that the future relations between Mussolini and Hitler would be those of vassal and lord.

The day after Ciano's departure from Berchtesgaden, Hitler and Ribbentrop put their cards on the table before the Spanish Foreign Minister, Serrano Suñer. On November 12 Hitler had ordered the preliminary moves for Operation "Felix", which was to capture Gibraltar. It was vital to waste no further time in establishing Franco's final intentions.

Suñer restated the arguments which had been put forward at Hendaye. The capture of Gibraltar, he declared, would not pay full dividends until the Italians had taken Port Said, the key to the other entrance to the Mediterranean. Moreover, Spain would need nearly 400,000 tons of cereals and two months to prepare for war. For all his powers of persuasion, Hitler failed to get Suñer to modify this point of view. Suñer left the Berghof without having accepted anything, but – and this was probably even more important – without having issued a flat refusal.

The Italian defeats at Koritsa and Taranto had certainly done much to influence Franco's decision. In less than a month, the further defeat at Sidi Barrani would confirm the Caudillo in his policy of non-belligerence.

CHAPTER 16
Italy's North African empire crumbles

In December 1940 Wavell not only abandoned the defensive to which he had been confined since June 25, but launched an offensive which won such a total success that Hitler was forced to send yet more German forces to help his tottering ally, now facing ruin only six months after his entry into the war. Wavell was also helped immeasurably in that his opponent Graziani made a considerable contribution to the defeat of his own forces.

Certain aspects of this episode would still be unknown were it not for the surprising information contained in the memoirs of Sir Anthony Eden. He was Secretary of State for War at the time, and what he has to say on the preparation for Wavell's attack on Sidi Barrani throws a very different light on the story told by Churchill's *The Second World War*.

"A good average colonel and would make a good chairman of a Tory association." That was how Churchill described Wavell after a visit by the latter to London between August 8–15, 1940. Worse still, he did not feel in him, as he wrote to Eden, "the sense of mental vigour and resolve to overcome obstacles, which was indispensable to successful war." Moreover, Churchill's readiness to scrutinise Wavell's dispositions, "to move this battalion here and that battalion there." left Wavell "clearly upset". He even considered offering his resignation.

In *The Second World War* Churchill chose to play down this clash, in which he was proved utterly wrong by the course of events. But whatever one thinks of Churchill's account, written years after the event, nothing can detract from the heroic decision he made at the time. Thirty days before the invasion which was anticipated for mid-September 1940, it was decided to weaken the British Home Forces in order to reinforce Wavell's command in Egypt.

In all there were three tank regiments (154 armoured vehicles), 48 anti-tank guns, 48 25-pounder field guns, and other infantry weapons which Churchill wanted to send to Egypt through the Mediterranean. As the Admiralty refused to accept responsibility, the risk being too great, these reinforcements were sent out round the Cape. On September 19 they entered the Red Sea, finding no challenge from the Italian naval forces based on Massawa. The British air forces in the Middle East were also being reinforced. Between the end of August and the end of December 1940, Hurricane fighters and Blenheim and Wellington bombers were taken by sea to the Gold Coast and flown across Africa by devious stages to Khartoum on the Nile. When French Equatorial Africa, and particularly the important staging-post of Fort Lamy, went over to de Gaulle's cause, it became possible to build up the Takoradi air route into a key supply line.

"What would happen if the Italians were not to attack?" asked Eden on October 15,

when he visited Wavell in Cairo. By way of reply Wavell brought in General Sir Henry Maitland Wilson, commanding the British forces in Egypt, and asked him to explain to Eden the plan of attack – or rather of strategic envelopment – which had been prepared against the Italian forces dug in at Sidi Barrani.

At this time, it should be noted the Italian attack on Greece had led to more tension between London and G.H.Q. Cairo. The British War Cabinet demanded effective aid for the Greeks; and very unwillingly, as their own resources were weak, Wavell and Air Chief-Marshal Sir Arthur Longmore, Air Officer Commanding Mediterranean and Middle East, agreed to send 63 fighters and 46 bombers to Greece in two months.

There was equal friction and conflict of interests between Rome and Tripoli. Mussolini was pressing Graziani to march on Mersa Matrûh without further delay, while Graziani wanted to wait until he had been supplied with three more motorised battalions, with armoured cars, and with water trucks. Exasperated, Mussolini warned Graziani on October 21 that if any further objections were raised he would not hesitate to accept Graziani's resignation. Nothing came of this, doubtless because of the catastrophe on the Greek front.

The Greek venture and its disastrous results for Italy rebounded as far as the Western Desert, for the emergency transport of supplies to the Albanian front which it necessitated cut down the reserves of mobile forces which might reasonably have been sent to North Africa before the resumption of the campaign. Thus Mussolini's share of the blame for the defeat of December 9 was great, but it did not excuse the mistakes of Graziani, Berti, and Gariboldi.

The Italian 10th Army was deployed in two main groups in fortified camps, the groups being separated by a 15-mile gap in their centre – a fundamentally unsound plan whose weakness the British command proposed to exploit. The coastal group of camps – Maktila, Tummar East and Tummar West, and Nibeiwa – were garrisoned by the 1st and 2nd Libyan Divisions and a mixed force including tanks under General Maletti, while the 4th Blackshirt Division lay to the rear in Sidi Barrani. The inland group of camps – Rabia and the three Sofafis, East, Northwest and North-east – were held by the "Cirene" Division. Further to the rear, between Sofafi and Halfaya lay the 62nd "Marmarica" Division. West of the Nibeiwa-Rabia gap in the Italian centre the 64th "Catanzero" was now taking up its position.

The British plan was daring and imaginative. After a secret approach march in the open desert, Lieutenant-General Sir Richard O'Connor's Western Desert Force would penetrate through

the gap in the Italian centre, swing north and attack the Italian coastal group of camps from the rear, beginning with Nibeiwa. While this attack was going in, 7th Armoured Division with its fast-moving cruiser tanks, would advance towards Buqbuq on the coast in order to cut Italian communications and prevent any help reaching the enemy forward positions. A secondary attack would be launched by a brigade under Brigadier A. R. Selby on the coastal camp at Maktila. The British force numbered only 36,000 men, but in training fighting spirit and armoured strength it was vastly superior to the Italian enemy.

Although Italian air reconnaissance had reported signs of increased British motor traffic in the Western Desert during November, the Italian command had interpreted this as evidence that the British were either relieving forward units or strengthening their defences against a further Italian advance. When at dawn on December 9 O'Connor's troops struck through the gap in the enemy centre, it was a total surprise.

The 4th Indian Division and the Matilda tank battalion attacked Nibeiwa, which was defended by the Maletti Motorised Group. Surprise was complete, for the uproar of the artillery and air bombardment drowned the noise of engines and tank tracks, and the British were attacking from the south-west and even from the west. Badly wounded, General Maletti fought on until he was killed at the head of his troops, but by 0830 it was all over. For the price of 56 dead, Major-General Beresford-Peirse, commanding 4th Indian Division, had taken 2,000 prisoners.

Encamped at Tummar, General Pescatori of the 2nd Libyan Division planned to march to the sound of the guns as soon as the British attack began. But 4th Indian Division and the Matildas saved him the trouble. Thrown back, Pescatori counter-attacked with spirit, but his forces were broken up by crushing British artillery fire. Tummar West fell in the afternoon while Tummar East did not surrender until dawn on the 10th.

In the evening of December 9, Brigadier J. A. L. Caunter's 7th Armoured Division reached the sea, cutting off the retreat of the survivors of the 2nd Libyan Division. Facing Sidi Barrani, Selby Force had thrown General Sibille's 1st Libyan Division (not without some trouble) out of its position at Maktila. The Italian pocket thus formed at Maktila was cleaned up with the assistance of British naval bombardment by the evening of the 11th.

During the same day Graziani ordered XXI Corps to fall back immediately to the Halfaya–Sollum–Capuzzo line on the frontier. The "Cirene" Division got the order in time and fell back without trouble. But this was not the case with General Spinelli's "Catanzaro" Division, thanks to an error in transmission. It was caught on the move between Buqbuq and Sollum and half annihilated.

This last defeat raised the losses of the Italian 10th Army to 38,000 prisoners, 237 guns, and 73 tanks, while the British losses amounted to only 624 killed, wounded, and missing. But O'Connor's force had no sooner won this glorious and virtually painless victory than it was seriously weakened by the withdrawal of the excellent 4th Indian Division, which was earmarked for the campaign against the Italians in Eritrea.

The 6th Australian Division (Major-General I. G. Mackay) replaced 4th Indian Division in XIII Corps. But General O'Connor did not wait for its arrival before launching an all-out pursuit against the beaten and disorganised Italian forces. On December 14 he crossed the frontier south of Capuzzo, swung his armoured and motorised forces to the north, and invested Bardia on the 18th. The Bardia perimeter, 24 miles in extent, was defended by General Bergonzoli's XXIII Corps, with the survivors of the "Catanzaro" and "Cirene" Divisions from Egypt, General Tracchia's "Marmarica" Division, and General Antonelli's "23rd of March" Black Shirt Division – a total force of 45,000 men and 430 guns.

On December 18, General Mackay's 6th Australian Division joined XIII Corps. Prospects for the Axis darkened with the fall of Bardia right at the beginning of 1941; not even the first major fire raid on London on the night of December 30–31 did much to redress the balance. In the occupied or threatened countries of Europe there was a widespread feeling that the defeat of Mussolini would only be a matter of time, and that that of Hitler would follow.

But in view of the military weakness of Great Britain and her Empire, this was very far from the truth . . .

By mid-December 1940 Germany could no longer ignore the successive land and sea defeats inflicted on the Italian forces in 1940 in Albania, at Taranto, and in

Bren-gun carriers advance on Derna

Libya. If the grave consequences of the military crisis precipitated by Mussolini were not eliminated promptly and efficiently, the Germans feared that a political crisis would also ensue, and bring about the downfall of the only man in Italy who had Hitler's confidence.

The disturbing after-effects of the Duce's defeats were already apparent. On November 11 a parade of students, all carrying symbolical rods, had marched down the Champs-Elysées in Paris under the gaze of a sympathetic crowd. A little later, at Menton on the Franco-Italian frontier, placards appeared with the message; "This is French territory; Greeks, don't pursue the Italians past this point." But the most alarming incident took place at Vichy on December 13, when Pierre Laval was ousted from power by military force. Now there was considerable apprehension in German circles that General Weygand would throw in his lot with the Allies: he had already been appointed Delegate General of the French Government in French North Africa on October 3, with authority over Algeria, Tunisia, Morocco, and Senegal.

Hitler had no intention of being taken unawares. On December 10 he signed his Directive No. 19, which ordered Brauchitsch, Raeder, and Göring to take all necessary steps for the annexation of Unoccupied France. For this purpose, one column was to march from the region of Dijon down the valleys of the Saône and the Rhône, occupy Marseilles and then move towards Béziers, where it would join up with a column coming from Bordeaux via Toulouse and Narbonne. Two Panzer and four motorised divisions would take part in this operation, which was given the appropriate code-name "Attila". In addition, the Luftwaffe and German Navy were ordered to prevent the French fleet from leaving Toulon.

But it was doubtful whether the annexation of the Unoccupied Zone would have made up for the reappearance of North Africa as a factor in the war. If a new Franco-British front had been formed between Alexandria and Agadir, Italy's

position, already critical, would have become almost desperate.

But meanwhile, in Albania, the Italians could rely on the bad weather of the winter and the rough conditions in the mountains to halt the impetus of the Greek counter-offensive. In the spring the Germans could therefore launch Operation "Marita", which would employ the German 12th Army (Field-Marshal List) and *Panzergruppe* Kleist, totalling five corps, made up of four Panzer divisions, one motorised division, two mountain divisions, and ten infantry divisions. In Libya, on the other hand, the débâcle at Sidi Barrani stressed the need for immediate action.

For this reason the Luftwaffe's X *Fliegerkorps* was sent south to bases in Sicily at the end of December 1940. Apart from its reconnaissance and fighter formations it consisted of two *Gruppen* of Junkers Ju 87 dive-bombers and two *Gruppen* of Ju 88 twin-engined bombers. The X *Fliegerkorps* was under the command of Luftwaffe General Geissler, who had harassed Allied shipping in Norwegian waters earlier in the year; its mission now was to close the Mediterranean to the British between Sicily and Tunisia and to engage in combat the British aircraft based on Malta. On January 10, 1941, X *Fliegerkorps* opened its account by launching heavy attacks against the British aircraft-carrier *Illustrious*.

On the 11th, Hitler issued 13 copies of his Directive No. 22: "German support for battles in the Mediterranean area". The introduction was worded as follows: "The situation in the Mediterranean area, where England is employing superior forces against our allies, requires that Germany should assist for reasons of strategy, politics, and psychology.

"Tripolitania must be held and the danger of a collapse on the Albanian front must be eliminated. Furthermore the Cavallero Army Group [in Albania] must be enabled, in co-operation with the later operations of 12th Army, to go over to the offensive from Albania."

Hitler therefore ordered O.K.H. to form "a special detachment [*Sperrverband*] sufficient to render valuable service to our allies in the defence of Tripolitania, particularly against British armoured divisions."

The preparations for the intervention of a German mountain division in Albania came to nothing: Mussolini actually declined its services. However, Operation *Sonnenblume* ("Sunflower"), which led to the creation of the *Afrika Korps*, went ahead.

It was intended to engage a German force in the defence of Tripoli, not to launch it on a campaign to conquer Egypt and seize the Suez Canal. The decision was taken because the German High Command curiously overestimated the strength of the British. The Germans took the assessment of their allies at face value: in fact, the Italians believed that Wavell had 17 full strength divisions, with another four in the process of embarking

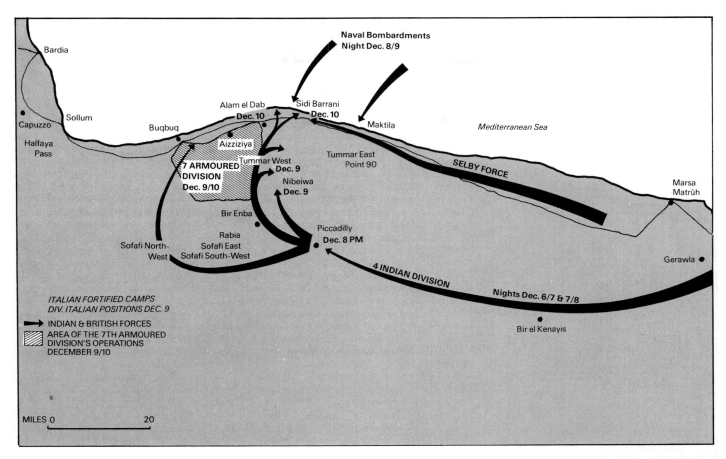

in Britain, and at least 1,100 aircraft.

Meanwhile, the German plans to seize the Rock of Gibraltar for the Axis were nearing completion. Field-Marshal von Reichenau was to command the operation, which was code-named "Felix". He had under his command two Panzer divisions, three motorised divisions, and a mountain division, supported by the Luftwaffe's VIII *Fliegerkorps*–eight Stuka *Gruppen*, two fighter *Gruppen*, and five reconnaissance squadrons. The question of Portugal remained to be settled; if, contrary to Hitler's expectations, President Salazar appealed to Britain, Reichenau's forces would leave their planned route (Irun-Burgos-Seville) at Cáceres and head for Lisbon.

The assault on Gibraltar was to be entrusted to the XLIX *Gebirgskorps* (General Kübler). According to the calculations of General Brand, head of artillery at O.K.H., the fortress had 154 guns, including 56 A.A. guns; and the neck of land connecting the Rock to the mainland was exposed to the fire of 14 guns in concrete casemates. General Kübler was therefore to be given about 50 heavy batteries with 8,500 tons of ammunition to strengthen his normal quota of artillery. In addition the Germans were planning to use hitherto untried weapons for this operation, including *"Mörser Karl"*: a self-propelled tracked vehicle with a 60-cm (23½-inch) mortar, which fired a 2.2-ton armour-piercing shell over a range of about 4½ miles. This huge 132-ton vehicle was powered by a 580-hp engine, and therefore had a certain mobility. Moreover, in his diary Halder

several times mentions a plan to cause explosions in the Rock's galleries.

Supported by this powerful artillery force and by General von Richthofen's Stukas, General Hubert Lanz's division would launch the final attack on the fortress. On the right the *Grossdeutschland* motorised regiment would take the port of Gibraltar with the help of assault-boats; on the left the 98th *Gebirgsjäger* Regiment (mountain troops) would capture the Rock, whose summit towers 1,400 feet above sea level.

Operation "Felix" would be completed when coastal batteries (15-cm and 24-cm) had been established at Ceuta and Tarifa, commanding the strait, while a Panzer division and a motorised division were sent into Spanish Morocco. Weygand and Pétain, it was confidently believed, would be powerless to intervene.

Admiral Canaris, head of the *Abwehr*, was instructed to go to Madrid at the end of December 1940 to explain Hitler's intention to Franco and to ask him to open the Spanish frontier on January 10; Reichenau would then be able to launch the attack on Gibraltar on February 8. Once again, however, Franco fell back on his previously-stated conditions; and on February 12 Mussolini, who had been charged by Hitler with the task of getting Franco to declare himself openly, was also unsuccessful in his mission when he met the Caudillo at Bordighera in Italy.

It should be stressed that Mussolini pleaded Hitler's case extremely gently. He told Franco what he had said to Hitler:

Wavell's attack took the Italian defences of Sidi Barrani in the flank and put the British on the Libyan border.

"I'll talk, but I won't exert any pressure"; and this was hardly likely to persuade Franco to take the decisive step. Moreover, Mussolini seemed to be offering a loop-hole which Franco was quick to take. According to the official Italian record of the meeting, Mussolini stated:

"The Duce reminds the Caudillo that he had always shown great discretion and consideration for the attitude of Spain. [This was a veiled criticism of Hitler.] He agrees with the Caudillo's view that Spain cannot remain neutral, but he believes that the timing and manner of Spain's entry into the war is entirely her own affair. Participation in war is too serious a matter for it to be precipitated by outside influences."

To explain Mussolini's strange behaviour one can only hazard a few guesses. It seems safe to assume that he did not want Operation "Felix" to be successful. If Gibraltar fell, Germany would replace Britain as the master of the western entrance to the Mediterranean; and Mussolini had laid down the neutralisation of the Strait of Gibraltar as one of Fascist Italy's war aims.

Hitler received an Italian memorandum giving the rather negative results of the interview, and on February 28 he noted Franco's evasion, which showed the classic skill of a bullfighter. Resentfully, Hitler stated to Mussolini:

"In any case the outcome of the Spaniards' lengthy chattering and their

Dishevelled Italian prisoners taken near Tobruk plod towards the British lines in January, 1941.

written explanations is that Spain doesn't want to go to war and will not do so. This is extremely irksome because for the moment the opportunity to strike England in the simplest manner possible, in her Mediterranean possessions, is lost."

This may well have been the case, but clearly the continued run of Italian defeats in Libya encouraged Franco to go on waiting.

The Italians did make some half-hearted attempts to put pressure on Spain to take an active part in Operation "Felix". An example is the following passage from a letter from Ciano to Suñer on June 3, 1941–particularly the curious postscript in which Mussolini left Franco an easy way out:
"My dear Ramon,
I am writing to you on my return from the meeting at the Brenner. I am sure you will be pleased to hear that both we and the Germans discussed Spanish matters with great interest, and that the Axis powers regard their friendship with your country as a matter of vital importance.

"The events of recent weeks are of great significance in the conduct of the war. The Balkans have now been cleared of British influence. The British Navy has lost many of its bases and is being caught in an increasingly closing vice by the Axis forces. A day will come–it's not far off–when the Mediterranean will be free of the presence of the British fleet. Can Nationalist, Falangist Spain remain indifferent and neutral in the face of these events which have such great significance for our lives and for the future of the Mediterranean countries? As a sincere and well-tried friend of Spain, I don't think so." A further plea by Ciano follows, and then the Duce's final, modest entreaty: "Spain must *at least* join the Tripartite Pact, and before other countries do so at that. In subscribing to the Tripartite Pact, Spain will be in a position to influence the future settlement of Europe."

On January 10, 1941, the British Western Desert Force was designated XIII Corps with its commander, Lieutenant-General O'Connor, directly responsible to G.H.Q. Middle East instead of to the G.O.C.-in-C. British troops in Egypt as heretofore. This simplified the chain of command and facilitated O'Connor's offensive into Libya. But unfortunately, the conflicting demands for men and material were to deprive the battle-hardened XIII corps of much of its efficiency.

On the 1st, XIII Corps was preparing to attack the fortress of Bardia, which was protected by a fortified perimeter 18 miles long. Small forts had been built at a distance of about 800 yards from each other along this perimeter, which consisted of an anti-tank ditch 13 feet wide and about 4 feet deep, behind which was a barbed-wire network and minefields. Behind this perimeter, which had been carefully strengthened along its southern face, was another defensive position.

Lieutenant-General Annibale Bergonzoli, commander of the Italian XXIII Corps, had been entrusted with the defence of Bardia in an urgent telegram from Mussolini. For this purpose he had the "Marmarica" Division (General Tracchia), the "23rd of March" Division (General Antonelli), some Fascist militia, plus survivors from the "Catanzaro" and "Cirene" Divisions.

General O'Connor's assault plan, as at Sidi Barranti, hinged on the heavy "I" tanks, of which 23 runners now remained. But this time it would be different in that the infantry would have to open a way through the lines of fixed defences first. The infantry of the 6th Australian Division would therefore have to cross the anti-tank ditch using a specially-built assault bridge, and clear the mines with the help of the sappers, to allow the remaining Matildas to exploit the breach thus made in the Italian defences.

The attack was launched at the western sector of the perimeter, which was not as strongly defended as the southern face. At 0530 hours on January 3 the Australians went into the anti-tank ditch; an hour later they had cleared two mine-free passages, and the tanks went through them towards Bardia town, which had been bombarded by the Royal Navy and the R.A.F. On the next day the victors reached the sea, having cut the Italian garrison in two. The Italians capitulated on January 5, surrendering to XIII Corps 45,000 prisoners, 460 guns, 131 (mainly light) tanks, and over 700 trucks.

At this point the question of British intervention in Greece was raised again. On November 2, 1940, during his visit to Cairo, Anthony Eden had received a message from Churchill asking him to reinforce General Papagos's air force at the expense of the Middle East theatre. Eden had irreverently scribbled over the despatch: "Egypt more important than Greece. Enemy air power in Libya unaltered."

After this the problem of British intervention had been shelved, as the Italians suffered successive defeats in Epirus and Albania. It was discussed again, however, when news reached London about the German concentrations in Rumania, and there was much speculation as to their possible objectives. Eden, who had just exchanged the War Ministry for the Foreign Office, found himself compelled to reverse his views on the relative importance of Greece and Egypt.

In Churchill's view, after the fall of Bardia, aid to Greece became more important than the operations in Libya, which were to be halted at Tobruk.

The capture of this deep-water port, built in a well-protected bay, would offer the British forces in Libya the opportunity of using the sea route for replenishing their supplies rather than relying on the 375 mile overland route between Alexandria and Tobruk. A single 6,000 ton merchantman can carry a cargo equivalent to the load of 600 to 1,200 trucks, each with a driver and his mate; this makes for a considerable saving in fuel as well as manpower. Moreover, near the Tobruk fortress lay El Adem, an important airfield which British aircraft could use as a forward base. The Tobruk defences were similar to those of Bardia, but they were still partly under construction and had a perimeter of about 40 miles. The garrison, under General Pitassi Mannella, commander of the Italian XXII Corps, consisted mainly of the "Sirte" Division (General Della Mura).

Without waiting for the fall of Bardia, O'Connor had sent the 7th Armoured Division to cut Tobruk's communications. After the 6th Australian Division had joined up with 7th Armoured, O'Connor started the attack on Tobruk at dawn on January 21. As he only had 12 Matilda tanks left, he supplemented them by mechanising a squadron of Australian cavalry, giving them some Italian M-13/40 tanks.

General Pitassi Mannella was apparently surprised by the speed with which O'Connor had prepared this new manoeuvre. In spite of a few energetic counter-attacks everything was over by nightfall, as the Italian artillery had been put out of action by the British armour. By the following afternoon O'Connor had added 25,000 prisoners, 208 guns, 23 medium tanks, and 200 trucks to his bag. He had advanced so rapidly that the sea-water distilling plant fell intact into the hands of the British, and the Tobruk port installations were working again in a few days. The 6th Australian Division lost 179 dead and 638 wounded in the attacks on Bardia and Tobruk, which were energetically conducted at all levels.

The British were firmly settled in Mussolini's North African empire. The small garrison in Egypt, which had embarked on a spoiling raid on the Italians, had become giant-killers.

After the capture of Tobruk, the question for the British was whether or not to go for Benghazi. Churchill did not exclude this possibility in the appreciation he drew up for the Chiefs-of-Staff Committee on January 6, 1941, but he regarded it as of secondary importance to supporting the Greeks and helping them to take Valona. In Section 13 of this lengthy document he wrote: "It would not be right for the sake of Benghazi to lose the chance of the Greeks taking Valona, and thus to dispirit or anger them, and perhaps make them in the mood for a separate peace with Italy. Therefore the prospect must be faced that after Tobruk the further westward advance of the Army of the Nile may be seriously cramped. It is quite clear to me that supporting Greece must have priority after the western flank of Egypt has been made secure."

But by January 10 Valona was no longer

the key objective. The German concentration in Rumania could no longer be interpreted as a manoeuvre in a war of nerves: it was clearly the first stage of a large-scale military campaign, and Greece seemed to be the inevitable objective. Faced with the threat of a new disaster in the Balkans, British military aid to the Greek Army became a matter of vital importance. Churchill therefore sent new instructions to General Wavell, from which we may quote an extract:

"You must now therefore conform your plans to larger interests at stake.
"3. Nothing must hamper capture of Tobruk, but thereafter all operations in Libya are subordinated to aiding Greece, and all preparations must be made from the receipt of this telegram for the immediate succour of Greece . . .
"4. We expect and require prompt and active compliance with our decisions, for which we bear full responsibility."

The Chiefs-of-Staffs Committee endorsed the text of this telegram, which revealed certain differences of opinion between London and G.H.Q. Cairo. But when the Greek Government declined to accept British aid under the terms offered, agreement between the two headquarters was restored for the time being.

General Wavell and Air Chief-Marshal Longmore flew to Athens on January 14 and conferred with General Metaxas, King George II of the Hellenes, and General Papagos on the subject of British aid.

According to Metaxas, if Germany should invade Bulgarian territory, neither Yugoslavia nor Turkey would abandon

their neutrality unless it were first violated by the Germans. Papagos then described the current military situation within this diplomatic and political context, and gave his own appreciation of the situation for the benefit of the two British commanders.

Twelve Greek divisions, three infantry brigades, and a cavalry division were holding the Albanian front. The 6th, 7th, 12th, and 14th Divisions were facing the Bulgarian frontier but the 6th was about to leave for the western Macedonian sector, as the Italians were increasing their strength there every day.

From all the information at the disposal of the Greeks, it appeared that the Germans had at least 12 divisions – including two or three Panzer divisions – in Rumania; in Bulgaria, under the direction of German officers in civilian clothes, the airfields were being improved, some new ones were being built, and the roads leading to the frontier were being repaired. It was clear from these preparations that in all probability the main force of the German or German-Bulgarian offensive would be aimed at eastern Macedonia, with Salonika as its main objective.

"I therefore concluded," states Papagos in his book *Greece at War*, "that in the present political and military situation, in order to have a stable defensive front the Greek armies would have to be reinforced as soon as possible by nine divisions and the appropriate aircraft from Great

The left hook by the 7th Armoured Division which trapped the Italians.

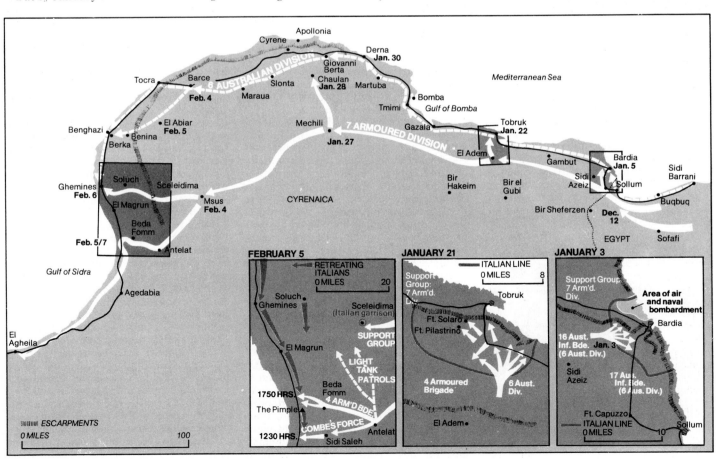

Britain." In addition, the Allies would have to act quickly to man the western Thracian and eastern Macedonian sectors before the German forces in Rumania had taken up their offensive dispositions along the Bulgarian-Greek frontier. Papagos also suggested a series of both logistic and defensive (anti-aircraft) measures which would, in his opinion, speed up operations and make up for the advantage gained by the Germans.

Wavel informed his allies that the only forces he could afford to dispatch immediately to the Greek theatre of operations consisted of an artillery regiment, a mixed A.A. and anti-tank regiment, and an armoured group with about 60 armoured cars. Generals Metaxas and Papagos were very much taken aback by the British proposals. The immediate dispatch to Greece of 24 field guns, 12 heavy howitzers, 24 anti-tank guns, 40 A.A. guns, and 65 light and medium tanks would not add to the defensive power of the Greek Army very much although it would give Hitler an excuse to bring forward his plans. They therefore politely declined the British offer and a note expressing their views was sent to the British Ambassador on January 18, 1941. Confirming the attitude of General Papagos, Metaxas noted in his preamble: "We are resolved to resist the German attack, if it is made, by every means and at any price; but we have no wish to provoke it in any way, unless the aid which Great Britain can lend us in Macedonia is sufficient for this purpose."

After receiving this reassuring confirmation of Greece's intentions, the British Government made no attempt to influence the Greek Government. On January 21, the very day of the attack on Tobruk, London, now free from any urgent Greek commitments, ordered G.H.Q. Cairo to resume its offensive towards Benghazi without further delay.

After the surprise attack on Sidi Barrani, Marshal Graziani had given his opinion that Cyrenaica could no longer be defended and that it would be advisable to withdraw to Tripoli, putting the Sirte Desert between his 10th Army and the Army of the Nile. When the Italian High Command recommended him to be more

Wavell arrives in Greece.

optimistic, Graziani set to work to improvise the defence of Cyrenaica – but it must be admitted that he did not make a very good job of it. His 10th Army was divided into three defensive groups: XXIII Corps at Bardia, XXII Corps at Tobruk, and the XX Corps (General Cona) holding the Mechili-Derna line. This disposition meant that it was highly likely that 10th Army could be defeated piecemeal by an enemy who was greatly inferior in overall numbers.

On January 9, despite the destruction of XXIII Corps in the battle for Bardia, Graziani was now showing optimism instead of his previous pessimism. In fact the Jebel Akhdar, the massif between Mechili and Derna which rises to a height of about 1,650 feet, was quite unsuitable for an attack by mechanised forces.

By putting an infantry division into the Derna position and the armoured brigade of General Babini into Mechili, Graziani thought he would have an excellent chance of halting the British advance towards Benghazi. But he was forgetting that those two formations would have to fight independently as they were separated by the Jebel Akhdar hills and could not reinforce one another.

On January 24 the 6th Australian Division approached the Derna position, while the 7th Armoured Division fell upon Babini's armoured brigade, in spite of the extremely poor state of the British tanks. The Italian 14-ton tanks were fighting the same number of 12.5-ton British cruiser tanks, and the battle ended badly for the Italians. They retreated into the Jebel Akhdar to avoid encirclement – but in so doing they gave the British a clear road to the main Italian supply-line along the Gulf of Sirte. For this reason Graziani decided to abandon western Cyrenaica on February 1. General Gariboldi was sent to Tripoli to organise the defence of the province, and General Tellera succeeded him as commander of 10th Army.

The distance between Mechili and Beda Fomm, near the Gulf of Sirte, is about 140 miles. Along the coast road between Derna and Beda Fomm the distance is about 225 miles. But the retreating Italians had the advantage of using the *Via Balbia*, the excellent coast road; the British, advancing from Mechili towards Beda Fomm, had only a poorly reconnoitred track, which was not clearly marked and which crossed a desert consisting either of soft sand or of areas strewn with large rocks.

"War is won with leftovers", Marshal Foch had once said. It is hardly likely that Generals O'Connor and O'Moore Creagh, commander of 7th Armoured Division, had ever heard of this dictum, but now they put it into practice with a vengeance. At 1500 hours on February 4 the 11th Hussars (Colonel Combe) were at Msus, only 60 miles from the *Via Balbia*. At dawn on the 5th, after they had been reinforced with some artillery, they took the track leading to Antelat and at noon reached their objective at Beda Fomm, half an hour before the first Italian

column retreating from Benghazi down the *Via Balbia*. Confused engagements were fought throughout February 6, with the Italians hitting out wildly as they came up against the British blocking their retreat.

Finally, at 0900 hours of February 7, O'Connor sent an uncoded signal for the information of Wavell and the edification of Mussolini: "Fox killed in the open." Badly wounded, General Tellera died a few hours later; the H.Q. of 10th Army, and Generals Cona and Babini, had been captured. General Bergonzoli had also been captured: he had managed to make his way through the Australian lines when Bardia fell. About 20,000 Italians were also captured, and the final count of the equipment seized by the British after this last battle amounted to 112 11- and 14-ton M 11 and 13 medium tanks, 216 guns, and 1,500 vehicles.

On February 3 the British had reached El Agheila at the bottom of the Gulf of Sirte. This was a very important position, for there was only a narrow gap about 15-20 miles wide through which tanks could pass between the desert and the sea. As the British XIII Corps now commanded this position, it was well placed to invade Tripolitania or defend Cyrenaica as required.

Wavell's original five-day raid had developed into a two-month campaign. In four pitched battles O'Connor had advanced 560 miles from his starting position. Although he never had more than two divisions under his command, he had destroyed one Italian army (four corps, or nine divisions) at a cost of only 500 dead, 1,373 wounded, and 56 missing. The "bag" of Italian prisoners amounted to 130,000 men, including 22 generals and one admiral, and O'Connor had seized or destroyed 845 guns and 380 tanks. For the third time in the war Guderian's words to Hitler had been proved true: "Tanks are a life-saving weapon".

On February 10 Marshal Graziani was ordered to hand over his command to General Gariboldi and to return to Italy. His conduct of operations was carefully examined by a commission of enquiry, which came to highly equivocal conclusions about them. But it was hard to assign him the total responsibility for this catastrophe without implicating the Duce himself. Undoubtedly, Graziani had not excelled himself; possibly, also, he still suffered from the effects of the hand-grenade which had been thrown at him in Addis Ababa in 1938. But above all he had been hampered by his shortage of modern weapons, just as had Gamelin in the French campaign a few months earlier.

On December 27, after the battle of Sidi Barrani, Graziani had attempted to explain matters to Mussolini. "From the harsh experience of these bitter days," he wrote, "we must conclude that in this theatre of war a single armoured division is more powerful than a whole army."

Coming events would prove these to be prophetic words.

CHAPTER 17
Germany intervenes in North Africa

At the end of December 1940, General Geissler of the Luftwaffe set up his H.Q. at Taormina. His squadrons were divided between the airfields at Catania, Comiso, Marsala, Trápani, Palermo, and Reggio di Calabria, along with 45 Italian bombers and 75 Italian fighters. Together with the 70 bombers and 25 fighters of the *Regia Aeronautica* based in Sardinia, the number of Axis aircraft capable of operating in the central Mediterranean, which narrows to under 90 miles between Cape Bon in Tunisia and Marsala in Sicily, was approximately 400.

Such a force should normally have been under the command of *Superaero*, the High Command of the Italian Air Force. But Göring had no intention of permitting this, for he deliberately kept "his" airmen under his own control and reserved to himself the right to give them orders. Thus it is fairly certain that he was responsible for continual interference and fraction in the conduct of operations.

The strength of the R.A.F. on Malta was far smaller. When X *Fliegerkorps* moved south, the British air defences of Malta consisted of a dozen Swordfish, 16 Hurricanes, 16 Wellington twin-engine bombers, and a few Martin Maryland bomber/reconnaissance aircraft built in the United States. Admittedly a new shipload of 16 Hurricanes was expected with the next convoy from Gibraltar, but this was still a drop in the ocean.

General Geissler and his aircrews got their first chance to distinguish themselves with the British Operation "Excess", which started on January 6. Admiral Somerville's task was to convoy four merchantmen (one for Malta, the others for Greece) from Gibraltar to the central Mediterranean. Admiral Cunningham in Alexandria would make use of the appearance of Force H in the Western Mediterranean to send two merchantmen into Malta. At the same time, two cruisers from his light forces would take troops there. After that he would take charge of the ships making for Greece from Gibraltar.

While the two British convoys converged on Malta from east and west, the Malta-based bombers struck at Naples on the night of January 8–9. Their target was the Italian battleships which had survived the Taranto raid. The *Giulio Cesare* suffered a leak as the result of a bomb explosion on the bottom of the harbour and had to steam to Genoa for repairs. The *Vittorio Veneto* escaped untouched, but *Supermarina* decided to transfer her to La Spezia, where she would be out of range of the Malta-based bombers. This, however, would prevent *Vittorio Veneto* from taking any useful action in the narrows between Tunisia and Sicily.

Force H completed its mission without incident. Somerville passed to the south of Sardinia on the evening of January 9 and returned to Gibraltar with the battleship *Malaya*, the battle-cruiser *Renown*, and the aircraft-carrier *Ark Royal*, leaving his charges under the protection of an A.A. cruiser, two heavy cruisers (*Gloucester* and *Southampton*, which had joined him after landing the troops they had brought from Alexandria in Malta), and five destroyers. At dawn on January 10 the *Gloucester* and *Southampton* sank the Italian torpedo-boat *Vega* which had tried heroically to attack them. During this action, the destroyer *Gallant* hit a mine and had to be towed to Malta. Repairs proved impossible, however, because of Axis air attacks.

But Cunningham's Mediterranean Fleet did not get off so easily. Towards 1230 hours Junkers Ju 87 and Ju 88 bombers appeared over the British fleet, which had joined the convoy soon after the sinking of the *Vega*, and launched a fierce attack on the aircraft-carrier *Illustrious*, in spite of sustained fire from the battleships *Warspite* and *Valiant*.

"There was no doubt we were watching complete experts," wrote Admiral Cunningham in his memoirs. "Formed roughly in a larger circle over the fleet they peeled off one by one when reaching the attacking position. We could not but admire the skill and precision of it all. The attacks were pressed home to point-blank range, and as they pulled out of their dives some of them were seen to fly along the flight deck of the *Illustrious* below the level of her funnel."

Illustrious was struck by two 550-lb and four 1,100-lb bombs in under 10 minutes, and but for her armoured flight deck she would most likely have suffered the same fate as many American and British aircraft-carriers in the Far East. Nevertheless she was badly damaged; her steering-gear was out of action and she had to steer with her propellers. Admiral Cunningham therefore ordered her to return to Malta for repairs.

On its return voyage the following day Cunningham's force was again attacked by the dive-bombers of X *Fliegerkorps*. The luckless *Southampton* was disabled and set on fire; she had to be abandoned by her crew and was sunk by torpedoes.

At Malta, workers and engineers laboured frantically to get *Illustrious* ready for action again. But on January 16 she received more damage from German bombs, which was patched up after a fashion. On the night of January 23 *Illustrious* left the Grand Harbour and returned to Alexandria, making the remarkable speed of 28 knots. Nevertheless, she had to be completely overhauled and set out on a long voyage to the American yards at Norfolk, Virginia, which undertook the work with the sympathetic agreement of President Roosevelt.

In the absence of *Illustrious* the Admiralty decided that the carrier *Formidable*, which was in the Atlantic, should proceed to Alexandria round the Cape of Good Hope. Without fleet air cover, Admiral Cunningham was unable to take any action in the waters south of Sicily until *Formidable* joined his flag, which she did, in spite of the Luftwaffe's attempts to mine the Suez Canal and the approches to Alexandria, on March 10.

Meanwhile the German bombers based in Sicily kept Malta under constant air bombardment. Heavy losses were inflicted on the island's aircraft, which were under the command of Air Vice-Marshal H. P. Lloyd. At the end of February the surviving Wellington bombers had to be brought back to Egypt; the fighters had been suffering similar losses, and on March 11 the Hurricanes, the only aircraft on Malta capable of tackling the Messerschmitt 109's and 110's on anything like equal

Sailors double across the flight deck of the Illustrious *after a hit by bombers of* X Fliegerkorps.

terms, were reduced to eight battle-worthy machines.

From March 1941, however, the need for air support for the *Afrika Korps* and for Operation "Marita" in the Balkans compelled General Geissler to divert a large number of his squadrons to these new operational theatres. The inevitable result was a slackening of the pressure put on Malta by X *Fliegerkorps*. Between April 3 and May 21 Force H was able to supply Malta with 82 Hurricanes, flown from the carriers *Ark Royal* and *Furious*.

It is true that the German High Command and the Italian *Comando Supremo* failed to take full advantage of the temporary local superiority in all neighbouring waters achieved by the transfer of X *Fliegerkorps* to Sicily. Nevertheless, the actions of X *Fliegerkorps* gave the Axis three months in which to transfer troops to North Africa for the defence of Tripolitania against the British, which was done with very little loss. From this point of view, the air and sea engagements between Sicily and Tunisia on January 10–11 had much more serious consequences than the destruction of the *Southampton* and the temporary disablement of the *Illustrious*.

Between February 1 and June 30, 1941, no less than 81,785 Axis troops were landed at Tripoli with approximately 450,000 tons of weapons, fuel, and ammunition. In February and March, with the temporary neutralisation of Malta, the troops were shipped with very few casualties. These increased slightly from April onwards, but until June 30 casualties totalled only 4.8 per cent of all the troops embarked.

First to arrive were the Italian "Ariete" and "Trento" Divisions, together with the German 5th Light Division, which was the first contingent of the *Deutsches Afrika Korps* or D.A.K.

On February 6, 1941, Lieutenant-General Erwin Rommel was received by Brauchitsch, who gave him instructions for his new mission. He was appointed to command the expeditionary corps which was to be sent to Africa, and received orders to proceed to Africa as soon as possible. Rommel's intention, as he noted in his diary, was to examine the possibilities of using the new formation. It was anticipated that the first German troops would arrive in mid-February and that the last unit of the 5th Light Division would be landed in mid-April. By the end of May the last detachments of the 15th Panzer Division should be in position, and the D.A.K. ready to move.

In his new rôle Rommel was to take his orders from Marshal Graziani. This was decided only after O.K.W. and *Comando Supremo* had agreed that the original plan for a close defence of Tripoli should be abandoned. The Italian and German forces, under Rommel's immediate command, would move further down the Gulf of Sirte and base their defence of Tripoli on Buerat. Rommel was authorised to

appeal to the German Army High Command over Graziani's head, if the latter's orders looked like endangering the safety of the expeditionary force or the honour of the German Army.

In the afternoon of the same day, Hitler received Rommel and told him that he would be accompanied to Africa by Colonel Schmundt, the Führer's personal aide-de-camp. On February 11, Rommel presented himself to General Guzzoni, acting Chief of the General Staff in the absence of General Cavallero at the Albanian front. After a quick review of the situation with General Roatta, Italian Army Chief-of-Staff, Rommel set off for North Africa via Catania, where he conferred with Geissler. On February 12 he arrived at Tripoli and reported to General Gariboldi, who had just relieved Graziani.

And thus this remarkable commander began his military career in Africa.

For 18 months, between March 1941 and September 1942, Erwin Rommel displayed outstanding ability to attack and to manoeuvre, learning to combine cunning with force. There is no doubt that the man who managed to rebound from a decisive defeat before Tobruk into an advance which took him to the gates of Alexandria must be counted among the truly great field commanders of all time.

But was his brilliance as a tactician matched by his strategic ability? This is not so clear. One firm criterion of sound strategy is that it must combine the different interests of land, sea, and air forces into a framework which Churchill described with the ugly word "triphibian". And Rommel repeatedly failed to do this.

During the summer of 1942, for example, Rommel constantly blamed *Comando Supremo* for the frequent breakdowns in his supply system, forgetting that after taking Tobruk on June 21 he had assured Cavallero that he would be able to reach the Nile with the help of the fuel and transport captured in Tobruk. He also forgot that although he was keeping Luftwaffe squadrons from the task of neutralising Malta, the British bombers, torpedo-bombers, and submarines based on the island were exacting a merciless toll on the Italian merchant tonnage in the central Mediterranean. In fact, it was on Rommel's urgent request – despite the protests of Kesselring and Cavallero – that Hitler and Mussolini gave up Operation "Hercules", which could and should have presented the Axis with Malta and Gozo.

Whatever one may think of Rommel in a historical context, his former subordinates and opponents all pay tribute to his nobility of character and his high moral code. Undoubtedly his task in fighting a "clean war" in the African desert was easier than that of his colleagues on the Eastern Front, who had the partisans and Hitler to deal with. But when slight scuffles broke out between his troops and Arab tribesmen, whom British agents were trying to enlist against the Italians, Rommel noted in his diary on September

16, 1942: "There is nothing so unpleasant as partisan warfare. It is perhaps very important not to make reprisals on hostages at the first outbreak of partisan warfare, for these only create feelings of revenge and serve to strengthen the *franc-tireurs*. It is better to allow an incident to go unavenged than to hit back at the innocent. It only agitates the whole neighbourhood, and hostages easily become martyrs."

In 1944 Rommel protested to Hitler in the same spirit of humanity, good sense, and true German patriotism against the appalling massacre of French civilians at Oradour-sur-Glane perpetrated by the S.S. *Das Reich* Panzer Division, and demanded exemplary punishment for those responsible for the crime. (The result was a coarse and violent rebuff.) The honourable treatment which Rommel offered to the Free French prisoners taken at Bir Hakeim in June 1942 should also be noted. It ignored the fact that the Franco-German armistice of 1940, according to the rules and usages of war, had deprived de Gaulle's Free French of the status and privileges of regular combatants.

Rommel was also an attentive husband, who wrote to his wife every day to keep her in touch with his fortunes. The following extracts come from two successive letters (the second contains a thinly-veiled reference to his new assignment in Africa).

"February 6, 1941

"Dearest Lu,

"Landed at Staaken 12.45. First to C.in-C. Army, who appointed me to my new job, and then to Führer. Things are moving fast. My kit is coming on here. I can only take barest necessities with me. Perhaps I'll be able to get the rest out soon. I need not tell you that my head is swimming with all the many things there are to be done. It'll be months before anything materialises.

"So 'our leave' was cut short again. Don't be sad, it had to be. The new job is very big and important."

"February 7, 1941.

"Slept on my new job last night. It's one way of getting my rheumatism treatment. I've got a lot to do, in the few hours that remain, getting together all I need."

This was typical of Rommel. And one can only conclude that when his widow and his son, Manfred, chose the title *War Without Hate* for the collection of letters and memoirs which he left, it was a perfectly appropriate decision.

While the advance units of the *Afrika Korps* were leaving Italy for Africa, General Wavell in Cairo was carrying out the orders he had received from London. The 6th Australian Division, the 2nd New Zealand Division (Major-General B.C. Freyberg) and over half the 2nd Armoured Division (Major-General M. D. Gambier-Parry), which had just arrived from England, were to be sent to help the Greeks.

Brigadier E. Dorman-Smith, an officer of G.H.Q. Middle East in Cairo, who had been at the front with O'Connor from

General Erwin Rommel: the celebrated German commander was a legendary figure, even to his opponents.

Mechili to Beda Fomm, returned to Cairo to see Wavell at 1000 hours on February 12 (a few hours, in fact, before Rommel called on Gariboldi in Tripoli), and heard about this new change of front from Wavell. Dorman-Smith remarked that while he had been away from G.H.Q. the usual maps of the Western Desert on the walls had been replaced by maps of Greece, and that Wavell commented sardonically: "You see, Eric, I'm starting my spring campaign."

On the previous day Wavell had in fact cabled Churchill after receiving a message from Lieutenant-General Sir Henry Maitland Wilson in Tobruk, informing him that the Italian forces were in a state of collapse. At the front, O'Connor stated that he was ready to move forward into Tripolitania if all available troops were sent to reinforce his 7th Armoured Division, and if the R.A.F. and Admiral Cunningham's Inshore Squadron (one monitor and three gunboats) could harrass the Italian-held coastline and give him the necessary support. On the latter

141

assumption he had planned amphibious operations against Buerat and subsequently against Misurata, further along the coast.

O'Connor's optimism was matched in Tripoli by Rommel's initial pessimism. The latter had just received a discouraging report from Lieutenant Heggenreiner, a German liaison officer in North Africa. Rommel noted that Heggenreiner "described some very unpleasant incidents which had occurred during the retreat, or rather the rout which it had become. Italian troops had thrown away their weapons and ammunition and clambered on to overloaded vehicles in a wild attempt to get away to the west. This had led to some ugly scenes, and even to shooting. Morale was as low as it could be in all military circles in Tripoli. Most of the Italian officers had already packed their bags and were hoping for a quick return trip to Italy."

General Gariboldi now had only five divisions under his orders: the "Bologna", "Brescia", "Pavia", "Sabratha", and "Savona" Divisions. Even on June 10, 1940, these had been considered "inefficient" and had since had to give up part of their equipment to the recently-destroyed 10th Army. But for the formal orders of the British War Cabinet, nothing could have kept O'Connor and the victors of Sidi Barrani, Bardia, Tobruk, Mechili, and Beda Fomm from driving through to Tripoli.

But Churchill had already made his decision, and it was adhered to. For once Sir John Dill, the C.I.G.S., supported the Prime Minister's view. But Brooke, still C.-in-C., Home Forces, believed that Churchill's decision overreached the possibilities of British strategy, considering the means then available. Brooke later

wrote: "This is one of the very few occasions on which I doubted Dill's advice and judgement, and I am not in a position to form any definite opinion as I was not familiar with all the facts. I have, however, always considered from the very start that our participation in the operations in Greece was a definite strategic blunder. Our hands were more than full at that time in the Middle East, and Greece could only result in the most dangerous dispersal of force."

Brooke's fears were certainly proved correct by the course of events. But the British felt themselves bound to go to the aid of the Greeks, quite apart from the fact that a refusal to do so would have been a gift for the Axis propagandists. There was always the possibility that without British help the Greeks might have been tempted to negotiate some arrangement with Hitler. On the other hand, the sending of a British expeditionary force to Greece proved to the world that Britain was not pursuing a policy of national self-interest. Despite the defeats in Greece and Crete, the attempt did much to save British prestige – more so than if it had not been made. During this period of the Desert War, Wavell was faced with a succession of conflicting demands on his already stretched resources; this seriously compromised the possibility of an early British victory.

As G.H.Q. Cairo was forced to give up the troops for this expeditionary force, it was left with only skeleton forces to "consolidate" its position in western Cyrenaica, according to orders. These forces consisted mainly of the understrength 2nd Armoured Division, which had been equipped with captured Italian vehicles

A British tank captured by the Germans and put into service.

to replace the tanks sent to Greece. But the Italian tanks were so poor that even good British crews could not improve their performance. The 9th Australian Division (Major-General L. J. Morshead) very short of transport, artillery and signals, lay at Tobruk and to the north-east of Benghazi. The 3rd Indian Motorised Brigade completed this set of poorly-equipped formations, which were now to take on Rommel's forces.

After the capture of Benghazi, Wavell had appointed General Maitland Wilson as military governor of Cyrenaica. But the latter was recalled to Cairo and put in charge of the Greek expeditionary force immediately after taking up his command. He was succeeded by Lieutenant-General Philip Neame, V.C., a newcomer to the desert theatre, who only had a few days to accustom himself to the terrain.

The 7th Armoured Division, which had been the spearhead of XIII Corps, had been brought back to the Delta by Wavell to be completely refitted. Churchill had protested violently against this decision, and it is clear that if the division's repair shops could have been set up in Tobruk after its fall, Rommel's task would have been much harder. But it must be remembered that this first British desert offensive had been the result of successive improvisations. On December 9, 1940, O'Connor had set out on a five-day raid. By February 6, 1941, he was over 500 miles further west, at El Agheila. It was not surprising that in these totally unexpected circumstances the base facilities had not kept up with the advance of the tanks.

In any event the dispositions made by Wavell show that he believed that any early large-scale counter-offensive by Rommel was highly improbable. Brauchitsch and Halder also believed that Rommel's attack on Agedabia could not take place until the end of May, after the last units of 15th Panzer Division had joined his force. Again, on March 19 Hitler, decorating Rommel with the Oak Leaves to the Knight's Cross, gave him no other instructions. According to his diaries this left Rommel, eager for action, "not very happy". Benghazi, the objective given him for his spring campaign, appeared to him to be indefensible by itself. The whole of Cyrenaica must be therefore recovered to ensure its security.

At dawn on March 24 the reconnaissance group of 5th Light Division attacked El Agheila – and the British units defending this key position pulled back without a fight. They took up new positions at Marsa Brega, between the Gulf of Sirte and salt marsh impassable to tanks, about 50 miles south-west of Agedabia.

Rommel felt that he could not stick to the letter of his orders and so leave the British with enough time to reorganise while he waited for the whole of the 15th Panzer Division to reach the front. If he attacked again without delay he had a chance of surprising the British with his small mobile forces and of dislodging them from what was an extremely strong defensive position.

He therefore attacked again on March 31. The British did put up some resistance at Marsa Brega, but, outflanked on the desert front, they were forced to give up the place to the 5th Light Division. By the evening of April 2 the German forces, followed by the "Ariete" Armoured Division and the "Brescia" Infantry Division, occupied the Agedabia region two months ahead of the schedule set by O.K.H. About 800 British prisoners were taken during this engagement. Rommel's cunning use of dummy tanks had added to the confusion of the British as they retreated; German reconnaissance aircraft saw disorganised columns streaming back towards Benghazi and Mechili.

Rommel has often been criticised for acting disobediently; but any subordinate is entitled to pursue his own objectives if he discovers that the ones he has been given by his superiors have been based on an incorrect appreciation of the situation. And this was precisely the position when Rommel and the *Afrika Korps* reached Marsa Brega at the end of the March 1941.

But in such a situation a subordinate is also supposed to inform his superiors without a moment's delay of the steps he feels himself obliged to take. Rommel failed to do so, and for days he played hide and seek with his superiors while he breathlessly exploited his initial success.

In his book on the war in Africa General Pietro Maravigna makes this quite clear. "The covering enemy troops were surprised by the attack and withdrew. They abandoned Bir es-Suera and Marsa Brega, which Rommel's advanced forces occupied on April 1, while the main body of the 5th Light Division took up its position to the east of El Agheila.

"In Tripoli, and even more so in Rome, this news came like thunder in a clear sky. Mussolini, who was very much put out, asked Rintelen for information. Rintelen had none to give. He then asked Gariboldi to explain matters. Gariboldi replied that Rommel had evaded all authority and was acting entirely on his own initiative. Moreover, Gariboldi disclaimed all responsibility, as he had only authorised Rommel to make a surprise attack on the British forces west of Marsa Brega to improve our own defences; the German general, carried away by his initial success, had exceeded his authority."

Gariboldi subsequently set off after Rommel with the intention of stopping him, but he was very abruptly received by his impetuous subordinate, especially as fresh successes had provided further justification for his actions; and the German High Command in Berlin signalled its approval. In fact, on the night of April 3–4 the reconnaissance group of the 5th Light Division entered Benghazi, and its main body drove onwards towards Mechili.

In Cairo the news of Rommel's escapade caused as much bewilderment as it had to *Comando Supremo*. Neame had been ordered not to let his position be endangered if the Axis forces attacked but to make a fighting retreat; but Wavell quickly realised that Neame had been overtaken by the sudden speed of events, and that the organised retreat he had had in mind was turning into a rout.

Wavell therefore decided to call upon the services of O'Connor, but the latter had not had time to take stock of the situation before suffering an appalling stroke of ill luck. O'Connor and Neame, accompanied by General Carton de Wiart of Narvik fame, were on their way to Tmimi for a staff conference when they were captured by a German patrol near Derna.

"He was half asleep when his driver braked suddenly," writes Anthony Heckstall-Smith. "An Afrika Korps soldier shone his torch inside the car and could not suppress a cry of astonishment. Perhaps the generals could have escaped in that fraction of a second, but the soldier was rapidly joined by his comrades from the machine gun battalion commanded by Lieutenant-Colonel Ponath. O'Connor realised, too late, that his driver had veered to the north instead of steering eastward towards Tmimi.

"A few months later people in Egypt were telling the story of O'Connor's arrival at Rommel's field H.Q., when Rommel was having breakfast with his staff. O'Connor looked them up and down and asked: 'Does anyone here speak English?

"A bespectacled officer leapt to his feet, clicked his heels, bowed deeply, and said 'I do, sir.'

"'Well, get lost.'

"The story is probably apocryphal, but the soldiers in the desert army are very proud of it."

At Mechili General Gambier-Parry, commander of the 2nd Armoured Division, was also captured, along with most of his divisional headquarters and much of the 3rd Indian Motorised Brigade.

When he thrust from Agedabia to Mechili, and from Mechili to Derna, Rommel was executing O'Connor's manoeuvre at Beda Fomm in reverse. But he was not so fortunate as O'Connor had been; when the advanced German units reached the Gulf of Bomba, the rearguard of the Australian brigade retreating from Benghazi had already fallen back on Tobruk and was strengthening the garrison. The Allies had escaped from the Axis net.

The decision to defend Tobruk at all costs was taken by Wavell on the advice of Air Chief-Marshal Longmore and Admiral Cunningham. The garrison consisted of the 9th Australian Division, reinforced by a brigade of the 7th, an armoured regiment with 45 armoured cars, and an A.A. brigade with 16 heavy and 59 light guns. All in all, there were about 36,000 men within the Tobruk perimeter.

The assault on January 21, in which Major-General Mackay had captured Tobruk, had been so rapid that the fortifications had fallen into the hands of the British almost untouched. The strongpoints, which were laid out in alternating rows, were protected by 3-foot thick concrete slabs which were proof against the heaviest guns (15-cm) the *Afrika Korps* had at this time. The anti-tank ditch was also intact and was still completely camouflaged with sand-covered planks.

But above all – if it is true that an army is as good as its commander – the strongest part of the Tobruk defences was Major-General Leslie Morshead, commander of 9th Australian Division. "There'll be no Dunkirk here!" he told his men. "If we should have to get out, we shall have to fight our way out. No surrender and no retreat."

Morshead, who had fought in World War I, had risen to the command of an infantry battalion at 20. For his bravery under fire he had been awarded the C.M.G., the D.S.O., and the *Légion d'Honneur,* and had been six times mentioned in despatches. His soldiers called him "the pitiless thing" because of his iron discipline. Another factor favouring the defenders was the comparative narrowness of the battlefield, which prevented Rommel from making his customary surprise manoeuvres.

On April 10 Rommel tried to storm Tobruk by launching a motorised detachment under General von Prittwitz, commander of the 15th Panzer Division, to cut the coast road. But the detachment was repulsed by heavy gunfire and its commander was killed by a shell. During the night of April 13–14, a battalion of the

5th Light Division succeeded in finding a way through the minefields and crossing the anti-tank ditch. Rommel stated, however, that:

"The division's command had not mastered the art of concentrating its strength at one point, forcing a breakthrough, rolling up and securing the flanks on either side, and then penetrating like lightning, before the enemy had time to react, deep into his rear." For this reason the Panzer regiment of the 5th Light Division was overwhelmed by the concentrated fire of the Australian artillery and was unable to support the battalion which had made a "finger-probe" advance into the defences. The latter battalion was counter-attacked and virtually destroyed, leaving 250 prisoners in the hands of the Australians. Rommel was incensed by this failure, which he punished by sacking General Streich.

The Italian divisions (the "Brescia" Infantry Division, "Trento" Motorised Division, and "Ariete" Armoured Division) were even less fortunate. On the other hand, the *Afrika Korps* units covering the rear of the troops attacking Tobruk reoccupied the former Axis frontier positions at Sollum, Halfaya, and Capuzzo and now stood on the Egyptian frontier. But they were considerably dispersed, and although 15th Panzer Division had now joined him, Rommel realised at last that he would only be able to capture Tobruk with a well-organised attack. He lacked the resources to do this, and the regrets he expressed to O.K.H. met with a chilly reception on the part of Brauchitsch and Halder.

Halder's note of April 23 shows this clearly. "I have a feeling that things are in a mess. He [Rommel] spends his time rushing about between his widely-scattered units and sending out reconnaissance raids in which he fritters away his strength . . . no one knows exactly how his troops are deployed, nor the strength of their fighting capacity . . . He has had heavy losses as a result of piecemeal attacks. In addition his vehicles are in a bad state because of the wear and tear caused by the desert sand and many of the tank engines need replacing. Our air transport can't meet Rommel's crazy demands; we haven't enough petrol anyway, and the planes sent to North Africa wouldn't have enough fuel for the return flight."

But whatever Halder thought, he could only express it in his private diary, as Hitler retained full confidence in Rommel. In these circumstances, and with the approval of Brauchitsch, he merely sent Lieutenant-General Paulus, the Quartermaster-General of O.K.H., out to the North African front to obtain first-hand information.

Paulus, Halder thought, because of his old friendship for Rommel, would "perhaps be capable of exerting some influence to head off this soldier who has gone stark mad". The special envoy of the German Army High Command carried out his delicate mission satisfactorily—but a few weeks later the entire North African theatre was transferred from O.K.H. to O.K.W. This change of the command structure eliminated any further causes of

An Afrika Korps *10.5-cm gun in action. Ammunition details are standing on the left ready to load more shells.*

friction between the impulsive Rommel and the methodical Halder. Halder has been criticised for being unduly cautious, because his fears did not materialise. But he had no way of knowing how small were the reserve forces at the disposal of the British C.-inC. Halder was relying on the information of his Intelligence experts, who estimated that Wavell had 21 divisions, six of which were actually fighting or in the area between Tobruk, Sollum, and Halfaya.

As already mentioned, the Axis convoys which carried the 5th Light Division to North Africa had suffered insignificant losses. But the ships which carried 15th Panzer Division had a harder time.

From the time of his first meeting with General Geissler of X *Fliegerkorps*, Rommel had asked that the efforts of the German bombers should be concentrated against the port of Benghazi. Later, X *Fliegerkorps* had given very efficient air cover to the advance of the *Afrika Korps* between Agedabia and Tobruk, making up to a large extent for the heavy artillery which Rommel lacked.

The inevitable result of this was that the former pressure being applied to Malta by these air forces became considerably lighter. Admiral Cunningham was not slow to exploit this welcome and unexpected respite. Early in April he transferred a flotilla of the most modern destroyers from Alexandria to Valletta. This small force, commanded by Captain

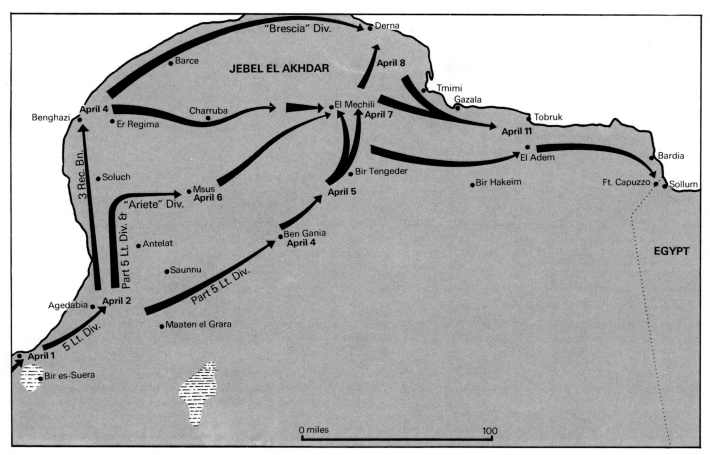

Rommel's counter-attack which caught the British off balance and sent them back to the borders of Egypt.

P. J. Mack, scored its first success on the night of April 14–15. It surprised an Axis convoy of five merchantmen escorted by three destroyers about 35 miles off Sfax. The convoy was silhouetted against the moon while Mack's ships were in darkness. Surprise was complete. The merchantmen were reduced to wrecks within a few minutes; 350 men, 300 vehicles, and 3,500 tons of equipment for the *Afrika Korps* were lost. The Italian destroyer *Baleno* was sunk, but Captain de Cristoforo of the *Tarigo*, with a leg shot off by a British shell, managed to launch three torpedoes before sinking with his ship – two of which hit and sank the British destroyer *Mohawk*.

The third Italian escort destroyer, the *Lampo*, was totally disabled and stranded on the shoals of the Kerkenna Bank, together with the German merchantman *Arta*. *Lampo* was recovered by the Italians in August and subsequently recommissioned – but in the meantime a group of French Resistance men from Tunisia had searched the derelicts by night, seized the ships' papers, and had passed on all information about the Afrika Korps' order of battle to Malta.

The work of the British destroyers was supplemented by that of the British submarines based on Malta and Alexandria. On February 25 the *Upright* (Lieutenant E. D. Norman) had scored a direct hit on the Italian light cruiser *Armando Diaz*, which sank in four minutes with

three-quarters of her crew. In a space of four months the British submarines in the Mediterranean sank at least a dozen Axis merchantmen, tankers, and transports between Messina and Tripoli.

The submarine *Upholder*, commanded by Lieutenant-Commander Malcolm Wanklyn, a brilliant submariner, particularly distinguished herself in these actions, on which the outcome of the Desert War so much depended. On the evening of May 25 *Upholder* sank the large Italian liner *Conte Rosso* (17,879 tons), and only 1,520 out of the 2,732 sailors and soldiers aboard were saved. In recognition of this Wanklyn received the Victoria Cross.

Yet another consequence of the first offensive of the *Afrika Korps* was to create serious tension between the Admiralty and Admiral Cunningham.

Cunningham had been ordered to bombard Tripoli's port installations with his battle fleet, but he doubted whether the fleet's guns would be able to inflict any serious damage. He pressed for the transfer of long-range heavy bombers to Egypt, to smash the installations from the air. But this would be impossible in the immediate future. Seeking a drastic solution to the problem of Tripoli, the War Cabinet and the Admiralty decided that Cunningham should sacrifice the battleship *Barham* and an A.A. cruiser. Manned by skeleton crews, these would be deliberately scuttled in the entrance to Tripoli harbour.

When Cunningham received this message on April 15 he reacted with an immediate objection. If he obeyed he would

not only lose one of his three vital battleships: it was also to be feared that the *Barham* and the cruiser would be sunk by the Italians before reaching their objective. Nor was there any guarantee that the crews, however small, could be recovered, and this would mean the additional loss of about 1,000 highly-trained officers, petty officers, and ratings. But Cunningham was ready to make a compromise. Reconsidering his first objections, he stated that he was prepared to bombard Tripoli.

The Admiralty agreed, and at dawn on April 21 the battleships *Barham*, *Valiant*, and *Warspite*, with the cruiser *Gloucester*, battered Tripoli harbour for three-quarters of an hour while Swordfish from the carrier *Formidable* and aircraft from Malta assisted the warships by bombing and illuminating the port. As Cunningham had anticipated, the actual damage inflicted was not severe and had no lasting effect; but the Italians were so slow to sound the alarm that the British squadron completed its hazardous mission without suffering any harm.

Churchill's own account in *The Second World War* suggests that the responsibility for this venture rests with Sir Dudley Pound. This, however, seems unlikely. Pound would hardly have issued such a drastic order without first referring it to the Minister of Defence, Churchill. Much more likely, the initiative for the idea to scuttle the *Barham* came from Churchill. And the fact that Pound retracted his order so promptly suggests that he was being influenced by Churchill again.

CHAPTER 18
Blitzkrieg in the Balkans

On December 29, 1940, General Ugo Cavallero, the new Chief-of-Staff of the *Comando Supremo*, was sent over by Mussolini to relieve General Ubaldo Soddu of his command and to take control of the Italian armed forces in Albania. The Duce defined Cavallero's task in a letter dated January 1: his forces were to move over to the offensive and prove, by their energy and resolve, that doubts abroad about Italian military prestige were baseless. "Germany," the letter went on, "is ready to send a mountain division into Albania and at the same time is preparing an army to attack Greece through Bulgaria in March. I am expecting, nay, I am certain, that your intervention and the bravery of your men will show that any direct support by Germany on the Albanian front will prove to be unnecessary. The Italian nation is impatiently waiting for the wind to change."

After the war General Halder drew attention to the vexing question of German reinforcements in Albania, on which Hitler and his generals never agreed:

"When the Italians got into trouble in Albania, Hitler was inclined to send help. The Army Commander-in-Chief managed to stop the plan from being put into action, as it would have been fruitless. It was a different matter when the German forces, which were actually intended for an attack on the Greeks, were ordered into Greece from Bulgaria to throw the British back into the sea. Hitler then ordered major units into northern Albania. This eccentric operation could have thrown into jeopardy any lightning success against Greece. But Hitler refused to give up his plan and his political will overrode all military objections. No harm was done, however, as the German High Command evaded executing the order, and events proved that they were right."

Before Cavallero could meet the Duce's wishes he had to prevent the Greeks reaching Valona and Durazzo. At this date, to cover a front of 156 miles, he had 16 divisions, some in very bad shape and most of them poorly supplied on account of Albania's virtually non-existent communications. It is true that the opposing forces, the Greeks, who had been on the offensive since November 14, had lost a fair number of men and had only 13 divisions or their equivalent. Until such time as they could make up their strength and repair communications, General Papagos decided to abandon temporarily any idea of an all-out attack and restricted himself to limited-objective offensives. It was during one of these operations that the Greek II Corps, working as usual in the mountains, captured the important crossroads at Klisura on January 9. In a heavy snowstorm they inflicted a severe defeat on the *"Lupi di Toscana"* (Wolves of Tuscany) Division (General Ottavio

Bollea), which had been force-marched to its objective. Papagos grouped his I and II Corps together under General Drakos as the Army of Epirus, but this was defeated at Telepenë in February. Not that the Greek troops lacked keenness or endurance (in his diary Cavallero says that their attacks were "frenzied"): they simply had no means of waging modern offensive warfare. This is clearly explained in the former Greek Commander-in-Chief's book on his army's operations:

"The presence among the Italian troops of a considerable number of tanks, and the fact that we had none at all and very few anti-tank guns, forced us to keep well clear of the plains, which would allow rapid movement, and to manoeuvre only in the mountains. This increased the fatigue of the men and the beasts of burden, lengthened and delayed our convoys and brought additional difficulties in command, supplies and so on. The enemy, on the other hand, thanks to the means at his disposal, was able to fall back rapidly on the plains and take up new positions without much difficulty. Taking advantage of the terrain, he was then able to hold up our advance in the mountains with a relatively small number of men. Also, the fresh troops which the Italians brought up during this phase of the war came to the front in lorries, whereas ours had to move on foot, reaching the front tired and frequently too late to be of any use. As a final point I must mention the difficulties we had in restoring the engineering works which were damaged by the enemy, and the superiority of the Italian Air Force which, after the limited daily sorties by Greek and British planes, were able to attack with impunity both our forward and our rear areas." General Cavallero's success in these defensive operations gave him enough respite to reinforce and rest his troops so as to go over to the offensive as Mussolini had ordered.

From December 29, 1940 to March 26, 1941 no fewer than ten divisions, four machine gun battalions, together with three legions and 17 battalions of Black Shirts crossed the Adriatic. When spring came the Italian land forces in Albania thus comprised: the 9th and the 11th Armies, the 9th now under General Pirzio-Biroli and the 11th still under General Geloso: six corps, with 21 infantry divisions, five mountain divisions and the "Centauro" Armoured Division. The Greeks, on the other hand, had only 13 to 14 divisions, all of them suffering from battle fatigue.

This goes to show that, though denied the Mediterranean, the Italian Navy still controlled the Adriatic. Only one difficulty faced General Cavallero: was he to give priority to bringing up reinforcements or to supplying his troops at the front, given that all the Albanian ports together, whatever might be done to increase their

capacity, could only handle 4,000 tons a day? One of the few units lost during these operations was the hospital ship *Po*, torpedoed in error in Valona harbour. Countess Edda Ciano, who was serving on board as a nurse, escaped with no more than a ducking.

As he had re-established numerical superiority, General Cavallero now set about his offensive operations. On March 9, 1941, watched by Mussolini, the 9th Army began attacking in the sector between the river Osum (called the Apsos by the Greeks) in the north-east and the Vijosë or the Aóos in the south-west. The area is dominated by the Trebesina mountains. General Geloso put in his IV, VIII and XXV Corps (Generals Mercalli, Gambara and Carlo Rossi respectively), comprising 11 infantry divisions and the "Centauro" Armoured Division. On D-day the Greeks had three divisions and the equivalent of a fourth, all from the II Corps (General Papadopoulos). At dawn the Greek positions were heavily shelled and bombed. From their observation point, at 0830, Mussolini and Cavallero could see the infantry moving up to their objectives over territory not unlike the Carso, where so many Italians had fallen in fruitless attacks between June 1915 and August 1917 during World War I.

The Trebesina offensive did not restore the Duce's prestige. Not because the Greek defenders equalled the Italian attacking force in strength, as Cavallero wrote in his diary in the evening of March 9, but because they were well organised and their morale was high. He went on: "The Greek artillery is powerfully deployed. All the elements of the defending forces are well organised in depth, using positions of strength which enable them to contain the offensive and to counter-

An unusual bust of Mussolini.

attack immediately and vigorously."

Forty-eight hours later, not only had there not been the expected breakthrough, but losses were mounting, the 11th Alpini Regiment alone reporting 356 killed and wounded, including 36 officers. Should the plan be abandoned after this discouraging start? Mussolini did not think so. That very day he said to General Geloso: "The directives of the plan must be adhered to at all costs. Between now and the end of the month a military victory is vital for the prestige of the Italian Army."

And he added, with an unusual disregard for his responsibilities in the matter of Italian military unpreparedness:

"I have always done my best to maintain the fame and the prestige of the Italian Army, but today it is vital to drive on with the offensive." They drove on, therefore, but attacks were followed by counter-attacks and General Papagos having, so to speak, thrown two divisions into the fray, the Italians were no further forward on the 15th than they had been on the 9th. When General Gambara was asked by Mussolini about the morale of his corps he replied, tactfully: "It cannot be said to be very high, but it remains firm. Losses, no territorial gains, few prisoners; this is hardly encouraging. All the same, morale is good enough not to prejudice the men's use in battle."

Mussolini and Cavallero finally drew the right conclusions from the situation and called off the attack. Mussolini returned to Rome without increasing his reputation. The three corps engaged in this unhappy affair lost 12,000 dead and wounded, or some 1,000 men per division. When it is realised that most of these losses were borne by the infantry it cannot be denied that they fought manfully.

The Greeks, on their side, however, suffered enormously and this defensive success, however honourable it might have been for their army, left them with only 14 divisions against 27.

Meanwhile, on January 29, 1941, General Metaxas, who had forged the victories in Epirus and Albania, died suddenly in Athens and King George nominated Petros Koryzis as his successor. Events were soon to bring tragic proof that the new Greek Prime Minister could not match his predecessor in strength of character. He was, however, no less resolved to oppose with force the Germans' aggressive intentions in Rumania, as he made known in a letter to London dated February 8. This led to the departure from Plymouth on the 14th in a Sunderland flying boat bound for Cairo of Anthony Eden and Dill, the Chief of the Imperial General Staff. General Wavell raised no objections in principle to aid for Greece, in spite of the serious risks involved. Eden was thus in a position to cable the Prime Minister on February 21:

"Dill and I have exhaustively reviewed situation temporarily [sic] with Commanders-in-Chief. Wavell is ready to make available three divisions, a Polish brigade

and best part of an armoured division, together with a number of specialized troops such as anti-tank and anti-aircraft units. Though some of these ... have yet to be concentrated, work is already in hand and they can reach Greece as rapidly as provision of ships will allow. This programme fulfils the hopes expressed at Defence Committee that we could make available a force of three divisions and an armoured division.

"Gravest anxiety is not in respect of army but of air. There is no doubt that need to fight a German air force, instead

Mussolini listens attentively to his new High Command Chief-of-Staff, General Ugo Cavallero.

of Italian, is creating a new problem for Longmore. My own impression is that all his squadrons are not quite up to standard of their counterpart at home . . . . . We should all have liked to approach Greeks tomorrow with a suggestion that we should join with them in holding a line to defend Salonika, but both Longmore and Cunningham are convinced that our present air resources will not allow us to

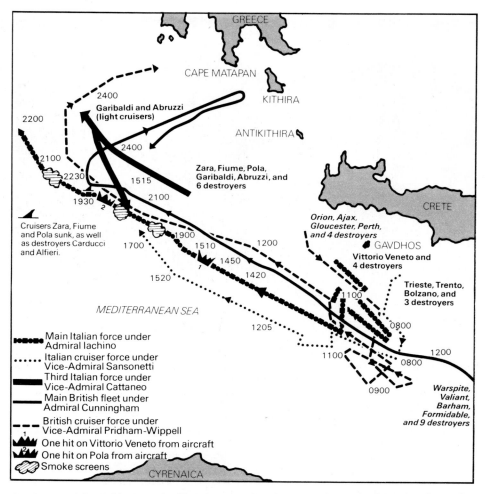

GREECE

CAPE MATAPAN

KITHIRA

2400
Garibaldi and Abruzzi
(light cruisers)

2200

2100

2230

1930

1515

2100

2400

ANTIKITHIRA

Zara, Fiume, Pola,
Garibaldi, Abruzzi, and
6 destroyers

CRETE

Cruisers Zara, Fiume
and Pola sunk, as well
as destroyers Carducci
and Alfieri.

1700

1900

1510

1200

Orion, Ajax,
Gloucester, Perth,
and 4 destroyers

GAVDHOS

1520

1450

1420

Vittorio Veneto and
4 destroyers

MEDITERRANEAN SEA

1205

1100

Trieste, Trento,
Bolzano, and
3 destroyers

0800

1100

1200

0800

Main Italian force under
Admiral Iachino

Italian cruiser force under
Vice-Admiral Sansonetti

Third Italian force under
Vice-Admiral Cattaneo

Main British fleet under
Admiral Cunningham

British cruiser force under
Vice-Admiral Pridham-Wippell

One hit on Vittorio Veneto from aircraft

One hit on Pola from aircraft

Smoke screens

0900

Warspite,
Valiant,
Barham,
Formidable,
and 9 destroyers

CYRENAICA

The battle of Cape Matapan in March 1941, when the Italians lost six ships.

do this ."

The truth is that the R.A.F. would find itself having to face not the Italian Air Force but the Luftwaffe, and that is why both Air Chief-Marshal Longmore and Admiral Cunningham doubted if the expeditionary force could fight on a front covering Salonika. These doubts were shared also by Sir John Dill. However, the matter was to be discussed with the Greeks at a secret conference on the following day (February 22) at the Royal Palace at Tatoi, near Athens. The results were to prove very dangerous. But at the time the British saw this as their chance to get back into Europe.

The conference was attended by King George II, Anthony Eden, Prime Minister Koryzis, the British Ambassador in Athens, Generals Dill and Wavell, Air Chief-Marshal Longmore, and the heads of the British Military Missions in Greece. General Papagos was asked to report on the latest situation.

After giving an account of the latest Intelligence information, he put forward the solution he would advocate if Yugoslavia were to remain neutral and refuse to allow German troops to cross her territory. In this hypothesis the defence of western Thrace and eastern Macedonia would seem to be inadvisable. Troops defending the Metaxas Line, the main bulwark against Bulgaria, would there-

fore be given the task of slowing down the enemy advance, holding out to the last round, but the troops supporting them opposite Yugoslavia (three divisions) would fall back on a position between the lower Aliákmon river and the Vérmion and Kaïmakchalán mountains, which rise respectively to 6,725 and 8,375 feet. If all went well this operation should take about 20 days. But Papagos thought that the German forces in Rumania would need only a fortnight to get to the Bulgarian-Greek frontier from the left bank of the Danube.

This is where General Papagos's version disagrees with that of Eden. According to Papagos, no firm decision was taken at the end of the Tatoi conference concerning the eventual evacuation of the two provinces mentioned above. "I emphasised, however," he writes, "that after taking such a grave decision as to withdraw our troops from Thrace and eastern Macedonia and to leave this whole sector of our national territory at the mercy of the enemy without even defending it, we had to be absolutely sure about the attitude of Yugoslavia and I suggested informing the Yugoslavs about the decisions we intended to take and which would depend on their reaction."

"The British delegation," he adds, "seemed to agree and it was decided that Eden would inform H.M. Ambassador in Belgrade by urgent coded telegram. The Greek Commander-in-Chief would define

his position according to the reply received. Whereupon Anthony Eden and Generals Dill and Wavell flew off to Ankara."

Eden's version is very different, though he affirms his statement on the evidence of General Wavell who died, it is true, in 1950. But, for all that, it appears that on this point, like many others, Eden's record is at variance with the events. When he got back from his fruitless journey to Ankara he sent a telegram to the Prime Minister on March 4, in which he said, among other things:

"General Papagos had on the last occasion insisted strongly that the withdrawal of all troops in Macedonia to the Aliákmon line was the only sound military solution. We expected that this withdrawal to the Aliákmon line had already begun. Instead we found that no movement had in fact commenced, Papagos alleging that it had been agreed that the decision taken at our last meeting was dependent on the receipt of an answer from Yugoslavia as to their attitude."

As we see, if this text establishes the good faith of Anthony Eden, it also shows that General Papagos's version was not thought up after the event. There was therefore a misunderstanding at Tatoi. However this may be, one thing is clear: the premature evacuation of Salonika, Yugoslavia's only possible access to the Aegean Sea, could only have a discouraging effect on Belgrade.

On March 1, 1941 Bulgaria joined the Tripartite Pact and the German 12th Army under Field-Marshal List crossed the Danube on pontoon bridges. In line with undertakings given on the previous January 18, this event decided the Athens Government to allow the entry into Greece of the expeditionary force organised in Cairo and put under the command of Sir Henry Maitland Wilson. But however strongly the British might have insisted, General Papagos refused to begin the anticipated withdrawal from Thrace and eastern Macedonia. It was already March 4 and everything inclined to the belief that if his three divisions on the Metaxas Line were given the order, they would now be caught in full movement.

From March 7 onwards the British Expeditionary Force began to land at the ports of Piraeus and Vólos. It was transported in 25 ships and no untoward incident occurred, as the Italian air forces based in the Dodecanese were not up to strength. Altogether 57,577 men and about 100 tanks were landed to form the 1st Armoured Brigade, the 6th Australian Division (Major-General Sir Iven Mackay) and the 2nd New Zealand Division, the latter under Major-General Bernard Freyberg, V.C., a hero of the Dardanelles and the Somme.

At the end of the month Maitland Wilson's troops were in position behind the Aliákmon and the Vérmion mountains. On the other hand, after negotiations which, in a telegram dated March 4,

Eden describes somewhat testily as "bargaining more reminiscent of oriental bazaars", the Greek High Command put under the B.E.F. three divisions (the 12th, the 20th, and the 19th Motorised) with seven battalions withdrawn from the Turkish border after reassurances from Ankara. The British expected more of their allies, but it should be noted on the other hand, that the 7th Australian Division (Major-General J. D. Lavarack) and the 1st Polish Brigade (General Kopanski), which should have been sent to Greece, never left the Middle East.

On February 14 at Merano, Grand-Admiral Raeder had recommended Admiral Riccardi to be more active. The transportation of the expeditionary force to Greece gave *Supermarina* the chance of intervening in the Eastern Mediterranean. The German and Italian G.H.Q.'s encouraged these impulses towards an offensive all the more keenly because on March 16 the X *Fliegerkorps* announced, wrongly as it turned out, that its planes had torpedoed two of the three battleships of the Mediterranean Fleet and put them out of action.

The plan was to sweep the Aegean and Mediterranean on D-day with two detachments as far as the island of Gávdhos, 31 miles south of Crete. The task force was put under the command of Rear-Admiral Angelo Iachino and consisted of the battleship *Vittorio Veneto*, six heavy and two light cruisers, and 13 destroyers. The operation also required considerable air support, both for reconnaissance and for defence against British bombers and torpedo-carrying aircraft.

Agreement was reached on joint air support with both the Italian Air Force and the Luftwaffe's X *Fliegerkorps*, but there was no time to test the arranged procedures in exercises. It is true that there were German and Italian liaison officers on board the *Vittorio Veneto*, but on the whole Admiral Iachino was sceptical of the results to be expected from this improvised collaboration, particularly concerning fighter support.

In the afternoon of March 27 a Sunderland flying boat spotted the squadron, which was then steaming through the Ionian Sea. The British had thus been alerted, as decoded messages subsequently confirmed, and it was now unlikely that any of their convoys could be intercepted. Yet the only offensive orders countermanded by *Supermarina* were those concerning the area north of Crete. That same evening Cunningham slipped out of Alexandria with three battleships and the aircraft-carrier *Formidable*, which had 37 aircraft on board. He had arranged a rendezvous south-east of Gávdhos with Vice-Admiral H. D. Pridham-Wippell's squadron of four cruisers from Piraeus.

First contact, at about 0800 hours, was between Admiral Sansonetti's three heavy cruisers and Pridham-Wippell's light cruisers. Though the British ships mounted only 6-inch guns against the Italian vessels' 8-inch, their evasive action, contrary to the Royal Navy's tradition of aggressiveness, led Iachino to think that they might be acting as bait for a large ship as yet out of sight. He therefore recalled Sansonetti. Pridham-Wippell then gave chase, only to find himself being fired on by the *Vittorio Veneto*'s 15-inch guns. The Italians loosed off 94 rounds but failed to score a hit. Then at about mid-day torpedo-carrying aircraft from the *Formidable* launched a first attack, but without success. Admiral Iachino thereupon headed back to base.

At 1510 hours, the Fleet Air Arm launched its second attack. At the cost of his life, Lieutenant-Commander J. Dalyell-Stead dropped his torpedo at very short range and severely damaged the *Vittorio Veneto*, causing her to ship 4,000 tons of water and putting her two port engines out of action. Thanks to the efforts of her crew the damaged battleship got under way again at a speed of first 17 then 19 knots.

By this time Cunningham, with the main body of his fleet, was about 87 miles away. The *Formidable*'s planes kept him fully informed of the Italian movements, whereas Iachino was in complete ignorance of Cunningham's, and was no

An Italian Bolzano-*class cruiser under attack by carrier-borne torpedo bombers during the battle of Matapan.*

better informed than he had been defended by the exiguous Axis air support. In despair, and relying on a radio bearing from *Supermarina*, Iachino admitted that he was being chased by an aircraft-carrier and a cruiser some 170 miles away.

As daylight faded he gathered about the damaged flagship his 1st and 3rd Cruiser Squadrons and the destroyers in case another attack was made by British aircraft. These had, in fact, been ordered to delay the *Vittorio Veneto* so that the British battleships could finish her off. Iachino's defensive tactics, including the use of smoke screens, prevented this, but towards 1925 hours the heavy cruiser *Pola* was torpedoed. Iachino ordered Admiral Cattaneo to stay with the *Pola*, taking her in tow if possible and scuttling her if this proved impracticable. The decision was later criticised, but was justified in the light of Iachino's estimate of the British position. However this may be, the luckless cruiser then came up on the *Ajax*'s radar screen. Pridham-Wippell took her for the *Vittorio Veneto* and signalled to Cunningham, who was closing with the *Warspite*, *Valiant*, and *Barham*. At about 2200 hours *Valiant*'s radar picked up Cattaneo's cruisers sailing blindly forward into the darkness. Some 30 minutes later the British squadron's 24 15-inch guns blasted them out of the water at point-blank range. The *Fiume* went down at 2315 hours, the *Zara*, which was sinking more slowly, was scuttled by her commander and the destroyers *Alfieri* and *Carducci* met a similar fate. Finally a British destroyer sank *Pola* after picking up her survivors.

That night and the morning after the battle, which took place 112 miles southwest of Cape Matapan, the British, with the aid of several Greek destroyers picked up just over a thousand survivors. The rescue operations were hampered by a Luftwaffe attack, but Cunningham generously signalled Rome, giving the area where further survivors might still

be found. The hospital ship *Gradisca* subsequently picked up another 160. Altogether 2,400 Italian seamen were lost, including Admiral Cattaneo and the commanders of the cruisers *Zara* and *Fiume*, Captains Giorgis and Corsi respectively. The only British loss was that of the heroic Dalyell-Stead.

Although Admiral Cunningham was not altogether satisfied with the outcome of the battle, since the *Vittorio Veneto* had got away and reached Taranto, Cape Matapan was a heavy defeat for the Italian Navy, which had lost at one blow three of its 12,000-ton cruisers, a loss which could not be made good overnight. This was what Mussolini had in mind when he received Admiral Iachino at the Palazzo Venezia.

"The operation promised well and might have been successful had it not been for the total lack of co-operation from the air arm. During the whole time you never had a single Italian or German plane over you. All the aircraft you saw were the enemy's. They chased you, attacked you, overpowered you. Your ships were like blind invalids being set upon by several armed killers."

Naval operations were impossible in British-controlled waters without proper reconnaissance and fighter support. Mussolini concluded, with what Iachino describes as the true journalist's capacity for summing things up: "And as fighter aircraft have a limited range, the ships must take their escorts with them. In a word, all naval forces must always be accompanied by at least one aircraft-carrier."

And so the Duce was going back on the point of view he had expressed in 1930, but late in view of a defeat which was to weigh heavily on Italian strategy. To

alleviate the consequences it was decided to convert two liners, *Roma* and *Augustus*, into aircraft-carriers and rename them *Aquila* and *Sparviero*. Until they came into service the fleet was forbidden to sail outside land-based fighter range.

The exploit of Lieutenant Faggioni and his five men in the battle of Cape Matapan deserves not to be forgotten. During the night of March 25–26 they managed to get into Suda Bay, on the north coast of Crete, in motor boats loaded with explosives. There they crippled the cruiser *York* and the oil-tanker *Pericles*.

The entry of German troops into Bulgaria, the import of which escaped no one in Europe, put Yugoslavia in a difficult position. In face of the claims on her territory by Italy, Hungary, and Bulgaria, was she to go on defying the Third Reich by refusing to join the Tripartite Pact? And had not Hitler said that he did not intend to pass through Yugoslav territory to invade Greece?

It has been said that this guarantee was a trap, but it seems unlikely. It must be remembered that when List and his H.Q. were told that they could in future use Yugoslav territory to turn the Metaxas Line they greeted the news with feelings of great relief. This permission must clearly have been denied to them previously, doubtless because Hitler looked upon the Yugoslav Army as the heirs of the Serbian Army of 1914–1918.

By joining the Tripartite Pact on March 25, the Regent, Prince Paul, and the Prime Minister, Dragisa Cvetković, did not choose to tread the hero's path, but before condemning them it must be realised that a discreet sounding of opinion in Athens had revealed to them

A German machine-gun post established on the Aegean coast.

that very little was to be expected of the British. On the other hand they were doubtless better informed of the ruinous situation within Yugoslavia than the military faction who overthrew them two days later.

Was the British Ambassador an accessory to the military plot in Belgrade on March 27, when the young King Peter's majority was proclaimed and General Simović assumed power? It was said so at the time and we know now that when he heard that the Regent had decided to sign the Tripartite Pact, Anthony Eden telegraphed Sir Ronald Campbell on March 24:

"You are authorized now to proceed at your discretion by any means at your disposal to move leaders and public opinion to understanding of realities and to action to meet the situation.

"You have my full authority for any measures that you may think it right to take to further change of Government or régime, even by *coup d'état*."

But did King George VI's representative in Belgrade have time to carry out these new instructions? It would appear not. However this may be, the new masters in Yugoslavia showed a marked lack of determination in both the diplomatic and the military field, and continued to hope that the crisis would be resolved without recourse to war. They thus took care not to provoke the Third Reich by, for instance, denouncing the Tripartite Pact or proclaiming general mobilisation. This gave Hitler time to seize the initiative.

Before the day of March 27 was over Hitler

Balkan Campaign

GRECO-ITALIAN FRONT ON APRIL 6, 1940
ITALIAN OPERATIONS
GERMAN ADVANCES
BOUNDARY BETWEEN 2ND AND 12TH ARMIES
METAXAS LINE
BRITISH MOVEMENTS
AIRBORNE OPERATIONS

had signed the 13 copies of his Directive No. 25. This declared in its first paragraph: "The military revolt in Yugoslavia has changed the political position in the Balkans. Yugoslavia, even if it makes initial professions of loyalty, must be regarded as an enemy and beaten down as soon as possible." Having defined the principle he went on to the means of execution. Two strategic groups, one from the Fiume-Graz front and the other from the Sofia area, would converge on Belgrade and wipe out the Yugoslav Army. A third group would attack Serbian Macedonia to secure a base for the Italo-German attack on Greece. An attempt would be made to bring in Hungary and Bulgaria by guaranteeing that their territorial claims would be met. Assurances of national self-determination to the Croats would intensify political tension in Yugoslavia.

On the same day Belgrade had 900,000 men under arms and a mobilisation decree would have brought in another 500,000.

But to carry out the Führer's orders within the time required to achieve surprise, a necessary condition for a quick success, the German High Command had to draw heavily on its preparations for "Barbarossa", thus delaying the attack on the Soviet Union from mid-May to late June. In fact Operation "Marita", revised and extended in next to no time by admirable staff work, involved two armies and *Panzergruppe* Kleist: ten corps, four of which were armoured – 32 divisions, including ten armoured and four motorised or their equivalent in all. Events moved so rapidly, however, that eight of these divisions could not get to the front in time.

As was to be expected, Mussolini welcomed Hitler's initiative, which would allow him to realise his long-cherished dream of crushing Yugoslavia. To this effect 2nd Army was concentrated in Venezia Giulia under the command of General Ambrosio, with four corps (14 divisions, including the "Pasubio" and "Torino" Motorised Divisions and the "Littorio" Armoured Division). Another division was to attack from Zara, while 11th Army in Albania would attempt to link up with the Germans in Serbian Macedonia.

On the promise that Hungarian claims on Yugoslavia would be met, Admiral Horthy felt obliged to join in the attack, in spite of the non-aggression pact he had signed a few weeks previously with Prince-Regent Paul. His Foreign Minister, Count Teleki, committed suicide over this breach of promise.

The defeat of Yugoslavia and her armed forces took 12 days. On April 6 units of *Luftflotte* IV under Colonel-General Alexander Löhr savagely bombed Belgrade while *Panzergruppe* Kleist began the assault. The XIV Motorised Corps (General von Meitersheim) advanced along a line Sofia – Niš, immediately took the Tsaribrod col and covered 312 miles in seven days along the Morava valley. On April 13, in the ruins of the unhappy

capital, it met the XLI Panzer Corps (General Reinhardt) which had advanced from the Timisoara area.

Except for its 5th Panzer Division, *Panzergruppe* Kleist then came under 2nd Army, which had concentrated in Carinthia and southern Hungary under the command of Colonel-General von Weichs. As soon as it was engaged in battle its XLVI Panzer Corps (General von Vietinghoff) launched a surprise attack on a bridge over the Drava at Barcs, captured it and opened the way for the headlong rush of this latest Blitzkrieg. Without stopping at Zagreb, the 14th Panzer Division made its first contact with the Italian 2nd Army at Karlovac, then sped on through Banja Luka towards Sarajevo, which it occupied on April 15. Between the Sava and the Drava the 8th Panzer and the 16th Motorised Divisions drove on just as easily through Novi Sad and Ruma, then up the Drina valley to join forces with the 14th Panzer Division. Meanwhile *Panzergruppe* Kleist had moved from Belgrade to Kruševac to block the escape route of any Yugoslav remnants trying to get from Bosnia into Macedonia.

The way the campaign developed shows that Peter II's armies not only had obsolete weapons but had been caught in indefensible positions. It must also be stated that Mussolini and Ciano's undermining of morale in Croatia over the years had at last borne its rotten fruit. There is proof of this in this note from Colonel-General Halder, who was in Wiener-Neustadt with Brauchitsch:

"April 11, Good Friday . . . Information gathered during the course of the day gives the impression that in the north of Yugoslavia the front is breaking up with increasing rapidity. Units are laying down their arms or taking the road to captivity, according to our airmen. One cycle company captures a whole brigade with its staff. An enemy divisional commander radios his superior officer that his men are throwing down their arms and going home."

One more indication, among others, of this lack of morale: the Yugoslav fleet never attempted to get into British-controlled waters, and even let most of its ships fall into Axis hands undamaged. In particular there were three destroyers which the Italian Captain Bragadin describes as "very modern" and of whose capture he boasts as a proud accession to the Italian Navy. The only vessel of this class denied to the Axis was the *Zagreb*, which her commander scuttled.

Under these conditions it is not surprising that on April 17, 1941 the Yugoslav Foreign Minister, Aleksander Cincar-Marković, and General Janković, the Deputy Chief-of-Staff, went to Belgrade to sign the instrument of surrender drawn up by Colonel-General von Weichs and the Italian Military Attaché. King Peter II boarded a Sunderland flying boat at Kotor and left for Egypt.

As a consequence of the surrender of April 17, 6,028 Yugoslav officers and

337,684 N.C.O.s and men became prisoners-of-war. Almost 300,000 men of the conquered army, mainly Serbs, succeeded, however, in escaping captivity. Many of them continued to fight under Colonel Draža Mihailović, who had played an important part in the *Putsch* on March 27. On the other side of the scales, the German High Command figures, confirmed after the end of the war, gave 151 killed, 15 missing, and 392 wounded. This is further proof of the causes of the Yugoslav collapse mentioned above.

Though they were no more able to escape defeat than the Yugoslavs, the Greeks nevertheless cut a much better figure, although uncertainties as to the eventual direction of Belgrade's policies continued to affect the decisions of the Greek High Command. On March 25, hearing that Cvetković had signed the Tripartite Pact, General Papagos ordered the Metaxas Line and Salonika to be abandoned. He countermanded this order on the 27th, when he learnt of the upsurge of patriotism which had carried Simović to power. During the night of April 4–5, accompanied by Anothony Eden and Sir John Dill, he met General Janković on the Greco-Yugoslav border. According to his account, the latter guaranteed that the Strumica area would be solidly defended; with this door to invasion securely locked and bolted, a concentric attack, in which both countries would share, would be mounted against Albania. His Yugoslav colleague's intention of defending an over-long frontier by 1920-type methods seemed to Papagos to be strategic heresy.

But advisers are not the ones who pay. Papagos could not persuade Janković to abandon two-thirds of his national territory in the interests of common defence. Yet reports were piling up in his headquarters to the effect that a German attack was imminent. Therefore on April 6, at 0100 hours, he ordered demolitions to be carried out between the Bulgarian frontier and the forward Greek defence positions.

Zero hour came at 0515. According to the plan, western Thrace, between the Greek frontier and the Néstos, was to be abandoned to its fate. On the other hand, the right bank of the Néstos was to be defended to the last man, as also was the Metaxas Line, so as to link up with the Yugoslavs in the area of Strumica. The force to be used was the Army of Macedonia (General Bakopoulos) comprising the "Evros" and the "Néstos" Divisions, the 7th Division, General Dedes's group (the 14th and the 18th Divisions), and the Kroúsia group, which was in touch with the Yugoslav forces. Resistance would be based on the Metaxas Line fortifications, which were modern, well-planned, and manned by an élite garrison.

Opposite these Greek forces, Field-Marshal List crossed the Greco-Bulgarian frontier with five divisions from the XXX Corps (General Ott) in the east and the XVIII Mountain Corps (General Böhme) in the west. The attack was supported

from the air by Stukas of VIII *Flieger-korps*. But, and this was unique in Europe, the fortifications of the Metaxas Line included A.A. turrets with 37-mm guns, which minimised the effect of the dive-bombers.

Wherever the Greeks had not previously been ordered to retreat, they held out desperately and often with success. When it reached the Néstos, the German XXX Corps was driven back as it tried to cross. In the Nevrokop basin the 72nd Division (Lieutenant-General Mattenklott) lost 700 killed and wounded in three days as it tried to break out towards Sérrai and Salonika; twice its pioneers got inside the outer defences at Perithórion and twice they were driven back. In the Rupel pass the reinforced regiment which was attacking lost a quarter of its men in fire from the fortifications and was unable to reach any of its objectives. The 5th and 6th Mountain Divisions under Generals Ringel and Schörner were more fortunate. The forts at Istibey and Kelkayia were too close to the Bulgarian frontier and were put partially out of action by shots fired through their embrasures by 5-cm anti-tank guns and 2-cm and 8·8-cm A.A. guns, which had been lined up before D-day but had not been attacked by the Greeks. Nevertheless, the Greeks defended the

approaches, then the main positions of their forts until they had been all but asphyxiated by the carbon dioxide released by numerous underground explosions. At Kelkayia, at mid-day on April 7, Captain Zakynthos surrendered 154 men, unwounded, but most of them poisoned, out of 264; at Istibey, before ordering them to lay down their arms at 1600 hours, Major Pitoulakis had lost 143 men killed and wounded out of a garrison of 457. For its part the 5th Mountain Division had lost the equivalent of a battalion. In the Kroúsia sector, which was less well organised, the 6th Mountain Division made good progress.

But the fate of the Greek forces fighting in Macedonia as well as the future of the Greek and Balkan campaign were being decided here and now and irrevocably by the successes of the 2nd Panzer Division (Lieutenant-General Vieil) at Strumica and of the XL Motorised Corps (General Stumme) on the Kyustendil col. Operating on the right wing of the XVIII Mountain Corps inside Yugoslavia, the 2nd Panzer Division had reached Strumica, over 19 miles from its point of departure, before nightfall, knocking out the "Bregalnica" Division on its way. At dawn on the 8th, having occupied the right bank of Lake Dojran, it crossed the Greek frontier. The

Greek prisoners trail past three German armoured cars. The famous Sd. Kfz-231 is on the right of the picture.

19th Motorised Infantry Division tried to block its path at Kilkís, but according to the history of this campaign published by G.H.Q. Athens, the division's equipment was "tragi-comical" and so, in the evening of the same day, after a dash of some 56 miles, Vieil occupied Salonika. With his communications cut, General Bakopoulos was ordered to surrender and he commanded his 70,000 men to lay down their arms at 1400 hours on April 9.

It took the XL Motorised Corps 48 hours to get its 9th Panzer Division from Kyustendil to Skopje and its 73rd Division to Kočani and Veles, demolishing on the way the "Morava" and "Ibar" Divisions. So complete was the surprise that seven Yugoslav generals fell into the hands of the Germans along with 20,000 men and at least 100 guns. Stumme then changed the *Leibstandarte Adolf Hitler*'s axis of advance from west to south and on April 9 it seized the important crossroads at Bitola or Monastir. Forty-eight hours later the "Chumadia" and "Vardar" Divisions had been put out of action, while the XL Motorised Corps made its

153

first contact with the Italian 9th Army in the area of Ohrid. The collapse of the Yugoslav 3rd Army brought the right wing of the German 12th Army up against the rear positions along the line Aliákmon – Vérmion – Kaïmakchalán, occupied by Maitland Wilson and his Anglo-Greek force. Air Vice-Marshal D'Albiac's Gloster Gladiators, which had swept Mussolini's Fiat C.R. 42's out of the sky, were now unfortunately being hounded by Messerschmitt 109's from *Luftflotte* IV as these opened the way for the Stukas.

On the ground, the British 1st Armoured Brigade had 100 tanks, most of them obsolete, against Field-Marshal List's possible 500 or even 600, when the 5th Panzer Division rejoined the XL Motorised Corps. All the evidence pointed to the necessity of retreat in both Macedonia and Albania. Perhaps General Papagos decided on it too late. What is certain is that the XVIII Mountain Corps crossed the Aliákmon after a fighting withdrawal by the 2nd New Zealand Division, skirted Mount Olympus and occupied Lárisa on April 18, while the XL Mountain Corps, adding to the outflanking movement, pushed forward along the line Flórina – Kozáni – Tríkkala. Through lack of mobile

German paratroopers enjoy a meal of wurst *after landing in Crete.*

reserves and insufficient co-ordination of movement between the two Allies, a breach opened up between the left of the B.E.F. and the right of the Greek armies slowly withdrawing from Albania.

The *Leibstandarte Adolf Hitler* reached and swept through Grevená, took the Métzovon col and, on April 21, captured Yanina in the rear of the Greeks. Against orders from Athens and over the head of his superior, General Drakos, the commander of the Army of the Epirus. General Tzolakoglou entered into negotiations with the Germans, an action in which he was supported by his corps commanders and the Bishop of Yanina.

The instrument of capitulation, which led to the surrender of 16 Greek divisions, was signed at Lárisa by a representative of the Greek Parliament and Field-Marshal List. Mussolini's anger at this rattled the window panes of the Palazzo Venezia. Hitler then ordered the commander of the 12th Army to organise a new signing ceremony to which the representatives of his friend Mussolini were to be invited. The derisory event took place at Salonika on April 24, 1941, and thus it was that the Fascist dictator came to triumph over the Greeks whom he had not conquered. Some 140,000 Greeks had capitulated under these terms.

Meanwhile, on April 19, a conference between the Allies had been held in Athens to take stock of the situation. King George II and Generals Papagos, Wavell, and Maitland Wilson were present and by common consent they decided that the British Expeditionary Force would evacuate the mainland of Greece.

The subsequent fighting at Thermopylai, then before Thebes, was aimed solely at covering this operation, the execution of which was entrusted to Rear-Admiral H. T. Baillie-Grohman. The Australians and New Zealanders left Attica from the little ports of Rafina, Pórto Ráfti and Mégara.

But on April 25, while a detachment of German paratroops was landing on the south bank of the Corinth Canal, the *Leibstandarte*, which had reached Náupaktos, was crossing the Gulf of Patras in makeshift craft and pouring out on to the roads in the Peloponnese. The British Expeditionary Force nevertheless managed to reach the open sea through the ports of Náuplion, Monemvasía (formerly Malvoisia) and Kalamáta.

In all, at the cost of four transports and two destroyers sunk by Stukas, Baillie-Grohman miraculously managed to re-embark 50,732 British, Australian and New Zealand troops.

Maitland Wilson's losses in this rapid and disastrous campaign were 12,712 killed, wounded and missing, including 9,000 prisoners, two-thirds of whom had been swept into the bag around Kalamáta. The Greeks, after a campaign lasting six months, had lost 15,700 killed and missing; 218,000 were taken prisoner by the Germans but these, apart from the officers, were released shortly afterwards.

On May 1 Hitler had good reason to gloat on the rostrum in the Reichstag. He had overrun Yugoslavia and Greece and, for the second time, had driven the British off the continent; and all this in 25 days of fighting and with losses of only 1,684 killed and 3,752 wounded – the equivalent, that is, of one third of one of the 24 divisions he had put into the campaign.

Mussolini, as can be realised, had less reason to boast. He took good care not to publish his losses at the time. But according to the statistics diligently compiled after the war by the historical service of the Italian Army we know that they amounted to more than 102,000 men. There were 13,755 killed, 50,874 wounded and 25,067 missing, most of whom were dead. To make up the total given above 12,368 cases of severe frost-bite must be added. No comment is needed on the desperate state in which the Duce's pseudo-military régime had left the man at the front.

Victors of the hour, the Führer and the Duce set up the "New Order" in the Balkan peninsula and brought in Hungary and Bulgaria to share the spoils of conquest.

Yugoslavia was forthwith dismembered. Slovenia was divided between Germany and Italy, which also took a large slice of the Dalmatian coast and the bay of Kotor. Montenegro got back her independence. Hungary got Bačka, north-west of Belgrade, and Bulgaria got Serbian Macedonia as far as Lake Ohrida, on whose shores King Boris's occupation troops found themselves at daggers drawn with those of his father-in-law, Victor Emmanuel III, King of Italy and Albania.

Mussolini and Ciano set up a Kingdom of Croatia into which they incorporated, quite illegally, the Serbian provinces of Bosnia and Hercegovina. The crown of this puppet state was handed by its new masters in Zagreb to Aymon, Duke of Spoleto, of the House of Savoy. But the new sovereign preferred the society of Rome to the company of General Kvaternik and Dr. Ante Pavelić and never set foot in his capital.

From what was left of Greece the conquerors took western Thrace, which, under the promises made by Hitler and Mussolini to King Boris, was awarded to Bulgaria, thus restoring her access to the Aegean, lost under the Treaty of Neuilly in 1919.

All these many alterations to the map of the Balkans were accompanied by frightful atrocities. In Bosnia and Hercegovina the Ustase, as Ante Pavelić's militiamen

were called, massacred whole villages of Orthodox and Muslim believers. In Bačka the brutal excesses of the Hungarian troops moved Horthy, the Regent, to indignation, but he was powerless to intervene as the authors of these atrocities claimed to be carrying out the orders of Hitler and Himmler. In their new provinces the Bulgars seemed to have exceeded the Hungarians and equalled the Croats in their savagery.

With Greece evacuated, should the Allies have continued to cling on to Crete? British critics of Churchill's war strategy have said on more than one occasion that the island should have been abandoned. Yet a glance at the map will show that whereas Crete is 500 miles from Alexandria, it is only 200 from Tobruk. Tobruk, the bastion of British resistance in the Middle East, could only be supplied by sea and the great danger was that it might be starved out if the Luftwaffe controlled the aerodromes at Máleme and Heraklion. If Churchill is to be criticised for wanting to fight the war on every front with insufficient means, this is not a front which should be held against him.

Hitler drew similar conclusions. His aims were defensive as well as offensive. Within a few weeks the unleashing of "Barbarossa" would deprive him (only temporarily he hoped) of Russian oil. What would happen if the R.A.F. on Crete were to wipe out all the production of Ploiești? That is why, on April 25, 1941, his Directive No. 28 ordered the three armies in Greece to prepare Operation "Mercury", which was to secure Crete for Germany.

Brauchitsch, Göring, and Raeder set to work with great energy. And it was no small matter to plan an operation of the size required in a country with such limited resources as Greece where, in particular, air bases had to be improvised. The task of planning the operation fell to General Kurt Student, the commander of XI *Fliegerkorps*, which included the 7th Paratroop Division, reinforced by three infantry regiments from 5th and 6th Mountain Divisions. Air support was to be provided by VIII *Fliegerkorps*, commanded by General Wolfram von Richthofen, 18 fighter and reconnaissance *Gruppen*, that is 228 bombers, 205 dive bombers, 119 single-engined and 114 twin-engined fighters, and 50 reconnaissance aircraft.

The first wave of paratroops was to be carried in 493 three-engined Ju 52's and 72 gliders, but the mountain troops who were to reinforce the paratroops would be ferried over in 63 motorised sailing ships and seven small steamers hastily requisitioned by Rear-Admiral Schuster. This flotilla was to be escorted by two destroyers and 12 torpedo-boats of the Italian Navy under Captain Peccori-Giraldi. The British enjoyed detailed forewarning of the German preparations through decoding German signals sent by the "Enigma" machines. London and Cairo agreed that Crete should be held, and feared German

Masters of the air: a German reconnaissance plane flies over a Greek city.

seaborne landings more than the initial airborne attack.

On the island itself, the defence on paper comprised 42,500 men, of whom 10,300 were Greeks. Its core was the A.N.Z.A.C. force, 6,540 Australians and 7,700 New Zealanders who had escaped from Greece but had had to abandon a great deal of material on the beaches of Attica and the Peloponnese. They were thus very short of vehicles, artillery, infantry weapons, ammunition, entrenching tools, barbed wire, blankets, and mess-tins, and were likely to remain so. They had only 68 heavy and light A.A. guns, which were clearly not enough to cover the 162-mile front from the eastern to the western end of the island. On May 1, 1941, the R.A.F. had 35 operational aircraft; on the 19th, after incessant bombardment by the Luftwaffe, it had only four Hurricanes and three Gladiators left in a state good enough to take off for Egypt. Abandoned aerodromes were merely obstructed and not put out of use, as it was intended to reoccupy them as soon as possible.

On April 30, Sir Archibald Wavell entrusted the command of this severely weakened defence force to General Freyberg. Whatever the eminent qualities of this commander, whose 27 wounds testified to his bravery in World War I, he was nevertheless the seventh British commander the island had had in six months and, when he arrived, he had only three weeks in which to familiarise himself with the situation.

Operation "Tiger", which had brought 238 tanks across the Mediterranean, had given the Admiralty the chance of rein-

155

German paratroops take a welcome opportunity for a quick cigarette and a drink.

forcing the Alexandria naval squadron with the battleship *Queen Elizabeth* and the cruisers *Fiji* and *Naiad*. London thought that this naval force would thus be in a better position to oppose Axis landings on the island from the continent. But Cunningham's only aircraft-carrier, the *Formidable*, had only a handful of Fulmar fighters which, even if there had been more of them, would have been no match for the Germans' Messerschmitts.

Throughout May 20 airborne troops from the 7th *Fliegerdivision* were dropped at Máleme, west of Canea, and in the areas of Réthimnon and Heraklion. The defenders had been expecting them for 48 hours and so the fighting was bitter. At Máleme General Meindl, gravely wounded, had to hand over his command to Colonel Ramcke; at Réthimnon the paratroops landed with no commander at all as the glider carrying General Sussman had crashed on the island of Aegina. The battle might have swung in General Freyberg's favour had he had time to reinforce the brigade defending Máleme airstrip against Ramcke, and if the Mediterranean Fleet had been able to destroy completely the convoys bringing in Lieutenant-General Ringel's mountain troops. But, for the few losses they inflicted on the Germans, the Royal Navy lost, in rapid succession from aerial bombardment by Stukas, the cruisers *Gloucester* and *Fiji* together with four destroyers, while the

Warspite and the aircraft-carrier *Formidable* were so badly damaged that they had to be sent for repair in the United States.

In spite of pressure from London, Admiral Cunningham had to give up operations north of Crete, where he was suffering heavy losses. On May 25, with admirably controlled air support, the 5th Mountain Division managed to break out of the Máleme perimeter held by the 2nd New Zealand Division and push on through Canea. The German breakthrough decided General Freyberg on May 27 to begin the evacuation of the island and to ask for help from the Mediterranean Fleet. This help was not refused him.

In spite of the risks involved and the losses already sustained, the Commander-in-Chief Mediterranean, Admiral Cunningham, did not hesitate a moment.

"We cannot let [the army] down," he signalled to the ships of his fleet which had been designated for this mission, and when one member of his staff seemed pessimistic he retorted, with a just sense of realities: "It takes the Navy three years to build a ship. It would take 300 years to re-build a tradition."

The evacuation of Crete, begun on the night of May 28–29, was carried out through the small harbour at Sphakia on the south coast and was completed by dawn on June 2. During the operation the A.A. cruiser *Calcutta* and the destroyers *Hereward* and *Imperial* were lost. But the heaviest losses of life were on board the cruiser *Orion*, Vice-Admiral Pridham-Wippell's flagship. One single German

bomb killed 260 men and wounded 280.

British Empire losses were nearly 1,800 killed and about 12,000 captured out of 32,000 men engaged. The Royal Navy lost 1,828 killed and 183 wounded. 18,000 troops were evacuated to Egypt. But the losses of General Student and XI *Fliegerkorps* had not been slight in spite of this. Though the Germans' casualties could not have reached the 15,000 given by Churchill in his memoirs, statistics published since the war show that, with 3,714 killed and missing and 2,494 wounded, the eight days of fighting on Crete had cost the Germans more than the whole three weeks of the Balkans campaign. The loss was the worse because it fell mainly on the experienced and well-trained airborne troops. Material losses had been high, too: at Maleme airfield alone, one aircraft in three had been lost. Crete was the last major victory for the German airborne army operating in its original role. It was not so risked again.

Was it because of these German losses that Hitler rejected General Student's suggestion to follow up the victory on Crete by capturing Cyprus? We do not know. But the memory of this blood-bath admittedly encouraged Hitler to abandon his operation "Hercules" (the capture of Malta from the air) in late June 1942, when Rommel thought he had convinced him that the Axis forces could get to the Nile and Suez.

These German victories had offset earlier Italian defeats, but at a price: the postponement of operation "Barbarossa"–the invasion of the Soviet Union. And this lost time could never be regained.

CHAPTER 19
Hitler turns East

In 1941 the war which had been confined mainly to Europe since September 1939 really became a world war.

In the summer and autumn of 1940, German warships had cruised in the South Atlantic, the Indian Ocean, the Pacific, and even as far as the Antarctic ice barrier. But irritating as these pinpricks were, their strategic effect was virtually nil; the German Navy could not make much play with its naval forces even in home waters, and in this war against mercantile tonnage the British Home Fleet did not bother with them as long as they kept clear of the British convoys.

But when Hitler invaded Russia on June 22, 1941, the war spread from the German-Soviet demarcation line drawn across Poland in September 1939 to Vladivistok and the Bering Strait. In December 1941 Japan's entry into the war extended the war by land, sea, and air across the enormous area stretching from east to west between the Hawaiian Islands and Ceylon, and from north to south between the Aleutian Islands and Guadalcanal. The war now became a direct sequel to the apparently endless war between China and Japan, which had been in progress since 1932. From 1941 this series of bitter hostilities can be called "World War II" in every sense of the term.

With the entry into the war of the United States and the Soviet Union, both of them industrial giants, the material and technical aspects of the war now became more significant. Obviously, not all the battles after 1941 were decided beforehand in the factories and the research laboratories. But it is certainly true to say that from 1941 every belligerent state was run on a war economy and an increasing mobilisation of industry, as is reflected by the continually rising production of every type of armament in Germany, Great Britain, the United States, and the Soviet Union.

In Germany, production of tanks increased twelve-fold (from 2,235 to 27,345 tanks) between 1941 and 1944. American aircraft production underwent an even greater increase. In 1941, 317 four-engined bombers came off the assembly lines; in 1943 and 1944, 25,946 were built, including about 4,000 Boeing B-29 Superfortresses. Clearly Germany and Japan, as well as Italy, could not match America and the Soviet Union in industrial capacity, and the consequences of this state of affairs dominated the war after 1941.

Firstly, Hitler, confronted by the Soviet Union, and Tojo, confronted by the U.S.A., would have to act quickly and strike a succession of devastating and decisive blows at their enemies; they could not permit the latter to recover from their first surprise and eventually bring their undoubted material superiority into play. Having decided to attack, Germany and Japan were therefore each compelled to adopt a bold strategy.

Secondly, their war policy was governed by the need to obtain strategic raw materials. In geographical terms this meant coal from the Donets basin, iron ore from Krivoy Rog, manganese from Nikopol, nickel from Petsamo, oil from the Caucasus, the Dutch East Indies, and Burma, and rubber from the Malay States. Hitler used this economic argument freely to justify his most daring and even his most absurd decisions to his generals. In any event, after June 22, 1941, Germany's entire strategy had to take these factors into account, although resources of all kinds had been made available by the victories of 1939 and 1940, and although commercial treaties had been concluded with satellite and neutral countries as a result of those victories.

For the same reasons, communications across the sea between Britain and America became of vital importance. It was essential for these two powers to be able to intercept raiders and to protect their communications by land and sea. From the time of Pearl Harbor – and even before, as far as Great Britain was concerned – the United States undoubtedly held the position of the "great arsenal of democracy". The consequences would have been serious if a half, or even a third, of the cargoes of arms and equipment from American factories had been sunk in the Atlantic or the Pacific.

In the latter half of 1940 Hitler and Göring were completely mistaken about the results to be expected from the Luftwaffe's night bombing offensive against the sources of Britain's war production. Equally so, Churchill and the Chief of Air Staff, Sir Charles Portal, were just as misguided about the damage which Bomber Command could do to Germany's war industries. In 1941 the destruction so wrought was negligible, and even at the beginning of 1943 it was hardly perceptible. From the summer of 1943, however, the Allied bombers did begin to make themselves felt, but even then they did not seriously curtail the production of German tanks and aircraft, which reached record heights in 1944.

The Third Reich's attack on the Soviet Union introduced into the war a new element which was at least as important as the others we have mentioned.

World War II had had a particularly ideological aspect right from its beginning, a factor which had been entirely lacking in World War I. The dictator states, headed by Hitler and Mussolini, were opposed by the democratic and parliamentarian states of central and western Europe. But the ideological character of the war became far more pronounced after the German invasion of Russia on June 22, 1941. From that day two equally totalitarian states, two inter-national organisations, (one might almost say two religions), faced each other on the battlefield.

Each of the two adversaries on the Eastern Front was fighting not only enemies but infidels: "German Fascists", according to the jargon used in Moscow, and "Jew Bolsheviks", as denounced by Hitler, Goebbels, and the Nazi propaganda machine. It was therefore not surprising that in these circumstances the German-Soviet war did not conform with the rules.

Hitler's order, issued before the outbreak of hostilities, to shoot the political commissars appointed by Moscow is well known. But there is no doubt that criminal directives of the same kind were also given by the Russians on their side of the front. The best evidence for this is the high mortality rate – around 85 per cent – of German, Italian, and Japanese prisoners-of-war in Soviet camps.

The German-Soviet war, like the Wars of Religion in the 16th and 17th Centuries, transcended the bounds of nationality. In this respect Hitler was less fortunate than Stalin. His European "crusade against Bolshevism" commanded only scanty support in France, Belgium, Holland, Denmark, and Norway; most of the volunteers from these countries were enlisted by the *Waffen-S.S.* in 1941. Stalin, on the other hand, right from the beginning of the war, commanded the unconditional and unlimited support of all the European Communist parties; these soon became the well-disciplined allies of the resistance movements.

Another aspect of the ideological side of the war is rarely mentioned and deserves brief notice. From 1941 onwards, Soviet espionage had the necessary facilities for infiltrating its agents into Britain and America. It appears to have escaped general attention that the great treason trials in Britain and the United States

Schulenburg, Hitler's Ambassador in Moscow in 1940-41.

157

German propaganda: the invasion of Russia as a crusade against Bolshevism.

during the period 1945–50 had their origins in the years when Stalin, Roosevelt, and Churchill were being photographed in apparent harmony during their meetings. The "anti-Fascist" mystique cultivated in Moscow, London, and Washington had an enormous attraction for some British and American citizens, both native and naturalised, and they therefore thought they were entitled to abandon the loyalty which bound them to their countries.

This is not to say that Roosevelt and Churchill ignored security precautions when they pledged their alliance to the Soviet Union in 1941. They would certainly have been acutely embarrassed if they had suspected the sinister facts: the Soviet missions which, in accordance with the Lend-Lease agreement, were requesting arms, munitions, fuel, raw materials, and food, were also engaged in secret recruiting and Intelligence work, in the belief that a third world war would immediately follow the downfall of Hitler and Mussolini.

Such excuses can reasonably be advanced only for the first two years of the tripartite alliance, which Churchill, thinking of the wars against Louis XIV, refers to in *The Second World War* as the "Grand Alliance". After the summer of 1943, however, the Allies' negligence became inexcusable.

Hitler's central role in the war remains unassailable. But no generals or politicians of his former entourage have ever reached

Mussolini and Hitler, with General Jodl at the Führer's elbow.

objective agreement about the Führer's ability as a military commander; and this deserves some study.

At the Nuremberg war crime trials after the war, Keitel and Jodl both described Hitler's strategic intuition, his prodigious memory, his precise knowledge of the most insignificant details of military history and technology, and his quickness in understanding the problems of the art of war. Rundstedt, on the other hand, once referred to him in private as a "Bohemian corporal", and since 1945 many leading generals have written memoirs which dwell at length on Hitler's political and strategic errors. But after the French armistice Hitler's sycophantic staff referred to him as *"Der grösste Feldherr aller Zeiten"* (the greatest general of all time).

Soviet historians regard this type of criticism of Hitler's errors, which is made with certain modifications by nearly all German generals, as a puerile attempt to conceal their own responsibility and to minimise their own mistakes in the conduct of the war. These generals tend to represent Hitler as the sole scapegoat for the sins of the German people in general and for those of the German General Staff in particular.

Clearly it would be absurd to put blind faith in all the stories about Hitler retailed by German writers; it would also be just as absurd to make Hitler alone responsible for the successive defeats which precipitated the final collapse of the Third Reich. It had already been pointed out that Rundstedt was as least as much to blame as Hitler for the issuing of the order on May 24, 1940, directing the Panzers to halt outside Dunkirk, thereby letting the B.E.F. re-embark for England.

But in fact these critics were not all influenced by Germany's defeat in 1945; nor were they relying on the fact that Hitler, Göring, Keitel, and Jodl were no longer alive to contradict their statements. A classic example can be found in the diaries kept by General Halder daily up to September 24, 1942, which have already been quoted on the subject of the campaign in France.

The following comment on the supreme master of the Third Reich's strategy dates from July 23, 1942, when Field-Marshal List's army group was approaching Rostov, the gateway to the Caucasus. "[Hitler's] continual under-estimation of the moves at the enemy's disposal is more and more grotesque, and is becoming dangerous. The position is now getting quite intolerable. It is no longer possible to get any serious work done. Hitler's idea of 'conducting operations' is to follow neurotic reactions based on momentary impressions and to show a total inability to appreciate the apparatus of command."

Certainly Hitler had a kind of intuitive grasp of the principles of warfare. This was strengthened by his reading of Frederick the Great, Clausewitz, Moltke, and Schlieffen. He had met Ludendorff and had discussed military problems with him; and it is true that he was always sustained by his belief in his mission, his implacable will-power, and his total lack of scruples and human feelings.

Unquestionably, the strategic conception behind the German victories of 1940 was Hitler's work. There was the daring shown in the decision to make five simultaneous landings in Norway, in the face of the Royal Navy's enormous superiority; and it will also be recalled how readily Hitler responded to Manstein's strategic plans for the attack on the West, and how quickly he assimilated them and made them his own. Hitler also conceived the idea of sailing the battle-cruisers *Scharnhorst* and *Gneisenau* through the Channel in daylight in February 1942.

Napoleon claimed that when he worked out a plan of campaign he experienced all the labour-pains of a woman giving birth to a child, but that as soon as the campaign began he was always imperturbable and determined, with eyes and ears open, ready to take immediate decisions. Hitler certainly seemed to initiate his plans with the sureness of a sleep-walker (to whom he sometimes compared himself); but he

159

tended to lack audacity when carrying out his plans. In fact he did not have the supreme quality of a military commander which Napoleon, who had it to a supreme degree, once called "courage at two o'clock in the morning".

For example, when Hitler heard that Commodore Bonte's destroyer flotilla had been destroyed at Narvik, he lost all self-control and wanted to order General Dietl to withdraw across the Swedish frontier with his men. A few weeks later, when the French campaign had begun, he kept interfering with the working of O.K.H., as he was terrified of a powerful counter-attack against Sedan from the direction of Rethel, although all Intelligence clearly showed that this assumption was absurd.

To sum up, Hitler was unsure of himself, indecisive, finicky, shuffling, and hesitant in execution, sticking obstinately to any thoughtless decision, and he was all the more sour and morose when he had hesitated a long time before taking such a decision. Moreover, as he had not been trained as a staff officer he was quite incapable, for all his undeniable strategic talents, of co-ordinating his operations according to a timed plan, or of adjusting his objectives to suit the resources available to him.

For this he was compelled to turn to his highly-qualified subordinates in the Armed Forces High Command (O.K.W.), and particularly in the Army High Command (O.K.H.). In addition, quite apart from his general mistrust of all and sundry, Hitler seems to have had the same aversion to staff officers that was shown many British, French, and German front-line soldiers in World War I.

With regard to his generals, Hitler undoubtedly had the situation better in hand in 1941 than in the first quarter of 1940. The Norwegian and French campaigns had clearly shown that those generals who had predicted defeat or even catastrophe if the Wehrmacht should be so ill advised as to move forward from the Siegfried Line had been completely mistaken. The atmosphere of dissension which had been spread by Blaskowitz, Witzleben, and Leeb had now been dissipated. Those who had had doubts in the previous winter, such as Brauchitsch and Halder, did not accept the basic principles of the régime, but they obeyed Hitler's directives more submissively than before. And Hitler, with his prestige enhanced by his victories, was now in a position to smash all opposition.

Many German generals, both at the Nuremberg trials and in their memoirs, claimed that they had been stunned when they heard of Hitler's decision to attack the Soviet Union. But none of the documents relating to that decision reveal any effective opposition within the German Army High Command to the venture. Hitler therefore imposed his will on everyone, and undoubtedly the enormous successes which he more or less forced on his generals made him even less ready to listen to their arguments.

In any event, the German Army remained poised for instant action on any front during the interval between the postponement of the invasion of England and Rommel's arrival in Libya. This alone suggests that, during the period in question, friction between the Supreme Commander of the German Armed Forces and the Army High Command was infrequent. Hitler exercised his authority by issuing general directives, and the Army High Command then converted them into plans for troop concentrations or operational orders with its customary efficiency and promptness.

But after the invasion of Russia in June 1941 there was renewed friction with O.K.H., and this led Hitler to take over command of the Army from Brauchitsch.

From then onwards the former Bavarian Army corporal combined in his own person the offices of Head of State (Führer), Chief of Government (Chancellor), Supreme Commander of the Armed Forces (O.K.W.), and Supreme Commander of the Army (O.K.H.). We should also bear in mind that he still retained his post as leader of the National Socialist Party. Thus Hitler combined in his own person a concentration of powers such as Ludendorff had recommended to the German people in his book *Total War* in 1936.

There was, therefore, no way in which Hitler could be relieved of his command, in the way that the younger Moltke had been by the Kaiser after the Battle of the Marne and Falkenhayn after Verdun. Nor had he any political superior whom the General Staff might persuade to replace him, as had happened to Bethmann-Hollweg in 1917. Nor, in the end, could Hitler find himself in the position of the Kaiser, driven to abdicate when the Chancellor and the General Staff had combined against him. Hitler, as it were, was Kaiser, Chancellor, and Chief of the General Staff, as though empowered to sign his directives "By Order of his Majesty the Kaiser".

It is also clearly doubtful whether or not Hitler was physically and intellectually capable of bearing his great responsibilities. There is much evidence to suggest that as early as 1944 he had no purpose or energy left. General Frido von Senger und Etterlin, who received the Oak Leaves to the Knight's Cross from Hitler after his successful defensive battle at Monte Cassino, gave the following description of the Führer in 1944:

"The ceremony for those who were to be honoured was far from impressive. Hitler made a really horrifying impression, and in spite of myself I wondered how the young officers and sergeants who were being decorated with me would react . . . . . . His unattractive figure, with his short neck, appeared more slovenly than ever. The skin of his face was flaccid, his complexion pale and creased by lack of sleep. The look in his blue eyes, which was said to have completely fascinated so many people, was vacant, possibly as a result of the stimulants which he was continually

given. His handshake was floppy. His left arm hung limp and trembling . . ."

It is not clear whether this was the result of illness or of the absurd diet to which Hitler kept. According to information that reached Switzerland in 1943 Hitler may have suffered from Parkinson's Disease; this would to some extent account for the trembling of his left hand, which had been noted by Senger und Etterlin and others before the bomb plot of July 20, 1944. Some writers have suggested that Hitler was an epileptic. Because of the secrecy in which the Führer's health was always shrouded a definite diagnosis is almost impossible. What is quite certain is that in 1939 Hitler used his excellent health as an argument against the advisers who would have preferred to postpone the launching of a war until 1945 or 1946. As Hitler had just celebrated his 50th birthday, it is possible that Hitler already felt that he was rapidly approaching a period of physical degeneration.

It is also certain that nobody could have endured a way of life like Hitler's for very long. After dealing with military matters in long sessions and allowing his generals to make little more than monosyllabic comments, he spent the night until 2 or 3 o'clock in the morning in haranguing his Party colleagues. (The shorthand record of his statements, made on the orders of Martin Bormann, makes up a large volume of ferocious and redundant banalities.) Then a few hours of sleep, a boiling hot bath, and Hitler was ready to hold forth again without pause as he studied the war situation map which had been brought up to date overnight.

Hitler relied upon Doctor Morell, who was regarded by his professional colleagues as a dangerous quack, to keep up his strength from one day to the next. This dubious figure gave his patient a good dose of sleeping pills after his exertions of the night; early in the morning Hitler was also given a strychnine injection which helped to revive him, and later a few benzedrine pills.

In any event this mental and physical decline was only just beginning in 1941. According to Halder's personal diary and the O.K.H. War Diary, Hitler was still extremely active, completely self-confident, and able to make everyone do exactly what he wanted. But these same documents also show clearly that he used to avoid an issue when a strategic decision was essential. In his relations with his generals Hitler used an ingenious deceptive technique: sometimes, when he had a favourable opportunity, he would turn the discussion on to subjects with which they were unfamiliar; at other times he would switch their attention to points of detail or historical analogies, where his amazing memory put him in full control of the situation.

When Hitler decided to take on the Soviet Union and destroy Stalin and his régime it was not because, like Napoleon, he had faced up to the impossibility of getting his armies across the Channel. He had already come to a preliminary decision on July 29, 1940, at a time, that is, when preparations for Operation "Sea Lion" were just getting under way.

During the "phoney war", under the Moscow treaties of August 23 and September 28, 1939, the two totalitarian powers had continued to give each other discreet but very valuable assistance.

But the agreement on the economic conditions of the Soviet-German Pact was not signed until February 11, 1940, after negotiations which had lasted throughout the autumn of 1939. The Russian delegation had been led by Molotov and Mikoyan, two very touchy and obdurate bargainers. In addition to the material provided for in August 1939 and now in the course of being delivered, the Soviet Union undertook to supply to the Reich between then and August 11, 1941 some 650 million marks' worth of raw materials and foodstuffs.

In exchange for these products, the Reich was to supply to the Soviet Union military material, as well as equipment, machinery, and plant for heavy industry. Moscow's negotiators were particularly interested in the production of synthetic petrol by the hydrogenation of coal and in the manufacture of synthetic rubber, called *Buna*, two processes which had been perfected in Germany.

In the supply of arms, Joseph Stalin's concern was chiefly for his navy. He asked for the uncompleted heavy cruiser *Lützow*, the plans for the battleship *Bismarck*, and for a destroyer armed with 6-inch guns, a complete 15-inch gun turret, designs for 11- and 16-inch turrets, and specimens of engine parts, torpedoes, magnetic mines, and periscopes. Then came demands for the delivery of some samples of certain army and air force material: Pzkw III tanks, all-purpose transport vehicles, 21-cm howitzers, 10.5-

Hitler, seen here in a more relaxed mood.

cm A.A. guns, Messerschmitt 109 and 110 fighters, Junkers 88 bombers, and plant for the production of explosives and ammunition.

The German delegation had to accept these demands. But, on Hitler's orders, the German war industry, already overstretched, showed no great alacrity in supplying these orders. In fact only the cruiser *Lützow* was handed over to the Soviet Union and she was uncompleted and remained so. The Soviet delegation in Berlin entrusted with seeing to the delivery of this material was not taken in by the delays, and a certain tension thus crept into the relations between the two capitals.

On April 9, 1940, diplomatic relations underwent a sudden improvement. When Schulenburg, the German Ambassador, told him of the measures which the Reich was taking against Denmark and Norway. Molotov readily agreed that Germany had had no alternative and, according to the Ambassador, he said "literally": "We wish Germany complete success in these defensive measures."

Was the People's Commissar for Foreign Affairs putting a good face on things? This was not Schulenburg's impression, and he was a very acute observer. In his despatch of April 11 he noted that in reply to Berlin's complaints about the temporary suspension of grain and oil deliveries, Molotov had been "affability itself" and had attributed these and other annoyances to "over-zealous minions".

Russian deliveries to Germany were resumed quickly and on May 10, 1940, the German Ambassador in Moscow, who had been instructed to inform Molotov of the invasion of Belgium, the Netherlands, and France, was able to telegraph his government: "Instruction *re* Molotov carried out. Molotov received communication in spirit of understanding, adding that he realised that Germany had to protect herself against Franco-British attack. He does not doubt our success."

The same tune again on June 18. On that day Molotov summoned Count von der Schulenburg to his office to explain to him what measures the Soviet Union had taken against the Baltic countries. But before he broached the subject, he wished to offer "his government's warmest congratulations on the splendid success of the German armed forces".

Molotov's remarks on the German armed intervention were accepted calmly by the Count, who was acting on instructions circulated by telegraph to all Heads of Missions of the Third Reich on the previous day by the Secretary of State for Foreign Affairs, Baron von Weizsäcker. This instruction ordered that Russia and the Baltic States should be left alone to work out the problem of their "co-operation".

At the Munich conference on June 19, 1940, the Führer spoke in similar terms to Count Ciano about the "incorporation" of Estonia, Latvia, and Lithuania into the Soviet Union. According to him it was a "natural and inevitable" event and, from their conversations on the subject, Ciano got the impression that Hitler was "not then contemplating action against Russia".

Eight days later the Kremlin sent a strongly-worded ultimatum to the Rumanian Government demanding that it should give up Bessarabia and Bukovina within 48 hours. In the secret protocol to the Soviet-German Non-Aggression Pact, the Reich had stated that it was totally unconcerned with the former province. But Bukovina was not mentioned in the pact and, as Berlin remarked, it had never been part of the Czarist Russian Empire.

Not wishing, however, to see war break out between the Dniestr and the Prut at a time when they thought they had halted it on the continent, Hitler and Mussolini reacted energetically, urging unquestioning acceptance of the Russian terms on Bucharest. In Moscow, Schulenburg, accepting the *fait accompli* in Bessarabia, merely drew attention to the fate in Bukovina of the 100,000 *Volkdeutschen* who lived there. But, in his triumphal speech to the Reichstag on July 17, the Führer proclaimed *urbi et orbi*: "The agreement signed in Moscow between the Reich and the Soviet Union has established precisely once and for all their respective areas of influence. Neither Germany nor Russia has so far set a single foot outside these areas." And so the most authoritative voice of the Third Reich made his partner's invasions of Finland, the Baltic States, and Rumania seem part of the Soviet-German Pact.

Was Hitler lying when he made this solemn declaration? Perhaps so, for he had ordered the transfer to the Eastern Front from July 20 onwards of the 18th Army (Colonel-General von Küchler), six corps strong: in all 15 infantry divisions and the 1st Cavalry Division. Yet there may have been good reason for this, as the German troops were very thin on the ground between the Carpathians and the Baltic, looking more like a series of customs posts, in face of the massive Russian occupying forces, than a strategically deployed army, albeit on the defensive. It was natural, therefore, that he should wish to thicken up the line. On the other hand, in the same period O.K.H. was ordered to reduce its strength from 155 to 120 divisions, though the latter included, it is true, 20 armoured and ten motorised divisions.

Hitler's decision to attack the Soviet Union can therefore be pinpointed to his stay in Berchtesgaden between July 20 and 29, 1940. It arose from a kind of inspired insight after a long period of solitary meditation. Even today it is difficult to see what processes of thought led him to this conclusion. It is reasonable to suppose that the presence of Soviet bombers within 30 minutes' flying time of the indispensable Ploiesti oil fields had a great deal to do with his decision. At the very least one might say that the rape of Bessarabia crystallised his inclinations towards aggression and brought him back to the ideology of *Mein Kampf*, which he had somewhat neglected since August 23, 1939.

However this may be, as described above, on July 29 General of Artillery Jodl came down from Berchtesgaden at the end of the day and gathered together his most important colleagues of the *Wehrmachtsführungsamt* (Armed Forces Operational Staff): Colonel Warlimont, Lieutenant-Colonel von Lossberg, Lieutenant-Commander Junge, and Major von Falkenstein of the Luftwaffe. They met in his Command H.Q. train, the *Atlas*, halted in Bad Reichenhall station and, enjoining on the others the strictest secrecy, Jodl revealed the Führer's determination to crush the Soviet Union.

"Hitler," Keitel said at Nuremberg, "wanted to know if something could be done immediately. The generals said 'no'. War against Russia simply could not be entertained in the autumn of 1940."

To have the army fight in Poland, transport it to the west to fight again, and then return it to Poland to fight once more was absolutely impossible. The troops needed to be re-equipped.

"But the question he asked was a fair indication of the workings of his mind. 'I was worried,' said Warlimont. 'I was worried,' said Jodl. 'I was worried,' said Keitel."

Hitler forestalled the objections he expected from those who counselled a prudent conduct of the war: would this not be reviving the risk of war on two fronts which had brought Imperial Germany to her final defeat in 1918 and which the Non-Aggression Pact of 1939 had so opportunely eliminated? To this he replied that he would be eliminating Great Britain's last possible continental ally and this would be done before the intervention of the United States in 1942 or 1943. From then onwards Russia would be crushed for ever.

Two days later, on July 31, Grand-Admiral Raeder and *Reichsmarschall* Göring, with their Chiefs-of-Staff, went up to the Berghof where Hitler told them of his decision: to his great regret an attack in the autumn was out of the question; the operation would therefore begin in May 1941. He saw the offensive developing as two main thrusts: one towards Kiev, the other towards Moscow.

Russia's organised forces were to be crushed within five months. The operation was subsequently to allow the rapid occupation of the Baku oilfields.

Halder's diary, normally so incisive as far as Hitler is concerned, records on this date no fundamental objection to the proposed operation. It is true that the principle of it was not discussed, but the impromptu decision which had been taken nevertheless brought the German High Command up against problems which it had very little time to solve.

As Britain was to be defeated by sea and air, the High Command had been called upon to demobilise or to send on leave 35 divisions. Hitler's oracular pronounce-

ment required the army to be increased to 180 divisions, the number of Panzer divisions to be doubled, and the large motorised formations to be increased from four to six. This meant the creation of some 40 divisions, plus the corps troops and H.Q.s to support and staff them. At the same time, the planning of the operation against the Soviet Union was entrusted to Major-General Marcks, who was replaced on September 3, 1940 by Lieutenant-General Paulus, then Deputy Chief of General Staff.

If even now Hitler had yet to make his final decision, a series of incidents arising from fortuitous circumstances caused German-Soviet relations to become further embittered. There was firstly the settlement at Vienna. When they had settled the conflict between Hungary and Rumania over Transylvania, neither Hitler nor Mussolini had intended to trick the Soviets. Nevertheless, to sweeten the bitter pill being offered to King Carol, Germany and Italy had to promise him their guarantee for what was left of his kingdom. Instructed to inform Molotov of the solution reached at the Belvedere Palace, Count von der Schulenburg had to put it to him that the two Axis powers had acted solely in the interests of peace and that the Reich still valued the friendship of the Russians as highly as ever.

Despite the placatory aspect of the account, Molotov retorted that he had only heard of the Vienna settlement through the newspapers and that, by keeping him in ignorance of the matter, the Reich had contravened Article 3 of the Non-Aggression Pact, which obliged both parties to consult each other. On the other hand, according to Grigore Gafencu, then Rumania's representative in Moscow, Molotov is said to have asked: "Why did you give this guarantee? You had been advised that we had no intention . of attacking Rumania." To this Schulenburg replied, with some presence of mind: "That is precisely why we gave it. You had told us that you had no claims on that country; our guarantee could not therefore embarrass you in any way."

The signature on September 27, 1940 of the Tripartite Pact between Berlin, Rome, and Tokyo also provoked requests for explanations from Moscow. The German Foreign Ministry claimed the pact was purely defensive and intended by the three powers to dissuade Washington from poaching upon the preserves of Germany in Europe and Africa, and of Japan in China and South-East Asia. But the Kremlin wondered if this public instrument aimed at American "warmongers" did not contain, as did the Soviet-German Pact of August 23, 1939, some more sinister secret protocol.

Another cause for alarm was Germany's receipt from Sweden and Finland, in September 1940, of permission to transport artillery through their territory for the reinforcement of Norway's arctic defences. At this period Soviet-Finnish relations were becoming daily more tense

on account of the Soviet Union's abusive interpretations of the peace treaty of the previous March 12. Was Germany going to interfere in this wolf-lamb dialogue?

Finally, the announcement that a German military mission accompanied by "demonstration troops" was about to undertake the training of the Rumanian Army caused no pleasure to the Soviets, who were attempting to increase their presence in the Danube delta, in the southern part of Bessarabia.

In the face of this persistent ill-humour and of the risk of seeing the Soviet Union suspend its deliveries of raw materials, Ribbentrop, acting on Hitler's orders, sent a long letter to Stalin on October 13. It took up the complaints made by Moscow, but in particular pointed out to Stalin the conclusion that "the four great powers, the U.S.S.R., Italy, Japan, and Germany, had the historic mission of adopting a long-term policy and guiding the future development of their peoples in the directions determined by the world-wide boundaries of their interests."

To this effect he suggested that Stalin send Molotov to Berlin. He would be welcome there and this would give the Führer an opportunity to explain his concept of future Soviet-German relations.

Was Ribbentrop trying to deceive Stalin, offering to enlarge on his behalf the concept of the tripartite system, while the German High Command was setting up Operation "Barbarossa", designed to bring about the final destruction of the Soviet state and government? It would rather seem that before deciding irrevocably, the leaders of the Third Reich wished to know the Kremlin's intentions about sharing out the planet. If Molotov accepted the delimitation of the spheres of interest proposed by Hitler and Ribbentrop the projected campaign might be unnecessary; otherwise it would be war.

On October 22 Stalin replied to Ribbentrop by letter, agreeing with his long-term proposals and delimiting the spheres of influence to be shared between Germany and the Soviet Union. Consequently Molotov would go to Berlin at a date to be fixed between November 10 and 12. Yet in September Field-Marshals von Bock, von Kluge, and List and the H.Q.s of Army Group "B" and the 4th and 12th Armies had already been transferred to the Eastern Front. These comprised four corps. in all ten infantry, one motorised, and three armoured divisions. Soon afterwards Field-Marshal von Leeb and the H.Q. of Army Group "C", stationed at Nancy, were recalled to Germany. On October 30 Field-Marshal von Brauchitsch's staff left its quarters at Fontainbleau to return to the quarters at Zossen Camp, south of Berlin, which they had left on the evening of the previous May 9.

In the evening of November 10 Molotov, accompanied by his deputy, left Moscow for Berlin. On November 12 at Anhalt Station, where Ribbentrop had gone to greet him, all the correct ceremonial was obeyed punctiliously.

Molotov had a preliminary conversation with his German colleague in the Foreign Ministry. A few hours later he was received by Hitler, who also gave up the following day to him. On the morning of November 14 Molotov took the train back to Moscow.

We have only the German version of these crucial talks, yet again from Paul Schmidt, as Molotov's conversations with Ribbentrop and Hitler are not even mentioned in the official *History of the Great Patriotic War of the Soviet Union.*

This is discretion indeed. But whatever the reason for the silence, Paul Schmidt's evidence shows that Molotov's conversation with Ribbentrop was limited merely to generalities.

As Germany had by now practically won the war, it was time to proceed to a division of the Old World, and to this effect Ribbentrop recommended that the four totalitarian powers should all drive southwards: Germany and Italy would take over Africa and Japan South-East Asia. This left a large area between the Caspian and Singapore which might without difficulty be allotted to the Soviet Union, giving the Russians an outlet to the open sea in the Persian Gulf and the Indian Ocean. Ribbentrop thus proposed to Molotov a system of four parallel thrusts to the south and, as parallels only meet at infinity, there was no risk in an agreement of this kind of any friction or even of encounter between Japan and the U.S.S.R. in the Far East or between the U.S.S.R. and Germany on the Bosporus or in the Middle East.

Ribbentrop also suggested that an arrangement be made between the three powers of the Tripartite Pact on the one hand and the Soviet Union on the other. By way of encouragement to Molotov, Ribbentrop said that Germany was prepared to replace the Montreux Agreements of 1936, governing the Bosporus and Dardanelles, by a new convention which Turkey would be called upon to negotiate, if that is the word, with Germany, Italy, and Russia. But Molotov took good care not to show his hand. He asked for a few explanations, but all the time gave it to be understood that his principal concern was an agreement between Germany and Russia, and that only after this was concluded would he consent to talk with Italy and Japan. According to Paul Schmidt, Molotov was visibly holding himself back for his meeting with the Führer.

With that peculiar psychological insight which characterised him, Adolf Hitler understood immediately that his usual tactics of intimidation would be of no avail against this old Bolshevik Vyacheslav Skriabin, of excellent Great-Russian bourgeois stock. It was not for nothing that his comrades in the party had nicknamed him the "Hammer" (Molotov). This was Schmidt's observation during these three long and difficult sessions. Peppered with precise questions by the Russian, the Führer contained himself: "He didn't jump into the air and he didn't rush to the door as he had done

in September 1939 when Sir Horace Wilson handed him Chamberlain's letter. Nor did he declare that further discussion was useless as he had done three weeks earlier to Franco at Hendaye. He was gentleness and courtesy personified."

But then, moving on from the generalities about the delimitation of spheres of influence and the exclusion of the United States from affairs in Europe, Africa and Asia, it became apparent that any agreement between Germany and Russia on the four points raised by Molotov was impossible:

1. The Soviet Government considered it to be its duty to settle once and for all the Finnish question. "No war in Finland," Hitler protested; "We need peace in Finland because of nickel and wood; a conflict in the Baltic might have unforeseen consequences on Soviet-German relations."

2. Was the disagreeable guarantee given to Rumania also valid against Russia? "Of course," Hitler replied. But he added, in the manner of his Ambassador in Moscow: "This question cannot become serious for you. You reached an agreement with the Rumanians a short time ago."

3. "In that case then," Molotov went on imperturbably, "would Germany agree to Russia's offering similar guarantees to Bulgaria and following them up with a strong military mission?" Hitler answered this question with another: "Has Bulgaria, like Rumania, asked for such a guarantee?" When Molotov replied "no", Hitler said he would have to consult Mussolini before coming to a decision on this matter.

4. Finally they came to the question of the Straits. As far as a guarantee against attack from the Black Sea was concerned, Molotov was not content with a paper revision of the Montreux Agreements. In addition to the security provided by the stationing of Soviet troops in Bulgaria, he also demanded the right to land and naval bases in the Bosporus and Dardanelles areas. Hitler, once again, refused.

And so Germany's attempt to divert Russia's traditional direction of advance, from south-west to south, had failed. As for the rest, it is not that Stalin and Molotov had scorned the prospects offered to them by Hitler and Ribbentrop in the direction of the Persian Gulf, but that they had connected these with their claims on Finland, Bulgaria, and Turkey. This view is supported by the draft agreement drawn up in the Kremlin listing the conditions under which the U.S.S.R. would join the Tripartite Pact. These were submitted to Berlin by Count von der Schulenburg on November 26.

In particular, giving his opinion on the articles of a draft German scheme aimed at revising the terms of the Montreux Agreements, Molotov wrote: "The draft protocol or agreement between Germany, Italy, and the Soviet Union must be amended to guarantee to the latter long-

Field-Marshal List, the man who conquered the Balkans—and by so doing secured Germany's southern flank for any subsequent moves against Russia.

term leases on light naval and land-force bases on the Bosporus and in the Dardanelles. It would guarantee the independence and territorial integrity of Turkey, the guarantee to be signed by the three states mentioned above, were she to express her wish to join the four-party pact. In the case of Turkey's refusal to join with the four powers, the above protocol should envisage the agreement of Germany, Italy, and the Soviet Union to prepare and execute appropriate military and diplomatic procedures. A separate agreement should be concluded to this effect."

Engaged as he was in a struggle to the death with Great Britain, Hitler allowed the conversation to drop. Already the presence in the Balkans of the lone, unfortunate cavalier Mussolini risked the intervention of Britain. An initiative by the Russians against Finland must not give the British an excuse to land at Petsamo. On the other hand, developments on the Albanian front made it seem likely that the Wehrmacht would have to go to the help of the Italian armies by manoeuvring through Bulgaria. In which case how could Russia be allowed the right to set up "strong military missions" in the Bulgarian ports of Varna and Burgas? Finally, the pressure which Molotov wanted him to bring to bear on Turkey might drive the Government of Ankara to open its frontiers to the British forces in the Middle East, the strength of which had given the German High Command some strange illusions.

Molotov did not on this occasion display his normal finesse. In the last analysis he had revealed to Hitler the next objectives

Hitler, Keitel and Jodl discussing German operations.

of Soviet policy and demonstrated quite clearly that Moscow's and Berlin's theses on the sharing out of the planet were and would remain irreconcilable. On the other hand he left for Moscow without suspecting the alternative with which he had been left. As a matter of fact, the soundings and the feelers he had used on the persons of Hitler and Ribbentrop did not reveal to him that in the event of disagreement with the programme set before him the result would be war. And it was to be a war which Moscow did not want at all, because of the state of world politics and because of the weaknesses of the Soviet armed forces.

During the last months of 1940, Hitler's intention to attack Soviet Russia grew firmer, especially after these negotiations with Molotov in Berlin in November. And so he wrote at the foot of each of the nine copies of his Directive No. 21–"Bar-

barossa"–of December 18, 1940:

"The German armed forces must be prepared, even before the conclusion of the war against England, *to crush Soviet Russia in a rapid campaign.*"

During this intended campaign, the task of keeping up activity against Great Britain would be the task of the German Navy principally. The Luftwaffe would aid the navy in blockade operations, while maintaining a solid defence against attacks by the R.A.F.

The army, leaving behind only such forces as were necessary for maintaining security in the occupied nations of the West, would launch an offensive against the bulk of the Soviet forces deployed in western Russia. These Russian forces were to be dislocated by savage armoured thrusts, which were to push on right into Russia and thus prevent Soviet forces from falling back into their vast rear areas. The final objective for Operation "Barbarossa" was fixed as the line Astrakhan'–the Volga–Gor'ky–Kotlas–Archangel.

The Luftwaffe was to take part in the campaign with the main weight of its effective force utilised thus:

1. To protect German concentrations and industries in the east of the Reich from attacks by enemy aircraft;
2. To ensure support for the army at its main points of attack; and
3. At the end of the offensive to put out of action the industrial installations of the Urals area.

The Führer envisaged three army groups, in two major concentrations, carrying out this gigantic operation:

1. South of the Pripet Marshes, which were to divide the western Russian theatre between the two major sub-units, Army Group "A" (Rundstedt) was to concentrate around Lublin and drive rapidly on Kiev and along the right bank of the Dniepr; and
2. North of the Pripet Marshes and up to the Baltic:
   a. The strongly equipped Army Group "B" (Bock) was to concentrate around Warsaw and take the area between the Dniepr and the Dvina, as far as Smolensk and Vitebsk; and
   b. The more lightly equipped Army Group "C" (Leeb) was to thrust out from East Prussia through Lithuania and Latvia in the direction of Leningrad.

Hitler then planned that, once it had taken Smolensk, Army Group "B" would turn from Moscow and advance towards Leningrad in support of Army Group "C". The fall of Kronstadt, which would follow upon that of Leningrad, would wipe out Russian naval forces in the Baltic. Then the two army groups would turn on Moscow together.

In this operation Hitler could count on the armed support of Rumania and Finland. With the latter's help a German detachment from Norway would seize Murmansk.

Master of the only Arctic port usable all the year round, he would be able to sever the most convenient link between the U.S.S.R., Great Britain, and the U.S.

The map exercises and studies carried out as a result of Hitler's decision of July 31 caused misgivings about the whole idea of the operation in the minds of certain members of the German High Command, notably Field-Marshal von Brauchitsch and especially Colonel-General Halder. They thought that as soon as the German forces had cleared the Dniepr-Dvina corridor, where the rivers run parallel to each other, the objective of Army Group "B" should be not Leningrad but Moscow. In this they were not looking for a mere prestige victory, but reckoned that the fall of Moscow would deprive the Russians of their administrative centre and important industrial resources. They were also influenced by the fact that Moscow was the centre of most of the lines of communication. Once the Germans had reached the other side of Moscow, the Russians would be left with no strategic

The Me-109, spearhead of the Luftwaffe fighter arm during the first part of the war on the Eastern Front.

mainline railway running north-south. The capture of Moscow would therefore also deprive the Soviet High Command of any possibility of large-scale manoeuvre.

Moreover, Brauchitsch, Halder, and Paulus thought that to score an initial victory on the Moscow front would have such an impact that the Russians would do everything in their power to stop any German advance in this direction. They would thus be forced to fight a delaying battle between Smolensk and their capital. Here the last organised forces of the Soviet Union would be engaged, attacked, out-manoeuvred, broken up, and wiped out in accordance with the strictest doctrine of Clausewitz and his school.

The last argument in favour of this direct attack on Moscow was that it would save time. By cutting out the flanking attack on Leningrad it was more likely that the tight schedule of "Barbarossa" could be adhered to. The Führer's directive had said that, once launched on May 15, the operation had to be concluded by October 15. There was all the more reason to make haste, as when the High Command had asked Hitler to lay in stocks of special equipment for a winter campaign he had refused, saying that industrial production was not to be overloaded and he had to avoid severe restrictions on the German people.

Field-Marshal von Brauchitsch and his chief-of-staff do not appear to have discussed their objections frankly with Hitler, not only from the fear of his sarcasm but also because they thought that the matter was not urgent, an opinion based on Moltke's statement that no plan of operations can be expected to provide any reliable forecast beyond the first engagement with the enemy's main forces. For the moment they had to succeed in their allotted task of concentration and then secure a resounding initial victory both in the Ukraine and in Belorussia. After this they would have time to think out how to exploit their victory and persuade the High Command to agree to a direct thrust towards Moscow.

They did not take into account Hitler's obstinacy, though it was well known.

Meanwhile a vast organisation programme was afoot in the German High Command. Fifty large new units had to be created and 3,400,000 men, 600,000 vehicles, and 600,000 horses transported and concentrated between the Black Sea and the Baltic, their on-the-spot feeding had to be arranged, and stocks of supplies sufficient to allow them to push forward at the required speed in a country with poor communications had to be amassed. And all this had to be done without prejudicing such demands as might arise from other theatres of war and without arousing any suspicions on the other side.

The concentration of these enormous quantities of men and material required the movement of 17,000 trains. To ensure secrecy this was staggered between early March and June 22, 1941.

By the end of February there were 25 divisions in the concentration area; seven more arrived in March, 13 in April, 30 in May, and 51 between June 1 and 22. These 126 divisions were increased by a further 19 from the High Command reserves which were moved up into battle after the outbreak of hostilities. At the same time the Luftwaffe, leaving 1,500 planes for operations against England, concentrated some 2,000 first-line aircraft to support "Barbarossa": 720 fighters, 1,160 high altitude and dive-bombers, and 120 tactical and strategic reconnaissance planes, all of which required, in Poland alone, the establishment or rebuilding of 250 airfields. To relieve O.K.H., which was to act as Operational G.H.Q. on the Eastern Front, Hitler gave O.K.W. authority over all the other theatres of war, including North Finland, where four German divisions were to force their way through the tundra towards Murmansk and the White Sea. The other theatres were held by 55 divisions, allocated as follows:

Norway and Denmark:	8
France, Belgium, and Holland:	38
The Balkans:	7
Libya:	2

Was this an "annoying frittering away of resources" as Colonel-General Guderian says in his book *Panzer Leader*? He would seem to be exaggerating, as out of these 55 divisions, 32 were so short of men and material as to be considered for the moment unfit for use at the front. Of the 21 armoured divisions, only the 15th and the 21st Panzer Divisions, allotted to the *Afrika Korps*, did not take part in the Eastern offensive. These two divisions had less than 300 tanks between them, whereas Kleist, Guderian, Hoth, and Hoeppner had exactly 3,332 on June 22, 1941.

Between Molotov's return to Moscow and dawn on June 22, Soviet policy described a curve, the summit of which was the signing of the Soviet-Yugoslav Treaty of Friendship during the night of April 5–6 in the Kremlin. This curve followed faithfully the vicissitudes of Axis strategy. It will be recalled that Hitler signed his "Marita" directive on December 13, 1940, committing him to a diversion in the Balkans.

This he would willingly have avoided as it caused him to cross Bulgarian territory, which the Soviet Union considered as one of its preserves. So, when he renewed the Soviet-German agreements on supplies, Molotov, at the first rumour that the Germans were preparing to cross the Danube, sent through *Tass* a very clear warning to the German Government.

The day after Bulgaria joined the Tripartite Pact, Molotov was not satisfied with the soothing explanations which the German Ambassador had been instructed, by the orders of the Wilhelmstrasse, to offer to him. On the basis of his communiqué of November 26 he pointed out that Moscow considered Bulgarian territory as coming within the Soviet security zone and that Berlin was well aware of this; that was why, his memorandum to Schulenburg concluded, "the German Government must realise that it cannot count on the support of the Soviet Union for its actions in Bulgaria."

As this memorandum contained no threat of reprisals, Hitler could afford to ignore it. King Boris's Minister in Moscow, Altinov, was severely reprimanded, and the reprimand was made public, while Molotov's remarks to the German Ambassador were not. On March 4 a communiqué from the People's Commissar for Foreign Affairs, and not a *Tass* despatch, stated that Altinov had received the following reply from Vice-Commissar Vishinsky: "The Soviet Government cannot agree with the Bulgarian Government that the latter's decision was correct, since this decision, whatever the desires of the Bulgarian Government, will help to spread and not to reduce the area of war and draw Bulgaria into the conflict. The Soviet Government, faithful to its policy of peace, cannot support the Bulgarian Government in its new policy."

A stinging rebuke, indeed, but one which carried no threat of action, or even suggestion of a threat.

The presence of the Wehrmacht on Bulgarian soil nevertheless led Moscow to encourage Turkey to resist. Statements were exchanged and published to this effect on March 25. Far from associating herself with an aggressor who would force the Turks to take up arms to defend their territory, the U.S.S.R., sticking to a Russo-Turkish non-aggression pact still in force, assured Turkey of her neutrality and her complete understanding, and the Ankara Government undertook similar promises in the event of the Soviet Union herself being attacked.

The Yugoslav Government which came to power after the coup d'état of March 27 decided to resume the friendly relations with Russia which had existed between Belgrade and St. Petersburg from 1903 to 1917. After some hesitation Stalin and Molotov replied, accepting the overtures brought to them by Peter II's Minister in Moscow, Milan Gabrilovic. And so, on the morning of April 6 the world learnt simultaneously of the signing of a Pact of Non-

King Peter III of Yugoslavia (left) stands by the former Regent, Prince Paul.

Aggression and Friendship between the two states and of the savage aerial attack on Belgrade, the first stage of the German onslaught.

The Soviet Government's only reaction to this latter event was a sharp reprimand from Vishinsky to the Hungarian Minister who, on April 13, had come to inform him that his country, notwithstanding its recently-signed non-aggression pact with Belgrade, supported the German action and would make no official recrimination. On the very same day, however, when the Soviet authorities were seeing off the Japanese Minister, Yosuke Matsuoka, who had just signed a non-aggression pact with Molotov, Stalin made it abundantly clear that he wanted friendly relations. The curious scene was recorded by Grigore Gafencu:

"When the Japanese Minister, surrounded by members of his mission, finally arrived at the station where diplomats, economists, and military attachés from the Axis powers were waiting for him, a second dramatic event occured. In the general commotion of astonished onlookers, bustling policemen and soldiers running up at the double, Stalin appeared at the top of the steps and walked forward to meet the Japanese. His appearance caused utter astonishment among the diplomats: the Russian ruler, whose public appearances were so rare, had never paid such an honour to a visiting guest. However, Stalin walked uncertainly, as though light-headed from the open air, contact with the people, and his own audacity. As if each onlooker were a brother, he shook the hands of travellers and employees standing around on the platform. Then, after greeting his Japanese guest, who stepped forward gravely to meet him, looking solemn and moved, he turned to the medal-bedecked group of military attachés and saluted all the officers who were presented to him. He stopped in front of Colonel Krebs of the German General Staff, standing stiffly at attention, put his arm round his neck and winked at him, saying 'We shall always be friends, eh?'"

A fortnight previously the tiny Japanese Minister had had another opportunity of

appreciating his own popularity when he had stayed in Berlin for important talks with Hitler and Ribbentrop.

"The clear-sounding name of this little statesman, who came on an official visit to Germany at the end of March 1941, was on every Berliner's lips. It so happened that they were able to pronounce it clearly, without distorting it . . . I often had the occasion to go out with Matsuoka in an open car through the streets of the city and I was able to see the reaction of the people at first hand. 'It's Matsuoka,' the crowds would say as they gathered either in front of the Chancellery or before the Bellevue Palace in the Tiergarten. 'Take care the little man doesn't fall under the car,' a fat Berliner shouted to me one day from among the crowd of spectators. Matsuoka thought the crowd was giving him an ovation and he raised his top hat with truly oriental solemnity."

As tension deepened, and the likelihood of war grew with German victories in the Balkans, Joseph Stalin, then Secretary of the Communist Party of the U.S.S.R., became Chairman of the Council of People's Commissars on May 7, 1941.

In this he replaced the intractable Molotov who, however, retained the Ministry of Foreign Affairs. This was the version Schulenburg gave the Wilhelmstrasse and it was very likely the right one. Anyhow, on the following day the Ministers of Belgium, Norway, and even the unfortunate Gabrilovic were ignominiously expelled from Soviet territory.

As quickly as possible Stalin attempted to get back to the spirit of the Soviet-German Pact of August 23, 1939 and hoped to succeed in appeasing Hitler. Amid the rumours of war circulating from the Atlantic to the Urals, on June 14 he dictated to the official *Tass* Agency the following communiqué which, after implicating the person of Sir Stafford Cripps, the British Ambassador to Moscow, brought everything back to its essentials and intensified Russian advances to the Third Reich:

"According to these rumours," *Tass* said:
"1. Germany has made economic and territorial demands on the U.S.S.R. and these are at present the subject of negotiations between Germany and the U.S.S.R. for the conclusion of a new and closer agreement;

2. The U.S.S.R. has rejected these demands and as a result Germany has begun to concentrate her troops on the frontier of the U.S.S.R. in order to attack the Soviet Union; and

3. The Soviet Union on its side has begun intensive preparations for war against Germany and has concentrated her troops along the German border.

"In spite of the evident absurdity of these rumours, responsible circles in Moscow have thought it necessary – because of the persistence of such false reports – to authorise *Tass* to state that the rumours are the clumsy product of a propaganda campaign by the enemies of the U.S.S.R. and Germany and who are interested in

spreading the war. *Tass* states that:
"1. Germany has made no claims of any kind and does not propose any closer agreement with the Soviet Union; for these reasons negotiations on this matter cannot have taken place;

2. According to Soviet information Germany is respecting the Soviet-German Non-Aggression Pact as scrupulously as is the Soviet Union. This is why Soviet circles consider that rumours to the effect that Germany is contemplating breaking this pact and attacking the Soviet Union are without any foundation. Recent movements of German troops liberated from the Balkan campaign to regions east and north-east of Germany have other purposes and do not affect Soviet-German relations;

3. In accordance with its policy of peace the Soviet Union has respected and intends to respect the conditions of the Soviet-German Non-Aggression Pact. Rumours that the Soviet Union is preparing for war against Germany are untrue and provocative; and

4. The summer mobilisation of the Red Army reservists and the manoeuvres which will follow continuously are intended merely for the training of the troops and the inspection of the running of the railways, as is done every year. To claim that these current measures by the Red Army are directed against Germany is, to say the least, absurd."

As usual the Soviet press echoed this communiqué and directed its bitterest attacks at Perfidious Albion's plutocratic warmongers, who fancied they could bring the two nations into conflict.

This explains Molotov's question to the German Ambassador at dawn on June 22, 1941. Schulenburg had come to inform him that, by reason of the insupportable pressure along the demarcation line of Russian troops on the Germans, the latter had been given the order to enter Soviet territory. Molotov replied: "It is war. Your planes have just bombed some ten open towns. Do you think we deserved that?"

History's answer must be "no". Everything goes to show that at this precise moment Communist Russia was earnestly searching for terms of a new and fruitful agreement with Nazi Germany.

At the same moment the Foreign Office sent the news to Chequers, where Churchill was peacefully asleep. This dramatic event is one more illustration of British phlegm, as the Prime Minister's private secretary's account shows:

"I was awoken at 4 a.m. the following morning by a telephone message from the F.O. to the effect that Germany had attacked Russia. The P.M. had always said that he was never to be woken up for anything but Invasion (of England). I therefore postponed telling him till 8 a.m. His only comment was, 'Tell the B.B.C. I will broadcast at 9 to-night.' He began to prepare the speech at 11 a.m., and devoted the whole day to it. . . . The speech was only ready at twenty minutes to nine."

CHAPTER 20

The military balance in the East

On June 22, 1941, at dawn, 3,400,000 Germans launched a surprise attack on the Soviet Union, defended by the 4,700,000 men of the Red Army, as Russia's army was called. In the numbers engaged and the losses suffered on both sides, this titanic struggle, unprecedented in human history, had no equal in any other theatre of operations in World War II. It would go on until the Wehrmacht was annihilated a fate expressed in the destruction of Berlin, and the signing of the instrument of unconditional surrender by Field-Marshal Keitel, followed by Grand-Admiral von Friedeburg and Colonel-General Stumpff of the Luftwaffe, in the presence of Marshal of the U.S.S.R. Georgi Zhukov, General Carl Spaatz of the United States Army Air Force, Air Chief-Marshal Sir Arthur Tedder of the R.A.F., and General de Lattre de Tassigny of France.

In the German army's war plans, the decisive stroke had been allotted to the armour. It is essential, then, to consider briefly the growth of this arm between May 10, 1940 and June 22, 1941, with the aid of the following table:

	1940	1941
Panzergruppen	1	4
Panzer or motorised corps	5	11
Panzer divisions	10	21
Motorised divisions	7	14

The number of armoured and motorised divisions had thus risen from 17 to 35. As a result of their battle experience in 1939 and 1940, the Germans had ceased production of the Pzkw I and II light tanks and up-gunned most of their 965 Pzkw III medium tanks with 5-cm guns. This tank and the Pzkw 38(t) formed the backbone of the *Panzerwaffe* or Armoured Forces. The number of Pzkw IV heavy tanks armed with the short 7.5-cm gun had been increased from 278 to 517. The German Army also possessed 250 self-propelled guns, and these were to give excellent service in infantry support and anti-tank operations. The Panzer division of 1941, however, had only one tank regiment as against two in 1940, and instead comprised two motorised infantry regiments as against one. This reduced its tank strength from an average of 258 to 196, but gave it greater tactical flexibility. The total German tank strength of 3,350 tanks was only 800 more than in the French campaign: there was little margin for heavy losses.

The German infantry, including mountain troops, totalled 129 divisions at the end of the French campaign. By June 22, 1941, it had increased to 162 divisions made up into 47 corps.

But Russia's strength of resistance lay not only with her regular armed forces. From information received by German Intelligence it was known that Moscow, if Russia were invaded, could also hurl the civil population of any areas overrun, organised into guerrilla units, against the flanks and communications of the invader. To combat this threat, O.K.H. formed nine Security Divisions (*Sicherungsdivisionen*) and allotted three to each army group. Though not capable of fighting regular troops in open country, they were nevertheless useful auxiliaries to front line troops, whom they relieved of the necessity of attending to their own security. The task of these divisions became more and more onerous as the Germans plunged deeper into Russian territory.

Including one cavalry division (1st Cavalry Division), which was removed from the front at the end of the year to be converted into an armoured division, the German Army could muster no less than 208 divisions in all theatres of war. Three-quarters of them, 153 to be exact, were engaged on the Eastern Front on June 22. Brauchitsch commanded 148 between the Black Sea and the Baltic deployed as follows:

1. *Right flank:* Army Group "South" (Rundstedt) with 42 divisions, including five Panzer and three motorised, divided between three armies and one *Panzergruppe*;
2. *Centre:* Army Group "Centre" (Bock), between Lublin and Suwałki, with 49 divisions, including nine Panzer, six motorised, and one cavalry, divided between two armies and two *Panzergruppen*; and
3. *Left flank:* Army Group "North" (Leeb) with 29 divisions, including three Panzer and two motorised, divided between two armies and one *Panzergruppe*.

In greater detail, these army groups broke down thus:
1. Army Group "South":
   Moldavia: 11th Army (Colonel-General E. von Schobert); Carpathians–Lublin area: 17th Army (Colonel-General K. H. von Stülpnagel), *Panzergruppe* I (Colonel-General von Kleist) with 750 tanks, and 6th Army (Field-Marshal von Reichenau);
2. Army Group "Centre":
   from south to north: *Panzergruppe* II (Colonel-General Guderian) with 930 tanks, 4th Army (Field-Marshal von Kluge), 9th Army (Colonel-General Strauss), and *Panzergruppe* III (Colonel-General Hoth) with 840 tanks; and
3. Army Group "North":
   East Prussia: 16th Army (Colonel-General E. Busch), *Panzergruppe* IV Colonel-General Hoeppner) with 570 tanks, and 18th Army (Colonel-General G. von Küchler).

Thus the front line forces contained 120 divisions, including 17 of the 21 Panzer divisions (3,090 tanks), and 12 of the 14 motorised divisions. In reserve, O.K.H. had 2nd Army (Colonel-General von Weichs) with five corps made up of the 2nd and 5th Panzer Divisions, two motorised divisions, and no less than 24 infantry divisions.

In contrast, the German forces in Finland came under O.K.W. command and totalled five divisions or their equivalent.

In its struggle against the Soviet Union, the Third Reich could count on the help of Rumania, Hungary, and Slovakia, as well as the collaboration of Finland which, though she never signed any formal agreement with Germany, waged war at her side in order to recover the territory which she had lost to Russia by the terms of the treaty of March 12, 1940.

Marshal Antonescu put the Rumanian 3rd and 4th Armies at the service of his ally. These totalled 12 infantry divisions and her mountain, cavalry, and tank brigades, the equivalent of another two divisions. Admiral Horthy, the Regent of Hungary, played a more modest part, for Hungary had no bone to pick with Russia. Only one Hungarian corps, composed of a motorised brigade and two cavalry brigades, took part in the first phase of the campaign. Slovakia could not remain neutral in such a conflict, and put a motorised brigade and two small infantry divisions under the command of Rundstedt, who also controlled the Hungarian and Rumanian contingents.

Between the Arctic Circle and the Gulf of Finland, Marshal Mannerheim took the field with 18 divisions, all eager for revenge after the Winter War.

It was not until the evening of June 21 that the Führer communicated his decision to invade Russia to his friend Mussolini in a long letter. Although Hitler made no request for aid, Mussolini proclaimed loudly that the dignity of Fascist Italy would not allow her to surrender her share in the "Crusade against Bolshevism". The *Corpo di spedizione italiano in Russia* (C.S.I.R.) was then formed under General Giovanni Messe with three infantry divisions: the partially motorised "Pasubio" and "Torino", and the "Celere". The corps formed part of the German 11th Army and went into battle on August 7, 1941.

At the news of the split between the allies of the Treaty of Moscow, General Franco authorised the recruitment of a Spanish infantry division, which was to repay the debt he had owed to Hitler since the Civil War. Composed of volunteers and named the *División Azul* (Blue Division), it went into line on the Novgorod front at the end of the summer of 1941 under General Muñoz Grande, who was later replaced by General Esteban Infantes.

Thus new satellites or associates had put about 50 divisions and brigades in the service of Germany. Nevertheless, with the exception of the Finnish Army, which did not belie its previous superb reputation, these allied forces were far less efficient than those of the Reich, in training, leadership, organisation, and equipment.

The major ground offensive was also to be supported from the air, the four air fleets

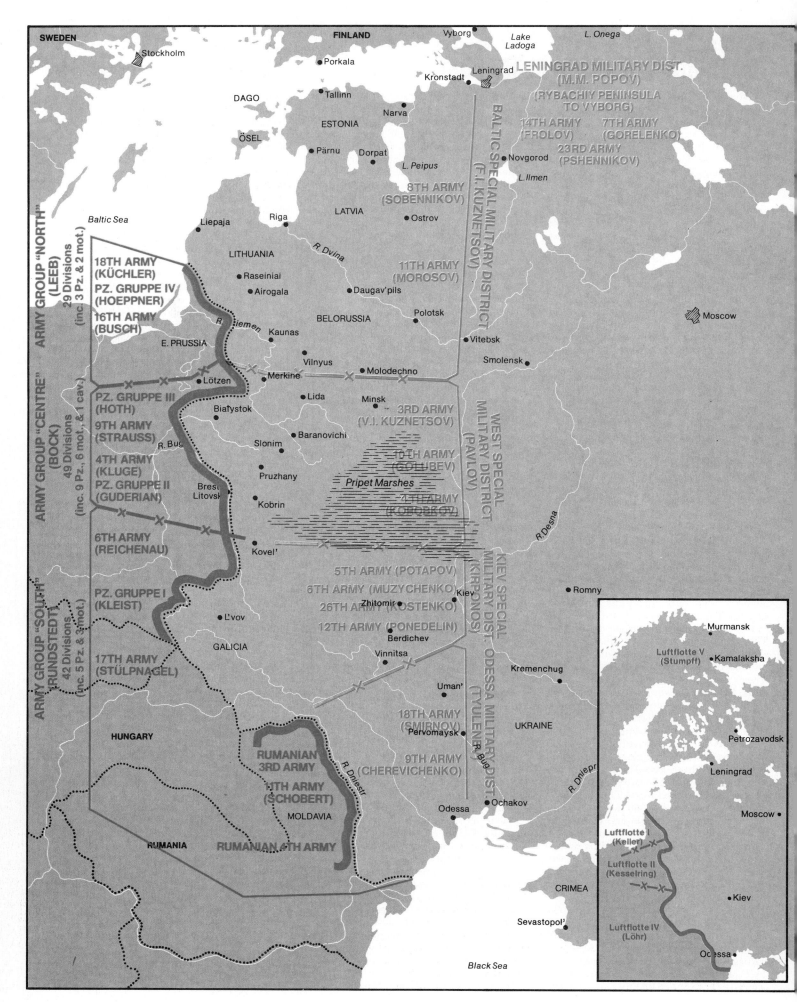

SWEDEN

FINLAND

Vyborg

Lake Ladoga

L. Onega

Stockholm

Porkala

Kronstadt

Leningrad

LENINGRAD MILITARY DIST.
(M.M. POPOV)

(RYBACHIY PENINSULA
TO VYBORG)

DAGO

Tallinn

Narva

14TH ARMY
(FROLOV)

7TH ARMY
(GORELENKO)

ÖSEL

ESTONIA

Pärnu

Dorpat

L. Peipus

Novgorod

L. Ilmen

23RD ARMY
(PSHENNIKOV)

BALTIC SPECIAL MILITARY DISTRICT (F.I. KUZNETSOV)

8TH ARMY
(SOBENNIKOV)

Baltic Sea

Liepaja

Riga

LATVIA

Ostrov

Moscow

ARMY GROUP "NORTH"
(LEEB)
29 Divisions
(inc. 3 Pz. & 2 mot.)

**18TH ARMY
(KÜCHLER)
PZ. GRUPPE IV
(HOEPPNER)
16TH ARMY
(BUSCH)**

R. Dvina

11TH ARMY
(MOROSOV)

LITHUANIA

Raseiniai

Airogala

Daugav'pils

Polotsk

R. Niemen

Kaunas

BELORUSSIA

Vitebsk

E. PRUSSIA

Vilnyus

Molodechno

Smolensk

Merkine

ARMY GROUP "CENTRE" (BOCK)
49 Divisions
(inc. 9 Pz., 6 mot., & 1 cav.)

**PZ. GRUPPE III
(HOTH)
9TH ARMY
(STRAUSS)
4TH ARMY
(KLUGE)
PZ. GRUPPE II
(GUDERIAN)**

Lötzen

Lida

Minsk

3RD ARMY
(V.I. KUZNETSOV)

WEST SPECIAL MILITARY DISTRICT (PAVLOV)

Białystok

Slonim

Baranovichi

10TH ARMY
(GOLUBEV)

R. Bug

Pruzhany

Pripet Marshes

R. Desna

Brest Litovsk

Kobrin

4TH ARMY
(KOROBKOV)

**6TH ARMY
(REICHENAU)**

Kovel'

5TH ARMY (POTAPOV)

Romny

6TH ARMY (MUZYCHENKO)

ARMY GROUP "SOUTH" (RUNDSTEDT)
42 Divisions
(inc. 5 Pz. & 3 mot.)

**PZ. GRUPPE I
(KLEIST)**

Kiev

Zhitomir

26TH ARMY (KOSTENKO)

L'vov

KIEV SPECIAL MILITARY DIST. (KIRPONOS)

GALICIA

12TH ARMY (PONEDELIN)

Berdichev

Vinnitsa

Kremenchug

**17TH ARMY
(STÜLPNAGEL)**

Uman'

18TH ARMY
(SMIRNOV)

R. Bug

UKRAINE

HUNGARY

R. Dniepr

Pervomaysk

9TH ARMY
(CHEREVICHENKO)

ODESSA MILITARY DIST. (TYULENEV)

**RUMANIAN
3RD ARMY**

R. Dniestr

**11TH ARMY
(SCHOBERT)**

MOLDAVIA

Odessa

Ochakov

RUMANIA

RUMANIAN 4TH ARMY

CRIMEA

Sevastopol'

Black Sea

Murmansk

Luftflotte V
(Stumpff)

Kamalaksha

Petrozavodsk

Leningrad

Moscow

Luftflotte I
(Keller)

Luftflotte II
(Kesselring)

Kiev

Luftflotte IV
(Löhr)

Odessa

involved being allocated as follows:

1. *Luftflotte* IV (Colonel-General Alexander Löhr) to Army Group "South";
2. *Luftflotte* II (Field-Marshal Albert Kesselring) to Army Group "Centre";
3. *Luftflotte* I (Colonel-General Alfred Keller) to Army Group "North"; and
4. *Luftflotte* V (Colonel-General Hans-Jürgen Stumpff) to the mountain corps attacking Murmansk.

The Luftwaffe performed its tasks brilliantly. By the end of the first day of the invasion it had wiped out the Red Air Force as a fighting force for months to come, leaving the skies open for the Stukas to repeat the successes of Poland, France, the Balkans, and Crete against minimal opposition.

During the period leading up to "Barbarossa", the Soviet Army was undergoing the turmoils of reorganisation. This was a consequence of the salutary lessons imposed by the Finnish war and, more immediately, of the German Blitzkrieg in the west. Russian theorists now realised that a coherent military doctrine was an urgent priority; a doctrine, moreover, that allowed for the crucial role of armoured formations in battle.

Colonel-General Pavlov, Stalin's armoured warfare expert, had previously denounced the use of large scale tank formations but in the light of recent developments he was forced to revise his views. Accordingly, in July 1940, orders were issued for the organisation of mechanised corps.

However, this revision of policy arrived too late to make possible the development of a tank force that could meet the German Panzers on equal terms. Most of the new formations were destroyed in the first few weeks of the campaign.

The Red Army like other Soviet institutions, was a victim of the confused and contradictory ideology that issued forth from the Kremlin. This made decisive reform virtually impossible. Retarding the progress of modernisation was the inadequate command structure of the army and the baleful influence of Stalin himself: he considered new initiative with a suspicion that sometimes could prove fatal. In summary, it can be said that while on the surface Russian military thought had comprehended the changes wrought by modern warfare, little had been done to implement these ideas at a practical level.

Between the Arctic and the Black Sea, the Red Army was deployed in five major groups:

1. Leningrad Military District (Rybachiy Peninsula to Vyborg, latterly Viipuri, some 750 miles), under Lieutenant-General M. M. Popov, was made up of:
   a. 14th Army (Lieutenant-General V. A. Frolov);
   b. 7th Army (Lieutenant-General F. D. Gorelenko); and
   c. 23rd Army (Lieutenant-General P. S. Pshennikov);

The line up of the forces (opposite).

2. Baltic Special Military District (Polanga to the southern frontier of Lithuania, some 200 miles), under Colonel-General F. I. Kuznetsov, was made up of:
   a. 8th Army (Major-General P. P. Sobennikov); and
   b. 11th Army (Lieutenant-General V. I. Morosov);
3. West Special Military District (southern frontier of Lithuania to northern frontier of the Ukraine, some 280 miles), under General D. G. Pavlov, was made up of:
   a. 3rd Army (Lieutenant-General V. I. Kuznetsov);
   b. 10th Army (Major-General K. D. Golubev); and
   c. 4th Army (Major-General A. A. Korobkov);
4. Kiev Special Military District (northern frontier of the Ukraine to Lipkany, some 500 miles), under Colonel-General M. P. Kirponos, was made up of:
   a. 5th Army (Major-General of Armoured Forces M. I. Potapov);
   b. 6th Army (Lieutenant-General I. N. Muzychenko);
   c. 26th Army (Lieutenant-General F. Ya. Kostenko); and
   d. 12th Army (Major-General P. D. Ponedelin); and
5. Odessa Military District (Lipkany to the Black Sea, some 300 miles), under General I. V. Tyulenev, which shortly after the opening of hostilities divided its forces into:
   a. 18th Army (Lieutenant-General A. K. Smirnov) and
   b. 9th Army (Lieutenant-General Ya. T. Cherevichenko).

The Soviet dispositions formed a long, undulating line along the western frontier. The organisation within the Military Districts was poor (with reserve units too far back to give effective support to the front line troops) and there was little real coordination between the Districts.

Although considerable effort had been invested in the construction of field fortifications in strategically vital areas (over 200,000 men were engaged in the task), the results failed to live up to expectations. In what was supposedly an interlocking system of defence, gaps 10 to 80 kilometres wide were apparent.

A further problem facing the Soviet commanders was Stalin's own curious attitude towards the possibility of war. Because of Stalin's refusal to heed the warnings of impending invasion he forbade his generals to mobilise their forces in anticipation of attack. He maintained that any sizeable troop movements would be construed by the Germans as "provocation".

The most serious flaw in the Russian dispositions was their forward deployment which made it quite impossible for the Soviet commanders to react effectively to the swiftness of the German invasion. The reasoning behind the decision to defend the frontier line of the Soviet Union was based on two erroneous assumptions: firstly, that a formal declaration of war would precede offensive operations, so that the Red Army would not be surprised, and secondly, that the enemy offensive would be opened with limited forces, thereby giving the army time to fight holding actions and allow a full mobilisation. The folly of these assumptions would soon be fully exposed.

If we consider the Red Army in more detail we see that it was quite unprepared for modern war. A fundamental problem acting against military efficiency was the absence of effective communications. Radio equipment was in short supply, especially so in the armoured formations and the air force. Basic communication was carried out through the civilian network so that in one instance, noted by Professor Erickson, the signals of the 22nd Tank Division were sent through a local post-office, the unit "plugging-in" to the civilian network and telegraph service!

Similarly in the fields of transport and supply the Russian armed forces were woefully deficient. The Motorised Transport branch was another victim of administrative ineptitude: its independent status was removed, being reassigned to the armoured forces. However, the armoured units proved incompetent in this additional role.

As professor Erickson explains, within the Red Army there was a general failure to put theory into practise:

"Throughout the whole of the Soviet military sector, from research and development to tactical training, the pressure was on, but its application was uneven, uncoordinated and in parts uncomprehending."

In terms of size, the Soviet tank force, was unchallengeable: the total mechanised force facing the Wehrmacht was 13 motorised divisions and 34 tank divisions. But by 1941 many of its tanks were obsolete and grossly unreliable.

A Waffen-S.S. cavalry patrol. Cavalry was used by both sides in Russia.

In a weapon as complicated as the tank, technical qualities are naturally more significant than in infantry equipment.

From this point of view, the numerous lessons learnt in the Spanish Civil War justify the belief that the Soviet T-26 and BT-7 light tanks, derived from original designs by Vickers of Great Britain and Christie of the United States, were superior to German machines of the same class and far better than Italian ones. On the other hand, they were greatly inferior to the medium and heavy tanks in service with the German Army.

The small number of T-35 and KV-2 heavy tanks, weighing 49 and 52 tons respectively, were to give the Germans some very unpleasant surprises in Lithuania and Galicia, but they were so clumsy that once the German infantry had got over their initial shock at the size of the tanks, they rapidly learned how to immobilise them with grenades before going in to attack them directly.

In contrast, M. I. Koshkin, A. A. Morozov, and N. A. Kucherenko had achieved in the T-34 the best combination of the three factors important in armour at the time: armament, armour, and mobility. The rate of fire of its 76.2-mm gun was superior to that of the 7.5-cm gun mounted by the heaviest German tank, the Pzkw IV, and its armour, in places 65-mm thick and well sloped, made it impervious to German anti-tank shells. Its mobility came from its 500-hp engine, wide tracks, and improved Christie-type suspension, and enabled it to tackle marshy or snow-covered ground in which its opponents bogged down.

At the same time as Soviet tacticians readopted Marshal Tukachevsky's theories, they kept the infantry tank, constructing the KV-1 for this purpose. Its speed was only 21 mph, compared with the 33 mph of the T-34, but this was not the disadvantage it might have been as the KV-1 was an infantry support weapon, and its lack of speed was compensated for by

its massive hull, which gave it a weight of 43.5 tons, compared with the 26.3 tons of the T-34.

With 967 T-34's and 508 KV-1's, the Red Army had an enormous *matériel* superiority over the Germans who, on June 22, could put only 439 20-ton Pzkw IV's into the field. Yet this advantage was cancelled by several circumstances. Firstly, Stalin's blindness about Hitler's intentions had obliged the Soviet High Command to adopt unsuitable strategic plans. Secondly, Russian equipment was badly maintained: according to the *History of the Great Patriotic War*, only 29 per cent of the Russian tanks were ready to move out at a minute's notice because of the shortage of spare parts. Lastly, radio equipment was in extremely short supply and functioned only poorly.

The remarkable development of Soviet armour had escaped Hitler's eyes entirely, and had raised no more than unformulated doubts at O.K.H. But in his book *Panzer Leader*, General Guderian records the "curious incident" about Germany's possible enemy which led him to entertain doubts about the Third Reich's alleged invincibility:

"In the spring of 1941 Hitler had specifically ordered that a Russian military commission be shown over our tank schools and factories; in this order he had insisted that nothing be concealed from them. The Russian officers in question firmly refused to believe that the Panzer IV was in fact our heaviest tank. They said repeatedly that we must be hiding our newest models from them, and complained that we were not carrying out Hitler's order to show them everything. The military commission was so insistent on this point that eventually our manufacturers and Ordnance Office officials concluded: 'It seems that the Russians must already possess better and heavier tanks than we do.' It was at the end of July, 1941, that the T-34

tank appeared at the front and the riddle of the new Russian model was solved."

Whatever the numerical superiority of the Red Air Force over the Luftwaffe, it merits only a brief mention in the calculation of Russian forces, since most of its few modern aircraft were surprised and destroyed on the ground in the first few hours of the campaign. In May 1941, Luftwaffe Intelligence estimated that the Red Air Force had 7,300 aircraft of all types, 4,000 of them first line, deployed in the west. It was later admitted that the figures were in error, greatly underestimating Soviet air strength.

Nevertheless, the Red Air Force would need at least a year to recover from the stunning blow inflicted on it by the Luftwaffe. In the interim, the Stukas of the Luftwaffe could attack Soviet armour and positions without hindrance, while the German A.A., now unemployed, could concentrate on anti-tank action, where its 8.8-cm guns achieved notable successes.

We have already noted Stalin's desire to build up a strong navy in the chapter on German aid to Russia. But on June 22, 1941, the Soviet Navy possessed no fewer than 139 submarines, distributed thus: Arctic Ocean 14; the Baltic 74; and the Black Sea 51. In other classes of vessel the Russian Navy was weak, having only a few modern cruisers and destroyers, but this submarine fleet was the largest in the world.

Its size was not, however, matched by its successes. Between June 22, 1941 and May 8, 1945, it sank only 292,000 tons of shipping, compared with Germany's 14.5 million tons, the United States' 5.5 million tons, and Great Britain's 1.8 million tons. It is true that the Arctic, Baltic, and Black Sea offered far less in the way of prey than the North Atlantic, Pacific, and Mediter-

German troops pass a dump of abandoned Soviet vehicles.

ranean, but all the same, not until the end of 1944 were Soviet submarines able to interfere significantly with the seaborne supply or evacuation of German troops, and with imports of Swedish iron ore.

It must be admitted, however, that Germany's main lines of communication lay on land, and thus even had they been more efficient, there would have been little that they could do.

The Soviet High Command had been the first in the world to recognise the value of airborne troops for operations in the enemy's rear, destroying his communications and cutting front line units off from their supplies and reinforcements. Under Tukachevsky's aegis, the first parachute units in the Red Army had been raised in 1935. But after the purges of 1937, the parachute forces were temporarily disbanded. In 1940–41, following German success with this arm, the old units were reconstituted. Yet by the summer of 1941 training was still in its infancy: only men of the 9th brigade had made two jumps and of the 214th brigade less than half had jumped at all.

Such were the strengths and weakness of the Soviet land, sea, and air forces. But the defeats which the Russians suffered in four continuous months, and the German's advance to the suburbs of Moscow, cannot be explained without mentioning the factor of surprise, of which the invaders made full use right from the beginning of the campaign. In fact, Hitler and O.K.H. had camouflaged as best they could the 153 German divisions which would go into the attack on June 22, and they had also made several diversionary feints.

"For two days," writes Paul Carell, "they had been lying in the dark pine-woods with their tanks and their vehicles. They had arrived, driving with masked head-lights, during the night of June 19–20. During the day they lay silent. They must not make a sound. At the mere rattle of a hatch cover the troop commanders would have fits. Only when dusk fell were they allowed to go to the stream in the clearing to wash themselves, a troop at a time.

"The regiment was bivouacking in the forest in full battle order. Each tank, moreover, carried ten jerricans of petrol strapped to its turret and had a trailer in tow with a further three drums. These were the preparations for a long journey, not a swift battle. 'You don't go into battle with jerricans on your tank,' the experienced tankmen were saying.

"A fantastic rumour swept through the field kitchens. 'Stalin has leased the Ukraine to Hitler and we're just going to occupy it.'"

Hitler himself had had his command post carefully concealed. "This great H.Q.," recalls Paul Schmidt, "was hidden in a thick forest near Rastenburg in East Prussia. One recalled the old tales of witches. Not without reason was the H.Q. known by the code-name of *Wolfsschanze* (Wolf's lair).

"The atmosphere of the post in the dark Prussian forest was depressing for people coming from sunnier parts.

"The rooms were tiny. You always felt constricted. The humidity which came from masses of concrete, the permanent electric light, the constant hum of the air-conditioning imposed an air of unreality on the atmosphere in which Hitler, growing paler and more flabby every day, received the foreign visitors. The whole place might easily have been the mystic retreat of some legendary spirit of evil."

Nevertheless, since the coming of spring, London, Vichy, Berne, Stockholm, Tokyo, and Washington had been expecting a decisive split between the signatories of the German-Soviet Non-Aggression Pact of August 23, 1939, and were already calculating the effect this immense extension of the war would have.

Only the Kremlin refused until the last moment to admit that Hitler was about to cross his Rubicon. Stalin took none of the measures which were clearly required if Russia was to be prepared for the imminent change in the political and military situation. The *Great Patriotic War* explains his strange blindness in this way:

"One of the reasons for the error made in the appreciation of the situation is that J. V. Stalin, who alone decided the most important political and military questions, was of the opinion that Germany would not break the Non-Aggression Pact in the near future. Therefore he considered all the reports of German troop movements merely as evidence of provocations, intended to force the Soviet Union into counter-measures."

The responsibility for Russia's inability to face a surprise attack must be shouldered by Stalin and his two "advisors", Kulik, the self-proclaimed artillery expert, and Mekhlis, the political commisar, who both supported the defence of the forward frontiers.

The blame assigned to General Zhukov, in the *Great Patriotic War* is unjustified. Zhukov, who had been ordered to prepare a plan of defence in the spring of 1941 found his hands tied by the strategical limitations imposed upon him by Stalin.

The "State frontier defence plan of 1941" was a general set of instructions issued to the Military Soviets of the frontier areas. It directed the Red Army to resist any intrusion by a hostile power on Russian territory and in the event of invasion, to carry out a stubborn defence, allowing time for the mobilisation and deployment of the Soviet forces. However, the means to fulfill this optimistic plan just did not exist.

There is nothing surprising in Stalin's refusal to believe Churchill's warning about an imminent German attack. The message that the British Prime Minister sent him on April 3 and which, for various reasons, was not handed him until the 22nd was not explicit enough to have made him change his views:

"*Prime Minister to Sir Stafford Cripps* [British Ambassador in Moscow]

"Following from me to M. Stalin, *provided it can be personally delivered by you:*

"I have sure information from a trusted agent [in fact decodes, by British Intelligence, of German signals sent via 'Enigma' machines], that when the Germans thought they had got Yugoslavia in the net–that is to say, after March 20–they began to move three out of the five Panzer divisions from Roumania to southern Poland. The moment they heard of the Serbian revolution this movement was countermanded. Your Excellency will readily appreciate the significance of these facts."

Stalin did nothing, fearing that Churchill, using all kinds of forged information, was trying to create a split between Berlin and Moscow and to divert the weight of German arms from Great Britain to the Soviet Union. Though history has shown these suspicions to be groundless, the man in the Kremlin cannot be blamed for being on his guard.

The fact remains, however, that the British message of April 3 was soon corroborated by a deluge of information which ought to have found more credence

The raw material of the Red Army.

German heavy artillery in action.

Moscow was told the names of all senior officers down to the corps commanders."

Never had a state been better informed than Russia about the aggressive intent of another. Never had the accuracy of the information been so highly guaranteed, since there could have been no collusion between Sorge and Rössler. But never had an army been so ill-prepared to meet the initial onslaught of its enemy than the Red Army on June 22, 1941.

With 138 rifle divisions and over 40 motorised and armoured divisions under arms between the frozen Arctic Ocean and the Danube delta, the Red Army could have been expected to hold the attack of some 200 German and satellite divisions, had it been properly deployed for a defensive campaign. But it was not. The troops of the Baltic Special Military District were dispersed between the Niemen and the Dvina to a depth of nearly 200 miles. It was worse in the West Special Military District where General Pavlov had placed divisions along the whole 300 mile line between Białystok and Minsk. The situation was slightly better, though still not satisfactory, in the Kiev District.

This dispersal of Soviet forces was the pattern the length of the German-Russian demarcation line. There is no getting away from the fact that the fronts were too long for the divisions detailed to garrison them. For instance, according to the *Great Patriotic War*, the Russians had only the 125th Division covering a 25-mile front facing *Panzergruppe* IV which, on June 22, put two motorised divisions and three armoured divisions into the field. The situation was the same in the sectors awaiting the onslaught of Hoth and Guderian, powerfully supported by Colonel-General von Richthofen's Stukas.

On June 18, a German deserter crossed into the Russian lines near Kovel' and reported the attack as coming on June 22. But this extra proof provoked no greater reaction from the Kremlin than the information it had previously received. Nevertheless, on the night of June 21, after midnight, the penny dropped and at 0030 hours the commanders of the military districts concerned were ordered to occupy their front line positions, disperse and camouflage their aircraft, and put the A.A. on full alert. But they were not to take "any other steps without special orders". This instruction, however, insufficient as it was, had not reached all commanders before they found themselves at grips with forces which were very much greater in numbers and in armament. Furthermore, the Russian communications with the rear had been cut by the German artillery bombardment, which began at 0335 hours that morning and destroyed the Russian telephone networks. At 0415 the barrage of shells was followed by the wide-ranging destruction of Russian barbed wire by German sappers. The Stukas, diving from high in the sky, alternated with the artillery in pounding the bewildered Soviet Union.

The war had come to Russia.

in Moscow, since it originated from Soviet spy networks in the Far East and Central Europe.

At the outbreak of war the *Frankfurter Zeitung*'s Far East correspondent, Richard Sorge, long in the pay of the Soviet Secret Service, had been sent as Press Attaché to the German Embassy in Tokyo. General Eugen Ott, Hitler's envoy to the Mikado, was well connected in Japanese circles and kept no secrets from Sorge.

So, on May 19, this informer, an old hand at his calling and particularly well placed, reported the concentration of nine armies (which was correct) and 150 German divisions (he underestimated by three) facing the Soviet frontiers. On June 1, he described the strategy the Nazis would use; and on June 15, he gave June 22 as the date of attack. "Too good to be true," it might have been thought, when the first revelations of Richard Sorge's exploits appeared some 20 years ago. The fact that in 1964 the Kremlin awarded him posthumously the title of "Hero of the Soviet Union" and issued a commemorative postage stamp, indicates the importance of his services to Russia.

In Switzerland there was a network known to the *Abwehr* as the "Red Trio" (or

"Lucy Ring") because of the three clandestine transmitters which it used to communicate from Lausanne and Geneva.

The three "musicians", as they were known in Moscow, were led by the German Rudolf-Rössler, known under the codename "Lucy", a German refugee of Christian Progressive hue who lived, ostensibly, as a bookseller in Lucerne. Where did this agent obtain the information that he communicated to Moscow? Even today this question is difficult to answer. From the value of the information he gathered and the three or four days he took to obtain it each time, it is reasonable to conclude that he got it from someone who took part in the most secret conferences of O.K.W.

A proof of this, in respect of Operation "Barbarossa", is the description of Rössler's information given by General Otto Heilbrunn in the book he wrote about the Soviet Secret Service. "Not only had the 'Red Trio' given the date of the attack to its Moscow control, but it had also supplied the German plan of campaign, the composition and numbers of Army Groups "North", "Centre", and "South", with precise details of the number of tanks and their distribution between the groups. What is more, Moscow now knew the intentions of the enemy, his directions of attack, and his precise objectives. Lastly

CHAPTER 21
Operation Barbarossa

On the evening of June 22, in the headquarters which German G.H.Q. had just taken over at Lötzen in East Prussia, Halder observed in his invaluable diary:

"The enemy has been taken unawares by our attack. His forces were not tactically in position for defence. In the frontier zone his troops were widely dispersed and his frontier defence was weak overall.

"Because of our tactical surprise, enemy resistance on the frontier has been weak and disorganised. We have been able to seize bridges over the border rivers and, slightly further on, to overwhelm enemy positions fortified by deep earthworks."

Stalin's failure to react until the very eve of the German attack is astonishing. Some validity can be given to the explanation given by one of the best-informed biographers of the Russian leader:

"At dawn on June 22, 1941," writes Emmanuel d'Astier de la Vigerie, "on the day before the anniversary of Napoleon's crossing of the Niemen, 120 divisions speed towards Kiev, Leningrad, and Moscow, where the theatre is performing *A Midsummer Night's Dream*.

"Stalin, living in a dream world of hope, has spurned warnings and refused advice. During the first hours of the attack he issued orders that German firing is not to be answered. He would like to think he is faced by nothing more than a provocative act from a few ill-disciplined German units. On June 21, a German Communist worker deserted and revealed the date and time of the attack. Stalin is told but refuses to believe the evidence. Fifteen years later Nikita Khruschev recounts the episode; and another historian adds that Stalin ordered Korpik, the deserting worker, who could in his view only be an *agent provocateur*, to be shot."

To the north of the Pripet Marshes, Soviet resistance had, from the early hours of that warm summer morning, been surprised and overcome more or less everywhere. The same fate had overcome reinforcements moving up to the front to obey People's Defence Commissar Marshal Timoshenko's broadcast message of 0715 hours:

"Our troops must hurl themselves with all their means and energy against the enemy and annihilate them in all places where they have violated our frontiers."

In Army Group "Centre's" area, Colonel-General Guderian had taken the bridges over the River Bug, above and below Brest-Litovsk, by storm, and by the evening his XXIV Panzer Corps (General Geyr von Schweppenburg) was in Kobrin and his XLVII Panzer Corps (General Lemelsen) in Pruzhany, 41 and 47 miles respectively from their jump-off points.

This enormous success by *Panzergruppe* II was equalled and even surpassed by that of *Panzergruppe* III. Not only had Colonel-General Hoth penetrated deeply into the Russian defences but his LVII Panzer Corps (General Kuntzen) and his XXXIX Panzer Corps (General R. Schmidt) had taken the bridges over the Niemen at Merkine and Olyta intact. The XXXIX Corps was in fact 59 miles over the demarcation line.

This ultra-rapid war of movement led at times to comic incidents such as this adventure of General Guderian:

"I next visited the front line in Slonim and then drove in a Panzer IV through no-man's-land to the 18th Panzer Division. At 15.30 hrs I was back in Slonim having ordered the 18th Panzer Division to push on in the direction of Baranovichi, while the 29th (Motorised) Infantry Division was instructed to hasten its advance towards Slonim. I then returned to my Group command post. This drive took me unexpectedly through the middle of Russian infantry, which had come up in lorries to the very outskirts of Slonim and was on the point of dismounting. I ordered my driver, who was next to me, to go full speed ahead and we drove straight through the Russians; they were so surprised by this unexpected encounter that they did not even have time to fire their guns. All the same they must have recognised me because the Russian press later announced my death; I felt bound to inform them of their mistake by means of the German wireless."

In Army Group "North", Field-Marshal von Leeb had no reason to be any less satisfied with the results of the first day of the campaign. *Panzergruppe* IV (Colonel-General Hoeppner) had also thrown the Russians into disorder; in particular, at about 1900 hours, the LVI Panzer Corps

Vehicles of a motorised artillery unit roll past a column of soldiers, on a dusty road in a Russian village.

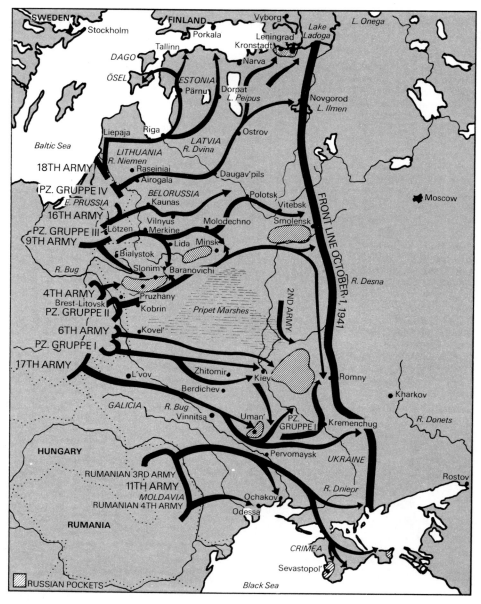

Barbarossa: the lightning German advance into Russia.

(General von Manstein) had boldly seized the important viaduct which crosses the Doubissa gorges at Airogala. He was about 50 miles from his starting point.

As for the Soviet Air Force, those planes which had not been destroyed on the ground in the first hour made a rather pitiful impression on General Kesselring:

"From the second day onward I watched the battle against the aircraft which were arriving from the depths of Russia. It seemed almost criminal to me that they should use formations which were so ridiculous from the point of view of aerial tactics, and machines obviously incapable of getting out of trouble in the air. In they came, one squadron after the other, at regular intervals, and one after the other they crashed, easy prey to our fighters. 'This is the massacre of the innocents,' I thought. So completely did we manage to crush the basis of any future bomber fleet that Russian bombers never appeared again throughout the whole campaign!"

In contrast, south of the Pripet Marshes,

the achievements of Field-Marshal von Rundstedt had been no greater than what German military theorists call an "ordinary victory", and it had not been possible to split off units from *Panzergruppe* I (Colonel-General von Kleist) to exploit the success.

Due to the fact that the Red Army was given a special responsibility for the Ukraine District, it was defended by 68 divisions, including ten armoured and five motorised, while Rundstedt had only 54 divisions under him, including 12 Rumanian, five Panzer, and three motorised divisions. Furthermore, following an order from Hitler, the German 11th Army (seven divisions), which had been concentrated in Moldavia, did not join battle on June 22. This allowed the Russians to assemble part of the forces they had aligned along the Rumanian frontier and use them profitably in Galicia. The Russian defences, however, would be unable to withstand the German onslaught.

Looking at the Soviet Army and the performance of its officers and men, the testimony of General Fedyuninsky, who

was fighting in Kovel' that day, may be useful. As his memoirs have not been translated into any Western language, they will be quoted in the translation given by Alexander Werth:

"Railway junctions and lines of communication were being destroyed by German planes and diversionist groups. There was a shortage of wireless sets at army headquarters, nor did any of us know how to use them . . . Orders and instructions were slow in arriving, and sometimes did not arrive at all . . . The liaison with the neighbouring units was often completely absent, while nobody tried to establish it. Taking advantage of this, the enemy would often penetrate into our rear, and attack the Soviet headquarters . . . Despite German air supremacy, our marching columns did not use any proper camouflage. Sometimes on narrow roads, bottlenecks were formed by troops, artillery, motor vehicles, and field kitchens, and then the Nazi planes had the time of their life." In such conditions the higher levels of the front line command often performed rather poorly. Certain commanders, such as General Boldin, performed heroically; he managed to blast his way through the German lines with 2,000 men of his XIII Corps; others, such as General D. G. Pavlov, who was shot, together with his chief-of-staff and General Korobkov of the 10th Army, lost their heads. Opposite *Panzergruppe* III a Lithuanian division went over to the Germans and, as Fedyuninsky points out, at first cannon shot many Ukrainian partisans rebelled against their September 1939 "liberators". In contrast, the Brest-Litovsk garrison, surrounded on the evening of June 22, held out to July 24, under a hail of bombs and artillery fire, among which were monster 2.2-ton shells fired by the 61.5-cm mortar *Karl*.

In many other sectors, once he had overcome his initial shock, the Russian soldier fought with a stubbornness and bravery admitted by most German combatants who have written about the campaign:

"The Russians again proved their mastery in forest fighting. With sure instinct they moved among the impenetrable undergrowth. Their positions, not on the forest's edge but deep inside, were superbly camouflaged. Their dugouts and foxholes were established with diabolical cunning, providing a field of fire only to the rear. From the front and from above they were invisible. The German infantrymen passed them unsuspecting, and were picked off from behind.

"The Russians were also very good at infiltrating into enemy positions. Moving singly, they communicated with each other in the dense forest by imitating the cries of animals, and after trickling through the German positions they rallied again and reformed as assault units. The headquarters staff of 247th Infantry Regiment fell victim to these Russian tactics.

"In the night, at 0200, the shout went up, 'Action stations!' There was small-arms fire. The Russians were outside the regimental head-quarters. They had surrounded it. With fixed bayonets they broke into the officer's quarters. The regimental adjutant, the orderly officer, and the regimental medical officer were cut down in the doorway of their forest ranger's hut. N.C.O.s and headquarters personnel were killed before they could reach their pistols or carbines.

"Lieutenant-Colonel Brehmer, the regimental commander, succeeded in barricading himself behind a woodpile and defending himself throughout two hours with his sub-machine-gun."

In Moscow, on June 22, the Praesidium of the Supreme Soviet announced the mobilisation of the reserves of the years 1925 to 1938, thus recalling 15 million men to the colours. The next day a new high command headquarters or Stavka was set up, composed of the Marshals of the Soviet Union, the Chief-of-Staff and the Chiefs of the Navy and Airforce. Additionally, in order to increase his power over the leadership of the army, Stalin had himself appointed to the post of Supreme Commander of the Soviet Armed Forces.

The general running of the war fell to the National Defence Committee. This was presided over by Stalin, and its members were Molotov, Voroshilov, Malenkov, and the sinister L. P. Beria in his capacity as head of the Soviet Secret Service or N.K.V.D.

On July 3, 1941, Stalin broadcast:

"Comrades, citizens, brothers and sisters, men of our Army and Navy! I speak to you, my friends!"

This sort of language from the tongue of the cruel master of the "purges" of previous years was unfamiliar, but nevertheless, as Alexander Werth has pointed out, it evoked an enormous response. Indeed it was this speech that brought Stalin out of the recesses of the Kremlin and into public life. Stalin stressed that this conflict must be a people's war, a war that would be essentially nationalist in character. Thus the role of the Communist Party was played down while the necessity of the masses fighting for the survival of Mother Russia was emphasised by the Soviet leader.

"A serious threat hangs over our country," he went on. "It can only be dispersed by the combined efforts of the military and industrial might of the nation. There is no room for the timid or the coward, for deserters or spreaders of panic, and a merciless struggle must be waged against such people. We must destroy spies, *agents provocateurs*, and enemy parachutists . . . On the spot court-martials will try anyone who, through panic or cowardice, hinders our defence, whatever his post or rank."

Stalin expressed himself in this way not only because he had to consider a possible Fifth Column, but also because he was hinting at anybody who might have been tempted to ask him to justify his policies over the previous two years. Whatever his intentions, he gave the order that, if the enemy push became stronger, the Russians should abandon only "scorched earth" to the invader:

"The enemy must not find a single railway-engine, not a wagon, not a pound of bread or a glassful of petrol. All the *Kolkhozes* [collective farms] must bring in their herds and hand their stocks of wheat over to official bodies to be sent to the rear. Everything that is usable but cannot be sent back (such as wheat, petrol, or non-ferrous metals) must be destroyed."

Lastly, he decreed the setting-up of partisan units which would take the war into the enemy rearguard and destroy his communications.

There was also a change in military organisation. The corps (the formation between the army and the division) was abandoned and, as already mentioned, the armoured, motorised, and mechanised brigades were no longer to be formed into divisions. Furthermore, infantry divisions were required to give up one of their artillery regiments. This enabled Russian G.H.Q. to organise large artillery units as the High Command's reserve of firepower.

However, before these various measures had had time to produce the desired effect, the situation between the Black Sea and the Baltic had developed at frightening speed, to the disadvantage and dismay of the Russians.

From the Black Sea to the Pripet Marshes, Army Group "South" had finally overcome Soviet resistance. L'vov fell on June 30 and on July 2, the German 11th Army, which included the Rumanian 3rd Army (General Dumitrescu), went over to the attack. Three days later, the German 6th Army (Field-Marshal von Reichenau) succeeded in punching a hole through the fortified positions constructed by the Russians near the old Polish-Soviet frontier; *Panzergruppe* I drove into the breach along the Berdichev-Zhitomir line and it is possible that its III Panzer Corps (General von Mackensen) would have taken Kiev and the Dniepr bridges if a sudden order from Hitler had not forbidden him to risk his tanks in this large city.

He was forced to wait outside Kiev to be replaced by the German 6th Army, and then wheel from the east to the south-east. On August 2, near Pervomaysk, on the Bug, the 6th Army linked forces with Colonel-General von Stülpnagel's 17th Army, which had arrived after forced marches from Vinnitsa. The Soviet 6th, 12th, and part of the 18th Armies had their lines of retreat cut off and were wiped out. The victors captured 103,000 prisoners, 317 tanks, and 858 guns, all that remained of seven corps (22 divisions). Rapidly exploiting their success, the Germans reached the Black Sea near Ochakov.

This success was notable but not as remarkable as that of Field-Marshal von Bock. By June 25, Guderian had arrived at Baranovichi and Hoth had reached Lida and Molodechno, both more than 125 miles east of Białystok, where the unfortunate Pavlov was still bottled up. On the next day the two *Gruppen* established first contact at Slonim, and at Minsk on the 29th the pincers closed behind the Russians, who had left the decision to retreat until too late. On July 8, according to Halder's diary, of the 43 divisions in the Soviet 3rd, 4th, 10th Armies, 32 could be taken as annihilated. The Germans counted close on 290,000 prisoners, as well as 2,585 tanks, 1,449 guns, and 246 aircraft captured or destroyed.

A second pincer movement was closed at Smolensk on July 16, when *Panzergruppe* II, which had advanced to Elnia after forcing the bridges over the Berezina and the Dniepr, met *Panzergruppe* III, which had sped from Polotsk to Vitebsk

Following up in the rear of the Panzers, the infantry: their job was to mop-up any remaining resistance.

French cars, requisitioned for the invasion. But they were not robust enough for Russian conditions.

and then wheeled south to meet Guderian. Here O.K.H. amalgamated the two *Gruppen* as the 4th *Panzerarmee* (Tank Army), with Kluge as its commander.

Unfortunately, Kluge could not get on with his impetuous subordinates, who accused him of failing to understand the tactical possibilities of tanks and restricting their initiative to an intolerable degree. Whatever the effect of this friction, the Smolensk sector was the centre of a furious struggle until August 8. The Russians trapped in the pocket tried to break through the perimeter which hemmed them in. From outside, Timoshenko and Lieutenant-General A. I. Eremenko tried to break through to the besieged Russian forces.

In the final analysis, all was in vain. Marshal Timoshenko was defeated at Roslavl' and Guderian took 38,000 prisoners, 300 tanks, and 300 guns. When fighting ceased in the "cauldron" of Smolensk, a communiqué from O.K.H. announced the capture of 310,000 prisoners and the capture or destruction of more than 3,000 armoured vehicles and 3,000 pieces of artillery. At Elnia, the Panzers were 200 miles from Moscow but, since June 22, they had travelled 440 miles, mostly on unmetalled roads, in dust which had scored their pistons and cylinders mercilessly.

In Army Group "North", *Panzergruppe* IV was counter-attacked strongly near Raseiniai on June 24 by the Soviet XII Armoured Corps, which launched 100 immense KV-1 tanks against the Germans. Even so, the Russians were cut to pieces and this success allowed LVI Panzer Corps to take Daugav'pils during the

course of the 26th without the Russians having time to destroy the bridges over the Dvina. Kaunas and Vilnyus fell to the 16th Army, Liepāja and Riga to the 18th. The Lithuanians and Letts welcomed the Germans as liberators, but Hitler had no intention of restoring their independence.

Beginning his push on July 2, Hoeppner reassembled his *Panzergruppe* on the right bank of the Dvina, moved up to the fortified Russo-Latvian frontier and forced it at Ostrov, opening the way for his XLI Panzer Corps (General Reinhardt) to capture the important centre of Pskov on the eastern shore of Lake Peipus on July 8, and his comrade Manstein to manoeuvre in the direction of Novgorod. Meanwhile, the 16th Army had established links with the 9th Army (Army Group "Centre") near Vitebsk and the 18th had established itself along a line from Lake Peipus, through Dorpat, to Pärnu on the Gulf of Riga.

From now on, the operations of Army Group "North" would slow down markedly, because of Soviet resistance and counter-attacks and also as a result of the swampy nature of the area and the heavy rain. Another reason was that Leeb had given different objectives to his *Panzergruppe* IV. Its LVI Panzer Corps was to drive on Novgorod while its XLI Panzer Corps moved towards Narva.

Though not everything had gone according to plan during this first phase of the campaign, the German Chief-of-Staff was nevertheless satisfied with the results that had been achieved. On July 3, he wrote in his diary:

"All in all, I can already say that we have carried out the task entrusted to us, which was to crush the mass of the Russian Army between the Dvina and the Dniepr rivers."

On July 8 his optimism was confirmed by the figures of Russian losses:

"Of the 164 infantry divisions which the Red Army mobilised, 89 have been completely or partially destroyed. Forty-six Russian divisions are still fighting and in reasonable condition. Eighteen are in other sectors (14 in Finland and four in the Caucasus) and a maximum of 11 are in reserve in the interior of the Soviet Union. Of the 29 armoured divisions mobilised, 20 have been completely or partially destroyed and nine are still fully fit for combat. The Russians can no longer offer a continuous front even using the best defensive positions."

In spite of the hecatombs of Minsk, Białystok, Uman', and Smolensk, it is true that, on August 8, O.K.H. had identified 143 Russian divisions arrayed against the 136 German divisions, but many of them existed in name and number only. By August 13, the 53rd day of the campaign, German losses had reached the total of 389,924 officers, N.C.O.'s, and men, of whom 98,600 had been posted killed or missing. Yet between September 1, 1939 and May 31, 1941, the Polish, Norwegian, French, North African, and Balkan campaigns had cost the Wehrmacht a total of only 218,109 casualties, of whom 97,000 were killed.

The figures for the Russian campaign indicated losses of 11 per cent of the effectives engaged on June 22, 1941. Colonel-General Halder then wrote on August 8, after listing the figures given above and estimating that 70 of the 143 Russian divisions were still barring the invaders' road to Moscow:

"This confirms my original belief that 'North' (Leeb) has sufficient forces to carry out its task, that all forces in the 'Centre' (Bock) must concentrate to crush the main mass of the enemy and that 'South' (Rundstedt) is strong enough to carry out its mission with success. It might even be able to help 'Centre'."

Evidently, O.K.H. still held to its original plan of attack. Once the Smolensk salient and the zone to its rear had been taken, the German Army would dash towards Moscow, stopping for nothing. It would not do this for the sake of vain prestige but because along that axis it would have the best chance of destroying the principal Russian forces. Hitler had never agreed with this strategy. During the planning of "Barbarossa" he had discounted the importance of Moscow. Hitler had always envisaged turning on Leningrad and possibly the Ukraine as well, once Smolensk was taken. Now he remained faithful to these ideas.

Between July 19 and August 12, he expressed his thoughts in four directives.

Tanks of Panzergruppe *Kleist move eastward. The wear on men and machines became a serious problem due to the huge distances and bad roads (opposite top). A Pzkw III fords one of the many rivers on the Eastern Front (opposite below).*

Finally he made his decision:

1. Army Group "Centre", which was now in a salient, would go over to the defensive temporarily, co-operating with Army Group "South" on its right and allow Army Group "North" to borrow from it as many units and resources as it needed for its task.
2. Army Group "South" would prevent the defeated Russians from establishing themselves on the left bank of the Dniepr and would gain control of the Crimea, which otherwise the Russians could use as an air base to attack the Rumanian oilfields. This group would also overrun the industrial basins of Khar'kov and the Donets.
3. Army Group "North" would continue its offensive in order to cut off Leningrad and link up with the Finnish Army.

This programme, definitely established in Directive No. 34 of August 12, 1941, changed Brauchitsch's and his Chief-of-Staff's dreams of an arrow pointing straight to the Soviet capital into an open fan with its southern end pointing towards Rostov and its northern tip towards Leningrad. Certainly, Hitler meant his powerful Army Group Centre eventually to advance to a winter line some 200 miles beyond Moscow – but only after Rundstedt and Leeb had attained their own objectives.

But would they? Was the year not too far gone already to tackle the decisive act of the campaign?

This argument was certainly important, but Hitler clung obstinately to his views.

A new order to O.K.H. on August 21 cut short any more discussion. It declared unequivocally:

"O.K.H.'s suggestions of August 18 concerning the conduct of operations on the Eastern Front do not correspond with my views. My orders are:

"1. The essential target to be achieved before winter is not the capture of Moscow but the conquest of the Crimea and the Donets coal and industrial basin together with the interruption of oil supplies from the Caucasus. In the north, Leningrad must be invested and German forces must link up with the Finns, etc . . ."

The order was accompanied by a note in which Brauschitsch was reproached for allowing himself to be influenced by individual views emanating from his army groups. Halder judged this accusation unjustified and offensive and wanted his superior to fight back by handing in his resignation, in which he offered to join him. But Brauchitsch did nothing.

On August 23, 1941, General Guderian, whose *Panzergruppe*, diverted from its original objective of Moscow, was to be launched against the line defending the Dniepr, visited Hitler in the presence of Field-Marshal Keitel, General Jodl, and Colonel Schmundt. In vain did Guderian protest that the operation as now planned would force him to make a detour of 600 miles when he was now less than 220 miles from Red Square:

"My generals understand nothing of the theory of war," was Hitler's unpleasant retort. In those conditions the only choices were to submit or to resign. But Guderian, like Brauchitsch and Halder, did not resign. He agreed to obey the orders he had been given.

For several weeks, events seemed to belie the pessimistic prognostications that Hitler's new plan had evoked in the German generals.

By the end of August, after a tough struggle, Rundstedt's 11th, 17th, and 6th Armies had established four bridgeheads on the left bank of the Dniepr and on September 11 Colonel-General von Kleist moved out of Kremenchug to link up with Guderian. Although the latter had suffered the subtraction of an armoured corps from his force and had faced incessant counter-attacks from east and west, he had already passed Romny. On his right, the German 2nd Army was east of Chernigov and pushing south-east.

On September 11, in face of a steadily increasing threat on both wings of the South-West Front and the meagre relief promised by Marshal Shaposhnikov, Marshal Budenny requested permission to evacuate the Kiev pocket:

"Any further delay in the evacuation of this front," was the conclusion of his report, "may lead to the loss of troops and enormous amounts of war material."

From Moscow Stalin coldly rejected this request, though it was reasonable in the circumstances:

"Kiev," he answered, "must be held at all costs." To be sure of being obeyed, he relieved Budenny of his command and replaced him with Timoshenko, who had taken over by September 13. The next day, Shaposhnikov noted signs of panic in a report from the South-West Front stating that the catstrophe could come about any day now. Twenty-four hours later, fears became facts as *Panzergruppe* I linked up with *Panzergruppe* II near Lokhvitsa on the River Sula.

On September 17, as the Panzer grip tightened, Shaposhnikov sent a signal to the encircled armies at Kiev authorising them to withdraw. The order had arrived too late, however: the hapless Russians were caught in the German trap. The following day Kiev itself fell to the Germans. A number of attempts were made to break out from the Kiev pocket but they were isolated and ill-organised, most ending in failure. Russian leadership was disintegrating and the broken Soviet units surrendered in droves to their German captors.

Colonel-General Kirponos, in command of the South-West Front, was killed in the collapse of his 5th, 21st, 26th, and 37th Armies, which totalled about 50 divisions. According to German historians, the full capture was 665,000 prisoners, 884 tanks and 3,718 guns. The *Great Patriotic War*

German infantry in action on the opening day of Hitler's invasion of Russia.

contests these figures, basing its argument on the fact that the South-West Front made ration returns for only 677,085 men at the beginning of September and that more than 150,000 of these, principally from the 38th and 40th Armies, managed to escape the prisoners' cages. This denial is worth recording but it should also be noted that for two months the Russians were incapable of slowing down the German advance towards Khar'kov and then Rostov-na-Donu.

Thanks to the arrival of reinforcements detached from the Army Group "Centre", particularly from XXXIX Panzer Corps, Field-Marshal von Leeb was able to give fresh impetus to operations in the Army Group "North" zone. His 16th Army reached the first spurs of the Valdai hills and succeeded in taking the ancient city of Novgorod, at the mouth of Lake Ilmen. On September 5, XLI Panzer Corps saw Leningrad for the first time but was ordered not to advance from the positions it had reached. The Germans had resolved to invest the city of Peter the Great, for O.K.H. judged that the feeding of its four million inhabitants would pose the Russians an insoluble problem. Therefore the 18th Army, to the east of Leningrad, advanced as far as the River Neva and took Petrokrepost' at the end of Lake Ladoga. However, to the west of the city, the Germans were unable to overcome the resistance of Oranienbaum, where the Russians maintained a bridgehead supported by the Kronstadt batteries and the guns of the fleet.

On September 4, the left wing of the 18th Army had completed mopping-up operations in Estonia, to the joy of its inhabitants. The *Kriegsmarine*, aided by the Finns, was now able to lay an anti-sub-

Panzergrenadiers, riding on a Pzkw III, move past burning Russian buildings. Note the extra baggage being carried on the tank (above).
Weary German soldiers take a rest, during a mopping-up operation early on in the campaign (left).
The sheer size and scale of the operation was beginning to tell on the German forces which were now stretched almost to breaking point.

marine net between Tallinn and Porkala, to reinforce the abundant minefields. In a daring series of amphibious operations, lasting from September 15 to October 22, the islands of Moon, Dago, and Ösel fell to XLII Corps (General Kuntze with the 61st and 217th Divisions), and thus opened the Gulf of Riga.

Hitler had given up the idea of taking Leningrad by force of arms, but Army Group "North" had not yet been able to establish a stranglehold on the city.

Nor had the Germans managed to link up with the Finnish Army, which had reached the right bank of the Svir' between Lakes Onega and Ladoga, reconquering the territory in the Karelian Isthmus which Finland had ceded to Russia by the Treaty of Moscow (March 12, 1940). But on September 11, in view of the imminence of Operation "Typhoon", Leeb had received orders to transfer *Panzergruppe* IV to his comrade Bock.

Though to the north of the Arctic Circle, General Dietl's mountain corps had safeguarded the Petsamo nickel mines from any possible Russian attack, his advance towards Murmansk had slowed down rapidly in the Arctic tundra. A similar fate had befallen the German forces whose target had been Kandalaksha on the White Sea.

179

CHAPTER 22
The battle for Moscow

Planned for September 15, Operation "Typhoon" could not be launched until October 2. The German Army Group "Centre" was reinforced to the strength of 78 divisions, with 14 armoured and eight motorised divisions. By this time these units were seriously depleted and the Panzers had less than half their establishment of tracked vehicles. Its objective was to wipe out the Bryansk Front (General Eremenko) and the West Front (General Konev), which contained, according to German information, 14 armies with 77 divisions, of which six were armoured and six cavalry.

The manoeuvre included a double pincer movement with the intention of cutting through and encircling the Soviet forces.

Panzergruppe II and the 2nd Army formed the southern pincer. The 4th and 9th Armies, which included *Panzergruppen* III and IV, formed the northern claw. *Luftflotten* I and II, reinforced with all of Richthofen's Stukas, would support this attack, as a result of which Moscow would fall to the Germans.

Emerging from the area of Glukhov, Guderian swept aside everything in his path. He sped through the gap made on October 1, and his XXIV Panzer Corps drove 90 miles north in two days to take Orel. This achievement allowed the XLVII Panzer Corps, which followed Guderian, to veer north-west, take Bryansk from the rear and link up with the 2nd Army, which had forced the Russian positions along the Desna. In this way, two encircling pockets were formed on either side of the city. Both had surrendered by October 25th.

On the first day of Operation "Typhoon", the 4th Army and *Panzergruppe* IV concentrated near Roslavl', hurled themselves against Konev's left wing, and broke it. On the next day, Colonel-General Hoeppner began to advance north-east to exploit his success. On October 7, his XL Motorised Corps (General Stumme) entered the city of Vyaz'ma to meet the spearhead of LVI Panzer Corps, which had come under the command of General Schaal as a result of General von Manstein's promotion. To the left of Army Group "Centre", the joint 9th Army and *Panzergruppe* III poured out of the zone north of Smolensk and easily pierced the right of the Russian West Front. So Colonel-General Hoth was immediately able to unleash his tanks, which reached Vyaz'ma by the date mentioned, after cutting round through Kholm. According to the Germans, the Bryansk and Vyaz'ma pockets yielded 663,000 prisoners from 67 infantry divisions, six cavalry divisions, and various armoured units, as well as 1,242 tanks and 5,412 guns. As usual, Soviet historians contest these figures and Marshal A. I. Eremenko does so in terms which are particularly insulting ("pure and simple lies") to the memory of Colonel-General Guderian, his direct adversary in those

The German advance on Moscow
The ravages of war in Russia (opposite).

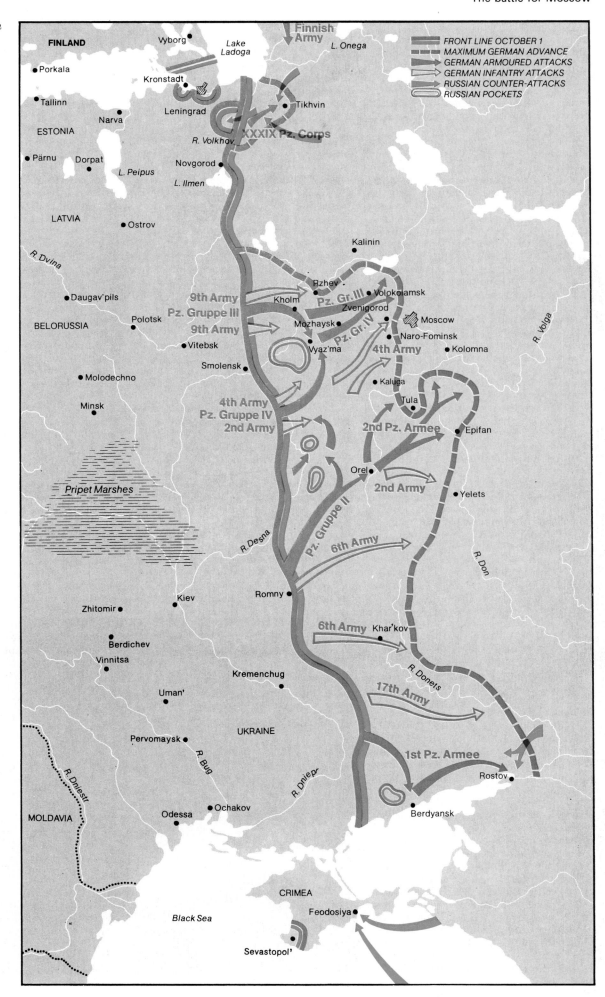

FINLAND

Porkala

Tallinn

Narva

ESTONIA

Pärnu Dorpat

LATVIA

Ostrov

R. Dvina

Daugav'pils

BELORUSSIA

Polotsk

Vitebsk

Molodechno

Minsk

Pripet Marshes

Zhitomir

Kiev

Berdichev

Vinnitsa

Kremenchug

Uman'

UKRAINE

Pervomaysk

R. Bug

R. Dniepr

MOLDAVIA

R. Dniestr

Odessa Ochakov

Black Sea

Sevastopol'

CRIMEA

Feodosiya

Vyborg

Lake Ladoga

L. Onega

Finnish Army

Kronstadt

Leningrad

Tikhvin

R. Volkhov

XXXIX Pz. Corps

Novgorod

L. Ilmen

L. Peipus

Kalinin

Rzhev

Kholm

Pz. Gr. III

Volokolamsk

9th Army
Pz. Gruppe III

9th Army

Zvenigorod

Mozhaysk

Pz. Gr. IV

Moscow

Naro-Fominsk

R. Volga

Vyaz'ma

4th Army

Kolomna

Smolensk

Kaluga

4th Army
Pz. Gruppe IV
2nd Army

Tula

2nd Pz. Armee

Epifan

Orel

2nd Army

Yelets

R. Desna

Pz. Gruppe II

6th Army

R. Don

Romny

Khar'kov

6th Army

R. Donets

17th Army

1st Pz. Armee

Rostov

Berdyansk

FRONT LINE OCTOBER 1
MAXIMUM GERMAN ADVANCE
GERMAN ARMOURED ATTACKS
GERMAN INFANTRY ATTACKS
RUSSIAN COUNTER-ATTACKS
RUSSIAN POCKETS

tragic October days.

It is only fair to admit that Eremenko's 50th Army was not totally annihilated in the pocket which had been formed to the north of Bryansk. Yet the truth is that, in order to regroup and cause some trouble to the 2nd *Panzerarmee* (ex *Panzergruppe* II) near Epifan on November 21, it had had to retreat 170 miles.

But since only 90,000 men could be mustered on the Mozhaisk line covering the approach to Moscow, it is plain that the Red Army had suffered appalling losses. Meanwhile von Kluge, with the German 4th Army, had left Roslav some three weeks ago, and presently he was to find himself outside Naro-Fominsk, nearly 200 miles from his starting point. So, without claiming absolute reliability for the German figures quoted above, it may safely be concluded that the Red Army had undergone a defeat of incalculable magnitude as a result of the opening moves of Operation "Typhoon". The Soviet capital was now directly threatened.

That was the conclusion reached in Moscow by Stalin, Molotov, Voroshilov, and Malenkov, who constituted the National Defence Council. And so, on October 10, a new West Front, barring the way to Moscow, was established and General G. K. Zhukov was called on to command it. He was given a first-class Chief-of-Staff in the person of Lieutenant-General Sokolovsky; as political adviser, the authorities appointed N. A. Bulganin. Some days later, the Soviet Government and the main organs of administration left the capital and set up house at Kuybyshev on the left bank of the Volga.

As is clear, in October 1941 there was less optimism in the Kremlin about the situation than would appear from Soviet historiography 20 years later. The state of affairs was even more serious because the departure of the authorities had given rise to serious disorder in Moscow. The evidence comes from A. M. Samsonov's work entitled *The Great Battle of Moscow*, in a version supplied in 1959 by the East German Ministry of Defence.

Speaking about the period from October 16 to October 20, Samsonov describes the Soviet capital thus:

"Those days also witnessed isolated difficulties among the population. There were those who spread panic, abandoned their places of work and fled hastily from the city. There were traitors who took advantage of the situation to pillage Soviet property and to try to sap the strength of the Soviet state, but everywhere these attempts were blocked by the resistance of the population."

The truth of this is not doubted for a moment, but the Soviet author continues:

"On October 18, the Executive Committee of the Moscow Soviet published a decree aimed at assuring order as rigorously as possible, maintaining normal commercial and public services, and providing for the feeding of the inhabitants of the city."

Does the decreeing of such measures prove their insufficiency? In any case, Samsonov writes:

"On October 20, following the decision of the National Defence Committee, a state of siege was declared in Moscow and the surrounding districts."

This decree ordered that those guilty of offences against public order should be tried without delay by military courts and also prescribed immediate execution for *provocateurs*, spies, and other enemies who incited the people to acts of disorder.

"The National Defence Committee," the decree reads, "appeals to all the workers of Moscow to observe order, remain calm and give their entire support to the Red Army in defence of the capital."

There is no reason to suppose that the powers decreed on October 20, 1941 were not applied with implacable rigour under Stalin's personal control, for the Russian leader had decided to stay on in Moscow.

The Soviet capital organised its defence at a speed that astounded the invaders. Five divisions were improvised from the factories of Moscow. In addition, 500,000 men and women, workmen, clerks, students, secondary school pupils, and housewives were conscripted to improvise a system of fortifications nine miles deep. Without repeating all Samsonov's figures, it may be noted that there were 62 miles of anti-tank ditches and 5,000 miles of trenches; 177 miles of barbed wire were laid and 45 miles of barricades were thrown up. But these defences alone would hardly have been sufficient.
Two circumstances came to the aid of the defenders of Moscow.

The magnificent weather which favoured the offensive at dawn on October 2 was followed, a few days later, by a long period of rain, sometimes mixed with snow. From October 20 onward, the German armies were literally wading in the mud of the steppes which, in Poland at the end of December 1806, Napoleon had described as the "fifth element". Off the roads, the terrain was generally impassible and, with rare exceptions, the roads themselves were dreadful sloughs where vehicles were seen to disappear completely. All the rivers were in flood, which made it a long and difficult operation to repair the countless bridges that the Russians had destroyed in their retreat.

Under these conditions wheeled motor transport was almost paralysed. The German units had to be amalgamated more and more frequently because of their losses. At the end of October, outside Kalinin, the 36th Motorised Division of *Panzergruppe* III had only one quarter of its regulation reserve of ammunition and the 6th Panzer Division had lost all its tractors. In the 2nd *Panzerarmee*, mud and the wear resulting from the Ukraine offensive combined to produce an even worse situation. On November 14, by grouping together all the tanks of XXIV Panzer Corps which were still functioning, General Guderian was able to improvise a "brigade" of only 50 machines, yet on June 22, 1941, the 3rd and 4th Panzer Divisions, which formed the XXIV Corps, must have totalled 350 tanks. Taken as a whole, the Panzers had lost the use of about half their effectives. In spite of this, Army Group "Centre" had taken the towns of Kaluga, Mozhaysk, and Rzhev and, by the end of October, it was fighting along the line Yelets–Tula–Naro-Fominsk –Volokolamsk–Kalinin.

Soviet historians of World War II have always rejected unanimously the view

Many Ukrainians welcomed the Germans as liberators but the insane brutality of the Nazis destroyed any goodwill.

that mud played any part in the final check of the German attack on Moscow. It cannot be denied that the massing of brigades of T-34 tanks at the front slowed down the Panzer advance but, on the other hand, there is abundant photographic evidence to illustrate this phase of the campaign and this shows mud up to the hubs of German vehicles, up to the bellies of their horses, and over the knees of their soldiers. This speaks for itself.

Alexander Werth's opinion is more balanced but, despite the distinction of this author,it cannot be advanced as true. Quoting Guderian's recollections, he writes:

"Guderian's argument that rain and mud interfered with the success of the first German offensive against Moscow seems futile, since it affected the Russians as much as the Germans."

This argument seems to ignore the fact that the Russians had all the resources of their railway network, while their adversaries were at a great disadvantage since the Soviets had carried out wide-scale demolitions and evacuated their rolling-stock. Furthermore, the bridges behind them were intact and they could draw supplies from depôts in the rear as they moved back. The pursuing Germans, on the other hand, were getting further from their logistic bases every day. Finally, as Kesselring remarks, in that season of torrential rain, the Luftwaffe was able to fly very few missions in support of the ground troops. Because of their losses, the Russians were in the same position.

However, by now a vitally important piece of news had reached Moscow. On September 14, Richard Sorge, the spy, had revealed that the Japanese Government had no intention of taking advantage of the military situation to associate itself actively with the German attack. Stalin had learned, from Sorge's warning about the attack of June 22, 1941, to appreciate the value of his information. Therefore he felt secure enough to draw freely from the garrisons in eastern Siberia, calculated at 20 to 25 divisions. As early as October 13, near Borodino, *Panzergruppe* IV had come up against the 32nd Division, which had left Vladivostok the previous month. In his diary on November 21, Colonel-General Halder noted the intervention in the Tula sector of "new Siberian divisions".

Such was the last but not the least of the services which Richard Sorge rendered the cause of the Soviet Union. He served Russia from the shadows for close on 15 years but, on October 18, 1942, he was arrested by the redoubtable Japanese counter-espionage service, which was not deterred by Sorge's status as Press Attaché in the German Embassy in Tokyo. He and his Japanese accomplice were condemned to death and executed in the autumn of 1943.

As autumn wore on, the ground hardened with frost, to the satisfaction of the German generals, who thought that they could get the offensive going again at the speed it had reached at the beginning of

October. But the drop in temperature was far greater than was tolerable for the tasks required of Army Group "Centre". On November 12, the temperature was −12 degrees Centigrade, the following day −13 degrees and, on December 4, the mercury fell to −35 degrees and a strong north-east wind made the biting cold even more painful. Winter equipment had been ordered too late, because of intervention by Hitler, but even that which had been manufactured had not crossed the Russo-German demarcation line. Even though the Russian railways had been relaid on the European gauge, the equipment was delayed on its way to the front by the effect of the cold on German locomotives and the ever more numerous and daring Russian partisan raids.

Badly worn by five months in the field, the clothing of the German soldier was, in any case, not at all suitable for the rigours of the Russian winter. It did not include a Balaclava helmet, earflaps, a padded tunic, fur gloves, or camouflage overalls. The infantryman's boots had room for only one pair of socks whereas, when Marshal Mannerheim inspected the 163rd Division in Helsinki, he observed to its commander that, to face the Finnish winter, each man should have boots two sizes too large. For these reasons there was a great increase in the number of men evacuated with serious frostbite: 400 in each infantry regiment in the 112th Division, Guderian noted on November 17.

For lack of anti-freeze, engines had to be left running all the time, which meant a considerable increase in fuel consumption. Crampons for the tank tracks had not yet reached the front, and the tracks were too narrow to carry the tanks over deep snow. Automatic arms jammed during combat and guns did not recoil properly after firing. Parts made of artificial rubber (*Buna*) became friable and took on the consistency of wood. Lastly, the army's livestock suffered terribly. The German horse does not have the same resistance to the harsh Russian climate as his Russian cousin who is accustomed to scratching out grass with his hoof.

Since the beginning of November, Hitler had been forced to recognise that the final objectives of Operation "Barbarossa" would not be achieved by the end of the year. He was thus compelled to fall back on a far more modest programme. According to the new plan:
1. Rundstedt would take Sevastopol' and Rostov, throw his armour across the Don, and conquer Maykop and the Kuban oil areas;
2. Bock would bring about the fall of Moscow by a pincer attack; and
3. Leeb would push east as far as Tikhvin, then wheel north and link up with the Finns on the Svir'; this would solve the problem of Leningrad.
The final objectives of the original plan had been to reach the Volga between Astrakhan and Gor'ky, and the Northern Dvina between Kotlas and Archangel, but this goal now became the target of a

General Erich von Manstein.

new attack to be launched in 1942 as soon as weather permitted. In spite of the delay, Hitler still felt optimistic. Though the enemy had not been literally annihilated, he had been decisively defeated. Hitler's optimism was misplaced. Although the Red Army had suffered a blow of staggering proportions, sustaining heavier numerical losses in six months than any other army in history, it was not finished. Stalin's ruthless control of the Soviet war effort and the fighting spirit of the Red Army had enabled Russia to survive the German onslaught.

The plans were now prepared for the offensive against Moscow, to be carried out by Army Group 'Centre' under von Bock.

In the fulfilment of its task, Army Group "Centre" put six armies into the field:
1. Covered on the right by the 2nd Army, the 2nd *Panzerarmee* would push north along the Tula-Kolomna line;
2. In the centre, the 4th Army would attack the Russians directly opposite in order to hold them and prevent them escaping encirclement; and
3. Covered on their left by the 9th Army, *Panzergruppen* IV and III would force a passage over the canal connecting Moscow with the Volga. Then turning south-east, they would meet Guderian as he fanned out from Kolomna.

Though he did not issue his generals with a peremptory order, the Führer's aim was to see his armies solidly installed along a line running from Ryazan', through Vladimir and Yaroslavl', to Rybinsk from where, with the spring, they would move towards Gor'ky, the ancient city previously known as Nishny-Novgorod.

In carrying out his task, Bock displayed energy that Keitel describes in his diary as "incredible". The fact remains, nevertheless, that by December 5, 1941, his army group had reached, in the words of the famous military theoretician Karl von Clausewitz, its "limit of strategic consumption". Any fresh movement forward was out of the question, as much because of the exhaustion of the troops as through the obstinate resistance of the Russians.

Unable to take the great industrial city of Tula, the 2nd *Panzerarmee* had tried to bring it to its knees by cutting it off, but the Germans had spread themselves over a front of 200 miles. In the centre, the 4th Army had been held up at Zvenigorod.

A section of German soldiers warm themselves during the first snowfalls on the Moscow front (left). A Pzkw III advances through the village of Bulchevo in December 1941 (above).

The 2nd Panzer Division of *Panzergruppe* IV had reached Krasnaya Polyana, 22 miles from Red square but, on December 4, a young artillery officer in the 2nd Motorised Division *Das Reich*, belonging to the *Waffen*-S.S., wrote to his mother:

"These Russians seem to have an inexhaustible supply of men. Here they unload fresh troops from Siberia every day; they bring up fresh guns and lay mines all over the place. On the 30th we made our last attack – a hill known to us as Pear Hill, and a village called Lenino. With artillery and mortar support we managed to take all of the hill and half of the village. But at night we had to give it all up again in order to defend ourselves more effectively against the continuous Russian counter-attacks. We only needed another eight miles to get the capital within gun range – but we just could not make it."

The view of this junior officer is in accord with that expressed by Colonel-General Guderian, who wrote to his wife on November 9:

"We have seriously underestimated the Russians, the extent of the country and the treachery of the climate. This is the revenge of reality."

A last effort by the 7th Panzer Division, once Rommel's division and now part of the *Panzergruppe* III, under the command of General Reinhardt since the end of October, brought it not only up to the Moscow – Volga canal, but also across it near Dmitrov. A vigorous counter-attack threw it back to the west bank and Reinhardt did not try to regain the lost ground. Besides, with the reversal of fortune, he and his comrade Hoeppner were in a dangerously exposed position and liable to possible flanking attacks by the Russians.

During the Stalin epoch, Communist sources claimed that this last offensive by Army Group "Centre" had cost it more than 55,000 dead between November 16 and December 6. However the statistics of O.K.H., preserved in Halder's diary, quote losses from November 16 to December 10 as less than 66,000 officers, N.C.O.s and men for the whole of the Eastern Front, and of these only 15,435 were killed or missing. It is true that these losses threw a terrible burden on the already seriously undermanned German units. For example, in the 7th Division, the infantry brigades consisted of about 400 men each by the end of November, and were commanded by lieutenants.

Whatever its mental anguish after the catastrophes of Bryansk and Vyaz'ma, the Soviet High Command had not given up the idea of taking the offensive. During October and November, no less than nine armies, totalling about 50 divisions, were being organised in the rear. On December 1, the Russians estimated that they had reached numerical par with their adversary. Though the Germans were still better equipped with armoured vehicles, they had nothing capable of emerging successfully from a clash with the redoubtable T-34 and KV-1 tanks. This is illustrated by an episode recounted by Colonel Pavel Guds, then a lieutenant and tank commander:

"Our target was a base outside Volokolamsk. The battalion commander ordered me to support the infantry attack with fire from my KV-1 tank. When our infantry were some way forward, the enemy unleashed a counter-attack, spearheaded by 18 tanks. Our men stopped, wavered, and broke in disorder. They needed help. I ordered my driver to move forward towards the German tanks and my gunner to open fire. Methodically, the Soviet tank destroyed its opponents one after the other. A few minutes later, ten mutilated and burning German tanks lay on the battlefield and the eight survivors were fleeing. On the same occasion, our machines rolled several anti-tank guns flat into the ground.

"When we had finished, we inspected our tank. It bore the marks of 29 impacts and yet it was in first-class condition."

It was also evident that the defenders of Moscow, and the reserves which came flowing in to reinforce them, were perfectly equipped to face the rigours of the climate. A few examples suffice for illustration of this point. The factories of Moscow alone delivered 326,700 pairs of Russian-style boots and 264,400 pairs of fur gloves. The only shortage was in transport, for the 8,000 lorries that the Russians possessed were not sufficient to supply the needs of the attack. The lack was made good by using long columns of trailers and sledges.

The troops who launched the attack on the Germans on December 5 and 6 seem to have had excellent morale. On November 7, the twenty-fourth anniversary of the November Revolution, Stalin had appealed to the patriotic glory of ancient Mother Russia. One after the other he rolled off the names of Alexander Nevsky, who defied the German knights on the frozen Lake Peipus in 1242, Dmitri Donskoy, who crushed the Tartars at Kulikovo in 1380, Minin the Butcher and Poyarsky the Boyar, who raised Moscow against the Poles in 1612, Alexander Suvarov, conqueror of Ismail, Warsaw, and Cassano, and of Mikhail Kutusov, who forced Bonaparte, the victor of Europe, to begin his retreat from Moscow in 1812.

The Soviet offensive on the Moscow front was part of a pattern of movement which aimed at destroying the three German army groups fighting between Lake Ladoga and the Kerch' Strait, which separates the Crimea from Kuban'. For the sake of clarity, and because of its great importance, the great battle which began on December 5 and 6, 1941, will be described first. It began, according to High Command orders, on the immense, 500-mile front which twisted and turned from Kalinin to Yefremov.

As Bock's order of battle has already been described and had not been changed in any important aspect since about November 15, there is no need to outline it again.

However, on account of the considerable losses suffered by the German infantry, the line was thinly held and nowhere were there sufficient troops to cover the front adequately. Army Group "Centre" had spent all its reserves and was by now, to use the expression applied by General Laffargue to the deployment that General Gamelin had tried to organise on May 10, 1940, in a state of "pre-rupture". Furthermore, the Germans, abandoning their attack on December 4, had only 24 or, at most, 48 hours, according to the sector, to carry out a defensive reorganisation of their newly-won positions. If this were not enough, a temperature of 34 degrees below zero made the ground so hard that no real fortification work was possible.

This last observation draws attention to the fact that the success of the first Soviet winter offensive can be partially explained by the speed with which the Red Army was able to put its plans into effect. On November 30, Stalin and Shaposhnikov approved the plans drawn up by Zhukov, nicknamed "vinegar-face" or "cropped-head", and the plans' effects became apparent less than one week later.

According to John Erickson in his book *The Road to Stalingrad*, Konev's Kalinin Front comprised 15 rifle divisions, one motorised rifle brigade, two tank battalions and one cavalry division; Zhukov's West Front 48 rifle divisions (plus three forming in the rear), three motorised rifle divisions, three tank divisions (two without tanks), 15 cavalry divisions, 18 rifle brigades, 15 tank brigades and a parachute corps; Timoshenko's South-West Front (right wing) 11 rifle divisions, one motorised rifle division, six cavalry divisions, one rifle brigade, two tank brigades and a motor-cycle regiment; a grand total of 718,000 men, 7,985 guns and 720 tanks. The Soviet Army's main advantage lay not in numbers, but in fresh, well-clad troops where the Germans were exhausted, ill-fed, demoralised and freezing.

Like Operation "Typhoon" of October 2, 1941, the Soviet attack launched on December 5 consisted of two pincers designed to crush the flanks of Army Group "Centre". When this result had been achieved, Bock's army group, trapped in front by holding attacks, would be cut off from its communications with Smolensk, surrounded, and annihilated.

To the north-west of Moscow, the salient bounded by the Zvenigorod–Krasnaya-Polyana–Dmitrov–Kalinin line, against which the last efforts of *Panzergruppen* IV and III and the German 9th Army had spent themselves, would undergo the concentrated assault of the 5th, 16th, and 20th Armies, the 1st Shock Army and the 30th Army of the Moscow Front, as well as the 31st and 29th Armies of the Kalinin Front, under the command of Generals L. A. Govorov, K. K. Rokossovsky, A. A. Vlasov, V. I. Kuznetsov, D. D. Lelyushenko, I. I. Maslennikov, and Y. Yushkevich respectively.

On the southern side, the forces in the 200-mile salient pushed through the Soviet line by the 2nd *Panzerarmee*, bordered by Tula, Kashira, Mikhaylov, and Yefremov, would be cut off from their base and crushed by the concentrated attacks of the 50th and 10th Armies (Generals I. V. Boldin and F. I. Golikov), of the Guard Cavalry Corps and the 13th Army (General Gorodnyansky), the latter forming the right wing of the South-West Front.

The Germans were surprised as much by their adversary's initiative as by the vigour and scale of its execution. In effect, by nightfall on D-Day, December 6, General Lelyushenko had penetrated 12 miles into the depleted lines of *Panzergruppe* III and, on the 11th, a special Kremlin communiqué was able to give details of 400 villages liberated around Moscow, including the small towns of Yakhroma, Solnechnogorsk, and Istra, and the defeat of 17 German divisions, of which ten were motorised.

The Volga was secured and would no longer hinder General Konev's forces. In spite of this advantage, they were less fortunate than those of the West Front in their attacks against the German 9th Army. Not till December 16 did they manage to retake Kalinin and fan out south-west. As a result the pincer did not grip the left wing of the German Army Group "Centre", as Moscow had hoped. But, though Hoeppner, Hoth, and Strauss managed to elude the encirclement that threatened them, they did so at the price of losing a large part of their equipment. When Generals Boldin, Golikov, and Belov were concentrating their attacks on the 2nd *Panzerarmee*, Colonel-General Guderian was trying to get out of the exposed position in which he had been left by the halt of the German offensive. To some extent he succeeded, but not without being forced to make painful sacrifices. In the course of their retreat, the 3rd and 4th Panzer Divisions abandoned most of their combat and transport vehicles in the deep snow, and the rout of the 10th Panzer was echoed even in the rarefied realms of the German Supreme Command, as Halder's diary records.

Worse was to come; under the blows of the converging thrusts of his adversaries, who retook Stalinogorsk and Venev on December 13, Guderian had to pull in his forces, which obliged him to break contact with his right (2nd Army) and his left (4th Army). And so enormous gaps appeared in the German line, which Bock could not fill for lack of men and which the Russians resolutely exploited towards both Kaluga and Kursk. Army Group "Centre" was now in great danger. The situation was even more serious for, though the fighting units retreated in as good an order as circumstances permitted, outbreaks of panic could be observed in the rear services not to mention the Luftwaffe ground crews, who left an enormous amount of material behind.

At the northern and southern ends of the immense Eastern Front, just as Leeb was not successful in carrying out the mission entrusted to him, Rundstedt, after having overrun the Eastern Ukraine and the Crimea, was also gradually forced onto the defensive by Soviet counter-attacks, which his troops, worn out by five months of sustained effort, could not withstand.

In Army Group "North", the XXXIX Panzer Corps forced the River Volkhov on October 16 near Chudovo and took Tikhvin on November 8, being hampered in its advance less by Russian action than by bad weather and soft ground. The corps did not manage to consolidate its position and less still to link up with the Finns. On December 8, suitably reinforced, the Soviet 54th, 4th, and 52nd Armies, under the command of Generals Fedyuninsky, Meretskov, and Klykov, forced the Germans to evacuate the salient. The Russians now crossed the Volkhov and established a 30-mile deep bridgehead on the left bank of the river. Of course the victors of Tikhvin had not achieved their ultimate purpose, which was to lift the siege of Leningrad, but henceforward the besiegers were to find themselves in a highly exposed position at Petrokrepost'.

Because so many units had been removed from his army group for Operation "Typhoon", Rundstedt's forces were reduced to 40 German divisions, to which four divisions and eight brigades of Germany's allies provided a rather feeble backing. However, the Kiev disaster had weakened the Russians so greatly between the Dniepr and the Don that for nearly two months, Army Group "South" did not feel the loss of its transferred units.

On September 12, Colonel-General von Schobert, commanding the 11th Army, was killed when his aircraft landed in a minefield, and Manstein was appointed to succeed him. The first exploit of the new commander, using the 1st *Panzerarmee* and the Rumanian 3rd Army, was to annihilate the Russian 18th Army (Lieutenant-General Smirnov); a pocket was created between Bol'shoy-Tokmak and Berdyansk on October 10. In it were trapped 100,000 men, 212 tanks, and 672 guns. Then the German 11th Army turned its attention to the strong position of the Perekop Isthmus which joins the Crimea to the Russian land mass and, on October 29, with the aid of the Stukas, battered the Russian 51st Army (Colonel-General F. I. Kuznetsov). Though he possessed no tanks, Manstein still conducted the Crimean campaign at Blitzkrieg pace. On November 16, his XLII Corps (General von Sponeck) was overlooking the Kerch' Strait and the bulk of the 11th Army was besieging Sevastopol', right at the south of the Crimea.

Meanwhile, the 1st *Panzerarmee* had arrived from Mariupol. Skirting the shores of the Sea of Azov, it took Rostov on November 21, while the 17th Army, now under Colonel-General Hoth, overran the western half of the Donets industrial and mining basin. To Halder's disappointment, the 5th Army's progress was less spectacular, for by the same date it had advanced only 30 miles from the great city of Khar'kov, abandoned by the Russians on October 24. These were notable successes all the same. It is true that between the Don at Rostov and the junction of Army Groups "Centre" and "South", Field-Marshal von Rundstedt was operating on a front of some 525 miles with only 32 German divisions, including only three armoured and two motorised.

The Russian High Command in Moscow now tried to use the situation to its best advantage. While the South Front (General Cherevichenko) took Rostov and pursued the invader back to the Dniepr, the Transcaucasus Front (General Kozlov) would send two armies into the Crimea, lift the siege of Sevastopol' and, crossing the Perekop Isthmus, spread out and harry the retreating Germans. On November 30, the 9th Army (General Kharitonov), the 17th Army (General Lopatin), and the 18th Army (General Kolpakchy), totalling 22 infantry divisions, nine cavalry divisions, and six armoured brigades (about 330 tanks), took Rostov after a grim struggle with Colonel-General von Kleist. Hitler refused to allow von Rundstedt to pull his men back to the river Mius, whereupon the general promptly requested to be relieved of his command. He was replaced by Reichenau, who made exactly the same demands as his predecessor and, what is more, had them accepted by Hitler himself. All the efforts of the Russian South Front to break the line failed with heavy losses.

The operations order issued for the Transcaucasus Front included two landings in the Crimea: the 51st Army (General Lvov) at Kerch', and the 44th Army (General Chernyak) at Feodosiya. On December 26, only 3,000 Russians were locked in combat with the 46th Division in the Kerch' Peninsula. At dawn on the 29th there were more than 17,000 Russians with 47 guns and 12 tanks, while at the same time advance units of the 44th Army were throwing the Germans into confusion at Feodosiya. Disobeying the express orders of his army commander, General von Sponeck, with his communications in peril, ordered his 46th Division to abandon its positions at Kerch'. When the order was obeyed, all the divisional equipment was left behind. But Generals Lvov and Chernyak, doubtless inhibited by over-rigid orders, were slow to take up fortune's favours and their hesitation gave Manstein time to bar their road over the Kamenskoye Isthmus.

However, to do this he had been obliged to abandon the attack on Sevastopol', with all its consequences. Relieved of his command, Sponeck was court-martialled on Hitler's orders. Without regard for his daring exploits at Rotterdam, where he had led the 22nd Airborne Division, he was sentenced to death. The Führer commuted the sentence to imprisonment in the fortress of Rastatt, where agents of Heinrich Himmler murdered him in the confusion at the end of March 1945.

Guderian gives us the following picture of the winter battle. He noted it at Tula, but it is true for the whole front:

"On the actual day of the offensive, the thermometer fell from −20 to −40 degrees. The sufferings of the troops were ghastly. All the automatic arms ceased to work because the oil in them froze. On the afternoon of the 5th all the armies called a spontaneous halt.

"There is nothing more dramatic in military history than the stunning assault of the cold on the German Army. The men had greatcoats and jackboots. The only additional clothing they had received consisted of a scarf and a pair of gloves. In the rear, the locomotives had seized up with cold. In the line, weapons were unserviceable and, according to General Schaal, the tank motors had to be warmed up for 12 hours before the machines could get going. One hideous detail is that many men, while satisfying the calls of nature, died when their anuses froze."

On December 20, General Guderian left for the Führer's H.Q. to try and obtain his consent to cease operations. All he got were renewed orders to attack:

"So greatly had the cold disorganised the army that the Führer's orders could not be obeyed. The Russians counterattacked as often as they could, for their own men were suffering badly, but they managed to endanger our forward lines

Soldiers of a ski battalion march through Moscow, armed with sub-machine guns.

which they trapped by circling round them from behind. Our communications were interrupted and our radio-transmitters put out of action by the snow.

On December 16, totally exhausted in mind and body, Field-Marshal von Bock asked to be relieved, on health grounds. In fact, he and Hitler had clashed over future strategy and the true state of the German army. Bock wished to withdraw west of Smolensk; Hitler refused to give any ground. The Führer allowed Bock to resign, and then appointed Kluge to succeed him as commander of Army Group "Centre". On December 19, Field-Marshal von Brauschitsch, who had suffered a severe heart attack on the night of November 6/7, left O.K.H., where he was succeeded by the Führer and Reich Chancellor, who remained in command of O.K.W. also. Hitler ordered Colonel-General Halder to stay at his post. These changes brought others in their wake between the second fortnight of Decem-

German gunners unload heavy ammunition. The cold affected the operation of guns as their recoil mechanisms froze-up.

ber 1941 and the end of January 1942:
1. In Army Group "South", the sudden death of Field-Marshal von Reichenau on January 18, 1942 brought Bock back into active service, though the 6th Army was entrusted to General Paulus, who thus left O.K.H. In addition, General Ruoff replaced Colonel-General Hoth at the head of the 17th Army;
2. In Army Group "Centre", Field-Marshal von Kluge's appointment brought in General Heinrici to command the 4th Army while General Model, with swift promotion, relieved Colonel-General Strauss in the 9th Army. Colonel-General Hoeppner, who had had the temerity to order the 4th *Panzerarmee* (from January 1, 1942) to disengage, without first asking Hitler, was dismissed from the Wehrmacht and was forbidden to wear uniform. On December 26 Guderian was relieved in his turn. He was replaced by General Rudolf Schmidt while Colonel-General Hoth was ordered to replace the unfortunate Hoeppner.
3. In Army Group "North", Field-Marshal von Leeb requested and obtained permission to go into retirement. Colonel-General von Küchler took

command of the group and was replaced in the 18th Army by General Lindemann.

By December 31, German losses on land had reached 830;903 officers, N.C.O.s, and men, or about a quarter (25.9 per cent) of the forces which had been allotted to Operation "Barbarossa" the preceding June. Of this total, 173,722 were dead and 35,875 were missing. But in spite of all these sacrifices, the objectives of the campaign as laid down in the order of December 18, 1942 had not been achieved, on the political, the economic, or the strategic level, for the Soviet Union had not collapsed, the Red Army was counter-attacking and, though the Germans held the rich wheatlands and mineral wealth of the Ukraine, the indispensable oil of the Caucasus still eluded them.

Between June 22 and December 6, 1941, Soviet losses in prisoners alone were of the order of 2,800,000 officers, N.C.O.s, and men. From Brest-Litovsk to the suburbs of Moscow, the Germans had covered a distance equivalent to that between London and Prague. But to help it withstand the blows that hammered it, the Red Army possessed two elements

German tanks halt in a Russian hamlet. The frozen ground enabled the Panzers to get back into action.

lacked by the nations which had been overrun in 1940: depth and resources. Regarding the latter, on December 1, 1941, Stalin is thought to have had at his disposal 200 infantry divisions, 35 cavalry divisions, and 40 armoured brigades (2,600 tanks) at the front, and another 80 formations (63 infantry divisions, six cavalry divisions, and 11 armoured brigades) in the rear. In spite of the difficulties inherent in an operation of that size, the evacuation of war industries to the other side of the Urals was successful and would begin to bear fruit in the spring of 1942. The Soviet Union was now no longer alone. The day after the Germans attacked, President Roosevelt announced that Russia would enjoy the benefits of "Lend-Lease". Winston Churchill shipped no less than 500 Hurricane fighters to his ally on Arctic convoys during the summer and winter of 1941. These supplies would be increased in the following year, in spite of heavy losses suffered by both merchantmen and warships in the convoys.

While the British were not able at this stage to open the "Second Front", it is none the less true that British activities in Libya and the Straits of Messina forced Hitler to issue his order No. 38 on December 2, 1941, in which he appointed Field-Marshal Kesselring "Supreme Com-

mander South" and ordered the transfer of a *Fliegerkorps* from the Eastern Front to come under Kesselring's orders in his North African and Italian bases.

This transfer of forces from east to west was tiny, yet it signified that Hitler now faced war on two fronts. Moreover Hitler's rash and foolish declaration of war on the United States after the Japanese attack on Pearl Harbor inevitably meant that Germany would now have to face America's enormous war potential. However, the three Allied powers were deeply suspicious of each other and it was not until May 1942 that the U.S.S.R., Britain and the U.S.A. formed a triple alliance against the Axis forces. Stalin in particular, demanded the opening of a second front in Europe in order to relieve the German pressure on Russia–an impossible request at the time.

On January 1, 1942, between Feodosiya, on the south side of the Crimea, and Oranienbaum on the Gulf of Finland, 12 German armies (with 141 divisions, six of them from satellite countries, plus five Hungarian and Rumanian brigades) were locked in combat with 22 Soviet armies (a total of 328 divisions or their equivalent).

Even temperatures of 30 and often 40 degrees below zero, recorded from one end to the other of the front, and 1,000 miles difference in latitude, did not force the Russians to seek winter quarters. On the contrary, during the month of January, Stalin would extend his offensive to the

left and right flanks of the front, no longer limiting himself to Army Group "Centre", against which Generals Konev and Zhukov continued to struggle, with 165 divisions confronting Kluge's 68.

In the face of this first Soviet winter offensive, Hitler, who had taken over control of O.K.H. and the Eastern Front from Field-Marshal von Brauchitsch, issued the following order to his armies on December 28.

"The abandonment without struggle of positions, even if they have been only cursorily prepared, leads, under present weather conditions, to intolerable losses in material and munitions. It weakens our fighting capacities and allows the enemy ever-growing freedom of action."

In order to exploit to the full the defensive situation to which he was for the moment reduced, he ordered every village and even every farmhouse to be made into a stronghold, with garrisons drawn from all fighting arms and also from the service échelons. Over a wide expanse of territory, this "quartering" of the terrain–to use General Weygand's expression of the end of May 1940–would force the enemy to bivouac in the open, prevent him using his road and rail network, and finally reduce him to impotence and famine.

Nevertheless, to redeploy in depth, as the order required, the heavily-stretched German units, who were already fighting on an excessively long front, were obliged to spread their resources even more thinly. And so the enemy was able to filter through

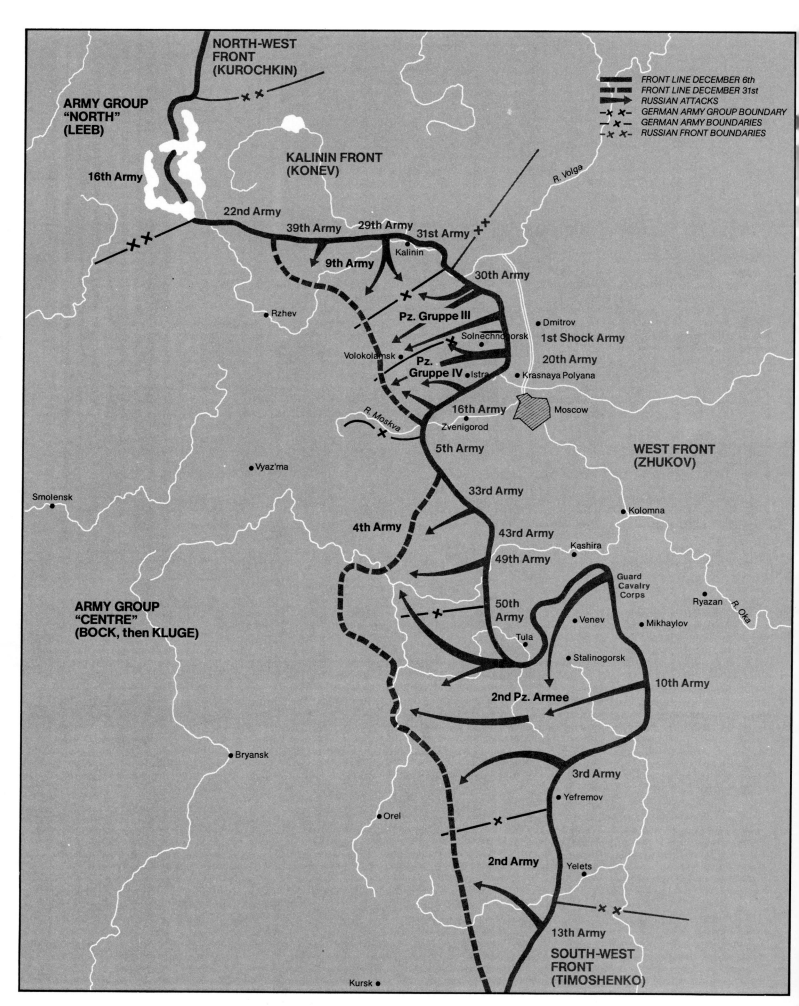

the gaps which inevitably opened in their lines. In fact the Russians were able to penetrate the German front even more easily than they would have been able to do in summer, because the extreme temperatures had frozen the lakes and rivers to the extent that they no longer formed obstacles. Their ice was so thick that it could even support 52-ton heavy tanks.

To stiffen the German line, which was buckling and threatening to break at any moment, Hitler called on troops from Occupied France and others who had just finished their training in Germany. Between the end of December 1941 and the end of March 1942, no less than 22 infantry divisions were moved from West to East for this purpose.

Moreover, the situation was so dangerous in certain sectors that they were thrown into action as soon as they detrained, in small groups and without time to distribute equipment and clothing to withstand the climate. For its part, the Red Army was reinforced in the first six months of 1942 by the addition of about 60 new divisions.

In a directive dated January 7, 1942, the Soviet High Command ordered Generals Konev and Zhukov, in command of the Kalinin and West Fronts respectively, to go over once more to the attack, with the intention of annihilating Army Group "Centre".

For this purpose the forces of the Kalinin Front would move forward along the Ostashkov–Volga line, attacking in a general south-westerly direction and, to the west of Vyaz'ma, would cut the road and railway between Minsk and Moscow, the life-lines of Army Group "Centre". Furthermore, using the gap which had been formed during the retreat to the south of Kaluga between the right wing of the German 4th Army and the left wing of 2nd *Panzerarmee*, the West Front would make its main effort in the direction of Vyaz'ma. This gigantic pincer-movement, aimed at bringing about the encirclement of the whole of Army Group "Centre", would be covered on its right by attacks by troops of the North-West Front and on its left by offensives by the Bryansk Front.

The offensive so planned made an excellent beginning on January 9 and 10, 1942. For three weeks, O.K.H. was seriously concerned that Konev and Zhukov should meet in the region of Dorogobuzh, some 16 miles south of the Moscow–Minsk railway.

In the north, the 4th Shock Army (General A. I. Eremenko), which formed the right of the Kalinin Front, took advantage of the thick ice on Lake Seliger, the boundary between Army Groups "Centre" and "North", to break through the German lines which, in this sector, were no more

The Russians fight back: despite its enormous losses the Soviet Army launched a mid-winter offensive against the Germans. For the first time, the initiative passed into Russian hands.

than skeletal. Eremenko pushed straight as far as Velikiye-Luki, more than 115 miles from his starting-point, replenishing his supplies from depôts which the Germans had built up at Toropets. In this way the Russians made up for the defects of the Soviet supply services, which had failed to keep up with the front line units. On February 1, however, 3rd *Panzerarmee* (Colonel-General Reinhardt) retook the line Demidov–Velizh–Nevel'–Velikiye-Luki and blocked the Russians' potentially dangerous advance to Vitebsk and Smolensk.

In the centre of the Kalinin Front, General Konev separated his 29th, 39th, and 30th Armies which, to the west of Rzhev, had succeeded in splitting the German 9th Army and isolating its left wing, which consisted of the XXIII Corps (General Schubert). The Soviet 29th Army exploited its breakthrough to the full, and, on January 27, was within tactical reach of the Minsk–Moscow road. But General Walther Model, who had just taken over command of 9th Army, was an astonishing military improviser. Ignoring the various concentrated offensives against Rzhev from the north and east, he counterattacked vigorously in a westerly direction and established contact with XXIII Corps at the end of the month. Now it was the turn of the Soviet 29th Army to find its communications cut. In the course of the subsequent furious battles, it lost 27,000 dead and 5,000 prisoners. Only 5,000 men, 800 of whom were wounded, managed to break out of the pocket and reach Soviet lines on February 15.

"German casualties, too, had been heavy," Paul Carell notes. "On February 18, when *Obersturmbannführer* Otto Kumm reported at his divisional headquarters, Model happened to be there. He said to Kumm: 'I know what your regiment has been through–but I still can't do without it. What is its present strength?'

"Kumm gestured towards the window. '*Herr Generaloberst*, my regiment is on parade outside.' Model glanced through the window. Outside, 35 men had fallen in."

Model's gift for manoeuvre and his prompt decision had therefore carried the day against Russian doggedness, for the Russian 39th Army was as sore-hit as the Germans. Nevertheless, Model's army was trapped in a tube-shaped pocket nearly 125 miles long and, in the region of Sychevka, barely 40 miles in width.

It was now vital that Rzhev be evacuated, if only to allow the 12 or so divisions earmarked for the summer offensive the chance to recuperate. Yet before he would consent, Hitler delayed until the reverse at Stalingrad put the seal on his defeat.

On the other hand, on January 15, in view of the speedy and dangerous advances by the 49th, 50th, and 10th Armies of the West Front into the breach which had been opened south of Kaluga, Hitler authorised Kluge to order the necessary withdrawals to permit the left of 2nd *Panzerarmee* to link-up firmly again with

the right of 4th Army:

"This is the first time in the war," his order concluded, "that I have ordered a withdrawal over a sizable section of the front. I expect the movement to be carried out in a manner worthy of the German Army. Our men's confidence in their innate superiority and their absolute determination to cause the enemy as much damage as possible must also condition the way in which this withdrawal is carried out."

In order to slow down enemy pursuit, the Germans, just as the Russians had done previously, applied a scorched earth policy to the areas they abandoned. Villages were razed, and even the stoves used to heat the Russian dwellings were destroyed at Hitler's express order.

General Zhukov's offensive followed a pattern similar to Konev's. A lightning jump-off took I Guard Cavalry Corps almost to Dorogobuzh, but there the advance was checked, causing a stabilised front to develop. At the end of February, Field-Marshal von Kluge had redeployed after his withdrawal and re-established a continuous front along the Kirov–Yukhnov line. As a result, General Pliev's I Guard Cavalry Corps was trapped and, slightly more to the north, a similar fate overtook the 33rd Army. Russian G.H.Q. in Moscow tried to get the operation moving again by parachuting two brigades behind the German lines and extending General Zhukov's authority to include the Kalinin Front. But Army Group "Centre" still maintained its positions along the Minsk–Vyaz'ma and Vyaz'ma–Rzhev lines.

The *History of the Great Patriotic War* does not conceal the slowing down of this winter offensive, from which Stalin had expected a decisive victory. It blames its failure on to the fact that the armies of the West Front wasted their shock value by attacking over fronts which were too long. This is very likely, but the question must be considered at a higher level than the one set by the *Great Patriotic War*. It would appear that the principles of concentration of force and convergence of effort were both insufficiently understood in the highest councils of *Stavka*, as Russian G.H.Q. was called.

Beginning on January 8, to the north of the Kalinin Front, General Kurochkin, commander of the North-West Front, badly mauled the German 16th Army, which formed the right wing of Army Group "Centre". The 16th Army broke under the assault of the 3rd Shock Army (General Purkaev) emerging from the Lake Seliger region, and the 11th Army (General Morosov), which swept over the frozen Lake Ilmen.

Certainly the latter, in spite of five furious attacks, was halted before Staraya Russa, but working its way up the Lovat' it succeeded, on February 8, in closing the trap around the German II Corps. This formed a 200 mile pocket around Dem'yansk, which was defended by five badly-worn divisions. But, under the

191

command of General Brockdorff-Ahle-feldt, they repelled every enemy attack, even when the Russians parachuted two brigades into the centre of the pocket. To supply the 96,000 men and their 20,000 horses, the Luftwaffe organised an air-lift. At a rate of 100 to 150 aircraft daily, it brought the besieged men more than 65,000 tons of foodstuffs, forage, muni-tions, and fuel, also flying out over 34,500 wounded and sick.

On March 21, General Seydlitz-Kurzbach moved out of Staraya Russa and attacked with four divisions in the direction of Dem'yansk. An unexpected thaw hamp-ered this movement and not till April 21 was he able to re-establish contact with II Corps across the Lovat'. Some 65 miles south-west of Dem'yansk, the little town of Kholm and its garrison, commanded by Major-General Scherer, was cut off by the 3rd Shock Army. The pocket was re-lieved just as it was about to fall.

Under the command of General Vlasov, 2nd Shock Army, six divisions strong, crossed the Volkhov on January 22 and pushed north-east, reaching the Lenin-grad–Novgorod railway. The attack was

to take place at the same time as an offen-sive by the 54th Army, emerging from the area south-east of Petrokrepost'. If the manoeuvre had succeeded, the salient formed here by the German 18th Army would have been liquidated and Lenin-grad relieved at the same time. But the 54th Army failed in the face of the resistance of I Corps (March 10, 1942).

From that moment on, Vlasov, who had been reinforced by the XIII Cavalry Corps and three armoured brigades and had de-ployed his forces fanwise, found himself in a very risky situation, for the handle of the fan was only 13 miles wide while his forward troops were 50 miles from the Volkhov. From March 15 to March 19, furious combat, in which the Spanish volunteers of the *División Azul* distin-guished themselves, allowed the German 18th Army to sever the line which joined the 2nd Shock Army to the main Soviet line. The mopping-up operations lasted until the end of May. Vlasov himself was not captured until the end of July.

In the southern theatre of operations, the sudden death of Field-Marshal von Reich-enau led Hitler to entrust the command of Army Group "South" to Field-Marshal

von Bock. As he entered his office at Poltava on January 18, the new com-mander of German operations in the Ukraine and the Crimea was received with two pieces of news. One was good: Feodo-siya had been recaptured by General von Manstein, who had also taken 10,000 prisoners. This would allow the siege of Sevastopol' to continue without fear of being surprised by Russian attack. The other news was disturbing: the 17th Army's front had been pierced near Izyum.

General von Manstein recalls the diffi-culties which arose at the time of the re-capture of Feodosiya and also his attitude about the treatment of Russian P.O.W.s:

"Everything seemed to have conspired against us. Extremely severe frosts affect-ed the airfields at Simferopol' and Yev-patoriya, which were used by our Stukas and bombers, and often prevented air-craft taking off in the morning to attack Feodosiya. The Kerch' Strait was frozen over and allowed free passage to enemy units.

"In spite of the difficulties, the army did its best to feed – sometimes even reducing

The crew of a Pzkw III thaw the frozen mud around their immobilised tank.

its own rations—the prisoners whom we had not sufficient transport to transfer north. Consequently, the mortality rate among the prisoners averaged only two per cent. This was an extremely low figure, considering that most of them were seriously wounded or absolutely exhausted at the time of their capture. One incident may serve to illustrate their feelings towards us. There was a camp for 8,000 prisoners close to Feodosiya when the Russians made their landing. The camp guards fled, but the prisoners, instead of running towards their 'liberators', set off, without guards, towards Simferopol', towards us, that is."

On the Donets, Marshal Timoshenko, in command of the South-West Front, had attacked seven German divisions with his 37th, 57th, and 6th Armies, totalling 21 infantry divisions, 11 cavalry divisions, and ten armoured brigades (about 650 tanks). The long-range object of this operation was Khar'kov and the railway between Dniepropetrovsk and Donetsk (Stalino), which supplied the German 17th Army and 1st *Panzerarmee*. In temperatures of 40 degrees below zero the Russians spread out behind the German line and, by January 26, were restocking their supplies from the stores which the 17th Army had established at Lozovaya. Two days later they reached Sinel'nikovo and Grishino, which were within gunshot of the railway they hoped to cut. Several

days later they were thrown back by *Gruppe* von Kleist which was an amalgamation of Kleist's own 1st *Panzerarmee* and the 17th Army.

The Russian attack then folded up. Army Group "South" had indeed had a nasty shock, but Timoshenko had not been able to widen the breach he had made on the Donets front on January 18. The Izyum salient, about 60 miles deep, would cause him the same tragic disaster as the Volkhov salient had brought on Vlasov.

From March 21, mud steadily replaced snow between the shores of the Baltic and the Black Sea, making any significant operations impossible for close on two months. This relative truce allowed the two adversaries to consider their achievements and lay their plans for the coming summer campaign.

According to statistics calculated by O.K.H., over the entire Eastern Front the Germans had lost, between January 1 and March 20, a little more than 240,000 men, of whom 51,837 had been killed and 15,086 were missing. This brought their losses since June 22, 1941 to 1,073,006 officers, N.C.O.s, and men, that is just under one-third of the effectives who had attacked on that date. It is true that the Wehrmacht had escaped the disaster which had just threatened it, but only just, and, to a large extent, because of the fact that *Stavka* had not been able to concentrate its efforts to

destroy Army Group "Centre".

And so Colonel-General Halder, not exhibiting at this time any sign of pessimism in general, recommended prudence to the new Commander-in-Chief of the German Army. But it was not for lack of caution that Hitler had dismissed Brauchitsch. Since the Soviet winter offensive had been more or less checked, all risks appeared laudable to the Führer and, for six months, he could be heard shouting as he stared at the campaign maps: "*Der Russe ist tot! Der Russe ist tot!* (Russia is dead! Russia is dead!)".

Even today information on Soviet losses in this period is unavailable. However, everything seems to indicate that these were considerable, even more so as the rear-guard services of the Red Army functioned very badly and the Russians were not so insensitive to the cold as their opponents thought. As Lieutenant Goncharov noted:

"January 25. 'You know, Comrade Lieutenant,' one of my men said to me yesterday, 'when one gets really cold one becomes indifferent to freezing to death or being shot. One only has one wish – to die as quickly as possible.' That's the exact truth. The cold drains the men of the will to fight."

Luftwaffe men dig their vehicle out of the snow in bitterly cold weather conditions.

CHAPTER 23
America draws near to war

On November 5, 1940 Franklin Delano Roosevelt was re-elected President of the United States of America for a third term by a popular vote of 27,241,939, against 22,327,226 for his Republican opponent Wendell Willkie.

This achievement was all the more remarkable in that the new representative of American democracy had for the first time broken with the sacrosanct tradition established by George Washington, first President of the United States, who withdrew from the political arena at the end of his second period of office. Furthermore, Roosevelt's opponent had based his campaign on a question of foreign policy, which was extremely pertinent: in his view, after sacrificing the needs of defence to the welfare conquests of the New Deal, President Roosevelt, against all logic, was now about to take the nation along a path which could only lead to intervention in World War II.

In fact, on the question of the military unpreparedness of the United States, Wendell Willkie and the Republican opposition were substantially correct; and Roosevelt, more than anyone else, was sensitive to criticism on that score, and with reason.

It is true that on June 16, 1940, Congress had voted a first Naval Expansion Bill, whereby the Navy's tonnage would be raised from 1,557,840 to 1,724,000 tons; on September 9 following, in the face of an international situation worsening as a result of the German victory and the threat from Japan, it adopted a supplementary programme known as the Two Ocean Programme, further increasing overall tonnage to a figure of 3,050,000. Yet the first ship to be built under these two armament programmes would not be ready for service before the end of 1942.

A week later, on September 16, 1940, Congress passed, by a comfortable majority, a bill of recruitment known as the Selective Service Act, which would affect more than 16 million American citizens. Nevertheless, no more than with the vote on conscription by the British Parliament in April 1939, this measure was not going to provide the industrial state with a large modern army overnight–especially since the supplies of war material agreed by Washington to Great Britain did not make American military preparations any easier.

In the case of the air force, the same lack of foresight had the same results. For all the publicity given at the time to the Boeing B-17 four-engined strategic bomber known as the Flying Fortress, we now know that on June 17, 1940, there were no more than 56 of these in service. Elsewhere even in spite of the tremendous effort by industry to step up production, it was the same story.

Naturally, Roosevelt felt obliged to allay public anxiety aroused on this score

by Republican propaganda. Speaking at Boston on October 30, he told his audience:

"And while I am talking to you mothers and fathers, I give you one more assurance.

"I have said this before, but I shall say it again and again and again.

"Your boys are not going to be sent into any foreign wars."

"Except in the event of attack," one of his collaborators endeavoured to make him add. This drew the following rejoinder from the President, for whom it went without saying:

"Of course, we'll fight if we're attacked. If somebody attacks us, then it isn't a foreign war, is it? Or do they want me to guarantee that our troops will be sent into battle only in the event of another Civil War?"

In this debate there can be little doubt that the President had no intention of being the first to open hostilities against the Axis Powers, still less of sending an expeditionary corps to Europe, as his opponents put about. Two facts are clear: on the one hand, according to his admirer, Robert E. Sherwood, the "terrifying weakness" of America's military preparedness was fully recognised by Roosevelt; on the other, on September 27 of that year, when concluding the Tripartite Pact in Berlin, Germany, Italy, and Japan, no doubt in order to deter outside intervention, sought the widest publicity for the extent to which the Pact bound them.

By virtue of Article 1 of the Treaty, Tokyo promised to "recognise and respect" the paramount right that Rome and Berlin sought to exercise with a view to establishing a "new order" in Europe, and, similarly, the two Axis powers, under Article 2, recognised Japan's right to fashion a new order of things in "the sphere of Greater Asia", which included China, French Indo-China, Thailand, Malaya, and the Dutch East Indies.

But above all, Article 3 of the Tripartite Pact made it clear what would happen should the interim victors in Europe, on the one hand, and the Japanese Empire, on the other, meet interference in the exercise of the right to a "new order" defined above; it declared, word for word:

"Germany, Italy, and Japan undertake to provide reciprocal support by all political, economic, and military means in the event of an attack on one of the three contracting states by a power which, as of that time, is not a participant in either the European war or the Sino-Japanese war."

Clearly, this article was aimed as much at the United States as at the Soviet Union, and perhaps even more, because in the circumstances prevailing in the autumn of 1940, Japanese expansion in South-East Asia afforded little occasion indeed for retaliation on the part of Moscow. But the occupant of the White House was left in no doubt at all that any action on the part of America that was hostile to

the Third Reich or Fascist Italy would automatically involve his country in a war on two fronts. Hence Roosevelt's resolve not to repeat the action of his predecessor, Woodrow Wilson, who had, on April 6, 1917, solemnly declared war on Imperial Germany.

But it can also be said that if a so-called "defensive war" is not a "foreign war" (as Roosevelt pointed out to his colleagues), it can be the inevitable result of a policy which presents two foreign powers, in the interests of a third power, with no alternative but to suffer a crushing defeat or to fire the first shot. We must therefore conclude that on October 30, 1940, in his Boston speech, Roosevelt did not speak "the whole truth and nothing but the truth" to the American "fathers and mothers" whose votes he was canvassing. But it was certainly difficult for him to conceal from them that he was steadfastly resolved to risk attack by Germany, on account of the ever-increasing support he had determined to give Britain.

Rear-Admiral R. A. Theobald has no scruple in further analysing President Roosevelt's motives in his book *The Final Secret of Pearl Harbor*. Calling his first chapter *Main Deduction: President Roosevelt Circumvents American Pacifism*, the author pleads the cause of Rear-Admiral Husband E. Kimmel, his ill-starred commanding officer at the time, with considerable passion. Admiral Theobald writes:

"There is every reason to believe that when France was overcome, President Roosevelt became convinced that the United States must fight beside Great Britain, while the latter was still an active belligerent, or later sustain the fight alone, as the last democratic stronghold in a Nazi world. Never, however, had the country been less prepared for war, both psychologically and physically. Isolationism was a dominant philosophy throughout the land, and the armed forces were weak and consequently unready for a major war.

"The United States not only had to become an active participant in democracy's fight as quickly as possible, but a people, completely united in support of the war effort, had to be brought into the arena. But, how could the country be made to fight? Only a cataclysmic happening could move Congress to enact a declaration of war; and that action would not guarantee that the nation's response would be the completely united support which victory has always demanded. This was the President's problem, and his solution was based upon the simple fact that, while it takes two to make a fight, either one may start it.

"As the people of this country were so strongly opposed to war, one of the Axis powers must be forced to involve the United States, and in such a way as to arouse the American people to wholehearted belief in the necessity of fighting.

uneasy at the prospect of being drawn into war merely to underwrite the conquests of her Axis allies in Europe. This explains the limits beyond which she was unwilling to pledge herself.

For his part, Hitler was resolved to put up with increasingly antagonistic treatment on the part of Roosevelt without taking the irrevocable step of declaring war on his dangerous transatlantic adversary, since he had no sure guarantee that Japan would feel bound to take up arms along-side the Reich, and in doing so go beyond the strict letter of the Pact. More than this, following the American occupation of Iceland, Hitler resisted representations made to him by Raeder and Dönitz that the submarine campaign was being rendered ineffective by warships flying the Stars and Stripes having unimpeded access to a sector of the Atlantic which had been declared blockaded. Consequently, on June 21, 1941, submarine captains received the following signal:

"The Führer orders that, in the course of the coming weeks and whatever the circumstances, action must be taken to avoid any incident with the United States. Until further notice, only capital ships, cruisers, or aircraft-carriers are to be attacked and then only if categorically recognised as enemy vessels. As to warships, the masking of navigation lights is insufficient proof of hostile intent."

Considering the number of vessels in Icelandic waters flying British and American flags, such an order prohibiting U-boats from attacking destroyers, corvettes, and other escort craft was tantamount, as Admiral Dönitz bitterly observed, to rendering them defenceless against their worst enemies, since they had no authorisation even to counter-attack. But above all, he further noted, such conciliation could only convince Roosevelt that he could do his utmost to help Great Britain without incurring any sort of retaliation other than verbal broadsides from Goebbels and the German propaganda ministry.

Thus went the argument of the White House. In consequence, there was no need to commit the United States to a war with Germany. Nor had Winston Churchill, with his unshakable optimism, requested any such thing, evidence of this being that on hearing the news that the House of Representatives had voted the Lend-Lease Bill, he had exclaimed in a broadcast speech on February 9, 1941: "Give us the tools and we will finish the job." But this utterance, which finds its place in Churchill's memoirs, was in fact followed by a passage which was there omitted but which is no less illuminating as to the matter that concerns us:

"It seems now to be certain that the Government and people of the United States intend to supply us with all that is necessary for victory. In the last war the United States sent two million men across the Atlantic. *But this is not a war of vast armies, firing immense masses of shells at one another.* We do not need the gallant

This would require drastic action, and the decision was unquestionably a difficult one for the President to make."

Then, after drawing attention to the conclusion of the Tripartite Pact between Berlin, Rome, and Tokyo, Admiral Theobald propounds the view that President Roosevelt and his chief collaborators, Secretary of State Cordell Hull, Secretary of War Henry Stimson, and Secretary of the Navy Frank Knox "were favourable to" the surprise attack at Pearl Harbor, knowing as they did that by virtue of this covenant: "War with Japan would lead *ipso facto* to war with Germany and Italy."

So it was that by the circuitous means of Japanese aggression which they had made possible, those responsible for American policy and defence attained the principal objective which since June 1940 had governed their" diplomatic strategy", war with Nazi Germany and Fascist Italy.

The causes of the surprise attack on December 7, 1941 and the attribution of

M-2 light tanks of the U.S. Army parade during pre-war manoeuvres.

responsibility both at Pearl Harbor and in Washington after the disaster will be discussed in a later chapter. But it should be stated here and now that the interpretation given by Rear-Admiral Theobald is not entirely plausible.

In the first place, it does not follow automatically that aggression on the part of Japan would necessarily lead to Italy and Germany going to war with the United States. In fact, Article 3 of the Tripartite Pact, quoted in full above, says no such thing; on the contrary, the implementation of the *casus foederis* was restricted to the specific circumstances of an aggression on one of the three states party to the Pact; hence the obligation incurred was less compelling than that contracted by Hitler and Mussolini under the terms of the Pact of Steel. And there may be grounds for thinking that Japan felt armies which are forming throughout the American Union. We do not need them this year, nor next year; nor any year that I can foresee."

As Robert E. Sherwood points out in his introduction to the Harry Hopkins papers, the sincerity of this declaration has been called into question. But he would seem to be right in dismissing any evidence of deception in a form of words that corresponds only too clearly with the ideas then prevailing in Churchill's mind as to the best means of achieving victory through a series of "marginal" operations. The defeat of Italy in North Africa, the Mediterranean, and the Balkan peninsula would lead to her collapse. As for Germany, the non-stop bombing of her industries would reduce her to impotence. To this end, what was required was not the despatch of a huge American army, but the delivery of American war material. Events were certainly to show up the specious element in his argument; nevertheless this was the argument that prevailed with Churchill's cabinet.

Looking at America's commitment to Britain in this light, there disappear the motives which might have encouraged Roosevelt and his advisers to favour an act of aggression on the part of the Japanese which, by rebound so to speak, would force the United States to declare war on the Axis powers. In any case, would the United States Government have invited an attack which could easily have destroyed U.S. carrier-borne air power and the oil stocks at Hawaii, and which in the event crippled the U.S. Pacific Fleet for months?

In any event, re-elected on November 5, 1940 to the Presidency of the United States, Roosevelt had a free hand until the next election campaign, and during this time would dispose of the enormous powers that the American Constitution vests in the occupant of the White House, who is at once head of State and head of the Government, and whose authority is greater still since the principle of ministerial solidarity, which is virtually sacrosanct in Western Europe, is unknown on the other side of the Atlantic.

It may be asked whether President Roosevelt was always wise in his choice of those with whom he collaborated. Certainly his ideological preferences inclined him to men whose views were very much to the left, even to the extreme left. First among these mention must be made of Harry Hopkins, known as the *"éminence grise* of the White House", who was so much under the spell of Stalin's personality that Stalin convinced him on May 26, 1945 that Hitler had left Germany on board a submarine "with the connivance of the Swiss Government"—and this without a twinge of disbelief on Hopkins' part. Stalin had incontrovertible proof at the time that the ex-Führer had perished in the downfall of the Nazi régime.

Then there was the Secretary to the Treasury, Henry Morgenthau, whose declared intentions of "pastoralising" Germany had the effect of galvanising the last-ditch resistance of the Third Reich in 1944 and giving Dr. Goebbels' propaganda machine a new lease of life. His deputy, Harry Dexter White, was also his close associate.

Nevertheless it would be a mistaken view to see Franklin Roosevelt as the pawn of the advisers he had chosen. In effect, neither in his written nor in his spoken utterances is there the slightest hint that he had wind of the darker possibilities latent in the situation prevailing in 1943 and 1944; namely that the cause of freedom for which he had fought so nobly might, once the Fascist and Nazi enemy had been cast down, find in Communism an adversary all the more dangerous in that under cover of the Lend-Lease Act Kremlin agents had established an espionage network across the length and breadth of the United States.

According to the American Constitution, the President of the United States, by virtue of his office, assumes supreme command of the federal armed forces, a prerogative that enabled Abraham Lincoln, during the Civil War, to intervene personally in the conduct of operations in a not always beneficial way.

How then did Franklin Roosevelt discharge his duties as war leader? His experience as Assistant Secretary of the Navy during World War I had given him some insight into the larger problems of strategy, but he never made this a pretext for involving himself personally in the conduct of operations, as his predecessor in office had done, or as his friend Winston Churchill so often did.

The course he adopted was to issue very general directives of a political and military nature, which he then relied on his Joint Chiefs-of-Staff to carry out, under the expert leadership of General George Catlett Marshall, with Admirals Stark and Ernest J. King representing the Navy and General H. H. Arnold the Air Force. Liaison between the White House and the Pentagon was in the capable hands of Admiral William D. Leahy, who after a period as Ambassador to the Vichy Government was on July 20, 1942 appointed Chief-of-Staff to the President. This system of organisation seems to have functioned with the minimum friction and maximum efficiency.

Such, with the benefit of hindsight, is the picture we have of Franklin Delano Roosevelt. The commanding part he played in the successive defeat of the three totalitarian powers, Italy, Germany, and Japan, cannot in truth be denied him, but one is bound to consider criticisms of his policy because of his responsibility for the ruthless subjection by Soviet Russia of 100 million Estonians, Latvians, Lithuanians, Poles, Rumanians, Bulgarians, Hungarians, and Germans. Beyond Europe, it is with Roosevelt's policies that a large part of the blame for the anguish and uncertainties that have troubled the world since 1945 must lie.

The President had not yet been officially inaugurated in his third term when Winston Churchill sent distress signals to the White House. Purchases of war material effected by Great Britain in the United States, on the basis of the Cash and Carry Bill, which became law on November 2, 1939, stood at more than 4,000 million dollars at the end of 1940. The British Treasury had not only exhausted its transatlantic monetary resources but had liquidated the private portfolios of American shares held in England of which it had been granted the right to dispose when hostilities commenced.

Hence if the President of the United States intended to continue to support Britain in her struggle against Nazi Germany and Fascist Italy—as the mass of opinion in America wished—a legal basis other than that of the system then in force had to be found. An altogether new bill had to be deliberated and approved by Congress. But might not Congress shy away from taking measures which without doubt would take the United States a little closer to intervention in the war, a course which officially, in line with public opinion, the White House wished to avoid at any cost? The problem was enormous, and President Roosevelt, rather than attacking it head on, got round it with a brilliant display of his expertise in manoeuvring opinion, employing for this purpose his technique of "fireside chats" which were broadcast to every home in America and which, with their calm and unaffected delivery, achieved a well deserved success.

As early as December 16, in the course of a press conference, when alluding to the financial difficulties of Great Britain and to the possibility of abandoning the Cash and Carry system in force, Roosevelt prepared the ground for an alternative system that was already in his mind. Speaking to the journalists present, he said:

"Now, what I am trying to do is eliminate the dollar sign. That is something brand new in the thoughts of everybody in this room, I think—get rid of the silly, foolish old dollar sign."

And to drive his point home more vividly, he drew the example of a "length of garden hose" which you willingly lend to your neighbour if his house catches fire and which he brings you back when he has put the fire out.

On December 29, addressing the American people, he evoked the sorry fate that would be theirs if, through a (misguided) desire for peace, they should stand by and let Britain be overrun by the Nazis (this was the first time he had used the term in a public address):

"We cannot escape danger, or the fear of danger, by crawling into bed and pulling the covers over our heads.

"A nation can have peace with the Nazis only at the price of total surrender.

"All of us, in all the Americas, would be living at the point of a Nazi gun loaded with explosive bullets, economic as well as military.

"We must be the great arsenal of democracy."

And even as these strong, uncompromising words were being pondered throughout the length and breadth of the land, eliciting less disapproval than was feared by his entourage, the President addressed a message to Congress on January 6, setting out the four liberties which the United States must guarantee throughout the world:

1. A nation's right of self-determination in the event of territorial change;
2. The right of every nation to choose its own form of government;
3. The guarantee to every nation of free and equal access to raw materials; and
4. The foundation of a lasting peace guaranteeing to every human being an existence free from poverty and fear.

Congress had no option other than to endorse a humanitarian programme of this kind, but clearly the four points would remain a dead letter unless Great Britain was equipped with the means of overcoming the totalitarian powers who had subjugated the European continent; such was the aim of the Lend-Lease Bill which was submitted for its approval (Greece and China being included as additional beneficiaries). The Bill authorised the President to agree deliveries of arms and military equipment to powers fighting in self-defence against Germany, Italy, and Japan, in exchange for payments to be determined by Congress on the recommendation of the Administration, on the understanding that the states benefiting from Lease-Lend undertook, at the conclusion of peace, to restore unused stocks of what had been supplied.

On February 8, 1941, the House of Representatives, by 260 votes to 165, adopted the text which had been submitted to it by the President; on March 8 following, the Senate in turn adopted it by 60 votes to 31. Promulgated without delay, the Lend-Lease Act came into effect immediately under Harry Hopkins, the former Secretary of Commerce, who had Franklin Roosevelt's entire confidence. From March 11, 1941 until August 31, 1945 the United States disbursed by way of Lend-Lease 50,690 billion dollars, which enabled them to produce, among other material, 17 million rifles, 315,000 guns, 87,000 tanks, 2,434,000 motor vehicles and 296,000 planes. Such, strictly in terms of equipment, was the contribution made to the combined victory of the Allied nations by the great American democracy. But these figures also give some idea of the prodigious activity undertaken by Harry Hopkins, who was a chronic invalid.

Prior to taking up his post as personal adviser to the President on the administration of Lend-Lease, Hopkins had spent a month in London for the purpose of making an evaluation of Great Britain's needs for the successful prosecution of the war. Winston Churchill's energy and resolution made a considerable impact on Hopkins, and the latter's practical sense and acumen so impressed Churchill that one day he promised him, once victory had been achieved, elevation to the peerage.

By the spring of that year, agreements were concluded between London and Washington concerning the exchange of scientific information on all subjects dealing with military technology, as well as the close co-operation of British and American information and security services. In addition, the American Pacific Fleet was ordered to make over to the Atlantic Fleet three battleships, an aircraft-carrier, four light cruisers, and 18 destroyers, all of which passed through the Panama Canal in the last days of March. Rear-Admiral Theobald considers this strategic movement to be one of the manoeuvres concocted by the White House in order to lure Japan on, but the date of this transfer of forces argues against such an interpretation of Roosevelt's motives.

By this action, Admiral Harold R. Stark, Chief of Naval Operations, intended merely to relieve the Royal Navy's burden by having United States units take over responsibility for security in the waters around Greenland and Iceland. Furthermore, with the prior agreement of Reykjavik, a brigade of U.S. Marines was stationed in Iceland on June 7, 1941, following the detachments which had on April 9, with Danish assent, established small bases in Greenland.

Convoys were organised to supply these strategic United States advanced posts. Thus it was that the security zone falling within Washington's sphere of responsibility was pushed eastwards, so as to include Iceland, while allowing the British to maintain their base at Hvalfjord. Moreover, on both the outward and inward passages, British merchant vessels received authorisation to join up with convoys that were, naturally enough, escorted by light units of the American Atlantic Fleet.

On June 16, German and Italian consulates in the United States were ordered to cease functioning, and measures were taken to prevent Axis merchant ships which had sought refuge in American ports from being scuttled in the event of hostilities. It is quite clear that between Washington on the one hand, and Rome and Berlin on the other, there existed from that time on a situation, deliberately created by the White House and the State Department, unknown to the conventional international law which stipulates the obligations of belligerents and neutrals. Since the Communist takeover in Prague in 1948, such a situation has become known as the "cold war".

For reasons previously given, Franklin Roosevelt was able to strike out all the more defiantly in this direction because

Churchill and Roosevelt with their aides at a church service held aboard Prince of Wales *in Placentia Bay during the conference of August 1941.*

Hitler and Mussolini were in no position – in the immediate and foreseeable future – to retaliate.

Hitler's attack on the Soviet Union brought a pledge from the American President to extend the provisions of Lend-Lease to her. And for this purpose, Harry Hopkins was despatched to the Kremlin, by way of London, aboard a reconnaissance plane, which landed him at Archangel. The President's envoy returned very much under the spell of Stalin and on August 4, at Scapa Flow, embarked on the battleship *Prince of Wales*, together with Winston Churchill, the Chief of the Imperial General Staff, Sir John Dill, and the First Lord of the Admiralty, Sir Dudley Pound. Thereupon, the ship set sail for Newfoundland, for which the cruiser *Augusta*, with President Roosevelt on board, was also heading. On August 9, the two statesmen met in the Placentia Bay.

August 10 was a Sunday. Winston Churchill and Franklin Roosevelt, seated side by side on the quarterdeck of *Prince of Wales*, attended divine service; the lesson for the day was taken from the Book of Joshua:

"There shall not any man be able to stand before thee all the days of thy life: as I was with Moses, so I will be with thee: I will not fail thee, nor forsake thee.

"Be strong and of a good courage: for unto this people shalt thou divide for an inheritance the land, which I sware their fathers to give them."

The sermon, delivered by the ship's chaplain, was preceded and followed by the hymns "God Eternal" and "Onward, Christian Soldiers", the first chosen by the American President and the second by the British Prime Minister.

Such was the imposing religious ceremony that inaugurated the Atlantic Conference, which would raise so many false hopes among the oppressed or threatened peoples of the European continent.

If Rear-Admiral Theobald were to be believed, it was on this occasion that the representatives of the United States and of Great Britain constructed the fatal trap into which the Japanese mouse was to be enticed. But in order to subscribe to this opinion, it would require for there to be documents in contradiction to those we actually possess.

Without anticipating the chapter that follows, it may be said that the situation pertaining between Tokyo, Washington, and London, on August 11, 1941, appeared as follows: consequent on the Japanese extending their occupation of French Indo-China, the British and Americans, together with the Dutch Government in exile, had taken various retaliatory measures against Japan, including, in particular, an embargo on her imports of oil products. The nature and manner of this reaction had made a keen impression on the Japanese Prime Minister, Prince Konoye, and he had instructed his ambas-

sador in Washington, Admiral Nomura, to resume talks. On August 6, Admiral Nomura had presented the American Secretary of State, Cordell Hull, with an overall plan to put an end to the conflict. President Roosevelt in fact considered the conditions which had been submitted to the State Department by Tokyo to be unacceptable, and agreed to further talks merely in order to gain time

It is true that on August 11, 1941 the point had not yet been reached between the two powers when extreme measures would be taken, and that President Roosevelt was fully aware of this as the decoding of Japanese diplomatic correspondence, which the Americans had been undertaking for the past year, revealed no immediate initiative on the part of Tokyo. In the last analysis, he was at liberty to employ a form of deterrence in his dealings with Prince Konoye, by indicating a *casus belli* which it was incumbent on the Japanese Prime Minister to avoid.

One of Churchill's main objectives at the Atlantic Conference was to obtain a public declaration from Roosevelt that Japanese aggression against Anglo-Dutch possessions in the Far East would bring them into collision with the United States. Churchill obtained a qualified declaration in the following form:

"Any further encroachment by Japan in the South-Western Pacific would produce a situation in which the United States Government would be compelled to take counter-measures even though these might lead to war between the United States and Japan.

But on his return from Placentia, Roosevelt handed the Japanese ambassador a fresh version in which U.S. solidarity with Britain and the Netherlands was replaced with an emphasis on U.S. interests alone.

The question of Portugal was also raised at Placentia Bay, on account of a letter addressed to Roosevelt by President Salazar; envisaging the possibility of a

German invasion, Salazar informed Roosevelt of his intention of withdrawing to the Azores, at the same time appealing to the age-old alliance between Britain and Portugal. But it was to be feared that, should such an occasion arise, British forces might be engaged elsewhere; in which case, Portugal would willingly accept protection from the United States. Although he considered this request favourably, President Roosevelt had not wanted to accede to it without obtaining the agreement of his British ally, who raised no difficulties. It was even decided that Washington's guarantee to Portugal should stand if Britain should, through a preventive occupation of the Azores, provoke the invasion of Portugal.

Agreement was also reached on a plan whereby the U.S. Navy should assume responsibility for the sector of the Atlantic between Newfoundland and Iceland. Thus, British destroyers and corvettes based on Halifax, Nova Scotia, could be relieved for anti-submarine and escort duties between Britain and Iceland.

But above all, following discussions about the preferential economic relations that Great Britain intended to maintain with her dominions, the two statesmen, on the afternoon of August 12, put their signatures at the bottom of the document, known to history as the "Atlantic Charter", in whose eight articles the four liberties set forth earlier by Roosevelt received further and more explicit definition. Although the text has remained a dead letter, this solemn declaration of intent may still be read with profit:

"The President of the United States of America and the Prime Minister, Mr. Churchill, representing His Majesty's Government in the United Kingdom, being met together, deem it right to make known certain principles in the national

President F. D. Roosevelt with Admiral Bloch, C.-in-C. U.S. fleet from January 6, 1940.

policies of their respective countries on which they base their hopes for a better future for the world.

"First, their countries seek no aggrandisement, territorial or other.

"Second, they desire to see no territorial changes that do not accord with the freely expressed wishes of the people concerned.

"Third, they respect the right of all peoples to choose the form of government under which they will live; and they wish to see sovereign rights and self-government restored to those who have been forcibly deprived of them.

"Fourth, they will endeavour, with due respect to their existing obligations, to further the enjoyment by all States, great or small, victor or vanquished, of access, on equal terms, to the trade and to the raw materials of the world which are needed for their economic prosperity.

"Fifth, they desire to bring about the fullest co-operation between all nations in the economic field, with the object of securing for all improved labour standards, economic advancement, and social security.

"Sixth, after the final destruction of the Nazi tyranny they hope to see established a peace which will afford to all nations the means of dwelling in safety within their own boundaries, and which will afford assurance that all the men in all the lands may live out their lives in freedom from want and fear.

"Seventh, such a peace should enable all men to traverse the high seas and oceans without hindrance.

"Eighth, they believe that all the nations of the world, for realistic as well as spiritual reasons, must come to the abandonment of the use of force. Since no future peace can be maintained if land, sea, or air armaments continue to be employed by nations which threaten, or may threaten, aggression outside of their frontiers, they believe, pending the establishment of a wider and more permanent system of general security, that the disarmament of such nations is essential.

They will likewise aid and encourage all other practicable measures which will lighten for peace-loving peoples the crushing burden of armaments."

Published on August 14, the Atlantic Charter was put forward for the adherence of all the nations at war with Italy and Germany, and, as from December 7, 1941, Japan. On January 1, 1942, at the White House, it was signed by the plenipotentiaries of 25 states who for the first time took the collective title the "United Nations". With Britain were the five self-governing states of the Commonwealth: the United States, five Central American republics, Cuba, Haiti, and the Dominican Republic; and eight governments in exile, namely Belgium, Greece, Luxembourg, Norway, Holland, Poland, Czechoslovakia, and Yugoslavia. All these signed the charter promising them the restoration of their independence and of their liberties. Finally, Mr. Soong signed the declaration in the name of China, and Maxim Litvinov in the name of the Union of Soviet Socialist Republics.

According to Winston Churchill, Soviet Ambassador in Washington "manifestly shook with fear" at the thought of asking the Kremlin for its adherence to a document proclaiming the principle of religious liberty to all the world, and it required all President Roosevelt's diplomatic skill to persuade him to transmit the eight articles which British and Americans had agreed in Newfoundland to Moscow. But Stalin gave him the order to sign "without batting an eyelid".

The settlement by which the United States Navy took over protection of convoys without distinction of flag, between Newfoundland and Iceland, had the result of provoking incidents between United States' ships and German U-boats and, in truth, this was inevitable and not altogether unwelcome to Roosevelt. The first such incident occurred in the course of

The United States destroyer Kearney, *victim of Roosevelt's policy of confrontation with U-boats.*

the morning of September 4, with *U-652* firing two torpedoes at the American destroyer *Greer*, which managed in fact to take evading action.

On September 11, President Roosevelt made a radio announcement to the effect that he had instructed the armed forces of the United States to fire on sight at Axis "pirates", both surface and submarine vessels. It is difficult to believe that he had not been aware when he made this declaration that for nearly four hours, in compliance with her orders to "obtain information but not attack", the *Greer* had maintained contact with *U-652*, signalled its whereabouts to all British escort ships and aircraft in the vicinity, and had been instrumental in an R.A.F. plane making an attack on it, though this was unsuccessful. In any event, on October 9, he seized upon this incident to request Congress to amend the Act of Neutrality on two fresh points, one regarding the arming of merchant ships, the other authorising them to navigate in waters declared to be within the zone of hostilities. The reception given by the two chambers to this new move by the President was somewhat cool; it received only 50 votes as against 37 in the Senate, and 212 as against 194 in the House of Representatives. These changes were enacted on November 7, 1941.

Meanwhile, two further incidents to the south-west of Iceland brought Germans and Americans face to face. In the course of action between U-boats and convoy S.C.48, the destroyer *Kearney* was hit by a torpedo and ten of her crew were killed; on October 17, less than a fortnight later, the aged *Reuben James* was sunk with 125 of her crew and all her officers.

On the strength of the order to fire on sight at "pirate" vessels that President Roosevelt had just promulgated, Grand-Admiral Raeder, accompanied by Dönitz, called on Hitler in order to ask him to reconsider the situation. But the Führer was adamant, and German U-boat crews continued to abide by the orders of June 21, which expressly forbade retaliation.

On November 30, however, there took place the event which resolved the dilemma facing Hitler and Ribbentrop as to the best means of responding to the increasingly hostile actions of the United States towards the Axis Powers. On that day, General Oshima, Japanese Ambassador in Berlin, received instructions to read out and comment on to the Führer a telegram which is here reproduced in the text supplied by the American decoding service.

"The conversation begun between Washington and Tokyo last April . . . now stands ruptured–broken . . . Say very secretly to them [Hitler and Ribbentrop] that there is extreme danger that war may suddenly break out between the Anglo-Saxon nations and Japan through some clash of arms, and add that the time of the breaking out of war may come quicker than anyone dreams."

On December 4, the Japanese Ambassador in Rome, Horikiri, asked to see the Duce to give him a similar message.

CHAPTER 24
Japan's road to war

When one looks at the phoenix-like recovery of the Japanese economy out of the débris of an empire which, on the day of its unconditional surrender–signed on the quarterdeck of the American battleship *Missouri* in Yokohama Bay–lay in total devastation after an overwhelming defeat, it is easy to talk about the Japanese miracle just as one does about the German miracle. When one considers this amazing upsurge, the might which Japan deployed with explosive force in her conquest of South-East Asia–territory which she considered to be rightfully hers–becomes more readily understandable today than it was in 1941, although it was, in fact, common knowledge in Europe and America that nearly half (49 per cent) of Japan's budgetary expenditure for the year 1941 went on armaments.

Knowing what one does now, one is stunned by the kind of irresponsible propaganda which was put out in the British and American press about Japanese military strength on the eve of Pearl Harbor; and there is no doubt at all this mirrored the blind optimism of the politicians and military chiefs in London and Washington. According to some scientists, it was a well-established fact that through a deficiency of vitamin C the Japanese lacked acuity of vision; hence, they would make poor air pilots and, at sea, would be no match for British and American sailors after sunset. Hence also the view held by British Intelligence, as reported by Captain Russell Grenfell, that Japanese planes and Japanese airmen were not worth half their British counterparts, and the view of Air Vice-Marshal C. W. H. Pulford, Air Officer Commanding, Far East, when he declared that American Brewster F2A "Buffalo" fighters, which absolutely no one in the European or African theatres of war would hear of having, were "good enough for Singapore".

A sober look at the situation reveals that the Japanese air forces had as many as 4,000 planes, that her aircrews were superbly trained for a whole range of offensive and defensive missions, and that their machines were as good as any in the world. In particular, the "Zero" fighter, designed by Jiro Horikoshi for the Mitsubishi firm, held its own for more than two years over all British and American rival planes until the United States Navy's Grumman F6F "Hellcat" came into service in September 1943. As in the case of the United States, there was no autonomous Japanese Air Force.

During the furious battles which took place between August 8, 1942 and February 11, 1943 off the Solomon Islands, the Americans discovered that their adversaries actually looked for night combat, and that their eyes were as efficient, if not more so, in the dark as the radar of the time. So much for the pronouncements made by the dietetics experts . . .

At all events, on December 7, 1941 the Imperial Japanese Navy entered the fray with ten battleships, ten aircraft-carriers, 38 cruisers (18 heavy and 20 light), 112 fleet destroyers, and 65 submarines. This exact balance between battleship and aircraft-carrier, or the "ship armed with planes" as the late Admiral Pierre Barjot aptly named it, was unique to the Japanese Navy; the proportion was one aircraft-carrier to two battleships in the Royal Navy, and one to three in the United States Navy. Advanced thinking in the Japanese Naval Air Force, inspired by Admiral Isoroku Yamamoto, took the view that the proportion should be still higher. Furthermore, Rear-Admiral Kishimoto and Captain Asakuma had developed a 24-inch torpedo which was far superior to the 21-inch weapon used by the Americans. The Japanese warhead contained 1,100 pounds of explosives as against the other's 668; but its chief advantage was that, being propelled by oxygen instead of compressed air, as were the British and American models, it left little trace of its path, thus rendering evading action very difficult. It was also considerably faster and possessed excellent speed/range ratios.

The Japanese merchant navy, at the moment of the attack on Pearl Harbor, amounted to nine million tons and, had it been used more rationally, would have been equal to the task of sustaining a war economy. But the Japanese High Command came to accept the necessity of sailing merchantmen in convoy too late, with the result that American bombers and submarines attained results in the Pacific which the U-boats and Luftwaffe just failed to reach in the Atlantic.

At the same moment, the Imperial Army had 51 divisions in service, of which 27 were involved in what for nearly ten years Tokyo had been calling "the liquidation of the Chinese incident". Thirteen other divisions were facing the Red Army on the Manchurian frontier. Hence it was not difficult for the Imperial General Staff to find the dozen or so divisions which, before the monsoon broke, would conquer the Philippines, the Dutch East Indies, Malaya, Thailand, and Burma, and manage this without waiting for the mobilisation decree, which would put an empire of 72 million people on a war footing, to begin to take effect.

When it comes to making an appraisal of the Japanese land forces one is put in a quandary. Whereas the publications of Commanders Fuchida, Hara, Hashimoto, and Okumiya provide first-hand evidence of great value on air and naval operations in the Pacific war, the accounts of Japanese military campaigns quoted in the bibliography of Giuglaris's *Le Japon perd la guerre du Pacifique* have none of them been so far translated into a European language. And so we have to make do with British and American sources which,

for all their probity, often fail to show us "the other side of the hill" as the late Captain Liddell Hart was fond of saying.

With these reservations, one factor is immediately apparent. While most of the top-ranking officers of the Japanese Navy had generally had a period as naval attaché at the embassy in London and Washington, the future army commanders had completed their experience in Paris or Berlin, as was indeed entirely normal in the years between the wars, but which at the same time gave them no chance of making an objective assessment of their future opponents.

In addition to this, the Japanese High Command had trained and developed its army to be a weapon of formidable fighting quality. But at a tactical level, it does not appear that middle-rank officers, in spite of the first-hand fighting experience which gave them an advantage over their enemies, showed as much initiative and resourcefulness as did the captains, majors, and colonels of the United States Army; proof of this being the failure of most of the counter-attacks by Japanese infantry during the Guadalcanal campaign, that is to say at a phase in the relentless fighting when there was little to choose between the two adversaries.

If it happened that, in December 1941 and January 1942, the 25th Army led by General Yamashita overcame the obstacles of the Malayan jungle with an ease that left his British adversaries speechless, the Japanese troops in New Guinea and the Solomon Islands sustained losses through disease equal to those which decimated European troops fighting colonial campaigns in the 19th Century, whereas the Australian and American troops got off relatively lightly. In fact, it would seem that the Japanese High Command gave insufficient attention to its medical service. As for sanitation and personal cleanliness, which were considered of such importance in English-speaking units, this would seem to have been non-existent or virtually so on the Japanese side.

Such were the strengths and weaknesses of the Japanese military machine which moved into action on December 7, 1941. There is every evidence that for a short-term war begun in an indescribable atmosphere of fanatical patriotic and imperial enthusiasm, the strong points easily outweighed the weak ones. Added to which, a veil of mystery shrouded the latest, superlative weapons in the Japanese armaments programme. A boy of 15 in Europe or America would in 1940 have been able to give more or less accurate details of the respective performances of the Messerschmitt Bf 109E or the Supermarine Spitfire; in the Pacific theatre and in Malaya, British and American pilots had their first introduction to the formidable Zero fighter when it came down at them out of the sky. Likewise the 1940 naval almanacs ascribed a tonnage of 12,000 to 15,000 to the aircraft-carriers *Zuikaku* and *Shokaku* which were then building, whereas we now know that fully loaded their displacement tonnage was nearly 30,000.

Even so, when in the course of the summer of 1941 Admiral Yamamoto, Commander-in-Chief of the Combined Fleet, was invited by Prince Konoye to provide an expert prognosis of the probable outcome of a war between Japan and the United States and British Empire, he made no secret of his pessimism if the war were not a short one.

Yamamoto put it as follows: "If you tell me that war with the United States is unavoidable, then I will unleash all I have in the first six months and promise you an uninterrupted sequence of victories. But I warn you, if hostilities continue for two or three years, then I have no confidence that ultimate victory will be ours."

Wise words indeed. The industrial pre-eminence of the United States in relation to Japan was not, as with population, of the order of two to one, but rather of five or six to one. And the supply to Japanese industry of the strategic raw materials which the conquest of South-East Asia was intended to make available, posed far more of a problem than had generally been anticipated in Tokyo, and became even more difficult with the increasingly heavy losses of tankers and cargo ships; so much so that in the early part of 1944, the fleet commanded by Admiral Ozawa made its anchorage off the island of Tawitawi, near the oil wells and refineries of Tarakan and Balikpapan on the east coast of Borneo.

Further still in this conflict between the Japanese and the Americans and British, factors of potential in terms of size and capacity were not the only ones where the Rising Sun found itself at a disadvantage. There is absolutely no question that Japanese armament experts proved in the main to be less inventive than their German allies and their American enemies.

What indeed was the point in undertaking the construction of 15 aircraft-carriers, if they were to be fitted with apparatus which American and British technology, involving unremitting radar innovation, improvement, and development, rendered yet more out of date every few months. As an illustration of this: while the Germans were trying to develop a weapon of reprisal at Peenemünde, the so-called V-weapons, and the Americans at Oak Ridge, together with their allies, were putting the final touches to the atomic bombs that would drop on Hiroshima and Nagasaki, the Japanese Navy, too, developed its secret weapon—a huge paper balloon which, when the wind was favourable, was launched from submarines some hundreds of miles off the American Pacific coast.

And indeed, this strange weapon managed to start a few forest fires in the States of Oregon and California, but it was certainly not the way to win the war,

any more than the appearance in autumn 1944 of the famous *Kamikazes* or those human torpedoes which were given the name of *Kaiten* by Tokyo. All things considered, there are grounds for agreeing with the American writer who sought to explain the final defeat of the Japanese by the fact that they failed to back up a display of quite exceptional courage with an intelligent direction of the conduct of the war.

The prime cause of the diplomatic rupture between Tokyo and Washington lies in the attempt by Japan to establish either direct or indirect rule on the Chinese mainland.

Without going back to the events which enabled the Japanese to set up the puppet government of Manchukuo at Mukden or compelled General Chiang Kai-shek to fall back on Chungking, it is necessary to point out that at the time of the "phoney war" Paris and London embraced the cause of China, motivated quite understandably by the desire to gratify Washington. Hence, arms, munitions, motor vehicles, and fuel oil were routed to Chungking via French Indo-China and Burma, either by the road linking Rangoon with Lashio or by rail from Tonkin.

The defeat of France and the isolation of Great Britain allowed Japan to seize the advantage and, on June 19, 1940, make representations to General Catroux, Governor-General of Indo-China, to the

effect that the Tonkin frontier be closed within the space of 24 hours and that a Japanese supervisory force should be set up to ensure its closure. General Catroux was relieved of his functions for having acceded to conditions of the Japanese ultimatum, but his successor, Admiral Decoux, was no more able than he to negotiate with Japan, so obvious were the French weaknesses, and, on September 22, he was forced to agree to a compromise arrangement whereby a contingent of the Japanese Army would be allowed entry into Tonkin, as well as the use of three airfields. The application of this agreement was the occasion of incidents involving bloodshed between French and Japanese, but tension soon subsided.

On July 2, 1941, the Imperial Council, meeting in Tokyo, decided not to cross the Manchurian frontier as the Soviet-Japanese Non-Aggression Pact of the previous April 13 required, and as Article Three of the Tripartite Pact allowed. Furthermore, in the words of Matsuoka, the Foreign Minister, to the German Ambassador Ott, when the latter called to inquire about the decision: "The Japanese effort to contain the United States and Great Britain in the Pacific is no less vital a contribution to the common cause than intervention by Japan in a war between Germany and the Soviet Union."

A Japanese officer leads his men into the Chinese town of Changsha.

But, seemingly justifying the statement above, the Imperial Council decided in the course of the same meeting to extend Japanese dominion over the whole of Indo-China; and on July 14, Kato, Japanese Ambassador in Paris, informed Admiral Darlan, then head of the Vichy Government, of a request to this effect from the Prime Minister, Prince Konoye. It was a case of organising the "joint defence" of the colony and this, Tokyo asserted, involved its entire occupation by an unlimited number of troops and, in addition, the right for the occupying force to set up bases wherever it pleased.

Within 24 hours, Darlan alerted Admiral Leahy, United States Ambassador in the capital of Unoccupied France. But from documents which have been published on the subject, it appears that, while encouraging Darlan and Marshal Pétain to resist this pressure on the part of Tokyo, Leahy, contrary to reliable sources of information, gave them no effective guarantee of aid in the eventuality of French intransigence resulting in the invasion of Indo-China.

According to the wording of a memorandum from Vichy to Washington, dated August 5, President Roosevelt's Ambassador, earlier on July 16, "in the course of conversations with Marshal Pétain informed him that there were no grounds for thinking that the American Government was disposed to reconsider the passive attitude adopted by the State Department following the first Japanese intervention in 1940."

In these conditions, Vichy bowed to the inevitable, and on July 29, 1941 an exchange of letters between Kato and Darlan ratified the agreement which had been signed in Hanoi by Admiral Decoux and the Japanese negotiators.

Just when Prince Konoye was trying to come to an agreement with Washington, and had in fact, in the hope of a settlement, sacrificed Matsuoka and installed Admiral Toyoda in his place, the news of the occupation of Saigon hit the United States with the force of a thunderbolt and obviated all Konoye's efforts.

And, indeed, if the establishment of Japanese bases in Cochin-China hardly constituted an act of war, it was nonetheless an act preparatory to war which threatened at one and the same time the British positions in Burma and Malaya, the Dutch in Indonesia, and the American in the Philippines. President Roosevelt's reaction was to freeze Japanese assets in the United States as from July 26 and to place an embargo on exports of oil to Japan. A few days later, the United Kingdom, Canada, and the Dutch Government in exile followed suit, thus straightway depriving Japan of any access to the Sumatra, Borneo, and Burma oilfields.

Nevertheless, these developments had no effect on the Japanese Government's attempts to restart negotiations, and, as has already been observed, President Roosevelt, whose policies were influenced by various considerations, was not unwilling to talk. To this end, Prince Konoye proposed a meeting with President Roosevelt in Honolulu, but he was

General Tojo (centre, in uniform) surrounded by his war Cabinet.

informed by Washington that it was desirable first to prepare the ground by diplomatic negotiation.

And indeed, with the embargo on oil, Franklin Roosevelt and Cordell Hull possessed a most effective means of exerting pressure, since it was estimated that Japanese stocks of oil would not last more than two years. But, in fact, this was a double-edged weapon; for it was idle to think that the exchange of diplomatic notes between Tokyo and Washington would be allowed to continue indefinitely at a time when the fleet of the Rising Sun might find itself incapacitated for lack of fuel oil. Especially when Tarakan and Balikpapan in Borneo and Palembang in Sumatra, not to mention the Burmese installations of Burmah Oil, might all be within striking distance. And so, Japan's military leaders, without rejecting attempts to obtain a negotiated settlement out of hand, insisted on a time limit being set to the negotiations, for it would not do to relinquish the considerable advantage the other party would obtain, if negotiations were broken off, simply by constant temporising.

On September 6, upon the covert refusal of President Roosevelt to meet the Japanese Prime Minister either in Honolulu or even in Juneau (Alaska), the Imperial Council met again to consider the situation; there was no avoiding the arguments that have just been summarised and the following conclusions were drawn:

1. Japan, "determined not to reject the possibility of a conflict", was likely to have completed her preparations for war between that time and the end of October;

2. "Parallel to and in tune with this", she would endeavour, "by all diplomatic means", to reach agreement with the United States and Great Britain on the basis of the programme which had been drawn up in Tokyo; and

3. "If, at the beginning of October, there was no longer any appearance of our demands being able to be met by means of negotiation, it would be resolved to go to war with the United States, Great Britain, and the Netherlands."

Accordingly, while the Japanese Foreign Minister was informing Ambassador Grew of his government's intentions, Admiral Nomura, the Japanese Ambassador in Washington, was conveying them on September 28 to Secretary of State Cordell Hull, who gave him a somewhat cold reception as it transpired from a reading of his memorandum of October 2.

The date fixed by the Imperial Council on September 6 fell without there being any issue from the diplomatic *impasse* and, on October 12, Prince Konoye summoned his Minister of Foreign Affairs, Admiral Toyoda, War Minister, General Tojo, Navy Minister, Admiral Okawa, and General Suzuki, the head of military planning, to his villa on the outskirts of Tokyo. According to the account of this meeting which has come down to us from

Giuglaris, words ran high between the head of the Japanese Government and his Minister of War:

Tojo: "Negotiations cannot succeed. In order for them to succeed, there must be concessions on both sides. Till now, it is Japan that has made the concessions, the Americans who have not budged an inch."

Okawa: "We're precisely balanced between peace and war. It is up to the Prime Minister to decide and to stand by his decision."

Tojo: "It's not as simple as that. It's not the Prime Minister alone who counts, there are the army and the navy."

Konoye: "We can contemplate a one- or two-year war with equanimity, but not so a war that might last more than two years."

Tojo: "That reflection is the Prime Minister's personal opinion."

Konoye: "I would rather a diplomatic solution than war."

Tojo: "The question of the Prime Minister's confidence in going to war should have been discussed in the Imperial Council. The Prime Minister attended that Council, did he not? There can be no question now of his evading his responsibilities."

Konoye: "Not only do I have no confidence in going to war but I refuse to take responsibility for doing so. The only action taken by the Imperial Council was to determine the measures to be taken should all diplomatic means fail. I still have confidence in a diplomatic solution."

With the benefit of the hindsight afforded the historian as compared with those who direct the course of events, one is at liberty to point out that both men were

wrong on October 12, 1941. General Hideki Tojo was in error in assuming that, given the maximum effect of surprise, the military potential of the Japanese Empire would in one fell swoop inflict a fatal blow on the American colossus. And, on his side, Prince Fumimaro Konoye was under a delusion in thinking that the country with which he was trying to reach agreement, invigorated by the anticipated effect of the oil embargo she had imposed, would lift it merely for Japan's assurance not to use Indo-China as a springboard for the conquest of South-East Asia.

Be that as it may, General Tojo was uttering no empty threat when he called his Prime Minister's attention to the state of opinion in the Army and the Navy, for, under the terms of the Japanese constitution, the ministers responsible for national defence were appointed by the Emperor and so escaped the rule of ministerial solidarity, and could at any time within the cabinet voice the censure of the military. In which case, the Prime Minister must tender his resignation; this in effect occurred on October 16, 1941, the instigator of the crisis then being called upon to resolve it.

As Prince Konoye's successor, Tojo kept the portfolio of War and entrusted Foreign Affairs to Shinegori Togo, who had previously been Japan's Ambassador in Moscow, and who was unattached at the time.

Japanese troops, in marching order and festooned with netting for personal camouflage, wade across a river during their severe field training.

At the time, this latest ministerial crisis in Japan caused no disquiet in the American Embassy in Tokyo; the military attaché, Lieutenant-Colonel Cresswell, commenting on the fact, wrote to the Secretary for War: "The composition of the new government is the very image of conservatism, but it is not thought that the resignation of the government led by Konoye will mark an abrupt change, at least not for the present. Certainly, General Tojo puts Japan before all else, but he is said to have a breadth of view which goes against his embarking on an extreme course."

Instancing the Emperor's pressing for a peaceful settlement, Ambassador Grew held approximately the same view as his military attaché. Nevertheless, on November 3, he put Secretary of State Cordell Hull on guard against imagining that Tojo would direct his conduct according to the norms of self-interest generally accepted in the West. "Make no mistake," he cabled, "the Japanese are capable of launching a suicide war with the United States. Self-interest should prevent them doing so; but Japanese national self-interest cannot be assessed according to the canons of our logic." The new Minister of Foreign Affairs in the Tojo Cabinet declared his earnest intention of enabling negotiations between Japan and America to succeed as soon as he took up office, and, on October 20, his Prime Minister declared that the maintenance of world peace was the first concern of his government's policy. But time was running out: throughout the Empire, stocks of liquid fuel were dwindling slowly but surely; moreover, the weather conditions prevailing in South-East Asia argued for action before December 15. The military necessities of the situation were now forcing the politicians' hands.

Confronted with these problems, Tojo called a cabinet meeting on November 1, to which were summoned the Chiefs-of-Staff of the Army (General Sugiyama) and of the Navy (Admiral Nagano) as well as their deputies. That day the debate was yet stormier than on October 12, witness the following extract of the proceedings taken from Giuglaris' book:

Togo (Foreign Affairs): "It is unlikely that the Germans will succeed in effecting a landing in England, even with our assistance. And, in any case, we should not delude ourselves about the contribution that collaboration between Germany and Italy can make to our cause."

Sugiyama: "We need the help of no one to achieve our objectives in our campaign in the south. Once that is over, China will be isolated and will capitulate. Next spring we shall turn our attention to the Soviet Union."

Kaya (Finance): "We have confidence in a war lasting two years. But not beyond."

Tojo: "Anyway, that gives us two years."

Togo: "Why take such a risk? The Western powers won't attack us, they

203

have enough on their plate with the war in Europe. It is to our advantage to maintain peace."

Nagano: "After two years at war, we shall have made all the conquered territory in the south impregnable. We shall not fear America, however strong she then is."

Kaya: "Defence is not the way to victory. When and how will victory come?"

Nagano: "Now. At once. We shall never have a chance like this again."

Sugiyama: "The first half of December is the right time to start active operations. We can temporise no longer with only a month to go. Let us break off diplomatic negotiations now and prepare unequivocally for war."

Tsukada (Deputy Chief-of-Staff, Army): "The decision to go to war should be taken at once."

Togo: "2,600 years of Japanese history cannot be dismissed so glibly."

Tsukada: "The Army must have an immediate decision."

Ito (Deputy Chief-of-Staff, Navy): "The Navy will be ready by November 20. Why not continue negotiations till then."

Tsukada: "The Army cannot wait longer than November 13. After that date the Government may be overturned. I propose that as from November 13 military action takes priority over diplomatic action."

Shimada (Navy): "Why not continue negotiating to within 24 hours of launching an attack?"

The debate concluded with the decision to let the military chiefs take command of the situation at midnight on November 30. Nevertheless, Togo had gained an ultimate respite of four weeks within which he hoped to get agreement by the United States for new compromise proposals that were to be submitted by Ambassador Kurusu. Kurusu, who was married to an American, was thought to have a better chance of being listened to in Washington. He arrived there on November 16 with Admiral Nomura. In fact, with the proposals contained in Plan B, the Tokyo cabinet made a few concessions to the American negotiators. These included the undertaking to withdraw the troops who had recently established themselves in the south of Indo-China to Tonkin, provided that Washington agreed to annul the economic sanctions decreed on the previous July 26. A further demand was that the United States should cease to supply arms to Chiang Kai-shek.

The last stipulation in the Japanese offer of November 20 was in fact unacceptable to the government and public opinion in America. But the counter-proposals for a *modus vivendi* that Cordell Hull handed to the two envoys, Kurusu and Nomura, on November 26, were for Japan still more unacceptable: the American Secretary of State posed as a prerequisite the evacuation not only of Indo-China, but of all China, the disowning of the puppet governments in Mukden and Nanking, the recognition of the sovereignty over China of Chungking alone, and finally an agree-

ment between Japan and America whereby Japan covertly abrogated the *casus foederis* as defined by the Tripartite Pact.

Were the American President and his Secretary of State so far from a true appreciation of the situation as to think that their ten articles of November 26 could really lead to a revival of peaceful intentions on the part of the Japanese? It is hardly credible, there being clear evidence that Japanese diplomatic correspondence was an open book to them. It cannot have escaped their notice that as the days passed and his anxieties grew, Togo notified his embassy in Washington that beyond a certain date limit, finally fixed for November 29, relations between Japan and America, in view of the inability to find a compromise, "would disintegrate in chaos", or that "events would occur of their own accord."

However, on November 25, the day before the American counter-proposals for a *modus vivendi* were handed to the Japanese envoys, the Defense Committee, presided over by President Roosevelt, and attended by the Secretaries of State, of War, and of the Navy, the Chief of the General Staff and the Chief of Naval Operations, held its weekly meeting. Afterwards, Harry Stimson, the Secretary of War, made this entry in his diary: "How could the Japanese be got into a situation where they would have to fire the first shot, and without leaving ourselves too exposed? That was the question."

And that is not all, because, on November 27, Knox, Secretary of the Navy, in a communication to his department heads, wrote:

"This dispatch is to be considered a war warning. Negotiations with Japan looking toward stabilization of conditions in the Pacific have ceased and an aggressive move by Japan is expected within the next few days."

Certainly, at the time that he sent out this warning, Knox might have been in possession of the decoded despatch which Kurusu and Nomura had sent to Togo the previous day, at the conclusion of which they made known the degree of amazement they felt at the Secretary of State's latest proposals. But it was not till the day following the warning reproduced above that the Japanese Minister of Foreign Affairs announced the imminent rupture of negotiations.

From the texts quoted above it appears that the American administration applied the "semi-positive" method in its relations with Japan, forcing on Japan responsibility for the last word which, in the view of President Roosevelt's entourage, would be war. And certainly in Washington this contingency was contemplated with complete optimism. Stimson, the Secretary of War, indeed wrote on October 21: "An extraordinarily favourable strategic situation has just developed in the South-West Pacific. All the strategic options open to us during the last 20 years have been totally transformed in the last six

months. Whereas we were unable before to change the course of events, suddenly we find ourselves possessed of enormous potential, whose full possibilities we are as yet unable to appreciate."

At all events, the ten articles of the *modus vivendi* proposed to Japan by the State Department played into the hands of General Tojo and those of his cabinet who were urging war against the United States, Great Britain, and the Netherlands. On November 29 an "Imperial Conference" assembled, consisting of ministers in office and the leading Japanese politicians of the past few years. The fateful decision was approved by a majority on a count of everyone present; Emperor Hirohito gave tacit consent, and on December 2 somewhere between the Kurile Islands and Hawaii, Admiral Nagumo, commanding the Air Attack and Support Forces, received the message agreed upon: "Climb Mount Niitaka", signifying the order to attack the fleet anchored at Pearl Harbor at dawn on Sunday, December 7, 1941.

Quite apart from the strictly military enquiries, the "mystery of Pearl Harbor" or, perhaps better, the mystery of the surprise at Pearl Harbor, has been the subject of a congressional enquiry in Washington whose proceedings, published in 1946, fill 40 volumes.

In regard to the controversy produced by Rear-Admiral R. A. Theobald's book, referred to above, use has been made of Volume III of the *History of United States Naval Operations in World War II*, whose author, Professor Samuel Eliot Morison, of Harvard University, enlisted in the United States Navy in 1942 as a historiographer with the rank of Lieutenant-Commander. In spite of its official character, it is a work which is totally objective and can be recommended both on account of its abundance and the reliability of its information.

More recently, in 1962, Mrs. Roberta Wohlstetter published a large volume at the University of Stanford, California, devoted to the same question. *Pearl Harbor* is a masterpiece of critical analysis, every significant document is examined, and the conclusions drawn are quite unbiased. The author is fully conversant with the different questions relating to the political and military information services, how they functioned, the constraints imposed upon them, and the extent and limit of their possibilities.

In short, the question that is most pertinent could be put as follows: bearing in mind that Colonel William S. Friedmann and his team of cipher experts in Washington had managed to "break" the Japanese diplomatic codes within the required time, how did it come about that the Pacific Fleet at Pearl Harbor did not receive warning of the stratagem that was being prepared to take them by surprise there where they lay at anchor?

To this, Rear-Admiral R. A. Theobald's reply is: because President Roosevelt and his advisers (principally, General Marshall and Admiral Stark) had made up their minds that the fleet should play the part of the goat that is left tethered to the post as bait for the Japanese tiger, and that the risk to which it was thereby exposed was the one means of provoking the attack which would bring the United States irrevocably into the war.

It is perfectly true that none of the five electronic machines built to decipher the "Purple Code" of the Japanese was allocated to Pearl Harbor, nor was Rear-Admiral Kimmel among those who received the "Magic" messages which recorded the transcription of Japanese secret despatches. But it is common knowledge that the secrecy surrounding the activity of decoding services is, in every country in the world, the most jealously guarded of all; increasing the circulation of "Magic" messages would have involved a serious risk of disclosure, which was at all costs to be avoided, and it is a fact that in July and August 1945, the "purple machine" was still unscrambling radio correspondence between the Japanese Ministry of Foreign Affairs and its representatives in Moscow, Stockholm, and Berne.

Besides, Togo's despatches contained nothing relating to Pearl Harbor for the excellent reason that he had no knowledge whatsoever of the operation entrusted to Admiral Nagumo. On the other hand, it would have been of use to Kimmel to know that, after the end of September, the Japanese consul in Honolulu received the order to communicate the exact moorings of all major American warships.

But this clue, which seems so obvious to us today, was just one among a host of others which singled out Malaya and the Dutch colonies as the single objective of Japanese aggression, and with such conclusiveness that some sources in Washington even forecast that the Philippines would be spared.

On the afternoon of December 6, the Navy's "purple machine" decoded Togo's final instructions to his envoys in Washington. They were followed by a message containing 13 points to be completed by a fourteenth on the following morning. The complete document was to be handed to the Secretary of State at 1300 hours on December 7; when it was shown to President Roosevelt, it drew from him the exclamation: "This is war!" And, in fact, the thirteenth paragraph included the statement:

"The (American) Proposal menaces the Empire's existence itself and disparages its honor and prestige. Therefore, viewed in its entirety, the Japanese Government regrets that it cannot accept the proposal as a basis for negotiation."

Yet nothing was done to alert the Pacific Fleet of the imminence of hostilities. But if Rear-Admiral R. A. Theobald interprets this silence as supporting his thesis, it can be advanced against him that the fleet had already, on November 27, been placed on the alert by the Chief of

Japanese fighter planes take off.

Naval Operations.

And this brings us to Pearl Harbor itself. There, on the previous March 31, a report drawn up by two senior officers, one Army, one Navy, drew attention to the danger to which the base was exposed from a carrier-borne aircraft attack. But this prediction was disregarded, Japanese naval concentration seeming to converge on points in South-East Asia. And this thesis appeared to receive confirmation in the "ultimatum" of November 27, according to which Siam, the Kra isthmus (the narrowest part of the Malay peninsula), North Borneo, and the Philippines seemed to be the particular points of possible attack. And, doubtless, it was thought that the huge Japanese aircraft-carriers, which had been out of radio contact for several weeks past, were to cover an amphibious campaign.

Within the Pacific Fleet, to have maintained a permanent state of readiness would have impaired the action training programme, and on that point Admiral Kimmel was not prepared to compromise, because the operational order *Rainbow 5* that it was his task to execute required him to lead his forces to attack the Marshall, then the Caroline, Islands.

In the Army Air Force, Major-General W. Short, commanding the military district of Hawaii had, on sight of the "ultimatum", been concerned above all to prevent acts of sabotage which were to be expected on the part of enemy agents introduced into the archipelago's large Japanese colony, and this led him to order his planes to be close-packed on airfields, rather than dispersed. Furthermore, reconnaissance patrols round Oahu Island suffered from the fact that the intensive training programme for fighters and bombers had left insufficient stocks of fuel for reconnaissance.

Finally, liaison between the naval and air force information services was insufficient and unreliable, while within the Pacific Fleet and the military district of Hawaii, radio communications left a lot to be desired.

But sooner than adopt Rear-Admiral Theobald's argument concerning Washington's responsibilities in the Pearl Harbor disaster, one is inclined to give credence rather to Professor Morison. He points out that the commanders of the U.S. armed forces may have fallen into a very simple but dangerous trap: that of considering what they thought the enemy was likely to do and formulating contingency plans based upon that, rather than assessing all the possibilities open to the enemy and being prepared for any eventuality. Though often pointed out, this is an error all too simple to fall into.

Seen in this light, the surprise attack on December 7, 1941 is the exact replica of that in the Ardennes on May 10, 1940. It follows, however, that Morison's judgement embraces Admiral Stark and General Marshall in Washington as well as Kimmel and Short in Honolulu.

Pearl Harbor's fate was set.

CHAPTER 25
Pearl Harbor and the Japanese blitzkrieg

It was early in January 1941 that Admiral Yamamoto, commanding the Combined Fleet, instructed a small group of staff officers to make a study of a surprise attack on Pearl Harbor, which would be made by carrier-borne aircraft. Until then, the Japanese Admiralty had contemplated adopting a defensive posture towards the American Pacific forces. But it became apparent that only a single devastating blow dealt at the enemy's principal naval formation at the beginning of hostilities would guarantee Japan the smooth conquest of her objectives in South-East Asia. Was the idea for such an enterprise suggested to her by the remarkable success of the Fleet Air Arm's attack on Taranto on November 11 of the previous year? It seems highly probable, in view of the fact that at the end of May 1941, a mission from the Japanese Naval Air Force visited Taranto and was given a detailed account of the course of events in Operation "Judgement".

In the following August, a series of strategic map exercises carried out under the supervision of Admiral Yamamoto provided the basis for Operational Order No. 1, which was signed on November 1. In the meantime, he had converted his colleagues to his plan, some of them having at first found it too risky, others objecting that the expeditionary corps destined for South-East Asia was being excessively weakened; but further and most important, Yamamoto had made his aircrews undergo a period of intensive training.

Under the orders of Vice-Admiral Chuichi Nagumo, the task force given the mission of attacking Pearl Harbor included: six aircraft carriers (*Kaga, Akagi, Hiryu, Soryu, Zuikaku,* and *Shokaku*) with a total complement of 432 planes; two fast battleships (*Hiei* and *Kirishima*); three cruisers (two heavy and one light); nine destroyers; three submarines, which were to patrol the itinerary plotted; and eight tankers to refuel the squadron at sea.

In the eventuality of Japan's deciding on war, the attack would take place at dawn on December 7, a Sunday, when the American fleet was normally at its moorings. In the words of Rear-Admiral Matome Ugaki, chief-of-staff of the task force, addressing his unit commanders, the attack on Pearl Harbor would be the Waterloo of the war that was to follow. Furthermore, the damage from the air attack would be added to by those delivered by the midget submarines which were to be transported close to the island of Oahu by ocean-going "parent" submarines.

On November 22, the 31 units commanded by Vice-Admiral Nagumo assembled in a deserted bay on the island of Etorofu, the southernmost of the Kurile chain. On the 26th, the Japanese task force

set sail, but, as has been said, the order to attack was to be communicated in a coded message and this came on December 2. The course charted ran east along the 43rd Parallel, thus, with the fog that prevails in those Pacific latitudes, rendering any accidental encounter with other ships unlikely.

On December 6, after nightfall, the formation set course for its objective. The news that no aircraft-carrier was present in Pearl Harbor caused some disappointment among the Japanese pilots. On the other hand, listening to the light-hearted radio programmes coming from Hawaii, it seemed quite clear that the Americans suspected nothing.

The following day, Sunday December 7, at 0615, Nagumo, who was by then 230 miles from Pearl Harbor, despatched a first wave of 214 machines, including 50 conventional bombers, 51 dive-bombers and 70 torpedo planes. One hour later, this formation appeared on a training radar screen, at a range of approximately 160 miles. But this information, which would have given 30 minutes warning to the Pacific Fleet, was not reported by the young air force officer to whom it had been passed because of the coincidence that a formation of Flying Fortresses coming from California was expected at the same time and from the same direction.

Lieutenant-Commander Nakaya, who was leading the fighters in the first wave, saw Pearl Harbor at about 0750:

"Pearl Harbor was still asleep in the morning mist. It was calm and serene inside the harbor, not even a trace of smoke from the ships at Oahu. The orderly group of barracks, the wriggling white line of the automobile road climbing up to the mountain-top; fine objectives of attack in all directions. In line with these, inside the harbor, were important ships of the Pacific Fleet, strung out and anchored two ships side by side in an orderly manner."

A few minutes later, two radio messages crossed: at 0753, Captain Fuchida signalled *Akagi:* "Surprise successful"; at 0758, Rear-Admiral Patrick Bellinger from his H.Q. on Ford Island sent out in plain language: "Air raid, Pearl Harbor – this is no drill."

Of the 127 ships under the command of Rear-Admiral Husband E. Kimmel, 94 were at berth and preparing for the ceremony of the colours. But the Japanese concentrated their efforts on the seven battleships moored in pairs alongside Ford Island, which stands in the middle of the roadstead. One 1,760-pound bomb blew up the forward magazine of *Arizona.* The ship settled quickly and went down with Rear-Admiral Isaac C. Kidd and 1,106 officers, petty officers, and other ranks out of a crew of 1,511. Struck by five torpedoes, *Oklahoma* capsized almost instantaneous-

ly, trapping below decks 415 men, some of whom survived until Christmas Eve. Had it not been for the extraordinary presence of mind of their crews in taking action to right the two ships, *West Virginia* and *California* would have met the same fate; *Nevada* was hit by a torpedo and two bombs but shot down three of her attackers. *Maryland* and *Tennessee* escaped relatively lightly and were able, after December 20, to leave Oahu for an American dockyard, together with *Pennsylvania,* which had been in dry-dock, and thus out of reach of torpedoes. Three cruisers and three destroyers also suffered damage.

The Japanese pilot Nuzo Mori gives the following account of his feelings as he flew his torpedo plane in to attack an American battleship:

"I manoeuvred in order to make my line of approach absolutely right, knowing that the depth of water in the harbour was rarely more than 35 feet. The slightest error in speed or altitude when firing might upset the mechanism of the torpedo and make it go to the bottom or break surface, undoing all my efforts either way.

"At the time, I was hardly aware of my actions. I acted like an automaton through force of habit which my long training had given me.

"The battleship appeared to leap suddenly into view across the front of my machine, looming huge like a vast grey mountain.

"Stand by! . . . . Fire! . . .

"All the while, I completely forgot the enemy fire and the throbbing of my own engine, totally absorbed by my manoeuvre. At the right moment, I pulled with all my strength on the release lever. The machine jolted violently as shells hit the wings and fuselage. My head was flung back, and I felt as though I'd just hit an iron bar head-on. But I'd made it! The torpedo-launching was perfect! My plane still flew and responded to my control. The torpedo was going to score a direct hit. I suddenly became conscious of where I was and of the intensity of the enemy fire."

At 0715, Nagumo launched his second strike, consisting of 54 bombers, 80 dive-bombers, and 36 fighters. Led by Lieutenant-Commander Shimazaki, it completed the work of the first wave in the harbour, then turned its attention to the naval installations on Ford Island, Wheeler and Hickham Fields (the air force bases), and the flying boat station at Kaneohe, destroying 65 aircraft out of the 231 on Oahu. In men, American losses for the day totalled 2,403 killed and 1,178 wounded.

This tremendous success cost Nagumo 29 planes and 55 airmen. After recovering the aircraft of the second strike, Nagumo set course north at 1300. The midget submarine attack was a complete failure,

A torpedo bomber (top right) climbs away from an American ship in Pearl Harbor.

however, and on December 10 one of the transport submarines was sent to the bottom by an aircraft from the carrier *Enterprise*. Moreover, the Japanese omitted to attack the vast oil storage tanks at Pearl Harbor, whose destruction would have incapacitated the U.S. fleet for months. American soldiers and sailors had acted so swiftly to re-establish the situation that Nagumo abandoned a third assault, as he thought that its cost in aircraft would be prohibitive – conclusive enough proof that Kimmel had shown energy and intelligence in training his crews.

Yamamoto – if one may be forgiven an analogy from boxing – had flattered himself that he would knock out the U.S. Navy in the first round; in fact, he had merely left it groggy but upright. The destruction of two battleships and the damage sustained by six others did not deprive it of its main striking force: its three aircraft-carriers were intact and with them 20 cruisers and 65 destroyers. Above all, the attack on December 7 mobilised all American resources and raised a mighty wave of indignation across the United States which with steadily mounting strength would break on Japan with colossal force.

"A date which will live in infamy," said Roosevelt, giving an account of the events before Congress. And, on the bridge of *Enterprise* as she headed back to Pearl Harbor on December 9, Rear-Admiral William F. Halsey echoed him when, at the sight of the wrecks obstructing the

fairway at Ford Island he made this, less academic, utterance: "Before we're through with 'em, the Japanese language will be spoken only in hell!"

In the spring of 1939, with the threat of war in Europe posed by Germany and Italy, the case of Japanese intervention on the side of the Axis powers was examined in the course of conversations between the British and French staff officers who drew up the Allied war plans. If Japan joined in the war, the French Navy was to assume responsibility for operations throughout the Mediterranean while the British naval forces based on Alexandria sailed to reinforce those at Singapore.

The armistice signed at Rethondes on June 22, 1940 caused reverberations as far as the Far East, because it was now out of the question for the British Mediterranean Fleet to abandon the Mediterranean to the Italian Navy. Thus the naval defence of South-East Asia against the emergent threat by Japan was reduced to an absolute minimum, even allowing for the small Dutch force based on the East Indies, which effectively took its orders from the British War Cabinet. Graver still, while in 1939 the British could still consider French Indo-China as the bastion of Malaya, two years later, the agreements forced on Vichy by Tokyo turned Saigon into a Japanese pistol aimed at Singapore; and already Japanese technical missions were finding their way into Siam.

It is clear that, faced with the defence of the Far East, on which in the last analysis depended that of Australia and New Zealand, the Imperial General Staff and the War Cabinet found themselves with an extremely difficult problem, in spite of

the fact that Roosevelt, at the Atlantic Conference, had given Churchill his guarantee that he would consider any new Japanese violation of territory in this global sector as a ground for war and that he would inform the Tokyo Government accordingly.

In view of this threat and of the choice of measures it required, did the British Premier give evidence of somewhat impulsive, dilettante decision-making rather than the sober appreciation of military reality that was called for? In his book *The Fall of Singapore*, Captain Russell Grenfell gives a clearly affirmative answer to this question, taking Churchill very severely to task in fact. The substance of his accusation is that with full knowledge of the deficiency in aircraft in the bastion of empire that was Singapore, Churchill, who had accepted the loss of 209 planes in Greece, nevertheless sent another 593 to the Soviet Union during the second half of 1941. Grenfell concludes:

"It follows that had the aircraft given or utilised for the benefit of foreign countries been sent to Singapore, the A.O.C. Malaya could by autumn have had a total of 802 modern aircraft instead of 141 old crocks. It is true that many of the 802 would have been fighters. But more and better fighters were Malaya's principal need."

To this it could apparently be replied that the failure to give due recognition to the technical and tactical capacity of the Japanese air forces was not only Churchill's but that of the highest ranking officers in the R.A.F. We have already seen that to confront the estimated 713 planes of his adversaries the unfortunate Pulford expressed himself content with 336. It is true that he did not receive even these and

207

that as the crisis loomed he was far less optimistic. Furthermore, it could be objected that by sending Stalin hundreds of Hurricane fighters, the British Premier acted in the conviction that he was defending Britain in the Russian sky. The real danger in the summer of 1941 was that the Red Army might collapse under the assault by the Wehrmacht, and that in the spring following the Wehrmacht would turn its full power against Great Britain. In that event her chances of survival would be slender, and Singapore would inevitably follow her into defeat.

It will also be recalled that, in the previous March, the British and American Governments had agreed to assume certain strategic risks *vis-à-vis* Japan in order the better to fight the Third Reich. There is therefore no doubt but that the transfer of war material to the Soviet Union agreed by the War Cabinet met with the approval of the White House. These, in the main, are the reasons that would militate against total acceptance of the point of view expressed by Captain Russell Grenfell.

Nevertheless, Russell Grenfell would seem to be entirely justified in the criticism he brings to bear on another initiative of Winston Churchill's: the despatch to Malayan waters of the new battleship *Prince of Wales* and the elderly battle-cruiser *Renown*.

On returning from his meeting with President Roosevelt in Newfoundland

waters, the Prime Minister, on August 25, made a suggestion to Pound which in his view would lead to an improvement in the situation in the Far East:

"I felt strongly that it should be possible in the near future to place a deterrent squadron in the Indian Ocean, and that this should consist of the smallest number of the best ships", including *Duke of York*, which was finishing her trials, a battle-cruiser, and an aircraft-carrier.

But the First Sea Lord did not believe in the "deterrent" effect such a formation might have and, from a strategic point of view, advised that a strike force, composed of the two *Nelsons*, *Renown*, and two or three aircraft-carriers, should be based on Trincomalee, the four old "R" Class battleships being assigned to escort duties in the Indian Ocean.

Churchill nevertheless was obdurate. In his view, *Resolution* and the others of her class were no more than "floating coffins", and Pound took insufficient account of the effect on the enemy of the detachment of one of the *King George V* class; and Churchill repeated on August 29:

"It exercises a vague general fear and menaces all points at once. It appears, and disappears, causing immediate reactions and perturbations on the other side."

The Foreign Office supported this argument which, it should be noted, went further than purely "preventive" mea-

A fuel tank explodes in a mushroom of flame, dwarfing the men at Ford Island Naval Air Station during the attack on Pearl Harbor.

sures, and the First Sea Lord deferred to Winston Churchill's evidently imperious wishes, prevailing upon him only to the extent of replacing *Duke of York* by *Prince of Wales*, whose crew was more highly trained. Admiral Sir Tom Phillips, hitherto Deputy Chief-of-Staff (Operations) at the Admiralty, was appointed C.-in-C. of this reduced squadron, which left the Clyde on October 25. On November 11, *Repulse* was ordered to join *Prince of Wales* in Ceylon. But, in the meantime, there was an unfortunate accident: the carrier *Indomitable*, which was to join the two capital ships, ran aground during a training exercise in the Caribbean.

Sir Tom Phillips arrived in Singapore on December 2; on December 5 he met General MacArthur and Admiral Hart, commanding the United States Asiatic Fleet, in Manila, and the three agreed that in the circumstances Singapore could not serve as the main base. From London, the Admiralty instructed Phillips to consider falling back on Port Darwin in Australia. Already, Winston Churchill's strategic conceptions were beginning to crumble.

The rest of the story is well known. On December 7 Japanese bombs fell on Singapore, proclaiming the beginning of hostilities. Could Admiral Phillips decently slink away when only a few days earlier it had been announced, with less concern for the truth than for flag-waving, that "*Prince of Wales* and other battleships" had arrived at Singapore to participate in the defence of this great bastion of the British Empire? However, on hearing the news that the Japanese had set foot in Singora on Siamese territory, not far from the Malayan frontier, he decided to try to take them by surprise while landing troops and supplies. Leaving his chief-of-staff in Singapore to try to arrange the vital fighter cover needed, Phillips weighed anchor at nightfall on December 8.

However, the following afternoon, he abandoned his plans when the appearance of Japanese planes in the sky overhead led him to believe that the enemy knew of his intentions. In fact this was not so, but his movements had been observed and signalled by two submarines, and even before dawn on December 10, Rear-Admiral Matsunaga despatched 11 reconnaissance planes, 52 torpedo planes, and 34 level bombers, belonging to his 22nd Air Flotilla, from Saigon.

At the same instant, the two British capital ships, escorted by three destroyers, were on course for Kuantan. Phillips had abandoned his plan to attack the Japanese landing force at Singora when his chief-of-staff had informed him that fighter cover was impossible, and decided to return to Singapore. *En route* he had been informed of possible enemy landings at Kuantan and concluded that he should investigate. Having ascertained that all was normal and that nothing untoward was happening, Sir Tom Phillips headed back for Singapore. At about 1100 hours, when he had Kuantan on his beam, the first enemy planes appeared in the sky. The fire from the British ships was as poor as the aim of the Japanese bombers, who managed to get only three out of 57 bombs on target; but the torpedo planes attacked with consummate skill, setting up a crossfire of torpedoes to defeat any attempt at avoiding action on the part of *Repulse* and *Prince of Wales*. The former sank half an

hour after noon, the latter less than an hour later.

What can be more tragic for a commanding officer than to witness his ship's agony? The following account by a British naval officer vividly conveys the intense personal drama of *Repulse*'s captain, W. G. Tennant, after he had given the order to abandon ship:

"As she heeled rapidly over, Captain Tennant clambered over the side of the bridge on to what had previously been a vertical surface and was walking unsteadily along it when the sea seemed to come up and engulf him. The ship must have rolled right over on top of him, for everything at once became pitch dark, telling him he was a long way down under water. The defeatist part of the mind that we all possess whispered to him that this was the end of things and that he might as well take in water and get it over. But another part of his brain bade him react against this advice, and he decided to hang on to life as long as possible; though he wondered if he could possibly hold his breath long enough to come up again. Lumps of wood hit him in the darkness. After what seemed a long, long time the water began to show a faint lightening, and suddenly he was on the surface in swirling water, luckily close to a Carley float, the occupants of which hauled him on board still wearing his steel helmet. The destroyers *Vampire* and *Electra* were coming up to pick up survivors and soon had them on board."

Of the 2,921 officers and other ranks who manned the two capital ships, 2,081 were picked up by the destroyers who went to their rescue with no concern for the risk to themselves; Admiral Sir Tom Phillips, however, went down with *Prince of Wales* as did her commanding officer, Captain J. C. Leach who, on May 24 of the same year, had been one of two survivors out of the 11 men on the bridge of his vessel when it was struck by a shell from *Bismarck*. Just as rescue operations were being completed, nine R.A.F. fighter

Japanese soldiers double past a burning oil storage depot in Hong Kong.

planes from the Singapore base appeared in the sky. In enumerating the causes of this disaster, unprecedented in the annals of the Royal Navy, Captain Russell Grenfell indicts principally:

"The presence in London of a Minister of Defence so convinced of his own individual competence as a master of naval strategy that he was prepared to ignore the advice of his professional naval experts and force upon them measures for the naval defence of Malaya which they clearly did not like."

And one is left no choice but to confirm this opinion. There is no doubt at all that the whole idea of committing two battleships to ill-defined operations without adequate air cover must have come from a totally mistaken appreciation of the situation. Does this judgement reflect on the First Sea Lord, too? Possibly; but it should be borne in mind that at the time he was suffering considerably from the brain tumour which was to cause his death on October 21, 1943 (the 138th anniversary of Trafalgar). As for the initiative taken by the ill-fated Sir Tom Phillips, it was that to be expected of a British sailor, bred in the tradition of taking the offensive and promoted to his high command by virtue of this very fighting spirit which was admired by all.

The loss of *Prince of Wales* and of *Repulse* was a considerable relief to the 2nd and 3rd Japanese Fleets who, under the command of Vice-Admirals Kondo and Takahashi, had the task of protecting, then supplying the 14th and 25th Armies, who would go on to conquer respectively the Philippines and the Malayan peninsula, including Singapore.

If the American, Dutch, and British cruisers and destroyers in this theatre of operations on December 10, 1941 were ineffective, being old and open to attack from the air, the 42 submarines under the orders of Admirals Helfrich at Surabaja and Thomas Hart at Manila did not perform much better; certainly, the Dutch registered some successes, but the Americans had the bitter experience of finding that their magnetic detonators worked no better than those carried by U-boats in 1940; this extract from a series of reports collected by Captain Edward L. Beach provides evidence of this:

"Fired three torpedoes, bubble tracks of two could plainly be seen through the periscope, tracked by sight and sound right through target. They looked like sure hits from here. No explosions. Cannot understand it."

In such advantageous conditions, it is hardly surprising that the amphibious operation set in motion by the Japanese High Command on December 8 proceeded as planned.

In the Philippines, General Douglas MacArthur disposed of rather more than 31,000 men (19,000 Americans) against General Homma's 14th Army, which began the assault with two divisions. It was the same story in the air, the attacking

force having 750 planes, the defence 300, at the moment, that is, when Clark Field was bombed, involving a loss of 17 out of 36 Flying Fortresses and several fighters destroyed on the ground. The lack of spare runways has been put forward as explaining the success of this operation, carried out only a few hours after Manila had received the news of Pearl Harbor.

On December 10, General Homma established a first beach-head at Aparri in the north of Luzon, with the intention of engaging the defence at this spot while effecting a second landing in the bay of Lingayen in order to outflank and destroy it. But MacArthur was too quick for him. At the first sign of the enemy's second manoeuvre, he disengaged, but far from trying to block the Japanese advance on Manila, he side-stepped, so to speak, placing his troops across the peninsula of Bataan, which shuts off the bay of Cavite, in positions prepared beforehand. When, on December 27, Homma got over his surprise, the Americans and Filipinos were so well dug in that it took the Japanese five months to drive them out of their last stronghold.

Hong Kong was the objective of General Sakai's 23rd Army. The defence of the island city of Victoria and Kowloon on the mainland devolved upon Major-General C. M. Maltby with 12,000 men; a force which was to be hardly adequate.

On the night of December 9–10 (thus

Japanese gains during December 1941.

giving the lie to the legend started by the British about their night-blindness), the Japanese stormed the defence of Kowloon peninsula and forced the British troops to fall back on to the island after three days severe fighting. On the 18th, again under cover of darkness, the Japanese 38th Division crossed the strait separating Victoria from the continent. In spite of vastly superior enemy forces, Major-General Maltby continued to resist until shortage of ammunition obliged him to accede to the third call to surrender. The cease-fire came on Christmas Day 1941.

On the day that the first Japanese landings took place at Singora, Air Chief-Marshal Sir Robert Brooke-Popham was C.-in-C. of combined British forces in the Far East. The planes at his disposal were woefully inadequate, as has already been observed. If the state of his troops, under the command of General Percival, was somewhat better, it was still far from satisfactory: no tanks, little artillery, and the infantry a mixture of British, Indian, Australian and Malay. In training and tactics Percival's forces could not compete with the enemy. Neither had the troops been positioned in the most effective manner.

The Japanese 25th Army's mission was to fly the Rising Sun over Singapore on D-Day plus 100, counting from the first landing, that is to say March 16, 1942. With three, subsequently four divisions (27, then 36 battalions), its numerical superiority over the British was only slight. The Japanese forces however were

crack formations and had the initial advantage of surprise. Furthermore, their abundant aircraft support would thwart British attempts to reform and regain the initiative. To this end, the numerous air-fields in the Malay peninsula which the R.A.F. had put into service proved invaluable. And the army had at its head an outstandingly dynamic and resourceful leader in General Yamashita–"Rommel of the jungle" as he was known. (Yamashita had a reputation for cruelty, but in other respects the resemblance was fully deserved.) Advancing by means of constant infiltration and outflanking movements, he forced Percival to abandon position after position, never leaving him time to entrench himself; many times, in order to further his objective, he "mixed" (his own description) his own commandos in with retreating British troops with the aim of preventing a "scorched earth" policy being carried out.

By the end of the year General Yamashita was ahead of schedule. The fall of Kota Bhara provided him with an excellent base for air attacks on Singapore, as well as an easy path to the Indian Ocean. Once there, he commandeered everything that would float, and, with a barrage of tiny amphibious operations prodding at the British rear areas, unnerved the British completely.

In Siam, General Iida, commanding the 15th Army, found every door opened for him by a collaborator government. By the end of December, after what may be described as a "route march", he reached the frontier with Burma to whose defence Lieutenant-General T. J. Hutton had just been appointed. The means at hand to do so were exiguous to say the least, and will be covered in a later chapter.

With the exception of Guam, the Mariana group of islands was transferred from Germany to become a Japanese mandate by the Treaty of Versailles in 1919. Hence the American island of Guam was left virtually indefensible and surrendered on December 10.

It remained for Wake Island, half way between Guam and Midway, to inflict a first reverse on the Japanese, whose offensive in other sectors was so successful and auspicious. An exceptionally timely reinforcement had arrived on December 4 in the shape of a squadron of Grumman F4F "Wildcat" fighter-bombers, and the atoll's garrison repelled a first assault, even managing to sink two Japanese destroyers. Exasperated by this humiliating setback, Yamamoto ordered Nagumo to detach the carriers *Hiryu* and *Soryu,* two cruisers, and two destroyers so as to contrive a fresh assault.

On December 21, the last Wildcat was shot down, but not before it had itself disposed of two Zero fighters. Then the dive bombers destroyed the batteries defending the island, reducing them one by one. On December 23, overwhelmed by the Japanese landings, the heroic garrison at Wake was compelled to surrender.

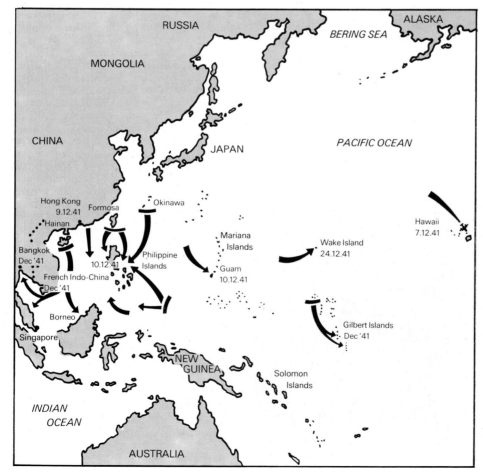

CHAPTER 26

Japan drives the Allies out of South-East Asia

On September 11, 1941, General Marshall and Admiral Stark sketched out to President Roosevelt the "main lines of the military policy" which they thought should be adopted, and proposed that these should be implemented without delay. In this extensive document they drew the President's attention to the enormous danger that the Third Reich would be to America if it were given the time to reorganise the continent of Europe as it liked. They therefore both agreed:

"The principal strategic method employed by the United States in the immediate future should be the material support of present military operations against Germany, and their reinforcement by active participation in the war by the United States while holding Japan in check pending future developments."

For this purpose, the "maintenance of an active front in Russia" appeared extremely important to them, and it was also imperative to "prevent Axis penetration into North Africa and the islands of the Atlantic" (Cape Verdes, Canaries, Madeira, and Azores).

These proposals, which were accepted by the President, also met the wishes of the British cabinet. In effect, Hitler and Mussolini, by declaring war on the United States, had saved Roosevelt the difficulty of persuading Congress that the best way to avenge Pearl Harbor would be to have two more new enemies on America's hands. Nevertheless, just when Churchill was preparing to put the case for Operation "Gymnast" (an American landing in Algeria in conjunction with an 8th Army drive into Tunisia) to the men responsible for American strategy, it was already apparent to the latter that their forces were unable to keep Japan at bay anywhere in the Far East.

But this order of priorities, in which the defeat of Germany would take priority over that of Japan, was not questioned by Roosevelt, Marshall, and Stark at the "Arcadia" Conference in Washington at the end of 1941. On the contrary, Marshall and Stark (the latter of whom was later replaced by Admiral Ernest J. King) took up an unequivocal position on the matter from the time of their first meeting with their British colleagues:

". . . notwithstanding the entry of Japan into the war, our view remains that Germany is still the prime enemy and her defeat is the key to victory. Once Germany is defeated the collapse of Italy and the defeat of Japan must follow."

Agreement was reached on the principle of such a landing on January 12, whereupon the plan was reworked as "Super-Gymnast". According to this new version, three British and three American divisions were to land in Morocco and Algeria from April 15 onwards. At the same time, three more American divisions would cross the Atlantic and relieve three British divisions in Northern Ireland. The latter would then be available for active operations.

It was maintained among General Douglas MacArthur's staff that this decision had been wrung from Roosevelt by Churchill's plausible eloquence. This was not in fact so; the American Chiefs-of-Staff, quite independently of the British and for purely national reasons, were already entirely in favour of the "Germany first" principle. However, it must be noted that in his memoirs MacArthur, the defender of the Philippines, claims that he was kept in ignorance of this important decision, and it is understandable that as a result of this omission he remained somewhat bitter against Marshall.

On the other hand, no great importance need be attached to the criticism MacArthur made of Admiral King, the new Chief of Naval Operations, when he wrote:

"Although Admiral King felt that the fleet did not have sufficient resources to proceed to Manila, it was my impression that our Navy depreciated its own strength and might well have cut through to relieve our hard-pressed forces. The Japanese blockade of the Philippines was to some extent a paper blockade. Mindanao was still accessible and firmly held by us. The bulk of the Japanese Navy, operating on tight schedules, was headed south for the seizure of Borneo, Malaya and Indonesia. American carriers having escaped destruction at Pearl Harbor could have approached the Philippines and unloaded planes on fields in Mindanao."

Writing about Pearl Harbor shortly before his death in 1966, Admiral Chester W. Nimitz, who must share with MacArthur the credit for the final defeat of Japan, said:

"No one regrets more than I our 3,000 dead when the Japanese attacked Pearl Harbor. But if Admiral Husband Kimmel, who at that time commanded the American forces at Pearl Harbor, had had information of the attack 24 hours in advance, he would have sent off all our forces to meet the Japanese.

"We had not one aircraft-carrier capable of opposing Admiral Nagumo's aircraft-carrier formation, and the Japanese would have sunk all our ships on the high seas.

"We would have lost 6,000 men and almost all our Pacific Fleet."

This was the position on the day of the attack. But on the next day, when the aircraft-carriers *Lexington* and *Enterprise* reached Pearl Harbor, there was no question of sending them out on an operation against six other carriers without the advantage of surprise. Moreover, the six aircraft-carriers of the Japanese striking force each carried at least 60 planes, all superior in performance to the 80 machines on each of the American carriers.

MacArthur's proposed operation would therefore in all probability have led to a second Pearl Harbor, but this time in mid-ocean, with no hope of rescue.

Faced with Japanese aggression that had been prepared and worked out at leisure, the "Arcadia" Conference hastily formed the A.B.D.A. command, the initials standing for the American, British, Dutch, and Australian forces fighting the Japanese in the Philippines, Malaya, Burma, and the Dutch East Indies. The establishment and appointments for this unified command, which Churchill cheerfully compared with Marshal Foch's appointment as Allied generalissimo on March 26, 1918, gave rise to hard talking among the conference delegates at the White House. The Americans wanted the commander-in-chief to be British and expressed a preference for Sir Archibald Wavell; the British refused to accept any responsibility for this, giving somewhat unconvincing reasons for their hesitation.

Though Churchill remained optimistic about the fate of Singapore, Sir John Dill, in a letter to Sir Alan Brooke, introducing him to his new duties as C.I.G.S., gave his views on the subject and put forward an argument, which he could obviously not pursue at an inter-Allied conference. He wrote, not mincing his words:

"It would, I think, be fatal to have a British commander responsible for the disasters that are coming to the Americans as well as ourselves . . . Never was a soldier given a more difficult task . . . It is of the first importance that we should not be blamed for the bloody noses that are coming to them."

However, General Marshall and President Roosevelt carried the day, with the result that on January 15, 1942, General Wavell started to set up his A.B.D.A. headquarters at Batavia. He was assigned three deputy commanders: General H. ter Poorten, a Dutch officer, for the land forces; Admiral Thomas Hart, C.-in-C. U.S. Asiatic Fleet, for the naval forces; and Air-Marshal Sir Richard Peirse for the air forces. Although the command structure appeared logical and workable, Wavell, seeing that the *matériel* resources of his command were poor and obsolete, noted sarcastically: "I had been handed not just a baby but quadruplets."

The Japanese offensive, making full use of its considerable *matériel* superiority, particularly at sea and in the air, was now in full spate, with its right wing threatening Burma and its left Australia. Success followed success.

Lieutenant-General A. E. Percival, G.O.C. Malaya, had III Indian Corps with which to try to oppose the Japanese advance. This corps, under the command of Lieutenant-General Sir Lewis Heath, disposed of three divisions, the 9th and 11th Indian in the line and the 8th Australian in reserve. Percival, faced with the problem of defending the Malay Peninsula, at places 175 miles wide, was forced to deploy his forces to cover the main axial roads, while the Japanese either infiltrated the British line through the jungle or bypassed the British positions by carrying out amphibious landings in their rear.

Although the British forces enjoyed a slight superiority in numbers over their opponents (88,000 allied troops to 70,000 Japanese), their formations were inferior in training. The crack Japanese divisions were more than a match for those troops facing them. The British, moreover, had deployed well forward in northern Malaya to cover airfields for which, in the event, no air cover could be found. To reinforce these stretched dispositions, it is true that convoys were bringing in considerable reinforcements: an Indian brigade on January 3, the 53rd Brigade of the 18th Division from Britain on the 13th, a second Indian brigade on the 22nd, and the rest of the 18th Division on the 29th. But the training of the Indian troops was entirely inadequate, and the British division, which had originally been intended for the Middle East and diverted to Malaya at the Cape of Good Hope, had declined in efficiency during its long sea passage.

Headed by a colour party, a Japanese company marches into Malaya.

Meanwhile, the Japanese Navy had also been moving forward, stretching out its tentacles to seize the bases it coveted, as Admiral Morison puts it. These tentacles consisted of the 2nd Scouting Fleet, 3rd Blockade and Transport Fleet, and 4th Mandate Fleet. The 2nd Scouting Fleet, commanded by Vice-Admiral Kondo, was to assist in the capture of Malaya and the reduction of the "impregnable" fortress of Singapore; the 3rd Blockade and Transport Fleet, under Vice-Admiral Takahashi, was ordered to gain possession of the Philippines, Borneo, and Celebes and then to join forces with the 2nd Scouting Fleet in order to take the Dutch East Indies, with their coveted oilfields; and the 4th Mandate Fleet, commanded by Vice-Admiral Inouye, was to take Guam and Wake. The attainment of these objectives would secure the perimeter of the Greater South-East Asia Co-Prosperity Sphere.

It should also be noted here that the Japanese land-based air forces co-operated very efficiently with the 2nd and 3rd Fleets, which had no carriers. From December 15, 1941 they operated from the base at Davao on the island of Mindanao; Kendari airfield, in the south of Celebes, was captured in record time on January 17 and was soon in full swing as a Japanese advanced base; Amboina, in the Moluccas, was captured on February 3. From these bases, the Japanese could wreak havoc

over the whole area of operations assigned to the 2nd and 3rd Fleets.

Besides being better trained than the Allied pilots opposing them, the Japanese had a distinct advantage in numbers and *matériel*. Most of the Hawker Hurricanes which had reached Singapore on January 14 were quickly overwhelmed in the air or destroyed on the ground, and a second consignment of these fighters, the only Allied aircraft in the theatre capable of taking on the Zero at anything like even terms, was diverted to Java. And thus the Japanese bombers had a field day at little cost. On February 3, Surabaja in Java was bombed for the first time; the next day the American cruisers *Houston* and *Marblehead* were both hit, the second badly enough to have to return to Australia for repairs.

The first Japanese landing on Borneo occurred at Miri, on December 16. The oil port of Tarakan, near the entrance to the Makassar Strait, and Manado, at the northern tip of Celebes, both fell on the same day, January 11, 1942. During the night of January 24, a division of American destroyers surprised the Japanese as they were landing an invasion force at Balikpapan, where most of Borneo's oil was refined, and sank four merchantmen, but this success could not alter the course of events. Without even taking into account the fall of Kendari and Amboina, or

waiting for the capture of Singapore, the Japanese invaded Sumatra, on February 14, and Timor on the 20th, without making any distinction between the Portuguese and Dutch parts of the island. This advance was of great strategic import, as it breached the "Malay barrier" and thus gave the Japanese the opportunity of cutting communications with Australia.

The situation was now beyond any hope of remedy, and on February 25 Wavell received orders to move his headquarters back to Ceylon, to which he had been preceded, on February 14, by Admiral Hart. Command of the Allied naval forces still operating against the Japanese had devolved upon the Dutch Vice-Admiral C. E. L. Helfrich, who was later to show exceptional courage in a disastrous situation.

Meanwhile, the Allied advanced headquarters at Bandung in Java had received information that two convoys, totalling 97 transports and with powerful escorts, had been observed off the Malay Peninsula and leaving the Makassar Strait. These were in fact the convoys carrying the Japanese 16th Army to the invasion of Java. With three divisions and one brigade, this force was far superior to the 30,000 trained troops with which General ter Poorten had to conduct the defence of Java.

Java's only hope lay in the destruction of the two convoys before they reached the island. To this end, the Allied naval forces in the area were dispatched under the Dutch Rear-Admiral Karel Doorman to the decisive Battle of the Java Sea. The Allied force, however, was at a distinct disadvantage as it had not had the time to learn to co-ordinate its efforts properly and to work out a common signalling code. Doorman's command consisted of two heavy cruisers, the British *Exeter* and American *Houston*; three light cruisers, the Dutch *De Ruyter* and *Java*, and the Australian *Perth*; and nine destroyers, four American, three British, and two Dutch.

On February 27, at 1500, Doorman was at sea off Surabaja when he received orders to intercept the Japanese convoy heading from the Makassar Strait towards Surabaja. Contact was made at about 1615 between the Allied force and the Japanese escort under Rear-Admiral Nishimura: the heavy cruisers *Nachi* (Rear-Admiral Takagi) and *Haguro*, the light cruisers *Naka* (Nishimura) and *Jintsu*, and 13 destroyers.

Though the Allies thus had a numerical superiority in cruisers, the range at which the action opened, more than 13 miles, meant that it was the numbers of 8-inch guns involved that was the critical factor. And here the Japanese prevailed, with 20 such weapons against the Allies' 12 (it should be remembered that *Houston* had been hit by bombs on February 4, and this had knocked out her after turret). The battle was to continue for almost seven hours without achieving concrete results, partly because the Japanese were

more concerned with the safety of their convoy than sinking Allied vessels, and partly because the Allied warships had no reconnaissance aircraft, and were thus forced, as Morison puts it, to play a kind of blind man's bluff.

During the first engagement, *Exeter* was hit in her engine room at 1708 and hauled out of the line, the cruisers following her doing the same under the impression that such a manoeuvre had been ordered by Doorman in *De Ruyter*, leading the Allied line. While the crippled British cruiser made for Surabaja, the Japanese launched a wave of 72 torpedoes, only one of which, remarkably, hit an Allied warship, the Dutch destroyer *Kortenaer*, which exploded and sank. While covering the retirement of *Exeter*, the British destroyer *Electra* was stopped by gunfire and hammered into a blazing wreck. During the night, Doorman searched in vain for the Japanese convoy, which had been ordered by Nishimura to retreat to the north during the action, without finding it. He was also forced to release his American destroyers, which had expended all their torpedoes and were running drastically short of fuel.

During his fruitless search for the Japanese transports, however, Doorman once again ran into their escort, in the form of the cruiser *Jintsu* and her seven destroyers, at 1930. Turning away from the Japanese cruiser, Doorman inadvertently

led his force over a newly-laid Dutch minefield, which cost him the British destroyer *Jupiter*. But time was running out for the Allied ships, for Japanese seaplanes had been keeping their cruisers informed of the Allied survivors' movements, and *Nachi* and *Haguro* were moving in for the kill. During the subsequent engagement, *De Ruyter* and *Java* were both hit and sunk by Japanese torpedoes. Doorman went down with his flagship. Immediately afterwards *Perth* and *Houston* broke off the action and returned to Batavia.

The crisis in Allied naval fortunes had yet further to run, however. After refuelling at Batavia, *Perth* and *Houston* received orders to retire southwards through the Sunda Strait. Here they ran into the second of the Japanese convoys mentioned above. This had sailed from Indo-China and was in the process of landing the first units of the Japanese 2nd Division in Banten Bay. The two Allied cruisers immediately went into the attack, and managed to sink one transport and force three others to beach themselves, as well as damaging one cruiser and three destroyers, before being sunk by the rest of the Japanese escort.

A few hours later, *Exeter* sailed from Surabaja with two destroyers to try to

A Japanese soldier advances warily during the fighting for Kuala Lumpur.

pass through the Sunda Strait. They were spotted by Japanese reconnaissance aircraft and sunk by four cruisers and three destroyers on March 1.

The naval defeat of February 27 sealed the fate of Java. The two vital centres of Batavia and Surabaja fell into Imamura's hands, and General ter Poorten asked the Japanese commander for armistice terms. As was to be expected, the victor demanded unconditional surrender, which he received at Bandung on March 10. Sherwood notes at this time:

"Churchill, who had won his greatest Parliamentary triumph a scant three weeks before, now faced the worst predicament of his career as Prime Minister. He made a broadcast speech in which he attributed the whole series of misfortunes in the Far East to the fact that America's shield of sea power had been 'dashed to the ground' at Pearl Harbor. There were numerous expressions of irritation at this statement in Washington, as though Churchill were attempting to escape censure by blaming it all on the U.S. Navy, but it did not bother Roosevelt at all. He merely remarked: 'Winston had to say *something*.'"

Under the keen and vigorous command of Lieutenant-General Tomoyuki Yamashita, the Japanese 25th Army smashed its way through the British defences in the north of Malaya. On January 1, 1942 Kuantan, on the east coast, fell to the swiftly-advancing Japanese, while on the other side of the country Kuala Lumpur, on the Slim river, succumbed on the 11th, after a period of fierce resistance. Seeing

his reserves melting away, Percival ordered his forces to fall back on Singapore on January 29, after asking for and receiving Wavell's authorisation. On January 30 the causeway linking the island fortress and the mainland was blown up.

But Singapore's garrison, its back to the wall, was in no position to offer a solid resistance for the great imperial base, which was intended to close the Indian Ocean to attack from the east and to ensure the safety of Britain's sea link with Australia and New Zealand. The Committee of Imperial Defence had recognised since the mid-1930's that the survival of Singapore in the face of a land attack depended upon the successful defence of the jungles of the Malayan hinterland – and that a Japanese attack via Malaya was quite probable. But now that the British defence of Malaya had collapsed, Singapore was indefensible.

In his memoirs, Churchill tells us of the "feelings of painful surprise" he had when reading Wavell's message of January 16, which emphasised Singapore's weakness as a fortress. Churchill adds:

"Moreover, even more astounding, no measures worth speaking of had been taken by any of the commanders since the war began, and more especially since the Japanese had established themselves in Indo-China, to construct field defences. They had not even mentioned the fact they did not exist." He summed up as follows:

"I do not write this in any way to excuse myself. I ought to have known. My advisers ought to have known and I ought to have been told, and ought to have asked. The reason I had not asked about this matter, amid the thousands of questions I put, was

General Percival (right) heads the British surrender delegation at Singapore.

that the possibility of Singapore having no landward defences no more entered into my mind than that of a battleship being launched without a bottom." It should be added, however, that Churchill had been a member of the Conservative cabinet in the 1920's when the Singapore base was planned and begun. There is, therefore, no reason why he should not have known the details then.

In the circumstances, it was not difficult for General Yamashita, on the night of February 8–9, to get his forces across the Strait of Johore and win a beach-head north-west of the city of Singapore. Immediately afterwards, the Japanese captured Tengah airfield and the reservoirs supplying the city's million inhabitants with water.

On February 15, the advanced guard of the Japanese 5th Division ran into the British delegation sent out to seek terms for surrender. General Yamashita refused to discuss terms, but insisted that General Percival come to see him personally. The Japanese commander told Percival that his forces "respect the valour of your army and will honour your dead", but then insisted on unconditional surrender. Percival hesitated for nearly an hour, and then signed the British surrender.

One of Yamashita's staff then asked if he was to prepare for a victory parade through the streets of Singapore, to which he received the dry reply:

"No. The war isn't finished. We have lost 3,300 men in the campaign. What have the survivors done to deserve it? We must first honour our dead. Then we'll prepare for future campaigns."

The disaster in Malaya provoked another crisis between the irritable Mr. Curtin and Churchill, following on their earlier disagreement about Tobruk.

Curtin had a majority of two in the Australian parliament and stubbornly refused to introduce the conscription necessary for the defence of Australia. This did not, however, prevent him from abusing Churchill for his lack of zeal in calling the home country to the defence of her Pacific dominions. On December 27, 1941, for example, the following virtual ultimatum appeared over Curtin's signature in the *Melbourne Herald*:

"Without any inhibitions of any kind, I make it quite clear that Australia looks to America, free of any pangs as to our traditional links with the United Kingdom.

"We know the problems that the United Kingdom faces. We know the constant threat of invasion. We know the dangers of dispersal of strength. But we know too that Australia can go, and Britain can still hold on.

"We are therefore determined that Australia shall not go, and we shall exert all our energies towards the shaping of a plan, with the United States as its keystone, which will give to our country some confidence of being able to hold out until the tide of battle swings against the enemy.

"Summed up, Australian external policy will be shaped towards obtaining Russian aid, and working out, with the United States, as the major factor, a plan of Pacific strategy, along with British, Chinese, and Dutch forces."

The reader will be spared the details of the somewhat acrimonious correspondence which followed. In the course of this the Australian Prime Minister went so far as to inform his British opposite number that after all the assurances that had been given to various Canberra governments for years: "the evacuation of Singapore would be regarded here and elsewhere as an inexcusable betrayal."

But it must be emphasised that Churchill, for all his normal impetuosity, made no attempt to modify his attitude to placate the Australian Prime Minister. Faced with the daily-growing threat of the Japanese advance, it was decided to withdraw the 6th and 7th Australian Divisions from the Middle East and incorporate them into the defence of Java and what British and American strategists called the "Malay barrier", separating the Indian Ocean from the Pacific.

Meanwhile, the defence of the Philippines had been concentrated in the Bataan Peninsula, west of Manila Bay. Here MacArthur had 15,000 Americans and 65,000 Filipinos, although only 10,000 of the latter could be considered as fully trained soldiers. MacArthur's foresight had provided the garrison with ample ammunition, but the position with food

supplies was a problem right from the beginning of the siege as the provisions for the garrison itself had to be spread to feed the thousands of refugees who had fled the Japanese advance and now seriously jeopardised the defence of Bataan. Notwithstanding, the American and Filipino forces on the peninsula held out for a very creditable period, not surrendering until April 9, 1942 after a siege of 98 days.

On January 10, Lieutenant-General Homma, the commander of the Japanese 14th Army, sent the following message to MacArthur:

"Sir,

You are well aware that you are doomed. The end is near. The question is how long you will be able to resist. You have already cut rations by half. I appreciate the fighting spirit of yourself and your troops who have been fighting with courage. Your prestige and honour have been upheld.

"However, in order to avoid needless bloodshed and to save the remnants of your divisions and your auxiliary troops, you are advised to surrender."

When this summons remained unanswered, the 14th Army attacked the American lines during the night of the 11th. After ten days of fruitless frontal attacks, the Japanese infiltrated the American lines across the slopes of Mount Natib, which the defenders had thought inaccessible, and thus forced the Americans to fall back to their second defence line across the peninsula. The retreat was conducted in an orderly fashion, however, and the American forces did not lose their cohesion. Homma, to his extreme chagrin, had to ask Tokyo for reinforcements.

On February 22, MacArthur received a message from the White House ordering him to quit Bataan, organise the defence of Mindanao to the south, and then proceed to Australia. MacArthur delayed in executing these orders, claiming that his departure would result in the immediate collapse of resistance in the Philippines. On March 10, however, Roosevelt cabled him: "Proceed immediately to Melbourne." General MacArthur could no longer ignore this direct order, and on the night of the 11th, he and his staff sailed from his command post on the island of Corregidor in four PT boats (motor torpedo boats). After an eventful three days at sea, MacArthur landed at Cagayan de Oro in Mindanao, flying from there to Australia on board a B-17 bomber. On this occasion he made his celebrated promise to the journalists waiting for him: "I shall return!"

Major-General J. M. Wainwright, who succeeded MacArthur as commander in the Philippines, visited his superior just before he left. Their conversation has been preserved by John Toland:

"'Jonathan,' [MacArthur] said as they shook hands, 'I want you to understand my position very plainly.' He was leaving he said, only because of insistent, repeated orders from Roosevelt. At first he had told his staff he would refuse, but they con-

vinced him that defying the President's direct order would bring disciplinary action. 'I want you to make it known throughout all elements of your command that I'm leaving over my repeated protests.'

"'Of course I will, Douglas,' said Wainwright.

"'If I get through to Australia, you know I'll come back as soon as I can with as much as I can.' Then he warned of the necessity of greater defense in depth. 'And be sure to give them everything you've got with your artillery. That's the best arm you have.'

"The two men were quiet for a moment. In the distance the dull rumble of battle from Bataan could be heard. Wainwright was thinking of the dwindling ammunition and food supply, his air force of two battered P-40's, of the spreading malaria and dysentery and lack of medicine. He said, 'You'll get through.'

"'And back,' MacArthur added with determination. He gave Wainwright a box of cigars and two large jars of shaving cream. 'Good-bye Jonathan.' They shook hands warmly. 'If you're still on Bataan when I get back, I'll make you a Lieutenant-General.'

"'I'll be on Bataan if I'm still alive.' Wainwright turned and slowly started back to his lunch."

Lieutenant-General Douglas MacArthur had a strong and somewhat theatrical personality. He was the object of passionate disagreement in his own country, not only in political circles, where he was regarded as a possible rival to Roosevelt, but also among his peers in the army and navy, among whom he aroused feelings of great admiration or great animosity. To describe him we may quote the evidence of a British officer who was far from indulgent when assessing the great American military commanders. On leaving Tokyo on November 22, 1945, where he had visited MacArthur, Lord Alanbrooke noted in his diary:

"MacArthur was the greatest general and best strategist that the war produced. He certainly outshone Marshall, Eisenhower and all the other American and British generals including Montgomery. As a fighter of battles and as a leader of men Montgomery was hard to beat, but I doubt whether he could have shown the same strategic genius had he been in MacArthur's position."

Alanbrooke believed that MacArthur, apart from his outstanding qualities as a war leader, also showed great political and diplomatic ability, and this view may certainly be correct. In fact, MacArthur succeeded in keeping the loyalty of the Filipinos during the Japanese occupation, remained on good terms with the intractable Curtin, and after the war won the friendship of Emperor Hirohito and helped the Japanese get over their defeat.

When he arrived in Australia, General MacArthur, who had been eating at the same mess as his men, noted that he had lost nearly two stones in weight at Bataan.

General Homma lands on Luzon during the Japanese invasion of the Philippines.

It is thus clear that the American garrison was severely weakened when Homma launched his final assault. Added to this physical debilitation was the loss of morale of the troops, to whom it was now abundantly clear that there was no possibility of a relief force reaching them. These facts, then, make it clear why General Wainwright was unable to galvanise his men to action. Moreover, the Japanese 14th Army had been reinforced with another division and brigade, and had improved its tactics, from now on combining frontal assaults with small-scale landings in the Americans' rear.

On April 1 Wainwright ignored a fresh summons from Homma to surrender and accept an "honourable defeat". The final Japanese attack started two days later, and three days after that the American defences were finally breached. After the failure of one counter-attack, General King, commanding on Bataan, considered that his men were at the end of their tether and sent emissaries to the Japanese to discuss terms on April 9. The surrender was signed the next day; 64,000 Filipinos and 12,000 Americans were taken prisoner.

There then followed the notorious "Death March", when the prisoners taken on Bataan were marched from Mariveles 55 miles to the railhead at San Fernando, under the most inhuman conditions. During the march, 2,330 Americans and between 7–10,000 Filipinos died. As the officer responsible, General Homma was tried after the war, found guilty, and executed. General MacArthur, turning down a final appeal for Homma, said: "I am again confronted with the repugnant duty of passing final judgement on a former adversary in a major military campaign ... I approve the finding of guilt and direct the Commanding General, United States Forces in the Western Pacific to execute the sentence."

But the American historian John Toland examined all the documents per-taining to the case and did not come to such definite conclusions about Homma's guilt, attaching blame more to the 14th Army's general staff for their irresponsibility than to Homma himself for criminal intent. The Japanese had expected to find 30,000 prisoners and got 76,000, all of them in poor physical condition. Twenty miles from Mariveles, transport had been provided for the rest of the journey, but only 230 trucks were available. Moreover, the behaviour of the Japanese guards towards their prisoners varied considerably: in some cases it was relatively humane, in others completely abominable. This seems to indicate that these guards were not obeying a general directive from their superiors.

The Japanese now controlled all of Luzon except the island fortress of Corregidor and the islets surrounding it. While the Americans held these, the Japanese were denied the use of Manila harbour. On May 4, the Japanese poured a barrage of 16,000 shells onto the island, and under the cover so provided landed a powerful assault force, which managed to secure a small beach-head. The American garrison numbered 15,000, but of these only 1,300 could be considered battleworthy. Homma urged Wainwright to surrender, but insisted that if he did so, the capitulation must also apply to all other American forces in the Philippines archipelago. The Japanese would thus be able to secure Mindanao and the islands around the Visayan Sea without firing a shot.

After a painful mental struggle, and despite MacArthur's intervention, Wainwright finally ordered his subordinates to terminate their resistance. The latter at first protested, but all American resistance finally ended on May 6, 1942. Wainwright was not condemned for ordering the capitulation by the American Govern-ment, General Marshall, and MacArthur. Indeed, with General Percival, who had surrendered Singapore, he was one of those invited to the Japanese surrender ceremony on September 2, 1945.

According to Churchill, it was not expected in London that the Japanese would invade Burma until they had finished with Malaya and conquered Singapore. As a result of this lack of foresight, the defences of this wealthy colony were extremely sparse. On December 8, 1941 they comprised troops totalling about a division – the 1st Burma Division, Burmese battalions stiffened by two British battalions and an Indian brigade. Towards the end of January 1942, the incomplete 17th Indian Division was shipped in. The whole was under Major-General T. J. Hutton. The R.A.F. was in an even worse position, with only four Bristol Blenheim light bombers and 32 superannuated Brewster Buffalo fighters, of which only 24 were airworthy.

Burma was as important to the Japanese as Malaya or India, not only for its oil and other natural resources, but because it contained the "Burma Road", which had only recently been completed and linked Lashio in Burma with Chungking in China. As President Roosevelt had just extended Lend-Lease to Nationalist China, the Japanese High Command considered it vital to sever this only artery supplying Generalissimo Chiang Kaishek's forces with war supplies from the "arsenal of democracy". The task of destroying this link was entrusted to the 15th Army, under Lieutenant-General S. Iida.

The invaders also had aid in Burma in the form of a large number of agents, whom the Japanese had been enlisting for years. The British knew of this, and on January 18, 1942 arrested the Prime Minister, U Saw. On the same day the Japanese 15th Army took the port and airfield of Tavoy in the south and moved on Moulmein, at the mouth of the Salween. This river, which formed a considerable natural barrier, did not slow the Japanese for long. Moulmein fell on the 31st, and the Japanese pushed on towards the Sittang. The critical phase of the campaign was reached when the Japanese arrived at this river before the retreating 17th Indian Division, under the command of Major-General J. Smyth, V.C. The bridge the division was to have used was blown prematurely, resulting in the loss to the Japanese of two-thirds of the division's men, most of its transport, and all its artillery. This defeat, on February 22, decided the campaign.

After the fall of Singapore, it had been decided, with the agreement of the Dutch Government, that the 6th and 7th Australian Divisions, which had previously been allocated to the defence of Java and Sumatra, should return to their own country. As the convoy in which the two divisions was sailing was off Ceylon at the time of the attack on Burma, Churchill wished to divert one, if not both, of them to Rangoon. The only result was another rebuff from Mr. Curtin on February 23:

"4. With A.I.F. troops we sought to save Malaya and Singapore, falling back on Netherlands East Indies. All these northern defences are gone or going. Now you contemplate using the A.I.F. to save Burma. All this has been done, as in Greece, without adequate air support.

"5. We feel a primary obligation to save Australia not only for itself, but to preserve it as a base for the development of the war against Japan. In the circumstances it is quite impossible to reverse a decision which we made with the utmost care, and which we have affirmed and reaffirmed."

In this situation there can be no question but that the Australian Prime Minister was right. In so critical a situation, Churchill and the Combined Chiefs-of-Staff Committee would only have been writing off the division or divisions that ventured into this hopeless theatre of operations.

On March 5, 1942, General Sir Harold Alexander arrived from England to take over command in Burma from Hutton. The decision to send out a new commander was, to some extent quite understandable. Alexander was an optimistic and determined officer, but within a short time of his arrival realised that he was faced by problems very similar to those by which he had been faced at Dunkirk.

The capital of Burma was defended by the remnants of the 17th Indian Division, while the 1st Burma Division, made up of native battalions with British and Indian strengthening, was operating against the invaders to the north. But the defenders were so short of men that a 125-mile gap had opened up between the two divisions, and through this the Japanese were infiltrating in considerable numbers. At first Alexander ordered that Rangoon must be held, but then came to Hutton's view that British forces were too weak for this task. He therefore decided to concentrate his troops for the defence of upper Burma and the retreat began. Rangoon was abandoned on March 7, the British retreating up the Irrawaddy valley to regroup their forces, now reinforced by the arrival of the British 7th Armoured Brigade, more infantry, and aerial reinforcements from Britain and China. Lieutenant-General William Slim was appointed to command these reorganised forces.

Alexander now decided that his primary strategic objective was the protection of the Yenangyaung oilfields, in which he was to be aided by the Chinese 5th and 6th Armies, under the command of Lieutenant-General "Vinegar Joe" Joseph Stilwell, the American officer who had been considered originally for the command of Operation "Super-Gymnast" but was now Chiang Kai-shek's military right hand. But co-operation with the Chinese proved difficult. A force equivalent in size to a British division was considered an army, and Chinese tactics bore very little resemblance either to Allied or Japanese ones. The following anecdote from Field-Marshal Lord Alexander's memoirs will serve to illustrate this:

"Before the battle of Mandalay I went round the front to inspect our defences and was much impressed to see how cleverly this Chinese Fifth Army had dug in its field guns, which were well sited and cleverly camouflaged. When contact had been gained with the advancing Japanese I again visited the front, and to my astonishment I found that the artillery had disappeared.

"When I asked the army commander what had happened to his guns he said that he had withdrawn them to safety.

" 'Then you mean,' I said, 'that they will take no part in the battle?'

" 'Exactly,' he replied.

" 'But then what use are they?'

"He said: 'General, the Fifth Chinese Army is our best army, because it is the only one which has any field guns, and I cannot afford to risk those guns. If I lose them the Fifth Army will no longer be our best.' "

A Japanese patrol marches through a small town in the Philippines.

In the circumstances, upper Burma was no more defensible than lower Burma. The Japanese 15th Army had been reinforced by two more divisions and more aircraft just before the capture of Rangoon, and the British-Chinese line south of Mandalay had not the resources to hold the Japanese advance. In the middle of April the Japanese took Yenangyaung, though the Allies managed to sabotage the oil wells before they arrived. At the end of the month, on the 29th, the Japanese drove the Chinese 5th Army back over the border into China and occupied Lashio. Alexander, with his left flank exposed by the defeat of the Chinese, was forced to evacuate Mandalay, and retreat towards India across the Irrawaddy and Chindwin rivers. When the monsoon began, his little army was safe in the Indian state of Manipur after the longest, and one of the most gruelling, retreats ever carried out by the British Army.

The Japanese capped their victory in Burma by occupying the Andaman Islands, in which Port Blair offered them an excellent anchorage.

The above advances by the Japanese land forces were matched by the successes of Vice-Admiral Chuichi Nagumo's Carrier Fleet. On January 20, planes from Nagumo's carriers bombed Rabaul on New Britain, and then this extremely important strategic point in the South-West Pacific was captured on the 23rd. Possession of this base gave the Japanese the choice of advancing either on New Guinea or the Solomons. On February 29, Japanese carrier-borne aircraft raided Port Darwin, on the north coast of Australia, sinking a dozen merchantmen in the harbour. A few days later, the Carrier Fleet was ordered to move south of Java, with the aim of preventing the evacuation of the island when the Japanese invaded from the north. Between March 3 and 5, repeated attacks were made on the port of Tjilatjap, causing the loss of three destroyers and 17 transports. On March 26, the Carrier Fleet sailed from Kendari, under the command of Vice-Admiral Kondo, to launch a surprise attack against targets on the island of Ceylon.

The Japanese fleet sent on this mission was a powerful one: five aircraft-carriers (with some 300 aircraft), four *Kongo*-class battleships (14-inch guns), two heavy cruisers, one light cruiser, and eight destroyers. As this force attacked Ceylon, another squadron, comprising the light aircraft-carrier *Ryujo*, six cruisers, and eight destroyers, was to carry out a raid in the Bay of Bengal, under the command of Vice-Admiral Ozawa. British reconnaissance aircraft had seen the beginning of this two-pronged attack, and the British War Cabinet became intensely worried lest the Japanese should try to obtain naval and air superiority in the Indian Ocean.

The question had, in fact, been discussed by the Japanese. In order to take maximum advantage of their recent run of brilliant

Two Japanese platoons prepare to advance during the fighting for the oilfields at Yenangyaung in Burma. Behind them are the wrecked oil derricks.

successes, this strategic aim appeared to be both possible and appropriate. Captain Kuroshima, head of the operations section of the Combined Fleet headquarters, supported the idea. In his opinion, it was advisable to make use of the respite gained by the neutralisation of the American forces in the Pacific to crush the British squadron in the Indian Ocean, conquer Ceylon, and advance on the Red Sea and Persian Gulf. The Japanese forces would then advance to meet their Axis partners sweeping down from the Caucasus and east from Suez.

Realising that this possibility was on the way to becoming a probability after the fall of Malaya, Admiral of the Fleet Sir Dudley Pound made every effort to frustrate this dangerous scheme. To this end he essembled in the area of Ceylon the elements of a new fleet, under Admiral Sir James Somerville, the former commander of Force H at Gibraltar. On the day that Kondo and Ozawa sailed from Kendari, the Eastern Fleet, as the new British fleet was called, consisted of three aircraft-carriers (*Indomitable*, *Formidable*, and the aged *Hermes*), five battleships (*Warspite*, which had just returned from repairs in the U.S.A., and the four *Royal Sovereign*-class vessels, with a total of 40 15-inch guns), two heavy cruisers, five

light cruisers (one of them Dutch), 16 destroyers, and seven submarines (two of them Dutch).

On his way out to take up his new command, Somerville wrote to Pound a masterly appreciation of the situation in the Indian Ocean: if the Japanese captured Ceylon "it will be extremely difficult, but not necessarily impossible, to maintain our communications to the Middle East. But if the Japanese capture Ceylon *and* destroy the greater part of the Eastern Fleet, then . . . the situation becomes really desperate."

The British had learnt the lessons of the loss of *Prince of Wales* and *Repulse*, and now had a better appreciation than before of the relative strengths of the forces which might come into contact. Somerville realistically decided that it could not be in the Royal Navy's favour. Admittedly, the British fleet's 40 15-inch guns were superior to Kondo's 32 14-inch weapons, but to use this advantage, the four *Royal Sovereigns* would have to maintain contact with the *Kongos*, which were five knots faster. But more important was the question of defence. The British ships had been built in World War I and had been little modified, resulting in inadequate deck armour and A.A. armament. The Japanese naval aircraft, which were in every respect superior to their British counterparts, would have made short work of them.

Somerville had only about 100 out-of-date bombers and fighters to put up against more than 300 superior Japanese machines, which also had excellent crews. This disparity was clearly shown in an engagement off Colombo on April 5, when a formation of 12 Fairey Swordfish torpedo-bombers was surprised by Japanese Zeros and completely destroyed.

On April 1, Somerville divided his fleet into two parts. The faster and more effective part, Force A, was to go on patrol, using Addu Attol, a new secret base in the Maldive Islands about 600 miles south-west of Ceylon, to refuel. The British fleet avoided exposure either to a fleet action of to air attacks, unable to match the superior striking power of the Japanese carrier force. The British position in the Indian Ocean was now seriously threatened.

Colombo was bombed on April 5, though the raid missed the cruisers *Cornwall* and *Dorsetshire*, which had sailed late on the 4th. On the morning of the 5th, however, they were spotted by Japanese aircraft. An attack by 80 planes swiftly mounted, and under a rain of bombs (about 90 per cent hit their targets) the two heavy cruisers sank. On April 9 *Hermes*, which had been launched in 1919 and was one of the world's oldest aircraft-carriers, was caught by a raid as she was leaving Trincomalee harbour with the Australian destroyer *Vampire*. Both vessels were sunk. At the same time, Ozawa was attacking merchant shipping further to the north, where he sank 23 vessels, dis-

placing a total of 112,312 tons. In the first ten days of the month, Japanese submarines operating in the area sank a further 32,404 tons. To the south again, the British were fortunate in evading Nagumo's aircraft, which were searching south-east of Ceylon, whereas the British fleet was in fact to the west of the island.

On April 7, however, the British Admiralty realised that the Japanese had not been deterred from advancing into the Indian Ocean by the Allied forces there, and authorised Somerville to withdraw to East Africa. Somerville decided to send his slower ships there while he himself, with the faster units, continued in the area. The withdrawal of the British fleet was a further humiliation for British seapower. Fortunately for the Allies, however, the Japanese forces did not exploit their opportunity, having already strayed beyond the limits they had set themselves beforehand.

So the crisis soon passed. On April 12 the Japanese Combined Fleet had returned to Kure to prepare for its next offensive operations. Kondo and Ozawa returned to the Pacific, and major Japanese units never again entered the Indian Ocean.

This marked the end of the first phase of Japan's military expansion in World War II. General Tojo had occupied the "South-East Asia Co-Prosperity Sphere" which had been his major objective since coming to power. And he had obtained it at little cost: five destroyers, eight sub-

marines, and 50,000 tons of merchant shipping at sea; and 10,000 dead and 4,000 wounded on land.

The Japanese advance into the Indian Ocean had presented the Allied command with the question of how to deal with the Vichy French colony of Madagascar, in particular the naval base at Diego-Suarez in the far north of the island. As long as Churchill hoped to persuade Marshal Pétain and Admiral Darlan to support Operation "Gymnast", he turned a deaf ear to General de Gaulle's exhortations to him to occupy Madagascar. But Rommel's success in Cyrenaica postponed any landing in North Africa indefinitely.

Laval's return to power, on the other hand, raised Allied fears that Vichy might agree to hand over Madagascar, which controls the Moçambique Channel, to the Japanese. Churchill decided to wait no longer, and Operation "Ironclad" was launched on May 5, when naval and land forces under Rear-Admiral E. N. Syfret and Major-General R. C. Sturges captured Diego-Suarez. Further landings were made between September 10 and 29, resulting in the surrender of the final Vichy forces on November 6.

In fact the Japanese had no real interest in the Indian Ocean, and the invasion of Madagascar did nothing but prevent a threat that never existed and further exacerbate relations between Vichy and Great Britain.

Japan's conquests early in 1942.

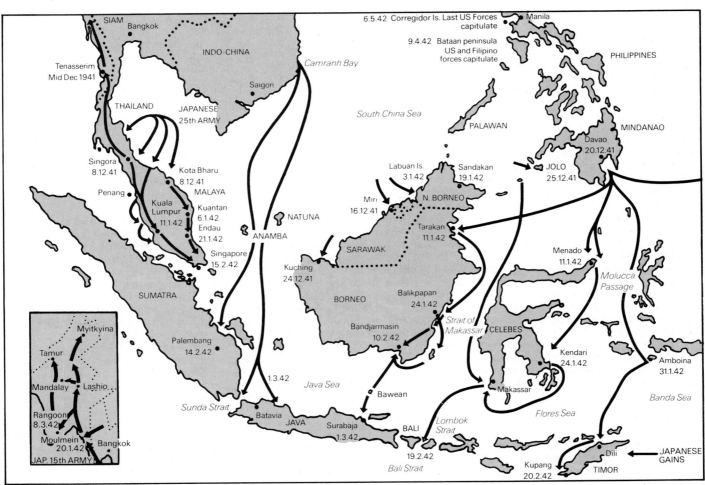

CHAPTER 27

Attack and counterattack in North Africa

We left Wavell and Rommel confronting each other along the fortified Tobruk perimeter, defended by the 9th Australian Division, as well as on the Egyptian-Libyan front. But before describing the battles which took place in this theatre of war between June 15 and December 31, 1941, we shall look at the campaign which brought Italy's East African empire to an end in its sixth year.

On June 10, 1940, Mussolini's empire included the old Italian colonies of Eritrea on the Red Sea, Somaliland on the Indian Ocean, and also the ancient empire of Abyssinia, wrested from Emperor Haile Selassie in spite of the League of Nations and its inoperative sanctions. Forming enclaves within this empire were the colonies of British and French Somaliland. The latter's capital, Djibouti, was linked to Addis Ababa by a narrow gauge railway.

King Victor Emmanuel's authority was vested in a Viceroy combining the functions of civil governor and commander-in-chief of the armed forces. Prince Amedeo, Duke of Aosta, who had held this position since 1938, was an active and able Viceroy, but was surprised and then soon overtaken by events. Mussolini in his memorandum to Hitler on May 30, 1939, had stressed the necessity of strengthening Abyssinia in order to begin operations on a wider scale in 1943.

On June 10, 1940, when Mussolini handed their passports to the British and French Ambassadors, the Viceroy had 290,000 troops under his command, including 90,000 metropolitan Italians. The land forces had no more than 24 notoriously unsatisfactory medium and 39 useless light tanks. In General Pietro Pinna's air force the modern equipment consisted of 34 Fiat C.R.42 fighters, already outclassed by even the R.A.F.'s Gloster Gladiator, let alone the Hurricane. In the Red Sea, Admiral Carlo Balsamo commanded seven destroyers, two torpedo-boats, and eight submarines, but, as has already been pointed out, the last were ill-adapted to operations in tropical climates, and in less than a fortnight, by June 23, 1940, four of them were out of action. From this time onwards, the Italian forces found themselves in a highly critical condition. Artillery shells were in short supply, fuel stocks even more inadequate, and new tyres virtually unobtainable. It was clear that the Duke of Aosta's 7,874 lorries and cars and 307 motorcycles would not be mobile for long. In addition, there were to be serious shortages of flour by the end of November and of olive oil by March 1941.

In Kenya and the Anglo-Egyptian Sudan, thousands of Abyssinian refugees were preparing to return home, armed, to join up with those of their fellow-countrymen, particularly in the Shoa and Amhara provinces, who had never given up the fight. Wavell entrusted the organisation and command of the partisans to the young Major Orde Charles Wingate, an outstanding leader whose taste for action had not been impaired by extensive scholarship in Greek, Sanskrit, Arabic, and Hebrew.

On June 25, 1940, French Somaliland was neutralised according to the terms of the Franco-Italian armistice. Colonel de Larminat, arriving from Syria by way of Alexandria and Cairo, failed to win over the garrison to the Free French cause. The port was thus subjected to the tight blockade imposed by the British fleet on the approaches to Italian East Africa.

In July, the Duke of Aosta captured, in the course of several skirmishes, Kassala, Gallabat, and Kurmuk in the Sudan, and with little difficulty took the Moyale salient in Kenya.

On August 1, Lieutenant-General Guglielmo Nasi, commanding an expeditionary force of five brigades (26 battalions and 21 batteries) began the invasion of British Somaliland. The defending forces were inadequate, and their commander, Major-General A. R. Godwin-Austen, received authority from Cairo to evacuate his troops through Zeila and Berbera. The Italians thus found these ports abandoned on the evening of August 19.

In Rome, Marshal Badoglio intended the Duke of Aosta to contribute to the big offensive being prepared by Graziani against Marsa Matrûh and Alexandria. The Duke's objective was to be Khartoum at the junction of the two Niles, or Port Sudan on the Red Sea. But the Viceroy maintained that these objectives would be impracticable unless he received, at the outset, 100 aircraft, 10,000 tons of fuel, and 10,000 tyres. Further, he reported to the Supreme Commander at the end of August:

"In view of my basic and essential mission—to maintain the political and territorial security of the Empire—I believe that the only possible course is to play a purely passive and defensive rôle, to avoid wasting our energy and to conserve our forces for as long as possible."

He was already preparing a plan, he added, to decentralise his reserves to avoid the situation in the future where, for lack of transport, he would not be able to deploy them to counter Allied initiatives. Eventually, Japan agreed to supply the Italians with 2,500 tons of petrol, 6,000 tyres, 1,000 tons of rice, 500 tons of sugar, and 200 tons of olive oil. But when the merchant ship *Yamayuri Maru* finally arrived at the Somali port of Kismayu, the British had already been in occupation for several days.

These circumstances explain how Wavell was able to regain the initiative at a time of his own choosing. In the Eritrean sector of this theatre, he organised an expeditionary force commanded by Lieutenant-General William Platt. It comprised two divisions: Major-General L. M. Heath's 5th Indian Division, already in the area, and Major-General N. M. Beresford-Peirse's 4th Indian Division, which had left the Western Desert immediately after Sidi Barrani. His forces also included a Free French Senegalese battalion and a regiment of the Foreign Legion. From January 15, 1941 the Italian forces, commanded by General Luigi Frusci, retreated towards Agordat and Barentu, to reform at Keren on February 1. Defensively, they were now in a very strong position and General Platt had to mount a full scale operation against this bitterly defended strongpoint. He also employed strike aircraft, to counter which the Italians had neither fighters nor anti-aircraft guns. However, by March 24 the operation was over and the British forces were able to push forward to Asmara.

In Kenya, Lieutenant-General Sir Alan Cunningham, younger brother of the commander of the Mediterranean Fleet, had been given the command of a force comprising the 11th and 12th African and the 1st South African Divisions. He had held Kismayu since February 14 and on February 19 he broke through Lieutenant-General Pietro Gazzera's line along the Juba. The operation was so successful that six days later his advance guard reached the Somaliland capital, Mogadishu.

From then on, General Cunningham's campaign assumed the character of a motorised raid, combined with an amphibious landing at Berbera on March 16. The victorious army had covered some 950 miles since Gelib; moving through Gabredarre and Jijiga, it broke through the Marda pass (6,200 feet) on March 30, intercepted the Djibouti railway at Diredawa and entered Addis Ababa in triumph on April 5. Losing no time, Cunningham moved north, then northeast, to meet General Platt hastening from Asmara.

Italian rule in Ethiopia had now collapsed. The British and Allied forces, including Wingate's partisans and Kenyan and Sudanese refugees, were now joined by thousands of Abyssinian deserters from the Duke of Aosta's army.

On May 12, Generals Platt and Cunningham met at the foot of the Amba Alagi heights. The Duke of Aosta sought refuge at the summit (over 9,300 feet); but without water or ammunition and subjected to heavy bombardment, he had to surrender on May 16 with 7,000 troops. His captors treated him with every military courtesy. He died in Nairobi on March 2, 1942, and Count Ciano wrote of him in his diary:

"The Duke of Aosta is dead. With him disappears the noble figure of a prince and an Italian, simple in his ways, broad in outlook, humane in spirit. He did not want this war. He was convinced that the Empire could only hold out for a few months, and, besides, he hated the Germans. In this conflict, which drenches the world with blood, he feared a German more than a British victory. When he left for Abyssinia in May, 1940, he had a premonition of his fate. He was determined to face it, but was filled with sadness. I communicated the news to the Duce, who expressed his regret laconically."

In the Galla-Sidamo province, Italian resistance was longer lived. However, more and more hard-pressed, General Gazzera had to seek a truce, on July 4, from the Belgian Major-General Gilliaert, commanding two Congolese regiments. The last Italian to give up the fight was General Nasi in the Gondar area, where he had made literally a last-ditch stand. He had to surrender to vastly superior forces on November 27.

In view of the worsening situation, the commander of the Italian Red Sea flotilla decided, in early March, to send his four remaining submarines to Bordeaux by the Cape route. Avoiding naval patrols in the Bab al Mandab straits, all four arrived at their destination after a voyage of over 16,000 miles. The colonial sloop *Eritrea*

Figurehead of the Allied counterstroke: Emperor Haile Selassie, escorted by British officers, returns to his capital.

and an auxiliary cruiser reached Kobe in Japan via the Sunda Strait without being boarded by the Dutch.

Being of limited range, Rear-Admiral Bonetti's destroyers could not follow this example. Rather than scuttle in the roads off Massawa when the British arrived, they launched a suicide attack on Port Sudan. Discovered by an R.A.F. patrol at dawn on April 3, two of them were accounted for by bombs before reaching their objective, and the three others scuttled themselves in the Red Sea off the Arab coast.

Although the British authorities restored Haile Selassie to his throne in Addis Ababa, they made considerable efforts to protect Italian colonists, established since 1936, against reprisals. During the summer of 1942, many colonists were repatriated under the terms of the agreement reached, with Switzerland acting as intermediary between the British and Italian Governments.

The conquest of Abyssinia allowed President Roosevelt to raise the ban on American shipping in the Red Sea, imposed on June 10, 1940. American merchant ships could now unload at Suez supplies sent from the United States to the British Middle East forces. This success also eliminated any threat to the Upper Nile and brought into full operation the important supply line through Takoradi and Fort Lamy to Khartoum. Prompted by the Governor-General, Félix Eboué, and with what General de Gaulle called "the firm but discreet support" of the Governor of the Belgian Congo, Mr. Ryckmans, French Equatorial Africa and the Cameroons had, in late August 1940, repudiated the Vichy Government and joined the Free French.

Colonel Leclerc was involved in these events and set up his H.Q. at Largeau. Seriously wounded as Captain Philippe de Hauteclocque on the Somme battlefield, he had later escaped to join General de Gaulle, and adopted the pseudonym Leclerc to prevent reprisals against his family in occupied France. The backbone of this famous commander's army was the Senegalese infantry, a highly mobile force which until January 1943 carried out commando-type operations in the Sahara desert, directed against supplies and installations. Leclerc could also count on the experience and enterprise of a first class team of officers, such as his chief-of-staff, Colonel Ingold, Lieutenant-Colonel d'Ornano, Major Dio, and Captains de Guillebon and Massu. Working with the British desert warfare specialist Major P. A. Clayton, he organised his first raid on Murzuk, capital of Fezzan, and its aerodrome on January 11, 1941. Several Italian aircraft were shot up and destroyed, but this success cost the life of Lieutenant-Colonel d'Ornano.

Several days later Major Clayton's car was bombed and he was taken prisoner. Leclerc's reaction to this incident was to lead his motorised column to attack Fort

Et Taj, dominating the Kufrah oasis, first having put out of action the flight control station directing Italian aircraft between Libya and Abyssinia. On March 1 Captain Colonna surrendered with 12 officers and 320 other ranks. When the tricolour was hoisted the victor declared: "We shall not stop until the French flag is flying over Metz and Strasbourg!"

Patriotic and dedicated as he was, Leclerc did not allow his crusading spirit to impair his tactical judgement. A good example was his instruction of July 19, 1941, which Liddell Hart, Rommel, Guderian, and other exponents of mechanised warfare would have fully endorsed. Drawing the lesson from the engagements which took place during the Kufrah raid, he expressed the following view on assault tactics:

"Wherever possible, attack from an unexpected direction and at an unexpected time. The commander should be well to the fore in order to make prompt decisions. Manoeuvre in wide, sweeping, outflanking movements. The battle should be brief, and if not decisive at one point, switched to another."

A final comment is taken from W. B. Kennedy Shaw's most interesting book *Long Range Desert Group*, about British patrols in the Sahara. This writer took part in the Kufrah operation and was with Leclerc at Fort Lamy. He remarks: "While we were waiting at Fort Lamy for transport to Cairo, I saw every day dozens of aircraft on the Takoradi-Khartoum-Cairo route. I then realised the great service our French allies had rendered in securing this vital line of communication."

We have no figures for aircraft movement in this area in 1941. But we know from General Ingold's writings that in 1942 no less than 2,999 British and American aircraft landed at Fort Lamy; while 6,944 Allied aircraft flew over this African re-routing point on their way to the Libyan front or, through Iraq and Iran, to the Soviet Union. Kennedy Shaw's remarks were thus not without justification. The Takoradi-Khartoum air route was a vital artery of British air power in the Western Desert theatre.

Until Pearl Harbor, developments in the North African campaign depended on the course of the naval/air war in the Mediterranean. This was affected to a great extent by the defensive and offensive capabilities of Malta, which relied on supplies sent from England and Egypt. It was a case of "triphibious" warfare, as Winston Churchill called it. The Italian Navy, whose task was to keep open the sealanes to the forces fighting in Libya and Egypt, was faced, from mid-July 1941, with an increasingly difficult situation. Already at a disadvantage as it lacked any naval airpower worthy of the name, its shortage of oil fuel was now assuming tragic proportions. It had entered the war with reserves of 1,880,000 tons, 600,000 of which had been consumed in the first six months of operations. Monthly consumption was reduced to 75,000 tons. But when

Wrecked shipping in Benghazi, the key Axis supply-port in western Cyrenaica. It was bombarded by three British destroyers and a cruiser on May 7-8, 1941.

it became clear that supplies from Germany would not exceed 50,000 tons a month, this meant, recorded *Supermarina*, that it would be impossible "to maintain forces in a state that was already inadequate for waging war".

But even these supplies could not be relied on, for when the yearly figures were established it was shown that supplies from Germany amounted to barely 254,000 tons, instead of the 600,000 tons expected. One can understand why, just before El Alamein, the Chief-of-Staff of the Italian *Comando Supremo*, Marshal Cavallero, wrote in his diary on October 23, 1942: "I have two major preoccupations–oil and Malta."

Thus it is clear that in this and many other respects Operation "Barbarossa" damaged the Axis potential in the Mediterranean. But as we have seen, Hitler did not agree that there was danger in war on two fronts. According to his directive of December 18, 1940, a 120-day Blitzkrieg would be sufficient to lay the Soviet colossus in ruins and to ensure that the bulk of the production of the Maykop, Grozny, and Baku oil wells would be supplying the needs of Nazi Germany and Fascist Italy. Moscow would be captured in 1942, and then the "tropical" Panzers, already being prepared, could be unleashed on Basra, Mosul, Suez, Alexandria, and Gibraltar, with the Luftwaffe concentrating on Malta.

The arrival in Africa of the 15th Panzer Division in the latter part of April caused alarm in G.H.Q. Cairo and in the British War Cabinet. General Wavell expected a strong force of German infantry to move up the line, and on April 20 he signalled to the C.I.G.S., Sir John Dill:

"I have just received disquieting intelligence. I was expecting another German colonial division, which disembarked at

Tripoli early this month, to appear in the fighting line about the end of the month. Certain units have already been identified. I have just been informed that latest evidence indicates this is not a colonial but an *armoured* division. If so, the situation is indeed serious, since an armoured division contains over 400 tanks, of which 138 are medium. If the enemy can arrange supply it will take a lot of stopping."

It is now known that Wavell overestimated considerably the strength of the Panzer division in the spring of 1941. Instead of the three or four tank battalions at the disposal of the large armoured units in action in the Balkans at this time, the 15th Panzer Division had only two, which comprised 168 tanks and 30 reconnaissance vehicles. It must be recognised, however, that this distinguished soldier was basing his assessment on reports not only from the British Intelligence service but also from its French, Belgian, and Swiss counterparts. These sources gave the Panzer strength as 488, including 122 heavy tanks.

In any case, once he had "digested" the information, Wavell informed Dill that he attached the highest priority to immediate reinforcement of his armoured strength. He had in reserve sufficient personnel to man six armoured regiments, and was insistent that the tanks he needed should be delivered before the 15th Panzer Division was in position and ready for action. Churchill overruled the objections of the C.I.G.S., who was reluctant to weaken the home front while there was still a possibility of a German invasion, excluded the Cape route in view of the urgency of the problem, and insisted that the First Lord of the Admiralty order delivery by the Mediterranean route. At the same time, the battleship *Queen Elizabeth* and the cruisers *Fiji* and *Naiad* were transferred from home waters to Alexandria. Two hundred and ninety-five tanks and 50 Hurricane fighters were loaded aboard five fast 15-knot merchant ships.

This convoy was escorted by Force H between Gibraltar and Cape Bon. During the night of May 7–8 one merchant ship struck a mine in the dangerous Sicilian Narrows, but the next day, 55 miles south of Malta, the convoy was taken over by Admiral Cunningham who, while he was about it, shelled Benghazi and sent three tankers and four supply ships to Malta. A few days later, the four remaining ships unloaded at Alexandria 43 Hurricanes and 238 tanks–135 Matildas, 82 cruisers, and 21 Mark VI's, small 5½-ton machines of relatively little value in battle. Apparently, the transfer of X *Fliegerkorps* from Sicily to Rommel in Africa had contributed considerably to the success of this daring operation–"Tiger" as it was named by Churchill.

The War Cabinet had learned from intercepts of "Enigma" signals that Rommel had various weaknesses. Wavell was therefore urged to attack with minimum delay, and to relieve the tired garrison of Tobruk. He had under his command XIII Corps, under Lieutenant-General Sir Noel Beresford-Peirse, including the 4th Indian Division (Major-General F. W. Messervy), the 7th Armoured Division (Major-General Sir Michael O'Moore Creagh), and the 22nd Guards Brigade (Brigadier J. Marriot).

However, recent engagements at Halfaya Pass had made him aware of a number of "black spots". In a message to the C.I.G.S. on May 28 he said:

"Our armoured cars are too lightly armoured to resist the fire of enemy fighter aircraft, and, having no gun, are powerless against the German eight-wheeled armoured cars, which have guns and are faster. This makes reconnaissance difficult. Our Infantry tanks are really too slow for a battle in desert, and have been suffering considerable casualties from the fire of the powerful enemy anti-tank guns. Our cruisers have little advantage in power or speed over German medium tanks. Technical breakdowns are still too numerous. We shall not be able to accept battle with perfect confidence in spite of numerical inferiority, as we could against Italians. Above factors may limit our success. They also make it imperative that adequate flow of armoured reinforcements and reserves should be maintained."

Did General Wavell exaggerate the weakness of his armoured forces? It is unlikely, since Rommel's account completely supports Wavell. Discussing his successful defensive action of June 15–17, 1941, Rommel wrote:

"But [Wavell] was put at a great disadvantage by the slow speed of his heavy Infantry tanks, which prevented him from reacting quickly enough to the moves of our faster vehicles. Hence the slow speed of the bulk of his armour was his soft spot, which we could seek to exploit tactically."

He also reveals that the Matilda tanks, which were supposed to sweep a path for the infantry through enemy defences, had only anti-tank armour-piercing shells. Against troops that were widely spread and well dug in one might just as well have used the iron cannon-ball of the Napoleonic wars. Finally, the *Afrika Korps'* commander used 8·8-cm anti-aircraft guns as anti-tank weapons. This 21-pounder gun was highly accurate, firing 15 to 20 rounds a minute at a velocity of over 2,600 feet per second. It thus outclassed all British armour, which could be knocked out even before the Germans were within range of their 40-mm guns. After the battle the British said they had been taken by surprise, but it was really nothing new. Colonel de Gaulle had been through the experience at the Abbeville bridgehead on May 30, 1940.

In these circumstances it was not surprising that the British offensive, Operation "Battleaxe", was a failure. Wavell had not even had the advantage of surprise. The plan was to take the Halfaya position in an encircling movement, with the 7th Armoured Division attacking the rear and the 4th Indian Division making the frontal assault. After an initial success by the 7th Armoured Division, which took Capuzzo, the whole operation went wrong.

For one thing, General Beresford-Peirse's command was apparently too remote and inflexible. Also, at Halfaya Pass, the battalion of the 15th Panzer holding the position put up a remarkable fight although almost completely surrounded. Its commander, Captain Wilhelm Bach, formerly a priest in Baden and conscripted in 1939, aided by Major Pardi of the Italian artillery, offered a determined and courageous resistance. Their gallantry gave Rommel the time to bring the whole of his forces to bear. By June 16 he had stabilised the situation, bringing the British to a halt with considerable casualties. But he was not the man to be satisfied with a merely defensive success. Assembling as much of his *Afrika Korps* as possible he struck south, reaching Sidi Omar, then east, hoping to surround and wipe out XIII

Corps. The British managed to withdraw, however, before their last lines of communication were cut, and on June 17 all was quiet again on the Halfaya escarpment.

Of the 25,000 men in the engagement, British casualties were 122 killed, 588 wounded, and 259 missing, most of whom were taken prisoner. Wavell's fears on May 28 were justified if one considers the losses in his armoured units. Of the 180 tanks which had set off at dawn on June 15, about 100 were lost. As for Rommel, he recorded the loss of 12 tanks totally destroyed and 675 men, including 338 dead or missing. His success was timely as he had many critics in O.K.H. and especially since on June 22 O.K.W. was to assume complete control over this theatre of operations.

The defeat of XIII Corps at Halfaya led to the removal of its commander. In London, Churchill decided that the G.H.Q. Cairo needed new inspiration and strength and so replaced Wavell by General Sir Claude Auchinleck, formerly Commander-in-Chief, India. Was Wavell really "exhausted", as Churchill claimed? He certainly had more responsibilities than he would have liked, in view of the lack of resources at his disposal. But nevertheless his successor, who took over on July 5, later told the British historian Corelli Barnett: "Wavell showed no signs of tiredness at all. He was always the same. I think he was first class; in spite of his silences, he made a tremendous impact on his troops. I have a very great admiration for him . . . but he was given impossible tasks."

Perhaps it should be noted that Auchinleck, after his own misfortune in 1942, was not enamoured of Churchill. And Sir Alan Brooke, C.-in-C., Home Forces, wrote in his diary on June 17, 1941 that he entirely disapproved of Churchill's strategy:

"The P.M. began with a survey of the world situation which was interesting. To my horror he informed us that the present Libyan operation is intended to be a large-scale operation! How can we undertake offensive operations on two fronts in the Middle East when we have not got sufficient for one? From the moment we decided to go into Syria we should have put all our strength in the front to complete the operation with the least possible delay. If the operation is not pressed through quickly, it may well lead to further complications."

In fact, Wavell's thinking corresponded exactly with Brooke's concerning orders to move troops to various foreign theatres (Balkans, Crete, Iraq, and Syria), with complete disregard for the principle of concentration of force, as applied in the main areas of Tobruk and Halfaya. Whereas Brooke could only write in his diary at his London H.Q. in St. Paul's School, Wavell would have been failing in his duty as commanding officer if he had not put before Churchill all the dangers involved in the latter's strategy.

This is exactly what he did, even offering to resign, in the hope of calling off the operation intended to win Syria from the Vichy régime. At the same time he was ordered to speed up preparations for "Battleaxe", of which the government expected no less than the rapid destruction of the *Afrika Korps*. As we know, Wavell finally gave in to Churchill and launched the operation, although disapproving of it in principle. His professional military judgement was, however, entirely vindicated.

It is worth noting that it took over a month for Lieutenant-General Maitland Wilson to overcome the resistance of General Henri Dentz who, in any case, had no intention of fighting to the last man. But the two divisions employed in this operation could profitably have been employed in the Western Desert. What would have happened if they had been in position at Sidi Omar to face Rommel? It is, of course, a matter of conjecture, but Rommel's flanking tactics on June 16 and 17 might have ended in failure.

Air Chief-Marshal Longmore, commanding the British air forces in the Middle East, was recalled to London and was then given the post of Inspector-General of the R.A.F. His place was taken by Air-Marshal Sir Arthur Tedder, later chosen by Eisenhower to be his Deputy C.-in-C. just before the Normandy landings. Also, the War Cabinet appointed Oliver Lyttelton, formerly President of the Board of Trade, as resident Minister of State in the Middle East. More fortunate than his predecessor, General Auchinleck, relieved of a host of political and administrative duties, was to be able to devote himself entirely to military matters in his own province.

Before examining Auchinleck's operations, we should look briefly at events in Iraq and Syria.

At the end of March 1941, the Emir Abdul Illah, Regent of Iraq and a strong supporter of friendship with Britain, had to leave his capital after a rebellion by his premier, Rashid Ali, and a mutiny in the army. On May 2 his partisans attacked Habbānīyah, the large air base on the right bank of the Euphrates some 30 miles from Baghdad. Were the rebels going to cut the pipeline taking oil from the Mosul fields to Haifa? Were they going to occupy Basra, within reach of the Kuwait oil wells and the Abadan refinery? It was a critical time for the British, but the events seemed to have taken both Hitler and Mussolini by surprise. Not until May 23 did the Führer sign his Directive Number 30, ordering the organisation and despatch to Baghdad of a military mission commanded by General Hellmuth Felmy. Its task was to prepare for action a unit each of Messerschmitt Bf 109 fighters and of Heinkel He 111 bombers. Mussolini's contribution was a promise to send a few fighters to Iraq.

But by this time Churchill had already seized the initiative. He was aware of

Wavell's doubts in Cairo, but in India the Viceroy, Lord Linlithgow, and General Auchinleck diverted to Basra an Indian division previously intended for Malaya. On May 19 a motorised division from Palestine arrived at Habbānīyah, where the rebel siege had been abandoned. On the rebels' surrender, a cease-fire was declared on May 30, and Rashid Ali left for Germany, by way of Iraq and Turkey.

Vichy had allowed German aircraft bound for Iraq to refuel at Beirūt, Damascus, and Aleppo. It was expected that the Germans, having taken Crete, would begin the invasion of Cyprus, and so it was not surprising that Churchill decided to force a solution to the Syrian problem. General de Gaulle supported the proposed operation and provided General Legentilhomme's brigade, comprising six infantry battalions, one field battery, and a light tank company.

For the reasons already mentioned, Wavell was much less forthcoming. Having finally given in to Churchill he ordered into Syria an expeditionary force, commanded by General Maitland Wilson and composed of the 7th Australian Division, the 1st Cavalry Division, the 5th Indian Brigade Group, and the Legentilhomme brigade. Since General Henri Dentz, Vichy commander in Syria, had two divisions, the British force could not be considered a strong one.

Mopping up in Syria: Australian troops jump from their Bren-gun carrier among the ruins of Palmyra.

In these circumstances, it was not surprising that the operation progressed slowly. It was launched at dawn on June 8, backed by a barrage of radio and other propaganda. Engagements took place at Sidon, El Quneitra, on the Damascus road, and around the Palmyra Oasis. The Vichy French troops proved a determined foe. To prevail, Wavell had to draw on some of his last reserves, two brigades of the British 6th Division and the motorised group he had sent to help the defenders of the Habbaniyah base. With these reinforcements, the Australians and Free French occupied the Syrian capital on June 21.

In his memoirs, General de Gaulle recalls this unhappy campaign:

"The memories evoked in me by the campaign we have been obliged to open are cruel ones. I can still see myself coming and going between Jerusalem, where I had fixed my head-quarters, and our brave troops as they advanced towards Damascus, or else going to visit the wounded in the Franco-British ambulance unit of Mrs. Spears and Dr. Fruchaut. And I heard, gradually, how many of our men, and of the best, were left on the field, – how, for instance, General Legentilhomme had been severely wounded, how Colonel Génin and Lieutenant-Commander Détroyat had been killed, how Majors de Chevigné, de Boissoudy, and de Villontreys had been badly hit, – and how, on the other side, many good officers and men were falling under our fire, – how, on the Litani on June 9th and 10th, before Kiswe on the 12th, and round

Quneitra and Izra' on the 15th and 16th, violent fighting had mingled French dead from both camps and those of their British Allies. I felt, towards those who were opposing us on a point of honour, mixed emotions of esteem and commiseration. At a time when the enemy held Paris under his boot. was attacking in Africa, and was infiltrating into the Levant, this courage shown and the losses borne in the fratricidal struggle imposed by Hitler upon leaders who had fallen under his yoke made on me an impression of horrible waste."

On July 10 Dentz, who had lost 6,500 men, most of his aircraft, the destroyer *Chevalier Paul* and the submarine *Souffleur*, sent General de Verdillac to Maitland Wilson, who offered the French representative very honourable terms. The surrender agreement was signed at Acre on July 14, but not without vigorous protest from General de Gaulle, who considered that he had been cheated of his share of the victory. An addition to the agreement, on July 24, gave him the right to the French forces' equipment in the Levant and facilities for recruiting among the 30,000 men who had surrendered. One hundred and twenty-seven officers and 6,000 men were thus induced to join de Gaulle's Free French forces. Writing of this division among the beaten French, de Gaulle said:

"But 25,000 officers, N.C.O.s and men of the French Army and Air Force were finally torn away from us, whereas the great majority would without any doubt have decided to join us if we had had the time to enlighten them. For those Frenchmen who were returning to France with the permission of the enemy, so giving up the possibility of returning there as fighters, were, I knew, submerged in doubt and sadness. As for me, it was with my heart wrung that I gazed at the Vichy transports lying in the harbour and saw them, once loaded, disappear out to sea, taking with them one of the chances of our country."

General de Gaulle had appointed General Catroux his "Delegate-General and Plenipotentiary in the Levant", giving him instructions to negotiate, with the Syrian and Lebanese authorities, a new statute granting the two countries independence and sovereignty but ensuring that they remained allies of France. But propaganda, intrigues and money were already being employed by, among others, Glubb "Pasha" at Palmyra, Commodore Bass in the Jebel ed Drūz, and the chief British liaison officer, General Spears, at Damascus and Beirūt to supplant Vichy and Free France alike. This caused new quarrels between Oliver Lyttelton and General de Gaulle. But there was nothing the French could do to prevent the appointment, in January 1942, of General Spears as Minister Plenipotentiary in Syria and the Lebanon. Spears was a former friend of de Gaulle and there is little doubt that what he had to do was not his own personal responsi-

bility but attributable to the Prime Minister and Anthony Eden. In 1945 it was thought in London that the celebrated Colonel T. E. Lawrence's dream of undivided British influence throughout the Arab world was about to become a reality. It did not take long for events to prove that there was no substance in this dream.

Relations between the new C.-in-C. Middle East and Churchill differed very little from those in Wavell's time. On his arrival in Cairo on July 1, Auchinleck received a letter from Churchill apparently giving him complete freedom of action in his own sphere of responsibility. But this was no more than a façade; Churchill neither expected the C.-in-C. in Cairo to have any other criteria with which to judge the situation than those applied in Downing Street, nor did he envisage any other plans than his own.

And no sooner had Auchinleck demanded three months of preparations and three or four extra divisions (two or three of them armoured), than these two equally determined men found themselves in violent disagreement. At the end of July Auchinleck was summoned to London to explain his views. His arguments were sound enough to win over the General Staff and the War Cabinet, but, as Churchill's memoirs show, he did not alter the Prime Minister's basic convictions. Nevertheless, Churchill had to bow to the majority and accept that Operation "Crusader", aimed at expelling Rommel from Cyrenaica, should be postponed until the period between September 15 and November 1.

Before zero hour on the desert front, the British and Australian Governments were involved in an incident with unfortunate consequences. Defeated in Parliament, Mr. Menzies' Liberal Government gave way to a Labour administration headed first by Mr. Fadden, then by Mr. Curtin. Australian opinion had become extremely sensitive following all kinds of alarmist rumours about Tobruk. Anxious to appease public feeling, the new cabinet demanded the immediate relief of the Australians in the garrison.

Whatever he said or did, the Prime Minister had to fall in with this demand, which was put forward in a most truculent manner, for however loyal the Dominions were to the United Kingdom, their relationship was between equals and decisions had to be negotiated, not imposed by Westminster.

Therefore, using periods of the new moon in September and October, a shuttle operation was organised, bringing into Tobruk General S. Kopanski's Polish 1st Carpathian Brigade and the British 70th Division, commanded by Major-General R. M. Scobie, and evacuating to Alexandria the 9th Australian Division and the 18th Australian Infantry Brigade Group. In spite of the loss of the fast minelayer *Latona,* the operation was completely successful.

Owing to the late arrival in Egypt of the 22nd Armoured Brigade, Auchin-

leck found that he was obliged to postpone his attack from November 1 to November 18. Churchill has been criticised for his irritation at the delay, but seen in the context of the overall situation, there was some rational justification on his side. He wanted Rommel attacked, beaten, and eliminated in Cyrenaica before a likely German victory in Russia permitted Hitler to drive his Panzers across the Caucasus towards the Persian Gulf and the Red Sea. This is precisely what the Wehrmacht was planning to do.

The new delay to "Crusader" had no adverse effect on the progress of the operations, thanks to the pressure exerted on Axis communications in the Mediterranean by the sea and naval air forces of Admirals Cunningham and Somerville. No harm can be done to these remarkable commanders' reputations by pointing out two circumstances which made their task easier. In the first place, after the Balkans campaign X *Fliegerkorps* did not return to its bases in Sicily but served with Rommel. In the second place, the Italian fleet was not permitted to operate beyond coastal waters. In these conditions, the three convoys sent to Malta during 1941 lost only one merchant ship out of the 40 which left Gibraltar. Force H came well out of these dangerous operations, losing only the cruiser *Southampton* and the destroyer *Fearless,* though the battleship *Nelson* was seriously damaged on the "Halberd" convoy in a torpedo attack by an audacious Italian pilot.

In the same period the aircraft-carrier *Ark Royal,* sometimes accompanied by the *Victorious,* despatched to Malta nearly 300 fighters, most of which reached their destination. Also, during the summer, the island's airfields were reoccupied by a small attacking force of Blenheim and Wellington bombers. Finally, on October 21, Captain W. G. Agnew's Force K – the light cruisers *Aurora* and *Penelope,* from Scapa Flow – anchored in the Grand Harbour. The situation around Malta now seemed sufficiently under control for the Admiralty to send the cruisers *Ajax* and *Neptune* to join them a few weeks later.

This succession of reinforcements explains why, from August onwards, supplies to the Axis forces in Libya became more and more unreliable. During September, 94,000 tons of equipment and fuel were loaded in Italy, but 26,000 tons of it went to the bottom. Submarines operating from Malta took the lion's share of this destruction. For example, on September 18 Commander Wanklyn in *Upholder* sank with five torpedoes the two 19,500 ton ships *Oceania* and *Neptunia.* Also taking part in this sea offensive were the Alexandria and Gibraltar flotillas, including two Dutch vessels.

The Italian defence was at a disadvantage in this fighting since their vessels had no asdic of the type used by British escorts. A few dozen sets were obtained from Germany during the

summer of 1941, but it took time for them to be installed and crews trained to use them, time which was not wasted by their opponents. On the other hand, minefields in waters around Malta and Tripoli accounted for five of the eight British submarines lost in the Mediterranean in 1941.

In October, losses of supplies between Italian ports and Tripolitania amounted to one fifth of the cargoes loaded, and of 12,000 tons of fuel bound for the Axis forces, 2,500 tons disappeared into the sea. November was even worse, and for a while it was thought that Rommel would be brought to a standstill. In fact, out of a total of 79,208 tons of supplies loaded in Italy, he lost 62 per cent (49,365 tons). Every episode in the first battle of the convoys cannot be described here, but the disaster of November 9 does deserve mention in some detail.

The convoy "*Duisburg*", composed of six merchant ships and a tanker, left from Messina on the afternoon of November 8. It was closely escorted by six destroyers, backed up by the 3rd Cruiser Squadron commanded by Vice-Admiral Brivonesi (*Trento, Trieste,* and four destroyers). At 1645 the convoy was sighted and reported to Malta by a Maryland on patrol. At nightfall Captain Agnew set out with his cruisers and the destroyers *Lance* and *Lively.* Other aircraft, in constant radar contact with the enemy, guided him to the convoy.

Towards 0100, about 155 miles east of Syracuse, the convoy appeared on the radar screens of the British ships, themselves still unseen by the Italians. Less than ten minutes later it was all over, after a barrage of shellfire and torpedoes. The seven merchant ships were sinking, and the destroyer *Fulmine* was going down with them, shattered by a salvo from the *Aurora.* The attack had been so rapid that the 3rd Cruiser Squadron, in any case badly equipped for battle at night, had not time to intervene. On top of all this, near dawn, the destroyer *Libeccio* was sunk by the tireless *Upholder.*

With losses mounting, *Supermarina* tried to ensure delivery of the fuel vital to the Libyan operations by using very fast light cruisers. As a result of this decision, there was another disaster during the night of December 13. Loaded with drums of oil, the cruisers *Alberico da Barbiano* and *Alberto di Guissano* had sailed for Tripoli from Palermo. They were sighted by Malta-based aircraft which transmitted the information to Commander G. H. Stokes, leading four destroyers, including the Dutch vessel *Isaac Sweers,* from Gibraltar to Alexandria. Stokes surprised the two Italian ships off Cape Bon. Their cargo caught fire immediately and most of their crews, including Admiral Toscano, perished. And as if this were not enough, during the same night two brand new merchant ships, *Filzi* and *Del Greco,* were sunk.

In short, post-war statistics show that in the second half of 1941 Italy lost no

less than 189 merchant vessels totalling 500,000 tons. On June 10, 1940, taking into account 500,000 tons of Italian shipping frozen in American ports, the Italian merchant fleet had totalled 3,300,000 tons. As a result of these losses, the situation for the Italians by the middle of December was, to say the least, very serious.

When one considers these events, so disastrous for the Axis, the question arises whether they were due to treason committed by a member of *Supermarina* in a key position. This question caused violent arguments in Italy, and ended in the courts. In his book *The Foxes of the Desert*, Paul Carell supports this view, but such serious naval historians as Bragadin and Admiral Bernotti refute it. Methodical modern techniques of enquiry, using evidence from continuous monitoring of enemy radio communications, tend to leave one sceptical of the theory. Moreover, there were one or more British submarines permanently on the watch outside every port where convoys were formed. Finally, the two incidents already described are proof of the excellent work done by reconnaissance aircraft, operating from Malta with complete impunity.

Italian ships bound for Tripoli had been used to hugging the Tunisian coast in order to avoid the perils waiting for them in the open sea. Thus they were spotted by French observers, who had already carefully recorded the wreckage of Axis units washed ashore at Kerkenna after the battle on April 15 and had also been the first to report the movement of the 15th Panzer Division to Africa. General de Gaulle's men were no longer the only ones passing information to the British. General Weygand, in his memoirs, reveals that Major Navarre, his head of Intelligence, had organised a secret Intelligence system to transmit as quickly as possible the information about Axis convoy movements to Tripolitania obtained on the Tunisian coast by air and naval observers. He was to continue this activity although General Weygand was relieved

of his post as the government's Delegate-General in Africa and replaced by General Juin on November 18, 1941.

Marshal Cavallero, Chief-of-Staff at *Comando Supremo*, had not waited until disaster was inevitable before grasping the importance of the port of Bizerta and Tunisian lines of communication. At a meeting at Brenner on June 2 he made his views known to Field-Marshal Keitel. His German colleague was very cool on this question, considering that Cavallero's inclination for strong action would result in the secession of the French Empire, whereas by bargaining with prisoners-of-war and by negotiation, Vichy should be amenable to further concessions. This was also Hitler's view.

Count Ciano met Admiral Darlan at Turin on December 9 and gave no support to the *Comando Supremo*. When Darlan brought up the question of the Tunisian ports the Duce's son-in-law cut him short. He wrote: "I interrupted him to say that I had no intention of talking about this subject and had no instructions to do so." There is no satisfactory explanation for Ciano's negative attitude, so clearly prejudicial to the campaign then being fought.

Since his victory at Sollum-Halfaya, Rommel had nurtured plans to capture Tobruk. The successes of Force K and Malta-based R.A.F. operations, however, forced him to postpone the attack from week to week. By November 4 everything was at last ready, and he revealed his plans to Marshal Cavallero in Rome.

To take advantage of the full moon, the operation would begin between November 20 and December 4. The evening before the chosen day, the "Brescia" Division would make a strong diversionary attack on the south-west front, thus drawing the defence's reinforcements. The following dawn Rommel would attack the fortress from the south-east with General Cruewell's *Afrika Korps* and General Navarrini's Italian XXI Corps. He calculated that it would be all over in 48 hours.

After the meeting, Cavallero wrote: "I

A Bf 110 fighter lands in a cloud of sand on an Italian-built air-field in North Africa (above). A motorcycle combination, spearhead of the 21st Panzer Division (opposite).

asked Rommel if he thought the enemy might be able to launch a full-scale attack. He thought not because the enemy would not want to expose their lines of communication to easier interception by the German and Italian divisions. He expected defensive action by relatively few ground forces but with air support."

Was Rommel unaware of General Auchinleck's offensive preparations or did he conceal them from the Italian Chief-of-Staff in case he should be ordered to remain on the defensive? In 1949 this was still an open question, and in the Italian official account we read:

"There was a striking difference in the information supplied by the German and Italian Intelligence services. For reasons that were not very clear, the Germans insisted that the British had no intention of taking the offensive, and considered their Italian colleagues to be 'excessively nervous Latins'." Again, on November 11, Major von Mellenthin, chief of Rommel's Intelligence, discussing the matter with an Italian liaison officer, said: "Major Revetria (chief of Italian Intelligence) is too jumpy. Tell him to calm down, because the British are not going to attack."

In 1955, however, Mellenthin, in his war memoirs, gave the key to the enigma, writing quite candidly: "To allay the fears of the Italians and prevent interference with his plans, Rommel instructed his staff to adopt a confident tone in all discussions with Italian officers, and in November—as the date of our attack drew nearer—I deliberately minimised the possibilities of a British offensive whenever I spoke to our allies."

Sir Claude Auchinleck had organised the troops taking part in "Crusader" into the 8th Army, commanded by Lieutenant-General Sir Alan Cunningham, who had just achieved fame for his lightning defeat of the Italians in Abyssinia. Auchinleck had thus some justification

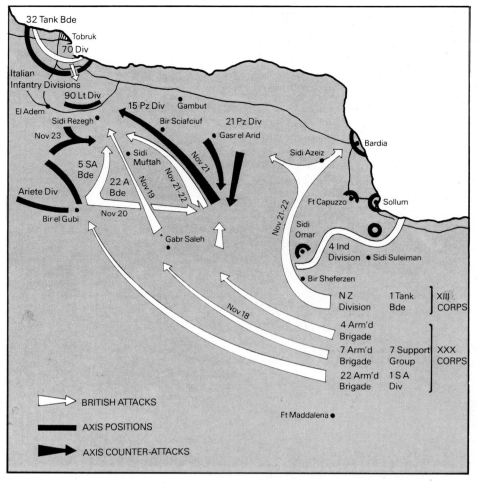

The opening of Operation Crusader (above). An 8.8-cm gun ready for action in the Western Desert (below).

for giving him precedence over his colleague Sir Henry Maitland Wilson, in spite of Churchill's disagreement. He had no idea that Cunningham would not be equal to the strain involved in directing a battle between armoured forces. On the day of the battle the 8th Army was deployed as follows:

Tobruk:

70th Division (Major-General R. M. Scobie, who also commanded the whole garrison); Polish 1st Carpathian Infantry Brigade Group (Major-General S. Kopanski); and 32nd Army Tank Brigade (Brigadier A. C. Willison);

Right flank:

XIII Corps (Lieutenant-General A. R. Godwin-Austen), made up of:

1. New Zealand Division (Major-General B. C. Freyberg);

2. 4th Indian Division (Major-General F. W. Messervy); and

3. 1st Army Tank Brigade (Brigadier H. R. B. Watkins);

Left flank:

XXX Corps (Lieutenant-General C. W. M. Norrie), made up of:

1. 7th Armoured Division (Major-General W. H. E. Gott);

2. 4th Armoured Brigade Group (Brigadier A. H. Gatehouse);

3. 1st South African Division (Major-General G. L. Brink); and

4. 22nd Guards Brigade (Brigadier J. C. O. Marriott).

This was a completely motorised and partially armoured force, spearheaded by the 7th Armoured Division, which had 469 tanks; this total included 210 Crusaders and 165 American M3 Stuarts.

The British had by no means given up using tanks as infantry support weapons, so the Tobruk garrison and XIII Corps each included an independent brigade equipped with either cruiser or Matilda tanks. In all, 8th Army had 713 gun-armed tanks and could count on over 200 more in reserve to replace any losses.

In the air, Air Vice-Marshal H. Coningham provided the 8th Army with support from the Western Desert Air Force's 16 fighter, eight bomber, and three reconnaissance squadrons. Finally there was Sir Andrew Cunningham, whose fleet's guns were there to give direct support to his brother's operations. This explains the British soldier's nickname for the operation—"Cunningham, Cunningham, and Coningham".

The Axis deployment might give the impression that Rommel's armour was under the command of General Ettore Bastico and that the "Italian Supreme Commander in North Africa" could control General Gambara's XX Corps. But the impetuous Panzergruppe Afrika commander had no intention whatsoever of respecting this chain of command, and went over Bastico's head to appeal directly to the Comando Supremo, or even to Hitler, when he did not agree with Cavallero's decisions. The deployment was as follows, under Bastico's command:

1. Italian XX Mobile Corps (General Gambara), made up of:
   a. "Ariete" Armoured Division (General Balotta) and
   b. "Trieste" Motorised Division (General Piazzoni); and

2. Panzergruppe Afrika (Rommel), made up of:
   i Afrika Korps (Lieutenant-General Ludwig Cruewell), composed of:
      a. 15th Panzer Division (Major-General Walther Neumann-Silkow);
      b. 21st Panzer Division (Major-General Johann von Ravenstein);
      c. Afrika Division (Major-General Sommermann); and
      d. "Savona" Division (General de Giorgis); and
   ii Italian XXI Corps (General Enea Navarrini), composed of:
      a. "Brescia" Division (General Zambon);

A dead German crewman lies before his captured Pzkw IV.

b. "Trento" Division (General de Stefanis);

c. "Bologna" Division (General Gloria); and

d. "Pavia' Division (General Franceschini).

Panzergruppe Afrika was formed on August 15 and this enabled Rommel to hand over command of the *Afrika Korps* to General Cruewell. The 5th Light Division was renamed 21st Panzer Division, but retained its original composition. The *Afrika* Division comprised only two infantry battalions, recruited from former German volunteers in the French Foreign Legion, to whom Hitler was offering a chance to "make good". At the beginning of December it was renamed the 90th Light Division.

While the Italian XXI Corps was to overrun Tobruk, the *Afrika Korps* – some German units and the whole "Savona" Division – would make contact with the British on the Sidi Omar – Capuzzo – Halfaya – Sollum front. Ready for any eventuality, the 15th and 21st Panzer Divisions were stationed in the Gambut area and further south. Finally, Gambara had placed the "Ariete" Armoured Division around the Bir el Gubi watering place and the "Trieste" Motorised Division around Bir Hakeim.

The Axis forces thus amounted to ten divisions, against the 8th Army's six divisions. But it should not be overlooked that the large Italian units were considerably under-strength and that Rommel's supplies of food and fuel were more and more uncertain. As for the armoured forces, General Cunningham had 713 gun-armed tanks, the Italians 146, and the Germans 174.

These are the approximate figures of the forces involved. But when one gets down to brass tacks the British superiority was reduced by certain technical factors. The Matilda had well-known defects and the Crusaders and other cruisers were subject to frequent mechanical faults. In addition the Stuart or M3, driven by an aero engine requiring a high octane fuel, displayed an alarming tendency to catch fire.

But this is not all. Whereas none of the British tanks had weapons more powerful than 40-mm (37-mm for the American M3), half of the *Afrika Korps'* 139 Pzkw III's were fitted with a 5-cm rather than 3.7-cm gun, and their 35 Pzkw IV's already had a 7.5-cm. Ballistically, the heavier the projectile the more consistent its speed, giving it a longer range and a greater armour-piercing potential. With their $4\frac{1}{2}$-pounder (5-cm) and 15-pounder (7.5-cm) shells, the Germans had an important advantage over their opponents' 40-mm shells, weighing only two pounds.

On the tactical level, it appears that the Germans had struck a better balance between tanks, infantry, and artillery than the 8th Army, and that their radio communications were more reliable. One should also remember Rommel's formidable defensive weapon – the 8·8-cm anti-aircraft gun. Used in an anti-tank role, it soon became a decisive factor on the battlefields of the Western Desert. The "88" as it was called by the British was notorious, and assumed the status of an all-purpose wonder weapon, which could destroy any British tank at any range. One British officer, captured and under interrogation, expressed the opinion that it was unfair to use anti-aircraft guns against tanks. His captors replied that it was equally unfair for the British to use tanks whose armour nothing but the "88" would penetrate!

According to Cunningham's planning, the leading role in "Crusader" was to be played by XXX Corps, which would cross the Egyptian-Libyan border near Fort Maddalena and deploy at Gabr Saleh. It was expected that while this was happening, Rommel would have arrived, and a tank battle would then take place, in which the more numerous and better equipped British and South Africans would have the upper hand. Meanwhile, from the south-east, XIII Corps would overrun the frontier position at Sollum – Sidi Omar. With the *Afrika Korps* toppled, XXX Corps would push on vigorously to Sidi Rezegh to join up with the Tobruk garrison, which, on the signal, would break out of the Italian XXI Corps' partial encirclement to meet the British forces advancing from the south-east.

Between Cunningham's two columns, however, there was a 20-mile gap, which would widen as Godwin-Austen's XIII Corps moved north and Norrie's XXX Corps headed north-west. Fearing an outflanking movement on his left, Godwin-Austen therefore demanded, and secured, an intermediary column, which was drawn, however, from Norrie's force. Norrie was far from pleased with this decision which, in the event, was an unfortunate one. The resulting diversion of the 4th Armoured Brigade meant that the 7th Armoured Division lost a third of its strength, 165 Stuarts, and was thus weakened in what was intended to be its decisive rôle.

This was the first setback to the operation, even before it had begun. When the attack got under way at dawn on November 18, in torrential rain, Rommel's reaction caused a second setback. Ready to attack Tobruk, he saw the British move as no more than a reconnaissance in strength and kept his armoured forces around Gambut, whereas Cunningham was waiting for him at Gabr Saleh. On top of all this, a third setback occurred with the capture of no less than the 8th Army operations orders, carelessly brought to the front by a British officer. This happened on November 19 when the 22nd Armoured Brigade, equipped with the new Crusader tanks (7th Armoured Division) was defeated in its attempt to take Bir el Gubi, bitterly defended by the "Ariete" Armoured Division. This fourth setback

cost the British about 50 tanks.

XXX Corps did, however, reach Sidi Rezegh, although weakened for the reasons already explained. There it met a counter-attack by the *Afrika Korps,* strengthened by the Italian XXI Corps, ordered in by Mussolini himself at Rommel's direct request. Saturday, November 22 was a black day for Willoughby Norrie. His 7th Armoured Brigade was reduced to 10 effective tanks, and the 22nd Armoured Brigade was little better off with only 34. On the next day, the German onslaught smashed into the 5th South African Brigade, the 22nd Armoured Brigade was reduced to some 12 tanks, and Sidi Rezegh was lost.

If Rommel had followed up this important success against XXX Corps he could probably have wiped it out. But this chance was not enough for him; he was after the destruction of the whole of 8th Army. To do this, he brought 15th and 21st Panzer Divisions under his direct command, left Lieutenant-Colonel Siegfried Westphal, head of the operations section, in charge of the *Panzergruppe* H.Q., and set off with his Chief-of-Staff, Major-General Alfred Gause, and 100 tanks to reach the Mediterranean by way of Sidi Omar and strike the British in the rear.

For Cunningham, in his Maddalena H.Q., the reversals occurring since November 19 were an immense strain, and seemed to offer sufficient justification for an order to retreat. But in the evening of the 23rd, Sir Claude Auchinleck appeared in his mobile caravan H.Q. and ordered him to continue the attack. Auchinleck later wrote: "My opinion was different from Cunningham's. I thought Rommel was probably in as bad shape as we were, especially with Tobruk unvanquished behind him, and I ordered the offensive to continue. I certainly gambled (in fact, by going on we might have lost all) and Cunningham might very well have proved to be right and I wrong!"

At the same moment, his opponent, writing to his wife, claimed to be "well, in excellent spirits and full of confidence." In spite of this, Rommel's raid in the British rear did not succeed in upsetting Auchinleck. "He is making a desperate effort but he won't get very far," he said to Cunningham on November 24. At the end of his order of the day to his troops he told them:

"His position is desperate, and he is trying by lashing out in all directions to distract us from our object, which is to destroy him utterly. We will NOT be distracted and he WILL be destroyed. You have got your teeth into him. Hang on and bite deeper and deeper and hang on till he is finished. Give him NO rest. The general situation in NORTH AFRICA is EXCELLENT."

But as he suspected that Cunningham was in no condition to carry out this aggressive plan, he replaced him, on

German troops in a half-track (opposite).

November 26, by his own Deputy Chief-of-Staff, Major-General Neil Methuen Ritchie. The former chief of Intelligence in the *Panzergruppe Afrika,* in his book *Panzer Battles,* said of this action by Auchinleck at this most critical moment: "This was certainly one of the most important decisions of the war. Auchinleck's will to attack and his strategy of penetration saved 'Crusader' and much else besides." This is a sound judgement.

Although Ritchie took over from Cunningham it was Auchinleck who directed the battle.

On November 25 Scobie received a telegram informing him that the New Zealand Division would attempt to take Sidi Rezegh the next day. The garrison was then expected to occupy El Duda. Scobie launched a new attack on the morning of November 26. After a fierce struggle his infantry overcame the final centre of resistance called "Wolf". But there was still no sign of the arrival of the New Zealanders. At 1300 hours the garrison saw tanks on the horizon, and from one of their turrets three red rockets soared into the blue sky.

The troops cheered wildly, for it was the recognition signal of the 8th Army. Reinforcements were at last in sight!

Writing to his wife on their silver anniversary, Rommel described his action behind the British lines as a "magnificent success" calling for a "special communiqué" from O.K.W. But he was undoubtedly alone in this view. For not only had he not overcome the 4th Indian Division's stubborn resistance or captured the 8th Army's supply dumps, but he had also left the *Panzergruppe* without orders for four days, unconcerned that a few hours after his reckless departure he had lost his mobile radio, broken down in the desert.

Liddell Hart's description of this incident in his presentation of Rommel's notebooks gives some idea of the life led in the desert by the commanders themselves:

"A wireless signal from Rommel summoned the commander of the Afrika Korps to the Panzer Group's forward H.Q., which was said to be located near Gambut. After searching for a long time in the darkness they finally discovered a British lorry, which General Cruewell's command car approached with great caution. Inside it, to his good fortune, were no British troops, but Rommel and his Chief-of-Staff, both of whom were unshaven, worn with lack of sleep and caked with dust. In the lorry was a heap of straw as a bed, a can of stale water to drink and a few tins of food. Close by were two wireless trucks and a few dispatch riders. Rommel now gave his instructions for next day's operations."

Meanwhile, XIII Corps had succeeded where XXX Corps had failed. The New Zealand Division, moving through Belhamed, had made contact with the Tobruk garrison, which itself had broken out at El Duda.

With the situation becoming more critical, Lieutenant-Colonel Westphal took it upon himself to pass over the head of his untraceable chief and recall to the Tobruk sector the 21st Panzer Division, which was unattached south of Sollum. When he returned to his H.Q. on November 27, Rommel tacitly endorsed this initiative and without any pause mounted a new operation designed to bring him victory. Some very confused engagements followed, during which the New Zealand Division was cut in two and part of it thrown back to Tobruk. The Germans were becoming exhausted, however, and the 21st Panzer Division's commander, General von Ravenstein, was captured in the confusion.

Auchinleck's reinforcement of the 8th Army had been timely, and the rapidly reorganised XXX Corps again made its presence felt in the battle. Rommel, on the other hand, had to rely on a mere handful of tanks in the decisive days that lay ahead. He had been warned that no supplies of any consequence could be delivered before the latter half of December. So on December 5 he withdrew his forces attacking east of Tobruk, and the next day, after a counter-attack had failed, gave the order for a general retreat. He left to the "Savona" Division the honour of holding out as long as possible in the Bardia–Sollum–Halfaya area.

The previous summer, while waiting for a British offensive, the Germans and Italians had agreed to make an all-out defensive stand on the heights of Aïn el Gazala if it became impossible to hold the frontier. General Bastico now wanted to stick to this plan, as it had the advantage of covering Benghazi. Rommel, however, insisted that to stand on this line would risk the loss of Tripolitania without even saving Cyrenaica. In his view, as a result of British superiority, the retreat should be extended to Derna–Mechili; but he really wanted to move back to the area of Mersa Brega, which he had left on March 31.

On December 8, 14, and 17 these differences of opinion led to dramatic exchanges between the two commanders and their general staffs. During the first of these Rommel became excited and, according to the testimony of Lieutenant-Colonel Ravajoli exclaimed "that he had fought to win for three weeks, and that now he had decided to take his divisions to Tripoli and seek internment in Tunisia."

In order to win over the Italians to his argument in favour of a retreat he had no hesitation in using false information— now 2,000 or 3,000 motor vehicles sighted south of Sidi Barrani, now a convoy reported in Tobruk waters. On December 17 he succeeded in obtaining freedom of action from Cavallero, who had arrived with Field-Marshal Kesselring from Rome. They both strongly opposed the retreat from Derna; Rommel, however, said that his orders had already been issued, and in some cases were actually being carried out.

Whatever judgement one makes about Rommel's methods, the basic soundness of his decision must be admitted. Moreover he conducted the retreat in a masterly fashion, dealing sharp blows to the British whenever they became too hurried in pursuit. On Christmas Day, General Ritchie's advance guard entered Benghazi. But as the year ended, the 8th Army had not succeeded in intercepting Rommel, although desert patrols had occupied the Jalo oasis. He was now securely in position behind the El Agheila – Marada strongpoint, leaving behind him 340 tanks destroyed since November 18. On January 17 the "Savona" Division, its food and ammunition exhausted, surrendered to General Villiers, commander of the 2nd South African Division, which had relieved the 4th Indian Division. 32,000 prisoners, 9,000 of them Germans, were taken by the 8th Army in two months. The 8th Army itself had lost 18,000 in killed, wounded and prisoners.

In Washington, Churchill was jubilant over this limited, but undeniable, victory. In a few weeks' time, he thought, Auchinleck would begin Operation "Acrobat", which would complete the destruction of the Axis forces in North Africa and take Ritchie from El Agheila to the Tunisian frontier. Then, under the agreement just reached with President Roosevelt, Operation "Gymnast" would be launched. With or without the consent of the Vichy Government, an Anglo-American expeditionary force would invade Morocco and Algeria.

For various reasons, the Mediterranean situation then changed, upsetting British plans.

First, Hitler was rightly concerned about the way things were developing and decided to send a submarine force there, just at the time when he seemed in sight of success in the battle of the Atlantic. From the outset, this move proved to be profitable, since on November 13 *U-81* (Lieutenant Guggenberger) sank the aircraft-carrier *Ark Royal* near Gibraltar just after she had despatched another load of fighters to Malta. As

Illustrious, Formidable, and *Indomitable* were still undergoing repairs in the United States, the only modern vessel in this class the Admiralty had was *Victorious.* Some 60 miles north of Sollum, *U-331* (Lieutenant von Tiesenhausen) succeeded in hitting the battleship *Barham* with three torpedoes, and this proud veteran of the Battle of Jutland disappeared in a terrible explosion, with 861 officers, petty officers, and men. Destroyers picked up 450 survivors, including Vice-Admiral Pridham-Wippell, who had distinguished himself at Cape Matapan. Finally, on December 14, not far from Alexandria, the light cruiser *Galatea* was destroyed by *U-557* (Lieutenant Paulsen).

Hitler's assistance to his ally did not stop there. With the Italians' agreement he signed Directive No. 38 on December 2, ordering a unified command of the Axis forces in the central Mediterranean under a Supreme Commander "South" (*Oberbefehlshaber Süd*).

This was Field-Marshal Kesselring, commander of *Luftflotte* II. He was given a three-fold task:

"To win mastery of the air and sea in the area between Southern Italy and North Africa in order to ensure communications with Libya and Cyrenaica, and particularly to neutralise Malta. Secondly, to co-operate with the German and allied forces operating in North Africa. Thirdly, to paralyse enemy movements in the Mediterranean, including supplies to Tobruk and Malta, working in close co-operation with the available German and Italian naval forces."

Kesselring took command of the Luftwaffe air and anti-aircraft units already in the Mediterranean, and was reinforced by II *Fliegerkorps* (General Loerzer), withdrawn from the Eastern Front. So the Soviet allies obtained some benefit from British strategy between Malta and Suez.

But these were only half measures by Hitler, for the Supreme Commander "South", or O.B.S. as he was abbreviated, was nowhere in the same class as Eisenhower, Nimitz, or MacArthur when

A British Crusader Mk.I stops by a burning German Pzkw IV tank.

it came to commanding a whole theatre of war. In fact, *Panzergruppe Afrika* refused to acknowledge his supreme authority, thus very likely prejudicing the outcome of Axis operations. It remained to be proved that this Bavarian, a former artilleryman turned pilot, had a better overall conception of modern combined operations than the Württemberger, a former mountain infantryman converted to tanks. In addition, subordinate to the *Comando Supremo,* O.K.W., and even *Reichsmarschall* Göring, Kesselring's position was a most ambiguous one. In spite of all this, he was still able to redress the balance in the central Mediterranean for a time.

Japan's entry into World War II, especially the invasion of Malaya and the threat to Singapore, also played its part in the change in the Mediterranean balance. In Washington, the American President and the British Premier decided that, in spite of the Pearl Harbor and the Kuantan disasters, Germany was still to be considered as the prime enemy. Therefore, until Germany was beaten, the Allies would adopt an opportunist, wait-and-see policy in the Far East war. The Australian Government did not share this view. If Roosevelt could impose his own policy on Admiral Nimitz and General MacArthur, it did not follow that Churchill could do likewise with Mr. Curtin's troublesome government.

So the 6th and 7th Australian Divisions, which it had been hoped would take part in Operation "Acrobat", left the Middle East for good, and the British 70th Division embarked for Singapore. Again, the formation of a new squadron, to defend communications in the Indian Ocean against possible action by the Japanese fleet, prevented the Admiralty from making good the considerable losses sustained by the Mediterranean Fleet.

During the night of December 18 and 19, Force K was pursuing an Italian convoy heading for North Africa when it ran into a minefield. *Neptune* struck four mines in succession and sank with all her crew except one leading seaman. *Aurora* and *Penelope* survived, but were so badly damaged that they remained unseaworthy for many long weeks. The destroyer *Kandahar* made a courageous attempt to help *Neptune* but her stern was blown off by another mine and she sank on the spot.

Also on December 18, at 2100 hours, with admirable precision, the Italian submarine *Sciré* (Lieutenant Valerio Borghese) managed to launch three manned torpedoes less than one and a half miles from the lighthouse overlooking Alexandria's main channel. Seated astride their machines, in pairs, the six daring men slipped in behind a returning group of destroyers and aimed for their allotted targets: De la Penne and Bianchi for *Valiant*, Marceglia and Schergat for *Queen Elizabeth*, and Martellota and Marino for the large tanker *Sagona*. Once under the hulls of their targets, they removed the explosive warheads of their torpedoes, suspended them from the bottom of the vessels and set the detonators. All this was done in pitch darkness over 30 feet below the surface.

Sagona blew up first, at dawn on December 20. Then came *Valiant*, with De la Penne and Bianchi aboard. They had been picked up during the night but had uttered no word about their mission, of which they might have been the first victims. At about 0625 hours, Admiral Cunningham was on the rear deck of *Queen Elizabeth* inspecting the damage to *Valiant* when the explosion from Marceglia and Schergat's torpedo flung him four or five feet in the air.

As Roskill points out, "both battleships were seriously flooded and incapacitated for many months. Fortunately it was possible to keep them on even keels and the enemy's . . . air reconnaissance failed to reveal the full measure of success achieved." But it would be months before they rejoined the fleet, and meanwhile, apart from destroyers Cunningham had no more than four light cruisers under his command, including the old anti-aircraft cruiser *Carlisle*. The Italian Navy, thanks to its mines and midget submarines, had gained, in a single night, a considerable advantage in the Mediterranean. It is true, however, that it did not have enough supplies of oil fuel to make use of this advantage, and so the situation continued to deteriorate in 1942. Taking a general view of all the theatres of operations, it can be concluded that between November 25 and December 20, 1941, the Anglo-American forces had lost five of their 33 major vessels, and eight others were out of commission for some months. It may be argued that aircraft-carriers were taking the place of battleships; but the Japanese navy was the leader in this field.

Rommel retreats (top).
Italian tanks move forward in the Western Desert (bottom).

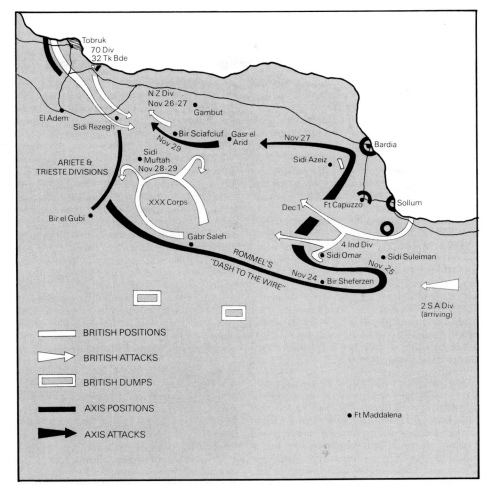

CHAPTER 28

The Battle of the Atlantic begins

In his memoirs, Winston Churchill sums up the strategic situation as he saw it at the end of 1941 thus:

"Amid the torrent of violent events one anxiety reigned supreme. Battles might be won or lost, enterprises might succeed or miscarry, territories might be gained or quitted, but dominating all our power to carry on the war, or even keep ourselves alive, lay our mastery of the ocean routes and the free approach and entry to our ports."

Though written after the war, these words are not the product of hindsight, but express exactly the feelings of the wartime British leader as he prepared to face up to the menace of the U-boats and the four-engined Focke-Wulf Fw 200 Condor; although this does not mean to say that all the measures he took to eliminate the threat were equally effective, as we shall have occasion to point out later. But Churchill was never the one to commit himself half-heartedly.

Proof of this is contained in his order of March 6, 1941, concerning the conduct of what he called "The Battle of the Atlantic", for the purpose of waging which he established that same day a standing committee. This brought together three times a week representatives of the Transport Department of the Admiralty, and of the Ministries of Transport and Shipping. To this new body fell the task of recommending measures necessary "to defeat the attempt to strangle our food supplies and our connection with the United States."

The Prime Minister naturally expected that among the means that Germany would use to attain these objectives, would figure prominently the renewed bombing by the Luftwaffe of Clydeside, Merseyside, and the Bristol Channel, since this was where American war supplies were being landed–and where the unloading and distribution operations were falling further and further behind schedule. Furthermore, one and a half million tons of merchant shipping were lying idle for lack of repair. Churchill therefore ordered the immediate strengthening of anti-aircraft defences in all west coast ports.

And indeed, during the early days of March, it certainly looked as if Hitler and Göring were going to follow this strategy. The results were sobering.

On March 13 and 14, Clydeside, which up till then had got off rather lightly, was subjected to the merciless attacks of the Luftwaffe; in fact, so fierce were the attacks upon Greenock and Glasgow that some shipyards remained closed until June, and others even until November. This "second edition" of the Blitz reached its height between May 1 and May 7, when, for seven successive nights, German bombers implacably pounded Liverpool and the adjoining Merseyside ports. Not only were there 3,000 dead and wounded as a result; in addition, 69 of the 144 mooring bays were put out of action, and the unloading capacity of the area reduced by 75 per cent for some weeks after.

Thus the shattering effects of this aerial bombardment of western port installations, combined with the successes achieved on the high seas by U-boats, Focke-Wulf Condors, and the surface raiders, added up to an effective reply to the "Lend-Lease" law promulgated by President Roosevelt on March 11, 1941. And yet, from May 13 onwards, after one last massive attack on London, the Luftwaffe relaxed the pressure it had–especially over the past few months, when the western ports had been the chief victims– been exerting on Britain. Some 43,381 civilians had been killed and 50,856 seriously injured; but the respite thus granted by the calling-off of the bombing was to last more than three years, until the launching of the first V-1 flying bombs on June 13, 1944.

It is of course, true that the implementation of Operation "Barbarossa" inevitably entailed the transfer of the bulk of the Luftwaffe from the West to the East, if the Russian giant was to be laid low before the onset of winter. Nevertheless, writing about this piece of good fortune in his memoirs, Churchill affirmed that if the Germans had continued their attacks against Britain, the Battle of the Atlantic would have been even more tightly fought.

The constant and vital chore on a submerged U-boat: keeping the ship's trim stable (below). Admiral Dönitz and his staff ponder their next move. He co-ordinated U-boat movements into an overall strategy (opposite).

And in 1954, discussing this aspect of the conflict, Captain S. W. Roskill, the Royal Navy's official historian, asked this question:

"If Hitler, instead of attacking Russia, had concentrated the full weight of his air power against our commercial ports, our docks and dockyards, our unloading and storage facilities, our coastal shipping and river estuaries, and had he kept the might of the Luftwaffe so directed for months on end if need were, could this country have survived?"

At all events, the Prime Minister, confronted with the growing menace of the Focke-Wulf aircraft, gave top priority to equipping the Merchant Navy with anti-aircraft weapons, the Admiralty providing the necessary gun crews. In addition, Fighter Command was given orders to release 50 fighters and pilots for convoy escort duty; these planes were to be installed on catapults on board merchantmen, from which they would take off on sighting a Condor; they would shoot it down and then ditch in the sea themselves, there to wait until one of the escort vessels came to pick them up – a procedure which inevitably resulted in the loss of the aircraft, and, very often, in that of the pilot's life. When escort aircraft-carriers, intended for convoy duty, came into operation, these expensive Catapult Aircraft Merchantmen were abandoned.

Facing up to Admiral Dönitz's U-boats in June 1941, the British defences were better equipped than a year earlier, thanks to the successful carrying out of the war production programme, and also to the additional help of the U.S.A. At his Liverpool base, where he had taken over command of Western Approaches on February 17, Sir Percy Noble had available for convoy escort duties 248 destroyers (59 of which were, in fact, being refitted and therefore unusable), 99 corvettes (small ships of 950 tons, admirably suited to this task, but the last word in discomfort), 48 sloops (ten of which had just been given to Britain by Washington under the recent "Lend-Lease" Act, for the duration of hostilities), and 300 miscellaneous small craft. It should be noted, however, that as a result of the arduous tasks they were called upon to perform, a large proportion of them were out of action at any one time.

The escort vessels were fitted with the first radar equipment, which, though rather primitive, was quite effective in countering the enemy submarines' favourite tactic – the night surface attack. We are thus poised on the threshold of that escalation of this campaign, in which the final word went to the Allies.

Though still part of the R.A.F., Coastal Command was placed under the operational control of the Admiralty from April 1941: a hybrid solution which goes far to explaining why Coastal Command was always at the end of the queue when it came to receiving new equipment, whether produced at home or supplied by the United States. A second explanation is that top priority was being given to Bomber Command, which was expected by the Chief of Air Staff, Sir Charles Portal, by the Air Minister, Sir Archibald Sinclair, and by the Prime Minister to cripple German industrial production, especially the submarine shipyards, in an impossibly short space of time.

In any case, the fight against the U-boat menace, though a high priority, was only one of the tasks which Coastal Command had to carry out. It had also to attack enemy shipping in the Channel and the North Sea, to observe and harry German ships sheltering in Brest harbour, to lay mines, and to weed out raiders operating in the Atlantic. In short, July 1941 saw Air Chief-Marshal Sir Philip Joubert de la Ferté, who had just taken over from Sir Frederick Bowhill as the head of Coastal Command, having to carry out a great variety of tasks with insufficient resources.

At the same time, R.A.F. Coastal Command's Short Sunderland and Consolidated PBY Catalina flying boats, as well as Lockheed Hudson bombers, were being fitted with radar, sometimes combined with a searchlight.

While Bomber Command made futile efforts to knock out German submarines lying at their bases – Bremen, Hamburg, and Kiel – it proceeded to ignore the U-boat shelters then being built at Lorient, Saint Nazaire, Brest, la Pallice, and Bordeaux, which might have been more profitable targets. When, via the Free French "Rémy" network, Lieutenant Philippon sent a message from Brest to London, pointing out the magnitude of the work being carried out, and how important it was to attack these sites, London loftily replied, according to Jacques Mordal: "These bases will be attacked when they are finished." In Mordal's opinion, this was a woeful error of judgement, since the horizontal protection to these pens comprised two 12-feet thick layers of concrete, and as the pens themselves were also well-protected with A.A. guns, they stood up to all that the British and American air forces could throw at them.

From a consideration of Great Britain's defences, let us now look at her losses, especially as we have the memoirs of Admirals Raeder and Dönitz, and also the historical works of Vice-Admiral Assmann and Captain Gerhard Bidlingmaier to help us.

Statistics published after the war, in the British official history, *The War at Sea*, demonstrate that the year 1941 cost Allied and neutral shipping 1,299 ships, displacing 4,328,558 tons, an increase of 240 ships and some 340,000 tons over 1940. If we split up these figures according to the way the losses were incurred, we find that losses to submarine action were down slightly, to 2,171,754 tons, as against the 2,186,158 tons of 1940. On the other hand the Luftwaffe considerably increased its total of tonnage destroyed, from 580,074 to over one million, though it has to be remembered that in April and May the evacuation of Greece, and then of Crete, had cost British shipping dear. This makes it easier to understand why, until the Stukas could be eliminated, the British High Command was so reserved in discussing plans for a European second front, which Harry Hopkins and General Marshall had submitted for its consideration, with the enthusiastic backing of President Roosevelt, as early as the spring of 1942.

The tonnage sunk by surface warships, including camouflaged surface raiders, was almost the same for both years, and the menace of the magnetic mine, which made its first appearance in November 1939, was greatly reduced and no longer represented a real threat: 13 per cent of all ships destroyed in 1940, but only $5\frac{1}{2}$ per cent in 1941.

Since Admiral Raeder's staff calculated that British and Canadian shipyards produced 1,600,000 tons annually, Allied shipping thus sustained for 1941 a net loss of 2,700,000 tons, excluding ships that were out of service for repair. However, the Japanese attack on Pearl Harbor and the declaration of war by Germany and Italy on the U.S.A. on December 11, 1941, placed the enormous resources of the American shipyards, estimated by the Germans at more than 5,000,000 tons for 1942, at the disposal of Great Britain—a major turning-point in the Battle.

At the beginning of 1942, Admiral Dönitz, from his command post at Kernével near Lorient, had 22 submarines operating under his orders, while another 67, based on Gotenhafen, as the Germans now called Gdynia, were carrying out their trials in the Baltic. For the first two months of the year, the heavy storms which lashed the North Atlantic severely limited the number of U-boat successes, just as they made it impossible for the British convoy escorts to sink a single submarine. March enabled the two adversaries to resume the struggle in more normal conditions; 41 British and Allied vessels (243,021 tons) were torpedoed and sunk by Dönitz's wolf packs.

This success was, however, dearly bought. Five U-boats were sunk, three of them by the five destroyers and two corvettes which, under the command of Captain Donald Macintyre, were escorting convoy H.X. 112. Besides these, on March 18, *U-47*, commanded by Günther Prien, famous for his Scapa Flow exploit and credited with 28 ships sunk as well as *Royal Oak*, was lost with all hands in an attack by the destroyer *Wolverine*. The first attack on the submerged submarine had bent its propeller shafts. According to Captain Macintyre's account:

"Surfacing after dark in the hope of escaping the destroyer, which had clung persistently to an intermittent asdic contact, the submarine's propellers emitted a rattle clearly to be heard on *Wolverine*'s asdic, leading her accurately to the target. Further depth-charge attacks shattered *U-47*'s hull. A vivid flash and an explosion from the depths told of her end, confirmed as wooden debris floated to the surface."

During the night of March 15–16, U-boats succeeded in sinking five of convoy H.X. 112's merchantmen and tankers. But the destroyer *Vanoc*, thanks to her radar, managed to locate, ram, and sink *U-100*, whose captain, Joachim Schepke, was killed in the collision. A particularly aggressive submarine commander, Schepke had been credited with the sinking of 39 ships totalling 159,130 tons. Almost simultaneously, the destroyer *Walker*, under Captain Macintyre, depth-charged *U-99*, which had used all its torpedoes; completely crippled, the German submarine was able to remain on the surface just long enough for its crew to escape. Wearing his officer's peaked cap and with his binoculars slung round his neck—the binoculars had been presented to him by Admiral Dönitz—Otto Kretschmer was the last man to be hoisted aboard *Walker*. With 44 ships totalling 266,629 tons to his credit, Kretschmer was the U-boat "ace of aces", and as such had been decorated with the Oak Leaves to his Knight's Cross of the Iron Cross. He spent the first stage of his captivity in Captain Macintyre's cabin, showing himself to be a fine bridge player.

May, with 58 ships sunk, a total of 325,492 tons, was the worst month for Great Britain in the Battle of the Atlantic; and if we add to this the losses incurred in the Aegean and Mediterranean Seas during the campaign in the Balkans we find that Allied shipping had lost nearly 1,200,000 tons in two months; Germany was within an ace of the figures Raeder and Dönitz had calculated as being necessary to bring Britain to her knees, without undertaking any other military action.

However, the second half of the year, as a simple comparison with the first half shows, was far from justifying the optimism felt in Dönitz's Kernével H.Q.: between July and December, for various political and strategic reasons, the monthly average of shipping sunk by the U-boats slumped by 50 per cent, to only 120,000 tons.

Firstly, the posting of American naval forces near Greenland and Iceland, and the inclusion of the North Atlantic between Iceland and eastern Newfoundland in the American security zone enabled the British Admiralty to release ships in that area for the strengthening of escorts in the eastern Atlantic. This was especially important; as we have mentioned earlier, Hitler had given strict instructions to avoid any trouble with the U.S.A. The U-boats had stuck to them, despite the fact that on September 11, 1941 the U.S. Navy ships in the Atlantic had been told to shoot on sight.

Secondly, although the number of submarines operational had increased from 22 in January to 65 in July, and to 91 by the end of the year, not all of them were employed on this vital task of destroying enemy shipping, despite Dönitz's frenzied pleas; with the increase in submarine numbers, Hitler seemed to think he could post them anywhere. Some of his decisions were correct, others much less so.

Thus the beginning of hostilities against the Russians seemed to him to demand the sending of four submarines to the Arctic. Because they found no targets there worthy of their torpedoes, they were recalled, but were not posted back to their essential task, for the Führer had decreed that Norway constituted a "zone of destiny", and would probably be Churchill's first objective. Dönitz thought such an enterprise out of the question. He was probably right, but it still remains a fact that Churchill gave Sir Alan Brooke, Commander-in-Chief, Home Forces, express instructions to cease all other activity and prepare a plan to attack Trondheim. It was only after a week's polite but steadfast objections that Brooke was able to note in his diary on October 12: "The meeting finished shortly after 8.30 p.m. and for the second time Winston had been ridden off Trondheim." All of which would seem to indicate that, in this case at least, Hitler was right and Dönitz wrong.

Dönitz's forces were further weakened by the continually worsening situation in the central Mediterranean. On the orders of O.K.W., six submarines passed through the Straits of Gibraltar at the end of September, being joined in Eleusis harbour by four more in November. In the last chapter we saw the useful contribution they made to the Italians' strategy, just when the southern theatre of operations was being gravely threatened. However, it had been agreed that once their mission had been accomplished, they would return to service in the Atlantic. But this was a meaningless phrase: the current in the middle of the Strait flows very rapidly from the Atlantic to the Mediterranean, which prevented the U-boats from returning underwater, while one night was not long enough to allow them to return on the surface. At the end of December the German Navy had no fewer than 23 U-boats in the Mediterranean, unable to play any part in the battle of the Atlantic (to say nothing of four submarines which had been lost while entering the Mediterranean).

Lastly, expecting an "Anglo-Gaullist" landing in French North Africa, Hitler sent an order to Admiral Dönitz on November 29 to post 15 U-boats on either side of the Strait of Gibraltar. Dönitz thought that the rumours upon which Hitler had based his decision were quite false, but when, at the end of December, Churchill and Roosevelt met in Washington for the "Arcadia" Conference, this was the very plan they agreed on: as soon as Operation "Crusader", then being carried out, had completed the destruction of Axis forces in Cyrenaica, General Auchinleck would implement Operation "Acrobat", bringing the British 8th Army quickly up to the Tunisian border; after which an expeditionary force, Anglo-American rather than Anglo-Gaullist as first envisaged, would carry out Operation "Gymnast", appearing unexpectedly on the Atlantic coast of Morocco and at suitable points in Algeria and Tunisia. The local French authorities and the Vichy Government would thus be given a last chance to choose between "a blessing or a cursing", as Churchill put it in a note of December 16. We know what happened to this plan, but it is clear that Hitler was right to be concerned about such an eventuality, and about the means of countering it.

On December 31, therefore, there were 91 U-boats available, split up as follows:

Mediterranean	26
West of Gibraltar	6
Norway	4
Available to Dönitz	55

Returning to this question in the light of the extra information available after the war, Captain S. W. Roskill comes down, with slight reservations, in favour of Dönitz's arguments:

"But the transfer [of U-boats] from the Atlantic brought us a most welcome ease-

Admiral Sir Percy Noble, C.-in-C., Western Approaches.

ment in that vital theatre. The German Staff, when it ordered the U-boats to the Mediterranean, did not know of the Japanese intention to attack on the 7th of December, and could not therefore have foretold that a new ally would assist greatly towards propping up Italy and saving the Axis armies in North Africa. But, in the long view, it may be doubted whether the redistribution of the enemy's U-boat strength brought him any advantage, because of the decline in his Atlantic offensive which it made inevitable."

With 55 U-boats at his disposal for the blockade of Britain, Dönitz would have done much better if he had been able to use them in co-operation with air and surface forces. He could of course rely on Lieutenant-Colonel Martin Harlinghausen, commanding *Kampfgeschwader 40* at Bordeaux, equipped with Focke-Wulf 200 Condors, adequate maritime reconnaissance/bomber machines. But the immense enthusiasm and intelligence of this former naval officer could not compensate for the very limited serviceability rate of his unit's aircraft–only two per day at the most, instead of the 12 that Dönitz would have liked. And yet, each time that aircraft and U-boats were able to co-operate, the results proved most encouraging, and this tiny handful of four-engined German bombers produced considerable consternation among Allied convoys.

With a little more diplomacy, would Dönitz have been able to bring home to the vindictive and presumptuous Hermann Göring a more accurate realisation of what was really needed for naval and air forces to co-operate successfully? This is most unlikely because, on Hitler's express instructions, Göring combined responsibility for the Wehrmacht's air operations with the industrial dictatorship of the Third Reich and the occupied countries, and flitted from one sphere of activity to the other with the most disconcerting frivolity, apparently quite incapable of setting his mind to a problem and carrying it through to a reasonable conclusion.

Another factor militating against the effective waging of the battle of the Atlantic was the pitifully small number of maintenance personnel available to Dönitz. And even these could not do all that they might have done as a result of several unforeseeable circumstances.

On March 23, 1941, at the end of a lightning raid, the battle-cruisers *Scharnhorst* and *Gneisenau* put in at Brest, being joined there on June 1 by the heavy cruiser *Prinz Eugen*, which had succeeded, in circumstances related below, in escaping from the battle which had resulted in the sinking of *Bismarck*. The concentration of three such powerful units in one place provoked a violent reaction from the R.A.F.

On April 6, an R.A.F. pilot succeeded in hitting *Gneisenau* with a torpedo, and after she had been towed back to harbour, she was hit again, this time by four bombs. On July 1 a British bomber hit *Prinz Eugen*, putting her out of commission for four months. Lastly, *Scharnhorst* was hit by five bombs while on trials off la Pallice.

In order to repair these surface warships as soon as possible, maintenance crews, despite Dönitz's strongest protests, were taken off submarine work in considerable numbers, and the overhaul and repair of U-boats consequently suffered.

Thus, at the end of the year, 60 per cent of Dönitz's U-boats were out of action, and of the 22 left, ten were in transit, leaving only 12 for operations over the whole theatre of operations from Cape Farewell in Greenland to the Azores.

Meanwhile, Admiral Sir Percy Noble's anti-submarine forces had increased both in quantity and quality. This is clearly shown by the results of the battle, from Gibraltar to Ushant, between U-boats and the escort for the 32 merchantmen of convoy H.G. 76 between December 14–23. The British Admiralty had gone to great lengths to protect this convoy, giving Captain F. J. Walker, commanding the escort force, an escort carrier, three destroyers, four sloops, and no fewer than ten corvettes.

After nine days of relentless combat, the losses were these:
1. Britain: escort carrier *Audacity*, lost to *U-751* (Lieutenant Bigalk) and destroyer *Stanley*;
2. Germany: two Focke-Wulf Condors, shot down by *Audacity*'s fighters, and five of the ten submarines involved. One of these was *U-567*, commanded by Lieutenant Endrass, whose total tonnage sunk was very close to the record set by Otto Kretschmer.

In short, the British had had the best of the engagement, especially as 30 of the 32 merchantmen reached their destination.

1941 had cost the Germans 35 U-boats, of which three had been lost in the Baltic and five in the Mediterranean. During the first half of the year, however, the shipyards of the Reich had been producing new U-boats at the rate of 13 a month, a figure that increased to 20 in the second half of the year. Thus the U-boat arm gained a total of 163 boats during the year (a production of 198 minus 35 boats lost). Dönitz therefore had no reason to be pessimistic, especially as the German and Italian declarations of war on the United States on December 11, 1941 left his boats free to attack American shipping. To complete the picture, it should be noted that the Italians lost eight boats in the battle of the Atlantic.

During the same period, Germany's surface warships destroyed 427,000 tons of Allied shipping, slightly less than one-fifth of the tonnage despatched by the U-boats. By this activity, however, the surface raiders tied down ships that could profitably have been used elsewhere. Battleships, for example, had to be escorted by four destroyers, and this weakening of the anti-submarine effort made Dönitz's task that much easier.

On January 1, 1941, there were six German disguised surface raiders (converted cargo or banana boats) at large on the high seas: two in the Pacific, two in

Shells from the secondary armament of the heavy cruiser Admiral Hipper *crash around an isolated merchantman. The* Hipper *was one of the more successful surface raiders of 1941.*

the Indian Ocean, and two in the South Atlantic. Operating either singly or in pairs, they scuttled their prey after taking off supplies for their own use or sent them off with a skeleton crew to one of the French Atlantic ports if their cargoes of food or industrial supplies could be of use to the Reich.

There were, for example, three Norwegian whaling factory ships captured by *Pinguin* off the Antarctic ice-pack on January 14–15. Slipping through the British patrols, they managed to reach Bordeaux. *Pinguin* had left Germany on June 22, 1940 and had sunk 28 merchantmen (137,000 tons) when she was surprised and sunk by the cruiser *Cornwall* on May 8, 1941, off Somaliland.

On November 19, 1941, another German raider, *Kormoran*, was sunk off the coast of Western Australia by the cruiser *Sydney*. But before going down with most of her crew, she torpedoed her attacker,

which sank with all hands. *Kormoran* had been at sea for more than ten months and had 11 ships (68,000 tons) to her credit.

Three days later Germany lost a further raider. *Atlantis* was caught while transferring supplies to a U-boat half way between Guinea and Brazil. She was sunk quickly by the 8-inch guns of the cruiser *Devonshire* after a cruise that had brought her 22 victims (146,000 tons) in 1½ years.

The three remaining raiders, *Komet, Thor,* and *Orion,* were luckier, and managed to get back to Germany under the very noses of the Allies. The most noteworthy of their cruises was probably that of *Komet,* commanded by Captain Eyssen, who was promoted to Rear-Admiral on the last day of 1940. *Komet* left Hamburg on June 6, 1940 and returned there on April 30, 1941, after cruising right round the world. With the aid of Russian icebreakers she had made the North-East Passage, skirted Siberia, and entered the Pacific via the Bering Strait. After taking her toll of Allied shipping in the Pacific in conjunction with *Orion,* she returned to Hamburg via the Cape of Good Hope, her whole cruise having taken her something like 100,000 miles.

From figures released after the war, it seems that *Komet, Thor,* and *Orion* accounted for 33 merchantmen totalling about 183,000 tons. In addition to these, *Thor* met and sank the British auxiliary cruiser *Voltaire* on April 4, 1941, picking up 196 survivors.

At the beginning of 1941, the pocket-battleship *Admiral Scheer,* a sister ship of the ill-fated *Graf Spee,* was operating in the South Atlantic in collaboration with *Pinguin,* which *Scheer* provided with the crews necessary to sail back to France the three factory ships mentioned above. On February 2 she sailed round the Cape of Good Hope and made contact with *Atlantis.* The two German vessels then operated together in the Moçambique Channel. Among their victims was the tanker *British Advocate,* whose cargo was naturally enough greatly prized by the two raiders.

On March 6, having sunk or captured 16 ships (99,000 tons) *Admiral Scheer* began her voyage home. She slipped past the two British cruisers on watch in the Denmark Strait. On April 1 she docked at Kiel, after 161 days at sea. During her cruise, *Admiral Scheer* had covered over 50,000 miles, a tribute indeed to her robust diesel engines and the magnificent spirit that Captain Krancke had instilled into his crew.

A month and a half earlier, the heavy cruiser *Admiral Hipper,* commanded by Captain Meisel, had also reached Kiel. She had sailed from Brest on February 1, and on the 12th intercepted a convoy from Gibraltar between the Azores and Madeira. In less than 90 minutes she sank seven merchantmen (33,000 tons) with her 8-inch guns and with torpedoes.

The return of these two warships was facilitated by Operation "Berlin"–the attacks carried out against British shipping in the North Atlantic by the battle-cruisers *Scharnhorst* and *Gneisenau.* Under the command of Admiral Günther Lütjens, the *Flottenchef* or Fleet Commander, the two battle-cruisers had sailed from Kiel on January 23 and passed through the Denmark Strait, after a few anxious moments, on the night of February 3. But their mission was dogged by crippling restrictions. Raeder had told Lütjens: "the essential task of the squadron is to be the destruction of enemy shipping . . . In the course of its attacks on enemy shipping it is on no account to engage an enemy of equal strength . . . it is also to avoid an engagement even if it encounters a single battle-cruiser armed with 15-inch guns."

On February 8, the German force spotted convoy H.X. 106, which had sailed from Halifax for Great Britain on January 31. The convoy was escorted by the old battleship *Ramillies,* however, and in accordance with his orders Lütjens broke off contact, despite the fact that the captain of *Scharnhorst* had offered to draw off the escort and thus give *Gneisenau* the opportunity to annihilate the convoy. The plan entailed little risk as *Scharnhorst* was a

The clean, elegant lines of the Hood *are shown as she lies at anchor in Scapa Flow.*

good 11 knots faster than *Ramillies*, but Lütjens stuck rigidly to his orders.

A fortnight later, off Newfoundland, the German squadron sank three cargo vessels and two tankers of an America-bound convoy that had scattered on being attacked. Then, heading south-east, the German ships found themselves on March 3 less than 300 miles from Tenerife in the Canary islands, well-placed to attack convoys on the Gibraltar–Freetown run. On the morning of the 8th, a dozen merchantmen came over the horizon, escorted, however, by the battleship *Malaya*, armed, like *Ramillies*, with 15-inch guns. Still obeying orders, Lütjens stood off, though he did try to direct towards the convoy the two U-boats operating in the area–no easy task, as German surface vessels and U-boats did not use the same code, and it was only by the roundabout route Paris–Kernével that he was able to pass on the information.

Then *Scharnhorst* and *Gneisenau*, accompanied by their two supply ships, moved off north-west again to intercept the Halifax–Great Britain route. Here they managed to avoid the attentions of the battleship *Nelson* while sinking or capturing 16 ships on March 15–16.

"As day broke on March 16," write J. Vulliez and J. Mordal, "the squadron was surrounded by merchantmen which, seeing the Germans, scattered in all directions. The hunt began with *Ermland* forcing a large cargo vessel within range of *Scharnhorst*, whose guns quickly sank her. Immediately afterwards *Gneisenau* sank an unidentified ship of 5,000 tons at long range. And so the hunt went on:

while *Scharnhorst* was sinking the 4,350-ton *Silverfix*, *Uckermark* forced five ships within range of *Gneisenau*, which picked them off one by one. Time was running out, and it was getting too late for the attackers to think of making any captures. At about 1500, just when the chase seemed over, the two battle-cruisers increased speed and caught one more merchantman."

It was about this time that Lütjens received orders to create a diversion, to enable *Admiral Hipper* and *Admiral Scheer* to slip through the Denmark Strait. With the choice of heading for the Azores or Brest, Lütjens chose the latter. He passed through the dangerous Iroise between the islands of Ushant and Sein at 0700 in March 22.

Dr. Goebbels' propaganda machine made great play with the warships' safe return, heaping scorn on the Royal Navy which, in spite of its overwhelming numerical superiority, had not even been able to engage the two German ships, let alone sink them. In reality, the situation was rather different and in no way justified such jubilation.

While it was true that the two raiders had sunk 22 merchantmen, totalling 116,000 tons, this very creditable result had its gloomy side in the disastrous state of their engines after two months' continuous cruising. And since the same comments were made about *Admiral Hipper*, one can only conclude that high-pressure turbine engines were the weak link in German marine engineering.

At all events, repairs to *Gneisenau's* engines took several weeks, and to *Scharnhorst's* even longer. It therefore became clear that neither could participate in Operation *"Rheinübung"*, which was to have consisted in a raid on British shipping

by *Bismarck* and the heavy cruiser *Prinz Eugen*, combined with a further sortie by the two battle-cruisers.

Although a great deal has been written in Great Britain and Germany about the four days which sealed the fates of the two giant warships *Hood* and *Bismarck*, together with most of their crews, the full circumstances of this tragic episode are still not clear. More than a quarter of a century later, the reasons for certain decisions remain wrapped in mystery; Admirals Holland and Lütjens have taken their secrets with them to the grave, and the survivors of the two ships (three from *Hood* and 115 from *Bismarck*), included only four junior officers (one British and three German), who could not give the reasons for their superiors' decisions.

What we do know is that the objective and execution of Operation *"Rheinübung"* were first described in a directive from Grand-Admiral Raeder on April 2, 1941.

In contrast with the orders given to *Scharnhorst* and *Gneisenau's* squadron would this time be allowed to attack escorted convoys, but *Bismarck* herself could take on an opponent of equal strength only to allow other members of the squadron to get at the merchantmen. "The essential objective," said Raeder in section four of his directive, "remains the destruction of enemy shipping. An attack on an enemy warship can take place only insofar as the success of the mission warrants it, and even then excessive risks are to be avoided."

Raeder's increased aggressiveness was justified by *Bismarck's* powerful offensive armament and superb defensive strength. The battleship's main armament consisted of eight 15-inch guns in four two-gun turrets and, beside the superb optical

Seamen of the British cruiser, Suffolk.

ranging equipment possessed by German warships, *Bismarck* was fitted with a "radiotelemeter", a 90-cm wavelength type of radar, for range calculating. The battleship's secondary armament consisted of twelve 5.9-inch, sixteen 4.1-inch A.A., and sixteen 3.7-cm A.A. guns. Defensively, she had a 12.6-inch belt of armour on the hull, turrets armoured to 14-inches thickness and decks 8 inches thick. Her great beam (118 feet) and large number of watertight compartments gave her a high degree of underwater protection, and her engines, developing 138,000-hp, enabled her to reach 30 knots.

Originally intended to displace 35,000 tons, *Bismarck* in fact displaced 41,700 tons when ready for service. She had been commissioned on August 24, 1940, and so as she made ready for her first and last sortie, had nine months of intensive training behind her. During this time, Captain Lindemann had brought both ship and crew to a high level of efficiency.

Prinz Eugen, commanded by Captain Brinkmann, was another brand new ship. Displacing 13,900 tons, she was armed with eight 8-inch guns in four two-gun turrets, twelve 4.1-inch A.A. guns, twelve 3.7-cm A.A. guns, and twelve 21-inch torpedo tubes. Her engines, which seem to have been more reliable than those of her sister ship *Admiral Hipper*, gave her a top speed of 32 knots. On April 23, however, she struck a mine in the Baltic, and "Rheinübung" had to be put off till May.

Since *Scharnhorst* and *Gneisenau* were undergoing repairs, they were unable to carry out the diversions assigned to them,

and Admiral Lütjens expressed the opinion that it would be better if the operation were postponed until the two battle-cruisers were once again ready for sea. He even went so far as to suggest that *Tirpitz*, *Bismarck*'s sister ship, should be commissioned first. The objection to that, however, was that the surface fleet would thus have been condemned to long weeks of inactivity. Raeder would have none of it, so Lütjens withdrew his objections.

On the evening of May 20, after passing through the Kattegat, *Bismarck* and *Prinz Eugen* emerged into the North Sea.

As early as the following morning, news that the two German warships had left the Baltic reached London. The Admiralty immediately alerted Admiral Sir John Tovey, C.-in-C. Home Fleet, and also informed him that the aircraft-carrier *Victorious* and battle-cruiser *Repulse* had been put at his disposal. Reconnaissance photographs the next day identified *Bismarck* and an *Admiral Hipper*-class heavy cruiser in Korsfjord, south of Bergen.

Without dismissing entirely such explanations for *Bismarck*'s move as an invasion of Iceland, Tovey was fairly sure that the real reason was a second German naval sortie into the Atlantic. Consequently he strengthened the patrols along the Orkneys–Shetlands–Faeroes–Iceland–Greenland line, and on the evening of May 21 ordered Vice-Admiral L. E. Holland's Battle-Cruiser Squadron (the battle-cruiser *Hood*, battleship *Prince of Wales*, and six destroyers) to sail from Scapa Flow to Hvalfjord. Tovey would thus be assured of a considerable superiority in fire-power over his adversary: eight 15-inch and ten 14-inch guns against eight 15-inch guns.

It is true, however, that *Hood*, for all her 42,100 tons displacement and 860-foot length, was beginning to show her age. Commissioned in 1920, she reflected World War I ideas of naval warfare. In particular her defences against plunging fire left a great deal to be desired. *Hood*'s companion capital ship in the squadron, *Prince of Wales* was fitted with a main armament of a calibre new to the Royal Navy, and had not yet proved herself. Two of her three gun turrets (one two-gun and two four-gun) had only been fitted on April 28. Indeed, when she weighed anchor, there were still workmen on board trying to iron out her teething troubles, and these civilians went to sea with her.

On May 22 another reconnaissance of Korsfjord made in abominable weather, showed that the two German ships had gone, so at 2245 the main fleet sailed from Scapa Flow under Admiral Tovey. Beside *King George V*, a sister ship of *Prince of Wales*, Tovey also had the aircraft-carrier *Victorious*, four cruisers, and seven destroyers. The battle-cruiser *Repulse*, coming from the Clyde, joined him later. Operation "Rheinübung" was under way.

Admiral Lütjens had a choice of two passages through which to break out into the Atlantic: the Denmark Strait between Iceland and Greenland, which

had been reduced to 60 miles in width by a minefield and pack ice, and the 300-mile wide gap between the Faeroes and Iceland. His staff advised him to choose the latter, but he opted for the former, as he knew it from an earlier sortie. Captain Bidlingmaier considers this choice to have been mistaken, pointing out that had they taken the route south of Iceland, the German ships could have slipped through the area between the Battle-Cruiser Squadron and the Home Fleet. As the British had only three cruisers on patrol in the area, Bidlingmaier is surely correct.

Perhaps the German admiral had reckoned on fog and rain to hide his movements; but if he did, he had reckoned without radar.

On May 23, at 1922, the cruiser *Suffolk* spotted *Bismarck* and her companion. She then dodged into a patch of mist to prevent *Bismarck* from firing on her, and sent out a report of the German ships' position, while shadowing them by radar. About an hour later *Suffolk* was joined by her sister ship *Norfolk* (Rear-Admiral W. F. Wake-Walker), which made the first enemy report received by Tovey. The two cruisers then shadowed the German squadron by radar.

At 0535 the following morning, using the information so ably provided by *Suffolk* and *Norfolk*, the Battle-Cruiser Squadron sighted *Bismarck* and *Prinz Eugen* off the starboard bow, in an excellent position in which they could be fired on by all turrets. Yet a few minutes later Vice-Admiral Holland altered course, with the result that the rear turrets of his ships could no longer bear: the British superiority in firepower which, as we have seen, was in the order of 18 to 8, had thus been reduced to 10 to 8, and after the first salvo 9 to 8, as one of *Prince of Wales*'s 14-inch guns could not be reloaded.

Holland's manoeuvre has given rise to a great deal of controversy, and many critics have taken him severely to task for going into battle with one hand tied behind his back, so to speak. Roskill, however, impartial as always, has pointed out that ballistic considerations may have dictated the change of course. For beyond a range of about 12,000 yards, the German shells, plunging down at a steep angle, would have torn straight through *Hood*'s inadequately armoured deck. By making directly for his enemy, Holland could get his ship inside the dangerous plunging trajectory of *Bismarck*'s shells to a position where any hits would be on the 12-inch belt rather than 3¾-inch deck.

At all events, at 0552 Admiral Holland gave the order to open fire, concentrating on the leading German ship. During the night, however, *Prinz Eugen* and *Bismarck* had changed places, with the result that the fire of *Hood* was now directed against the former. *Bismarck* was correctly identified by *Prince of Wales*, which thus fired on the second ship. But this meant that the anticipated superiority in guns of 18 to 8 had now become an inferiority of 5 to 8.

The crisis of the battle occurred at 0600. Just as the British squadron began to turn to port, in order to bring their after turrets to bear, and with *Hood* about to open fire on *Bismarck*, a 15-inch salvo landed on the British battle-cruiser. Lieutenant-Commander Jaspers, *Prinz Eugen*'s gunnery officer, describes the scene thus:

"As a whole salvo of 15-inch shells from the German flagship reached its target, there was an explosion of quite incredible violence, between the second funnel and the mainmast. The salvo seemed to crush everything under it with irresistable force. Through huge holes opened up in the grey hull, enormous flames leapt up from the depths of the ship, far above the funnels, and blazed for several seconds through an ash-coloured pall of smoke, which spread terrifyingly towards the ship's bows. And this grey mass fringed with red, composed of smoke, fire, and steam, was seen to form two billowing columns spreading upwards and outwards, while just below them formed a kind of incandescent dome, whose initial low flat curve rose higher and higher, finally culminating in an explosion of burning debris. The aft magazine blew up, shooting into the air a molten mass the colour of red lead, which then fell back lazily into the sea–it was one of the rear gun turrets that we thus saw rising into the air for several yards. All the inflammable objects in the area at the time–rafts, boats, and deck planking–broke loose, and even as they drifted continued to burn.

"And in the midst of this raging inferno, a yellow tongue of flame shot out just once more: the forward turrets of *Hood* had fired one last salvo."

In the circumstances, it is not surprising that out of a total complement of 95 officers and 1,324 men, there should be only three survivors, the senior being Midshipman W. J. Dundas.

Having disposed of *Hood*, *Bismarck* and *Prinz Eugen* turned their attention on *Prince of Wales*, which had as yet not been fired on. In the space of only a few minutes, the German ships landed four 15-inch and three 8-inch shells on the British battleship. One shell hit the compass platform, killing or wounding everyone on it except the ship's captain, Captain Leach, and a signaller. *Prince of Wales*'s plight was increased by the fact that breakdown followed breakdown in the turrets. As a result, Captain Leach broke off the engagement under a smoke screen at 0613 and retired.

Having fired only 93 15-inch shells–less than ten per cent of her stock of main-calibre shells–*Bismarck* had obviously achieved brilliant results. But she had also been hit by two of *Prince of Wales*'s 14-inch shells. Considering the teething troubles of her main armament, *Prince of Wales* may be said to have performed very creditably. More important, one of the British shells had hit a fuel bunker, causing it to leak. This contaminated the fuel with sea water, seriously affecting *Bismarck*'s performance, and also caused an enormous ribbon of fuel to trail out behind her. At 0801, therefore, Admiral Lütjens informed his superiors that he intended to make for Saint Nazaire. *Prinz Eugen* had escaped from the clash unscathed, despite several near misses, and later carried out her original orders for operations in the Atlantic.

Admiral Lütjens' decision was discussed at the Berghof by Hitler and Grand-Admiral Raeder on June 6. The Führer was puzzled by two decisions in particular. Firstly, why had Lütjens not returned to a German port after the engagement with *Hood*, and secondly, why had he not pressed

The awesome power of a 15-inch salvo: Bismarck *silhouettes herself from stem to stern in her own gun flashes.*

home the attack on *Prince of Wales* and destroyed her? Even if the latter had led to the loss of *Bismarck*, the net result would have been the destruction of two British capital ships for one German.

Raeder's answer was, to say the least of things, tortuous. If *Bismarck* had tried to return via the Denmark Strait, as her captain had vainly suggested to Lütjens, nothing would have prevented her safe return to Korsfjord, so far as one can see. This would have meant abandoning her original mission, but this would probably have been inevitable had she tried to finish off *Prince of Wales*, since "she would have been very much the worse for wear, even if she had come off best," as Raeder put it, "and this would certainly have prevented her from continuing her attack on merchant shipping. Her mission compelled her to stand and fight only if the enemy stopped her attacking such shipping."

It is clear that Raeder was using his knowledge and authority to shield his hapless subordinate. All the same, he may have been right, as chance rather than planning played a large part in the ensuing catastrophe.

Vice-Admiral Wake-Walker's message that *Hood* had blown up, followed by the co-ordinates, was a real bombshell both for *King George V*, then about 450 miles south-east of the position radioed, and for the Admiralty.

But by mid-day, Sir Dudley Pound and his deputy, Vice-Admiral Sir Tom Phillips, had embarked on a whole series of measures designed to remedy the situation and restore the prestige of the

Royal Navy. To quote but one example, they had set on *Bismarck*'s tail two battleships, one battle-cruiser, one aircraft-carrier, three cruisers, and nine destroyers, not hesitating to rob Atlantic convoys of their escorts in the process. Thus new orders were received by Force H, which had sailed from Gibraltar at 0200 on May 24, and *Rodney*, which was escorting, with four destroyers, the liner *Britannic* to New York.

Off the eastern coast of Greenland, Wake-Walker had taken under his command *Prince of Wales* and the destroyers of the Battle-Cruiser Squadron, and continued to shadow *Bismarck* by radar. Since Lütjens was steering south-west, Tovey closed on an interception course that would allow him to engage the two German ships at some time the following morning, even if they tried to return to the North Sea by passing south of Iceland or to put in at a French port, because of the oil leak, rather than pursue their original plan of hunting down Atlantic merchant shipping. To slow down his opponent, Tovey decided to send in the Swordfish from *Victorious*.

But both *Victorious* and her aircrew were as untried as *Prince of Wales* and, more important, the weather had turned foul. Despite the weather, however, Lieutenant-Commander Esmonde led his Swordfish on an attack on *Bismarck*, he himself landing a hit on the German battleship's armour belt. Unfortunately for the British, this torpedo hit did little but damage the paintwork. In the depth of night all the attacking aircraft managed to relocate *Victorious* and land safely, much to the relief of the aircraft-carrier's captain, Captain H. C. Bovell.

Swordfish torpedo-bombers on the flight deck of the aircraft carrier Victorious. *Their early strikes were unsuccessful.*

Meanwhile, events had been moving swiftly. First of all Lütjens ordered *Prinz Eugen* to leave *Bismarck* and operate independently, and then, much to Tovey's consternation, *Suffolk* lost contact with *Bismarck*. Matters were not improved by the fact that a long radio message sent by Lütjens at 0400 on May 25 was intercepted by the British. But its bearing was incorrectly plotted and led Tovey to believe that the Germans were attempting to move back into the North Sea. Another serious problem for the British was the fact that hardly an hour passed without one of the Royal Navy's vessels having to withdraw to refuel, some to Iceland, some to Newfoundland, and some even to Gibraltar. In fact, of the 15 units which had sailed on May 22, *King George V* was the only one left in the central Atlantic.

On May 26, however, a patrolling Catalina of Coastal Command spotted *Bismarck*, heading south-east, about 690 miles from Brest:

"'George' (the automatic pilot) was flying the aircraft," said the pilot, "at 500 feet when we saw a warship. I was in the second pilot's seat when the occupant of the seat beside me, an American, said: 'What the devil's that?' I stared and saw a dull black shape through the mist which curled above a very rough sea. 'Looks like a battleship,' he said. I said: 'Better get closer, go round its stern.' I thought it might be the *Bismarck*, because I could see no destroyers round the ship and I should have seen them had she been a British warship. I left my seat, went to the wireless operator's table, grabbed a piece of paper and began to write out a signal."

It was now 1030, and though Admiral Tovey, as a result of the plotting error of the night before, was not in a position to intercept, Sir John Somerville, commander of Force H, was able to send in a strike of Swordfish torpedo-bombers from

Ark Royal. If they could only succeed in slowing down *Bismarck* before midnight, the battle would be won; otherwise, *King George V* and *Rodney* would be forced to turn back for lack of fuel.

The first strike was launched in squally showers at 1450, but was a total failure. The Swordfish mistakenly attacked the cruiser *Sheffield*, which Admiral Somerville had sent on ahead to keep tabs on *Bismarck*. Fortunately for *Sheffield*, the attack achieved nothing apart from another demonstration of British torpedoes' inefficiency: the Fleet Air Arm pilots saw their weapons, fitted with magnetic detonators, exploding as soon as they touched the water. The second strike flew off at 1910, armed with torpedoes fitted with contact pistols and set to run at a shallower depth.

As the 15 aircraft took off, they were observed by Lieutenant-Commander Wolfahrt of *U-556*. In his log he wrote:

"1908 hours: Alert. A battleship of the *King George V*-class and an aircraft-carrier, probably *Ark Royal*, are coming up astern, travelling at great speed. Deflection 10 degrees right. If only I had torpedoes! I am in the perfect position to attack – no need even to manoeuvre. No destroyers, no zig-zags! I could slip between them and fire on both simultaneously. Torpedo planes are taking off from the aircraft-carrier. Perhaps I could have helped *Bismarck*."

Apart from the error of identifying *Renown* for a *King George V*-class battleship, there is no reason to doubt the validity of Wolfahrt's narrative.

Despite a hail of fire from all *Bismarck*'s guns, the Swordfish strike went in successfully between 2047 and 2125 and scored two hits. The first struck *Bismarck*'s armour belt and caused no damage, but the second hit aft, damaging her propellers, wrecking her steering gear, and

jamming her rudders. After desperate but unsuccessful efforts to free them, Lütjens sent the following message: "No longer able to steer ship. Will fight to last shell. Long live the Führer."

After describing two complete circles, the luckless *Bismarck* headed slowly north-north-west, straight towards *King George V* and *Rodney*. But before she met these two battleships, she ran into five destroyers led by Captain Vian, which had been taken off convoy duty to act as an anti-submarine screen for Sir John Tovey's main fleet. Seeing *Bismarck*'s drastically reduced speed, Vian decided to attack. So heavy was the sea running, and so accurate *Bismarck*'s fire, that of the 16 torpedoes fired by the one Polish and four British destroyers, possibly only two of them struck home.

The following morning, *King George V* and *Rodney*, guided by *Norfolk*, arrived on the scene. The two battleships opened fire on *Bismarck*, which was moving at seven knots, at 0847 and 0848 respectively, at an initial range of 25,000 yards, but soon closing to 16,000. The British battleships blasted *Bismarck* with their ten 14-inch and nine 16-inch guns until 1015, when Tovey broke off the engagement to head back north to refuel. By this time *Bismarck* was a battered hulk, ablaze from stem to stern, with all her guns silenced but her flag still flying proudly. Russell Grenfell has described the German battleship's end in vivid terms:

"By 10 am the *Bismarck* was a silent, battered wreck. Her mast was down, her funnel had disappeared, her guns were pointing in all directions, and a cloud of black smoke was rising from the middle of the ship and blowing away in the wind. Inside, she was clearly a blazing inferno, for the bright glow of internal fires could be seen shining through numerous shell and splinter holes in her sides. Her men were deserting their guns, and parties of them could be seen running to and fro on the upper deck as shells continued to rain in, and occasionally jumping over the side, to escape by a watery death from the terror on board. Captain Patterson would have ceased fire earlier had he known of this, but the *Bismarck*'s port side was so screened by a wall of shell splashes along her whole length that it was none too easy to notice what was happening on board her."

It should be pointed out here that there is a difference of opinion between British and German historians about the last few minutes of *Bismarck*'s life. The British claim that the German battleship was finally sunk by two torpedoes from *Dorsetshire* at 1036. German historians do not dispute the time, but claim that *Bismarck* was scuttled by her crew, after all her armament had been knocked out, to prevent her falling into the hands of the British. What does seem clear, however, is that none of the British shells succeeded in penetrating *Bismarck*'s belt or deck armour.

In any event, the conclusion of Sir John Tovey's report must command general

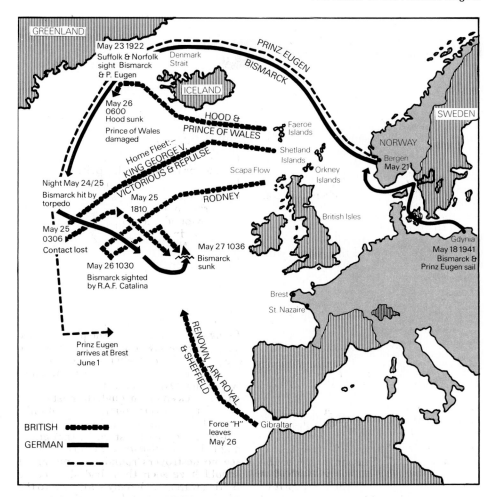

agreement: "*Bismarck* fought an extremely courageous battle against greatly superior forces; in the best tradition of the old Imperial German Navy, she went down with her colours flying."

Dorsetshire and the destroyer *Maori* picked up 110 survivors, *U-74* three more who were clinging to a raft, and the German supply ship *Sachsenwald* two more. On hearing of the result of the engagement, General Franco sent the Spanish cruiser *Canarias* to the area, but no further survivors were found.

The following points should be made in conclusion:

1. What would have been the result if the aircraft-carrier *Graf Zeppelin*, which had been launched in 1938, had been with *Bismarck*? Her Messerschmitt Bf 109T fighters would have made mincemeat of the British aircraft, and her Stukas could have played havoc with the British warships.

2. Without such an aircraft-carrier, the Luftwaffe was powerless to save *Bismarck*: the first Heinkel 111 to arrive on the scene did so a few minutes after *Bismarck* had gone down. The following day, however, German aircraft were able to sink the destroyer *Mashona*.

3. *Bismarck*'s and *Prinz Eugen*'s sortie had forced the British Admiralty to send in pursuit eight battleships and battle-cruisers, 11 cruisers, 22 destroyers, and six submarines, thus proving that Admiral Raeder's "Z-Plan" was basically sound. But what he did not

The epic chase of Bismarck, *the greatest air-sea pursuit in British naval warfare, covering the entire North Atlantic.*

possess in May 1941 was a combat force capable of utilising this forced redeployment of the Allied naval forces.

4. Throughout the 141 hours that the chase lasted, the fact that the Royal Navy lacked tankers able to refuel its warships at sea was, logistically and tactically, a constant headache both for Tovey and the Admiralty. It is in this light that Lieutenant-Commander Wolfahrt's exclamation "no destroyers, no zig-zags" takes on its full significance. Compare the British situation with Raeder's. At the same time, and in considerably more difficult circumstances, he had no fewer than 13 supply ships operating in the Atlantic, loaded with fuel, spare parts, and ammunition for *Bismarck*'s squadron, U-boats, and the disguised surface raiders.

Now alerted, the Admiralty sent out powerful forces, including the aircraft-carriers *Eagle* and *Victorious*, against them. Between June 5 and 18, nine of these supply ships were sunk, the four others managing to return to port but never to go to sea again.

Prinz Eugen, after leaving *Bismarck*, continued south and thence to Brest, where she arrived on June 1. Such was the baptism of fire of this cruiser, which was later to be blown up by the third atomic bomb on December 16, 1946.

CHAPTER 29
Coral Sea and Midway

The question of whether the neutralisation of the American aero-naval forces based on Pearl Harbor should be exploited by a landing on the island of Oahu had been discussed in Tokyo during the detail planning for the December 7 attack. The answer had been "no". Those responsible for Japanese strategy were content with knocking out the main U.S. fleet, thus gaining the time necessary for their forces to overrun South-East Asia. After that they would consider the matter again.

And so, after the capture of Guam and Wake, in the south-eastern Pacific theatre, the Japanese contented themselves with the occupation of the Gilbert Islands, on which they based their major defensive hopes.

Pearl Harbor was a fatal blow to Operation "Rainbow", the American conquest of the Marshall and the Caroline Islands and the organisation of an American base at Truk. The Pacific Fleet had had an offensive mission; now it was on the defensive, but this was only for the time being and there was no danger that it would become a passive force. This was the idea which Rear-Admiral Husband E. Kimmel expressed in a note to Navy Secretary Knox on December 11, 1941 when the latter arrived in Pearl Harbor:

"With the losses we have sustained, it is necessary to revise completely our strategy of a Pacific war. The loss of battleships commits us to the strategic defensive until our forces can again be built up. However, a very powerful striking force of carriers, cruisers and destroyers survives. These forces must be operated boldly and vigorously on the tactical offensive in order to retrieve our initial disaster."

In support of this opinion it should be said that on that same day the Pacific Fleet still had in fighting trim the aircraft-carriers *Lexington*, *Saratoga*, and *Enterprise*, 16 cruisers, 44 destroyers, and 16 submarines, some at sea, others in bases at Pearl Harbor and Bremerton (Washington State). Also, when he heard of the Japanese attack, Vice-Admiral Stark, Chief of Naval Operations, ordered the Atlantic Fleet to send *Yorktown*, a carrier of the same class as *Enterprise*, through the Panama Canal to the Pacific—a vital reinforcement.

Scarcely had Kimmel formulated his rather optimistic plan than he was relieved of his command and replaced, on Roosevelt's personal choice, by Rear-Admiral Chester W. Nimitz: "a tow-haired, blue-eyed Texan, of the Naval Academy class of 1905. Tactful and modest, sound in his judgement of men and events, he was to prove a thoroughly fortunate choice." Such is the opinion of E. B. Potter, a professor at the Annapolis Naval Academy, with whom Nimitz later wrote books on naval warfare in World War II. On December 27 Nimitz took over as Commander-in-Chief Pacific Fleet, or

Cincpac, with promotion to Admiral, whilst in Washington Admiral Ernest J. King was appointed head of the U.S. Navy, replacing Vice-Admiral Stark. King thus became Cincus, Commander-in-Chief United States Fleet, and addressed his first order to Cincpac, defining his mission in these terms:

"1) Covering and holding the Hawaii–Midway line and maintaining communications with the west coast.

2) Maintaining communications between the west coast and Australia, chiefly by covering, securing, and holding the Hawaii–Samoa line which should be extended to include Fiji at the earliest practical date."

The execution of this order postulated the setting up of an air-sea front running from Dutch Harbor (Alaska) to Midway, including New Caledonia and hinging on Port Moresby in New Guinea. Nimitz could, of course, call upon all possible facilities in the British and Australian possessions in the Pacific. The French territories had gone over to de Gaulle in the summer of 1940 and in the following year an agreement reached between the Free French leader and the American Government gave the same facilities to the Americans in the case of aggression by the Japanese. The Pacific Fleet's task, therefore, was to engage and repel all enemy forces which attempted to force the front described above. But it was not to be restricted within this perimeter. On the contrary it was, as Admiral King is said to have put it, "to hold what you've got and hit them when you can".

Admiral Nimitz set about his task as best he could, in spite of the temporary loss of *Saratoga*, damaged by a torpedo on January 11, 1942 and out of service for five months thereafter. On February 1, groups commanded by Rear-Admiral F. J. Fletcher and Vice-Admiral W. F. Halsey, each built round one carrier, "struck", the one in the Gilbert archipelago and the other in the Marshall Islands, to such effect that the Japanese High Command thought it necessary to withdraw the aircraft-carriers *Zuikaku* and *Shokaku* from the fleet then preparing to operate in the Indian Ocean. During another undertaking by Halsey, planes from *Enterprise* bombed Wake Island on February 24, then Marcus Island. The latter was only about 1,100 miles from the Japanese capital.

Annoying though they were, these were only pinpricks, and during this phase of the campaign they were less important than another victory which the Americans won over their enemy. This came about in the shade of an office in Pearl Harbor and was never the subject of any special communiqué. By dint of much patience and perspicacity, the code-breaking unit attached to the Pacific Fleet succeeded in deciphering the Japanese naval code. From then onwards, now that it was

known what the enemy was going to do, the enemy was going to be undone, to paraphrase an old proverb.

Aboard the battleship *Nagato*, flying the flag of Admiral Yamamoto in Hiroshima Bay, the Combined Fleet's Chief-of-Staff, Rear-Admiral Ugaki, had been concerned since late January about what the next Japanese naval operations should be. In his opinion, it was important to take advantage immediately of the superiority of the naval and naval air forces enjoyed by Japan to crush the American fleet and seize Hawaii. Among the arguments which seemed to him to point to this conclusion we mention one:

"Time would work against Japan because of the vastly superior natural resources of the United States. Consequently, unless Japan quickly resumed the offensive–the sooner the better–she eventually would become incapable of doing anything more than sitting down and waiting for the American forces to counter-attack. Furthermore, although Japan had steeled herself to endure a prolonged struggle, it would be obviously to her advantage to shorten it if at all possible, and the only hope of so doing lay in offensive action."

But Rear-Admiral Ugaki was unable to convince his Chief of Operations, Captain Kuroshima, who considered that a new attack on Hawaii would no longer have the benefit of surprise. Quite to the contrary, and a Japanese fleet operating in these waters would now have to deal not only with the enemy's naval forces but also with his air force and coastal batteries. In the face of these difficulties Kuroshima opted for an offensive westwards: the destruction of the British fleet in the Indian Ocean, the conquest of Ceylon, and the establishment of contact with the Axis powers. These were the objectives he recommended.

Direct co-operation between Japan, Germany, and Italy soon had to be abandoned as the links between the three totalitarian allies were very tenuous. Kuroshima's proposal was nevertheless examined very carefully both by Admiral Yamamoto and at the highest level of the Naval General Staff by Admiral Nagano. This was the state of things in late February when the Army, under the pretext of the Soviet pressure on Manchukuo, refused their co-operation in any attack on Ceylon.

Meanwhile the headquarters of the Combined Fleet had been set up on board the giant battleship *Yamato*. Here Ugaki's arguments against any expectations of assistance seemed still to prevail. So, turned away from Ceylon by the Army's unwillingness, no time was lost in turning the offensive eastwards. Account was taken of the objections against a direct attack on Hawaii and it was therefore decided to mount an operation for the capture of Midway. This objective was far enough away from Oahu to prevent interference by land-based American aircraft; it was also important enough to compel the enemy fleet to fight, and without land-based support this would allow the Japanese battleships and aircraft-carriers to use their as yet undoubted superiority.

Admiral Yamamoto approved the plan submitted to him for the attack on Midway and sent it forward on April 2 for approval by the Naval High Command. But in Tokyo, among Nagano's colleagues, it ran into opposition from the Operations Section, where Admiral Fukudome was insisting on an attack against Australia. According to Commander Fuchida, whose account of the matter we have drawn on, the "Australian School", as the supporters of an offensive in this area were called, put forward the following arguments:

"Australia, because of its size and strategic location on the Japanese defensive perimeter, would almost certainly become the springboard for an eventual Allied counter-offensive. This counter-offensive, they reasoned, would be spearheaded by air power in order to take full advantage of American industrial capacity to produce planes by mass-production methods, and the effective utilisation of this massive air strength would require the use of land bases in Australia. Consequently, there would be a weak spot in Japan's defensive armour unless Australia were either placed under Japanese control or effectively cut off from the United States."

It is true that the Army had refused the Navy the one division thought necessary to overrun Ceylon, and it had all the more reason to refuse to put ten into an operation such as this. They would content themselves, therefore, with isolating Australia and this would be done by the progressive occupation of New Guinea, the Solomon Islands, New Caledonia, New Hebrides, Fiji, and Samoa.

Admiral Yamamoto did not agree with this line of reasoning. In his opinion the G.H.Q. plan would not give him the great naval battle which he thought so necessary for swift victory. Admiral Nagano supported him, though very much against his better judgement. These differences of opinion continued up to the day of the operation, but on April 18 an event occurred which decided the argument: the bombing of Tokyo by a handful of North American B-25 Mitchell twin-engined bombers under the command of Lieutenant-Colonel James H. Doolittle.

These planes weighed 13 tons fully loaded and nothing so heavy had ever taken off from an aircraft-carrier before. Lengthy preparations were therefore necessary. On April 13 the aircraft-carrier *Hornet*, with 16 of these B-25's on board, rendezvoused with Task Force 16, under Halsey, which was to escort her. The plan was that Doolittle and his companions were to take off some 500 miles from Japan, carry out their mission, and land

in Nationalist China, deck landings by B-25's being impossible. Some 200 miles east of the area from which the planes were to take off, Halsey's force fell in with an enemy patrol and the American admiral had to order Doolittle to take off at once as the necessary secrecy could no longer be guaranteed.

A few tons of bombs were shared out between the Japanese capital and the large cities of Nagoya and Kobe from 1300 hours on April 13, and no appreciable damage was done. But nonetheless the psychological impact of Doolittle's raiders on the Japanese people and on the Japanese armed forces was immense. The Emperor's own palace had been exposed to the danger of a direct attack.

Of the 16 twin-engined B-25s which took part in the raid, one landed on the aerodrome at Vladivostok and was seized by the Soviet authorities. The pilots of the remaining 15, running out of fuel, either crash landed or ordered their crews to bale out.

In the face of this air-raid, which was the bitterest humiliation for the whole Navy, there was no further disagreement over Yamamoto's plan. He offered his personal excuses to the Emperor. The Admiral was incensed by the American raid and he was bent on destroying the U.S. Pacific fleet by advancing to Hawaii. So on May 5 the Chief of Naval Operations issued "Naval Order No. 18 of the Grand Imperial Headquarters" requiring that before June 20 the Commander of the Combined Fleet should "proceed to the occupation of Midway Island and key positions in the Western Aleutians in collaboration with the army".

Meanwhile the 4th Fleet (Vice-Admiral Inouye), suitably reinforced, was to occupy Port Moresby on the south coast of eastern New Guinea and the little island of Tulagi in the Solomon archipelago opposite Guadalcanal. At the beginning of July they were expected to seize strategic points in New Caledonia and Fiji. As we shall see, the "Australian School" had not given up its preferences, but Yamamoto took no notice, as meanwhile the conquest of Midway would give him the chance to wipe out the American fleet.

In April, at its base in Truk in the Caroline Islands, the Japanese 4th Fleet had been reinforced by two heavy cruisers and three aircraft-carriers, two fleet ones (*Zuikaku* and *Shokaku*, 25,700 tons each) and one small (*Shoho*, 11,300 tons). Acting on orders received, Vice-Admiral Shigeyoshi Inouye divided his Task Force "MO", based on the 4th Fleet, into a Carrier

A B-25 bomber of Colonel Doolittle's strike force takes off from Hornet.

Striking Force, two Invasion Groups, a Support Group, and a Covering Group. The Tulagi Invasion Group occupied its objective without opposition on May 3. On the following day 14 transport vessels of the Port Moresby Invasion Group set sail.

Under an agreement of March 17 between London and Washington, the United States had agreed to take charge of the defence of the whole of the Pacific, including Australia and New Zealand. Alerted in time by his code-breakers, Admiral Nimitz sent Task Force 17 (Rear-Admiral Fletcher) towards Port Moresby. The force was centred on two aircraft-carriers, *Yorktown* (Rear-Admiral Fletcher) and *Lexington* (Rear-Admiral A. W. Fitch) and was joined south of the Solomon Islands by an Australian task force of cruisers under Rear-Admiral J. C. Crace. The fact remains, however, that for the accomplishment of his mission Cincpac had no authority over the 300 American planes based in northern Australia and Port Moresby. These were under the Supreme Commander South-West Asia, General MacArthur, and hence there was a certain lack of co-ordination.

The ensuing actions between the opposing forces on May 6–8 came to be called the Battle of the Coral Sea. We have already remarked that the engagement marks a date in naval warfare as it was the first time that two fleets fought from over the horizon without ever being in sight of each other, and attempted to destroy each other by bombs and aerial torpedoes.

The eminent naval historian Professor Morison has called this action the "Battle of Naval Errors". He cannot be gainsaid, in view of the many mistakes committed by the airmen on both sides, errors both in navigation and in the identification of the enemy's ships, as well as in the assessment of aerial bombing and torpedoing. In their defence, however, it must be pointed out that rapidly alternating sunshine and heavy squalls over the Coral Sea could not have made their task easy. Tactically, success went to the Japanese, since against the loss of the light carrier *Shoho*, one destroyer, one minelayer, and three minesweepers, they sank the American *Lexington* (33,000 tons), the oiler *Neosho*, which they took for another aircraft-carrier, and the destroyer *Sims*.

"The *Yorktown*, which came first under attack, successfully evaded the torpedoes launched at her and took only a single bomb hit, which did not significantly impair her fighting effectiveness. But the *Lexington*, larger and less manoeuvrable, fell victim to an 'anvil' attack on both bows simultaneously and took two torpedoes on the port side, which flooded three boiler rooms. Two bomb hits, received at almost the same time, inflicted only minor damage. The list caused by the torpedo hits was quickly corrected by shifting oil. Her engines were unharmed, and her speed did not fall below 24 knots.

"But at 1445 there was a severe explosion. Fires passed rapidly out of control and the carrier was forced to call for assistance. The *Yorktown* took aboard the *Lexington* planes that were in the air, but there was no opportunity to transfer those already on the *Lexington*. With the ship burning furiously and shaken by frequent explosions there was no choice but to 'get the men off'."

Strategically, however, the advantage was on the Allies' side, as the serious damage done to *Shokaku* and the losses of the aircraft from *Zuikaku* forced Inouye to give up the idea of landing at Port Moresby.

Worse still, the several Task Forces of the Combined Fleet had to set off for Midway and the Aleutians by May 26 and it was not possible, in the short time available, either to repair *Shokaku* or to replace the aircraft lost by *Zuikaku*. On the other hand, the Japanese grossly exaggerated their successes. They claimed that *Yorktown* had met the same fate as *Lexington*, whereas she had been hit by only one 800-lb bomb. Hence the "spirit of imprudence and error" which seized Yamamoto. This is shown by the war game, or map exercise, carried out to test out Operation "Midway". The director of the exercise, Rear-Admiral Ugaki, did not hesitate to cancel such decisions by the referee as seemed to him unfavourable to the Japanese side.

However, until the ships yet to be built under the American budgets of 1939 to 1941 came into service, the Japanese fleet enjoyed considerable superiority over its enemy. This is shown in the table at right, in which we give only the ships which took part in the actions of June 3–6 between Midway Atoll and Dutch Harbor in the Aleutians.

The Japanese aircraft-carriers had between them 410 planes, those of Admiral Nimitz 233. But Nimitz could also call upon the 115 concentrated on the airstrips at Midway in case of enemy attack. Yet these figures must not make us lose sight of the fact that the American inferiority in ships and planes was not only quantitative but qualitative as well. The Grumann F4F Wildcat fighters were less manoeuvrable and had a slower rate of climb than the Japanese Mitsubishi A6M Zeros. The torpedo bomber then in service with the U.S. Navy, the Douglas TBD-1 Devastator, with a top speed of only 206 mph, was entirely at the mercy of the Zero, Japan's standard carrier-borne fighter, which could reach some 340 mph.

Also, the American air-dropped 21-inch torpedo was so slow to reach its target that the victim had a good chance of taking avoiding action. It is nevertheless true that the Japanese Commander-in-Chief threw away recklessly the enormous chances which, for the last time, his superiority in *matériel* gave him.

For the operation designed to seize the islands of Attu and Kiska in the Aleutians, Yamamoto assembled a task force whose lavish size was out of all proportion to the strategic value of the objective: three heavy cruisers, three light cruisers, 13 destroyers, and the aircraft-carriers *Ryujo* and *Junyo* with between them 82 planes on board. In view of the impending threat to this theatre, however, the Americans sent out five cruisers and 13 destroyers (Task Force 8) under Rear-Admiral R. A. Theobald.

But there was a very serious and fundamental defect in the Japanese plan for the Midway operation. The Combined Fleet was split up into a number of separate task forces. They were deployed at considerable distances from each other, but the plan called on them to operate according to a rigid and complex timetable and yet to co-operate with each other in overcoming the Americans. The Japanese failed to concentrate their forces.

Admiral Yamamoto was convinced that his planned bombardment of Midway Island on June 4 and the assault on the atoll next day would provoke Nimitz into bringing out his fleet so that the engagement at sea, all being well, would take place on June 7 or 8. This would give Nagumo time to recover his liberty of action and the Japanese Commander-in-Chief to draw in his scattered forces. To leave nothing to chance, on June 2 two squadrons of submarines were to station themselves along all the routes the Americans might take on their way to assist Midway. Logical this might have been, but there was a basic error in its reasoning, as Professor Morison has pointed out:

"The vital defect in this sort of plan is that it depends on the enemy's doing exactly what is expected. If he is smart enough to do something different—in this case to have fast carriers on the spot—the operation is thrown into confusion."

But Yamamoto, of course, had no idea that the Americans knew his movements, and could act accordingly. So everything was decided on June 4 between Vice-Admiral Nagumo's four aircraft-carriers (272 planes) and Rear-Admirals Fletcher and R. H. Spruance's three (233 planes) supported by 115 planes from Midway. On the decisive day nine battleships, including the colossal 64,200-ton *Yamato*, 11 cruisers, and 32 destroyers never fired a shot and the 41 planes on board the light aircraft-carriers *Zuiho* and *Hosho* took no part in the action.

There was a somewhat tense atmosphere in Pearl Harbor in spite of the breaking of the Japanese codes. Men began to wonder if in fact they were not getting

involved in some diabolical deception about the objective of the next Japanese move. Their last doubts were dispelled by a ruse thought up by Commander J. Rochefort, head of the Combat Intelligence Unit at Pearl Harbor: the commander in each of the areas where a Japanese attack might be expected was required to signal some deficiency in his equipment. The Midway commander chose his seawater distillation plant, and a few days later the Americans intercepted a report from a Japanese listening post announcing that it had heard "AF" report such a deficiency. "AF" had been mentioned as the objective of Japan's present move, and Rochefort now knew for certain that Midway was the target about to be attacked.

The whole archipelago of Hawaii had been in a state of alert against a landing ever since May 14. The little Sand and Eastern Islands, the only land surfaces of any size in Midway Atoll, were rightly the object of particular care and attention and were so well reinforced with A.A. guns, reconnaissance planes, and fighter planes that the commanders on Midway, Commander Cyril T. Simard and Marine Lieutenant-Colonel Harold Shannon (soon promoted to Captain and Colonel respectively) had just over 3,000 men and 115 planes under them.

Not counting Rear-Admiral Theobald's squadron, Admiral Nimitz's forces were divided into two groups:
1. Task Force 16, based on the aircraft-carriers *Enterprise* and *Hornet*, together with six cruisers and nine destroyers. Vice-Admiral Halsey was now in hospital and so command of this force was given to Rear-Admiral Raymond A. Spruance, whose intellectual powers were so formidable as to earn him the nickname of "electric brain".
2. Task Force 17, still under the command of Rear-Admiral F. J. Fletcher, based on the aircraft-carrier *Yorktown*, together with two cruisers and five destroyers. The damage sustained by *Yorktown* on the previous May 8 would have taken two months to repair in peacetime. The 1,400 men of the Pearl Harbor dockyards did it in less than 48 hours. This allowed Fletcher to set sail on the morning of May 30, behind Task Force 16 which had left on May 28.

And so when the Japanese submarines, which were behind schedule anyway, reached the watching stations assigned to them, Admiral Nimitz's ships had already gone, and they were thus unable to report the enemy's dispositions or strength. On June 3 at 0900 hours, when the first enemy sighting reports reached them, Fletcher and Spruance were north-east of Midway and in a good position to act against the Japanese forces from the flank. On leaving Pearl Harbor they had received the following warning from Cincpac in anticipation of the enemy's superior strength:

"You will be governed by the principle of calculated risk, which you shall inter-

American torpedo bombers of 6 squadron on the Enterprise. *Only four were to return.*

pret to mean the avoidance of exposure of your force to attack by superior enemy forces without good prospect of inflicting, as a result of such exposure, greater damage on the enemy."

But as Professor Potter and Admiral Nimitz point out. "to fight cautiously, to meet a superior enemy force without unduly exposing one's own is difficult in the highest degree. That Fletcher and Spruance were able to carry out these orders successfully was due primarily to their skilful exploitation of intelligence, which enabled them to turn the element of surprise against the Japanese."

Even before the Japanese fleet left its bases. Rear-Admiral Ryunosuke Kusaka, Nagumo's chief-of-staff, made the following observation to Yamamoto: so as not to hinder take-off and landing on the flight decks, the aircraft-carriers had had their masts shortened to such an extent that their radio aerials were incapable of intercepting any enemy wireless traffic. Thus the carrier forces which would be the first to make contact would be deprived of an essential source of information. It was therefore suggested that the battleship *Yamato* should accompany the aircraft-carriers, but this was rejected by the Commander-in-Chief.

Even so, the Japanese admiral's flag-ship intercepted in the single day of June 1 180 messages from Hawaii, 72 of which were classified "urgent". This sudden intensification of radio traffic, as well as the great increase in aerial reconnaissance, could mean that the enemy forces were now at sea or about to set sail. Should Nagumo, sailing on more than 600 miles ahead of *Yamato*, be alerted? This would mean breaking the sacrosanct radio silence and Yamamoto could not bring himself to do it, although the Americans already seemed to have penetrated the secret of Operation Midway. In such a situation the Germans would have said *"Wirkung geht vor Tarnung"*, or "effectiveness comes before camouflage".

It was shortly after 0900 on June 3 when the first contact with the enemy was reported. A Catalina searching 470 miles to the south-west of Midway had been fired on by two Japanese patrol craft. Further confirmation that the Japanese were moving on Midway came when another Catalina spotted the convoy and escorts of the Midway Occupation Force. In Walter Lord's words:

"Farther to the west, Ensign Jack Reid piloted another PBY across an empty ocean. He had started earlier than the rest, was now 700 miles from Midway, nearing the end of his outward leg. So far, nothing worth reporting. With the PBY on automatic pilot, Reid again studied the sea with his binoculars. Still nothing–occasional cloud puffs and a light haze hung over the Pacific, but not enough to bother him. It was shortly before 9:25 A.M., and Ensign Reid was a man with no problems at all.

"Suddenly he looked, then looked again. Thirty miles dead ahead he could make out dark objects along the horizon. Ships, lots of them, all heading toward him. Handing the glasses to his co-pilot Ensign Hardeman, he calmly asked, 'Do you see what I see?'

"Hardeman took one look: 'You are damned right I do.'

"Commander Yasumi Toyama looked up from his charts on the bridge of the light cruiser *Jintsu*. For once all the transports were keeping in column, but the destroyer on the port side forward was raising a fuss. She hoisted a signal, then fired a smoke shell. Toyama rushed out on the bridge wing, and there was no need to ask what had happened. Everyone was looking and pointing. There, low and well out of range on the horizon, hovered a PBY."

That afternoon the convoy was attacked by a formation of Flying Fortresses.

At dawn Nagumo had reached a position 280 miles north-west of Midway island. He turned his force into the wind. Then the carriers *Akagi, Kaga, Hiryu,* and *Soryu* unleashed 36 level bombers, 36 dive-bombers, and 36 fighters. At the same time six seaplanes took off to reconnoitre for American warships, followed half an hour later by a seventh, delayed by a break-down in the catapult gear on the cruiser *Tone*.

Captain Simard on Midway was alerted in time to put up all his planes, but his 26 fighters were no match for the Japanese Zeros, which knocked out 17 of them and

The target: Midway Atoll, two insignificant specks of land with their vital air-field.

crippled seven others to such an extent that they had to be written off. The Japanese lost only six. The Midway air force was not silenced for all that. Lieutenant Joichi Tomonaga, who led the first wave, signalled back to Nagumo that in his opinion a second attack was necessary.

The Japanese admiral acted on Tomonaga's report and ordered that the torpedo-carrying bombers of the second wave (108 planes), armed to attack any U.S. ships that might appear, should have their torpedoes replaced by bombs, and the dive-bombers their armour-piercing bombs by high-explosive ones. This decision seemed justified by the ferocity of the Midway air force's counter-attack. It is true that Captain Simard's pilots pressed their charges home, as the saying was in the days of cavalry; it is also true that the training of the men on the one side and the efficiency of the machines on the other were unequal to the courage displayed. Thirty-nine torpedo-carrying aircraft and dive-bombers had attacked the Japanese without causing any damage to their ships; 17 of these planes had been shot down and seven were declared beyond repair on their return. A squadron of Flying Fortresses then bombed the enemy convoy from a height of 21,000 feet, also without success. Though these attacks had been fruitless, Admiral Nagumo nevertheless threw in his second wave of fighters.

Meanwhile, at 0728 hours, *Tone's* seaplane signalled that it had spotted ten enemy ships 240 miles away, steaming south-south-east. Not until 0820 hours did the pilot see, and then only vaguely, that there was an aircraft-carrier with them. Though this report was far from clear, it put

Nagumo in a very embarrassing position. If he sent up his second wave dive-bombers (36 planes) to attack this formation, they would be without fighter escort and would take a heavy beating. The same danger faced *Akagi's* and *Kaga's* torpedo-bombers, which were now loaded with bombs instead of torpedoes. These were less likely to be successful against warships. If he waited for the first wave to land on his carriers when they returned from Midway he would then be able to attack with all his forces. And so at 0855 hours Nagumo signalled his squadron: "After landing, formation will proceed north provisionally. We expect to make contact with the enemy and destroy him."

Whereupon the armourers of the aircraft-carriers again threw themselves into the task of changing the weapons on the aircraft, replacing H.E. bombs with torpedoes and armour-piercing bombs. As time was short, they piled up the bombs alongside the aircraft in the hangars.

At 0552 hours on June 4 a message to Admirals Fletcher and Spruance announced that the enemy forces with four aircraft-carriers were 230 miles to their south-west. Fletcher, the senior of the two officers and therefore in command of the whole force, gave the order to attack. From 0702 hours Task Force 16, now sailing towards the enemy, sent up 116 planes. *Yorktown,* in Task Force 17, waited until 0838 hours before launching her 35.

It has been said that Rear-Admiral Spruance had calculated the time so as to surprise the enemy aircraft-carriers just when their flight-decks would be cluttered up with planes returning from Midway. With admirable, almost unprecedented modesty he himself has denied the flattering legend in his preface to Commanders Fuchida's and Okumiya's book, *Midway.*

"When I read the account of the events of June 4, 1942 I am struck once more by the part played by chance in warfare. The

authors congratulate us on having chosen the moment of our attack on the Japanese aircraft-carriers when they were at their most vulnerable, that is with their flight-decks encumbered with planes ready to take off. We did not choose this moment deliberately. For my part I had only the feeling that we had to achieve surprise and strike the enemy planes with all the strength at our command as soon as we met them."

The first U.S. Navy squadron to attack, 15 TBD Devastator torpedo-bombers under Lieutenant-Commander John Waldron, from *Hornet,* appeared at about 0930, skimming over the tops of the waves. A few minutes later they had all been shot down and only one out of their total crew of 30 survived. They were slow and vulnerable to enemy fire. Fuchida and Okumiya described this unsuccessful but heroic attack in the following words:

"The first enemy carrier planes to attack were 15 torpedo bombers. When first spotted by our screening ships and combat air patrol, they were still not visible from the carriers, but they soon appeared as tiny dark specks in the sky, a little above the horizon, on *Akagi's* starboard bow. The distant wings flashed in the sun. Occasionally one of the specks burst into a spark of flame and trailed black smoke as it fell into the water. Our fighters were on the job, and the enemy again seemed to be without fighter protection.

"Presently a report came in from a Zero group leader: 'All 15 enemy torpedo bombers shot down.' Nearly 50 Zeros had gone to intercept the unprotected enemy formation! Small wonder that it did not get through."

The squadrons of Devastator torpedo-bombers from *Enterprise* and *Yorktown* were almost as unfortunate: they lost 20 out of 26 planes to the Japanese fighters and A.A. guns. Worse still, not a single one of their torpedoes reached its target.

So by 1015 hours Nagumo was winning. At the cost of six of his own planes he had destroyed 83 of his enemy's and at 1030 hours he would unleash on the American squadron a wave of 102 planes, including 54 torpedo-bombers and 36 dive-bombers. He was confident that they would destroy the Americans.

By 1028 hours, however, the Rising Sun had been decisively defeated.

The American planes had encountered difficulties during their approach, as the position they had been given was erroneous, the Japanese ships having changed direction. This caused an unwelcome detour. Some Wildcat fighter squadrons lost the torpedo-carrying aircraft they were supposed to be escorting. The massacre described above was the result. But the heroic sacrifice of Waldron and his men payed off a few minutes later. The Zero fighters were so busy tracking down Waldron's planes at low level that they were too late to prevent an attack by Douglas SBD Dauntlesses, which dive-bombed the Japanese aircraft-carriers from a height of nearly 20,000 feet. On the carriers themselves, the Japanese were too busy warding off torpedoes to see the second attack.

This was one of the most decisive moments of World War II, and yet it was over in a flash, almost before the Japanese knew what had happened.

The scene has been described by an eyewitness on the flight-deck of the ill-fated *Akagi*:

"I looked up to see three black enemy planes plummeting towards our ship. Some of our machine guns managed to fire a few frantic bursts at them, but it was too late. The plump silhouettes of the American 'Dauntless' dive-bombers grew larger, and then a number of black objects suddenly floated eerily from their wings. Bombs! Down they came straight towards me! I fell intuitively to the deck and crawled behind a command post mantlet.

"The terrifying scream of the dive bombers reached me first, followed by the crashing explosion of a direct hit. There was a blinding flash and then a second explosion, much louder than the first. I was shaken by a weird blast of warm air. There was still another shock, but less severe, apparently a near-miss. Then followed a startling quiet as the barking of guns suddenly ceased. I got up and looked at the sky. The enemy planes were already gone from sight . . .

"Looking about, I was horrified at the destruction that had been wrought in a matter of seconds. There was a huge hole in the flight deck just behind the amidships elevator. The elevator itself, twisted like molten glass, was drooping into the hangar. Deck plates reeled upwards in grotesque configurations. Planes stood

tail up, belching livid flame and jet black smoke. Reluctant tears streamed down my cheeks as I watched the fires spread."

A few minutes later a series of explosions from petrol and the loose piles of bombs rocked the huge ship from stem to stern, causing widespread fires and destruction. *Akagi*'s radio was out of action, and Vice-Admiral Nagumo and his staff left the ship at 1046 hours.

"As the number of dead and wounded increased and the fires got further out of control, Captain Aoki finally decided at 1800 that the ship must be abandoned. The injured were lowered into boats and cutters sent alongside by the screening destroyers. Many uninjured men leapt into the sea and swam away from the stricken ship. Destroyers *Arashi* and *Nowaki* picked up all survivors. When the rescue work was complete, Captain Aoki radioed to Admiral Nagumo at 1920 from one of the destroyers, asking permission to sink the crippled carrier. This inquiry was monitored by the combined fleet flagship, whence Admiral Yamamoto dispatched an order at 2225 to delay the carrier's disposition. Upon receipt of this instruction, the captain returned to his

The shattered wreck of the Japanese cruiser Mikuma, *caught while escaping from Midway; she was sunk by bombing.*

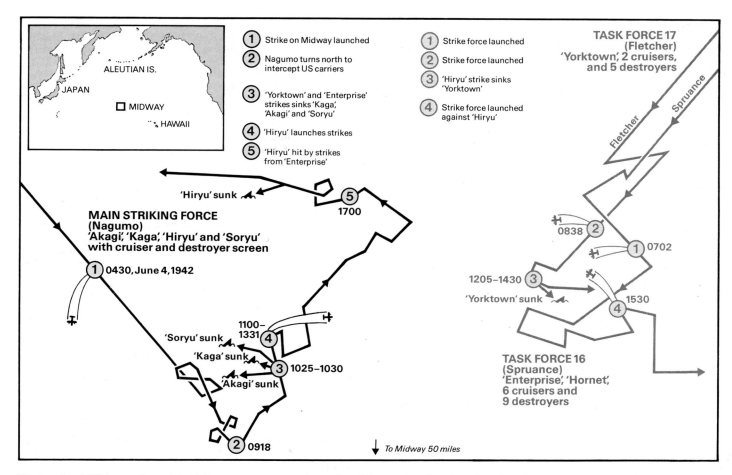

①	Strike on Midway launched
②	Nagumo turns north to intercept US carriers
③	'Yorktown' and 'Enterprise' strikes sinks 'Kaga', 'Akagi' and 'Soryu'
④	'Hiryu' launches strikes
⑤	'Hiryu' hit by strikes from 'Enterprise'

①	Strike force launched
②	Strike force launched
③	'Hiryu' strike sinks 'Yorktown'
④	Strike force launched against 'Hiryu'

The battle of Midway, June 4-6, 1942. Through this great victory the Americans gained the strategic initiative in the Pacific theatre of war.

carrier alone. He reached the anchor deck, which was still free from fire, and there lashed himself to an anchor . . .''

A few miles away, *Kaga*, hit by four bombs, had also become a raging inferno and her crew were attempting to control the flames amidst explosions which were causing widespread death and destruction. The ship had been attacked by *Enterprise*'s and *Hornet*'s Dauntless dive-bomber squadrons, led by Lieutenant-Commander Clarence W. McClusky. *Soryu* was bombed by planes led by Lieutenant-Commander Maxwell Leslie and by formations from *Yorktown*. By 1040 hours *Soryu*'s rudder and engines were out of action and her crew were surrounded by fires and explosions.

The only unit of the Japanese Carrier Striking Force now fit to fight was *Hiryu*. In accordance with Nagumo's order she sent off some 40 planes in two waves to attack Task Force 17. At mid-day, 18 dive-bombers appeared above *Yorktown*. The American fighters, warned in time by radar, and the A.A. wiped out 12 of them, but two bombs reached their target and the powerful vessel was brought to a standstill at 1220 hours. She had got under way again, but not at full speed, when *Hiryu*'s aircraft pressed home their attack through a seemingly impenetrable barrage of fire and scored hits with two torpedoes. Seeing his ship in danger of capsizing, her

commander ordered her to be abandoned and taken in tow. This was to be *Hiryu*'s last action. Only 15 of her planes, including six fighters, returned. At 1630 hours, Spruance sighted her and sent in 24 Dauntlesses under McClusky. The Japanese vessel whipped her speed up to 33 knots, but she was hit by four bombs at 1700 hours. All the planes on the flight deck were set on fire and all means of escape from the ship were cut off. At dusk Task Force 16 set course eastwards as Spruance did not care to risk a night battle with an enemy force containing the battleships *Haruna* and *Kirishima*, against which he was clearly at a disadvantage.

Between 1900 and 1930 hours, *Soryu* and *Kaga* both disappeared beneath the waters of the Pacific. In the morning of the following day Nagumo, with the authority of Admiral Yamamoto, finished off the wrecks of *Akagi* and *Hiryu* with torpedoes. The commander of the second, Rear-Admiral Tamon Yamaguchi, obstinately refused to leave his ship and, to ensure that he went down with her, tied himself to the bridge.

On board *Yamato*, the Commander-in-Chief of the Combined Fleet could do no more than admit his powerlessness to redeem the situation now that his various detachments were so widely scattered. After a series of orders and counter-orders, on June 5 he finally confirmed the abandonment of operations against Midway and the return to their bases of his several detachments.

This was not to be done without further

loss, however. In the 7th Cruiser Division, *Mogami* was in collision during the night with *Mikuma*. Hounded by enemy planes in the daylight, the former was further damaged and put out of action for a year. The latter went down at about noon on June 6. A few hours later the Japanese submarine *I-168* (Lieutenant-Commander Yahachi Tanabe), which had shelled Midway on the night of June 4–5, surprised *Yorktown* as she was being towed slowly back to Pearl Harbor. Manoeuvring swiftly and decisively it sank her with two torpedoes and cut the destroyer *Hammann* in half with a third.

This was the end of one of the most decisive battles of World War II, the effects of which were felt far beyond the waters of the Pacific. It deprived Japan of her freedom of action and it allowed the two Anglo-Saxon powers to go ahead with their policy of "Germany first", as agreed between Churchill and Roosevelt.

The Americans had lost 307 dead and 147 planes. The Japanese lost 4 fleet carriers, 332 planes and 3,500 dead, and these heavy losses included the cream of her naval air forces. The results show that, though they had been dealt a worse hand than the enemy, Nimitz, Fletcher, and Spruance had played their cards better than Yamamoto and Nagumo. Chance had played her part too, though. What would have happened if *Tone*'s seaplane had not been half an hour late in taking off? We shall never know.

On June 6–7 the Japanese occupied the undefended islands of Kiska and Attu in the Aleutians.

CHAPTER 30

The economic balance between Allies and Axis

From the documents available today it is evident that the fortunes of war in the early months of 1942 were evenly matched between the two great alliances.

By July 1, 1942, in spite of their disappointments of the previous year, Hitler and Mussolini felt close to victory. It is true that they must have suspected that success had not crowned Admiral Yamamoto's recent venture at Midway on June 4, but Tokyo had hidden the extent of the Japanese defeat from the other two partners in the Axis, and the general situation thus appeared excellent: Sevastopol' was being mopped up, while the offensive which was aimed at taking the Wehrmacht on to Stalingrad, Baku, and Batumi had begun brilliantly, sweeping the feeble Russian defences before it; in the Mediterranean, Malta seemed to have been definitely reduced to impotence and the Duce, who had travelled to Derna bringing with him the conqueror's white horse, was impatiently expecting any hour the telegram from Field-Marshal Rommel which would enable him to make a triumphal entry into Cairo.

Three months later the German 6th Army had begun its exhausting street battle in the centre of Stalingrad, while in the Caucasus the 1st Army was advancing towards Groznyy only in fits and starts, and the first snow had appeared on the mountain crests.

At the same time, the aircraft based on Malta were beginning to exact a steadily more greedy toll of the supplies destined for the Axis forces which were still held up before El Alamein. These German and Italian troops, still nursing their wounds after their attempt to reach the Suez Canal, were aware that the enemy was growing stronger with every day that passed. Finally, in the Pacific, the Japanese, far from taking their revenge for Midway, had been reduced to the defensive in the jungles of Guadalcanal.

To sum up, 1942 was not to see the fulfilment of spring's promises in any theatre in this gigantic conflict.

On August 27, as he came away from the funeral of the son of Admiral Horthy, Regent of Hungary, who had been killed in an aircraft accident, Count Ciano wrote in his diary that his German opposite number had lost some of his previous boastful confidence:

"Ribbentrop's tone is moderate, even though he continues to be optimistic. The German: 'The war is already won' of the old days has now become: 'We cannot lose this war'. He is obviously coming off his high horse. He gave no particulars, but he judges Russia to be a hard nut, very hard, and thinks that not even if Japan should attack her would she be entirely knocked out. He makes no forecasts on the length of the war; it might have a rapid conclusion, 'but one must not count too much on that'."

The fact is that, if Ribbentrop was thinking along these lines, he had lost sight of the plan upon which his Führer had decided in the summer of 1940, which was to complete the annihilation of the Soviet Union in 1941. And this was based on the assumption that he could rule out the intervention of the United States on the side of Britain until 1942. Yet Hitler and Mussolini had not kept to this timetable. Four days after Pearl Harbor, giving the *casus foederis* of the Tripartite Pact a generous interpretation, they had not waited for the Russian campaign to achieve a decisive result before declaring war against the United States, to President Roosevelt's great satisfaction.

Since the war on two fronts would continue without any reasonable possibility of forecasting its length, the industrial might of the United States would weigh more and more heavily in the balance of the opposed forces. During the "Arcadia" Conference, which took place between December 23, 1941 and January 14 of the following year, President Roosevelt and the British Prime Minister met at the White House. Churchill, backed up by Lord Beaverbrook, and with the determined support of Harry Hopkins, persuaded his ally to revise the war industries' programme to which Roosevelt had agreed on the day following the Japanese attack. In every class of material, the figures would be substantially increased, and the results achieved reveal the size of the effort which the eloquence and the persuasive powers of his friend Winston Churchill had inclined the President to undertake.

In addition, it was decided to raise the production figure for American merchant shipping to eight million tons deadweight by 1942 and to aim at a figure of ten million for 1943. And thus it is not at all difficult to understand why Churchill, summarising these figures, wrote to Clement Attlee, who was deputising for him in London, these words at the end of his letter of January 4, 1942:

"Max [Lord Beaverbrook] has been magnificent and Hopkins a godsend. Hope you will be pleased with immense resultant increase in programme."

Even though these figures had appeared in the message addressed by the President to Congress when he applied for the necessary supplementary credits, they aroused only incredulity and even derision among the leaders of the Third Reich. This was the origin of Ribbentrop's optimism. Yet *Reichsmarschall* Göring himself, who as commander of the Luftwaffe and head of German industry ought to have been more alert, shared the general casualness about the war potential of the United States. This was noted with bitter irony by Erwin Rommel in the light of his recent experiences in North Africa. Leaving

O.K.W. after a visit at the end of September 1942, he noted:

"During the conference I realised that the atmosphere in the Führer's H.Q. was extremely optimistic. Göring in particular was inclined to minimise our difficulties. When I said that the British fighter-bombers had shot up my tanks with 40-mm shells, the *Reichsmarschall*, who felt himself touched by this, said: 'That's completely impossible. The Americans only know how to make razor blades.' I replied: 'We could do with some of those razor blades, *Herr Reichsmarschall*.'

"Fortunately, we had brought with us a solid armour-piercing shell which had been fired at one of our tanks by a low-flying British aircraft. It had killed almost the entire crew."

But if Göring was so open in showing his scepticism about the American plan to build 45,000 warplanes in 1942, the reason was that he had on his desk the figures for the aeronautical industry of the Third Reich. In the same 12 months, with everything included, it delivered only 15,556 planes to the Luftwaffe. Göring based his opinion on this figure. In his mind, if Germany could, by stretching its energies to the limit, produce only 1,300 machines per month, the figures quoted in President Roosevelt's message to Congress could represent nothing more than a flight of pure imagination.

In this he was mistaken for, in 1944, Germany herself, under a terrifying hail of bombs and incendiary devices, would manufacture about 40,600 aircraft of all types, including more than 25,000 fighters.

Göring was even more misinformed for, in this war of alliances, account must be taken of the aircraft production of the powers allied to Germany and to the United States. For all kinds of reasons, in 1942 British and Russian production was far greater than that of Italy and Japan. The Allied war effort was far more evenly balanced than that of the Axis.

As regards armoured equipment, the figures were even more out of proportion since Hitler, by his decision of January 23, 1942, had thought it sufficient to increase production to 600 vehicles a month (7,200 per year) while, in the same year, the U.S.S.R. put 20,000 into service, Great Britain constructed 8,611, and the United States 24,000. To sum up, at this period of the war, the powerful industry of the Reich was not yet mobilised to the same degree as that of its adversaries.

At this point in its development, World War II must be considered from another angle: since two alliances are concerned, the relations – good or bad – between the allies in both blocs should come under examination.

Hitler continued to have full confidence in his friend Benito Mussolini. In fact, the Italian dictator was probably the only man to receive the Führer's

A Lockheed Hudson, bound for Britain, is loaded onto a ship in a port on the American eastern seaboard.

respect and even affection. However, Mussolini was no longer in a position to refuse anything to his ally in the Pact of Steel. Certainly, in private, he sometimes complained about the Germans and about the behaviour of their troops in Italy, and he would shout, as he did in the presence of his son-in-law on February 20: "Among the cemeteries, I shall some day build the most important of all, one in which to bury German promises."

He could, however, no longer refuse to believe the prophecies communicated to him by the German dictator, either in person, as at Klessheim on April 29 and 30, or by letter, as after the fall of Tobruk, or through an intermediary such as Lieutenant-General von Rintelen, the German liaison officer attached to *Comando Supremo*.

In fact, Fascist Italy counted negatively in the balance sheet of the Third Reich and required, if she were to be kept in action, military investments that Germany found increasingly burdensome. The growing participation of the Wehrmacht in operations in the Mediterranean and North Africa provided increasing possibilities for friction and bitterness between the Italian and German generals. General, later Marshal, Ugo Cavallero, did indeed strive to maintain Italian strategy along German lines, but he met ferocious opposition from the very heart of the government. Count Ciano, for instance, described him in his diary as a "perfect buffoon", "servile lackey", "clown", "imbecile" and, the day after the defeat at El Alamein, as "really the one responsible for all our troubles". These accusations will be examined in more detail in their correct context, but it will be noted for the moment that the Duce's

Minister of Foreign Affairs did not fail to receive those generals who came to him to protest about decisions taken by the Chief-of-Staff of the *Comando Supremo*.

It is very difficult to divide the responsibilities fairly between Germans and Italians in the growing tension which became increasingly evident as the year wore on.

For a start it is clear that, like many French generals in 1940, a number of the Italian military leaders in 1941 thought that they would have to do no more than adapt their experiences of 1918 to the new conflict. Yet, from another point of view, though one may have the greatest admiration for the tactical vision, the decision, and the valour of Rommel, one must admit that he had none of the qualities needed in a good leader of allied forces, in the manner of Foch in 1918 or Eisenhower from 1942 onwards. One only has to read his letters and his war diaries to understand the hostile feelings he aroused in officers of the Italian Army. In contrast, Kesselring knew how to gain their trust. It has also been seen how Rommel did not play fair with them and was capable of going over the head of the *Comando Supremo* and appealing directly to *Oberkommando der Wehrmacht*.

If he had been at the peak of his physical powers, would Mussolini have been able to control the situation? It is unlikely, considering his lack of method and his changes of mood. However, after a few alarms in the spring, he had to face a new challenge in September: that of his health, which was affected by a painful stomach ulcer and complicated by an amoebic infection. As a result, he was forced to allow his son-in-law to represent Fascist Italy at the Axis conferences that were held to discuss the implications of the Anglo-American landings in North Africa, and Count Ciano no longer believed in Hitler's star.

The last touch to the picture of Italo-German relations is added by the fissures that grew steadily deeper in the monolith of the Fascist Party itself, and were revealed by the crisis of July 25, 1943, when Mussolini was sacked. By then, outside the Party, the German alliance had as many opponents in Italy as there were Italians.

It was more difficult to reach agreement on a war plan between the Axis and Japan than between the two English-speaking governments and the Soviet Union. For one thing, Berlin and Rome were given very little information on the strategic intentions of their Japanese ally. Not until March 15, 1942 does Ciano mention the subject in his diary. On that day he notes:

"In a conference with Indelli [Italian Ambassador in Tokyo] the Japanese have defined their plans. No attack on India, which would disperse their forces in a field that is too vast and unknown; no attack on Russia; an extension of the conflict towards Australia, where it is evident that the Americans and British are preparing a counter-attack."

Then the curtain fell again and, on May 9, the Italian Foreign Minister was reduced to looking at communiqués published in the press in order to obtain some idea of what had really happened in the Battle of the Coral Sea. Ciano records his perplexity, since the bulletins issued by the Japanese General Staff affected the honour of the Emperor himself:

"Therefore, they should not lie, although war lies are more or less like those that do not compromise the honour of a woman – permissible lies."

In fact, it seems that Tojo, in imitation of Mussolini, had never envisaged any other form of belligerency than "parallel war". He would fight with his allies but admitted no possibility of any strategic co-operation. His absolute ambition was limited to conquering what the Japanese called the perimeter of Greater Asia, which would place the "Greater East Asia Co-Prosperity Sphere" out of the range of any Anglo-American counter-attack and would allow it to expand in peace.

At one moment, it might have been believed that Hitler, Mussolini, and Tojo were fighting as a team. This was at the beginning of April 1942 when the Japanese fleet under Admiral Kondo steamed into the Indian Ocean and launched its aircraft to bomb Colombo and Trincomalee, in Ceylon. Were the Japanese preparing for an invasion of Ceylon, or of Madagascar, where the base of Diego-Suarez, if captured, would have allowed them to cut the vital supply line linking the British 8th Army to its base in the United Kingdom? This was the question being asked in London and Washington. But, as early as April 10, Kondo had set course for Japan and, on May 26, the very day that Rommel's Panzers thrust eastwards towards Tobruk, Vice-Admiral Nagumo's aircraft-carriers sailed in the same direction, their objective being Midway.

Nevertheless, on August 3, Marshal Cavallero met the Japanese military mission in Rome and took the opportunity to explain his views to General Shimazu. Of course, collaboration between the Japanese Empire and the Axis could only have been indirect in most cases. Yet there was one place where it could have been of immediate value: the Indian Ocean. But, according to the notes which he took after the meeting, the Japanese general reserved his opinion. Besides, after the disaster at Midway, of which Cavallero had not been informed, it was too late.

Relations between Japan and the Soviet Union were still conditioned by the clauses of the Non-Aggression Pact of April 13, 1941. By virtue of this agreement, Russian cargo vessels, crammed with war material furnished under the terms of Lend-Lease, sailed from ports on the Pacific Coast of the United States and, even after Pearl Harbor, continued to use the short cut to Vladivostok through the Japanese archipelago. This was not to say that Tojo had seriously given up his secret ambitions over the northern part of the island of Sakhalin and the maritime province of eastern Siberia. But, for his hopes to be realised, he would have to wait until the Wehrmacht had made his task easier by crushing and eliminating the Red Army.

As has been seen, the Japanese war effort was based on entirely egoistic considerations and, from the second half of 1942 onward, would allow the enemies of the Tripartite Pact Powers steadily increasing freedom in their choice of objectives. It would permit them to apply, with ever-greater effectiveness, the principle laid down between the British and the American Chiefs-of-Staff at their earliest consultations: "Germany First".

To sum up: in the totalitarian camp, the strategic maxim of the concentration of effort was not put into effect between the Axis Powers. This would have serious consequences.

In the Allied camp, the machinery of the alliance did not function without some moments of friction, but generally it ran much more smoothly and satisfactorily. Churchill put it thus:

"The enjoyment of a common language was of course a supreme advantage in all British and American discussions. The delays and often partial misunderstandings which occur when interpreters are used were avoided. There were however differences of expression, which in the early days led to an amusing incident. The British Staff prepared a paper which they wish to raise as a matter of urgency, and informed their American colleagues that they wished to 'table it'. To the American Staff 'tabling' a paper meant putting it away in a drawer and forgetting it. A long and even acrimonious argument ensued before both parties realised that they were agreed on the merits and wanted the same thing."

Apart from their telephone conversations and their written correspondence,

the British Premier and the President of the United States met no fewer than eight times between the end of December 1941 and February 1945, accompanied by their principal military, political, and administrative aides, to review the situation and make decisions about their common purpose. Since none of these conferences lasted for less than a week, it is reasonable to conclude that, every time they met, the two statesmen went over all outstanding questions. In this Anglo-American dialogue, it is evident that the last word belonged to Franklin D. Roosevelt but, for all that, Winston Churchill was not reduced to the pitiful rôle played by Mussolini in his talks with Hitler. In 1942 and 1943 Churchill's opinions on the second front convinced the American President and in addition, at a later date, the latter would show a rare spirit of military comradeship towards his ally.

As regards the conduct of operations, from the day following Pearl Harbor, the Chiefs-of-Staff committee began to function. In it, on the British side, were General Sir Alan Brooke, appointed Chief of the Imperial General Staff on November 13, 1941, Admiral of the Fleet Sir Dudley Pound, and Air Chief-Marshal Sir Charles Portal. On the American side there were General George Catlett Marshall, Admiral Ernest J. King, recently promoted

Head of Naval Operations in place of Admiral Stark, and General Henry H. Arnold of the United States Army Air Force. This committee formed what came to be known as the Combined Chiefs-of-Staff Committee.

Agreement was not always easy between these six high-ranking men, and discussion at times could be stormy. Was Admiral King an anglophobe, as was often declared in London? This would be overstating the case, but it seemed to him that British naval supremacy belonged to the past and he did not hesitate to tell Sir Dudley Pound so. Furthermore, the "Germany First" plan appealed to him much less than to General Marshall. Disagreements between the latter and Sir Alan Brooke, though not so bitter, were still very serious, for they were based on questions of principle. These two generals may have spoken the same tongue, but not the same language.

Like the majority of American generals, Marshall held to a classical system of war on the Napoleonic model, consisting of wiping out the main enemy forces, without bothering about what, in the

An American official checks a shipment of American-produced food destined for Russia.

language of debate, would be called "side issues". Brooke was far less definite; certainly he opposed Winston Churchill's preference for "small parcels", but the system of "direct strategy", in which his American colleague believed, did not seem to him to be the only road to victory; particularly so, since from that time until the moment when the Allies would be able to mount a large-scale attack, they ought not to allow the enemy to enjoy full and entire freedom of action. And hence, it seemed to Brooke, they should go in for minor and pinpricking operations which would begin on a small scale and grow steadily larger.

Winston Churchill's views were similar. In one of the notes which he composed on *Duke of York* for President Roosevelt he wrote, underlining the passage:

"What will harm us is for a vast United States Army of ten millions to be created which for at least two years while it was training would absorb all available supplies and stand idle defending the American continent."

In this controversy, Marshall referred to the precedent of the first war of continental dimensions in which the U.S.A. had been involved, its own Civil War of 1861–1865, while Brooke, naturally enough, quoted the method by which Great Britain had defeated Napoleon in one great battle, the last. Nevertheless,

Russian Industrial production: Ilyushin Il-2 Shturmovik fighter-bombers await completion.

it still remained to be seen whether the Russian campaign would have the same effect on the Wehrmacht as it had had on the armies of the French Emperor 120 years earlier.

In spite of these differences, co-operation between the British and American staffs was maintained permanently by the British Military Mission stationed in the American capital and headed by Sir John Dill from the end of December 1941. In that way a satisfactory and even neat solution was found for the chronically irritating conflict which had arisen between the ex-Chief of the Imperial General Staff and Churchill since the former's appointment some time earlier. His successor would have a task which was relatively easier because Winston Churchill no longer had the right to make decisions on his own on an impulse or momentary flash of inspiration.

In spite of these inevitable differences of view, the Chiefs-of-Staff Committee did excellent work and co-operated with absolute loyalty. Yet it should not be assumed that Great Britain was the only partner to benefit from their co-operation. Actually, the United States owed her ally a great debt in tactical and technical expertise. The fact that the Prime Minister put the whole of the progress achieved by Great Britain in the field of nuclear arms into the President's hands, alone demonstrates the importance of the British contribution to the alliance.

With the Axis astride Europe from the North Cape to the Gulf of Sirte, relations between the Western Allies and the Russians were not easy. Churchill made his first contact with Stalin in August 1942, travelling from Cairo to Moscow. Then came the inter-Allied meetings at Teheran in November 1943, Yalta in February 1945, and Potsdam in July 1945, during which the three men responsible for the policies and strategy of the great Allied powers took the opportunity to put their points of view on the war and how it should be fought. This history will include discussion of the controversies which arose between Churchill, Roosevelt, and Stalin concerning the second front and the Arctic convoys.

However, generally speaking, military co-operation between the British, the Americans, and the Russians produced satisfactory results from the outset. Leaving aside the *matériel* of all kinds supplied to the U.S.S.R. under the Lend-Lease agreement, which will be described later, a simple comparison of two figures makes it clear that, on the eve of the invasion of Normandy, the strategy devised by the Combined Chiefs-of-Staff had already caused serious harm to the forces of the Wehrmacht fighting the Red Army.

On June 22, 1941, of his 208 divisions, Hitler had left 55 in occupied Europe and Libya, between the North Cape and Half-aya Pass. On June 5, 1944, though German land forces had in fact increased to 304 divisions, the defence of Norway, Denmark, the Netherlands, Belgium, France, Italy, the Balkans, Crete, and Rhodes absorbed 108 of them. This was not all, for, though the beginning of "Barbarossa" brought 34 out of 36 armoured and motorised divisions into action against Russia, on the day of Operation "Overlord", O.K.H. could deploy only 30 such units between the Black Sea and the Baltic, while O.K.W. controlled 12 in France and six in Italy. It does not seem unreasonable to state that these figures speak for themselves.

As has been seen, on the technical side there were no secrets between the British and the Americans. They kept hardly any from their Soviet ally. This is revealed by General John R. Deane, who directed the American Military Mission in Moscow, under Ambassador W. Averell Harriman, from November 1943:

"Our policy was to make any of our new inventions in electronics and other fields available to the Russians once we had used such equipment ourselves, had exploited the element of surprise, and were satisfied that the enemy had probably gained knowledge of the equipment as a result of its having fallen into his hands. Each month I would receive a revised list of secret American equipment about which the Russians could be informed in the hope that, if it could be made available, it might be used on the Russian front. We never lost an opportunity to give the Russians equipment, weapons, or information which we thought might help our combined war effort."

But General Deane confesses that this collaboration was one-way only. The

Russians grew steadily less inclined to give information even on the nature and quality of material captured from the Germans.

The British, for their part, were stupefied when faced with Moscow's blank refusal to allow them to set up a hospital at Archangel where British medical staff would have tended sailors wounded aboard cargo ships bringing arms and munitions, through extreme danger, to Britain's Soviet ally.

From 1942 the conflict between the two mighty alliances became more bitter.

On June 9, 1941, two weeks before he unleashed Operation "Barbarossa", Hitler informed his generals that, in the struggle he was leading against Bolshevism, he could not consider himself bound by those rules of international law which attempt to ease the harsher aspects of war. Certainly, he said, the enemy would not respect them. Consequently he refused to grant prisoner-of-war status to commissars of the Red Army who fell into German hands, and ordered that they were to be shot on the spot.

It is true that this order came up against the opposition of the majority of German generals, who, like Manstein, considered that it was "contrary to the military spirit" and, if carried out, "would not only stain the honour of the troops but affect their morale". So they concealed the order and permitted their subordinates to do likewise. But this instruction, which shocked officers brought up in the old military tradition, received the enthusiastic approval of the Nazis in charge of administering the conquered territories and of the S.S. units responsible for enforcing the "New Order".

On its side equally, the guerrilla warfare which had flared up behind the German lines did not respect the customs of war as prescribed by international law. Nor could it be expected to do so, for it would be difficult to expect the partisans, not wearing uniform, fighting a war of ambushes and sabotage hundreds of miles behind the lines, to organise prisoner-of-war camps regularly inspected by delegates of the International Red Cross! And so there followed a hideous war which, on both sides, usually involved the killing of the wounded and of prisoners.

In Yugoslavia, war was now widespread, mainly in Serbia and Montenegro. On one side, supported by King Peter II and the Yugoslav Government in exile, General Draža Mihailović, who had never surrendered, continued to wage guerrilla war against the invaders of his country. On the other, the German attack of June 22, 1941 had authorised Comrade Josip Broz, alias "Tito", an ex-recruiting sergeant for the Popular Front in Paris and member of the *Comintern*, to emerge from the calm tranquility with which he had contemplated the national catastrophe of the previous spring.

But General Mihailović's *Četniks* and the partisans of the future Marshal Tito were themselves sworn enemies, for the latter were aiming not merely at the defeat of the German invaders but also at installing a Communist régime in Belgrade. So, from the end of 1941, Yugoslavia suffered a pitiless civil war grafted on to its war against Germany. On Hitler's orders, the Germans did not differentiate between *Četniks* and communist partisans, and waged a war of extermination against both. Meanwhile, General Roatta, commander of the Italian 2nd Army, attempted to establish some sort of understanding with the *Četniks*, who were not deaf to his blandishments. This difference in their treatment of the Yugoslavs gave rise to acrimonious correspondence between the two Axis partners.

In the Scandinavian and western European countries occupied by the Germans, the main activity of the resistance movements up to then had been the gathering of information and aiding British or Polish personnel stranded by the tide of war. Great importance must be attached to the information about the Germans discovered by the Norwegian, Danish, Dutch, Belgian, and French networks. Briefly, from 1941 onwards, Hitler could not move a division or a warship, or begin fortification work, without London learning of it in the minimum of time.

On June 22 of the same year, the Communist parties of the occupied countries went over to resistance, following the German attack just launched on the Soviet Union. Their contribution was without doubt of vital importance. The unquestioning discipline of their adherents, their unshakable determination to serve Moscow, the fact that they were accustomed to working clandestinely, and their long practice in espionage made them redoubtable fighters in this secret war; on the other hand, there is reason to doubt the efficiency of all the actions against the invader undertaken by such forces.

The murder of some German soldiers or officers in a passage in the Paris Metro or in a dark street in Nantes had not the slightest effect on the capacities of the Wehrmacht, but for the French people it signified frightful reprisals. Furthermore the enforcement of security measures that such murders brought in their wake itself hindered the action of the resistance fighters. Similarly, there are legitimate doubts about the advantages of assassinating Reinhard Heydrich, Chief of the Reich Security Head Office, which comprised the *Gestapo*, S.P., and S.D. Heydrich was the abominable successor to Baron von Neurath at the head of the "Protectorate" of Bohemia and Moravia. Yet the death of this undoubted criminal, once dismissed from the *Kriegsmarine* for misconduct, was paid for by savage reprisals, including the extermination of the entire male population of the Czech village of Lidice.

Up to this moment, the war between the armies of Germany, France, Britain, Belgium, Holland, and Norway, though

S.S. men and their victims at Lidice.

brutal, had not gone past the limits set by the Geneva Convention. But in 1942 British raids against Saint Nazaire (on March 28), Dieppe (on August 19), and Tobruk (on the night of September 13-14) so exasperated Hitler that, on October 18, he issued his famous order regarding commandos. Claiming that these units were recruited in United Kingdom prisons and that they had received orders to execute their prisoners, the Führer ordered the same treatment to be applied to them:

"From now on, all enemy personnel taking part in operations described as 'commando', against German forces in Europe and North Africa, are to be executed to the last man, whether they are soldiers wearing uniform of sorts, or demolition groups armed or unarmed, fighting or in flight."

Of course, nobody would deny that British troops were not gentle in their fighting techniques; but, between neatly stabbing or strangling a sleepy sentry and coldly ordering the shooting of a helpless prisoner, there is all the difference between an act of war which is cruel but legitimate and perhaps necessary, and a war crime specifically proscribed by the Geneva Convention.

On December 13, 1942, this criminal order was applied to Lieutenant Mackinnon of the Royal Marines and four of his companions who had paddled up the Gironde river in two-seater kayaks and blown up with limpet mines five German cargo ships moored in Bordeaux harbour. But all the evidence goes to show that such cases were exceptional or almost so, as German troops found these evil procedures repugnant.

Nevertheless the order of October 18, 1942 was still held against Field-Marshal Keitel and Colonel-General Jodl by the International War Crimes Tribunal at Nuremberg. These two men had countersigned Hitler's order and transmitted it for action by their subordinates. It contributed in no small way to the death sentence which was pronounced on them.

Chapter 31
Crisis in the naval war

For the Allies, upon whom Roosevelt had conferred the somewhat grandiose title of "United Nations", 1942 had begun badly in South-East Asia, when the Japanese got within striking range of Australia. But still greater disaster was to strike them in the Atlantic, on the American east coast and in the Caribbean, extending well into 1943. This was, of course, the new U-boat offensive, which between January 1942 and March 1943 would account for 1,673 merchant ships, totalling about 8½ million tons.

On December 8, 1941, with the attack on Pearl Harbor by the Japanese, Hitler had lifted all the efficiency-limiting restrictions which he had imposed on the use of U-boats in the Atlantic. Three days later, the American *chargé d'affaires* was summoned to the Wilhelmstrasse and handed his passport. Dönitz was now free to fight the "tonnage war" in any way he pleased, with efficiency his only criterion, instead of being confined to those theatres where the tactical and technical countermeasures of the Royal Navy were becoming daily more effective.

At the end of 1941, Dönitz, as *Befehlshaber der Unterseeboote* or B.d.U. (Commander of Submarines), had 249 U-boats available, of which, however, 158 were undergoing trials or training in the Baltic; of the remaining 91 combat U-boats, various postings, at which Dönitz had protested vigorously but which had been ordered directly by the Führer, had deprived him of another 36 (of which 23 were caught in what Dönitz described as the "Mediterranean mousetrap"). Thus only 55 boats were left for duty in the vital Atlantic, a number still further reduced because some were under repair or being overhauled in their bases. Dönitz was left with only about a dozen units for active service in the Atlantic.

However, the crews of these units were magnificently trained, and the U-boats themselves were well-designed craft, tough, manoeuvrable, possessing a fair turn of speed and excellent endurance–at an average speed of 12 knots, Type IXC boats had a range of over 11,000 miles, sufficient to allow them to operate on the Atlantic coast of America for two or three weeks before returning to France. But all these qualities would have been useless had not the technical difficulties in the firing mechanism of their torpedoes, which had been a source of trouble, and even of danger, in 1940 and 1941, been finally remedied.

From December 9, 1941, therefore, Dönitz decided to unleash Operation *"Paukenschlag"* ("Kettledrum-roll") against American merchant shipping, to cash in on the latter's inexperience. But instead of the 12 Type IXC boats that he had hoped to have in this operation, he could send out only five in the period between December 16 and 25, since Grand-Admiral Raeder, sticking very closely to

the Führer's orders, refused to allow Dönitz to use any of the boats around Gibraltar, where six were on observation duty. The five boats actually sent out crossed the Atlantic undetected, and arrived at their stations on January 13. Two days later, four more Type IXC boats left Brest and Lorient to join them.

From January to June, these German raiders, operating singly on the American eastern seaboard, achieved results that can only be compared with those of a pack of wolves let loose among a herd of sheep, although little more than a month had elapsed between Hitler's declaration of war on the United States on December 11 and the beginning of *"Paukenschlag"* in January. Many aspects of World War II remain controversial, but upon this, opinion is unanimous: America was totally unprepared to take part in a ruthless struggle of this nature and her merchant shipping suffered greatly.

The defence of the American east coast from Canada to Florida, was the responsibility of the American Atlantic Fleet, commanded by Admiral R. E. Ingersoll, who took over from Admiral King when the latter became Commander-in-Chief of the United States Fleet and set to work to remedy the effects of Pearl Harbor. Under Admiral Ingersoll's overall authority, the responsibility for the defence of this enormous coastline fell upon Vice-Admiral Adolphus Andrews who never ceased calling attention to the woefully deficient resources available to him and to his command. His task was to be almost impossible because of this striking material weakness.

Indeed, the fact is that when war was declared on America, Andrews had under his command only 12 surface vessels, three of which dated from World War I, and 103 aircraft, of which most were unfit for combat duty. Furthermore, whereas the British Admiralty was formally empowered to issue orders to R.A.F. Coastal Command, the same was not true in America, where, by a law dating from 1920, the U.S. Navy had authority only over aircraft of the U.S. Marine Corps and aircraft taken on board a ship, all other land-based aircraft coming under the orders of the Army. The consequences have been described by Captain Macintyre:

"U.S. Army pilots were neither trained in shipping protection duties nor to bomb small moving targets such as submarines. Nevertheless, at the outbreak of war it was upon aircraft of the U.S. Army that the U.S. Navy had to rely for anti-submarine patrols and searches. The inexperience and lack of training of the pilots no doubt made the shortage of aircraft of less consequence; but, in fact, in January 1942 the air effort in the area of the Eastern Sea Frontier, covering some 600 miles of the Atlantic coast, consisted

of two daylight sweeps every 24 hours by six short-range Army bombers."

Even Churchill, in his memoirs, comments discreetly "... it is remarkable that no plans had been made for coastal convoys and for multiplying small craft."

Such lack of preparation must be blamed, not only on the American military chiefs, but also upon members of the Washington administration, beginning with Navy Secretary Frank Knox and President Roosevelt himself, who by the terms of the constitution was the Commander-in-Chief of all the American armed forces. But it must be said that Admiral King himself was slow to grasp the extent and seriousness of the crisis, and to recommend the tried and tested British remedies necessary to overcome it. On March 19, at a time when American losses were causing Churchill and Pound serious concern, King asserted that "a convoy with only an inadequate escort is worse than no convoy at all". The results of such a strategy made themselves felt with dramatic speed: proceeding individually along the coast and in the Caribbean, American tankers and cargo vessels were sunk individually, while Admiral Ingersoll's destroyers carried out utterly pointless daily offensive patrols.

Indeed, although on April 1 a com-

A U-boat in harbour.

A Sunderland takes off. These flying-boats played a vital role in the anti-submarine war.

muniqué from the Secretary of the Navy announced that 28 U-boats had been sunk by the Atlantic Fleet since January 1, post-war documents show that the first U-boat to be sunk in this particular sector was not claimed until January 14, when the American destroyer *Roper* accounted for *U-85*, commanded by Lieutenant Greger. By that date, other Allied escorts had eliminated no less than seven U-boats.

One of the reasons why King was slow to adapt to the new conditions created by the German operations, and benefit from the Royal Navy's great experience in this field since September 1939, was that he felt little esteem for Great Britain or her navy. King was deeply anti-British in prejudice and, therefore, refused to profit from British experience and all the wealth of information and advice the British made available to the American Navy.

On the German side, Dönitz has described the first phase of his new Atlantic offensive in the following words:

"Our success was complete. Ships sailed as if it was still peace-time. There was no black-out on the coast, the cities remaining brightly lit; the only exceptions were the lighthouses and buoys, whose lights were slightly reduced. Ships were still normally lit. Although war had been declared nearly five weeks before, no serious anti-submarine measures appeared to have been taken. Destroyers did, of course, patrol the shipping lanes, but with such clockwork regularity that our boats got to know when they would be coming round, and in between these times would be perfectly safe. There were a few depth-charge attacks, but they were never kept up long enough, although the shallow water would have given a high success rate. Their aircraft crews were completely inexperienced.

"Merchant ships were completely free with the use of their radios, often indicating their positions, and so giving our raiders valuable information. It was glaringly obvious that ships' captains had no idea of the circumstances in which

they might be attacked, and never dreamed that night surface attacks might be made on them.

"Our U-boats soon found the best tactics: by day they would remain on the sea-bed at a depth of between 150 and 300 feet, a few miles off the shipping lanes; and then at dusk they would move in towards the coast, and when it was quite dark they would surface in the middle of the enemy shipping." Small wonder, then, that this period was known to the German Navy as "the happy time".

The large Type IXC boats which formed the initial attacking group were soon joined by some smaller Type VIIC craft which, thanks to the enthusiasm and skills of their crews, managed to attain ranges hitherto thought impossible. The result was that from mid-February Dönitz was able to include the Caribbean in his offensive, and to attack tankers leaving Venezuela, Trinidad, and Curaçao – U-boats even fired on the refineries on the two islands.

On April 22, 1942 the new U-boat *U-459*, commanded by Lieutenant-Commander von Wilamowitz-Mollendorf, supplied its fellow submarines 500 miles north-east of Bermuda, a new idea to extend the operational radius of the active boats. Soon other German submarines were fulfilling the same task. These large 1,688-ton Type XIV "milch cow" submarines possessed only anti-aircraft guns in the way of armament, but were able to carry 700 tons of oil fuel, sufficient to replenish the tanks of a dozen U-boats in the Caribbean, or four if they went down as far as the latitude of the Cape of Good Hope. Thus Dönitz was able to keep 27 boats at sea between Nova Scotia and British Guiana, while the "milch cows" doubled the endurance of the U-boats in their area.

To sum up, during the first half of 1942, the only man capable of threatening the success of Operation *"Paukenschlag"* was Adolf Hitler who, for reasons best known to himself, had returned to his obsession of the previous autumn – that Norway was the "zone of destiny". On January 22 he declared that "we must send reinforcements there, both submarines and surface vessels, neglecting all other considerations if necessary." He thought better of

it soon afterwards, but on February 6 he ordered that eight U-boats be posted around the shores of Norway. Dönitz's reaction was to retort that the best way of defeating any possible attempt on Norway was to sink Allied shipping in the North Atlantic. His arguments, however, were not backed up by his superior, Grand-Admiral Raeder, and he had to submit to Hitler's wishes. Thus six U-boats, with their well-experienced crews, which Dönitz had been about to send off to the richly-promising American east coast, were sent off on patrol between Iceland and the Faeroes, on the look out for non-existent invasion forces.

Such was the effect of the Führer's "Norwegian complex", if it may be so called, on the strategy of the *Oberkommando der Kriegsmarine* (O.K.M.) or Navy High Command. And this was also a time when a single-minded application of the principle of concentrating one's energies on one object would have paid handsome dividends.

Captain Roskill's summing-up of this episode must command general agreement:

"Inevitably the weight of the offensive off the American coast declined, just at a time when it had proved highly profitable. In actual fact, the U-boats stationed between Iceland and the North Channel accomplished little in February and March, though two homeward convoys (S.C. 67 and H.X. 175) and two outward ones (O.N. 63 and O.N.S. 76) were attacked in those waters."

On the conning tower of a U-boat, two observers scan the seas.

According to Admiral Dönitz, the untimely and quite useless depletion of his forces resulting from Hitler's decision about Norway meant that the German submarine forces sank half a million tons of shipping less than they would otherwise have done between January and June 1942. Even so, the U-boats were doing as well now as they had been at the height of the previous year.

But the figures above take no account of the losses incurred in the Mediterranean, Indian Ocean, or Pacific, in which theatres, according to Roskill, losses amounted to 287 ships of 625,000 tons. Furthermore, during the first quarter of 1942, 30 new U-boats entered service with the German Navy, whereas only 11 were sunk by the Allies. The situation was becoming hourly more desperate.

Churchill's alarm when faced by this situation was perfectly understandable. On February 10 he took the initiative in offering the U.S. Navy ten corvettes and 24 trawlers fitted with the latest asdic. On March 12 he decided to inform the President of British fears, which he did via Harry Hopkins. Presenting Hopkins with the grim statistics, he further added:

"The situation is so serious that drastic action of some kind is necessary, and we very much hope that you will be able to provide additional escort forces to organise immediate convoys in the West Indies-Bermuda area by withdrawing a few of your destroyer strength in the Pacific, until the ten corvettes we are handing over to you come into service."

To convince the President still further, Churchill enclosed with his letter an eloquent map, graphically illustrating the absolute massacre of Allied shipping by U-boats in January–March 1942.

On March 18, Roosevelt acknowledged this letter:

"My Navy has been definitely slack in preparing for this submarine war off our coast. As I need not tell you, most naval officers have declined in the past to think in terms of any vessel of less than two thousand tons. You learned the lesson two years ago. By May 1, I expect to get a pretty good coast patrol working. . . ."
The Royal Navy, in fact, directed a corvette group from the Atlantic to the Caribbean to aid the Americans.

In June, Marshall pointed out to King that the whole of the U.S.A.'s war policy was being undermined by the ruthless German offensive.

"The losses by submarines off our Atlantic seaboard," he wrote in his historic memorandum to Admiral King, "and in the Caribbean *now threaten our entire war effort*. The following statistics bearing on the subject have been brought to my attention:

"Of the 74 ships allocated to the Army for July by the War Shipping Administration, 17 have already been sunk.

"Twenty-two per cent of the bauxite fleet has already been destroyed. Twenty per cent of the Puerto Rican fleet has been lost.

"Tanker sinkings have been 3.5 per cent per month of tonnage in use.

"We are all aware of the limited number of escort craft available, but has every conceivable improvised means been brought to bear on this situation? *I am fearful that another month or two of this will so cripple our means of transport that we will be unable to bring sufficient men and planes to bear against the enemy in critical theatres to exercise a determining influence on the war.*"

On April 1, the U.S. Navy had at last organised its first convoys along the east coast. But lacking adequate escorts the convoys had to anchor each night in protected harbours, after daily stages of less than 150 miles. Continuous convoys between Halifax, Nova Scotia, and Key West in Florida could not be instituted until the end of May.

Faced with this new situation, Dönitz, though continuing with attacks by single U-boats in the Gulf of Mexico and in the Caribbean, where convoys could not be formed, recalled his U-boats operating off the east coast of the U.S. to the middle of the Atlantic, where they again began to hunt in packs, as before. He had great success in the second quarter of 1942, especially as the number of U-boats under his command was growing continuously and the trans-Atlantic convoys had been somewhat weakened by the organisation of the convoys from Halifax to Key West. Consequently, Allied losses in the spring of 1942 were even heavier than in the previous winter, this causing General Marshall to write to Admiral King the memorandum quoted above. No less than 455 ships, of more than two million tons total displacement, including a catastrophic proportion of tankers, were sunk – and this in the Atlantic and Caribbean alone, and excluding all but losses to U-boats.

In his answer to General Marshall, Admiral King now took up an attitude diametrically opposed to that which he had adopted in March, when he had cast grave doubts on the efficacy of the convoy system. On June 21 he wrote:

"Escort is not just one way of handling the submarine menace; it is the *only* way that gives any promise of success. The so-called patrol and hunting operations have time and again proved futile."

What was needed, therefore, was a large number of escort vessels capable of crossing the Atlantic, backed up by the new escort carriers. The alarm expressed by Marshall also gave King the chance to ask for a decision in his favour in the argument raging between himself and General Arnold about the allocation of anti-submarine aircraft. King estimated his needs as 1,350 aircraft, but the Army Air Force intended to supply him with only 500 medium-range bombers. Given these ships and aircraft, trans-Atlantic convoys could be covered during their whole crossing. Finally, King insisted that all operations in any way connected with the battle of the Atlantic should be

centralised under his direct command.

Thus King, once he had realised his earlier mistakes, set to work to remedy the situation with a rational and well-balanced programme carried out energetically and clear-sightedly. Even so, nearly a year was to pass before his measures could begin to take effect, and much could happen in the interval. For example, none of the destroyer escorts ordered in the autumn of 1941 would come into service before the spring of 1943. But meanwhile the Allies would have to make do with the means at their disposal, and these were far from satisfactory as they stood.

In Paris, to which he had transferred his H.Q. after the St. Nazaire raid in March, Dönitz was also a worried man. To replace the 12 U-boats lost in the Atlantic in the first six months of the year, he had received 41 new craft, of which Hitler had taken 26 for the defence of Norway and two for the Mediterranean. The policy of dispersion of effort was still, therefore, being practised in Germany. But this was not all: while the U-boats in the Caribbean were having an easy time of it against the Americans, their fellows in the central and north Atlantic were running into greater and greater difficulties against British convoys whose escorts were growing ever stronger and more experienced.

On June 17, Dönitz radioed the following question to Lieutenant Mohr, commander of *U-105* and one of Germany's ablest U-boat captains, just as he was attacking a convoy sailing from Nova Scotia: "Have you personally noted the use by the enemy of surface detection apparatus?"

Mohr's negative reply was only partially reassuring, for U-boats sailing on the surface in the Bay of Biscay *had* been subjected to air attacks in circumstances admitting of no other explanation, despite the scepticism of German electronics experts. Dönitz notes in his memoirs:

"Aircraft came in from behind the sun, or suddenly emerged from behind a cloud, a fact which led us to believe that they had taken up position out of sight of the U-boat, whose position must therefore have been known. In June some of our vessels were bombed during the darkest nights. A searchlight would suddenly come on 1,500 to 2,000 yards away, illuminate the target immediately, and then the bombs would start to fall almost straight away. Three U-boats damaged in such attacks had to return to base."

Although he managed to obtain the use of 24 Junkers Ju 88's from the Luftwaffe to counter the activities of Coastal Command, on June 24 Dönitz was forced to order his boats not to surface while passing through the Bay of Biscay except to recharge their batteries. This had the unfortunate consequence for the Germans of greatly reducing their U-boats' operational radius.

Until they could be fitted with radar

similar to that fitted to surface vessels, the U-boats were equipped with *"Metox"* apparatus, which recorded the British radar impulses and could thus tell the U-boats' captains when they had been spotted. But the *"Metox"* apparatus was designed to receive on the 150-cm wavelength, whereas the British and Americans were in the process of installing new equipment which operated on the 10-cm wavelength. This allowed the Allied anti-submarine patrols to spot the conning tower of a U-boat at a range of up to five miles. Thus, good as the German *"Metox"* was, it was obsolete by the standards of the improved British radar.

Dönitz was luckier with the *"Pillenwerfer"* (pill-thrower), which on several occasions enabled his U-boats to throw their pursuers off the scent. As soon as a U-boat commander heard the "ping" of Allied asdic on the hull of his boat, he would discharge a *"Bold"*, or cylinder filled with calcium carbide, which made the sea literally boil in its wake. For a quarter of an hour the boiling sea would send back false echoes, and give the U-boat a chance to escape. With time, however, the asdic (or sonar as it was called in America) operators became more skilful at distinguishing between *"Bold"* echoes and the real thing, and could no longer be tricked.

The tactic of hunting in packs presupposed a continuous exchange of information between U-boats at sea, and also between U-boats and their bases. But the British and Americans were able, however, to take advantage of this from the autumn of 1942 onwards by fitting their escort craft with H/F D/F (High Frequency Direction Finder or "Huff-Duff"), which enabled them to fix the position of a U-boat transmitting, up to a range of 25 miles away. Thus when a U-boat was discovered in the vicinity of a convoy, it was a simple matter to alter course away from the area, while sending in an escort to attack the U-boat. Meanwhile, the convoy, with the rest of the escort, would be steaming away from the place where the pack might be expected.

It was Churchill who described this closely-contested technological conflict as the "wizard war". But the most decisive element in the struggle was to be the air power which the Allies could call into play. On August 21, faced with the constantly increasing number of British and American aircraft now helping in convoy duties, Dönitz noted in his diary:

"The difficulties to be expected from that direction could lead to heavy, even disastrous, losses, to less successful results; and therefore to a lessening of the possibility of success in the submarine war."

For Coastal Command was increasing its strength, though less quickly than its commander, Air Chief Marshal Sir Philip Joubert de la Ferté, would have liked, as Bomber Command had higher priority. Nevertheless, by mid-1942 Coastal Com-

mand did have 709 aircraft available, of which 16 were of the new Consolidated B-24 Liberator type. And at the same time the Americans and Canadians were increasing their anti-submarine air forces. Little by little, the "North Atlantic gap" was being plugged.

Following instructions from the German Foreign Ministry, U-boats operating in the South Atlantic now extended their attacks to Brazilian shipping, and on August 22 the Brazilian Government reacted to these acts of aggression with a formal declaration of war. Both Dönitz and Roskill maintain that the Germans committed a grave error–American aircraft could now be based at Pernambuco and Natal, in Brazil, thus tightening Allied control of the South Atlantic by co-operating with R.A.F. aircraft from Freetown, Bathurst, and Takoradi in West Africa.

The turn for the worse that events had taken only served to increase Dönitz's attacks on Allied merchant shipping. Between July 1942 and May 1943 the balance swayed first one way, then the other, until Dönitz was forced on the latter date to admit defeat, for the time being àt least. His forces had, in fact, fought magnificently, and his crews, their increased numbers notwithstanding, had performed miracles of skill and courage.

During this second half of 1942, the German U-boats turned their attentions away from the Caribbean and the American east coast to three sectors of the Atlantic: the area between the Newfoundland Bank and Iceland; off Freetown and Cape Green; and off the mouth of the River Orinoco and around Trinidad. In all these areas they exacted a heavy toll of Allied shipping. A few examples will suffice to show this:

Between August 5 and 10, convoy S.C.94, made up of 36 merchantmen and

Sinking a merchantman with gunfire– far cheaper than using torpedoes and just as effective.

six escorts, lost 11 cargo vessels in the North Atlantic, though the Germans lost two U-boats;

On the same route, between October 10 and 15, convoy S.C.104, of 44 ships, was attacked by a pack of 13 U-boats and lost eight vessels, seven of them to *U-221* (Lieutenant Trojer); in reply, the escort of two British destroyers and four Norwegian corvettes sank two U-boats, *U-619* and *U-353;*

Worse was to follow: between October 26 and 30, convoy S.L.125, *en route* from Freetown to London, was attacked between the Canary and Madeira islands, and lost 13 of its 37 ships. The escort was unable to claim a single kill. However, as Captain Roskill has pointed out, the U-boats which converged on this convoy left the way open for the first transport vessels for Operation "Torch".

Finally, between October 1 and November 7, and at the cost of only one U-boat sunk off French Guiana by an American bomber, 25 tankers and cargo vessels were sunk by U-boats in the waters around Trinidad.

Taking into account the production capacity which his department credited to the British, American, and Canadian shipyards, Dönitz reckoned that for the battle of the Atlantic to be won decisively by the Germans, 700,000 tons of Allied shipping would have to be sunk each month. This figure was reached in June (700,235 tons), and improved upon slightly in November (729,160 tons). In December, however, because of the new theatre of operations opened up in North Africa by the "Torch" landings, and the consequent need to post a considerable number of U-boats in the approaches to the Strait of

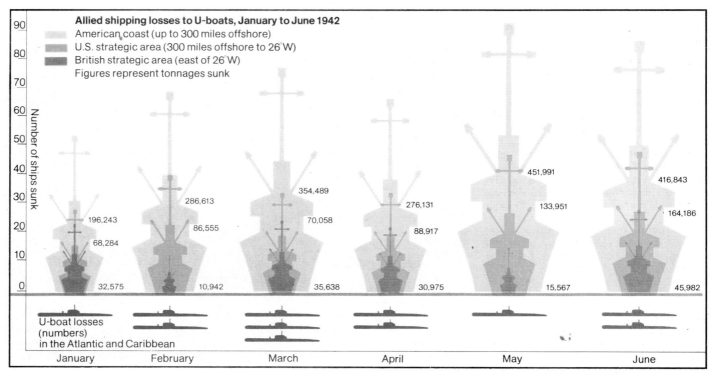

Allied shipping losses to U-boats, January to June 1942
American coast (up to 300 miles offshore)
U.S. strategic area (300 miles offshore to 26°W)
British strategic area (east of 26°W)
Figures represent tonnages sunk

For the U-boats "Happy Times" returned with successes in the new hunting grounds of the United States.

Gibraltar, less than half the required tonnage was sunk (330,816). But the Atlantic was not the only area in which the tonnage war was being fought out, nor was the U-boat the only weapon in the Axis arsenal.

In all, during 1942 Allies and neutrals lost a total of 1,664 ships (7,790,967 tons), of which 1,160 ships (6,266,155 tons) were sunk by German and Italian submarines. To this figure must be added a million tons of shipping unavailable as it was under repair. During the same period, only 7,000,000 tons of new shipping were built.

This explains why British imports in 1942 fell to less than 34 million tons, two-thirds of the tonnage that had been imported in 1939; as imports of consumer goods had been severely controlled from the beginning of the war, it was clearly vital war commodities that were being seriously threatened at this time, Captain Roskill tells us, the state of Britain's fuel oil supplies were beginning to give grave grounds for fear:

"In mid-December there were only 300,000 tons of commercial bunker fuel in Britain, and consumption was running at about 130,000 tons a month. The Admiralty held another million tons which could be used in an emergency, but if the naval stocks were allowed to run down the fleet might be immobilised. 'An ample reserve of fuel on this side of the Atlantic is the basis of all our activities,' reported the Admiralty; and when the Prime Minister was given the figures quoted above, he minuted on the paper 'This does not look at all good . . .' "

In November, Admiral Sir Percy Noble, having served his term as Commander-in-Chief, Western Approaches, handed over to Admiral Sir Max Horton a first-class organisation. Horton, a seasoned submarine commander in World War I, devoted the priceless commodities of experience and enthusiasm to his task.

In the German camp, Dönitz was faced by a problem: he had lost 87 U-boats, two in accidents, 15 in the Mediterranean, and 70 in the Atlantic. Only 17 of this last category had succumbed to American vessels and aircraft. However, as the number of U-boats built greatly exceeded that of losses, at the end of the year Dönitz had 212 craft instead of the 91 with which he had started the year, and 20 new boats were being commissioned each month.

Closer scrutiny of these figures justifies a less optimistic assessment of German success in the event of a prolonged war. Recovering from Operation *"Paukenschlag"* quickly, the Allies had begun to counter-attack vigorously, with the result that U-boat losses in the second half of the year were four times greater than in the first half: 14 between January and July, 56 between July and December. Etienne Romat has given a most graphic description of the scene in a sinking submarine:

"A dreadful drama unfolds inside the submarine: the water gushes in through a hole in the mess-room forward of the control room. The batteries are flooded; the salt water comes into contact with their sulphuric acid and gives off dense, stifling fumes of that terrible chlorine gas, which is sucked up into the engine room by the still-functioning diesel engines. The men's lungs are burnt out even before the order to abandon ship reaches them.

"Slowly the poisonous fumes reach the forward positions. Commander Hoeltring, who has been taken on board after his own submarine has been sunk, leaps up from his bunk and dashes to the control room, where one of his men, too seriously hurt to move, is dying. The chloride fumes arrive just as he does so. Knowing that he is finished, the young sailor begs his captain to finish him off quickly; Hoeltring obeys: taking out his pistol he first shoots the sailor then, half-suffocated, puts a bullet through his own brain.

"In the control room there is a wild rush towards the fresh air. Throwing discipline to the winds, ratings and officers fight madly with fists and spanners to get up the ladder to that little round opening framing the blue sky."

The contribution made by the German Navy's surface warships to the battle of the Atlantic was smaller than it had been previously, either because the loss of *Bismarck* had made Raeder more cautious about the use of his surface vessels, or – more probably – because the possibility of an Anglo-American landing in Norway had led Hitler to refuse to sanction the posting of any major vessels away from Germany. The contribution of the disguised raiders was also modest: from March to November, only 30 ships of 194,265 tons were sunk.

On January 14, *Thor* slipped out of the Gironde estuary. By the end of February she was in the Antarctic on the lookout for more whaling factory ships like those *Pinguin* had so profitably captured the year before. Drawing a blank there, however, *Thor* returned to the South Atlantic, where she made a few captures. During the summer, she moved into the Indian Ocean and after creaming off the ships plying between Ceylon and Australia, she passed through the Sunda Strait, preceded by her prizes, and docked in Yokohama on October 9.

Michel sailed from Germany on March 20 and managed to slip through the English Channel as the northern escape routes appeared impossible. For nine months, thanks to the system of supply ships organised by the navy, she prowled the waters of the South Atlantic and Indian Ocean. Although she only just missed the big French liner *Pasteur*, which had been requisitioned by the British as a troopship, she did capture or sink 14 other Allied vessels of 94,362 tons. She arrived in Yokohama on January 1, 1943.

The third and last raider to reach the open sea was *Stier*, which sailed from Stettin on May 20, 1942. She reached the South Atlantic without difficulty via the English Channel and Bay of Biscay. Between July and September she sank two cargo ships and two American tankers. But on September 27 her fifth victim, the American ship *Stephen Hopkins*, proved her undoing. Although she had only one 4-inch gun against *Stier*'s six 5.9-inch weapons and two torpedo tubes, *Stephen Hopkins*, under the command of Lieutenant Kenneth Willett, took on *Stier* and managed to sink her, though she herself was also sunk. The crew of *Stier* were picked up by the German supply ship *Tannenfels*, but that of *Stephen Hopkins* had to face four weeks in their life-boat before reaching Brazil. There were only 14 survivors from the American vessel.

On October 14 *Komet*, which was trying to join *Michel* and *Stier* in the South Atlantic, was intercepted and sunk by a force of five destroyers off Cape de la Hague in the Channel.

While Hitler's fantasy about an imaginary Allied threat to Norway greatly damaged Dönitz's U-boat offensive, it must at the same time be recognised that it led to a redeployment of the German Navy's surface forces which created considerable alarm in Great Britain and the United States, as their new positions constituted a powerful threat to the Allies' Arctic convoy route.

On the night of January 14, the battleship *Tirpitz*, which had completed her training in the Baltic, left Wilhelmshaven for Norway. On the 16th she reached Aasfjord, some 20 miles south of Trondheim, where her crew immediately camouflaged her and laid anti-torpedo booms and nets. The appearance of *Bismarck*'s sister ship in Norwegian waters caused no little panic at the Admiralty, as Sir John Tovey, commanding the Home Fleet at Scapa Flow, had only *King George V* with which to engage *Tirpitz*, *Rodney* being too slow, *Renown* too unprotected, and *Duke of York* untrained. When he heard the news, Churchill breathed fire and slaughter. "The whole strategy of the war," he wrote to the chiefs-of-staff on January 25, "turns at this period on this ship, which is holding four times the number of British capital ships paralysed, to say nothing of the two new American battleships retained in the Atlantic. I regard the matter as of the highest urgency and importance. I shall mention it in Cabinet tomorrow, and it must be considered in detail . . ."

He therefore demanded the immediate planning of an attack on *Tirpitz* by the R.A.F. A torpedo attack was out of the question because *Tirpitz* was anchored in a part of the fjord where the attackers would not be able to make their run-in, so the attack was carried out by nine Handley Page Halifax and seven Short Stirling four-engined bombers of Bomber Command on the night of January 29. Not a single bomb hit its target.

The *Tirpitz* was to spend the rest of the war in Norway. She remained a threat to British convoys to Russia and was a constant target for air attack; but not until November 1944, after 16 attempts, was she finally put out of action.

In November 1941, Raeder had been summoned to Supreme Headquarters in Berlin. Here he had proposed to Hitler that the heavy cruiser *Prinz Eugen*, which had lain idle in Brest since June, might return to Germany via the English Channel. "Why not the other two?" had been the Führer's immediate reaction, referring to the battle-cruisers *Scharnhorst* and *Gneisenau*, which were sharing *Prinz Eugen*'s enforced idleness. Hitler had not pressed the point at the time as Raeder objected to the idea strongly. But the question was raised again at the beginning of 1942, as Hitler wished to build up around Trondheim a force capable of countering any Allied attack on Norway.

On January 12, at a conference at Rastenburg, Raeder was forced to admit that an escape to Germany via Iceland was out of the question, the three crews

The fate of a straggler: a lone merchantman blazes after a bombing attack by the Luftwaffe.

no longer being at peak efficiency. And any attempt to break out up the Channel seemed to him to be pushing audacity to the point of folly. Vice-Admiral Ciliax, Lütjens's successor as *Flottenchef*, was less pessimistic; he thought that it could be done provided that absolute secrecy could be maintained and that the Luftwaffe could lend powerful air support from dawn to dusk on the day chosen for the operation. Colonel-General Hans Jeschonnek, Göring's chief-of-staff, and Adolf Galland, the General of Fighters, were both able to give their assurance for the second condition, and Hitler decided in favour of the operation.

"To come through the Channel is risky, but to stay in Brest is even more so," he said. "In any case the element of risk can be reduced if we take the enemy by surprise, which we can do if we send the ships through in broad daylight.

"The British are not capable of lightning decisions; and in any case, let us try to put ourselves in their place: what would we do if we were informed that an English squadron was sailing up north via the Pas-de-Calais? Could we, in the space of just a few hours, get together the aircraft necessary for a concerted attack? With our ships blockaded in Brest, we are in the position of a man ill with cancer; the operation is dangerous, but it is the only chance of survival, and therefore must be tried."

Bringing the meeting to a close, he declaimed: "You will see; Operation 'Cerberus' will be the greatest naval exploit of the whole war."

Admiral Ciliax's first condition—secrecy—could not be fulfilled, since in Brest Lieutenant Philippon was taking time off from his duties as officer in charge of the Navy's vegetable gardens to pass on information to London about the activities of the German warships there, and about their probable plans. On February 7, he sent this message: "Sailing imminent. Keep close watch at period of the new moon."

0028: German squadron passes Ushant, having left Brest shortly after midnight, February 11.

0114: Squadron swings east into Channel.
0530: Squadron passes Alderney.
0850: Low level fighter escort joins squadron north of Le Havre.
1042: Squadron sighted by Spitfire.
1219: Dover guns open fire.
1245: Esmonde's Swordfish attack is repulsed.
1431: *Scharnhorst* hits mine. Ciliax transfers to a destroyer.
1505: *Scharnhorst* under way again.
1547: British destroyers from Harwich attack unsuccessfully.
c. 1830: Last British air attacks on squadron, off Dutch coast.
1955: *Gneisenau* hits mine.
2134: *Scharnhorst* hits second mine.
Dawn, February 13: *Gneisenau* and *Prinz Eugen* arrive at Brunsbüttel.
0930: Ciliax returns to *Scharnhorst*.
1030: *Scharnhorst* arrives at Wilhelmshaven.

The fact that Operation "Cerberus" was successful is not due, as some have stated, to any scepticism at the Admiralty about this message, for Lieutenant Philippon was known as an absolutely reliable source of information; rather was it because the Admiralty interception plan assumed that the Germans would approach the Pas-de-Calais at night, and at high tide, which presupposed that they would leave Brest the previous afternoon. In fact, Admiral Ciliax left on February 11 at 2215; it so happened that the Coastal Command aircraft on patrol outside Brest harbour had a radar breakdown at that vital moment, and by a strange coincidence, a similar mishap befell the aircraft which was patrolling the Ushant-Brehat sector.

At 0730 on February 12, the German warships caught their first glimpse of Galland's supporting fighters. It was not until three hours later, as they were passing Le Touquet, that they were at last identified by a British Spitfire. At 1256 they entered the North Sea in line ahead and escorted by four destroyers, ten torpedo boats, numerous small craft, and covered by a very powerful air umbrella, organised by Adolf Galland.

Admiral Ciliax, the German commander in Operation "Cerberus".

When the Spitfire's report made what was happening crystal-clear, the British were totally unprepared, and their reaction was piecemeal, not to say quite unco-ordinated. In spite of the ten protecting fighters, the six Swordfish aircraft of Lieutenant-Commander Esmonde, who had previously distinguished himself in the encounter with *Bismarck*, were all shot down almost before they had time to launch their torpedoes. Their attack had bordered on the suicidal. A little later two flotillas of destroyers were thrown into the attack, but never got within striking distance. As for the R.A.F., 71 of the 398 aircraft which took part were lost, without a single bomb reaching its target, mainly because the Pas-de-Calais had an immense concentration of anti-aircraft guns, and the weather was deplorable.

Mines, however, were more successful; at 1431 *Scharnhorst* hit her first mine off the Scheldt estuary, and a second one in the evening as she passed Terschelling. With a thousand tons of water in her hull, and almost out of control, she nevertheless reached Wilhelmshaven, thanks to the coolness and excellent seamanship of Commander Hoffmann. Later that same evening *Gneisenau* struck a mine, but nevertheless managed to reach the Heligoland Bight.

British public opinion was furious at the success of Operation "Cerberus", and the War Cabinet was violently attacked in the press—*The Times*, for example, going as far as to say that "Vice-Admiral Ciliax has succeeded where the Duke of Medina Sidonia [commander of the Spanish Armada] failed . . . Nothing more mortifying to the pride of sea-power has happened in home waters since the 17th Century."

The Times did not seem to realise that the German Navy's brilliant exploit—the result, be it remembered, of one of Hitler's happier inspirations—masked a strategic retreat, the abandonment of any further attempt to throw its capital ships into the tonnage war.

Nor was this all; *Scharnhorst* only managed to get back into Norwegian waters in March 1943, whilst *Gneisenau*, which was being repaired at Kiel, was so badly damaged by an R.A.F. bombing raid on February 26 that she was put into mothballs. *Prinz Eugen* came out of all this unscathed, and received orders, together with the pocket battleship *Admiral Scheer*, to get back to Trondheim, but was torpedoed *en route* by the submarine *Trident* (Commander G. M. Sladen), and had to turn back.

On March 21 the heavy cruiser *Admiral Hipper* reached "the zone of destiny", and on May 26, the pocket battleships *Lützow* and *Admiral Scheer* dropped anchor at Narvik.

Thus Hitler had recreated in Scandinavian waters a naval force of reasonable size, but quite unable to pass north of a line Scapa Flow–Iceland, since it would, in that event, have to face up to the Home Fleet, and behind that, the American Atlantic Fleet. Yet it posed a considerable threat to the Arctic convoys.

According to Soviet historians, not only had their Anglo-Saxon allies broken their promise to the Soviet Union to open a second front in Europe but also had done no better when it came to furnishing the arms, equipment, petrol and raw materials which Russia had been assured of receiving.

But it is only proper to note that this accusation can only be made to stand up by comparing the number of tanks, planes etc. that Churchill and Roosevelt had promised to Stalin with those that actually arrived in Russia, while in justice the comparison ought to be made between the quantities promised and those which were embarked in American and British ports. For what was lost *en route* can scarcely be attributed to bad faith on the part of London or Washington. To get such supplies to the Soviet Union, Britain and America had the choice of three routes:

1. They could go via Vladivostok, through which Britain, before Pearl Harbor, could send sizable quantities of tin and rubber from Malaya to Siberia. After the opening of hostilities in the Far East, as we have noted, the Japanese did not stop Russian vessels plying between Vladivostok and America's Pacific ports. However, the Trans-Siberian Railway was capable at this time of carrying little more than it had been able to do at the beginning of the century.

2. There was the Persian Gulf route, which had become available on the occupation of Persia by Anglo-Soviet forces at the end of August 1941. This gave them control of the rail and road links between the Persian Gulf and the Caspian Sea. But supplies flowed along these two lines very feebly and thought was now given to making significant improvements in them by sending out a large contingent of American engineers and technicians. Nevertheless, the Allied merchantmen taking this route and sailing from New York or Liverpool still had to round the Cape of Good Hope, which put the American Atlantic ports at 73 days sailing from Bandar-e-Shahpur on the Persian Gulf.

3. Lastly, there was the Arctic route to Archangel and Murmansk. Situated on the estuary of the northern Dvina at the southern edge of the White Sea, the first of these two ports is inaccessible in winter and, anyway, was badly equipped in 1942. The other, thanks to the Gulf Stream, is open all the year round and, given the circumstances, was somewhat better fitted out. It was, however, dangerously exposed to heavy air attack from the Luftwaffe.

During the winter, Allied Arctic convoys benefited from the cover of the long Arctic night. On the other hand, the advance of pack ice towards the south forced them to round North Cape at a distance which laid them open to short-range German attacks. In summer, the retreat of the ice allowed the convoys to stand further off from the Norwegian coast, but for 24 hours out of 24 they were, if discovered, an easy prey to dive-bomber, torpedo aircraft, and submarine attacks.

On the outward journey these convoys were distinguished by the letters P.Q. followed by their sequence number. The ships, which were unloaded at Murmansk and Archangel, waited there until they were numerous enough to be regrouped as a Q.P. convoy, and raised anchor when the escort ships of an incoming convoy could accompany them on the voyage home.

Convoy P.Q.1 set sail from Scottish waters on September 29, 1941, and before the end of the year five others had followed it, landing in all 120,000 tons of supplies at Murmansk, including 600 tanks, 800 aircraft, and 1,400 motor vehicles. Opponents of Winston Churchill's war strategy claim that these supplies would have sufficed to check the Japanese at Singapore and to defeat Rommel at Tobruk. Whatever the truth of this assertion, it has to be admitted that the Germans found themselves considerably embarras-

Before the British woke up to the fact that the big ships were out, Scharnhorst, Gneisenau, *and* Prinz Eugen *were almost into the straits of Dover. Once in the channel they were protected by a multi-level air umbrella of German fighters.*

sed by these first convoys, which they had not foreseen. It is also noteworthy that between September 28 and December 31, 1941, all 55 vessels of the first six convoys reached their destination safely.

During the first half of 1942 no less than ten convoys made the Arctic run, and of their 146 cargo vessels, 128 reached port despite the increasing opposition of the German Navy. As we have already seen, Hitler had feared an Anglo-American landing in Norway and in consequence had stationed the 43,000-ton battleship *Tirpitz*, the pocket battleships *Lützow* and *Admiral Scheer*, the heavy cruiser *Admiral Hipper*, and a dozen U-boats between Trondheim and Narvik. And, at the return of spring, *Luftflotte* V had at its bases around the North Cape more than 250 machines, including 130 Junkers Ju 87 and 88 bombers and 60 land and seaplane torpedo aircraft.

Faced by this concentration of forces, the Admiralty was forced to provide the same protection for the Arctic convoys as for the Mediterranean ones. Yet at the same time it was the Admiralty which had to bear the brunt of the battle of the Atlantic—and after having just improvised another fleet for the Far East.

In consequence, the situation was very precarious, especially since Roosevelt continued to urge Churchill to intensify and speed up the provisioning of the Soviet Union. And to this end he attached Task Force 99 (Rear-Admiral R. C. Giffen)

to the Home Fleet, with two 35,000-ton battleships, the aircraft-carrier *Wasp*, two heavy cruisers, and a flotilla of destroyers.

At the beginning of March *Tirpitz* came out to intercept and destroy the convoys P.Q. 12 and Q.P. 8, a total of 31 cargo vessels, but because of inadequate aerial reconnaissance the powerful battleship failed to locate her prey. The hunter now became the hunted, since the Home Fleet, which had been detailed to provide strategic cover for the operation, had not failed to notice *Tirpitz*'s movements; and on the morning of March 9 she was attacked by 12 torpedo-planes from *Victorious*. However, the undeniable bravery of the Fleet Air Arm pilots did not make up for their lack of training. None of the torpedoes hit its target.

The next convoy to arrive at Murmansk, between March 30 and April 1, lost five ships on the way. The U-boats and the Luftwaffe claimed two each, and the fifth went to a division of destroyers which had put out from the port of Kirkenes. But the Germans paid for this success with the loss of the destroyer *Z-26* and the U-boats *U-585* and *U-655*. In the course of the encounter that led to the sinking of *Z-26* the British cruiser *Trinidad* was damaged by one of her own torpedoes and had to put into Murmansk.

At the end of April the protection of P.Q. 15, with its 15 merchant vessels, occasioned the loss of the cruiser *Edin-*

The 8-inch guns of the German heavy cruiser Hipper *frame her destroyer escort as they steam through the gloom of Norway's coastal waters (above). Map (right) shows the Arctic convoy routes, with days out of Scapa Flow and the German and Allied bases.*

burgh, torpedoed by *U-450* and finished off two days later by destroyer attack. For its part, *Trinidad* left Murmansk again only to be sunk by a Junkers Ju 88, and to crown misfortunes, in the fog, the battleship *King George V* attacked the destroyer *Punjabi*, which sank within a few minutes, though not before her exploding depth-charges had damaged *King George V* severely.

As the days lengthened the losses of the convoys mounted, despite the reinforcement of their escorts with anti-aircraft vessels bristling with A.A. guns, and C.A.M. ships, merchantmen from which a Hurricane fighter could be catapulted into the air. Of the 35 vessels that made up P.Q. 16, which set sail from the base at Hvalfjord, north of Reykjavik, seven fell into the ambushes prepared for them by the Luftwaffe and U-boats, with losses that have been tabulated by Captain S. W. Roskill as follows:

	Loaded	Lost
Tons	125,000	32,400
Tanks	468	147
Aircraft	201	77
Vehicles	3,277	770

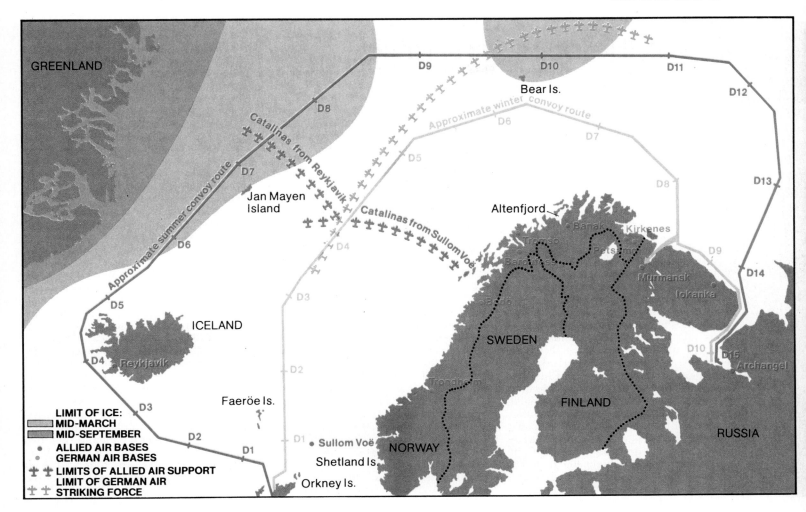

However disappointing they may have been, these losses were slight when compared with the catastrophe which overtook P.Q. 17, a disaster not only on account of the strength of the attack to which it succumbed, but also because of the unfortunate intervention of the First Lord of the Admiralty, Admiral of the Fleet Sir Dudley Pound.

Convoy P.Q. 17 was composed of 35 vessels, 22 of which were American, eight British, two Russian, two Panamanian, and one Dutch. It set sail from the Bay of Reykjavik on June 27, 1942, with an escort of six destroyers, four corvettes, four armed trawlers, three mine-sweepers, two submarines and two auxiliary anti-aircraft vessels. Further support was given by Rear-Admiral L. H. K. Hamilton's squadron, which comprised four heavy cruisers, two of which were American, and three destroyers. Finally, Admiral Sir John Tovey had ordered the Home-Fleet to sea, bringing together under his command the battleships *Duke of York* and *Washington* (U.S.N.), the aircraft-carrier *Victorious*, the cruisers *Nigeria* and *Cumberland*, and 14 destroyers. The Admiralty had done things in style.

Discovered on July 1, the convoy lost three merchant vessels on July 4, all to torpedoes dropped by German Heinkel 111's. By the evening of that same day the convoy was still about 280 miles away from Archangel by way of the North Cape – for Murmansk had been almost com-

pletely destroyed by repeated bomber attacks by *Luftflotte* V.

The Admiralty was now informed that *Tirpitz* had joined *Scheer* and *Hipper* in Altenfjord, which led to the inference that a powerful enemy formation would attack the convoy and Rear-Admiral Hamilton's supporting escort around dawn next day and would swiftly destroy them. Upon which, after brief deliberation, Sir Dudley Pound sent out these three messages, which sealed the convoy's fate.

"2111 Hours: Most immediate. Cruiser force withdraw to westward at high speed.

"2123 Hours: Immediate. Owing to the threat of surface ships convoy is to disperse and proceed to Russian ports.

"2136 Hours: Most Immediate. My 2123 of the 4th. Convoy is to scatter."

On receiving these orders Rear-Admiral Hamilton retired at the indicated speed, taking with him the six escort destroyers. The convoy dispersed as ordered. But of the 30 merchantmen which were left to make Archangel by themselves only 11 arrived at their destination between July 11 and July 25, some of them having made off eastwards towards Novaya Zemlya to escape their pursuers. Nine cargo ships fell prey to air attack from *Luftflotte* V and ten to the 82 torpedoes fired by the U-boats involved. The Germans lost only two bombers, three torpedo planes, and two reconnaissance aircraft.

Tirpitz and her companions, escorted by six destroyers, left Altenfjord at 1100

hours on July 5, more than 12 hours after Hitler had given his permission. But they did not get far, for the same day, at 2200 hours, they were ordered to return to base immediately.

As may be expected, this tragic episode gave rise to passionate dispute in Great Britain, and, as Captain Roskill judiciously points out, it is undeniable that in thinking it possible to exercise direct operational control from London over distant naval forces, the First Sea Lord was inviting just such a nemesis. Roskill concludes: "it is hard to justify such an intervention made in such a way."

The table of losses occasioned by the P.Q. 17 disaster is as follows:

	Loaded	Lost
Tons	156,492	99,316
Tanks	594	430
Aircraft	297	210
Vehicles	4,246	3,350

We may easily understand now that despite Stalin's exhortations, when faced with these figures, Winston Churchill should have waited until September before permitting P.Q. 18 to set out. And even though it was provided with a powerful escort – including the escort carrier *Avenger* – 13 of the 40 vessels that then sailed from Hvalfjord were lost. But on the German side losses were not light: four submarines and 41 aircraft. The struggle in the Arctic waters was now draining the strength of both sides. As in the Atlantic, this was proving a battle of attrition.

CHAPTER 32

German triumphs in North Africa

If the insolent passage through the Straits of Dover by Vice-Admiral Ciliax's squadron provoked such an outburst of discontent in Britain, it was also because, coming only three days before the fall of Singapore, it had followed on the defeat, as unexpected as it was remarkable, of the 8th Army in North Africa. This latter had brought the Axis forces from the El Agheila–Marada line to a line Gazala–Bir Hakeim. And what would British opinion have made of it all if it had also been informed of the enormous successes of Admiral Dönitz between Cape Sable in Nova Scotia and the Mississippi delta?

Under the influence of the pessimism caused by this succession of bad news, some put it about in the corridors of the House of Commons that it was time that Winston Churchill's duties were reduced merely to those of Prime Minister and that the Ministry of Defence should be entrusted to another person, such as Anthony Eden. In his memoirs Churchill makes no mention of this intrigue and, as can well be imagined, those responsible for it took good care not to boast about it.

Churchill had his own very personal way of illustrating his theories, as is shown by this story he told about the effect of surprise, which could all too often be decisive during the course of a battle:

"I have often tried to set down the strategic truths I have comprehended in the form of simple anecdotes. One of them is the celebrated tale of the man who gave the powder to the bear. He mixed the powder with the greatest care, making sure that not only the ingredients but the proportions were absolutely correct. He rolled it up in a large paper spill and was about to blow it down the bear's throat. But the bear blew first."

These intrigues against the Prime Minister are, however, revealed to us in Sir Arthur Bryant's "presentation" of Lord Alanbrooke's war note-books. Sir Arthur's reputation as a scrupulous and independent historian is well known.

To the great good fortune of Britain and the Commonwealth, and therefore to the nations who were their allies, this scheme was nipped in the bud; had it succeeded it would probably have caused a series of political crises. In fact, one can hardly imagine the Prime Minister confining himself to the figurehead rôle envisaged for him, convinced as he was that he incarnated that sense of strategy which had amounted to genius in his ancestor John Churchill, Duke of Marlborough. He could not have failed to interest himself in the conduct of operations, and his Minister of Defence would never have tolerated the daily intrusion of the Prime Minister in his sphere of responsibilities. Further conflicts would have been inevitable.

On the other hand, when the two great warring coalitions were balanced on the knife-edge of destiny, Britain and the United Nations would have been without the drive of the man whose part in the Allies' final victories Sir Arthur Bryant has defined by saying:

"When it came to the political direction of war–to seeing and expressing its broad, fundamental truths in terms that men and nations could understand and translate into action–the Prime Minister had no equal."

It is quite clear that at the beginning of this year of 1942, British strategy in the Middle East most disastrously reflected the increasing menace of events in the Far East.

We have seen how, when it reached the Cape, the 18th Division, originally intended for General Auchinleck, was redirected to Singapore, where it arrived just in time to be swallowed up in the capitulation of February 15. The 5th Division was also diverted from the Eastern Mediterranean theatre and split up into brigades, some to be used against Diego-Suarez (Operation "Ironclad") and others in Burma.

In addition to these failed expectations, G.H.Q. Cairo also had taken away from it, on orders from London, 150 tanks and three divisions: the 70th, which had defended Tobruk and was sent to Ceylon, and the 6th and 7th Australian which, as we have seen, were sent home at the urgent request of Prime Minister Curtin.

Far from receiving the reinforcements he thought he could count on, Air Chief-Marshal Tedder, Air Officer Commanding Middle East, had to lose four fighter squadrons. Finally, owing to the Japanese threat to the Indian Ocean, the Admiralty was quite unable to repair the terrible damage caused to the Mediterranean Fleet. Sir Andrew Cunningham had therefore to do as best he could without battleships, aircraft-carriers, and heavy cruisers.

As far as concerns the forces which Sir Arthur Tedder deployed with such skill, their failed expectations arose not only from the fact that new theatres of operations in the Far East were being equipped with formations due to them on the eve of Pearl Harbor, but also because hundreds of fighters and light bombers for the R.A.F. were sent to Murmansk and Archangel, and U.S. military aid to Russia meant that the delivery of planes to Great Britain had had to be slowed down.

But for all that and in accordance with the decisions taken at the "Arcadia" Conference, Auchinleck was still required to mount Operation "Acrobat", which was to take the 8th Army from Agedabia to the Tunisian frontier. Naturally he argued that for the moment, his supply difficulties and the depletion of his forces ruled out any early renewed offensive.

The forward troops of the 8th Army were in positions hardly suited to even a defensive action, but G.H.Q. Cairo did not consider the enemy strong enough for an early counter-offensive.

The last days of 1941 had seen a complete reversal of the situation in the Central Mediterranean: the destruction of Force K, based on Malta, the battering of the island-fortress by the concentrated efforts of the Italian Air Force and II and X *Fliegerkorps* of the Luftwaffe, the weakening of the Mediterranean Fleet–all this had reopened the route to Tripoli to the Axis convoys. Whereas in December, taking into account losses of 19 per cent, only 39,902 tons of war *matériel* and fuel had been landed, in January 100 per cent of all replacements and supplies loaded in Italy got through to Africa. These amounted to 43,328 tons of *matériel* and 22,842 tons of liquid fuel. On January 5 one convoy brought in for the *Afrika Korps* 54 Pzkw III and IV tanks, 20 armoured cars, and some self-propelled guns, Russian 76.2-mm guns on Czech tank chassis, all complete with their crews. For its part, the Italian Mobile Corps, now under the command of General Zingales, got two groups of *semoventi*, Italian-made 75-mm self-propelled guns which proved very effective. Altogether the Axis armoured strength taken by Rommel out of the El Agheila–Marada line, which was henceforth held by only the Italian XXI and X Corps, was 84 German medium and heavy tanks and 89 Italian medium tanks on January 11, 1942. A further 28 German tanks, newly arrived at Tripoli, were expected to join him soon.

Rommel therefore decided to counterattack, taking advantage immediately of his enemy's scattered forces and hoping thus to catch him by surprise, thin on the ground. He issued the following order of the day to his troops:

"German and Italian soldiers:

"You have already endured hard battles against an enemy vastly superior in numbers to yourselves. Your fighting spirit has not been daunted. We now have material superiority over the enemy in front of us. The army will go over to the attack today to wipe him out.

"I expect every man to give of his best in these decisive days. Long live Italy! Long live Greater Germany! Long live their leaders!"

Surprise was complete, not only at the front for the British XIII Corps but also for G.H.Q. at Cairo. On the Axis side, however, Rommel's move came as a shock for General Bastico and at Rome both for the *Comando Supremo* and for Field-Marshal Kesselring. In the entry in his diary for January 21 Rommel explains his silence in terms which give cause for reflection:

"I had maintained secrecy over the Panzer Group's forthcoming attack eastwards from Marsa Brega and informed neither the Italian nor the German High Command. We knew from experience that Italian Headquarters cannot keep things to themselves and that everything they wireless to Rome gets round to British ears. However, I had arranged with the Quartermaster for the *Panzergruppe*'s order to be posted up in every Cantoniera (Road Maintenance Depot) in Tripolitania on the 21st January—the day the attack was due to take place."

Without expressing an opinion of the danger of the leaks in Rome which he feared, and which in his view entitled him to deploy the Italian troops under him without reference to General Bastico, we would observe that he did not need to fear such leaks at O.K.W. If Rommel kept his intentions secret from his superiors it was because he feared they would forbid him from carrying them out.

In the first part of this battle Rommel found himself facing the British 1st Armoured Division. Newly arrived in Africa, it had only 150 tanks, and had been split into three groups which could not be self-supporting. The same dispersion was evident at the next level upwards, XIII Corps: the 4th Indian Division which, for logistic reasons, had got no further forward than Benghazi, could not help the 1st Armoured, and the latter was even less likely to get help from the 7th Armoured Division, which had been sent back to Tobruk to be brought up to strength.

Moving forward along two axes of attack with five armoured and motorised divisions, the Italian Mobile Corps along the Via Balbia and the *Afrika Korps* further inland, Rommel had no difficulty in sweeping before him the 22nd Guards Brigade and, in the evening of January 22, he camped at Agedabia, having advanced 56 miles in 48 hours. In particular he had cut the road to Benghazi, to the surprise and dismay of his enemy. The following day he set about the destruction of the opposing forces by an encircling movement. Whilst General Zingales engaged the bulk of the 1st Armoured Division in the west, he drove the *Afrika Korps* northeast towards Antelat then turned southeast, and due south from Saunnu. However, in its haste to close the trap round the enemy, his vanguard left Saunnu before the head of the 15th Panzer Division reached it and the British escaped through the gap, though in a bad state and leaving a great deal of *matériel* behind.

Meanwhile, alerted by Bastico, Marshal Cavallero, sent by plane to the battlefront by Mussolini, appeared in Rommel's headquarters to tighten the reins on this bold *Panzerwaffe* charger. In a directive dated January 23 he drew Rommel's attention to the general situation:

"The conduct of the war in Tripolitania is a function of the situation in the Mediterranean. It is possible that, owing to a shortage of diesel oil, our convoys might be reduced or even stop altogether

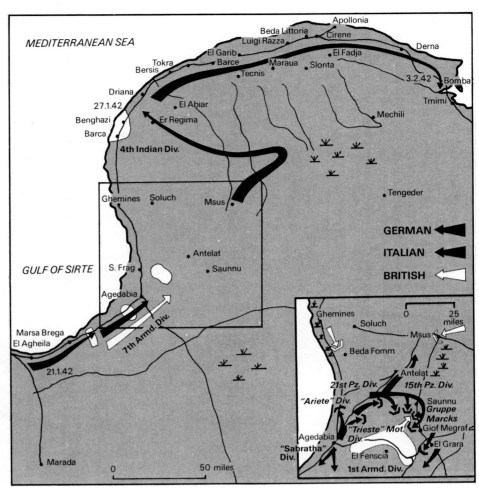

Rommel's drive to the Gulf of Bomba in January and February 1942.

from mid-February. It must be expected, however, that the effects of our intensive action on Malta will help considerably the despatch, already under way, of isolated ships by the western route, but this will scarcely be enough to ensure the normal feeding of our colony and no more troops or *matériel* can be expected."

Taking into account possible enemy action, including an "Anglo-Gaullist" landing in Tunisia or on the Libyan coast, or even of an attack from the Sahara, Cavallero, acting in the name of the Duce, drew up the following instructions based on the above premises:

1. In the east the line of resistance was still Mersa Brega–Marada, which the major infantry units were not to pass.
2. As for the mobile forces, intended to disorganise the enemy's preparations for attack, they would carry out "limited range operations" whenever the opportunity arose.

If he had obeyed these instructions, Rommel would have had to send his mobile forces back over the Mersa Brega–Marada line. He did nothing of the kind, arguing that the situation had overtaken the orders and, making a show of driving towards Mechili, where, remembering his first offensive, General Ritchie was waiting for him, he appeared unexpectedly outside Benghazi in the evening of January 27, cutting off the 4th Indian Division, which managed to break out. On February 3, the forward units of the *Afrika Korps*, after bypassing Derna,

reached the Gulf of Bomba. The offensive halted before the new British positions at Gazala. The 8th Army had lost about 1,390 men, 72 tanks and 80 guns. Rommel's devastating offensive had wrested the initiative from the 8th Army.

From all evidence, General Ritchie, C.-in-C. 8th Army, had been caught unprepared and then overtaken by events; the orders and counter-orders which had been showered on Lieutenant-General Godwin-Austen caused him to ask to be relieved of his command. Major-General Frank Messervy had just taken over command of the British 1st Armoured Division from his wounded colleague Lumsden; he cannot therefore be held responsible for the misadventures which Rommel inflicted on the division.

On the Axis side, the "limited range offensive operation" envisaged in the January 23 directive had taken Rommel more than 375 miles from his base. This act of insubordination had certainly been crowned with success, but its author was only going to be more inclined to ignore the advice, even when better motivated, of *Comando Supremo*. This was all the more likely because the Führer had promoted his *Panzergruppe* to the grade of *Panzerarmee* (though without giving him any more men or *matériel*) and had promoted him Colonel-General, thus giving

Admiral Vian's Malta convoy.
A painting by Charles Pears.

him virtual equality with his Italian colleagues.

The successes of the Axis forces in Cyrenaica resounded like a thunderclap on the banks of the Thames. On January 25, the Prime Minister, "much disturbed" by the report that the 8th Army was intending to evacuate Benghazi and Derna, cabled General Auchinleck:

"It seems to me this is a serious crisis, and one to me quite unexpected. Why should they all be off so quickly? Why should the 4th (British-) Indian Division not hold out at Benghazi, like the Huns at Halfaya? The kind of retirement now evidently envisaged by subordinate officers implies the failure of 'Crusader' and the ruin of 'Acrobat'." In his memoirs, Churchill says that he refused to accept General Auchinleck's explanation that the "only" reason for this defeat, which was "so serious and heavy with consequences", had been the mechanical unreliability of the British armour about which Auchinleck had complained previously. Churchill's anger is understandable, but no one could deny that this very real inferiority of the British tanks compared with the Panzers weighed heavily in the balance. But again, what so irritated the Prime Minister in the event was not only that "Acrobat" (the advance on Tripoli) had to be postponed, but that there was also now the greater

danger to Malta after the 8th Army's retreat to the Gazala–Bir Hakeim line, and this at a time when the Luftwaffe's II and X *Fliegerkorps* and the Italian Air Force were pounding the island.

From the airstrips in the Benghazi area, some 420 miles from Valletta, or, at a pinch, from Derna (530 miles), the R.A.F. could give continuous support to convoys from Alexandria supplying the beleaguered island. This was impossible from Tobruk (580 miles) and, to make matters worse, the "bump" of Cyrenaica, retaken by Rommel, was only 190 miles from Crete. The seas between were thus at the mercy of Axis cross-fire. Nevertheless, in January Admiral Cunningham succeeded in getting through to Malta three merchant ships and the supply-ship *Breconshire* for the loss of only one vessel. But February's convoy was a total failure: out of three merchant ships which left Alexandria, one had to be sent in to Tobruk because of the damage caused by enemy bombs, a second was sunk, and the third had to be scuttled.

Admiral Cunningham could not abandon Malta to her dire fate. He therefore organised another convoy of three merchant ships and the supply-ship *Breconshire*, which had meanwhile returned from Valletta. Rear-Admiral Philip Vian, of *Altmark* fame, who had commanded the previous convoys, was put in charge of this risky operation and, on March 20 he set sail from Alexandria with an escort of

four light cruisers, ten destroyers, and six *Hunt*-class destroyer escorts. At dawn on the 22nd he was joined by the cruiser *Penelope* and the destroyer *Legion* which had come out from Malta to bring the merchant ships in. But Vian's movements had been spotted off Derna by the Italian submarine *Platino* and at midnight on the 21st the battleship *Littorio*, flying the flag of Admiral Iachino, sailed from Taranto, whilst an hour later the cruisers *Gorizia*, *Trento*, and *Bande Nere* left Messina. Each of these two detachments was escorted by four destroyers. At 1427 hours Rear-Admiral Parona's three cruisers made contact with the enemy, whereupon Vian made his convoy turn south-west, covered by the guns of the anti-aircraft cruiser *Carlisle* and the *Hunts*, and engaged the Italians with the rest of his forces. The Italians would not join battle, but preferred to await the arrival of the battleship *Littorio*, which appeared on the scene towards 1640 hours.

Admiral Iachino's plan was to get between Malta and the convoy and then wipe out the ships, but the sirocco, blowing in gusts from the south-east, allowed Vian to take cover behind a smoke-screen, which the Italians, having no radar, could not penetrate. When one of the British cruisers did appear out of the smoke, the enemy could not engage it because of the spray and the smoke which obscured their range-finders. Thus the Italians' enormous superiority in firepower was of little avail to them. At nightfall Iachino made a last attempt to get near to the convoy but he had to withdraw, driven off by the volleys of torpedoes fired off at him by the British destroyers as they counter-attacked and, as none of his ships was equipped for night-fighting, he had to abandon the action a little before 1900 hours.

The result of this second battle of Sirte was not as disappointing for the Italians as it might at first have seemed. Admiral Cunningham had lost the destroyers *Havock* and *Kingston*, which had been heavily damaged and had had to make for Malta. The convoy, having had to sail south-west for hours, could not now reach Valletta before dawn on the 23rd. This caused the loss by bombing of the *Breconshire* and one merchant ship: the two survivors reached harbour but were sunk as they were unloading. And so, out of the 26,000 tons of supplies which had left Alexandria only 5,000 reached their destination. On the other hand two Italian destroyers, ploughing on through the storm, sank with most of their crews. The light cruiser *Bande Nere* was so severely damaged in the same storm that she had to be sent to La Spezia for repairs. On the way there she was sunk by the submarine *Urge* (Lieutenant-Commander E. P. Tomkinson). This was a compensation for the loss of the light cruiser *Naiad*, which had gone down under Rear-Admiral Vian on February 11 in the previous year, torpedoed off the coast of Egypt by U-*565*.

The bombardment of Malta, which had been intensified from mid-December 1941 to the end of February, became in March a veritable ordeal by fire: in 31 days 4,927 bombing sorties were flown against the island, and in April no fewer than 9,599 dropped 6,700 tons of bombs. In the Grand Harbour three destroyers, including *Kingston* were sunk and the valiant *Penelope* was so riddled with shrapnel that her crew facetiously renamed her *Pepperpot*. To avoid destruction, the submarines of the 10th Flotilla had to submerge by day with reduced crews.

For its part, the island's air force was decimated in battles in the air or wiped out on the ground. On January 31 there were only 28 fighters left; a fortnight later, there were only 11. In this almost desperate situation help came from the west, that is from Force H, now commanded by Rear-Admiral E. N. Syfret who had taken over from Sir James Somerville. On March 6 the old *Argus*, the first "flat-top" of any navy in the world, and the *Eagle* sent 15 Spitfires, more capable than the Hurricanes of dealing with the Messerschmitt Bf 109F's of X *Fliegerkorps*. This operation was successfully repeated on March 21 and 29.

To speed up the reinforcement of Malta's defence, Winston Churchill appealed to President Roosevelt. On April 1, after describing the tragic situation of Malta's defenders, who had only 20 to 30 fighters as against the 600 of the Axis, and the difficulties of sending them enough Spitfires on the carriers at his disposal, he added:

"Would you be willing to allow your carrier *Wasp* to do one of these trips provided details are satisfactorily agreed between the Naval Staffs? With her broad lifts, capacity and length, we estimate that *Wasp* could take 50 or more Spitfires. Unless it were necessary for her to fuel, *Wasp* could proceed through the Straits at night without calling at Gibraltar until on the return journey, as the Spitfires would be embarked in the Clyde. Thus, instead of not being able to give Malta any further Spitfires during April, a powerful Spitfire force could be flown into Malta at a stroke and give us a chance of inflicting a very severe and possibly decisive check on the enemy. Operation might take place during third week of April."

President Roosevelt responded to his ally's request in a fine spirit of comradeship. Thus on April 20 *Wasp*, which had got within 620 miles of Malta, sent off 47 Spitfires; these were reduced to six four days later after redoubled attacks by the Luftwaffe. Churchill had therefore to ask for a second run by the American aircraft-carrier and he did this with an argument worth mentioning. He cabled the President on April 20:

"Without this aid I fear Malta will be pounded to bits. Meanwhile its defence is wearing out the enemy's Air Force and effectively aiding Russia."

Roosevelt responded again with help and *Wasp* went back into the Mediterranean on May 9. Together with *Eagle* she sent off 64 Spitfires to Malta; these were lates in his memoirs:

"It may be well here to complete the story of the *Wasp*. On May 9 she successfully delivered another important flight of Spitfires to struggling Malta. I made her a signal: 'Who said a wasp couldn't sting twice?' The *Wasp* thanked me for my 'gracious' message. Alas, poor *Wasp*! She left the dangerous Mediterranean for the Pacific and on September 15 was sunk by Japanese torpedoes. Happily her gallant crew were saved. They had been a link in our chain of causation."

The fact remains, however, that the population and the garrison of the island-fortress were put on short rations and that their supply of flour was due to run out on about June 15.
followed by a further 17 on May 18 from the British carrier alone. Churchill re-

For a long time now Grand-Admiral Raeder had been maintaining to the Führer that the war would be won at Suez and Basra, but that the capture of these two objectives depended on the seizure of

An Axis petrol dump. Scarcity of fuel was a major problem for Rommel.

Malta. The day after Admiral Ciliax had forced a passage through the Straits of Dover, Hitler was somewhat more receptive to these ideas and, at the end of February, Field-Marshal Kesselring could write to Marshal Cavallero without fear of repudiation:

"The Führer is in complete agreement with the Italian Command for definite action against the island of Malta. He is following the development of this action with great interest; he will give it all possible support unless Britain attempts a landing on such a scale that it would require a maximum concentration of our forces."

And a few days later, Keitel, the Chief-of-Staff of O.K.W., wrote along the same lines to his Italian opposite number, who welcomed the news as he had long been in favour of this operation, which he considered risky but necessary. Hence on April 12 a Planning H.Q. was set up under General Fassi. The two dictators met on April 30 at Klessheim near Salzburg, and Cavallero, warmly supported by Kesselring, put forward his plan. This produced no practical or theoretical objections, Hitler merely remarking that "an operation like this must be planned down to the smallest detail for if it fails there can be no going back to the beginning." On this agreement and the promise of substantial German support, the Chief-of-Staff of the *Comando Supremo* drew up his plan for a simultaneous attack on the islands of Malta and Gozo by:

1. Naval and air forces consisting of:
    a. 1,506 combat planes, including 666 from the Luftwaffe;
    b. Admiral Iachino's naval forces;
    c. Admiral Tur's 12th Naval Division (with all the means for landing); and
    d. 14 groups of submarines.
2. Land forces, under General Vecchiarelli, consisting of:
    a. the Luftwaffe's XI *Fliegerkorps* (General Student), a German parachute division, the "Folgore" parachute division, and the "Spezia" airborne division;
    b. XVI Corps (General Carlo Rossi), the "Assieta" Division and the "Napoli" Division; and
    c. XXX Corps (General Sogno), the "Superga", "Livorno", and "Friuli" Divisions.

The operation was called "Herkules" by the Germans. They also contributed a number of heavy tanks and some 300 transport aircraft. The Axis powers would thus have eight divisions against the Allies' garrison on the two islands of 30,000–35,000 men under Lieutenant-General Sir William Dobbie.

It had been originally planned that the assault on Malta should precede Rommel's offensive. This was to start from the line Sollum–Halfaya–Sidi Omar. The need to train the "Folgore" Division paratroopers, however, compelled Cavallero to reverse this order of priority and the resultant delay was to have incalculable consequences.

Had Operation "Herkules", which the Italians called *Esigenza "C3"*, any chance of success? The Duce's Chief-of-Staff did not doubt it, nor did Kesselring and Admiral Weichold, Raeder's liaison officer at *Supermarina*. On the other hand, at Leghorn, where he was conscientiously training the "Friuli" Division for its assault on the cliffs of Malta, General Giacomo Carboni considered that the enterprise was some new folly imposed on Italy by the Germans because of the servility of Cavallero. Nor did he keep this opinion to himself. In particular he spoke to Count Ciano of his pessimistic conclusions. Ciano often went to the great Tuscan port and Carboni had become friendly with him.

"I had a long and interesting conversation with Carboni," Ciano noted in his diary on May 31. "At the moment he is commanding one of the assault divisions which is to participate in the Malta operation. He is decidedly against it. He is convinced that we shall have heavy losses and that nothing will come of it. He takes it out on Cavallero, whom he considers to be an intriguer and a man of bad faith. He is also very pessimistic about the Russian Front. He doesn't think that the Germans can undertake any operations of far-reaching proportions during the summer. It is a war of position rather than anything else. From this he draws the most sinister conclusions about the German future. Carboni is a general of great ability. One must not forget, however, that he was dismissed by the Secret Military Intelligence for his anti-German attitude, and that he is the son of an American mother."

It was the same story again on June 20. "General Carboni has come to Rome to talk over the Malta enterprise, which is set for the next new moon. He is convinced, technically convinced, that we are heading for an unheard-of disaster. Preparations have been childish, equipment is lacking and inadequate. The landing troops will never succeed in landing, or, if they land they are doomed to total destruction. All the commanders are convinced of this, but no one dares to speak for fear of reprisals by Cavallero."

But the commander of the "Friuli" Division went further than these talks with Ciano in what he calls his "preparatory fire against the General Staff". He did not hesitate, in fact, to inform the Prince of Piedmont of his misgivings. The Prince, as the relevant army group C.-in-C. had been called upon to supervise the operation. The memorandum sent to him by Carboni late in May 1942 covers two pages in the Prince's memoirs and we will give the reader only the introduction and the conclusion:

"The Malta operation, carried out with the inadequate means at our disposal, takes on the appearance of a new folly, the consequences of which will be not only a new loss of military and political prestige to us and an irreparable loss of men, ships, and planes but will also have another effect.

"There is reason to fear that the enemy might take advantage of a defeat on Malta by landing in Italy and that our ally might seize on this 'new confirmation of our strategic and tactical weakness' to take over command and ravage our country. And so the Malta expedition will be in every way profitable to the Germans. It has certain similarities with the operation at Sidi Barrani in the sense that it might have the same consequences for our country as Sidi Barrani had for Libya: it would bring the British or the Germans here, and perhaps both of them together."

After the heir to the throne, General Carboni approached the King himself during a royal inspection of his division, but apparently without any more success. The fact remains, however, that these complaints, which were not made through the proper channels, brought no sanctions on their author, though General Ambrosio, the Army Chief-of-Staff, was not unaware of them. Not only did General Carboni remain in command of the "Friuli" Division but in December 1942 he was appointed commander of the corps occupying Corsica. *Esigenza "C3"* was cancelled for reasons which we shall examine later. It is naturally difficult to decide who would have been right, Cavallero or Carboni, the optimist or the

Italians guard British troops, victims of Rommel's Afrika Korps.

pessimist. There are, however, two observations to be made on this controversy:

1. That the Malta undertaking was not in any way imposed on the Chief-of-Staff of the *Comando Supremo* by the Germans, as the former commander of the "Friuli" Division states. From the beginning to the end of this affair, all the initiatives point to Cavallero rather than to O.K.W. It would seem that those concerned were only too glad to take advantage of Rommel's victories to climb down from the undertakings that had been made; and

2. It cannot be denied that the means at the disposal of General Vecchiarelli were "inadequate" for the execution of his mission, at least to some extent. But Carboni in his argument makes no allusion to the state in which a surprise attack might have found the defenders. Neither General Dobbie on the spot nor the Chiefs-of-Staff Committee in London were very optimistic about holding Malta without a prompt and vigorous offensive by the 8th Army.

As we have quoted Count Ciano and General Carboni, witnesses for the prosecution in this historic dispute, it is only right that we should hear the witness for the defence, Admiral Vittorio Tur who, it will be remembered, had been put in charge of the landing operations proper. He wrote of Marshal Cavallero:

"I can state that the Marshal was a true leader for whom I had the highest esteem and devotion and whose end showed the firmness of his character and the uprightness of his conscience; a leader who always encouraged and appreciated the preparatory work which had been done, giving sound advice and intelligent orders, and who never had the slightest doubt about the outcome of the operation."

These considerations naturally bring us to Operation "Venezia", started by Rommel in the evening of May 26, 1942. It was no doubt going to set the seal on his indisputable tactical genius, but it was also to show, by the way in which he went too far in insisting on freedom of action, a certain incapacity on his part to rise to the level of a total conception of warfare

and to sacrifice his own initiative to this. The reverse also deserves consideration, however: that is, if *Comando Supremo* did not manage to impose on Rommel the strategic zig-zag of Tobruk–Malta–Tobruk–Suez which it wanted, it was because it did not have the tactical means of forcing its will on its German ally. Finally the double subordination of the *Panzerarmee Afrika* to both *Comando Supremo* and the *Oberkommando der Wehrmacht* made it easy for its commander to adopt the rôle of the lonely knight of destiny which, within four months, was to turn a resounding victory into an irreparable defeat.

The mobile forces of the Axis, having taken on their own initiative a position on the line Gulf of Bomba–Bir Temrad–Rotunda Segnali, could not be left to face alone the British 8th Army, which was regrouping and falling back on the line Aïn el-Gazala–Bir Hakeim. So Cavallero agreed to bring forward towards these mobile forces his X and XXI Corps and to put them, as the tactical corps troops (now XX Corps) already were, under the command of Colonel-General Rommel. To relieve the tension which had now become obvious between the latter and Marshal Bastico, the Italian C.-in-C. North Africa, he recalled General Gambara to Rome and replaced him by General Barbasetti di Prun as Chief-of-Staff in Tripoli.

As for the immediate future, the commander of the *Panzerarmee Afrika* was of the opinion that the enemy's preparations for a new offensive had to be forestalled, and on April 30 he submitted to Marshal Bastico, Field-Marshal Kesselring, Admiral Weichold, and *Comando Supremo* through Rintelen, an initial outline of his plans:

"The commander of the *Panzerarmee Afrika*, taking advantage of the balance of forces which is at present in our favour, intends to attack in the early days of June (the moon then being favourable) the British forces at present in the area Bir el Gubi–Tobruk–Aïn el-Gazala–Bir Hakeim and annihilate them. Following on this action he proposes also to take Tobruk, by a surprise attack if possible."

An encircling movement by his motorised forces as they broke out on each side of Bir Hakeim towards Acroma would compel the enemy to fight on a reverse front and his complete defeat would be assured in the evening of the second day. Forty-eight hours should be enough to prepare the assault on Tobruk and Rommel could expect to be ready to advance on the Sollum–Bardia front on about the sixth day. This attack should take place, in his opinion, after the taking of Malta, but if the Malta operation could not be launched before June 1 he might have to take the initiative; otherwise it would pass to the enemy.

Cavallero, who had gone to Cyrenaica on May 5, raised no objection to the plan submitted to him. But although he approved it in his directive dated that day, he still placed it in the more general framework of operations in the Mediterranean theatre. Because of its intelligent assessment, it is worth quoting two points from this document:

"1. *Objective:* to defeat the enemy's mobile forces west of Tobruk. If outcome successful, prompt attack on Tobruk.

"Capture of Tobruk is categorical condition for advance of our forces; if this condition fulfilled, we advance to the line Sollum–Halfaya–Sidi Omar which the main body of the armour must not pass. If the occupation of Tobruk is not successful, the objective after the battle will not be beyond the Gazala line . . .

"4. *Time available for the operation.* Operations cannot continue beyond June 20 since by this date the supporting air and naval units at present in Cyrenaica will have to be withdrawn, all of them being destined for other use by this date. A resumption of operations must be expected in the autumn."

As he explained in his diary, the Duce's Chief-of-Staff wanted to avoid involving the Axis forces in a war of attrition such as they had had to fight the previous year when they had to maintain at the same

Spitfire V's on stand-by on a Malta airfield. They are part of the reinforcements flown in from Eagle.

time the siege of Tobruk and their frontier positions. But he wrote in particular:

"The operations in Marmarica must not compromise the preparation and the execution of *Esigenza 'C3'* [Malta] which is essential for the later development of the war in the Mediterranean."

So it was important for the air detachments in Cyrenaica to be sent back to Sicily and prepared for further action. Rommel was limited by both time and space. In acting thus, Cavallero was obeying considerations of a strategic nature, which he had explained to Field-Marshal Kesselring on March 18 in the following terms:

"After the capture of Tobruk there must be absolutely no further advance. There must be a break. Tobruk–the Nile: it's only a dream."

It is odd that these documents are not mentioned at all in the papers Rommel left behind; indeed there is a gap from April 28 to May 12, 1942. But it is plain that the commander of the *Panzerarmee Afrika* had received clear and sensible orders from *Comando Supremo* and that he was wrong to ignore them.

In London, meanwhile, the Prime Minister was getting more and more irritated at General Auchinleck's reluctance to launch an offensive. As far back as February 26 he had taken him to task over this, evidencing the supposed superiority of the 8th Army in tanks, planes, and other weapons. Cairo disputed this and claimed that no operation on any worthwhile scale could be started before June 1, although it was proposed to strengthen as much as possible the line from Gazala to Bir Hakeim, extend the Marsa Matrûh railway down to El Adem, south of Tobruk, build up an armoured striking force, establish more forward ordnance depôts and, if the situation warranted it,

make a limited attack to recover the airstrips in the Derna–Mechili area. This programme was not to Churchill's liking, and on March 8 he sent a message to summon the British C.-in-C. Middle East to London to confer with him about the situation. When the latter refused, he took up his pen again on the 15th and wrote him a long letter, of which we quote the fourth and last paragraph:

"4. I have done everything in my power to give you continuous support at heavy cost to the whole war. It would give me the greatest pain to feel that mutual understanding had ceased. In order to avoid this, I have asked Sir Stafford Cripps to stop for a day in Cairo about 19th or 20th on his way to India, and put before you the views of the War Cabinet. He will be joined by General Nye, who is proceeding separately, and is fully possessed of the Chiefs of Staff's opinion."

But to the Prime Minister's great displeasure both the Lord Privy Seal and Sir Archibald Nye were won over to Auchinleck's view, which also had the support of Air Chief Marshal Tedder. Both had to agree that neither the situation in the air nor the performance of the tanks could guarantee the success of any large-scale offensive operation for the moment. Perhaps the canny Scot Auchinleck might have been thought to have pulled the wool over the eyes of the civilian Sir Stafford Cripps; if so, he could hardly have done the same with Lieutenant-General Nye, an experienced military man and, moreover, Deputy C.I.G.S. The latter nevertheless got a most disagreeable letter, to say the least, from Churchill:

"I have heard from the Lord Privy Seal. I do not wonder everything was so pleasant, considering you seem to have accepted everything they said, and all *we* have got to accept is the probable loss of

Malta and the Army standing idle, while the Russians are resisting the German counter-stroke desperately, and while the enemy is reinforcing himself in Libya faster than we are."

This debate, which died down for a time, flared up again at the beginning of May when Auchinleck asked for further delays. Churchill sent a telegram to Auchinleck on May 10, in the name of the War Cabinet, the Defence Committee and the Chiefs of Staff, instructing him to attack in May, or at the latest in June. As chairman of the Chiefs-of-Staff Committee, Sir Alan Brooke did his best to keep the peace. But although he could be a severe critic of the Prime Minister, on this occasion he felt that Auchinleck too was at fault. On May 10, Brooke noted in his diary:

"We framed a proposed policy at C.O.S. in which we laid down that we considered that the value of Malta was underestimated, whilst his argument against attack was not very convincing. Finally we suggested that he should be allowed to wait to take advantage of possible limited German offensive for Tobruk to put in a counter-stroke, but that the June convoy to Malta should be the latest date, as this afforded the last opportunity of assisting in the supply of Malta."

Auchinleck had been given a choice between obeying and resigning. He chose to obey, and to prepare his forces to attack Rommel. But it was to be Rommel who struck first, using his armoured units to spearhead the assault.

In fact, on May 27 Ritchie had some 994 tanks, compared with Rommel's 560. On both sides of the balance-sheet there were non-starters to be deducted (Italian

"An 8th Army Brigade preparing for an attack", by the artist, Edward Bainbridge Copnall.

An infantry section in a camouflaged dug-out.

M13's, German Pzkw II's, British Matildas, Valentines, and Crusaders), giving a slight advantage to the *Panzerwaffe*. Rommel had 282 Pzkw III's and 40 Pzkw IV's with respectively 5- and 7·5-cm guns and against them were just 167 M3 Grants, the only tanks which could match them. This American tank had a 75-mm gun with a longer range than the Pzkw IV's 7.5-cm weapon. The Grant was very similar to the French B1 *bis* but its gun was mounted in a casemate on the driver's right, which greatly restricted its field of fire–the whole tank had to be aimed by means of its tracks whenever the enemy appeared even marginally on its left. Its high silhouette made it visible from some distance by the low-slung Panzers, whose turret-mounted guns were capable of all-round fire.

This was not all, however: the new 6-pounder anti-tank gun with which the British infantry were being re-equipped had reached the 8th Army in very small numbers: only 112 were available. The main anti-tank defence was still the 2-pdr gun, a weapon outmatched by the 5-cm guns of the German tanks which, choosing their distance, could pick off the British like sitting ducks.

The 8th Army's air support was also clearly inferior in both quantity and quality. The Messerschmitt Bf 109F's and G's were noticeably better than the British Hurricanes or the American Curtiss Warhawks and Kittyhawks. Moreover, the training of the Luftwaffe pilots seems to have been better than that of the R.A.F.'s, as shown by the 158 victims accredited to Captain Hans-Joachim Marseille, killed in an accident on September 30 over El Alamein. In these conditions, the Stukas could take up again their rôle of flying artillery without the R.A.F.'s bombers being able to get their own back on the armoured columns of the *Panzerarmee*.

These serious British weaknesses could be seen more clearly from Cairo than from London and justified Sir Claude Auchinleck's caution in face of Winston Churchill's fiery exhortations. But the development of the battle was going to reveal further weaknesses which the

C.-in-C. British Forces in the Middle East was far from suspecting.

On May 26, General Ritchie had deployed the 8th Army from Gazala inland as follows:

1. XIII Corps, now under the command of Lieutenant-General W. H. E. Gott, had its 1st South African Division (Pienaar) blocking the Via Balbia opposite Gazala and its 50th Division (Ramsden) blocking the track running parallel to the coast road 18–19 miles further south; the 1st and 32nd Army Tank Brigades were in support with their 276 Matildas and Valentines.

   In second echelon XIII Corps had the 2nd South African Division and the 9th Indian Brigade as the garrison of Tobruk; and

2. XXX Corps (Lieutenant-General Willoughby Norrie) had in its first line the 1st Free French Brigade occupying the base point of Bir Hakeim and the 3rd Indian Motor Brigade extending from this area south-eastwards. The 1st and 7th Armoured Divisions (under Major-Generals Lumsden and Messervy respectively) were nine miles either side of "Knightsbridge", a focus of good tracks leading to Gazala, Sidi Muftah (50th Division), and Bir Hakeim. Finally, the 29th Indian Brigade had been placed in the rear at Bir el Gubi.

Stretching from Gazala on the coast to the south of Bir Hakeim was an enormous minefield which ran round the French position and turned north up to the surroundings of Bir Harmat. Behind this obstacle XIII Corps' divisions had deployed their brigades, reinforced by anti-tank weapons, A.A., and artillery in a number of all-round defence strongpoints. These dispositions did not entirely please General Auchinleck. He would have liked XIII Corps to assume responsibility for the whole of the defensive front so that XXX Corps could devote itself entirely to its job of counter-attacking. In addition, he would have liked the 1st and 7th Armoured Divisions to close in on each other so that they could have been used as a single entity. But the advice which he gave to Ritchie along these lines was never put into the form of an order, and so was never acted upon.

On the opposing side Rommel divided his forces into two parts. Under the command of General Cruewell, the Italian XXI Corps ("Trento" and "Sabratha" Divisions under Navarrini) and X Corps ("Pavia" and "Brescia" Divisions under Gioda), reinforced by some German units, would engage the 8th Army in a frontal attack to prevent its manoeuvring.

Rommel himself would have under his command the mobile forces of the Axis army, i.e. the Italian XX Corps ("Trieste" Motorised Division and "Ariete" Armoured Division under Baldassare) and the two divisions of the *Afrika Korps*: 15th and 21st Panzer plus 90th Light.

Rommel set out at dusk on May 26 on the outflanking attack which was to pass north and south of Bir Hakeim and take

his tanks into the rear of the 8th Army. On his right the 90th Light Division was to make a feint towards El Adem, then turn back to Acroma and cut the Via Balbia, the enemy's last line of communication.

The day of May 27 was for both sides an inextricable mixture of successes and reverses which left them uncertain of the way the battle was going. On the right the *Afrika Korps* overran the 3rd Indian Motor Brigade and then routed the 7th Armoured Division, whose two brigades were caught, separated and unsupported, by the 15th and 21st Panzer Divisions, which attacked in close formation; even so the German tanks were considerably damaged by the Grants. On the left, however, XX Corps was completely stopped. The "Trieste" Motorised Division slipped out of Baldassare's control and was lost but, more important, the "Ariete" Armoured Division was thrown back in front of Bir Hakeim, losing 32 of its 163 tanks. General Koenig, commanding the 1st Free French Brigade, had had 50,000 mines laid around his positions and also had 55 25-, 47-, and 75-mm anti-tank guns. In this trap was captured, wounded, Colonel Prestissimone, the commander of the Italian 132nd Armoured Regiment; he was pulled out of a tank, the third which he had had blown up under him, evidence of the determination of the "Ariete" Armoured Division's attack. At the end of the day, Rommel's mobile forces, being counter-attacked more and more closely by the British XXX Corps, far from cutting the 8th Army's communications, were finding their own communications in danger. They were also short of fuel. Then too, the frontal attacks of the Italian X and XXI Corps did not have the diversionary effect the German commander expected. On the whole, General Auchinleck in Cairo and Winston Churchill in London had every reason to be pleased, all the more since on May 29 General Cruewell had made a forced landing behind the British lines and been captured.

But they were reckoning without Rommel. On May 28 his scouts had made contact with the forward elements of the "Trieste" and "Pavia" Divisions and together they made a narrow gap through the minefields, restoring communications, albeit precariously, with his rear areas. Then, covering himself in the "Knightsbridge" area against an attack from the British XXX Corps, he threw the mass of his armour against the strongpoint at Got el Oualeb, held by the left flank of the British 50th Division of XIII Corps. Caught also on their western flank by the Italian X Corps, the British 150th Brigade and the 1st Army Tank Brigade capitulated on June 2; Rommel took 3,000 prisoners, 124 guns, and 101 armoured vehicles.

The fall of Got el Oualeb opened a ten-mile wide gap in the minefield, allowing the *Panzerarmee Afrika* to reunite its forces and Rommel to regain the initiative. This he used to close the pincers round Bir Hakeim. As can be seen, the reaction of the British 8th Army had been slow and indecisive, and between May 29 and June 2 several occasions had arisen to exploit the risky situation into which the enemy had got himself, but these were purely and simply wasted. It would seem unjust to blame all this on General Ritchie. From all evidence his radio communications were bad and only gave him out-of-date news of the battle, and the Germans, combining with greater skill their tanks, infantry, anti-tank guns, and mines, were as inaccessible on the defensive as they were aggressive in attack.

The battle of what the British called "The Cauldron" ended in a fresh defeat for Ritchie. Skilfully laid minefields protected by batteries of 8.8-cm guns thwarted the most valiant attacks of the XIII and XXX Corps whose various units, unfortunately, were widely dispersed and sometimes out of contact one with the other. Then at a given point Rommel redoubled his armoured attack with the 15th Panzer and the 90th Light Divisions, which drove hard into the enemy's rear. As night fell on the "Knightsbridge" battlefield the Germans counted 4,000 prisoners, and the 32nd Tank Brigade alone had lost 50 out of the 70 tanks it had had at dawn. It was the defeat of this badly co-ordinated British counter-stroke which marked the turning point of the battle.

In spite of this defeat, which robbed it of all hope of relief, the garrison at Bir Hakeim kept up its resistance under repeated bombing by Stukas and drove back the daily attacks of the 90th Light Division and the "Trieste" Motorised Division. General Koenig also had to cope with a delegation of Italian emissaries who got through to his command post to urge him to capitulate.

"On the stroke of 1030 hours." writes Jacques Mordal, "the officer commanding the 2nd Battalion of the Foreign Legion telephoned his Brigade Headquarters that a car flying a flag of truce was at the east gate. Two Italian officers got out and were led blindfolded to the General's headquarters by Captain de Sairigné. One of them said in Italian that he had come in the name of his own leader and in that of General Rommel, 'the great victor of Libya' to ask for a surrender so as to avoid useless bloodshed. . . . Was it not also in the interest of the defenders to be taken prisoner by the Italians, well known for their consideration, rather than to risk falling later into the hands of the Germans who would very likely show them little respect? . . . General Koenig did not seem impressed by the pertinence of this remark and merely replied very politely in French that there was absolutely no question of his surrendering. Upon this the two emissaries stood at attention and saluted. 'Grandi soldati' they said as they withdrew."

Water and ammunition were running short and so the 1st Free French Brigade was ordered to evacuate the position it had so valiantly defended. More than 3,000 French, led by General Koenig, reached the British lines during the course of the night June 10–11, leaving behind 984 missing, of whom 500 were taken prisoner.

Three nights later, when it was on the point of being surrounded, XIII Corps also disengaged. Ritchie's intention was to regroup to form a coherent force based on Tobruk. But he was reduced to 100 tanks and, slower than his adversary, he was driven back to the frontier and denied all contact with the fortress, whose defences were now derelict since G.H.Q. Cairo had decided in January that it should not be held again as an isolated fortress, and had informed London accordingly.

At dawn on June 20, whilst the 90th Light Division and the "Littorio" Armoured Division, recently arrived in the battle area, covered the 8th Army, or what was left of it, Rommel attacked Tobruk with his two Panzer divisions and the Italian XX Corps. The attack was from the south-east and was supported by Stukas. By 0800 hours the forward troops of the 15th Panzer Division had bridged the anti-tank ditch so that the armour could immediately exploit the breach, and by mid-day the ships at anchor in the harbour were being pounded by heavy artillery. The battle raged until nightfall around the Solaro and Pilastrino forts, where finally the 21st Panzer Division hoisted the Swastika flag.

In these desperate conditions, at 0940 hours on June 21, Major-General H. B. Klopper surrendered to General Navarrini the garrison of Tobruk, that is 33,000 men of the 2nd South African Division, the 11th Indian Brigade, the 32nd Army Tank Brigade, and the 201st Guards Brigade. A considerable number of vehicles and 2,200,000 gallons of petrol fell into Axis hands. A few hours later, Rommel, quoting the 45,000 prisoners taken since May 27, together with 1,000 armoured vehicles, and 400 guns, addressed a glowing order of the day to his men. He ended with this meaningful appeal:

"Soldiers of the *Panzerarmee Afrika*!

"Now for the complete destruction of the enemy. We will not rest until we have shattered the last remnants of the British 8th Army. During the days to come, I shall call on you for one more great effort to bring us this final goal."

And he designated Sidi Barrani as the next objective for his victorious troops.

It had, however, been agreed that the bulk of the *Panzerarmee* would not go beyond Halfaya Pass and that from June 20 some of its detachments would be withdrawn so that *Esigenza "C3"* or Operation *"Herkules"* could be started on August 1. Cavallero in Rome was still keeping to what had been agreed at Klessheim, and on the very day when Rommel announced his intention of disobeying his directive of May 5, he had the Duce sign a letter reminding Hitler of the great importance he attached to an early solution of the Malta question, asking the Duce to say in particular:

"This action against Malta is more imperative than ever. The truly remark-able effects of the mass action by the Axis air forces, and in particular of *Luftflotte* II in April, were still being felt in May. But in June Malta was being constantly re-supplied with planes and it has recovered its offensive powers so that now our sea-borne routes towards Libya are again under threat. As things stand, we must be able to conduct our transport operations with sufficient security if the results achieved in Marmarica are to be maintained and our future needs met."

But at German headquarters Hitler had become much less enthusiastic over the Malta enterprise. In his reply dated June 23 he never even mentioned it. He urged his ally not to imitate the British, who in the previous year had gone off chasing shadows in Greece when they could have occupied Tripoli. And, moreover, there was the danger of U.S. heavy bombers based in Egypt attacking Italy. Finally the conquest of Egypt, combined with the effects of the campaign which had started with the attack on Sevastopol', would be the end of British rule in the Middle East. At this historic hour, which would not return, the Führer advised the Duce to order Rommel to pursue the enemy's forces to complete annihilation. "In war," he noted sententiously, "the goddess of Fortune visits captains only once. He who does not grasp her at such a moment will never reach her again."

Mussolini gave in to his ally's point of view and his Chief of General Staff had to agree. When Hitler was addressing this exhortation to his friend the Duce, Rommel, who had just been promoted Field-Marshal, had already driven beyond Sidi Barrani. And so in Derna, where Cavallero, accompanied by Kesselring and Weichold, had come to talk to him, the discussion was not about the alternative, Malta or Suez, but whether a pause was desirable before the El Alamein gap or whether they should try to rush through it. Forgetting his saying "Tobruk–the Nile: it's only a dream", Cavallero finally gave in to the more ambitious solution of his German colleagues, who thought they saw victory in sight.

At the same time the Panzers were approaching Marsa Matrûh, where Lieutenant-General Ritchie was preparing for a last-ditch stand. Sir Claude Auchinleck then took over from Ritchie's hesitant hands the reins of the 8th Army. Both at the time and since, much has been said about Ritchie's responsibility for the defeats of January and June 1942. We will merely state that the last time he had led troops was in 1938, as the commander of an infantry battalion, and that he had therefore little experience of the tactical and technical considerations required in army operations. It should also be stated that when commanding a corps in the 1944–1945 campaign he satisfied so demanding and punctilious a leader as Field-Marshal Montgomery who, as we know, could easily be displeased.

Auchinleck nevertheless managed to get X Corps (Lieutenant-General W. G. Holmes) out of the trap at Marsa Matrûh. This formation was newly arrived from Britain. It was not to be without loss, however, as the New Zealand Division, which took up the fighting again, was very hard pressed and its commander, Major-General Freyberg, was severely wounded. Even so, having a few days' start on the enemy, the remains of the 8th Army were able to take up position at El Alamein, where they were joined by the 9th Australian Division from Syria and the 4th Indian Division from Cyprus.

Tactically, this lightly-fortified position stood between the Mediterranean and the Qattara Depression, an area of salt marshes and quicksand impassable even to a loaded camel, which excluded any large-scale turning movement. Strategically, it left Rommel the difficult job of supplying his army over the 250 miles of desert behind him via a single road continually harassed by Air Vice-Marshal Coningham's fighter-bombers. One of these had already killed General Baldassare, commander of the Italian XX Corps.

The Axis advance had been so fast from Halfaya to El Alamein that on July 1 Rommel had only some 6,400 men, 41 tanks (14 of which were Italian), and 71 guns under his command to face the British position. Nevertheless he ordered an immediate attack. But all the dash of his experienced troops could not prevent this act of rashness from being crowned by failure. The following week he had 30 battalions under his command, but between them they had fewer than 5,000 infantrymen. On July 17 his four armoured divisions only had 58 German and Italian tanks between them.

To put it bluntly, Rommel had overstretched himself. The British were constantly reinforcing their positions and beginning to launch local offensives directed principally against Italian units, the weakest point of Rommel's army. And so it was that one after the other the "Ariete" Armoured Division, and the "Sabratha", "Trento", and "Brescia" Divisions were severely trounced: on July 22 Auchinleck was able to report the capture of 7,000 prisoners in three weeks. In his notes Rommel uses hard words against his allies. According to him, for example, the "Ariete" "gave in" on July 3, whereas we know from official sources that when it did fall back it was reduced to the strength of one small company. What is certain is that the new Field-Marshal, who had invited Marshal Bastico to dine with him in Cairo on June 30 when they were at the Derna conference, had well and truly lost his optimism. On July 17 he wrote to his wife:

"Things are going downright badly for me at the moment, at any rate in the military sense. The enemy is using his superiority, especially in infantry, to destroy the Italian formations one by one, and the German formations are much too weak to stand alone. It's enough to make

one weep". And the next day, the same story:

"Yesterday was a particularly hard and critical day. We pulled through again. But it can't go on like it for long, otherwise the front will crack. Militarily, this is the most difficult period I've ever been through. There's help in sight, of course, but whether we will live to see it is a question. You know what an incurable optimist I am. But there are situations where everything is dark. However, this period too, will pass."

In this pessimistic view of things on July 23 he went so far as to envisage retreat, but Mussolini, Cavallero, and Bastico intervened and on the next day, having repulsed with losses a new attempt by Auchinleck to break through his front, he recovered his calm. The victor of Tobruk, in reporting that he was checked, blamed the haphazard supplies he got in North Africa during this decisive period from *Comando Supremo*. This complaint seems ill-founded for two reasons:

1. because in Rome the logistic services of *Comando Supremo* had calculated Rommel's requirements on the basis of the situation agreed with him in late March 1942 and confirmed by the directive of May 5, that is that the proposed offensive would have as its objective Halfaya by June 20 at the latest; and

2. because the effort of improvisation demanded of *Comando Supremo* had

A German Pzkw IV ploughs on through the desert. Armed with the short 7.5 cm gun the Pzkw IV proved superior to its undergunned and frequently unreliable British rivals.

coincided with renewed air activity from Malta. It was not Cavallero's fault if Hitler had transferred to the Eastern Front by mid-April a good half of the X *Fliegerkorps* and if several squadrons of the II *Fliegerkorps* had been kept in North Africa and Crete after June 20.

On April 25 Winston Churchill offered Lord Gort, then in command at Gibraltar, the job of Governor of Malta. Gort accepted the post, and all its burdens, without a moment's hesitation. When he arrived at Valletta he found the situation as follows: air attacks on the island's installations were decreasing, for reasons which we have seen, and this allowed the R.A.F. to send back there a small number of Wellingtons and Beaufort torpedo-carrying aircraft. But, because of the blockade, the population was reduced to ten ounces of bread a day and petrol was so scarce that contemporary photographs show us the new governor inspecting his command by bicycle. A new supply operation was all the more urgent because further Axis attacks were expected at any moment, and the defences could not be caught short of fuel and ammunition. The

Admiralty therefore decided to send two convoys to Malta, one from Gibraltar and the other from Alexandria. This would cause the enemy to split his attack.

In the west, under the codename "Harpoon", a convoy of six merchant ships entered the Mediterranean during the night of June 11–12 escorted by the A.A. cruiser *Cairo* and nine destroyers. In support was Vice-Admiral A. T. B. Curteis with the battleship *Malaya*, the old aircraft-carriers *Eagle* and *Argus*, three light cruisers, and nine destroyers. The minelayer *Welshman* operated independently because of her greater speed.

On June 14, Axis aircraft attacked the convoy. 17 enemy aircraft were shot down but a Dutch merchant ship was lost and the cruiser *Liverpool* was so badly damaged that she had to be towed back to Gibraltar. As night fell, the supporting heavy ships turned back abreast of Bizerta and the convoy with its escort entered the Skerki Channel. At dawn on June 15 they ran into the Italian 7th Naval Division (Admiral A. da Zara) which *Supermarina* had very opportunely sent to patrol off Pantellaria. This Italian force consisted of the light cruisers *Eugenio di Savoia* and *Raimondo Montecuccoli*, together with five destroyers.

In spite of the Italian cruisers' superior fire-power, Captain C. C. Hardy, now the escort commander, turned to face the enemy and ordered the convoy to sail close to the Tunisian coast. During the ensuing battle the cruiser *Cairo* was slightly damaged but the destroyer *Bedouin*, totally disabled, was finally sunk by a torpedo-carrying aircraft. Again the British used smoke screens very effectively against the Italian ships, which had no radar, but they could not hide the convoy from the Axis aircraft which hurled themselves at their target. One merchant ship was sunk by bombs, while another and the American petrol-tanker *Kentucky* were disabled and later sunk by da Zara's guns.

Hardy reached Valletta during the night but he still had to reckon with Italian mines, which sank the Polish destroyer *Kujawiak* and caused such damage to the British merchant ship *Orari* that part of her cargo was lost. In all only 15,000 out of 43,000 tons of supplies reached Malta. *Welshman* acquitted herself well with her usual speed and discretion.

On the previous May 20 Admiral Harwood had succeeded Sir Andrew Cunningham as the new C.-in-C. Mediterranean. He was now given the task of directing Operation "Vigorous", designed to get through to Malta a convoy of 11 merchant ships with an escort of seven light cruisers, one A.A. cruiser, and 26 destroyers under Rear-Admiral Sir Philip Vian. But "Vigorous" was no luckier than Operation "Harpoon" in escaping the well-planned attentions of the enemy. On June 12 the Axis bombers scored a first point in forcing a merchant ship to drop out of the convoy and then finishing it off. On the 14th, after seven attacks by waves of 60 to 70 Junkers Ju 88's, a second mer-

chant ship was sunk off Derna. Towards 2300 hours Vian learned the dramatic news that Admiral Iachino had left Taranto with his two 41,000-ton battleships and four cruisers, two of them heavy ones. At this news Vian turned about, calculating that on his present course contact would be established at dawn and, with 16 hours of daylight in front of him, there would be no escape. During this manoeuvre a German E-boat sank the destroyer *Hasty* and damaged the cruiser *Newcastle*.

In the headquarters which he shared with Admiral Harwood, Sir Arthur Tedder tried to hold off Iachino, unleashing against him all the aircraft at his command, notably eight four-engined B-24 Liberators manned by Americans and 40 torpedo-carrying aircraft. These relayed with the Malta-based aircraft which had been attacking since the previous night. However, except for the cruiser *Trento*, damaged by a torpedo, no Italian ship had been severely damaged, although the British believed that both Italian battleships had been hit several times. This false information encouraged Harwood in his decision to order Vian to make for the

South African prisoners-of-war wait by a captured Marmon-Herrington armoured car following the rapid capture of Tobruk by the Afrika Korps.

island once more.

At 1400 hours, however, *Supermarina* recalled Iachino, who now had no chance of engaging the enemy before nightfall. Vian, however, was unable to make use of this withdrawal, as he had already used up two-thirds of his A.A. ammunition and had to return to Alexandria.

Submarines and torpedo-carrying aircraft now harassed the retreating enemy. The British lost the cruiser *Hermione* and also the destroyers *Nestor* and *Airedale*. On the other side, the *Trento* blew up after a hit from the submarine *Umbra* (Lieutenant-Commander Maydon), whilst the battleship *Littorio* was damaged, though not severely, by a torpedo from an aircraft. Malta thus got about 15 per cent of the supplies sent by the Admiralty. This undoubted success by the Axis powers had its reverse side, however: having used up 15,000 tons of diesel oil during three days of high speed operations, the Italian Navy was soon to be laid up through lack of fuel.

CHAPTER 33
Planning the Allied counteroffensive

Although in the last 20 years Soviet historiography has made some progress in its treatment of military operations, the same cannot be said for it where inter-Allied relations are concerned. There, no advance at all has been made on the hostile attitude adopted in the Stalinist era – an attitude which we notice whenever it touches on the help given to Moscow by London and Washington in assisting the Red Army's fluctuating struggle against the German invaders. No one will deny that when it came to supplying equipment and *matériel* and to opening a second front, the two Anglo-Saxon powers were able to do little for their Soviet ally. But could they really have done any more in view of the other aspects of their strategic situation, which could not but occupy their attention? And can it really be correct to see a sinister plot secretly hatched out between the London and Washington Governments in this quite relative and temporary lack of assistance?

The second volume of *The Great Patriotic War* makes no bones about giving an affirmative answer to the second of our two questions.

But while its official nature constrains the satellite countries and the Communist parties of Western Europe to accept the thesis as an article of faith affirmed by Moscow, it need carry no weight with impartial historians such as ourselves. And if we apply to it standard tests of historical exactitude we see that it crumbles away and dissolves, leaving witness only to the extreme naïvety of those who, on this side of the Iron Curtain, believe it.

Dealing with the question of a second front, the *Great Patriotic War* quotes Eisenhower as saying that such a front should be delayed until German morale cracked. But the quotation only makes sense if it is put back into its proper context. What was Eisenhower talking about? Simply that "This was a very definite conviction, held by some of our experienced soldiers, sailors, and airmen, that the fortified coast of western Europe could not be successfully attacked. Already much was known of the tremendous effort the German was making to insure integrity of his Atlantic Wall."

Moreover, bearing in mind the capacity of the Luftwaffe, the strength of the Army, and the submarine and mine-laying potential of the German Navy, all of which would have been used to oppose an attempted landing, Eisenhower writes in his *Crusade in Europe*: "Many held that attack against this type of defence was madness, nothing but military suicide. Even among those who thought direct assault by land forces would eventually become necessary, the majority believed that definite signs of cracking German morale would have to appear before it would be practicable to attempt such an enterprise."

Admittedly, he says, General Marshall, who was Chief of General Staff, and Major-Generals J. T. MacNarney and Carl A. Spaatz (U.S. Army Air Force) were less pessimistic, but they were almost alone in their views. Be that as it may, it should be emphasised that the objections raised by the American military to establishing a second front in Western Europe in 1942 were based on technical and tactical considerations, and not on political ones. In fact, it was a general tendency of Allied commanders to ignore the vital political elements in warfare.

The Great Patriotic War attempts to rebut this line of argument by appealing to the success of Operation "Torch": "The English and American Governments justified this delay by insisting that they did not have the men and the means to land on the French coast. That this piece of reasoning is senseless can be seen from the fact that the United States and Great Britain engaged considerable forces in North Africa in November 1942 and succeeded in landing both in Morocco and in Algeria."

A peculiar argument, we may reply, which quite ignores the serious military and political preparatory work carried out in North Africa by the American and English secret services as soon as a decision had been taken to land to the south of the Strait of Gibraltar.

As for the undertakings the London and Washington Governments are supposed to have given Moscow, they were far less onerous than the Russians would today have us understand. Certainly, at the conclusion of the visit to the two Allied capitals made by Molotov, an agreed communiqué published in June 1942 said:

"In the course of these discussions complete agreement was reached on the urgency of opening a second front in Europe during 1942."

But in fact, this was a Russian draft first accepted by Roosevelt without consulting the British. Churchill went along with it in order to avoid embarrassment to the Western Allies. However, he himself made it quite plain to Molotov that Britain was in no way committed to opening a European Second Front in 1942. He stated expressly:

"We are making preparations for a landing on the Continent in August or September 1942. As already explained, the main limiting factor to the size of the landing force is the availability of special landing-craft. Clearly however it would not further either the Russian cause or

American Infantry undergoing training in Northern Ireland during March 1942.

that of the Allies as a whole if, for the sake of action at any price, we embark on some operation which ended in disaster and gave the enemy an opportunity for glorification of our discomfiture. It is impossible to say in advance whether the situation will be such as to make this operation feasible when the time comes. *We can therefore give no promise in the matter*, but provided that it appears sound and sensible we shall not hesitate to put our plans into effect."

At the White House on the preceding May 30, President Roosevelt had gone somewhat further. According to the account of the meeting given by Professor Samuel H. Cross, who acted as interpreter for the American delegation, Molotov had told his host:

"'If you postpone your decision you will have eventually to bear the brunt of the war, and if Hitler becomes the undisputed master of the Continent, next year will unquestionably be tougher than this one.'

"The President then put to General Marshall the query whether developments were clear enough so that we could say to Mr. Stalin that we are preparing a Second Front. 'Yes,' replied the General. The President then authorized Mr. Molotov to inform Mr. Stalin that we

American mountain troops in training for the day when Europe would be invaded.

expected the formation of a Second Front this year."

Even though these words cannot be regarded as giving any explicit formal undertaking, it will scarcely enter anyone's head to suggest that President Roosevelt, advised by Harry Hopkins and General Marshall, would have offered his Russian partner deliberately false assurances. In fact, at this time American military opinion was still hoping that a landing in Western Europe in 1942 might be possible, whereas the British were convinced that the Allies would not be strong enough to attempt such an operation before 1943.

Nevertheless, Hitler was still very worried about the possibility of a cross-channel attack. On July 9, less than a month after the publication of the communiqué quoted above, he despatched an identically-worded directive to Army, Navy, and Air Force, the first paragraph of which contained his assessment of the situation and deserves note.

"Our swift and massive victories may force Great Britain to choose between launching a large scale invasion, with a view to opening a second front, or seeing Russia eliminated as a military and political factor. Hence it is highly probable that we shall soon face an enemy landing within the O.K.H. command area."

In danger, he thought, were:

"(a) In the first place the Pas de Calais, the sector between Dieppe and Le Havre,

and Normandy, because these regions are within range of enemy guns and within reach of most of their transport vessels. (b) Secondly, southern Holland and Brittany."

On August 8 following, Hitler touched on the same subject in a long letter to Mussolini, in which he expressed both his contempt for his adversary and his confidence in his own resources.

"I consider the second front quite insane, but since in democracies decisions are taken by majority and therefore tend to derive from human incomprehension, one must always be ready for the fools to carry the day and to try to establish a second front." However, as he went on to explain to the Duce, everything was already set up both in Norway and in the West to give the invader the warmest of receptions. On the Channel coast and the Strait of Dover, fortifications were progressing apace and included numerous gun batteries of all sizes.

Whatever is said on this subject in Moscow, Hitler was alive to the danger and remained alert. He even proposed to go in person to the Western Front in the event of a landing and to assume command of operations on the spot.

"Any captain who attacks a shore battery is a madman," said Nelson, and that great sailor paid highly for his knowledge, losing his right eye at Calvi (1795) and his right arm two years later at Santa Cruz de Tenerife.

The experience of the Great War seemed to offer striking confirmation of Nelson's views. In the Dardanelles, English and French battleships, among them the powerful *Queen Elizabeth*, firing her 15-inch guns for the first time, had not succeeded in silencing the Turkish batteries which blocked the strait. The Navy had therefore requested the Army's aid in their destruction. But the landing of April 25, 1915, had run into a succession of disappointments and disasters, and the troops who were put ashore were soon to discover how weak, to say the least, was the cover and support supplied by the Navy's firepower.

During the period between the wars, a few men in France and Great Britain still interested themselves in the problems posed by landing powerful forces away from a large port. To this end they envisaged the construction of motorised landing-craft fitted with drop-gates in the bows over which to land their troops.

In France, three vessels of this type had been built by May 10, 1940. On May 14 the Royal Navy's landing craft put General Béthouart's *légionnaires* and tanks ashore near Narvik, and a little later 11 of these vessels had taken part in the evacuation of Dunkirk. The experience gained from these small-scale operations was encouraging enough to prompt the British Admiralty to order 178 of these craft from English shipyards and another 136 from American sources. For since the Americans foresaw a war in the Pacific, their Navy too had been concerned with the problem of making effective large-scale

landings in strength.

On the day of "Overlord", taking together all the military theatres throughout the world, there were about 9,500 craft of all sizes and types under the British and American flags.

As these figures indicate, the Anglo-Saxon powers had committed themselves to an amphibious form of warfare needing enormous industrial and economic efforts which for a long time to come left their mark in one way or another on the general development of war-time operations.

That this was so gradually became obvious later on, but neither Major-General Dwight D. Eisenhower, recently appointed to strategic planning, nor General Marshall were aware of it when, on April 1, 1942, they presented a plan of war to President Roosevelt. These comprised three separate operations:

1. Operation "Bolero" was to be initiated immediately, ensuring that within the period of a year 30 American divisions, of which six were to be armoured, should be moved across the Atlantic. These troops were to be complemented with air power whose task it would be to offer effective tactical support as well as to play its part in the R.A.F.'s strategic offensive against the industrial base of the Third Reich.

2. Once this logistic operation was completed, a major invasion of Western Europe would be launched in spring 1943. This operation was known as "Round-up". It would involve 30 American and 18 British divisions, of which three were to be armoured. A vanguard of six divisions, reinforced by parachute regiments, would land between Le Havre and Boulogne. Strengthened at the rate of 100,000 men a week, this Anglo-American offensive would have as its primary objective the capture of the line Deauville – Paris – Soissons – St. Quentin – Arras – Calais. Later on the line would be extended in the direction of Angers.

3. However, if the German army became suddenly greatly weakened by Russian victories, then the Western Allies should be ready to seize a limited bridgehead in the Cherbourg peninsula by September 1942. This scheme was called "Sledgehammer".

These plans were enthusiastically recommended by Defense Secretary Harry Stimson, always afire, despite his 72 years of age, and by Harry Hopkins, mindful as ever of Soviet interests. President Roosevelt too, without totally abandoning his old preference for a North African enterprise, finally came round and sent Hopkins and General Marshall to lay the plan before the British War Cabinet and the Chiefs-of-Staff Committee. On April 4 they left Baltimore by plane and on the evening of the 8th they met Winston Churchill, General Brooke, Anthony Eden (the Foreign Secretary), and Clement Attlee (Deputy Prime Minister since February 18, 1942).

These first conversations that General Marshall had with his British colleagues were reassuring. As Winston Churchill wrote in this regard:

"We were all relieved by the evident strong American intention to intervene in Europe, and to give the main priority to the defeat of Hitler. This had always been the foundation of our strategic thought."

As often happens, it was not clear at the time to the two parties that they were not speaking the same language. Nor was it clear that the difficulties between them would come to light as soon as active decisions had to be taken. More than their allies, the British were concerned with the total strategic situation throughout the world, and at a time when a powerful Japanese fleet was at large off the coast of Ceylon they thought it important not to relegate the defence of the Indies and the Middle East to second place, and certainly not to sacrifice it to the initiation of a second front, which the American plan now envisaged for spring 1943. Such was the tenor of Brooke's speech on behalf of the Chiefs-of-Staff Committee to a meeting with Roosevelt's representatives summoned by the British Prime Minister on April 14. Sir Hastings Ismay records him as saying:

"The Chiefs-of-Staff entirely agreed that Germany was the main enemy. At the same time it was essential to hold the Japanese and to ensure that there should be no junction between them and the Germans. If the Japanese obtained control of the Indian Ocean not only would the Middle East be gravely threatened, but we should lose the oil supplies from the Persian Gulf. The results of this would be that Germany would get all the oil she required, the southern route to Russia would be cut, Turkey would be isolated and defenceless, the Germans would obtain ready access to the Black Sea, and Germany and Japan would be able to interchange the goods of which they stood so much in need."

At the end of the meeting Churchill announced that the overall plan could be unanimously accepted and that the two Anglo-Saxon powers, as brothers in arms, would nobly march together in the attainment of their common aim, a final victory. The next day Hopkins wired the White House that London had agreed to the essentials of the American plan.

As a matter of fact, only Operation "Bolero" had met with the full agreement of the British War Cabinet and the Chiefs-of-Staff Committee.

As expounded to him by General Marshall, the "Round-up" project did not appeal to Brooke in the least. In his diary he writes:

"But, and this is a very large 'but', his plan does not go beyond just landing on the far coast. Whether we are to play *baccarat* or *chemin de fer* at Le Touquet... is not stipulated. I asked him this afternoon – Do we go west, south or east after landing? He had not begun to think of it."

Maybe General Brooke was exaggerating a little. Nonetheless, "Round-up" certainly looked a rather ill-conceived idea. For landing between Le Havre and

U.S. assault craft practise for the real thing.

Boulogne, at the start of operations the British and Americans would have been confronted by natural obstacles serious enough to make the defensive bluff that overlooked Omaha Beach look like a trivial inconvenience of terrain. The German 15th Army, entrusted with the defence of the area, had received favoured treatment with regard to its equipment and could rely on more solid fortifications than were to be found anywhere else – not to speak of the enormous gun batteries which pounded the English coast between the North Foreland and Dungeness.

Besides, the best proof that this plan met heavy criticism is that it was abandoned and never heard of again.

As for the projected attack on Cherbourg, it was no more warmly received by Winston Churchill than by General Brooke. But while the British had time to wait and see before finally abandoning "Round-up", if they were to block "Sledgehammer" they would have to act quickly, for that plan was due to be set in motion by September.

Nonetheless, in this connection Winston Churchill was careful to avoid saying anything that might upset Roosevelt. So he offered no overt resistance, and was content to let the facts speak for themselves. Thus he wrote:

"But I had little doubt myself that study of details – landing-craft and all that – and also reflection on the main strategy of the war, would rule out 'Sledgehammer'. In the upshot no military authority – Army, Navy, or Air – on either side of the Atlantic was found capable of preparing such a plan, or, so far as I was informed, ready to take the responsibility for executing it. United wishes and goodwill cannot overcome brute facts."

Was the British Prime Minister guilty of overstating his case in order to discourage the White House? Not if it is true that, taking together all the landing equipment available at any one time in Great Britain, it would have been impossible to move more than 4,000 men. And everything goes to show that matters were not much further forward in this field on the other side of the Atlantic either.

Moreover, it must be admitted that it would be hard to find a less suitable base

A U.S. paratrooper armed with an M1 Thompson sub-machine gun poses by two billowing parachutes.

from which to mount an invasion of the Continent than the Cherbourg peninsula, which was quite appropriately known in the Middle Ages as the "Cotentin enclosure". Its base is effectively cut off by a network of small rivers, marshes, and fields, which can easily be flooded by the operation of two or three sluice-gates. Nothing would have been easier for the enemy, once he had recovered from his initial surprise, than to block the paths of exit from the peninsula at its narrowest point—on the right at Carentan and on the left at Lessay.

These were the arguments which Churchill and Brooke persuasively and validly pressed against their American allies. And, apart from all these matters, it is undeniable that the British were naturally resistant to any such strategy as that proposed by General Marshall. For the British military authorities remained, on doctrinal grounds, as opposed to the teachings of Clausewitz and Napoleon as are British jurists to the legal code of Justinian. There were also the lessons of World War I to be taken into account. Nineteen months of war in 1917–1918 had cost only 50,510 American lives, and the United States entered World War II without their taste for offensive action tempered in the least. For the British, matters were quite different. On the Western Front alone the British Empire had lost 684,000 men from August 1914 to November 11, 1918. The futility of this warfare had profoundly influenced opinion in Britain. Hence Churchill and Brooke sought to achieve a relatively easy initial victory which was clearly not to be had between the Cape de la Hague and Barfleur Point.

Until now the British Prime Minister and his C.I.G.S. had been as one. But scarcely had General Brooke succeeded in thwarting what he believed to be the disastrous Operation "Sledgehammer" than Churchill laid before him another, codenamed "Jupiter". The aim of this project was to capture the aerodromes from which German bombers took off to harass the Allies' Arctic convoys.

"If we could gain possession of these airfields and establish an equal force there not only would the Northern sea route to Russia be kept open, but we should set up a second front on a small scale from which it would be most difficult to eject us. If the going was good we could advance gradually southward, unrolling the Nazi map of Europe from the top. All that has to be done is to oust the enemy from the airfields and destroy their garrisons."

The Chiefs-of-Staff were not impressed by the Prime Minister's reasoning, and on July 13 he came back to his theme in a memorandum which, while purely formal in composition, manifested clear signs of considerable irritation.

"The following note on 'Jupiter' should be read by the Planning Committee in conjunction with my previous paper on the subject. The Planners should set themselves to making a positive plan and overcoming the many difficulties, and not concern themselves with judging whether the operation is desirable or not, which must be decided by higher authority."

Despite this rebuff, "Jupiter" turned out as still-born as "Sledgehammer". And for very good reason, as the conquest of the German air bases was even less realisable than the attack on Trondheim which the Chiefs-of-Staff had vetoed in the previous autumn.

Among other considerations, one of the most powerful was that successful provision of air cover for the amphibious forces to be used in the assault depended on a number of somewhat tenuous assumptions. Churchill in fact thought that he could provide this support by basing six fighter and two or three bomber squadrons at Murmansk, but it now seems that this supposed too optimistic an assessment of the logistic possibilities which that base then offered.

Be this as it may, on June 17, Winston Churchill and his C.I.G.S. flew to Washington to finalise the Anglo-American strategy for 1942 and 1943. In the American capital, however, neither Roosevelt nor Harry Hopkins harboured any further illusions about still being able to convert their ally to the establishment of a second front in Europe in the autumn. Yet neither of them was disposed to keep the American troops destined for this purpose on an idle war footing until "Round-up" in spring 1943, and even less were they ready to see them used for operations in the Pacific theatre, as Admiral King had suggested. So if the principle of "Germany first" were to be adhered to, a principle which formed the keystone of White House policy, Operation "Gymnast" would have to be revived, even though the Hopkins-Marshall mission in April had given it scant attention.

And this is indeed what happened, al — though one may say that it happened somewhat obliquely. For on July 21 it was agreed between the English and Americans, without however committing themselves to any definite decision, that Winston Churchill's favourite project should be re-examined. As the last paragraph of General Ismay's minute at the conclusion of the meeting records:

"The possibilities of French North Africa (Operation 'Gymnast') will be explored carefully and conscientiously, and plans will be completed in all details as soon as possible. Forces to be employed in 'Gymnast' would in the main be found from 'Bolero' units which have not yet left the United States ... Planning of 'Bolero' will continue to be centred in London. Planning for 'Gymnast' will be centred in Washington." On the same day Churchill met Eisenhower.

"At five o'clock therefore Major-Generals Eisenhower and Clark were brought to my air-cooled room. I was immediately impressed by these remarkable but hitherto unknown men. They had both come from the President, whom they had just seen for the first time. We talked almost entirely about the major cross-Channel invasion in 1943, 'Round-up' as it was then called, on which their thoughts

As German propaganda saw it:
Roosevelt and Churchill
struggle for control of Africa.

had evidently been concentrated. We had a most agreeable discussion, lasting for over an hour... At that time I thought of the spring or summer of 1943 as the date for the attempt. I felt sure that these officers were intended to play a great part in it, and that was the reason why they had been sent to make my acquaintance."

But after Churchill's return to London, he and his advisers agreed that "Sledgehammer" was impractical for 1942, and that "Gymnast" should be adopted. When this news reached Washington, it naturally angered Marshall and King. Roosevelt, therefore, sent them both to London under the leadership of his confidant Harry Hopkins to undertake a final examination of the situation together with the American military mission stationed in London and with his ally's Chiefs-of-Staff. And on Saturday, July 18, beside the Thames, they met Generals Eisenhower and Spaatz and Admiral Stark.

In appearance options were still open, but only in appearance. For it was now scarcely possible to complete the preparations necessary for a cross-Channel descent on the Cherbourg peninsula before the September equinox. After that date local weather conditions might very well make the whole enterprise impossible for weeks on end. On this point American naval experts were no less pessimistic than their British colleagues, and in *The White House Papers of Harry Hopkins* Robert Sherwood has well summarised the

discussion which finally settled the issue. "There was sufficient unanimity on the British side and a large enough fragment of doubt on the American side to make it impossible to push through the agreement for SLEDGEHAMMER."

Foreseeing this check, President Roosevelt, in one of the orders he had signed as Commander-in-Chief, expressly put out of court the Pacific venture favoured by General Marshall and Admiral King. And they were then asked to choose between reinforcing the British Army in the Middle East with American troops and attempting a landing in French North Africa under American command.

Naturally enough, Marshall and King opted for the second alternative, which was ratified by an inter-Allied agreement on July 24, 1942. But since the plans for Operation "Gymnast" had seen the inside of too many offices since the "Arcadia" Conference, it was decided to rechristen it Operation "Torch" for reasons of security. It was planned that this operation should be launched under the command of Eisenhower sometime before October 30.

Meanwhile, contact with the French authorities in North Africa favourable to the Allies was to be established.

It was Winston Churchill's job, as he was the driving force behind the Western Allies' change of plan, to explain to the Russians the reasons which had led the British and American Governments to give up all intentions of landing in Europe

in 1942 and demonstrate the advantage to the coalition as a whole of a successful Anglo-American landing in French North Africa. Nevertheless, on his request, it was decided by President Roosevelt that Averell Harriman would go to Moscow with him and would help in what the British Prime Minister called "a somewhat raw job."

It had to be shown to Stalin that the new plan being submitted to him resulted not from the lone initiative of the British Cabinet and the Imperial General Staff, but from an inter-Allied decision and that the American leaders were in full agreement with it.

When they were in Teheran, Churchill and Harriman had agreed to hand over the running of the trans-Persian railway to the Americans. This railway, linking the Persian Gulf to the Caspian Sea, had been laid by a British firm and had just been opened to traffic. It could only handle three trains a day in each direction, however (from 300 to 350 tons of goods), and war *matériel* destined for the Soviet Union was piling up on the platforms at Bandar-e-Shāhpūr. As the British were unable to remedy this state of affairs by the delivery of sufficient amounts of rolling stock or by providing enough men to run the line, the Americans got the agreement of their Allies to take over from them, and did the job with complete success. This was the first takeover from the United Kingdom by the United States in this part of the world. The post-war period was to see an acceleration of this process when an exhausted Great Britain's sphere of influence in Turkey and Greece was taken over by the United States.

At 1900 hours on August 12 Winston Churchill, accompanied by the British Ambassador in Moscow and Averell Harriman, were received in the Kremlin by Stalin, flanked by Molotov and Marshal Voroshilov. We have no record at all from Soviet sources of this or subsequent conversations and we are therefore restricted to the account left us by the Prime Minister, filled out with the aid of Lord Alanbrooke's notebooks, although the Chief of the Imperial General Staff did not arrive in the Soviet capital until the 13th. According to Churchill's memoirs, his explanations of the abandonment of Operation "Sledgehammer" and his promises to put into execution Operation "Round-up" from April 1, 1943 with 48 divisions, 27 of which would be American and 21 British, caused Stalin to "look gloomy", "more and more glum", then to "become restless". The argument that Hitler had not risked crossing the Channel when he was at the height of his power and England had only 20,000 trained men, 200 guns, and 50 tanks, did nothing to calm his irritation.

After an interlude during which he spoke of the bombing of Germany, the British Premier then went on to Operation "Torch" which aroused "intense interest" in Stalin. "In September we must win in

Egypt," Churchill said, "and in October in North Africa, all the time holding the enemy in Northern France. If we could end the year in possession of North Africa we could threaten the belly of Hitler's Europe and this operation should be considered in conjunction with the 1943 operation. That was what we and the Americans had decided to do."

And he adds: "To illustrate my point I had meanwhile drawn a picture of a crocodile and explained to Stalin with the help of this picture how it was our intention to attack the soft belly of the crocodile as he attacked his hard snout. And Stalin, whose interest was now at a high pitch, said, 'May God prosper this undertaking'."

With a startling quickness of mind the Soviet dictator took in the strategic advantages of the conquest of North Africa which, in his opinion, were as follows:

1. it would hit Rommel in the back;
2. it would keep Spain neutral;
3. it would produce fighting between Frenchmen and Germans in France; and
4. it would expose Italy to the whole brunt of the war.

Churchill then put forward a fifth argument in favour of "Torch", which was more familiar to him as a former First Lord of the Admiralty than to the Georgian Stalin: the reopening of the Mediterranean to Allied shipping would avoid the interminable detour round the Cape. This would also benefit the Russians, in view of the measures agreed between the British and the Americans to develop traffic on the trans-Persian railway.

"Torch", according to Churchill, pleased everyone; so, after four hours of talks, they separated in a more cordial atmosphere. On the morrow, however, there was a moment when they thought they would have to begin all over again.

On August 13, the Anglo-American delegation, now joined by Generals Brooke and Wavell and Air-Marshal Tedder, was received in the Kremlin at 11 o'clock in the evening. This was to hear read out to them by Stalin a memorandum in which, armed with the Anglo-Soviet communiqué of June 12 (announcing the forthcoming opening of a second front in Europe), he expressed in rather offensive terms his regret at the decision taken on this matter by his Anglo-Saxon allies. "Naturally," he pointed out, "the Soviet High Command was planning its summer and winter operations in relation to this second front. It is easy to grasp that the refusal of the Government of Great Britain to create a Second Front in 1942 in Europe inflicts a mortal blow to the whole of Soviet public opinion; it complicates the situation of the Red Army at the front and prejudices the plans of the Soviet command. I would add that the difficulties arising for the Red Army as a result of the refusal to create a Second Front in 1942 will undoubtedly be detrimental to the military situation of England and all the

remaining Allies. It appears to me and my colleagues that the most favourable conditions exist in 1942 for the creation of a Second Front in Europe."

But to his great regret he had to state that he had not been able to convert the British Prime Minister to this view and that the representative of the United States had taken the British side on all these points. He interspersed his reading with questions such as the following, which Brooke noted: "When are you going to start fighting? Are you going to let us do all the work whilst you look on? Are you never going to start fighting? You will find it is not too bad if you once start!"

Indignant at these spiteful imputations, says Brooke, "Winston crashed his fist down on the table and poured forth one of his wonderful spontaneous orations. It began with: 'If it was not for the fighting qualities of the Red Army . . .' Stalin stood up, sucking on his large bent pipe and, with a broad grin on his face, stopped Winston's interpreter and sent back through his own: 'I don't understand what you're saying, but, by God, I like your sentiment!' " Had he, as Churchill supposed, been taken to task by his colleagues in the Supreme Soviet for having too easily accepted the fact of "Torch" or, as Brooke thought, had he tried to see just how far he could go with this man whom he was meeting for the first time? We cannot know. In any case, the British Prime Minister could not let pass Stalin's statement that the Anglo-Soviet communiqué of June 12 was a formal engagement by his Government. He reminded him of the aide-mémoire which he had handed to Molotov when the latter came to London and, so that there should be no mistake about it, he confirmed this point of view in a memorandum of August 14:

"3. No promise has been broken by Great Britain or the United States. I refer to paragraph 5 of my aide-mémoire given to Mr. Molotov on June 10 which distinctly says: 'We can therefore give no promise.' We cannot admit that the conversations with M. Molotov about the second front, safeguarded as they were by reservations both oral and written, formed any ground for altering the strategic plans of the Russian High Command."

Stalin did not refer to the subject again and the rest of the conversations between the two statesmen and their military experts were about the supplies of Anglo-American war *matériel* to the Soviet Union, the defence of the Caucasus, which Stalin claimed was assured by 25 divisions, and the eventual transfer to that area of a number of British bomber squadrons.

In the morning of August 16, after a long evening in Stalin's villa in the company of Molotov, who "could drink", the Prime Minister flew off to Cairo. He was returning from this first encounter with the Soviet dictator on the whole "definitely encouraged", as he wrote to President Roosevelt.

CHAPTER 34
Alamein—the turning point in North Africa

It was on the afternoon of June 21, in the elegant White House study of President Roosevelt, that Winston Churchill first learnt of the fall of Tobruk. According to Churchill's memoirs, on learning of the catastrophe, the President dropped everything and immediately summoned General Marshall. Lord Alanbrooke, on the other hand, in the 1946 additions to his war diaries, would have us believe that it was General Marshall himself who delivered the bad news to the two statesmen, as they conferred in the Oval Room of the White House.

"I can remember this incident as if it had occurred yesterday. Churchill and I were standing beside the President's desk talking to him, when Marshall walked in with a pink piece of paper containing a message of the fall of Tobruk. Neither Winston nor I had contemplated such an eventuality and it was a staggering blow. I cannot remember what the actual words were that the President used to convey his sympathy, but I remember vividly being impressed by the tact and real heartfelt sympathy which lay behind these words. There was not one word too much nor one word too little."

But Roosevelt did not stop at mere eloquent expressions of sympathy; quite spontaneously, he immediately asked what he could do to temper the effects of the disaster inflicted upon the British Army. His first idea was to send out the American 1st Armoured Division to the Middle East, but the carrying out of such a project would have created enormous difficulties; he and General Marshall, therefore, in a spirit of comradeship rarely known in coalitions, offered to refit the 8th Army, by giving it the 300 Sherman tanks that had just been distributed to the American armoured units. To complete this most generous gift, 100 self-propelled 105-mm guns were also offered. But even that was not all, for when the cargo vessel carrying the 300 tank engines was torpedoed and sunk off Bermuda, "without a single word from us the President and Marshall put a further supply of engines into another fast ship and dispatched it to overtake the convoy. 'A friend in need is a friend indeed.'"

The entry into active service of the 31-ton M4 Sherman tank upgraded the hitting power of the 8th Army in the Battle of El Alamein. Its long-barrelled (37.5 calibre) 75-mm gun was almost as good as the shorter (24 calibre) 7.5-cm gun generally fitted to the heaviest tanks (the Pzkw IV) of the *Panzerarmee Afrika*; secondly it had a less obtrusive shape than its predecessor, the M3 Grant; finally, the latter's awkward sponson was replaced in the Sherman tank by a turret capable of traversing through 360 degrees.

For diplomatic reasons it was not revealed at the time that the Sherman was what General Sir Brian Horrocks, commander of XIII Corps at El Alamein, later

in his memoirs called "a brilliant example of Anglo-American co-operation". American engineers were in charge of the tank's mechanical features (engine, transmission, and tracks), whilst the armament derived from researches carried out by a British team. It was, apparently, because he wanted the aid the Americans were so generously giving to receive full public recognition, that Churchill suppressed the extent of British participation.

At the same time (summer 1942), the Italo-German air forces fighting in North Africa finally lost their last remnants of superiority over the R.A.F., now being regularly reinforced by deliveries of American and British aircraft, which, technically and tactically, were of the highest quality: there was, for example, the Supermarine Spitfire Mark V interceptor and the Hawker Hurricane IID fighter-bomber, nicknamed the "tin-opener", because its 40-mm armour-piercing shells tore through the thickest Panzer armour with considerable ease. Later came the excellent North American P-51 Mustang fighter capable of 390 mph, and with a ceiling of 31,000 feet. Roosevelt's sympathetic understanding of Britain's needs also made it possible to increase to 117 the number of strategic bombers posted to this theatre, when the four-engined American Consolidated B-24 Liberator bomber joined the British-built Handley-Page Halifax.

It therefore follows that the R.A.F. not only recovered, conclusively and permanently, mastery of the air, but also that it was able to give the 8th Army, in both its defensive and offensive rôles, support that daily became more powerful and better organised. In his book on the war in the air, Air Vice-Marshal J. E. Johnson has traced this development very precisely:

"Slowly, by trial, error, and the foresight of gifted men, not only airmen, the pattern of air support for the soldiers again took shape. Fighters to grind down the enemy bomber and fighter forces; fighters which could then be armed with bombs to attack the enemy ground forces; fighters which, armed or not with bombs, were always capable of protecting themselves and providing protection for the bombers. A bomber force which was as capable of bombing enemy airfields and installations as of attacking troops on the ground. A reconnaissance force to be the eyes of both Army and Air Force Commanders."

Among the "gifted men" whom the author mentions, pride of place must go to General Bernard Law Montgomery, who on taking over command of the 8th Army, set up his H.Q. next to that of Air Vice-Marshal Coningham, commanding the Desert Air Force, as the Middle East's tactical air force was called.

We have already seen that, since June 25, General Sir Claude Auchinleck had been

at the head of both the 8th Army and the Middle East Land Forces, a situation of which Churchill fully approved, as is shown by his message of June 28; and on July 4, when he learnt that the 8th Army was not only standing its ground, but even counter-attacking, he again showed his satisfaction: "I must tell you how pleased I am with the way things are shaping," he wrote that day. "If fortune turns I am sure you will press your advantage, as you say, 'relentlessly'."

And yet, three weeks later, Churchill had decided, if not actually to dismiss him, at least to deprive him of his command in Egypt, Palestine, and Syria, thus limiting him to Iraq and Persia. Quite clearly, Churchill was once more itching to attack, whereas lack of resources, and the need to wait for the reinforcements which were coming around the Cape of Good Hope, made G.H.Q. Cairo wish to refrain from any large-scale offensive initiative until mid-September. And when it is realised that co-operation between armour and infantry was still very poor in the 8th Army, and that the new command team of Alexander and Montgomery waited until October 23 before attacking, it is difficult not to accept the view of Cairo command.

On the other hand General Brooke, whose sturdy independence vis-à-vis Churchill is well known, never stopped saying, in his war diaries, that "It was quite clear that something was radically wrong but not easy at a distance to judge what this something was, nor how far wrong it was . . . The crisis had now come and it was essential that I should go out to see what was wrong. But for this I wanted to be alone."

To help us interpret these somewhat veiled remarks, we have available the testimony of two very different personalities: Field-Marshal Smuts, the Prime Minister of South Africa, and Field-Marshal Montgomery. They criticised Sir Claude Auchinleck for an inability to choose his subordinate officers. Montgomery expressed himself on this subject with his usual directness.

"A good judge of men would never have selected General Corbett to be his Chief of Staff in the Middle East. And to suggest that Corbett should take command of the Eighth Army, as Auchinleck did, passed all comprehension.

"Again, nobody in his senses would have sent Ritchie to succeed Cunningham in command of the Eighth Army; Ritchie had not the experience or qualifications for the job and in the end he had to be removed too." A brutal judgement, certainly, but on August 4, 1942, Smuts had spoken in a similar vein to General Brooke during the latter's visit to Cairo.

At all events, the C.I.G.S., General Brooke, went to Cairo, inspecting Gibraltar and Malta on the way—but not alone, as he would have liked; Churchill had also decided to go out and see for himself what

British soldiers with their Bren Carrier.

the situation was like, and had summoned General Wavell, C.-in-C. India, and Field-Marshal Smuts, both men whose opinion he valued, to meet him in Cairo.

"Had General Auchinleck or his staff lost the confidence of the Desert Army? If so, should he be relieved, and who could succeed him?" According to his memoirs, these were the two big questions that brought Churchill to Cairo, where he landed on the morning of August 4, only a few minutes before the C.I.G.S. In reality his mind was already made up, as is proved by the fact that on August 6, at dawn, he went to see Brooke, just as the latter was getting up ("practically naked"), and told him that he had decided to split the Middle East theatre into two. Relegated to Basra or Baghdad, Auchinleck would be given the new Persia and Iraq Command, separated from the rest of Middle East Command, which Churchill now offered to Brooke. The latter asked not to be appointed on the grounds that this was no time to disorganise the Imperial General Staff, and that in any case he had no knowledge of desert warfare. But that evening he confided to his diary:

"Another point which I did not mention was that, after working with the P.M. for close on nine months, I do feel at last that I can exercise a limited amount of control on some of his activities and that at last he is beginning to take my advice. I feel,

therefore, that, tempting as the offer is, by accepting it I should definitely be taking a course which would on the whole help the war least. Finally, I could not bear the thought that Auchinleck might think that I had come out here on purpose to work myself into his shoes."

Brooke having thus refused, for the most honourable of reasons, Sir Harold Alexander was asked that very evening, on Brooke's recommendation, to take over the Middle East Command. A happy choice, for the new commander had shown the same imperturbability and resourcefulness at Dunkirk as later in the Burma jungle, and, in addition, wore his authority easily. "Calm, confident and charming – as always" was the impression the difficult Montgomery received on their first meeting at G.H.Q. Cairo. Alexander had just been appointed deputy to General Eisenhower, as commander of the British 1st Army taking part in "Torch", and Eisenhower now had to be asked to release him for this new post.

Originally, and in spite of Brooke's opposition, General W. H. E. Gott had been appointed to command the 8th Army, but the aircraft in which he was travelling was forced down by two German fighters; whilst he was helping other passengers caught in the wreckage, a second attack caused the plane to explode, leaving no survivors, and his successor, Brooke's candidate, took over and was told to get out to Cairo immediately. This was Lieu-

tenant-General Bernard L. Montgomery – who had just introduced himself to Eisenhower as Alexander's successor as commander of the 1st Army. Small wonder that on being deprived of his second deputy in 48 hours, Eisenhower cynically asked, "Are the British taking 'Torch' seriously?"

To replace General Corbett, Alexander chose as his chief-of-staff Lieutenant-General R. McCreery; he was very popular, and Alexander wrote of him that "he was one of those officers who is as successful at H.Q. as at the head of his troops" and "faithful friend and companion" to him personally. Thus was formed the brilliant team which, with Air Chief Marshal Sir Arthur Tedder and Admiral Sir Henry Harwood, led the 8th Army from El Alamein to Tripoli in less than nine months.

General Auchinleck, relieved of his command because he had refused to attack before mid-September, accepted his disgrace with dignity, but refused the consolation prize that Churchill offered.

On August 10 the British Prime Minister, accompanied by Generals Wavell and Brooke, flew to Moscow to inform the Russians of the Anglo-American decision to abandon Operation "Sledgehammer" in favour of Operation "Torch". But before leaving Cairo, Churchill had sent Alexander hand-written instructions, fixing his tasks in the following manner:

"1. Your prime and main duty will be to take or destroy at the earliest opportunity the German-Italian Army commanded by Field-Marshal Rommel together with all its supplies and establishments in Egypt and Libya.

2. You will discharge or cause to be discharged such other duties as pertain to your command without prejudice to the task described in paragraph 1, which must be considered paramount in His Majesty's interests."

Whilst Churchill and his advisers were setting off for Moscow via Teheran, 14 merchant ships slipped through the Straits of Gibraltar under cover of dense fog. The interruption of convoys to Archangel had allowed the Admiralty to devote considerable resources to this new operation of supplying Malta: three aircraft-carriers, *Eagle*, *Victorious*, and *Indomitable* with their 72 fighters; the two battleships *Nelson* and *Rodney*; seven cruisers, one of which was an anti-aircraft vessel; 24 destroyers; two tankers; four corvettes; and eight submarines. In addition, the old aircraft carrier *Furious*, with an escort of eight destroyers, was able to fly off 38 Spitfires to Malta. The convoy had 14 merchantmen.

This considerable naval force was under the overall command of Vice-Admiral Sir Neville Syfret, commanding Force H. Rear-Admiral H. M. Burrough, with four cruisers and 12 destroyers, was the convoy's immediate escort; bearing in mind what had happened the previous June, he was to escort the convoy as far as Malta.

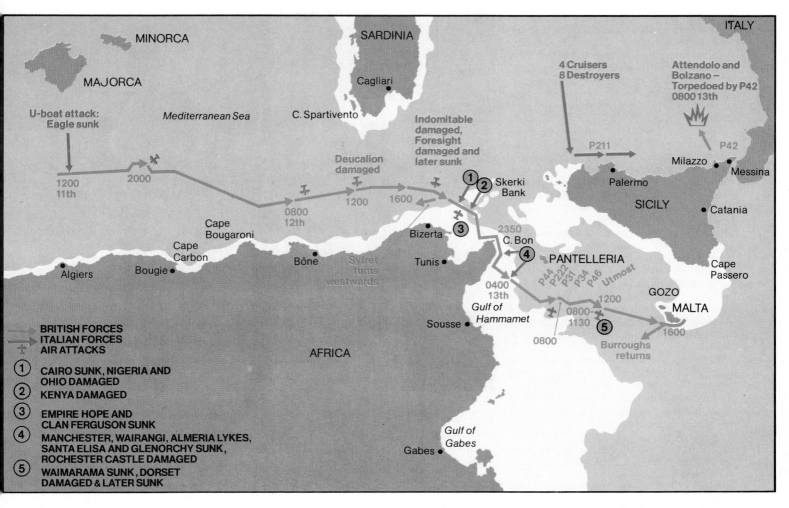

MINORCA

MAJORCA

U-boat attack:
Eagle sunk

Mediterranean Sea

1200
11th

2000

SARDINIA

Cagliari

C. Spartivento

ITALY

4 Cruisers
8 Destroyers

Attendolo and
Bolzano —
Torpedoed by P42
0800 13th

Deucalion
damaged

0800
12th

1200

1600

Indomitable
damaged,
Foresight
damaged and
later sunk

① ② Skerki
Bank

③

*Syfret
turns
westwards*

Bizerta

2350

C. Bon ④

P211

P42

Milazzo

Messina

Palermo

SICILY

Catania

PANTELLERIA

Cape
Bougaroni

Cape
Carbon

Algiers

Bougie

Bône

Tunis

AFRICA

Sousse

Gabes

*Gulf of
Gabes*

*Gulf of
Hammamet*

0400
13th

P44 P222 P31 P34 P46

Utmost

0800
1130

0800

⑤

1200

*Burroughs
returns*

GOZO

MALTA

1600

Cape
Passero

BRITISH FORCES
ITALIAN FORCES
AIR ATTACKS

① CAIRO SUNK, NIGERIA AND
OHIO DAMAGED

② KENYA DAMAGED

③ EMPIRE HOPE AND
CLAN FERGUSON SUNK

④ MANCHESTER, WAIRANGI, ALMERIA LYKES,
SANTA ELISA AND GLENORCHY SUNK,
ROCHESTER CASTLE DAMAGED

⑤ WAIMARAMA SUNK, DORSET
DAMAGED & LATER SUNK

Such were the outlines of "Pedestal".

However, it was all the more difficult to keep such a large-scale undertaking secret as the Italian secret service had paid informers in the Bay of Algeciras, and the Germans and Italians were able to prepare, right down to the smallest details, a plan to intercept and destroy the "Pedestal" convoy. This shows the close co-operation which now existed between *Supermarina*, under Admiral Arturo Riccardi, *Superaero* (General Rino Corso Fougier), and the Germans, Field-Marshal Kesselring and Admiral Weichold. However, they had to recognise that they would not be able to use the four battleships available to them, so great had the fuel crisis become since June 15. The attack would therefore be carried out by the following aerial and naval forces:

1. sixteen Italian and five German submarines, which would share the task of attacking the enemy between the Straits of Algiers and the Sicilian Channel with 784 aircraft (447 bombers, 90 torpedo aircraft, and 247 fighters);

2. eighteen motor torpedo boats, which would be lurking between Cap Bon and the island of Pantelleria; and

3. six cruisers and 11 destroyers which, in combination with the aerial forces, would finish off the convoy.

It was Lieutenant Rosenbaum (*U-73*) who opened the Axis score when, early on the afternoon of August 11, a salvo of four

torpedoes struck the aircraft-carrier *Eagle*, and sank her in eight minutes, thus ending the career of this fine old ship, which had played so vital a part in the supplying of Malta. On the Allies side, a few hours later the destroyer *Wolverine* rammed and sank the Italian submarine *Dagabur* as it was trying to torpedo *Furious*, which, having accomplished her mission, was returning to Gibraltar.

Throughout August 12, the Hurricanes of the three aircraft-carriers repulsed successive attacks from some 200 dive-bombers and torpedo-carrying planes, which had taken off from the Sardinian bases of Elmas and Decimomannu; in conjunction with the anti-aircraft fire of the convoy, the Hurricanes destroyed 28 aircraft, so that during this second phase of the battle, the successes of the Axis air forces were meagre indeed: one cargo ship, damaged by a bomb, lagged behind the convoy and was finished off during the night by a motor torpedo boat, while three German Ju 87's scored hits on the flight deck of *Indomitable*, whose planes were then taken on board *Victorious*. The destroyer *Foresight*, which had received a torpedo hit, was scuttled by her own crew, while the destroyer *Ithuriel* sank the Italian submarine *Cobalto*.

At 1900 hours, having reached a point north of Bizerta, Syfret, in accordance with instructions, headed for Gibraltar with his support force, wishing Burrough and his convoy a safe journey, a wish

*Operation "Pedestal", the convoy of
14 merchantmen which, though subject
to heavy attacks, reached Malta in 1942.*

which was never granted, for the third and fourth acts of this aero-naval tragedy firmly established the victory of the Axis forces, and especially the Italian Navy.

The last acts of the tragedy started just after 2000 hours, when, near Cape Bon, the two submarines *Axum* and *Dessié* (commanded by Lieutenants Ferrini and Scandola) fired eight torpedoes, five of which struck home, sinking the anti-aircraft cruiser *Cairo*, and causing serious damage to one of the convoy's cargo ships (the tanker *Ohio*) and the cruiser *Nigeria*, Admiral Burrough's flagship. In the ensuing confusion a further air attack damaged two more merchant ships, which were sunk in the night by Italian naval forces. In addition, at about 2200 hours, the submarine *Alagi* (Lieutenant Puccini) damaged the cruiser *Kenya* and sank yet another cargo ship. In the early hours of the 13th the Italian motor torpedo boats, prowling between Cap Bon and Pantelleria, fell upon the remnants of the convoy and attacked continuously until sunrise, sinking four more merchantmen and the cruiser *Manchester*.

But at the same time an equally fierce battle was being waged within the Axis Supreme Command, between Admirals Riccardi and Weichold on the one hand,

and Field-Marshal Kesselring and General Fougier on the other; the question at issue was the following: on August 13, should the fighter cover be given to the two squadrons of cruisers charged with finishing off the convoy south of Pantelleria, or should they protect the bomber squadrons, since they would not be able to protect both at the same time?

Unable to decide between the two rival claims, Marshal Cavallero put the question to Mussolini, who decided that the fighters should protect the bombers: a bad decision as the Stuka bombers and torpedo planes sank only one ship, whereas the six cruisers and 11 motor torpedo boats originally due to go into action would almost certainly have finished off the five ships still left of the convoy. To make matters worse, the Italian naval squadron was intercepted on the way back to base by the submarine *Unbroken*, commanded by Lieutenant Alastair Mars, who scored two direct hits on the *Bolzano* and the *Attendolo*, damaging them so badly that they remained out of action till September 1943.

Bragadin's conclusion on this episode is that "the battle of mid-August 1942 marked the swan-song of the Italian Navy, and the last important victory of the Axis in the Mediterranean conflict". How right he was is seen from the fact that of the 85,000 tons of supplies loaded in the Clyde, 53,000 tons went to the bottom but the 32,000 tons that got through to Valletta were sufficient to see the island fortress through till November; and thanks to the admirable devotion to duty of Captain Dudley W. Mason and the crew of *Ohio*, which in impossible conditions managed to get through 10,000 tons of fuel, the torpedo planes and submarines stationed at Malta were able to engage their offensive against the Italian Navy with renewed vigour, until Rommel was finally and comprehensively defeated.

The last Panzer offensive towards Cairo, Alexandria, and the Suez Canal gave rise to two battles. The first was lost by Rommel between August 31 and September 5, 1942; the second, less conclusive, was the verbal battle fought after the war by Churchill and Montgomery on the one hand, and Auchinleck and his chief-of-staff (Major-General Dorman-Smith, who shared his chief's fall from grace in August 1942), on the other. This quarrel has been revived by Correlli Barnett who, in his book *The Desert Generals*, has passed harsh judgement on both the British Prime Minister and Field-Marshal Montgomery. According to the latter, when he was received at Mena House on August 12, Auchinleck was anything but determined to defend the El Alamein position at all costs if there were an Italo-German offensive. Montgomery writes in his memoirs:

"He asked me if I knew he was to go. I said that I did. He explained to me his plan of operations; this was based on the fact that at all costs the Eighth Army was to be preserved 'in being' and must not be destroyed in battle. If Rommel attacked

in strength, as was expected soon, the Eighth Army would fall back on the Delta; if Cairo and the Delta could not be held, the army would retreat southwards up the Nile, and another possibility was a withdrawal to Palestine. Plans were being made to move the Eighth Army H.Q. back up the Nile."

Auchinleck has categorically denied ever having uttered such words to Montgomery, and Montgomery's own publishers later made a disclaimer. Naturally, Auchinleck had considered the possibility of withdrawal. This did not mean, however, that Auchinleck would have deliberately retreated as soon as Rommel had begun his first large-scale manoeuvre, as Montgomery implies. On the contrary, everything seems to indicate that he fully intended to face up to an attack at El Alamein, in accordance with the plans drawn up by Major-General Dorman-Smith. Furthermore, it is fair to ask whether or not the new team at the head of the 8th Army, however determined it might be to fight, would have condemned it to destruction in the event of one of Rommel's typical outflanking movements. In fact, both under Auchinleck and later under Montgomery and Alexander, contingency plans were made to meet the "worst possible case" of a German breakthrough past the Alamein position. The problem of how to cope with such a breakthrough was naturally discussed by the successive sets of command.

Was Dorman-Smith's plan, adopted by Auchinleck, taken over without reference or acknowledgement by Montgomery? This is the claim put forward by Correlli Barnett. In reality, such a plan was forced upon both generals by Rommel's probable tactics, and also by the nature of the terrain, which dominated the surround-

General Montgomery surveys his disposition from the top of a Crusader tank.

ing countryside by nearly 200 feet and did not lend itself to the German general's usual outflanking tactics. To this plan, however, Montgomery added personal qualities of dynamism and cunning, which justify him calling the battle his own.

Faced with an opponent whom he knew to be getting stronger day by day, Rommel realised he had to attack, and quickly, otherwise he would soon be overrun by an opponent superior in numbers and equipment. He had been able to motorise his 90th Light Division, and had been reinforced by the 164th Division flown in from the Balkans–but without its vehicles; this was also the case with the parachute troops of the German Ramcke Brigade, and the Italian "Folgore" Division.

In the notes which he has left us, Rommel lays the blame for the failure of his last offensive on the way he was let down by the *Comando Supremo*, whose head, Marshal Cavallero, never stopped making him the most alluring promises. But it is difficult to accept this criticism, since it was no fault of Cavallero's that Malta was not neutralised and then besieged, instead of the boats of the British 10th Submarine Flotilla being once more able to use Malta's large harbour from the beginning of July. As a result, Italian supplies lost in transit, about six per cent in July, shot up to 25 per cent of equipment and 41 per cent of fuel in August; indeed, Cavallero's diary for the period reads like an obituary:

"August 25. The *Pozarica* is torpedoed. August 27. The *Camperio* is set on fire. August 28. The *Dielpi* and the *Istria* are both sunk, the latter with all her crew. August 30. The *Sant'Andrea* is sunk with 1,300 tons of fuel for the D.A.K."

Another point is that Rommel's criticisms take no account of the fact that his supply lines had become far too long. To get from the front to Benghazi took a week, with a further five days to get to Tripoli for supplies. It is true that Tobruk was better placed, but it could only take small ships of up to 600 tons, and in any case had suffered very heavy attacks at the hands of the R.A.F. The responsibility for this state of affairs was Rommel's alone since, despite the doubts of Bastico, Cavallero, and Kesselring himself, he had insisted on exploiting his victories by going headlong after the enemy.

Rommel's plan of attack included some decoy movements by the Italian X and XXI Corps, reinforced by German elements. These would engage the enemy head-on and prevent him getting wind too soon of the plan of attack. These dummy attacks were to begin at 0200 hours, giving Rommel the whole night to take his armoured forces (consisting of the Italian XX Corps and the *Deutsches Afrika Korps*) through the left wing of the enemy's lines, and up to 30 miles past their starting point. After this he would regroup his armour and wheel to the north, with the intention of reaching the Alexandria road behind the 8th Army, which would thus be cut off from its communications, caught on the retreat, and annihilated. There would then be a threefold pursuit of the enemy:

1. the Bismarck group (the 21st Panzer

A 40-mm Bofors anti-aircraft gun moves up towards the front. Such weapons were now less essential, however, as British superiority in the air became assured.

Division and the 164th Division) would make for Alexandria;
2. the *Afrika Korps* (the 15th Panzer Division and the 90th Light Division) would cross the Nile at Cairo and immediately head for the Suez Canal; and
3. the Italian XX Corps (the "Ariete" and "Littorio" Armoured Divisions) and the "Trieste" Motorised Division would clean up any resistance in the Wadi Natrun area.

As Paul Carell has said, this plan had Rommel written all over it. And Colonel Bayerlein, chief-of-staff of the *Panzerarmee* at this time, has confirmed that it was a tried and tested Rommel tactic, which he had used at Tobruk, Gazala, and Marsa Matrûh. All very true—but the point was that it had been used so often that it was now worn out, and was too typical not to be seen through quite easily. In fact, both the Auchinleck/Dorman-Smith team and General Montgomery made their plans on the assumption that Rommel would do something like this: a deep eastward push into the southern sector of the El Alamein position, followed by a rapid turn up towards the Mediterranean.

When Montgomery assumed command (48 hours earlier than he was supposed to), the 8th Army was deployed as follows:

1. on the right, blocking the way to Alexandria, was Lieutenant-General William H. C. Ramsden's XXX Corps, made up of the 9th Australian, 1st South African, and 5th Indian Divisions; and
2. on the left, Lieutenant-General Brian Horrocks' XIII Corps had the New Zealand Division in the line with the 7th Armoured Division further south, for the purpose of slowing up Rommel's initial push and then making a flank attack as soon as he turned north.

These dispositions did not altogether please Montgomery; he thought in particular that Alam el Halfa ridge was too lightly defended, so he brought in the 44th Division, under Major-General I. T. P. Hughes, and also two armoured brigades of the 10th Armoured Division (a perfect example of the Montgomery "dynamism" mentioned earlier on). All in all, on August 31, the 8th Army had available 712 serviceable tanks, though this figure includes 164 Grants.

In spite of these reinforcements, Montgomery imposed an essentially defensive strategy upon his army. He thought that too often in the past the British tanks had been launched into attacks or counterattacks that Rommel had cunningly channelled so as to bring them up against his redoubtable anti-tank guns. This battle would therefore be essentially an artillery duel, with tank movements restricted to exceptional cases; so his tanks dug in. "Don't let yourself get bitten!" he never tired of repeating to Horrocks, upon whose corps the brunt of the Axis offensive was soon to fall.

An element of cunning was brought into the operation by Montgomery's chief-of-staff, Brigadier Francis de Guingand, who made up a false map seeming to show the condition of the tracks, the positions of the areas of soft sand unusable by vehicles, and the minefield positions for XIII Corps' sector—all put in with more than a dash of fantasy. The next step was to fake in no-man's land an incident which would lead to the capture of this spurious document in such a way as not to arouse suspicion about its authenticity. This was brought about at the instigation of General Horrocks who, on being told that the precious map had disappeared from the wreck of the armoured car in which it had been left, telephoned Guingand thus: "Is that you Freddy? They've taken your egg away. Please God that they hatch out something from it." And, according to Colonel Fritz Bayerlein, they tended it with loving care until it did indeed hatch out on the night of August 30.

To launch his attack Rommel would have liked to take advantage of the full moon of August 26, but the supply difficulties mentioned above led to its postponement until August 30. That evening, just before H-hour, which had been fixed for 2200 hours, a stirring order of the day was read out to the troops, reminding them of their glorious past exploits, and exhorting them to the decisive effort:

"Our army, reinforced by new divisions, is moving in to annihilate the enemy.

"In the course of these decisive days, I expect every man to give of his best.

"Long live Fascist Italy! Long live Germany! Long live our glorious leaders!"

But Rommel was less certain of a successful outcome to the operation than his own proclamation indicated. Writing to his wife a few hours earlier, he had told her, after pointing out the deficiencies that still remained in his army:

"I've taken the risk, for it will be a long time before we get such favourable condi-

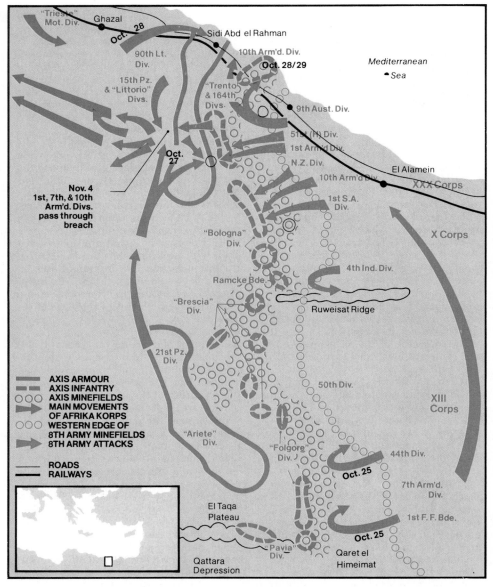

MAP LABELS:

"Trieste" Mot. Div.
Ghazal
Oct. 28
Sidi Abd el Rahman
10th Arm'd. Div.
90th Lt. Div.
Oct. 28/29
Mediterranean Sea
15th Pz. & "Littorio" Divs.
"Trento & 164th Divs.
9th Aust. Div.
Oct. 27
51st (H) Div.
1st Arm'd Div.
N.Z. Div.
Nov. 4 1st, 7th, & 10th Arm'd. Divs. pass through breach
10th Arm'd. Div.
El Alamein
XXX Corps
1st S.A. Div.
"Bologna" Div.
X Corps
4th Ind. Div.
Ramcke Bde.
"Brescia" Div.
Ruweisat Ridge
21st Pz. Div.
50th Div.
XIII Corps
"Ariete" Div.
"Folgore" Div.
44th Div.
Oct. 25
7th Arm'd. Div.
El Taqa Plateau
1st F. F. Bde.
Oct. 25
"Pavia" Div.
Qaret el Himeimat
Qattara Depression

LEGEND:
AXIS ARMOUR
AXIS INFANTRY
AXIS MINEFIELDS
MAIN MOVEMENTS OF AFRIKA KORPS
WESTERN EDGE OF 8TH ARMY MINEFIELDS
8TH ARMY ATTACKS
ROADS
RAILWAYS

The battle of El Alamein, October 23–November 4, 1942. Montgomery outwitted Rommel and crushed him, using his great material superiority to grind the Axis forces down and then to mount the decisive attack on the coastal sector.

tions of moonlight, relative strengths, etc., again. I, for my part, will do my utmost to contribute to success.

"As for my health, I'm feeling quite on top of my form. There are such big things at stake. If our blow succeeds, it might go some way towards deciding the whole course of the war. If it fails, at least I hope to give the enemy a pretty thorough beating."

At 0200 hours on the 31st, the Italo-German motorised column reached the first British minefield. The D.A.K., consisting of the tough 15th and 21st Panzer Divisions, was in the lead, followed by the Italian XX Corps, now commanded by General de Stefanis. Bringing up the rear was the 90th Light Division, which remained in close contact with the Italian X Corps, holding a pivotal position in the Axis line. All in all there were 515 tanks, of which 234 were German machines,

including 26 of the new mark of Pzkw IV's mounting a 7.5-cm 43-calibre gun. The D.A.K. also had available 72 mobile 8.8-cm guns, but these were hardly used in an anti-tank role, because the 8th Army had learnt its lesson, and tanks were dug in as supplementary artillery. By 0300 hours on the 31st, it had dawned on Rommel that things were not going with their usual smoothness. Fired on by the guns of the 7th Armoured Division, and bombed by the Desert Air Force, some German tanks were coming up against unmarked minefields, whilst others were getting bogged down in bad going to the south of the Allied position. So that instead of making a push of 30-odd miles into the enemy's lines, the Axis mechanised forces had only covered about ten. Rommel would consequently have to give up the wheel he had intended to make after an initial deep push; but if he turned north now, he would come under fire from the crest of Alam el Halfa ridge, where XIII Corps, with 64 artillery batteries, 300 anti-tank guns, and the same number of tanks, was waiting.

Shortly afterwards, even worse news reached Rommel: Major-General Georg

von Bismarck, commanding the 21st Panzer Division, had been killed by a mine, and Lieutenant-General Walther Nehring, commanding the *Afrika Korps*, had been badly wounded in an air attack and replaced in the field by Colonel Bayerlein.

It was therefore no surprise that the D.A.K. attack on Hill 132, the highest point of the Alam el Halfa ridge, was repulsed; on its left, the Italian XX Corps fared no better–inevitably–in view of its light equipment; and the 90th Light Division, in the pivotal position, opposite the New Zealand Division, had its commander, Major-General Kleeman, seriously wounded in an air attack. The R.A.F., in fact, was everywhere, and on September 1 Rommel himself nearly met with the same fate as Nehring and Kleeman. Furthermore, despite the assurances showered on him by Cavallero and Kesselring, fuel supplies for the *Panzerarmee* were coming up more and more slowly. Accordingly, on the morning of September 3, Rommel took the decision to withdraw his troops.

Preoccupied with his plans for a general offensive, Montgomery decided not to exploit this defensive success. It had cost the 8th Army 1,750 men and 67 tanks, whilst Axis losses were 536 dead, 1,760 wounded, and 569 missing, together with 49 tanks, 55 guns, and 395 trucks captured or destroyed. These are the figures for the battle of Alam el Halfa, which General Mellenthin has described as follows:

"8th Army had every reason to be satisfied with this victory, which destroyed our last hope of reaching the Nile, and revealed a great improvement in British tactical methods. Montgomery's conduct of the battle can be assessed as a very able if cautious performance, in the best traditions of some of Wellington's victories."

The day after his victory, Montgomery wrote to a friend:

"My first encounter with Rommel was of great interest. Luckily I had time to tidy up the mess and to get my plans laid, so there was no difficulty in seeing him off. I feel that I have won the first game, when it was his service. Next time it will be my service, the score being one-love."

At about this time, Rommel, whose health was poor, went on sick leave. The Goebbels propaganda machine greeted him rapturously, and put all sorts of optimistic forecasts into his mouth; and on visiting Hitler he received the most alluring promises: the *Afrika Korps* would soon be strengthened by the 10th Panzer Division, by the S.S. *Leibstandarte Adolf Hitler* Motorised Division, then stationed in France and also by the 22nd Airborne Division which had just left the Crimea for Crete. He could also have a brigade of *Nebelwerfer* rocket-launchers, and 40 56-ton Pzkw VI Tiger tanks, which in firepower and protective armour far outclassed even the newest of Allied tanks. It is a sad fact, however, that by the fateful day of October 23, none of these reinforcements had reached him, whilst fresh troops and equipment were reaching the Allies at an ever-increasing rate.

Early September saw the arrival in Egyptian ports of the 300 Sherman tanks and 100 self-propelled 105-mm guns that a generous President Roosevelt had provided; of course, this equipment could not be used immediately as sand filters had to be fitted to the tanks, and the British crews had to be trained to get the best out of these American tanks which they had never seen before. Almost simultaneously, two new divisions fresh from Great Britain disembarked at Suez: the 51st Highland Division, soon to add El Alamein to its battle honours, and the 8th Armoured Division, which had only a short existence.

Middle East aerial forces were also being built up: four squadrons of two-engined North American B-25 Mitchell bombers, with a range of more than 1,200 miles, were delivered to Egyptian bases, and the Vickers Wellington bombers of Sir Arthur Tedder—and even the Fleet Air Arm's Fairey Albacores—underwent training to enable them to take part in the 8th Army's operations. The advantage in "flying artillery" thus passed over to the Allies, and played the same vital rôle in the offensive as it had done at the time of the Blitzkrieg.

These then, were the preliminaries of the Battle of El Alamein, which as we shall see in the next chapter, was to complement Operation "Torch".

In his headquarters at Burg el Arab, Lieutenant-General Montgomery was carrying on with his preparations for Operation "Lightfoot", as G.H.Q. Cairo called the third British offensive in North Africa. First of all, in the light of experience gained at Alam el Halfa, Montgomery demanded new leaders for XXX Corps and the 7th Armoured Division. For the former he got Lieutenant-General Sir Oliver Leese, formerly commander of the Guards Armoured Division in Britain, and for the latter Major-General A. F. Harding. These were excellent choices, as can be seen from the later careers of these officers: Leese went on to command an army group in Burma and Harding became a Field-Marshal after the war.

One of Montgomery's early decisions was where to make his first attack. So far, Wavell, Rommel, and Auchinleck had all manoeuvred over the desert in order to drive the enemy into the Mediterranean. But by launching his attack in the northern sector, that is between Ruweisat Ridge and the sea, Montgomery thought that there was a good chance that Rommel would be surprised – provided, of course, that he still believed that Montgomery himself would stick to the tried and tested tactics used by his predecessors and the Germans. Also, if he moved in from the north, the desert in the south would play the same part as the sea in offering a complete obstacle in the event of a breakthrough. Originally Montgomery had stuck to the tactics laid down by the British and German military doctrine of the period: if the enemy's tanks could be

A mine explodes beside a British truck as it skirts a German minefield.

knocked out at the beginning, his infantry was at your mercy. He was courageous enough to state that in open ground, given the training of their crews, the Panzers were more manoeuvrable than the British tanks and had a good chance of tearing them to pieces. Montgomery was also determined, if at all possible, to adhere to one of the most basic rules of desert warfare. He had no intention of allowing his own tanks to attack Rommel's anti-tank guns, unless they were supported by Allied infantry.

So a change of method was needed and Montgomery has explained this perfectly clearly in his memoirs: "My modified plan now was to hold off, or contain, the enemy armour while we carried out a methodical destruction of the infantry divisions holding the defensive system. These un-armoured divisions would be destroyed by means of a 'crumbling' process, the enemy being attacked from the flank and the rear and cut off from their supplies. These operations would be carefully organised from a series of firm bases and would be within the capabilities of my troops."

Thus Rommel was due for a second surprise. Already deceived about the sector where the 8th Army would make its main thrust, he would also be caught out by his enemy's sudden change of tactics. It could be assumed that he would not remain inactive in face of the danger of seeing his divisions fall apart and then disintegrate. He could be expected to launch counter-attack after counter-attack, but it would only be to find his Panzers deprived of all freedom of movement in the middle of the innumerable minefields protecting the British infantry positions and being fired on by the British

armour, waiting steadfastly for them as they had done at Alam el Halfa.

The successful execution of this plan in which nothing was left to chance, required the organisation of a third corps, in addition to XIII and XXX.

This was to be X Corps, under the command of Lieutenant-General Herbert Lumsden. It consisted of armoured divisions and its job was to be the immediate exploitation of the infantry's advance along the line of the main thrust; then, once a breach was made, to pursue the enemy. Originally it was to have had the 1st, 8th, and 10th Armoured Divisions, but, to the great chagrin of its commander, Major-General C. H. Gairdner, the 8th had to be disbanded to make up the tank strength of the other two.

The headquarters and communications units played an equally important part in the execution and success of Operation "Bertram". This was the name given by the 8th Army to the deceptions carried out under Major Charles Richardson to convince the enemy that the threat of attack was increasing in the south. To this end the 8th Army used a large number of dummy vehicles, made of rubber and inflated by compressed air. No vehicle left the south for the northern sector without being replaced by a dummy. In the same sector Axis reconnaissance aircraft could watch the laying of a pipe-line, also a dummy, and calculate from the progress of the work that the expected attack would not start before November 1. Finally radio messages from the pseudo-8th Armoured Division made *Panzer-*

armee H.Q. think that there was another armoured division between the Qattara Depression and the Ruweisat Ridge.

All this ingenuity would have been of little avail, however, if in the northern sector, where Montgomery was preparing to attack with seven divisions, the 8th Army's camouflage units had not successfully hidden from prying enemy aircraft the thousands of vehicles and enormous storage depôts, and if the secret of Operation "Lightfoot" had not been jealously guarded. In fact, lower-ranking officers, N.C.O.s, and men were not informed of the offensive until two days before the attack.

Parallel with this enormous effort of organisation, there was an intensive training programme for the troops by Montgomery, a first-class instructor. All this activity explains why, in spite of the Prime Minister's impatience, it was out of the question for the 8th Army to attack before full moon in October, which fell on the 23rd. We may therefore conclude that in once more tempering the ardour of Winston Churchill, General Sir Alan Brooke showed himself to be a truly great servant of his country and one of the architects of her final victory.

On the other side, Rommel had left Africa and handed over command of the *Panzerarmee* to General Georg Stumme, who had played an important part at the head of the XL Motorised Corps in Greece and then maintained his high reputation in Russia. This new posting relieved him of the disgrace into which he had fallen with the Führer as a consequence of his corps' operations orders falling into the hands of the Russians on the eve of Operation *"Blau"*, Germany's 1942 Russian offensive. He had merely a holding role, however, and was not allowed to take much initiative, having to content himself with the programme left him by Rommel.

The armoured elements of the *Panzerarmee* had been withdrawn from the front as the force went over to the defensive. This left the Ramcke Brigade and five infantry divisions, including the German 164th Division and the Italian "Folgore" Airborne Division, in fixed defences. To the rear, in the northern sector, were the tough and mobile "Ariete" Armoured Division and 21st Panzer while in the southern sector were the 15th Panzer Division and the "Littorio" tank Division. In army reserve, the 90th Light Division and the "Trieste" Motorised Division were deployed in depth along the coastal road. Thus the 164th Division and two battalions of the Ramcke Brigade together with the Italian XXI Corps held the position where the enemy attack was expected, while two battalions of paratroopers were stationed with X Corps south of the Ruweisat Ridge.

The time taken to mount Operation "Lightfoot" was naturally not wasted by the Axis forces, which were deployed in depth and considerably strengthened.

The units were contained within closed strongpoints protected by more than 445,000 mines, of which 14,000 were anti-personnel ones intended to discourage the enemy's engineers. Under the direction of Colonel Hecker, Rommel's chief of engineering, Italian and German engineers had also contrived booby traps of truly diabolical imagination, using even aeroplane bombs. These defences were naturally covered by machine guns and anti-tank guns. As regards the latter, on October 23, 1942 the D.A.K. had 86 8.8-cm weapons and 95 Russian 7.62-cm guns, of which 30 had been mounted on Czech tank chassis. The British considered these almost as deadly as the famous "88".

It was a hard nut to crack. But between the opposing shores of the Mediterranean, traffic conditions had not improved. Far from it, though Cavallero had thrown in everything he could get hold of. In September 40,465 tons of war *matériel* and 31,061 tons of petrol reached North Africa, 80 per cent of the supplies loaded in Italy. But in October losses rose to 44 per cent and the Axis forces opposing Montgomery got only 12,308 tons of liquid fuel. Cavallero asked Kesselring to put pressure on Malta; he replied by recalling some bomber squadrons from Libya. Although 300 twin-engined German bombers took part in this renewed offensive, it was a total failure and the losses were so heavy that Göring, going over the head of *Comando Supremo* on October 20, ordered it to stop.

At 2140 hours on October 23, 1942, the El Alamein front lit up with a blaze of gunfire over its whole length. Between the sea and Ruweisat Ridge 456 guns opened fire to blast the way open for XXX Corps. In the south XIII Corps had 136 guns.

The attack was a complete surprise: at the time the battle started the commanders of the Italian XXI and X Corps (Generals Navarrini and Nebbia respectively) were on leave in Italy and only got back to their H.Q.s at the same time as Rommel. This was the curtain-raiser for 12 days of battle fought out between 12 Axis and ten Allied divisions, though these numbers are misleading: Montgomery had the advantage in both men and *matériel*. In round numbers Montgomery deployed 195,000 men against some 50,000 Germans and 54,000 Italians. The following table, taken from the British Official History, gives the comparative figures for the two sides:

Strengths of the forces engaged on the El Alamein front on October 23, 1942
(Italian figures in brackets)

	Panzer-armee	8th Army
Infantry battalions	71 (40)	85
Field and medium guns	460 (260)	908
Anti-tank guns	850 (300)	1,451
Tanks	496	1,029
Armoured cars	192	435

This table does not show that the defenders were short of ammunition and fuel,

whereas Montgomery was more than abundantly supplied. Also, the Axis had nothing to compare with Sir Arthur Tedder's 1,200 planes, in particular Air Vice-Marshal Coningham's 550 light bombers and fighter-bombers.

The 8th Army's artillery barrage lasted 15 minutes. It effectively silenced the enemy's batteries and damaged his telephone communications and minefields, where many of the aircraft bombs were blown up. At 2200 hours the sappers advanced into no-man's-land, using the first mine-detectors to reach North Africa. Behind the sappers there were a small number of "Scorpion" tanks, special adaptations of ordinary tanks, designed to set off mines with whirling flails attached to a drum in front of the tank.

Behind these followed the infantry, with fixed bayonets.

In the southern sector, XIII Corps (Sir Brian Horrocks), whose rôle was to put on a diversionary attack, had been ordered to hold back its 7th Armoured Division. The advance of its major infantry formations, 44th Division (Major-General I. T. P. Hughes) and 50th Division (Major-General J. S. Nichols) was consequently limited and secured at heavy cost against the determined resistance of the "Pavia" and "Brescia" Divisions and the paratroops of the "Folgore", commanded respectively by Generals Scattaglia, Brunetti, and Frattini. On the left flank, the 1st Fighting French Brigade confirmed its fighting spirit on the Qaret el Himeimat, but had to yield some of the ground it had won. Horrocks' objective had been reached: to prevent the enemy from deploying the "Ariete" Armoured Division (General F. Arena) and the 21st Panzer Division (Major-General von Randow) in support of the rest of the Axis forces in the northern sector.

In the northern sector, XXX Corps' job was to make an inroad along two "corridors" in the minefields. The right-hand corridor was given to the 9th Australian Division and the 51st (Highland) Division, newly arrived in North Africa and commanded by Major-General D. N. Wimberley; the left-hand corridor went to the New Zealand Division. None of these divisions reached the objectives marked for them on the map, but their action began the destruction of the enemy infantry, as foreseen by Montgomery. The "Trento" Division (General Masina) was very badly mauled and the 164th Division (Major-General Lungershausen) had two of its battalions virtually wiped out. But since the British infantry had failed to clear corridors right through the enemy minefields, the tanks of X Corps were jammed up in the enemy's defences. Montgomery ordered Lumsden to punch a way through but the attempt failed with considerable losses in men and machines. On the other side, General Stumme, who was roaming the battlefield alone, had a heart attack and fell from his vehicle without his driver noticing it. His death was a considerable blow to the Axis forces and his command was taken over in the evening of the 24th by the commander of the D.A.K., Lieutenant-General Ritter von Thoma.

On October 25 Montgomery ordered XIII and XXX Corps to press home their attacks. But they both failed to reach their objectives and so, with great coolness and resolution, Montgomery began to organise a fresh onslaught.

When he got back to his H.Q. in the evening of October 26, Rommel realised exactly how serious the situation was. It had been saved only by the engagement of the 90th Light Division and the armoured group in the northern sector. Major-General von Vaerst's 15th Panzer Division had only 39 tanks left and General Bitossi's "Littorio" Armoured Division only 69. He therefore ordered the 21st Panzer Division with its 106 tanks to move north of Ruweisat Ridge. Once he had concentrated his remaining armour Rommel tried to regain the initiative. He led the Axis tanks in a counter-stroke against the British penetrations. However, Montgomery's forces were ready to meet him. A heavy toll was taken of the Axis troops by bombers of the Desert Air Force and an anti-tank screen which contained many of the new 6-pounder anti-tank guns. Rommel was repulsed and this was a major success for Montgomery and the 8th Army. In XXX Corps, the 9th Australian Division struck north-west and trapped the 164th Division against the sea. The 1st South African Division (Major-General D. H. Pienaar) and the 4th Indian Division (Major-General F. I. S. Tuker), which formed Sir Oliver Leese's left flank, made a deep penetration into the positions of the "Bologna" Division (General Gloria). On October 29 Rommel wrote to his wife: "The situation continues very grave. By the time this letter arrives, it will no doubt have been decided whether we can hold on or not. I haven't much hope. At night I lie with my eyes wide open, unable to sleep for the load that is on my shoulders. In the day I am dead tired. What will happen if things go wrong here? That is the thought that torments me day and night. I can see no way out if that happens." Rommel's army was being torn apart.

In London, however, Winston Churchill could not contain his impatience and summoned General Brooke to his office the same day. "What," he asked, "was *my* Monty doing now, allowing the battle to peter out? (Monty was always *my* Monty when he was out of favour.) He had done nothing now for the last three days and now he was withdrawing troops from the front. Why had he told us that he would be through in seven days if all he intended to do was to fight a half-hearted battle?"

As usual the Chief of the Imperial General Staff was able to placate Churchill and was well seconded in this by Field Marshal Smuts, who enjoyed the Prime Minister's special confidence. Montgomery had, in fact, withdrawn one brigade each from the 44th, 50th (XIII Corps), and 51st (XXX Corps) Divisions and given them to the New Zealand Division which, under Major-General Freyberg, was to be the spearhead of Operation "Supercharge" for the decisive breakthrough. Meanwhile XXX Corps had continued to hammer the enemy and forced Rommel to engage the "Ariete" Armoured Division and the "Trieste" Motorised Division, his last reserves.

"Supercharge" was being followed in London with some anxiety: "During the morning," Montgomery records, "I was visited at my Tactical H.Q. by Alexander and by Casey who was Minister of State in the Middle East. It was fairly clear to me that there had been consternation in Whitehall when I began to draw divisions into reserve on the 27th and 28th October, when I was getting ready for the final blow. Casey had been sent up to find out what was going on; Whitehall thought I was giving up, when in point of fact I was just about to win. I told him all about my plans and that I was certain of success; and de Guingand spoke to him very bluntly and told him to tell Whitehall not to bellyache."

"Supercharge", unleashed on November 2, gave rise to battles of a ferocity unheard of in this theatre. Italian anti-tank guns fired on British tanks at a range of 20 yards and General Freyberg's 9th Armoured Brigade was reported to have lost 70 out of the 94 tanks it had started with. At the end of the day, and in spite of repeated attacks by the Desert Air Force, what remained of the Axis army had managed to form the semblance of a front, but this was the end. Rommel was now aware that his forces had reached the limits of effective resistance. The *Afrika Korps* had only 35 tanks left. These were far too few to stop the 8th Army's advance. Rommel drew his conclusions from the situation and ordered his troops to withdraw. The movement had just begun when, on November 3 at 1330 hours a message from Hitler, a *Führerbefehl*, reached him. It was drawn up in the following terms:

"To Field-Marshal Rommel,

"In the situation in which you find yourself there can be no other thought but to stand fast and throw every gun and every man into the battle. The utmost efforts are being made to help you. Your enemy, despite his superiority, must also be at the end of his strength. It would not be the first time in history that a strong will has triumphed over the bigger battalions. As to your troops, you can show them no other road than that to victory or death."

As the disciplined soldier that he was Rommel cancelled his order and instructed his troops to hold their positions. Fortunately for Rommel, Montgomery failed to exploit the opportunity given to him by the *Führerbefehl* by driving swiftly on and surrounding the Axis troops. In the afternoon of November 4 the 8th Army made a breach 15 miles wide in the thread-

An Axis soldier, dead beside his trench at Alamein.

like front of the enemy in the area of Tell el Aqqaqir. The tanks of X Corps broke through, demolished the "Ariete" Armoured Division in spite of heroic resistance and captured the commander of the D.A.K., General von Thoma, as he leapt out of his blazing vehicle. The mechanised units of Rommel's *Panzerarmee* managed to escape to the west, just as a fresh order arrived from Berlin sanctioning a withdrawal westwards after all. The whole of the Italian infantry, however, (the "Trento", "Bologna", "Brescia", and "Pavia" Divisions) were left stranded, as were the "Folgore" Airborne Division and the headquarters of X Corps. 104,000 troops took part in this battle: the Axis powers lost 25,000 killed and wounded and 30,000 prisoners, including nine generals and 7,802 Germans. A thousand guns and 320 tanks were destroyed or captured by the victors. The Allies lost 13,560 men, of whom 4,610 were killed or missing; most of the missing turned out to be dead. 500 Axis tanks were put out of action and many of them were irreparable. At Alamein not only had Axis strength in North Africa been broken for ever but so was Rommel's morale, so that not for a moment did he consider making another stand at Halfaya and El Agheila, as *Comando Supremo* ordered. This gave rise to new friction between the Axis partners which was to bear fruit in 1943.

El Alamein was over. Rommel now started on his long retreat to Tunis, followed steadily by Montgomery's 8th Army, that was to see the end of Axis power in Africa.

CHAPTER 35
Operation Torch

Some people still believe that President Roosevelt favoured an invasion of North Africa solely because he thought that a military success by American troops would enhance his Democratic Party's showing in the Congressional elections on November 3, 1943. Although it is true that he hoped "Torch", as the invasion was called, would take place before the voting, the amphibious forces involved had to delay their departures for North Africa, mainly because they awaited delivery of landing ships and craft; they came ashore on November 8, five days after the elections. Yet the President never put pressure on his military leaders to launch the operation before it was ready.

Actually, there were sounder reasons why the President approved the landings. The most important consideration was probably his wish to indicate to the Russians, who were under extreme duress in 1942, that the Anglo-American members of the Grand Alliance fighting the Axis nations were making an active contribution to the war effort. In all the discussions revolving around strategic decisions, the Western Allies consistently sought to assist the Russians by taking action that would draw German forces away from the Eastern Front.

Roosevelt, moreover, wished to demonstrate the feasibility of combined Anglo-American operations. He hoped to transmit at once the close co-operation and mutual high regard that existed at the highest levels of government to the armed forces of both nations. Making coalition ventures work was a vital prerequisite for eventual victory, and the sooner they started, the better were the chances for quick development of coalition unity and *esprit*.

Finally, the President wished to divert the interest and the will of the American people, stunned and shocked by the Japanese attack on Pearl Harbor, from the Pacific area and to arouse and direct their attention to the European side of the conflict. For even before the United States was at war, Roosevelt and his strategic advisers had decided in conversations with British military officials that if the country became involved in war against the Axis, the United States would follow a "Germany first" strategy, as we have seen. In other words, the United States would remain on the defensive against Japan while exerting every effort to crush the military forces of Germany and Italy first. Among the factors supporting this policy was the logistical fact that it took many more ships to maintain forces in the Pacific than it did in the Atlantic.

Thus, offensive operations were required in Europe. The best way to commit American energies to that part of the war was to have an early encounter with the European enemies.

According to American strategic thought and doctrine, the most appropriate method to defeat an enemy was by the direct approach: grapple with the main enemy forces and crush them in battle. Applied to the situation in Europe, this meant coming to grips with and concentrating against Germany first. To do this, Allied troops had to enter upon the European continent. A quick and crushing victory over Germany would bring about the surrender of Italy. The Americans could then turn to the Pacific and eliminate Japan.

From the beginning, this was, in essence, the strategic concept of General George C. Marshall. Although he constantly sought to implement his view, the desires of the British and the condition of the American military establishment would dictate a postponement of what has come to be regarded as the American strategic approach.

No sooner had Pearl Harbor brought America into the war than Churchill and some of his advisers travelled to Washington, D.C., to confer with the President and his military officials. In a series of talks in December 1941 and January 1942, known as the "Arcadia" Conference, Churchill discovered to his immense relief that the Americans had no intention of adopting anything but a "Germany first" strategy. Marshall reiterated that Germany was the main enemy and "the key to victory". His principal assistant, Dwight D. Eisenhower, said: "We've got to go to Europe and fight . . . we've got to begin slugging with air at West Europe; to be followed by land attack as soon as possible."

The commitment was heartening to Churchill, but the enthusiasm to fight the Germans immediately seemed unrealistic. For the American military forces were in the process of expanding, organising, and training for combat; they were hardly a match for a strong and veteran foe, particularly in major operations. According to Sir John Dill, the United States "has not–repeat not–the slightest conception of what the war means, and their armed forces are more unready for war than it is possible to imagine".

In these circumstances Churchill, before returning home, spoke somewhat vaguely of the possibility of launching a relatively small Anglo-American operation in Norway. He also suggested landings in French North Africa, a plan he codenamed "Gymnast".

The Americans saw these as diversionary efforts that would interfere with a quick strike against Germany. As early as February 1942, Eisenhower outlined the American strategic objectives as being to maintain the present position in the Pacific and "to develop in conjunction with the British a definite plan for operations against North West Europe". What was required, he believed, was an Ameri-

can build-up of resources–men and *matériel*–in the United Kingdom, followed by an Anglo-American cross-Channel attack in 1942.

But Roosevelt, perhaps better than his military chiefs, estimated that American forces could not hope to carry out a programme of this sort. Like the British, he thought that a cross-Channel attack of any size could not be mounted probably until 1943. He talked of joining the British in the Middle East or the Mediterranean.

To resolve the differences in outlook between him and his military strategists, Roosevelt directed Harry Hopkins, his close adviser, and Marshall to go to London to confer with Churchill and his military staff. As the result of discussions in April, the coalition partners tentatively agreed on "Bolero", codename for building up a concentration of American forces and supplies in the United Kingdom; on "Round-up", an eventual cross-Channel attack of major proportions; and on "Sledgehammer", a limited attack in 1942 to seize a bridgehead in France.

All firmly recognised the need for "Bolero", and indeed U.S. forces were already beginning to arrive in Northern Ireland, but the British had serious reservations with respect to the other ventures, primarily because they would have to shoulder a preponderant portion of the burden. The United States, it was estimated, could have ready and available for action in 1942 no more than three and a half combat divisions. This was hardly enough for what was being contemplated.

Even Eisenhower, who was sent to confer with British authorities on establishing the arrangements for "Bolero", had to agree that cross-Channel operations in 1942 were impractical. The spring of 1943 was more likely. Nevertheless, if there was ever to be a cross-Channel invasion, "Bolero" had to be implemented, and late in June 1942, Marshall appointed Eisenhower to be Commanding General, European Theatre of Operations, U.S. Army. His task was to make sure that American forces shipped to the United Kingdom would be ready, trained, and supplied when the decision was reached to invade the continent and engage the Germans.

About that time, Churchill arrived in Washington for additional strategic discussions. Having concluded that major attacks were impossible in the near future, he recommended "preparing within the general structure of 'Bolero' some other operation by which we may gain positions of advantage and also directly or indirectly take some of the weight off Russia."

Although American military officers still opposed what they called sideshows, Roosevelt liked the idea of an early commitment in the European theatre of war, particularly since he had promised Foreign Minister Molotov that the Western Allies would take some action in Europe that year. In this context, "Gymnast" seemed attractive.

The loss of Tobruk in June and the British withdrawal to El Alamein reinforced the President's desire, even though Marshall continued to say that "Gymnast" would be indecisive and a heavy drain on the "Bolero" resources. Furthermore, Marshall said, "Gymnast" would jeopardise the chance of Russian survival and undermine commitments made to the U.S.S.R. "Sledgehammer", he felt, was necessary to keep the Soviet Union in the war.

To gain final agreement on a combined Anglo-American operation in 1942, Roosevelt sent Hopkins, Marshall, and Admiral Ernest J. King, Chief of Naval Operations, to London in July. When the British and Americans found themselves deadlocked – the former favouring North Africa, the latter inclining toward a cross-Channel endeavour – Hopkins cabled Roosevelt for instructions. Late in July, Roosevelt agreed to a landing in North Africa, now called Operation "Torch".

Already the Allies had agreed that an invasion of French North Africa had to be, in appearance, a completely American operation. The French remained bitter about what they considered the less than all-out British contributions, particularly in air forces, to the campaign of 1940. They still resented the British attacks on the French fleet shortly after the French surrender. Although the armistice provisions carried a pledge that the French would fight to repel any invasion of North Africa, they presumably remained essentially anti-German. Given the long ties of Franco-American friendship dating from Lafayette's contribution to the American side in the War of Independence, would the French, who would certainly oppose a British landing, permit American troops to come ashore against only token resistance? The Allies hoped so. But since the Americans lacked the means to invade without the British, "Torch" would have to be a combined invasion. A solution was found in having the initial landing waves consist solely of American soldiers. The commander of the overall operation would also have to be an American.

Since the "Bolero" build-up would have to be diverted, at least in part, to "Torch", Eisenhower became the Allied Commander-in-Chief. He had never been in combat, but he had impressed all his superiors – including Douglas MacArthur, for whom he had worked in the Philippines before the war – with his quick mind, his thorough grasp of military matters, and his ability to make people of different backgrounds work together in harmony. Yet he was an unknown quantity, and "Torch", a complicated venture to be undertaken in considerable haste, would be a serious challenge. As it turned out, he grew in stature and self-confidence as the war progressed, measuring up repeatedly to the increasing demands of his position.

As his Deputy Commander-in-Chief, Eisenhower chose Major-General Mark W. Clark, a hard-driving and energetic infantryman who had been wounded as a young officer in World War I. Just before America entered World War II, Clark had become the right hand man of Lesley J. McNair, who directed the training of the U.S. combat forces. Clark had worked indefatigably to prepare American soldiers for battle. He had then accompanied Eisenhower to England. There he commanded II Corps, which consisted of the U.S. combat forces in the United Kingdom. As Eisenhower's deputy, Clark would prove to be an invaluable help, not only in the planning and execution of "Torch" but also in dealing with the French in North Africa. He would also become a more than competent comman-

American troops of the Centre Task Force land in the Gulf of Arzew, near Oran on November 7.

der of high rank in his own right.

For his Chief-of-Staff, Eisenhower asked Marshall to make available from Washington Major-General Walter Bedell Smith, a tough and uncompromising organiser, manager, and administrator. He would run Eisenhower's headquarters, known in North Africa as Allied Force Headquarters, with an iron hand, and he would carry out his chief's instructions to the letter so that British and American staff officers worked together on an integrated and Allied, rather than on a separate nationalistic, basis.

As an example of the unity upon which Eisenhower insisted, when an American officer during a heated argument called his counterpart a "British son of a bitch", Eisenhower sent him home to the States. Calling him simply a son of a bitch would have been tolerable.

Using her own derricks an American ship unloads part of her cargo of trucks and guns in North Africa.

The original idea of "Torch" was to have two landings, thus requiring two major ground forces, one British, the other American. Lieutenant-General Sir Harold Alexander was initially selected to command the British part, then Lieutenant-General Bernard L. Montgomery; but when these two were assigned to the Western Desert, Lieutenant-General Kenneth Anderson was given the job. For the American ground force commander, Marshall unhesitatingly chose and Eisenhower enthusiastically accepted Major-General George Patton.

Flamboyant in his personal life style, Patton was a thoroughly professional soldier. Older than Eisenhower and Clark, he had served with Pershing in Mexico and in France. He had become America's foremost tank protagonist in World War I by organising and leading a brigade of light tanks in the St. Mihiel battle and the Meuse-Argonne offensive, where he was wounded. In 1941, he took command of the 2nd Armoured Division, was soon advanced to head I Armoured Corps,

and in 1942 was in charge of the Desert Training Centre where infantrymen, tank crew, gunners, and others learned the techniques of battle. Patton was aggressive and experienced in combat, and he would soon become known as America's best fighting leader.

At the end of July, Marshall summoned Patton from the south-western part of the United States to Washington to start planning for "Torch". Early in August, Patton's headquarters, known variously as I Armoured Corps, Provisional Task Force A, and finally Western Task Force, was set up in the War Department directly under Marshall's Operations Division.

Meanwhile, planning had started in London. A Combined Planning Staff of British and American officers, responsible to Eisenhower, worked under Alfred M. Gruenther. Patton flew to London to help and stayed for two weeks, conferring and collaborating with Eisenhower, Clark, and British participants. But hammering out a plan suitable to both nations and taking into account the available resources was extremely difficult.

The aim of "Torch" was to seize Morocco, Algeria, and Tunisia, and the problem of where exactly to land had to be measured against the considerable threats posed by U-boats in the Atlantic and the Mediterranean, enemy aircraft operating from Sicily and southern Italy, possible French opposition, and conceivable Spanish intervention on the side of the Axis.

Although there were no Axis troops in French North Africa, as agreed in the armistice of 1940, the proximity of Tunisia to Sicily made it extremely likely that German and Italian forces would be dispatched to counter Allied landings. To forestall such action, some planners argued that the invasion should take place as far eastward in French North Africa as was reasonably safe. Others felt that landings entirely inside the Mediterranean would be too dangerous because the Straits of Gibraltar might be blocked to Allied shipping. They wished to make at least one landing on the Atlantic coast.

Not until early September was agreement finally reached that "Torch" would consist of three major landings. The Western Task Force was to be wholly American in composition. Patton would command the ground troops, Vice-Admiral Henry Kent Hewitt, a solid, no-nonsense sailor, the ships. They would sail from Hampton Roads, in Norfolk county, Virginia, and come ashore near Casablanca in French Morocco.

The Centre Task Force was to consist of American ground troops transported from the United Kingdom in British ships to Oran in Algeria. The ground force commander was Major-General Lloyd R. Fredendall, a rough-talking and blustering man superficially similar to Patton. Fredendall had commanded II Corps in the United States, and when Clark became Eisenhower's deputy, Fredendall

flew to London to reassume that command. Several months after "Torch", he would prove incapable of keeping firm control over his troops in the battle of Kasserine Pass in Tunisia, and would be relieved.

The Eastern Task Force was also formed in the United Kingdom. It was to be predominantly British in composition, and was to land near Algiers. As a façade, and therefore making the initial landings, would be a relatively small American force under Major-General Charles W. Ryder, commander of the 34th Division. A competent soldier, he would remain at the head of his division for most of the war.

Following the American landings at Algiers, British troops under Anderson would come ashore in force, as the 1st Army, dash eastward to Tunis, and prevent Axis forces from entering the country.

The mission of all three major task forces was to gain control of French North Africa, hopefully with French assistance. The Allies had no wish to displace the French presence; instead, they wanted to sustain and enhance French authority over the potentially restless native populations. This would enable the Allies to fulfil their military requirements—rush to Tunis, establish a great supply base, begin to rearm and re-equip the French military forces, which had obsolete weapons—without having to divert troops to guard military installations and to patrol the countryside. The Allies also desired to intimidate Franco's Spain and prevent it from entering the conflict. They expected to forestall an Axis occupation of Tunisia.

A larger strategic result was envisaged in plans to co-ordinate Eisenhower's forces with the British Middle East forces under Alexander. Specifically, the 8th Army under Montgomery was to launch an offensive against Rommel in Egypt shortly before the "Torch" landings. If the British could dislodge Rommel's Italo-German army from El Alamein and send it reeling back across Libya, the "Torch" landings, combined with an 8th Army push into Tunisia, would close the trap on Rommel's forces.

The elimination of these Axis troops would give the Allies complete control over the northern shore of Africa and open the possibility of further operations across the Mediterranean into the European continent.

But where were sufficient well-trained and well-equipped American troops to be found for "Torch"?

The Regular Army in 1939 had numbered only 145,000 officers and men. They were scattered among 130 posts in the continental United States, mostly in parcels of battalion size. Field army commands hardly existed, and corps area commands were administrative in nature. Nine divisions were authorised, but only three were anywhere near being up to strength; the others were nothing more than brigades.

In November 1939, two months after the outbreak of World War II, Congress authorised an army of 280,000 men. This would bring all nine Regular divisions up to strength and permit the formation of two more corps headquarters and certain other miscellaneous units, groups, and headquarters. Not until May 1940, when the Germans launched their attack on the Low Countries and France, did President Roosevelt request authority to call the National Guard into Federal service and to order individual members of the Organised Reserve Corps to active duty. Late in August, Congress granted that authority, but with the proviso that non-Regular forces could remain in active Federal service for only one year.

By the Selective Service Act, passed in September, Congress authorised an army of 1,400,000 men—a ten-fold increase over the previous year; but again, the conscripted men were to serve for only 12 months. America's geographical isolation had promoted a spiritual isolation, and although Americans were generally sympathetic to Great Britain and France—they were shocked by the collapse of France—public opinion indicated that World War II was none of America's concern.

Meanwhile, the rapidly expanding Army created a General Headquarters in July 1940. Marshall, while remaining U.S. Army Chief-of-Staff, became Commanding General; McNair was his chief-of-staff "to direct and support the train-of the troops". The new organisation prompted some changes in the methods for teaching soldiers to be effective military men. Formerly, all recruits had received their basic training in the units to which they were assigned. Now, the system was improved by giving individuals military training at General and Specialised Service Schools and by giving key individuals, both enlisted and commissioned, advanced and specialised training in specifically designated small units.

Nevertheless, preparation for war proceeded slowly. Not until March 1941 were four American defence commands activated, much in the manner of the British area commands. At the same time several Replacement Training Centres were opened to handle the large influx of citizen soldiers known as selectees or draftees. Designed for mass production, the system provided that new soldiers rotated in cycles through special centres devoted to individual basic and special training. This relieved the field units of responsibility for individual training, allowing them to concentrate on unit exercises, and also made possible a steady flow of partially trained men to tactical units.

Training thus became standardised in the early stages of indoctrination. The result was that the field units could depend on a common foundation among their incoming recruits, who had been trained in combat specialities such as infantrymen, tank crew, gunners, or in administrative specialities such as cooks, clerks, and radio operators. Not long afterwards, ten Officers Candidate Schools were opened.

Yet preparations for war were half-hearted and bumbling, with little sense of urgency, little appreciation of the nature of the war, little thought that, if America became involved, there would be precious little time to get ready for combat. Some of this could be ascribed simply to growing pains and inexperience, for the Army at the end of 1941 consisted of 1,700,000 troops organised into 37 divisions and 67 air combat groups, a sizable increase.

Pearl Harbor swept away all the uncertainty, much of the red tape, and the congressional restriction on keeping men in uniform for only 12 months. A thorough reorganisation, in March 1942, modernised and streamlined the Army. The War Department functioned as before, but immediately below that echelon were created three major commands at home, Army Air Forces, Army Service Forces, and Army Ground Forces. The last, under McNair, was responsible for preparing individuals and units for overseas deployment.

A.G.F. quickly formed a Replacement and School Command, an Armoured Force, a Tank Destroyer Command, an Anti-Aircraft Centre, eight unit training centres, 14 replacement training centres, and seven service schools. By then the authorised strength of the Army had been raised to a goal of 4,500,000 by the end of the year. Similar augmentations affected the Navy and the Marine Corps.

The Army had held a series of great practice manoeuvres in 1941, exercises larger in scope and in the numbers of men involved than had ever been done before in peace-time. These had revealed serious deficiencies in the combat expertise of the units. To remedy the defects, a more systematic schooling of certain officers and enlisted men was undertaken. These key persons became cadres or nuclei around which new units were built and trained.

By 1942, the typical training period consisted of 17 weeks for individuals, 13 weeks for units from squad to regiment, and 14 weeks for exercises by the combined arms. Thus, training was progressive. Men proceeded from individual basic and special training to small-unit training, to larger exercises, and finally to manoeuvres involving large forces.

The difficulties of raising, equipping, and training a large military establishment for all the services were enormous. Camps, barracks, installations of all kinds, and training grounds had to be built or enlarged all over the United States. Shortages and obsolescence of equipment hampered instructors and students, who were forced to rotate weapons and other *matériel* among various groups and who were compelled to improvise—for example, using broom sticks as rifles. Recently formed units were frequently stripped for cadres to activate other units or to make up shortages in formations assigned overseas. Veteran N.C.O.s and officers who could carry out efficient and effective training programmes were in terribly short supply.

Yet somehow vast numbers of civilians were transformed into military personnel. The essential training philosophy was to make soldiers learn by doing. The emphasis in practices and rehearsals was on realistic battle conditions. So rigorous was the training that many troops finding themselves in combat for the first time commented, "Hell, this is no worse than manoeuvres."

All sorts of tests were devised to measure the proficiency of individuals and units. When passing grades were attained, the delivery of trained and equipped formations to ports of embarkation culminated the training process. Although most units received additional training overseas before entering combat, theoretically when they were released to port commanders for staging and shipping, they were ready for combat.

Yet chronic shortages of personnel and equipment complicated procedures. Usually when a unit was earmarked for movement, a hurried draft on other organisations for men and *matériel* was necessary. This cycle of robbing certain units to replenish others led to a condition where partially trained and equipped men were often a large component of the formations sent overseas. It also had an adverse effect on the units that had been stripped.

For example, to mount "Torch" General Marshall had to order certain non-participating units to furnish men and equipment in order to fill shortages in the Western Task Force. This reduced eight divisions completing the training cycle to such low levels that six to eight months were required to restore them. There was simply not enough to go around during the swift expansion of the American armed forces.

When the War Department gave notice that certain numbers of various types of units were required overseas, A.G.F., A.A.F., and A.S.F. designated the specific units to perform the final preparations for overseas movement, which became known as "POM". In order to transport men, equipment, and supplies to the port, immense co-ordination was needed, and as August 1942, McNair wrote to Marshall: "The whole question of staging areas is confused and rather complicated."

Part of the complication for "Torch" came from the impetuous nature of Patton, who often acted independently and disregarded proper channels of liaison and of command. One A.G.F. officer explained the confusion by saying, "Individuals in Washington"—he meant Patton—"have called units direct and have given instructions. There have been times when we didn't know whether they were official, personal, or what."

Another wrote; "Frequent changes of instructions on troop movements have been normal . . . This condition appears to be getting worse . . . The condition was aggravated by the introduction of . . . General Patton's headquarters, here in Washington, which dealt directly with the Desert Training Centre and issued certain instructions at variance with those issued by the office [A.G.F.] without notifying this office . . . In addition to this, the Services of Supply issued directives to its supply agencies to ship equipment direct to the units."

Although the training of the Western Task Force was Patton's responsibility, his units were actually prepared for amphibious warfare while assigned to the Amphibious Force, Atlantic Fleet, which had constructed a training centre during the summer and autumn in the Norfolk area, with schools for commanders and staffs and for various specialists. Army and Navy instructors taught men to serve as transportation quartermasters, as members of shore fire control teams and of beach parties, as boat operators, and the like.

Problems inevitably arose between Patton and the Navy. As Marshall later recalled: "Patton and the Navy were in a scrap all the time. He would get off a wild punch and the Navy would fire up." At one point Admiral King talked to Marshall about replacing Patton with another commander. But Marshall insisted that the qualities that made Patton an outstanding combat leader made him difficult to work with.

Before leaving on the invasion, Patton expressed doubt to Marshall that the Navy would be effective in putting his troops ashore. But two days before the landings, while still at sea, Patton wrote to the Chief-of-Staff:

"I should like to call your attention to the fact that the relations between the Army and Navy in this convoy could not possibly be more satisfactory. Admiral Hewitt and his Chief-of-Staff, Admiral John L. Hall, [have] shown the utmost co-operation and the finest spirit. My doubts have been removed."

Much of the confusion in the Norfolk area attending the preparations and the shipment of Patton's Western Task Force stemmed simply from the fact that it was the largest combat-loaded force, 60,000 men, ever to sail from the United States. Facilities were strained to the utmost. Men were lodged in a variety of camps, posts, and stations along the eastern seaboard, some quite distant from the port of embarkation.

The 1st Infantry Division completed amphibious training in the summer of 1942 and sailed for the United Kingdom to become part of the Centre Task Force. The 9th Infantry Division, less its 39th Regimental Combat Team, which also sailed for England to join the Centre Task Force, moved in and underwent the amphibious training cycle. The 3rd Infantry Division trained on the west coast and arrived at Camp Pickett, Virginia in mid-September. The 2nd Armoured Division rehearsed at Fort Bragg, North Carolina and elsewhere on the east coast.

These formations—the 2nd Armoured and 3rd and 9th Divisions—were the major components of the Western Task Force, and their training was harassed by incessant withdrawal of men for assignment to Officers Candidate Schools or to cadres for new units. The air forces were expanding so swiftly that they could not spare enough aircraft and personnel to train with the ground troops to achieve effective air-ground co-ordination.

Meanwhile, officers were making frantic inspections of combat readiness while others were checking equipment and supplies. Throughout the various preparations for combat, men had to be fed, clothed, cared for medically, and seen through a host of what would otherwise have been routine measures.

The whole preliminary period came to an end late in October, as the official historian has written, "in an atmosphere of unrelieved improvisation and haste, an unavoidable consequence of the determination to undertake an operation which stretched resources to the limit".

More than 100 ships transported Patton's men, and this was too large a convoy to go from a single port without attracting attention. They left in small packets at various times from various places, ostensibly bound for different destinations, and then assembled at sea. They were discovered by a U-boat during the crossing, but they managed to get off the shore of Morocco at the designated time. There a high surf, a more or less normal condition in those waters, threatened to end the invasion before it started.

In the United Kingdom, the units comprising the Centre and Eastern Task Forces prepared for "Torch" in similarly exasperating circumstances. The 1st Armoured Division, commanded by Major-General Orlando Ward, the 1st Infantry Division, headed by Major-General Terry Allen, and the 34th Infantry Division were the major American components, and they had skimpy amphibious training because time was lacking. Nor were there enough ships and boats, or even suitable training sites, to provide thorough rehearsals for the forthcoming combat. Armoured formations trained in Northern Ireland while some elements worked in Scotland and much of the staff was involved in planning in London. The infantry had equally frustrating experiences.

It could well be said, as the official historian remarks, that what the Allies were attempting to do was "the best thing possible within the limitations imposed by inexperience, uncertainty, and the shortness of time, rather than trying to turn out a force completely ready".

The assault ships of the Centre and Eastern Task Forces loaded in Liverpool and Glasgow late in September. In convoys, which proceeded toward Gibraltar. It moved safely through the straits during the night of November 5-6.

Deep within the Rock of Gibraltar, in damp and restricted quarters, Eisenhower, Clark, and the principal staff members of Allied Force Headquarters – who had flown there from the United Kingdom – listened for news of the impending contest. Eisenhower and Clark also awaited the arrival on November 7 of General Henri Giraud, who was brought secretly by submarine from southern France to discuss whether, and how, he could contribute to the operation.

In what seemed like interminable conversations, Eisenhower was unable to persuade Giraud to go to North Africa and try to rally the French authorities, who were loyal to the government of Marshal Pétain, over to the Allied side. Giraud would do so only if he received supreme command of the Allied expedition then under way and if he could divert part of it directly to a landing in southern France. This was, of course, hardly practical for a number of reasons.

After the invasion Giraud agreed to help. By this time, the Allies were negotiating with Admiral Darlan, Pétain's second in command, who by chance had happened to be in Algiers visiting his sick son in hospital there. Darlan was the highest governmental official on the scene, and he represented the legal authority of France. The Darlan deal, as the arrangements were later called, would prevent a protracted Allied struggle with the French in North Africa. But this could hardly be envisaged as the Allies made ready to assault the coast.

All three task forces were to land simultaneously in order to make the maximum impression on the French. Although the military were sure to offer at least token resistance, some French officers had promised to help the Americans come ashore. These had learned vaguely of the planned invasion from Robert Murphy, an American diplomat stationed in Algiers, and from General Clark who, two weeks before the landings, made a secret and hazardous trip by submarine to a clandestine meeting with sympathisers at Cherchell in Algeria. Unfortunately, security considerations made it impossible to inform the French of the exact time and places of the landings. As a consequence, the assistance that was given so forthrightly was poorly co-ordinated and of small concrete value.

The amphibious forces were to hit the beaches before dawn November 8. Yet each task force commander had discretion to set his exact time because of differing conditions of tide, moonlight, wind, and sunrise at the various sites. The Eastern and Centre Task Forces adopted an H-hour of 0100 hours, Greenwich time; the Western 0400.

The Western Task Force planned to anchor its troop transports several miles offshore, there to release the landing craft already swinging from davits. These boats would assemble alongside the transports to take aboard the troops. Thus loaded, the landing craft would circle nearby until a signal was given for them to form into waves at a line of departure marked by two control vessels. Escorted by guiding vessels equipped with radar and other navigational aids, the landing craft would then proceed on a predetermined schedule toward the shore. There was to be no preliminary shelling, but fire support ships were to take stations from which to shell shore targets if necessary. The waves of landing craft would go in at intervals to allow each wave to unload and pull back from the beach in time to make room for the wave following behind. The first troops to land were to capture the beach and prepare to receive succeeding waves. Later arrivals would reconnoitre inland, expand the beach-head, and penetrate the interior to reach special objectives.

Patton, who had read the Koran during the voyage, issued a circular to his men. "The local population," he said, "will respect strong, quiet men who live up to their promises. Do not boast nor brag, and keep any agreement you make." To his officers he said, "There is not the least doubt but that we are better in all respects than our enemies, but to win, the men must KNOW this. It must be their absolute belief. WE MUST HAVE A SUPERIORITY COMPLEX!"

During the night of November 7, the Western Task Force split into three attack groups and took sub-task forces to positions off the beaches of Safi, Fedala, and Mehdia. Although Patton's objective was Casablanca, the city was too strongly fortified and defended to be taken by frontal assault from the sea. He had therefore divided his troops into three landing forces. Those going ashore at Mehdia were to capture the airport at

Men of Patton's Western Task Force clamber down scrambling nets.

Salé; the other two forces, after establishing beach-heads, were to converge on Casablanca from the landward side.

Up to virtually the last minute, the surf conditions made landings dubious. But when final readings indicated that the weather might moderate, Hewitt decided to gamble and go. Instead of finding a heavy swell, the troops sailed the last few miles to their beaches in almost a flat calm. In a letter to Marshall about a week later, Patton explained why this had happened. "In spite of my unfortunate proficiency in profanity," he wrote, "I have at bottom a strongly religious nature. It is my considered opinion that the success of the operation was largely dependent on what people generally call 'luck', but what I believe to be Divine help."

Major-General Lucien Truscott was in charge at Mehdia, with about 9,000 men from the 2nd Armoured and 9th Divisions. A cavalryman who had accompanied the Canadian troops in the ill-fated Dieppe raid, he showed the competence and dash that would lead him eventually to division, corps, and army command. With his usual proficiency, he took in hand the members of his force, which had become somewhat disorganised in the initial landings at five different points along the shore. French resistance was immediate and strong, and an air bombardment of the ships offshore at dawn of November 8 delayed and reduced the prompt reinforcement and support that had been planned.

At nightfall of D-day, the Americans were in precarious positions. Hard fighting carried them through the second day. Not until the late afternoon of November 10 was the airfield objective taken and secured. As the battle was about to start again on November 11, word came that a cease-fire had been arranged in Algiers.

To obtain the airfield and seaplane base judged to be required for control of the area, Truscott's men had sustained considerable casualties, including 79 killed.

The Safi landings were under Major-

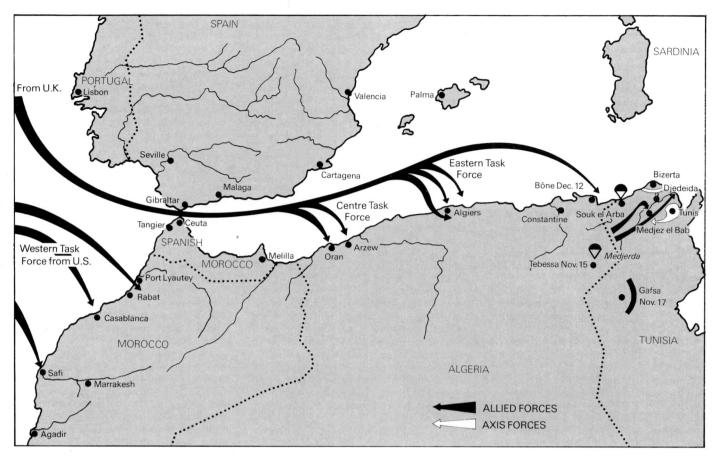

The "Torch" landings, November 7, 1942.

General Ernest N. Harmon, a cavalry and tank officer who commanded the 2nd Armoured Division. A bluff and rather rough fellow who was a fighter through and through and who would eventually command a corps, Harmon had a force of about 6,500 men from the 2nd Armoured and 9th Divisions. Their limited training and experience showed at once as they left their transports and moved ashore. There was considerable disorganisation.

On the beaches the Americans met strong opposition from the French. But they fought inland and established a beach-head. On the following day, at Bou Guedra, they met a French force marching from Marrakesh to engage them, and a serious battle ensued. Not until November 10, after blocking the French troops, could Harmon start north toward Casablanca. He took Mazagan on the coast on the morning of November 11 and was starting for Casablanca, 50 miles away, when he learned of the cease-fire.

At Fedala, Major-General Jonathan Anderson, the 3rd Division's commander, headed a force of 16,000 men built around his division. The same difficulties of getting ashore were encountered, and the same strong French opposition from naval batteries and ground forces was met. The Americans established a beach-head and extended it by heavy fighting, then started toward Casablanca. On the morning of

November 11, as they were about to open a bombardment of the city as a preliminary for assault, news came of the armistice.

There had been serious fighting at all three landings of Western Task Force, the assumption or the hope that the French were anxiously awaiting their liberation by the Allies proving completely wrong. Patton, a long-time friend of the French, had attempted to negotiate a local armistice throughout the fighting, but his efforts had failed until a general settlement was arranged. After three days of combat in Morocco, American casualties totalled about 550, including 150 killed.

At Oran, the Centre Task Force, numbering about 22,000 men, was to come ashore in three major operations involving seven different amphibious groups. In general, the 1st Armoured Division, only about half of which was present, was to thrust inland before daylight and close on the city from the south. The 1st Infantry Division was to encircle the city from the west and east and block the arrival of possible French reinforcements.

The assault convoys found their beacon submarines around 2130 hours on November 7, and sent motor launches to pick up pilot officers. Then the transport groups, preceded by minesweepers, headed for their assembly positions. Landing craft organised themselves into waves and carried men to the beaches of Marsa bou

Zedjar, les Andalouses, and the Gulf of Arzew.

The landings were uniformly successful, although the number of troops ashore at the end of the first day was somewhat less than expected. Arzew was captured intact, as was an airfield. The French naval installations and ships at Oran and Mers el Kébir offered weak opposition, and French air efforts were negligible. Only a frontal assault on the Oran harbour, a suicide mission, and an airborne attack on Tafaraoui airfield miscarried.

French forces counter-attacked on the second day, and there was serious fighting. On the third day, an attack on Oran resulted in a sudden armoured penetration into the city. The French authorities surrendered at noon.

The seizure of Oran had been accomplished in less than three days by military means alone. This was the only action wholly won by force of arms. Surprise had taken the men ashore without significant French opposition. Sheer determination had carried them inland and to their main objectives rapidly. American casualties totalled about 275 killed, 325 wounded, and 15 missing.

Algiers was the most important objective of "Torch" because it was closest to Tunis, the ultimate goal. In addition, the port, railway terminal, two airfields, space for a supply base, city facilities for headquarters, and the fact that Algiers was the seat of government for all of French North Africa made it a great prize.

The Eastern Naval Task Force divided into three columns, one heading for Cape Matifou, two toward Cape Sidi Ferruch. Because there were insufficient Americans for the landings, 7,200 British troops of the 11th Infantry Brigade Group came ashore west of Algiers near Castiglione. The operations went smoothly. French units in the area said they had been instructed not to resist.

Part of the U.S. 34th Division landed closer to the city on its western side. Components were scattered by landing craft along 15 miles of the coast, and all met some French resistance. But the force of 4,350 American and 1,000 British troops took Blida airfield and a small group entered the city.

The 39th Regimental Combat Team, of about 5,700 Americans reinforced by 200 British Commandos, landed successfully east of Algiers and moved to their assigned positions.

A suicide group of 650 Americans and several British officers in American uniforms made a direct assault on the harbour. By 0800 hours on November 8, they had taken their objectives, an electric power station, a petroleum storage depôt, a seaplane base, port offices, docks, and moles. They were then surrounded by French military units, and had to surrender.

Meanwhile, Algiers had come briefly under control of pro-American irregulars of the French Resistance, who held the important centres of communication. They were dispossessed, however, and French Army units took over.

The presence of Darlan in the city was fortuitous. Having to decide whether French North Africa would pass to the Allies with or without bloodshed, he radioed Pétain for instructions and received authority to act freely. Around 1600 hours, with Allied troops closing in on the city, Darlan authorised General Alphonse Juin to negotiate for an armistice in Algiers, but not for all of French North Africa. Two and a half hours later, agreement was reached to halt the fighting.

On the following day, Clark arrived in Algiers to negotiate with Darlan a settlement for the rest of North Africa. They reached agreement late on November 10, and hostilities between the French and the Allies ended.

By then, General Anderson had arrived in Algiers on November 9, and was getting his 1st Army's movement eastward organised and started. Tunis, along with Bizerta, was 380 miles away, and the Axis nations had already started to pour troops into the north-eastern corner of Tunisia by sea and air. French forces offered no resistance, for officers and men were anguished by the conflict between their strong sense of duty to Pétain and Darlan and by their strong desire to join the Allies and fight the Axis. While negotiations took place in Algiers, French officers waited for instructions on whether to collaborate with the Axis or with the Allies. Meanwhile, considerable numbers of German and Italian troops arrived through the ports and airfields of Bizerta and Tunis and established a strong beach-head. Not until mid-November could French ground troops form a thin defensive line to keep the Axis units somewhat bottled up while Anderson's forces rushed to their aid.

Given the distances, the poor roads, and the rough terrain, the Eastern Task Force, predominantly British, made excellent progress. By November 20, Anderson's formations were in contact with Axis units. Five days later, the British, reinforced by a relatively few American units known as Blade Force and by French forces, attacked. But combat strengths on both sides of the front were equal, and Anderson was at a disadvantage. His line of communications was weak, a depôt system was lacking, and air support was difficult to obtain.

Anderson was not to blame. Allied planners had long been aware that the precipitous advance to Tunis on a shoe-string would be a gamble. Although Anderson tried for another month to crack the enemy defences, increasingly bad weather, including heavy rains, made it obvious that the Allies could not force a favourable decision before the end of the year.

Eisenhower had done all he could to help. He had sent U.S. units from Algiers and Oran, indeed as far away as Morocco, to reinforce Anderson. He had put pressure on the airmen and logistics experts to give Anderson as much support as possible. But on December 24, after visiting Anderson, Eisenhower had to agree that an immediate attempt to capture Bizerta and Tunis would have to be abandoned. A stalemate disappointing to the Allies now set in.

This brought "Torch", the landings and the sweep to the east, to an end. The assassination of Admiral Darlan on the same day, December 24, underscored the conclusion of the operation. A new political situation now had to be dealt with. There were also new military conditions. Rommel's forces had been driven from Egypt and across Libya and were about to enter southern Tunisia.

"Torch" represented the first successful Anglo-American combined offensive, and it set the pattern for Allied unity and cohesion in subsequent coalition ventures. Largely improvised, "Torch" was a triumph of planning and execution, for it required an unprecedented effort to build up an American task force in the United States, separated by 3,000 miles from the other two task forces and from Eisenhower's headquarters, then to arrange for the entire force to converge simultaneously on the North African coast.

If "Torch" did not immediately bring American troops into contact with the armed forces of Germany, the last two months of 1942 placed them in proximity

U.S. soldiers march through Oran, wearing small replicas of the Stars and Stripes produced for the landings.

to Germans and Italians on the field of battle. That confrontation would take place in 1943, probably earlier than could have been expected if the initial operation had been launched elsewhere. But the quick success that the Americans had enjoyed over the French was unfortunate, for as a result an overconfidence, even an arrogance, arose in the ranks. Many American soldiers came to believe that they were invincible. They had but to appear before the Germans, they thought, to win. The battle of Kasserine Pass in the following year would expose how terribly inexperienced they really were.

The hope of securing a quick cessation of French resistance, not only to facilitate the landings but also to enhance the subsequent operations into Tunisia, had worked. The French had fought bravely despite their outmoded weapons and equipment. Many were wounded, and more than 650 were killed in the fighting. They could with honour enter into the Allied camp and join in the continuing struggle to liberate Europe from the power of Nazi Germany.

Finally, "Torch" was the first of a series of large-scale coalition amphibious landings – Sicily, southern Italy, southern France, Normandy – that would lead the Allies to the final battle with the enemy.

CHAPTER 36
The German advance to Stalingrad

There have naturally been many books published, in French, German, English, Italian, and Russian, about the events on the Eastern Front between May 8 and November 1942. There are general accounts of the Soviet-German conflict; histories of particular episodes or army units; and biographies, or the "I was there" type of story, based on personal experiences. Finally, one must take into account the collections of documents from German military archives, painstakingly prepared for publication by the historians Hans-Adolf Jacobsen, Hans Dollinger, Andreas Hillgruber, Walter Hubatsch, and Helmut Huber.

There is absolutely no question about the decisive nature of the defeat inflicted on Germany by the counter-stroke launched on November 19, 1942. On November 5 Montgomery had smashed four German divisions at El Alamein. On November 23, no less than a whole army (five corps or 20 divisions) of the German forces were surrounded in the Stalingrad pocket. German and Soviet commentators do not dispute the importance and the consequences of these great events, but there are differences about their causes and those responsible for them.

All the German accounts concentrate almost exclusively on the evil genius of Adolf Hitler, but this is somewhat exaggerated. Most Russian publications assert that the German generals must also share the blame. This is borne out by a typical extract, written by Marshal A. I. Eremenko, who commanded near Stalingrad:

"The beaten Fascist generals may seek vainly to prove to their new masters, the American leaders, that they are not responsible for the failure of the Hitlerian adventure, and that it was all due to Hitler's mistaken directives, but they will not succeed. Can anyone fail to see that Hitler's directives, and all his strategy, were prepared by the German General Staff, those who are now criticising his plans? It is understandable that it is in the interest of the German generals to argue that the defeat was due to the wild caprices of a madman, rather than frankly admit the bankruptcy of their military doctrine, the superiority of Soviet generalship, and the stronger morale of the Soviet fighting man."

This is not a convincing argument. Since taking over O.K.H. (while still retaining control of O.K.W.), Hitler's interference in operations had become more and more extensive, and any objectors were silenced or ruthlessly eliminated. On July 15 he relieved Field-Marshal von Bock of command of Army Group "B"; and on September 9 Field-Marshal List suffered a similar disgrace. But the Führer, not content with dismissing List, then assumed personal command of the latter's Army Group "A", with the declared intention of leading it in the conquest of the Caucasian oilfields. Finally, on September 24, Colonel-General Halder was dismissed, since as head of O.K.H. he still refused to show the slightest enthusiasm for the Führer's intuitions.

On December 19, 1941, taking over supreme command, Hitler had declared: "Anyone can provide the limited command required for the conduct of operations. The task of the commander-in-chief is to create a National-Socialist Army. I know of no general capable of doing this, therefore I have decided to take command myself." On the day of General Halder's dismissal, he had also revealed his innermost thoughts: "The dictator complained bitterly of the constant and strong opposition he had encountered. He even quoted exact dates when this opposition had caused dramatic scenes and had deeply hurt him. This perpetual struggle had robbed him of much of his nervous energy. It was not worthwhile, however. To carry out the army's remaining tasks it was no longer a question of 'technical possibilities', but of National-Socialist ardour', which could not be expected of an officer of the old school. He even declared that 'the secret of Moltke's victories was to be found in his unshakable faith in the monarchy'."

Halder, however, almost as if replying in advance to Marshal Eremenko's accusations mentioned above, noted in his diary on July 23, 1942, apropos of a reverse in the Rostov sector destined to have important consequences:

"I have made known my express warnings, and now the results are only too apparent – we have fits of mad rage and violent accusations levelled at the commanders; his constant under-estimation of the enemy's capabilities is becoming increasingly absurd and dangerous; in short, the situation is more and more intolerable. It is no longer possible to talk seriously about our work. Unsound reactions based on fleeting impressions, with a total inability to assess the potential of his commanders – this is what he calls directing operations."

Just before the German summer offensive, the Third Reich's land forces amounted to 233 divisions of all kinds – that is, 25 more than when Operation "Barbarossa" was launched (according to Halder's table of June 16, 1942). Three of them had just completed their training in Germany, while 46 were on fronts of secondary importance – nine less than on June 22, 1941:

Norway and Denmark	12 instead of	8
West	26 ,,	38
Balkans	5 ,,	7
North Africa	3 ,,	2

It can be seen that naval forces were not the only ones affected by the Führer's "Norwegian complex", as it can be called, because Colonel-General von Falkenhorst, commanding in Norway, acquired a Panzer division. Moreover, Army Group "D" in Western Europe had to give up 15 divisions, but received the 6th, 7th, and 10th Panzer Divisions; Rundstedt took over command of Army Group "D" from Field-Marshal von Witzleben on March 15, 1942.

Operations on the Eastern Front were therefore carried out by 184 divisions: five of these formed the 20th Army in Lappland under Colonel-General Dietl, and were controlled by O.K.W., like units in other secondary theatres. O.K.H. authority covered the other 179 divisions in action between the Gulf of Finland and the Kerch' peninsula. These included:

122 infantry divisions
> (+18 compared with 1941)

3½ *Gebirgsjäger* divisions
> (+1½ compared with 1941)

6 light divisions
> (+2 compared with 1941)

19 Panzer divisions
> (unchanged)

11 motorised divisions
> (unchanged)

5½ S.S. motorised divisions
> (+1½ compared with 1941)

12 security divisions
> (+3 compared with 1941)

What stands out in the above table is the fact that the highly mobile Panzer and motorised units gained very few reinforcements. Those which benefited were the infantry and mountain troops, and also the security units – because of the increasing activity by Soviet partisans behind the German lines.

But if the *Panzerwaffe* did not benefit numerically, it did improve its *matériel* considerably. Not only had the production of light tanks been abandoned, but the medium and heavy vehicles were better armed: the Pzkw III was given a 5-cm gun of 60 calibres barrel length, and the Pzkw IV a 7.5-cm gun of 43 calibres barrel length, firing armour-piercing shells at a muzzle velocity of 2,700 and 2,428 feet per second respectively. The 5-cm had the longer range. Of course these improvements meant more weight to be carried, but this did not affect the Panzers' tactical mobility. It is evident therefore that during the year the Germans had surmounted the crisis caused by the unexpected appearance of the Russian T-34.

At the same time, the increased number of tracked cross-country vehicles allowed the *Panzergrenadier* infantry to follow more closely behind the tanks. Thanks to their vehicles' light armour and cannon, the troops were able to do some of their fighting behind the tanks without leaving their vehicles.

Also, the Wehrmacht's Panzer and motorised divisions had begun to receive various infantry support weapons, anti-tank guns and even conventional artillery, fitted onto tracked chassis. For street fighting and assault on fortified positions they had a flame-throwing tank based on the Pzkw III with an 85-yard range. The little remote controlled "Goliath" tank, first used at Sevastopol', also had the same purpose. It was a wire-controlled tracked vehicle (modelled on the French Cloporte, produced experimentally at la Seyne in September 1939) capable of delivering a 180-pound explosive charge in front of an obstacle. The Panzers had thus made progress, but the other arms had not been standing still.

At this time the infantry acquired a new machine gun, the MG42, firing over 1,000 rounds a minute, and capable of repulsing massed infantry attacks on its own. The first rocket launching batteries also made their appearance, their official name being *Nebelwerfer* (smoke thrower).

Before the war both the Russians and the Germans had made great efforts to produce rocket artillery. The Russians were ready first, having settled for a fairly primitive piece of equipment, the BM8 "*Katyusha*". These "Stalin organs", as the Germans called them, fired their first shots with great psychological effect on July 15, 1941. The Germans replied with a weapon consisting of six 15-cm barrels arranged hexagonally on a split-trail mounting. It fired salvoes of 80-pound rocket shells a distance of well over 7,000 yards, and those on the receiving end found them unpleasantly effective.

Whatever the improvements in its weapons, two questions caused concern in O.K.H. The first was over numbers of troops. On May 1, 1942 units on the Eastern Front were 308,000 men below strength. But it was calculated that men called up in 1942 would be arriving by August 1 to make up the losses expected in the summer campaign.

The second problem was that of keeping this increasingly mechanised and motorised army supplied with fuel. In spite of increased production of synthetic petroleum and supplies from Austrian, Hungarian, Rumanian, and Polish oilfields, the problem was becoming increasingly serious. On June 13 General E. Wagner, the Quartermaster General, head of the supply section of O.K.H., informed the Führer of his concern at the situation. In his view there was a great risk of supplies drying up by mid-September. Operations should therefore be limited according to supplies. "I couldn't expect any other answer from one of my generals," was Hitler's biting rejoinder. And yet Wagner had been optimistic rather than pessimistic, since from the end of July whole units were immobilised for days by lack of fuel. It is clear that Hitler's strategy found itself in a vicious circle: he needed oil to conquer the Caucasus, and at the same time he needed the Caucasus to obtain oil.

At a higher level, at O.K.W., another no less worrying problem was emerging. The development of R.A.F. Bomber Command, and the appearance over Holland on July 4 of the first American aircraft, forced Hitler and Göring to commit more and more forces to the defence of German

A Russian rifleman and DP M1926 light-machine gunner dug in near Stalingrad.

ports and the Ruhr industrial basin. At the end of the year, three-quarters of German fighter strength were in the West. Fighter protection for bomber squadrons in the East was thus correspondingly weak, so it was more and more difficult for these bombers to play their part in the thick of land operations. In the autumn, faced with the Russian Air Force, continually reinforced by Lend-Lease deliveries, the Luftwaffe no longer enjoyed its numerical superiority of the year before.

In the name of the "crusade against Bolshevism" that he had proclaimed on June 22, 1941, and of what he called the defence of "Europe", Hitler called upon all his allies and satellites to increase their contribution to the Russian campaign.

As a result of losses during the winter of 1939–1940, Finland could keep its 18 divisions in action only between the Arctic circle and the Karelian isthmus; General Franco did no more than maintain the *Azúl* Division in the Novgorod sector; and the Slovak contingent which took part in the Caucasus invasion was reinforced by a motorised division. Rome, Budapest, and Bucharest made a more positive response to the German appeal, as shown by the numbers of their troops on the Eastern Front in 1941 and 1942:

	November 15, 1941	November 15, 1942
Italy	3 divisions	10 divisions
Hungary	3 brigades	10 divisions
Rumania	15 divisions	25 divisions

Instead of the 52 satellite divisions and brigades fighting with the Germans from June 22, 1941, there were, just before Stalingrad, 65 allied divisions on the Eastern Front. Forty-six of these were wholly or partially involved in some way or another in the great catastrophe that began on November 19, 1942.

OK.H. calculated that, given their differences in arms and equipment, three allied divisions were the equivalent of two German divisions. On this basis, the contribution of Hitler's allies in this phase of the campaign was the equivalent of 44 German divisions. And on July 1 Field-Marshal von Bock commanded in the Crimea and the Ukraine 29 such divisions, of which 12 were Rumanian, ten Hungarian, six Italian, and one Slovak.

These were Hitler's forces at the opening of the German summer offensive. They amounted in all to some 215 divisions (184 German, plus 46 satellite divisions, i.e. 31 in German equivalents)–on paper 35 more than on June 22, 1941.

One would like to be able to give with the same precision the numbers of Red Army troops involved when operations again became possible. But even today, Russian historians maintain a peculiar silence on this subject. Of course from time to time we are given the order of battle and varying fortunes of some division which participated in a particular action during this second phase of the "Great Patriotic War". But there is not enough information to obtain an overall view. As for western historians' calculations, they are all based, in the end, on the situation tables prepared at intervals for his superiors by Colonel R. Gehlen, who had succeeded General E. Kinzel as head of "Section East" of O.K.H. Intelligence early in April 1942. These by no means settle all the uncertainties.

There is more information, however,

Russian 120-mm mortars under production.

about the structural reorganisations carried out by the Russians in the light of the preceding year's experience, which, in general, was correctly interpreted. The infantry division was reduced considerably in numbers. It now contained no more than about 10,000 men, that is almost half the number in a corresponding German division; and its organic heavy artillery regiment was also withdrawn. Thanks to the widespread use of individual automatic weapons, the infantry's firepower was still not significantly inferior to that of the Germans. In addition, their anti-tank weapons were increased, including 210 14.5-mm anti-tank rifles and 102 57-mm anti-tank guns. But to judge by the ease with which the Panzers broke through all resistance between May and July, it seems clear that these reinforcements were far from complete when Hitler launched his three attacks. Finally, the various services attached to the Russian division were reduced to an absolute minimum.

As for the armoured units, the independent tank brigades still existed. There were one or two of them in each army to use their weight and firepower in an infantry support rôle. The Russians were still, and would remain, attached to the tank support system in spite of its apparent failures during two years of Blitzkrieg operations. These brigades each had three battalions, 60 T-34's, with a squadron of T-70 light tanks for advanced reconnaissance work. As integral parts of each brigade there were also a battalion of motorised infantry, plus supply, maintenance, and repair services.

It was a 1942 innovation to group them in two's with a motorised infantry brigade to form tank corps, which were, in a sense, a Front (army group) commander's personal strike force. He would send them in to widen and deepen breaches in enemy positions made by infantry units and their organic armour. But, as Moscow H.Q. repeated incessantly, such actions should avoid wild onslaughts and any engagements whatsoever with enemy tanks. Communications between armour, infantry, and artillery had to be maintained throughout the attack.

Transporting infantry was a difficulty for the Russians, as they had no tracked cross-country vehicles, but they got over the problem by carrying troops on tanks. The T-34 carried between 20 and 30, and therefore an armoured brigade could transport a whole battalion. In the same year the first self-propelled guns also made their appearance in the Red Army, though only in small numbers.

It has already been mentioned that the infantry divisions had to give up their 122-mm and 152-mm guns and howitzers. *Stavka* thus built up an enormous reserve of guns from which it would soon form its famous artillery divisions. Like the armoured, mechanised, and motorised corps, these were allocated to Front commanders as the need arose. It was also at this level of command that one found the brigades of *Katyushas*, as they were known to the Russian troops, rocket launchers with 24 or 36 ramps mounted on vehicles, with an electrical firing mechanism for their 35-pound projectiles. At the same time, anti-tank brigades were being formed. Between July 5 and 13, 1944 they were to prove themselves very potent indeed on the Kursk battlefield.

It must be emphasised that this is in no way a definitive account of the many aspects of Russian organisation, or of the numbers of Red Army troops involved. Russian sources are too imprecise. But one cannot fail to be impressed by the scope and originality of the efforts made by the Soviet political, administrative, and military authorities.

"In Russia the winter campaign is coming to an end. Thanks to the extraordinary bravery and spirit of sacrifice displayed by our troops, the defensive battle on the Eastern Front is proving a most striking success for German arms." This was the statement that introduced Hitler's Directive No. 41, dated April 5, which set out the Wehrmacht's objectives for 1942 in the Eastern theatre of operations. Undoubtedly it was not far from the truth at that time. But he did not stop there, and his second paragraph contained an appraisal of the situation that was very wide of the mark. "The enemy have suffered enormous losses of men and *matériel*. In attempting to exploit their apparent initial successes, they have exhausted during this winter the mass of their reserves, which were intended for later operations."

It was on this basis that Hitler's directive was drawn up, giving not only the objectives of the summer offensive but even the lines on which it was to be conducted. This document occupies no less than five pages in Hubatsch's *Hitlers Weisungen für die Kriegsführung,* but need only be summarised here. Hitler set his armies the task of destroying the last remaining enemy forces and, as far as possible, of capturing the main sources of the raw materials on which their war economy depended. To this end, but without prejudice to a Leningrad offensive, all the available German and allied forces would be concentrated in the southern sector. Their mission was to annihilate the

enemy on the Don, to conquer the Caucasian oil areas, and to capture the passes giving access to the southern slopes of the Caucasus mountains.

The operation was to be divided into several phases. First, the left flank of Army Group "South" would move from Kursk on the Don to Voronezh and, moving down the river, close a pincer by meeting the 6th Army from Khar'kov (second phase). In the third phase, Field-Marshal von Bock's right flank, now commanded by Field-Marshal List and renamed Army Group "A", would force the Donets in the Voroshilovgrad area and move up the Don through Rostov to meet the rest of Army Group "South", which in the interval would have become Army Group "B". This new pincer movement would close on Stalingrad, either taking the city or, at least, eliminating it as an industrial and communications centre.

Then Bock, with his right flank on the Volga and his left in contact with Army Group "Centre" in the Kursk area, would cover List's rear while the latter, reinforced by the 11th Army (after forcing the Kerch' Strait) pressed forward to invade the Caucasus. With this aim, the Rumanians, Italians, and Hungarians would position themselves on the Don between the bend at Kalach and the Voronezh area, while the German 2nd and 6th Armies, on the flanks, would be moved to the sectors where the defence would have no river obstacle to help them. This would be the fourth and final phase of the summer campaign that was intended to win the war in the East for the Third Reich.

Was this grandiose plan feasible? Some deny it; but if it is to be given any credibility at all, one has to be convinced that Hitler would have carried it out carefully and methodically. This is just what he did not do. He repeatedly departed from his original plan by intervening personally, sometimes in fits of his well-known megalomania and other times in fits of weakness (less well-known), as a result perhaps of alternating states of euphoria and depression brought on by Dr. Morell's drugs.

Was the Führer aiming still higher? It has not gone unnoticed that in his letter to Mussolini on June 22 he used the attack on Sevastopol' as an argument to encourage his ally to exploit the Tobruk victory and push on into Egypt. Anyhow, his navy chiefs seem to have urged him to complete Rommel's expected success in the Middle East and East Africa as well as the victory in the East. Thus on June 12 Vice-Admiral K. Fricke, Chief of Naval Staff (Operations), and Captain Assmann put such a plan to the meticulous Halder, who was unimpressed and noted in his diary: "These people are dreamers on a continental scale. On the basis of their experience of the army so far, they readily admit that it depends on our enthusiasm and effort whether the Persian Gulf is to be reached overland through the Caucasus, or the Suez Canal from Cyrenaica through Egypt. They talk of land operations through Italian Africa (Abyssinia), aiming for the East African coast." After having received his guests for dinner, he concluded with this somewhat sarcastic remark: "much ado about nothing".

However, before launching Operation "Blau", the codename for Army Group "South"'s general offensive, Directive No. 41 required Bock to take the last remaining positions in the Crimea and to wipe out the irksome Izyum salient, carved into the German lines on the right bank of the Donets during the Soviet winter offensive.

At dawn on May 8 the German 11th Army, by substituting as many Rumanian troops as possible for German ones in LIV Corps besieging Sevastopol', moved over the Kamenskoye isthmus to attack the positions covering Kerch' with nine divisions, including three Rumanian and the newly formed 22nd Panzer Division, against the Russians' 17 divisions and three brigades, with two cavalry divisions and four armoured brigades. But if the Russians had a numerical advantage, the German 11th Army enjoyed superiority in the air, having Colonel-General Löhr's *Luftflotte* IV, including VIII *Fliegerkorps*.

On the evening of May 8, XXX Corps had made an opening in the Soviet 44th Army's line (Lieutenant-General S. I. Chernyak). The next day its 50th, 28th *Gebirgsjäger*, and 22nd Panzer Divisions gained enough ground eastwards to turn north and drive eight Russian divisions back to the Sea of Azov on May 11; on May 16 a pursuit force reached Kerch'. On May 20 the remnants of the Caucasus Front retreated across the strait linking the Black Sea and the Sea of Azov, leaving behind them 170,000 prisoners, 1,138 guns, and 258 tanks.

Not wishing to belittle his victory, Manstein describes his enemy in his memoirs in much more moderate terms than does the *Great Patriotic War*, which vigorously criticises their bad positioning, inertia, and lack of communication, at the critical moment, between air and land forces. It reads: "The bureaucratic spirit which dominated the conduct of the campaign had disastrous consequences. The troops received orders which had absolutely no bearing on the real situation at the front. At the critical moment, instead of energetically leading their troops, the front commander, Lieutenant-General Koslov, and Army Commissar 1st class L. Z. Mekhlis wasted precious time in long and inconclusive councils of war." Consequently Mekhlis, who was also Vice-Commissar for Defence, was replaced and demoted, against which no one in the Red Army protested, for this man had taken an active part in the 1937 and 1938 purges. Lieutenant-General B. T. Koslov was dismissed, as were Generals S. I. Chernyak, K. S. Kolganov, and J. M. Nikolayenko, who commanded, respectively, the 44th Army, the 47th Army, and the air force on the Caucasus Front.

In his H.Q. at Poltava, Bock had chosen May 18 for Operation *"Fridericus I"*, a pincer movement intended to take the Izyum salient as ordered. But at dawn on May 12 he learned that his 6th Army (General Paulus) was itself being heavily attacked around Khar'kov. A few hours later it became clear that it was not simply a local attack but a major strategic offensive employing dozens of divisions and hundreds of tanks.

At the end of the winter, Stalin and his advisers in Moscow had refused to accept that they should remain on the defensive when spring came. On the contrary, they intended to attack. The *Great Patriotic War* includes this justifiable comment on their decision: "The Supreme Command G.H.Q. exaggerated the success of the counter-attack and ordered a general offensive in all important sectors, thus scattering their reserves."

Anyhow, at the end of March, *Stavka* rejected, because of lack of reserves, a plan put forward by Marshal Timoshenko which would have brought Russian forces back to the Dniepr between Gomel' and Cherkassy, and between Cherkassy and Nikolayev on the right bank of the river. Instead, they placed the South and South-West Fronts under his command, and gave him the much more modest objective of Khar'kov.

Timoshenko divided his forces into two. North, in the Volchansk area, the 28th Army (Lieutenant-General D. I. Ryabyshev) reinforced to 16 infantry and three cavalry divisions, and six armoured brigades, was to break through the German front and exploit its success towards the south-west. In the south, the 6th Army (Lieutenant-General A. M. Gorodnyansky: 11 infantry and six cavalry divisions, and 13 tank brigades) would break out of the Izyum salient, attack south of Khar'kov, and having broken through, then converge on the north-west, moving in front of Ryabyshev. Finally, cavalry and armoured forces would advance quickly on Dniepropetrovsk.

In the Volchansk sector, the 28th Army's attack, launched on May 9, was checked after having pushed out a salient of some 20 miles into the enemy lines. In the south, on the other hand, Gorodnyansky set General Paulus and Field-Marshal von Bock a very worrying problem. On May 14 VIII Corps was nearly in ruins; on May 16 the Russians arrived at Merefa and Karlovka on the heels of the 454th Security Division, which had given ground, and a Hungarian division which had done no better. Sixty-four guns had also been lost.

In these circumstances, could Operation *"Fridericus"* retrieve the situation? Paulus and Bock doubted it very much, and on May 14 the latter noted in his diary: "Although I am most unwilling to do this, I can only propose, as far as the Army Group is concerned, to grab from Kleist [right prong of the *"Fridericus"* pincer] everything we can get hold of, say three or four divisions, one of them armoured, and transport them to XI Panzer Corps' left flank. From there they will attack the southern flank of the enemy pocket."

A German light anti-tank gun moves forward during the May 9 assault.

In agreement for once, Hitler and Halder were intractable. Colonel-General von Kleist managed to save a day on his timetable and counter-attack at dawn on May 17. He fell on the Russian 9th and 57th Armies (South Front) under Major-General F. M. Kharitonov and Lieutenant-General K. P. Podlas, who had to protect the offensive by the South-West Front from surprise attacks. It is true that Kharitonov had only four divisions to hold a 65-mile front and that *Luftflotte* IV was applying its usual great pressure.

It took no miracle therefore for *Gruppe* von Kleist, with 15 divisions, including four Rumanian, to reach the Donets within 48 hours. Faced with this unexpected reversal, Timoshenko asked the Supreme Command to authorise the abandonment of the Khar'kov attack. This was refused, so he appealed to Stalin through N. S. Khruschev, political member of the council of South-West Front. During the 20th Congress of the Communist Party of the Soviet Union in February 1956, Khruschev explained this fruitless attempt.

"Against all good sense Stalin rejected our proposal and ordered that the Khar'kov operation must continue; and yet several of our army units were already threatened with encirclement and extermination . . . I telephoned the Chief-of-Staff, Vasilevsky, and begged him to explain the situation to Comrade Stalin. But Vasilevsky replied that Comrade Stalin wanted to hear no more about it. So I telephoned Stalin at his villa. It was Malenkov who replied. I said I wanted to speak to Stalin personally. Stalin's answer was that I could speak to Malenkov. Again I asked for Stalin himself. But he continued to refuse, though he was only a few steps from the telephone. After having 'listened', so to speak, to our request Stalin ordered: 'Leave things as they are.' And what was the result? The worst one could expect – our armies were surrounded by the Germans and we lost hundreds of thousands of men."

Khruschev's account may be somewhat embroidered but there is no doubt about Stalin's *"niet"*, and the results were disastrous. Unleashed at its appointed place, III Panzer Corps (General A. von Mackensen) moved up the right bank of the Donets, thrusting vigorously into the Russians' rear, and sealed off the Izyum bridgehead. On May 23 in the Balakleya area it joined up with LI Corps (General von Seydlitz-Kurzbach), thrown in by Paulus to meet it from the south-east of Khar'kov. Caught in the trap, the Russian 6th and 57th Armies counter-attacked furiously towards Izyum in the hope of breaking free. But in vain, for on May 28 the German 6th Army crushed the last centres of enemy resistance. Twenty infantry and seven cavalry divisions, and 13 armoured brigades had been wiped out, losing 214,000 prisoners, 1,246 tanks, and 2,026 guns. General Gorodnyansky was killed while fighting in the front line, and his colleague Podlas committed suicide with all his staff to escape captivity. Army

Russian prisoners at Sevastopol'

Group "South" losses at this time were no more than 20,000, according to Field-Marshal von Bock.

While Stalin was still alive, Soviet historians did their best to conceal this major disaster. Since the sensational declarations by Khruschev at the Kiev Congress, there has been less reticence about its causes and consequences. In fact, on a throw of the dice, Stalin had wasted his strategic striking force, and before he could rebuild it Paulus reached the Volga and Kleist was threatening Groznyy. The military historian V. P. Morosov, explaining Timoshenko's position just before Operation *"Blau"*, writes: "The reserves of the South-West Front were insignificant, since most of them had been used in previous battles in the Khar'kov sector."

The striking victory at Kerch' had freed the German 11th Army from any pressure on its rear, so Manstein was able to start the attack on Sevastopol' on June 7. He had received very strong reinforcements: three assault gun units, 24 *Nebelwerfer* rocket-launching batteries, and most of the siege artillery in general reserve.

Amongst the last were two 60-cm *Karl* mortars and the 80-cm super-heavy *Gustav* railway gun, which fired seven-ton shells at the rate of three an hour. This monster's barrel was 100 feet long and weighed 130 tons. In addition, the Luftwaffe had provided 600 aircraft, including General von Richthofen's Stukas.

It was, nevertheless, a hard nut to crack. Commanded by General I. E. Petrov, the Sevastopol' garrison had seven divisions, plus one unmounted cavalry division and Vice-Admiral F. S. Oktyabrsky's three brigades of marines. It depended on 3,600 permanent or temporary fortified positions set up in depth over some 15 miles. Amongst these was the Maxim Gorky fort, with four 305-mm guns in two turrets. The Russians had no opposition for the enemy's overwhelming air power, however.

Manstein's attack involved three corps, including the Rumanian mountain corps, in all nine divisions, including two Rumanian. LIV Corps had the main task, to attack on the northern front, while XXX Corps with stronger forces took the southern front. It has been calculated that the German artillery fired about 46,700 tons of shells, and that the Luftwaffe dropped 125,000 bombs during 25,000 sorties in one month. But for all that, the defenders were not intimidated. Each attack had to be decided by close hand-to-hand combat. When German infantry and pioneers had overrun the portions of any particular fort above the ground, they had then to overcome resistance in the labyrinth of underground installations, with the risk of being blown up with the defenders. And with destroyers and submarines the Black Sea Fleet worked hard to reinforce and supply the garrison. But although the German 11th Army's progress was slow, it was still sure and relentless.

On June 27, LIV Corps reached the north side of North Bay, and during the night of June 28 and 29 got its 22nd Airborne Division across in motor assault craft. XXX Corps had taken the dominating heights of Sapun. Sevastopol' was lost, but the defenders still gave the 11th Army a hard task. On July 4 Hitler had made Colonel-General von Manstein a Field-Marshal, but he had to wait until July 9 before the last stubborn resistance in the Khersonesskiy peninsula was overcome, fighting to the last cartridge and the last drop of water.

The Germans lost 24,111 killed and wounded, but captured 95,000 prisoners and 467 guns. The Germans were now in possession of the whole Crimea except the southern mountains, where there were still partisans, and the 11th Army was now available for other tasks.

Meanwhile the German 6th Army, not satisfied with having overcome the Izyum and Volchansk bridgeheads, itself crossed the Donets to secure a good jumping off position on the Oskol, the left bank tributary of this important waterway. This part of *"Fridericus"* brought in 45,000 prisoners, 266 tanks, and 208 guns.

According to Halder's table, already referred to, Field-Marshal von Bock had on June 16, between the Kerch' Strait and the Kursk area, 73 divisions of all types, including nine Panzer, seven motorised (two of them *Waffen* S.S.), and 26 satellite divisions. If the *Great Patriotic War* is to be believed, Stalin drew no conclusions from this impressive concentration of forces. Thus we read: "The Soviet High Command of course thought it possible that the Wehrmacht might attack in the south. It considered however that the enemy would not make its main attack on Stalingrad and the Caucasus but, with its forces before Moscow, would try to outflank the centre groups of the Red Army and take Moscow and the central industrial area."

Hence, in this author's view, *Stavka*'s mistaken decisions during the first part of the summer campaign. Priority was given to reinforcements for the Bryansk Front which, if broken, would have let the enemy through to Tula and the capital. There is no doubt that this is what happened. But according to Accoce's *La guerre a été*

gagnée en Suisse, the Soviet agent Rudolf Rössler had, from Lucerne, transmitted the text of Directive No. 41 to his superiors in Moscow. This was on April 14, ten days after Hitler had signed it. On May 3 Colonel-General Halder wrote this note: *"Exchange Telegraph* in Moscow is sending out surprising reports about our intentions."

Also, on June 20, eight days before the attack, a Fieseler *Storch* crashed behind the Russian lines while on its way back to the 23rd Panzer Division H.Q. In the aircraft, Major Reichel had apparently been carrying completely detailed operations orders for XL Corps. One can conclude that Stalin had therefore received more than enough information about enemy intentions from his Intelligence, but that he had ignored their reports. Why? Perhaps he thought he was being deliberately misled by the enemy, and clung more than ever to the belief that Moscow was to be the main objective of the coming German offensive.

On June 28 *Gruppe* von Weichs attacked on a 90-mile front with its left south of Orel and its right at Oboyan. Colonel-General von Weichs sent in his own 2nd Army, the 4th *Panzerarmee* (Colonel-General Hoth), and the Hungarian 2nd Army (Colonel-General Jany), in all 23 divisions, including three Panzer and two motorised.

Two days later it was the turn of Paulus's 6th Army, which extended the attack another 50 miles, with 18 divisions, including two Panzer and one motorised. Paulus's XL Corps (3rd and 23rd Panzer Divisions and 29th Motorised Division) was to close the pincer with Hoth. It was a striking success. The left of the Bryansk Front (General Golikov) and the right of the South-West Front were broken. On July 1 the Panzers were at Stary-Oskol and reached Valuyki on July 3, while one of General Hoth's divisions stormed a bridge over the Don and pushed into Voronezh. This created a pocket in which 30,000 Russians were taken prisoner.

The Don-Donets corridor was therefore opened up according to the plan adopted on April 5. The Germans were to exploit this opening with Hoth and Paulus rolling through it to meet the 1st *Panzerarmee* (Colonel-General von Kleist), preparing to attack north-east across the Donets. Though fearing a counter-attack on his flank, Bock nevertheless kept his 4th *Panzerarmee* around Voronezh. This act of timidity cost him his command; on July 15 Colonel-General von Weichs took over Army Group "B", leaving his own 2nd Army, already in defensive positions on the Orel-Voronezh front, to General H. von Salmuth.

In spite of this error the 6th Army still moved on towards the great curve of the Don and threatened to overrun the South-West Front. This brought an order from Timoshenko on July 7 for a retreat. It meant that Army Group "A", attacking two days later, met only rearguards when crossing the Don. Field-Marshal List's

forces, from left to right, were the 1st *Panzerarmee* (Kleist) and *Gruppe* Ruoff (17th Army and the Italian 8th Army) that is another 24 German, five Rumanian, three Italian, and one Slovak (including four Panzer and four motorised) divisions.

At the same time, Paulus was arriving at Rossosh' and a gigantic pincer movement was taking shape between Voronezh and Rostov, involving 52 divisions, including 18 armoured and motorised (about 2,300 tanks). On July 12 List extended his operation to the Sea of Azov, broke through the enemy lines at Krasnyy Luch, and five days later took Voroshilovgrad. This new setback, to say the least, forced Stalin to order Lieutenant-General R. Ya. Malinovsky, commander of South Front, to fall back in his turn. He perhaps intended to bar the enemy's way to the bend of the Don along a line from Voronezh to Rostov, but in this case he had not appreciated the weakened state of his own forces and the offensive momentum of the Panzers.

So on July 15 Hoth and his *Panzerarmee* took Millerovo, having covered half the distance to Stalingrad in three weeks. In view of this situation, the next day Halder called together the heads of his Intelligence and Operations sections to discuss the possibility of lunging for Stalingrad without waiting for the fall of Rostov. He was thus remaining faithful to the spirit of the April 5 directive, while Hitler was moving further away from it.

Fearing that the 1st Army might run into difficulties at Rostov, the Führer, from July 13, had placed Hoth, now reinforced by XL Corps, under Army Group "A"; then he had ordered it to swing from east to south-east. This brought it on July 17 to Tsimlyansk, upstream from the junction of the Donets and the Don, while Kleist himself had forced the Donets at Kamensk-Shakhtinskiy. Hitler remained deaf to the warnings from Halder and thought he was going to be able to pull off a massive encircling movement as successful as those at Kiev and Bryansk-Vyaz'ma in 1941, thus opening up the way to the Caucasus.

An enormous bottleneck and major supply difficulties then built up. But above all, without XL Corps' armoured and motorised strength, the 6th Army remained the only force still making for Stalingrad, instead of the two army groups as originally planned. Hoth's transfer prevented him from exploiting his newly-won bridgeheads on the southern Don and striking to the Volga. Paulus, having to depend on his own resources, was forced to mark time while the enemy were using every means in their power to organise quickly a new Stalingrad Front.

Moreover, Paulus himself was far from overjoyed with the situation. Talking after the battle with his son Ernest Alexander, who had been wounded in a tank, he told him: "You can see the damage your tanks inflicted on the Russians. There are heaps of their tanks destroyed on the battlefield. We were told this story by a captured Russian officer—

The crew of an anti-tank gun surrender.

Timoshenko had been watching a tank battle from an observation post, and when he saw the rate at which his tanks were literally shot to pieces by their opponents he went pale and left, muttering 'It's frightful, frightful'." However, the wounded son sensed concern rather than satisfaction behind his father's spirited account of events. Paulus was certainly wondering what new reserves might be produced by the enemy who seemed, like Lerna's hydra, to sprout new heads as soon as the old ones were cut off.

On July 23 Rostov fell to Colonel-General von Kleist, but did not yield the expected amount of prisoners and booty. Hitherto in a state of depression, Hitler, again for no good reason, became once more optimistic. Hence his Directive No. 45, to carry out Operation *"Braunschweig"*. It was signed on July 23 at his new H.Q., set up at Vinnitsa in the western Ukraine to enable him to keep a closer watch on the current offensive. In his preamble he proclaimed: "In a three-week campaign the main objectives I had indicated behind the southern wing of the Eastern Front have been achieved. Only remnants of Timoshenko's armies have managed to escape encirclement and reach the south bank of the Don. It must be admitted that they will be reinforced from the Caucasus. The concentration of another group of armies is taking place near Stalingrad, where the enemy is likely to make a stubborn defence."

It was on these ill-conceived premises that he based the following orders for his army groups:

"A" was to:

1. occupy the east coast of the Black Sea from the Taman' peninsula, opposite Kerch', to Batumi, inclusively;
2. take the Maykop and Armavir heights,

and by successive wheeling movements through the west Caucasian passes overcome enemy resistance in the coastal area; and
3. simultaneously launch a fast mobile force (1st and 4th *Panzerarmee*) towards Groznyy and then Baku. The Italian Alpine Corps would be used in this operation, blocking the central Caucasian passes.

"B" was to:

1. defend the Don between Voronezh and the great river bend at Kalach;
2. destroy the enemy forces concentrating at Stalingrad and take the town;
3. extend the line of defence between the bend of the Don and the Volga, upstream from Stalingrad; and
4. launch a fast mobile force towards Astrakhan' and block the Volga, downstream from Stalingrad.

The July 23 directive has since the war found no defenders on the German side. All the West German military historians' accounts consulted agree that the disaster which followed was the direct result of the decision imposed on the High Command by Hitler. To quote just one writer, the former chief-of-staff of LII Corps, Major-General Hans Doerr, who took part in the campaign with Army Group "A": "This July 23 must be considered as the day it became clear that the German Supreme Command abandoned standard principles of warfare to adopt peculiar new approaches stemming rather from Adolf Hitler's irrational and diabolical power than from methodical and realistic military practice. Once again history proved that Faith and the Devil triumphed over Reason. The trained soldiers around Hitler were virtually impotent, under the spell of the Devil."

Of course Russian historians do not agree with Major-General Doerr's view. One can only quote here the opinion of

Marshal A. I. Eremenko, former commander of the Stalingrad Front. He writes: "German generals will not succeed in proving that if Hitler had not forced them to get bogged down in the battle for Stalingrad they would have achieved victory and in any case would have taken the Caucasus in the autumn of 1942. The most important issue was not that Hitler was thrusting simultaneously towards both Stalingrad and the Caucasus, but that he had insufficient forces to fight both battles successfully. He had imposed this impossible task on his army to prove to satellites and potential allies the strength of the Wehrmacht (it was thus assumed that victory at Stalingrad and in the Caucasus would force Turkey, in the south, and Japan, in the Far East, to declare war on the U.S.S.R.)."

Eremenko's argument is not convincing. The "important issue" was quite simply that in ignoring the aim set down in Directive No. 41–first Stalingrad, then the Caucasus–Hitler ordered simultaneous and, what is worse, divergent attacks on the two objectives.

But this is not all, for the Führer made ruinous reductions in the army groups intended to complete Operation *"Braunschweig"*. In particular, the 9th and 11th Panzer Divisions were removed from the 2nd Army's inactive front and assigned to Field-Marshal von Kluge. An O.K.W. decision, dated July 9, ordered the S.S. *Leibstandarte* Motorised Division, which Hitler had not wanted to transfer, to France to repel any possible invasion landing. The excellent *Grossdeutschland* Division, held up at Rostov, would have joined them if it had not been sent on a futile errand to reinforce Army Group "Centre". Finally, though it had been planned that the whole 11th Army should cross the Kerch' Strait, it was decided that only XLII Corps and the 46th Division would take part in this movement, while six other divisions were dispersed to the four winds.

Eventually Army Groups "A" and "B", which had had 68 divisions on June 28, had no more than 57 on August 1. It is true that List and Weichs then had 36 satellite divisions instead of the initial 26, but it must be re-emphasised that these were not capable of taking the offensive. With reduced forces–besides the usual wastage from battle casualties–List and Weichs saw their two fronts lengthening inordinately before them:

500 miles on June 28;
750 miles on July 25, after reaching the Voronezh – Tsimlyansk – Rostov line;
Over 2,500 miles, after reaching their final objectives, along the line Voronezh – Stalingrad – Astrakhan' – Baku – Tbilisi – Batumi – Kerch' Strait.

Even subtracting 1,100 miles of coast from the last figure, the remaining 1,400 miles suffice to show that the July 23 directive was the product of megalomania, of a sick mind.

What would have happened if the Führer had stuck to the April 5 plans? Without going as far as saying that he would have taken Stalingrad in his stride, one can draw up the list of the opposing forces that clashed on July 22 at the great bend of the Don, between Kletskaya in the north and Verkhne-Kumskiy in the south, over a 130-mile front:

1. On the German side, six Panzer and three motorised divisions from the 4th *Panzerarmee* and the 6th Army, followed by the best German infantry divisions.
2. On the Russian side, the 61st and 62nd Armies of the Stalingrad Front, which, on July 12, came under the orders of Marshal Timoshenko on the South-West Front.

According to the *Great Patriotic War*, on July 22 the 62nd Army had six divisions in the line and the 64th only two; three more were moving up quickly by forced marches. But in the open plains 11 divisions extended over 130 miles could provide no more than an unsubstantial piecemeal defence. Also, the successive defeats sustained by the Red Army from the fall of Kerch' to the capture of Rostov had been a severe blow to morale, and a certain defeatism seemed to be gaining ground in its ranks. Soviet historians have been very discreet about this crisis, which reached its height about July 25. But it was serious enough for Stalin to issue his order of the day of July 28, of which the most important passages are reproduced below, as published in A. M. Samsonov's work on the Stalingrad campaign. Summing up 13 months of war, Stalin wrote:

"Since the loss of the Ukraine, White Russia, the Baltic States, the Donets basin and other areas, our territory is decidedly smaller at present, and so any reserves of men, grain, metal, and factories are much weaker. We have lost 70 million inhabitants and an annual production of 13 million tons of grain and 10 million tons of metal. We have now lost our superiority in reserves of manpower and cereals. To continue to retreat is to give up ourselves and our country for lost.

"Every inch of territory we concede strengthens the enemy and weakens the defence of our country. We must oppose pitilessly the view that we can retreat indefinitely because our country is rich and large, our population immense, and our grain always abundant. Such statements are untrue and harmful; they weaken us and strengthen the enemy, since if we do not stop the retreat we shall be left with no grain, fuel, metal, raw materials, workshops, factories, or railways. Therefore the moment has come to stop the retreat: not another step back! This must be our watchword. Every position and every yard of Soviet territory must be defended tenaciously and to the last drop of our blood. We must hang on to every piece of Soviet land, and defend it at all costs."

Stalin spoke of the satisfactory progress of Soviet war production and Hitler's mounting difficulties as he tried to achieve his objectives. He continued:

"What do we need? Order and discipline in our companies, battalions, regiments, divisions, armoured units, and air force squadrons. This is our greatest weakness. If we want to defend and save our country we must impose much stricter discipline and order in the army. Cowards and panic-mongers will be executed on the spot. Henceforth every commander, soldier, and political officer must be subject to iron discipline. Not a step back unless ordered by the supreme commander!"

Perhaps Stalin wanted his subordinates to be blamed for the grim consequences of his own mistaken conduct of the operations. In any case, at the same time there was a whole series of changes and reshuffles of commands, both at front and at army level, which could indicate only a certain disarray amongst the generals.

Whatever the weakness of the Soviet forces barring his way to Stalingrad, Field-Marshal von Weichs, as a result of the July 23 directive, had only the 6th Army to break through them. But even this was not complete since Paulus was waiting for the Italian 8th Army (General Gariboldi) to extend the line from the Hungarian 2nd Army (General Jany) on the Don, and meanwhile had to cover his flank with his own forces. Again, fuel was in short supply and he could not use all his armour at once. This explains his slow progress from the bridgehead he had taken on July 20 at Bokovskaya on the Chir. On July 30 Hitler returned the 4th *Panzerarmee* to Army Group "B", but

Hoth, on receiving his new orders, was over 90 miles to the south-west of Tsimlyansk, and his orders were to move towards Stalingrad by the left bank of the Don.

On August 4 the 6th Army was nevertheless at Kalach at the top of the river bend, but the Russian 1st Tank Army (Major-General K. S. Moskalenko) got across the river and put up a stubborn resistance which lasted a week. Paulus finally overcame it with a pincer movement. His XIV Panzer Corps (General G. von Wietersheim) pushed from north to south to meet the XXIV Panzer Corps (General W. von Langermann und Erlenkamp) in the enemy's rear. A brilliant success, but the 6th Army was not able to exploit it until August 21.

On that day LI Corps, magnificently supported by *Luftflotte* IV and with insignificant casualties, established two bridgeheads on the eastern bank of the Don, upstream of Kalach. On the evening of August 23 the 16th Panzer Division, leading the XIV Panzer Corps, arrived at Rynok on the west bank of the Volga after a thrust of over 30 miles. Wietersheim was counter-attacked furiously from north and south and wanted to retreat. Consequently he received the order to hand over his corps to Lieutenant-General Hube, commander of the 16th Panzer Division. A well-timed action by VIII Corps (General W. Heitz) relieved XIV Panzer Corps and made a defensive front

The advance to Stalingrad, summer 1942.

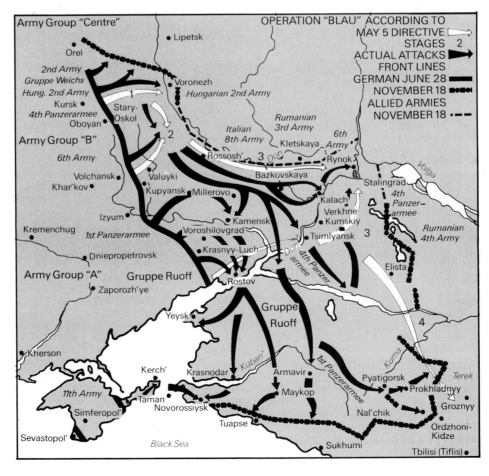

possible between the Don and the Volga upstream from Stalingrad. LI Corps followed up its success towards the south-east, which allowed Paulus to combine his operations with Hoth's.

Making for the bend in the Volga by way of the left bank of the Don, Hoth had been reduced to six divisions, of which one was armoured and one motorised. It is not surprising therefore that with such slender resources he was stopped at the exit from Abganerovo on August 10. As Army Group "B" had no reserves it was up to Paulus to help them out, and he transferred his 297th Division and 24th Panzer Division. This was made possible by his success at Kalach. This reinforcement meant that the 4th *Panzerarmee* could renew the attack on Tinguta, but it was not enough for them to reach the heights overlooking the Volga downstream from Stalingrad. Failing further reinforcements, Hoth switched XLVIII Panzer Corps from his right to his left and pushed it due north. On September 2 he made contact with the 6th Army's right at Voroponvo.

In his attack orders on August 19, Colonel-General Paulus assigned the objective of the south and centre of Stalingrad to LI Corps, and the northern districts to XIV Panzer Corps. The latter could spare only a fraction of its forces for this task because, with VIII Corps, it had to cover the 6th Army in the Volga-Don isthmus. It was not appreciated that this town, which then had 445,000 inhabitants, extended over 20 miles along the Volga and that, in places, there were five miles between the river banks and the western edge of the town.

This makeshift attack could only succeed if it met an enemy which was not only beaten but whose morale was extremely low. From the very first engagements in the streets of Stalingrad it was clear to the Germans that the Russians had recovered beyond anyone's expectations, and that the Russians' slogan "The Volga has only one bank" was no empty boast. On September 16 Colonel-General von Richthofen, now commander of *Luftflotte* IV, complaining of the lack of spirit in the 6th Army, wrote in his diary: "With a little enthusiastic effort, the town should fall in two days." Less than a week later, he noted, more justly: "September 22. In the town itself progress is desperately slow. The 6th Army will never finish the job at this rate. Above all because it is threatened from the north by the Russians and because reinforcements arrive only in dribs and drabs. We have to fight endless engagements, taking one cellar after another in order to gain any ground at all."

At the same time, in the Caucasus, Army Group "A"'s offensive reached what Clausewitz called a falling-off point, beyond which wear and tear take over from the initial drive and energy.

The day after the fall of Rostov, Field-Marshal List's only worries were about supplies. It was impossible to satisfy the needs of 26 advancing divisions, some moving south-west, some south, and some south-east—so much so that Colonel-General von Kleist jested: "No Russians in front of us; no supplies behind us!" Jerricans of petrol dropped from Junkers Ju 52 transports had to be brought to the Panzers by camel transport.

In spite of these logistic difficulties *Gruppe* Ruoff (German 17th Army and Rumanian 3rd Army) occupied simultaneously on August 9 the port of Yeysk on the south bank of the Sea of Azov, Krasnodar on the Kuban', and Maykop (whose oil wells had been so thoroughly sabotaged that they were not in operation again until four years after the war). On the same day the 1st *Panzerarmee* took Pyatigorsk at the bottom of the first foothills of the Caucasus; on its left, the 16th Motorised Division positioned itself at Elista in the centre of the Kalmuk Steppe and sent out patrols towards Astrakhan'. On August 21 a combined detachment (to avoid jealousies) of the 1st and 4th *Gebirgsjäger* Divisions scaled Mount El'brus (over 17,000 feet), while at the end of the month Kleist crossed the Terek not far from Prokhladnyy, some 80 miles from the Groznyy oil wells.

It is true that the nearer they got to their respective objectives (Batumi and Baku), the more List's two groups became separated, and thus found themselves unable to co-ordinate their operations. In addition, Ruoff's outflanking movements over the mountains, intended to overcome resistance on the coast, became increasingly difficult as he moved south-east. On September 6 he succeeded in taking Novorossiysk, but he then had to reorganise his forces before tackling Tuapse.

Irritated by this lack of progress, Hitler blamed the local commanders. He therefore sent Colonel-General Jodl to Field-Marshal List to put matters right. But however loyal he was to his leader, Jodl knew his job, and when he was fully in the picture he approved the decisions taken by the Army Group "A"'s commander. On his return to Vinnitsa he made his report accordingly, but could not prevent the dismissal of List, who left his Krasnodar H.Q. on September 9. Moreover, Hitler was so furious with the report that Jodle himself came very close to being ignominiously dismissed and replaced by Paulus. On September 24 Colonel-General Franz Halder had to hand over to General of Armoured Troops Kurt Zeitzler.

The new Chief-of-Staff of O.K.H. was said to be a National Socialist. Whether or not this was the case, it should be noted that, formerly chief-of-staff of the *Panzergruppe* von Kleist in 1940 and 1941, and then of the 1st *Panzerarmee*, he had only been appointed to this second post on March 15, 1942. On the same day he had moved to France with Field-Marshal von Rundstedt to become chief-of-staff of the latter's Army Group "D" at its headquarters in Saint Germain-en-Laye. He had thus been able to follow only from afar the disappointing progress of the second German summer offensive, and was not in a position to appraise the causes of its undeniable breakdown. Hitler was therefore able to do just as he pleased with him, whereas Halder had for a long time kept out of his reach.

The Führer not only removed his Chief of General Staff; he also did not appoint a successor to List but proposed himself to direct operations on the Caucasus front. But all the genius and dynamism he credited himself with were unable to improve their progress. This was hardly surprising. Army Group "A" had had to reassign 4th *Panzerarmee* to Army Group "B" and had not received the promised 11th Army, and so was reduced to 20 divisions. Fifteen of these were exhausted German troops, there were only 300 tanks, and the campaigning season was rapidly drawing to an end on the slopes of the Caucasus . . .

At the headquarters of the Soviet 62nd Army (Lieutenant-General V. I. Chuikov), defending Stalingrad, the officer who kept the army's war diary made the following entries on September 14, 1942:

"0730: the enemy has reached Academy Street.

0740: 1st Battalion 38th Mechanised Brigade is cut off from our main forces.

0750: fighting has flared up in the sector of Matveyev-Kurgan hill and in the streets leading to the station.

0800: the station is in enemy hands.

0840: the station is in our hands.

0940: the station has been retaken by the enemy.

1040: the enemy has reached Pushkin Street, 500 yards from the Army's Battle Headquarters.

1100: two regiments of infantry supported by 30 tanks are moving towards the Technical Institution."

These brief notes, taken from the *Great Patriotic War*, are sufficient without further comment to show how bitter was the struggle between the Russians and the Germans, first in the streets, then in the ruins of Stalingrad. This struggle was now a grim conflict indeed.

On September 14, weakened by the battles in the great curve of the Don, the 62nd Army had only 50,000 fighting men left. On the following night, however, a Regiment of the 13th Guards Division was sent hurriedly across the Volga in reinforcement and this enabled Lieutenant-General Chuikov to retake Matveyev-Kurgan hill. On September 17 more men, an infantry brigade, and an armoured brigade also crossed the river on ferries to take part in the defence of Stalingrad.

These reinforcements did not, however, prevent the German 6th Army, powerfully supported by *Luftflotte* IV, from scoring victories. By September 20 they had reached the banks of the Volga, slightly downstream of the station which they had finally occupied. This cut off the 62nd Army on its left from the 64th (Major-General M. S. Shumilov), and trapped it against the river for some 15 miles.

There is no doubt that in the battle for Stalingrad, Paulus had numerical and *matériel* superiority, but if he could not take advantage of it as he did on the Don, it was because the nature of the street fighting deprived him of most of the advantages of his tanks and planes. In his memoirs, Chuikov, later a Marshal, gives a clear indication of this: success "did not depend on strength, but on ability, skill, daring, guile. Buildings split up enemy formations like breakwaters, forcing them to follow the line of the streets. That is why we clung to the most solid ones, with small units capable of all-round defence. These buildings allowed us to set up centres of resistance from which the defenders mowed down the Nazis with their automatic weapons."

In this connection it must be recalled that the Russians had followed more closely than the Germans the fighting between the Spanish Nationalists and Republicans in December 1936 in the outer suburbs and, especially, the University City in Madrid. Experience had shown that large, modern concrete buildings were all but proof against medium artillery fire. And there were many such buildings in Stalingrad, especially large factory buildings, of which Marshal Chuikov said that their "solid construction in metal and concrete and the development of their underground installations allowed prolonged and bitter resistance".

At the request of Paulus, Colonel-General von Richthofen, the commander of *Luftflotte* IV, strove to make up for the lack of artillery by heavy bombing. But the only effect of this was to create enormous amounts of rubble in the streets, which prevented the use of armour, and the German engineers of the time had no bulldozers to clear such rubble away under enemy fire. This was the lesson of experience, but let us note in passing that the Western Allies made the same mistakes both at Cassino and in Normandy.

The German tanks themselves were split up into units of some 15 to 20, but these were prevented from using the range of their guns in the streets, whereas the Russians, in attic windows, cellars, and manholes were able to attack them at a range of a few yards with Molotov cocktails, anti-tank grenades, and 14.5-mm anti-tank rifles, which would have been no good in open country.

The German infantry, moreover, was no better off than its comrades in the Panzers for, Chuikov writes, "the defenders of Stalingrad let the tanks come within range of their guns and anti-tank rifles, and this, at the same time, kept the infantry away from the tanks so that the enemy's normal order of battle was upset. The infantry were wiped out separately as the tanks went ahead of them. And without infantry the tanks were not much good on their own: they were stopped and suffered heavy losses when they pulled back."

In street fighting, rifles, machine guns, and sub-machine guns came into their own, but mention must also be made of the marksmen who, with their semi-automatic rifles fitted with telescopic sights, decimated German detachments.

Hitler's directive of April 5, 1942 had left open the question as to whether Stalingrad should be taken or whether Germany should be content with wiping it out as a centre of war production and of communications. Did Hitler see in Stalingrad a symbol? Or did the elimination of this Soviet bridgehead on the west bank of the Volga seem to him necessary for the successful outcome of the operations then taking place in the Caucasus? We do not know. What is certain, however, is that Paulus received an unequivocal order to complete the conquest of the city at whatever cost. To help him, five battalions of sappers were dispatched to him by air.

This gave new impetus to the attack, whilst increased support was given by the Stukas of the Luftflotte's VIII *Fliegerkorps*. The Orlovka salient was reduced and then, on a front of only two and a half miles, the 94th and 389th infantry, the 100th Jäger and the 14th and 24th Panzer Divisions hurled themselves on to the great industrial complexes known as the "Dzerzinsky" and the "Barricades" on October 14. For the 62nd Army this was a day of crises and severe tests, as its war diary shows:

"0800: enemy attack with tanks and infantry. Battle raging over whole front.

0930: enemy attack on Tractor Factory repulsed. Ten tanks on fire in factory yard.

1000: tanks and infantry crush the 109th Regiment of the 37th Division (Major-General Zheludov).

1130: left flank of 524th Infantry Regiment of the 95th Division smashed in. Some 50 tanks are rolling up the Regiment's positions.

1150: enemy has occupied stadium at Tractor Factory. Our units cut off inside and fighting their way out.

1200: commander of 117th Regiment, Guards Major Andreyev, killed.

1220: radio message from unit of 416th Regiment from hexagonal block of flats: 'Surrounded; have water and cartridges; will die rather than surrender.'

1230: Stukas attack General Zheludov's H.Q. General in his collapsed shelter without communications. We are liaising with elements of his Division.

1310: two shelters collapse at Army H.Q. An officer trapped by legs in rubble. Can't free him.

1525: Army H.Q. guard now fighting in battle.

1635: Lieutenant-Colonel Ustinov, commanding infantry regiment, asks for artillery fire on his H.Q. He is surrounded by enemy with sub-machine guns."

From the opposing side, Major Grams offers us confirmation of the terrible battles of October, in which he took part as

General Chuikov with his staff officers in an underground command post.

commander of a motorised battalion in the 14th Panzer Division. In his history of this famous unit he writes: "It was an appalling and exhausting battle at both ground level and underground in the ruins, the cellars, the drains of this large city. Man to man, hero to hero. Our tanks clambered over great mountains of rubble and plaster, their tracks screeching as they drove their way through ruined workshops, opening fire at point-blank range in narrow streets blocked by fallen masonry or in the narrow factory yards. Several of our armoured colossi shook visibly or blew up as they ran over mines."

The worst thing for the Germans to bear, according to Grams, was the fact that every night hundreds of ferries brought in reinforcements across the Volga and there was no way of stopping them. In fact, during the night of October 16–17, the Soviet 138th Division (Colonel I. I. Lyudnikov) arrived at a very opportune moment to bolster up the defence of the "Barricades" factory sector. LI Corps under General von Seydlitz had occupied the Tractor Factory itself, and had even reached the river bank but, faced with the Russians' continuous and insurmountable resistance, their attacks petered out, as previous ones had done.

Meanwhile Hitler, who was in Munich to celebrate the eighteenth anniversary of the abortive 1923 *Putsch* among the faithful, considered the battle for Stalingrad, and with it the war in Russia, as won. "I wished," he shouted in his raucous voice,

A Soviet 76-mm gun in action in the streets of Stalingrad in autumn 1942.

"to get to the Volga and at a certain time and a certain place. It happens to be named after Stalin himself. But do not think that that is why I directed our efforts against it; it could have had quite a different name. No. It is because this is a particularly important place. This is where 30 million tons of traffic comes to be sorted out, including some nine million tons of petrol. This is where all the cereals from the huge regions of the Ukraine and the Kuban' pass through on their way to the north. This is where manganese ore is sent. This is where there are huge transshipment facilities. I wanted to take it and let me tell you, for we are modest, we have it!" This message had more effect on the party members crowded into the Munich Beer Cellar than on the fighters on the Stalingrad front. They knew what the real truth was, and it was them Hitler now told to "finish it off". It also shows that the Führer did not know – or pretended not to know – about the railway linking Astrakhan' and Saratov, bypassing Stalingrad and the Volga's great western bend.

Yet on November 11, the German LI Corps, still fighting in the breach, renewed its assaults with armour and sappers; at the cost of incredible effort it succeeded in isolating from the rest of the Russian 62nd Army the defenders of the "Barricades", whose courage still remained steadfast, and in overrunning the workers' quarters attached to the "Red October" factory. They got inside the factory itself, but then the attack ground to a halt. The 6th Army had worn itself out: its infantry companies were down to 80 or even 60 men, and the three divisions of its XIV Panzer Corps had only 199 tanks left

of which many were inferior Czech types. The situation on the other side had also worsened considerably. On the west bank of the Volga the Russian 62nd Army only had 300 to 1,000 yards behind it. The river was beginning to bring down icefloes large enough to prevent supplies or reinforcements from crossing. The fact still remains, however, that by now Chuikov knew secretly that he had won a sufficient margin of time, albeit a small one, for Russia, and that within ten days or so the enemy would have something else to think about.

Some of the famous units of the Red Army which distinguished themselves in the defence of Stalingrad have already been mentioned. To these must also be added the 112th and the 308th Divisions, commanded respectively by Colonels I. Zh. Ermolkin and L. N. Gurtiev. Mindful of the soldier in the front line, we quote the tribute to this gigantic struggle by Marshal Eremenko, then in command of the Stalingrad Front.

"The epic of Stalingrad brought out particularly the high and noble qualities of the Soviet people and their heroic army: fervent patriotism, devotion to the Communist cause, fighting comradeship between soldiers of all nationalities, inflexible courage and self-sacrifice, unshakable firmness in defence, forceful bravery in attack, constant liaison and unfailing help between the front and rear areas, brotherhood between soldiers and workers in the factories and the fields. The heroic spirit which has breathed over Stalingrad has borne illustrious testimony to the power of the great Communist Party to guide and inspire our lives and to adapt itself to every circumstance, trustee as it is of the eternal ideas of Lenin."

It will be recalled that Hitler had assumed direct command of Army Group "A" in the Caucasus on September 10. Reduced

to some 20 divisions since the transfer of the 4th *Panzerarmee* to Army Group "B", the Germans ended up in late autumn by failing at their last objectives also, just as Stalin had forecast to Winston Churchill. In the Black Sea area, autumn was drawing in and *Gruppe* Ruoff had not got beyond the foothills of the Caucasus. It was thus unable to complete that encircling movement which the Führer had calculated would have given him at best the ports of Tuapse and Sukhumi. The defenders were helped by the forests, the altitude, the rain, and then the snow, all of which showed up the lack of training of the German mountain troops who, however, had been driven very hard. Colonel-General von Kleist had reached Prokhladnyy on the River Terek, which flows out into the Caspian, on August 27. He was no luckier than the others. Held some 50 miles from the Groznyy oilfields, he rallied his III Panzer Corps (General von Mackensen) and swung his attack upstream. This seems to have caught the defence by surprise and he took Nal'chik on October 25 and Alagir on November 5 but failed at Orzhonikidze as he was crossing the Terek. Worse still, this finger that he had rashly thrust into the enemy's positions was all but cut off in counter-attacks, and he nearly lost his 13th Panzer Division. Though it escaped, its near loss put an end to the 1st *Panzerarmee*'s offensive for good and all.

The North Caucasus and the Trans-Caucasus Fronts were now being reinforced week by week, so that on about November 15 the 22 Axis divisions (15 German, six Rumanian, and one Slovak) were opposed by almost 90 major formations, including 37 infantry and eight or nine cavalry divisions, and eight armoured brigades. The tide was about to turn on Germany's effort to secure Caucasian oil.

CHAPTER 37

The annihilation of the Sixth Army

During their conversations in August, Stalin had told Winston Churchill that he intended to launch a great offensive as winter approached. So during the first fortnight in September Colonel-General A. M. Vasilevsky, replacing the sick Marshal Shaposhnikov as Chief-of-Staff, and his colleague General N. N. Voronov, head of the Red Army's artillery, were sent to the banks of the Volga to deal with the situation. When they returned to *Stavka* it was decided that the forthcoming operation should be in the hands of General G. K. Zhukov. It was expected to engage several Fronts or army groups. Colonel-General Eremenko then had to be relieved of some of his large command, on the South-East and Stalingrad Fronts. The former was renamed the Stalingrad Front and remained under his control; the second became the Don Front, under the command of Lieutenant-General K. K. Rokossovsky.

By the beginning of September 1942 the Soviet Supreme Command saw that the German reserves were becoming exhausted. They knew that the time had come when they could launch a major counter-attack against their opponents.

Zhukov and Vasilevsky discussed these questions with *Stavka*, and they went to the Volga Front to judge the situation for themselves before drawing up a plan for a counter-offensive against the Axis forces. They were told to keep the purpose of their visit secret. At Stalingrad Zhukov ascertained the 6th Army's strength and calculated the numbers of men, tanks and guns the Russians would require for a successful offensive. He also reconnoitred the bridgeheads held by the Russian forces to the south of the River Don at Kletskaya and Serafimovich. Vasilevsky went to the south of Stalingrad to see sectors of the front held by the Russian 51st and 57th Armies between Krasnoarmeysk and Lake Barmantsak. On their return to Moscow *Stavka* invited the General Staff's Operations Directorate to help them to work out the details of a practical plan. *Stavka* took a direct control of the two new fronts (Staligrad and Don) which were to conduct the counter-attack. By the end of the month they approved the plan and the General Staff were engaged in working out the operational details. Vasilevsky commanded the Stalingrad Front and Zhukov was given charge of the Don Front and the newly created South-West Front. The attack was to consist of a concentric movement north and south of Stalingrad against the thinly held flanks of the 6th Army, the Rumanian 3rd and 4th Armies and the underequipped 4th Panzer Army. The attack would then link up to the west of Stalingrad, thus trapping the 6th Army and destroying it. By the second half of October the plans were complete for this attack on a 250-mile front.

When these decisions had been taken, the next step was to transport men and *matériel* to their concentration areas. The 5th Tank Army (Lieutenant-General P. L. Romanenko) was recalled from the Bryansk Front to become the spearhead of Vatutin's attack. IV Mechanised Corps (Major-General A. G. Kravchenko) and XIII Mechanised Corps (Major-General Tanichikhin) occupied the lake area under strict camouflage precautions as part of Eremenko's front.

In view of the decisive result expected from the campaign, *Stavka* did not hesitate to call upon half its reserve of artillery. Vatutin, Rokossovsky, and Eremenko thus got an additional 75 artillery regiments, bringing their total up to 230, or 13,540 guns and mortars. They were also sent 115 *Katyusha* batteries, with a total of 10,000 launchers. Two air armies were sent to the South-West Front and one each to the Don and Stalingrad Fronts, so that the three fronts had a total of 1,000 planes, including 600 fighters, to call on. This weight of equipment was to batter a hole in the thinly-held German fronts.

These troop and equipment movements were usually carried out at night and the strictest orders were given to preserve secrecy. This was also secured by manoeuvres designed to deceive the enemy. Radio operators on the Bryansk Front, for instance, continued to transmit messages for the benefit of enemy listening-posts long after the troops had left the area, and did not rejoin their units on the Don Front until the very last moment.

Can we conclude with Marshal Eremenko that if the German Supreme Command admitted the likelihood of a Russian counter-attack, "it still did not know precisely where or when it would take place"? Eremenko was no doubt basing his opinion on the authority of Colonel-General Jodl, who is said to have declared after the capitulation of the Third Reich: "We had no idea of the gigantic concentrations of Russian forces on the flank of the 6th Army. We did not know in what strength the Soviet troops were massing in this sector. Shortly before the attacks, there was nothing there and suddenly we were struck a massive blow, a blow which was to have far-reaching, even fatal, consequences."

We should remember, however, that at O.K.W. Jodl enjoyed only a partial view of the Eastern Front. From mid-October, both in the German 6th Army and the Rumanian 3rd Army, there was constant concern about enemy activity in the bridgeheads he controlled and on the right bank of the Don in the areas of Kletskaya and Serafimovich. Similar signs of movement had been noticed in the sector of the 4th *Panzerarmee*, which extended the right flank of the 6th Army, and Colonel-General Paulus deduced that the enemy was preparing some pincer movement which would be all the more dangerous for the Germans as the Ru-

German soldiers advance through the power station in Stalingrad.

311

manians on the flank were very poorly equipped with anti-tank weapons. · He therefore strengthened his left flank by bringing over the Don the armoured units of his 14th Panzer Division into General Strecker's XI Corps, but he could do no more as he had the strictest orders from Hitler to hold Stalingrad at all costs.

Paulus naturally informed Colonel-General von Weichs, commanding Army Group "B", of the way he thought things were going and Weichs passed this on, together with his own appreciation of the situation, to O.K.H. Here General Zeitzler was sufficiently impressed to propose to Hitler that the attack on Stalingrad should be abandoned and the German 6th Army brought back into the great loop of the Don, whilst the 4th *Panzerarmee* blocked the Stalingrad–Novorossiysk railway opposite Kotel'nikovo.

Hitler, however, came out with another solution. This was recorded in the O.K.W. diary, then being kept by the historian Helmuth Creiner. The entry for October 26 reads: "The Führer again expresses his concern over a large Soviet attack, perhaps a winter offensive starting in the sector held by our allied armies on the Don and aimed at Rostov. This concern is based on strong troop movements ob-

served in the area and on the number of bridges the Russians have thrown over the river. The Führer orders each of the three allied armies to be stiffened with fighting divisions from the Luftwaffe. This will allow a number of divisions to be withdrawn from the front and, together with other units to be sent to the area, these will build up a reserve behind our allied armies."

This text, the authenticity of which is beyond doubt, is interesting from more than one point of view. First of all it shows that, contrary to what Marshal Eremenko says in his pamphlet against the German generals, O.K.H.'s new Chief-of-Staff had adopted the conclusions reached by Paulus and Weichs and had brought them to the knowledge of the Führer. Especially, however, it shows Hitler's favoured form of reasoning: he discards the approved method which, piecing together information received, consists in asking: "what are the possibilities for the enemy?" to ask the questions such as one might hear at a café-table discussion: "wherein lies the enemy's greatest advantage?" or again: "what would I have done if I had been Stalin?" Now an attack towards Rostov was markedly more advantageous to the Russians than the pincer movement adopted by *Stavka* since, when it had

Russian soldiers counterattack in the snow-covered ruins of the city centre.

reached its objective, it would have meant the destruction not only of five of Weichs' seven armies, but also of the whole of Army Group "A" right down in the Caucasus. If Stalin had been Hitler he might have adopted this risky solution, but he was not and went for prudence.

The Rostov hypothesis, however, meant that the Italian 8th Army had to be strengthened. This would take the first brunt of any attack in this direction. It was reinforced by the XLVIII Panzer Corps under its recently-appointed commander, Lieutenant-General F. Heim. A few days later Hitler, no doubt on the receipt of further information, seems to have been converted as a very last extreme to Zeitzler's view. It is a fact that on November 16, that is on D-day minus three, XLVIII Panzer Corps received the order to move from Boguchar to Perelazovskiy in the area behind the Rumanian 3rd Army. These two places are 110 miles apart. Too late! We must therefore conclude that, if we accept Marshal Eremenko's view that "Hitler's command" was caught out by the event, this really meant only the Hitler-Keitel-Jodl trinity.

"How many divisions has the Pope?" Everyone knows this question, put by Stalin to one of his western visitors. But if, 30 years after the event, we ask the authors of Volume III of the *Great Patriotic War* how many divisions Stalin threw into the Stalingrad counter-offensive on the dates indicated, we have to state that no precise reply is obtainable, whereas we know down to regimental level the order of battle of Army Group "B" for November 15, 1942. On that day, in his headquarters at Star'obel'sk Colonel-General von Weichs held a front from Elista in the Kalmuk Steppe to Kursk, a distance of 710 miles, with 80 divisions, four of which were for the protection of his rear areas, the other 76 being fighting units. The latter were divided into types and nationalities as follows:

	Inf.	Cav.	Mot'd	Arm'd	Total
German	31	–	4	5	40
Italian	6	1	2	–	9
Rumanian	13	4	–	1	18
Hungarian	8	–	–	1	9
Total	58	5	6	7	76

The fact remains, it is true, that on November 19 and 20 the Soviet pincers bit into only seven German and 15 Rumanian divisions from the 4th *Panzerarmee*, XI Corps (6th Army), XLVIII Panzer Corps, and the Rumanian 3rd and 4th Armies. On the same dates Generals Vatutin, Rokossovsky, and Eremenko were able to deploy over a million men, divided into nine armies, which had 66 rifle divisions, five tank corps, and a mechanised corps: a comfortable superiority.

The same superiority was apparent in *matériel*. According to the *Great Patriotic War* the following was the picture on the Don battlefield and on the Steppe:

	Russians	Axis	Ratio
Armoured vehicles	894	675	1.3:1
Guns and mortars	13,540	10,300	1.3:1
Aircraft	1,115	1,216	1:1

These figures cannot be accepted, however. According to an entry in the O.K.W. war diary dated November 6, 1942, out of 1,134 Luftwaffe aircraft available over the whole front, *Luftflotte* IV disposed of only 600 which, moreover, had to meet the demands of both Army Group "A" and Army Group "B". As for tanks, the 6th Army's XIV Panzer Corps was reduced to 199 on the day the battle started, as we have seen, and on the day it arrived on the scene XLVIII Panzer Corps only had 84. When we add to these a handful of tanks the 27th Panzer Division and the Hungarian 1st Armoured Division, both of them units in the course of formation, we have scarcely reached the half of the Soviet historian's figure. Moreover, this figure cannot have taken into account the fact that the Panzers included a high proportion of Czech Pzkw 38(t)'s, whose obsolete 37-mm guns had no effect on the thick plating of the T-34's and KV-1's now making up the major part of the Red Army's armoured formations.

Even before the start of the battle which was to bring about the final destruction of his army group, Colonel-General von Weichs was not optimistic about the outcome after the adverse reports of his Intelligence units. On the preceding October 10, the Rumanian 3rd Army (General Dumitrescu) had taken up positions between the left flank of the German 6th Army and the right flank of the Italian 8th Army (General Garibaldi). This was in execution of the directive of April. 5, which laid down that the Don front should be defended by the satellite powers.

But between the right flank of the Rumanian 3rd Army, which adjoined the left flank of the German 6th Army, and the left flank of the Hungarian 2nd Army (Colonel-General Jany) which adjoined the German 2nd Army, the Don front was some 310 miles long. The three satellite armies which were being asked to defend it had between them some 30 divisions. All of them were somewhat weak in infantry, lacking in mobility and, especially, very badly equipped both qualitatively and quantitatively to meet armoured attack. The Rumanian 3rd Army was particularly badly situated as it faced the two bridgeheads at Kletskaya and Serafimovich, where the Russians had held out in the previous summer against all attacks and, without being able to take advantage of the river obstacle, the Rumanian battalions each had an average front of over three miles.

Marshal Antonescu, the Rumanian dictator, had not failed to draw Hitler's attention to the extreme danger of the situation. In particular he had asked Hitler for 5-cm anti-tank guns to replace the earlier 3.7-cm weapons with which the Rumanians were equipped and which were recognised as completely obsolete. The Führer had promised to supply these without delay, but his promise remained empty words and a catastrophe became inevitable. Army Group "B" was thus in a position of "pre-rupture".

The position was further blackened by the fact that the strategic reserves available to Weichs consisted of only four divisions, two German infantry divisions, and the two armoured divisions of the XLVIII Panzer Corps. One of these two, however, the Rumanian 1st Armoured Division (Radu) had never been in action, and both were under strength.

The operation, under Zhukov's overall command, had been baptised "Uranus" in Moscow and was launched in two phases.

At 0730 hours on November 19, after a general rocket barrage the artillery of the South-West and the Don Fronts opened up on the German-Rumanian positions north-west of Stalingrad with about 90 guns per mile of front. According to the Russians, the density of this concentration was made less effective by a thick fog. Be that as it may, the entire telephone network of the Rumanian 3rd Army was put out of action as the wires were cut by the shelling. The fog also

helped the surprise effect. At 0848 the Soviet barrage moved forward, and infantry and tanks flung themselves into the assault.

On the South-West Front, the 5th Tank Army (Lieutenant-General P. L. Romanenko) had as its task the annihilation of the Rumanian defence facing the Serafimovich bridgehead, but it met such resistance that its commander had to use up in the breakthrough some of the tanks he had planned to hold back for exploitation of the breach. But then the defence collapsed. At nightfall, two Soviet tank corps, protected on their flanks by corps of cavalry, broke through the breach and poured into the enemy's rear, causing fearful panic.

Further to the east, the Soviet 21st Army broke out of the Kletskaya bridgehead on a front of nearly nine miles. Under the command of Major-General I. M. Chistyakov, it also had to use its armoured forces to overcome the resistance of the Rumanians. By the end of the day it had had the same success as the 5th Tank Army. The Rumanian V Armoured Corps (General M. Lascar), which was holding out between Kletskaya and Serafimovich, saw that it was doomed to encirclement.

On the Don Front, the Soviet 65th Army (Lieutenant-General P. I. Batov), attacking from the Kletskaya bridgehead towards Vertyachiy, where the Germans had bridged the Don, was caught at a disadvantage in deep ravines. It also ran up against the XI Corps, which formed the left flank of the 6th Army, and was counterattacked furiously by the 14th Panzer Division. It was therefore able to make only modest advances. The 24th Army (Major-General I. V. Galanin), which had been ordered to advance along the left bank of the Don, was similarly held up. The 66th Army (Lieutenant-General A. S. Zhadov) was to make a diversion in the Don-Volga isthmus, stubbornly defended by the VIII Corps (General W. Heitz).

On the Axis side, the XLVIII Panzer Corps, on stand-by since dawn, rumbled off at 0930 hours towards Kletskaya, where it was thought that the main Russian effort was being made, with orders to engage it without worrying about the flanks. Towards 1100 hours, in the light of new information, General Heim was ordered to drive towards Serafimovich – a switch from north-east to north-west. In the fog this counter-order produced confusion, contact was lost, and both the 22nd Panzer Division (Major-General Rodt) and the Rumanian 1st Armoured Division ran blindly into the Soviet 5th Tank Army. In the evening Heim was surrounded and his troops were in a very bad way.

On November 20, to the south-west of Stalingrad, the second phase of the Soviet offensive opened under Colonel-General Eremenko, from a line Lake Tastsa–Lake Sarpa–Krasnoarmeysk, with the 64th 57th, and 51st Armies under the command respectively of Major-Generals M. S.

Shumilov, F. I. Tolbukhin and N. I. Trufanov. To exploit the expected breakthrough, Eremenko had put the XIII Mechanised Corps (Major-General T. I. Tanichikhin) under 57th Army, whilst the 51st Army had been given the IV Mechanised Corps and the IV Cavalry Corps (Major-Generals V. T. Volsky and T. T. Shapkin). On the other side, all Colonel-General Hoth had left of his former *Panzerarmee* was IV Corps (General E. Jaenecke), but he did have the Rumanian 4th Army, of which General C. A. Constantinescu was about to take over the command. He thus had seven infantry divisions (two of which were German), and two Rumanian cavalry divisions. He held in reserve the excellent 29th Motorised Division.

Delayed by fog, the attack started at 1000 hours, but by early afternoon the breakthrough had come in the sector of the Rumanian VI Corps whose 1st, 2nd, and 18th Divisions were virtually wiped out. The 29th Motorised Division tried to restore the situation and scored some early victories. But as the only unit capable of counter-attacking amidst the general rout, it soon had to abandon the positions it had won for fear of being surrounded. Eremenko was not long in letting loose his cavalry and mechanised units, and on the following day, at 1030 hours, IV Cavalry Corps galloped into the village of Abganerovo, a station on the Stalingrad–Novorossiysk railway line. A few minutes later Nikita Khruschev was on the scene, bringing congratulations and encouragement.

In the great sweep of the Don on this same November 20, Vatutin and Rokossovsky energetically exploited their successes of the day before. The former used his 5th Tank Army and the latter his IV Tank Corps (Major-General G. P. Kravchenko) and his III Guards Corps (Major-General I. A. Pliev). Meanwhile the 21st Army completed the encirclement of the Rumanian V Corps, which then turned south and fought with some tenacity.

But how could it face an attack by some 900 tanks and two cavalry corps? At dawn on November 20, at Perelazovskiy, the staff of the Rumanian II Corps was so taken by surprise that when the patrols of the XXVI Tank Corps (Major-General A. G. Rodin) reached their headquarters they found tables laden with maps and documents, cupboards open, keys in the locks of chests, teleprinters still connected, and officers' caps still hanging on their pegs. XLVIII Panzer Corps, as a result of a breakdown in radio communications, was out of touch with the Rumanian 1st Armoured Division, but managed to break out of the encirclement. In the evening of November 20 it would have obeyed Weichs' order to retreat had it not had, through a *Führerbefehl*, the overriding order to extricate the Rumanian V Corps. This was an impossible task, and once again XLVIII Corps was surrounded. Yet it finally managed to reach the German lines, though at the cost of its 22nd

Panzer Division, which was reduced virtually to scrap.

The day of November 22 had not yet dawned before destiny had given her verdict. The night before, the Soviet XXVI Tank Corps, forming General Romanenko's left-hand column, was within striking distance of Kalach after covering over 62 miles in three days. The disorder had to be exploited at once and so General Rodin decided to take the bridge over the Don by surprise. He put under the command of Colonel Philippov of the 14th Motorised Brigade a detachment of two infantry companies. They were to advance behind five captured and restored German tanks each carrying 12 men armed with submachine guns. Rumbling forward with all their lights on, as the Germans did, Philippov's detachment overwhelmed the bridge guard then drove off the German counter-attacks. The defence was further confused by the shooting-match going on at the same time between the tanks of the 6th Army and those of the Soviets.

Meanwhile Eremenko had eagerly exploited his victory of November 20. Driving his IV Cavalry Corps along the railway from Kuban', he moved his IV Mechanised Corps north-west until at 1030 hours on November 23 it linked up with the IV Tank Corps from the Don Front in the village of Sovetskiy some 18–19 miles south east of Kalach. This completed the encirclement of the Axis troops in the Stalingrad area. The following day Khruschev came in person to congratulate Generals Volsky and Krav-

chenko and to enquire about the needs of the troops. This same day (November 24) saw the end of all Rumanian resistance in the Don pockets. The previous evening General Lascar, who had just been awarded the Iron Cross with Oak Leaves by Hitler, had had to surrender through lack of ammunition. On the 24th General Stenesco did the same and 33,000 Rumanians took the road to captivity.

Events of November 19 found Hitler at Berchtesgaden, whereas O.K.W. was in Salzburg and O.K.H. had for some weeks now been in East Prussia. The Führer's only contacts for three days were by telephone with Zeitzler, and his first reaction was to give command of Army Group "A" to Colonel-General von Kleist, which brought in its train the nomination to the command of the 1st *Panzerarmee* to General von Mackensen, the son of the famous Field-Marshal of World War I. On November 22, however, Hitler decided to go back to Rastenburg. He had already decided the fate of the 6th Army. When the news reached him that afternoon that it was encircled between the Don and the Volga he ordered, over the heads of Colonel-General von Weichs and General Zeitzler: "The 6th Army will take up a hedgehog position and await help from outside."

Operation "Uranus", the Soviet counter-attack at Stalingrad, November 19, 1942. The two thrusts linked up near Sovietskiy and trapped the 6th Army.

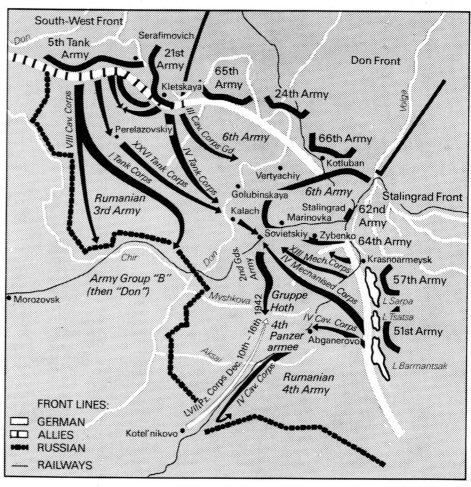

A Soviet rocket exploding in Colonel-General Paulus's headquarters could not have had a more staggering effect on the mind of the commander of the 6th Army than this *Führerbefehl*, revealing as it did its author's complete misunderstanding of the tragedy which he was at that moment living. He had just had to evacuate in haste his headquarters at Golubinskaya in the loop of the Don. After consulting four of his five corps commanders he appealed to the Führer in the evening of November 23 on the grounds that he was "better informed".

"Since receipt of your telegram of evening of November 22 events have developed very quickly here. Enemy has not yet succeeded in closing the gap to west and south-west. But his preparations for attack are becoming evident.

"Our ammunition and petrol supplies are running out. Several batteries and anti-tank units have none left. Supplies not expected to reach them in time.

"Army heading for disaster if it does not succeed, within very short time, in pulling together all its strength to deal knockout blow against enemy now assailing it in south and west.

"For this it is essential to withdraw all our divisions from Stalingrad and northern front. Inevitable consequence will be that army must be able to drive through in south-west, neither north nor east fronts being tenable after this withdrawal . . ."

At Star'obel'sk Colonel-General von Weichs was still linked to the 6th Army by a telephone line which had escaped the attention of the Russians. When he was told of Paulus's intentions, he vigorously supported them in a message to O.K.H.

"Fully conscious of the unusual seriousness and implication of the decision to be taken," he sent over the teléprinter, "it is my duty to advise you that I consider that the withdrawal of the 6th Army as suggested by General Paulus is necessary." He based his opinion both on the impossibility of supplying by air an army of 22 divisions and on the fact that the offensive needed to liberate the 6th Army could not possibly start before December 10 at the earliest. On the other hand, the fighting strength of the 6th Army seemed indispensable to him when it came to rebuilding a front and organising a counter-offensive. This strength had to be regained at all cost. With the help of this brief, which he energetically defended, Zeitzler did so well that at 0200 hours on November 24 he was able to assure the chief-of-staff of Army Group "B" that as soon as he awoke Hitler would sign the withdrawal order asked for by Paulus and recommended by Weichs.

The hours passed. But, instead of the expected confirmation, the radio at Star'obel'sk received a new *Führerbefehl* aimed directly at the 6th Army: "The 6th Army is temporarily surrounded by Russian forces. My intention is to concentrate it in the area north of Stalingrad – Kotluban – Hill 137 – Hill 135 – Marinovka – Zylenko – south of Stalingrad. The

Army must be persuaded that I shall do all in my power to supply it adequately and to disengage it when the time is convenient. I know the valiant 6th Army and its Commander-in-Chief and that every man will do his duty.

Signed: Adolf Hitler."

Shaken by the forceful argument of General Zeitzler, the Führer had been restored to vigour by the exuberant assurances of *Reichsmarschall* Hermann Göring. These were received in silence by Colonel-General Hans Jeschonnek but had the support of Field-Marshal Keitel and Colonel-General Jodl. The 6th Army reckoned that it needed 700 tons of supplies a day. This meant the necessary food, animal fodder, petrol, and ammunition to keep going, albeit at a reduced rate, 250,000 men, 8,000 horses, 1,800 guns, and 10,000 vehicles. With a carelessness that can only be called criminal, Göring undertook to assure them of 500 tons a day. He based this on the successful supply of the far smaller pockets at Kholm and Dem'yansk where, for five months from January 1942, 100,000 Germans had held out thanks to supplies from the air. But he was forgetting that:

1. the transport squadrons of the Luftwaffe were no better equipped in November 1942 than they had been the preceding winter;
2. the pocket whose maintenance he was guaranteeing would be 125–250 miles away, or three times the distance of Kholm and Dem'yansk from their supply airfields;
3. the Soviet Air Force, almost non-existent in the first quarter of 1942, had been considerably reinforced since then, particularly in fighters;
4. it would take time to assemble personnel and *matériel* on the bases to be used for this operation; and
5. with the onset of winter, the weather would deteriorate very rapidly.

Indeed, as Colonel-General von Richthofen, the man on the spot, had predicted from the outset, the supplying of the 6th Army by air was a complete and disastrous failure. In actual fact, from December 1 to 12 deliveries to the Stalingrad pocket amounted to an average of 97.3 tons of petrol and ammunition a day. From December 13 to 31 this increased by some 40 tons, then fell again as a consequence of the progressive deterioration of the strategic position and the weather. The average over the whole 70 days of the airlift was 91.16 tons a day, so that Göring's shortfall may be reckoned at 81 per cent. The loss of 488 planes, including 266 Junkers Ju 52's and 1,000 aircrew must also be included on the debit side. On the credit side, 25,000 sick and wounded were evacuated.

In the Stalingrad pocket, to which Paulus had transferred his headquarters, the *Führerbefehl* of November 23 had been the object of bitter argument at the highest level. General von Seydlitz (LI corps) held that it should be ignored as Hitler did not know the realities of the situation,

and that a breakout should be attempted along the line of the railway to Kuban'. Major-General Arthur Schmidt, chief-of-staff of the 6th Army, held the opposite view, both out of respect for orders and because he reckoned that the movement advised by the commander of LI Corps would end in catastrophe compounded by a complete breakdown of discipline. Paulus, though feeling little conviction, decided that his chief-of-staff was right. The German 6th Army thus dug itself into a pocket measuring some 37 miles between Stalingrad and its western perimeter and 25 miles from north to south. The day after the breakthrough at Lake Tsatsa, IV Corps had come under 6th Army command, though XI Corps, as it retreated across the Don after the surprise attack at Kalach, had taken with it the Rumanian 1st Cavalry Division. Paulus thus commanded five corps, in all 15 infantry divisions, three motorised divisions, three Panzer divisions, and one division of cavalry. These totalled some 278,000 men including the units left outside the pocket.

Hitler entrusted the mission of freeing the beleaguered troops in Stalingrad to Field-Marshal Erich von Manstein.

A few days after his victory at Sevastopol', the new Field-Marshal, with four divisions of his 11th Army and the great guns which had demolished the Soviets' emplacements, was transferred to Army Group "North" for, in spite of Halder's objections, Hitler had decided to seize Leningrad without waiting for a solution on the Stalingrad front. This offensive, called *"Nordlicht"*, never got started, as the Russians moved first and the 11th Army found itself from August 27 to October 2 using up its strength to bolster up a weakened 18th Army, which had given way, and then having to iron out the salients knocked into the front.

On November 21, when he was in Vitebsk, Manstein received the order to take over forthwith the command of a new army group, Army Group "Don", which would contain the 6th Army, *Gruppen* Hoth and Hollidt, and the Rumanian 3rd Army. Its task was defined as follows: "To arrest the enemy's attacks and to regain the ground lost since the beginning of his offensive."

On the 24th he was at the headquarters of Army Group "B", now reduced to the Italian 8th Army, the Hungarian 2nd Army, and the German 2nd Army. Colonel-General von Weichs informed him of the state in which he would find the units allotted to him. Now cut off, the German 6th Army had lost all freedom of movement. Along the line Stalingrad – Novorossiysk, *Gruppe* Hoth was, if the phrase may be permitted, no more than a strategic expression. Having lost its IV Corps and its 16th Motorised Division, immobilised on the Kalmuk Steppe by the express order of Hitler, the 4th *Panzerarmee* was reduced to a handful of Rumanian divisions which had escaped the *débâcle* of November 20. In the great loop of the Don, General Hollidt somehow improvised a defensive line behind the Chir so as to deny to the enemy the defence of the main river.

On November 26 Field-Marshal von Manstein set up his headquarters at Novocherkassk. On the 27th, 78 trains from France arrived in Kotel'nikovo station, 100 miles south-west of Stalingrad, bringing in the first units of the 6th Panzer Division (Major-General E. Raus). These were greeted by artillery fire and began their career on the Eastern Front by driving off the Soviet IV Cavalry Corps. This included a brigade of troops mounted on camels and recruited in Central Asia. Naturally enough, it was virtually wiped out.

Yet it was not before December 10 that the 4th *Panzerarmee*, part of *Gruppe* Hoth, was able to go over to the offensive. It was in fact reduced to nothing more than LVII Panzer Corps (General F. Kirchner), as the Rumanian VI and VII Corps could not be relied on. The 6th Panzer Division was soon up to its full strength with 160 tanks, a battalion of half-tracks, and 42 self-propelled guns. Not so the 23rd Panzer Division (Lieutenant-General von Boineburg-Lengsfeld) hurriedly brought up from the Caucasus, which went into action with only 20 tanks. These figures are important in view of the claims of Soviet historians that Manstein went into action in what they pompously call his "counter-offensive" with 460 armoured vehicles.

On December 12–13, LVII Panzer Corps nevertheless forced a crossing of the Aksai in spite of resistance from the Russian 51st Army of the Stalingrad Front. The valiant Eremenko thought this serious enough to appeal to Supreme Headquarters. "I reported it to J. V. Stalin," he wrote. "Alarmed by this information he sent a message 'Hold out. We will send you reserves immediately.' And he added 'Supreme Headquarters has finally realised what danger you were in.' The situation was becoming very serious: the reserves might be too late." This was why he threw in his XIII and IV Mechanised Corps, in spite of their being worn out. They counter-attacked furiously whilst the Germans put in their 17th Panzer Division, which had only 30 tanks, from the Orel front. The Panzer division's commander, Major-General F. von Senger und Etterlin signalled Hoth: "Situation regarding *matériel* very bad." Hoth replied: "Some divisions up front are even worse off. Yours has an excellent reputation. I am counting on you." The attacks started again and on December 15 Eremenko had to sound the alarm a second time. *Stavka* promised him the prompt aid of the 2nd Guards Army (Lieutenant-General R. Ya. Malinovsky). This army did, in fact, succeed in preventing Kirchner from breaking out of the bridgehead

A party of German soldiers surrender in a shell-blasted hole on the Eastern Front.

he had won on the north bank of the Myshkova. Hoth had thus won 50 miles in eight days and was within 30 miles of his objective. But he had worn out his men. Conscious of his subordinate's difficulties, Manstein planned to bring over the XLVIII Panzer Corps from the north to the south bank of the Don, which would allow him to take up again the advance towards Stalingrad, from which Paulus now said he could not break out through lack of fuel. But things turned out very differently.

On December 16, the Soviet High Command set in motion Operation "Saturn" intended as a pincer movement by the South-West and the Voronezh Front (Lieutenant-General F. I. Golikov) to wipe out the Rumanian 3rd Army and the Italian 8th Army and open the way to Rostov. Co-ordination of the attack was entrusted to General Zhukov. The artillery preparation at dawn on D-day required the concentration of 5,000 guns and mortars. On the South-West Front the Russian 3rd Guards Army (Lieutenant-General D. D. Lelyushenko) soon overcame the resistance of the Rumanian 7th and 11th Divisions and forced the XVII Corps to abandon its positions. This done, it exploited its success in the rear areas of the Italian 8th Army (General Gariboldi), whose 230,000 men in nine divisions were deployed on a front of 170 miles. And the Don was now frozen hard enough for tanks to cross. Not only that, but the catastrophe of November 19 had forced Hitler to withdraw its "stays" (the 62nd and 294th Divisions). It had only 380 47-mm guns to defend itself against the enemy tanks, but even twice this number would still have been unable to pierce the Russian armour. Finally, the Italians had only 55 tanks, and these were obsolete. So the army which the boastful Mussolini had flung defiantly at the Russians was now the mere shadow of a real force.

General Golikov had massed in the Verkhne Mamon bridgehead the 1st Guards Army (Lieutenant-General V. I. Kuznetsov) and the 6th Army (Lieutenant-General F. M. Kharitonov). Between them they had 15 infantry divisions supported by many tanks, which operated at battalion strength. Opposite them was the Italian II Corps, with the "Cossiera" and the "Ravenna" Divisions. In such conditions of inequality, the breakthrough took only 48 hours and on December 18 no fewer than five armoured corps poured through the breach which Colonel-General von Weichs was striving in vain to close. How could he have done this when his 27th Panzer Division had only 50 tanks?

At Novocherkassk the defeat of Army Group "B" forced Manstein not only to countermand the order to XLVIII Panzer Corps to go to the rescue of the LVII, but on December 23 to order Kirchner to pull the valiant 6th Panzer Division back across the Don. This latter was the only complete formation in the forces designated to free Paulus. It therefore meant that the whole enterprise had been abandoned; This was on a day when the temperature was 30 degrees Centigrade below zero and the men's menu was:

Midday: rice and horsemeat.

Evening: 8 ounces of bread, two meatballs (horse) à la Stalingrad, 12 ounces of butter and real coffee.

Extras: 4 ounces of bread, an ounce of boiled sweets, and 4 ounces of chocolate.

Tobacco: one cigar and two cigarettes.

The significance of this was conveyed by Paulus to a young major from *Luftflotte* IV attached to his staff. His words betray his emotion and despair: "We couldn't even pull in our outposts, as the men were falling down from exhaustion. They have had nothing to eat for four days. What can I reply, I an Army Commander, if a soldier comes up to me and says, 'Please, Colonel-General sir, a little bit of bread'? We have eaten the last horses. Could you ever imagine soldiers falling on a dead horse, cutting off its head, and devouring its brains raw? How can we go on fighting when the men haven't even got winter clothing? Who is the man who said we would be supplied by air?"

Kirchner was now down to his 17th and 23rd Panzer Divisions with less than 60 tanks between them. Could he hold the Myshkova line? It was unlikely now that the enemy had thrown in the 2nd Guards Army with its numerous powerful armoured formations. The order of December 23 was therefore a sentence of death on the German 6th Army. Also the loss of the aerodromes at Tatinskaya and Morozovsk meant that their supplies had to travel an extra 125 miles.

Manstein could not avoid involvement in this disastrous state of affairs. If Vatutin and Golikov got to Rostov, it would not be only the 6th Army which would be wiped out, but the catastrophe would spread to what was left of Army Groups "Don" and "A". We can only conclude that a system of operations is doomed to destruction when it subjects the commanders to such a dilemma.

"In war, a great disaster always pins great guilt on one man" said Napoleon. In obedience to this dictum Hitler had the commander of the XLVIII Panzer Corps, Lieutenant-General Heim, dragged before a court-martial presided over by Göring. He was condemned to death. Secretly imprisoned in the Moabit Gaol in Berlin, he was released without a word of explanation in May 1943 then, the next year, although banished from the army, nominated commander of the fortress at Boulogne.

On December 24, 1942, the South-West Front's offensive against Rostov forced the Luftwaffe formations which were supplying the Stalingrad pocket to make a hurried departure from their bases at Morozovsk and Tatsinskaya and establish a new base at Sal'sk, and obliged them to fly over 200, instead of 120, miles to carry out their missions. The retreat of the 4th *Panzerarmee* along the Stalingrad–Novorossiysk railway forced them to withdraw further on January 4, 1943. Now they had to take off from Shakhty and Novocherkassk, some 275 miles from the 6th Army's aerodromes. In this way the development of the strategic situation aggravated the consequences of the criminal irresponsibility with which Göring had boasted of being able to supply the so-called "fortress" at a rate of 500 tons a day. In fact there were only six days between January 4 and 21 during which the unfortunate forces of the besieged army received more than 100 tons of supplies.

The supplying of Stalingrad by air was therefore a failure and one of the most important causes of the surrender. This theme recurs constantly in Field-Marshal Paulus's notes: "You are in fact addressing yourself to men who are already dead", he wrote in answer to a suggestion that he make sorties. "We have stayed here on the orders of the Führer. The Air Force has left us in the lurch and has never kept its promises."

A decision was reached on three drop zones for parachuting supplies behind the divisional sectors, but Paulus objected: "If you insist on parachuting supplies, this army is finished. You must land because our most absolute need is for fuel."

Later, there is a diatribe against Göring: "At the same time I learn from Manstein and Zeitzler that, during a vital meeting, the *Reichsmarschall* said that re-supplying was not going so badly out there! . . . He has big boots so it wouldn't do him any harm to come here himself and see the situation! Clearly my reports have not been passed on to him or he has not taken them seriously. In the old days I should have made my decision at once but now they treat you like a naughty child and what else can you do but grin and bear it?"

The situation was serious, as is shown by a note in the O.K.W. war diary, written by its editor at the time, Helmut Greiner. The daily ration of the troops, which Paulus, it must be stressed, also lived on, was by January 10, 1943 as little as: $2\frac{1}{2}$ ounces of bread, 7 ounces of horsemeat (bones included), $\frac{2}{5}$ of an ounce of fats, $\frac{2}{5}$ of an ounce of sugar, and 1 cigarette.

The ordeal of hunger was increased by that of the cold, because, for reasons which have not been elucidated, the winter kit of the 6th Army had not got further than the railway stations of Khar'kov and Kiev. But for weeks, under a bitter north-east wind, the thermometer read between 25 and 35 degrees Centigrade below zero. Artillery ammunition and fuel were in very short supply, which excluded all but very localised counter-attacks.

At the turn of the year, *Stavka* revised its order of battle between the Don and the Volga. Colonel-General Eremenko was required to give up his 57th, 62nd, and 64th Armies to the Don Front which, now consisting of seven armies in all, would take on the task of liquidating the German forces besieged in the Stalingrad pocket.

The Russian commander, Lieutenant-General K. K. Rokossovsky, therefore had under his command about 90 brigades and divisions against the 22 decimated and starved divisions of the German 6th Army. Attached to his staff, as representative of *Stavka*, was Colonel-General N. N. Voronov, for whom the destruction of the Germans would mean the baton of a Marshal of Artillery. The 16th Air Army (Major-General S. I. Rudenko) gave the Don Front efficient support and challenged the aircraft of the Luftwaffe which attempted to supply the 6th Army in ever more difficult conditions.

Preparations for the attack had been completed, when, on January 8, two Soviet officers, carrying a flag of truce, crossed the siege lines, not without some difficulty, and submitted conditions for surrender to Paulus. These had been drawn up and dictated by Voronov and Rokossovsky in the most formal and proper terms.

"In view," they wrote to him, "of the hopeless situation of the German forces, and to avoid unnecessary loss of life, we suggest the following terms of surrender:

1. All German troops who are besieged, including yourself and your staff will cease all resistance.

2. All members of the Wehrmacht will surrender by units. All arms, equipment and other property of the Army are to be handed over in good condition.

"We guarantee the lives and safety of all officers, non-commissioned officers and other ranks who cease fire, and, after the war, their free return to Germany or the country of their choice, according to the wishes of the prisoners.

"Wehrmacht troops who surrender will retain their uniforms, rank insignia, decorations, and objects of value. Senior officers will be permitted to retain their swords or daggers. Officers, non-commissioned officers, and other ranks who surrender will receive normal rations at once. Medical care will be given to the wounded, sick, and victims of frostbite."

Previously, Eremenko had tried to use captured German pilots for this purpose. He describes their reaction in these words:

"I brought them together in my headquarters and suggested that they should be sent back to Paulus. 'Make your report and say that you have been shot down and made prisoners, that you have had an interview with the Russian commander of the Stalingrad Front and that Eremenko has promised to guarantee the lives of the whole garrison of Stalingrad, if they surrender.' The pilots asked for a few minutes to consider my proposal. A lively argument arose among them. Some of them were inclined to accept my suggestion but the majority were opposed to it and soon the former came around to their point of view. Finally, one of the prisoners asked permission to ask a question. I gave it. He said. 'Sir, what would be your reaction if a Russian officer came to you and suggested that your troops should surrender?' 'I should have sent him for court martial,' I replied. 'Well,' he said, 'if we do so, one single mention of surrender and we should be shot out of hand. With your permission we shall not go back to Paulus but shall stay as prisoners, however unpleasant conditions may be.'"

No reply was made to the Russian proposals. But should one accuse Paulus of inhumanity, following the line of historians behind the Iron Curtain, because of his silence and because by that date there was no further point in the 6th Army resisting? This question may be answered perfectly well by another: what would have happened to the German forces on the Eastern Front as a whole if the defenders of the Stalingrad pocket had laid down their arms on January 9? And the answer given by Field-Marshal von Manstein in his memoirs should be recorded:

"The army had to go on fighting, even if it had no future itself. Every day it gained was of decisive importance for the rest of the German front. It would be quite incorrect to say that the war was finally lost and it would have been better to bring it to a swift end so as to spare suffering. Such a statement would simply be being wise after the event. At that time, it was not at all certain that Germany would lose the war by force of arms. A negotiated peace remained within the realm of possibility, but, in order to achieve this, we had to stabilise the situation on this part of the front, which we did in the end. To achieve this, the 6th Army had to hold down enemy forces locked in battle with it for as long as it could. Cruel necessity forced the High Command to demand this last sacrifice on the part of the valiant troops."

"Die, but save your brother," proclaimed General Dragomirov, one of the leading lights of the Tsarist Army in the 1880's. Nevertheless, there is no doubt that this pitiless command was imposed on Paulus because of the unbelievable errors committed in the conduct of operations by Hitler and Göring. The *Great Patriotic War* records the reception encountered by the Communist refugees Walter Ulbricht, Erich Weinert, and Willi Bredel in their attempts to suborn the besieged troops with leaflets and radio appeals. It writes: "The men continued to obey Fascist discipline unquestioningly They did not have the strength to make up their own minds to surrender over the heads of their officers and General."

The only question that arises after reading this is what would the writer of this passage have recorded about the Russian garrison of Brest-Litovsk if it had behaved any differently in July 1941 than did the 6th Army in Stalingrad.

On January 10, 1943, at 0805 hours, the entire artillery of the Don Front, grouped under the command of Lieutenant-General M. I. Kazakov, with more than 7,000 guns and mortars, opened a torrential fire on the positions of the 6th Army. At 0900 hours, the barrage started to creep forward, thus giving the Soviet 65th and

Two Russian T-34 tanks roar westwards across the plains of the Don steppe.

21st Armies (Lieutenant-General P. I. Batov and Major-General I. M. Chistyakov) the signal to attack. Within three days they had wiped out the Marinovka salient in concentric assaults. By January 17, unleashing his 24th and 57th Armies (Generals I. V. Galinin and F. I. Tolbukhin) on the left and the right, Rokossovsky, who had arrived at Voroponvo, had reconquered two-thirds of the pocket and, most importantly, had taken the aerodrome at Gumrak, the last one still left in German hands, thus preventing German aircraft from landing.

From then on, the remains of the 6th Army were supplied as far as possible by dropping containers. But the end was close, for the physical and moral resistance of the defenders was becoming rapidly exhausted and, at 1600 hours on January 22, Paulus transmitted the following message to Hitler:

"After having repelled at the outset massive enemy attacks, wide and deep gaps torn in the lines of the XIV Panzer Corps and the IV Corps noon on 22. All ammunition has been exhausted. Russians advancing on both sides of Voroponvo on a 6-kilometre front. Flags waving here and there. No longer any chance of stemming the flood. Neighbouring fronts, also without any ammunition, contracting. Sharing ammunition with other fronts no longer feasible either. Food running out. More than 12,000 wounded in the pocket untended. What orders should I issue to troops who have no more ammunition and are under continuous attack from masses of artillery, tanks, and infantry? Immediate reply essential as signs of collapse already evident in places. Yet confidence still maintained in the command."

Manstein pressed Hitler to answer this telegram, which hinted at surrender, by giving his permission to Paulus to lay down his arms. But three-quarters of an hour of telephoned appeals did not succeed in weakening the Führer's savage obstinacy. And so, on January 26, as the 21st Army

exploited its success of January 22 by pushing eastward, it linked up on Mamaev-Kurgan hill with the Soviet 62nd Army (Lieutenant-General V. I. Chuikov) which had so bravely defended the ruins of Stalingrad. And thus the German pocket was split in two.

In the southern pocket, General von Hartmann, commander of the 71st Division, rashly exposed himself to fire and was killed rifle in hand, while General Stempel of the 113th committed suicide. Their fellow commanders Drebber and Dimitriu surrendered the 297th Division and the Rumanian 20th Division; General von Seydlitz-Kurzbach, commander of the LI Corps, followed their example.

Paulus, on whom, as the end approached, the Führer had conferred the supreme distinction of promotion to Field-Marshal, was by dawn on January 30 trapped in the basement of the large department store in Stalingrad where he had set up his final headquarters. Together with his staff he accepted the inevitable. General M. S. Shumilov, commanding the Soviet 64th Army, gives the following account of his surrender:

"As our officers entered the room, Paulus was sitting on his bed. According to the accounts given by members of the Russian group, he gave the impression of a man in the last stages of exhaustion. The staff of the 6th Army was given one hour to move out. At that moment Major-General Laskin, Chief-of-Staff of the 64th Army, arrived, with my order to bring Paulus and Schmidt, his chief-of-staff, to 64th Army headquarters at Beketovka.

"A tall, wasted, greying man, in the uniform of a Colonel-General, entered the room. It was Paulus.

"Following the custom under the Hitler régime, he raised his arm as if he were about to give the regulation '*Heil Hitler*' cry.

But he stopped himself in time, lowered his arm, and wished us the usual German 'Guten Tag'.

"General Shumilov requested the prisoner to show his identity documents. Paulus took a wallet out of his pocket and handed the Soviet army commander his military paybook, the usual document carried by German officers. Mikhail Stepanovich looked at it and then asked for other identification confirming that Paulus was in fact the commander of the German 6th Army. Holding these documents, he then asked if it was true that Paulus had been promoted *Generalfeldmarschall*. General Schmidt declared:

"'By order of the Führer, the Colonel-General was promoted yesterday to the highest rank in the Reich, *Generalfeldmarschall*.'

"'Then can I tell our Supreme Command Headquarters that *Generalfeldmarschall* Paulus has been taken prisoner by troops of my army?' insisted Shumilov, addressing himself to Paulus.

"'*Jawohl*,' came the reply, which needs no translation."

All the same, the northern pocket continued to hold out until February 2, and General Strecker, commanding the XI Corps, was the last to surrender.

When he heard the news, Hitler flew into an indescribable rage, the effects of which fill no less than eight pages of the stenographic record that was taken of his statements from 1942 onwards. In Hitler's words, Paulus and his staff had dishonoured themselves by preferring surrender to suicide: "When you have a revolver," he exclaimed to Zeitzler, "it's quite easy. How cowardly you must be to flinch before such a deed! It would be better to allow yourself to be buried alive! It's even worse. Paulus was in a position where he knew that his death would make the other pocket resist even more fiercely. After all, when you give the sort of example he has given, you can't expect men to go on fighting." Zeitzler replied: "There's no excuse. When you feel that you're losing your nerve, then you ought to blow your brains out first." Hitler agreed. "When your nerves give way, there's nothing else for it but [to say] 'I'm at the end of my tether' and kill yourself. One could also say: 'That man must kill himself just as in the old times [leaders] used to rush on their swords when they saw that their cause was irretrievably lost. It's self-evident. Even Varus ordered his slave to kill him.'"

It would not be out of place to reply to this tirade by pointing out that the reincarnation of the foolhardy Varus should be sought not in the cellar of the Stalingrad department store, but in the temporary headquarters at Rastenburg.

In spite of the violent anger which he showed when he heard of the German capitulation at Stalingrad, Hitler for once assumed entire responsibility, as Manstein recalls:

"On February 6 I was summoned to the Führer's headquarters, although pre-viously I had had no reply to all my requests for Hitler to observe what was going on in our front with his own eyes, or to send for that purpose at least the Chief of the General Staff or General Jodl.

"Hitler began the meeting by saying: 'As for Stalingrad, I alone bear the responsibility. I might perhaps say that Göring gave me an inaccurate picture of the Luftwaffe's capabilities of supplying the Army from the air and so I could possibly make him take some of the blame. But I myself have appointed him to succeed me and so I must accept the responsibility entirely myself.'"

The cold facts of the matter were that the Russians buried 147,200 German and Rumanian dead in the Stalingrad pocket, while they themselves suffered 46,700 dead, according to Marshal Eremenko. These figures illustrate the savagery of that final battle. The five corps and the 22 divisions (two Rumanian) which perished left in Russian hands slightly more than 91,000 prisoners, including 24 generals and 2,500 officers, as well as more than 6,000 guns and 60,000 motor vehicles. The only troops to escape the trap by being flown out were 24,000 sick and wounded and 18,000 specialists or high-ranking officers marked down for promotion. Of the 91,000 prisoners, very few were still alive in 1950.

After the surrender, the Russians celebrated their victory. Recalling the moment, Marshal Eremenko recounts the following story:

"During the evening, at the very modest dinner to which the city council entertained us, General Shumilov, commander of the 64th Army, whose units had taken Field-Marshal Paulus prisoner together with his Staff, handed the German's personal weapon over to Nikita Sergeivich [Khruschev], saying: 'The weapon of

A Russian officer at the 64th Army headquarters salutes the German surrender delegation on January 30, 1943.

the defeated Field-Marshal belongs by right to the commander of the Stalingrad Front, which has taken all the weight of the Nazi attack and also an important part in our counter-offensive.'

"Nikita Sergeivich came to see me on his way back to the front headquarters. I was in bed, with constant and cramping leg pains. Comrade Khruschev gave me an account of his day and then handed me a small burnished metal revolver: 'It's Field-Marshal Paulus's personal weapon. The Commander of the 64th Army hands it over to the commander of the Stalingrad Front, now happily no longer in existence. I consider that it is yours by right, Andrei Ivanovich.'

"So I took the pistol gratefully, as a symbol of the unforgettable days of the great battle."

As described above, the defeat of the Rumanian 3rd Army and the Italian 8th Army in the great bend of the Don had forced *Gruppe* "Hoth", which was moving towards the pocket, to suspend its offensive on the evening of December 23, 1942. Already extremely weakened, it was thrown back by Colonel-General Eremenko, who had just been opportunely reinforced by the 2nd Guards Tank Army (Lieutenant-General R. Ya. Malinovsky.) On December 29, Hoth lost Kotel'nikovo, two days later Elista, on the Kalmuk Steppe, and, on January 2, moved back behind the Tsimlyansk–Remontnoye line. Of course, in the battles themselves Hoth had not lost the 571 tanks that the special Moscow communiqué claimed he had, for he had never more than 200 under his command. All the same, the troops of the Russian South Front now saw the road to Rostov open to them. The South Front had replaced the Stalingrad Front on January 2, under the same commander, Eremenko. Conditions were worsening day by day.

After a long struggle, on the night of December 27–28, Colonel-General Zeitzler had managed to get Hitler to sign an order to Army Group "A", fighting in the Caucasus between Tuapse, Nal'chik, and Mozdok, to begin a full-scale retreat. On January 5 Eremenko was holding Tsimlyansk on the left bank of the Don and was thus 165 miles from Rostov, while Colonel-General von Mackensen's 1st *Panzerarmee* had only just recrossed the Terek, at Prokhladnyy, 365 miles from the same point. In this situation the commander of Army Group "Don", Manstein, would have preferred his fellow-general Kleist to speed up, whereas the latter was retreating slowly and methodically in order to keep his *matériel* and evacuate his depôts properly.

Two circumstances, however, spared Army Group "A" and Colonel-General von Kleist the fate of Paulus and his 6th Army. In the first place, there was no real aggressive pursuit by the Transcaucasus Front's troops, fighting under the command of General I. V. Tyulenev. His Northern Group (Lieutenant-General I. I. Maslennikov), consisting of four armies and two corps of Cossack cavalry, did not succeed in troubling the 1st *Panzerarmee's* retreat to any serious degree, and the Black Sea Group, (Lieutenant-General I. E. Petrov) with its three armies, in spite of a few local successes, was not able to interfere with the withdrawal of the German 17th Army.

But the most important point was that Manstein's able manoeuvring, on the left bank of the Don and along the Stalingrad–Novorossiysk axis, had put a very successful brake on the advance of Colonel-General Eremenko, which had been very serious for a short time. On January 21, the 2nd Guards Tank Army forced the Manych at Proletarskaya only to be thrown back on the 25th by the 11th Panzer

The broken remnants of the 6th Army troop through the ruins of Stalingrad.

Division, sent in at the right moment by the army group commander under Lieutenant-General H. Balck's excellent leadership. A few days later the German 1st and 4th *Panzerarmee* moved back over the bridges at Rostov together and without too much of a delay. On Hitler's orders, the 17th Army, with eight German and three Rumanian divisions, established itself on the Taman' peninsula, with its right at Novorossiysk, vainly attacked by Petrov in an amphibious operation, and its left backed up against the Sea of Azov.

In fact, Hitler had not given up his Caucasian dream; sooner or later, he thought, the chance would come for him to break out of the bridgehead and seize the Kuban' oil-wells. In vain did Manstein try to put him on his guard against detaching these troops. Since the Hungarian 2nd Army had collapsed completely, broken on the Voronezh Front, the last days of January were ominous with the threat of a second Stalingrad, menacing not only Army Group "A" but also Army Group "Don" and Army Group "B"–in other words all those German and satellite forces fighting between Novorossiysk and Kursk.

Manstein had his work cut out trying to prevent the armies of the South-West Front (Lieutenant-General N. F. Vatutin) from engulfing *Gruppe* "Hollidt" and crossing the Donets near Kamensk-Shakhtinskiy and Voroshilovgrad, which would have opened the way dangerously towards Taganrog. So the defeat of Army Group "B" burst upon him like a thunderbolt in his headquarters at Stalino.

Overall command of this third act of the Soviet winter offensive had been entrusted to Lieutenant-General F. I. Golikov, commanding the Voronezh Front. His left wing, positioned in the region of Kantemirovka, faced the Italian Alpine Corps, and his right, to the north-west of Voronezh, was in contact with the German 2nd Army (Colonel-General von Salmuth.) On December 20, 1942 Golikov received orders from *Stavka* to crush the enemy forces between Kantemirovka and Voronezh, principally the Hungarian 2nd Army under Colonel-General Jany.

For this purpose, Golikov divided his forces into three main attack groups. On his left, the 3rd Tank Army (Lieutenant-General P. S. Rybalko) would move out from a line stretching from Kantemirovka to Novaya Kalitva and push in a north-westerly direction towards Alekseyevka; there it would make contact with the 40th Army of Major-General K. S. Moskalenko, which in its turn would move off from the bridgehead that the Russians had kept at Storogevoye on the right bank of the Don, 100 miles south of Voronezh. In that way the Hungarian 2nd Army would be caught in a pincer while, by using the bridgehead at Bobrov, the XVIII Corps (Major-General Sykov) would attack in the centre and try to cut through the enemy's rear and meet Rybalko's right wing. Although it is true, as the *Great Patriotic War* states, that the attacking forces had superiority only in artillery and armour, their superiority in these two arms must have been considerable.

With two armoured corps and eight armoured brigades, Golikov must have had about 900 tanks to face the 19th and 27th Panzer Divisions and the Hungarian 1st Armoured Division (15 tanks). As for the artillery, it should be noted that when the Russian 40th Army moved out of the Storogevoye bridgehead, its advance was heralded by a barrage laid down by 750 guns and howitzers and 672 mortars, in other words by 179 guns per mile. Furthermore, one-fifth of the Russian artillery, including medium calibre 122-mm and 152-mm guns, fired directly at enemy positions which had been pinpointed for a long time. On January 13, after a ferocious two-hour bombardment, the armour of the Soviet 3rd Tank Army was seen to move forward, 48 vehicles to each mile of front. Success was total. Not only did the Hungarian 2nd Army disintegrate under the powerful thrust, but the XXIV Panzer Corps and the Italian Alpine Corps, on the right, were also swept away in the defeat. As a result, by January 19 Rybalko's tanks were already close to Valuyki on the Oskol, 75 miles from their jumping-off point. In addition, the Hungarian rout endangered the German 2nd Army, which was positioned between the Don above Voronezh and the region north of Kursk, linking Army Group "B" with Army Group "Centre" (Field-Marshal von Kluge). To sum up, the break-up of the German front had taken place in a few days over a front of more than 215 miles from Livny to Kantemirovka, while Manstein had no firm positions left on the Donets above Voroshilovgrad.

At that moment, Colonel-General A. M.

Vasilevsky, who had overall command of the Voronezh and South-West Fronts, slipped the leash on his two subordinate commanders. Golikov crashed through the remains of Army Group "B" while Vatutin, on his left, received orders to attack Army Group "Don" across the Donets. Golikov moved swiftly west and south-west and, on February 8, his 60th Army (Major-General I. D. Chernyakhovsky) took Kursk, which had been held against all attacks the previous winter, while his 40th Army moved through Belgorod and Volchansk, and his 3rd Tank Army, further to the south, described a pincer movement which would give it Khar'kov. Vatutin, passing through Kupyansk, reached the Donets on February 7, crossed it the following day at Izyum and Balakleya, and fanned out south of the river. All in all, the style of campaign of May 12, 1942 was being repeated, but with better chances of success than the previous year for, on one hand, the German armies had been bled white and on the other, the Russian forces of the South-West Front had Manstein in a trap, both on the Mius front and on the Donets at Voroshilovgrad. In those circumstances, Stalin thought that, on February 6, he could safely order the South-West Front to "Seize Sinel'nikovo with the 6th Army and then, with all speed, Zaporozh'ye, so as to cut the enemy off from all possibility of retreat on the west bank of the Dniepr over the bridges at Dniepropetrovsk and Zaporozh'ye."

In the same tone an order was dispatched to the Voronezh Front to press energetically on to Poltava so as to reach the Dniepr near Kremenchug. But, as the *Great Patriotic War* correctly points out, this *ukase* took no account of the losses suffered by Golikov and Vatutin during six weeks of attacks which had taken them 200 and 240 miles respectively from their supply bases. Some armoured brigades, for example, had been reduced to six tanks and some infantry battalions to 20-odd men. Even the better off units were absolutely exhausted.

To consider Stalin's order feasible would also imply a complete lack of respect for the readiness, determination, and boldness of Field-Marshal von Manstein. In circumstances which were close to tragic, Manstein showed himself to be one of the most outstanding tacticians of his time, more than anything because to extract his armies from the serious situation in which they were trapped, he had to fight on two fronts; against the Russians and, moreover, against Hitler. The obstinacy of the latter was no less difficult to combat than the determination of the former.

We have already seen how the wills of Hitler and Manstein had clashed concerning the mission to be entrusted to the 1st *Panzerarmee* as it retreated from the Caucasus. It was, of course, true that the commander of Army Group "Don" had obtained permission from the Führer to engage it on the Donets after *Gruppe*

"Hollidt" had been withdrawn; but it had been obliged to leave behind some of its forces, including the 13th Panzer Division, on the Taman' peninsula. This allowed Vatutin to pursue his outflanking manoeuvre towards Mariupol' on the Sea of Azov.

On February 6, following the defeat of Army Group "B", Hitler summoned Field-Marshals von Kluge and von Manstein to his headquarters at Rastenburg to study the situation. Without making too many difficulties, he authorised Kluge to carry on with Operation *"Buffle"*, which he had been refusing for months. This operation consisted of methodically evacuating the Rzhev salient. With the troops recuperated in this way, he could extend the 2nd *Panzerarmee* southward. It would link up again with the 2nd Army and prevent all enemy attempts to exploit the victories on the Voronezh Front and the Bryansk Front (Lieutenant-General M. A. Reiter) by taking Orel in an outflanking move.

Hitler's discussion with Manstein was more heated. In the latter's opinion, the situation demanded the urgent evacuation of the Don–Donets salient between Rostov and Voroshilovgrad, except that Hollidt would defend the original Mius position and the 4th *Panzerarmee*, once reformed after being evacuated from the salient, would move swiftly behind the 1st *Panzerarmee* and take up position on its left. In that way there would be a link-up with the *Waffen* S.S. I Panzer Corps, which was arriving at Khar'kov precisely at that moment. The enemy would be prevented from penetrating in the direction of Dniepropetrovsk. However, the decision had to be taken there and then for, given the state of communications,

The frozen corpse of the German soldier lies where he died by the road.

Colonel-General Hoth would need a fortnight to get his forces into place. To all this Hitler replied with involved arguments that the shortening of the front would also benefit the enemy, which was untrue, for the Germans had the advantage of interior lines of communications. Hitler also added that the thaw would once more make the Don and the Dniepr natural obstacles, and so on. In the end, Manstein got his way, but only just.

On February 12, O.K.H. announced that Army Group "B" had been dissolved. This decision placed the 2nd Army, retreating west of Kursk, under Kluge's orders and gave Manstein authority over the Khar'kov sector, where the *Waffen* S.S. Panzer Corps was in great danger of being encircled by the armies of General Golikov. Should the capital of the Ukraine be evacuated or not? This question gave rise to another tense situation between Army Group "South", which had replaced Army Group "Don", and the Führer's headquarters at Rastenburg. In this case, however, it was settled over the heads of the parties on the initiative of General Hausser, commander of this armoured force, who abandoned the city during the course of February 15 and fell back on the Krasnograd–Karlovka region.

Two days later, accompanied by Field-Marshal Keitel and Generals Jodl and Zeitzler, Hitler arrived at Zaporozh'ye, to which Manstein had transferred his headquarters. There was a large map of the campaign marked as follows:
1. in the new 6th Army (ex-*Gruppe* "Hollidt") zone, the enemy had crossed the Mius at Matveyev-Kurgan;
2. in the 1st *Panzerarmee* zone, a cavalry corps had reached the railway junction at Debal'tsevo while at Grishino an enemy armoured column had cut the Voroshilovgrad – Dniepropetrovsk railway line. However, the Soviet drives had been contained in the end and were even being pushed back. By contrast there was a gap of more than 60 miles between Pavlograd and Krasnograd, through which Russian armour was advancing, clearly directed against the elbow of the Dniepr. It was true that with the 4th *Panzerarmee* in line or almost, this corner could be nipped off by pushing the I *Waffen* S.S. Panzer Corps to join Colonel-General Hoth as he moved in.

Hitler was slow to admit this reasoning as, for reasons of prestige, he would have preferred the *Waffen* S.S. to begin its campaign by recapturing Khar'kov. Manstein, however, answered Hitler's points by indicating that the thaw was moving from south to north and a counter-attack in a southerly direction was urgent, leaving aside the question of retaking Khar'kov. Without a southward attack, even if the city was retaken, the Germans risked being hemmed in by mud. For the third time, Manstein won the battle of words. But even so, in the meantime, General Vatutin's flying columns had reached Novomoskovsk, only 20 miles

German machine gunners on the outskirts of Khar'kov

from Dniepropetrovsk, and also Sinel'nikovo, 40 miles from Zaporozh'ye. Therefore Manstein sighed with relief when the Führer and his retinue returned to Rastenburg by air on the afternoon of the 19.

Army Group "South" unleashed a counter-offensive on February 21. In this it broke the rule which seemed, in the judgement of the most prudent, to sum up the experience of 1918: contain, and only then counter-attack. It is true that there were insufficient numbers of infantry available for containment and that Manstein had command of 13 divisions of armour or of *Panzergrenadiers,* in all about 800 tanks, including a considerable number of Pzkw VI Tigers. But the Russians misunderstood the reshuffling of Manstein's forces. This is how the *Great Patriotic War* describes the situation:

"Both the South-West Front command and Soviet Supreme Command were led to believe from the enemy's retreat from the lower Donets to the Mius and the transfer of his armoured and motorised divisions from around Rostov to near Konstantinovka, that the Germans intended to evacuate the Donets basin and retire behind the Dniepr. That is why Supreme Headquarters kept to its decision to develop its attack as soon as possible".

The result of this error of judgement and of the German initiative was a series of battles and clashes in which the clumsier Russians did not come off best.

On February 22, attacking due south from Krasnograd, the S.S. I Panzer Corps (1st *"Leibstandarte" Panzergrenadier* Division and 2nd *"Das Reich" Panzergrenadier* Division) crushed the Russian forces attacking Novomoskovsk as they advanced; then, reinforced by the 3rd *"Totenkopf" Panzergrenadier* Division of the *Waffen* S.S., the corps pushed on hard towards Pavlograd where it came under the 4th *Panzerarmee*, which Manstein was pushing towards Lozovaya at the same speed. During these strategic moves, Lieutenant-General M. M. Popov's

armoured force was utterly destroyed and, with its defeat, the entire South-West Front behind the Donets was forced into flight.

Though retreat was justified in the circumstances (General Vatutin had lost 32,000 killed and captured, 615 tanks, and 423 guns), it nevertheless exposed the left wing of the Voronezh Front, which was now threatened halfway between Khar'kov and Poltava. On March 5, the 4th *Panzerarmee* hit the Soviet 3rd Tank Army hard near Krasnograd. Then a pincer attack enabled the S.S. I Panzer Corps to "lay Khar'kov at the feet of the Führer" on March 14, 1943. *Gruppe* "Kempf", to the north of the city, drove forward at the same time and, on March 18, its *Panzergrenadier* division, the *"Grossdeutschland"*, reoccupied Belgorod.

The III and XL Panzer Corps of the 1st *Panzerarmee* mopped up the Debal'tsevo, Makeyevka, and Kramatorskaya pockets. The result of this drive was that the VII Guards Cavalry Corps (Major-General Borisov), the IV Guards Mechanised Corps (Major-General Tanichikhin), and the XXV Tank Corps (Major-General Pavlov) found themselves trapped and then surrounded. The bridgehead at Matveyev-Kurgan, on the west bank of the Mius, was retaken by the 6th Army.

About March 18, the thaw and the resultant mud caused operations to come to a halt between Kursk and the Sea of Azov. On that day, an O.K.W. communiqué proclaimed that Manstein's counter-attack had cost the enemy more than 50,000 killed, 19,594 prisoners, 3,000 guns, and 1,410 tanks. Without even questioning the figures, it is easy to put them into proportion by revealing that, in contrast, the Red Army had destroyed between 40 and 45 German and satellite divisions – a quarter of the forces the Russians had before them – in four months.

CHAPTER 38
The situation in the Mediterranean

The year 1943 was marked in the Mediterranean by the exploitation of the British victory at El Alamein, the American triumph at Midway, and the Russian recapture of Stalingrad. Not only had the three totalitarian powers failed to achieve their aim of winning the war by 1943, but the reverses that all three of them had suffered obliged them to go on to the defensive and to do this at a time when the American and Soviet colossi were applying the almost inexhaustible resources of their manpower, industry, and other resources to the war effort.

Only in Berlin, or rather in the headquarters at Rastenburg, did anybody in the Tripartite Alliance believe that the war could be won on two fronts. Hitler explained this to Mussolini, via Ribbentrop, on February 25, 1943: the Russians had lost 11,300,000 men while the Wehrmacht had lost only 1,400,000 killed, wounded, and missing. His decision was immutable, Hitler wrote to Mussolini, in a letter which took four hours to read:

"I therefore intend to continue fighting in the East until this colossus finally disintegrates, and to do it with or without allies. For I regard the mere existence of this peril as so monstrous that Europe will know not a moment's peace if, heedlessly balancing on the edge of the abyss, she forgets or simply refuses to face reality ... I shall fight until the enemy himself admits defeat."

On the question of the British and Americans, Hitler granted that they had "temporarily" achieved certain advantages but, he went on, "what matters is if they succeed in the long run in holding such points by keeping them supplied ... The continued menacing and obstruction of their sea supply lines is bound sooner or later to lead to catastrophe. I have therefore taken all possible steps to put our U-boat warfare on a virtually indestructible footing."

But in Rome Mussolini did not see the situation in the same light. In his opinion, everything pointed to the British and the Americans making a major effort in the Mediterranean in order to crush Italy. Thus the thing to do was to transfer south of the Alps the bulk of the Axis forces that Hitler insisted on keeping in the Don steppes. Who knew? Holding Bizerta and Tunis as they did, the Italians and the Germans might be able to inflict a major defeat on General Eisenhower, which might even allow the Axis powers to wrest control of French North Africa from the hands of the Allies. For Mussolini, of course, was mainly concerned with the troops of Eisenhower's Allied armies, now so near to Italy and probably planning a landing in his country.

The fact remains that this reversal of Axis strategy would have entailed a complete reappraisal of the Third Reich's attitude towards the Soviet Union. Mus-

solini's health did not permit him to go to Rastenburg where Hitler had summoned him; so he ordered Ciano, in instructions dated December 16, 1942, to put forward the following point of view, when the Führer let him get a word in:

"Mussolini is especially anxious that Hitler should know, as he had already spoken of it to Göring, that he considers it extremely advisable to come to an agreement with Russia, or at least to fix upon a defensive line which could be held by small forces. 1943 will be the year of the Anglo-Saxon effort. Mussolini considers that the Axis must have the greatest number of divisions possible to defend itself in Africa, the Balkans, and perhaps in the West."

At the meeting on December 18, 1942, Count Ciano followed his father-in-law's instructions, which also expressed his own point of view. But when he told the Führer that, in the Duce's opinion, the signing of a peace treaty would be an "ideal solution", Hitler repeatedly shouted that when Molotov had visited Berlin in November 1940, he (Hitler) had tried in vain to lead the discussion towards Central Asia but every time he had brought up this idea his guest had mentioned Finland, Rumania, Bulgaria, and the Dardanelles. This was perfectly true, in fact, and Hitler's conclusion was:

"The Russia of Stalin still follows the path chosen by Peter the Great for the expansion of his people to the North and South-West. Russia has in no way shown herself prepared to follow the course proposed to her towards India and the Persian Gulf because she regards these aims as secondary. If she were first assured of hegemony over Europe, the rest would follow of its own accord."

Moreover, in his lengthy letter of February 25, Hitler did not restrict himself to repeating to Mussolini that he had no intention of following his advice to make diplomatic soundings in Moscow. He left Mussolini in no doubt that he had also no intention of giving up the Russian campaign which would crush the Soviet giant for ever. Of course, the Axis had to throw back attempts at landings in Corsica, Sardinia, the Peloponnese, Crete, Rhodes, and the Dodecanese, all of which he considered possible in the near future. In other words, what was required was to hold the British and Americans in check while the war in Russia was won.

But what means were available to dispel the threat looming in the Mediterranean? It was quite clear to Mussolini, to the Under-Secretary of State, Bastianini, and to General Ambrosio, who had just replaced Count Ciano at the Foreign Ministry and Marshal Cavallero at *Comando Supremo* respectively, that the offensive

Even in adversity the two dictators remained friends.

General Oshima, the Japanese ambassador, confers at Rastenburg with Ribbentrop about Togo's mediation plans.

mentality which reigned at *Oberkommando der Wehrmacht* would not permit the Germans to deprive the Russian front of the land and air forces which might give the Axis the means for a successful defence of the southern theatre of operations. In fact, the only subject to arise at the conference held in the Palazzo Venezia on February 25–28, in which Ribbentrop, accompanied by General Warlimont, representing O.K.W., explained the Führer's point of view to his Italian hosts, was the military situation in the Balkans and particularly in Croatia and Montenegro.

If, after the evacuation of Tripoli and the destruction of the German 6th Army at Stalingrad, the Duce expected that the problem of the war as a whole would be discussed as between equal allies, he must

have been terribly disappointed. Having got over the few general questions just mentioned, almost all the rest of the conference was devoted to the support, in any case somewhat limited, that the Italians were giving to General Mihailović and his *Cetniks* in the open struggle in which they were engaged against Tito and his Communist partisans. In Hitler's view, there was no difference between them as both were animated by hate for Germany and Italy, and would join the British and Americans if the latter landed on the Yugoslav coast. General Ambrosio, who had commanded the Italian 2nd Army in Croatia, had the temerity to disagree and brought down the rage of the easily-offended Ribbentrop on his head.

And so the Palazzo Venezia conference was characterised by Mussolini's acquiescence in all the opinions that Ribbentrop communicated to him from Hitler. Certainly the Italian dictator, after his illness, was a shadow of his former self, and could not make his voice heard in the argument. But perhaps he realised in his heart that Fascist Italy no longer had the chance to separate herself from the Third Reich, so fast were Italy's means of defence and industrial resources being exhausted. In his diary, Ciano describes the state of depression into which Mussolini had fallen after the Italian defeat in Tripolitania:

"I have seen the Duce again after three days and find him looking worse. But in my humble opinion, what is doing his health more harm than anything else is his uneasiness about the situation. He has rage in his heart over the abandonment of Tripoli, and suffers for it. As usual, he hurled bitter words at the military, who do not make war with the 'fury of a fanatic, but rather with the indifference of the professional'."

He also emphasises the anxiety of the party leaders:

"I have lunch with Bottaï and Farinacci. Both are furious. In speaking of the loss of Libya, Bottaï says: 'After all, it is another goal that has been reached. In 1911 Mussolini uttered his "away with Libya". After thirty-two years he has kept his word.'"

In Japan, General Tojo, the dictatorial head of the Japanese Government, with the Army united behind him, seems during this same period to have preserved all his confidence in German military might. He was still convinced that the defeat at Moscow and the Stalingrad disaster were only temporary setbacks. Once these were victoriously overcome, the Third Reich would annihilate the last organised forces of the Soviet Union and this would allow the Empire of the Rising Sun to claim its part of the spoils cheaply enough. In particular, the Japanese wanted a foothold at Vladivostok, the northern part of Sakhalin, and Kamchatka.

There was somewhat more caution in the Japanese Foreign Ministry. Before Smetanin, the Soviet Ambassador, returned home on January 1, 1942, Shinegori

Togo told him outright and requested him to repeat to Molotov that:

"The present nature of Japanese-Soviet relations in the midst of a world conflict resembles a ray of sunlight shining through a rainstorm; and I hope it will illumine the whole world. If the Soviet Government wishes for peace to be re-established, Japan is ready to offer herself as a mediator and to use all the means at her disposal."

The idea of Japanese mediation between the Soviet Union and the Third Reich was the subject of a discussion at a co-ordination conference held in July 1942 by the principal ministers of Tojo's cabinet and the Army and Naval Chiefs-of-Staff. The following month, Togo instructed the Japanese Ambassador in Moscow, Sato, to sound out Molotov's attitude. However, on September 1, Togo was moved from the Ministry of Foreign Affairs to the Ministry of Greater Asia, and there is reason to suppose that his suggestions regarding Japanese mediation in the Soviet-German war were in some way responsible for this disguised fall from grace.

Ever since the first Soviet winter offensive, the Naval Staff had been thinking along the same lines as the Foreign Ministry. According to a report by the German Ambassador in Tokyo, dated March 14, 1942:

"The Japanese official concerned pointed out that 'the desire' of the Japanese Navy that Germany should postpone her differences with Soviet Russia, and reach an agreement with the Russians, stemmed from the wish that Germany could then turn all her efforts to destroying British forces in the Far East, and the British position in the Eastern Mediterranean, and in this way and as quickly as possible implement a direct collaboration between the Axis powers and Japan."

Clearly, the result of the Battle of Midway and the operations centred on the island of Guadalcanal could only confirm the Emperor's admirals in their point of view, even more so because the period after which Yamamoto had said that he could no longer guarantee Japanese victory was fast approaching its end.

Though it had been so poorly supported, Togo's initiative had nevertheless provoked the irritation of Ribbentrop. On August 31, he summoned Ambassador Oshima to the *Wilhelmstrasse*:

"The rumour in the world of a separate peace between Germany and Russia has not died down. Unfortunately we have to state that once again it was also Japanese sources which nourished this rumour. It gives strong support to Stalin's propaganda, and he uses it to spur the British to greater efforts. If Japan is using the rumour as cover, to lull the Russians into false security before attacking them, then Ribbentrop has nothing against it. But if not, would Oshima tell his government that 'rumour of a separate peace merely helps our enemy'."

In spite of this outburst, the question came up again a few months later during a conference of Japanese ambassadors to European countries. But in the final analysis, as Oshima told the German Foreign Minister on December 11, if Russia could not make peace on the conditions that Germany laid down, consideration should be given to the situation when "Stalin–having been thoroughly beaten militarily–being finally ready to [make peace] because of the fear of internal revolt, his Japanese government asked to be speedily informed . . . This would be very important to Tokyo as the Army under Yamashita, the conqueror of Singapore, stood on the permanent alert in Manchuria."

Ribbentrop seemed satisfied with this clarification, which indicated that Tokyo had given up any attempt at mediation. Furthermore, several weeks later, Tojo proclaimed before the Diet:

"Japan takes an oath to fight to the end, shoulder to shoulder, until a common victory is won, side by side with her German and Italian allies to whom she will give aid and assistance!"

Events would completely belie this foolhardy proclamation later. But, at the moment when the Japanese Army was evacuating Guadalcanal, Rommel was falling back on the Mareth Line, and the defenders of Stalingrad, besieged and starving, were fighting the final battle, should Tojo be accused of deceiving his audience about the coming disaster? Not at all, if account is taken of the unbelievable nonsense that was supplied to him by his Intelligence services concerning losses suffered by the enemies of the Rising Sun during the first year of the Pacific War.

During that year, according to a triumphant communiqué issued in Tokyo on December 7, 1942, 3,798 British, Dutch, and American planes had been shot down or damaged. This was obviously a grossly exaggerated figure, if the air weakness of the three victims of Japanese aggression is considered. The 1947 edition of the *Annuaire de Flottes de Combat*, scrupulously compiled by Henri Le Masson, lists Japanese exaggerations about Allied naval losses as follows:

	Communiqué	Real losses
Battleships	11	4
Aircraft-carriers	11	5
Cruisers	46	14
Destroyers	48	35
Submarines	91	11
	207	69

From this it may be concluded that General Tojo was the victim of his own propaganda.

The German defeats on the Eastern Front at the end of the autumn of 1942, followed by the near annihilation of the Hungarian 2nd Army near Voronezh in January 1943, had been followed by deep disappointment and heart-searching in government circles in Bucharest as well as in Budapest.

The defeat of the Rumanian 3rd Army on the Don had already given rise, on November 25, to a heated exchange about the responsibilities for this setback between General Steflea, Chief-of-Staff to Marshal Antonescu, and General Hauffe, leader of the German military mission to the Rumanian Army. At the beginning of January, Hitler demanded the raising of 19 new Rumanian divisions. Consequently, Mihaï Antonescu, the *Conducator's* nephew and Foreign Minister, summoned Bova-Scoppa, the Italian Ambassador, and asked him to convey a memorandum to Count Ciano in which he revealed the serious fears he felt concerning the future development of the political and military situation. In his opinion, as his uncle and he himself had verified in their recent visit to O.K.W., Hitler appeared obsessed by the Soviet problem. In order to preserve the eastern border of Fortress Europe, he was ready to hurl the flower of European youth into the furnace. When Antonescu had asked Ribbentrop for his opinion on "the immense moral and political problems posed in Europe", the latter had replied that he could give no opinion until Russia had been defeated and added: "Europe must hold. That is the main point."

This blind obstinacy evoked these observations from the Rumanian Foreign Minister:

"Under these circumstances I think that one should assist the German leaders to clarify the situation. If the position in the East gets still worse, Hitler will send all his reserves to that Front, and then the state of affairs in the Mediterranean and the Balkans will deteriorate. My conviction is that England and America have no interest in letting the Russians into Europe and I have precise information to that effect. The Turkish Ambassador came specially to tell me that America and particularly England were pressing on into Europe in order to bring the war to an end, but that they wished at all costs to avoid the collapse of the European system in favour of Russia. I have received similar reports from Portugal."

For all this, Mihaï Antonescu did not reach any positive conclusion. But since Germany, obsessed by her own problems, had no interest in thinking about the future of Europe, Italy became the only country Rumania could call on, and this made Antonescu decide: "Ask Count Ciano to inform me of the Italian point of view through you, if I cannot manage to see him".

On January 19, Bova-Scoppa carried out the mission with which he had been entrusted, receiving a most friendly welcome from Count Ciano. On the same day, the Italian Foreign Minister noted in his diary:

"The latter [Antonescu] was very explicit about the tragic condition of Germany and foresees the need for Rumania and Italy to make contact with the Allies in order to establish a defence against the bolshevization of Europe."

But Mussolini received his son-in-law's suggestions coldly and confirmed in the clearest terms that he had made his mind up to march to final victory shoulder to shoulder with the Third Reich.

However, on January 29, a long handwritten report from Filippo Anfuso, Ciano's ex-Principal Private Secretary and now Italian Ambassador in Budapest, revealed that the Hungarian leaders were thinking along the same lines as Mihaï Antonescu: "We are told," Admiral Horthy, Regent of Hungary, had informed him, "that we are a German satellite. Very well. But if Germany cannot defend us against the Slavs, what will become of us? . . . I still believe that a common Italo-Rumanian front against the Germano-Slav waves would be a sure guarantee of safety for us. We shall continue to fight, but we live in a state of tension . . .'"

And Nicholas de Kallay, the Hungarian Prime Minister, went even further than Horthy. "In the midst of the Flood," he wrote, "the politicians of the kingdom of Saint Stephen crowded round the portholes of their Noah's Ark, hoping to see land, and asking 'what is Italy doing?'" He continued:

"In these questions . . . lies the naturally understandable anxiety of those who asked themselves whether the Slavs of the South and North will not slaughter the ten or twelve million Magyars before any English, American, Italian, or German military police arrive to save them. In order to imagine this panic state of affairs, it is sufficient to reflect on what has happened recently: the dogs and cats of the Carpathian plain – the Hungarians and the Rumanians – have decided to negotiate with each other again, because they realize they are neither Germans nor Slavs, and fear to be devoured by them."

In the end, just like his enemy Mihaï Antonescu, he appealed to Count Ciano, whose friendship the Hungarians had been able to appreciate at the time of the Belvedere arbitration.

If truth be told, the news of the rapprochement of Hungary and Rumania was not exactly a surprise for the Italian Foreign Minister, as Ambassador Bova-Scoppa had already informed him of it on January 10. On the other hand, a plan of Kallay's and the commentary on it by Anfuso in his "intelligent and clearsighted letter" seemed to have disturbed him more. On January 29 he noted:

"There are no actual facts as yet, but many indications lead one to believe that Hungary has already had some contact with the Anglo-Saxons. Besides, Mariassy [Hungarian ambassador] asked d'Aieta [Ciano's Chief of Cabinet] with a good deal of anxiety if it were true that the Rumanians had been negotiating with the British and that conversations were under way in Lisbon. D'Aieta denied this, but, in reality, what do we do about it?"

In fact, Admiral Horthy's memoirs reveal what Ciano could only suppose in 1943. First contact was made with the British by the Budapest Government in summer 1943 and the two governments reached, doubtless in autumn 1943, a

Former Prime Minister Ivanoë Bonomi (top). Monsignor Montini (above).

secret agreement, according to whose terms Allied aircraft flying over Hungary would not be attacked and, in their turn, would not engage in any hostile act against the territory of the Kingdom of Hungary. Then the talks led by Kallay on the Hungarian side turned to the heart of the problem. Horthy writes:

"Between Kallay and myself there was a tacit agreement that granted him (without informing me of every detail) the necessary freedom to take initiatives which, though apparently maintaining normal relations with Nazi Germany, would strengthen our friendship with the Anglo-Saxons, and yet not help the Soviets. It was a delicate task, made particularly difficult, if not impossible, by Roosevelt's policy towards Stalin."

Actually Hitler knew what to expect from Kallay, and Admiral Horthy realised this during his visit to Hitler in April 1943. At that time Hitler was staying at Klessheim:

"He was more than usually irritable," Horthy writes in his memoirs. "My visit had been preceded by Mussolini's. The Italian leader had been accompanied by Ciano's successor, Secretary of State Bastianini, and by the Rumanian Marshal Antonescu. They had all stated they were in favour of negotiating peace. Mussolini, after the now inevitable defeat in North Africa, feared an invasion of Sicily and wanted an agreement with Stalin, while Antonescu, who wanted to make a grand union of all forces to stem the tide from the East, had come out in favour of an agreement with the Western Allies. This 'defeatism', to use the term preferred by the Nazis, shown by two men for whom he felt particular respect, had greatly irritated Hitler and this had not disappeared by the time I arrived and contributed to the way in which I was received. Even Goebbels, who in his heart of hearts was most evilly disposed towards Hungary and myself, noted in his diary that 'Hitler had treated Horthy too severely'."

The Italian Foreign Minister was not at all indignant at the news which his representatives in Budapest had conveyed to him, with the usual diplomatic reserve, concerning the possible contact made by Hungarian leaders with the British and Americans. The fact was that since El Alamein, Algiers, and Stalingrad, Ciano had seen the defeat of the Axis clearly written on the wall. Besides, since Hitler obstinately refused to cut his losses, that is to negotiate with the Soviet Union as Mussolini advised him, Ciano saw Italy defenceless or almost so in face of the British and the Americans; already the bombing of Genoa, Milan, and Turin, which had accompanied Montgomery's African offensive, was giving him a foretaste of what 1943 could be like. But Ciano, the son of Admiral Costanzo Ciano, Count of Cortellazzo, scion of a famed and wealthy family of Leghorn, did not feel any of that violent hatred and scorn for the "capitalist" states of Great Britain and the United States, that his father-in-law Mussolini, the ex-schoolmaster and revolutionary agitator from Forlì, had only just recently proclaimed to the Chamber of Deputies once again. Thus one may well believe that Mussolini and his Foreign Minister did not see the situation from the same viewpoint.

Mussolini's African and Atlantic ambitions made him quite naturally consider Britain, and after her, America, as his main enemy while Ciano, concerned with maintaining Italian influence in the Danube basin and the Balkans, saw danger in the unexpected expansion of Soviet power.

Thus it was that he conceived the idea of replacing the North–South (or Berlin–Rome) Axis, from which he could expect nothing more, given Hitler's incurable blindness, with a new one, running East–West (Bucharest–Lisbon) which Rumania, Hungary, Croatia, Italy, France, Spain, and Portugal would be invited to join.

In that way a line of neutral, mainly Latin and Catholic powers, would be formed. Here it seems very likely that Count Ciano shared the opinion or the dream of his Rumanian colleague, that the American President and the British Prime Minister would not look favourably on the establishment of "Bolshevism" in Central Europe. Contrary to his father-in-law, he now thought the moment had come to seek a reconciliation with the United States and Great Britain.

Even today there is still some obscurity about the feelers put out by Ciano to try to execute his plan; his famous diary does not mention them at all and, as may well be imagined, he did not use the normal diplomatic channels. It is thought that there were talks in Lisbon soon after El Alamein and in Berne some weeks later.

What is known for sure is that the secret services of the Third Reich managed to obtain some information about the web that Ciano was trying to spin behind Mussolini's back. According to information given in the early 1960's to the British historian F. W. Deakin by Mr. Allen Dulles, at the time Head of United States "Strategic Services" in Switzerland, the cryptographers of the *Abwehr* had managed to break the code which the United States legation in Berne was using at the time; and a dispatch from their transmitter in January 1943 had reported that an anti-German faction was in existence in Rome, with Marshal Badoglio, Ciano, and Count Dino Grandi as its leaders.

Is this statement reliable? It seems so, for at the same time, the late Nicholas Lahovary, Rumanian Minister in Switzerland and himself a great supporter of the "neutral front" was relieved of his post by Marshal Antonescu on the express orders of Hitler and Ribbentrop.

This would explain why, on February 5, Mussolini, who had received, with Hitler's compliments, a copy of the American cable, "changed guard" as he called it and reshuffled his ministers, excluding from his new government those who supported Italy's quitting the war.

"What would you like to do now?" the Duce asked his son-in-law when he received him in his office in the Palazzo Venezia. The latter later noted:

"Among the many personal solutions that he offers me I decisively reject the governorship of Albania, where I would be going as the executioner and hangman of those people to whom I had promised brotherhood and equality. I choose to be Ambassador to the Holy See. It is a place of rest that may, moreover, hold many possibilities for the future. And the future, never so much as to-day, is in the hands of God."

Fearing – as in fact happened – that Mussolini might go back on his offer, Ciano requested the *placet* of the Vatican that same day and immediately received it. This was only to be expected, for Pope Pius XII's Under-Secretary of State, Monsignor Montini (later Pope Paul VI) seems to have known of his plan to take Italy out of the war. For the same reason, King Victor Emmanuel III said he was "very happy" at the appointment, and the Duke of Acquarone, Minister of the Royal Household, was "delighted".

Count Ciano describes his last interview with the Duce before taking up his new duties in the Vatican:

"He thanks me for what I have done and rapidly enumerates my most important services. 'If they had given us three years longer we might have beeen able to wage war under different conditions, or perhaps it would not have been at all necessary to wage it.' 'Yes,' I answered. 'I have them all in order, and remember, when hard times come—because it is now certain that hard times will come—I can document all the treacheries perpetrated against us by the Germans, one after another, from the preparation for the conflict to the war on Russia, communicated to us when their troops had already crossed the frontier."

Ciano's successor, Giuseppe Bastianini, was reduced to the status of Under-Secretary of State in the Foreign Ministry. He had been out of touch with diplomacy, the last important position he had held being Ambassador to Great Britain, which he had been up to June 10, 1940. All things considered, therefore, he imagined that his new appointment was intended to allow him to prepare discreetly for Italy's withdrawal from the war, a war which he had spoken against from the beginning. But as he pushed open the door in the Palazzo Venezia on February 10, 1943, he might well have read Dante's line "Abandon hope, all ye who enter here."

For at the first word he mentioned on the subject to the Italian dictator, the latter replied quite sharply:

"It seems to me that you are making a mistake; my intentions are not those which you imagine. We are at war. I am the Foreign Minister. You have specific duties to carry out, but the direction of foreign affairs is in my hands, and my conception is very simple; when one is at war, one stays with one's ally until the end."

However, the Duce had not only taken over the Foreign Ministry but had also kept control of the portfolios of the Interior, War, the Navy, and the Air Force. To these administrative responsibilities must be added the burden of the *Comando Supremo* and the leadership of the Fascist Party. Clearly even the fittest man would have found it difficult to fulfil so many obligations satisfactorily. Then the stomach ulcer which he had thought healed at the end of December flared up again under the influence, it appears, of the bad news which flowed in endlessly from North Africa and the Russian front. So the despotic power which he had taken on himself was equalled only by his inability to exercise it efficiently.

One further remark concerning Mussolini's declaration: the Duc de Saint-Simon once wrote that one of King Victor Emmanuel III's ancestors, the Duke of Savoy, could never be found on the same side at the end of a war as when it had been declared, unless he had changed camps twice. In contrast, the Duce considered that he had to respect the conditions of the Pact of Steel to the letter, because it concerned his personal honour, that of the Fascist Party, and of his country. His partner, on the other hand, had brazenly violated it twice, first by attacking Poland on September 1, 1939 and then by invading the Soviet Union on June 22, 1941, without having consulted his ally. "Nobody is obliged to sacrifice himself on the altar of an alliance," stated Prince Bismarck in a similar situation.

These were the arguments advanced by the exhausted Italian ministers on February 5, 1943, when faced by Hitler's obstinate determination to persevere with war on two fronts. One of those men, Dino Grandi, leaving the Palace on February 12, 1943, after the audience traditionally granted to resigning ministers, said to the King's senior aide-de-camp, General Puntoni:

"One must not have any illusions. Italy should attempt little by little to unhitch her wagon from that of Germany to make the crash less painful. I have always been a supporter of a policy of understanding with Great Britain, and within the limits of my power have always sought to oppose the thrust in the direction of Germany...On the home front, in face of the apathy of the great mass of the people, a general lack of confidence in their leaders, there is resentment of many of the old Fascist elements, who have been frustrated in this desire to make and serve the country. For them, Fascism should be an instrument of redemption. At any moment, in the face of military disaster, a political movement could take shape with a social basis which

Mussolini in the days of his pre-war ascendancy—a far cry from early 1943.

RAF and USAAF raids on Italy gave an added spur to the anti-war faction.

the Communists would at once exploit. Only the King at the right moment could restore things to their place. It would, however, be a most difficult and dangerous operation. For my part, I am with the King.''

Puntoni naturally passed on the offer of service to the King, who replied by conferring on Grandi, as President of the Fascist Chamber, the Collar of the Annunziata, the highest decoration in the gift of the House of Savoy and which, very usefully, gave its holder free access to the Quirinal Palace. Thus the distinction constituted an encouragement to Grandi and furnished him with the means of continuing his talks with the King.

In fact, as the King said in a letter to the Duke of Acquarone, since January 1943 he had ''definitely decided to end the Fascist régime and dismiss Mussolini''. He was being insistently urged to do so by the old Marshals Badoglio and Cavaglia and by the young Generals Carboni and Castellano. Nevertheless the monarch countered these demands by arguing that a military *coup d'état* would allow the Duce to hide behind the ramparts of the constitution and to mobilise the paramilitary forces of the Fascist militia. In this case, there would be civil war, and everything pointed to Germany's siding with Mussolini, the only man in Italy that Hitler trusted.

On the other hand, if the opposition within the Fascist Party itself could be stirred up, Mussolini would gradually find himself in a minority among his own supporters. This change of heart would bring on a political crisis to which the monarch and, if it became necessary, the Army would find a solution which could be seen to be within the letter of the

constitution. This way of doing things would, the King thought, morally disarm the Duce's private army and remove any excuse for intervention by the Third Reich, since the matter would be purely domestic. That was the reason for the great importance that the prudent King attached to his relations with Grandi, who was to play an essential part in the process of undermining and wearing away the régime.

In the Fascist Grand Council, Count Grandi was supported in his rebellion by Ciano and Bottaï. The latter had just been ousted from the Ministry of Education. Even so, as has just been seen, Victor Emmanuel III had set himself the task not only of ridding himself of Mussolini as head of the government, but also of putting an end to the totalitarian régime that had been instituted in Italy following the ''March on Rome'' at the end of October 1922. Clearly he could not talk about this to the disgruntled Fascist ex-ministers. At the most, he thought he could work with them in the same way as Carboni.

In his plans to overthrow the régime, the King spoke to prime ministers of the Liberal era such as Victor Emmanuel Orlando and Ivanoë Bonomi in private audiences at the Quirinal Palace. But both were in their eighties and had been away from public life for more than 20 years. Besides, the opportunity presented by some ''military disaster'', which would precipitate the movement, as Grandi mentioned to General Puntoni after his audience with the King on February 12, was a great deal more difficult to seize than he had somewhat lightly imagined.

With every fresh defeat suffered by Italian arms, several thousand more Germans crossed the Brenner Pass into Italy. Certainly, their primary task was to help in the defence of Corsica, Sardinia, Sicily, and southern Italy against landings which

were expected from their mutual enemy. But German troops were sent also with the intention of preventing Italy from drawing the obvious conclusions from the increasingly hopeless strategic situation. The ''whalebone stiffeners'', as Hitler described German reinforcements, had become prison bars . . .

The position, however, was worse still. There is no doubt that the defeats foreseen by Grandi would remove the small amount of prestige that Mussolini still enjoyed among the Italian people. At the same time they would bring about the destruction of those military forces on which, in the event of an armistice following Mussolini's downfall, the new régime was counting to oppose, if it became necessary, the ever-growing number of German troops in Italy. It is thus easier to understand, though General Carboni in his memoirs does not, the fears which held General Ambrosio, Cavallero's successor as head of *Comando Supremo*, while he awaited Italy's change of course, as dangerous as it was vital.

The situation grew more serious as the gradual reinforcement of the Wehrmacht in Italy gave Hitler a multitude of pretexts for infiltrating hundreds of secret agents into the country and for recruiting generously-paid informers from the highest level of the State administration and the Fascist hierarchy. *Wilhelmstrasse* archives demonstrate quite clearly that some of the Duce's closest associates did not hesitate to report to Mackensen on the secret debates of the Italian Cabinet.

Was Mussolini unaware of these dealings? Was he also ignorant of the web being spun between the Royal Palace, the Army, and the opposition wing in his own party, in order to oust him from power? It is difficult to believe that he was. Yet, after the reaction marked by the ''Changing of the Guard'' on February 5, his behaviour between that date and the famous session of July 25, 1943, was characterised by a strange apathy.

Some remarks by Mussolini's wife are pertinent at this point.

''Two months before the Allied landings in Sicily, a lady of the Court informed me that secret meetings aimed at overthrowing my husband were being held at Castelporziano. The leaders of the plot were Grandi, Bottaï, and Federzoni, but the person who held the strings was none other than our cousin Badoglio, who intended to sacrifice not only Mussolini but the King and the dynasty as well.

''From what I have been told, Galeazzo [Ciano] was also in the plot. And yet my husband held him in great respect and appreciated his quick intelligence. Nevertheless he reproached him for allowing himself to be influenced by certain sectors of the Roman aristocracy that Benito and I had always avoided. I, for my part, was well aware of my son-in-law's opinion of me. He thought I was too *petit-bourgeois* and down-to-earth. On my side I certainly could not approve of his uncontrolled ambition and his liking for golf courses and society gatherings.''

CHAPTER 39
The Casablanca Conference

In his speech at the Lord Mayor's Banquet at the Mansion House on November 10, 1942, Winston Churchill commented on the recent successes of Anglo-American strategy from Montgomery's victory at Alamein to the successful Operation "Torch" landings in French North Africa. At the close of his address, which Sir Alan Brooke described as "very good", the War Premier said cautiously and with some reserve:

"This must not be taken as the end; it may possibly be the beginning of the end, but it certainly is the end of the beginning."

But the British and American governments still had to discuss and decide how best to exploit these considerable achievements; to hammer out finally the strategic shape of their joint effort in 1943. Such was the purpose of the Casablanca Conference (codenamed "Symbol"), which was attended by Churchill, Roosevelt and their chiefs-of-staff from January 14 to 23, 1943.

The two principals were luxuriously housed in adjoining villas in sub-tropical gardens; their staffs in a nearby hotel; the entire site being isolated and easily guarded. Full communications facilities were afforded by the British headquarters ship HMS *Bulolo*. Alan Brooke has left a colourful picture of Churchill at his ease amid the splendours of his borrowed villa:

"I had frequently seen him in bed, but never anything to touch the present setting. It was all I could do to remain serious. The room must have been Mrs Taylor's bedroom and was done up in Moorish style, the ceiling was a marvellous fresco of green, blue and gold. The head of the bed rested in an alcove of Moorish design with a religious light shining on either side; the bed was covered with a light blue silk covering with a 6-in wide *entre-deux* and the rest of the room in harmony with the Arabic ceiling. And there in the bed was Winston in his green, red and gold dragon dressing-gown, his hair, or what there was of it, standing on end, the religious lights shining on his cheeks, and a large cigar in his face!"

Churchill and Roosevelt had chosen Casablanca in preference to the mooted alternatives for various reasons. Iceland, though geographically convenient, did not attract for a midwinter meeting. As Roosevelt wrote to Churchill, "I prefer an oasis to the raft at Tilsit" (a reference to Napoleon's meeting with the Tsar Alexander in 1807). Constitutional considerations made it impossible for the President to travel as far as Cairo or Khartoum. On the other hand he could justify a visit to French North Africa on the score of inspecting the American forces there in his rôle as Commander-in-Chief.

It had been Roosevelt's original idea that the conference should be limited to

the heads of the armed services and that Soviet Russia should participate. Churchill, however, pointed out that only Stalin counted in Russian circles, and that, therefore, mere service leaders could not deal with him, nor fend off the kind of searching questions he would pose concerning the relative Anglo-American contribution to the struggle against Nazi Germany. Likewise, Churchill wanted there to be a preliminary meeting between British and Americans so that the Western Allies could present an agreed strategic package to the Russians. The President was against such a meeting, "because I do not want to give Stalin the impression that we are settling everything between ourselves before we meet him." In fact on December 6, 1942 Stalin courteously declined the invitation to take part in the summit on the grounds that the war situation (the battle against the trapped German 6th Army at Stalingrad was then at its height) made it impossible for him to leave the Soviet Union. He made it clear at the same time, however, that for him the salient question for the British and Americans to decide was the opening of a Second Front in Europe by the spring of 1943.

Thus it came about that the Casablanca Conference was a purely Anglo-American affair in which heads of governments as well as service chiefs took part.

In Britain and the United States alike there had already been long and wearisome argument as to the shape of future strategy. Thanks to the close-knit planning organisation forged in Britain by the pressures of war and the personal involvement of Churchill as Minister of Defence, all this hard discussion of projects and available resources had finally resulted in an agreed strategy buttressed by facts, figures and a closely argued case. But the American side came to Casablanca with no similar agreed strategy of its own. Since in certain fundamental respects the conference finally came round to agree with the British analysis, a legend arose in America after the war that the cunning British had "conned" the innocent Americans. The record belies this: the arguments turned in the end on the realities of available logistical resources and fighting strength, not on a simple British-versus-American line-up. This is not to say that there were not underlying differences of national temperament and approach, or lurking suspicions as to the sincerity behind an apparent commitment.

At the heart of the conference discussions on grand strategy lay two inter-related questions: the proportion of resources to be allotted respectively to the war against Germany and the war against Japan, and the rival merits of making the main Allied effort against Germany in 1943 in the Mediterranean or across the

Channel (Operation "Round-up"). The war against Japan—except for the Burma front—had become an exclusively American preserve controlled by Admiral Ernest J. King, the U.S. Chief of Naval Operations, a man blunt of speech and powerful of will. Grappling as he was with the problems of "Triphibious" warfare at the end of 3,000 miles of sea communications against a formidable enemy, King believed that the Pacific theatre was being dangerously starved of resources in favour of the German war with the consequent risk that the Japanese could dig themselves into a perimeter defence so strong that the allies might have great difficulties later in overcoming it. King, therefore, demanded a higher proportion of resources, even mentioning a percentage of 30 per cent as against the present 15 per cent. This would permit him to proceed with a series of step-by-step offensives aimed at retaining the initiative over the Japanese.

The British, being understandably pre-occupied with Germany and enjoying little or no say over operations in the Pacific, suspected King of seeking to overturn the order of strategic priority decided at the Washington Conference in December 1941, whereby Germany was to be beaten first, and then Allied resources switched to Japan. They wanted to see this priority clearly re-affirmed, with only minimum force going to the Pacific theatre until Germany had been defeated. None the less, there was a certain refusal to face facts in so believing that the Japanese war could be virtually kept on ice in the meantime.

With regard to strategy against Germany, the British had come to the conclusion—Churchill had taken a lot of convincing—that the Allied plan agreed in the summer of 1942 (to follow the conquest of North Africa with a cross-Channel invasion in 1943) was not a practicable operation of war. Instead they wished the principal Allied effort for 1943 to take place in the Mediterranean, exploiting the victories already being won in that theatre.

Sir Alan Brooke presented the British case at the opening session of the Combined Chiefs-of-Staff Committee on the morning of January 14. He pointed out that victory over the U-boat was essential to the war against Germany: "The shortage of shipping was a stranglehold on all offensive operations, and unless we could effectively combat the U-boat menace we might not be able to win the war." On land, he went on, Germany now lay on the defensive both in Russia and North Africa, while her allies were losing heart. It was not impossible that she could be brought down in 1943. The best means of achieving this lay in affording all possible aid to Soviet Russia, stepping up strategic bombing of the German home-

Churchill and Roosevelt have a word while they address reporters at the conference. Their relations with the press were generally very good.

land, and in launching amphibious operations. The latter, in the British analysis, should take place where poor communications made it most difficult for the Germans to concentrate and maintain large forces. Whereas excellent rail communications enabled the Germans to switch seven divisions at a time from Russia to Western Europe in 12–14 days, the Alps bottleneck meant that they could only move one division at a time into Italy. In the Balkans too, communications were scanty and exposed. With such scattered territories to defend along the northern shores of the Mediterranean, the Germans would be forced to disperse their strength. An offensive in the Mediterranean would thus maintain unremitting pressure, bring more effective support to Russia than a risky cross-Channel attack, and open up possibilities of forcing Italy out of the war and bringing Turkey in. Brooke nevertheless conceded–partly in deference to Churchill's fiercely held wishes– that the Allies should stand ready in England later in the summer to land in Europe if Germany should show signs of cracking up.

In the afternoon Admiral King argued his case for strengthening the Allied effort against Japan. The offensive in the

Solomons had been undertaken in order to clear the Japanese threat away from the main line of communications between Australia and the United States, but due to shortage of reserves, it could not be pressed beyond Guadalcanal and Tulagi. A further advance, however, opened up the possibility of advancing deep into the Japanese perimeter either via the Netherlands East Indies, or via Truk and the Marianas. King contended that it was essential to maintain constant pressure in order to prevent the Japanese consolidating their defences at leisure, but that his present forces were quite inadequate to achieve this.

Thus King opened up the debate on basic strategic priorities that lay at the heart of the conference. Probing questions by Brooke and Air Chief Marshal Portal, the Chief of Air Staff, as to exactly what would be entailed by maintaining pressure on Japan revealed British uneasiness lest King's requests led to an open-ended commitment that would decisively weaken the Allied effort against Germany. King, with characteristic directness, voiced a counter-suspicion that, once Germany was defeated, Britain would leave American to finish off Japan alone. On a suggestion by Portal, it was agreed to direct the Combined Staff Planners to examine and report on "what it was we had to prevent the Japanese from doing, and what forces we should require for the purpose".

But after four days of work the Combined Planners remained deadlocked and, therefore, wrote separate national papers instead of a joint one. Even though the British saw the force of the American argument that the Japanese must be pushed further north away from the Australia–America line of communications, they still wished to allot the minimum resources to the Japanese conflict necessary to achieve certain tightly defined and limited objectives. The American paper argued for a much more flexible attitude by which "Germany is recognised as the primary, or most powerful and pressing enemy, and that the major part of the forces of the United Nations are to be directed against Germany in so far as is consistent with the overall objective of bringing the war to an early conclusion . . ." It was necessary, contended the American planners, to keep the initiative over Japan by forcing battles on her and so denying her the opportunity of launching offensives at times and places of her own choosing. They therefore considered that in 1943 the Allies could and should carry out offensives from their present positions in the Solomons and New Guinea aimed at reaching New Britain and the Japanese advanced base at Rabaul on New Ireland and the Lae-Salamau Peninsula on New Guinea. In the Central Pacific area, the American planners proposed a thrust through the Gilbert, the Marshall and the Caroline Islands aimed at the Japanese main fleet base of Truk. A subsidiary offensive in the Aleutians should yield Kiska and Agattu. At the same time there should be an offensive in Burma to re-open the lower Burma road in order to bring succour to Chiang Kai-shek's China, which American opinion (and in particular Roosevelt) persisted in regarding as a powerful and effective ally. The American planners also wanted a seaborne invasion of Burma (codenamed Operation "Anakim"). To carry out this strategy would, the American planners reckoned, demand an extra 210,000 men, 500 aircraft and a million and a quarter tons of shipping.

Their British colleagues, inured to waging war with scant resources, felt that this American strategy–born of a buoyant sense of America's immense industrial and human resources–was over-ambitious. They argued that only the offensives in the Solomons towards Rabaul and on New Guinea towards Lae, together with limited operations in Burma against the port of Akyab and to open a road route to China were really necessary in 1943; and that although planning for the further offensives should be put in hand, a decision as to their launching should be delayed until late in the year. In particular the British planners contended that simultaneous operations against Truk and Burma ("Anakim") "cannot but react adversely on the early defeat of Germany".

Here the British put their fingers on the basic factor in a global amphibious war such as Britain and America had to wage–the availability of assault and supply shipping and the naval forces to cover them, and above all the availability of landing craft. Since the United States were overwhelmingly the principal producer of landing craft, and since the disposition of American landing craft lay entirely with Admiral King, the British did not enjoy the strongest bargaining position.

On January 18, the Combined Chiefs-of-Staff met to grapple with the problem of composing the differences between the two papers. In the meantime, however, they themselves had been arguing about the rival merits of an offensive in the Mediterranean or across the Channel as the more effective means of relieving pressure on the Russians and weakening Nazi Germany. In these discussions, differing national traditions and attitudes to strategy again manifested themselves. Since the fall of France and the end of the Western Front in 1940, the British had had to contend with the conundrum of how to wage war with heavily outnumbered land forces against a great Continental power; a conundrum they had encountered many times before in their history. The traditional British answer lay in maritime landings in peripheral areas where the enemy could not deploy his full strength because of poor land communications. Only in the Great War had the British fielded a mass army and engaged the main body of the enemy army in protracted battles; an experience which had made a lasting and profoundly discouraging impression on British soldiers and statesmen alike. Therefore, although Sir Alan Brooke offered a convincing (and in retrospect, entirely justified) case for postponing a major cross-Channel landing until 1944 in favour of an offensive in the Mediterranean in 1943, there underlay the British position a deep unwillingness to risk directly taking on the German army until operations elsewhere (above all on the Russian Front) had decisively weakened it.

The American tradition of warfare, on the other hand, derived from Continental European models, together with an awareness of America's huge resources. The American mind was less pragmatic than the British; it preferred a clear-cut "over-all strategic concept" into which everything fitted neatly. General Marshall, therefore, thought in almost opposite terms from Brooke; his instinct was to engage the main body of the German army in the West at the earliest possible moment and by the most direct route–across the Channel. He was highly suspicious of the British preference for an "indirect approach" of strategic bombing and attacking via the Mediterranean. He had unwillingly accepted the necessity for the "Torch" landings in 1942 in place of "Round-up" (crossing the Channel), fearing nevertheless that "Torch" could lead on to further commitments that would continued to prejudice "Round-up". Now at Casablanca he saw the British arguing for exactly such a further involvement in the Mediterranean. Just as the British themselves feared that Admiral King's strategy for the Pacific could become an open-ended commitment prejudicing the war against Germany, so Marshall feared that the British Mediterranean strategy would prove equally open-ended, delaying and perhaps even preventing an eventual invasion of France. While conceding that one of the strongest arguments in favour of the Mediterranean was that "there will be an excess of troops in North Africa once Tunisia has been cleared of Axis forces", he wanted to know whether a Mediterranean offensive would be an end in itself or a means to an end.

Brooke had already spent wearisome weeks convincing his Prime Minister that a cross-Channel landing in 1943 was simply beyond Allied resources, and he was, therefore, prepared to argue with Marshall. He pointed out in detail that the Allies would lack the land forces in the United Kingdom and the landing-craft lift to have a chance of defeating the 44 divisions the Germans could concentrate for the defence of the West without even weakening the Russian Front. Better, therefore, in his analysis, to invade Sicily from North Africa and force Italy out of the war, so compelling the Germans to find troops for the occupation of Italy and in replacement of the Italian forces garrisoning the Balkans. Brooke was not, however, looking beyond the conquest of Sicily at this time. Far from advocating a campaign on the Italian mainland, he specifically warned the Combined Chiefs-of-Staff against "accepting any invitation to support an anti-Fascist insurrection. To do so might only immobilise a considerable force to no useful purpose".

In his discussion with Marshall, Brooke was acting as spokesman for a carefully planned set of policy decisions, whereas General Marshall's arguments were merely expressing a personal view. His own air colleague, General Arnold, agreed with Air Chief Marshall Portal that operations in the Mediterranean would better force the Germans to disperse their air power than "Round-up", and that the collapse of Italy would open the way for the destruction of German oil resources and other key targets from the air. Admiral King, himself a maritime war expert, likewise saw the force of the British case in favour of the Mediterranean especially on the grounds that since the Allies had the troops in the theatre they might as well make use of them. He favoured Sicily rather than Sardinia as an objective, and promised the necessary naval support. President Roosevelt, worked on in private by Churchill, also came to favour the Sicily operation. Even some members of Marshall's own staff recognised that hard facts told against "Round-up" in 1943. Marshall, therefore, yielded to the consensus. It was decided that there would be no "Round-up" that year except in the event of a sudden German disintegration, and the principal Allied effort would be made against Sicily. The Cross-Channel attack had to wait until 1944.

Nevertheless this Mediterranean strategy did come under further discussion at the Combined Chiefs-of-Staff meeting on January 18, when it had to be married to a final agreement on the balance of

George Catlett Marshall, the director of much of America's war effort, here decorating an American soldier.

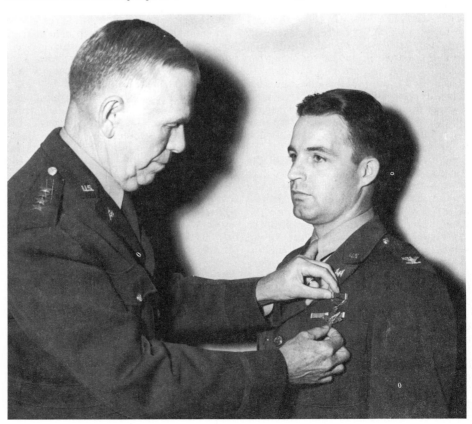

priority between the German war and the Japanese war. Brooke, deploying yet again the British arguments in favour of a fixed minimum allotment of resources to fighting Japan until after Germany had been beaten, emphasised the need for constant pressure on Germany to prevent her from recovering from her present setbacks; that was, by operations in the Mediterranean. Marshall now voiced an anxiety lest this should mean that large forces would sit around in the United Kingdom throughout the year waiting for some problematical German collapse, for such forces could be better employed in the Pacific. He was, he said, "anxious to get a secure position in the Pacific so that we knew where we were".

It was Air Vice Marshal Slessor who helped break the deadlock by drafting a compromise formula which, put forward by Brooke that afternoon, was accepted by the American side, and made possible the drawing up of the final Memorandum on the Conduct of the War in 1943, formally agreed by the Combined Chiefs-of-Staff next day and later approved by the President and Prime Minister.

This memorandum constituted the strategic fruit of the Casablanca Conference, the basis of all subsequent detailed planning. "Operations in the European Theatre," it stated, "will be conducted with the object of defeating Germany in 1943 with the maximum forces which can be brought to bear on her by the United Nations." Then came the balancing clause: "In order to ensure that these operations and preparations are not prejudiced by the necessity to retrieve an adverse situation elsewhere, adequate forces shall be allocated to the Pacific and Far Eastern Theatres." In those theatres operations were to continue with the forces allocated, with the object of maintaining pressure on Japan, retaining the initiative and attaining a position of readiness for the "full scale offensive against Japan by the United Nations as soon as Germany is defeated". The memorandum laid down that such interim operations "must be kept within such limits as will not, in the opinion of the Combined Chiefs-of-Staff, jeopardise the capacity of the United Nations to take advantage of any favourable opportunity that may present itself for the decisive defeat of Germany in 1943". Within the broad Far Eastern and Pacific strategy the memorandum gave priority to the "Anakim" operation (the seaborne invasion of southern Burma) in 1943 over the drive through the Marshall and Caroline islands on Truk, unless, in the event, time and resources permitted both. So far as strategy against Germany was concerned, the memorandum laid down, as agreed, that the Mediterranean was to be the scene of the principal effort and Sicily the first objective; the general object being to divert German pressure from the Russian front, increase the pressure on Italy and if possible draw Turkey into the war. However, such forces

as could be built up in the United Kingdom after satisfying the needs of the Mediterranean operations and the Japanese war were to stand ready to re-enter the Continent "as soon as German resistance is weakened to the required extent". Otherwise offensive action from the United Kingdom was to take the form of an intensified strategic air offensive against the German economy.

On two fundamental grand-strategic questions there had been no argument among the Combined Chiefs-of-Staff. As the opening two paragraphs of the final memorandum put it, "defeat of U-boat remains first charge on resources", and "Russia must be sustained by greatest volume of supplies transportable to Russia without prohibitive cost in shipping".

Hindsight casts its own light on the basic strategic decision taken at Casablanca to make the main Allied effort against Germany in 1943 in the Mediterranean rather than across the Channel. Marshall's misgivings, shared by some members of his own staff like General Wedemayer (who bitterly claimed after the war that, "We even lost our shirts" to the British), that the Mediterranean option could lead to an ever deeper involvement was to be fully borne out when the Allies embarked on the long slog up the mountainous spine of Italy. Yet the British calculation that the Allies would not be strong enough to launch a victorious cross-Channel invasion in 1943 was shown to be correct by the relatively narrow margin by which the Normandy invasion succeeded even a year later. With regard to the British fear that the Japanese war could suck in an ever greater quantity of Allied resources, the course of events was to demonstrate just such a tendency to slippage, and despite the firm statement agreed at Casablanca whereby clear priority was accorded to beating Germany.

It remained to put the operational flesh on the strategic bones; a task which occupied the last five days of the Casablanca Conference, as the Joint Planners worked out a series of detailed planning papers to be amended and agreed by the Combined Chiefs-of-Staff. As the Memorandum on the Conduct of the War in 1943 has stated, defeat of the U-boat was crucial—and at that moment the U-boat was winning. During 1942 a total of 7,790,697 tons of Allied shipping had been sunk, the bulk of it by submarine, while only 7 million tons had been turned out by Allied shipyards, so that year by year Allied shipping resources were being progressively whittled down. Moreover Germany was producing U-boats faster than the Allies were destroying them, so that the number of operational boats had risen during the last year from 91 to 212. The key to defeating the U-boat, as the Conference agreed on the basis of the Joint Planners' paper, lay in convoy escort ships and Atlantic air cover. However the shortfall in escort ships, in

view of the competition for such craft offered by amphibious operations in the Mediterranean and Pacific, meant that it would be late summer before the Atlantic convoys could be given the protection they needed. At Admiral Sir Dudley Pound's suggestion, the Combined Chiefs-of-Staff added a rider to their Memorandum on the Conduct of the War to the effect that they recognised this danger. In its resolution on the Battle of the Atlantic the Conference agreed that the U-boat must be beaten firstly by attacking its building yards and bases with heavy bombers; secondly by Britain and America combing their existing allocations of escort vessels for other purposes in order to meet without delay half the present shortfall on the Atlantic; thirdly by providing light escort carriers to afford convoys air cover in the mid-Atlantic "air-gap" as quickly as possible, and lastly supplying very-long-range aircraft for the same purpose.

The global shortage of escort vessels also affected the question of the number of Arctic convoys that could be run to Russia. The Combined Chiefs-of-Staff were determined that "supplies to Russia shall not be continued at prohibitive cost to the United Nations effort", but Churchill, mindful of Stalin's likely disappointment at there being no Second Front in 1943, argued that "no investment could pay a better military dividend" than aid to Russia, and so secured an assurance from the Chiefs-of-Staff that everything possible would be done to keep the convoys flowing even while the invasion of Sicily was under way.

Discussion of the paper on the Allied strategic air offensive against Germany brought fresh problems of clashing demands on limited available resources. Air Chief Marshal Portal, supported by General Brooke, argued that if too literal an interpretation were made of the priority accorded in the Memorandum on the Conduct of the War to bombing U-boat yards and bases, it would seriously reduce the general bombing of the German war economy. British and American airmen stood united in a faith that the bomber could play a key role in bringing Germany to her knees, even though the British air marshals were sceptical about the American belief in daylight precision bombing by unescorted bomber fleets—rightly, as it turned out. Admirals King and Pound retorted that in view of the shortage of surface escorts it was more than ever necessary to concentrate air strength against the U-boat. The final Conference Directive for the Bomber Offensive attempted to compromise between the sailors and the airmen by reaffirming the bomber-offensive's objective as "the progressive destruction and dislocation of the German military, industrial and economic system, and the undermining of the morale of the German people, to a point where their capacity for armed resistance is fatally weakened", while at the same laying down that U-boat building yards must be the priority target, followed by the German aircraft industry, transportation network and oil resources.

The way was clear for the combined British and American bomber offensive which in 1943 was to inflict grievous but never decisive damage on the German economy and end in the clear, if short-lived, defeat of both Bomber Command and the U.S. Eighth Air Force at the hands of the enemy air defence. However, despite the Chiefs-of-Staff's statement that the U-boat must be the priority target, the airmen were to prove profoundly reluctant to release aircraft from the general bombing of Germany, and the battle of the Atlantic was for some months to be starved of very-long range aircraft equipped with the new 20-cm radar–another case where conference decisions failed to be fulfilled completely.

During the general strategic debate earlier in the Conference, it had been decided to invade Sicily (Operation "Husky") rather than Sardinia (Operation "Brimstone"), which had been the preference of the British Joint Planners and the Chief of Combined Operations, Lord Louis Mountbatten. Both Churchill and Roosevelt as well as the Combined Chiefs-of-Staff themselves favoured Sicily. The argument now turned on the planners' draft operational plan for "Husky" and its timing. Given that Tunisia would be finally captured by April, the Joint Planners reckoned that the necessary air, sea and land forces for "Husky" could not be assembled and trained before August 30. They envisaged a British invasion force based solely on Middle East ports landing on the south-

east corner of Sicily while the American force, based on French North African ports, landed on the south-western coast and at Palermo. Churchill was outraged by the proposed D-Day, which meant that the Allied forces would be standing idle for four months after the conquest of Tunisia. As a result of his urging, the Combined Chiefs-of-Staff hammered out a fresh schedule by which the Allies would seek to launch "Husky" during the July moon period. General Eisenhower, the Supreme Commander Designate, was to report back not later than March 1 as to whether this would be possible or whether "Husky" would have to be delayed into August. But Churchill was still not satisfied. With the skill born of years of cross-examining generals and admirals, he demanded convincing reasons why the operation could not be launched still sooner. Nevertheless, the Combined Chiefs-of-Staff remained adamant that if the Allies were not to risk a disastrous repulse adequate forces could not be concentrated and trained in a shorter time. Churchill would not have it. At his and Roosevelt's insistence the directive to Eisenhower carried the rider that "an intense effort" was to be made during the next three weeks to study whether "by contrivance and ingenuity" the invasion could not be launched during the June moon period; and they returned to the charge at the end of the Conference in a note to their advisers stressing the importance of not leaving Allied forces idle beyond June. In the event the invasion of Sicily began on July 10, some six weeks earlier than the date first suggested; an instance where, as Michael Howard points out in *Grand Strategy*, Vol IV

(HMSO 1972), Churchill's impatient prodding proved of great benefit to the Allied war effort.

The remaining strategic question discussed at the Casablanca Conference was that of the rate of build-up of U.S. land forces in the United Kingdom ("Bolero") for a possible limited cross-Channel operation late in 1943 ("Sledgehammer"). On January 20 Churchill, in reporting conference decisions to the War Cabinet, wrote: "At home 'Bolero' is to go ahead as fast as our commitments allow, with a view to a 'Sledgehammer' of some sort this year or a return to the Continent with all available forces if Germany shows definite signs of collapse." Thus, just as General Marshall had always feared, the original decision for "Torch" and the fresh decision at Casablanca for "Husky" were at the expense of the creation of a mighty invasion from the UK. In July 1942 it had been expected that there would be over half a million American troops in Britain by the end of the year; in fact there were fewer than a hundred thousand, excluding troops earmarked for "Torch". As with all aspects of Allied strategy the key factor in "Bolero" lay in shipping space. Nevertheless, on January 21 the Casablanca Conference began to tackle the problem of how to maintain the momentum of "Bolero" during 1943 despite all other commitments. General Marshall expressed the hope that American forces in Britain might be increased to some 400,000 by the beginning of July, giving five to six divisions

De Gaulle, the embodiment of French nationalism; he resented his peremptory summons to Casablanca.

Roosevelt addresses the press conference which closed proceedings, making his "unconditional surrender" statement.

for a "Sledgehammer" landing in France by the beginning of August; four extra divisions could be supplied in time for a mid-September attack. However, a detailed study of shipping space by Lord Leathers and General Somerwell proved much less sanguine: four American divisions in Britain by mid-August, seven by mid-September, 15 by the end of the year. And although Churchill in his eagerness to launch some kind of "Sledgehammer" late in the summer criticised these estimates as too pessimistic, the event was in fact to prove them too optimistic.

In any case, staff studies of possible "Sledgehammer" operations gave little scope for optimism. The Cotentin Peninsula, the planners thought, was "the only area with a short and easily defensible line within a reasonable distance of the beaches, and one which, at the same time, permits reasonable air support". The minimum strength needed to seize a bridgehead and defend it against the calculated flow of German reserves was put at five brigade groups supported by ten parachute battalions and an airborne division, with reinforcements of eight more divisions in the first forty-eight hours. But the expected total of available landing craft would only be sufficient to lift a fraction of this force. The Joint Planners, therefore, concluded that "Sledgehammer" would not be feasible in

1943 unless the German reserves had first been greatly worn down. The Conference, therefore, decided merely that planning should continue for a contingency operation by August 1 to exploit some sudden German weakness. Far more important, it was decided to accept the recommendations of the Joint Planners in their paper ponderously entitled "Proposed Organisation of Command, Control, Planning and Training for Operations for a Re-entry to the Continent across the Channel beginning in 1943" that the Allies should plan for a full-scale invasion in 1944, and that either a Supreme Commander or a Chief-of-Staff, with a nucleus staff, should be appointed without delay. The British Lieutenant-General F. E. Morgan was, therefore, appointed COSSAC, Chief-of-Staff to the (as yet undesignated) Supreme Allied Commander, with the task of planning the invasion. Here was the first step along the path of complex preparation that eventually was to lead to D-Day on June 6, 1944.

Grand strategy and operational planning were not, however, the only matters to be tackled by the President and the Prime Minister and their advisers at Casablanca; there were political questions too, the thorniest being that of the future government of French Africa, spiky as this was with the susceptibilities of Generals de Gaulle and Giraud (High Commissioner in North Africa in succession to the assassinated Admiral Darlan). The British and American governments wished to create gradually a

single administration for the former Vichy colonies in Africa and those which had rallied to de Gaulle's Free French Movement; and eventually a single French national organisation, or shadow French government. This entailed in the first place getting agreement between General Giraud and de Gaulle, the head of the French National Committee in London, and both leaders were, therefore, invited to Casablanca. While Giraud readily agreed to come, de Gaulle refused. He felt slighted at not having been privy to the "Torch" landings, and was highly suspicious of any deal with former Vichy elements wished on him by the Anglo-Saxons. As Churchill wrote later: "I understood and admired, while I resented his arrogant behaviour. Here he was–a refugee, an exile from his country under sentence of death, in a position entirely dependent on the goodwill of the British Government, and now also of the United States . . . He had no real foothold anywhere. Never mind; he defied all. Always, even when he was behaving worst, he seemed to express the personality of France–a great nation, with all its pride, authority, and ambition."

In order to get de Gaulle to Casablanca Churchill finally instructed Eden, the British Foreign Secretary, to warn him that if he failed to come, "The position of His Majesty's Government towards your Movement while you remain at its head will also require to be reviewed. If with your eyes open you reject this unique opportunity we shall endeavour to get on as well as we can without you". And

Churchill advised Eden: "For his own sake, you ought to knock him about pretty hard."

So on January 22 de Gaulle duly arrived in Casablanca. A three-hour conversation with Giraud produced no acceptance of the Anglo-American plan for a combined French leadership and administration, but instead a characteristic Gaullist public statement by the two generals:

"We have met. We have talked. We have registered our entire agreement.

"The end to be achieved is the liberation of France and the triumph of human liberties by the total defeat of the enemy.

"This end will be attained by the union in war of all Frenchmen fighting side by side with all their allies."

So, resolutely and skilfully, de Gaulle went his own way; a way that was to end in the 1960s with himself as leader of a resurgent France dominating western Europe, from which high position he was to pay Britain and America back in full for wartime humiliations.

The last formal proceedings of the Casablanca Conference took place on Sunday, January 24, 1943–a press conference given by Roosevelt and Churchill, to the astonishment of journalists who until then had had no inkling that they were absent from Washington and London. Yet it was this final press conference which of all the transactions at Casablanca led to perhaps the most lasting controversy. The American President added at the end of his address: "... I think we had all had it in our hearts and heads before, but I don't think that it has ever been put down on paper by the Prime Minister and myself, and that is the determination that peace can come to the world only by the total elimination of German and Japanese war power.

"Some of you Britishers know the old story–we had a General called U.S. Grant. His name was Ulysses Simpson Grant, but in my, and the Prime Minister's early days he was called 'Unconditional Surrender Grant'. The elimination of German, Japanese and Italian war power means the unconditional surrender by Germany, Japan and Italy. . . This meeting may be called 'the unconditional surrender meeting'."

The controversy over this "unconditional surrender" policy has turned on the strategic wisdom of leaving the enemy nation no recourse but resistance to the bitter end, so, it is argued, binding them indissolubly to the fortunes of their fascist régimes, and hence prolonging the war. Certainly, as the Casablanca Conference records make clear, the possible strategic consequences of such a policy were never analysed and discussed. Nevertheless it remains impossible to establish how much, if at all, the demand for unconditional surrender in fact lengthened the resistance of the three enemy states, especially in view of the tight grip in which the German and Japanese régimes in particular held their peoples. It must also remain a matter of historical doubt

whether it would have been of greater benefit to future peace and stability if the Allies had negotiated an armistice with some alternative German or Japanese government. The 1918 Armistice with Germany does not offer a favourable precedent.

But in any event "unconditional surrender" no more than expressed the will and wish of the British and American, as well as the Russian, peoples that this time German military power should be demonstrably and unambiguously crushed into the dust and the whole of Germany occupied. Hindsight must also take account of the deep anger felt at the time of peoples who had been wantonly attacked, bombed and occupied.

However, controversy also centres on the actual timing of the President's announcement of the policy of "unconditional surrender", and on the degree of prior consultation with his British colleague. Roosevelt himself said later that the thought came to him impromptu in the very course of the press conference:

"We had had so much trouble getting those two French generals together that I thought to myself that this was as difficult as arranging the meeting between Grant and Lee (at the end of the American Civil War in 1865, so that Lee might surrender his army)–and then suddenly this press conference was on, and Winston and I had no time to prepare for it, and the thought popped into my mind that they called Grant 'Old Unconditional Surrender' and the next thing I knew, I had said it."

But this could not have been so, because Roosevelt spoke from notes in which the famous words appear several times.

Churchill's own later recollections of the matter seem equally at fault. In his war memoirs he wrote that although he loyally spoke up in the press conference in support of Roosevelt's announcement of "unconditional surrender", he had himself heard the President's words "with some feeling of surprise". In point of fact, it was Churchill who, at a meeting with the President and the Combined Chiefs-of-Staff on January 18, had suggested that a public statement be issued after the conference "to the effect that the United Nations are resolved to pursue the war to the bitter end, neither party relaxing its efforts until the unconditional surrender of Germany and Japan has been achieved." This was, according to Michael Howard the British official historian, the first time the phrase occurs in the official record. Furthermore Churchill referred the proposal to the War Cabinet in London, which not merely fully concurred but recommended the inclusion of Italy as well. Thus the British War Premier and War Cabinet fully and freely supported the "unconditional surrender" policy and its announcement at Casablanca.

The truth is that "unconditional surrender" had as much to do with appeasing mutual suspicions among the Allies as

with impressing enemies. In the first place, the British and Americans recognised that Stalin could only regard Sicily as a poor substitute for a Second Front in 1943, and might well doubt the Western Allies' commitment to Nazi Germany's defeat. "Unconditional surrender" served publicly to re-assure Stalin on this point. Secondly, Admiral King had voiced during the Conference a lurking American suspicion that once Germany had been beaten the British would not prove very keen on fully participating in the war against Japan. Churchill's suggestion at the meeting of January 18 of a public statement about "unconditional surrender" was intended to allay this American mistrust; in fact, he had even offered to enter into a solemn public treaty if the Americans so desired.

Perhaps the real danger of the "unconditional surrender policy" lay in that it crystallised a British, and even more an American, concentration on winning the war, to the detriment of far-sighted consideration of the shape of post-war Europe and the post-war world. Stalin, for his part, had been looking ahead to an eastern Europe under the Soviet thumb since the autumn of 1941, a time when the German panzers were approaching Moscow. The Spanish dictator Franco, a no less shrewd and subtle politician, wrote to Sir Samuel Hoare, the British Ambassador in Madrid, a month after the Casablanca Conference about the dangers of a Russian takeover of Germany:

"If Germany had not existed Europeans would have invented her and it would be ridiculous to think that her place could be taken by a confederation of Lithuanians, Poles, Czechs and Rumanians which would rapidly be converted into so many more states of the Soviet confederation."

Sir Samuel Hoare replied in confident terms that Soviet power would be balanced after the war by the economic strength and the resources of fresh troops enjoyed by Britain and America. "We shall not shirk our responsibilities to European civilisation", he wrote, "or throw away our great strength by premature unilateral disarmament. Having, with our Allies, won the war, we intend to maintain our full influence in Europe, and to take our full share in its reconstruction." Events were to belie this assurance: not until 1944 did Churchill really awaken to the menace of Soviet expansionism in eastern Europe, while it was not until 1945, after Roosevelt's death, that American policy ceased to look on Soviet Russia as a friendly ally with whom it would be easy to get along. The years 1945–48 were to witness just that consolidation of Soviet empire in eastern and central Europe against which Franco had warned Hoare in February 1943, and just that unilateral disarmament by the Western Allies which Hoare assured Franco would not take place. The "unconditional surrender" policy announced at Casablanca encouraged the Western Allies to see victory as an end in itself.

CHAPTER 40
The American build-up

The year 1943 was to see the young army of the United States engaged successively in Tunisia, in Sicily, and then in southern Italy; hence it is important for the reader to know its most original features.

On the day that World War II began, September 1, 1939, the American land forces were as unprepared in terms of men and *matériel* as they had been in August 1914. Six years later, on September 2, 1945, the day that Shigemitsu, the Japanese Prime Minister, and General Umezu, Chief of the Imperial General Staff, signed the terms of surrender for the Japanese Empire, they had put into service four army groups, nine armies, 23 corps, 89 divisions (including 67 infantry, one cavalry, 16 armoured, and five airborne). These were supported, covered and moved by 12 air forces totalling 273 air combat groups which, on the day of the surrender of the Japanese Empire, were divided into five very heavy bomber, 96 heavy bomber, 26 medium bomber, eight light bomber, 87 fighter, 24 reconnaissance, and 27 transport groups.

On the same day, the United States Army had 7,700,000 officers, N.C.O.s, and other ranks, including 100,000 W.A.C.s (Women's Army Corps), serving under the colours. It counted for just over half of the 14 million young Americans who were, in one respect or another, affected by the general mobilisation order which was the response to the attack on Pearl Harbor.

Compared with the 17 million Germans who donned one of the several uniforms of the Wehrmacht or of the *Waffen* S.S., out of a total population of between 80 and 90 millions, the figure of 14 million Americans seems insignificant. Likewise in comparison with the 22 million men and women whom the Soviet Union hurled into the heat of the conflict between June 22, 1941 and September 15, 1945.

But these comparisons are only part of the truth. It will be remembered that on September 1, 1939 Hitler had at his disposal 108 fully trained, officered, and equipped divisions, and that on June 22, 1941 Stalin was able to call on at least 178 to face the German aggressor alone, whereas when the war began in Europe, the Regular Army of the United States comprised only five divisions, numbering about 188,500 men and 14,400 officers. Hence everything (in every sphere – recruitment, training, equipment) had to be built up from this minute nucleus.

Furthermore, we must not forget that the "great arsenal of democracy" was not exclusively at the service of the American armed forces. By virtue of the Lend-Lease Act, war material had to be supplied to powers allied to the United States. According to the final two-yearly report addressed to the Secretary of State for War on September 1, 1945, military equipment worth more than 20,000 million dollars

was made over to Great Britain, the Soviet Union, China, France, etc., enough, it assures us, to equip fully no fewer than 2,000 infantry or 588 armoured divisions. These Lend-Lease supplies could only act as a brake and restriction on the American armed forces, both in view of the personnel required in their manufacture and transport overseas, and because of the delays consequently imposed on the organisation and training of units.

Mention has already been made of the irritation felt by General MacArthur at the thought of all the *matériel* President Roosevelt was sending to the Soviet Union, when he was left virtually destitute in the Philippines; one might also allude to the case of the armoured division stripped of the 300 Sherman tanks it had only recently received, so as to re-equip the British 8th Army, which had lost most of its tanks in the heavy fighting between Bir Hakeim and Tobruk. But what alternative was there? None it seems, judging by the fact that, in the main, General Marshall, Army Chief-of-Staff and Chairman of the Joint Chiefs-of-Staff Committee, never came into conflict on this issue with Franklin Roosevelt or Harry Hopkins, for like them he firmly believed in the principle of "Germany first".

Taking into account all the constraints that stood in the way of the natural growth of the American land forces, one is all the more astounded at the tremendous effort made between 1939 and 1944.

Credit for this is due to General of the Army George Catlett Marshall, whom President Roosevelt, so discerning in the choice of men so long as political considerations were not involved, had called to the post of Chief of the General Staff on September 1, 1939.

In the words of Sir John Dill, head of the British military delegation in Washington, writing to the Chief of the Imperial General Staff at the end of March 1942, he was "a man who improved immensely on acquaintance–straight, clear-headed, and loved by all: not a strategist, full of character and humour."

Lord Alanbrooke wrote as follows about his American colleague in 1946:

"There was a great charm and dignity about Marshall which could not fail to appeal to one; a big man and a very great gentleman who inspired trust but did not impress me by the ability of his brain."

We shall let Field-Marshals Dill and Alanbrooke bear the responsibility for their judgement as to Marshall's shortcomings as a strategist, which have all the appearance of being attributable to a quite divergent conception of the general conduct of operations, but the testimony of Sir Arthur Bryant is of value here the better to point the characteristics of the man he calls the "great Virginian":

"Without the great Virginian's strength of purpose and administrative ability the

American armies could never have been made so swiftly the instrument of victory they became. Between Pearl Harbor and D-Day Marshall did for America, and on a far vaster scale, what Carnot did for Revolutionary France and Kitchener for Britain."

Yet an army, be it large or small, is something other than an administrative or organisational entity. It is also a pyramidic structure of human beings, most of them attached to the military concept of duty, all of them subject to the rigours of military discipline. From this comes the importance attached to officer selection, to every aspect of officer training, and to appointments to high command.

In this respect, it has sometimes been unrecognised outside America that military staff training in the United States had been revolutionised as a result of the 1918 campaign, when the inadequacy of the rear area troops so contrasted with the *élan* of the front-line troops. There is no question at all that the Infantry School at Fort Benning and the Command and General Staff School at Fort Leavenworth were quite comparable with similar institutions in France, Germany, and Great Britain.

Nevertheless, although military leaders are never found among those who fail to pass out of staff college, the cream of any one year are not all military leaders; so of necessity there is a final stage in promotion, the most vital of all, and one is bound to recognise that Marshall's discernment here was unequalled. A close examination of the orders of battle of the different belligerents in World War II provides evidence that, in relation to other armies, American generals relieved of their command during active service were relatively few, thus vindicating Marshall's appointments.

And yet the task before him was a gigantic one: namely to move from a small professional army of five divisions to a great national army numbering 89, without the quality suffering from such a rapid rate of increase. One example will suffice to justify this statement: an example taken from the memoirs of General of the Army Omar Nelson Bradley, who is here describing the difficulties of every kind that he encountered during 1942, in the organisation and training of the 28th Infantry Division:

"The 28th Division was then undergoing the troubles that plagued so many National Guard divisions during mobilisation. Like others called into federal service in 1940 and 1941, the 28th Division had been cannibalized again and again for cadres in formation of new divisions. In addition, hundreds of its finest non-commissioned officers had been sent to officer training schools. Many more of its best-qualified men transferred to the air corps as flying cadets. These vacancies in the divisions were then filled with periodic transfusions of draftees, leaving the divi-

West Point cadets take part in a grenade practice during the early days of the war. Much of the junior leadership of the expanding United States Army was to devolve on officers from this academy.

sion in a constant state of unpreparedness. In June, 1942, I was ordered from the 82nd to take command of the 28th, whip those unbalanced units into a trim division, and ready it for the field.

"For months afterwards the 28th Division continued to be bled both for cadres and officer candidate quotas. The constant turnover in personnel gutted our progress in training, and throughout the entire division we became desperately short of junior officers and noncoms. Only too often companies were commanded by second lieutenants assisted by sergeants.

"Finally when IV Corps called for still another cadre to form a new division, I said, 'Fine, we'll send you one. But then suppose you send us a cadre so we can get along here.' "

Lord Alanbrooke, as we have seen, describes General Marshall as a "very great gentleman". Let this be the final touch to his portrait. And indeed a man who was able to live on good terms with a colleague as awkward as Admiral King and command the respect of a subordinate as difficult as General MacArthur, must have been distinguished by outstanding qualities of balanced leadership, tact, evenness of temper and shining integrity. Furthermore, in his capacity as chairman of the Joint Chiefs-of-Staff, which constituted a sort of link between the military command and the government, he enjoyed the entire confidence of Secretary of War Henry Stimson and of President Roosevelt. In addition to this, he was held in esteem by, and had ready access to, the Senate, which was not unimportant in view of

the Senate's watching brief on the appointment of general officers.

Let us now attempt to describe the larger military formations of the American army, with emphasis less on what they had in common with, than on what distinguished them from the formations we have already encountered. In both the Red Army and the Wehrmacht, as we have seen, the basic tank or armoured formation altered from the brigade or division to the corps or army (between 1939 and 1941 in the case of the Germans, 1940 and 1942 for the Russians). There was no such development with the Americans, where the norm remained the division. Was this a defect of organisation, as has been suggested?

The American infantry division was completely motorised, numbering 1,440 vehicles for 14,253 officers, N.C.O.s, and other ranks. Hence in attack it was possible within a corps to couple armoured and infantry formations without their disintegrating once they started moving, as occurred on so many occasions on the Eastern Front, where infantry or horse-drawn units found it hard going to keep up with advancing mechanised units. Thus of 328 German divisions that had been or were being formed on October 4, 1943, there were no more than 46 that could be considered as armoured or motorised. It is nevertheless true that if wholly motorised units proved their worth in the plains of France and Germany, they were to give plenty of trouble to the Americans in the mountainous regions of southern Italy, where communications were poor. During the winter of 1943/4, the American 5th Army, incapable of manoeuvring across the mountains, was reduced–with the negative results that are common knowledge–to pounding away at the fortress of Cassino.

Taken altogether, with its three infantry regiments (nine battalions), artillery regiment consisting of four groups each of 12 howitzers (three of 105-mm and one of 155-mm weapons), engineer battalion, signals company, medical battalion, and supply and maintenance units, the American infantry division was in no essential way different from its European and Japanese counterparts.

On the other hand, it is quite another story with the armoured division in the form given it at Fort Knox (the American "tankodrome") by General Chaffee, with the influential support of General Marshall; it was Chaffee who in the United States played the rôle of Colonel de Gaulle and General Guderian.

Its order of battle consisted of a reconnaissance battalion, four battalions of medium tanks, three battalions of infantry in half-tracks, three battalions of self-propelled 105-mm howitzers (18 in each), an engineer battalion, a separate engineer company, a medical battalion, a repair and maintenance battalion, and other rear formations. The whole comprised, in its 1942 form, 159 medium M4 Sherman type tanks, 68 light M3 Stuart tanks, 68 8-ton armoured cars, and rather more than 1,100 wheeled all-purpose vehicles for the division's 651 officers and 10,248 N.C.O.s and other ranks.

Compared with the Panzer division in its 1943 form, the American armoured division had 227 tanks as against 160. Its three infantry battalions moved up into the combat zone in lightly armoured half-tracks, whereas the Germans were only able to mechanise one battalion in every four. With artillery the picture is the same. The Americans equipped the three artillery battalions with self-propelled guns based on Sherman chassis, whereas the Panzer division had only one of its artil-

The backbone of the Army: a G.I.

lery regiments equipped with self-propelled guns.

But above all, the originality of the American armoured divisions lay in the fact that they were flexibly assembled in tactical groups whose composition was fixed; known as Combat Commands, these incorporated at regimental level one tank battalion (17 Stuart and 51 Sherman tanks), one battalion of motorised infantry, and a battalion of self-propelled howitzers, under a single commander supported by a staff. An armoured division had two combat commands, the rest of the division's forces forming the commander's reserve. This system of organisation, which simplified the exercise of command by decentralising it, produced such good

results that for the 1944 campaign it was decided to organise a third combat command in each division.

Finally, it should be said that unlike parallel European units, the American division had neither an anti-tank nor an anti-aircraft detachment as part of its equipment. These were allocated on a temporary basis from a higher échelon as the situation demanded; even so, every Sherman tank and every self-propelled howitzer was armed with a .5-inch anti-aircraft machine gun, quite sufficient to hold off low-flying aircraft.

The American Army faced the test of battle with equipment that was wholly new and, with very few exceptions, well suited to combat conditions – strong and sturdy, easy to learn to handle and to maintain, and designed for mass-production: for instance the Jeep and the Walkie-Talkie radio.

Certainly the standard American army tank, the M4 Sherman, even with its 75-mm (40 calibre) exchanged for a British-made 76.2-mm (58 calibre) gun, was no match for German machines of the same year of manufacture. But it must be remembered that if it had had to be prematurely discarded in favour of a more powerful, hence heavier machine, the transportation plans for Operation "Round-up", subsequently "Overlord", would have required total revision, and this would have involved discarding several hundred landing craft which had been built around the Sherman's specifications.

General Marshall, replying to certain criticisms, vindicated his action here in seemingly irrefutable terms:

"Our tanks had to be shipped thousands of miles overseas and landed on hostile shores amphibiously. They had to be able to cross innumerable rivers on temporary bridges, since when we attacked we sought to destroy the permanent bridges behind the enemy lines from the air. Those that our planes missed were destroyed by the enemy when he retreated. Therefore our tanks could not well be of the heavy type. We designed our armour as a weapon of exploitation. In other words we desired to use our tanks in long range thrusts deep into the enemy's rear where they could chew his supply installations and communications. This required great endurance – low consumption of gasoline and ability to move great distances without 'break-down.

"But while that was the most profitable use of the tank, it became unavoidable in stagnant prepared-line fighting to escape tank-to-tank battles. In this combat, our medium tank was at a disadvantage, when forced into head-on engagement with the German heavies."

In the face of the enemy's tanks, the American infantryman possessed a weapon that was both sturdy and ingenious. The "bazooka" got its name from a musical instrument then popular in the United States. Its punch was the

result of using a hollow charge warhead, whose effect on armour-plating was well known, before the war, to ordnance experts in both continents. On May 10, 1940 the Germans tried it out for the first time when they detonated charges of this type against the casemates of Fort Eben-Emaël. At the same time, a grenade-firing rifle, working on the same principle, had been ordered as a standard weapon by the French Army, and indeed had its production been accelerated there is no doubt that the Panzer divisions would not have found it so easy to cross the Meuse.

However, the file concerning this invention, which originated in Switzerland, was transferred to Washington by Vichy, in addition to that of the B1 *bis* tank. Then an American inventor had the idea of fitting a rocket-launcher to the base of the hollow charge grenade and of firing it through an open ended tube. The weapon's range was up to 400 yards, which left the infantryman only 30 seconds to take aim, but it was capable of penetrating five inches of armour plate and, if the right circumstances presented themselves, of blowing up the tank's supply of petrol and ammunition.

Evidence of their destructive power was to be seen after the war, for example in Normandy and Alsace where the wrecks of armoured vehicles were still strewn across the 1944 and 1945 battlefields.

In the infantry regiments, the M3 37-mm anti-tank gun had to be replaced almost on the spur of the moment by the British 57-mm 6-pounder, which had come into service, with highly successful results, on the El Alamein front during the previous summer. But at army and corps level, there were still anti-tank battalions equipped with the M5 75-mm gun firing a $12\frac{1}{2}$-lb armour-piercing shell at a muzzle velocity of 2,800 feet per second. Initially it was fitted onto half-tracks, but the results were so discouraging that the weapon acquired the name of Purple Heart Box after the American medal for wounds received in action. It was quickly abandoned in favour of a device given the designation number M10; mounted in an open turret on a Sherman chassis, it was completely satisfactory.

It has been alleged, sometimes in print, that the United States Army was too lavishly equipped and that its rear formations operated on a gigantic scale. They certainly contained laundering companies and shower units, naturally enough motorised. But before ridiculing an organisation that took certain things to extremes, it should be clearly understood that the Americans conceived the war they were fighting as, in General Eisenhower's words, a "Crusade in Europe". Forced as they were to operate among peoples who had been cruelly impoverished by enemy occupation, they had no wish to requisition from those they liberated.

Finally, a few remarks must be made on the subject of those who constituted an army which, following a brief period of being broken in, would acquit itself so magnificently in the liberating mission it had been entrusted with.

Its successes are ample demonstration of the quality of the American fighting soldier, his courage under fire, endurance, and devotion to duty. Better still, looking down the list of names of an American company where Anglo-Saxon names, Scottish, Irish, German, Scandinavian, Italian, Spanish (some of Indian ancestry), Slavonic, Greek, and even Japanese, are to be found side by side, tribute is due to the system of education in the United States which has shown itself capable of moulding the son of every immigrant into a citizen and a patriot, whatever his social class, his race, or his religion.

General Marshall himself made the following statement as to the methods by which the American soldier received his training:

"Not only were men taught to handle their weapons with proficiency in the replacement training centres, but they were taught to take care of themselves personally. There was intense instruction in personal sanitation, malaria control, processing of contaminated water, cooking, and keeping dry in the open and all the other lore that a good soldier must understand. But most important, our replacements were taught the tricks of survival in battle.

"Problems of street fighting, jungle fighting, and close combat were staged in realistic fashion with live ammunition, and men learned to crawl under supporting machine-gun fire, to use grenades, and advance under live artillery barrages just as they must in battle."

For the officer corps, the climate of competition and free enterprise in America, and its corollary in terms of personal initiative and responsibility, and the massive growth of big business throughout the United States provided a source of hundreds of thousands of reserve officers capable not only of commanding a company or a battalion, but also of undertaking general staff duties. This was helped by the fact that the abilities of every man in civil life were judiciously put to use; an ingenious system of temporary promotion enabled each man to find the post where he would be most effective. There is a significant remark by General Bradley in this connection. Speaking of the lack of enthusiasm felt before the war by fellow comrades of the Regular Army who found themselves posted to information services, and of the errors or miscalculations suffered in consequence in the early stages of the war, he writes:

"Had it not been for the uniquely qualified reservists who so capably filled so many of our intelligence jobs throughout the war, the army would have found itself badly pressed for competent intelligence personnel."

A knocked out Pzkw VI Tiger (top) testifies to the prowess of American armour in North Africa. Recruits practise landing on a hostile shore (below).

CHAPTER 41
Victory in North Africa

In an earlier chapter we left the newly promoted General Montgomery exploiting his brilliant victory of November 5, 1942. Despite the torrential rains which, by all accounts, characterised the last weeks of that autumn, and despite the logistical difficulties inherent in such a prolonged pursuit of the enemy, on November 13 he was by-passing Tobruk; on November 20 he had retaken Benghazi; and on December 13, having covered more than 700 miles in five weeks, he stood before the defensive position of Marsa el Brega-Marāda, which had hitherto thwarted all the attacks of his predecessors. During this time he had put Lieutenant-General Brian Horrocks in command of X Corps, in place of Lieutenant-General Herbert Lumsden, whom he considered insufficiently aggressive, with Lieutenant-General Miles Dempsey taking command of XIII Corps.

A German tank blows up as a shell hits its ammunition store.

Allied strategy in the closing months of 1942 had been extremely successful. Montgomery's overwhelming victory against the *Panzerarmee Afrika* at El Alamein and the Anglo-American landings in French North Africa ("Operation Torch") had been devastating blows.

These operations had led to many bitter arguments between Hitler, Rommel, Göring, Kesselring and the Italian Marshals Bastico and Cavallero. At the front in Tunisia, Field-Marshal Rommel thought that all was irreparably lost in Italian North Africa, and had already decided on the Wadi Akarit, to the north of Gabès, as the halting point of the retreat he had begun on November 5. However, he had no intention of holding this line, or the rest of Tunisia, at all costs. His thinking at that time is summed up in the notes he wrote when he got back to Europe: "Our object in Tunisia would again have to be to gain as much time as possible and get out as many as we could of our battle-tried veterans for use in Europe. We knew by experience that there would be no hope of supplying and equipping an Army Group in Tunisia, which meant that we would have to try to reduce the fighting troops there to fewer but well-equipped formations. If a major, decision-seeking offensive were launched by the Allies, we would have to shorten the front step by step and evacuate increasing numbers of troops by transport aircraft, barges and warships. The first stand would be in the hill country extending from Enfiddaville round Tunis, the second in the Cape Bon peninsula. When the Anglo-American forces finally completed their conquest of Tunisia, they were to find nothing, or at the most only a few prisoners, and thus be robbed of the fruits of their victory, just as we had been at Dunkirk."

Rommel had, therefore, to reach Tunisia as quickly as possible, so as to be able to surprise the Anglo-American army which had just arrived in Algeria, and inflict a severe defeat on it, which would allow him to gain time. This was the plan he put forward to Hitler in the presence of Field-Marshal Keitel and Generals Jodl and Schmundt. But his final remark, "If the army were to remain in Africa, it would be destroyed", was the spark which set off the powder keg. "The Führer flew into a fury and directed a stream of completely unfounded attacks upon us."

At the end of this interview, Rommel, who was travelling in the special train which was taking Göring to Rome, had to put up with the *Reichsmarschall's* presumptuous and sarcastic remarks, and expressed himself quite frankly. "I was angry and resentful at the lack of understanding displayed by our highest command and their readiness to blame the troops at the front for their own mistakes. My anger redoubled when I was compelled to witness the antics of the *Reichsmarschall* in his special train. The situation did not seem to trouble him in the slightest. He preened himself, beaming broadly at the primitive flattery heaped on him by imbeciles from his own court, and talked of nothing but jewellery and pictures. At other times his behaviour could perhaps be amusing – now it was infuriating.

"He gave birth to the absurd idea that I was governed by moods and could only command when things went well; if they went badly I became depressed and caught the 'African sickness'. From this it was argued that since I was a sick man anyway, it was necessary to consider whether to relieve me of my command."

Hitler, feeling it politically necessary to retain a firm bridgehead in North Africa, accordingly gave Rommel orders to hold the defensive position of Marsa el Brega.

For his part, Field-Marshal Kesselring, although he in no way shared the O.K.W.'s illusions, was equally critical of what he considered to be the haste with which Rommel wanted to leave Libya. He expected no rapid action from Eisenhower's inexperienced troops, and thought that Montgomery, who was faced with severe logistical problems, would play for safety. It therefore seemed to him quite possible to make the enemy pay dearly, in terms of time, for the advance along the 700-mile road from Marsa el Brega to Gabès. As he wrote in his memoirs:

"Of course, it would not be an easy task, but it would have been worthy of a Rommel! And in spite of all the difficulties, it could have been accomplished if Rommel had not been fundamentally opposed to it. His desire to get to Tunisia, and from there, to cross into Italy and the Alps, took precedence over the objectives and orders of his superiors."

As may very well be imagined, Marshal Cavallero, in Rome, and Marshal Bastico, in Tripoli, went even further than Kesselring in their criticisms; it is also undoubtedly true that Rommel took no notice of the orders he received from either *Comando Supremo* or the Italian command in Libya, *Superlibia*. It is probably true that it was quite impossible for him to carry out the order he had received to re-establish his position at Sollum-Halfaya, but he also abandoned his defensive line at Marsa el Brega on the pretext of making a stand at Buerat, at the other end of the Gulf of Sirte. He reached this position on about January 1, but he had no intention of defending it.

Rommel was only too well aware that the *Panzerarmee Afrika* was in no condition to stand and fight. It had been starved of reinforcements and supplies. It was short of petrol and it had been totally unable to make good the losses it had suffered in men, guns and tanks at El Alamein. So the "Desert Fox" knew that to stand firm on a position once Montgomery had built up his overwhelming strength in men and *materiel* would be to invite his own defeat at the 8th Army's hands.

But, as Rommel wrote in his diary: "The British commander had shown himself to be overcautious. He risked nothing in any way doubtful and bold solutions were completely foreign to him... I was quite satisfied that Montgomery would never take the risk of following up boldly and overrunning us, as he could have done without any danger to himself."

It was fortunate for Rommel and his men that the British general was so cautious. Montgomery's caution was in large part responsible for Rommel and his army being able to conduct a brilliant retreat to Tunisia.

The reason the Allies had to wait from November 8, 1942 until May 13, 1943 before Axis resistance in North Africa was finally crushed, and the last remnants mopped up at Sainte Marie du Zit, was that all sorts of pressures influenced Eisenhower's operations.

The "Torch" plan had specified that all landings had to be covered by fighters, but these had only a limited endurance. Hence no landings were to take place east of Algiers, so that Tunis, the objective of Operation "Torch", was almost 400 miles away from the nearest Allied troops.

Secondly, there was what can only be described as the "Spanish obsession", which haunted both the Foreign Office and the State Department. As a result of faulty intelligence from British and American agents in Madrid, three months elapsed before the Allies abandoned the theory that there would be a German counter-offensive, with German troops passing freely through Spain to invade Morocco. This menace, imaginary though it turned out to be, had to be countered by posting the American 5th Army, four divisions strong, on the borders of the two protectorates – which until mid-February reduced the strength of the American troops in the theatre of operations to three divisions.

In Algiers, General Eisenhower allowed himself to be drawn into the quicksands of politics, whilst General Giraud, appointed Civil and Military High Commissioner after the assassination of Admiral Darlan on December 24, 1942, saw his authority disputed. His rallying-cry: "One aim, victory!", and his indifference to political considerations cut very little ice with those for whom victory was not the only aim, and he had to fight on two fronts – against the enemies of his country, and against those who challenged his authority.

Finally, Allied operations at the front suffered from a certain lack of co-ordination, for though apparently well integrated, and on excellent terms with each other, the French, American and British units fighting between the Ouargla oasis and the Mediterranean did not come under a single overall command.

General Delay, commanding the East Saharan Detachment at Fezzan, and Lieutenant-General A. Juin, commanding the French troops in Tunisia, were both under the command of General Henri Giraud, whilst General Eisenhower had overall command of the British and American forces of the British 1st Army, commanded by Lieutenant-General K. A. N. Anderson. But both Eisenhower and Giraud were daily inundated by a host of non-military questions they had to solve; to such an extent that Lieutenant-General L. M. Koeltz, who turned to writing the history of the campaign after having played a leading part in it, could write:

"In Algiers, the two commanders rarely saw each other; they communicated through liaison officers whom General Giraud had attached to Eisenhower. As for Franco-British co-operation at the front itself, it was purely fortuitous, the result of instant and very often hasty agreements."

Not wanting the French troops to take their orders from the British 1st Army, General Giraud was content with a "two-headed" arrangement, and General Eisenhower could hardly ask his French opposite number to go back on the terms of the compromise which he himself had proposed at the end of their stormy Gibraltar discussion, and which, according to General Beaufre, laid down that:

"Upon French territory the French command and the Inter-Allied United Nations command were equal. Each command gave orders to its own troops, but acted by common agreement, and consulted with each other on all important questions. If operations involving a mixed body of troops were carried out, command went to the general whose troops were in the majority."

At the front, however, this sharing of high command created serious difficulties. Although he had previously been severely reprimanded by his superior for having argued the case for a unified command, General Juin, in a long letter on January 1, 1943, brought the matter up with General Giraud once more, putting the case with courage and common sense. It was true, he stated, that for some time he had been able to count on the help of General Anderson. "But that doesn't solve the problem", he added, "for it is once more essential to insist upon there being a single overall commander. There is little point in my having British troops available to me for a single operation, if the essential act is left undone, i.e., if there is no co-ordination of our efforts. I might achieve a local success in drawing the bulk of the enemy's reserves, but the overall objective will not have been achieved. We must therefore have one single command, and if you have not got this matter in hand, as would be desirable, or if for political reasons, or because of previous promises that Eisenhower has hinted at to me, it *has* to be Anderson, then we must agree, as I am willing to do myself, to place the French army under Anderson's command. That would be a lot better than the present highly ambiguous situation, especially as Anderson is an understanding and honest man; with your persuasion from above and mine from below, he could be prevailed upon to act reasonably."

Events were to show how correct this was, but the lesson cost the Allies dear.

The Anglo-American troops entering the front line between Gafsa and the Mediterranean were covered by the French North African Land Forces. Consisting of troops formerly stationed in Tunisia and the Moroccan Infantry Division, the Barré Group was in positions astride the Medjerda river and level with Medjez el Bab, whilst the French XIX Corps (commanded by General Koeltz and consisting of the "Constantine" and "Algiers" Infantry Divisions, and the "Algiers" Light Armoured Brigade) first positioned itself east of Tébessa and then on the Eastern Dorsale, a mountainous fold dominating the coastal plain with its towns of Kairouan, Sousse, and Sfax. To carry out these tasks, General Giraud and his staff were by no means reduced to the forces that the Rethondes agreement of June 25, 1940 had allowed France to keep in North Africa. Thanks to the endeavours of Generals Weygand and Juin, there were 70,000 more troops–officers, N.C.O.s, and men–than the number stipulated; furthermore, out of hiding-places of which the Armistice Commissions were quite unaware, were brought 55,000 rifles, 4,000 automatic weapons, 210 mortars, 43 anti-tank guns, and 82 75-mm guns with ammunition. It should be remembered, however, that since 1939 arms manufacture had made immense strides and that the greater proportion of the arms that the French forces used were out of date, especially the anti-tank guns, and the D1 and Somua tanks with which the light armoured brigades were equipped.

Moreover, the few motorised vehicles available were at their last gasp, and most could not be repaired for lack of spare parts. On the other hand – and in stark contrast with the *Afrika Korps*– the Americans got delivery of the most modern equipment in record time. When Eisenhower asked for a large consignment of army lorries, he received them in North Africa less than three weeks later. "General Somerwell was still at my headquarters when the message came from the War Department that the last of the trucks had been shipped." The telegram, written by General Somerwell's assistant, Major-General Wilhelm D. Styer, described eloquently the unceasing labour that had gone into the rapid preparing of the convoy, whilst its last few words

An Italian M13/40 knocked out by Allied artillery.

contained a veiled reproach: "If you should happen to want the Pentagon shipped over there, please try to give us about a week's notice." At all events Eisenhower, taking into account the heavy rains and the state of the terrain, ordered the British 1st Army on December 24 to suspend its offensive towards Tunis for the time being, and a few days later General Giraud was told to dig in on the positions he had already taken up. As soon as possible it was intended to throw in the American II Corps (which was under the command of Major-General Lloyd R. Fredendall and consisted of the 1st Infantry Division and the 1st Armoured Division) to the right of the French XIX Corps; pushing through to Sfax, it would cut the communications route linking Tunis and Tripoli, thus splitting the Axis forces into two groups which could then be successively annihilated.

This was to be Operation "Satin". It seemed a logical plan, but it would take a long time to execute, and took little or no account of the enemy's capabilities and determination.

On December 31 the Axis forces in Tunisia stood at just over 47,000 German troops and nearly 18,000 Italians, formed since December 8 into the 5th *Panzerarmee* or Pz. A.O.K. 5, commanded by Colonel-General Hans-Jürgen von Arnim. Under him, on the German side, were the 10th Panzer Division (Major-General Wolfgang Fischer), which had been stationed in France the previous summer, the 334th Infantry Division (Major - General Friedrich Weber), the Broich Division (Major-General Freiherr Fritz von

Broich), which was only of regimental size, and the 501st Tiger Tank Battalion; the Italians provided the XXX Corps (General Vittorio Sogno), comprising the "Superga" Infantry Division (General Dante Lorenzelli), a special brigade, and a few miscellaneous units.

As can be seen, this was an armoured force of very modest dimensions, but to compensate for that, the Luftwaffe had for a few weeks managed to regain mastery of the air above Tunisia. This had two results: firstly, Anglo-American reconnaissance planes were unable to fly over the enemy lines and so did not get wind of Arnim's intentions until it was too late; and secondly, German bombers destroyed everything on the routes along which Allied supplies and reinforcements attempted to travel.

This destruction has been painted for us in the memoirs of General Beaufre, who at the beginning of January 1943 left General Giraud's H.Q. to take command of a battalion of crack Moroccan *tirailleurs:* "By day, the roads were the graveyards of vehicles, long lines of which lay riddled with bullets. If you travelled you kept an anxious eye permanently open for enemy planes and dashed for the nearest ditch at the first sign of danger. By night, travelling without lights on badly marked dirt roads, journeys seemed endless and reduced even further the efficiency of our modest forces."

In contrast with Rommel, who was very critical of him, Kesselring, as shown in his memoirs, had nothing but praise for the way in which Colonel-General von Arnim had grasped the purpose of his task and adapted himself to the situation. In

A Churchill, the main British tank.

his opinion, if Pz. A.O.K. 5 had consisted solely of German troops, Arnim would have been able to push Eisenhower back beyond the Tunis-Algiers border, either as far as the line Bône – Souk Ahras – Tébessa – Tozeur, which would have given the Axis a virtually unassailable position in North Africa, or, failing that, as far as the line Cape Serrat – Béja – Teboursouk – Chott Djerid, where the Germans would have been able to resist the Allies for a very long time.

Such is Kesselring's opinion. What is certain is that Arnim could not allow the French forces to remain in possession of the Eastern Dorsale, where an Allied offensive might be unleashed at any moment towards the Gulf of Hammamet. Therefore, on January 18, 1943, the *Gruppe* Weber, comprising the 334th Infantry Division and a few tank units, attacked the positions held by the Moroccan Infantry Division (Brigadier-General Mathenet), which formed the right wing of the Barré Group.

This attack did not really surprise the French, but it did catch them unprepared, for they were very short of reserves (General Giraud, engrossed in his project of forming a powerful North African liberation army, was extremely niggardly in sending reinforcements). Furthermore, against the Weber detachment's brand new tanks, French anti-tank equipment proved quite useless, as is shown by this account of a duel that took place on January 19, between a 55-ton Tiger tank

and a 75-mm anti-tank gun:

"Two men worked the gun, Captain Prévot on the elevating-wheel and Sergeant - Major Pessonneau on the sights. When the first tank was 50 yards away, they opened fire. Eight shells either ricocheted off the armour plate, or broke up harmlessly against it. They were about to fire the ninth, when the enemy retaliated with 8·8-cm tracer shells: a shell exploded behind the anti-tank gun, killing the sergeant-major, breaking the captain's left leg, wounding the rest of the gun crew, and overturning the gun."

The Moroccan Infantry Division was badly shaken by this powerful offensive, so Arnim tried to exploit his success by pushing towards the south and south-west and rolling back the XIX Corps' positions facing east. However, an effective, if delayed, counter-attack by Brigadier-General Paul Robinett's Combat Command "B" from the U.S. II Corps prevented the German commander from exploiting at the strategic level an undeniable tactical success which had brought him 4,000 prisoners.

Whilst this fighting was taking place in Tunisia, the Casablanca Conference took place in Morocco, leading to a reorganization of the Allied command structure in the Mediterranean.

Under General Eisenhower's supreme authority, an 18th Army Group was created, consisting of the 1st and 8th Armies, and commanded by General Sir Harold Alexander, whose post as commander in the Middle East was taken

over by General Sir Henry Maitland Wilson. The Allied naval forces in the same theatre of operations were to remain under the command of Sir Andrew Cunningham. Air Chief Marshal Tedder's authority now extended to all Allied air forces in the Mediterranean; in North Africa, particularly, he would have command of Major-General James H. Doolittle's strategic bombers, part of the Western Air Command, and the tactical support formations of Air Marshal Sir Arthur Coningham's North African Tactical Air Force.

However logical this structure seems, it should be noted that it was never repeated. Both before and after the Normandy landings Eisenhower obstinately resisted the British suggestion that he should have a deputy who would command the Allied land forces, and in this refusal he had the full weight of General Marshall's authority behind him.

At the front, and more or less unknown to General Giraud, the French army detachment was dissolved, and XIX Corps absorbed into the British 1st Army – as had the American II Corps since it had come into the front line. Freed from command, General Juin now took on the job of organising the future French Expeditionary Corps, which he later commanded. Giraud, who had just received from President Roosevelt and General Marshall the promise of enough American aid to equip an army of 11 divisions, acquiesced in this reorganisation of the Allied command: "It was a very big decision to take," wrote General Beaufre later, "since it marked the end of the Gibraltar agreement. The French army now came under Allied command, but had no representation at the highest level, and this situation lasted until 1945." A slightly bitter remark, no doubt, but it must be remembered that the fighting had continually shown the drawbacks of the Gibraltar agreement, and both Generals Koeltz and Juin asked for nothing better than a unified, and hence more effective, command.

On January 23, 1943, Rommel withdrew from Tripoli; on January 26 he was in Tunisia, inspecting the Mareth Line, whose reinforced concrete defences had been disarmed in accordance with the Franco-Italian Armistice.

Marshal Cavallero's intention was to place the Axis forces which had just withdrawn from Tripoli (ex - *Deutsch - Italienische Panzerarmee,* ex - *Panzerarmee Afrika*) under Italian command, by placing at their head General Giovanni Messe, who had commanded the Italian XXXV Corps in Russia. Though Cavallero was replaced on January 30 by General Vittorio Ambrosio, his plan was kept, and the very next day General Messe arrived in Tunis as the commander of the new Italian 1st Army or Pz. A.O.K. 1. Rommel wrote of him: "Like most people who came from Russia, he looked on things with considerable optimism. I did not intend to hand over the army until I

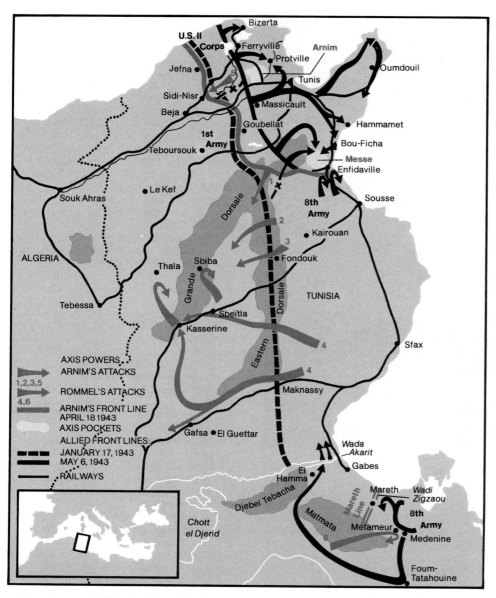

AXIS POWERS
ARNIM'S ATTACKS
1,2,3,5 ROMMEL'S ATTACKS
4,6
ARNIM'S FRONT LINE
APRIL 18 1943
AXIS POCKETS
ALLIED FRONT LINES:
JANUARY 17, 1943
MAY 6, 1943
RAILWAYS

Mopping up in North Africa: the last stages of the Allied thrust which drove Axis forces out of Tunisia.

could feel that its position was reasonably firm for some time ahead."

And in fact it was not until February 20 that General Messe was able to issue his first directive concerning the defence of the Mareth Line. Rommel, however, felt somewhat encouraged to take up this attitude because O.K.W. had not ordered him to return to Germany.

It was in these rather ambiguous circumstances that Rommel launched the last offensive engagement of his African campaigns, and although it resulted in defeat, it nevertheless exemplified his great flexibility as well as his determination as a military leader. Noting that Montgomery was taking his time in making contact with the German forces at Mareth, he decided to utilise the time thus given to him to deliver a heavy blow on the American II Corps.

Rommel was not unduly dismayed by the approach of American forces close to his line of retreat. His own numbers were

slowly increasing although most of his German formations were still seriously below strength: they had only about a third of the tanks, a quarter of the anti-tank guns and a sixth of the artillery they ought to have possessed. But Rommel planned to exploit his central position between the British and American forces by striking at the Americans before the 8th Army could come to their aid.

The Italian XX and XXI Corps, as well as the German 90th and 164th Light Divisions were left on the Mareth Line to hold up the 8th Army. Rommel then concentrated an armoured force consisting of the 10th and 21st Panzer Divisions and the Italian "Centauro" Armoured Division near the town of Sfax. This powerful mobile force was divided into two parts. On the right the two German Panzer divisions were placed under the command of General von Arnim's chief-of-staff, Lieutenant-General Heinz Ziegler. Rommel intended to use them to launch a surprise attack on the Faïd Pass which cuts through the Eastern Dorsale. On the left the "Centauro" Division and the *Afrika Korps* were under Rommel's own direction. He intended that they should make a quick dash for Gafsa

via Maknassy. The attack was launched on February 14: the new offensive took the Allies in North Africa by surprise and for a time they were thrown into confusion.

Stretched out across a very long front, as ordered by the 1st Army, American II Corps had not foreseen where the enemy would make his attack; and in addition, according to a remark made by Eisenhower himself the day before the attack was launched, there existed at H.Q. an atmosphere of complacency which boded no good. There was a rude awakening. To begin with, Ziegler forced the 1st Armoured Division (Major-General Orlando Ward) out from the Faïd Pass and inflicted such a heavy defeat that Fredendall had to order his corps to withdraw into the Grande Dorsale. This in turn led to the hasty evacuation of Gafsa, captured by Rommel's mechanised column on the afternoon of February 15 without a shot being fired. From Faïd and Gafsa, the two Axis columns converged upon Sbeitla and attempted to capture the Grande Dorsale.

Although the 21st Panzer Division failed to take the Sbiba Pass, being beaten back on February 20 by the French XIX Corps, the 10th Panzer Division, reinforced by a detachment of the *Afrika Korps,* got through the Kasserine Pass and headed for Tébessa. This further defeat created much tension within the Allied high command; in accordance with the instructions he had received from General Anderson, Fredendall decided to prevent the enemy moving towards Thala, even if that meant surrendering Tébessa which, according to Juin, "was the very nerve centre of his supply system, and plunging north into the mountainous Ouenza region – in heaven knows what disorder. The way to the Constantine region would thus have been opened to Rommel's forces, and he would still have taken Thala and then le Kef."

In vigorous yet appealing terms, Juin prevailed upon Fredendall to abandon this disastrous idea, whilst at the same time the British 6th Armoured Division (Major-General Charles Keightley) and the artillery units of the American 9th Division, coming from Morocco ahead of their infantry, entered the line to reinforce the Allies' right wing.

In the Axis camp, the twin successes of Faïd and Gafsa sparked off disputes nearly as bitter as those that had taken place among the Allied commanders.

In Arnim's opinion, the Kasserine Pass ought to be considered the final objective of the counter-attack. If it were successful, he would then withdraw the 5th Panzer Division and use it to give himself a little more elbow room in the western and central sectors of the front held by Pz. A.O.K. 5. Rommel, on the other hand, saw bigger and further. He explains his point of view in his notebooks: "I was convinced that a thrust beyond Tébessa by the combined armoured and motorised forces of the two armies would force the British and Americans to pull back the bulk of their forces to Algeria, thus greatly delaying their offensive preparations. The essential conditions for the stroke to succeed were that it should be made at once and that the striking force should be strong enough to overcome any reviving enemy resistance rapidly and break through to the open road. The thrust northwards had to be made far enough behind the enemy front to ensure that they would not be able to rush their reserves to the passes and hold up our advance. I was satisfied that by holding a number of passes and strategic points on the roads we would be able to contain the attacks we could expect on our flank. But whether or not the enemy main body would lose the race with my striking force was nevertheless open to question."

In other words, Rommel, once he had taken Tébessa, would have pressed his attack towards Bône, cutting clean through the British 1st Army's communications; and Kesselring, who had landed in Tunis the previous day, approved his plan, rejecting Arnim's proposals. However, the following evening the *Comando Supremo* made known its final decision—an attack towards the line Thala–le Kef. "This was an appalling and unbelievable piece of shortsightedness, which did, in fact, ultimately cause the whole plan to go awry," Rommel noted. "A thrust along that line was far too close to the front and was bound to bring us up against the strong enemy reserves."

And it is a fact that Rommel's attack on Thala failed, the British 6th Armoured Division fighting superbly, and the guns of General Koeltz and the American 9th Division pounding his forces unceasingly. But this failure does not necessarily mean that Rommel would have been successful on a front Tébessa–Bône. The weather was very bad indeed and all the Axis forces were seriously short of vital supplies, particularly ammunition and petrol. But on February 23, Rommel received a letter appointing him—a little late?—commander of a new Army Group "Africa".

This series of engagements had cost the American II Corps 7,000 men (of whom 4,026 had been taken prisoner), 235 tanks, and 110 self-propelled guns and reconnaissance vehicles; but above all, it was clear that Fredendall had lost the confidence of his men, and on March 6 he handed over his command to Major-General George S. Patton: an excellent choice, for despite his affectation of truculence he was a great leader of men.

On February 20, 1943 General Alexander, whose new command had got off to such a bad start, called upon Montgomery to lend a hand in easing the enemy pressure on the British 1st Army. Eager to help, Montgomery, whose 51st Division and 7th Armoured Division had just taken the Tunisian townships of Ben Gardane, Foum Tatahouine, and Medenine, pushed his advanced forces almost as far as the Mareth Line, which General Messe was holding with six Italian and two German divisions. But on February 22, Rommel,

leaving the "Centauro" Armoured Division to cope with the American II Corps, had left Thala and dashed southeast with the 10th and 21st Panzer Divisions.

The final plan was not Rommel's but Messe's and Ziegler's. The Italian 1st Army would engage the British head on, whilst an armoured force consisting of the 10th, 15th, and 21st Panzer Divisions, plus the 164th Light Division, would strike from the Matmata mountains and head for Métameur and Medenine, attacking the enemy from the rear, and driving to the Gulf of Gabès. In other words, a repeat performance of Gazala and Alam el Halfa. But this time the three Panzer divisions, with only 141 tanks, were two-thirds below strength, and air support, provided by 160 planes (of which 60 were Bf 109 fighters and 20 Stukas), was very meagre. Neither Messe nor Rommel had any great illusions about the eventual success of their attack, which was due to be launched on March 5.

Did the Allies get wind of this Operation "Capri"? Kesselring implies this, and Paul Carell, in his *Foxes of the Desert,* puts forward the same theory. But there is no need to fall back upon such a hypothesis to explain the defeat of the Axis forces in this, their last attempt to secure a change of fortune.

Montgomery knew his Rommel well, and at the first hint of an attack, he regrouped his 2nd New Zealand Division, two other infantry brigades, and two armoured brigades, and positioned them on a front all of 43,000 yards long, at right angles to Rommel's expected line of attack. 810 medium, field and anti-tank guns, including many of the brand new 17-pounder anti-tank guns being used in battle for the very first time, lay waiting for the moment to open fire.

Firing a series of concentrated and accurate salvoes at the slightest sign of enemy movement within range, the British artillery forced Rommel to break off contact, with the loss of 52 tanks and 640 men killed, wounded, or missing. The British lost one Sherman tank and 130 men. Montgomery expressly forbade his men to pursue the enemy, who retreated behind the Matmata mountains. Paul Carell has described this battle of March 6 grippingly. "The grenadiers, laden with ammunition boxes, had pushed their steel helmets on to the back of their heads. Many of them had cigarettes in the corners of their mouths. They had looked exactly the same in front of the Maginot Line, on the Bug, on the Dniepr, and before Stalingrad.

"When General Cramer visited the tactical headquarters of the 21st Panzer Division, its commander, Major-General Hildebrandt, stood under shell fire with his armoured reserve looking very grave. 'We're making no progress,' he said. But Cramer could see for himself that ahead lay a heavy barrage of fire. British batteries kept up an infernal bombardment against the attacking armour. The

stony ground produced a rain of shrapnel with deadly effect on grenadiers and gunners. Major Schlickes' men of the 326th Observer Detachment lay ahead with their sound-rangers and rangefinders, trying to pinpoint the artillery positions. The question posed by all the commanders was 'where's all this awful artillery come from?'"

Two days later Rommel left Africa for good, but his departure was kept secret, so as not to jeopardise German morale and encourage the enemy. Colonel-General von Arnim succeeded him as C.-in-C. of Army Group "Africa", and tank specialist General Gustav von Vaerst took command of Pz. A.O.K. 5, Major-General Fritz Bayerlein going to General Messe's Italian 1st Army as chief-of-staff.

Meanwhile, O.K.W. had transferred to North Africa the "Hermann Göring" Panzer Division, the "Manteuffel" Division, and the 999th Division, recruited from among military prisoners, who were thus offered the chance of rehabilitating themselves.

But these reinforcements, which raised the number of divisions under Arnim's command to 16, should not deceive us. A number of the divisions were worn out, and the stubbornness of the two dictators forced them to defend a front nearly 400 miles long. Furthermore, it was becoming more and more difficult to supply them from Europe. The Italian merchant navy was, in fact, at its last gasp, as can be seen from the figures which the Communications Minister, Vittorio Cini, laid before Mussolini on March 3, 1943, and which can be summed up as follows:

Situation	Ships	Tons
On June 10, 1940	772	3,292,584
Additions up to March 1943	129	563,068
Total	901	3,855,652
Losses as of March 1943	568	2,134,786
Remaining	333	1,720,866

Deducting further the number of ships absent from the Mediterranean, liners and ships used for civil and military transport in the Tyrrhenian, Adriatic, and Aegean Seas, and those ships which were being repaired, less than 300,000 tons were available for the army. And, Cini added, despite the Tripoli evacuation, merchant navy losses through Allied action were continuing at an alarming rate: 87,818 tons in January, 69,438 tons in February.

In March and April the Sicilian Channel lived up to the reputation of the "route of Death" which the Italians had given it. During these two months, out of 132,986 tons of supplies and *matériel* which sailed from Italy, only 77,984 tons got to Bizerta and Tunis, just over a quarter of what Rommel considered necessary to allow the Axis troops to resist a major Allied offensive. This being so, the order given by Hitler and Mussolini to Arnim, after their Klessheim meeting of April 8, 1943, to hold Tunisia at all costs, was pure wishful thinking.

However, the view held by Rommel, and later by Arnim, that some of the Axis forces engaged between Mareth and Cape Serrat could be evacuated from Tunisia to Italy, was also rather unrealistic.

On February 21, as the battle for Thala was at its height, General Alexander was briefing his commanders on his strategic aims. To destroy the enemy forces engaged in Tunisia, he planned that the necessary operations should be subdivided into two phases: firstly the 8th Army would break through at Gabès and join up with the British 1st Army; then together they would crush the enemy by a careful and overwhelming concentration of land, sea, and air power.

The problem was not so much the size of the forces available, which were increasing week by week, but the time limit it imposed on Alexander. If, as the Casablanca Conference had laid down, the Allies were to land in Sicily during the July full moon, the North African campaign would have to be decided by May 15 at the very latest.

On March 14 Alexander completed his briefing with a general directive whose chief quality was its great good sense. It ordered the regrouping of the American, British and French in separate sectors, the withdrawal of the tanks from their advanced positions, the creating of reserves, and the training of troops. The second part of the directive was devoted to a discussion by Air Marshal Coningham of air questions, and the co-operation of the air and land forces.

On March 20 Montgomery addressed a rousing order of the day to his 8th Army, now up to complete strength. Two of its points are quoted below:

"3. In the battle that is now to start, the Eighth Army:
(a) Will destroy the enemy now facing us in the Mareth position.
(b) Will burst through the Gabès Gap.
(c) Will then drive northwards on Sfax, Sousse, and finally Tunis.

4. We will not stop, or let up, till Tunis has been captured, and the enemy has either given up the struggle or has been pushed into the sea."

At 2230 hours on the same day, the 8th Army's artillery opened fire on General Messe's forces: from right to left, i.e. from the Matmata mountains up to the Gulf of Gabès, these comprised the XXI and XX Corps commanded by Generals Berardi and Orlando. Thirty minutes later, the British XXX Corps (Lieutenant-General Oliver Leese) attacked the enemy along its coastal sector.

This frontal attack was to be accompanied by a flanking attack carried out by Lieutenant-General Freyberg's New Zealand Corps which, advancing along the corridor bounded on the left by the Grand Erg and on the right by the Matmata mountains, would take the El Hamma pass, held by General Mannerini's Sahara group, and dash for Gabès, where it could cut the Italian 1st Army's lines of communication; since El Hamma was

120 miles away from Foum-Tatahouine, Freyberg had begun to advance on March 18. His 2nd New Zealand Division was reinforced by the 8th Armoured Brigade and Leclerc's column. Such was the general aim of Operation "Pugilist".

The results, however, fell far short of the aims proclaimed in Montgomery's order of the day. On the afternoon of the first day, heavy rain had made a quagmire of the Wadi Zigzaou, which flowed in front of the Mareth positions and formed an anti-tank ditch 40 yards wide and 4 yards deep, so that by dawn on March 21, only six of the 50th Royal Tank Regiment's tanks had managed to get through to the opposite side and support Major-General J. S. Nichols's 50th Division, which was having a very bad time under the concentrated fire of the "Giovani Fascisti" Division under General Sozzani. An attempt by the Royal Engineers' bulldozers to breach the bank of the Wadi Zigzaou fared no better. Then the 15th Panzer Division (Major-General Willibald Borowietz), which was being held in reserve, counter-attacked with great vigour: by March 23 the attackers had only one foothold on the left bank.

Faced with this heavy setback, Montgomery became convinced that he would have to change his plan.

Instead of using the New Zealand Division in a subsidiary operation he decided that Freyberg's men would make his main thrust. Whilst the 4th Indian Division under Major-General F.I.S. Tuker was attacking the Matmata range on Messe's flank, X Corps and the 1st Armoured Division (Major-General R. Briggs) had been released in the wake of the 2nd New Zealand Division, and in order to deceive the enemy still further, Major-General G. W. E. J. Erskine's 7th Armoured Division had been brought into the front line. Truth to tell, this ruse did not have as much success as had been hoped for it, for by March 21 General Messe had already got wind of Freyberg's move, and had sent the 164th Light Division and the 21st Panzer Division towards El Hamma.

At 1600 hours on March 26, only 20 minutes after the 1st Armoured Division's last tank had entered the line, Lieutenant-General Horrocks gave the signal for the attack, greatly helped by the sun and a violent sandstorm, which blinded the enemy. The trump card, however, was probably the Desert Air Force, which hurled itself at the defence with devastating effect, making use of 22 squadrons of Spitfires, Kitty-bombers, and Hurricane anti-tank fighters, and operating in an area beyond the range of the artillery. "In that area every vehicle", writes Montgomery, "and anything that appeared or moved, was shot to pieces. Brilliant and brave work by the pilots completely stunned the enemy; our attack burst through the resistance and the battle was won."

The Allied breakthrough at El Hamma took place too late to enable X Corps to reach Gabès before the bulk of the Italian army could be withdrawn. Whilst the loss

Lieutenant-General K. A. N. Anderson, commander of the British 1st Army. He played a prominent part in the final victory in Africa.

of 16 infantry battalions, 31 guns, and 60 tanks was a heavy blow, Messe was nevertheless able to regroup his forces in a very strong position along the Wadi Akarit. Here he had only to defend the narrow eight-mile front that lay between the Gulf of Gabès and the lake of Chott el Djerid, and included three hills standing nearly 1,000 feet above the deep furrow that the wadi's high waters had cut into the plain.

Quite rightly, Messe discounted the possibility of a daylight attack on such a strong position; wrongly, however, he supposed that Montgomery would wait for the next full moon, April 19–20, before attacking.

Since, as we have seen, time was of the essence, XXX Corps attacked at midnight on April 5, taking advantage of the darkness of the new moon. To avoid any errors they pushed forward in a single line. There was a moment of panic and confusion before the defence steadied itself and inflicted heavy losses on Major-General D. N. Wimberley's 51st (Highland) Division, going over itself to the counter-attack as dawn came up. The following day, at about midday, X Corps' tanks entered the fray, and a few hours later Arnim decided to retreat, a decision

The burning wreckage of an American P-38 Lightning in Tunisia. Such Axis successes were now few.

he stuck to in spite of Messe's opinion that they were not yet beaten. The battle of Mareth–El Hamma had given the Allies 10,000 prisoners, and Wadi Akarit brought in 7,000 more.

Arnim's decision was probably justified, as a result of the threat that was looming up on the Italian 1st Army's right flank. Here the dynamic General Patton had not taken long to instil a new spirit into both officers and men of his new command. On March 17 he captured Gafsa, and straightway pushed forward toward El Guettar, Maknassy, and Sbeïtla. On April 8, on the Gabès–El Guettar road, he joined up with the 8th Army, whilst on his left, the French XIX Corps moved towards the Eastern Dorsale. But neither of them was able to intercept the Italian army as it retreated north towards Enfidaville via Sfax and Sousse. This was because of the vast numbers of land-mines that Italian and German sappers had laid, one of which, on April 6, killed the bold aggressive Major-General Edouard Welvert, commanding the "Constantine" Motorised Division, as they were entering Kairouan.

On April 15, Army Group "Africa" was established along a 135-mile front marked by Cape Serrat, Jefina, Sidi Nsir, Medjez el Bab, Bou Arada, the Djebel Garci mountains, Takrouna, and Enfidaville on the Gulf of Hammamet. To defend this line Arnim had 16 divisions. But what kind of divisions? The Italian Army's historical department, in its work on the Tunisia campaign, gives us the answer.

The "Spezia" Infantry Division and the "Centauro" Armoured Division had been all but destroyed; the "Giovani Fascisti" and the "Pistoia" Infantry Divisions, and the "Trieste" Motorised Division, could muster only 11 battalions and 84 guns between them. The army's total artillery strength consisted of 17 105-mm and 149-mm guns. Nor were the German units under Messe's command any better off: four battalions and a few guns for the 90th Light Division, two battalions and no artillery for the 164th, a dozen or so tanks and three decimated battalions for the 15th Panzer Division. The nine German divisions comprised only some 60,000 men and 100 tanks. Furthermore, petrol was in such short supply that radio communication was cut down for lack of fuel to drive the generators.

And what of the Allies? During the winter, the British 1st Army had been increased by one corps (IX Corps, under Lieutenant-General J. T. Crocker), and two infantry divisions (the 1st and the 4th). The 8th Army had lost XIII Corps, the 44th Division, the 1st South African Division, and the 9th Australian Division, but had gained the two French divisions, commanded by Major-Generals de Larminat and Leclerc respectively. So including the American II Corps and the French XIX Corps, General Alexander could count on 20 divisions, all equipped (except for the French) with new *matériel* and abundant supplies. This was also the period when the British Churchill Mk. IV tank made its first appearance with the British 6th Armoured Division; it weighed 39 tons, and had a 57-mm gun, whilst its heavy armour allowed it to be used to support the infantry.

The American II Corps' advance had not yet taken it beyond the Gafsa – Fondouk – Maknassy region, whereas ahead of it the French XIX Corps had made contact with the left wing of the 8th

Army. Under Alexander's plan for eliminating the Axis Tunis–Bizerta bridgehead the main thrust was to be made by the 1st Army and the U.S. II Corps. The latter was transferred from the right to the left flank of General Anderson's forces – a delicate operation involving as it did the movement of 110,000 men and 30,000 vehicles over a distance of between 150 and 250 miles, through the 1st Army's rear. Begun on April 10, it was concluded without any serious difficulties by April 19, which speaks volumes for the administrative efficiency of Patton's H.Q.

However, on April 15, Patton took leave of II Corps, being ordered to Rabat, where Eisenhower had entrusted him with the organisation of America's share in Operation "Husky". It was therefore his second-in-command, Major-General Omar Bradley, who was given the glittering prize of Bizerta to aim for; besides his four American divisions, he also commanded a French unit consisting of the African Rifle Brigade and the Moroccan mountain troops of Colonel de Monsabert.

The lie of the land had led Alexander to entrust the starring rôle in this final operation to the British 1st Army. He decided to make it the 8th Army's task to engage the enemy and immobilise its remaining slender reserves by making a strong attack on the southern half of the bridgehead extending from Bizerta to Tunis. April 21 marked a definite setback for the 8th Army which, it is true, captured Enfidaville and Takrouna, but could not break out, being beaten back on the slopes of Djebel Garci, which rise to a height of about 1,600 feet. But the slopes were not the only reason for the defeat. The Axis forces hung on grimly, fighting desperately to maintain their positions. Alexander later wrote of the episode:

"The enemy counter-attacked continuously and, at the cost of very heavy casualties, succeeded in holding the attack. It was noticed that the Italians fought particularly well, outdoing the Germans in line with them . . . In spite of severe losses from our massed artillery fire the enemy kept up his policy of continuous counter-attacks and it became clear that it would cost us heavily to advance further into this tangled mass of mountains. General Montgomery therefore decided late on the 21st to abandon the thrust in the centre and concentrate on forcing the coastal defile."

On the other hand, the French XIX Corps, of three divisions, had succeeded in overcoming enemy resistance in the Djebel Fifrine massif (3,000 feet), and on the morning of May 5, approached the western outskirts of Pont du Fahs. At the centre of the British 1st Army, the IX and V Corps had been attacking both banks of the Medjerda river since April 23, and although they had not defeated the enemy, they had at least beaten the Axis forces from the most favourable defensive posi-

Smiles of victory as the Axis resistance ends and the Allies celebrate.

tions; but each British attack provoked a German counter-attack, such as the "Hermann Göring" Panzer Division's thrust during the night of April 21–22, which cost it 34 out of the 70 tanks it had thrown into the action near Goubellat.

At the head of his II Corps, Major-General Bradley showed himself to be as good a tactician in practice as he had been in theory when an instructor at Fort Benning. By manoeuvring on the heights, he got the better of resistance in the Tine Valley and thus, at just the right moment, was able to release his 1st Armoured Division to cut the Tunis–Bizerta railway line at Mateur, on May 5. And on that same day, on his left, the 9th Division (Major-General Manton Eddy) and the African Rifle Brigade reached the north shore of Lake Achktel, less than ten miles from Bizerta.

On May 6 General Alexander was to deliver the blow which would finally drive the Axis forces from North Africa.

On April 30, Alexander had detached the 4th Indian Division, the 7th Armoured Division, and the 201st Guards Brigade

In rough country even the Americans used horse transport.

from the 8th Army, and allocated them to IX Corps, which had taken up a position between Lake Kourzia and the south bank of the Medjerda; with the wounding of Lieutenant-General Crocker at this time, Lieutenant-General Brian Horrocks, who has given us a colourful description of the episode, took over from him at a moment's notice. To disguise the direction of the attack still more from the enemy, the 1st Armoured Division, operating in the Goubellat area, was reinforced by a large number of dummy tanks. At 0300 hours on the first day of this attack, christened Operation "Strike", IX Corps began to advance on a very narrow front, less than two miles wide; the initial attack would be carried out by the 4th Indian Division and the 4th Division (Major-General J. L. T. Hawksworth); 6th and 7th Armoured Divisions were to form the second wave. Artillery preparation consisted of the concentrated fire of 100 batteries, whose psychological effect on the enemy was increased by the massive intervention of the whole of the Desert Air Force. Under such a battering, the resistance of the 334th Division and the "Hermann Göring" Panzer Division – or rather what was left of them – soon disintegrated. At 0730 hours, General Horrocks told his armoured divisions to head the advance; that evening there was one last skirmish when 20 tanks of the 15th Panzer Division tried to counter-attack in the Massicault area.

In the early afternoon of May 7, the 11th Hussars, forming the advance guard of the 7th Armoured Division, entered Tunis. At the same time, the American 9th Division liberated Bizerta, and the 1st Armoured Division bypassed Ferryville and headed for Protville to meet up with the 7th Armoured Division. This link-up, carried out on May 8, led General von Vaerst, the commander of the Axis 5th Army, to ask Bradley for an armistice. And on the next day, Vaerst surrendered unconditionally. "The fall of Tunis and Bizerta clearly came to the German Command both in Africa and Berlin, as a most severe shock," Alexander wrote. "It was not until the evening of the 8th May that the High Command issued a statement that Africa would now be abandoned and

the 'thirty-one thousand Germans and thirty thousand Italians remaining' would be withdrawn by sea. I commented in a report to General Eisenhower that night that the Navy and Air Forces would interfere with this programme, which in any event depended on the enemy holding a firm bridgehead in Cape Bon, and reminded him of Mr Churchill's words in August 1940: 'We are waiting, so are the fishes.'"

Thus fell the Axis' northern stronghold, which according to Arnim's order should have prolonged Axis resistance in Africa. The southern stronghold, which included the Cape Bon peninsula and the Zaghouan mountains, was cut in two by a raid carried out by the 6th Armoured Division, which found the Hamman-Lif pass undefended and on May 10 reached the Gulf of Hammamet in the rear of the Italian army. That same day the British V and the French XIX Corps surrounded the Zaghouan mountains and mopped up the remnants of the *Afrika Korps*. Having exhausted its ammunition, the "Superga" Division surrendered to the "Oran" Motorised Division (Major-General Boissau) at Sainte Marie du Zit, and in the Zaghouan mountains the "Morocco" Motorised Division finished off the 21st Panzer Division, and forced the Italian XXI Corps to surrender to General Koeltz. However, XX Corps continued to offer valiant resistance to the British 8th Army. When, on the evening of May 12, the 90th Light Division was crushed at Bou Ficha and forced to surrender, the knell of the Axis 1st Army sounded. In the circumstances, at 1935 hours, Mussolini sent a telegram to General Messe: "Cease fire! You are appointed a Marshal of Italy! You and your men have fought the good fight." Arnim was captured by troops of the 4th Indian Division under the command of Major-General "Gertie" Tuker after very heavy fighting.

The exact number of prisoners taken by the Allies is not known. But on May 25 they held 238,243 unwounded prisoners, including 101,784 Germans, 89,442 Italians and 47,017 of unspecified nationality. Of the once-mighty Axis forces, only 638 soldiers succeeded in reaching Italy, among them Lieutenant-General Alfred Gause, Rommel's former chief-of-staff, Bayerlein, Major-General Josef Schmid, commander of the "Hermann Göring" Panzer Division, and General Sogno, commander of the Italian XXX Corps. The Allies, during this seven months' campaign, had suffered 42,924 killed and wounded. 11,104 lost their lives: 2,156 Frenchmen, 6,233 British and Empire troops and 2,715 Americans.

On May 13, two days earlier than planned at the Casablanca Conference, General Alexander could send the following restrained but joyful telegram to London:

"Sir, It is my duty to report that the Tunisian Campaign is over. All enemy resistance has ceased. We are masters of the North African shores."

CHAPTER 42
Assault on Italy

If the catastrophe which befell the Axis forces in Tunisia was a defeat of some magnitude and of so far unforeseeable consequences for the Third Reich, for Fascist Italy it was nothing less than a death sentence, without appeal or reprieve.

The mobilisation decree of June 10, 1940 had given *Comando Supremo* an army of 75 divisions. Since that date 20 more had been raised, but these were not enough to make up for the losses sustained since June 10, 1940.

Two divisions had disappeared with the Italian East African empire and 25 more went in the Libyan, Egyptian, and Tunisian campaigns between December 8, 1940 and May 13, 1943. Of the divisions which had fought in the ranks of the Italian Expeditionary Force (later the Italian 8th Army) which Mussolini, over-riding all objections, had sent to join the "crusade against Bolshevism", only straggling remnants had returned. Through Mussolini's Russian 'adventure' the Italian army had suffered 84,830 casualties from an original force of 229,000 men, not counting the 30,000 wounded. An inglorious end to Mussolini's hollow boast.

Less than three years of hostilities had therefore cost Italy more than a third of her field army. Even so, on the date in question, no fewer than 36 divisions were immobilised outside Italy and her island dependencies, occupying France or re-pressing guerrillas in the Balkans.

The situation from Crete to the Italian–Yugoslav frontier as laid down on April 6, 1940 was clearly not improving. Far from it. A communiqué from Rome gave 10,570 killed, wounded, and missing among the Italian occupation troops in the first five months of 1943. The maquis were organising in Savoy and the Dauphiné, whilst in Corsica arms were reaching the resistance fighters via the underwater shuttle-service run by Lieute-nant-Commander L'Herminier in the sub-marine *Casabianca*. No massive recoup-ment of losses could therefore be made from these 36 divisions.

The defence of the Italian peninsula, Sardinia, and Sicily was thus entrusted to some 30 divisions, but not all these were immediately available. Two armoured divisions, including the Black-shirt "M" Armoured Division, equipped with German tanks, had not yet finished training. A great effort was therefore made to reconstitute the "Ariete" and the "Centauro" Armoured Divisions, which had escaped from Russia under conditions which we have already described. And so *Comando Supremo* had only about 20 divisions (with equipment no better than it had been in 1940) with which to face the threatened invasion. Its pessimism, in view of the Anglo-American preparations in North Africa, can well be imagined. No reliance could be placed on the so-called "coastal" defences (21 divi-sions and five brigades) which, as their name indicates, were to offer an initial defence against the enemy landing on the beaches. These units had only local recruits, all in the top age-groups, and they were very poorly officered. Mussolini quoted the case of Sicily, where two battalions were commanded by 2nd Lieu-tenants retired in 1918 and only recently recalled to the colours. The weapons and equipment of these formations were even more deficient than those of any other divisions. To ease the only too evident shortages, the Duce was counting on the *matériel* coming to him under the Villa Incisa agreement and on what could be pillaged from the now disbanded Vichy French army. But the weapons he did get from these sources often reached him without ammunition or accessories: some-times they had been astutely sabotaged. Finally, the units were strung out along the coast like a line of customs posts. In Sicily there were 41 men to the mile.

If we remember that the R.A.F.'s defeat of the Luftwaffe in 1940 caused the abandonment of Operation "Sea Lion", it is pertinent to ask what was the state of the Italian Air Force at this time. On June 14, 1943, in the presence of General Ambrosio, Chief of the Italian General Staff, and of the Commanders-in-Chief of the three armed forces, Mussolini had stated unequivocally: "We have neither a powerful bombing force nor the fighters to protect it."

No doubt things would tend to improve in the second half of 1944, but at first it would merely be a drop in the ocean. That is why, Mussolini went on, "it is *absolutely essential* for Germany to supply our needs for A.A. defence in our homeland, that is planes and guns." In calling blithely on the services of his Axis partner, Mussolini was relying on the good will of the Führer, and quite properly. But did he know that the Luft-waffe was then in very dire straits and likely to remain so? On the one hand the Germans had lost all air superiority in the East; on the other they were having to fight off increasing air attacks by Anglo-American bombers on their war in-dustries. There was thus little that could be done to make good the deficiencies in the Italian air strength. Moreover, the aerodromes of Sicily, Sardinia, and southern Italy were regularly being ham-mered by the Allies.

By May 13, 1943, 35 months of war had caused the deaths, by killing or drowning, of 35,000 officers and men and the loss of the following ships: one battleship, five heavy cruisers, seven light cruisers, 74 destroyers, and 85 submarines.

It had, of course, proved impossible to build enough new ships to make up for all these losses. Admiral Riccardi, Chief-of-Staff at *Supermarina,* still had, it is true, six battleships, a dozen cruisers, some 60 destroyers and torpedo-boats and the same number of submarines. The smaller surface vessels, however, were worn out after three years' hard escort service. The day after the Battle of Matapan the Duce had decided that until the converted liners *Roma* and *Augustus* came into service as aircraft-carriers, the fleet would not venture outside the radius of action of land-based fighters. No-one had foreseen that the day would come when there was to be no fighter support at all. When the Anglo-Americans set up a powerful bombing force in North Africa, Admiral Riccardi had been compelled to move his squadrons away from their moorings at Taranto, Messina, and Naples. On April 12 the cruiser *Trieste* was sunk by air attack as she lay at anchor in the roads at La Maddalena off the north coast of Sardinia. On June 5 a raid by Flying Fortresses on La Spezia caused varying degrees of damage to the big battleships *Roma, Littorio,* and *Vit-torio Veneto.* The fuel crisis had now become critical, and to economise on supplies the cruisers *Duilio, Doria,* and

A Goumier of the Free French Forces sharpens his bayonet in preparation for a night attack. Goums recruited from North Africa were noted for their prowess with this weapon.

German paratroopers on the look-out as the Allied invasion of Sicily gets under way.

Cesare were laid up, the first two at Taranto and the third at Pola.

Faced with this disastrous state of affairs, Mussolini came to the following conclusions on point 2 of the note on which he commented on June 14 to his Chiefs-of-Staff:

"In the present state of the war the Italian forces no longer hold any possibility of initiative. They are forced onto the defensive. The army no longer has any possibility of initiative. It lacks, amongst other things, room to manoeuvre. It can only counter-attack the enemy who lands at one point on our territory and drive him back into the sea."

We shall comment no further on Mussolini's remarks on the possibilities open to the Italian Navy and Air Force, as these have been mentioned already. It should be noted, however, that in asking the Army to counter-attack the enemy as he landed and throw him back into the sea, Mussolini had overlooked the report made to him on May 8 by the Chief of the General Staff after an inspection in Sardinia.

After noting certain differences of conception in the organisation of defences against landings, General Ambrosio recommended the adoption of what he called the "modern technique". This was to break up the landing on the beaches or, even better, crush the opposing forces whilst they were still at sea. The advanced defensive position therefore had to have guns capable of dealing with ships, landing-craft, personnel, and tanks, not only to stop the mechanised columns which might break through the first defence line, but also to knock out approaching flotillas and all the troops who managed to set foot ashore. "It is all the more necessary to stop the attack on the beach before it can secure a foothold as, not having enough armour, we shall

not be able to halt a well-equipped adversary once he has landed and started to make his way inland."

Thus Ambrosio did not believe, any more than Rommel was to in 1944, in a counter-attack from inland against an enemy who had secured an extensive beach-head. His scepticism was backed by a decisive argument: the Italians did not have in their army any powerfully-equipped shock force to carry it out. Had the Duce any more faith in it? Probably not. In his note to his four Chiefs-of-Staff he had sensibly written: "It has been said that the artillery wins the ground and the infantry occupies it." He did not hesitate to apply to Sicily the very recent precedent of Pantelleria. Against Ambrosio it must be remembered that nowhere did the coastal units have the weapons he was recommending and that he was well aware of this. Thus there was no way of driving any invasion force back into the sea or of counter-attacking it as it was striking inland. In other words they had reached the situation covered by the saying quoted by Mussolini on June 14: "He who defends himself dies!"

But was it necessary to die? As we have seen, Mussolini was counting on German aid to drive back the invaders. But even within his own party, a majority of its leaders thought that Hitler's intentions were less to defend Italy than to defend Germany in Italy, and that the final defeat of the Third Reich was written in the stars anyway. The peninsula must therefore not be allowed to become a battlefield. Italy must get out of the war one way or another—and immediately, as she had already lost the war irremediably. We have seen that Ciano, Grandi, and Bottaï, all three former ministers of the Duce, shared this opinion with Marshals Badoglio and Caviglia, with the "young" Generals Castellano and Carboni, with the former Prime Ministers of the liberal era Orlando and Bonomi, and with those

close to the King. The Chief of the General Staff accepted the principle of a rupture of the Axis and a cessation of hostilities but, as he continually urged him, preferred Mussolini to take the initiative for this change of tack. Failing this he envisaged arresting the Duce. Finally, General Chierici, Chief of Police, and General Hazon, Commander of the Corps of Carabinieri, also declared themselves in favour of an eventual show of force.

The King, however, hesitated to give the signal. We would impute this not to lack of personal courage but to the fear of provoking indescribable chaos if the elimination of Mussolini, which he thought would be necessary, were to be carried out by other than legal means. In particular the presence in the Lake Bracciano area, some 25 miles from the capital, of the Blackshirt "M" Armoured Division, militated against any ill-considered gesture, and whilst Germany was reinforcing her strength in the peninsula, she could be counted upon to react with some force.

The King's reserve caused Count Grandi to lose patience. On June 3, recalling to Victor Emmanuel III the ups and downs of the House of Savoy, he said: "Your Majesty, there is no choice: either Novara, namely abdication, or a change of front in the style of Victor Amadeus II who, when he realised the mistake of the alliance with the King of France, saved Piedmont and the dynasty at the last moment, by going over to the Imperial camp."

Marshal Badoglio felt the same way on July 17, when he said to Senator Casati: "Either the King accepts the solution which, in agreement with us, he has already anticipated, or he resigns himself to waiting for another moment. In the second case each one of us can choose the way he wishes to follow."

Hitler thought that the first objective of the Anglo-American invasion would be Sardinia. General Ambrosio's inspection of the island's defences in early May would seem to indicate that the *Comando Supremo* agreed with the Führer. After the event, Marshal Badoglio gave it as his opinion that the strategists in London and Washington had made a great mistake in preferring the easier way of a landing in Sicily.

This would be correct if the two Western powers had proposed an immediate conquest of Italy, for the occupation of Sardinia means that the peninsula south of a line La Spezia–Ancona cannot be defended and allows, through Corsica and after landings in Liguria, the turning of the Apennine bastion.

But when plans were being drawn up for Operation "Husky", the Anglo-Americans were proposing nothing of the sort. They anticipated, first of all, clearing the Sicilian Channel, and then securing a bridgehead, including Naples and Foggia, whose great aerodromes would allow bombing raids on the Rumanian oilfields. But at the "Trident" Conference on May 12-25 in Washington, attended by Roosevelt and Churchill, which was to decide on the follow-up to "Husky", the Americans expressed their conviction that the British had "led them down the garden path by taking them into North Africa". "They also think," continued Alanbrooke in his diary, "that at Casablanca we again misled them by inducing them to attack Sicily. And now they do not intend to be led astray again."

And the American President agreed, apart from a few minor reservations, with the thinking of the Pentagon. According to Alanbrooke, Roosevelt admitted, it is true, "the urgent need to consider where to go from Sicily and how to keep employed the score or more of battle-trained Anglo-American divisions in the Mediterranean. But the continuing drain involved in any attempt to occupy Italy might prejudice the build-up of forces for a cross-Channel invasion, and, though there now seemed no chance of the latter in 1943, it would have to be launched on the largest scale in the spring of 1944."

After long arguments between the British and Americans, it was agreed that while an invasion of France in late spring 1944 remained the principal Allied operation against Germany, the Allied forces in the Mediterranean after "Husky" were to mount "such operations as are best calculated to eliminate Italy from the war and to contain the maximum number of German divisions".

For "Husky" General Eisenhower kept the same team which had brought him victory in Tunisia. Under his control General Alexander would direct the operations of the 15th Army Group, the number being the sum of its two constituent armies, the American 7th (Lieutenant-General Patton) and the British 8th (Montgomery): an experienced and able high command.

According to the original plan, the British 8th Army was to land between Syracuse and Gela and the American 7th Army on each side of Trapani at the other end of the island. Montgomery, however, objected because, as he wrote to Alexander on April 24: "Planning to date has been on the assumption that resistance will be slight and Sicily will be captured easily . . . If we work on the assumption of little resistance, and disperse our effort as is being done in all planning to date, we will merely have a disaster. We must plan for fierce resistance, by the Germans at any rate, and for a real dog fight battle to follow the initial assault."

The original plan had therefore to be concentrated so that the two Allied armies could give each other mutual support if either ran into trouble. Credit is due to both Eisenhower and Alexander for having accepted without too much difficulty Montgomery's reasoning. The revised plan set Scoglitti, Gela, and Licata as Patton's first objectives, whilst

German troops watch an artillery bombardment in the midday heat.

Montgomery moved his left flank objective over from the Gela area to Cape Passero so as to be able to seize this important promontory at the southeastern tip of Sicily in a pincer movement.

The British 8th Army comprised the following:
1. XIII Corps (Lieutenant-General Dempsey), made up of the 5th Division (Major-General Bucknall), the 50th Division (Major-General Kirkman), and the 231st Brigade (Brigadier-General Urquhart); and
2. XXX Corps (Lieutenant-General Leese), made up of the 51st Division (Major-General Wimberley) and the 1st Canadian Division (Major-General Simmonds).

The American 7th Army comprised the II Corps (Lieutenant-General Bradley), made up of the 45th Division (Major-General Middleton), the 1st Division (Major-General Allen), and the 2nd Armoured Division (Major-General Grittenberger), plus also the 3rd Division (Major-General Truscott), unattached to a corps.

Each army had an airborne spearhead of brigade strength, and one division held provisionally in reserve in North Africa.

An armada of 2,590 ships, large and small, took part in Operation "Husky" under the command of Admiral Cunningham. Under him Admiral Sir Bertram H. Ramsay was in command of the landings. Ramsay's experience went back to the Dunkirk evacuation, and this time he had 237 merchant vessels and troop transports and 1,742 motorised landing-craft to bring ashore the men, tanks, and supplies. The fighting units had two missions: to neutralise by gun fire all resistance on the shore and to deal with the Italian fleet. They had therefore

351

On the alert as the Allied armada heads for the Sicilian beaches.

been given generous support: six battleships, two fleet aircraft-carriers (both British), three monitors, 15 cruisers (five American), 128 destroyers (48 American, six Greek, and three Polish), and 26 submarines (one Dutch and two Polish).

An enormous concentration, but during the first phase of the operation 115,000 British and Canadians and more than 66,000 Americans had to be put ashore.

As for the Allied air forces, they had 4,000 planes under Air Chief-Marshal Tedder. By D-day they had virtually wiped out the enemy's defences. Over Sicily the opposition was a mere 200 Italian and 320 German planes.

On June 12 the *matériel* and morale effect of the air bombardment of Pantelleria was such that Admiral Pavesi surrendered this island fortress of 12,000 men to the Allies after losing only 56 killed and 116 wounded. According to Mussolini, Pavesi had deceived him by giving the reason for his request to surrender as lack of water. According to Admiral Bernotti it was not so much the water which was short as the means of distributing it. There were only four

American tanks hit the beach at Licata.

tanker-lorries and three wells for 10,000 civilians and 12,000 troops. Add to this the physical shock of the explosion of 6,550 tons of bombs in six days and it will be seen that the capitulation of June 12 was understandable.

At the same time, the Allied air forces redoubled their attacks on Sicily, particularly on the aerodromes and the harbours. Messina alone received 5,000 tons of bombs. Communications with the mainland were severely affected and feeding the civilian population began to bring enormous problems to the administration. At the end of June there were only 30 days' supplies of flour left.

On June 8, Generals Eisenhower and Alexander and Admiral Cunningham went to Malta. All was going well apart from the deteriorating weather. The meteorological office reported Force 4 to 5 winds over the sea but there was no going back.

Let us now go over to the other side. On June 1 General Guzzoni succeeded General Roatta in command of the Italian 6th Army, with the task of defending Sicily to the last. According to Mussolini, the enemy was to be wiped out before breaking through inland or "as he took off his bath-robe and before he had had time to get dressed".

As soon as he was informed of the Anglo-American invasion preparations, the Duce, said Marshal Badoglio, "had rushed to make a speech to the nation; the stupidest he ever gave. Later it became known as the 'bath-robe' speech."

The plan adopted for the defence corresponded so closely to the invasion plan abandoned at the request of Montgomery that it can be asked if in fact the Anglo-Americans had not leaked it on purpose. Guzzoni established his headquarters at Enna in the centre of the island and divided his forces into two:

1. west of the line Licata (inclusive)– Cefalú: XII Corps (H.Q. at Corleone) to defend Marsala, Trapani, and Palermo. Commanded by General Arisio it comprised the "Aosta" Division (General Romano) and the "Assietta" Division (General Papini) with the 207th, 202nd, and 208th Coastal Divisions; and
2. east of this line: XVI Corps (H.Q. at Piazza Armerina) to defend Gela, Syracuse, Catania, and Messina. Commanded by General Rossi, it had the "Napoli" Division (General Gotti-Porcinari), the 206th and 213th Coastal Divisions, and the 18th and 19th Coastal Brigades.

The "Livorno" Division (General Chirieleison) was held in army reserve at Mazzarino.

Including the Fascist Militia there were thus 230,000 men and 1,500 guns in the Italian 6th Army which, however, was not very mobile as there were very few motorised units among its formations. The coastal units had tremendous stretches of land to defend: the 206th Division (General d'Havet) had nearly 83 miles between Cassibile and Punte Braccetto, and the 18th Brigade (General Mariscalco) 36 miles between Punte Braccetto to east of Licata. These two units were to take the brunt of the six British and American divisions, while the American attack by 3rd Division was to face only two battalions of the 207th Division (General Schreiber).

The Italian 6th Army was supported by two German divisions, the 15th *Panzergrenadier* (Major-General Rodt) and the "Hermann Göring" Panzer Division (Lieutenant-General Conrath). The first of these was only partially motorised and the second had only two battalions of infantry and fewer than 100 tanks, though these included a company of Tigers. O.K.W. had appointed Major-General von Senger und Etterlin as liaison officer to General Guzzoni.

When Hitler received Senger und Etterlin on June 22 he did not disguise his mistrust of the Italian court, society, and high command. In spite of this he was optimistic about the outcome of the operations as, he assured Senger und Etterlin, the Allies "by neglecting to attack Sicily immediately after their landings in North Africa had virtually thrown away the war in the Mediterranean!"

General Warlimont, Chief of the Operations Staff at O.K.W., did not share these illusions. "He laid the situation clearly before me" wrote Senger und Etterlin, adding: "the best solution to the mission entrusted to me was to be, in case of heavy enemy attacks, to bring back to the mainland the majority of the troops stationed in Sicily. He recognised that we could not expect to bring back the bulk of our war *matériel*. This appreciation of the situation and the definition of my mission was a corrective to Hitler's viewpoint."

At Enna, where he had gone together with Field-Marshal Kesselring, the question of the intervention of the German units in the battle, now expected any day, gave rise to somewhat confused discussions. In the end the 15th Panzer Division, less one detachment, was relegated to the western tip of the island whilst the "Hermann Göring" Panzer Division was divided between the plain of Catania and the Caltagirone area.

The landing on July 10 came as no surprise. The evening before, Axis aircraft had spotted six Allied convoys leaving Malta and, towards five o'clock in the morning, Enna H.Q. reported that several parachutists had landed. These landings were unfortunate, as the men were widely scattered by the wind; nevertheless they succeeded in harrassing the enemy's movements. Brigadier-General Lathbury, at the head of a hundred or so British troops, seized the bridge at Primosole south of Catania and held out there for five days, preventing its destruction until the arrival of the 8th Army.

At dawn, naval guns and tactical aircraft pounded the Italian coastal defences whilst many landing-craft, loaded with men and tanks, advanced on to their objectives in spite of a choppy sea. D.U.K.W.s, American amphibious trucks, were the first vehicles to land. Franz Kurokowski's monograph on the Sicilian campaign tells of numerous acts of heroism by men of the 206th Division and the 18th Brigade, but faced with companies, battalions, and regiments supported by tanks they were overrun and virtually wiped out. In the evening General Guzzoni ordered the 15th Panzer Division to move towards Enna and the "Hermann Göring" Panzer Division, together with the "Livorno" Division, to mop up the American bridgehead at Gela. In the morning of July 11 the Panzers ran into the forward posts of the 1st American Division in the area of Niscemi but when they had got to within 2,000 yards of the beach they were caught by fire from the cruisers *Boise* and *Savannah* and six destroyers, which together loosed off no fewer than 3,194 6- and 5-inch shells at them and wiped out 30 tanks. The "Livorno" Division was also very badly knocked about. On the same day Montgomery occupied, without a shot being fired, the two harbours of Syracuse and Augusta, which had been abandoned by their garrisons in somewhat obscure circumstances.

On July 14 the American 7th Army and the British 8th Army met. This gave them the aerodromes at Ragusa and Comiso, which were put back into shape in record time. Was Montgomery going to race the enemy to Messina and force a surrender, as he had planned? No. Kesselring managed by a great feat to bring over to Sicily two paratroop regiments and the 29th *Panzergrenadier* Division (Major-General Fries). On July 17 General Hube and the staff of XIV Panzer Corps took command of all German fighting troops in Sicily and resistance stiffened on both sides of Mount Etna. The 8th Army was stopped at Catania and so attacked west of Etna, upsetting the advancing Americans.

Patton, by a miracle of improvisation, then threw his army against Palermo, which fell on July 22, having overcome on the way the "Assietta" Division. He then resumed his advance towards Messina, hoping, like Montgomery, to get there before the Germans. Once

The view from Russia: a despondent Mussolini, about to slip off the ripped and crumbling boot of Italy, awaits the worst. He was deposed on July 25.

again, however, Hube parried and on July 23 the forward units of the American 7th Army were stopped in front of the little town of Santo Stefano on the coastal road. Meanwhile the 1st Canadian Division, which formed Montgomery's left flank, after bypassing the important crossroads at Enna, tried to turn the Etna massif from the north-west.

Meanwhile the American 9th Division (Major-General Eddy), which had landed at Palermo, and the British 78th Division (Major-General Keightley), now ashore at Syracuse, brought the number of divisions in the 15th Army Group to 11 and gave the Allies an enormous superiority. Hube therefore began to withdraw, and did it so well that two-thirds of his forces got across to Italy.

Messina and the straits were bristling with A.A., which made life very difficult for Anglo-American aircraft. At 0530 hours on August 17 the commander of XIV Panzer Corps embarked on the last assault-boat leaving for Calabria. Three hours later the Americans and the British were congratulating each other in the ruined streets of Messina.

In his final communiqué, General Alexander announced the capture of 132,000 prisoners, 260 tanks, and 520 guns, and we know from General Faldella, former Chief-of-Staff of the 6th Army, that today there are 4,278 Italian and 4,325 German dead in the war cemeteries in Sicily. On the Allied side, out of 467,000 men in Operation "Husky" the losses were 5,532 killed, 2,869 missing and 14,410 wounded.

Though the battleships *Caio Duilio* and *Andrea Doria* had been brought back into service late in July, the Italian fleet, through lack of sufficient escort and air support, played only a passive rôle in the operation. Furthermore the bulk of the fleet, stationed as it was in La Spezia, was badly placed to intervene in the waters round Cape Passero. Admiral Riccardi thus limited his support to submarines, torpedo planes, and fast patrol boats. At the high cost of nine of their numbers sunk, the Italian submarines torpedoed and damaged the cruisers *Newfoundland* and *Cleopatra*, and sent to the bottom four merchant-vessels and a tanker. The American destroyer *Maddox* was sunk by aerial bombardment on July 10.

On July 16, after reading the communiqués, Count Grandi was moved to write the following letter to General Puntoni, King Victor-Emmanuel's senior A.D.C.:

"Dear Puntoni:

The news from Sicily has caused deep and poignant grief to my Italian heart. Almost 100 years after the day on which King Charles Albert promulgated the constitution of the kingdom and, with the *Risorgimento,* gave the signal for the struggle for the liberty, unity. and independence of Italy, our motherland is now on the road to defeat and dishonour."

As we have said, the King was hesitating over the best way to remove from power not only Mussolini but the whole Fascist Party, a plan which he could not reveal to Grandi. On July 19 there had been a meeting at Feltre, a small town in Venetia, between the Duce, the Führer, Bastianini, the Under-Secretary of State for Foreign Affairs, Ambassadors Alfiere and Mackensen, Field-Marshal Keitel, and Generals Ambrosio, Warlimont, and Rintelen. The outcome of this meeting had convinced the King that he had to cross his Rubicon, and soon, if Italy was to be spared further ruin and misfortune. The Feltre conference opened at 1100 hours and consisted essentially of an interminable monologue by Hitler, exhorting his Italian listeners to stiffen their resistance to the enemy as they were doing in Germany, where boys of 15 were being called up to

serve in A.A. batteries. When it came to the support in tanks and planes for which his allies asked he was vague: the most he could offer them was to bring LXXVI Panzer Corps, the 26th Panzer Division, and the 3rd *Panzergrenadier* Division down through the Brenner Pass, and even then he imposed certain conditions. According to Ambassador Alfieri he, Bastianini, and General Ambrosio took advantage of a break in the meeting to urge Mussolini to stop being so passive and to tell Hitler either to take it or leave it. Ambrosio had reported that within a month at most further organised resistance by the army would be out of the question. Hitler had therefore to be given the following alternative: the Third Reich must give Italy all the support she was asking for, or the latter would be compelled to withdraw from the war.

"Mussolini," Alfieri went on, "gave a start, then, pulling himself together, agreed to discuss the matter. He even asked us to sit down, a most unusual courtesy. 'Perhaps you think,' he said with some emotion, 'that this problem has not been troubling me for some long time? To you I may appear calm and collected but underneath I am suffering heart-rending torment. I admit the possible solution: break away from Germany. It looks easy: one fine day, at a given time, a radio message is broadcast to the enemy. But what will happen then? The enemy will rightly ask for capitulation. Are we prepared to wipe out at one go 20 years of government? To destroy the results of labours which have been so long and so bitter? To recognise our first military and political defeat? To disappear off the world stage? It's easy to say, you know... break away from Germany. What will be Hitler's attitude? Do you suppose he will leave us free to act?'"

Regardless of the force of these arguments, the Italian dictator could find no words capable of convincing his German colleague, either because he was ashamed of revealing the state of his military forces or because in his innocence he believed Hitler's hitherto secret reprisal measures: after the end of August new weapons would reduce the British capital to rubble in a matter of weeks and Dönitz would continue his war on Allied shipping with revolutionary submarines. It was true that these new weapons were being built, but it was a downright lie to state that they were ready to be put to use. The Feltre conference, which the interpreter Paul Schmidt called extremely "depressing", finally fizzled out. The two dictators, Deakin relates, said goodbye to each other on the aerodrome at Treviso: "As Hitler's plane took off, the Duce stood with his arm raised at the salute and remained thus until the machine was out of sight. His advisers approached him on the runway. 'I had no need to make that speech to Hitler,' he said, 'because, this time, he has firmly promised to send all the reinforcements which we need.' And turning to Ambrosio, 'Naturally our requests must be reasonable and not astronomic.'

Ambrosio and Bastianini travelled in the same car from the airport to Treviso railway station. The former suddenly burst out, 'Did you hear what he said to Hitler after my warning of this morning? He asked him yet again for that war material which they will never send, and he did not take my words seriously. He is mad, I tell you, mad. What I told him is serious, very serious.'"

General Ambrosio, who had only had airy promises from Field-Marshal Keitel, left the conference in a state of high indignation and determined to draw the necessary conclusion from the Duce's culpable debility. As Mussolini had not been able to convince his ally of the tragic dilemma in which Italy was now implicated, this had to be resolved without him and against him. In effect, to defend Italy which, now that Sicily was overrun, would very likely be the enemy's next objective, Army Group "South" had only seven divisions and 12 low-quality coastal divisions, although the 16th Panzer Division, reconstituted, like the 29th *Panzergrenadier* Division, after Stalingrad, had recently arrived in the peninsula: the Italians were nevertheless at the end of their tether.

It was in this atmosphere of bitterness and defeat that the meeting of the Fascist Grand Council, called by Mussolini, opened at 1700 hours on Saturday July 24 in the Palazzo Venezia. Strange as it may seem, the dictator does not appear to have got wind of the plot hatched against him or of the fact that a majority of the Council was now against him. This was borne out by Kesselring, who in his memoirs tells how the Duce had received him on the eve of the meeting and had gaily told him as he stepped into the dictator's office: "Do you know Grandi? He was here a moment ago. We had a clear and frank discussion; we think the same way. He is faithful and devoted to me."

Despite information he was receiving from within the Fascist Party, Ambassador von Mackensen was similarly optimistic and said so to Ribbentrop. The conspirators within the Grand Council were much less reassured than Mussolini as they went in, to such an extent that some had been to confession first. Mussolini's speech restored their spirits. "In a voice without either inspiration or conviction," Alfieri tells us, "the Duce spoke for two hours, disclaiming his responsibilities, blaming Badoglio, accusing the General Staff of 'sabotaging' the war and singing the praises of Germany." Grandi was as brief and penetrating as Mussolini had been irrelevant and long-winded and was supported by Bottaï, Ciano, Federzoni, and old Marshal de Bono, who had been cut to the quick by Mussolini's attacks on his comrades. After a brief adjournment and new exchanges the agenda was voted on and Grandi's motion came out top with 19 votes against eight with one abstention, that of Suardo, the President of the Senate. One of the majority withdrew before dawn; this saved his life at the Verona trial. It was almost three in the morning when Mussolini declared the meeting closed without, it would seem, having himself said one memorable thing during the whole session. The final scene of the Fascist Grand Council is described thus by F. W. Deakin: "Grandi addressed the meeting briefly. He then handed his motion to Mussolini. The names of the nineteen signatories were appended. The Duce put the paper in front of him with 'affected indifference.' And then 'without another word or gesture and in a relaxed and resigned manner' he called on Scorza to put Grandi's motion to a vote.

"Scorza stood up, and starting in order of priority round the table with De Bono, he called the roll of the names of those present. In an oppressive silence he counted. Nineteen in favour; seven against. Suardo abstained; Farinacci supported his own motion, on which no vote was taken. The Duce gathered his papers and stood up. According to his subsequent account he said: 'You have provoked the crisis of the régime. The session is closed.' Scorza attempted to call for the ritual salute to the Duce who checked him, saying: 'No, you are excused,' and retired to his private study."

Of the rather long text drawn up by Count Grandi we quote the final paragraph, which invited "the Head of the Government to request His Majesty the King, towards whom the heart of all the nation turns with faith and confidence, that he may be pleased, for the honour and salvation of the nation, to assume the effective command of the armed forces on land, on the sea and in the air, according to the article of the Statute of the Realm, and that supreme initiative of decision which our institutions attribute to him and which, in all our national history, have always been the glorious heritage of our august dynasty of Savoy."

As can be seen, this text, in spite of its verbosity, was cleverly drawn up since, without actually opening up a government crisis, it put the onus on the dictator to go to the King and hand over the command of the Italian armed forces. Moreover, the party hierarchy's formal disavowal of its leader by a majority of nearly eight to three authorised the sovereign to remove Mussolini from power.

Mussolini's attitude on the day following his defeat was incomprehensible. The Japanese Ambassador Hidaka, whom he received during the morning of July 26, found him full of confidence, and when the Duce went on to his audience with the King he took with him documents designed to show, as he wrote later, that "The Grand Council's motion committed nobody as this body was purely consultative."

What followed is well known. Mussolini presented himself at the Villa Savoia at 1700 hours and was informed by the King that it was his intention to relieve him of his powers and to appoint Badoglio

Jubilant Romans celebrate the fall of their erstwhile leader.

as head of the government. Twenty minutes later the fallen dictator was requested to leave in an ambulance and was taken to a military police barracks.

Marshal Badoglio reported the King's account to him of this meeting with the Duce: "Mussolini asked for an audience which I arranged to be held here at 1700 hours. At the time in question he presented himself and informed me as follows: the Grand Council had passed a motion against him, but he did not think that this was binding. I then told him that I could not agree because the Grand Council was a body of the State set up by him and ratified by the two houses of the Italian Parliament and that, as a consequence, every act of this Council was binding. 'So then, according to your Majesty, I must resign?' Mussolini said with evident effort. 'Yes,' I replied, 'and I would advise you now that I am accepting without further discussion your resignation as head of the government.'

"His Majesty then added: 'At these words Mussolini bent forwards as if he had received a violent blow in the chest and muttered: 'This is the end then.'"

There was sensation in Rome and throughout Italy, but no reaction in favour of the Duce either among the population in general or within the party. With rare exceptions, such as that of Roberto Farinacci who reached Germany dressed in a Wehrmacht uniform, everyone rallied to the new government. The new Foreign Minister was Baron Guari-glia, formerly Italian Ambassador in Ankara. His was the job of getting Italy out of the war. But as everyone was afraid of Hitler's reaction there was an immediate proclamation: "The war goes on!" As for the Fascist conspirators of July 25, they were kept away from all participation in the new government. Count Ciano thought it wiser to seek refuge in Germany. The Fascist Party seemed to have melted away like snow.

When Hitler heard at Rastenburg that his ally Mussolini had been ousted, he realised at once what this meant and Badoglio's proclamation came as no surprise to him. In his evening report on July 25 he had exclaimed, according to his secretary's shorthand notes: "That's just the way people like that would behave. It is treachery. But we too will go on and play the same game: get everything ready to make a lightning grab at the whole clique and put them all away. Tomorrow morning I'll send someone over there to give the commander of the 3rd Motorised Division the order to go into Rome without more ado, arrest the King, the whole bag of tricks, the Crown Prince and seize the scum, especially Badoglio and his gang. You'll see, they'll collapse like pricked balloons and in two or three days there'll be quite a different situation."

Mussolini prepares to board a Fieseler Storch on the Gran Sasso during his liberation by the Germans.

Whatever may be said about the coarseness and exaggeration of Hitler's words, the fact nevertheless remains that he and his collaborators reacted against this event, which took them by surprise, with all the promptness and the implacable resolution which they had shown in late March 1941 when the coup d'état in Belgrade had taken Yugoslavia out of the Tripartite Pact.

Field-Marshal Kesselring received orders to withdraw XIV Panzer Corps, now up to strength at four divisions, from Sicily and to move over to Corsica from Sardinia the 90th *Panzergrenadier* Division, which had replaced the 90th Light Division, torn to pieces in Tunisia. That same evening, Field-Marshal Rommel, who had just landed in Salonika on a tour of inspection, was ordered to drop everything and to go at once to O.K.W. Here he was given command of Operation *"Alarich"*, a plan which had been ready for some months against an eventual Italian defection. By the 29th he was installed in his Army Group "B" headquarters in Munich, and he moved the lot over to Bologna by about August 15.

Within a few days, LI and LXXXVII Corps, amounting to eight divisions, including the 24th Panzer and the *"Leibstandarte Adolf Hitler"*, had come down from France through the Brenner and Tarvis Passes and taken up positions north of the Apennines.

Kesselring, still the commander in the field, was south of this mountain barrier and was reinforced by the 2nd Parachute Division, which had landed unexpectedly in the area of Pratica di Mare some 15 miles south of Rome. All this goes to show that Hitler was not as short of men and *matériel* as he had given out at the Feltre conference. On August 6 Ribbentrop and Field-Marshal Keitel met Guariglia and General Ambrosio at Tarvis. On the 15th Jodl, accompanied by Rommel, met General Roatta, the Italian Army Chief-of-Staff, in Bologna. As can well be imagined, all these conversations went on in an atmosphere of mutual reticence and suspicion. Furthermore, the plan which was to liberate Mussolini and bring him back to power was being hatched in great secrecy under Hitler himself.

Guariglia was the first to admit this duplicity, but excused himself on the grounds of state: "Finally Ribbentrop revealed his hand and asked me solemnly if I could give him my word that the Italian

Government was not in the act of treating with the Allies. A single moment's hesitation could have gravely compromised all that I had painstakingly built up during the last two hours. Fortunately this was not to be and I replied at once that I could give him my word, but I confess that for a long time the lie weighed heavily on my conscience even though I tried to excuse it to myself by thinking that at that precise moment negotiations properly speaking had not yet begun in Lisbon and that we were still only at the stage of overtures. Be that as it may, my conscience is still subject to the ancient adage: *Salus Reipublicae suprema lex.*"

Rommel, in his notes of the meetings, and Kesselring, in his memoirs, both comment harshly on the behaviour of their ex-ally. In retrospect General von Senger und Etterlin judged the matter more calmly and he probably gave it the right tone when he wrote: "Historically—and not from the point of view of the disappointed ally—Victor Emmanuel III did his people as great a service in pulling out of the war in time as he had done after Caporetto in showing such a spirit of resistance. The fact that he was unable to take this decision

The Allied invasion of Sicily and Italy: Operations "Husky" and "Avalanche".

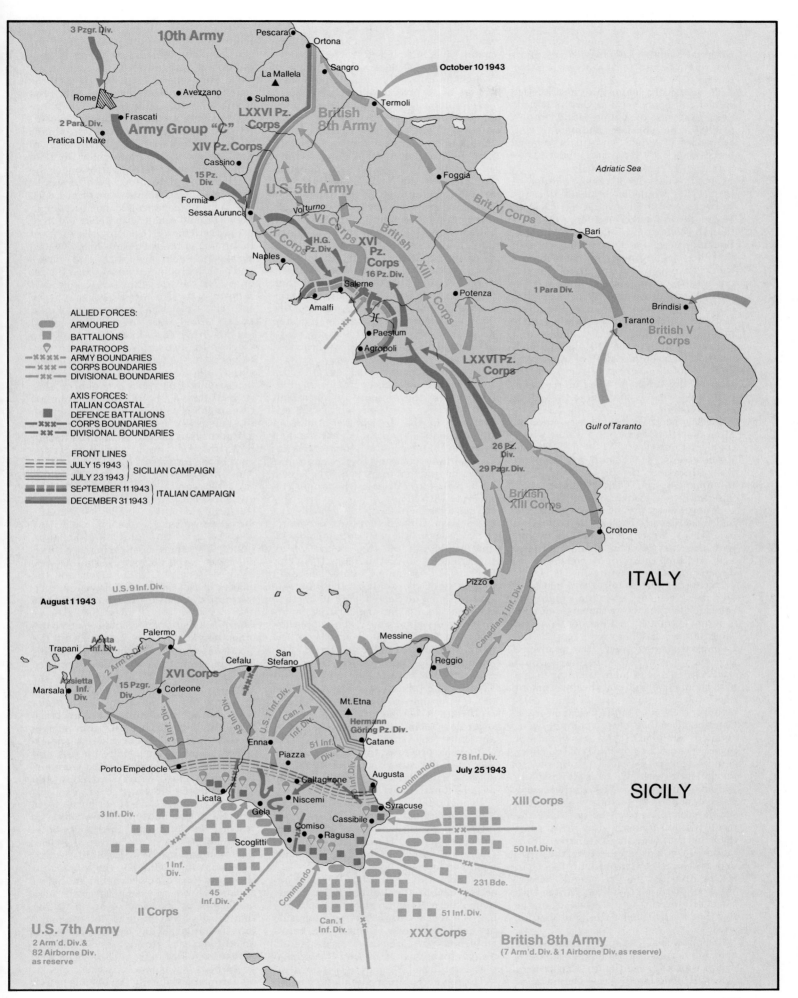

ALLIED FORCES:
- ARMOURED
- BATTALIONS
- PARATROOPS
- ──xxxx── ARMY BOUNDARIES
- ──xxx── CORPS BOUNDARIES
- ──xx── DIVISIONAL BOUNDARIES

AXIS FORCES:
ITALIAN COASTAL DEFENCE BATTALIONS
- ──xxx── CORPS BOUNDARIES
- ──xx── DIVISIONAL BOUNDARIES

FRONT LINES
- JULY 15 1943 } SICILIAN CAMPAIGN
- JULY 23 1943 }
- SEPTEMBER 11 1943 } ITALIAN CAMPAIGN
- DECEMBER 31 1943 }

3 Pzgr. Div.

10th Army

Pescara
Ortona
Sangro
La Mallela ▲
October 10 1943

Rome
Avezzano
Frascati
Sulmona
Termoli

2 Para. Div.
Army Group "C"
LXXVI Pz. Corps
British 8th Army

Pratica Di Mare
XIV Pz. Corps
15 Pz. Div.

Cassino
U.S. 5th Army
Foggia
Adriatic Sea

Formia
Sessa Aurunca
Volturno
VI Corps
Brit V Corps

X Corps
H.G. Pz. Div.
XVI Pz. Corps
British XIII Corps
Bari

Naples
Salerne
16 Pz. Div.

Amalfi
Potenza
1 Para Div.
Brindisi

Paestum
Taranto
British V Corps

Agropoli
LXXVI Pz. Corps

Gulf of Taranto

26 Pz. Div.
29 Pzgr. Div.
British XIII Corps

ITALY

Crotone

Pizzo

August 1 1943
U.S. 9 Inf. Div.

Palermo
Messine

Trapani
Aosta Inf. Div.
2 Arm'd. Div.
Cefalu
San Stefano
Reggio
Canadian 1 Inf. Div.

Assietta Inf. Div.
XVI Corps
Corleone

Marsala
15 Pzgr. Div.
Mt. Etna ▲

3 Inf. Div.
45 Inf. Div.
U.S. 1 Inf. Div.
Can. 1 Inf. Div.
Hermann Göring Pz. Div.

Porto Empedocle
Enna
Piazza
Catane

51 Inf. Div.
78 Inf. Div.
July 25 1943

Licata
Niscemi
Caltagirone
Augusta
Commando
XIII Corps
SICILY

3 Inf. Div.
Gela
Comiso
Cassibile
Syracuse

1 Inf. Div.
Scoglitti
Ragusa
50 Inf. Div.

45 Inf. Div.
Commando
231 Bde.

II Corps
Can. 1 Inf. Div.
51 Inf. Div.

U.S. 7th Army
2 Arm'd. Div. & 82 Airborne Div. as reserve

XXX Corps
British 8th Army
(7 Arm'd. Div. & 1 Airborne Div. as reserve)

openly and in agreement with his National-Socialist ally was a result of the relations of that ally with other powers."

The fact still remains that the armistice signed on September 3 at Cassabile near Syracuse was to plunge Italy into a tragedy, the physical and moral consequences of which were to be remembered for a very long time; indeed they may even be remembered still.

Could events have taken a different turn? That would have meant that the Italian armed forces would have had to be greater in number and less exhausted than they were on the day when Marshal Badoglio proclaimed the armistice, and that his Anglo-American counterparts would have had to attach greater importance to the complete and total occupation of the peninsula. Remember that at "Trident" both President Roosevelt and General Marshall had shown little inclination to push beyond Naples and Foggia. Finally, the 46 days which elapsed between the fall of Mussolini and the announcement of the armistice allowed the Germans to reinforce their positions in Italy, and this to the extent of 17 divisions.

On August 12 Generals Castellano and Montenari left Rome for Lisbon, where they met General W. Bedell Smith, Eisenhower's chief-of-staff, and General Kenneth Strong, the British head of his Intelligence staff. The Italians were handed the text of an armistice which had been approved at the end of July by London and Washington. On the 27th, Badoglio's delegates returned to the Italian capital with this text, a radio set and a cipher key so that they could communicate directly and secretly with Allied G.H.Q.

During the discussions there had been less disagreement over the conditions asked for by the victors than over quite a different problem: before laying down their arms, Eisenhower reports, the Italians wished to have "the assurance that such a powerful Allied force would land on the mainland simultaneously with their surrender that the government itself and their cities would enjoy complete protection from the German forces. Consequently they tried to obtain every detail of our plans. These we would not reveal because the possibility of treachery could never be excluded. Moreover, to invade Italy with the strength that the Italians themselves believed necessary was a complete impossibility for the very simple reason that we did not have the troops in the area nor the ships to transport them had they been there. Italian military authorities could not conceive of the Allies undertaking this venture with less than fifteen divisions in the assault waves. We were planning to use only three with some reinforcing units, aside from the two that were to dash across the Messina strait."

Eisenhower's reaction is understandable but so also is Badoglio's anxiety, which was quite legitimate. Expecting a powerful reaction by the Germans, it

was important for him to know, as Commander-in-Chief, if the Anglo-American landings would be south or north of Rome and in what strength, and if there would be a diversion in the Adriatic, preferably at Rimini. This was the point of view expressed by Castellano on August 31 when he met General Bedell Smith in the latter's tent at Cassabile. But Bedell Smith maintained an icy silence. It was, however, agreed that on the night of the armistice an airborne division would land on the outskirts of Rome whilst an armoured formation would disembark at the mouth of the Tiber.

Castellano thus returned to Rome with this proposition and on the following day, in accordance with the agreed instructions of the King, Marshal Badoglio, Foreign Minister Guariglia, and General Ambrosio, Castellano sent the following message to Bedell Smith: "Reply affirmative repeat affirmative stop person known will arrive tomorrow Sept 2 at time and place agreed stop confirmation requested."

Thus on September 3, 1943 at 1715 hours the Cassabile armistice was signed in triplicate in the presence of Macmillan and Murphy, the representatives respectively of the British and American Governments. When the signatures had been exchanged, Castellano relates, "Eisenhower came up to me, shook my hand and said that from then on he looked upon me as a colleague who would collaborate with him."

Then a serious difficulty arose. Whereas the Italian Government was expecting the landings to take place on September 12, and would put off the declaration of the armistice until this date, D-day for Operation "Avalanche" had been fixed for the 9th. General Maxwell Taylor was sent to Rome on September 8 to arrange the final details for the landing of his airborne division, and it was doubtless from him that Badoglio learned that the newly-signed armistice would be announced that very evening. He tried to gain time, but in vain, for, wrote General Eisenhower, "the matter had proceeded too far for me to temporize further. I replied in a peremptory telegram that regardless of his action I was going to announce the surrender at six-thirty o'clock as previously agreed upon and that if I did so without simultaneous action on his part Italy would have no friend left in the war."

Badoglio had to comply and broadcast a proclamation. This took place an hour later, but within minutes of his leaving the microphone Hitler had launched Operation "Achse", the new name for what had formerly been "Alarich".

Though expected, the German reaction caught the Italians off balance. In northern Italy Rommel put into the bag the ten divisions serving alongside his own. In Rome General Carboni's motorised and armoured corps melted away into the dust of the 3rd *Panzergrenadier* and the 2nd Parachute Divisions.

The Royal family, the Badoglio govern-

ment, and *Comando Supremo* set off for Bari whilst old Marshal Caviglia concluded a cease-fire with Kesselring.

On September 9, at 0300 hours, three battleships, six light cruisers, and nine destroyers left La Spezia for Malta in accordance with the armistice agreement. At 1550 hours, whilst it was off Asinara island, north-west of Sardinia, the convoy was spotted by 15 Dornier Do 217's which had taken off from Istres under the command of Major Jope with orders to intercept. These planes were armed with PC 1400 radio-controlled bombs, weighing a ton and a half with about 770 lb of explosive. One of these hit the forward fuel tanks of the battleship *Roma* (46,000 tons) which went down with 1,523 officers and men, including Admiral Carlo Bergamini. Her sister ship *Italia*, formerly *Littorio*, was also hit. However, on the 10th the La Spezia squadron anchored in the Grand Harbour, where it joined another from Taranto consisting of two battleships, two cruisers, and two destroyers. On the following day the battleship *Giulio Cesare*, which had succeeded in escaping from Pola, announced that it had joined the forces of Admiral Cunningham who was able to telegraph the Admiralty as follows: "Be pleased to inform your Lordships that the Italian Battle fleet now lies at anchor under the guns of the fortress of Malta."

In the Balkans, 19 German divisions surprised and disarmed 29 Italian divisions. The "Acqui" Division (General Gandin) held on the island of Cephalonia until September 22, when it had to lay down its arms through lack of ammunition; it was then almost completely wiped out after capitulating. A similar fate awaited General Cigala-Fulgosi and the officers of the "Bergamo" Division, who were guilty of defending Spalato for 19 days against the *Waffen* S.S. *"Prinz Eugen"* Division. Thousands of survivors of this horrible butchery joined Tito or the Greek resistance in the Pindhos mountains and the Peloponnese. The navy managed finally to get 25,000 of them across the Adriatic.

Churchill was quite unable to argue Roosevelt into supporting Italian resistance in the Dodecanese archipelago, though he did get 234th Brigade (Brigadier-General Tinley) put ashore on Cos and Leros. The result was that the Germans counter-attacked with paratroops and on November 18 it was all over.

On September 12, a glider-borne force from the commando led by Otto Skorzeny rescued Mussolini from the remote hotel in which he was being held in the Gran Sasso mountains. In Mussolini's words:

"At dawn on Sunday the summit of the Gran Sasso was covered in heavy clouds. However, some aircraft were heard passing overhead. I had a feeling that this day was going to determine my fate. Towards mid-day the clouds cleared and the sun came through. I was standing with arms folded in front of my open window when—it was precisely two o'clock—an aeroplane suddenly landed a hundred yards away. Four or five men dressed in khaki and carrying two machine guns jumped out of the cockpit and ran towards the villa. A few seconds later, other aircraft landed nearby and their crews all did the same thing. All the carabinieri, brandishing their arms, rushed to the road to cut off the attackers. At the head of the attackers was Skorzeny. The carabinieri were preparing to fire when I spotted amongst the Germans an Italian officer whom I recognised as General Soletti. In the silence just before the shooting began I suddenly shouted: 'What are you doing? Can't you see? You're going to fire on an Italian general! Don't shoot!' As they saw the Italian general approaching they lowered their weapons."

Mussolini was thus able to proclaim the Italian Socialist Republic on September 18. But none of the neutrals, not even Spain, agreed to set up diplomatic relations with it; in Rome Cavallero committed suicide after Kesselring had offered him the command of a new Fascist army; when the snow had made the Alps impassable no fewer than 18,400 Italians in Venetia, Lombardy, and Piedmont had got themselves interned in Switzerland; and in Italy some opposed the new régime by strikes and sabotage, others by armed resistance. Allied operations were soon to benefit from the information fed through by brave and efficient networks of guerrillas.

As we have seen, in the case of defection by the Italians, Field-Marshal Kesselring was ordered to withdraw the 90th *Panzergrenadier* Division from Sardinia and send it across the Bonifacio channel to join the forces defending Corsica. To this effect, O.K.W. put the troops stationed on the two islands under the command of General von Senger und Etterlin, who arrived in Ajaccio on board a Dornier Do 17 on September 7.

On Sardinia General Basso, who was in command of the island, had under him XVI and XXX Corps (two infantry and three coastal defence divisions), plus the "Bari" Division and the "Nembo" Parachute Division. This would appear to have been more than enough to deal with the 90th *Panzergrenadier*. It should not be forgotten, however, that the German formation, being in reserve, was concentrated in the centre of the island, completely motorised and commanded by a man of high quality, Lieutenant-General Lungershausen. It also had the high morale of all former *Afrika Korps* units.

On the opposing side the Italians had half their forces scattered along the coastline, whilst their "mobile" reserves simply lacked mobility and their anti-tank guns were no use against the Panzers. Under these conditions all General Basso could do was to follow the 90th *Panzergrenadier* as it withdrew. At the end of the day on September 18, the German evacuation of Sardinia was complete. The Germans had left behind them 50 dead, 100 wounded, and 395 prisoners,

against the Italians' 120.

On Corsica the Axis forces under General Magli comprised VII Corps ("Cremona" and "Friuli" Divisions), two coastal defence divisions, and an armoured brigade of the *Waffen* S.S. *Leibstandarte*. On the announcement of the Italian armistice the resistance forces which, since December 1942, had received by submarine or air-drop more than 10,000 automatic weapons, occupied Ajaccio, joined General Magli and appealed for help to Algiers. Meanwhile the Germans were able to drive their former allies out of Bonifacio and Bastia.

General Giraud in Algiers did not turn a deaf ear to the appeal from Corsica. With the help of Rear-Admiral Lemmonier, he improvised a small expeditionary force whose forward units reached Ajaccio on the night of September 12-13. These were 109 men of the famous Shock Battalion, who had crammed themselves aboard the submarine *Casabianca* which was still under the command of L'Herminier. On the following day the large destroyers *Fantasque* and *Terrible* landed over 500 men from the battalion and kept up the shuttle service together with the destroyers *Tempête* and *Alcyon;* then the cruisers *Montcalm* and *Jeanne d'Arc* joined in, despite the Luftwaffe's latest glide bomb.

But on September 12 O.K.W. changed its mind and orders were sent to Senger und Etterlin to abandon Corsica and evacuate the 90th *Panzergrenadier* to Piombino. This move was completed by October 4. The 5,000 infantry and *goums* of the 4th Moroccan Mountain Division, with the help of their new Italian allies, had managed to repel the German rearguard but were quite unable to cut off the main force. The British and Americans, busy south of Naples, were too late to get to this miniature Dunkirk, which rescued some 28,000 men for the Wehrmacht.

Only a partial success, in spite of the sacrifice of 222 Frenchmen and 637 Italians, the occupation of Corsica nevertheless gave the Allies a strategic position of the first importance, with 17 aerodromes capable of taking and maintaining 2,000 planes which the American air force moved onto the island within a

matter of months. As the armed forces of the Third Reich had by now spilt copious amounts of Italian blood, Marshal Badoglio's government declared war on it on October 13 and received from the "United Nations", as Roosevelt called them, the status of "co-belligerent." This raised the hackles of Harry Hopkins but was fully approved by Stalin.

"Salerno: A near disaster" was the title given by General Mark Wayne Clark, commander of the American 5th Army, to the chapter of his memoirs in which he described the landings at Salerno. The whole affair was indeed nearly a disaster and that the Allies did in fact win through was the result not only of Clark's obstinacy and Montgomery's promptness but also, and perhaps more so, of the bad relationship between Rommel and Kesselring.

The plan drawn up by Generals Eisenhower and Alexander, Air Chief Marshal Tedder, and Admiral Cunningham involved a diversionary action by the 8th Army across the Strait of Messina to pin down the enemy's forces. When this had been done, the 5th Army was to land in the Gulf of Salerno.

On September 3, under cover of fire from a naval force led by Vice-Admiral Willis, and from some 600 8th Army guns the British XIII Corps made a landing on the coast of Calabria north-west of Reggio di Calabria. It met no serious resistance as the 29th *Panzergrenadier* Division which, with the 26th Panzer Division and the 1st Parachute Division, formed the LXXVI Panzer Corps (General Dostler), had received orders not to get caught up in any engagement. General Dempsey thus had no difficulty in pushing his 5th Division up to Pizzo and his 1st Canadian Division to Crotone. This withdrawal by the enemy had not entered into the plans of the Allied 15th Army Group.

On September 8 Kesselring learned at his H.Q. in Frascati that a powerful Anglo-American fleet was now in the waters of the Tyrrhenian Sea and concluded that a landing must be imminent, though there was nothing to show whether it would be in the Gulf of Salerno, in the

The Italian battleship Roma, *now fighting with the Allies, is hit by a German bomb.*

American troops help secure the beach-head at Salerno on September 9, 1943.

Bay of Naples, or on the beaches opposite Rome. To oppose it he had had under his command since August 8 the 10th Army (General von Vietinghoff), the units of which were deployed as follows:
1. XIV Panzer Corps, back from Sicily, had its 15th *Panzergrenadier* at Formia, its "Hermann Göring" Panzer Division in Naples, and its 16th Panzer Division (Major-General Sieckenius) in the Salerno area (by August 22, Hitler had told Vietinghoff to regard Salerno as "the centre of gravity", and this was why 16th Panzer had been moved there);
2. LXXVI Panzer Corps, as we have seen, was engaged in Calabria; and
3. Though earmarked for Operation *"Achse"*, the 2nd Parachute Division and the 3rd *Panzergrenadier* Division were well placed to cover the Italian capital.

The curtain rose at dawn on September 9 when the first elements of the American VI Corps (Major-General Ernest W. Dawley) and the British X Corps (Lieutenant-General Richard L. Mc-Creery) landed between Paestum and Maiori, on either side of Salerno. The naval forces assigned to the operation (codename "Avalanche") were somewhat similar to those used against Sicily: they included seven aircraft-carriers for first-line support and were led by the American Vice-Admiral H. Kent Hewitt.

Attacked on a front of some 25 miles, the 16th Panzer Division had to give ground but did not disintegrate. By the end of the day the American 36th Division had got five miles inland, but the British X Corps had not reached all its objectives and fighting continued in the streets of Salerno. Sieckenius still controlled the high ground which overlooked the coastal strip from a distance of 600 to 1000 yards. The American 45th Division was landed and this allowed Clark to extend and deepen his bridgehead, which on September 11 was 11 miles inland at its furthest point and stretched from Agropoli to Amalfi with a circumference of over 43 miles.

"Avalanche" was off to a good start. In Frascati, however, Kesselring had remained calm and XIV Panzer Corps was ordered to concentrate and counterattack. LXXVI Corps also came to the rescue, leaving Montgomery facing only its 1st Parachute Division and part of the 26th Panzer Division. The capture of Rome enabled Kesselring to give the 3rd *Panzergrenadier* Division (Lieutenant-General Graeser) to the 10th Army, so that by September 12 Vietinghoff had five and a half divisions, admittedly understrength, against his enemy's four, scattered over a wide front. This led to a crisis that did not end until September 15.

Profiting from the fact that the British right flank (56th Division) had made slower progress than the American left (45th Division), the Germans attempted to get a pincer movement round the latter, cut the British off from the Americans, and destroy both piecemeal. The crux of this battle was at Ponte Bruciato, where Clark threw in everything he had, including two artillery battalions, a regimental band, and his H.Q. orderlies and cooks. The German advance was slowed down and eventually stopped some five miles from the beach, where it was pinned down by the concentrated fire of the fleet which Admiral Hewitt had brought as close inshore as possible. Although the capture of Rome by the Germans had freed the 3rd *Panzergrenadier* Division for Kesselring, it also released the American 82nd Parachute Division (Major-General Ridgway) which was to have landed in support of the Italians; during the night of September 13-14 a first paratroop regiment reached the bridgehead.

What would have happened if, on the morning of the 9th, Rommel had put at Kesselring's disposal his 24th Panzer Division and the *"Leibstandarte Adolf Hitler"*, and Kesselring had then used them at Salerno? The question cannot be answered as the Führer refused to reinforce the 10th Army, having been advised by Rommel that Italy could not be defended south of a line La Spezia–Rimini. In face of the threat to the American 5th Army, Alexander called on Montgomery to come up in haste and catch the forces attacking the bridgehead. Montgomery managed to do this, though in his memoirs he gallantly states that it was more or less all over on September 16 when his 5th Division got to Agropoli. On that day the 5th Army had five divisions or their equivalent engaged in the battle and had lost 5,674 officers, N.C.O.s, and men, including 756 killed and 2,150 missing. In addition, the British battleship *Warspite* and the cruiser *Uganda*, as well as the American cruiser *Savannah*, had been badly damaged by the Luftwaffe's new radio-controlled bombs. After this crisis, Clark got Eisenhower's permission to relieve VI Corps' commander and replaced him by Major-General John P. Lucas. The British Army was assigned the province of Apulia and the Cassibile armistice allowed the uneventful landing of its V Corps (Lieutenant-General Allfrey) in the well-equipped ports of Taranto and Brindisi.

The final defeat of the German 10th Army at Salerno and the threat to his rear forced Kesselring to disengage on September 16, but this brought a renewed conflict with Rommel, who wanted to abandon Rome, whereas Kesselring maintained that the Eternal City could be covered from a line running roughly Formia–Cassino–Pescara, using the Garigliano and the Rapido valleys and the Abruzzi mountains, which

reached over 9,000 feet at La Malella. On November 21 Hitler recalled Rommel and moved Kesselring from his position as C.-in-C. South to head a new Army Group "C", thus leaving him in complete command in Italy.

Hitler transferred the 24th Panzer Division and the S.S. "Leibstandarte" Division to the Eastern Front. Kesselring allotted three divisions to the 10th Army and the balance of Army Group "B" in northern Italy went to form a new 14th Army under General von Mackensen.

Meanwhile Vietinghoff, turning to great advantage the demolition and destruction which had been caused and the heavy autumn rains which, according to Montgomery, covered the roads in "chocolate sauce", did not allow his forces to get caught anywhere, either at Termoli on October 4, in spite of a commando landing behind his left flank, or on the Sangro on November 27 when the three divisions and an armoured brigade of V Corps broke out of the bridgehead and advanced along the line Sulmona–Avezzano to wipe out his 65th Division (Lieutenant-General von Ziehlberg). The rubble left after artillery shelling and aerial bombardment by the British, which their own tanks then had to get through (a sight which was to recur in the Caen campaign) made any exploitation impossible and in a couple of days

Vietinghoff was making a stand again and stopping the Allied advance.

In spite of the evacuation of Naples on October 1, it was the same thing along the way to Rome through Cassino and through Formia. When it had got through Venafro and Sessa-Aurunca, the 5th Army came up against the mountains and the deep valley of the Garigliano. The reinforcements which the 5th Army had just received, II Corps and the 1st Armoured Division, were not the most likely formations to cross these obstacles. Invited by General Clark to give his opinion, General Juin stated on October 1: "The whole way along the road from Salerno to Naples we kept running into the British 7th Division in close formation and incapable of getting off the road and deploying in the completely mountainous terrain. I had immediately concluded, along with Carpentier [his chief-of-staff], that the mechanisation of the British and American armies could actually hinder our rapid progress up the Italian peninsula. There is no doubt that the North African divisions would be very welcome . . ."

And indeed from November 22 onwards the French Expeditionary Corps did begin to land in Italy. It consisted of the 2nd Moroccan Division and the 3rd Algerian Division, totalling 65,000 men, 2,500 horses and mules, and 12,000 vehicles. But the corps was not used as such. Its 2nd Moroccan Division (General Dody)

A Red Cross nurse tends German wounded while stretcher bearers hurry to load them onto Junkers Ju 52 transports for evacuation to the north.

was attached to VI Corps which was trying to break out of the Mignano area, and General Lucas used it on his right some seven miles north of Venafro. The fortified position at Pantano was his first objective. This was defended by 305th Division (Lieutenant-General Hauck), a division which, wrote Marshal Juin "could never be caught napping". By December 18 the 2nd Moroccan Division, which had never before been under fire, had got the better of the difficult terrain and the strong enemy resistance. On the 26th it had a further success when it took Mount Mainarde and this enabled General Juin to claim a permanent position for his French Expeditionary Corps. He was successful, and the corps was allocated a position on the right of 5th Army's VI Corps.

All the same, Kesselring's strategy had to a large extent imposed itself on his enemy, so that unless a completely new offensive were to be mounted at once, the victory in Sicily, in spite of the Italian armistice, would now run out of steam. On December 24 Generals Eisenhower, Montgomery, and Spaatz flew to London and the Italian theatre of operations was relegated to the background.

Chapter 43
Defeat of the U-boats

On the morning of December 31, 1942 an engagement took place in the Barents Sea which had no important strategic consequences, but should be mentioned as it provoked a crisis in the German high command. The occasion was the passage off the North Cape in Norway of convoy J.W. 51B; its 14 merchant ships and tankers were taking 2,040 trucks, 202 tanks, 87 fighters, 43 bombers, 20,120 tons of oil fuel, 12,650 tons of petrol, and 54,321 tons of various products to Murmansk.

This large convoy was escorted by a minesweeper, two trawlers, two corvettes, and six destroyers (shortly reduced to five, as one had to give up after its gyroscopic compass had broken down). The small escort was commanded by Captain Robert St. V. Sherbrooke, a direct descendant of the famous Admiral Jervis who became Lord St. Vincent after his victory in 1797 over the Spanish fleet. Under the command of Rear-Admiral R. L. Burnett, a veteran of the Arctic run, the cruisers *Sheffield* and *Jamaica,* from Kolos were also sent in to help. Lastly, nine submarines (including the Polish *Sokol* and the Dutch *O 14*) provided a protective screen for the convoy as it passed the Norwegian coast. However, because of the winter ice floes the convoy J.W. 51B was sailing in single file about 240 miles from the German base at Altenfjord and its position had been signalled to Grand-Admiral Raeder by the *U-354* (Lieutenant Herschleb). Raeder acted very quickly on receiving this signal, as Hitler had recently made some extremely unflattering remarks about the Kriegsmarine. Therefore on that same evening of December 30, the pocket battleship *Lützow,* the heavy cruiser *Admiral Hipper,* and six destroyers put out to sea to intercept and destroy the convoy the following dawn. For this purpose, Vice-Admiral Kummetz, who was in command at sea, sent off his two major units in a pincer movement. But as he weighed anchor, he received a message from Admiral Kübler, the commander of the northern sector, which was clearly not calculated to spur him on:

"Contrary to the operational order regarding contact against the enemy [you are] to use caution even against enemy of equal strength because it is undesirable for the cruisers to take any great risks."

Here Kübler was merely repeating the instructions sent to him by the chief of the *Oberkommando der Kriegsmarine* through Kiel and Admiral Carls. But Raeder was following a standing order promulgated by the Führer after the sinking of the *Bismarck,* and that evening Vice-Admiral Krancke, who had informed Hitler that the two ships and their escort vessels had sailed, wrote:

"The Führer emphasised that he wished to have all reports immediately since, as I well knew, he could not sleep a wink when ships were operating.

"I passed this message subsequently to the Operations Division of the Naval Staff, requesting that any information be telephoned immediately."

Hitler's anxiety was certainly peculiar, since he did not lose any sleep over the terrible fate of the 230,000 Germans encircled in the Stalingrad pocket.

On the next day, at about 0915, Kummetz, who had chosen *Hipper* as his flagship, came into contact with the rear of the convoy. But *Onslow* (Captain Sherbrooke) fearlessly attacked the Germans, followed by three other destroyers. Meanwhile a fifth destroyer, which was under enemy fire, covered the merchant ships withdrawing towards the south-east under a smokescreen. In spite of his impressive superiority in guns, the German admiral did not dare to launch a full-scale attack, as he was afraid that in the prevailing half-light he would not be able to defend himself against the torpedoes which the British would certainly use against him if he came within range. At 1019 the first 8-inch shell hit *Onslow;* three more hits followed, killing 14 men and wounding 33, including Captain Sherbrooke, who lost an eye and had his nose fractured, but continued leading his division.

Lützow appeared a little later and tried to attack the convoy from the rear whilst *Hipper* engaged the escort vessels; however, as visibility was poor and her commander too unenterprising, her six 11- and eight 6-inch guns were hardly fired once. At 1130, the balance of the engagement changed; Rear-Admiral Burnett, who had been alerted by Sherbrooke, appeared on the scene just at the right time; as he was north of *Hipper,* he was able to take advantage of the light to the south while remaining in the darkness himself. Moreover *Sheffield* and *Jamaica,* which both remained unscathed, scored three hits on the German flagship, which retreated with a boiler room flooded with a mixture of sea water and oil fuel.

We shall not describe the game of blind man's buff that followed; during the engagement, the destroyer *Friedrich Eckholdt* was sunk by the British cruisers, which she took for *Lützow* and *Hipper. Lützow* fired 86 11-inch and 76 6-inch shells, but none of them scored a direct hit. When the darkness increased, Kummetz broke off contact and the convoy set off again, reaching Murmansk without further mishap. Apart from the damage done to *Onslow,* the convoy had also lost the minesweeper *Bramble* and the destroyer *Achates,* which had heroically sacrificed herself in protecting the front of the convoy.

At Rastenburg, Hitler was awaiting news of the engagement with feverish impatience. At 1145 a message from *U-354* was intercepted and this appeared to indicate a major success; then, a few minutes later, came Kummetz's order to abandon the operation. But on his return journey Kummetz quite properly observed radio silence, and when he had anchored in the Altenfjord a whole series of fortuitous incidents combined to delay the transmission of his report, with the result that at 1700 on January 1 the Führer had nothing but the British communiqué to hand concerning the previous day's engagement. He violently upbraided Admiral Krancke:

"He said that it was an unheard of impudence not to inform him; and that such behaviour and the entire action showed that the ships were utterly useless; that they were nothing but a breeding ground for revolution, idly lying about and lacking any desire to get into action.

"This meant the passing of the High Seas Fleet, he said, adding that it was now his irrevocable decision to do away with these useless ships. He would put the

A U-boat returns to base after a successful cruise against the merchant shipping of the Allies.

362

good personnel, the good weapons, and the armour plating to better use."

He received Kummetz's report a few hours later, but it failed to placate him. Far from it, for according to Krancke:

"There was another outburst of anger with special reference to the fact that the action had not been fought to the finish. This, said the Führer, was typical of German ships, just the opposite of the British, who, true to their tradition, fought to the bitter end.

"If an English commander behaved like that he would immediately be relieved of his command. The whole thing spelled the end of the German High Seas Fleet, he declared. I was to inform the Grand-Admiral immediately that he was to come to the Führer at once, so that he could be informed personally of this irrevocable decision."

He added: "I am not an obliging civilian, but the commander-in-chief of all the armed forces."

In this long diatribe, the argument that Vice-Admiral Kummetz had not pursued the engagement to its conclusion was perfectly correct. But it was hardly seemly for Krancke to call Hitler to account for the paralysing effect that his orders had had on the movements of the fleet on that occasion. Grand-Admiral Raeder arrived at Rastenburg on January 6, 1943 and was immediately faced with an indictment which began with the part played by the Royal Prussian Navy in the war over the Duchies of Schleswig and Holstein (1864) and went on for over 90 minutes; Hitler's tone was bitterly hostile throughout and he used arguments which, according to Raeder, were so incompetent that they seemed to show the influence of *Reichsmarschall* Hermann Göring.

"Battleships," raged Hitler, "to which he had always devoted his full attention and which had filled him with so much pride were no longer of the slightest use. They required the permanent protection of planes and small ships. In the event of an Allied attack on Norway, these planes would be more usefully employed against the invasion fleet than protecting our own fleet. Large battleships no longer served any purpose and therefore must be taken out of commission, after their guns had been removed. There was an urgent need for their guns on land."

Raeder was, however, authorised to submit to Hitler a memo expressing his objections. Feeling himself offended and discredited by Hitler's manner of addressing him, Raeder, who was over 66 years old, asked for and obtained his retirement. On January 30, 1943 he therefore gave up the high command he had held for 15 years and took over an honorary inspectorate-general. But before handing over the command of the German Navy to Admiral Dönitz, he regarded it as his duty to inform the Führer of the disagreeable but inevitable consequences of discarding the Grand Fleet.

The Royal Navy would obtain at no cost to themselves the equivalent of a great naval victory. But even more important,

Hitler had overlooked the fact that the application of his "irrevocable decision" would perceptibly affect the balance of forces in the Mediterranean, the Indian Ocean, and the Pacific. In fact, as soon as the potential threat of the German major warships in the North Atlantic disappeared, the Admiralty, recovering full freedom of action, would profit by it and crush Japan.

Events showed that Raeder saw clearly. It is now known that Churchill was impatiently waiting for the time when the elimination of German surface warships would allow the Navy to appear in the Far East again; he was determined to restore British prestige there, impaired as it had been by the loss of Singapore; and Churchill doubtless had no wish to concede the monopoly of victory over Japan to the Americans, as he was well aware of the fanatical anti-colonialism displayed by Roosevelt. Hitler's whim, if it had been acted upon, would therefore have benefited only the Allies. This is shown by the fact that the Admiralty had to attach a force of battleships and aircraft-carriers to the Home Fleet, thus giving it a wide margin of superiority in any circumstance. Thus when the powerful *Richelieu* had been refitted and sailed from Brooklyn dockyard, the Admiralty ensured that in November 1943 she joined the other ships at Scapa Flow.

The Onslow *returns home, having suffered four hits from the* Hipper *which knocked out two guns.*

Although he was a U-boat officer, the new Grand-Admiral deferred to the arguments of his predecessor, and Hitler was hardly in a position to thwart him immediately after his appointment.

In these circumstances, by a decision taken on February 18, 1943, the old battleships *Schlesien* and *Schleswig-Holstein,* which had been launched in 1906, the heavy cruiser *Admiral Hipper,* and the light cruisers *Köln* and *Leipzig* were merely declared obsolete, and the radical measures advocated by Hitler were not carried out. In fact, even this decision was only partially carried out; in autumn 1944 some of these units were to appear again in the Baltic to give gunfire support to Army Group "North" in its defence of the Kurland bridgehead.

Captain Sherbrooke had the exceptional distinction of winning the Victoria Cross for his exploit in the Barents Sea.

"The balance sheet of profit and loss in mercantile tonnage was one of the most disturbing issues which confronted the Casablanca Conference when it opened on the 14th of January 1943. Until the U-boats were defeated the offensive strategy to which the Allies were committed could not succeed. Europe could never be invaded until the battle of the Atlantic had been won, and the latter purpose had therefore to be made a first charge on all Allied resources."

Thus Stephen Roskill, the Royal Navy's official historian, begins his chapter describing the decisive phase of this merciless struggle, and one can only confirm his judgement. There is no doubt that even after this battle had been won, the Western Allies would still have gained nothing until the European continent had been invaded, but if this first battle had been lost, all would have been lost with it.

When he took over the command of the German Navy, Karl Dönitz probably made no attempt to disown responsibility for the battle of the Atlantic; he knew what was at stake better than anyone else on the German side. Therefore the new commander-in-chief of U-boats, Rear-Admiral Godt, whom Dönitz himself selected, became even more closely subordinate to the latter's authority than the latter himself had previously been to Raeder. Consequently Dönitz was responsible for all the successes and defeats in this campaign, both before and after his promotion to the command of the Kriegsmarine, though one must make allowances for the fact that he was never free of Hitler's interference.

On January 1, 1943, the German Navy had 212 operational submarines, more than double its strength compared with the same date in 1942, when it had 91. In addition it had another 181 in the Baltic, either training or on trials. Moreover, the Third Reich's shipyards produced 23 or 24 submarines a month in 1943, in spite of Anglo-American bombing. However, as they lacked crews, the U-boats stayed longer and longer in the dockyards when they returned from their cruises; at the end of 1942 they averaged two months in dock to 40 days at sea.

At the beginning of 1943, in this decisive year, the 212 operational submarines were distributed as follows:

Atlantic: 164

Mediterranean: 24

North Sea: 21

Black Sea: 3, moving down the Danube from Regensburg.

In the main theatre of operations, 98 units were at sea at this time. However, 59 of them were in transit. These were forbidden to attack when they left harbour, unless in exceptional circumstances, and they very often had no torpedoes on the way back. They still used pack tactics, and the strength of their packs had doubled and even tripled since the beginning of 1942. In February and March 1943 there were sometimes 10, 12, or even 16 submarines attacking the same convoy for days on end. Their effectiveness was much strengthened by the fact that German Naval Counter-

Intelligence managed continually to decipher Allied communications. "Thus we obtained," Admiral Dönitz wrote at this time, "not only information about the convoys but also, in January and February 1943, the 'U-boat positions', communicated from time to time by the British Admiralty to the commanders of convoys at sea to show them the confirmed or conjectured positions of our warships in their sector. This was extremely valuable, as we often asked ourselves what the enemy knew about us."

Even today, it is hard to explain the reasons why Dönitz was allowed to read, so to speak, over his enemy's shoulder; the British in fact knew nothing of this for three years and never took the appropriate counter-measures.

When they returned from their cruises, the U-boats were sheltered in the concrete pens at Lorient and la Pallice from December 1941, and later at Brest, St. Nazaire, and Bordeaux; the pens' 22-foot thick roofs were capable of withstanding the heaviest bombs. As has been mentioned, the R.A.F. did not attack them while they were being built, and when it did so, in accordance with a decision taken at Casablanca, there was no military result. From January to May 1943 English and

Because of the desperate shortage of inshore escort craft, hundreds of trawlers were converted to handle depth charges.

Admiral Karl Dönitz was now promoted to take command of the whole of the Kriegsmarine: a thankless task.

American bombers dropped about 9,000 tons of bombs and incendiaries on the German Atlantic bases, all to no effect; in vain they destroyed Brest, Lorient, and St. Nazaire without obtaining a single hit on their real targets. The only U-boat sunk at anchor was *U-622,* which was destroyed at Trondheim by a U.S. plane on July 24, 1943. And whilst the French population suffered very severely in these badly directed operations, they cost the Allies 98 planes. One final point: it appears that Raeder's successor was now reduced to using anything that came to hand for sustaining the enormous effort of the submarine war. Unquestionably, his fleets became more and more accident-prone. There were three in 1942 and nine in the following year, seven of them training in the Baltic.

Moreover, the new Grand Admiral had to withstand the weight of this campaign alone. He could not expect any assistance from the Luftwaffe. In fact, during 1943 R.A.F. patrols sank 41 U-boats in the Bay of Biscay without any serious interference from the Germans. It is not surprising that Dönitz, exasperated by the frequent criticisms of the German Navy continually made by Hermann Göring to Hitler, permitted himself a

tart reply: "Herr *Reichsmarschall,* kindly spare me your criticisms of the Kriegsmarine. You have got quite enough to do looking after the Luftwaffe!"

We shall now consider the Allies' defence against the U-boats.

During 1943 the Western powers' anti-U-boat weapons production was sufficient to meet the extent and urgency of the threat, but the Allied effort was not as one-sided as the German as it placed more importance on the aerial side of naval warfare. However, one must have many reservations about the use the British and Americans made of their air forces in their campaign against the U-boats.

This effort was from now on mainly American. Admittedly, the tactics and technology were mostly British, but the mass production needed to get them into action was predominantly American. The difference in industrial power between the two countries was enormous; the United States, moreover, which had suffered neither Blitz nor black-out, made tremendous innovations in prefabrication.

Amongst escort ships, the British frigate corresponded in its general features to the escort destroyer of the U.S. Navy. But from 1943 till the end of hostilities, Great Britain, with the help of Canadian dockyards, produced 100 frigates, whilst

the Americans in the same space of time built 565 escort destroyers; 78 of these were handed over to Britain under Lend-Lease, while eight went to Brazil and six to France. These ships were a little faster than the corvettes of 1940; they had considerable freedom of movement and were profusely armed and equipped for their specialised rôle.

The story of escort carriers is similar. The British had commissioned their first such carrier, *Audacity,* in November 1941; she was sunk on December 21, 1941, but had performed such signal services that the Admiralty decided to build half a dozen similar ships. The British could not produce as many as the Americans, however, who built 115 between the summer of 1942 and the capitulation of Japan, on new hulls or by converting cargo ships or tankers. But again these 7,000 to 12,000 ton ships were produced quickly and promptly by the prefabrication methods previously referred to. One may take as examples the aircraft carriers *Bogue, Card,* and *Core:*

	Laid down	Launched	Commissioned
Bogue	Oct. 1, 1941	Jan. 15, 1942	Sept. 26, 1942
Card	Oct. 27, 1941	Feb. 21, 1942	Nov. 8, 1942
Core	Jan. 2, 1942	May 15, 1942	Dec. 10, 1942

Considering their escort rôle, a speed of not more than 20 knots was acceptable for carriers of this type. As a result of this feature and the restricted length of their flight decks, catapults had to be installed to launch the planes, of which there were about 20 (fighters and torpedo-bombers). In addition, escort carriers were employed in landing operations as aircraft transports, and as tankers; as they served so many purposes and in such large numbers, they were nicknamed "Woolworth carriers".

By July 1943, the American fleet already had 29 escort carriers in service. Their usefulness soon became evident: by December 31 in the same year they had already destroyed 26 U-boats, and the *Card* alone had accounted for eight of these. Thirty-eight of the 115 escort carriers built by the Americans fought under the British flag.

Owing to the increase in the number of escort ships, the convoys were now reinforced; later, "support groups" were also formed as a strategic reserve. The work of the Department of Operational Studies facilitated this development; it was initiated by the Admiralty under the direction of P. M. S. Blackett, professor of physics at Manchester University and Nobel prizewinner in 1948. This organisation also made a most important deduction concerning merchant ship losses; as Captain Macintyre puts it:

"Whereas the number of ships lost in a convoy battle depended, as might be expected, upon the number of U-boats attacking and the size of the escort, it was quite independent of the size of the convoy."

When he demonstrated that the number of escort ships was being built up much more slowly than that of the ships to be escorted, Professor Blackett proved thereby, and in the face of most people's idea of common sense, that large convoys were proportionately less vulnerable than small ones. An important conclusion followed. Macintyre puts it thus:

"Then, as has been said, the economy of force, achieved by reducing the number of convoys to be defended, provided a surplus of warships which could be formed into Support Groups. These themselves resulted in a further economy. For, provided that the convoy escort could be reinforced during the passage of the most dangerous areas, a smaller escort could safely be given for the remainder of the convoy's voyage. Thus Operational Research, too often neglected or ignored, was responsible for a revolution in organisation, which came about in March 1943 with an adjustment of the North Atlantic convoy cycle, whereby fewer and larger convoys were sailed each way."

To the best of our knowledge, this was the first application of what is today called operational research, which is now essential, with the aid of computers, not only in military operations but also in sociology, economics, industry, and commerce.

As regards anti-submarine equipment, we may mention that centimetric wavelength radar equipment was installed on Allied ships and planes; its pulses could

The U-boat pens at Trondheim in Norway were the main base for the packs operating against the Arctic convoys.

not be picked up by the detection apparatus installed by German engineers on all U-boats. In July, however, an R.A.F. bomber carrying this most modern radar equipment was brought down over Rotterdam. Grand-Admiral Dönitz thus learned the secret of the defeat he had suffered, but it was now too late.

H/F D/F (High Frequency Direction Finder), goniometric radio equipment, nicknamed "Huff Duff", was undoubtedly another factor in the Allies' success in the Battle of the Atlantic. This had the capacity to detect U-boats whenever they were compelled to transmit. Thus the convoy could be directed away from the area where a pack of submarines was gathering, and a support group of "Hunter-Killers", as the Americans called them, could be launched against them. The U.S. Navy and Army Air Force ordered no less than 3,200 sets of this equipment.

At the beginning of 1943, the "Hedgehog" was put into general use. This was a projector, fitted in the bows of an escort vessel, which fired a pattern of 24 contact-fused bombs to a range of 250 yards. Thus the pursuer did not have to pass vertically over the top of the submerged target before firing its depth charges.

Finally the rockets which were successfully used by Montgomery's fighter-bombers against the Panzers were also used with the same redoubtable efficiency against the U-boats by the R.A.F.'s, U.S.A.A.F.'s, and U.S.N.'s anti-submarine

patrol aircraft.

On May 23, 1943 the new weapon was first used with success by a Swordfish from the British escort carrier *Archer*. In his excellent book on fleet air arm warfare Admiral Barjot gives the following description:

"On the morning of May 23, the convoy was in sight off Newfoundland and the first wave started to attack. The Swordfish B 819 then took off and almost immediately had the good fortune to surprise *U-572*, which had surfaced to keep up with the convoy. The eight rockets lanced off towards the U-boat, holing it so that it had to surface again quickly, as its batteries were flooded. It tried to use its guns, but the fight only lasted a few minutes. A Martlet fighter arrived and machine gunned the U-boat, killing its captain and several men. The rest of the crew lost hope and abandoned ship, the U-boat sinking almost immediately. A few Germans were picked up later by the destroyer *Escapade*."

Following a decision at the Casablanca Conference, the R.A.F.'s Bomber Command and the bomber groups of the American 8th Air Force in England redoubled their attacks against the German shipyards where submarines were under construction. Thus it was hoped to eliminate the danger at its source. In fact, according to Roskill, between May 1 and June 1 the British and American heavy squadrons carried out 3,414 sorties and dropped 5,572 tons of bombs and 4,173 of incendiaries on these targets, now recognised as of prime importance.

But in spite of the loss of 168 planes, the efforts were virtually fruitless. Even worse, this air offensive, which had been so warmly recommended by Churchill and Roosevelt, frustrated the British and American effort in the Atlantic; Bomber Command's requests for reinforcements and replacements could in fact only be satisfied if a parsimonious policy was maintained towards Coastal Command, at least as regards long-range four-engined aircraft for convoy protection.

Professor Blackett realised this perfectly clearly. In 1943 he extended his criticism to all R.A.F. Bomber Command operations:

"From the figures on the effectiveness of air cover, it could be calculated that a long-range Liberator operating from Iceland and escorting the convoys in the middle of the Atlantic *saved* at least half a dozen merchant ships in its service lifetime of some thirty flying sorties. If used for bombing Berlin, the same aircraft in its service life would drop less than 100 tons of bombs and kill not more than a couple of dozen enemy men, women and children and destroy a number of houses.

"No one would dispute that the saving of six merchant ships and their crews and cargoes was of incomparably more value to the Allied war effort than the killing of some two dozen enemy civilians, the destruction of a number of houses and a certain very small effect on production.

"The difficulty was to get the figures believed. But believed they eventually were and more long-range aircraft were made available to Coastal Command."

In fact in February 1943, Air-Marshal Sir John Slessor, who succeeded Sir Philip Joubert de la Ferté as head of Coastal Command, had only ten four-engined B-24 Liberators, whilst the American Navy had only 52. On July 1, however, the figures had risen to 37 and 209 respectively.

The early months of 1943 were a time of changing fortunes in the Battle of the Atlantic. January was relatively favourable to the Allies, as winter storms raged over the North Atlantic; in fact they only lost 50 merchant vessels (261,359 tons) against 106 (419,907 tons) in the same month of the previous year.

West of the Canaries, however, a pack of eight submarines skilfully directed to its rendezvous by Dönitz attacked a convoy of nine tankers heading for North Africa; seven of these were sunk; this was a remarkable feat for which Dönitz duly received General von Arnim's congratulations. In February, Allied losses increased and were slightly over 400,000 tons (73 ships). Nonetheless, between the 4th and 9th of this month, the slow convoy S.C. 118 (63 merchantmen and ten escort vessels) fought off 20 U-boats for four successive nights. A survivor from a previous attack, picked up by *U-632,* had been criminally indiscreet and drawn the attention of his captors to the convoy: the survivor's remarks caused the loss of several hundreds of his comrades' lives.

In fact 13 cargo-boats were sunk at dawn on February 9, but as Grand-Admiral Dönitz stated, the defence was keen:

"It was", he wrote, "perhaps the worst battle of the whole submarine war. Honour to the crews and commanders who waged it in the harsh winter conditions of the Atlantic! It went on for four successive nights, and the captains were unable to leave their bridges for the whole period. Their ships' safety often depended on the speed of their decisions. It is hard to imagine the self-discipline that is required after a terrible depth-charge attack, to give orders to surface, to approach the convoy, and to bear down on it through its protective screen, bristling with steel, with the alternative of success or destruction. The submarine commanders never performed such a colossal feat in the course of both world wars."

This opinion can be confirmed. The loss of the 13 cargo vessels previously mentioned was countered by that of three U-boats sunk by the escort vessels. They included *U-609* (Lieutenant Rudloff) which was sunk by a depth charge from the French corvette *Lobelia* (Lieutenant de Morsier). In other engagements, a further 16 U-boats were lost during February; on February 28, for the first time since hostilities began, the number of U-boats lost almost equalled the number completed by German yards.

In view of this slaughter and the escape, which was often noted, of the convoys from the U-boat onslaught, Dönitz thought for a time that a spy or even a traitor must have penetrated his own staff. The *Abwehr* conducted a search to locate him, but without success. This was not surprising, as, when they changed course to avoid packs, the British and the Americans relied on the contact signals transmitted by their opponents and picked up by their Huff Duff devices. Huff Duff operators had now had so much experience that they were no longer content only to spy out the enemy, but as they were personally involved in operating the device, they also often managed to identify him. In fact the Kriegsmarine only got to the bottom of the mystery in 1945.

In 1956 the official historian of the Royal Navy came to the following conclusion about the sea engagements of March 1943:

"Nor can one yet look back on that month without feeling something approaching horror over the losses we suffered. In the first ten days, in all waters, we lost forty-one ships; in the second ten days fifty-six. More than half a million tons of shipping was sunk in those twenty days; and, what made the losses so much more serious than the bare figures can indicate, was that nearly two-thirds of the ships sunk during the month were in convoy."

Had the system of convoys, begun in September 1939, outlived its usefulness? This was the question which the Admiralty was now anxiously debating. Captain Roskill quotes the following

comment from one of its reports, drawn up at the end of 1943:

"The Germans never came so near to disrupting communications between the New World and the Old as in the first twenty days of March 1943."

Between March 7 and 11, the slow convoy S.C. 121 lost 13 of its ships, and these losses remained unavenged. The submarines were not so lucky when they engaged the fast convoy H.X. 228; four merchant ships were destroyed at the cost of two U-boats. During this engagement, according to Captain Macintyre, the commander of the cargo vessel *Kingswood* almost rammed a German U-boat:

"In the darkness and the gale, as he peered anxiously out from his bridge, his eye was caught by what seemed to be a particularly heavy breaking sea on his port bow. Then he saw that the white flurry was travelling with some speed towards him. 'It's a torpedo,' he shouted to the mate standing beside him. But almost at once he realised that he was in fact looking at the wash of a submarine travelling at high speed on the surface. He ran to the telegraph and gave a double ring, calling for the utmost emergency speed and steered to ram. 'I really felt we could not miss,' he recorded.

"'Collision seemed inevitable. About this time I heard the U-boat's engine and a voice in the distance. I was sort of hanging on waiting for the crash when I saw the submarine's wake curling round—the voice I heard must have been the U-boat's commander shouting "Hard a Port" in German. The submarine's wake curled right under my stem—how its tail missed us I still do not know.'"

On March 11, the destroyer *Harvester* (Commander A. Tait) rammed *U-444* (Sub-Lieutenant Langfeld) which was then sunk by the French corvette *Aconit* (Lieutenant Levasseur). *Harvester,* however, had her propellers badly damaged and became an easy target for *U-432* (Lieutenant Eckhardt). When he saw the column of smoke that indicated *Harvester*'s end, Levasseur returned to the fray and managed to avenge Tait, who had gone down with his ship. From March 16 to 19, the battle reached its high point, pitting 38 submarines against the two convoys H.X. 229 and S.C. 122: in the three nights 21 cargo vessels were sunk whilst the attackers lost only one U-boat.

In all, 102 merchant ships and tankers, a total of 693,389 tons, were sunk by German action during March: a serious situation for the Allies.

The U-boats had much less success during April, however. Less than half the number of merchant ships were destroyed (344,680 tons), for the same number of submarines sunk (15). Moreover, the support groups and escort-carriers began to pursue the enemy more and more closely. The results were clear in May. In that month, at least 47 U-boats were destroyed: 41 were sunk in the North Atlantic, whilst Allied losses fell to below 300,000 tons.

Donitz inspects some more of the volunteers for U-boat service.

"The situation was changing," wrote Dönitz, acknowledging defeat. "Radar, particularly in aircraft, virtually cancelled out the ability of our submarines to attack on the surface. The previous tactics of our submarines could now no longer be employed in the North Atlantic, a theatre where air reconnaissance was too strong for us. Before using such tactics again, we had to restore our submarines' fighting abilities. I drew my own conclusion and we evacuated the North Atlantic. On May 24 I ordered the submarines to rendezvous in the area south-west of the Azores, taking all the necessary precautions. We had lost the Battle of the Atlantic."

Captain Roskill warmly praises the British captains and crews and summarises the episode as follows:

"In its intensity, and in the certainty that its outcome would decide the issue of the war, the battle may be compared to the Battle of Britain of 1940. Just as Göring then tried with all the forces of the Luftwaffe to gain command of the skies over Britain, so now did Dönitz seek to gain command of the Atlantic with his U-boats. And the men who defeated him–the crews of the little ships, of the air escorts and of our tiny force of long-range aircraft–may justly be immortalised alongside 'the few' who won the 1940 battle of the air."

Amongst these "few", Captain F. J. Walker's name should be mentioned; by March 14, 1944 his 2nd Escort Group had sunk 13 U-boats.

The first five months of 1943 had cost the Allies 365 ships (2,001,918 tons); in the following seven, the losses were reduced to 232 (1,218,219 tons). July was the only month in which the tonnage destroyed (365,398 tons) recalled the position in the first six months, but the Germans paid heavily for this.

Thirty-seven U-boats were lost, one per 10,000 tons sunk, whilst in March the proportion had been one to 46,200 tons. As the British squadrons were rein-forced by Coastal Command and suppor-ted by U.S. planes, they went over to the offensive in the Bay of Biscay. Dönitz thought he could ward off this threat by fitting quadruple 2-cm cannon on the conning towers of his U-boats. However, he was underestimating the danger of planes which were kept informed by radar and armed with heavy machine guns, rockets, bombs, and depth-charges. His failure to understand the situation cost him 22 U-boats between June 1 and September 1, 1943: he was therefore compelled to order his captains to sub-merge by day when they passed through these dangerous waters; thus their cruises took considerably longer. At night, when they recharged their batteries, his raiders still had to reckon with the enemy bombers, which were fitted with powerful radar-aimed Leigh searchlights.

In bringing the submarine war to the south-west of the Azores, the Grand-Admiral came up against the American defences.

At the Pentagon (which had just been built), Admiral Ernest J. King had appoin-ted Rear-Admiral Francis Low as deputy chief-of-staff specially entrusted with anti-submarine problems. On receiving his report, King set up a 10th Fleet on the following May 20, which by his decision on that day "was to exercise (under the direct command of COMINCH [C.-in-C. U.S. Fleet]) unity of control over U.S. antisubmarine operations in that part of the Atlantic under U.S. strategic control."

Low therefore only acted by King's delegation, whilst King retained com-mand of the organisation. On the other hand, in contrast with what was happen-ing on the other side of the Atlantic, where Sir Max Horton, C.-in-C. Western Approaches, had ships and marine air-craft, the 10th Fleet in Washington controlled neither boats nor planes. In the action it was directing, it therefore had to make use of the aircraft and formations of the Atlantic Fleet, to which it was not allowed to give any orders. This was the reason for what Ladislas Farago, the historian of the 10th Fleet, has called "an impressive flowering of periphrases" in its relations with Admiral Ingersoll, such as "suggest that you ...", "it is recommended that you ...", "would it be possible for you to ...?"

In spite of its paradoxical situation this organisation worked extremely efficiently from the beginning. In July and August the loss of 35 out of the 60 German submarines sunk in all theatres of war was undoubtedly due to the Americans. In the South Atlantic, where the U.S. 4th Fleet was operating, the groups centred on the escort carriers *Core, Santee, Card,* and *Bogue* (under the command respec-tively of Captains Greer, Fisk, Isbell, and Short) took a prominent and praiseworthy part in this success. The result was that in his commentary on this period of the merchant navy war, Admiral Dönitz wrote: "Every zone in the South Atlantic was closely watched by long-range four-engined planes or by planes from American aircraft-carriers which were specially deployed to hunt submarines in the central and southern Atlantic. The same strict observation was practised even in the Indian Ocean, although not on such a wide scale. The planes of the two great naval powers therefore took a considerable part in the pursuit of our U-boats, and this continued till the end of hostilities.

"The situation was similar in more distant operational sectors.

"West of the Azores, our ships were still able in mid-June 1943 to refuel from a submarine tanker without interference, before operating in their sectors, which extended from the Straits of Florida to south of Rio de Janeiro and from Dakar to the interior of the Gulf of Guinea. Each commander had a vast area in which to operate as circumstances permitted. We systematically avoided any concentration in order not to provoke a parallel defence concentration. At first the results were favourable, as 16 enemy vessels were sunk initially. But air observation in-creased rapidly and the boats, particu-larly those off the American coast, had difficulty in maintaining themselves in their sectors. Similarly, naval refuelling became so dangerous that we had to give it up, thus considerably shortening the length of operations."

Amongst the U-boats destroyed in this sector we may mention some returning from Penang in Malaya, which had valuable cargoes of raw materials.

The episodes of the submarine war are often moving, irrespective of one's sympathies. Ladislas Farago tells one story which may be found amusing. Lieutenant Johannsen's *U-569* had been put out of action by a plane from *Bogue:*

"Johannsen ordered his men to hoist the time-honoured symbol of surrender but the hapless submariners could not find anything white on the boat whose curtains, tablecovers and sheets were all made of some oil resistant drab green cloth. They waved what they had, but those improvised green surrender flags, whose colour blended with that of an angry sea, could not have been made out by Roberts who kept up his fire. However, they were spotted by the Canadian des-troyer *St. Laurent* and such evident eagerness to surrender induced her skipper to make preparations for board-ing the sub to capture. Johannsen's engineer officer spoiled the scheme. In the last moment he slipped below, opened the flood-valves and went down with the boat, leaving but twenty-four U-boat men for the *St. Laurent* to capture.

"Citing the *U-Johannsen's* fate, we recommended that the U-boats carry something white on board because our pilots could not be expected to distinguish any green cloth waved at them from the level of the green sea. Our suggestion was promptly heeded. A few weeks later the *U-460* was in Johannsen's predicament. Its crew waved that 'something white' we had recommended to keep handy for

A torpedo is loaded aboard the submarine depot ship Forth *(top); later the torpedo is loaded into a submarine.*

such emergencies. The 'surrender flag' turned out to be the skipper's dress shirt."

On October 8, 1943 the agreement between the Portuguese and British Governments granting the British naval and air forces the right to establish a base in the Azores was a new blow for German naval strategy; a few months later, moreover, the Americans were granted the same concession. Thus the "Atlantic gap" was finally closed.

On December 31, 1943, the German submarine flotillas consisted of only 168 operational units; there had been 212 on the preceding January 1. During the year they had lost 237 U-boats and their crews. Eight of these were the result of accident, 75 were sunk by the Americans, five by the French, one by the Russians, and the remainder (148) by the Royal Navy and Coastal Command squadrons. As against these losses, we must put the losses of all kinds of Allied merchant vessels in 1943: they amounted to 3,220,137 tons, made up of 597 ships. These figures may appear very large, but they are nevertheless 4,570,000 tons and 1,067 ships less than the figures in 1942. During the same period merchant ships and tankers of about 13 million tons were launched in British, Canadian, and

American shipyards. Here again the predominance of the U.S.A. became apparent. Their Liberty ships, which were succeeded by their Victory ships, were built with prefabricated parts by methods recommended by the industrialist Henry Kayser, an organiser of genius; they played a distinguished part in the Allied victory of 1945 and the reconstruction of Western Europe, including Germany and Italy, after the close of hostilities. But in spite of this Dönitz did not give up. He believed that new arms would bring victory in 1944, and in the meantime he counted on forcing the enemy to squander his effort within the bounds of the Atlantic; otherwise the Allies would concentrate their resources even more against the industrial might of the Third Reich.

From January 1 to December 31, 1943, more than 680,000 Allied combatants were disembarked in Great Britain and Northern Ireland by 66 convoys as a part of Operation "Bolero", whilst about 127,000 left the British Isles for Africa, Sicily, and Italy. As a general rule the troops crossed the Atlantic without a convoy on fast liners which managed to elude U-boat ambushes. Using the "hot berth" system (two berths for three soldiers), the *Queen Elizabeth* and the *Queen Mary* transported 15,000 men per crossing, whilst the French ship *Pasteur* accommodated 4,500.

Nevertheless the rations, fighting equipment, vehicles, fuel, and ammunition for these 680,000 men went via the usual convoy route, and most of the bombers for the U.S. 8th Air Force and all the fighters reached Britain by sea. Even if they had crossed the Atlantic by air, or via Iceland, their fuel supply could only have been secured by the use of tankers. For this reason, we may conclude that if the German submarine raiders had not been defeated in 1943, there would have been no Second Front in Western Europe in 1944.

At the end of March 1943, the battle-cruiser *Scharnhorst* joined the battleship *Tirpitz* and pocket battleship *Lützow* at Trondheim, and then together the three reached Kåfjord, a small section of the Altenfjord about halfway between Tromsö and the North Cape. From this position they could harass the Allied convoys in the Arctic or even resume the war against the merchant ships in the Atlantic. As the Sicilian operations and the Salerno landing required six British warships in the Mediterranean, the Home Fleet, as whose commander Admiral Tovey had been succeeded by Sir Bruce Fraser in June 1943, had some difficulty in intercepting the German ships.

In addition, the Admiralty in London organised Operation "Source" under the command of Rear-Admiral C. B. Barry, Flag Officer Submarines. The purpose of this operation was to destroy this dangerous German force at anchor by using six 30-ton midget submarines; their armament consisted of two 2-ton charges which could be released to sink under the hull of the target, exploding when set off by a clockwork mechanism. A squadron of reconnaissance planes made Murmansk their base and gave the attackers all possible Intelligence about the obstacles and defences around the anchored German ships.

On September 11, six midget submarines (each manned by four men and towed by conventional submarines), left an unobtrusive harbour in the north of Scotland and sailed towards Altenfjord. One of them *(X-8)* was to attack *Lützow*, two *(X-9* and *X-10) Scharnhorst*, and the remaining three *(X-5, X-6,* and *X-7) Tirpitz*. But *X-9* was lost with all hands during the crossing, and *X-8* had to be scuttled because it was heavily damaged. The four remaining submarines suffered mishaps of all kinds; even if their compasses managed to work, their periscope tubes filled with water or the electrical engine used for raising them failed.

In spite of all this, at dawn on September 22 Lieutenants Cameron and Place managed to steer *X-6* and *X-7* below *Tirpitz* and release their charges. When *X-6* accidentally surfaced, the huge warship was alerted and had enough time to slew round at her anchorage, thereby managing to escape the worst. But two of her 15-inch gun turrets were immobilised and her engines were badly damaged, and she was out of action for several months. *X-5,*

The Scharnhorst *at sea, showing its formidable armament.*

which followed *X-6* and *7,* was shelled and sunk. Cameron with his crew of three and Place with only one other survivor were taken prisoner on the ship they had crippled; they were treated in a way that did credit to their heroism. *X-10* was scuttled on its return journey as it was found to have the same defects as its companion submarines. It had missed *Scharnhorst,* its intended victim, because the battle-cruiser was engaged in target practice off the Altenfjord, but it lost nothing by waiting.

On December 22 a Luftwaffe reconnaissance plane spotted an enemy convoy 465 miles west of Tromsö; in fact this was J.W. 55B, which consisted of 19 merchant ships and ten destroyers; it was due to pass R.A. 55A, bringing back 22 empty ships from Murmansk, in the neighbourhood of Bear Island. Vice-Admiral Burnett was responsible for protecting this two-way passage with the heavy cruiser *Norfolk* and the light cruisers *Sheffield* and *Belfast.* In order to provide distant cover, Sir Bruce Fraser, flying his flag on the battleship *Duke of York,* with the light cruiser *Jamaica* and four destroyers, sailed from the Akureyri, the Allied base on the north coast of Iceland, on December 23.

When it received the first signal of an enemy convoy, the German naval group at Kåfjord, as whose commander Rear-Admiral E. Bey had just succeeded Vice-Admiral O. Kummetz, had been put at the alert; on the evening of December 25 it was ordered to attack the convoy. A few hours later, a message from Dönitz arrived to confirm its mission:

"1. By sending the Russians a large consignment of food supplies and *matériel,* the enemy is trying to make our army's heroic struggles on the Eastern Front even more difficult. We must go to the help of our soldiers.
2. Attack the convoy with *Scharnhorst* and destroyers."

Though the mission was clear, the Grand-Admiral followed it with contradictory instructions. Bey should not be satisfied with a "half-success", but should seize the opportunity of "attacking in force". Nevertheless he was allowed the option of breaking off the engagement, and he was reminded that the "essential thing" was always to avoid any "engagement against superior forces".

While Bey was ploughing on and pursuing the enemy, in these bitterly cold northern waters, the Admiralty was able to send a signal to Fraser that *Scharnhorst* was probably at sea. At approximately 0400 on December 26 the Home Fleet commander ordered convoy J.W. 55B to withdraw to the north, with Vice-Admiral Burnett covering its withdrawal. Fraser himself increased to 24 knots to close *Scharnhorst,* which he placed about 250 to 275 miles from *Duke of York.*

At 0840 *Belfast's* radar identified a large enemy warship about 20 miles to the north-west and at 0924, at a distance of eight miles, *Belfast* fired her first star-shell, illuminating *Scharnhorst.* During a brief engagement, *Norfolk,* without being hit, obtained two direct hits with 8-inch shells and destroyed the radar rangefinder in *Scharnhorst's* bows. Bey withdrew, doubtless hoping to circle round the British detachment and attack the convoy which, it will be recalled, was

his chief target. This manoeuvre was frustrated by Burnett, who in the meantime had requested the convoy to lend him four destroyers. These moves led to a second engagement at approximately 1230, and this time the light favoured the battle-cruiser; one of her 11-inch shells put *Norfolk's* aft gun-turret out of action, whilst *Sheffield* was covered with shell splinters.

In spite of this success, the German admiral retreated for the second time at a speed of 28 knots. In his memoirs, Dönitz shows moderation in his comments on the movements of his unfortunate subordinate, but clearly they do not meet with his approval. However, it is only fair to point out that Bey kept strictly to Dönitz's instruction not to endanger his ship; he would have disobeyed this order had he ventured further with his radar not functioning in the half-light of the Arctic day. On the other hand a message from a plane was signalled to him at 1100: "Five ships north-west of North Cape." As none of *Scharnhorst's* 36 survivors had a hand in the decision which was to lead to its destruction, one must be careful in one's comments.

When he headed for his base at about 1430, the German admiral, who was pursued by Burnett at the limit of radar range, had no idea that he was about to meet the Home Fleet; moreover he did not know that the plane message received at 1100 had an important passage missing: "Including probably one heavy ship." In fact, at 1617 *Scharnhorst* appeared on *Duke of York's* radar screen $25\frac{1}{2}$ miles to the north-north-east, approaching rapidly. At 1650 the English warship, at a range of less than $6\frac{1}{2}$ miles, opened fire on her adversary, who was lit up by *Belfast's* star-shells. Total surprise was achieved. The German battle-cruiser turned north again, and then meeting Burnett, tried to escape in an easterly direction. During this engagement she had been hit by three 14-inch shells; one of them exploded in a boiler room, and another put the forward 11-inch turret out of action. Although disabled, *Scharnhorst* managed to break contact at 1820 when Bey signalled: "We shall fight to the last shell." By this time the battleship *Duke of York* had ceased fire, but Sir Bruce Fraser's four destroyers attacked *Scharnhorst* on both sides. Although she managed to avoid *Scorpion's* and *Stord's* torpedoes, she laid herself open to the wave of 12 torpedoes launched at her by *Savage* and *Saumarez* at point-blank range. Three hit their mark a little before 1850.

Crushed by *Duke of York's* shells and all the light ships' torpedoes, *Scharnhorst* sank at 1945 on December 26. The victors picked up only 36 out of a crew of just under 1,900 men; both Rear-Admiral Bey and his flag captain, Captain Hintze, were lost. According to Stephen Roskill, 13 14-inch shells and 11 torpedoes were necessary to sink this heroic ship. "Once again the ability of the Germans to build tremendously stout ships had been demonstrated."

Chapter 44

The situation on the Eastern Front

The catastrophe of Stalingrad, which reached its climax on February 1, conditioned the evolution of the German Army during the year 1943. To its effects were added those produced by the defeat of the Axis in North Africa, the collapse of Fascist Italy, and the gathering threat of invasion from across the Channel.

To the annihilation of the German 6th Army, comprising five army corps and 20 divisions of the German army, Goebbels replied by ordering "total war" throughout the Third Reich. Hundreds of thousands of men were called up from offices, businesses, and factories, their places being taken by women or foreigners. At the same time, as this was being done the production of consumer goods for the German civilian population and their freedom to travel on the railways was subjected to draconian restrictions. A year earlier Albert Speer had taken the place of the celebrated Dr. Todt as Reich Minister of War Production and Armaments. Already he had brought about a considerable rise in production. Now he doubled his efforts, with the result that production surged upwards between 1942 and 1943, as the figures below show:

	1942	1943
Rifles	1,370,000	2,244,000
Automatic weapons	317,000	435,000
Mortars	10,500	23,400
Field guns (above 7.5-cm)	12,000	27,250
Tanks	9,395	19,885

With the Luftwaffe, figures tell the same story. During 1942, aircraft output had been 15,556 of all types; for 1943 the figure was 25,527. It is worth noting in this connection that if the figure for bomber output from one year to the other was up by under ten per cent, that of fighters was more than doubled, 11,198 as against 5,565. The air force of the Third Reich had finally switched from an offensive to a defensive rôle, as confirmed by the following figures for the production of anti aircraft weapons: 15,472 2-cm, 3.7-cm, 8.8-cm, and even 10.5-cm for 1942; 26,020 for 1943.

During 1942, R.A.F. Bomber Command, virtually on its own, had dropped 43,000 tons of bombs on the Reich and occupied territories. In 1943, with the help of American strategic bombing, this figure would rise to 157,160 tons. But in spite of the near complete destruction of Hamburg in July and successive bombing raids on targets, civil, military and industrial, the Allied air offensive against German industrial production did not achieve the hoped-for decisive victory.

On January 23, 1943, Hitler addressed an appeal "to all workers in tank production" urging them to intensify their efforts; on February 17 he summoned Colonel-General Guderian, who had been unemployed since December 26, 1941, by telephone to his H.Q. in Vinnitsa.

Hitler's purpose was to ask him to assume the functions of Inspector-General of Armoured Troops, in accordance with certain conditions which, at his own request, Guderian was allowed to draw up.

"I was sent a message summoning me to a conference with Hitler at 15.15 hrs. that afternoon. I was received punctually at that hour; to begin with Schmundt was present, but later Hitler and I withdrew to his study where we were alone together. I had not seen Hitler since the black day of December 20th, 1941. In the intervening fourteen months he had aged greatly. His manner was less assured than it had been and his speech was hesitant; his left hand trembled. On his desk lay my books. He began the conversation with the words: 'Since 1941 our ways have parted: there were numerous misunderstandings at that time which I much regret. I need you.'"

It was impossible for Guderian not to accept the post offered him at that time of crisis, particularly as the terms of his appointment, which he had Hitler sign on February 28 following, gave him almost complete autonomy:

"The Inspector-General of Armoured Troops is responsible to me for the future development of armoured troops along lines that will make that arm of the Service into the decisive weapon.

"The Inspector-General of Armoured Troops is directly subordinated to myself."

Contrary to other generals directing different arms, the new inspector of the *Panzerwaffe* came outside the authority of the Chief-of-Staff at O.K.H.; he might of course have had to seek his agreement on questions affecting training and organisation within the armoured units, but he was not placed under his command. This situation naturally enough led to a certain amount of friction between Guderian and General Zeitzler. Furthermore, in arranging that he should be directly subordinate to Hitler, Guderian probably imagined that he had given himself a free hand, seeing the many and possibly conflicting political and military burdens that Hitler had taken on. He little realised how mistaken he was.

At all events, the German armoured corps, which both Hitler and Guderian were willing to consider as the decisive

Goebbels addresses a group of recently decorated soldiers, the men who were fighting desperately on the Eastern Front.

Reich Minister for War Production, Albert Speer, test-drives an experimental tank hull across a shallow river bed.

weapon of the war, received a powerful initial impulse, because the man who created the *Panzerwaffe* was not only a theorist of imagination and an experienced tactician, but also an outstandingly practical man to boot. The year 1943 saw the mass production of a new and almost final development of the Pzkw IV, the H model. This was fitted with a 7.5-cm (48 calibres) gun and carried steel aprons to protect its tracks. It gave a good account of itself on different battlefields during the second part of the war, despite the fact that weight had risen from the original model's 17.3 tons to the H's 25 tons.

The production of the Pzkw V or Panther tank was at a less advanced stage. This tank weighed 43 tons and carried a very

long (70 calibres) 7.5-cm gun, which gave its anti-tank shot a muzzle velocity of 3,068 feet per second. The Panther also had beautifully sloped armour, and this proved very effective in defence as it caused projectiles hitting it to ricochet rather than explode or penetrate. The British and Americans were correct in estimating this tank to be the most formidable brought into German service.

It had been intended to equip the Panzer divisions with one battalion of Pzkw IV's and one battalion of Pzkw V's, which would have given it between 136 and 172 machines, according to whether it had 16 or 22 tanks per company. But these plans were not adhered to.

As for the Pzkw VI or Tiger, mention of which has already been made, its lack of speed ($23\frac{1}{2}$ mph) and its meagre range (under 65 miles), precluded its use at divisional level. Battalions of them were

formed, then reserve regiments. But, despite its excellent 8.8-cm gun, the Porsche assault-gun version, the Ferdinand or *Elefant*, had the disadvantage of being unsuitable for close combat as it lacked a forward-firing machine gun.

"Once they had broken into the enemy's infantry zone they literally had to go quail shooting with cannons. They did not manage to neutralise, let alone déstroy, the enemy rifles and machine-guns, so that the infantry was unable to follow up behind them. By the time they reached the Russian artillery they were on their own."

The mechanisation and motorisation of the armoured divisions' anti-tank guns and artillery also occupied Guderian's attention. In carrying through this programme he had Hitler's approval. On the other hand, he opposed Hitler in regard to the proliferation of "assault gun" battalions which had been surreptitiously removed from his authority, and for which, it seemed, the Führer nourished a special, quite unjustified affection. These self-propelled assault guns were intended to support motorised infantry. Guderian was afraid that their manufacture, on the scale intended by Hitler, would adversely affect the production of tanks and tank destroyers, and also that they would be entirely unsuitable for armour versus armour combat as their protection had not been designed with this in mind and was thus poorly shaped ballistically.

Guderian reports that Hitler abounded with more or less nonsensical ideas that he stood out against. For example, the new Inspector-General writes:

"For street fighting Hitler ordered the construction of three Ram Tigers, to be constructed on Porsche's chassis. This 'knightly' weapon seems to have been based on the tactical fantasies of armchair strategists. In order that this street-fighting monster might be supplied with the necessary petrol, the construction of fuel-carrying auxiliary vehicles and of reserve containers was ordered. Hitler also ordered the construction of multiple smoke mortars for tanks and declared that the helicopter was the ideal aircraft for artillery observation and co-operation with tanks."

Moreover, it was not over a purely technical question that the two men were in conflict. There were divergencies from the very beginning in two far more important areas: between Hitler, the amateur strategist, and Guderian, the professional soldier.

First, there was the overall conduct of the war. Guderian's opinion, voiced at a conference on March 10 at Vinnitsa, was to withdraw the main Panzer units from the front and reorganise them in the rear, and to hold the new weapons described above in reserve until enough of them had been moved up to allow the cumulative effect of mass and surprise to be utilised; hurling them into battle in bits and pieces would achieve no more than betray the secret of their superiority and encourage the enemy to take effective counter-measures. This argument could certainly not be faulted, though its corollary in Guderian's mind was to defer the major offensive until 1944 and be satisfied with strictly limited objectives in 1943.

Hitler held the opposite view. He was determined to avenge Stalingrad by launching an operation in the spring with the aim of destroying the Soviet forces that had ventured into the Kursk salient. The German military leaders were split between the two conceptions. Field-Marshal von Manstein and Colonel-General Model reached conclusions similar to those of Guderian, though in fact for different reasons; General Zeitzler, Chief-of-Staff at O.K.H., and Field-Marshal von Kluge, commanding Army Group "Centre", urged an offensive. With these divergences, the Führer's point of view predominated.

In this controversy it is difficult to vindicate Colonel-General Guderian because he was only interested in the

Eastern Front, and showed no consideration for what the Americans and British might attempt in the summer of 1943 or, with far more likelihood, according to reckoning at the time, in the spring of 1944. So much so that in notes he made preparatory to the Vinnitsa conference, he even states the desirability of "abandoning the policy of sending any tanks of recent design to secondary theatres of operations, and relying there on tank units captured from the enemy."

What would have been the outcome had the Führer adopted this proposition? Simply that Montgomery would have broken the front at Caen with the ease of a circus girl on horseback diving through a paper hoop. But Guderian's having been wrong does not mean that Hitler was right: if he found himself forced to take offensive action on the Eastern Front in 1943, without any chance of success being guaranteed him, the reason is that the failure of his strategy of war had left him quite without any freedom of choice and action. In a further sphere, too, there was no possible hope of understanding between Hitler and Guderian. In his views of the

organisation of the army, however, Guderian had the support of his fellow officers in their entirety, both on the staff and in the field. In his memorandum dated March 10, 1943 he had protested against the kind of megalomania to which Hitler was addicted and which led Manstein to write that, obsessed with sheer size and intoxicated by figures, "Hitler constantly ordered the creation of new divisions. The increase in number of our divisions was certainly desirable, but this was done at the expense of existing divisions, which received no reinforcements, and hence were completely drained. Whereas the new divisions paid for their lack of experience with a heavier toll of lives. The most striking instances of this were the Luftwaffe infantry divisions, the S.S., which were always being increased, and finally those known as the *Volksgrenadier* divisions."

Nor was Manstein guilty of exaggera-

German artillerymen load a 21-cm howitzer. This weapon was fitted with a dual-recoil mechanism, which made it very steady.

tion. At this time, there were cases of divisions being kept at the front even after their battalions, whose full establishment was some 900 officers, N.C.O.s, and other ranks, had been reduced to 100 and even less, without the slightest attempt being made to bring them up to strength.

Manstein also levels a further criticism at the Führer concerning his directives on weapons:

"His interest in anything technological led him to exaggerate the effect of armament. For example, he imagined himself to be able with the help of a few battalions of self-propelled artillery or new Tiger tanks to redress situations where only the engagement of several divisions held out any hope of success.

"There is no question that within the sphere of armament and weapons he was dynamic and intelligent. But belief in his own superiority here had fatal consequences. His constant interference prevented the Luftwaffe from realising its potential in time and his influence certainly delayed the development of rockets and atomic weapons."

It was this persistent and fateful wrongheadedness that made Guderian write:

"It is better to have a few strong divisions than many partially equipped ones. The latter type need a large quantity of wheeled vehicles, fuel, and personnel, which is quite disproportionate to their effectiveness; they are a burden, both to command and to supply; and they block the roads." And he concluded that salvation lay in "avoiding the establishment of new formations: the cadres of the old Panzer and motorised divisions consist of trained men with a sound knowledge of their equipment and are an incalculable asset in re-forming their divisions. New formations can never be of equivalent value." He returned to his theme later, and advocated "the abandonment of plans for the formation of new armoured or motorised divisions, both in the Army and in the *Waffen* S.S., and the assimilation of these divisions, and of the 'Hermann Göring' Division to the war establishment."

But nothing was done about it, as is shown by the following figures, taken from the war diary of O.K.W.

On January 1, 1943, the land forces of the Wehrmacht, taken with the *Waffen* S.S., had 286 divisions, including 27 armoured and 14 motorised, at the front. On the following October 4, there were 328, 282 of them distributed over the different operational theatres (197 on the Eastern Front) and 46 undergoing training of different degrees in Germany and the occupied territories.

Without dwelling further on the question of the infantry, let us turn our attention to the armoured and motorised units. Out of 41 divisions in this category that figured in the German order of battle on January 1, 1943, six were destroyed at Stalingrad (14th, 16th and 24th Panzer Divisions, and 3rd, 29th and 60th Motorised Divisions) and four (10th, 15th and 21st Panzer Divisions and the "Hermann Göring"

Panzer Division) in Tunisia. On October 4, we find 39 Panzer and *Panzergrenadier* divisions counted as operational. Hence eight had been reconstituted, while seven others were in the process of being reformed. The advice and warnings contained in Guderian's memorandum quoted above could not be any further neglected.

But the consequences were suffered, for it was impossible to make up the losses, amounting to some 500 tanks a month, that were being sustained by the armoured divisions fighting on the Eastern Front. Such losses were compounded by the fact that the Panzer divisions had been thrown into the Battle of Kursk the previous July 5 without having been restored to full strength. So it came about that by the end of the year most of them were no more than shadows of themselves; their little blue flags pinned up on the vast operational map recording the day-to-day situation at O.K.W. nevertheless enabled the so-called Führer to "conduct operations", just as if they still possessed some offensive potential, however slight.

In Italy it was the same story. On the evidence of its own commanding officer, Lieutenant-General Lemelsen, on October 1 the 29th *Panzergrenadier* Division, which had been hurriedly formed from the 29th Motorised Division, was short of the following standard weapons: 33 out of 58 8.1-cm mortars, 17 out of 31 medium and heavy anti-tank guns, 26 out of 42 tracked self-propelled guns and 29 out of 42 pieces of artillery.

And it was just the same with infantry divisions.

There is also the fact that Hitler continued to acquiesce in the development of the private armies that his fellow Nazis, *Reichsführer* S.S. Heinrich Himmler and *Reichsmarschall* Göring, had set up.

At the end of December 1942, there were eight *Waffen* S.S. divisions; a year later there were 17, both operational and in the process of formation, ten of them armoured or motorised (*Panzergrenadier*), comprising around half a million men. With such a rate of increase they could no longer count merely on volunteer recruitment as had been the rule initially. So Himmler got a certain quota of the conscript force made over to him, his recruiting sergeants creaming off any young men over 5 feet 9 inches tall.

Applied to this date and later, the Allies' decision to approximate the *Waffen* S.S. to a criminal association loses any foundation in law, since, in order for there to be such an association, it would have had to be voluntary. This it was not. In any event, when it came to *matériel* and equipment, the S.S. divisions had first claim, and this did not always correspond to their degree of training. Nevertheless, given their army training, and without in any sense exonerating those among them who perpetrated atrocities, it can truthfully be said that the S.S. fought well.

During the winter of 1941/2, Hitler ordered Göring to prune the Luftwaffe of its excessive numbers so as to put some

hundreds of thousands of men at the disposal of the Army. But the *Reichsmarschall* chose to understand the order differently; without its being exactly possible to evade it altogether, he prevailed upon Hitler to let him maintain his authority over the divisions that would thus be formed, so far as training and personnel were concerned. Hence the origin of the "Luftwaffe field divisions" (*Luftwaffenfelddivisionen* or L.F.D.), of which the least that can be said is that, as regards the quality of their leadership and their fighting qualities, they were far inferior to the Army's infantry divisions.

Even so, 20 of them were formed, and these enjoyed the same priorities in equipment as the *Waffen* S.S., at a time when weapons and *matériel* were becoming scarce at the front. In addition to this, Göring sought and received permission to set up a "paratroop armoured" division under his authority, the "Hermann Göring" Panzer Division, which up till the time Guderian put some order into it, had expanded (like its patron) until there were 34,000 men on its roll.

By adding the Göring divisions to the Himmler divisions, we arrive at a total of 39 out of the 328 divisions comprising the land forces, all of them independent of O.K.H. Was it Hitler's intention thus imperceptibly to replace the old reactionary and aristocratic army by a new National-Socialist army? Such a hypothesis cannot be written off right away.

Faced with Hitler's incurable misguidedness in spite of all the advice wasted on him, the generals and senior staff officers became restive. They realised that Hitler's obstinate refusal to appreciate the realities of the situation would bring the army to catastrophe and render the country defenceless before a Soviet invasion; they set about ways and means of eliminating his pernicious influence without causing too much damage. Field-Marshals von Manstein and von Kluge held the view that he would have to be forced to abandon supreme command of the army; but while agreeing as to the aim, they differed as to the means of achieving it.

Manstein wished to use persuasion, and indeed on three occasions he endeavoured to lead Hitler to a more rational appreciation of military command, yet without actually asking him to make way for someone else: "I knew perfectly well," he wrote, "that Hitler would never accept surrender of command officially. As dictator he could not do so without a loss of prestige that was for him unacceptable. My aim was thus to induce him to continue as supreme commander only nominally, to agree to hand over the actual direction of military operations in all theatres to a chief of general staff responsible to him, and to appoint a special commander-in-chief on the Eastern Front. I shall say more about these attempts which unfortunately remained fruitless. They were particularly delicate for me, since Hitler knew perfectly well that several sections of the army would have liked to see me hold the post of chief of the general staff or commander-in-chief in the East myself."

At all events he refused to resort to force, if rational argument was ineffective in face of the blind resolve of the despot, it being his opinion that a *coup d'état* could only result in a collapse at the front and chaos in Germany. Kluge, on the other hand, did not exclude the use of force, and for this purpose made contact with Colonel-General Guderian, through Major-General von Tresckow, one of his staff officers, whom he trusted entirely. Guderian owed his temporary disgrace in December 1941 to Kluge and declined to see the emissary for reasons of prudence, for he had no confidence in Kluge's integrity. In any case he had other ideas about the reorganisation of the German high command and well before Tresckow's approach to him (at the end of July 1943) he had acquainted Goebbels with his suggestions on the subject, on March 6 during a visit to Berlin. It was his opinion that in view of the confusion caused by the different command responsibilities of O.K.W., O.K.H., *Oberkommando der Marine*, *Oberkommando der Luftwaffe*, the *Waffen* S.S. high command, and the Ministry of Armaments, it was necessary that Hitler should have a better qualified chief-of-staff than the inconsistent Field-Marshal Keitel.

He did not get his way any more than Manstein had, nor any more than the latter did he consider taking the final plunge when faced by Hitler's blindness.

In any case, the intellectual and moral crisis that we have just described did not spread to the front, where the troops continued to fight with skill and tenacity.

But the circumstances were tragic, as German forces were outnumbered and virtually devoid of air cover.

On November 8, 1943, the day following the 25th anniversary of the October Revolution and two days after the liberation of Kiev, a decree of the Praesidium of the Supreme Soviet instituted one more of its large number of distinctions and decorations: the Order of Victory. This order, made of white enamel and encrusted with diamonds, was given only to Front commanders and those who led front-line units.

Apparently, Stalin and his colleagues anticipated the unconditional surrender of the Third Reich by 17 months. Even so, the year 1943 emphasised and added to the defeat suffered by the German armies at Stalingrad and in the great curve of the Don between November 19 and December 31, 1942.

Consideration of the number of days each side was on the offensive during 1943 is clear enough proof of the altered balance of initiative on the Eastern Front: O.K.H. managed 69 days, *Stavka* slightly over two and a half times as many, with 185 days.

Furthermore, it must be remembered that by January 1, 1943 the second Soviet winter offensive had been under way for 43 days, and the third, unleashed on

December 24, 1943 would not cease until April 24, 1944, along the line Kovel' – Buchach – Carpathian mountains. In other words, between November 19, 1942 and April 24, 1944, the Russians were on the attack for more than 11 months (334 days).

In addition, O.K.H.'s objectives were becoming more and more modest. It was a long way from Operation *"Blau"* to Operation *"Zitadelle"*, and between the latter and the counter-attack launched on November 16, 1943 by Field-Marshal von Manstein in the Zhitomir sector. In 1944, there would be no German summer offensive.

The change in the situation was due to the enormous increase in the size of the Red Army during 1943. On June 22, 1941, it had 4,700,000 men under arms. The following December 31, with 2,300,000 men, its numbers had fallen to their lowest level. Two years later they had grown to 5,100,000. Similarly, the number of divisions had increased at the same rate, as is shown in the following table, based on information extracted from Sir Basil Liddell Hart's *The Red Army:*

	June 1941	End of 1942	End of 1943
Infantry divisions	175	442	513
Armoured and mechanised brigades	78	186	290
Cavalry divisions	30	35	41

It must be noted, however, as regards infantry figures, that the figures for 1942 and 1943 include many brigades within the numbers of divisions, so that the effectives available in this arm were far from having tripled, as it might appear at first glance.

Furthermore, the number of guns, in spite of the heavy losses of the 1942 campaign, increased from 5,900 to 19,000, which enabled the Russians to organise 29 artillery divisions, large-scale bodies of artillery unknown in Western armies. These may be said to have been the sledge-hammers used by the front commanders.

As for tanks, in February 1943 there were 7,100 in forward areas, compared with 5,200 at the same time the year before. Moreover, Soviet armour was changing with the entry into service of the T-34/85, in other words a T-34 redesigned so as to be able to mount an 85-mm/53 calibre gun. This fired a 20·4-lb shell at a muzzle velocity of 2,600 feet per second and could pierce German armour at all normal ranges. Of course, the T-34/85 was somewhat heavier than the basic model, but even so, on the road it could still maintain a speed of 32 mph and carry enough petrol for a range of 220 miles. In the Korean war, this tank showed its superiority over the improved Sherman tank with which the South Korean army was equipped; not till 1958 did Soviet factories stop manufacturing it.

Just like Hitler, Stalin attached great importance to the self-propelled gun, so 1943 saw the appearance of the SU-152, a JS chassis armed with a 152-mm gun/

howitzer. Its thick armour allowed it to advance in the front line, beside the infantry which it was designed to support with direct fire. However, its weight was 43 tons and its speed was only 15 mph. Of course, its primary task did not require any more of it. Besides the SU-152, there were other calibres of artillery on self-propelled mountings, among which should be noted the SU-85, which was used as an anti-tank gun and can be compared with the "Ferdinand" of the German Army, though much smaller in size.

Though armoured forces had developed so greatly, as the table above shows, the cavalry also made progress and increased in numbers from 30 to 41 divisions between June 1941 and the end of 1943. Forest and marshy regions, where tanks cannot be used, are far more extensive in Russia than anywhere else in Europe. Furthermore, cavalry is ideal for rainy seasons. When earth roads become mud-sloughs, the cavalry can be given major tasks quite impossible for infantry or armoured units. In any case, right until the end of the war, the Soviet Army had no all-purpose cross-country vehicle, comparable with the *Panzergrenadierwagen* or the American half-track. Therefore it was not uncommon for large division- or even corps-size cavalry units to be more useful and speedy at exploiting tank break-throughs than the supposedly more sophisticated motorised infantry.

Many German historians of this campaign are surprised at the ease with which their enemy crossed river obstacles as sizable as the Don, the Donets, and the Dniepr and renewed road communications. They would have been less surprised if they had known that the Red Army had paid considerable attention to its sappers and had created Pioneer and Bridge-builder Brigades. From 17 in the autumn of 1942, their number rose to 46 by the beginning of 1943 and 55 the following summer.

The Soviet land forces possessed an excellent machine for support both in

A Russian 120-mm mortar crew.

The Soviet Order of Victory, given to commanders at the front.

attack and defence: the Ilyushin Il-2m3 "Shturmovik". The armoured bottom of its fuselage could resist 20-mm A.A. shells while it strafed enemy troops with its 23-mm or even 37-mm cannon, bombs, and the rockets with which it was the only aircraft to be armed at the time. The Russians also had the Yakovlev-1 and 9 fighters, the Lavochkin LaGG-3 fighter, and Mikoyan MiG-3 fighter, as well as the excellent Tupolev SB-2 and Petlyakov Pe-2 medium and light bombers. The only Russian four-engined heavy bomber to see widespread service was the Petlyakov Pe-8, but on the whole the Russians stuck to tactical rather than strategic bombing. Only after 1945 did the Soviet Union make a timid entrance into this latter field.

The question of the support provided by Great Britain and the United States in the gigantic Russian war effort comes in here. At the time, neither of the two enemies at grips on the Eastern Front was very forthcoming in this respect: the Germans so as not to alarm home public opinion by admitting that the U-boat blockade was not as complete as Dr. Goebbels claimed, and the Russians because they have always wished to keep the credit for final victory for the Red Army and the Soviet worker alone.

So, though since then ex-Wehrmacht generals in their memoirs and West German writers in historical works have described the importance of Anglo-American supplies quite openly, the Soviet authors that have been consulted obey an order from on high, thus mentioning the subject only rarely and then somewhat delicately. Occasionally they will make a contemptuous remark concerning the quality of the war *matériel* sent and about the paucity of supply and the slowness of dispatch.

But the truth, according to statistics quoted by Alexander Werth, at the time *Sunday Times* correspondent in Moscow, is that no less than 9,214 armoured vehicles, 12,230 aircraft, and 4,111 20-mm

and 40-mm A.A. guns were supplied to the Soviet Union under the Lend-Lease agreement, all of it, of course, with an adequate supply of ammunition and spare parts. These supplies came from the following countries:

	Tanks	Aircraft	A.A. guns
Great Britain	4,292	5,800	4,111
United States	3,734	6,430	
Canada	1,188		
Totals	9,214	12,230	4,111

It is true, nevertheless, that the Valentines, Matildas, and Grants did no better on the Russian steppes than they had in North Africa against generally superior German tanks. The Sherman tank, as explained above, was not as good as the T-34, even though the armour thicknesses were about the same. The Germans did, however, report large numbers of them in action in the Kurland offensive during the summer and autumn of 1944.

But mechanised warfare is not restricted to armoured and tracked vehicles. By delivering 434,000 trucks, 28,000 jeeps, 5,500 artillery tractors, and 330,000 field telephones, each with three miles of cable, the British and Americans contributed in no small way to increasing the mobility of Soviet land forces.

In the air, the Hawker Hurricanes supplied by the British, the Curtiss P-40 Kittyhawk and Bell P-39 Airacobra fighters and fighter-bombers supplied by the United States, as well as thousands of twin-engined bombers, reinforced the air forces of the Allies' Eastern partner.

These supplies of war *matériel* were accompanied by deliveries of fuel in corresponding amounts: 2,670,000 tons of petroleum products, of which 476,000 tons were high-octane aviation spirit.

Furthermore, with five and a half million pairs of boots and over 25 million yards of cloth for uniforms, the Americans supplied enough to shoe and clothe the entire Red Army once over. With its generous deliveries of flour and tinned food, the U.S.A. were to a large extent responsible for safeguarding its daily rations.

There was more to come, and this would be even more important. It is true that the arms sent under the Lend-Lease agreement totalled only ten or perhaps 15 per cent of those manufactured in Russia, but can it really be believed that Soviet war production could have reached the record figures that Communist historians boast of today, and with good reason, without massive imports of explosives and strategic raw materials, as we call them today? Actually, without relaxing their own armament programmes, the British, Americans, and Canadians supplied the Soviet Union with:

218,000 tons of various explosives
1,200,000 tons of steel
170,000 tons of aluminium
217,000 tons of copper
29,000 tons of tin
6,500 tons of nickel
48,000 tons of lead
42,000 tons of zinc

103,000 tons of rubber
93,000 tons of jute.

Finally, under the industrial heading, can be added 26,000 machine-tools and, from the United States, 1,045 locomotives and 8,260 wagons, built especially for the Soviet Union's broad gauge railways.

Yet these figures do not show all, for certain statistics used do not include shipments after December 31, 1944. Leaving this aside, there is every reason to state that the aid provided was considerable and generously given, particularly so because the safe routes through Persia and Vladivostok were less used than the dangerous and difficult Arctic passage.

In all, 42 convoys went to Murmansk and Archangel between August 1941 and May 1945. Their vicissitudes are shown in the following table:

	Convoys	Ships dispatched	Ships arrived
1941	9	64	62
1942	13	256	185
1943	6	112	105
1944	10	251	242
1945	4	160	158
Totals	42	843	752

Of the 91 which did not reach their destination, 33 had to leave their convoys because of breakdowns and various other reasons. So only 58 ships were destroyed on the way out, but to these must be added those which perished on the way back, 27 in all, plus six merchant ships travelling alone and five more, victims of Luftwaffe bombing raids on the port of Murmansk. This gives a total of 96.

In warships, convoy escort cost the Royal Navy two cruisers, seven destroyers, and six or seven smaller ships. Such was the price paid by the Western Allies of the Soviet Union to get their convoys to Russia. The least that can be said is that Stalin never understood the enormity of the sacrifice.

Alexander Werth frequently refers to the mutual misunderstandings between the Soviet Union and the Allies over the implementation of the Lend-Lease Act, notably when Admiral Standley complained of the lack of gratitude shown by the Soviet Union towards America:

"It is true that Americans paid for Russian blood with powdered egg and other surplus food. The Russian soldiers liked spam, but they called it, not without some bitterness, 'Second Front'."

In his diary for 1943, Alexander Werth noted on March 9:

"The Russian censorship, after five hours' high-power telephoning, passed the text of the Standley statement. The people at the press department looked furious. Kozhemiako, the chief censor, was white with rage as he put his name to the cable. His mother had died of starvation in Leningrad.... Another Russian remarked tonight: 'We've lost millions of people, and they want us to crawl on our knees because they send us spam. And has the "warmhearted"

Congress ever done anything that wasn't in its interests? Don't tell me that Lend-Lease is *charity!*"

"What nettled the British and Americans even more was that, after paying a warm tribute to Soviet Industry, Stalin should have made no mention at all of Lend-Lease and other Western supplies which were now beginning to arrive in very substantial quantities, partly along the newly-reorganised Persian route."

Whatever the quality and quantity of its weapons, the value of an army will always depend to a large measure on the morale, high or low, of the men who serve in its ranks. In terms of this, an examination of the morale factor of the Red Army at the time of the great change in its fortunes of the winter of 1942–1943 is called for.

It would seem that the phrase "Great Patriotic War" goes back to this time. The expression has remained the official name given by Moscow to the German-Soviet hostilities of the years 1941–1945. Government propaganda appealed to all the traditional values of the Russian nation to hurl itself against the "German invader", who was not yet described as "German-Fascist" as he is today. Nobody, not even the Orthodox Church, was exempt from being solicited in this way and, as was its duty in canon law, the Church did not remain heedless of the call. The proof of it is the column of tanks that it financed through collections, offered to the Russian Army, and baptised after the great prince "Dimitri Donskoi" of Russia who vanquished the Tartars in 1389 on the field of Kulikovo.

Soon the Komintern (or Third International, set up in 1919 to work for world communism) would be dissolved. Though this was certainly a measure aimed at reassuring Roosevelt and Churchill about the purity of Stalin's intentions, and to frustrate Hitler's efforts to involve Europe in a "Crusade against Bolshevism", it was also intended to free the "Great Patriotic War" from any overtone of "Cosmopolitanism", as the Communists use the term. Doubtless it was for the same reason that the *Internationale* was replaced by a specifically Russian national anthem. In the same patriotic mood, the old battleship *Pariskaya Kommuna* was renamed *Sevastopol,* her original name when launched from the St. Petersburg shipyards in June 1911.

On October 9, 1942 a decree of the Praesidium of the Supreme Soviet dissolved the Corps of Political Commissars, who supervised the actions of commanders down to divisional level and countersigned their orders. In this way a form of surveillance which was always very suspicious, often incompetent, and which seems to have been hated by most of the military hierarchy, was removed. But even so the Commissars were not demobilised; from among them many capable of command were selected to become 200 regimental and 600 battalion commanders, enough men to officer more than 66 infantry divisions by the Western standards of the time.

Moreover, the officers had received back their insignia of rank and their long Tsarist-style shoulder boards. A hail of decorations was showered over their uniforms and stimulated their ambition. Six orders were created for the Army and the Air Force and two for the Navy in 1942 and 1943, without counting the Order of Victory mentioned at the beginning of this chapter and the supreme distinction of "Hero of the Soviet Union" dating from 1943. N.C.O.s and privates could be awarded two of these orders as well as a score of medals struck to commemorate the victories of the Red Army.

According to the American historian Raymond L. Garthoff, who may be taken as correct, the total number of decorations awarded by the Soviet authorities in the "Great Patriotic War" was 11 million while the United States paid their debt of honour to their fighting men with 1,400,049.

On June 22, 1941, the Soviet Army had three Marshals (Voroshilov, Budenny, and Timoshenko); by the end of the hostilities, there were 30 of them, among their number 13 Marshals of the Soviet Union who appear to take precedence over Marshals designated within their branch of the Service: Air Force, eight; Artillery, three; Armoured Forces, four;

German fitters strip down the engine of a Pzkw IV during a break in the fighting.

A laughing Russian airman holds a bomb inscribed "A present for Hitler!"

Engineers, one; and Signals, one. Similarly Admirals Kuznetsov and Isakov were promoted to the rank of Admirals of the Fleet.

Besides these individual distinctions, there were the collective citations which allowed units deserving of it to call themselves "Guards". But this title, which corresponds to the *"fourragère"* lanyard of the French Army, is not only symbolic. For the units which merited it it brought considerable advantages in the form of pay supplements and other issues.

It can be seen that nationalism was in full flood, the traditional military virtues were restored and set on pedestals and the Army was represented as the complete embodiment of the national spirit. And yet the military had very little scope for the Party did not relax its grip on the Army in the slightest. Far from it; the Communist Party had officially recognised cells in all units and bodies of troops, holding meetings even in the cellars of Stalingrad, printing regimental newspapers, recruiting new members, and corresponding with rear organisations. All of these were activities that one would be surprised to see in any Western army but which, it must be stressed, were to the advantage of the military hierarchy. Among the troops Party members were a minority, but they were enjoined to show an example and were only accepted when they had given evidence under fire of possessing solid military qualities. When necessary, they sought the opportunities to show their ability. So, by September 1, 1944, of 5,400 "Heroes of the Soviet Union" created since the beginning of hostilities, 2,970 were Party members or had applied for membership.

The Communist organisations working within the Army took on another task, that of maintaining permanent liaison between the front and the rear. For example, they used the system of having their battalion or regiment adopted by a certain village, factory, or collective farm. Also, by means of continuous correspondence, they tried to maintain good relationships between the fighting men and what is called the Home Front. Between the military hierarchy and the Communist Party hierarchy, liaison at each level was maintained via Political Officers, who must not be confused with the Commissar for, at least officially, the former had no control over the military commanders. Their task consisted of indoctrinating the troops. Before any important action, the psychological preparation which they carried out was, in all the accounts given, considered as important and mentioned in the same way as the preparations of the staff and of the various technical branches.

One single quotation will be sufficient to illustrate this term. It comes from the monograph written by Colonel V. P. Morosov on the events of the great attack launched on January 13, 1943 by the forces on the Voronezh Front against the Hungarian 2nd Army and the Italian 8th Army:

"The main task of political work," he writes, "consisted of preparing the troops on the basis of the experience of combat obtained in the Stalingrad counter-offensive.

"The political officers of the Front had prepared a plan aimed at ensuring the political security of the attack, by organising the effort of propaganda and agitation.

"First of all, they had to reinforce the strength of the Party and its Youth *(Komsomol)* at all levels. By gaining new Party and *Komsomol* members, new organisations were formed and existing ones were strengthened. The best soldiers and officers joined the Party or the Communist Youth before the battle. The Communists were redistributed among the units in the line. In addition, units and establishments in the rear were required to furnish the front with a certain number of their militants. In this way, the Party's organisations were strengthened within the companies.

"The main mission of the agitation and propaganda was to remind every soldier of the demands of the Party and the Soviet Government: to be ready to inflict a crushing defeat on the enemy. Political agitation was intended to awaken the aggressive spirit in the men and officers and to ensure that tactical orders were successfully obeyed. In the front-line and army newspapers, just as in the sheets produced in the individual companies, the combat mission of the Soviet Army was clearly defined: to free the Soviet homeland from the Fascist conqueror."

At the summit of this double political and military hierarchy stood one man, like the keystone of an arch: Stalin, self-appointed Marshal and Generalissimo of the Soviet Armed Forces on one hand, and on the other Secretary-General of the Communist Party of the U.S.S.R. Did the master of the Kremlin, the greatest opportunist of his time, see further than the needs of the moment when he imposed this form of organisation? The very least that can be said is that once Germany had been defeated no other system would have been better able to guarantee his power, his person, and the régime against the danger of the Soviet military claiming all the credit for the victory and profiting from it.

The extreme rigour of this double discipline should be stressed; in the Red Army, the surrender of a soldier was something absolutely forbidden and in theory inconceivable. This was the cause of the total lack of concern shown for those who had in fact become prisoners. Raymond Garthoff quotes Eisenhower on the subject:

"While talking to a Russian general I mentioned the difficult problem that was imposed upon us at various periods of the war by the need to care for so many German prisoners. I remarked that they were fed the same rations as our own soldiers. In the greatest astonishment he asked: 'Why did you do that?' I said: 'Well, in the first place my country was required to do so by the terms of the Geneva Convention. In the second place the Germans had some thousands of American and British prisoners and I did not want to give Hitler the excuse or justification for treating our prisoners more harshly than he was already doing.' Again the Russian seemed astounded at my attitude and he said: 'But what did you care about men the Germans had captured? They had surrendered and could not fight any more.'"

CHAPTER 45

The battle of Kursk and the Russian counterattack

Operation *"Zitadelle"* was launched on July 5 against the Kursk salient and constituted the final attempt by the German Army to recover the operational initiative on the Eastern Front. But before turning our attention to this, it is desirable to examine briefly the events that occurred during the first three months of 1943 along the somewhat circuitous front line running from north of Kursk to Lake Ladoga. These were deliberately omitted from Chapter 83 so as to give full effect to the account of the Battle of Stalingrad and its consequences.

On this front Army Groups "Centre" and "North", still commanded by Field-Marshals von Kluge and von Küchler respectively, were composed of seven armies (23 corps of 117 divisions or their equivalent on January 1, nine of them Panzer and eight motorised). The extremely winding course of the line on which the Germans had stabilised their positions at the end of March 1942 meant that it could not be held in any depth. To make matters worse, the lakes, rivers, and marshy tracts, so characteristic of the region, freeze hard and allow not only infantry and cavalry to pass over them but also lorries, artillery, and even tanks.

On January 4, the 3rd *Panzerarmee* on Kluge's left flank was broken through by troops of the 3rd Shock Army (Kalinin Front) on either side of Velikiye-Luki. A fortnight later, after every attempt to relieve the citadel of the town had failed, its defenders, reduced to 102 in number, managed to find their way back to the German lines, leaving 200 wounded behind them.

Of graver consequence was the defeat inflicted on the German 18th Army (Colonel-General G. Lindemann) to the south of Lake Ladoga. At O.K.H. this sector was known as the "bottleneck" on account of the pronounced salient formed by the front between Mga and the southern shore of the lake. But to evacuate it would have meant abandoning the siege of Leningrad; and for this reason Hitler had always opposed any suggestion that it should be done. XVI Corps (General Wodrig) held the salient and was hence liable to be cut off as soon as the Neva, which covered its left flank, no longer constituted an obstacle to the enemy.

The task of co-ordinating the combined action of the Leningrad Front (Lieutenant-General M. A. Govorov) and the Volkhov Front (General K. A. Meretskov) was entrusted to Marshal K. Voroshilov. Govorov's 67th Army (Lieutenant-General V. P. Sviridov) was ordered to make contact with the 2nd Shock Army (Lieutenant-General I. I. Fedyuninsky) and the 8th Army (Lieutenant-General F. N. Starikov) both under the command of General Meretskov. According to a chart drawn up in Moscow, the operation involved 12 divisions and one infantry brigade taking on four German divisions. And whereas the Soviet divisions in all probability numbered some 10,000 men each, those of the Reich were severely reduced. In particular, the Russians could deploy almost 100 guns and mortars per mile, and each of the two fronts had its own air cover and support.

Hence the Russian attack on January 12, 1943 was backed by massive firepower and followed a sustained artillery bombardment lasting 90 minutes. Nevertheless, XVI Corps held the attack, with Lindemann, then Küchler, soon coming to its aid. Consequently it took a full week for the 2nd Shock Army advancing from the west and the 67th Army from the east to fight their way across the ten miles that divided them. On January 17, General Sviridov's troops entered Petrokrepost'; the following day, the entire population of Leningrad, delirious with joy, learnt that after 17 months' trials and privations borne with fortitude and stoicism, the siege had been broken. On February 6, railway communications between Peter the Great's capital city and the outside world were re-established. But the Russians were halted short of Mga, which meant that Leningrad's lifeline was restricted to a corridor six to seven miles wide. Stalin, however, was so pleased with the result that 19,000 decorations were awarded to the victorious troops who had raised the siege of Russia's second city.

This disaster, in which the 41st and 277th Infantry Divisions were almost entirely destroyed, and still more the rapid and tragic succession of defeats suffered south of Kursk, induced Hitler to agree to certain adjustments to the front line which he had obstinately refused to allow his generals to make the previous year, on the grounds that enormous quantities of *matériel* might be lost in the course of withdrawal.

With this authorisation, O.K.H., between the 19th and the end of February, effected the evacuation of the "fortress" of Demy'ansk, which was linked to the 16th Army's front line only by a narrow corridor under constant threat. The withdrawal was an orderly one and permitted a front line economy of seven divisions.

Next, starting on March 2, Operation *"Buffle"*, whereby 30 divisions of the German 4th and 9th Armies withdrew 100 miles, was set in motion. Once again, the actual manoeuvre failed to justify the Führer's apprehensions, feigned or real. Rzhev, Gzhatsk, then Vyaz'ma were one after the other evacuated in the course of a manoeuvre which lasted more than three weeks, without the Russians, who in the event were considerably delayed by numerous minefields, showing themselves particularly aggressive. The evacuation of the salient, which had a front of 410 miles, was completed on March 25. Field-Marshal von Kluge was thus able to deploy his armies along a front slightly less than half as long (230 miles), thus releasing 14 divisions.

Two comments seem appropriate here. Firstly, that the 21 divisions pulled back out of salients, in February and March 1943, were more or less equivalent in numbers to the Rumanian 3rd Army and the Italian 8th Army, whose destruction had sealed the fate of the German 6th Army in the Stalingrad pocket. What might the result have been if it had been they who were called on to reinforce Army Group "B" when Paulus reached the Volga? The question is one of pure speculation, however. Secondly, if the Rzhev salient was defended by one division for every 16 miles of front, Operation *"Buffle"*, which left Kluge with 16 divisions in order to hold 240 miles, made no appreciable difference to his own situation (15 miles per division). And proof of this would be given no later than July 13 following, on the occasion of the Soviet offensive directed against the Orel salient. But how could anything else have been done?

In any event, this agonising question did not preoccupy Hitler who, on April 15, put his signature to the 13 copies of Operaational Order No. 16. The document is a long one, as are all those which Hitler wrote, and the following extract will serve to illuminate the events that subsequently took place:

"I am resolved, as soon as the weather allows, to launch Operation *'Zitadelle'*, as the first offensive action of this year," were his opening words. "Hence the importance of this offensive. It must lead to a rapid and decisive success. It *must* give us the initiative for the coming spring and summer. In view of this, preparations must be conducted with the utmost precaution and the utmost energy. At the main points of attack the finest units, the finest weapons, the finest commanders will be committed, and plentiful supplies of munitions will be ensured. Every commander, every fighting man must be imbued with the capital significance of this offensive. The victory of Kursk must be as a beacon to the whole world.

"To this effect, I order:

1. Objective of the offensive: by means of a highly concentrated, and savage attack vigorously conducted by two armies, one from the area of Belgorod, the other from south of Orel, to encircle the enemy forces situated in the region of Kursk and annihilate them by concentric attacks.

"In the course of this offensive a new and shorter front line will be established, permitting economies of means, along the line joining Nejega, Korocha, Skoro-

dnoye, Tim, passing east of Shchigry, and Sosna."

Under Point 2, the Führer went on to define the conditions necessary for the success of the enterprise:

"(a) to ensure to the full the advantage of surprise, and principally to keep the enemy ignorant of the timing of attack;

(b) to concentrate to the utmost the attacking forces on narrow fronts so as to obtain an overwhelming local superiority in all arms (tanks, assault guns, artillery, and rocket launchers) grouped in a single echelon until junction between the two armies in the rear of the enemy is effected, thereby cutting him off from his rear areas;

(c) to bring up as fast as possible, from the rear, the forces necessary to cover the flanks of the offensive thrusts, thus enabling the attacking forces to concentrate solely on their advance;

(d) by driving into the pocket from all sides and with all possible speed, to give the enemy no respite, and to accelerate his destruction;

(e) to execute the attack at a speed so rapid that the enemy can neither prevent encirclement nor bring up reserves from his other fronts; and

(f) by the speedy establishment of the new front line, to allow the disengagement of forces, especially the Panzer forces, with all possible despatch, so that they can be used for other purposes."

Then the Führer fixed the parts to be played by Army Groups "Centre" and "South" and the Luftwaffe, apportioned the means at their disposal, and laid down certain requirements for misleading the enemy as to the German intentions, and for the maintenance of secrecy. As from April 28, Kluge and Manstein were to be ready to launch the attack within six days of receiving the order from O.K.H., the earliest date suggested for the offensive being May 3.

Hitler's initiative, which in fact stemmed from Colonel-General Kurt Zeitzler, Chief-of-Staff at O.K.H., nevertheless elicited varying reactions amongst the generals. Kluge gave determined support to Operation *"Zitadelle"*, but many others raised objection to it, some categorically, others only provisionally.

On May 2, Hitler had summoned the top commanders concerned in the enterprise, plus Colonel-General Guderian, to Munich. In his capacity as Inspector-General of Armoured Troops, Guderian put forward a whole series of impressive arguments against the projected offensive, which he sums up as follows in his memoirs:

"I asked permission to express my views and declared that the attack was point-

A "Marder" self-propelled gun (top) on the move near Belgorod, and a Pzkw III (below) emerging from a grass fire. By now the Pzkw III was quite out of date. The battle of Kursk and the Russian counter attack (opposite) completely changed the situation in the East.

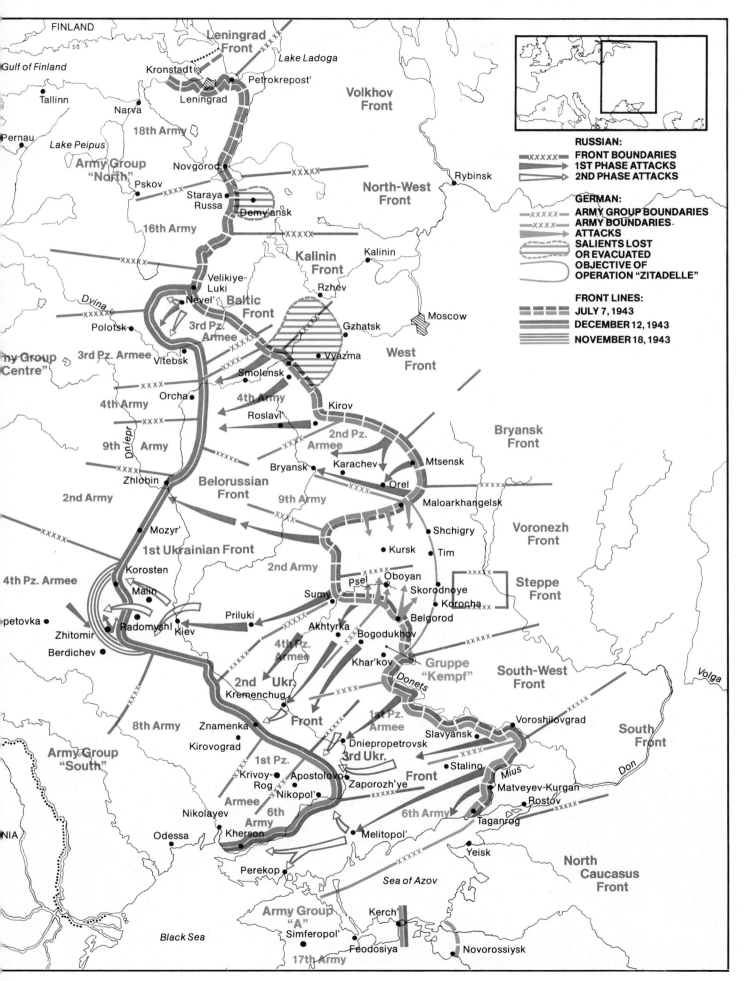

FINLAND

Gulf of Finland

Tallinn

Pernau

Lake Peipus

Narva

Kronstadt

Leningrad

Petrokrepost'

Lake Ladoga

Leningrad Front

Volkhov Front

Rybinsk

18th Army

Army Group "North"

Novgorod

Pskov

Staraya Russa

Demy'ansk

North-West Front

16th Army

Velikiye-Luki

Kalinin Front

Rzhev

Kalinin

Moscow

Dvina

Nevel'

Baltic Front

3rd Pz. Armee

Gzhatsk

Polotsk

3rd Pz. Armee

Vitebsk

Vyaz'ma

West Front

ny Group "Centre"

Smolensk

4th Army

Orcha

4th Army

Kirov

Roslavl'

Bryansk Front

9th Army

2nd Pz. Armee

Karachev

Mtsensk

Zhlobin

Belorussian Front

Bryansk

Orel

Maloarkhangelsk

2nd Army

9th Army

Voronezh Front

Mozyr'

Shchigry

1st Ukrainian Front

2nd Army

Kursk

Tim

Korosten

Psel

Oboyan

Skorodnoye

Steppe Front

4th Pz. Armee

Malin

Sumy

Korocha

petovka

Priluki

Akhtyrka

Belgorod

Zhitomir

Radomyshl

Kiev

Bogodukhov

Berdichev

4th Pz. Armee

Khar'kov

Gruppe "Kempf"

South-West Front

Volga

2nd Ukr. Front

Donets

Kremenchug

1st Pz. Armee

Voroshilovgrad

South Front

8th Army

Znamenka

Slavyansk

Kirovograd

Dniepropetrovsk

3rd Ukr.

Stalino

Don

Army Group "South"

1st Pz. Armee

Krivoy-Rog

Apostolovo

Zaporozh'ye

Front

Mius

Matveyev-Kurgan

Nikopol'

Rostov

Armee

6th Army

6th Army

Taganrog

Nikolayev

Kherson

Melitopol'

Yeisk

Odessa

North Caucasus Front

Perekop

Sea of Azov

NIA

Army Group "A"

Kerch'

Black Sea

Simferopol'

Feodosiya

Novorossiysk

17th Army

RUSSIAN:
FRONT BOUNDARIES
1ST PHASE ATTACKS
2ND PHASE ATTACKS

GERMAN:
ARMY GROUP BOUNDARIES
ARMY BOUNDARIES
ATTACKS
SALIENTS LOST OR EVACUATED
OBJECTIVE OF OPERATION "ZITADELLE"

FRONT LINES:
JULY 7, 1943
DECEMBER 12, 1943
NOVEMBER 18, 1943

less; we had only just completed the reorganisation and re-equipment of our Eastern Front; if we attacked according to the plan of the Chief of the General Staff we were certain to suffer heavy tank casualties, which we would not be in a position to replace in 1943; on the contrary, we ought to be devoting our new tank production to the Western Front so as to have mobile reserves available for use against the Allied landing which could be expected with certainty to take place in 1944. Furthermore, I pointed out that the Panthers, on whose performance the Chief of the Army General Staff was relying so heavily, were still suffering from many teething troubles inherent in all new equipment and it seemed unlikely that these could be put right in time for the launching of the attack."

Manstein had during the previous February and March declared his preference for a plan of operations radically different to that outlined in the order of April 15. He had told Hitler of this on the occasion of the Führer's visit to his H.Q. in Zaporozh'ye. In substance, his idea was to await the offensive that the enemy was bound to launch in order to recover the Donets basin. Once this had got under way, the Germans would conduct an orderly retreat to the Melitopol'–Dniepropetrovsk line, while at the same time a powerful armoured force would be assembled in the Poltava–Khar'kov region. Once the Russians had been led into the trap, this force would counter-attack with lightning speed in the direction of the Sea of Azov, and the superiority which German commanders had always shown over their Russian counterparts in mobile warfare would bring them victory.

"The guiding principle of this operation was radically different from that of the German offensive in 1942. We would attack by a counter-stroke at the moment when the enemy had largely engaged and partially expended his assault forces. Our objective would no longer be the conquest of distant geographical points but the destruction of the Soviet southern wing by trapping it against the coast. To prevent his escape eastwards, as was the case in 1942, we would entice him to the lower Dniepr, as it would be impossible for him to resist this.

"If the operation succeeded, with the consequent heavy losses he would sustain, we could perhaps strike a second blow northwards, towards the centre of the front."

Certainly Manstein was under no illusion that the method he advocated could decide the war in favour of the Third Reich; but at least the situation would again be in Germany's favour and she would obtain what Manstein terms a "putting off" and Mellenthin a "stalemate", enabling her to bide her time. But Hitler did not agree with this line of argument, countering it with his usual economic arguments: Nikopol' manganese, for instance–"to lose Nikopol' would be to lose the war" was his last word, and at the meeting in Munich, Manstein did not raise his plan again.

The Soviet authorities still deny the implication of Manstein's criticism of the Red Army high command, yet the counter-offensive which had recently given Khar'kov back to the Germans seems to furnish abundant proof of Manstein's point.

Nonetheless, there is no certainty that Manstein's plan would have been as successful as he claimed it would. Indeed, just as with the offensive directed against the Kursk salient, it had little chance of securing the advantage of surprise. For never before had the direct line linking O.K.W. and O.K.H. with the Soviet agent Rudolf Rössler functioned so surely and swiftly.

At all events, when he opened proceedings, Hitler had made reference to a report that had been sent him by Colonel-General Walther Model, whose 9th Army was to supply the north-to-south thrust of the operation. It is beyond question that a commander of Model's dynamic energy approved of the offensive in principle, but he registered concern at making an attempt in May that should have been made in March, for the enemy forces in the Kursk salient had not meanwhile been wasting their time. According to Guderian, "Model had produced information, based largely on air photography, which showed that the Russians were preparing deep and very strong defensive positions in exactly those areas where the attack by the two army groups were to go in. The Russians had already withdrawn the mass of their mobile formations from the forward area of the salient; in anticipation of a pincer attack, as proposed in this plan of ours, they had strengthened the localities of our possible

Pzkw IV's move through the outskirts of a Russian town.

break-throughs with unusually strong artillery and anti-tank forces. Model drew the correct deduction from this, namely, that the enemy was counting on our launching this attack and that in order to achieve success we must adopt a fresh tactical approach; the alternative was to abandon the whole idea."

Some weeks earlier, Colonel von Mellenthin, in his capacity as chief-of-staff of XLVIII Panzer Corps, which had been given an important part to play in the plans, had voiced the same opinion to General Zeitzler. By holding up the offensive until a first brigade of Panther tanks had been formed, as Hitler intended, the Russians would be given time to recover from the losses inflicted on them. For this they only needed a month or two, and the operation would then be a far more difficult, and hence costly, one. Although Manstein had been lukewarm in his attitude towards the operation at the outset, once it had been decided he pronounced against any procrastination: "Any delay with 'Zitadelle' would increase the risk to Army Group 'South's' defensive front considerably. The enemy was not yet in a position to launch an attack on the Mius and the Donets. But he certainly would be in June. 'Zitadelle' was certainly not going to be easy, but I concluded that we must stick by the decision to launch it at the earliest possible moment and, like a cavalryman, 'leaping before you look', a comparison which I quickly realised made no effect on Hitler, who had little appreciation either of cavalrymen or horses."

Model's line of reasoning made its due impression on Hitler, who had total confidence in him. On May 10, Hitler told Guderian: "Whenever I think of this attack my stomach turns over." And he was all the more disposed to let the date of the offensive be decided by the state of preparedness of the Panthers. On information that 324 Panthers would be ready on May 31, he settled D-day for June 15, in spite of Manstein's advice. But there were further delays, and Operation "Zitadelle" was not begun until July 5, a delay of two months on the original timetable.

As had been pointed out above, the left flank of the offensive was drawn from Army Group "Centre" and the right from Army Group "South". Manstein had concentrated *Gruppe* Kempf, reinforced by one Panzer corps and two infantry corps in the Belgorod sector; its rôle as it moved northwards was to guard the eastward flank of the armoured units of the 4th *Panzerarmee* (Colonel-General Hoth) upon which the main task would devolve; he therefore transferred to it the II *Waffen* S.S. Panzer Corps (General Hausser) with its three *Panzergrenadier* divisions: "Leibstandarte", "Das Reich", and "Totenkopf", as well as XLVIII Panzer Corps, which under the command of General O. von Knobelsdorff included an infantry division, the 3rd and 11th Panzer Divisions, and the "Grossdeutschland" *Panzergrenadier* Division, whose 190

Soviet infantry and tanks on the attack.

tanks and self-propelled guns were supported by a brigade of 200 Panthers. XXIV Panzer Corps (17th Panzer Division and "Wiking" *Panzergrenadier* Division) were held in reserve.

In Army Group "Centre", the 9th Army, to the south of Orel, had organised itself as a wedge. In the centre, XLVII Panzer Corps (General Rauss), with five Panzer divisions, constituted its battering ram; it was flanked on the right by XLVI Panzer Corps and XX Corps, on the left by XLI Panzer Corps and XXIII Corps; this flank, which was exposed to counter-attacks from the east, had been reinforced by the 12th Panzer Division and the 10th *Panzergrenadier* Division, under the command of XLI Panzer Corps. General Model's reserve consisted of one Panzer and one *Panzergrenadier* division.

Taken together, "Zitadelle" involved 41 divisions, all of them German, including 18 Panzer and *Panzergrenadier* divisions. Manstein had at his own disposal 1,081 tanks and 376 assault guns; air support was given by *Luftflotte* IV, as whose commander Manstein would have liked to see Field-Marshal von Richthofen, who was kicking his heels in Italy. But Hitler was obstinate in his refusal to transfer him. Model, whose eight Panzer divisions had been brought up to a strength of 100 tanks each, had as many vehicles as he could use. His air support was provided by *Luftflotte* VI.

According to a perfectly correct comment in the *Great Patriotic War*, when spring came round again, Stalin had more than sufficient means at hand to take the initiative. But confronted by the German preparations against the Kursk salient reported to him by General N. F. Vatutin, new commander of the Voronezh Front, from April 21 onwards Stalin felt, the same work assures us, that it "was more expedient to oppose the enemy with a defensive system constructed in due time, echeloned in depth, and insuperable. On the basis of propositions made to it by the commanders at the front, Supreme Headquarters resolved to wear the enemy

out decisively in the course of his assault, by defensive action, then to smash him by means of a counter-offensive."

Hence, by a curious coincidence, Stalin came round to the idea of "return attack" at the very time that Hitler refused to let Manstein attempt to apply it. With the Panzers smashed in the salient around Kursk, it would be a far easier task to defeat Army Groups "Centre" and "South" and attain the objectives that had been set for the end of autumn 1943: Smolensk, the Sozh, the middle and lower Dniepr, and Kerch' Strait, thus liberating the eastern parts of White Russia and the Ukraine, the Donets basin, and what the Germans still held in the Kuban'.

It is true that in adopting these tactics, Stalin had the advantage of detailed information as to the strength and intentions of the adversary and that he followed the "Zitadelle" preparations very closely: "Rössler," write Accoce and Quiet, "gave them full and detailed description in his despatches. Once again, *Werther*, his little team inside O.K.W., had achieved a miracle. Nothing was missing. The sectors to be attacked, the men and *matériel* to be used, the position of the supply columns, the chain of command, the positions of reinforcements, D-day, and zero hour. There was nothing more to be desired and the Russians desired nothing more. They simply waited, confident of victory."

And their confidence was all the greater because first-hand information and reports from partisans confirmed the radio messages of their conscientious informer in Lucerne. Accoce and Quiet make no exaggeration. From a memo of the period it appears that in July 1943 Stalin believed he had 210 enemy divisions, excluding Finns, facing him. The official O.K.W. record for July 7 of that year gives 210 exactly, plus five regiments.

Hitler's delays allowed the Russians to organise the battlefield on which the attack was anticipated and to do so to a depth of between 16 and 25 miles. A cunning combination of minefields was intended to channel the German armoured units onto what the Russians called "anti-tank fronts", solid defence sectors particularly well provided with anti-tank guns.

The defence of the Kursk salient, which had a front of about 340 miles, was entrusted to the Central and Voronezh Fronts. The Central Front, under the command of General Rokossovsky, had five armies deployed forward, a tank army in second echelon, and two tank corps and a cavalry corps in reserve. The Voronezh Front (General Vatutin) had four armies forward, two more armies (one of them a tank army) in second echelon, and two tank and one rifle corps in reserve. The Steppe Front (Colonel-General I. S. Konev), positioned east of Kursk, constituted the *Stavka* reserve, and comprised five (including one tank) armies, plus one tank, one mechanised, and three cavalry corps in reserve.

Air support was provided by some 2,500 planes from the 2nd and 16th Air Armies.

The crew of a T-34 surrender to a German soldier. But such German successes were limited and had no effect on the outcome of the battle.

Even now, Soviet historians, who are so precise in the case of the German Army, decline to tell us the number of divisions and tanks involved in this battle; nevertheless, if we take a figure of roughly 75 infantry divisions and 3,600 tanks, this would appear to be about right. The *Great Patriotic War*, however, drops its reserve in speaking of the artillery. If we believe what we read, and there is no reason not to do so, Rokossovsky and Vatutin could count on no fewer than 20,000 guns, howitzers, and mortars, including 6,000 anti-tank guns, and 920 rocket launchers. For example, in order to bar the axis along which it was expected that Model's main thrust would be developed, Rokossovsky allocated to Pukhov's 13th Army a whole additional corps of artillery, totalling some 700 guns and mortars. The defensive potential of the Red Army thus surpassed the offensive potential of the Germans, and their complete knowledge of Field-Marshals von Kluge's and von Manstein's dispositions and proposed axes of advance enabled the Russians to concentrate their artillery and armoured

units so as to prevent them moving in the direction intended. In the evening of July 4 a pioneer from a Sudeten division deserted to the Russians and revealed the zero hour for Operation "Zitadelle".

Now that most of the pieces on the chessboard are in place we can deal quickly with the actual sequence of events in the Battle of Kursk which, on July 12, ended in an irreversible defeat for the Wehrmacht. Far from taking the enemy by surprise, the German 9th Army, following close on the desertion mentioned above, was itself surprised by a massive artillery counter-barrage, which struck its jump-off points in the final stages of preparation 20 minutes before zero hour. By evening, XLVII and XLI Panzer Corps, consisting of seven armoured divisions, had advanced only six miles across the defences of the Soviet 13th Army, and their 90 "Ferdinands" or "Elefants", being without machine guns, were unable to cope with the Russian infantry. More important, XXIII Corps, guarding the left flank, was stopped short of Malo-Arkhangelsk. On July 7, spurred on by the vigorous leadership of General Rauss, XLVII Panzer Corps reached the outskirts of Olkhovatka, less than 12 miles from its start line. There the German 9th Army was finally halted.

Army Group "South's" part of "Zitadelle" got off to a better start, thanks largely to impeccable co-ordination between tanks and dive-bombers. In the course of engagements which Manstein in his memoirs describes as extremely tough, *Gruppe* Kempf succeeded in breaking through two defence lines and reaching a point where it could intercept Steppe Front reinforcements coming to the aid of Voronezh Front. On July 11 the situation might be thought to be promising.

For 48 hours the 4th *Panzerarmee* met a solid wall of resistance of which General F. W. von Mellenthin, at that time chief-of-staff to XLVIII Panzer Corps, provides the following description in his book *Panzer Battles:*

"During the second and third days of the offensive we met with our first reverses. In spite of our soldiers' courage and determination, we were unable to find a gap in the enemy's second defence line. The *Panzergrenadier* Division "Grossdeutschland" (Lieutenant-General Hoerlein) which had gone into battle in extremely tight formation and had come up against an extremely marshy tract of ground, was stopped by prepared fortifications defended with anti-tank guns, flame-throwers, and T-34 tanks, and was met by violent artillery fire. For some time it remained unable to move in the middle of the battlefield devised by the enemy. It was no easy task for our pioneers to find and fix a passable route through numerous minefields or across the tracts of marshland. A large number of tanks were blown up by mines or destroyed by aerial attacks: the Red Air Force showed little regard for the fact of the Luftwaffe's superiority and fought the battle with remarkable determination and spirit."

On July 7, however, XLVIII Panzer Corps and on its right II *Waffen* S.S. Panzer Corps found themselves unopposed, after repulsing heavy counter-attacks by tanks which developed as pincer movements. Thus on July 11, after establishing a bridgehead on the Psel and getting close to Oboyan, the 4th *Panzerarmee* had advanced 18 to 20 miles through Vatutin's lines, while *Gruppe "Kempf"*, without having been able to land on the western bank of the Korocha had nevertheless managed to fulfil its primary task of protecting the 4th *Panzerarmee's* right flank. Two days later, Manstein reported that since D-day he had taken 24,000 prisoners and destroyed or captured 100 tanks and 108 anti-tank guns, and intended to move up his reserve, XXIV Panzer Corps.

These, however, were limited successes and *"Zitadelle"* was a serious reverse for Hitler. Between the spearhead of the 4th *Panzerarmee*, on the edge of Oboyan, and the vanguard of the 9th Army, forced to halt before Olkhovatka, the gap between the two armies remained, and would remain, 75 miles.

Far from feeling discouragement, Vatutin made known to *Stavka* in the evening of July 10 his intention of counter-attacking, and bringing up for this purpose his 5th Guards Tank Army (Lieutenant-General P. A. Rotmistrov) with its 850 tanks and assault guns, as well as the 1st Tank Army (Lieutenant-General M. E. Katukov).

On the other side of the battlefield, Rokossovsky addressed the following rousing order of the day to his troops on July 12: "The soldiers of the Central Front who met the enemy with a rampart of murderous steel and truly Russian grit and tenacity have exhausted him after a week of unrelenting and unremitting fighting; they have contained the enemy's drive. The first phase of the battle is over."

And indeed, on that same July 12, the Soviet armies of the Bryansk and West Front, following a predetermined plan, proceeded to launch a major offensive against the German-held Orel salient.

With the unexpected development of the situation in the Kursk area, Hitler summoned Kluge and Manstein to his H.Q. at Rastenburg on July 13. Kluge left the Führer with no illusions: the 9th Army, which had lost 20,000 men in a single week, was both incapable of advancing further and at the same time obliged to relinquish part of its remaining strength to bolster the defence of the Orel salient. Manstein was less pessimistic, yet in order for him to be able to compel the Russians to continue to fight, as he proposed, on this altered front in the Kursk region, Kluge had to pin down the maximum Soviet forces in his sector. The argument was thus circular.

Hitler decided matters by simply abandoning the operation. Yet – and this has been insufficiently remarked upon – his decision was motivated not so much by the local situation or by the Russian

offensive in the Orel salient as by the fact of the Anglo-American landings in Sicily.

According to Manstein, the Führer took a particularly gloomy view of the immediate outlook in this new theatre of operations: "The situation in Sicily has become extremely serious," he informed the two field-marshals. "The Italians are not resisting and the island will probably be lost. As a result, the Western powers will be able to land in the Balkans or in southern Italy. Hence new armies must be formed in these areas, which means taking troops from the Eastern Front, and hence calling a halt to *'Zitadelle'*." And there is the proof that the second front in the Mediterranean, derided by President Roosevelt, by Harry Hopkins, and by General Marshall, achieved what none of them expected of it: relief for Russia.

Thus ended the Battle of Kursk which, involving as it did more than 5,400 armoured and tracked vehicles, must be counted the greatest tank battle of World War II.

Some commentators have compared it with the ill-starred offensive launched by General Nivelle which ground to a halt on April 16, 1917 on the steep slopes up to the Chemin des Dames. But it would seem to bear greater similarity to Ludendorff's final attempt to give victory to the German Army. On July 15, 1918, the Quartermaster-General of the Imperial German Army was brought to a stand-still in Champagne by Pétain's system of defence in depth, and this failure allowed Foch to detach Mangin and Degoutte in a French offensive against the Château-Thierry salient. Subsequently the new Marshal of France extended his battle-line to left and to right and the German retreat lasted until the armistice of November 11.

There is one difference between these two sets of circumstances. On August 10, 1918, on receiving the news that Sir Douglas Haig's tanks had scattered the German defence in Picardy, Wilhelm II declared to Hindenburg and to Ludendorff: "This to my mind is the final reckoning", and this flash of common sense spared Germany the horrors of invasion. In July 1943, Hitler, the head of state, was incapable of making a similar observation to Hitler, the war leader, still less of parting company with him as the Kaiser parted company with Ludendorff on October 26, 1918.

The Panzer defeat in the Kursk salient has had its historians in both camps, but it also had its prophet, who in the spring of 1939 mused on the question of what might be the result should an army of tanks collide with a similar army given a defensive function. And in the course of examining this hypothesis which he declared had been neglected at the following conclusion and another question: "On land, there does exist a means of halting a tank offensive: a combination of mines and anti-tank guns. What would happen to an offensive by

tank divisions which encountered a defence composed of similar tank divisions, but ones which had been carefully deployed and had had time to work out a considered fire-plan on the chosen battle-field, on which anti-tank firepower was closely co-ordinated with natural obstacles reinforced by minefields?"

Thus, three or four months before the war broke out, Marshal Pétain expressed himself in a preface to General Chauvineau's book *Is an Invasion Still Possible?* that is often quoted and never read. And the event itself would prove him right – but on a scale beyond the wildest imaginings in 1939: to stop 1,800 German tanks it required 3,600 Soviet tanks, 6,000 anti-tank weapons, and 400,000 mines!

Just as Foch, once he had reduced the Château-Thierry salient in 1918, never ceased to widen his battle-front, so Stalin was to proceed after taking the bastion of Orel. This meant that nine out of his twelve Fronts or army groups would now be engaged. From July 5 his order of battle was to comprise the following Fronts, stretching from the Gulf of Finland to Novorossiysk on the Black Sea:

Kalinin (A. I. Eremenko)
West (V. D. Sokolovsky)
Bryansk (M. M. Popov)
Central (K. K. Rokossovsky)
Voronezh (N. F. Vatutin)
Steppe (I. S. Konev)
South-West (R. Ya. Malinovsky)
South (F. I. Tolbukhin)
Transcaucasus (I. E. Petrov)

The commanders' names are worth more than a passing glance, as they make up a team which was to remain remarkably stable right through to the end of the war. Others were to be added (those of Bagramyan and Chernyakhovsky for example), but the top echelons of the Red Army experienced none of that avalanche of disgraces and dismissals which characterised the Wehrmacht after the spring of 1944. Stalin could rightly trust his generals.

On July 12, as we have seen, Generals Sokolovsky and Popov started the Soviet summer offensive by attacking the Orel salient from the north and east along a front of some 190 miles. The line was defended by the 2nd *Panzerarmee* (Colonel-General Rudolf Schmidt) with 12 divisions up and two in reserve, one of which was *Panzergrenadier*. It is true that since the front had stabilised in this sector the Germans had greatly strengthened their positions. So on the West Front the 11th Guards Army (Lieutenant-General I. Kh. Bagramyan), responsible for the main thrust towards Orel, got 3,000 guns and 400 rocket-launchers. It also had 70 regiments of infantry, compared with Rokossovsky's 34 for the final attack on the Stalingrad pocket. It is not to be wondered at, therefore, that Bagramyan's offensive, supported, it is true, by 250 tanks, covered over 15 miles in 48 hours. On the Bryansk Front the 61st Army (Lieutenant-General P. A. Belov) attacked Mtsensk, whilst further south the 3rd and 63rd Armies (Lieutenant-Generals A. V. Gorbatov and V. Ya. Kolpakchy) came to grips with the German XXXV Corps (General Rendulic), which was stretched out to the tune of 24 battalions on 75 miles of front, and made a gap in it from seven to ten miles wide. Through the breaches made by artillery and infantry the armour poured in.

Right away a pincer movement began to form, threatening to close in on the defenders of the salient. So Field-Marshal von Kluge relieved Model of the majority of his motorised divisions in order to keep gaps plugged. This sufficed for the immediate danger, but did not halt the Red Army's advance. Furthermore, the armies on the Central Front moved forward and threatened Model's already weakened position. Alexander Werth has left an account of what this gigantic battle was like between not only men determined on victory but also weapons of terrifying power:

"By July 15, after three days' heavy fighting, the Russians had broken through the main lines of the German defences round the Orel salient. There had never been, (said General Sobennikov, commander of the garrison of Orel) such a heavy concentration of Russian guns as against these defences; in many places the fire-power was ten times heavier than at Verdun. The German minefields were so thick and widespread that as many mines as possible had to be blown up by the super-barrage, in order to reduce Russian casualties in the subsequent break-through. By July 20, the Germans tried to stop the Russian advance by throwing in hundreds of planes; and it was a job for the Russian anti-aircraft guns and fighters to deal with them. In the countless air-battles there were very heavy casualties

The "Russian steamroller" surges on, with infantrymen snatching rides to the front on two T-34 tanks.

on both sides. Many French airmen were killed, too, during those days."

The partisans, as Werth also relates, played an equally important rôle in these operations: "On July 14, 1943, the Soviet Supreme Command ordered the partisans to start an all-out Rail War. Preparations for this had obviously already been made, for on July 20-21 great co-ordinated blows were struck at the railways in the Bryansk, Orel, and Gomel areas, to coincide with the Russian offensive against Orel and Bryansk following the Kursk victory. During that night alone 5,800 rails were blown up. Altogether, between July 21 and September 27, the Orel and Bryansk partisans blew up over 17,000 rails . . .

"Telpukhovsky's semi-official History claims that in three years (1941-4) the partisans in Belorussia killed 500,000 Germans including forty-seven generals and Hitler's High-Commissioner Wilhelm Kube (who, as we know from German sources–though the Russians for some reason don't mention this–had a partisan time-bomb put under his bed by his lovely Belorussian girl-friend)."

And so on July 29, 1943 there appears for the first time in communiqués from the Wehrmacht the expression "elastic defence" which might have been thought banned for ever from Hitlerian terminology. This was a delaying tactic which allowed Army Group "Centre" to evacuate the Orel salient, systematically burning the crops behind it, and to regroup along a front line covering Bryansk from the high ground round Karachev. This movement, completed around August 4, provided only temporary respite, as the comparative strengths of the opposing forces remained unchanged.

The situation was worse still between the area from north-west of Belgorod to the Sea of Azov, over a front of about 650 miles defended by Manstein:

"On July 17 our 29 infantry and 13 armoured or motorised divisions were

facing 109 infantry divisions, nine infantry brigades, ten tank, seven mechanised and seven cavalry corps, plus 20 independent tank brigades, 16 tank regiments and eight anti-tank brigades. Between that date and September 7 these forces were increased by 55 infantry divisions, two tank corps, eight tank brigades, and 12 tank regiments, most of them brought over from the Central and the North Fronts. All in all we must have been outnumbered by seven to one.

"This superiority allowed the Russians not only to go on to the offensive with overwhelming power, often in several places at once, but also to make up their losses, even when very heavy, in an astonishingly short space of time. Thus between July and September, they were able to withdraw from the front 48 divisions and 17 tank corps and reform them, some of the formations even twice, as well as providing reinforcements for all their divisions of up to ten per cent of their fighting strength."

This, according to the Soviet command, was the tally of the Red Army's strength on the South, South-West, Steppe, and Voronezh Fronts: 21 armies facing the one German Army Group "South". Manstein, whose 1st *Panzerarmee* was being driven back at Slavyansk as Tolbukhin was trying to make a breakthrough over the Mius river, was now driven to certain extremes. At Rastenburg, however, Hitler's answer to the strategic problems now arising was to argue economics and politics: the Donets coalfields, the manganese at Nikopol', the indispensable iron ore at Krivoy-Rog, Hungarian morale, the opinion of Bucharest, Bulgarian troop positions, Turkish neutrality, and so on.

This reached such a point that at the end of July Manstein was emboldened to write to Zeitzler: "If the Führer thinks he has at hand a C.-in-C. or an Army Group with nerves stronger than ours were last winter, capable of greater initiative than we showed in the Crimea, on the Donets, or at Khar'kov, able to find better solutions than we did in the Crimea or during the last winter campaign, or to foresee better than we did how the situation will develop, then I am ready to hand over my responsibilities. But whilst these are still mine I reserve the right to use my brains."

In effect, faced with the concentric offensive launched on the South and the South-West Fronts, which threatened to involve the new German 6th Army (Colonel-General Hollidt) in a disaster equal in magnitude to that of Stalingrad, Manstein had decided to evacuate the Donets basin, which would have the additional advantage of shortening his front. Yet Hitler had expressly forbidden such a step, just as he had refused Colonel-General Jaenecke permission to bring his 17th Army back over the Kerch' Strait into the Crimea, even though its 17 German and Rumanian divisions would have been more useful to the defence of the Donets than the Kuban' peninsula.

Under the circumstances imposed on him, Field-Marshal von Manstein was forced to make a dangerous move: to weaken his left flank between Belgorod and Sumy so as to strengthen his right in the hope (which was not fulfilled) of being able to make a stand before Konev and Vatutin were able to seize the opportunity offered to them. In fact the transfer of XXIV Panzer Corps (General Nehring) to the 1st *Panzerarmee* allowed the latter to plug the breach at Slavyansk, and the intervention of III Panzer Corps (General Breith) and the S.S. Panzer Corps gave General Hollidt the chance of inflicting a serious defeat on the South Front, which by July 30 had crossed back over the Mius, leaving behind 18,000 prisoners, 700 tanks, and 200 guns.

On August 3, however, more swiftly than Manstein can have supposed, Colonel-Generals Vatutin and Konev, considerably reinforced in artillery and rocket-launchers, made an attempt to drive a wedge between *Gruppe* "Kempf" and the 4th *Panzerarmee*. By the afternoon they were through and had pushed two mechanised armies into the gap. August 5 saw the liberation of Belgorod; on the 7th the Russian 1st Tank Army reached Bogodukhov, nearly 70 miles from its starting point. This breakthrough was now developing in the most dangerous direction for the German forces between the Sea of Azov and Khar'kov: towards Dniepropetrovsk. And so, to keep down his losses Manstein again switched the *Waffen* S.S. Panzer Corps and III Panzer Corps to this front, whilst on the orders of O.K.H. his comrade Kluge gave him back the "Grossdeutschland" Panzergrenadier Division which, on the day after "Zitadelle", had been engaged in the Orel salient. As we can see, the Panzers roamed all over this immense battlefield from one point of conflagration to another, just as the firemen were doing during the same period in German towns.

By throwing in its recently-arrived divisions, the 4th *Panzerarmee* finally closed the gap which, in the Akhtyrka region, was now 35 miles wide. It was all over at Khar'kov, however, and the city fell on August 22 under the combined blows of the 5th Tank Army (General Rotmistrov) and the 53rd Army (Major-General I. M. Managarov). On August 30 Khruschev, General Vatutin's political aide, received the ovations of this second city in the Ukraine. According to the *Great Patriotic War*, which followed him all the way, he cried in tones full of profound Bolshevik fervour: "Let us now get back to work! Let us remain firmly united! Everything for the front; all for victory! Let us further close our ranks under this banner which has brought us victory! Onwards to the West! Onwards for the Ukraine!"

At Army Group "South" H.Q. on that same August 22, General Wöhler and the staff of a new 8th Army started to take over from *Gruppe* "Kempf" south of Khar'kov. Forty-eight hours later, re-

duced to 25 divisions, including three Panzer, fighting on a front of over 1,300 miles and with ever-shrinking strength, the 6th Army and the 1st *Panzerarmee* reeled under the blows of Tolbukhin's and Malinovsky's 60 infantry divisions and 1,300 tanks. No fire-brigade operation by the Panzers could stop this now and new threats were growing on the left flank of Army Group "South". The German 2nd Army was violently attacked by Rokossovsky who had come back into the battle. By September 7 Manstein's Panzer and *Panzergrenadier* forces had only 257 tanks and 220 assault guns left. There was thus nothing for it but to retreat, even if this meant the loss of the Donets basin and all its industrial wealth.

On September 9 Hitler went to Zaporozh'ye on the Dniepr bend to take stock of the situation with Field-Marshal von Manstein. After eight days of wearying argument, first one way then the other, permission was given for the army group to be withdrawn behind the deep valley of the Dniepr which, with its right bank overlooking the left, lends itself easily to defence. This meant evacuating the bridgehead in the Kuban' where Field-Marshal von Kleist's Army Group "A" and the 17th Army were being hard pressed by an enemy superior in numbers and *matériel*. On September 10 in particular, a combined amphibious

Soviet troops at one of the Dniepr bridgeheads established in autumn 1943.

operation by Vice-Admiral L. A. Vladimirsky, commander of the Black Sea Fleet, and Lieutenant-General K. N. Leselidze, commander of the 18th Army, put the Russian troops ashore in the port of Novorossiysk. Amongst the heroes of the day was the army's Chief Political Administrator, Leonide E. Brezhnev, today General Secretary of the Communist Party of the U.S.S.R.

The evacuation of the Taman' peninsula was begun in the night of September 15-16 and completed on October 9. The operation was commanded by Vice-Admiral Scheurlen, to the entire satisfaction of his chief, Dönitz, who goes on in his memoirs to give the figures: 202,477 fighting troops, 54,664 horses, 1,200 guns, and 15,000 vehicles ferried across the Kerch' Strait by the German Navy. In a statement which challenges the figures given by General of Mountain Troops R. Konrad, formerly commander of XLIX Mountain Corps, the *Great Patriotic War* claims that the retreat of the 17th Army cost the Germans thousands of men as a result of attacks both by the Red Army land forces and the Soviet Air Force, which sank 70 barges in the Straits. Of these two opposing versions, that of Dönitz and Konrad is more likely to be true since the Russian version fails to mention any of the equip-

Tank-borne Russian infantry move forward on the Kalinin Front.

ment captured between September 16 and October 9. Now back in the Ukraine, Field-Marshal von Kleist and H.Q. Army Group "A" received into their command the 6th Army, by which Manstein's burden had been lightened.

To get his troops across the Dniepr, Manstein had six crossing points between Zaporozh'ye downstream and Kiev upstream. The withdrawal was completed in ten days under cover of rearguards whose job it was to create scorched earth areas 15 miles deep on the left bank of the great river. Army Group "South", behind this obstacle, had been brought up to a strength of 54 divisions (17 Panzer and *Panzergrenadier*) but most of them were worn out. On its right was the 6th Army holding the front Zaporozh'ye–Sea of Azov through Melitopol'. On its left was the 2nd Army (General Weiss),back again under the orders of Kluge. Its right flank came down to the confluence of the Dniepr and the Pripyat'.

In his memoirs Manstein defends the systematic destruction of the land behind him, saying: "We had recourse to the 'scorched earth' policy used by the Russians during their retreat in the previous year. Anything which could be of use to the enemy in an area 12 to 18 miles deep in front of the Dniepr was systematically destroyed or carried away. It was, of course, never a question of plunder. The whole operation was strictly controlled to prevent abuse. Furthermore we only took away goods and chattels belonging to the State, never those privately owned.

"As the Russians, in any land they reoccupied, immediately conscripted any men under 60 capable of carrying arms and forced the remainder of the population to do military work, the German High Command ordered the local inhabitants to be transported over to the other bank of the Dniepr. This in fact was restricted to men who would at once have become soldiers. Yet a great part of the population joined in our retreat voluntarily to escape the Soviet authorities, whom they feared."

August and September were months as fatal to Kluge as they were to his colleague Manstein. This is not surprising, since by September 7 he was down to 108 tanks and 191 assault guns.

At the beginning of August Stalin went to H.Q. Kalinin Front. His inspection was recorded thus by the Soviet official historian: "This was the only occasion during the war when Stalin went to visit the troops at the front. At this period it was relatively quiet. This visit had virtually no effect on preparations for the operation against Smolensk." Of greater encouragement no doubt was the visit of N. N. Voronov, delegated to Eremenko by *Stavka* and, after the Stalingrad victory, promoted Marshal and Commander-in-Chief of Artillery.

The battle opened at dawn on August 7, but for four days the German 4th Army, better commanded by General S. Heinrici, beat off the Russian attacks. On August 11 a breach was opened at Kirov and exploited by Eremenko towards Yel'nya and Dorogobuzh, which fell at the end of the month.

On September 19 the West Front met the southward advance of the Kalinin Front and on September 25 the armies entered the important city of Smolensk on the border of Belorussia.

Further south still, Colonel-General Popov had defeated Model's attempts to deny his advance to Bryansk. On September 19 this important centre of communications on the Desna had been recaptured by troops from the Front which bore its name.

The respite gained by Manstein in bringing his troops (the 1st *Panzerarmee,* 8th Army, and 4th *Panzerarmee*) over to the west bank of the Dniepr was shortlived, for Vatutin, Konev, and Malinovsky literally followed at their heels without noticeable hindrance from either the autumn rains or the destruction caused by the retreating Germans. Communications were restored with a speed which aroused everyone's admiration. The engineering and signals commanders, Colonel-Generals Vorobliov and Peresypkin were promoted Marshals of their respective arms of the service by a decision of February 22, 1944.

Hardly had the Russians reached the river than they began to establish bridgeheads on the right bank on either side of Kiev, between Kremenchug and Dniepropetrovsk and up-river from Zaporozh'ye. By October 1 one of these, secured by General Konev, was nearly ten miles deep and over 15 miles wide, thus putting the whole of the river in this area out of range of the German artillery. Magnificent exploits were accomplished by the soldiers, who earned between them 10,000 decorations and 2,000 citations for "Hero of the Soviet Union". On the other side, however, the infantry divisions of Army Group "South" were reduced to a few thousand men each. Manstein's losses had been mounting steadily during the clashes since mid-July but he had only received 33,000 men in replacement, and as usual it was the "poor bloody infantry" who came off worst.

It took the Russians just about ten days to renew their offensive in this theatre of operations. They threw their armies in simultaneously on the Voronezh, Steppe, South-West, and South Fronts, which for this offensive were renamed the 1st, 2nd, 3rd, and 4th Ukrainian Fronts respectively.

From September 26 the German 6th Army of Army Group "A" found itself under attack from the four armies of the 4th Ukrainian Front. It held out until October 9 then between the 10th and the 20th the battle swayed to and fro for the capture of Melitopol'. The bitterness of the resistance, which did honour to the defence, was also the reason why, after the final collapse, Tolbukhin was able to advance unopposed from Melitopol' to the estuary of the Dniepr. Furthermore, the completely bare and featureless landscape of the Nogayskiye Steppe greatly favoured the headlong advance of the tanks and the cavalry of the Soviet 51st

Army (Lieutenant-General V. F. Gerasimenko).

At the beginning of November troops of the 4th Ukrainian Front were outside Kherson. The German 17th Army had failed to force a passage across the Kamenskoye peninsula and was thus trapped in the Crimea. It was now threatened from the rear as Colonel-General Petrov was striving to get his 18th Army across the Kerch' Strait. At the same time, Army Group "South" narrowly escaped disaster twice and only recovered thanks to its commander's powers of manoeuvre. Operating on both sides of the bend in the Dniepr, Colonel-General Malinovsky's intention was to wipe out the Zaporozh'ye bridgehead and at the same time, by breaking the 1st *Panzerarmee*'s front above Dniepropetrovsk, exploit the breakthrough along the axis Krivoy-Rog–Apostolovo in the general direction of the river below Dniepropetrovsk. He was not short of men or *matériel*: the 3rd Ukrainian Front had no fewer than eight armies, or a good 50 divisions. Though Hitler had helped the Russians by refusing Manstein permission to withdraw from Dniepropetrovsk, the Soviet manoeuvre did not entirely succeed. On October 14 Zaporozh'ye was taken by a night attack, which brought distinction to General Chuikov, the heroic defender of Stalingrad, and his 8th Army, but after a lightning start under the most favourable of forecasts, General Rotmistrov and his 5th Guards Tank Army, having reached the outskirts of Krivoy-Rog, were held and counter-attacked concentrically by XL Panzer Corps, reinforced by the 24th Panzer Division freshly arrived from Italy. By October 28, their ammunition having failed to follow up in time, they had withdrawn over 15 miles and left behind them 10,000 dead, 5,000 prisoners, 357 tanks, and 378 guns.

This last minute success by the Germans stabilised the situation again, and allowed them to get their troops out of the Dniepropetrovsk salient without much difficulty. They were thus all the more startled to hear, on November 3, the guns of VIII Artillery Corps telling Manstein that Vatutin was preparing to break out of the bridgehead he had won above Kiev. Once more the Russians had managed things well: 2,000 guns at over 500 per mile. Yet contemporary photos show that they were all strung out in a line without the least pretence of camouflage. Where was the Luftwaffe? Nothing more than a memory now.

Under the moral effect of the pulverising attack of 30 infantry divisions and 1,500 tanks, the 4th *Panzerarmee* shattered like glass and during the night of November 5-6, VII Corps hastily evacuated the Ukrainian capital. The sun had not yet risen on this historic day when Colonel-General Vatutin and his Council of War telegraphed *Stavka:* "Have the joy to inform you that the mission you entrusted to us to liberate our splendid city of Kiev, the capital of the Ukraine, has been

A German light flak emplacement at Kerch'.

carried out by the troops of the 1st Ukrainian Front. The city of Kiev has been completely cleared of its Fascist occupants. The troops of the 1st Ukrainian Front are actively pursuing the task you entrusted to them." The 3rd Guards Tank Army (General Rybalko) dashed in at lightning speed to exploit the situation. By November 12 the bridgehead up-river from Kiev had widened to 143 miles and at its deepest beyond Zhitomir it was 75 miles beyond the Dniepr. The rapidity of this advance is perhaps less striking when it is realised that the 11 infantry divisions of the 4th Army were about one regiment strong and its 20th *Panzer-grenadier* Division was soon wiped out.

Perhaps General Vatutin had exaggerated the extent of his victory: as it was, he threw in his columns at all points of the compass between north-west and south-west and this dispersal of the Soviet resources gave Manstein the chance to have another go at him. Refusing to be put off by the Russian manoeuvre, he made a last switch of his armour and brought XLVIII and LVII Panzer Corps into the Berdichev–Shepetovka area, reinforcing them with three armoured divisions and the *"Leibstandarte" Waffen*-S.S. *Panzer-grenadier* Division, putting them under the command of the 4th *Panzerarmee* (General E. Raus, an Austrian officer). General H. Balck, who had again taken up command of XLVIII Panzer Corps, would have liked to see a counter-offensive with Kiev as its objective, thus providing the opportunity for turning the tables on the Russians. Raus spoke up for an attack on Zhitomir first, a cautious move but one with less potential, and Manstein supported him. Considering the alternating freezing and thawing characteristic of November weather in the Ukraine, the Zhitomir solution admittedly seemed the most likely to succeed immediately, wheareas a move towards

Kiev was a long-term gamble which Manstein could not risk.

As it was, the 4th *Panzerarmee* attacked from the south in a northerly direction and on November 15 cut the Kiev-Zhitomir road. During the night of the 17th-18th, XLVIII Panzer Corps took Zhitomir after a neat swing from north to west. The 3rd Guards Tank Army was taken by surprise and, attempting to regain the initiative, had its I Cavalry Corps, and V and VII Tank Corps caught in a pincer. Escape cost it 3,000 killed and the loss of 153 tanks and 70 guns. On December 1, LVII Panzer Corps (General Kirchner), which formed General Raus's left flank, returned to Korosten. Some days later Balck, daringly exploiting his success, recaptured Radomyshl' on the Teterev and Malin on the Irsha. Then, in collaboration with Kirchner, he attempted to encircle three tank corps and a dozen infantry divisions which were trying to block his advance eastwards. The German pincers, however, were too slow in closing round the enemy, who managed to slip away. On December 23 Manstein was able to draw up a balance-sheet of this operation: he had got back to within 25 miles of Kiev, and had killed 20,000 of the enemy and captured or destroyed 600 tanks, 300 guns, and 1,200 anti-tank weapons, but had only taken 5,000 prisoners. Bad weather and low cloud had, however, helped the operations of the 4th *Panzerarmee,* shielding it from observation and from attack by the Red Air Force. German air support was now so rare that the time was past when the generals hoped for long spells of fine weather.

On the other hand this partial success brought a grievous reversal of fortune. To prevent a collapse on his left flank, Manstein had been compelled to draw

A Katyusha rocket battery is prepared for action. The massive fire-power of the Katyusha made it invaluable.

on his strength in the centre. Here the 8th Army had been deprived of five divisions, including four Panzer, and was thus forced to give way under the pressure of the 2nd Ukrainian Front. On December 10 the important rail junction of Znamenka fell to Colonel-General Konev. On the 14th he took Cherkassy on the Dniepr in spite of stiff resistance by the German 72nd Division and the "Wiking" Waffen-S.S. *Panzergrenadier* Division.

Events on the Central Front were not quite as dramatic, though during the autumn of 1943 they severely tested Field-Marshal von Kluge and his commanders. The enemy was superior in men and *matériel* and kept up his attacks relentlessly.

On October 6 the Kalinin Front, which was to become the 1st Baltic Front on the 20th, opened up an attack on the 3rd *Panzerarmee* at the point where Army Group "Centre" joined Army Group "North". Colonel-General Reinhardt's lines were very thin on the ground and the troops of the 2nd and 3rd Shock Armies were able to break through at Nevel'. The Russians then attempted to drive forwards from the ground they had won north of the Dvina, one arm thrusting towards Polotsk, the other towards Vitebsk. If they won these objectives, the way would then be open to the Baltic coast.

The Germans, however, made a determined stand and counter-attacked, discouraging any further advance by Eremenko's troops, who nevertheless were able to establish a position south of the Vitebsk–Polotsk railway. In the German 4th Army sector General Sokolovsky and his West Front made repeated attempts to force a crossing of the narrow strip of land between the Dvina at Vitebsk and the Dniepr at Orsha. Each attempt was repulsed with heavy losses to the Russians, who advanced on a narrow front and were massacred by General Heinrici's heavy concentrations of artillery, which in places amounted to 70 batteries under unified command. A Polish division, the "Tadeusz Kosciuszko", under Colonel Zygmunt Berling, fought in this battle wearing Red Army uniforms. By the turn of the year the 2nd Baltic Front, formerly the Bryansk Front, under Popov, had reached the Dniepr in the area of Zhlobin and the Belorussian Front, formerly the Central Front (Rokossovsky), was engaged at Mozyr', 56 miles beyond the Dniepr and in contact on its left with the 1st Ukrainian Front.

And so, for the German Army operating on the Eastern Front, 1943 was ending with an outlook as gloomy as that of 1942. There had been no new Stalingrad but between Kursk and Zhitomir the German resistance was on the verge of a breakdown. Since July, they had lost 104,000 men, half of these wounded. A remarkable inconsistency in the figures published at this time was revealed when

the Russians claimed 900,000 of the enemy had been killed and 1,700,000 wounded in this same period. More remarkable still was that on November 6, Stalin made a statement to the effect that the Germans had lost four million men in the past year. If this had been remotely true, the war would have been over.

It is undeniable, however, that the remorseless attacks of the Red Army were inexorably flattening the German armies along a 1,250-mile front.

Hence the growing pessimism in the German Army among the generals and chiefs-of-staff. In the preceding spring Field-Marshal von Manstein could still think that, if there were a reform of the high command, the Wehrmacht could still draw even. Six months later, when Lieutenant-General von Choltitz, acting commander of XLVIII Panzer Corps, spoke to his chief-of-staff, Mellenthin, it was not about drawing the game, or even of stalemate. According to the latter, Choltitz, as if in a vision, described the situation as waves of Soviet troops pouring over every breakwater Germany could contrive, possibly reaching Germany herself. Mellenthin thought Choltitz unduly pessimistic.

In fact Choltitz was not a congenital or professional pessimist. He merely saw the seriousness of the situation: in the East O.K.H. was throwing in exhausted troops; in the other theatres of war the divisions at the disposal of O.K.W. were "untouchable", as in Germany no-one doubted that the invasion would come sooner or later. On December 26, 1943, German divisions were deployed as follows:

East	192	(33 Panzer and *Panzergrenadier*)
Norway	10	
Denmark	2	
West	43	(4 Panzer and *Panzergrenadier*)
Italy	16	(5 Panzer and *Panzergrenadier*)
Balkans	15	

Thus on that day 86 of the 278 German divisions deployed between Rhodes and Narvik were unavailable for the Eastern Front and these included nine of the 42 Panzer and *Panzergrenadier* divisions.

That same autumn General Guderian, convinced of the need for a change in the high command, went to G.H.Q.:

"I went to see Jodl, to whom I submitted my proposals for a reorganisation of the Supreme Command: the Chief of the Armed Forces General Staff would control the actual conduct of operations, while Hitler would be limited to his proper field of activities, supreme control of the political situation and of the highest war strategy. After I had expounded my ideas at length and in detail Jodl replied laconically: 'Do you know of a better supreme commander than Adolf Hitler?' His expression had remained impassive as he said this, and his whole manner was one of icy disapproval. In view of his attitude I put my papers back in my briefcase and left the room."

CHAPTER 46
The situation in the Pacific

In the Pacific the year 1943 was marked, as far as Admiral Nimitz and General MacArthur were concerned, by a series of limited offensives which, whilst gradually wearing down the Japanese forces, were to give the Americans and their Australian allies the necessary bases for the decisive offensive of 1944. The objective of this latter offensive was the complete and final destruction of the Japanese military machine. No more than with the Germans were the Washington political and military leaders prepared to accept, with or without Tojo, anything less than Japan's total and unconditional surrender.

Any change of opinion over these radical aims would have aroused the opposition of the American public. When he held supreme command, Mussolini several times complained that his fellow citizens did not whole-heartedly support him in his war effort. The war against Japan was deeply felt by the American people and, in Churchill's entourage, during the conferences which took him across the Atlantic, it was often noticed that the reconquest of some obscure copra island in the far corner of the Pacific raised as much enthusiasm in New York and Washington as did a whole battle won in Africa or Italy. The White House and the Pentagon had to take these feelings into account.

Along with the concern shown by Roosevelt and Hopkins for the U.S.S.R., a concern which caused them to urge the opening of a second front, there was also the fact that the Americans did not look favourably on their hero MacArthur being kept short of men and *matériel* whilst in Europe U.S. forces stood idle on the wrong side of the Channel. In the Joint Chiefs-of-Staff Committee, that was the sentiment of the rugged Admiral Ernest J. King: instead of giving complete and immediate support to the principle of "Germany first", the centre of gravity of American power should be shifted over to the Pacific. To forestall this reversal of strategy the President and General Marshall were therefore constrained to set in motion Operation "Round-up", which was to become "Overlord".

On the ways to get to Tokyo and the means to be employed there was, to put it mildly, lively discussion between Admirals King and Nimitz on the one side and General MacArthur on the other. This is not surprising, as each of these leaders was a man of strong character and not given to compromise solutions of which his conscience would not approve. It fell to General Marshall to pronounce judgement on their arguments and, in the last resort, to impose a solution. We shall see under what circumstances he did this, but let us say at once that it was done with both authority and a sense of opportunity.

In the last biennial report he presented to the Secretary of War on September 1, 1945, General Marshall had entitled his chapter on the Pacific campaign in 1943 "Relentless Pressure". He introduced it in the following terms:

"It had always been the concept of the United States Chiefs-of-Staff that Japan could be best defeated by a series of amphibious attacks across the far reaches of the Pacific. Oceans are formidable barriers, but for the nation enjoying naval superiority they became highroads of invasion".

We must now consider the means put at the disposal of the commanders to exert this pressure and to crush the "advances" made by the enemy in the Pacific during the first half of 1942.

1. The South-West Pacific Area

At the headquarters of the C.-in-C. South-West Pacific, General MacArthur, they complained of having to fight a war "stony broke", a "Cinderella War", and being driven to "sling and arrow operations". Even so, on July 1, 1943, MacArthur had the Australian Army (ten divisions), a New Zealand contingent, and four American divisions (to be raised to eight by the end of the year). He was supported by the U.S. 3rd Fleet (Admiral William F. Halsey), although this was not put expressly under his command. Finally he had authority over Major-General George F. Kenney's 5th Air Force, which at the same date of July 1 had 150 four-engined bombers. Some months later the Pentagon allotted him the 13th Air Force (Major-General Nathan F. Twining). From this it will be concluded that the South-West Pacific theatre of operations was less deprived than General MacArthur's entourage might have led one to believe. The opposing forces were no stronger.

However, MacArthur did not complain of the scarcity of his resources and then sit back and do nothing: on the contrary he manoeuvred his divisions, his squadrons, and his warships with considerable determination and skill.

2. The Central Pacific Area

In the Central Pacific theatre, under the command of Admiral Nimitz, Lieutenant-General Robert C. Richardson Junior had on July 1 nine Army and Marine divisions and was energetically training them for amphibious operations which, during the forthcoming autumn and winter, would give the Americans possession of the enemy's forward defensive posts on the Tarawa, Makin, Majura, and Eniwetok atolls. This offensive, like MacArthur's, evidently depended on the naval or, even better, the naval-air superiority of the United States over Japan.

We must say something of the Americans' enormous naval effort, just as we have dealt with the development of their land forces.

Programmes completed in 1941 and 1942 had aimed particularly at replacing obsolete battleships and destroyers. In 1943 ships of all types brought into service were:

2 fast battleships of 45,000 tons
6 fleet aircraft-carriers of 27,000 tons
9 light aircraft-carriers of 11,000 tons
24 escort carriers
4 heavy cruisers (8-inch guns)
7 light cruisers (6-inch guns)
128 destroyers
200 submarines

and many auxiliary units and supply vessels. Of course, except for specialist anti-submarine vessels, this great effort went as a priority towards building up the Pacific theatre of operations.

The new units which came under Admiral Nimitz's command had all benefited from the experiences of the tough year of 1942. Naval architects in the immediate pre-war years had not taken sufficiently into account the threat to the surface vessel of the dive-bomber and the torpedo-carrying aircraft. Battleships, cruisers, and destroyers built under the new programme were to come out of the yards bristling with A.A. weapons of all shapes and sizes. The following table shows how a battleship was equipped before and after Pearl Harbor:

	West Virginia (1923)	New Jersey (1942)
5-inch	8	20
3-inch	4	0
40-mm	0	80
20-mm	0	50
.5-inch	10	0

In addition, the combined work of the Carnegie Institute in Washington, the John Hopkins University, and the National Bureau of Standards had produced a radio-electric fuse for the shells used by the Army and the Marines. This fuse, known as the proximity or V.T. (variable time) fuse, considerably increased the effectiveness of A.A. fire.

The V.T. fuse was first used in open sea in case it failed to go off and fell into enemy hands. On January 5, 1943 it scored its first success in the waters around the Solomon Islands, when two salvoes from the 5-inch guns of the cruiser *Helena* were enough to shoot down a torpedo-bomber. During the V-1 attacks on London the proximity fuse's efficiency against these 435 mph missiles reached 79 per cent under favourable conditions.

Naval-air engagements in 1942 cost Admiral Nimitz no fewer than four aircraft-carriers. Between January 1, 1943 and September 2, 1945 he used a succession of 27 (18 fleet and nine light) and lost only one in 32 months of ceaseless offensives. Yet these U.S. carriers were the prime target of the famous Kamikaze from October 1944 onwards. During the battle for Okinawa (April 1-June 7, 1945) six carriers were the victims of these suicide attacks, but not one was sunk, thanks to their sturdy construction and to the efficient fire-fighting services on board.

The reconquest of the Pacific and the defeat of Japan after Guadalcanal required many landing operations, supported by naval fire designed to crush the Japanese land defences regardless of the cost in ammunition. But, Admiral King tells us in his second report covering the period March 1, 1944 to March 1, 1945:

"At the time of the attack on Pearl Harbor, the Navy had virtually no high capacity ammunition (so-called because it contains an extremely high amount of explosive). Since then, production of this type of projectile has risen rapidly, and currently accounts for 75 per cent of the output of shells from six to sixteen inches in calibre. Monthly naval production of all types of major calibre ammunition now exceeds the total quantity delivered during World War I."

This supporting fire-power was given by the old battleships which had escaped at Pearl Harbor, suitably refitted and heavily reinforced with A.A. weapons.

Because of the huge area of the Pacific, Admiral King gave Nimitz an enormous number of supply-vessels comprising troop transports, ships carrying *matériel*, ammunition, food of all kinds, tankers, hospital ships with homely names such as *Comfort, Mercy, Consolation, Hope,* or *Tranquillity,* aircraft supply-ships, destroyers, submarines, and even floating docks capable of berthing the longest ships in the fleet. This great collection of vessels, known as the Maintenance Fleet, was to allow Halsey, Spruance, and Kinkaid to operate at sea for weeks at a time, relying only on temporary bases in the atolls.

As can be seen, in this field as well the American leaders, with no historical precedent to guide them, had seen big, wide, and far, whereas their enemy had relied on time-honoured methods of supply for his troops. The rapid build-up of the American air and sea offensive, resulting from the logistic organisation which we have just described in brief, secured in addition a devastating effect.

These material achievements of the U.S. Navy, remarkable though they were, would have been of little avail if they had not been accompanied by a similar build-up in the quality and the quantity of the men who were to benefit from them.

On the day after Pearl Harbor the American Navy had 337,274 officers, petty officers, and other ranks. Twelve months later there were more than a million (1,112,218 to be exact); this figure had increased by nearly 930,000 by the end of December 1943, and had reached about three million on the same date in the following year. This enormous recruiting and training effort required some 947 Instruction Centres which in June 1944 were being attended each day by 303,000 men of all ranks and specialities.

According to Admiral King in the report quoted above, the number of men on active service on the day the Japanese began their aggression was only a tenth of those available. In particular there had to be intensive training of nearly 300,000 officers, 131,000 of whom came straight from civilian life. "Nothing succeeds like success," says an old adage. In the event the methods used by the Navy in selection, basic instruction, specialised

An amphibious D.U.K.W. storms ashore.

training, posting, and promotion for all these men were close to perfection and gave the United States fleets well-manned ships which incurred only a minimum of accidents at sea.

The crews must on the whole have been like those described by J. Fahey, who has left us a fascinating diary of the Pacific campaign, through which he served on board the light cruiser *Montpelier* between February 1943 and August 1945 from Guadalcanal to the Ryukyu Islands. The daily entries made by this young sailor show him to be patriotic, a keen fighter, a skilled and conscientious gunner, cheerfully accepting chores, a good companion and one singularly well aware of the sense and the implications of the actions in which his ship was engaged. Furthermore, Leading Seaman Fahey's snap judgements on Admirals "Tip" Merrill, "Thirty-one knots" Burke, "Bull" Halsey and Mitscher, the "terrific guy" have all been borne out by history. Others have maintained that the Americans overcame their adversaries in Europe and Asia by sheer weight of *matériel*. This is to a large extent true, but the fact remains that this *matériel* was handled by well-trained, well-disciplined personnel.

In Japan the year's events bore out Admiral Yamamoto's prediction that his country would not be able to withstand the strains of a prolonged war. In contrast with the United States' steel production of 90 million tons in 1943, Japan made only 7.8 million tons, which in itself was over two millions short of what the government had planned. Also, in spite of the conquest of Borneo, Sumatra, and Burma, as well as the severe restrictions imposed on civilian consumption, fuel supplies for the Imperial armed forces were by no means fully assured. The British and Dutch refineries had been sabotaged, but the Japanese did not restore them, contenting themselves with shipping the crude oil to Japan for refining, then sending the fuel oil and petrol out again to the combat area, thus incurring heavy expense in freight and fuel itself. American submarines were already beginning to take their toll of Japanese shipping and this was not being replaced rapidly enough by the Imperial shipyards.

Let us now have a look at the types and numbers of the warships put into service in the Pacific on both sides during 1943. It will be immediately evident that, without a miracle, the war was already virtually over for Japan:

	U.S.	Japan
Battleships	2	–
Combat aircraft-carriers	15	1
Heavy and light cruisers	11	2
Destroyers	128	11
Submarines	200	58
Totals	356	72

The American naval air forces had got rid of the types of aircraft which had shown up so badly over Midway, in spite of the

courage of their crews, but the Japanese had hardly improved their equipment at all. Whereas the Americans were also prepared to go to any lengths in risk and cost to recover a handful of pilots lost at sea, the Japanese cared little for the survival of their flying crews. The American airmen did not, it is true, at this time report any sign of despondency amongst their adversaries, but from now on there was to be evidence of a lessening of their fighting spirit. So little regard was given by the Japanese to what we call "human material" that there was now no time left to retrain the men for their rôle.

The morale of the Japanese was unaffected by the fact that they were now on the defensive.

According to Admiral de Belot, whose judgement remains valid today although his book *La guerre aéronavale du Pacifique* appeared in 1948, the fierce fighting in the Solomon Islands, New Guinea, the Aleutians, and the Gilbert Islands brought in only three to four hundred prisoners to the Americans up to the end of 1943, and up to the capitulation of Japan ordered by the Emperor, no Japanese general officer ever fell into the hands of his enemy alive.

There were 2,600 Japanese in the garrison of Attu Island (Aleutians) at the end of May 1943, but the 11,000 Americans of the 7th Division who captured it took only 28 prisoners. When the defenders had used up all their artillery ammunition and most of their cartridges, they assembled by night to the number of about 1,000 and charged, using only their side-arms. The 500 or so who survived were driven off and began all over again the next night. At dawn on May 30 the few who were left committed suicide, some with revolvers, others with grenades, after finishing off the sick and the wounded. This bloody affair cost the Americans 600 killed and 1,200 wounded. On November 10 in the waters south of Bougainville, Leading Seaman Fahey witnessed a chilling and awesome scene which he described as follows in his diary:

"This afternoon, while we were south of Bougainville and just off Treasury Island, we came across a raft with four live Japs in it. Admiral Merrill sent word to one of our destroyers to pick them up. As the destroyer *Spence* came close to the raft, the Japs opened up with a machine gun on the destroyer. The Jap officer put the gun in each man's mouth and fired, blowing out the back of each man's skull. One of the Japs did not want to die for the Emperor and put up a struggle. The others held him down. The officer was the last to die. He also blew his brains out . . . All the bodies had disappeared into the water. There was nothing left but blood and an empty raft. Swarms of sharks were everywhere. The sharks ate well today."

We could quote page after page of macabre examples like this. Those we have chosen may perhaps suffice for us to offer the following remarks: those Japanese fighting men who did not hesitate to finish off their wounded comrades to spare them

the inexpiable dishonour of captivity had no consideration either for the enemy prisoners who fell into their hands, even though the Japanese Government had signed the Geneva Convention and had respected it on the whole during the Russo-Japanese War of 1904-1905.

Another observation must be made here concerning the intellectual outlook of the Japanese Army and Navy: they showed unreasonable optimism almost throughout the war about the losses they inflicted on their enemy on land, on sea, and in the air. During 1943, for every action in the waters around the Solomon and Gilbert Islands, G.H.Q. Tokyo's spokesmen blew the victory trumpets and broadcast, as they had done during the previous year, the unlikely lists of battleships, aircraft-carriers, and heavy and light cruisers of the U.S. Navy which they had sunk.

We know from documents which became available after the war that during 1943 the U.S. Navy lost only the cruiser *Helena*, sunk on July 6 in Kula Bay (New Georgia) and the escort-carrier *Liscombe Bay*, sunk on November 24, the day after the successful attack on the Tarawa and Makin atolls in the Gilbert Islands.

Must these clumsy and absurd exaggerations be blamed on General Tojo's Intelligence services alone? Most of them, clearly, but this policy of boasting was continued even after the loss of even the Marianas (July 15-19, 1944). When we see the Imperial G.H.Q. basing its operations on enemy losses reported by its combat forces, as it was still doing after the battle of Leyte (October 1944), we must conclude that there was a peculiar spirit of braggadocio among the staffs at the front or at least a complete inability to see the situation coolly and to weigh up its every feature. The hastily-trained observers of the Japanese naval air force seem to have added confusion at this time by their errors of identification.

At the same time as the American Joint Chiefs-of-Staff Committee was deciding upon a limited offensive in the Pacific, Imperial G.H.Q. in Tokyo, far from taking

A Japanese navy pilot and his reconnaissance seaplane.

into account the defeats at Midway and Guadalcanal, adopted a defensive-offensive strategy which Washington had just abandoned. In May 1943 a Plan "Z" was issued. This defined the rôle of the Japanese armed forces as follows:

"a. A defensive front (bounded by the Aleutians, Wake, the Marshall Islands, the Gilbert Islands, Nauru, the Bismarck Islands, New Guinea, and the Malay Barrier) will be established. Local commands will be set up and charged to take defensive measures. The Combined Fleet will be stationed at Truk and on neighbouring islands.

b. In case of attack the enemy will be drawn towards the main force and destroyed by the combined action of land-based and carrier-based aircraft.

c. Enemy aircraft-carriers will be counter-attacked as often as possible.

d. During engagements the enemy aircraft-carriers are the primary objective, followed by his troop transports.

e. If the enemy attempts to land he must be stopped on the shore. If his landing is successful and he can exploit it, then he must be continuously counter-attacked."

Briefly then, the resistance of forward strategic posts under "a" had to last for some time and cause considerable damage to the enemy so that the Combined Fleet, kept concentrated at the hinge of the fan, could have the time necessary to move in on the enemy and overwhelm him. The atolls or islands on the perimeter of this defensive system were thus so many unsinkable aircraft-carriers. This directive went back to the strategic thinking which had dominated the Imperial Navy between 1920 and 1940. In the situation as it was in 1943, it could still have worked if the Americans had stuck to the means and methods of attack expected to be used about 1930. Then each of the strong-points between the Aleutians and Malaya would have had sufficient aircraft to drive off with losses a battleship squadron protected by one or two aircraft-carriers, giving time for the light surface vessels and the submarines to get the first nibble at the enemy fleet which, thus weakened, would be crushed by the main force of the Combined Fleet.

But it was now 1943. For his attack on the objectives in the Gilbert group, the American 5th Fleet (Vice-Admiral Raymond A. Spruance) had six 27,000-ton aircraft-carriers, five 11,000 ton light carriers and eight escort-carriers with between them some 700 fighters and bombers. This would allow him not only to attack Makin and Tarawa with overwhelming strength, but also to keep up a continuous attack on the Japanese bases in the Marshall Islands to prevent the Japanese from sending help from there to the Gilbert group. The strength of the U.S. force therefore nullified point "b" of the directive above which envisaged the "combined action of land-based and carrier-based aircraft of the Imperial Fleet", for the former were to be destroyed before the latter could intervene.

Such were the disastrous consequences of the dispersion under Plan "Z" of the Imperial forces. Nimitz and MacArthur simply abstained from attacking any enemy positions not immediately on their line of advance towards each other. There was worse still, however: the organisation, then the supply, of this vast chain of support points stretching from the North Pacific to the Indian Ocean demanded a logistic effort by the Japanese command, the cost and the extent of which seem at the time completely to have escaped them. The Japanese were short of ships, fuel, and aviation spirit, and the U.S. submarine fleet, ever expanding, more seasoned, and equipped with better torpedoes, made life very hazardous for transport vessels. At the time of Japan's final capitulation, the Japanese support-points which had been spared by the American strategy were virtually starving and for many months had ceased to have any effect on the outcome of operations in the Pacific, just like the German forces left in Norway or in odd pockets on the Atlantic coast.

In our chapter on Kursk we said that Manstein's "return attack" plan, which he had advocated in vain to Hitler, depended on the enemy's not discovering the Germans' intentions. It was the same with Plan "Z" and the success expected of it in Tokyo. The reader will remember that the Japanese naval code had yielded to the efforts of the American code-breakers and that the Japanese G.H.Q. and Admiralty had continued to believe that the transmissions were still secret. This was to provide a final reason for the course events in the Pacific were to take.

At the turn of the year General MacArthur, not content with the success he had had in denying the enemy access to Port Moresby in New Guinea, had now assumed the initiative which he was to retain until the end of hostilities.

He put his 32nd and 41st Divisions under the command of Lieutenant-General Robert L. Eichelberger and sent two columns over the Owen Stanley range in the direction of Buna on the north coast of Papua. At the same time there were to be airborne and amphibious landings close to the objective. On December 14, 1942 Buna fell, but it took General Eichelberger until January 2, 1943 to wipe out the last remnants of resistance. He was then able to write to MacArthur on that day:

"At 4.30 p.m., I crossed the bridge (from the Island) after 'C' Company had passed and I saw American troops with their bellies out of the mud and their eyes in the sun circling unafraid around the bunkers. It was one of the grandest sights I have ever seen . . . the 127th Infantry found its soul."

"Life in the virgin forest was atrocious," explains Marcel Giuglaris. "Every night trees fell; as the earth shook with the bombing their slender roots gave way and the darkness was filled with the thunder of the forest collapsing about you. There were also the poisonous scorpions whose sting sent you mad, the lack of food, malaria, typhoid, snakes, and nervous illnesses. Fighting in the jungle was equally terrifying, merciless, neither side taking prisoner. The Japanese counter-attacked regularly at night, screaming in Banzai charges. The Americans then changed their tactics: they began to lay the ground waste a hundred square yards at a time. The Japanese were astonished that they were still holding out. Every day the number of dead increased, every man fought until he was killed. The end came when Eichelberger's Marines had no more men facing them."

The reconquest of New Guinea, which was completed in mid-January, cost MacArthur dear and, in view of his losses and the enemy's tenacity, he decided to soften down his methods, as he wrote in his memoirs:

"It was the practical application of this system of warfare–to avoid the frontal attack with its terrible loss of life; to by-pass Japanese strongpoints and neutralise them by cutting their lines of supply; to thus isolate their armies and starve them on the battlefield; to as Willie Keeler used to say, 'hit 'em where they ain't'–that from this time guided my movements and operations.

"This decision enabled me to accomplish the concept of the direct-target approach from Papua to Manila. The system was popularly called 'leap-frogging', and hailed as something new in warfare. But it was actually the adaption of modern instrumentalities of war to a concept as ancient as war itself. Derived from the classic strategy of envelopment, it was given a new name, imposed by modern conditions. Never before had a field of battle embraced land and water in such relative proportions . . . The paucity of resources at my command made me adopt this method of campaign as the only hope of accomplishing my task . . . It has always proved the ideal method for success by inferior but faster-moving forces."

Briefly, MacArthur was applying the "indirect approach" method recommended in the months leading up to World War II by the British military writer Basil Liddell Hart and practised also by Vice-Admiral Halsey in his advance from Guadalcanal to Bougainville and in the following autumn by Admiral Nimitz in the Central Pacific Area. This also comes out in the following anecdote from Willoughby and Chamberlain's *Conqueror of the Pacific:*

"When staff members presented their glum forecasts to MacArthur at a famous meeting which included Admiral Halsey, the newly arrived General Krueger, and Australia's General Thomas Blamey, MacArthur puffed at his cigarette. Finally, when one of the conferees said, 'I don't see how we can take these strong points with our limited resources,' MacArthur leaned forward.

'Well,' he said, 'Let's just say that we won't take them. In fact, gentlemen, I don't want them.'

Then turning to General Kenney, he said, '*You* incapacitate them.'"

The results of this method were strikingly described after the end of the war by Colonel Matsuichi Ino, formerly Chief of Intelligence of the Japanese 8th Army:

"This was the type of strategy we hated most. The Americans, with minimum losses, attacked and seized a relatively weak area, constructed airfields and then proceeded to cut the supply lines to troops in that area. Without engaging in a large scale operation, our strongpoints were gradually starved out. The Japanese Army preferred direct assault, after the German fashion, but the Americans flowed into our weaker points and submerged us, just as water seeks the weakest entry to sink a ship. We respected this type of strategy for its brilliance because it gained the most while losing the least."

This could not be better expressed; nevertheless, MacArthur's method demanded perfect collaboration of the land, sea, air, and airborne forces under the command of the C.-in-C. of the South-West Pacific theatre of operations. He handled them like some great orchestral conductor.

According to the decisions taken at Casablanca, Nimitz's ultimate objective was Formosa via the Marshall and Caroline Islands. When he reached there he was to join MacArthur, who would have come from the Philippines, reinforced in the vicinity of the Celebes Sea by the British Pacific Fleet, which meanwhile was to have forced the Molucca passage. From Formosa, the Allies could sever Japanese communications between the home islands and the newly-conquered empire, as a preliminary to invading Japan itself.

A few weeks after Casablanca, the American Joint Chiefs-of-Staff defined as follows the immediate missions that were to be carried out by General MacArthur and Vice-Admiral Halsey:

"South Pacific and Southwest Pacific forces to co-operate in a drive on Rabaul. Southwest Pacific forces then to press on westward along north coast of New Guinea."

General MacArthur was therefore empowered to address strategic directives to Admiral Halsey, but the latter was reduced to the men and *matériel* allotted to him by the C.-in-C. Pacific. This included no aircraft-carriers. In his memoirs MacArthur complains at having been treated from the outset as a poor relation. We would suggest that he had lost sight of the fact that a new generation of aircraft-carriers only reached Pearl Harbor at the beginning of September and that Nimitz, firmly supported by Admiral King, did not intend to engage *Enterprise* and *Saratoga,* which were meanwhile filling the gap, in the narrow waters of the Solomon Islands.

Moreover, the situation was made even more precarious because of the new Japanese air bases at Buin on Bougainville and at Munda on New Georgia. This was very evident to Leading Seaman James J. Fahey, who wrote on June 30:

"We could not afford to send carriers or battleships up the Solomons, because they would be easy targets for the land-based planes, and also subs that would be hiding near the jungle. We don't mind losing light cruisers and destroyers but the larger ships would not be worth the gamble, when we can do the job anyway."

As we can see, all ranks in the Pacific Fleet were of one mind about tactics.

In the meantime, whilst at Port Moresby General MacArthur was setting in motion the plan which was to put a pincer round Rabaul and allow him to eliminate this menace to his operations, the U.S.A.A.F. was inflicting two very heavy blows on the enemy. After the defeat at Buna, the Japanese high command had decided to reinforce the 18th Army which, under General Horii, was responsible for the defence of New Guinea. On February 28 a first echelon of the 51st Division left Rabaul on board eight merchant ships escorted by eight destroyers. But Major-General Kenney unleashed on the convoy all he could collect together of his 5th Air Force. The American bombers attacked the enemy at mast-height, using delayed-action bombs so as to allow the planes to get clear before the explosions. On March 3 the fighting came to an end in the Bismarck Sea with the destruction of the eight troop transports and five destroyers.

MacArthur's biographers write:

"Skip bombing practice had not been wasted. Diving in at low altitudes through heavy flak, General Kenney's planes skimmed over the water to drop their bombs as close to the target as possible.

"The battle of the Bismarck Sea lasted for three days, with Kenney's bombers moving in upon the convoy whenever there was even a momentary break in the clouds.

"'We have achieved a victory of such completeness as to assume the proportions of a major disaster to the enemy. Our decisive success cannot fail to have most important results on the enemy's strategic and tactical plans. His campaign, for the time being at least, is completely dislocated.'"

Rightly alarmed by this catastrophe, Admiral Yamamoto left the fleet at Truk in the Carolines and went in person to Rabaul. He was followed to New Britain

The Americans supplied armour such as these Grant tanks to the Australians.

General Douglas MacArthur, wearing his characteristic dark glasses and cap, visits the front.

by some 300 fighters and bombers from the six aircraft-carriers under his command. Thus strengthened, the Japanese 11th Air Fleet, on which the defence of the sector depended, itself went over to the attack towards Guadalcanal on April 8 and towards Port Moresby on the 14th. But since the Japanese airmen as usual greatly exaggerated their successes, and as we now have the list of losses drawn up by the Americans, it might be useful to see what reports were submitted to Admiral Yamamoto who, of course, could only accept them at their face value. Yet it must have been difficult to lead an army or a fleet to victory when, in addition to the usual uncertainties of war, you had boastful accounts claiming 28 ships and 150 planes. The real losses were five and 25 respectively.

But this was not all, for during this battle the Japanese lost 40 aircraft and brought down only 25 of their enemy's. The results were therefore eight to five against them. Had they known the true figures, Imperial G.H.Q. might have been brought to the conclusion that the tactical and technical superiority of the famous Zero was now a thing of the past. How could they have known this if they were continually being told that for every four Japanese planes shot down the enemy lost 15?

CHAPTER 47

The campaign to secure New Guinea

The battles of the Coral Sea and Midway had turned the tide in the Pacific, and made possible the Allied advances of 1943. But before the Allied offensive could get into top gear, two crucial land campaigns had to be decided. These were the battles for New Guinea and the Solomon Islands. Both campaigns had begun in 1942, but were not completed until well into 1943. It is to these long, hard-fought struggles that we must now turn our attention.

In January 1942, the Japanese Army's South Seas Detachment (Major-General Tomitaro Horii) supported by the 4th Fleet (Vice-Admiral Shigeyoshi Inouye) had captured Rabaul, with its excellent harbour, on the island of New Britain in the Bismarck Islands.

The Japanese found Rabaul "a nice little town", with wide-eaved bungalows surrounded by red hibiscus. General Horii, the conqueror of Guam, rounded up the white civilians and sent them off to Japan in the transport *Montevideo Maru* (they were all lost *en route* when the ship was sunk by an American submarine). Then he began building an air base. Admiral Inouye helped to make the base secure by occupying Kavieng on New Ireland to the north. To the southeast, bombing took care of Bougainville, northernmost of the long string of Solomon Islands.

The towns of Lae and Salamaua, in the Huon Gulf in the east of New Guinea, had been heavily bombed in the preliminary attack on Rabaul on January 21. The civilians fled, some on foot to the wild interior, some in native canoes down the Solomon Sea, hugging the New Guinea coast. One party, after a voyage of about two weeks, put in at Gona, an Anglican mission on the coast in Australia's own Territory of Papua, in the south-east of New Guinea.

The arrival of the refugees from the Mandated Territory was long remembered by Father James Benson, the priest at Gona. The big sailing canoes against a flaming sunset sky brought through the surf "thirty-two woefully weatherbeaten refugees whose poor sun- and salt-cracked lips and bearded faces bore evidence of a fortnight's constant exposure." With only the clothes they fled in, "they looked indeed a sorry lot of ragamuffins". Next morning they began the five-day walk to Kokoda, a government station about 50 miles inland. From there planes could take them to Port Moresby, the territorial capital on the Coral Sea, facing Australia.

Planes flying from Kokoda to Port Moresby had to skim the green peaks of the Owen Stanley Range, the towering, jungle-covered mountain chain that runs the length of the Papuan peninsula. After a flight of about 45 minutes they put down at a dusty airstrip in bare brown foothills. From the foothills a road descended to

Port Moresby, in peacetime a sleepy copra port with tin-roofed warehouses baking in the tropical sun along the waterfront. A single jetty extended into a big harbour; beyond, a channel led to a second harbour large enough to have sheltered the Australian fleet in World War I.

Because of its fine harbour and its position dominating the populous east coast of Australia, Port Moresby was heavily ringed on military maps in Tokyo. On orders from Imperial General Headquarters the first air raid was launched from Rabaul on February 3. The bombers did a thorough job and returned unscathed. Port Moresby's handful of obsolete planes and small anti-aircraft guns was no match for modern Japanese aircraft.

Star of the Japanese air fleet was the Mitsubishi A6M Zero fighter-bomber, one of the best planes of the war. Armed with two 20-mm cannon and two 7.7-mm machine guns, it could carry 264 pounds of bombs and was fast and agile. Its range of 1,150 miles and ceiling of 32,800 feet also made it invaluable for reconnaissance.

To facilitate the bombing of Port Moresby, some 550 miles from Rabaul, Tokyo ordered General Horii to occupy Lae and Salamaua, Lae to be used as an advanced air base, Salamaua to secure Lae. At 0100 hours on the morning of March 8 a battalion of Horii's 144th Regiment made an unopposed landing at Salamaua–the first Japanese landing on New Guinea. An hour later Inouye's Maizuru 2nd Special Naval Landing Force (S.N.L.F.) marines occupied Lae. The naval force, which included engineers and a base unit, then took over at Salamaua. Horii's infantrymen returned to Rabaul to await orders for the next move in the south-west Pacific.

When Lae and Salamaua were captured, the next move was being hotly debated at Imperial General Headquarters in Tokyo. The Navy, flushed with its easy victories in south-east Asia, wanted to invade Australia. During operations against the Dutch/Portuguese island of Timor, from February 19 carrier aircraft had repeatedly bombed Australia's northwestern coast, with little opposition. The east coast was lightly defended, since the bulk of the Australian Army was still in the Middle East. Naval officers believed that the invasion would need only five divisions.

Army officers objected, arguing that to conquer and hold the vast continental area would require 12 divisions and a million tons of shipping–far more than the Army could afford. The Navy warned that the Allies would use bases in Australia for counter-attacks on Japanese bases. This point was reinforced by the news in late March that Mac-Arthur had arrived in Australia from the Philippines.

The argument went on for two weeks, at times coming close to blows at the Army and Navy Club. At the end of March a compromise was reached. Australia would not be invaded, but Port Moresby would be captured. This move, with the conquest of Samoa, Fiji, and New Caledonia out in the South Pacific, would isolate Australia by cutting her supply line from the United States.

On April 20 the south Pacific operations were postponed in favour of an ambitious Navy-sponsored plan to take Midway and the Aleutians; but preparations went forward for an amphibious assault on Port Moresby, codenamed Operation "MO". General Horii issued the orders on April 29, an auspicious date, for it was the Emperor's birthday. The landing was to take place on May 10.

On May 2, while the South Seas Detachment was boarding its transports, a force left Rabaul harbour for the small island of Tulagi in the southern Solomons to establish a seaplane base in support of Operation "MO". It landed without opposition the following day, and a few days later put a construction unit ashore on the large island of Guadalcanal to build an airfield.

The Port Moresby invasion force steamed south from Rabaul on May 4 in five transports, well escorted. Off Bougainville the convoy was joined by the light carrier *Shoho*, with six cruisers. Two fleet carriers, *Shokaku* and *Zuikaku*, stood by south of the Solomons. As the invasion convoy was nearing the eastern point of New Guinea on May 7, the carrier *Shoho*, in the lead, was attacked by U.S. carrier planes and sunk, along with a cruiser. Admiral Inouye then ordered the transports back to Rabaul.

The following day the Battle of the Coral Sea was fought between the U.S. carriers *Lexington* and *Yorktown* and the Japanese *Shokaku* and *Zuikaku*–the first carrier battle in history. One Japanese carrier was damaged, the other lost most of her planes. The *Lexington* was sunk. The battle was therefore not a clear-cut victory for either side; but the invasion of Port Moresby had been blocked. For this, credit was due to the U.S. Navy cryptanalysts in Hawaii who had cracked the Japanese fleet code and thus enabled the Allies to intercept the convoy.

Operation "MO" was not abandoned, only postponed; and the release of Japanese forces from the Philippines after the surrender of Bataan and Corregidor on May 6 made an expanded operation possible, with the Yazawa and Aoba Detachments at Davao and the Kawaguchi Detachment at Palau added to the South Seas Detachment, all to come under the 17th Army (Lieutenant-General Harukichi Hyakutake), which was established on May 18.

In Tokyo, euphoria was at its height.

At Army headquarters in late May, Seizo Okada, a war correspondent assigned to the South Seas Detachment, had to fight his way through a crowd of "provincials" (Japanese Army slang for civilians) clamouring for permission to go abroad with the Army. After receiving his credentials from a major, Okada asked for a pair of army boots. "Behind a screen that stood by the Major some staff officers were talking and puffing at cigarettes. One of them, as plump as a pig, broke in, 'Hey, what are you talking about? Boots? Don't worry about your boots. You'll get lots of beautiful ones out there–damned beautiful enemy boots'.

"The mocking words drove the other officers into a fit of boisterous laughter. They too, like myself or any other Japanese, were puffed up like toy balloons by the 'brilliant initial success' of the Pacific War."

A week later came news of the first crushing setback. At Midway on June 7 the Japanese Navy was decisively defeated by the U.S. fleet, with a heavy loss of carriers.

Plans for operations in the southern Pacific had to be revised. Assaults against New Caledonia, Fiji, and Samoa were postponed indefinitely; and, for lack of carriers, Operation "MO" was changed from an amphibious assault to a land attack on Port Moresby over the Owen Stanley mountains, to be made by the South Seas Detachment with the help of the 15th Independent Engineer Regiment (Colonel Yosuke Yokoyama).

An advance echelon under Colonel Yokoyama, consisting of the engineers, a battalion of Horii's 144th Infantry Regiment, a company of marines of the Sasebo 5th S.N.L.F., and some artillery, anti-aircraft, and service units, in all about 1,800 men, was to land between Gona and Buna, an Australian government station about ten miles down the coast, advance inland to capture Kokoda, and prepare the way for Horii's main force to cross the Owen Stanley Range. Reconnaissance Zeros had spotted a red ribbon of earth winding over the mountains and assumed it to be a road. The engineers were to put it into shape to take trucks, if possible, or at least pack horses.

While the Yokoyama Force was embarking in Rabaul harbour, General Hyakutake on July 18 prepared a plan to assist Horii with a flanking seaplane attack based on Samarai at the entrance to Milne Bay, the 20-mile long, 7-mile wide bay at the eastern end of New Guinea. The Navy was to seize Samarai on August 25 with the help of a battalion of the Kawaguchi Detachment. In this latest version of Operation "MO", the Yazawa Detachment, consisting mainly of the 41st Infantry Regiment (Colonel Kiyomi Yazawa), was allocated to Horii.

Late on the afternoon of July 21, the Yokoyama Force, in three heavily-escorted transports, began landing on the New Guinea coast just east of Gona. Allied planes arrived and damaged two transports, but only 40 men were lost, and there was no other opposition. At Gona the missionaries had fled, and Buna was found to be deserted when the marines arrived next day to start building an airfield. Colonel Yokoyama concentrated his army troops at a point about half-way between Gona and Buna, where a corduroy road led inland for about 15 miles.

On the evening of the landing the infantry battalion (Lieutenant-Colonel Hatsuo Tsukamoto) and a company of engineers began the march inland, about 900 men with torches, some on bicycles, with orders to "push on night and day to the line of the mountain range".

Half-way to Kokoda they were fired upon by a few Australian and native soldiers, but these were easily dispersed. The natives melted away into the jungle. The Australians, part of a company of raw militiamen, tried to stop the invaders by destroying the bridge that carried the road over the Kumusi river, but when the Japanese threw up a bridge and pressed on, they retreated. On the night of July 28, in a thick mist, Tsukamoto bombarded Kokoda with mortars and a mountain gun and drove the defenders out.

The Japanese were puzzled by the weakness of the opposition. They did not know that the Allies, after recovering from the surprise of the landing, had persuaded themselves that the object of the landing was only to establish airfields in the Buna area. The Australians found it impossible to believe that the Japanese would attempt an overland attack on Port Moresby. The "road" over the mountains was only a native footpath, two or three feet wide.

Known as the Kokoda Track, the path crossed a range of mountains described graphically by an Australian who had made the crossing on foot: "Imagine an area of approximately one hundred miles

The American Stuart light tank was equally at home in desert or jungle.

long. Crumple and fold this into a series of ridges, each rising higher and higher until 7,000 feet is reached, then declining in ridges of 3,000 feet. Cover this thickly with jungle, short trees and tall trees, tangled with great, entwining savage vines." The days were hot and humid, the nights cold; frequent afternoon rains made the track "a treacherous mass of moving mud".

By August 21, when the main Japanese force got ashore under cover of a storm, Horii had landed on the New Guinea coast a total of 8,000 Army troops, 3,000 naval construction troops, and some 450 marines of the Sasebo 5th S.N.L.F. At the head of a formidable body of fighting troops he rode into Kokoda astride his white horse on August 24.

He found that Colonel Tsukamoto's infantry had already pushed up the Kokoda Track for several miles and taken the next village, Deniki, from which the Australian militiamen, evidently reinforced, had been trying to retake Kokoda. Defeated at Deniki, they had withdrawn up a steep slope to Isurava. This was to be Horii's first objective. He began shelling it on August 26.

Horii's men had two 70-mm howitzers, outranging any Australian weapon on the Kokoda Track, and light enough to be manhandled over the mountains. They had an efficient machine gun, the *Juki*, with a rapid rate of fire. They knew how to use their weapons to best advantage, outflanking and encircling prepared positions. They had been taught that they must not be captured, even if wounded. Their manual read, "Bear in mind the fact that to be captured means not only disgracing the Army but that your parents and family will never be able to hold up their heads again. Always save the last round for yourself." They would fight to the death.

They were adept at night operations and preferred to attack in the rain. The manual told them that "Westerners–

being very haughty, effeminate, and cowardly–intensely dislike fighting in the rain or mist or in the dark. They cannot conceive night to be a proper time for battle–though it is excellent for dancing. In these weaknesses lie our great opportunity." In night attacks the Japanese smeared their faces with mud; officers wore strips of white cloth crisscrossed on their backs so their men could follow them in the dark, or doused themselves with perfume and issued orders to "follow your noses".

The Allied advance continues (below), past the wreckage caused by a recent bombardment. Troops have a keen look (bottom) at a knocked-out Japanese tank.

The Japanese soldier was admirably equipped for jungle warfare. He was camouflaged by a green uniform and green leaves stuck in a net on his helmet; under his helmet he wore a cloth to keep sweat from running into his eyes. He had been instructed to add salt to his tea and salt plums to his rice. He was used to carrying heavy loads–the infantryman about 100 pounds–consisting of rice, powdered bean paste, powdered soy, hand grenades, rifle ammunition, a shovel, a pickaxe, and tenting; the artilleryman and engineer carried some 16 additional pounds.

Seizo Okada, arriving at Kokoda with Horii's headquarters, observed that the soldiers had made "a kind of woodman's carrying rack" for their load and "like pilgrims with portable shrines, carried it on their backs. Now they plodded on, step by step, supported by a stick, through those mountains of New Guinea".

At Isurava, Horii met unexpected resistance. From ground so high that the Japanese referred to it as "Mt. Isurava", the Australians poured down a heavy fire that stopped him for three days. On August 28 his casualties were so heavy that a Japanese officer wrote in his diary, "The outcome of the battle is very difficult to foresee."

That evening, at his command post on a neighbouring hill lit by fires in which his men were cremating their dead, Horii learned the reason for the repulse: the untrained Australian militiamen of the 39th Battalion had been reinforced by experienced regulars of the 21st Brigade, brought home from the Middle East. Horii ordered his reserve forward from Kokoda and on the afternoon of August 29 launched an onslaught that drove the defenders out of Isurava. By the evening of August 30 the Australian forces were in full retreat up the Kokoda Track.

General Horii subjected them to constant pressure, using alternately his 144th (Colonel Masao Kusunose) and his 41st (Colonel Yazawa) Infantry Regiments. Following closely to keep the Australians off balance he gave them no time to prepare counter-attacks, outflanking them from high ground, and bombarding them with his mountain guns at ranges they could not match. His troops crossed mountain after mountain, "an endless serpentine movement of infantry, artillery, transport unit, infantry again, first-aid station, field hospital, signal unit, and engineers".

Between the mountains, swift torrents roared through deep ravines. Beyond Eora Creek the track ascended to the crest of the range, covered with moss forest. "The jungle became thicker and thicker, and even at mid-day we walked in the half-light of dusk." The ground was covered with thick, velvety green moss. "We felt as if we were treading on some living animal." Rain fell almost all day and all night. "The soldiers got wet to the skin through their boots and the undercloth round their bellies."

Coming down from the crest on the morning of September 7, slipping and sliding on the muddy downward track, the Japanese vanguard found the Australians preparing to make a stand on the ridge behind a ravine at Efogi. During the morning Allied planes came over, strafing and bombing, but in the thick jungle did little damage. The following day before dawn the Japanese attacked, and by noon, in bitter hand-to-hand fighting that left about 200 Japanese and Australian bodies scattered in the ravine, they pushed the defenders off the ridge.

In mid-September the Australians, reinforced by a fresh brigade of regulars, the 25th, tried to hold on a ridge at Ioribaiwa, only 30 miles from Port Moresby, so near that when the wind was right the drone of motors from the airfield could be heard. But on September 17 the Japanese, who still outnumbered them, forced them to withdraw across a deep ravine to the last mountain above the port, Imita Ridge.

At Ioribaiwa, Horii halted, his forces weakened by a breakdown in supply and by Allied air attacks. In any case, he had orders not to move on Port Moresby until an advance could be made by sea from Milne Bay.

Bad luck dogged the Milne Bay operation from the start. The second week in August, the battalion of the Kawaguchi Detachment assigned to the 8th Fleet (Vice-Admiral Gunichi Mikawa) for the operation was sent instead to help clear Guadalcanal in the Solomons, where U.S. Marines had landed on August 7. A replacement battalion could not arrive in time. Admiral Mikawa, who had won a brilliant naval victory at Guadalcanal on August 9, would have no help from the Army at Milne Bay.

At the last minute the target was changed. Reports from reconnaissance planes in mid-August that the Allies were building an airfield at the head of Milne Bay near Gili Gili led planners to change the landing from Samarai, at the mouth of the bay, to Gili Gili.

The Japanese knew little about the Gili Gili area, in peace-time the site of a coconut plantation. Low-lying rain clouds usually protected it from reconnaissance. Estimating that it was held by not more than three infantry com-panies and 30 aircraft, Mikawa allotted only about 1,500 men to the invasion. Most of them were to come from Kavieng: 612 marines of the Kure 5th S.N.L.F. (Commander Shojiro Hayashi), 362 16th Naval Pioneer Unit troops, and 197 marines of the Sasebo 5th S.N.L.F. The Kavieng convoys were to sail up Milne Bay and land at Rabi, about three miles east of the Gili Gili jetty. At the same time, 353 marines of the Sasebo 5th S.N.L.F. at Buna, carried in seven big, wooden, motor-driven barges, were to land at Taupota on the Solomon Sea side and march over the mountains to Gili Gili.

The overland force was the first casualty of the operation. As it chugged down the coast under cloud cover on August 24 it was sighted and reported by a "coastwatcher"–one of the Australian organisation of planters and officials who had taken to the hills with wireless sets. The following day the marines beached the barges on Goodenough Island and went ashore to eat lunch. At that moment the clouds parted and 12 Australian P-40 fighter planes swooped low and destroyed the barges. The Buna marines were left stranded.

Two cruiser-escorted transports with Commander Hayashi and the first echelon of the Kavieng marines arrived safely at the head of Milne Bay in a downpour on the night of August 25. Shortly before midnight Hayashi began the landings at

Australian troops fording a river in New Guinea.

a point he believed to be Rabi. But he had no reliable map, and in the darkness and rain he landed about seven miles to the east on a swampy coastal shelf where the mountains came down almost to the water. His only means of advance westward toward Gili Gili was a muddy 12-foot track.

Hayashi was a stickler for night operations. He waited until darkness fell on August 26 to attack his first objective, a plantation astride the track at K. B. Mission, lightly held by Australian militia. Preceded by a flame-thrower, his troops tried to outflank the defenders by wading into the bay on one side and the swamp on the other. By dawn they had almost succeeded; but at first light they retired into the jungle.

The following night the attack was resumed in greater force, the second echelon from Kavieng having arrived. This time the Japanese used two small tanks–the first tanks to be landed on the New Guinea coast. They each had a strong headlight which, shining through the rain, enabled them to illuminate the Australian positions while the attackers remained in darkness. With the help of the tanks, Hayashi's men cleared K. B. Mission, crossed the Gama river beyond, and before dawn on August 28 were attacking an airstrip that U.S. engineers were building between Rabi and Gili Gili. There, lacking the tanks, which had bogged down in mud and had had to be abandoned, they were stopped by heavy fire. At daylight they withdrew into the jungle.

Commander Hayashi had already asked Admiral Mikawa to send him reinforcements. He had been deprived of his overland force and had lost a considerable part of his food and ammunition when Allied aircraft sank the steel barges ferrying it ashore. He had met ground opposition greater than he expected and found the terrain worse than anything he could have imagined. Reinforcements landed on the night of August 29 under cover of a heavy mist. They were 568 marines of the Kure 3rd S.N.L.F. and 200 of the Yokosuka 5th S.N.L.F., all under Commander Minoro Yano who, being senior to Hayashi, took command of operations.

Before one o'clock on the morning of August 31 the combined Japanese forces launched a furious assault on the airstrip. They were beaten back by intense fire from anti-tank guns, heavy machine guns, and mortars, expertly sited with a clear field of fire and backed by heavy artillery positioned in the rear. Before day broke, three Japanese bugle calls rang out, the signal for retreat.

The Australians pursued. By nightfall on September 1 they had retaken K. B. Mission. Commander Yano, setting up defences on the track to block the pursuit, cabled Admiral Mikawa on September 3 for permission to withdraw from Milne Bay. He himself had been wounded; Hayashi had been killed; he had lost 600 men and had more than 300 wounded on his hands. The rest of the men, most of them suffering from trench foot, jungle rot, and tropical fevers, could not hold out.

Mikawa sanctioned the evacuation. By dawn of September 6, Japanese ships, carrying the 1,300 men remaining of the 1,900-man invasion force, were on their way to Rabaul.

The crowning misfortune of the Milne Bay invasion was the miscalculation of the strength of the defenders. Unknown to the Japanese, the Allies had landed at the head of Milne Bay between June 25 and August 20 some 4,500 Australian infantrymen, supported by about 3,000 Australian and 1,300 American engineer, artillery, and service units.

On September 20 General Horii called together his commanders and praised them for their success in crossing "the so-called impregnable Stanley Range". At the proper time they were "to strike a crushing blow at the enemy's positions at Port Moresby". The halt at Ioribaiwa would give the tired troops, many of them wounded and ill, a chance to regain their fighting strength. Most were hungry; little or no rice remained in the dumps. Horii had already ordered detachments

The confidence of victory: an Australian platoon on the march.

to dig up native gardens in the area and sent parties over the mountains to bring up provisions from the rear. To block an Australian attack, he ordered his engineers to build a stockade of tree trunks.

The Australians did not attack; but no supplies came from the rear, no Zeros flew over. "An atmosphere of uneasiness," noted Okada, "stole over the mountain, a feeling that things were not going well at Guadalcanal. On September 24 in a night of drizzling rain the blow fell. A signal commander came into Horii's tent with a message from Imperial General Headquarters ordering Horii to withdraw his force from the Owen Stanleys to the coast at Buna."

The reason for the order was a major defeat at Guadalcanal on September 15, in which the Kawaguchi Detachment had been virtually wiped out. Imperial General Headquarters decided to subordinate everything to the retaking of Guadalcanal. Once that had been accomplished, it would be possible to resume Operation "MO". In the meantime, Horii's mission was to defend the Buna beach-head.

For Horii, the order "to abandon this position after all the blood the soldiers have shed and the hardships they have endured" was agonising. He sent his chief-of-staff, Lieutenant-Colonel Toyanari Tanaka, to break the news to the battalion commanders. Some of them almost rebelled, urging a desperate, single-handed thrust into Port Moresby.

On September 25 the movement back over the mountains began. The order to withdraw had crushed the spirit of the soldiers, which, Okada reported, "had been kept up through sheer pride". For a time they remained stupefied. "Then they began to move, and once in retreat they fled for dear life. None of them had ever thought that a Japanese soldier would turn his back on the enemy. But they were actually beating a retreat!"

As soon as they accepted this bitter fact, "they were seized by an instinctive desire to live". Each tried to flee faster than his comrades. Passing by bodies of men killed in the fighting of early September, already rotting and covered with maggots, the soldiers stopped only to dig for taroes or yams. They found little; the fields had been dug up almost inch by inch. By the time they reached the crest of the Range, they were fleeing from starvation, a greater menace than the Allied planes roaring overhead or enemy guns rumbling in the rear.

To delay the Australian pursuit, which began on September 27, Horii ordered a rearguard battalion to make a stand on the heights above Eora Creek. There it was attacked by troops of the Australian 16th Brigade on October 21. Reinforced from Kokoda and Buna, it held out for seven days, long enough for Horii to evacuate Kokoda and set up his last defences, at Oivi and Gorari in the foothills between Kokoda and the Kumusi river.

At Oivi, strongly fortified by Colonel Yazawa, the Australians attacking on November 5 could make no headway; but at Gorari, where Colonel Tsukamoto was in command (Colonel Kusunose having been evacuated because of sickness and wounds), an Australian assault on November 10 succeeded, after heavy fighting. Yazawa's position was now untenable. He withdrew his 900-man force after dark that evening over a little-known track leading north-east to the mouth of the Kumusi. With him was General Horii, who had been on an inspection trip to Oivi.

The rest of the South Seas Detachment, about 1,200 men, began crossing the Kumusi river on the night of November 12, guided by the light of a bonfire. They had no bridge. Incendiary bombs dropped from Allied planes had burned the wooden bridge built in August by the Yokoyama Force and defeated all attempts to replace it. The soldiers crossed in six-man folding boats, then pushed on in the darkness toward Buna.

Seizo Okada crossed with the vanguard. Stopping at a newsmen's hut about half-way to Buna, he watched the "men of the mountains" as they moved along the road, day and night, toward the coast. "They had shaggy hair and beards. Their uniforms were soiled with blood and mud and sweat, and torn to pieces. There were infantrymen without rifles, men walking on bare feet, men wearing blankets or straw rice-bags instead of uniforms, men reduced to skin and bone plodding along with the help of a stick, men gasping and crawling on the ground."

The stretcher-bearers, themselves too weak to carry stretchers, dragged the sick and wounded to the overcrowded field hospital near Buna and laid them on straw mats in the jungle. "The soldiers had eaten anything to appease hunger – young shoots of trees, roots of grass, even cakes of earth. These things had injured their stomachs so badly that when they were brought back to the field hospital they could no longer digest any food. Many of them vomited blood and died."

Later, Okada learned that General Horii had drowned while on the march northwards with Yazawa. Horii, anxious to rejoin his men at Buna, tried to cross the lower Kumusi river on a log raft. In the swift current the raft carrying him and Colonel Tanaka overturned.

So ended, in tragedy, the overland march on Port Moresby. Misgivings about it had been felt by at least one officer at Imperial General Headquarters, Colonel Masanobu Tsuji, who warned, "Cross the mountains and you will get the worst of it." At the end his verdict was, "a blunder".

Though the Buna beach-head was reinforced from Rabaul and held out for several months, Operation "MO" was never resumed. Beginning early in October, the attention of Imperial General Headquarters was diverted from New Guinea and focused on Guadalcanal.

CHAPTER 48

Battle for the Solomons

Allied resources in the Pacific were stretched to the limit in the summer of 1942, and the greater part of the American war effort was directed toward the European theatre and the defeat of Germany. The Japanese, checked only by the crucial naval Battle of Midway in June 1942, were riding a tide of victory and easy conquests. Tulagi Island, site of the headquarters of the British Solomon Islands Protectorate, was not on the original schedule of targets the Japanese had projected for the South Pacific, but it too was taken as the victory tide swept onward. The seaplane base and radio station that the Japanese had established on Tulagi did not particularly worry the Allies, but reports in June 1942 that Japanese troops had begun levelling an aircraft runway on the kunai grass plains of the Lunga river on the large island of Guadalcanal, 20 miles south across Sealark Channel from Tulagi, were a different story. Here was a clear threat to the shipping lifeline stretched across the South Pacific from the U.S. to New Zealand and Australia.

At the time the Japanese moved to Tulagi, the nearest American troops were on the outposts of Espiritu Santo in the New Hebrides, 550 miles away. An airfield was rushed to completion there, to be ready by the end of July to support operations against the Japanese. The American Joint Chiefs-of-Staff, urged on by the Navy's leader, Admiral Ernest J. King, had decided to mount a ground offensive to halt the enemy drive to the south and to provide a base for offensive operations against Rabaul, the Japanese area headquarters and nerve centre on New Britain in the Bismarcks.

Guadalcanal and Tulagi were the objectives, and the assault force was the only amphibious trained division readily available, the 1st Marine Division. It was, in fact, the only unit of its size that was available. Commanded by Major-General Alexander A. Vandegrift, a veteran of the jungle fighting of the Banana Wars in the Caribbean, the 1st Division had been formed in 1940 and included many veteran Marines in its ranks as well as a number of men without combat or expeditionary experience. Its forward echelon had just arrived in Wellington, New Zealand, for six months of intensive combat training when the word was passed that it would go into battle instead. Some troops were still at sea; one of its regiments, the 7th Marines, was committed to the defence of Samoa and the 2nd Marines of the 2nd Marine Division had to be sent out from San Diego to replace it. Other major elements to be attached to the 1st Division were located on New Caledonia and in the Hawaiian Islands. All had to be alerted, equipped, and assembled in less than a month's time to meet a D-day of August 7, 1942.

Working around the clock and overriding New Zealand dock workers who wanted to invoke union labour rules, the Marines in Wellington unloaded transports as fast as they arrived, sorted and repacked equipment and supplies for combat, and loaded ship again. There was not enough room for all the division's motor transport and most of the heavier trucks had to be left behind. Only 60 days of supplies and rations, ammunition for 10 days' heavy fighting (units of fire), and the bare minimum of individual equipment were taken.

The amphibious task force which would transport, land, and support the Marines was commanded by Rear-Admiral Richmond K. Turner; overall commander of the naval expeditionary force, including carriers and their escorts, was Rear-Admiral Frank J. Fletcher. Since this was to be a naval campaign and the landing force was to be of Marines, Admiral King had insisted that it be conducted under naval leadership. Accordingly, the Joint Chiefs-of-Staff shifted the boundary of Vice-Admiral Richard H. Ghormley's South Pacific Theatre northward to include all of the 90-mile-long island of Guadalcanal, which precluded the possibility that General Douglas MacArthur, the South-West Pacific Area commander, would control operations.

The plan for the seizure of the objective, codenamed "Watchtower", called for two separate landings, one by the division's main body near Lunga Point on Guadalcanal and the other at Tulagi by an assault force made up of the 2nd Battalion, 5th Marines and the 1st Raider and 1st Parachute Battalions. In all, General Vandegrift had about 19,000 men under his command when the transports and escorts moved into position on D-day. They had come from a rehearsal at Koro, in the Fiji Islands, where the inexperienced ships' crews and the polyglot Marine units reinforcing the 1st Division had combined to take part in a run-through that General Vandegrift called a "complete bust".

Behind a thunderous preparation by cruisers and destroyers and under an overhead cover of Admiral Fletcher's carrier aircraft, the landing craft streaked ashore at both targets. Surprise had been achieved; there was no opposition on the beaches at either objective. True to preliminary Intelligence estimates, however, the Japanese soon fought back savagely from prepared positions on Tulagi.

It took three days of heavy fighting to wrest the headquarters island and two small neighbouring islets, Gavutu and Tanambogo, from the Japanese naval troops who defended them. All three battalions of the 2nd Marines were needed to lend their weight to the American attacks against Japanese hidden in pillboxes and caves and ready to fight to the death. The garrison commander had radioed to Rabaul on the morning of August 7: "Enemy troop strength is overwhelming. We will defend to the last man." There were 27 prisoners, mostly labourers. A few men escaped by swimming to nearby Florida Island, but the rest of the 750 to 800-man garrison went down fighting.

On Guadalcanal, the labour troops working on the airfield fled when naval gunfire crashed into their bivouac areas. Consequently, there was no opposition as the lead regiment, the 1st Marines, overran the partially completed field on August 8. Japanese engineering equipment, six workable road rollers, some 50 handcarts, about 75 shovels, and two tiny petrol locomotives with hopper cars, were left behind. It was a good thing that this gear was abandoned, for the American engineering equipment that came to Guadalcanal on Turner's ships also left on Turner's ships, which departed from the area on August 9. Unwilling to risk his precious carriers any longer against the superior Japanese air power which threatened from Rabaul, Admiral Fletcher was withdrawing. Without air cover, Turner's force was naked. Japanese cruisers and destroyers and flights of medium bombers from Rabaul had made the amphibious task force commander's position untenable.

Almost constant Japanese air attacks, which began on the afternoon of August 7, thoroughly disrupted unloading as the transports and escorts manoeuvred to escape the rain of bombs. The Marines did not have enough shore party troops to handle the supplies that did reach the beach. Ships' captains in a hurry to empty their holds and inexperienced coxswains combined forces to dump an unprogrammed jumble of ammunition, rations, tentage, vehicles, and assorted supplies on the shoreline, offering another tempting target for the Japanese planes. When Turner reluctantly sailed south to Espiritu Santo and New Caledonia, only 37 days' supply of rations and four units of fire had been landed. Vandegrift had 16,000 men ashore, 6,000 on Tulagi, with the rest still on board ship when the task force departed.

After this event, the commanding general of Army forces in the South Pacific, Major-General Millard F. Harmon, was far from optimistic about the chances of success for the Guadalcanal venture. On August 11 he wrote to the Army's Chief-of-Staff in Washington, General George C. Marshall:

"The thing that impresses me more than anything else in connection with the Solomon action is that we are not prepared to follow up . . . We have seized a stategic position from which future operations in the Bismarcks can be strongly supported. Can the Marines hold it? There is considerable room for doubt."

Cast loose, or at least promised only a tenuous lifeline to Allied support bases, the 1st Marine Division made do with what it had. The completion of the airfield that the Japanese had begun was crucial; without it there was little ground for hope that the Marines could stay on Guadalcanal. Japanese engineering equipment was used to the fullest extent; captured Japanese weapons were included in defensive positions; Japanese rations were added to the Marines' meagre stocks; and Japanese trucks were used to supplement the small American motor pool. The airfield was ready for use on August 18; it was named Henderson Field after a Marine pilot killed in the Battle of Midway. On the day that the runway was finished, the Japanese took their first step toward wresting control of the island back from the Americans, landing a battalion of the 28th Regiment to the east of Vandegrift's perimeter. This was to be the first of many runs by the "Tokyo Express," a cruiser–destroyer transport force commanded by Rear-Admiral Raizo Tanaka, which was largely responsible for the reinforcement and resupply of the Japanese on Guadalcanal.

The red letter day for the Marines was August 20. Two squadrons flew in to Henderson Field from the escort carrier *Long Island,* 19 Grumman F4F Wildcat fighters from Marine Fighting Squadron 223 and 12 Douglas SBD-3 Dauntless dive-bombers from Marine Scout-Bomber Squadron 232. The planes came just

in time to help with the destruction of the Japanese battalion that had landed two days before. Making a night attack headlong against the positions of the 1st Marines' battalion holding the west bank of the Ilu River, which marked the eastern edge of Vandegrift's perimeter, the Japanese were ground up in a fury of artillery, machine gun, and 37-mm canister fire. When daylight came, a Marine battalion mopped up the remnants of the attacking force, helped by strafing attacks by the newly arrived Wildcats. The Japanese commander, Colonel Kiyono Ichiki, disheartened by his failure, committed suicide; 800 of his men had died in the fighting.

Colonel Ichiki, like his superior in Rabaul, Lieutenant-General Harukichi Hyakutake, commanding the 17th Army, had underestimated both the strength and the determination to hold of the Marines. Time and again, the Japanese were to repeat Ichiki's error, sending thousands of men from Rabaul but never enough at one time so that Vandegrift could not handle them. The troops available to Hyakutake in August and September more than enough to overwhelm the Marine defences, but these troops were never committed in sufficient force to sustain a determined attack.

General Vandegrift never lost sight of his primary mission of defending Henderson Field. He was aggressive and mounted a number of limited objective offensives; he kept strong combat and reconnaissance patrols forward of his lines constantly. But he always kept his perimeter intact,

always maintained a reserve, and showed a marvellous ability for meeting strength with strength. The Japanese pattern of reinforcing Guadalcanal, and the impetuosity of Japanese leaders once they reached the island, played right into the American general's hands. Typically, a few thousand Japanese troops would be landed at night by Tanaka's Tokyo Express a few miles to either side of the Marine perimeter and they would attack almost without delay. The action would be furious at the point of contact, sometimes the Marine lines would be penetrated, but then the fire-brigade would arrive–a fresh infantry battalion, a platoon of tanks, the fire of an additional reinforcing artillery battalion, a flight of dive-bombers, perhaps all of these at once, and the Japanese would be thrown back, decimated by their own relentless courage in the face of killing fire.

The same fate that befell the Ichiki battalion was met by a 6,000-man brigade under Major-General Kiyotaki Kawaguchi, which landed on both sides of the 9,000-yard-wide perimeter in early September. The main body, about 4,000 men, mostly of the 124th Infantry, pressed inland under cover of the jungle to attack from the south against the inland perimeter toward the airfield. That portion of the Marine line was thinly held, as the greatest danger was expected from attacks along the coast or from the sea.

Fortunately, Vandegrift had moved the

The moment of truth: U.S. Marines storm ashore at Guadalcanal.

original assault force at Tulagi across Sealark Channel to bolster the Marine defences. Combining the raider and parachute battalions under one commander, Colonel Merritt A. Edson, he placed this unit astride an open, grassy ridge that led directly to the division command post and the airfield. The 2nd Battalion, 5th Marines was one mile away in reserve and a battalion of 105-mm howitzers from the division's artillery regiment, the 11th Marines, was in direct support. The Kawaguchi force lightly probed Edson's position on September 12, while a Japanese cruiser and several destroyers shelled Henderson Field, a frequent accompaniment to Japanese ground attacks. On the 13th, Edson tried a counter-attack but was forced back to his original positions; the Japanese were too strong.

That night in driving rain that severely limited visibility, the Japanese poured out of the jungle, smashing into the ridge position and forcing the American flanking companies back on the centre of the ridge. There the Marines held, the artillery smothered the attacking columns and troop assembly areas, and reinforcements from the 5th Marines joined the raiders and paratroopers in their foxholes. In the morning there was little left to do but mop up. Only about 500 of Kawaguchi's men struggled back alive through the jungle. A pair of diversionary attacks, mounted against the coastal perimeters while Kawaguchi struck, died in the face of stubborn Marine fire.

Another much needed respite had been gained by the Japanese failure to appreciate the Marines' strength. The 1st Marine Division had received no reinforcements or ammunition since the landing in August, the troops were eating only two meals a day and part of those were Japanese rations, and tropical diseases, particularly malaria, were beginning to fell large numbers of men. The "Cactus Air Force", so named by its pilots after the island's codename, was now a battered collection of Army P-40's, Navy fighters and dive-bombers from damaged carriers, and Marine Corps aircraft. Plane availability was often less than 50 and all types were woefully short of fuel and parts. The forward echelon of the 1st Marine Aircraft Wing under Brigadier-General Roy S. Geiger controlled the motley air force, but its attrition rate was heavy from its constant clashes with the Japanese and operational accidents caused by the primitive condition of the runways, and Geiger was hard put to it to provide replacement aircraft.

For both the ground and air elements of Vandegrift's force, then, September 18 was a day for celebration. The 7th Marines arrived from Samoa to rejoin the division; with its reinforcing artillery battalion of 75-mm pack howitzers, the regiment stood at 4,262 very welcome men. Moreover, the ships that Admiral Turner sent forward with the regiment also carried over 3,000 drums of aviation spirit, 147 vehicles, engineering equip-

ment, 1,000 tons of rations, and about ten units of fire for all weapons. Things were looking less bleak for Vandegrift's men.

The newly arrived regiment soon got a chance to test its mettle in combat. The Japanese were building up their forces west of the Marine perimeter and on the 23rd Vandegrift sent the 1st Battalion, 7th Marines inland toward Mt. Austen, which overlooks the Lunga plain, with the mission of crossing the jungle-covered foothills and turning north to patrol to the mouth of the Matanikau River. It was a hotly contested advance and the 2nd Battalion, 5th Marines came up to reinforce and help evacuate casualties. The Raider battalion moved along the coast to probe across the Matanikau. The Japanese made a stand at the river mouth and the action escalated. Colonel Edson, who now commanded the combined force, decided on a landing behind the Japanese position and chose the 7th Marines battalion for the job. Using the landing craft that had been left at Guadalcanal by damaged and sunken transports, the Marines made a shore-to-shore movement and drove inland to a ridge about 500 yards from the beach. The Japanese closed in behind them and cut them off from their boats. The battalion's radio was inoperative, but an SBD pilot overhead saw its predicament and repeatedly attacked the encroaching Japanese troops. Offshore, the destroyer *Ballard* used her 5-inch guns to blast a path to the beach and cover the landing craft. The battalion fought its way out of the trap, taking 24 dead and 23 wounded Marines with it. The coxswains of the landing craft made the evacuation despite a constant hail of enemy fire and considerable casualties.

This fight was just the first of a series of violent clashes, as Vandegrift sought to drive the Japanese away from the perimeter. Heavy artillery, 150-mm howitzers, had been landed near Kokumbona, the Japanese headquarters, and these guns could now shell Henderson Field and a fighter strip which had been completed nearby. If the Cactus Air Force could be kept from flying, the Japanese transports and bombardment ships could

Japanese bodies lie on the beach, shattered and half buried by American bombardment before the Marines landed.

have an unmolested run-in with reinforcements. As long as the mixed bag of American fighters and bombers could stay aloft, Sealark Channel was virtually shut off to the Japanese during daylight hours.

On October 7, the Marines set out again in force with two battalions of the 5th Marines to engage the Japanese at the mouth of the Matanikau. Inland, two battalions of the 7th Marines, the 3rd Battalion, 2nd Marines, and the division's scout-sniper detachment were to drive west and then south after crossing the Matanikau upstream to pin the Japanese against the coast. Three battalions of artillery were in direct support of the attack. The advancing Marines ran into the Japanese 4th Infantry Regiment, which was also moving forward to the attack. The resulting action spread over two days in the rain-swept jungle. The Americans trapped one sizable pocket of Japanese near the coast; only a few escaped death. Another force of 1,500 men was isolated in a deep ravine inland. There, while Marine riflemen on the high ground picked off the hapless enemy soldiers as they struggled up the steep slopes, artillery shells methodically blasted the floor of the ravine. Vandegrift broke off the action on October 9 when Intelligence indicated that a strong Japanese attack would be mounted from the Kokumbona area. When the Marine battalions retired to the perimeter, they took with them 65 dead and 125 wounded, but they left behind 700 Japanese dead.

The Intelligence was correct. General Hyakutake himself had landed on Guadalcanal on October 9 to take personal charge of the Japanese effort. He brought with him heavy reinforcements, the rest of the 2nd Division to join those elements already on the island, two battalions of the 38th Division, and more artillery. By mid-October, Hyakutake's strength was about 20,000 men, but Vandegrift had 23,000, for on October 13, the first

American Army troops arrived on Guadalcanal, the 164th Infantry of the Americal Division from New Caledonia. The night after the 164th arrived, Japanese battleships fired a 90-minute bombardment against Henderson Field, partly to cover a daylight run of Tanaka's transports carrying Hyakutake's reinforcements. Although only 42 of Geiger's 90 planes were operational when the bombardment ended and Henderson Field was a shambles, the pilots used the fighter strip as soon as the sun rose and made the muddy runway firm enough to take off from. Any plane that could carry a bomb or torpedo, including General Vandegrift's lumbering PBY flying boat, attacked the transports. Three were left burning and beached and the other two fled, but some 4,000 men of the 2nd Division were able to get ashore.

Hyakutake's plan was to attack the inland perimeter as Kawaguchi had done with some 6,000 men of Lieutenant-General Masao Maruyama's 2nd Division, while another 3,000 men simultaneously struck along the Matanikau, where the Marines now maintained a strong forward position. On October 16, Maruyama's column began cutting its way through the jungle, using the impenetrable cover of the giant trees to escape American observation planes. The march inland was a nightmare for the Japanese: all heavy equipment, including artillery, had to be abandoned and the time schedule kept slipping backwards. On the 19th, when the two-

pronged attack was to have been launched, the serpentine column had not even reached the upper reaches of the Lunga river. Hyakutake set the date back to October 22, but even that was not enough, and further days were added.

But the Japanese commander at the Matanikau got his signals crossed and attacked one day early, launching a tank-led thrust across the mouth of the Matanikau on the 23rd. Marine 37-mm guns stopped the tanks dead in their tracks and artillery massacred the following infantry. One result of this abortive attack, however, was that a battalion of the 7th Marines was pulled out of the inland defensive perimeter to reinforce along the Matanikau.

On October 24, therefore, the 1st Battalion, 7th Marines held 2,500 yards of jungle front anchored on the ridge, now generally known as Edson's Ridge or Bloody Ridge, which the raiders and parachute troops had defended so gallantly in September. To the Marine battalion's left, the 2nd Battalion of the 164th Infantry held the portion of the line that curved back toward the coast. The two American battalions held the area that was to be the focal point of Japanese attacks. When Maruyama's soldiers surged forward from the jungle after nightfall on the 24th, they were met by a solid wall of Marine and Army small

The ordeal of Vandegrift's Marines, penned in the narrow beach-head.

arms fire, canister shells from 37's, and a deadly rain of artillery and mortar fire. As soon as it became apparent that the main thrust of the attack was aimed at Edson's Ridge, the 3rd Battalion, 164th Infantry, in reserve, was started forward to reinforce the Marines. Slipping and stumbling through the rainy darkness, the soldiers were fed into the Marine positions as they arrived and wherever they were needed. The lines held and they held again the next night as Maruyama made another attempt with his dwindling forces. Then it was over, and all Japanese attempts to penetrate the 1st Division's lines had failed; 3,500 of the enemy lay dead in, around, and in front of the American positions, including the 2nd Division's infantry group commander and two regimental commanders. One of these, Colonel Sejiro Furumiya of the 29th Infantry, had made a pledge to his men when they landed on Guadalcanal, that if they were unsuccessful in capturing the island "not even one man should expect to return alive".

Things were looking up for Vandegrift's troops. Despite the horrendous losses that the Allies had suffered in sea battles in the waters off Guadalcanal, a steady stream of supplies and men continued to be landed on the island under the protective cover of the "Cactus" pilots. And on October 18, the vibrant and aggressive Vice-Admiral William F. Halsey relieved Admiral Ghormley as Commander, South Pacific Area and brought with him a resolve that Guadalcanal would be held and the Japanese driven off. In that determination he was supported by President Roosevelt, who personally ordered the tempo of aid to the defenders to be stepped up. The 25th Infantry Division in Hawaii was alerted for a move to Guadalcanal, and the rest of the 2nd Marine Division and the Americal Division were also ordered forward.

Heartened by the promise of reinforcements, Vandegrift continued to keep the Japanese off balance with the troops he had. On November 3, six battalions under Colonel Edson probed forward and trapped a Japanese force near Point Cruz and eliminated another 300 men of Hyakutake's army. At the same time, on the eastern side of the perimeter, a reconnaissance in force by the 7th Marines, backed up by two battalions of the 164th Infantry, punished a 1,500-man Japanese reinforcement group from the 38th Division which landed near Koli Point, driving the enemy soldiers into the jungle. Partly as a result of this action, Hyakutake decided to abandon the concept of the two-sided attack on the American position and ordered the 38th Division's troops to move overland to Kokumbona. Five hundred of the retreating Japanese failed to complete the trip. They were hunted down and killed by the Marines of the 2nd Raider Battalion who landed at Aola Bay 40 miles west of the Lunga on November 4. These men were part of a project dear to Admiral Turner's heart, an attempt to set up another airfield on Guadalcanal. Vandegrift wanted nothing to do with any scheme that dispersed American ground forces on Guadalcanal, but lost the argument to his naval superior. He did, however, get permission for the raiders to patrol overland to the Henderson Field perimeter and they accounted for the Japanese straggling through the jungle.

The further landing of 38th Division troops on Guadalcanal was part of a massive reinforcement effort which included the daylight landing of Japanese forces on November 14. While shore-based aircraft and planes from the carrier *Enterprise* sank seven of 11 transports carrying the Japanese soldiers, Tanaka's destroyers were able to rescue many of the men and Hyakutake had 10,000 fresh troops. But Vandegrift had two new reinforced regiments too, the 8th Marines from Samoa and the 182nd Infantry from New Caledonia, and he retained his numerical advantage. He continued to pressure the Japanese, repeatedly probing and jabbing toward Kokumbona in November, using many of his newly arrived Army and Marine battalions.

The Marine general needed the fresh men. His own division, after four months of fighting in the jungle heat and humidity, was worn out; over half the men had contracted malaria or other tropical diseases. His original Marine units had suffered nearly 2,000 casualties, 681 of them killed in action or dead of wounds. The decision was made to withdraw the 1st Marine Division to Australia for rest and rehabilitation. On December 9, 1942, General Vandegrift turned over command of the troops on Guadalcanal to Major-General Alexander M. Patch of the Americal Division, and the 5th Marines boarded ship to leave the island, leading the exodus of the 1st Division.

Patch's mission was to drive the Japanese off Guadalcanal, and his forces were increased substantially to give him the means to carry out this task. Major-General J. Lawton Collins' 25th Infantry Division began landing on Guadalcanal on December 17 and the last elements of the 2nd Marine Division came in on January 4 under command of Brigadier-General Alphonse de Carre. New Army and Marine squadrons swelled the ranks of the Cactus Air Force and the situation was grim indeed for the Japanese.

By the beginning of January, General Patch had 50,000 men of all services under his command. Hyakutake's 17th Army troops amounted to about 25,000 men, but they were now cut off from effective reinforcement or resupply by Allied air power and a resurgent naval effort. His men were on short rations and low on ammunition; many were sick with the same tropical diseases that had ravaged the Marines of Vandegrift's division, but there were not enough medical supplies to aid them back to health. While the Japanese were still capable of hard fighting, they could not sustain a serious offensive effort. The decision was made in Rabaul about mid-December to abandon the ill-fated attempt to recapture Guadalcanal and to rescue as many of Hyakutake's men as possible.

General Patch unwittingly reinforced the Japanese decision to get out. Commander since January 2 of a newly organised XIV Corps run by a skeletal staff from the Americal Division, he used his three divisions to drive unrelentingly west from the Lunga perimeter. Using Collins' 25th Division inland and de Carre's 2nd Division along the coast, he hammered steadily at the Japanese. The defenders fell back slowly, fighting hard but unable to hold any position long before the American troops, who used massive artillery, air, and naval gunfire support, drove them out. Kokumbona, so long the objective of Vandegrift's attacks, was occupied by the 25th Division on January 23. Here Patch held up the attack, anxious because reports of a Japanese shipping build-up at Rabaul and in the Shortland Islands presaged another attempt to take Guadalcanal. Actually, this was the Japanese destroyer force that was intended to evacuate Hyakutake's men.

Patch cautiously resumed his advance on January 30. He had a small blocking force in the mountain passes inland to prevent the Japanese crossing to the other side of the island, and he sent an Army battalion around Cape Esperance to the western coast to block that route of escape also. By February 5, when the advance was held up again by reports of a large Japanese flotilla lurking in the northern Solomons, the lead Army regiment, the 161st Infantry, had reached positions 3,500 yards west of Tassafaronga and 12 miles from Cape Esperance.

On the night of February 7-8, Japanese destroyers under the command of Rear-Admiral Koniji Koyonagi executed a masterly evacuation of 13,000 Japanese troops from Guadalcanal. Many of these men would fight the Americans again on other battlefields in the Solomons and on New Britain. But there were many others who would fight no more. Casualties had been high on both sides in this bitterly fought contest in the jungles and malaria infested swamps of Guadalcanal. However, thanks to their superior medical facilities and greater regard for human life, American casualties were correspondingly lower.

On January 8, 1943, with the fighting for Guadalcanal already decided, Major-General Patch could report "the complete and total defeat of Japanese forces on Guadalcanal." After the struggle for control of the island was decided, the Japanese never again advanced in the Pacific. The staggering Japanese losses of ships, planes, and pilots that were equally a feature of the Guadalcanal campaign with the bitter ground fighting were not replaceable in kind. Admiral Tanaka, whose Tokyo Express had done so much to sustain the Japanese on the island, considered that "Japan's doom was sealed with the closing of the struggle for Guadalcanal".

By February 9, 1943 the battle for Guadalcanal was over. The campaign had cost the Japanese some 24,000 lives, including more than 2,000 skilled pilots and aircrew, who could probably never be replaced. American losses were about 1,600 men killed and over 4,000 wounded. Japanese aircraft losses, still difficult to assess precisely, were probably well over 800, far outnumbering American planes destroyed. Both sides suffered heavily in numbers of ships sunk, but the Americans could build new ones more readily.

The final action in the Guadalcanal campaign was the seizure of the Russell Islands, just north-west of Guadalcanal. The U.S. 43rd Infantry Division landed unopposed in the Russells at the end of February. As on Guadalcanal, the invaders quickly began the construction of air and naval bases to support the projected advance up the Solomons.

The American victory at Guadalcanal was matched by similar gains in eastern New Guinea by General MacArthur's forces. By early 1943, then, the situation in the South Pacific had changed sufficiently for both sides to reassess their strategy. The Japanese, determined to hold the area at all costs, strengthened their defences and rushed in fresh troops, planes, and ships. Hoping to blunt the force of the Allied offensive, in April they launched a major air effort to destroy American bases, aircraft, and shipping in both the lower Solomons and New Guinea. Results were poor, however, and although Japanese pilots returned with great tales of success, the attackers actually sustained far greater losses than they inflicted – losses, again, that they could ill afford.

Perhaps the most damaging blow to the Japanese cause fell in mid-April. Gratified by the exaggerated reports of Japanese success, the commander of the Combined Fleet, Admiral Isoroku Yamamoto, planned to visit the island of Bougainville, in the northern Solomons, on a combination inspection-morale building tour. As Japan's foremost sailor, architect of the Pearl Harbor attack, and a source of inspiration for all, his arrival would be a major event. So, while security required the utmost secrecy, it was still necessary to inform local commanders. The appropriate messages accordingly went out. Unfortunately for Yamamoto, these messages were intercepted by American listeners, promptly decoded, and passed on to Admiral Halsey. The South Pacific commander now knew exactly when Yamamoto would arrive, his route of approach, and the number and types of planes in the flight. He immediately prepared an aerial ambush with Guadalcanal-based fighters.

Bougainville was at extreme range from Henderson Field, but Yamamoto had a reputation for punctuality, so the American pilots planned to waste no time at the fatal rendezvous. At 0930 on the morning of April 18, just as Yamamoto's plane began to land, and his own fighter escort turned to leave, the attackers struck.

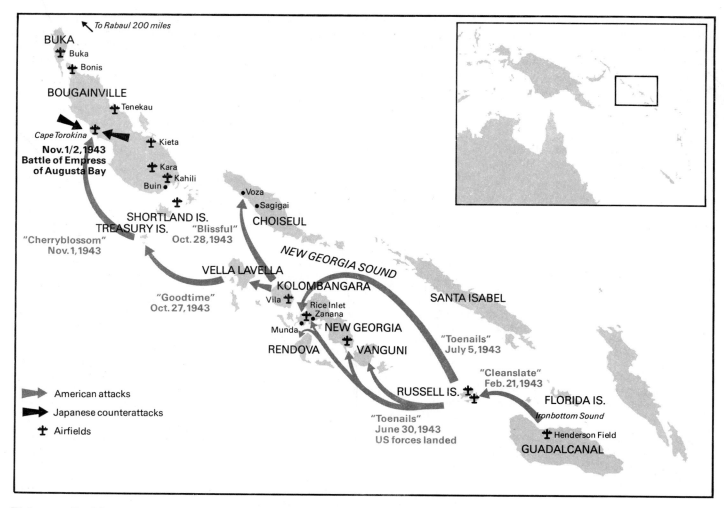

The battle for the Solomons in 1943.

Eighteen Lockheed P-38 Lightnings swooped down on the two bombers carrying the admiral and his staff. Brushing aside the remaining Japanese fighters, they quickly struck down their targets. Yamamoto died in the wreckage of his bomber, a victim of able Intelligence work and skilful timing.

The admiral's death was a great shock to Japanese morale, and an even greater loss to Japan's naval leadership. "There was only one Yamamoto," commented a saddened colleague, "and no one is able to replace him." His talents would be sorely missed in the coming months when the Americans resumed their offensive.

The details of this offensive had already been worked out. Despite the requirements of other areas, the two-pronged offensive against Rabaul would continue, with MacArthur advancing in New Guinea, and Halsey, still under Nimitz but subject to MacArthur's strategic direction, climbing the ladder of the Solomons. Halsey's objective was Bougainville, but to reach it he would first have to seize intermediate fighter bases from which to cover his final advance. So his initial target was New Georgia, in the central Solomons, with its vital airstrip at Munda.

New Georgia posed a difficult problem. The centre of a small group of islands, shielded by coral reefs and accessible only through narrow channels, it was all but

impossible to assault directly. Munda Point, moreover, site of the airstrip, could not be approached by large ships. It was clear to Halsey that he would first have to seize bases in the islands around New Georgia from which to mount and support his main attack. Making his task no easier were the Japanese defenders of the central Solomons, some 10,000 army and navy troops deployed in scattered detachments to deny airfields and harbours to any invader. Rabaul-based air and naval forces were also ready to assist these units.

The operation began late in June, with small unopposed American landings at the south end of New Georgia and on adjacent Vangunu Island. Then, on the night of June 29-30, some 6,000 troops of Major-General John H. Hester's 43rd Infantry Division went ashore on Rendova Island, just across the channel from Munda Point and ideally located to support the final assault on the airstrip. The few defenders on Rendova were surprised, and offered little resistance, but Japanese airstrikes proved a nuisance and coastal defence guns on Munda Point dropped heavy shells on the American beach-head. Rendova, nevertheless, was securely in American hands.

The landings on New Georgia began on July 2, when the bulk of Hester's division splashed ashore without opposition at Zanana, on New Georgia's south shore, about five miles east of Munda.

On the 5th, a small second force of soldiers and Marines landed at Rice Anchorage, on the island's north shore. While this group sought to cut off the approaches to Munda, the larger forces at Zanana struck out directly to capture the airstrip.

Almost immediately things went wrong. The fierce heat, jungle terrain, and stubborn Japanese resistance proved too much for the attackers. The 43rd Division's troops, in combat for the first time, suffered heavy casualties and morale dropped badly. Relieving one of the regimental commanders did little to help, nor did the arrival of reinforcing elements of the 37th Division. By July 7, the southern drive on Munda had halted, while the advance from Rice Anchorage, after some initial gains, was also stopped.

Major-General Noboru Sasaki, the Japanese commander on New Georgia, was so encouraged by his success that he began planning a counter-landing on Rendova. Higher headquarters overruled him, however, and instead decided to make a major effort to reinforce Sasaki's troops on New Georgia. As a result, for nearly two weeks the waters of the central and northern Solomons were violently disturbed by clashes between American warships and Japanese vessels engaged in a renewal of the "Tokyo Express". Two major battles, the Battles of Kula

Gulf (July 5-6) and Kolombangara (July 12-13), were slight tactical victories for the Japanese. More important, they managed to land about 2,000 reinforcements, which made the American ground advance all the more difficult.

This advance continued to stumble against the fierce Japanese resistance. The thick tropical vegetation and intense heat proved effective allies of Sasaki's men, who provided a bitter lesson in jungle warfare to the green American troops. If the Japanese were stubborn foes during the day, they were even more effective at night. Testing the American perimeters, throwing hand grenades, shouting, and dropping harassing fire on the exhausted men of the 43rd Division, they kept up a constant pressure. The inexperienced Americans, bewildered by the weird noises and intense darkness of the jungle night, were often terrified by their own imaginations. They mistook the slithering sound of land crabs for Japanese soldiers crawling to attack them, the phosphorescence of rotting logs for enemy signals, and the sick, dank smell of the jungle for poison gas. Fearing the nocturnal enemy who, it was said, would drag them from their foxholes with hooks and ropes, or at the least would knife or bayonet them while they slept, American troops fired wildly at the least sound, hurled grenades at each other, and suffered badly from combat neurosis.

Gradually they became accustomed to the worst aspects of fighting in the jungle, but they still made little progress in their efforts to reach Munda. By mid-July, despite another landing between Zanana and Munda, the main drive had advanced less than halfway to the airfield. To put new life into the offensive, therefore, Major-General Oscar W. Griswold, the new XIV Corps commander, took direct charge of the New Georgia operations. He immediately asked for reinforcements and set about reorganising for a major attack, in order, as he put it, "to crack [the] Munda nut".

It was ten days before he was ready. Then, on July 25, supported by artillery, airstrikes, and naval bombardment, the American infantry renewed its attack. Progress remained frustratingly slow, however, and on the 29th Griswold relieved General Hester and put Major-General John H. Hodge, a veteran of Guadalcanal, in command of the 43rd Division. Perhaps because of this change, or maybe because of a simultaneous Japanese decision—under the pressure of increasing casualties—to fall back toward Munda, the American drive gradually began to accelerate. By August 1, there was little doubt of the outcome. Three days later, the 43rd Division's troops overran the airfield. The surviving Japanese made their way to other nearby islands or sought shelter elsewhere in the New Georgia jungles. Munda airstrip, after hasty reconstruction and widening, was in operation on August 14. By the end of the month, with the help of the newly arrived 25th Infantry Division, the entire island had been cleared of Japanese.

There remained one more island in the central Solomons with a strong Japanese garrison and a useful airstrip. This was Kolombangara, just north-west of New Georgia, where General Sasaki now had his headquarters and about 10,000 troops with which he hoped to counter-attack the Americans on New Georgia. To help in this projected operation, the Japanese had been trying to run troops in from Rabaul. On the night of August 1, they succeeded in landing a few bargeloads of reinforcements. When American motor torpedo boats from Rendova tried to stop them, a Japanese destroyer ran down the PT boat commanded by Lieutenant John F. Kennedy. Thrown into the water, the future president of the United States not only escaped with his life, but also succeeded in rescuing most of his crew through a combination of bravery, determination, and several exhausting swims.

Five nights later, four fast Japanese troop-carrying destroyers again attempted to reinforce Kolombangara. Intercepted by American destroyers just as they were approaching their destination, three of the Japanese warships succumbed to a surprise torpedo attack before they knew what had hit them. The fourth made good its escape, but nearly two battalions of reinforcements drowned in the warm waters of Vella Gulf.

Sasaki's forces, nevertheless, still constituted a formidable challenge, for capture of the Kolombangara airstrip was the next scheduled operation. To Admiral Halsey, the prospect of another long and costly land battle against Sasaki seemed less and less palatable. After some consideration, and a daring advance reconnaissance, an alternative solution offered itself. This was to bypass Kolombangara in favour of seizing lightly-defended Vella Lavella, about 20 miles to the north-west, and building an airstrip there. From Vella Lavella and a few other small islands, Kolombangara could easily be cut off and neutralised. And since Vella Lavella was closer to Bougainville, its airstrip would be better located to support the subsequent invasion of the latter. Thus, a principle to be followed whenever possible for the rest of the Pacific war was established: it was easier to carve a new airstrip out of the jungle than to wrest one already built from its stubborn Japanese defenders.

Just after daylight on August 15, a reinforced regiment of the 25th Division landed on the beaches of southern Vella Lavella. Japanese dive-bombers and fighters constituted the only resistance, and these inflicted little damage on the invaders. Unloading proceeded rapidly. The troops quickly established a defensive perimeter and then struck inland to secure the island. A few hundred Japanese survivors of the ill-fated August 6 destroyer run, and some other escapees from New Georgia, were the only enemy troops on the island. The Americans had more trouble finding them than defeating them. There was some Japanese discussion of making a counter-landing, but wiser heads at Rabaul suggested that this would simply be like "pouring water on a hot stone", and the idea died quickly.

The Japanese thus limited themselves to hit-and-run air raids on the beachhead and on American ships bringing supplies to Vella Lavella. These were a constant danger, inflicting some casualties on troops unloading supplies and damaging a few ships. But despite such problems, the end of September saw the island all but secured, by which time the airstrip was in action and New Zealand units had replaced the American troops. An attempt by the Japanese to evacuate survivors on the night of October 6 led to

Moving up supplies through the mud of Rendova in July 1943.

another fierce destroyer engagement. This time the Japanese got the better of the fight, rescuing their compatriots and inflicting greater losses on the American warships.

The decision to bypass Kolombangara proved to be doubly sound. For even as the Americans were securing Vella Lavella, General Sasaki, under orders from Rabaul to save his troops for another day, was shifting the Kolombangara force to Bougainville. On three nights at the end of September and in early October, Japanese barges, landing craft, and torpedo boats, escorted by destroyers and aircraft, managed to evacuate more than 9,000 troops. Attempts by American destroyers to thwart the withdrawal were frustrated by the Japanese escorts.

The fight for the central Solomons thus ended with New Georgia and all of the islands around it in American hands. More than 1,000 Americans had died in the battle, and nearly four times as many had been wounded. Japanese casualties probably totalled around 10,000, of which at least a quarter had been killed. Furthermore, continuing Japanese air and naval losses emphasised the growing attrition of these valuable resources. Still, the four months' defence of the central Solomons meant that much more time to prepare Rabaul for its final defence. And on Bougainville the Japanese hoped to delay the Americans even further.

The importance of this was greater than perhaps they realised. Halsey's victories in the Solomons had been matched by impressive advances by MacArthur in New Guinea. As a result, the Joint Chiefs-of-Staff had concluded that it would be more advantageous to bypass and neutralise Rabaul than to capture it, thus freeing large forces for a more rapid drive on targets closer to Japan itself. This decision, ratified by Allied military leaders in late August 1943, left Bougainville as the last obstacle for Halsey to overcome before he could push on beyond Rabaul.

While American heavy bombers struck fiercely at Japanese air bases in the Bougainville area in late September, Halsey was planning his assault. There were about 40,000 Japanese soldiers on Bougainville, commanded by General Hyakutake, of Guadalcanal fame, as well as an additional 20,000 navy troops. Allied Intelligence had a fairly good appreciation of this strength, and Halsey, after his successful bypassing of Kolombangara, decided to attempt a similar strategy on Bougainville. What he sought was an air base from which Rabaul could be neutralised and from which the Japanese supply line between Rabaul and the Solomons could be severed. It was not necessary to crush all of Hyakutake's forces: only to bypass and isolate them. And this is exactly what Halsey proposed to do.

With most of the Japanese concentrated in southern Bougainville and at the island's northern tip, the practically undefended Empress Augusta Bay area,

midway up the west coast, seemed an attractive target. The landing date was set for November 1, with the I Marine Amphibious Corps under General Vandegrift, who had led the US Marine Corps at Guadalcanal, given the assignment.

During October, American bombers continued to punish Japanese airfields on Bougainville, knocking out the last of them by the end of the month. To confuse the Japanese further, in the pre-dawn hours of October 27, a small force of New Zealand troops occupied the Treasury Islands, south of Bougainville. Then, later in the day, a battalion of U.S. Marines landed on the large island of Choiseul, to the east. This was merely a raid, to mislead the Japanese about American intentions, but in the week before they were evacuated the Marines stirred up enough trouble to make the defenders believe they had come to stay.

Whatever the effect of the Treasury and Choiseul landings, when the 3rd Marine Division landed on the north shore of Empress Augusta Bay early on November 1, there was very little opposition. Since the terrain around the bay was low and wet, the Japanese thought it unsuitable for offensive operations by an invader and thus ruled out the chances of an American landing there. General Hyakutake had stationed less than 300 men in

A brisk fire-fight between Marine Raiders and concealed Japanese snipers.

the area, and these outnumbered troops were quickly overwhelmed by the attacking Marines. Within a few hours, Vandegrift's men had secured the area.

The Japanese counter-attack came by air and sea. Almost immediately, Rabaul-based bombers and fighters struck at the landing force, only to be driven off with heavy losses by defending American aircraft. At the same time, a strong cruiser-destroyer force sped down from Rabaul, hoping to smash American warships in a repeat of the Savo Island victory of the Guadalcanal campaign. The naval attack was also intended to cover the landing of Japanese ground troops at Empress Augusta Bay. But this time the Americans were ready. In the Battle of Empress Augusta Bay on the night of August 1-2, the Japanese were driven off, with slightly heavier losses than those sustained by the American vessels. Repeated Japanese air attacks the next day were also defeated.

Then it was the American's turn. Learning of a heavy Japanese naval build-up at Rabaul, Halsey despatched his fast carrier units against the enemy base. In two daring airstrikes, on November 5 and 11, the American carrier planes smashed

Japanese naval and air targets at Rabaul. So effective were these blows, that they forced the surviving Japanese warships to retreat north to other bases, thus ending the chances of further attacks on the Marine beach-head from the sea.

Japanese air strength also suffered badly. A sustained air attack on Empress Augusta Bay, lasting for ten days after the Marine invasion, was a dismal failure. The Japanese sustained heavy losses, with little to show for them. By November 12, with the Japanese fleet withdrawn from Rabaul and little or no air strength left there, the great Japanese base was no longer an offensive threat.

The Americans were thus free to enlarge their beach-head. Army troops of the 37th Infantry Division–had begun landing on November 8, and within a few days there were more than 34,000 Americans at Empress Augusta Bay. By the beginning of 1944, the Army's Americal Division had replaced the Marines, and the two army divisions, with strong artillery support, were defending a large beach-head that included a naval base, three airfields, and extensive supply installations.

Attempts by General Hyakutake to crush the American perimeter were to no avail. Japanese forces, pushing overland through the heavy Bougainville jungle and cut off from outside assistance, were unable to mount a co-ordinated and sustained offensive. There was considerable fighting during November and December, but Hyakutake's efforts were futile, and the American beach-head gradually expanded. Content to hold this beach-head, the Americans made no further effort to enlarge it after the end of the year.

On March 9, 1944, Hyakutake launched his last attack. This was an all-out assault, with at least 15,000 troops, and what the Japanese lacked in air and naval support, they made up in ferocity. In a bitter struggle that lasted until the end of the month, the Japanese threatened but never succeeded in breaking the American lines. When the fight ended, Hyakutake had lost some 6,000 troops. He continued to peck away at the American perimeter, but the threat had ended. The Japanese on Bougainville were no longer a force to be reckoned with. Defeated and isolated from support or resupply, weakened by hunger and disease, they were doomed to sit out the rest of the war. The Americans, meanwhile, soon to be replaced in their perimeter by Australian units, were free once again to push on to other conquests.

The fight on Bougainville brought to a close the long struggle up the Solomons ladder from Guadalcanal. In conjunction with MacArthur's efforts in the New Guinea area, the successful campaign had isolated and neutralised Rabaul. That once important Japanese bastion no longer posed any danger to the great Allied Pacific offensive, and could be left to wither and rot away. No less important was the damaging attrition the

Japanese had suffered in men and *matériel*. Thousands of soldiers had been killed or left to die in the Solomons. Even more crushing were the losses in warships and transport, which, at this stage of the war, could never be replaced. And finally, perhaps most significant of all, the tremendous Japanese losses in aircraft and trained pilots were decisive.

Japanese naval air power, which had once made the Combined Fleet one of the most effective fighting forces in the history of modern seapower, had now been all but wiped out. Without it, the Japanese would be unable to oppose the great central Pacific offensive that the Americans were now about to launch. Nor, for that matter, could they mount an effective air defence against MacArthur's projected drive to retake the Philippines. In this sense, the American victory in the Solomons was decisive, hastening and ensuring Japan's ultimate defeat.

American tank men have a break to take on ammunition (above).

Countering a Japanese ambush in the jungle (below).

CHAPTER 49
Allied planning and problems

The Anglo-American summit conference at Quebec in August 1943 ("Quadrant") was born out of a need to take fresh grand-strategic decisions in view of the fast-changing situation in the Mediterranean after the fall of Mussolini – and also out of underlying mistrust between the Western Allies. Churchill had proposed the summit to Roosevelt, partly because he had been informed by Averell Harriman that Roosevelt was thinking of convening a purely Soviet-American meeting. As the Prime Minister telegraphed to the President: "I do not underrate the use that enemy propaganda would make of a meeting between the heads of Soviet Russia and the United States at this juncture with the British Commonwealth and Empire excluded. It would be serious and vexatious and many would be bewildered and alarmed thereby." (Michael Howard, *Grand Strategy* Vol IV, 559) Roosevelt replied that he had only intended to explore informally with Stalin the question of postwar Russian policy, and suggested that in the meantime he and the Prime Minister should confer in Quebec. Nonetheless here was the shadow of the future – Roosevelt's burgeoning belief that he could settle the postwar world with "Uncle Joe" on the basis of personal deals in mutual trust; the emergence of two super-powers, the U.S.A. and Soviet Russia, and the relegation of Britain to the second division, against which Churchill was to struggle with all the force of his personal prestige in a frantic but hopeless fight.

Yet while this political mistrust before the Quebec Conference was no more than a whisper, military mistrust between Britain and the United States had now reached crisis point. It turned on the perennial issue of the correct relationship between a Mediterranean strategy and a cross-Channel invasion (Operation "Overlord", as "Round-up" had been renamed). The American Joint Chiefs-of-Staff, and especially General Marshall and his own staff, were convinced that the British were seeking to overturn the decisions first reached at Casablanca and confirmed at Washington in May whereby the Mediterranean was unequivocally subordinated to "Overlord". They feared that the British would drag them into an ever-deeper morass of involvement in the Mediterranean, so weakening and perhaps even ruling out "Overlord". They did not believe in fact that the British meant to attack across the Channel at all. The United States Secretary of War, Henry Stimson, reported to Roosevelt after a visit to London:

"We cannot now rationally hope to be able to cross the Channel and come to grips with our German enemy under a British commander. His Prime Minister and his Chief-of-Staff are frankly at variance with such a proposal. The shadows of Passchendaele and Dunkerque still hang too heavily over the imagination of these leaders of his government. Though they have rendered lip-service to the Operation, their heart is not in it. . . ." (Henry L. Stimson and McGeorge Bundy *On Active Service in Peace and War*).

In particular Marshall's staff, educated in the American military tradition to think only in narrow military terms and to regard political considerations as irrelevant, believed that the British *penchant* for the Mediterranean was inspired more by postwar British political interests than by wartime strategy. The American Chiefs-of-Staff therefore went to Quebec in militant mood. That this would be the case was well known to the British delegation, for they had been forwarned by their Joint Staff Mission in Washington that they would encounter "some serious difficulties".

The four-day voyage amid the pre-war luxuries of the Cunarder *Queen Mary* gave Churchill and the British Chiefs-of-Staff an opportunity to clear their own minds. In fact, they had a great deal to discuss, for there appears to have been a divergence between the Prime Minister and his military advisers. Sir Alan Brooke apparently remained completely committed to "Overlord" as the primary war-winning strike against Germany, while still believing that German resistance must first be weakened by further operations in the Mediterranean which would exploit the opportunity now presented by Mussolini's fall and the impending collapse of Italy. But Churchill's imagination now encompassed the possibility of actually deciding the whole war by offensives in the Mediterranean and the Balkans. The Balkans had fascinated him as a potential theatre of war ever since 1915. If there was to be an invasion of Europe launched from Britain, Churchill favoured Norway as the objective (Operation "Jupiter") rather than France. As it happened, Hitler too was preoccupied by Norway and the Balkans. However, Churchill, in the chapters on the Quebec Conference in his war memoirs, makes no mention of Norway or of his far-reaching Balkan ideas, but gives the impression that his mind was wholly upon how to ensure the ultimate success of "Overlord", to which an advance up Italy at least to the line Leghorn-Ancona would be an essential ancillary. But in fact he had written to the Chiefs-of-Staff in July 1943:

"I have no doubt myself that the right strategy for 1944 is:

(a) Maximum post-'Husky'; certainly to the Po, with option to attack westwards in the South of France or north-eastward towards Vienna, and meanwhile to procure the expulsion of the enemy from the Balkans and Greece.

(b) 'Jupiter' prepared under the cover of 'Overlord'."

The Chiefs-of-Staff, and in particular Brooke, spent the voyage to Canada arguing the Prime Minister out of these propositions, but, as it proved, with only partial success since he was to insist on putting forward "Jupiter" late in the Conference. With regard to the Mediterranean, the agreed British case to be put at Quebec was that a campaign in Italy constituted an essential preliminary to "Overlord", both by dispersing and consuming German land forces and by providing bases from which Allied bombers could destroy fighter factories in south Germany.

On August 11 Churchill and his party, which included Brigadier Orde Wingate the Chindit leader (who, being a romantic and eccentric figure offering an unorthodox, offensive nostrum, much impressed Churchill), arrived in the Citadel at Quebec. The role of the Canadian Government was limited to that of host, for Roosevelt had feared that if Canada took part, other American allied states such as Brazil would expect to be present too. On August 14 the British and American Chiefs-of-Staff met in battle, Churchill himself having gone off to visit Roosevelt at his home, Hyde Park, while the military men hammered out an agreed paper for the political leaders to consider.

The Americans laid down their own views in a forthright memorandum submitted to their British colleagues the day before. They insisted that there must be no renunciation of the decisions reached in Washington, but on the contrary an end to what they called "opportunist strategy". "We must not jeopardise," they wrote, "our second overall strategy simply to exploit local successes in a generally-accepted secondary theatre, the Mediterranean . . ." They demanded that "Overlord" be given "whole-hearted and immediate support". Nevertheless they had no objection to further operations in Italy aimed at weakening German strength, bringing about an Italian collapse and at establishing airfields at least as far north as Rome. But they were careful to emphasise that, as between Operation "Overlord" and operations in the Mediterranean, "when there is a shortage of resources 'Overlord' will have an overriding priority". With regard to more distant objectives, any surplus Allied forces in Italy should, they stated, be allotted to the invasion of southern France rather than to the Balkans or a march on Vienna.

When in the meetings on August 14 and 15 Brooke and Air Chief Marshal Portal argued that the American proposals failed to acknowledge adequately the importance of an advance in Italy as an essential preliminary to "Overlord", especially in making it possible to bomb German fighter production, they merely exacerbated the profound American mis-

trust of British intentions. A key issue lay in the seven Allied divisions which it had been agreed at Washington should be transferred from the Mediterranean to the U.K. by November 1943 as part of the "Overlord" build-up. The American paper wanted this decision re-affirmed, while the British argued that these divisions should be retained in the Mediterranean where they would be more useful.

On August 16 the American Joint Chiefs-of-Staff sent the British a formal memorandum couched in plain language:

"The discussion in the Combined Chiefs-of-Staff Meeting yesterday made more apparent than ever the necessity for decision now as to whether our main effort in the European Theater is to be in the Mediterranean or from the United Kingdom. The United States Chiefs-of-Staff believe that this is the critical question before the Conference ..."

They proposed that the Conference formally reaffirm the decision to launch "Overlord" and "assign it an overriding priority over all other operations in the European Theater". They added that they believed that "the acceptance of this decision must be without conditions and without mental reservations".

Thus came to a head the underlying differences of approach and military tradition that had divided the two allies ever since Marshall reluctantly accepted "Torch" as the operation for 1942 instead of "Roundup"; a matter now not so much

for strategic argument as for candid talk about American suspicion of British good faith. The candid talk took place unrecorded in a closed session. According to Brooke's account, he went over "our whole Mediterranean strategy to prove its objects which they had never fully realised' and finally I had to produce countless arguments to prove the close relations that exist between the cross-Channel and Italian operations. In the end I think our arguments did have some effect on Marshall." (Arthur Bryant *The Turn of the Tide*).

Next day, August 17, after more talk, a compromise strategic statement was agreed, but based largely on the American paper submitted at the start of the Conference. Instead of the original American phrase "'Overlord' will have an overriding priority" [over the Mediterranean in allotting limited resources], a British alternative was substituted, to the effect that "Available resources will be distributed and employed with the main object of ensuring the success of 'Overlord'. Operations in the Mediterranean theatre will be carried out with the forces allotted at 'Trident' [the Washington Conference in May 1943], except insofar as these may be varied by the decisions of the Combined Chiefs-of-Staff." Nevertheless, as Michael Howard points out, while the British had succeeded in getting written in a greater measure of flexibility as between "Overlord" and the Mediterranean, they gave up their own proposal that the seven battle-hardened divisions

The Allied leaders and their military advisers meet at Quebec in August 1943.

due for return to the U.K. should instead stay in the Mediterranean.

So the Quebec conference was witnessing Anglo-American discord break forth again. Was the American suspicion about the sincerity of British intentions in regard to "Overlord" due to a misunderstanding, or was it in fact justified? Churchill certainly hoped that opportunities would now open up in the Mediterranean and the Balkans which would render unnecessary what he saw as a highly risky cross-Channel invasion. What of Brooke himself? At the time of the Quebec Conference his arguments in the meetings and the entries in his diary alike express a belief in "Overlord" as the paramount Allied stroke. Yet, as Michael Howard notes in *The Mediterranean Strategy in the Second World War*, Brooke wrote in his diary only a few months later, on October 25:

"Our build-up in Italy is much slower than that of the Germans and far slower than I expected. We shall have to have an almighty row with the Americans who have put us in this position with their insistence to abandon the Mediterranean operations for the very problematical cross-Channel operations. We are beginning to see the full beauty of the Marshall strategy! It is quite heartbreaking when we see what we might have done this year if our strategy had not been distorted by the Americans . . ."

And his diary entry for November 1 is even more revealing:

"When I look at the Mediterranean I realise only too well how far I have failed. If only I had had sufficient force of character to swing those American Chiefs-of-Staff and make them see daylight, how different the war might be. We should have had the whole Balkans ablaze by now, and the war might have finished by 1943." (Arthur Bryant *Triumph in the West*)

Light is cast on this whole question by the matter of the appointment of an Allied supreme commander for "Overlord". It had long been understood between Brooke and Churchill that Brooke should be that commander. At Quebec, however, Churchill told Brooke that because of the preponderance of American over British land forces in "Overlord" after the first few weeks, the appointee must be American. In his war memoirs Churchill states that "I myself took the initiative of proposing to the President that an American commander should be appointed for the expedition to France. He was gratified at this suggestion, *and I dare say his mind had been moving that way*." [author's italics]. When Stimson's warning to the President about the prospects for the invasion under a British general is taken into account, it seems possible that it was not only the ultimate preponderance of American strength that dictated an American commander, but also the deep, ineradicable and perhaps justified American mistrust of Brooke's personal commitment to "Overlord".

The plenary sessions with Churchill and Roosevelt duly ratified the agreement on strategy in the European theatre reached by their military advisers. The intention was confirmed to advance as far north in Italy as possible in order to weaken the Germany army before "Overlord", and with a view to invading southern France. Meanwhile the bomber offensive against the German economy (Operation "Pointblank") was to be stepped up. In regard to the Far East and Pacific, however, it was not mistrust between allies but the variety of strategic options that caused the problems.

This was especially true of Burma. Sir Claude Auchinleck, the Commander-in-Chief in India and at present responsible for Burma operations, found himself – as in the Middle East in 1941 – acting as the unwelcome voice of realism. He had told London that poor rail and road communications, now severely interrupted by floods, necessarily laid tight logistic restrictions on strategy. He recommended a complete cessation of offensive operations until 1944, concentrating in the meantime on improving communications and building up supplies. Churchill reacted to this as he had to Auchinleck's similar advice in the Middle East – by writing Auchinleck down as a low-spirited obstructionist. Instead he lent a willing

ear to the splendid scenario outlined by Orde Wingate for air-supplied long-range penetration offensives behind the Japanese front in northern Burma; a scenario which would have drawn in much of Allied resources in troops and aircraft and virtually handed over operations in Burma to Wingate himself. The Prime Minister also strongly favoured Operation "Culverin", a plan for seizing the northern tip of Sumatra in 1944, which he saw as "the 'Torch' of the Indian Ocean". The British Joint Planners favoured a seaborne attack against the Burmese port of Akyab. The Americans simply wanted to re-open a land route between Burma and China; they also saw the Akyab operations as the touchstone of whether the British really meant to lend a hand in 1943 in the war against Japan at all. The British Chiefs-of-Staff had no very clear ideas, except that seaborne operations against Burma would be impossible without draining landing craft and naval forces from the European theatre, which they were determined must not occur. It was finally agreed by the Conference, though somewhat nebulously, that land operations should be pushed on in Upper Burma in order to press the Japanese and bring relief to China, Wingate playing a prominent part; but no conclusions were reached as to further operations.

However, the Quebec Conference did come to the major decision, originating from a proposal by Churchill, to set up a South-East Asia Command under Vice-Admiral Lord Louis Mountbatten to run the Burma campaign and any other operations in the region. The Commander-in-Chief in India became responsible only for providing the new command's main base and training facilities. The directives of the Allied governments were to reach Mountbatten via the British Chiefs-of-Staff, so that the new organisation became the British equivalent of the American-controlled Pacific and South-West Pacific areas. "Vinegar Joe" Stilwell became Mountbatten's deputy as well as continuing as Chief-of-Staff to Chiang Kai-shek.

With regard to the Pacific, the Conference merely blessed the now agreed American strategy of two separate but converging axes of advance, one under MacArthur via the northern coast of New Guinea and the other under Nimitz via the Gilberts, Marshalls and Carolines, aimed at establishing a base on the Chinese mainland from which an invasion of Japan could be launched. Likewise the British acquiesced without much argument in the American proposal to set the target date for the final defeat of Japan at twelve months after the defeat of Germany.

So once again the two Allies had composed their differences and emerged with agreed formulas of strategy. In particular, if "Overlord" had indeed been in doubt, the British had now committed themselves to it morally and verbally more firmly than before, whatever reservations individuals might still hold.

However, one of the most portentous decisions reached at Quebec, certainly in the long term, was not even recorded in the Conference proceedings, so secret was it. This was the so-called "Quebec Agreement" between Roosevelt and Churchill over the future of nuclear research and the development of the atom bomb. Up to early 1942 the British had been ahead in terms of original research, thanks to brilliant work done in British universities under the auspices of the Maude Committee in following up a paper drafted in spring 1940 by two German-born physicists at Birmingham University, Professor Rudolf Peierls and Dr Otto Frisch, which had first laid down how an atom bomb might be made. But by 1942 the sheer size of American research resources, especially in terms of experimental equipment, meant that the British lead was being fast overtaken. In July 1942 the British "Tube Alloys" (the codename for nuclear development) Council reported to the Prime Minister that if there were to be a merger between the two countries' efforts, it had better be effected quickly while the British side still had something to offer as part of a bargain. In the ensuing months the British found themselves more and more excluded from American information. In 1943 the Americans reached agreement with the Canadian Government for the entire Canadian output of uranium and the Canadian heavy-water plant, upon which the British themselves had been counting. Moreover, the British themselves, upon investigations, had come to realise that they could not spare the industrial resources in wartime to continue with their own nuclear development. It was therefore inevitable that Britain would have to accept that future research and development must be concentrated in the United States, albeit making use of British scientists and the fruits of British work.

So even in this uncharted field of the future Britain dwindled to the second rank of power, dependent on American resources and American good will.

As previously explained, the military situation, as it appeared at the time of the "Quadrant" Conference, was sufficiently hopeful to make the British and the Americans begin to think of the future of the European continent and its balance of power after German military might, which had changed the entire pre-war picture, had been reduced to dust and ashes.

There are two documents to be taken into account in this question. One comes from the pen of a senior American officer whom Robert E. Sherwood, editing the Harry Hopkins papers, could not identify. The other comes from a letter that Churchill sent to Field-Marshal Smuts personally on September 5, 1943.

When Harry Hopkins went to Quebec, he carried with him a note entitled "The Russian position", in which the anonymous American officer gave his views concerning post-war prospects in Europe and the chances of obtaining the help of Russia in the struggle against Japan:

"Russia's post-war position in Europe will be a dominant one. With Germany crushed, there is no power in Europe to oppose her tremendous military forces. It is true that Great Britain is building up a position in the Mediterranean *vis-à-vis* Russia that she may find useful in balancing power in Europe. However, even here she may not be able to oppose Russia unless she is otherwise supported.

"The conclusions from the foregoing are obvious. Since Russia is the decisive factor in the war, she must be given every assistance and every effort must be made to obtain her friendship. Likewise, since without question she will dominate Europe on the defeat of the Axis, it is even more essential to develop and maintain the most friendly relations with Russia.

"*Finally, the most important factor the United States has to consider in relation to Russia is the prosecution of the war in Pacific.* With Russia as an ally in the war against Japan, the war can be terminated in less time and at less expense in life and resources than if the reverse were the case. Should the war in the Pacific have to be carried on with an unfriendly or negative attitude on the part of Russia, the difficulties will be immeasurably increased and the operations might become abortive."

Churchill saw things in much the same light. His old South African friend, disappointed by the results of the Quebec Conference, which slowed down the war in the Mediterranean, cabled him on September 3:

"To the ordinary man it must appear that it is Russia who is winning the war. If this impression continues what will be our post-war world position compared with that of Russia? A tremendous shift in our world status may follow, and will leave Russia the diplomatic master of the world. This is both unnecessary and undesirable, and would have especially bad reactions for the British Commonwealth. Unless we emerge from the war on terms of equality our position will be both uncomfortable and dangerous."

Two days later, Churchill replied "after profound reflection", in a cable outlining eight points. Only the sixth is quoted here because it deals in particular with the question under discussion:

"I think it inevitable that Russia will be the greatest land Power in the world after this war, which will have rid her of two military Powers, Japan and Germany, who in our lifetime have inflicted upon her such heavy defeats. I hope however that the 'fraternal association' of the British Commonwealth and the United States, together with sea- and air-power may put us on good terms and in a friendly balance with Russia at least for the period of rebuilding. Farther than that I cannot see with mortal eye, and I am not as yet fully informed about the celestial telescopes."

So, it is evident that neither the anonymous American officer's memorandum nor the man responsible for British policy

were fundamentally opposed to the opinions expressed on February 21, 1943 by General Franco in his letter to Sir Samuel Hoare, at the time British Ambassador in Madrid, on the consequence of the military collapse of the Third Reich. But, in contrast to the report entitled *The position of Russia,* Churchill could not so easily accept the upsetting of the balance of power, and took some care to think about easing its most unpleasant consequences. So, in his opinion, after the war it would not be a good policy to loosen the Anglo-American ties which would have helped to win it. On September 6, with this in mind, he spoke to the staff and students of Harvard University, which had just conferred on him an honorary doctorate. He recalled the linguistic, literary, and legal heritage common to the two English-speaking democracies and, speaking beyond his immediate audience, exhorted Great Britain and the United States to strengthen their common purpose even more. In particular, he expressed the wish that the "marvellous" system of the Combined Chiefs-of-Staff Committee would not wind up, once the last shot had been fired.

"Now in my opinion it would be a most foolish and improvident act on the part of our two Governments, or either of them, to break up this smooth-running and immensely powerful machinery the moment the war is over. For our own safety, as well as for the security of the rest of the world, we are bound to keep it working and in running order after the war–probably for a good many years, not only until we have set up some world arrangement to keep the peace, but until we know that it is an arrangement which will really give us that protection we must have from danger and aggression, a protection we have already to seek across two vast world wars."

But President Roosevelt acted on the advice of Harry Hopkins and had no intention of following Churchill's plans. This would mean engaging the United States in a "special relationship" with Great Britain after the war. And so, in his memoirs, Churchill concludes, speaking of the rejection of his suggestion: "Alas, folly has already prevailed!"

At this point, should the ghastly charnel-house of Katyn be recalled? Here, six miles west of Smolensk, on April 13, 1943 the Germans found piled up 12 deep, the mummified bodies of 4,143 Polish officers, all felled by pistol shots in the back of the neck. It has been maintained that when

A horrifying sight: the rows of victims of the massacre.

413

the British and Americans learned of this example of Stalinist ferocity, they should have taken clear warning and had their eyes fully opened to the real nature of Soviet tyranny. Examination of the facts and the evidence require some modification of this opinion, however.

In fact, at the time neither Churchill nor Roosevelt had sufficient evidence to make a firm judgement as to Soviet responsibility for the affair. Stalin was, of course, quick to issue a denial of German claims, and whatever their suspicions about the Russian dictator, Churchill and Roosevelt had direct evidence of many Nazi atrocities, of which Katyn might well be another. Yet certainly, neither believed Stalin's grossest lies, such as when he told them on April 21, 1943, that Moscow was breaking off relations with the Polish Government-in-Exile. The terms used merit quotation:

"The fact that the anti-Soviet campaign has been started simultaneously in the German and Polish press and follows identical lines is indubitable evidence of contact and collusion between Hitler – the Allies' enemy – and the Sikorski Government in this hostile campaign.

"At a time when the peoples of the Soviet Union are shedding their blood in a grim struggle against Hitler's Germany and bending their energies to defeat the common foe of freedom-loving democratic countries, the Sikorski Government is striking a treacherous blow at the Soviet Union to help Hitler's tyranny."

It seems likely that Churchill never believed the Moscow version of the facts, which blamed the mass murder on the Germans. Perhaps it was the indignation caused by his conclusions on the massacre that was one of the motives which caused him to change his mind on the chances of co-operation between the Stalinist East and the Democratic West. But in the final analysis it had no influence on Anglo-American discussions.

However, the historian of today must note that Katyn was introduced, during the summer of 1945, into the charges preferred against the German leaders accused of war crimes before the Nuremberg International Military Tribunal, and that this was done at the request of the Soviet prosecutor. Furthermore, after long discussions, all the zeal of Colonels Pokrovsky and Smirnov could not establish conclusive proof, and the charge of the murder of 11,000 Polish officers was not even mentioned in the Tribunal's verdict on the condemned men.

And so it is valid to conclude that the Soviet accusation did not risk trying to contradict the report which had been signed by 12 forensic experts on April 30, 1943. These latter had been invited to Berlin to visit the charnel-house at Katyn and had been authorised to conduct post-mortems freely on whichever bodies they chose. With the exception of Professor Naville of the University of Geneva, they all belonged to occupied or German satellite countries. Yet, with the exception

of a Bulgarian, later acquitted after a pitiful self-accusation before a Sofia court, and a Czech, none of the 12 signatories agreed to go back on the declaration he had made in 1943.

In spite of the accusations made against him by a Communist deputy from Geneva, Professor Naville confirmed his evidence in September 1946, and was completely exonerated by the cantonal authorities of the suspicions that Moscow had tried to throw on his scientific reputation and professional probity. In 1952, Dr. Milosavić, once Director of the Institute of Criminology and Forensic Medicine of Zagreb, Professor Palmieri of the University of Naples, and Dr. Tramsen, Head of Medical Services of the Royal Danish Navy, deported for acts of resistance by the Gestapo in 1944, maintained their statements before the American Committee of Enquiry, as did Professor Orsōs, of the University of Budapest.

After having examined the bodies, their clothing and the documents found on them, they came to the unanimous conclusion that the crime of Katyn could not be dated later than the beginning of spring 1940. The Russians, on the other hand, claim that the massacre had been perpetrated during August 1941, that is just after the battle in which the Germans overran the entire Smolensk region.

These separate opinions, from Europe and from America, are confirmed absolutely independently by the evidence of Colonel van Vliet of the United States Army, in a report dated May 22, 1945. As a prisoner of the Germans he had been taken to the mass graves at Katyn, together with some other prisoners-of-war. He made the following observations which he revealed to nobody before his release:
1. The bodies wore winter uniforms.
2. The victims' boots and clothing were of excellent quality and showed no signs of wear.
3. "This was the way I saw it," continued van Vliet in his own words. "If the Germans had been responsible for the murders, they would have taken place at the time when the Germans invaded

The international committee at work, examining the personal effects found on the bodies.

the Smolensk area, in other words in July and August 1941, and then the clothes and shoes would have looked much more used because they would have been worn for two years more. I had had personal experience in that connection. I wore out two pairs of shoes in two years while I was a prisoner (and they were army issue!), and those two years represent more or less the difference in time between the German and the Russian claims for the date of the massacre. So I was convinced without any doubt of Soviet guilt."

General Bissel, head of the United States Information Services, stifled the report by Colonel van Vliet and went as far as ordering him to make absolutely no mention to anybody of his observations on the slaughter-house of Katyn. But did the former act on his own initiative, basing his decisions on reasons of major state interest about which he was not competent to judge? It seems reasonable to doubt this and to doubt it very strongly, because such a procedure is at variance with the normal practice of secret services.

Furthermore, and to bring this macabre question to a close, the extreme wariness shown by Soviet historical writing recently is noteworthy. When dealing with the breaking-off of diplomatic relations between Moscow and the Polish Government-in-Exile, the *Great Patriotic War* tells us simply that the U.S.S.R. could no longer tolerate the campaign of calumny indulged in at her expense by General Sikorski and his colleagues. But the history is very careful not to inform its readers of what these calumnies consisted and the name of Katyn is not even mentioned.

Not only was the question of the massacre removed from the attention of the Nuremberg court, but in Moscow, historians still attempt to remove it from the judgement of history!

CHAPTER 50

The conferences at Cairo and Teheran

In the last two weeks of November and the first week of December 1943 took place two linked summit conferences in Cairo and Teheran which, taken together, decided the strategic shape of the remaining stages of the Second World War and traced the first vague outlines of the postwar world. For the first time too.the Soviet and Chinese-Nationalist leaders were drawn into joint discussions with both the United States President and the British Prime Minister.

Like earlier purely Anglo-American summits, Cairo and Teheran witnessed the paradox of cordial personal relations between heads of state and between military staffs coupled with mistrust and manoeuvring behind the smiles because of differing national attitudes and interests. The British, as before Casablanca, had wanted there to be a preliminary exclusively Anglo-American summit in order to agree a basic grand-strategic package to put to Stalin. But Roosevelt, again as before Casablanca, wished to avoid giving any impression of an Anglo-American line-up that left the Russians on one side, for his ideas had further burgeoned with regard to a global postwar settlement, and he wanted to win Stalin's support for them. After some highly complicated correspondence between all the parties in order to find a *locale* and evolve arrangements agreeable to everyone, it was decided after all to hold an Anglo-American summit in Cairo, into the middle of which would be sandwiched a tripartite conference with Stalin in the Iranian capital Teheran; Stalin being unable to travel further because he was conducting major offensives against the German army in the East. Yet disagreements rumbled on between Churchill and Roosevelt. The President wanted to invite a Russian military observer to Cairo, but this was successfully resisted by the Prime Minister; the President also wanted Chiang Kai-shek, the Chinese leader, to take part in the conference, this being unwillingly accepted by the Prime Minister. But Churchill still desired that at least he and Roosevelt might meet privately in Malta before the main conference opened with Chiang among those present. This the President refused.

On November 12 Churchill set sail from Plymouth in the battlecruiser *Renown*, taking with him the American ambassador John Winant, as well as the Chiefs-of-Staff and Joint Planners. His daughter Sarah served as his ADC. As he wrote in his war memoirs: "I was feeling far from well, as a heavy cold and sore throat were reinforced by the consequences of inoculations against typhoid and cholera. I stayed in bed for several days." The new battleship *Iowa* raised anchor in Hampton Roads at 0001 hours next morning with Roosevelt, Admiral Leahy, Harry Hopkins and the Joint Chiefs-of-Staff aboard. Leahy records:

"President Roosevelt had no superstitions about the figure '13', which many people regard as an ill omen, but he did share the sailors' superstition that Friday is an unlucky day on which to start a long voyage. So the huge USS *Iowa* remained at her berth Friday night, November 12, 1943, and did not get under way for Oran, first leg of the trip to Cairo and Teheran, until 1201 am Saturday, November 13."

In Oran Roosevelt was able to confer with Eisenhower about operations in Italy before flying on to Cairo; Churchill had already paused in Malta likewise to confer with Eisenhower and Alexander.

The Cairo Conference ("Sextant") took place at Giza, where the Sphinx provided an object lesson to the participants on how to smile and yet remain inscrutable. As at Casablanca the VIPs were housed in luxurious villas amid palm-shaded gardens; the staffs were hardly less comfortable in the Mena House Hotel. Admiral Mountbatten, the Allied Supreme Commander South-East Asia, had flown in, as had his deputy "Vinegar Joe" Stilwell, also Chief-of-Staff to Chiang Kai-shek, whom Stilwell customarily referred to as "the Peanut". In the British delegation opinions on Chiang varied. The Prime Minister was impressed by his calm, reserved, and efficient personality. Sir Alan Brooke, however, was less impressed. "The Generalissimo", he wrote with the background knowledge of a keen naturalist, "reminded me of a cross between a pine-marten and a ferret. A shrewd, foxy sort of face. Evidently with no grasp of war in its larger aspects, but determined to get the best of all bargains." More important from the British point of view, Chiang's presence upset the order of priority of subjects to be discussed. The British were concerned above all with the question of the Mediterranean and its relationship with "Overlord". They had in mind further operations in Italy and in the Aegean: action to induce Turkey to enter the war. But instead, after item one on the agenda–"Reaffirm Overall objective, Overall Strategic Concept and Basic undertakings . . ."–it was South-East Asia that came next, with "Overlord" and the Mediterranean third. South-East Asia also took up a great deal of conference time. As Churchill testily wrote in his memoirs:

"All hope of persuading Chiang and his wife to go and see the Pyramids and enjoy themselves until we returned from Teheran fell to the ground, with the result that Chinese business occupied first instead of last place at Cairo."

When the first plenary session of the Cairo Conference opened in the President's villa on Tuesday, November 23, 1943, the topic for discussion was therefore South-East Asia in regard to China. Chiang Kai-shek did not stint himself with demands. He wanted an airlift of 10,000 tons over "the Hump" into China from India every month, an allied land offensive in 1944 aimed as far as Mandalay, and a naval operation to coincide with ground operations. In Chiang's words, "the success of the operation in Burma depended, in his opinion, not only on the strength of the naval forces established in the Indian Ocean, but also on the simultaneous coordination of naval action with the land operations." The "naval action" being considered by the British and American Chiefs-of-Staff was Operation "Buccaneer", an amphibious attack on the Andaman Islands, which had replaced the now abandoned "Culverin" (an attack on northern Sumatra). The United States President, determined to bring aid to Chiang, was strongly in favour of "Buccaneer"; the American Chiefs-of-Staff, falling in with their President's view, had submitted a paper before the Conference which urged that "Buccaneer" be mounted as soon as possible and that the Combined Chiefs-of-Staff direct Mountbatten to submit plans for approval. But the British were by no means so keen. They considered that the final strategy for defeating Japan should be drawn up before deciding on an incidental operation like "Buccaneer", which might or might not fit in with that strategy. They also feared that "Buccaneer's" need for landing craft would have adverse repercussions on the Mediterranean and "Overlord". This question proved in fact to be the crux of the whole "Sextant" conference.

British and Americans alike swiftly rejected Chiang's demand for a monthly airlift of 10,000 tons, pointing out that there were insufficient aircraft both for that purpose and for sustaining land operations in Burma. Mountbatten made it clear to the Chinese also that an advance to Mandalay would be beyond his strength, especially in aircraft. Chiang settled for a lift over "the Hump" of 8,900 tons a month for the next six months, and for the already agreed offensive in northern Burma with the limited objective of gaining a line Indaw–Katha. But "Buccaneer" remained a controversial issue. The British succeeded in persuading the Conference to delay a final decision on it until it could be placed in the world picture of amphibious operations. However, as John Ehrman points out, suspending a decision did not mean that it was not still discussed. Throughout the Conference, therefore, discussion of the far East and of the Mediterranean and "Overlord" proceeded day by day in parallel sessions with much overlap.

The British, mindful of current setbacks in the Aegean and, as they saw it, of missed opportunities in the Balkans during 1943, proposed further Mediterranean operations even at the expense of

The Generalissimo and Mme. Chiang, with their son Major Chiang Wei-Kuo, watch a demonstration by Chinese troops.

delaying "Overlord" from May to July 1944. Their strategy was well summarised by the Prime Minister: ". . . Rome in January, Rhodes in February, supplies to the Yugoslavs, a settlement of the Command arrangements and the opening of the Aegean, subject to the outcome of an approach to Turkey; all preparations for 'Overlord' to go ahead full steam within the framework of the foregoing policy for the Mediterranean." The American Chiefs-of-Staff did not, as might have been expected, pounce on this fresh British plea in favour of the Mediterranean, but accepted their ally's proposals as a basis for discussion with the Russians, subject to one proviso: that the Rhodes and Aegean operations "would in no way interfere with the carrying-out of 'Buccaneer'." General Marshall even expressed willingness to see "Overlord" postponed if that were necessary in order to make "Buccaneer" possible, and he revealed that President Roosevelt took a personal interest in the operation. In fact, during the conference Roosevelt went behind his British ally's back to promise Chiang that "Buccaneer" would take place. As John Ehrman writes: "On the eve of the Teheran Conference, the position seemed to be that the Americans (given the appropriate Russian pressure) might accept the British strategy for Europe, if the British would accept the Americans' strategy for south-east Asia."

The old question of the right relationship between "Overlord" and the Mediterranean came up at Cairo in a novel form. The United States Joint Chiefs-of-Staff submitted a long and elaborate paper arguing that a single Allied supreme commander "be designated at once to command all United Nations operations against Germany from the Mediterranean and the Atlantic under direction from the Combined Chiefs-of-Staff", in other words, much as in Nato today. They also wanted a single "strategic air force commander" to direct both Bomber Command and the U.S. 8th Air Force. The

remainder of their proposals sketched a tidy organisational pyramid of the kind also now familiar in Nato. However, the British Prime Minister and Chiefs-of-Staff reacted vigorously against the American proposals, which they believed were clumsy and would produce confusion. Even Marshal Foch in the Great War had only been in command of the Western and Italian fronts, not the Aegean and Balkan, they pointed out. In a cogently argued memorandum the British Chiefs-of-Staff said that because total war was a matter of politics and economics as much as of purely military decisions, "it seems clear that the Supreme Commander . . . will have to consult both the United States and the British Governments on almost every important question. In fact, it boils down to this, that he will only be able to make a decision without reference to high authority on comparatively minor and strictly military questions, such as the transfer of one or two divisions, or a few squadrons of aircraft, or a few scores of landing-craft, from one of his many fronts to another. He will thus be an extra and unnecessary link in the chain of command." They could see no reasons for making a "revolutionary change" in the existing and well-tried machinery of Allied command, let alone by such cumbrous means as inserting a whole new command layer.

Churchill, in a paper of his own, deftly tackled the political aspects of the American scheme. Since in May 1944 Britain would be fielding larger forces than the U.S.A. on all fronts against Germany, it "would therefore appear that the Supreme Command should go to a British officer. I should be very reluctant, as head of His Majesty's Government, to place such an invidious responsibility upon a British officer." Moreover, he went on, a Supreme Commander, be he British or American, who took a major decision which one or other Allied government believed seriously damaged its interests, "would therefore be placed in an impossible position. Having assumed before the whole world the responsibility of pronouncing and being overruled by one Government or the other, he would have little choice but to resign. This might bring about a most serious crisis in the harmonious and happy relations hitherto maintained between our two Governments."

In Teheran, Stalin and Churchill took up residence in the adjacent Russian and British embassies, which were protected by a single perimeter under British and Russian guard. But Roosevelt, in the American embassy, lay a mile or so distant, entailing the inconvenience, if not the danger, of mutual journeyings to meet in session. Molotov, the Russian foreign minister, suggested that Roosevelt come to live in an annexe to the Russian embassy; Churchill backed the idea; and the President and his staff duly moved in. With hindsight and knowledge of Russian skills in "bugging", it may be surmised

that Molotov was not only prompted by emotions of hospitality and concern for the President's safety; certainly the Russian delegation was to show itself acutely aware of the differences over strategy and policy between the British and Americans. Harry Hopkins wrote:

"The servants who made their beds and cleaned their rooms were all members of the highly efficient NKVD, the secret police, and expressive bulges were plainly discernible in the hip pockets under their white coats. It was a nervous time for Michael F. Reilly and his own White House secret service men, who were trained to suspect *everybody* and who did not like to admit into the President's presence anyone who was armed with as much as a gold toothpick."

On the afternoon of November 28 the first plenary session of the Teheran Conference ("Eureka") opened in the Russian embassy under, as with all the sessions, President Roosevelt's chairmanship. Flanked by Molotov and Marshal Voroshilov, Stalin was resplendent in a uniform, according to Lord Moran, "that looks as if it has not been worn before, and gives the impression that it has been specially designed for the occasion. It looks, too, as if the tailor has put on it a shelf on each shoulder, and on it dumped a lot of gold lace with white stars. And there is a broad red stripe down the trousers, which are immaculately creased. All this is crowned with a dreadful hat, smothered with gold braid." Gaudily uniformed or not, Stalin dominated the conference from the start. In his very opening statement he announced that after Germany's defeat Russia would join in the war against Japan, a development that at once threw Anglo-American grand strategy in the Pacific and Far East into the melting-pot.

Churchill followed by putting forward the British concept for the war against Germany: "Overlord" in the late spring or the summer of 1944, to be undertaken by 35 strong divisions, of which 16 would be British; the capture of Rome and an advance to the Pisa–Rimini line, with the option of advancing later either into southern France or north-eastward towards the Danube; an attempt to bring Turkey into the war, followed by the capture of the Dodecanese. Hereupon Stalin moved in masterfully by cross-examining Churchill not only about the details of these operations, but also about the depth of the British commitment to launch "Overlord". In the first place he wanted to know the proportion of Allied land forces to be allotted to "Overlord" and the Mediterranean. Churchill confirmed that "Overlord" would have 35 "very strong" divisions, leaving 22 in the Mediterranean region. After questioning the Prime Minister further about the present state of plans for invading southern France and the number of divisions thought necessary for the support of Turkey and the capture of the Dodecanese (should Turkey enter the war), Stalin proceeded to lay down unequivocally his own conception of the right strategy for

the Western Allies. According to the conference record:

"Marshal Stalin thought it would be a mistake to disperse forces by sending part to Turkey and elsewhere, and part to southern France. The best course would be to make 'Overlord' the basic operation for 1944 and, once Rome had been captured, to send all available forces in Italy to southern France. These forces could then join hands with the 'Overlord' forces when the invasion was launched. France was the weakest spot on the German front. He himself did not expect Turkey to enter the war."

In a further exchange with Churchill, Stalin agreed that it was worthwhile taking the Dodecanese if this involved only three or four divisions, but "repeated that 'Overlord' was a very serious operation and that it was better to help it by invading the South of France ..."

All this was congenial enough to Roosevelt, who now suggested that Stalin's suggestion of invading southern France two months before D-day should be examined by the military experts. Stalin added:

". . . the experience gained by the Soviets during the last two years of campaigning was that a big offensive, if

undertaken from only one direction, rarely yielded results. The better course was to launch offensives from two or more directions simultaneously . . . He suggested that this principle might well be applied to the problem under discussion."

Thus, to the surprise of both Americans and British, Stalin had placed all the weight of the Soviet Union and his own formidable personality behind the American strategy of concentrating on "Overlord" and abjuring wider commitments in the Mediterranean and Aegean. Churchill, however, did not agree with them and he resorted to bluster about the size of British-Empire forces in the Mediterranean area:

". . . he did not disagree in principle with Marshal Stalin. The suggestions he [Churchill] had made for action in Yugoslavia and in respect of Turkey did not, in his view, conflict in any way with that general conception. At the same time, he wished it to be placed on record that he could not in any circumstances agree to sacrifice the activities of the armies in the Mediterranean, which included 20 British and British-controlled divisions, merely in order to keep the exact date of the 1st May for 'Overlord' . . ."

President Roosevelt now suggested that

The line-up for the Cairo conference included (seated, left to right) Chiang Kai-Shek, Roosevelt, Churchill, and Mme. Chiang.

the question should be referred to the staffs for study and report. This vital session took place next day, when Marshal Voroshilov, following Stalin's line, unmistakably sided with the Americans against the British. Sir Alan Brooke found himself the victim at Voroshilov's hands of the kind of suspicious cross-examination about the sincerity of the British commitment to "Overlord" that he had been forced to endure from his American colleagues at earlier summit conferences.

"Marshal Voroshilov said he understood from General Marshall that the United States High Command and United States Government considered 'Overlord' to be an operation of the first importance. He said he would like to know whether Sir Alan Brooke considered this to be an operation of the first importance; whether he both thought the operation was necessary and that it must be carried out, or whether, alternatively, it might be replaced by another operation if Turkey came into the war."

When Brooke answered that Mediterranean operations were designed to ensure "Overlord's" success, Voroshilov did not disagree, but insisted that any such operations must be secondary to "Overlord" and not compete with it. He went on: ". . . the suggestion made yesterday by Marshal Stalin was that, at the same time as the operation in Northern France, operations should be undertaken in Southern France. Operations in Italy and elsewhere in the Mediterranean must be considered of secondary importance, because, from those areas, Germany could not be attacked directly with the Alps in the way. Italy . . . offered great possibilities for defence. Defences should be organised there with the minimum of troops. The remaining troops would be used for the South of France in order to attack the enemy from two sides."

Voroshilov added that "Marshal Stalin did not insist on an operation against the South of France, but that he did insist that the operation against the North of France should take place in the manner and on the date already agreed upon".

That afternoon the second plenary session of the conference saw Stalin press even more strongly the Russian case for total concentration on "Overlord". Firstly, he wanted to know the name of the Allied supreme commander for the operation; an embarrassing question since the American proposal at Cairo for a super supremo had put the former appointment in the melting-pot. Roosevelt answered that a staff officer with an Anglo-American staff had already brought plans and preparations for "Overlord" to an advanced stage. But Stalin, justifiably enough, observed that the commander might want to alter such plans, and should therefore be appointed at once so he could become responsible for the planning and execution of the operation. It was agreed that this appointment should be made within two weeks and the Russians informed of the name of the new supreme commander. In this case too, therefore, Stalin's intervention proved decisive.

When in the same plenary session Churchill tried yet again to make a case for the British Mediterranean strategy, Stalin simply ploughed on remorselessly:

"In his view there were three main matters to be decided. First, the date of the operation ['Overlord'] should be determined. This should be some time in May and no later. Secondly, Operation 'Overlord' should be supported by a landing in the South of France . . . He regarded the assault on the South of France as a supporting operation which would be definitely helpful to 'Overlord'. The capture of Rome and other operations in the Mediterranean could only be regarded as diversions.

"The third matter to be decided was the appointment of a Commander-in-Chief for the 'Overlord' operation. He would like to see this appointment made before the conclusion of the present conference. If this was not possible, at least within a

week."

Churchill, still game, brought up the question of available landing-craft in relation to the timings of "Overlord", the invasion of southern France and "Buccaneer", and put in a last plea for his favourite Aegean and Turkish strategy. On his suggestion, amended by Roosevelt, it was agreed to refer the subsidiary operations to an *ad hoc* military committee (in fact the Combined Chiefs-of-Staff) which was to submit detailed recommendations for approval. But Stalin, like the Americans before him, was now deeply suspicious of the sincerity of the British belief in "Overlord". At the close of the session, according to the British official record:

"Marshal Stalin said . . . he wished to pose a very direct question to the Prime Minister about 'Overlord'. Did the Prime Minister and the British Staffs really believe in 'Overlord'?

"The Prime Minister replied that, provided the conditions previously stated for 'Overlord' were to obtain when the time came, he firmly believed it would be our stern duty to hurl across the Channel against the Germans every sinew of our strength."

The British sense of isolation was enhanced by President Roosevelt's own conduct since arriving in Teheran. Churchill relates in his memoirs how he, Churchill, was led at this juncture to seek a personal interview with Stalin on account of the fact that "the President was in private contact with Marshal Stalin and dwelling at the Soviet Embassy, and he had avoided ever seeing me alone since we left Cairo, in spite of our hitherto intimate relations and the way our vital affairs were interwoven." In this interview, which took place on Churchill's 69th birthday, the Prime Minister sought to destroy "the false idea" forming in Stalin's mind "that", to put it shortly, "Churchill and the British Staff mean to stop 'Overlord' if they can, because they want to invade the Balkans instead". Churchill argued that if Roosevelt could be persuaded to call off Operation "Buccaneer" in the Indian Ocean, there would be enough landing-craft both for the Mediterranean and a "punctual" (*sic*) "Overlord". And yet, given Churchill's predilections earlier in 1943 for a major Anglo-American effort to bring about a collapse of the German position in the Balkans, and given also the bitter regrets Sir Alan Brooke was confiding to his diary only a month before the Teheran Conference about the chances missed for achieving this, was Stalin's mistrust unjustified?

At four o'clock that afternoon the final plenary session ratified the recommendations agreed after exhaustive argument by the military committee in the morning:

"(a) That we should continue to advance in Italy to the Pisa–Rimini line. (This means that the 68 LST's which are due to be sent from the Mediterranean to the United Kingdom for 'Overlord' must

be kept in the Mediterranean until 15th January.)

"(b) That an operation shall be mounted against the South of France on as big a scale as landing-craft will permit. For planning purposes D-day to be the same as 'Overlord' D-day.

"(c) . . . that we will launch 'Overlord' in May, in conjunction with a supporting operation against the South of France . . ."

The military committee reported, however, that they were unable to reach agreement about operations in the Aegean until they received fresh instructions from the President and Prime Minister.

Thus, thanks to Stalin, the Western Allies had finally agreed on their strategy against Germany in 1944. In military terms Teheran had been Stalin's conference all the way. Sir Alan Brooke, by now a connoisseur of politicians at war, later recorded his appreciation of Stalin's qualities:

"During this meeting and the subsequent ones we had with Stalin, I rapidly grew to appreciate the fact that he had a military brain of the highest calibre. Never once in any of his statements did he make any strategic error, nor did he ever fail to appreciate all the implications of a situation with a quick and unerring eye. In this respect he stood out compared with his two colleagues. Roosevelt never made any great pretence of being a strategist and left either Marshall or Leahy to talk for him. Winston, on the other hand, was more erratic, brilliant at times, but too impulsive and inclined to favour unsuitable plans without giving them the preliminary deep thought they required."

It may be that Stalin so strongly urged concentration on "Overlord" at the expense of Italy and the eastern Mediterranean because Russia as a great land power had a natural affinity with America in preferring a massive offensive proceeding along one major axis, in contrast to the British preference for opportunistic, peripheral and relatively small-scale operations. Nevertheless, the decisions taken at Teheran at Stalin's instigation, by shepherding the Western Allies away from the Balkans and making it less likely than ever that the Anglo-American army in Italy would eventually advance northeastward towards the Danube, also paved the way for the unhindered extension of Russian dominion over Rumania, Hungary, Bulgaria and Yugoslavia.

Although no far-reaching political decisions were reached at Teheran, Stalin proved hardly less the master in this sphere than in the purely military. In particular, his ruthless and farsighted sense of Russia's postwar interests contrasted with Roosevelt's naïve idealism and goodwill. Much of the political talk took place informally at mealtimes, or in private à deux–Roosevelt courted Stalin behind Churchill's back, Churchill courted Stalin behind Roosevelt's back. After dinner on the opening night of the conference, Churchill led Stalin to a sofa and suggested that they should talk about the postwar world. Stalin agreed, and proceeded to outline a profound fear of Germany's capacity for recovery, citing her prewar resurgence despite the Versailles Treaty. When Churchill asked him how soon he expected such a recovery, Stalin answered: "Within fifteen to twenty years." The Prime Minister remarked:

". . . Our duty is to make the world safe for at least fifty years by German disarmament, by preventing rearmament, by supervision of German factories, by forbidding all aviation, and by territorial changes of a far-reaching character. It all comes back to the question whether Great Britain, the United States, and the USSR can keep a close friendship and supervise Germany in their mutual interest."

When Stalin noted that control of this kind had failed after the last war, Churchill suggested that Prussia should be dealt with more harshly than the rest of Germany, and be isolated and reduced, while Bavaria might join Austria and Hungary in a broad, harmless Danubian confederation. But Stalin commented, "All very good, but insufficient."

The topic of postwar Germany came up for formal discussion at the very last plenary session of the Conference on December 1. Roosevelt put forward a plan to divide her into five self-governing parts, plus two areas–Kiel–Hamburg and the Ruhr/Saar industrial regions–under direct United Nations control. Churchill said again that the most important thing was to isolate and weaken Prussia; he believed Roosevelt's five independent German states would be too small to be viable, and that they should be attached to larger non-German groupings. In particular he put forward his idea of a Danubian confederation including southern Germany, whose population he reckoned to be less ferocious than the Prussians. However, in Stalin's estimation, north and south Germans, and Austrians, were equally ferocious. He expressed the fear that Germans would come to dominate Churchill's proposed Danubian confederation, and therefore he wanted there to be no more large combinations in Europe once Germany was broken up. The Germans themselves, even if split up, would always seek to re-unite themselves, a process Stalin thought must be neutralised by economic measures and if necessary by force. Churchill then asked Stalin if he contemplated a Europe of disjointed little states with no large units; a good question. According to Churchill's memoirs, Stalin replied that "he was speaking of Germany not Europe. Poland and France were large States, Rumania and Bulgaria were small States. But Germany should at all costs be broken up so that she could not reunite." Finally it was agreed to set up a special three-power committee under the European Advisory Commission to study the matter.

Tightly linked to these questions of the postwar anatomy of Germany and Stalin's anxiety over a revived German threat to Russia's western frontier was the question of Poland. Churchill brought the topic up unofficially during his conversation with the Soviet leader after dinner on the first night of the conference, proposing that the three powers should agree future Polish frontiers between themselves and put the result to the Poles. He suggested that Poland might sidestep westwards, giving up territory in the east to Russia in exchange for German territory; an idea which, in Churchill's words, "pleased Stalin". But postwar Poland, like postwar Germany, did not figure in official discussions until the final plenary session on December 1. Roosevelt opened the topic by expressing the hope that the Soviet and Polish governments would resume diplomatic relations (broken off by the Soviet Union because the Polish Government-in-exile in London had associated itself with the German claim that the Polish officers whose corpses had been found at Katyn had been murdered by the Russians). Churchill reminded his hearers of the importance to Britain of Poland's future, since Britain had originally gone to war on her behalf. He repeated his suggestion that Poland should be sidestepped westwards and reminded Stalin of his own remark earlier that he would not object if Poland reached the Oder. Stalin, however, now shrewdly drew a distinction between discussing the frontiers of a future Poland and discussing a future Polish government. According to Churchill's account, Stalin went on:

"Russia, even more than other States, was interested in good relations with Poland, because for her it was a question of the security of her frontiers. Russia was in favour of the reconstruction, development, and expansion of Poland mainly at the expense of Germany. But he separated Poland from the Polish Government-in-exile. He had broken off relations with the Polish Government-in-exile, not on account of caprice, but because it had joined with Hitler in slanderous propaganda against Russia. He would like to have a guarantee that the Polish Government-in-exile would not kill Partisans, but, on the contrary, would urge the Poles to fight the Germans . . . He would welcome any Polish Government which would take such active measures, and he would be glad to renew relations with them. But he was by no means sure that the Polish Government-in-exile was ever likely to become the sort of Government it ought to be."

In this statement were all the essential clues to the policy Stalin was to pursue towards Poland in the coming years, and which would reduce her to a Russian satellite. At Teheran, however, neither western leader challenged Stalin's comments about the Polish Government-in-exile or seemed to perceive their significance. Instead the discussion turned to Poland's future frontiers. After much consultation of maps and dispute as to the exact course of the Curzon Line of 1920, fixing the Russo-Polish frontier, the three leaders and their advisers agreed to a formula

Churchill presents Stalin with a sword forged to commemorate the Russians' successful defence of Stalingrad.

devised by Churchill that "it was thought in principle that the home of the Polish State and nation should be in between the so-called Curzon Line and the line of the Oder, including, for Poland, East Prussia and Oppeln, but the actual line required careful study . . ." Stalin's only caveat was to state that Russia also wanted Königsberg. All this was duly to come to pass.

At a private meeting on November 29 with Stalin and Molotov, Roosevelt had unveiled his ideas for a world peace-keeping organisation after the war which would avoid the built-in weaknesses of the League of Nations created by his predecessor President Woodrow Wilson. The preservation of peace would be entrusted to the "Four Policemen": the Soviet Union, the United States, Great Britain and China. But Stalin, more realistic than Roosevelt about the status of Chiang Kai-shek's China as a great power, did not respond to the President's visionary scheme. He doubted whether China would be very powerful after the war; he thought that European states would in any case resent being policed by China. Instead he suggested regional committees for Europe and the Far East, the Soviet Union, the United States and Britain being members of both. This, as Roosevelt acknowledged, tied in with a similar idea of Churchill's, although the Prime Minister wanted a supreme United Nations Council as well (an item which Roosevelt omitted to pass on to Stalin). But Roosevelt went on to tell the Soviet leader that the American Congress would be unwilling to sanction American participation in an exclusively European committee, which might demand the despatch of American troops to Europe. When Stalin pointed out that the same objection applied to the President's own concept of the "Four Policemen",

Stalin with his Foreign Minister, Molotov. They were a formidable diplomatic team.

Roosevelt, in an unguarded admission potentially dangerous for the future, answered that he had only considered committing American air and sea power; it would be up to Britain and the Soviet Union to find the land forces to deal with a future threat to peace in Europe. No doubt all this was carefully stored away in Stalin's memory and helped formulate his postwar policy.

The Teheran Conference concluded with a dinner at which friendly and flattering mutual toasts were exchanged by the three leaders, expressing the satisfaction felt by all of them at the results of their meetings; indeed expressing at that moment a true comradeship in the face of the enemy. But beyond the joint strategy and operations now agreed for the defeat of Germany and Japan lay the undecided questions of postwar Europe and the postwar world. Churchill wrote later in his memoirs: "It would not have been right at Teheran for the Western democracies to found their plans upon suspicions of the Russian attitude in the hour of triumph and when all her dangers were removed." But with hindsight it might be argued that it would have been just as "right" for the Western democracies to look shrewdly to their own long-term interests as it was for Stalin to look to those of Soviet Russia.

On December 2, 1943, Roosevelt and Churchill arrived back in Cairo to thrash out with the Combined Chiefs-of-Staff the details of the operations agreed on at Teheran and to settle the question of the supreme command. Once again the military staffs and the plenary sessions grappled with the old question of available landing-craft in relation to "Buccaneer", "Overlord", the invasion of southern France and the residual operations in the eastern Mediterranean. Fresh examination of the "Overlord" plan in the light of the experience of the invasion of Sicily and Italy suggested that a larger initial assault force was desirable, and that meant yet more landing-craft. The British Chiefs-of-Staff therefore once more sought to get "Buccaneer" abandoned, and with it the planned concurrent land offensive in northern Burma; their American opposite numbers nevertheless still argued that these operations were politically and militarily essential. Three days of discussion led only to deadlock. But on the evening of December 5, after hard thinking in private, Roosevelt came to a difficult decision. He sent Churchill the terse message "Buccaneer is off" Next day he signalled Chiang that European commitments left no margin for the operation. According to Robert Sherwood, this was the only time during the war that Roosevelt overruled his chiefs-of-staff.

There remained the question of a supreme commander for "Overlord". In the face of the strong British objections, the Americans had quietly given up their idea of a super supremo responsible for all operations everywhere against Germany. Yet only such a post would have been important enough to warrant moving General Marshall from Washington, where he was a key figure, and without giving the impression of a demotion. Roosevelt therefore came to another hard decision, this time one taken against the advice of Hopkins and Stimson as well as the known preference of Churchill and Stalin. He told Marshall, "I feel I could not sleep at night with you out of the country." Next day Roosevelt informed Churchill that Eisenhower would command "Overlord". It had already been agreed to create a single Mediterranean theatre command under a British supreme commander, who was named on December 18 as General Sir Maitland Wilson.

Thus the "Sextant" and "Eureka" conferences, when taken together the longest, toughest inter-Allied meeting ever held, came to an end with all the great strategic issues at last resolved. For all the arguing and bargaining, the British and Americans parted in amity, as the concluding remarks of the final session record:

"Sir Alan Brooke said he would like to express on behalf of the British Chiefs of Staff their deep gratitude for the way in which the United States Chiefs had met their views . . .

"General Marshall said that he very much appreciated Sir Alan Brooke's gracious tributes . . ."

On his way home Roosevelt summoned Eisenhower to Tunis, and as soon as Eisenhower had joined him in his car, he said: "Well, Ike, you are going to command 'Overlord'!" Eisenhower replied:

"Mr. President, I realise that such an appointment involved difficult decisions. I hope you will not be disappointed."

CHAPTER 51
The Russians clear the Ukraine

The first five months of 1944 were marked by new Red Army offensives to the south of the Pripet Marshes. The offensives led to the liberation of the Ukraine and Crimea as well as to the conquest of the northern part of Rumanian Moldavia, while in the Leningrad region they succeeded in throwing the Germans back from a line linking Oranienbaum–Volkhov–Novgorod–Lake Ilmen onto one linking Narva–Lake Peipus and Pskov. At the same time, the Western Allies were also putting more and more pressure on Germany.

Further south, General Sir Henry Maitland Wilson, new Allied Commander-in-Chief in the Mediterranean, endeavoured to carry out the limited mission which had been entrusted to him in implementation of decisions recently taken at the Teheran Conference. Two days before the Normandy landings, the advance guard of his 15th Army Group under General Sir Harold Alexander had entered Rome hard on the enemy's heels. Thereby the allies had achieved their strictly geographical objective, but arguably at the price of sacrificing their strategic objective in Italy, namely the destruction of the enemy forces.

Parallel to this, in Great Britain the preparations for Operation "Overlord", with all their attendant difficulties, were rapidly approaching their climax. While the divisions taking part in the landings by sea and by air were undergoing intensive training, in London Generals Eisenhower and Montgomery were putting the final touches to the invasion plans drawn up by the American and British Combined Chiefs-of-Staff, C.O.S.S.A.C., and submitted for their approval by General Morgan.

Anglo-American bomber formations intensified their missions by day and by night over the Third Reich as well as over occupied Europe. Most probably the results obtained over the first six months were no more significant in their impact on German war production than during the previous year. However, systematic pinpointing of synthetic oil plants from spring onwards, as well as of the Ploieşti oil-wells, enabled the Allied air forces for the first time to influence events on land directly by precipitating an extremely serious fuel crisis in the Wehrmacht. Furthermore, in the western and southern theatres British and American fighter-bombers and medium bombers constantly pounded the enemy's communications system. In France and Belgium their aim was to obstruct rapid reinforcement of the German 7th Army, which was in position on the coast between Cabourg and St. Nazaire; in Italy their main targets were the Po bridges and the course of the Adige, the route by which enemy supplies and reinforcements moved after crossing the Brenner Pass. Moreover, the Luftwaffe

was being forced to sacrifice itself against the mass American daylight raids escorted by long-range fighters.

On June 22, 1941, Hitler became involved unwisely in a "war on two fronts" such as had cost Wilhelm II his throne, in spite of the fact that the Emperor's ghost might have seemed to have been exorcised by the Soviet-German Pact of August 23, 1939. And now on January 1, 1944, the Third Reich and its Führer were in a position of having to conduct a "war on all fronts" (*Allfrontenkrieg*).

The only way in which Germany might have escaped the inevitable consequences of the powerful efforts of the Allies to surround and close in on her, would have been to resume the U-boat offensive in the Atlantic with the same success as in 1942. But for all his energy, intelligence, and experience, Grand-Admiral Dönitz was unable to stem the swelling tide of troops, war *matériel,* and supplies converging on Europe from America.

The facts are made clear in the following table, based on figures supplied by Captain Roskill, of Allied mercantile losses in 1942 and 1944 in the North Atlantic:

	1942		1944	
	tonnage	ships	tonnage	ships
January	276,795	48	36,065	5
February	429,891	73	12,577	2
March	534,064	95	36,867	7
April	391,044	66	34,224	5
May	576,350	120	0	0
Totals	2,208,144	402	119,733	19

The figures show the extent to which Britain and America recovered complete supremacy in the North Atlantic, with consequent complete freedom of manoeuvre and strategy. Although Grand-Admiral Dönitz was keeping new and unpleasant secret weapons up his sleeve, but they were not as yet ready, and until they were there was a great deal that could happen.

The immediate consequences of this complete reversal of the situation were perfectly clear to Hitler. One only needs refer to the arguments propounded on November 3, 1943 in support of measures prescribed by his Directive No. 51, as regards the conduct of the war; in his own words:

"The hard and costly struggle against Bolshevism during the last two-and-a-half years, which has involved the bulk of our military strength in the East, has demanded extreme exertions. The greatness of the danger and the general situation demanded it. But the situation has since changed. The danger in the East still remains, but a greater danger now appears in the West: an Anglo-Saxon landing! In the East, the vast extent of the territory makes it possible for us to lose ground, even on a large scale, without a fatal blow being dealt to the nervous system of Germany.

"It is very different in the West! Should the enemy succeed in breaching our defences on a wide front here, the immediate consequences would be unpredictable. Everything indicates that the enemy will launch an offensive against the Western front of Europe, at the latest in the spring, perhaps even earlier.

"I can therefore no longer take responsibility for further weakening the West, in favour of other theatres of war. I have therefore decided to reinforce its defences, particularly those places from which the long-range bombardment of England will begin. For it is here that the enemy must and will attack, and it is here–unless all indications are misleading–that the decisive battle against the landing forces will be fought."

On December 20 following, Hitler returned to the question in the presence of his generals. It appears from the short-hand account of his statement that, while he was convinced that the invasion would take place, he was less than convinced that the British would have their hearts in it:

"It stands to reason that the English have less confidence in this enterprise than has Eisenhower. Eisenhower has effected one [*sic*] successful invasion, but this was solely due to the work of traitors. Here with our soldiers he will find none to help him. Here, we mean business, make no mistake! It is a totally different matter to invade North Africa and be greeted by Monsieur Giraud or be confronted by the Italians who for the most part stay in their holes without firing a single shot, and to set foot in the West in the face of unrelenting fire. And so long as a battery is capable of firing, it will continue firing. That is a certainty."

The above extract from Directive No. 51 is interesting from more than one aspect. Its third paragraph adds a further reason to those normally advanced by way of explaining why O.K.W. situated the centre of gravity of its western defensive system between Le Havre and the Pas-de-Calais. The argument at Rastenburg ran as follows: the fact that the launching sites for the V-1 and V-2, whose effect was directed against Britain, were in this area would in all probability lead the British to urge their allies that this was the best place to make the landings. This argument was plausible enough, but its effectiveness required one condition, namely that the Germans should be the first to open fire. Yet Hitler knew perfectly well that the V-1 missiles (let alone V-2) would not be operational before the date when he expected his enemies to attempt invasion across the Channel.

Furthermore, insisting as he did on the peril that was looming in the West to the extent of giving it priority in the short run over the Soviet threat, Hitler's judgement was correct. On the basis of this eminently reasonable view of the situation, seen from the perspective of O.K.W., Hitler went on to deduce that the Anglo-American attempt at invasion would fail so long as he did not, as he had done during the winters of 1941–2 and 1942–3, prop up the now tottering Eastern Front with troops from among those guarding the Atlantic battlements.

Thence it follows that he to whom the directive of November 3, 1943 was principally addressed, that is Hitler himself, this time in his capacity as commander-in-chief of German land forces, would draw the logical conclusions from the premises he had just himself stated in his office at Rastenburg.

At O.K.H., Colonel-General Zeitzler perhaps flattered himself for several weeks that he would be given more freedom of action than hitherto in the conduct of operations. Was it not there in writing, in Hitler's own hand, that if it were a case of absolute necessity on the Eastern Front, withdrawals on a fairly considerable scale could be countenanced without necessarily putting the "nervous system" of the Third Reich in mortal danger?

But when it came down to it, the Russians' third winter offensive, the Führer showed the same persistent and mistaken obstinacy as he had done in the previous years, bringing his familiar arguments of high politics and the war economy to bear against his army group commanders every time one of them sought to advise him of a suitable chance to disengage in the face of the sheer weight, regardless of cost, of the Soviet onslaught.

And evidence of this came with the fresh disasters that occurred, principally to the south of the Pripet Marshes, when towards the end of January 1944 Kanev and Korsun' and, on the following May 13, Sevastopol' found their doleful place in the annals of German military history. So it was again a case of immediately arresting the possible consequences of these new defeats sustained by the Third Reich and, since the few reinforcements still available on the Eastern Front were quite inadequate, Hitler the head of O.K.H. sought help from Hitler the head of O.K.W. in order to avert imminent catastrophe. In these circumstances, born of his quite inexcusable obstinacy, Hitler the supreme commander had no alternative but to depart from the principle he had laid down in his Directive of November 3, 1943. At the end of the winter of 1943, the *Waffen*-S.S. II Panzer Corps had to be transferred from the Alençon sector, and hence missed the rendezvous of June 6, 1944 in Normandy.

The Soviet winter offensive began on December 24, 1943 on either side of the Kiev-Zhitomir road and within a few weeks involved the whole of Army Group "South" which, at that time, stretching as it did between the estuary of the Dniepr and the Mozyr' region, comprised the 6th Army (General Hollidt), the 1st *Panzerar-*

mee (General Hube), the 8th Army (General Wöhler), and the 4th *Panzerarmee* (General Raus). The entire group, commanded as before by Field-Marshal Erich von Manstein, was made up of 73 of the 180 understrength divisions that were then engaged between Kerch' Strait and the Oranienbaum bridgehead on the Baltic.

In particular, 22 of the 32 Panzer and *Panzergrenadier* divisions on the Eastern Front were allocated to Army Group "South".

The 18th Artillery Division had also been assigned there, with its eight tracked or motorised battalions, comprising nine 21-cm howitzers, plus 30 15-cm, 48 10.5-cm, and 12 10-cm guns. This was a new formation, based on similar ones in the Red Army, and much was expected of it. But it proved disappointing and was disbanded after a few months. A total of 73 divisions seems impressive, but the figure is misleading. Between July 31, 1943 and July 31, 1944, Manstein lost 405,409 killed, wounded, and missing, yet in the same period his reinforcements in officers, N.C.O.s, and other ranks amounted to only 221,893. His divisions, particularly the infantry ones, were thin on the ground. It was the same story with the Panzer divisions, which in spite of increased production of tanks, were 50 to 60 per cent below complement. And the front to be defended, in the Führer's words "with no thought of retreat", measured a good 650 miles.

As has been noted, the 1st Ukrainian Front (General N. F. Vatutin) inaugurated the Soviet winter offensive on December 24. With fire support from four artillery divisions and ten artillery regiments (936 guns and howitzers) assigned from general reserve, Vatutin launched an attack on an 18-mile front in the direction of Zhitomir, with 18 divisions (38th Army and 1st Guards Army) backed by six armoured or mechanised corps. The XXIV Panzer Corps (General Nehring: 8th and 19th Panzer Divisions and *Waffen*-S.S. 2nd Panzer Division *"Das Reich"*) put up a stubborn resistance for 48 hours, then, in spite of being reinforced by XLVIII Panzer Corps (General Balck) broke under the impact. The 3rd Guards Tank Army (General Rybalko) stormed through the breach and on the last day of the year recaptured Zhitomir and by January 3 reached Novograd-Volinskiy, over 85 miles from its jumping-off point. Further to the right, the Soviet 60th and 13th Armies, comprising 14 infantry divisions, had retaken Korosten and were close to the Russo-Polish frontier of the pre-war period. On Rybalko's left, Vatutin's centre was overwhelming the defenders of Berdichev.

Hence the defeat of the 4th *Panzerarmee* took on a strategic dimension, and in the event of Vatutin exploiting his success to the south-west resolutely and with vigour, could have led to the total destruction of Army Groups "South" and "A". As early as December 25, Manstein

had been aware of the possibility of such a danger and had alerted O.K.H. to this effect, confronting it with the following dilemma: "The 4th Army was no longer capable of defending the flank of Army Groups 'South' and 'A'; effective reinforcements were vital. If O.K.H. was unable to provide these, we would be obliged to take five or six divisions at least from our right wing, which clearly could not then maintain its positions inside the Dniepr loop. We sought our liberty of movement for that wing."

During the period when he was writing his memoirs, Manstein had no knowledge of the disobliging, indeed absurd, comments that his report had drawn from the Führer: that Manstein had inflated the enemy numbers knowingly in the hope of imposing his personal decisions on O.K.H. Furthermore, the troops were bound to mirror their commander's attitude, and if some divisions failed to measure up to the standards needed, it was because Manstein, lacking in conviction, had failed to galvanise them with the necessary determination.

Hitler went on, in the presence of Zeitzler, who must have been somewhat dumbfounded, about the heroic times when the party assumed power, capturing in turn Mecklenburg, East Prussia ("refractory and reactionary"), Cologne ("red and black"), and–according to the stenographic account of the meeting– "Thuringia was dyed a deep red, but then I had a Koch at the time I wanted him, at another time a Ley or a Sauckel. There were men for you. When, by some mischance, I didn't have the right men at hand, there was trouble. I took it as axiomatic that good *Gaus* made good *Gauleiters*. And it's not a jot different today."

In any case, whatever the parallel between the situation of the Nazi Party in its electoral campaigns and the Russian campaign, Manstein, who had been offered two or three divisions by Hitler with which to plug the two breaches, each 45 to 50 miles' in width, to right and left of the 4th *Panzerarmee,* proceeded on December 29 to carry out the manoeuvre he had proposed in his report of December 25. The 1st *Panzerarmee* command was moved from right to left of the 8th Army, transferring III Panzer Corps (General Breith) with its four divisions from the Dniepr loop and completing the movement by shifting VII Corps and XXIV Panzer Corps, which formed Raus's right flank, to the south-east of Berdichev. This manoeuvre, which was approved by O.K.H., provided some relief for Army Group "South", added to the fact that Vatutin failed to exploit his opportunity to drive to the Dniestr from Kamenets-Podolskiy. Hitler, however, had not let pass without response Manstein's proposal to evacuate the Dniepr loop and the

Russian attacks and German counterattacks from the end of 1943 until May 1944.

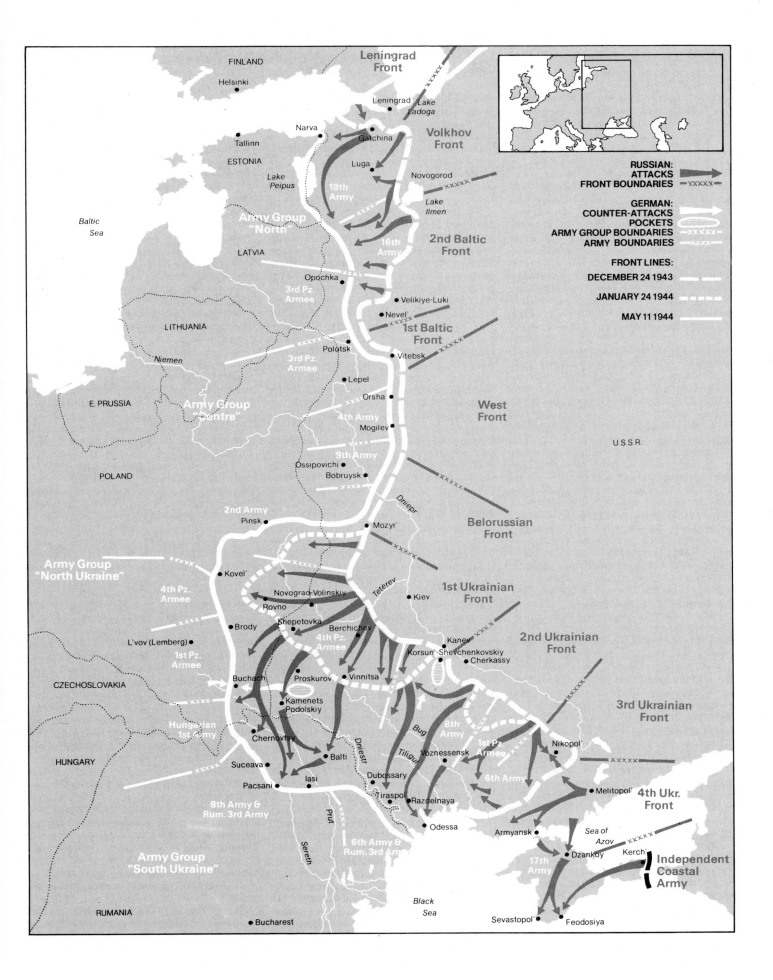

FINLAND
Helsinki

Leningrad
Front

Leningrad
Lake
Ladoga

Narva
Gatchina
Volkhov
Front

Tallinn
Luga

ESTONIA
Novogorod

Lake
Peipus
18th
Army
Lake
Ilmen

Baltic
Sea

Army Group
"North"
16th
Army
2nd Baltic
Front

LATVIA

Opochka

3rd Pz.
Armee
Velikiye-Luki

Nevel'

LITHUANIA
1st Baltic
Front

Niemen
Polotsk
Vitebsk

3rd Pz.
Armee
Lepel

E. PRUSSIA
Orsha
West
Front

Army Group
"Centre"
4th Army
Mogilev

U.S.S.R.

9th Army

POLAND
Ossipovichi
Bobruysk

Dniepr

2nd Army
Belorussian
Front

Pinsk
Mozyr'

Army Group
"North Ukraine"
Kovel'

4th Pz.
Armee
Novograd-Volinskiy
Teterev
Kiev
1st Ukrainian
Front

Rovno

2nd Ukrainian
Front

Brody
Shepetovka
Berchichev

L'vov (Lemberg)
4th Pz.
Armee
Kanev
Korsun'-Shevchenkovskiy
Cherkassy

1st Pz.
Armee

CZECHOSLOVAKIA
Buchach
Proskurov
Vinnitsa

3rd Ukrainian
Front

Kamenets
Podolskiy

Hungarian
1st Army
Bug
8th
Army
1st Pz
Armee
Nikopol'

HUNGARY
Chernovtsy
Tiligul
Voznessensk
6th Army

Suceava
Balti
Dniestr

Pacsani
Iasi
Dubossary
Tiraspol
Razdelnaya
Melitopol'
4th Ukr.
Front

8th Army &
Rum. 3rd Army
Prut
Odessa
Armyansk
Sea of
Azov
Dzankoy
Kerch'
Independent
Coastal
Army

Army Group
"South Ukraine"
6th Army &
Rum. 3rd Army
Sereth
17th
Army

RUMANIA
Black
Sea
Sevastopol'
Feodosiya

Bucharest

RUSSIAN:
ATTACKS
FRONT BOUNDARIES XXXXX

GERMAN:
COUNTER-ATTACKS
POCKETS
ARMY GROUP BOUNDARIES XXXXX
ARMY BOUNDARIES XXXX

FRONT LINES:
DECEMBER 24 1943
JANUARY 24 1944
MAY 11 1944

423

Nikopol' bridgehead. It so happened that on January 3, General Konev himself launched an attack in the Kirovograd sector, where the German 6th Army had just relieved the completely exhausted 1st *Panzerarmee*.

A clear decision was called for and with the object of obtaining one, Manstein went to Rastenburg in person, hoping that he would carry more weight with the Führer than his teletype messages. He put his case as follows:

"If the high command could not bring up strong reinforcements immediately, our Southern wing would have to fall back, abandoning Nikopol', and hence the Crimea, simply in order to make good the deficiency; and this in our opinion was only a first step. We had reconnoitred positions in the rear and given orders for their preparation. These positions more or less followed the course of the Bug, making use of any high ground that seemed advantageous, up to a point south of the sector where our Northern wing was at the moment engaged in fighting. Occupation of these new positions would reduce the 600 mile front by almost half, held too thinly by the 6th and 8th Armies. Such a drastic reduction, and the availability of the 17th Army once it was withdrawn from Crimea, would enable us to achieve the degree of consolidation required in the Northern wing."

And anticipating the likely objection of the Führer, he added: "Naturally the Russians would also benefit by the operation, but since our front would thereby achieve greater solidity, its defensive capacity would be enhanced – and this is the greatest asset in war – so as to be able to resist even massive assault. Furthermore, the destruction of the railway system would prevent the enemy moving the forces now available to him with sufficient speed to allow him to maintain his superiority to west of Kiev."

Hitler stubbornly opposed the propositions made to him in these terms. The need for Nikopol' manganese, whose mining had been suspended for several weeks, prohibited him from abandoning the Dniepr loop. And as for evacuating the Crimea, the idea should be totally excluded; it could well bring about the defection of Bulgaria and a declaration of war on Germany by Turkey. Nor was there any question of finding reinforcements from Army Group "North": if Field-Marshal von Küchler was forced to abandon his positions dominating the Gulf of Finland, Russian submarines would operate freely in the Baltic and cut the supply lines for Swedish iron-ore between Luleå and factories in Germany.

Manstein returned, disabused and empty-handed, to his H.Q. at Vinnitsa. From one of his several meetings with Hitler, the Field-Marshal took away the following impression of the dictator's face gripped, as was then the case, with inner fury:

"I saw Hitler's features harden. He threw me a glance which signified 'there is no further argument'. I cannot remember ever in my life having seen anyone portray such force of character. One of the foreign ambassadors accredited to Berlin speaks in his memoirs of the effect produced on him by Hitler's eyes. Alone in a coarse and undistinguished face they constituted the single striking feature, certainly the only expressive one. Those eyes fixed me as if they would annihilate me. The comparison with a Hindu snake-charmer suddenly struck me. For the space of a few seconds a kind of mute struggle took place between us. That gaze told me how he had contrived to dominate so many people."

The intervention of the 1st *Panzerarmee*, under the command of the gallant General Hube, may have allowed Manstein both to contain the centre of the 1st Ukrainian Front and even make it give ground a little after sustaining heavy casualties (during the second half of January on the furious Pogrebishche sector), but General Raus's northern wing, which presented a ragged line northwards to the Pripet Marshes, proved unable to resist the pressure applied on it by General Vatutin's right wing. On the previous January 4, in the course of his visit to O.K.H., Manstein had urged Hitler to build up a strong reserve in the Rovno region. His advice had not been followed, and this important fortress-town fell to the Russians on February 5, 1944. Since its breakthrough on December 24, the 1st Ukrainian Front had thus far advanced 170 miles westwards, with the result that the line Army Group "South" was required to hold was vastly lengthened from its furthest point at Nikopol', without receiving proportionate reinforcement. Also, lines of communication were increasingly under threat to the extent that the Russians exploited their gains in the direction of Tarnopol', only 90 miles to the south of Rovno.

In the immediate future, the situation was still more serious. On Hitler's express orders, the right of the 1st *Panzerarmee* and the left of the 8th Army were maintained on the banks of the Dniepr between Kanev and upstream of Cherkassy. With Vatutin's advance as far as Zhachkov and with Konev in possession of Kirovograd on January 10 a dangerous salient 100 miles wide and some 90 miles deep had formed in this sector, which gave the enemy the opportunity for a pincer movement. The reduction of the front (on the lines proposed to the Führer by Manstein at their meeting on January 4 at Rastenburg, a course which he continued to advocate in notes and personal letters) brooked no further argument; and subsequent events show that the whole manoeuvre, delicate though it was, might well have succeeded with the least cost; reckoning from January 4, there was an effective delay of three weeks, while the 1st and 2nd Ukrainian Fronts together cut off the area between Kanev and Cherkassy; of almost four weeks before the 3rd Ukrainian Front (under General Malinovsky) attacked the Nikopol' bridgehead; and of nearly five weeks before General Vatutin's armoured and mechanised advanced units reached the Rovno–Shepetovka line.

Soviet commentators attribute the relatively slow progress of the Russians to the constant changes in temperature and alternation of rain and snow recorded in the west of the Ukraine during the months of January and February 1944.

Writing in 1956, Colonel A. N. Grylev of the Soviet Army has this to say:

"Unfavourable weather conditions created more difficulties for our troops than did the crossing of rivers. An unusually early spring caused the snow to melt as early as the end of January. Rain and melting snow aggravated the difficulties. Rivers overflowed their banks. Roads and tracks became as impracticable for vehicles as was the terrain for infantry. These various factors had a considerable effect on our military activities, limiting the possibility of manoeuvre and hampering supplies of food, fuel, and munitions."

Lest it should be felt that the writer is trying to excuse the purely relative failure of the Soviet armies to annihilate the German army groups facing the four Ukrainian Fronts, Colonel Grylev's testimony is borne out in detail by General von Vormann, who was in the same area as commander of the hard-pressed XLVII Panzer Corps:

"The *rasputitsa* (thaw) had set in astonishingly early; everywhere it is spring mud . . . Worked on by the sun, the rain, and the warm winds, the heavy, black Ukraine earth turns into thick sticky mud during the day. There is not one metalled road in the country. On foot you sink down to your shins and after a few steps lose shoes and socks there. Wheeled vehicles stall and get stuck. Suction by the mud tore away the too-narrow tracks of our all-purpose transports. The only machines capable of making any headway were the tractors and the tanks, which rolled their way forwards at a maximum speed of 3 miles an hour but at the cost of tremendous strain on the engine and huge petrol consumption."

At all events, it is clear that the mud worked more to the disadvantage of the Russians than of the Germans, since in their task of attack and pursuit they also had to cope with the battlefield debris left by the retreating enemy, who destroyed everything of any value behind him.

In Manstein's dispute with Hitler, are there grounds for accusing the former – as has been alleged from time to time – of having been obsessed with withdrawal in the face of any build-up in enemy strength or else of having been unjustifiably alarmed by the spectre of encirclement?

It is clear that at this juncture Manstein no longer displayed the genius for bold moves that had characterised his performance between 1941 and 1943; yet it is also abundantly clear that he was no longer in a position where he could act boldly. Apart from XLVI Panzer Corps, which had recently been assigned to him, he knew that he could expect no further reinforcements from the west and that on the Eastern Front it was a case of robbing Peter to pay Paul. The liquidation of a pocket containing half a dozen divisions would mean not only the loss of some 60,000 men and most of their *matériel,* but, further, a breach of 75 to 90 miles in his now dangerously reduced defensive system. The battle of Korsun'-Shevchenkovskiy would show that his appreciation of the situation – and he had vainly tried to prevail on Hitler to accept it – was the correct one.

On January 25, Marshal Zhukov, who had been delegated by *Stavka* to co-ordinate operations, threw the troops of the 1st and 2nd Ukrainian Fronts into an assault on the Kanev salient. General Vatutin brought his 40th Army (Lieutenant-General E. F. Zhmachenko) and 27th Army (Lieutenant-General S. G. Trofimenko) to bear on the western front of the salient. They had a considerable job in overcoming German resistance so as to open a breach for brigades of the 6th Tank Army (Lieutenant-General A. G. Kravchenko) to move south-eastwards. The 2nd Ukrainian Front, under General Konev, seems to have had an easier task; delivering its attack at the point of junction of XLVII Panzer Corps and XI Corps, the 4th Guards Army (Major-General A. I. Ryzhov) and 53rd Army (Major-General I. V. Galanin) swiftly broke through the lines held by the 389th Infantry Division, thus enabling the 5th Guards Tank Army, under the command of General P. A. Rotmistrov, to be unleashed without further ado.

"There could be no other adequate analogy. The sea-dikes had given and the tide, interminable and vast, spread across the plain, passing either side of our tanks which, with packets of infantry round them, had the appearance of reefs rising from the swell. Our amazement was at its peak when in the afternoon cavalry units, galloping westwards, broke through our screen of fire in close formation. It was a sight long-forgotten, almost a mirage – V Guards Cavalry Corps, with the 11th, 12th, and 63rd Cavalry Divisions under the command of Selimanov." Thus, in a monograph dealing with this episode, the former commander of XLVII Panzer Corps describes the breakthrough at Krasnosilka (30 miles north-west of Kirovograd). In these conditions, it is not surprising that Vatutin's and Konev's tanks effected a meeting on January 28 in the region of Zvenigorodka. XI Corps, which formed the left of the German 8th Army, and XLII Corps, on the right of the 1st *Panzerarmee,* were caught in the trap along with four infantry divisions (the 57th, 72nd, 88th, and 389th), the 5th S.S. *Panzergrenadier* Division "Wiking" and the S.S. *Freiwilligen Sturmbrigade "Wallonie",* which Himmler had recruited in the French-speaking provinces of Belgium. By virtue of seniority over his comrade

Lieutenant-General T. Lieb, General W. Stemmermann, commander of XI Corps, assumed command of those encircled.

Hitler was determined to defend the Kanev salient at all costs, as he considered it the base for launching an offensive which would force the Russians to cross back over the Dniepr in the region of Kiev. Hence orders were given to Stemmermann to hold his positions and to establish himself so as to be able to repulse any attacks from the south; to General O. Wöhler, commanding the 8th Army, to hurl his XLVII Panzer Corps, reinforced to a strength of five Panzer divisions, at the eastern face of the pocket; and to General H. V. Hube, to drive his III Panzer Corps, comprising four Panzer divisions (among them the 1st S.S. Panzer Division *"Leibstandarte Adolf Hitler"*) at the western face of the pocket.

Such a plan, involving the concentration of nine Panzer divisions against the Kanev pocket, was nevertheless doomed to failure within the time limit imposed by the defenders' capacity to hold out, though an airlift was being organised to keep them in supplies. Moreover, most of the Panzer divisions designated by Hitler were already engaged elsewhere, and hence it was a case of relieving them, pulling them out of line, and moving them to their jump-off points. Furthermore, they were far short of complement; in particular their grenadier regiments were reduced to only several hundred rifles, and there were grounds for feeling some apprehension that they lacked the resilience necessary for a rapid thrust. Yet in counter-attacks speed is all.

Indeed, on February 2, XLVII and III Panzer Corps still had only four Panzer divisions and, what is more, one of them was immediately withdrawn from General N. von Vormann's XLVII Panzer Corps by special order of the Führer, on receipt of the news that units of the 3rd Ukrainian Front were advancing on Apostolovo, which lies half-way between Nikopol' and Krivoy-Rog. The following night, the *rasputitsa* arrived, covering the western Ukraine with the sea of mud described above. Now the unseasonable weather worked to the advantage of the Russians, delaying their enemy's movements still further. When the earth grew hard again, around February 10, the Soviet encirclement of the Korsun' pocket was consolidated to such an extent that III Panzer Corps only managed to reach the area of Lysyanka, eight miles from the lines held by the besieged forces.

General Stemmermann, as one might expect, had not succeeded in forming a front to the south as he had been enjoined to do in his orders from Rastenburg, without at the same time abandoning Kanev and the banks of the Dniepr, which would have been in defiance of these orders. On February 8 he gave no reply to a summons to capitulate trans-

German prisoners on the Eastern Front.

mitted to him from General Konev, under orders to reduce the pocket. Both Stemmermann and his subordinates turned a deaf ear to the exhortations made to them by representatives of the "Committee for a Free Germany" who had been conveyed to the battlefield on Moscow's orders and were led by General von Seydlitz-Kurzbach, former commander of LI Corps, who had been taken prisoner at Stalingrad. The tracts and individual free passes scattered among the soldiers with a view to encouraging surrender were equally ignored.

Notwithstanding, the airlift worked poorly in the face of an abundant and highly effective Soviet fighter force, and those encircled at Korsun' saw their strength diminish further each day. It was inevitable that the order should come to attempt to break out towards III Panzer Corps, which had been conclusively halted by the mud. It was the only chance left.

To this effect, General Stemmermann reassembled the remnants of his two corps round the village of Shanderovka and organised them in three echelons: at the head the grenadiers, bayonets fixed, next the heavy infantry units, and then finally the artillery and service troops. The 57th and 88th Infantry Divisions protected the rear and showed themselves equal to the sacrifice they were called upon to give. The attempt took place in the night of February 16–17, but at first light Soviet artillery, tanks, and aircraft were able to react with vigour and immediate effect:

"Till now," writes General von Vormann, "our forces had dragged all their heavy equipment across gullies filled with thick, impacted snow. But then enemy shelling proved our undoing. Artillery and assault guns were abandoned after they had exhausted their ammunition. And then the wounded moving with the troops met their fate . . . Veritable hordes of hundreds of soldiers from every type of unit headed westwards under the nearest available officer. The enemy infantry were swept out of the way by our advancing bayonets; even the tanks turned in their tracks. But all the same Russian fire struck with impunity at the masses, moving forward with heads down, unevenly and unprotected. Our losses multiplied . . . "

This hopeless charge by 40,000 men foundered on the natural obstacle of the Gniloy-Tikich, a stream which had thawed only a few days previously, and was now 25 feet wide and just deep enough for a man to drown in. And it heralded a fresh disaster, which the Belgian Léon Degrelle, fighting in the ranks of the S.S. *Sturmbrigade "Wallonie"*, describes in unforgettable terms:

"The artillery teams which had escaped destruction plunged first into the waves and ice floes. The banks of the river were steep, the horses turned back and were drowned. Men then threw themselves in to cross the river by swimming. But hardly had they got to the other side than they were transformed into blocks of ice, and their clothes frozen to their bodies. They tried to throw their equipment over the river. But often their uniforms fell into the current. Soon hundreds of soldiers, completely naked and red as lobsters, were thronging the other bank. Many soldiers did not know how to swim. Maddened by the approach of the Russian armour which was coming down the slope and firing at them, they threw themselves pell-mell into the icy water. Some escaped death by clinging to trees which had been hastily felled . . . but hundreds were drowned. Under the fire of tanks thousands upon thousands of soldiers, half clothed, streaming with icy water or naked as the day they were born, ran through the snow towards the distant cottages of Lysyanka."

In short, between February 16 and 18, III Panzer Corps at Lysyanka retrieved only 30,000 survivors, unarmed for the most part; among them, General Lieb, commander of XLII Corps. The valiant Stemmermann had been killed by a piece of shrapnel. According to the Soviet historian B. S. Telpukhovsky, of the Moscow Academy of Sciences, on this one occasion the Russians accounted for more than 52,000 dead and 11,000 prisoners but his German colleagues Hillgruber and Jacobsen take issue with him: "Just before the investment occurred the two German corps numbered 54,000 all told, including rear area troops, some of whom escaped encirclement."

Allowing for the 30,000 or 32,000 survivors of this 21-day tragedy, German losses in the sector could barely have risen to more than one third of the total claimed by Moscow nearly 15 years after Germany's unconditional surrender. Hillgruber's and Jacobsen's figures are beyond question.

Alexander Werth quotes the account of a Soviet eye witness of these tragic events which confirms General von Vormann's account. On the day following, Major Kampov told Werth:

"I remember that last fateful night of the 17th of February. A terrible blizzard was blowing. Konev himself was travelling in a tank through the shell-shattered 'corridor'. I rode on horseback from one point in the corridor to another, with a dispatch from the General; it was so dark that I could not see the horse's ears. I mention this darkness and this blizzard because they are an important factor in what happened . . .

"It was during that night, or the evening before, that the encircled Germans, having abandoned all hope of ever being rescued by Hube, decided to make a last desperate effort to break out . . .

"Driven out of their warm huts they had to abandon Shanderovka. They flocked into the ravines near the village, and then took the desperate decision to break through early in the morning . . . So that morning they formed themselves into two marching columns of about 14,000 each . . .

"It was about six o'clock in the morning. Our tanks and our cavalry suddenly appeared and rushed straight into the thick of the two columns. What happened then is hard to describe. The Germans ran in all directions. And for the next four hours our tanks raced up and down the plain crushing them by the hundred. Our cavalry, competing with the tanks, chased them through the ravines where it was hard for the tanks to pursue them. Most of the time the tanks were not using their guns lest they hit their own cavalry. Hundreds and hundreds of cavalry were hacking at them with their sabres, and massacred the Fritzes as no one had ever been massacred by cavalry before. There was no time to take prisoners. It was the kind of carnage that nothing could stop till it was all over. In a small area over 20,000 Germans were killed."

In connection with this episode, General von Vormann, in the study mentioned above, raises an interesting question. Observing that the encirclement of XI and XLII Corps on January 28 had opened a 65-mile breach between the right of III Panzer Corps and the left of XLVII, he considers why the Soviet high command failed to exploit the opportunity of a breakthrough afforded. In his opinion, on that day there was nothing to prevent Stalin driving his armoured units towards Uman' and across the Bug, assigning to them distant objectives on the Dniestr, the Prut, and in the Rumanian Carpathians. This not impossible objective would have sealed the fate of Army Groups "A" and "South".

This question was raised in 1954, but it is still impossible to provide an answer which documents can verify. We must be content with the supposition that Stalin acted with extreme prudence, by annihilating the Korsun' pocket before embarking on more hazardous enterprises, and it should be noted that 12 months from then Chernyakhovsky, Rokossovsky, Zhukov, and Konev had far more freedom of action. But by then, from Tilsit to the Polish Carpathians, the German Army was little more than a ruin.

What is certain is that Stalin showed himself eminently satisfied by the way in which Zhukov and those under him had conducted the business; the proof of it being that on February 23, 1944 a decree of the Praesidium of the Supreme Council of the U.S.S.R. conferred upon General of the Army Konev the title of Marshal of the Soviet Union and upon General Rotmistrov that of Marshal of Tank Forces.

No sooner had the Russians closed the ring around XI and XLII Corps, than Field-Marshal von Manstein, just installed in the H.Q. which he had had transferred from Vinnitsa to Proskurov, learnt that the 3rd and 4th Ukrainian Fronts' forces had begun a combined attack on the Nikopol' bridgehead. But he was soon spared the anxiety of having to wage two defensive battles simultaneously, for on February 2, by order of O.K.H., the 6th Army, which was fighting in this sector, was transferred from Army Group "South" to Army Group "A".

Due to Hitler's obstinacy, Manstein left a rather poor legacy to Field-Marshal von Kleist, since the four corps comprising the 6th Army were completely worn out and, in addition, were firmly held in a pincer movement between the 3rd and 4th Ukrainian Fronts' forces; though the thick mud would soon thwart Generals Malinovsky and Tolbukhin in their attempt to benefit strategically from the tactical advantages which their superior resources had given them.

On February 3, General Malinovsky's 46th and 8th Armies reached Apostolovo, 30 miles from Nikopol', at the same time as the 4th Ukrainian Front's forces were going in to storm this latter town's defences on the left bank of the Dniepr. Whereupon a command from the Führer ordered General von Vormann to send in his 24th Panzer Division; but this formation, though most ably commanded by Lieutenant-General M. von Edelsheim, arrived too late to plug the gap in the line at Apostolovo, as Wöhler and Manstein had tried to tell Hitler it would.

Against the Nikopol' bridgehead General Tolbukhin sent in no fewer than 12 infantry and two armoured divisions; General F. Schörner defended it with six infantry divisions and the two Panzer divisions of his XXX Corps. However, the strength of the former had been reduced to that of just one regiment, whilst on the day of the attack, the Panzer divisions had only five sound tanks. Despite the strong Nazi convictions which imbued Schörner and made him resist with great courage, he was pushed back from the right bank of the Dniepr, leaving behind him large quantities of *matériel;* on February 9, the 4th Ukrainian Front's forces liberated Nikopol', though the important engineering centre of Krivoy-Rog was not taken by the 3rd Ukrainian Front forces until February 22. By the end of the month the German 6th Army, in considerable disarray, had taken up positions behind the Ingulets, a tributary of the Dniepr, which flows into it just east of Kherson.

Whilst the 6th Army's retreat considerably shortened the line that Kleist now had to hold, Manstein's stretched between Vinnitsa and Rovno; furthermore, there had been heavy losses in the fighting at Korsun', Nikopol', and Krivoy-Rog, with the Panzer divisions in particular being reduced to an average of about 30 tanks, about 20 per cent of their normal strength of 152 Pzkw IV and V tanks.

According to the calculations of Army Group "South", January and February had been expensive months for the enemy, who had lost 25,353 prisoners, 3,928 tanks, and 3,536 guns; but as Manstein rightly points out in his memoirs: "These figures only served to show the enormous resources at the Red Army's command. The Russians were no longer merely hurling in infantrymen–the drop in the number of prisoners to the amount of arms captured or destroyed showed either that they had been able to save men by sacrificing arms and equipment, or that they had suffered enormous losses in manpower."

At Rastenburg, the Germans were counting upon the combined effects of these losses and of the thaw to slow down, then halt, the Russian advance. The staff sections of Army Group "South" were much less optimistic: the Russians still had 50 to 100 tanks per tank corps, making a total of 1,500 against less than 400 for the Germans. Secondly, radio Intelligence showed that between Rovno and Mozyr' another front, the 1st Belorussian Front (commanded by General Rokossovsky) was coming into being. Faced with this information, Manstein reformed as best he could to reinforce his 4th *Panzerarmee,* which barred the enemy's advance towards Ternopol' and Chernovtsy. Thus Generals Wöhler and Hube were forced to give up five Panzer divisions to Raus, who also received three infantry divisions from O.K.H.

Despite these reinforcements, the 4th Army was destroyed on the very first day – March 4 – of the new offensive launched by the 1st Belorussian Front's armies, now commanded by Marshal Zhukov. What, then, had happened to his predecessor, General Vatutin? The only thing one can state for sure is that he died at Kiev on April 14, 1944. But how? At the time of his death, a Moscow communiqué stated that it was from the after effects of a chill caught at the front. But the Soviet academician Telpukhovsky affirms "that this ardent defender of his socialist mother-country, this eminent general and Soviet army commander" – a judgement with which none will disagree – died as the result of bullet wounds inflicted by the enemy. In November 1961, however, during the twenty-second Congress of the Russian Communist Party, Nikita Khruschev, who had been Vatutin's political aide, revealed to an astonished audience that the liberator of Kiev had

committed suicide whilst suffering from a fit of nervous depression. This is the version related by Michel Garder in his book *A War Unlike The Others,* published in 1962. It should be noted, however, that he does not accept this story himself, and in fact declares it to be highly unlikely. Finally, Alexander Werth, who during the war was the *Sunday Times'* Russian correspondent, brought out yet another explanation. According to him, Vatutin had been ambushed and killed by a band of Ukrainian nationalists: a version which has the advantage of explaining why Khruschev, himself a Ukrainian, might have distorted the facts.

At all events, Zhukov, on going into battle on March 4, 1944, had under him three tank and six rifle armies, i.e. about 60 divisions and at least 1,000 tanks. Attacking on both sides of Shepetovka on a front of about 120 miles, he gained between 15 and 30 miles in less than 48 hours, so that by March 6 his 3rd Guards Tank Army was approaching the L'vov–Odessa railway line at Volochisk, the last but one communication and supply link for Army Group "South" before the Carpathians.

By March 9, having covered some 80 miles in less than six days, General Rybalko's tanks came up against the hastily improvised Tarnopol' defences. At the same time, the 1st *Panzerarmee* and the German 8th Army were being severely mauled by the left wing of Zhukov's forces and the 2nd Ukrainian Front, numbering seven rifle and two tank armies. Immediately the forces of Generals Hube and Wöhler, which had not yet recovered from their losses at Korsun', and had had part of their Panzer units transferred to Raus, buckled under the shock. In particular, the 8th Army was forced to withdraw towards Uman'.

Manstein, however, was not surprised by this new Russian offensive, whose purpose he saw only too clearly. *Stavka's* aim was, in fact, nothing less than the

cutting off of Army Groups "South" and "A" from the rest of the German troops fighting on the Eastern Front, pushing them south-west, as far as Odessa on the Black Sea, where they would stand no more chance of being evacuated than the defenders of the Crimea at Sevastopol'.

Faced with such an overwhelming threat, Manstein did not hesitate. First, he ordered Generals Hube and Wöhler to withdraw immediately; then he decided to mass his troops around General Raus to stop Zhukov taking the most threatening route across the Dniestr to the Carpathians via Chernovtsy. With his XIII Corps covering L'vov in the Brody region, he ordered XLVIII Panzer Corps, then fighting 120 miles to the east, southwest of Berdichev, to go to the defence of Tarnopol'. To carry out such an order, it first had to slip through the columns of the northbound 1st Ukrainian Front armies and do so without being engaged by the enemy. That it succeeded was due to the coolness and skill of its commander, General Balck, and also to errors committed by the Russians. Mellenthin, chief-of-staff of XLVIII Panzer Corps makes the following remark in this connection: "Since Russian attacks were nearly always aimed at large centres –probably because the Soviet generals wanted to attract attention to themselves by having their names inserted in special communiqués–we avoided such centres like the plague." Their manoeuvre was successful, and Manstein was able to ward off the catastrophe that had seemed so near, making the Russians fight for more than a month before they could enter Tarnopol'. However, it was not his responsibility to impose his views on Kleist, and he was not going to abandon his fellow-officer, just when the latter's 6th Army was locked in battle with the 50 or 60

Most Russians, like the women at lower right, welcomed the arrival of the Red Army's tanks and infantry.

*A dead German infantryman
lies beside a knocked-out
Pzkw IV.*

divisions of the 3rd and 4th Ukrainian Fronts' armies.

At O.K.H., where the actions of the two army groups ought to have been co-ordinated, Hitler obstinately refused to allow the 6th Army to abandon the Bug line and strengthen Manstein's right wing. The consequence was that on March 13 Marshal Konev had pierced the defences that the 8th Army had hastily improvised on the right bank of the Bug, and had crossed the river on a 100-mile wide front. This breakthrough cruelly exposed the right wing of the *1st Panzerarmee*, whilst its left wing was being mercilessly hammered by Marshal Zhukov.

Ordered to Obersalzberg on March 19 to take part in a ceremony during which Rundstedt, on behalf of his fellow officers, presented vows of loyalty to the Führer, Manstein took advantage of the occasion to put his point of view: in his opinion four decisions had to be made, and quickly: "1. Immediate withdrawal of the 6th Army behind the Dniestr. The salient it occupied on the Bug was still much too pronounced and demanded too many troops for its defence. It was Kleist himself, commanding Army Group 'A', who had proposed this;
2. The units thus freed would then be rapidly transferred to the area between the Dniestr and the Prut, preventing the 8th Army from being pushed back from the Dniestr towards the south-east;
3. Army Group 'A' to be given the clear responsibility, in liaison with Rumanian forces, for covering Rumania on the Dniestr or the Prut; and
4. A rapid strengthening of the northern wing of Army Group 'South', to prevent its being pushed back into the Carpathians, or to prevent a Russian advance on L'vov."

But Hitler remained intractable; there were to be neither substantial rein-forcements, nor freedom of manoeuvre for his generals.

Meanwhile, in the 2nd Ukrainian Front's sector, operations were taking place at Blitzkrieg speed, and even so far-seeing a commander as Manstein was being left behind by events. Almost at the same time as he was suggesting to Hitler that the 6th and 8th Armies be withdrawn behind the Dniestr, Marshal Rotmistrov's 5th Guards Tank Army and General Kravchenko's 6th Army reached and crossed the river on either side of the town of Soroki.

Worse still, on March 21, Marshal Zhukov, who had regrouped his forces after his moderate success at Tarnopol', attacked the point just where the commands of General Raus and Hube came together. Throwing three tank armies into the attack, he broke through and immediately advanced south; by the 23rd his forward troops had reached the Dniestr at Chernovtsy, with the resultant danger that the 1st *Panzerarmee*, fighting near Proskurov on the Bug, would be cut off. It had to be ordered to move west and try to make contact with the 4th Army, for already the only means of supplying it was by airlift.

After a whole day spent in sending and receiving a series of curt telephone calls, Manstein was peremptorily summoned to the Berghof. Here he was received by Hitler at about noon on March 25, and it was only after hours of discussion, and Manstein's threat to resign his command, that Hitler gave in on the two points he was most insistent upon: firstly, he was authorised to tell Hube to fight his way through to the west, and secondly he was assured that he would very soon be reinforced by the *Waffen*-S.S. II Panzer Corps which, in case there was a cross-Channel landing, was stationed near Alençon.

But this meeting had lost the Germans 48 hours, of which the Russians took full advantage: on March 27, the Russian 1st and 4th Tank Armies, commanded respectively by Generals D. D. Lelyushenko and K. S. Moskalenko, joined up at Sekiryany, on the Dniestr's right bank, and behind the 1st *Panzerar-mee*. Hube was thus caught in a trap near Skala-Podolskaya with about ten divisions, including three Panzer divisions, there is no doubt that everything south of the Pripet would have collapsed if this brave general, who had lost an arm in World War I, had not shown such optimism, resolution, and skill, and inspired such confidence in his troops, both officers and other ranks.

Did Hitler regret having agreed to Manstein's suggestions, or did he think him less capable than General Model of lessening the damage that his own stubbornness had caused in the first place? Whatever the reason, on March 30, Manstein, the victor of Sevastopol' and Khar'kov, took the plane to Obersalzberg, where at one and the same time, he was awarded the Oak Leaves to the Knight's Cross of the Iron Cross and relieved of the command which he had assumed in such grim circumstances on November 24, 1942.

"For a long time Göring and Himmler had been conspiring towards my downfall," wrote Manstein. "I knew this. But the main reason was that on March 25 Hitler had been obliged to grant me what he had previously, and in public, refused me. On shaking hands to take leave of him, I said 'I hope your decision today will not turn out to be mistaken.'

"Kleist was received after me and dismissed in like fashion. As we left the Berghof, we saw our successors, Colonel-General Model, who was going to take over my army group which would now be called Army Group 'North Ukraine' and General Schörner, Kleist's replacement, already waiting at the door!"

And so, on April 2, Colonel-General Walther Model, in whom Hitler recognised the best repairer of his own mistakes, took command of what a few days later was rather pompously re-christened Army Group "North Ukraine".

Major-General Mellenthin who, as chief-of-staff of XLVIII Panzer Corps, got to know Model well, describes him as a "small thin man, jovial and lively, whom one could never have imagined separated from his monocle. But, however great his single-mindedness, his energy or his courage, he was very different from Manstein. In particular, Model was only too prone to busy himself with every tiniest detail, and to tell his army commanders, and even his corps commanders, where and how they were to draw up their troops. General Balck, for example, the commander of XLVIII Panzer Corps, considered this tendency in his new chief to be most irritating."

At the same time as Hube's "mobile pocket" was painfully fighting its way west, Zhukov had crossed the Dniestr and reached the foothills of the Carpathians, first having captured Chernovtsy, Kolomyya, and Nadvornaya. It was at this time that the II S.S. Panzer Corps, comprising the 9th and 10th *"Hohenstaufen"* and *"Frundsberg"* Panzer Divisions, arrived in the L'vov region, under the command of Colonel-General P. Hausser. In addition Hitler had made available to Army Group "South" the 367th Division and the 100th *Jäger* Division, which had taken part in the occupation of Hungary. Thanks to these reinforcements, Generals Model and Raus succeeded on April 9 in re-establishing contact at Buchach on the River Strypa (one of the Dniestr's left bank tributaries) with the 1st *Panzerarmee* which, despite a retreat of some 120 miles through enemy territory, and having to cross four rivers, had managed to save most of its equipment. A few days later Hube was killed in an air accident *en route* to receive promotion from Hitler.

On March 30, like his colleague Manstein, Kleist had at the same time been decorated and dismissed; fortunately his successor, General Schörner, was a man after his own heart. A few days earlier, the 8th Army had been transferred to Army Group "A", which a week later was renamed Army Group "South Ukraine". But by the end of the month Schörner no longer held a square inch of Ukrainian territory–in fact, he considered he had done well to save the 6th and 8th Armies from complete disaster.

The Dniestr having been forced by Konev's armour, the 8th Army was soon face to face with the prospect of being cut off from all contact with Army Group "South", and of being pushed right back to the mouth of the Danube. Thanks, however, to the rapidity with which Marshal Antonescu moved his Rumanian 4th Army into the line, and to the splendid tactical sense of General Wöhler, not only was this disaster avoided, but also a break between Model and Schörner, who maintained contact at Kuty, 40 miles west of Chernovtsy.

This success, however, was obtained at the cost of northern Bessarabia and Moldavia, for the Prut was no more successful than the Dniestr in halting the Soviet tank advance. In fact, all that the stiffening of Germano–Rumanian resistance managed to accomplish, in mid-April, was to stop the Russians in front of Chișinau in Bessarabia and Iasi in Moldavia, though the towns of Botoșani, Pașcani, and Suceava fell into their hands.

The German 6th Army, which by Hitler's command had been kept on the lower Bug beyond all reasonable limits almost suffered the same fate near Odessa as had its predecessor at Stalingrad. Malinovsky and the 3rd Ukrainian Front tried to turn a good situation to their advantage by pushing through the gap that had been made between the 6th Army's left flank and the right of the 8th Army as a result of the Uman' breakthrough, with the obvious aim of cutting it off from the Dniestr; and it has to be admitted that

it had plenty of resources to accomplish this.

However, Hitler, judging by the directive he issued on April 2 to the commanders of Army Groups "A", "South", and "Centre", did not seem to think the situation so dangerous, since he ordered Schörner to hold "for the time being, the line of the Tiligul estuary to Dubossary on the Dniestr until such time as it would be possible to supply the Crimea independently of Odessa. The retreat to the Dniestr ought, however, still to be prepared."

The position to be occupied by the 6th Army between the estuary of the Tiligul and Dubossary on the Dniestr's left bank, level with the city of Chișinau, was about 120 miles long. With the completely worn-out troops that General Hollidt had, such a line could not be held indefinitely, even if he had been allowed sufficient time to dig himself in and organise himself.

The enterprising Malinovsky took good care, however, to allow him no time; on April 5, supported by the guns of a whole corps of artillery, he captured the Tiligul position, whilst the squadrons and tanks of the Kuban' Cavalry Corps, commanded by Lieutenant-General Pliev, took the railway junction of Razdelnaya by surprise, thus cutting off the enemy's access to the Dniestr crossings at Tiraspol. Faced with these reverses, which placed him in a catastrophic position, the 6th Army's commander took it upon himself, on April 9, to evacuate Odessa. Crossing the Dniestr, his troops, in collaboration with the Rumanian 3rd Army, organised the defence of the river's right bank, between the Black Sea and the Dubossary region. North of Chișinau, Hollidt's left flank once more made contact with General Wöhler's right. In Stalin's special communiqué, which described the liberation of Odessa in particularly glowing terms, the honour of this victory went to the gallant defenders of Stalingrad: Colonel-General Chuikov and his 62nd Army.

A Waffen-S.S. motorised unit pauses beside the road during the long retreat from the Dniepr front.

The April 2 directive, from which we have just quoted, showed Hitler's resolution to defend the Crimea at all costs. Less than a week later, the storm clouds which Kleist and Manstein had seen gathering burst with irresistible force. Within Army Group "A", it was the German 17th Army, under the command of Colonel-General C. Jaenecke, and comprising V and IL Corps and the Rumanian I Mountain Corps, themselves made up of five German divisions and seven Rumanian divisions, which had the task of defending the peninsula. It must, however, be said that two of the Rumanian divisions were in action against the partisans who, since November 1943, had held the Krimskiye massif, whose peaks dominate the southern coast of the Crimea. The key to the Crimea, the Kamenskoye isthmus, was held by IL Corps (General R. Konrad), who had established his 50th, 111th, and 336th Divisions in soundly fortified positions defending this tongue of land, whilst the Rumanian 9th Cavalry Division kept watch on the Black Sea, and the Rumanian 10th and 19th Divisions performed the same task on the shore of the Sivash Lagoon. V Corps (General K. Allmendinger) kept an eye on the small bridgehead which the Russians had taken the previous autumn beyond the Kerch' Strait, a task in which it was helped by the 73rd and 98th Divisions, and the 6th Cavalry Division and 3rd Mountain Division of the Rumanian Army.

Stavka's plan to reconquer the peninsula meant the simultaneous action of the 4th Ukrainian Front and a separate army, known as the Independent Coastal Army. The first, with 18 infantry divisions and four armoured corps, would storm the Kamenskoye isthmus, whilst the second, 12 divisions strong, would break out of the Kerch' bridgehead, and they would then together converge upon Sevastopol'. As will be noted, the Russians had ensured a massive superiority in men and *matériel*.

On April 8, General Tolbukhin unleashed the offensive, the 4th Ukrainian Front attacking under an air umbrella as large as it was powerful.

On the right, the 2nd Guards Army, under Lieutenant-General G. F. Zakharov, was hard put to it to storm the Kamenskoye defences, and took 48 hours to reach the outskirts of Armyansk. On the left, breaking out of the small bridgehead on the Sivash Sea, which it had succeeded in linking to the mainland by means of a dike, the 51st Army, commanded by Lieutenant-General Ya. G. Kreizer, which had the main task, had in fact a much easier job, faced as it was by only the two Rumanian divisions. By midday on April 9, the 10th Division was submerged, and its collapse enabled the Soviet tanks to capture two days later the important junction of Dzhanskoy, where the railway leading to Sevastopol' divides from that leading to the town of Feodosiya and the port of Kerch'.

On April 11, in the Kerch' peninsula, the Independent Coastal Army, under General Eremenko, attacked in its turn; and when one realises that Hitler, a prey to hesitation, thought he could conduct the Crimea campaign from Obersalzberg, it was little short of a miracle that General Jaenecke was able to withdraw his troops to their Sevastopol' positions without being intercepted by the combined forces of Tolbukhin and Eremenko, who had linked up on April 16 near Yalta. To defend its 25-mile long front before Sevastopol', the 17th Army could now count only upon the five German divisions already mentioned above. But they had been reduced, on average, to something like a third of their normal strength and were already tired. Therefore Schörner flew to see the Führer personally and put the case for the evacuation of his troops. In vain, however, and when Jaenecke, in his turn, went to Berchtesgaden to put the same arguments, he was even refused permission to return to Sevastopol', and was succeeded as head of the 17th Army, on April 27, by General Allmendinger.

On May 7, after artillery had softened up the positions for 48 hours, the 2nd Guards Army attacked the northern flank, as Manstein had done in 1942; but the Germans were too few to rival the heroic exploits of General Petrov's men. Thus, when General Allmendinger finally received a message on May 9 from the Führer authorising evacuation, it was already too late for it to be properly organised, especially since the Soviet Air Force, completely dominating the air, fired at anything that tried to take to the sea. On May 13, all resistance ceased in the region around the Khersonesskiy (Chersonese) peninsula, now (as in 1942) the last defence position.

The evacuation of the Crimea gave rise to dramatic scenes such as those described by Alexander Werth:

"For three days and nights, the Chersonese was that 'unspeakable inferno' to which German authors now refer. True, on the night of May 9–10 and on the following night, two small ships did come and perhaps 1,000 men were taken aboard. This greatly encouraged the remaining troops." But the Russians had no intention of letting the Germans get away by sea:

"And on the night of May 11–12 the *katyusha* mortars ('the Black Death' the Germans used to call them) came into action. What followed was a massacre. The Germans fled in panic beyond the second and then the third line of their defences, and when, in the early morning hours, Russian tanks drove in, they began to surrender in large numbers, among them their commander, General Böhme, and several other staff officers who had been sheltering in the cellar of the only farm building on the promontory.

"Thousands of wounded had been taken to the tip of the promontory, and here were also some 750 SS-men who refused to surrender, and went on firing. A few dozen survivors tried in the end to get away by sea in small boats or rafts. Some of these got away, but often only to be machine-gunned by Russian aircraft. These desperate men were hoping to get to Rumania, Turkey, or maybe to be picked up by some German or Rumanian vessel."

The 17th Army's losses were very heavy. On April 8 it had comprised 128,500 German and 66,000 Rumanian troops; of these, 96,800 Germans and 40,200 Rumanians were evacuated, leaving behind 31,700 German and 25,800 Rumanian dead or missing. But it must be remembered

Crouching behind a Pzkw IV, a Panzergrenadier *awaits a Stuka attack in support of German armour.*

that of the 137,000 evacuated, more than 39,000 were wounded and all their equipment lost.

Let us now turn from the Soviets' winter offensive south of the Pripet to the campaigns which, between January 15 and March 15, resulted in the complete relief of Leningrad through the rout of Army Group "North".

At the beginning of the year, Field-Marshal von Küchler, with his right flank at Polotsk and his left up by the Gulf of Finland, to the west of Oranienbaum, was holding a front of more than 500 miles with 40 divisions, all infantry. This line of defence was dangerously exposed, both at Oranienbaum and south of Leningrad, as well as on the left bank of the Volkhov. Which is why, on December 30, the commander of Army Group "North" suggested to Hitler that he withdraw his 16th and 18th Armies to the "Panther" position which was then being prepared; this would reduce the front by more than 60 miles; and of the remaining 440 miles, more than 120 miles consisted of Lake Peipus and 50 of the expanse of water formed by the junction of the Gulf of Finland with the mouth of the Narva.

Although such a withdrawal would have saved eight divisions, Hitler rejected Küchler's suggestion, for he was fully aware that the Russian and Finnish Governments had resumed diplomatic contact at Stockholm; thus to abandon the positions held by Army Group "North" might encourage Finland to bow out of the war.

In the meantime, on January 14 the Leningrad Front's armies, under General Govorov, attacked the left wing of the German 18th Army, commanded by Colonel-General von Lindemann. According to German authorities, Govorov commanded a force of 42 infantry divisions and nine tank corps, though these figures cannot be checked since Soviet historians such as Telpukhovsky give no information on the strength of the Red Army forces on this occasion. Simultaneously, General Meretskov's Volkhov Front forces, with 18 infantry and 15 tank divisions, attacked the right wing of the 18th Army in the Novgorod sector.

Thus this offensive planned by *Stavka* took the form of a pincer movement, with Govorov and Meretskov trying to meet at Luga, so catching Lindemann's 18 divisions in the trap.

On the Leningrad Front, the Soviet aim was to reduce the Peterhof salient, and to this end, General Fedyuninsky's 2nd Shock Army, from the Oranienbaum bridgehead, and General Maslennikov's 42nd Army were to aim for the common objective of Gatchina. The Germans, behind well-established defensive positions, put up a very stubborn resistance, and held out for nearly a week. But once the 126th, 170th, and 215th Divisions collapsed, a large gap was opened up in the German positions. On January 26, Govorov reached Pushkin, formerly Tsarskoye-Selo, and extended his offensive right

up to the Mga region, a victory which enabled the Russians to capture large quantities of arms, in particular 85 guns of greater than 10-inch calibre.

On the Volkhov front, General Meretskov's capture of Lyuban' enabled direct railway communication between Moscow and Leningrad to be re-established; whilst north of Lake Ilmen, his left flank, comprising the 59th Army, commanded by General Korovnikov, punched a gaping hole in the German defences, recaptured Novgorod, and speeded up its advance towards the west. On January 21 the plan prepared by Marshal Zhukov entered the phase of exploitation.

With both wings of his army in disarray, and no reinforcements except the single 12th Panzer Division, Küchler realised the necessity of withdrawing the 18th Army to the Luga as a matter of urgency, only to see himself immediately relieved of his command in favour of Colonel-General Model. Monstrously unjust as this decision was, it nevertheless helped to save Army Group "North", since Hitler showed himself more ready to listen to a commander of working-class origin than to the aristocratic Küchler; and the day after his appointment, Model was given two more divisions.

On the whole, Model, a capable soldier, adopted the arrangements made by his predecessor, and moreover managed to get them approved by Hitler. However, hardly had he got his army from out of the clutches of Govorov, than the latter, enlarging the radius of his activities, crossed the River Luga to the left of the town of the same name; Pskov, the main supply base of Army Group "North" seemed to be the objective of this push, but at the same time it seriously exposed Colonel-General Lindemann's rear. Furthermore, the left wing of General Hansen's 16th Army was beginning to wilt under the attacks of General Popov and his Baltic Front, and to make matters worse, was in great danger of being flooded by the waters of Lake Ilmen.

This last extension of the Soviet offensive forced Model to abandon his intention of placing his 18th Army as a defensive barrier between Lake Ilmen and Lake Peipus. He asked for, and obtained, permission from O.K.H. to withdraw all his forces back to the "Panther" line, which, stretching from a point west of Nevel', passed through Opochka and Pskov, then followed the western bank of Lake Peipus, finally reaching the Gulf of Finland at Narva. Begun on February 17, this withdrawal was concluded by mid-March without any untoward incident. When Model was called upon to replace Manstein a fortnight later, Lindemann succeeded him at the head of Army Group "North", being in turn succeeded at the head of the 18th Army by General Loch.

For the German Army, therefore, the first quarter of 1944 was marked by a long series of reverses, which, although their worst effects had been avoided, had

nevertheless been very costly in terms of men and materials. And many reports originating at the front showed that reinforcements were arriving without the necessary training.

Furthermore, the protective glacis of "Festung Europa" was being seriously encroached upon. Bucharest and the vital oil wells of Ploieşti, Budapest and the Danube basin, Galicia with its no less vital wells at Borislaw, Riga and the central Baltic, were all coming within the compass of Soviet strategy. So that these further defeats of the Third Reich had far more than merely military significance, and encroached upon the diplomatic and political plane.

As we have seen, Hitler was afraid that the withdrawal of Army Group "North" to its "Panther" defensive position might tempt Finland, which he knew to be engaged in discussions with Russia, to get out of the war and conclude a separate peace. Küchler's defeat and the battered state in which the 16th and 18th Armies reached the "Panther" line encouraged the Finns to continue their negotiations. These were broken off, however, on April 1, when the Russians insisted that all German troops should be evacuated or interned within 30 days, and that the Finns should pay them 600 million dollars in reparations, to be paid in five annual instalments.

A few days earlier, however, on March 27, whilst Hitler was talking to Admiral Horthy at Klessheim about the new "arrangements" that would have to be made in view of the line taken by the Kallay cabinet, 11 German divisions, carrying out Operation *"Margarethe"*, proceeded to occupy Hungary.

"What was I to do?" asks the former Regent in his memoirs. "It was quite clear that my abdication would not prevent the occupation of Hungary, and would allow Hitler to install a government entirely composed of Nazis, as the example of Italy clearly showed. 'Whilst I am still Regent,' I told myself, 'the Germans will at least have to show some consideration. They will be forced to keep me at the head of the army, which they will not be able to absorb into the German Army. Nor will they be able to place at the head of the government Hungarian Nazi puppets, who would hunt down, not only many Hungarian patriots, but also 800,000 Jews, and tens of thousands of refugees who had found shelter in our country. I could very conveniently have abdicated at that time and saved myself many criticisms. But I could not leave a sinking ship which at that moment had the greatest possible need of its captain.'"

In line with this reasoning, Horthy accepted the *fait accompli,* and on March 23 swore in a new cabinet, whose prime minister was General Dome-Sztojay, his ambassador in Berlin. But Hitler's Klessheim trap freed him from any obligation *vis-à-vis* the Third Reich, and henceforth the old Admiral was to embark upon a policy of resistance.

CHAPTER 52
Clearing the Gilbert and Marshall Islands

We have already seen, in Chapter 46, how American power in the Pacific was built up. Its continuing reinforcement allowed Admirals E. J. King in the Pentagon, C. W. Nimitz at Pearl Harbor, and Vice-Admirals W. F. Halsey, R. A. Spruance, and T. C. Kincaid at sea to take risks which would have been unthought of at Guadalcanal. The increase in the numbers of fast aircraft-carriers available would, however, not have been as effective had not the U.S. at the same time rebuilt it naval air force.

This became possible thanks to the gradual replacement of the 325 mph Grumman F4F Wildcat fighter by the 375 mph Grumman F6F Hellcat. Similarly, the Curtiss SB2C Helldiver dive-bomber supplemented the older Douglas SBD Dauntless. Finally, the Vought F4U Corsair was to prove an excellent all-round machine, sturdy and easy to maintain, as its long post-war career subsequently demonstrated. All this gave the lie to the opinion that ship-borne planes were always inferior to the enemy's land-based aircraft.

By September 2, 1945, of the 90 divisions raised by the U.S., the Pentagon had allocated six Marine and 21 Army divisions to the Pacific theatre. Because operations in this theatre were amphibious, troops had to be given massive landing capabilities: whereas on the day "Overlord" started there were 4,748 landing-craft operating in the Channel and the Mediterranean, on that same date Admiral Nimitz and General MacArthur had 3,866 between them.

In addition to the naval air force there was also the Army Air Force. The Central Pacific Area (Nimitz) had the tactical and strategic formations of the 7th Air Force (Major-General Willis H. Hale), and the South-West Pacific Area had the 5th Air Force under the brilliant command of Major-General C. Kenney. The entry into service of the four-engined Boeing B-29 Superfortress was to give the U.S. air forces a heavy bomber with the hitherto unequalled range of 3,250 miles. These planes, the heaviest in World War II ($53\frac{1}{2}$ tons on take-off), were allocated to a special force: the 20th Air Force under Major-General Nathan F. Twining.

In addition to his own forces, General MacArthur also controlled the land, sea, and air formations which Australia and New Zealand had put into the war.

In September 1943, Admiral Sir James Somerville, C.-in-C. Eastern Fleet, left Kilindini near Mombasa on the east coast of Africa for Colombo. With the *Tirpitz* out of action, the *Scharnhorst* destroyed, and the Italian Navy in Allied hands, the British Admiralty was able to send him reinforcements. And so by March 1944 he had 59 vessels, including the battleships *Queen Elizabeth* and *Valiant* (both now repaired after damage sustained in

Alexandria on December 19, 1941), the battle-cruiser *Renown*, the aircraft-carrier *Illustrious*, 14 cruisers (including the Dutch *Tromp*), 24 destroyers, and 17 submarines. On April 10, these were joined by the French battleship *Richelieu* and later by the U.S. carrier *Saratoga*.

In Burma, under the energetic command of Lieutenant-General William Slim, the British 14th Army had two corps of ten British and Indian divisions. On the Burma-China border, Slim also commanded U.S. Lieutenant-General Stilwell's group of five small Chinese divisions. All these forces were supported by transport and fighter aircraft virtually unopposed by the Japanese.

In his book on the bombing during the night of March 9-10, 1945, in which Tokyo suffered some 130,000 casualties, the American Martin Caidin writes:

"The Japanese failed because their men and officers were inferior, not in courage, *but in the intelligent use of courage.* In a predicted situation which could be handled in an orthodox manner, the Japanese were always competent and often they were resourceful. Under the shadow of frustration, however, the obsession of personal honor blinded the Japanese to reality and extinguished ingenuity."

This opinion is confirmed by the Bonze Daisetzu Suzuki, a well-known Zen Buddhist, who writes in a history of the *kamikaze* operations by Captain Inoguchi and Commander Nakajima:

"When we examine the *kamikaze* tactics, they reveal a grave shortcoming in the Japanese people: the lack of scientific thinking. The Japanese have tried to make up for this with moral and physical strength: hence the *kamikaze* tactics. When military leaders, not to say their fellow-citizens also, are incapable of scientific thought and rely only on human material, they can only conceive suicide tactics which, far from bringing glory to the Japanese people, must be regarded as ignominious."

It is evident that by November 20, 1943, the war was lost for Japan and Tojo, just as it was for Germany and Hitler, as the economic and industrial resources of the U.S. were now so much greater, in spite of early Japanese victories, than they had been in the winter of 1941-2. Yamamoto's pessimistic forecast that the war would go badly for Japan if it lasted longer than six months was now beginning to come true. The fact remains,

American Marines storm up the sides of a Japanese bunker on Tarawa.

however, that such forces as he did control were badly managed by Tojo because he was unable to solve the cardinal problem of sea transport. As E. B. Potter of the U.S. Naval Academy and Admiral Nimitz have pointed out, this was a particularly difficult problem for Japan, which, "having no industry in her resource areas and no resources in her industrial area, had to bring all raw materials to Japan for manufacture and then distribute them to the ultimate consumers which, in war, were the forces in the field.

"In other words, Japan's shipping pattern took the form of an inverted V with the apex in the home islands, whereas a delta-shaped pattern would have resulted in a more efficient use of available ships."

The inferiority of the Japanese at sea must also be attributed in part to the success of Admiral Nimitz's submarine war, waged after Pearl Harbor without regard to the restrictions in Article 22 of the London Naval Treaty of April 22, 1930. From December 8, 1941, to the same date in 1943, the number of U.S. submarines operating in the Pacific rose from 51 to 120. In 1944, in spite of the loss of 24, there were 200 under the command of Vice-Admiral Charles A. Lockwood, in Pearl Harbor, Midway, and the Western Australian base of Fremantle. The acute shortage of torpedoes which had so badly affected operations until the summer of 1944 had now been overcome thanks to the introduction of the excellent and reliable Mark 18 electric torpedo.

Japan's answer to this mortal threat was late and hesitant. Like Admiral King early in 1942, Japanese sailors hated convoys because of their defensive character. King had changed his mind in time, but it was November 1943 before the Japanese Admiralty came round to the idea of creating a large "escort command". Even then it went only half way and did no research to prove that it was in Japan's interest to assemble large convoys of 50 merchantmen or more, as the Americans and the British were doing at this time.

All Lockwood had to do, therefore, was to organise small packs of three or four submarines to decimate the small Japanese convoys and their feeble escort. He was so successful that by September 2, 1945, he had destroyed 1,178 Japanese merchantmen, totalling 5,320,000 tons. At the beginning of the war, the Japanese had had 2,583 ships, totalling 6,336,380 tons. In addition, they lost some two million tons of shipping to the U.S. and Allied air forces. Vice-Admiral Fukudome would appear to have been right when he said: "The losses we suffered from U.S. submarines were very high and it is not too much to say that they were the final blow to Japan."

The cost to the Americans was 52 boats and to the Japanese Navy 135, including six in the Indian Ocean, as the Americans kept up their pressure relentlessly. The reason for this disparity is to be found in the doctrinal error of the Japanese in making their prime target their enemy's fighting ships, usually well-protected, and not his convoys, which were much more vulnerable. In fact, according to Commander Hashimoto, the Allies lost a mere 125 merchantmen as a result of all Japanese attacks on convoys.

Harping back to the Bonze Suzuki's remark – in both offensive and defensive operations, the Japanese detection devices (sonar and radar) were greatly inferior to those of the Allies. Two typical episodes in the Pacific war illustrate this admirably:
1. From May 19 to 31, off New Ireland, the escort destroyer *England* (Lieutenant-Commander W. B. Pendleton) alone sank six Japanese submarines.
2. On June 6-7, 1944, in the waters between Borneo and the Philippines, the submarine *Harder* (Commander Samuel D. Dealey) torpedoed five Japanese destroyers, sinking three of them.

The same was true for air warfare. Not only was Japanese aircraft production unable to keep up with the Americans', but the types coming into service in 1944-5 were only slightly better than those which had done wonders at Pearl Harbor and off the coast of Malaya. Not only had there been no technical progress, but the training of pilots had lagged disastrously behind because of a shortage of fuel.

The American plan, under General Marshall and Admiral King, was to cut Japan's industries off from their sources of supply. Faithful to the principle of concentration of effort, the two leaders opted first of all for a single drive across the Central Pacific along the general axis Pearl Harbor–Marshall Islands–Caroline Islands–Marianas. This took no account of the impetuous MacArthur's prestige and personality. He did not see himself reduced to a secondary rôle or having to break his promise to liberate the Philippines. The Pentagon thus had to resign itself to a double thrust: Nimitz as above, plus MacArthur along a line New Guinea–Mindanao. MacArthur was required to see priority given in supplies to the Central Pacific forces; he agreed and neither Marshall nor King had any reason to regret giving him the go-ahead. They had, of course, given the enemy the advantage of an inner line, but the Japanese Combined Fleet, with Admiral Mineichi Koga in command (he took over from Yamamoto in late April 1942) was never in a position to profit by it.

The J.C.S. gave the Central Pacific forces the Marshall Islands as their first objective. Nimitz had this changed to the Gilberts. If these were not taken first, he assured Washington, the attack on the Marshalls could be caught in flank by the enemy from bases on the Tarawa and Makin atolls. Also, he could get the support of the bomber formations of the 7th Air Force on Funafuti in the Ellice Islands. King agreed.

The two archipelagos of the Gilbert and Marshall Islands have common characteristics, and Morison describes them as groups of atolls, each composed of between 20 and 50 islets and reefs. If one threw 20 necklaces of different lengths and sizes into a shallow tank of water, one would have an accurate impression of the Marshalls. One of the atolls in this archipelago is "Kwajalein, the largest atoll in the world, [which] encloses a lagoon over 60 miles long by 30 miles wide, but some of the smaller atolls are only a few hundred yards in diameter. A ten foot rise in the Marshalls is accounted a hill, and the highest point in the archipelago is only 21 feet above sea level."

Operation "Galvanic", which was to give the Americans possession of the Gilbert Islands, was led by Vice-Admiral Raymond A. Spruance, a commander of "outstanding intellect and an austere and demanding officer", as Nimitz describes him. On November 20, Spruance had no less than 139 vessels under his command. These included 29 troop-transports carrying V Amphibious Force (Major-General Holland M. Smith: 2nd Marine and 27th Divisions).

The Assault Force, led by Rear-Admiral Richmond K. Turner, had seven old battleships with 14- and 16-inch guns, eight heavy and light cruisers, 35 destroyers, and eight escort carriers (218 aircraft). Turner's job was to pulverise the enemy defences before the landing, then to support the troops on the ground with shelling and bombing. In this he had the collaboration of the 7th Air Force.

Task Force 81 (Rear-Admiral C. A. Pownall) consisted principally of five new battleships and the 11 fast carriers then available. It thus had 45 16-inch guns and a little over 700 planes, with which it was required to protect Operation "Galvanic" from all outside interference. It was ready to attack the Combined Fleet if the Japanese attempted to come to the rescue of the Gilbert Islands and crush their air bases. This was looking ahead, as by giving strategic cover to one operation, the next one was also being prepared for. From now on the Task Force split up into Task Groups, each with various types of warship. The nerve-centre of each group was one or more carriers, the capital ships of the Pacific war.

The aircraft ranged up to 225 miles from their carriers, which sailed inside a ring of protecting battleships and cruisers. Further out was a second screen of destroyers, about a dozen in number, providing anti-aircraft and anti-submarine protection in all directions. This second ring was normally about five miles in diameter, but in the event of a major air attack, the destroyers would move in closer to the battleship and cruiser ring. The normal interval between Task Groups, from carrier to carrier, was about 11 miles.

These tactics dominated the second half of the Pacific campaign. Meanwhile, as American offensive and Japanese

Marines prepare to storm Betio's airfield (above). The maps (opposite) show American progress in clearing the islands.

defensive capabilities both increased, in October 1944 the Japanese resorted to the suicide planes *(kamikaze)* of what they called the Special Strike Force.

In September 1943, Tokyo adopted a "New Operational Policy". An immovable defence line along the line Timor–west New Guinea–Biak Island–the Carolinas –the Marianas was set up. All forces outside this ring were to hang on, to buy time during which Japan's naval and air strength could be built up for a final, decisive, offensive.

Tokyo entrusted the defence of the Gilbert Islands to Rear-Admiral Keiji Shibasaki, who acted with great zeal to improve the defences of this strategically important advanced position. In particular, in the south-west corner of the triangle of the Tarawa atoll, the islet of Betio was turned into a veritable fortress, almost completely surrounded by a protective barrier of coconut-palm trunks covered by automatic weapons, mortars, and emplaced guns. Facing the sea there were eight medium guns, including four 8-inch guns captured at Singapore. Though over two miles long, Betio is less than half a mile wide and its 4,500-man garrison had been ordered to dig in on the coastline.

At dawn on November 20, three battleships, four cruisers, and nine destroyers under Rear-Admiral H. W. Hill opened fire simultaneously and rained 3,000 tons of shells on to this narrow strip of land within two and a half hours. At the same time it was bombed by aircraft from Funafuti. By 0845 hours it was on fire from end to end and covered with a thick pall of smoke and dust.

But when the first amphibious vehicles, called "amphtracks", came out of the lagoon and the 2nd Marine Division's landing-craft approached the shore, they came under a hail of accurate and withering fire. The ensuing fighting fell on lieutenants and their men, as radio communication between the command post at sea and the three beaches where the Marines landed was very bad. In the afternoon, the divisional commander, Major-General Julian C. Smith, threw in his reserve regiment, but in spite of this the Americans advanced only 150 yards at the most.

It took a further 48 hours of infantry fighting with flame-throwers, explosives, and grenades to snuff out the last dying kicks of the defence. The entire Betio garrison perished except for one subaltern, 16 men, and 129 Korean labourers. Of the 16,798 U.S. officers and marines who fought at Tarawa, 1,069 were killed and 2,050 wounded, giving losses of some 17 per cent. When it was all over this tiny island had 5,500 dead on it. Nevertheless, as the first assault launched by Central

Pacific Area, it provided valuable lessons for the future.

Some 85 miles south-east of Tarawa the Abemama atoll fell without incident into the hands of a company of Marines. The 27th Division, under Major-General Ralph C. Smith, lost 64 killed and 150 wounded in the capture of the Makin atoll to the north-west: much heavier losses than had been expected.

In the expectation of an attack on the Gilbert Islands, the Japanese high command had drawn up a plan for a counter-offensive, bringing in Vice-Admiral Kondo's 2nd Fleet and major supporting air forces. It never got started, however. Rear-Admiral Pownall's forces pounded the Japanese air bases on Nauru Island and Mili atoll in the Marshall Islands, which were well placed to support Tarawa. MacArthur's offensive in the South-West Pacific prevented any meaningful intervention by the Japanese against the U.S. 5th Fleet. On November 6, planes from *Saratoga* and *Princeton,* on loan from Spruance to Halsey, and awaiting the start of Operation "Galvanic", seriously damaged seven Japanese cruisers and two destroyers in harbour at Rabaul. The Japanese aircraft based on New Britain and Bougainville were literally decimated by fighters from the U.S. 5th Air Force.

Yet the Japanese scored a few victories. On November 20, the light carrier *Independence* was damaged by a torpedo-carrying aircraft and on the 24th, the

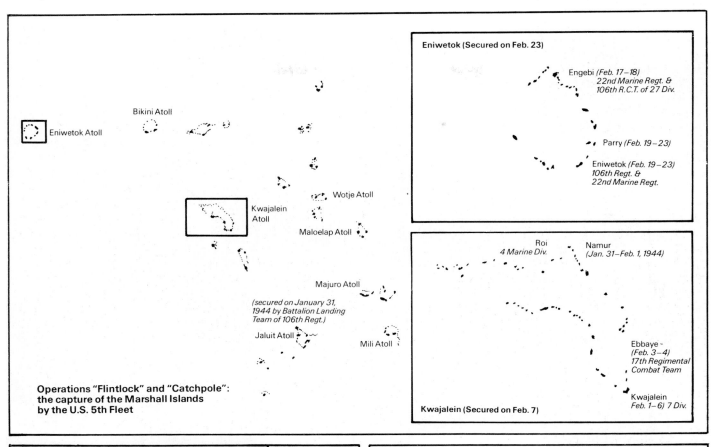

Operations "Flintlock" and "Catchpole": the capture of the Marshall Islands by the U.S. 5th Fleet

Bikini Atoll

Eniwetok Atoll

Kwajalein Atoll

Wotje Atoll

Maloelap Atoll

Majuro Atoll

(secured on January 31, 1944 by Battalion Landing Team of 106th Regt.)

Jaluit Atoll

Mili Atoll

Eniwetok (Secured on Feb. 23)

Engebi *(Feb. 17–18)*
*22nd Marine Regt. &
106th R.C.T. of 27 Div.*

Parry *(Feb. 19–23)*

Eniwetok *(Feb. 19–23)*
*106th Regt. &
22nd Marine Regt.*

Roi
4 Marine Div.

Namur
(Jan. 31–Feb. 1, 1944)

Ebbaye –
*(Feb. 3–4)
17th Regimental
Combat Team*

Kwajalein
Feb. 1–6) 7 Div.

Kwajalein (Secured on Feb. 7)

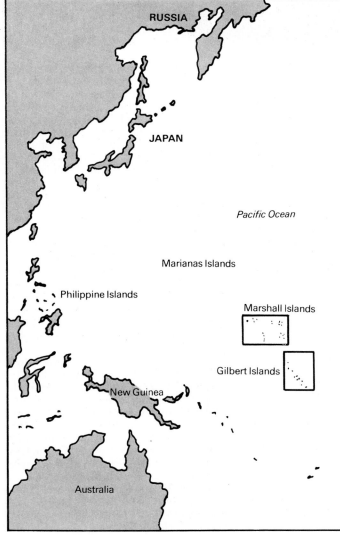

RUSSIA

JAPAN

Pacific Ocean

Marianas Islands

Philippine Islands

Marshall Islands

Gilbert Islands

New Guinea

Australia

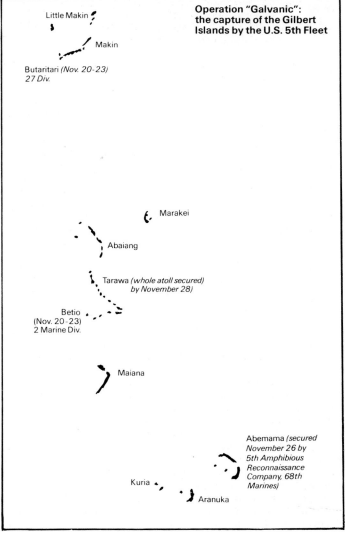

Operation "Galvanic": the capture of the Gilbert Islands by the U.S. 5th Fleet

Little Makin

Makin

Butaritari *(Nov. 20-23)
27 Div.*

Marakei

Abaiang

Tarawa *(whole atoll secured)
by November 28)*

Betio
*(Nov. 20-23)
2 Marine Div.*

Maiana

Abemama *(secured
November 26 by
5th Amphibious
Reconnaissance
Company, 68th
Marines)*

Kuria

Aranuka

A Marine prepares to hurl a grenade from his machine gun emplacement on Tarawa.

escort carrier *Liscome Bay* blew up after being hit by a torpedo from the Japanese submarine *I-175* (Lieutenant-Commander Tabata). The latter caused heavy casualties: Rear-Admiral H. M. Mullinnix, Captain I. D. Wiltsie, and 642 other officers and ratings.

"The Marshalls: offensive in high gear" is the title given by Fletcher Pratt, the Marine Corps historian, to the chapter of his book dealing with the 5th Fleet's capture of the Majuro, Kwajalein, and Eniwetok atolls in the Marshall Islands. The day following the capture of the Gilbert Islands, the 5th Fleet got three fast battleships, including the *Iowa* and the *New Jersey* (45,000 tons and 33 knots), three fast carriers (two "*Essex*" class fleet carriers and one "*Independence*" class light carrier), and two escort carriers.

The 5th Fleet's Task Force 58 now had 12 carriers with a total of 715 fighters, dive-bombers, and torpedo-bombers. The normal change-round in command gave this formidable unit to Rear-Admiral Marc A. Mitscher. It was divided into four groups, of which TG 58.3 (Carrier Task Group 3, Task Force 58) is typical. Under the command of Rear-Admiral F. E. Sherman, it comprised:
1. Fleet carrier *Bunker Hill* (89 aircraft), light carrier *Monterey* (34 aircraft), and light carrier *Cowpens* (33 air-

craft);
2. Battleship Division (Batdiv) 7, under Rear-Admiral O. V. Hustvedt, with battleships *Iowa* and *New Jersey,* and heavy cruiser *Wichita;* and
3. Destroyer Squadron (Desron) 46, under Captain C. F. Espe, with nine destroyers.

In the event of a naval engagement, Sherman thus had 31 dive-bombers, 49 torpedo-bombers, the 18 16-inch guns (40,000-pound broadside weight) of his battleships, the nine 8-inch guns of the heavy cruiser, and 90 torpedo tubes of his destroyers. In the air he had 87 fighters and 700 A.A. guns of 20-mm, 40-mm, and 5-inch calibre. The other Task Groups were basically similar.

Rear-Admiral R. T. Turner's amphibious force comprised 300 warships and transport vessels. Its task was:
1. to land by sheer force in the Marshall Islands the 53,000 men of V Amphibious Force (4th Marine Division under Major-General Harry Schmidt and 7th Division under Major-General Charles H. Corlett), and then
2. to land 31,000 holding troops to ensure the defence and exploitation of the conquered atolls.

After the murderous experience of Tarawa, Spruance, Turner, and General Holland M. ("Howling Mad") Smith reckoned that the operation should be split in two: firstly to overcome the resistance of the eastern atolls of the Marshall Islands, then to attack Kwajalein. Nimitz

agreed that a simultaneous attack on Wotje, Maloelap, and Kwajalein was now no longer possible, but being bold where he had been advised to be cautious, he decided to put onto the third of these objectives the whole of his V Amphibious Force and leave the neutralisation of the first two to Task Force 58. It was a good thing that he did, as the Japanese high command, thinking along the same lines as Nimitz's subordinates, had reinforced Maloelap and Wotje at the expense of Kwajalein.

Spruance carried out this task with complete success. From January 29 to February 11, 1944, his air forces made 6,232 sorties and dropped more than 1,150 tons of bombs on their objectives. This was combined with operations in support of the Army and Marine forces ashore on the Gilbert Islands, where another 1,600 tons were dropped. He also occupied Majuro lagoon and atoll, where the smooth stretch of water 25 miles long and 12 miles wide gave Nimitz a base for subsequent operations two-thirds of the way from Pearl Harbor to the Marianas.

Meanwhile, V Amphibious Force had seized Kwajalein atoll in the centre of the group at very little cost. By February 4, the Americans had lost 372 killed and 1,582 wounded out of the 42,000 men engaged. Japanese losses amounted to 7,870 killed, including Rear-Admiral Akiyama, C.-in-C. of the defence forces. And this was the first time the 4th Marine Division had been in action.

Marines shelter in a hollow on Parry Island in the Eniwetok atoll.

The Tarawa experience had borne fruit, and in record time too. Communications between troops on the ground and support ships worked satisfactorily and in the assault on the twin islands of Roi–Namur, Rear-Admiral R. L. Conolly's battleships came to within a mile of the coast to rain down shells on an area of two square miles. In the first assault wave there were now more amphtracks with better armour. Faced with this proliferation of *matériel,* Admiral Turner, as if replying to critics, notes that "maybe we had too many men and too many ships for the job, but I prefer to do things that way. It saved us a lot of lives."

As V Amphibious Force's reserve had so far not been used, Spruance launched it against Eniwetok on February 17. This was 360 miles north-west of Kwajalein. With the same kind of superiority over the Japanese as was generally thought necessary in these operations, he was able to take it with the losses of only 195 killed and 521 wounded, whereas the Japanese lost 2,677 killed out of a total defence force of 2,741. As at Kwajalein they were beaten to a standstill. This letter from a marine shows how:

"That night was unbelievably terrible. There were many of them left and they all had one fanatical notion, and that was to take one of us with them. We dug in with orders to kill anything that moved. I

kept watch in a foxhole with my sergeant and we both stayed awake all night with a knife in one hand and a grenade in the other. They crept in among us, and every bush and rock took on sinister proportions. They got some of us, but in the morning they lay about, some with their riddled bodies actually inside our foxholes. Never have I been so glad to see the sun."

On February 23, all resistance ceased on this atoll, which is some 3,000 miles west-south-west of Pearl Harbor, 660 miles north-east of Truk in the Carolines, and 1,000 miles from Saipan in the Marianas, Nimitz's next objective. As for the atolls of Wotje, Maloelap, Mili, and Jaluit in the same archipelago, they were left to their sad fate and the Japanese troops stationed on them lived as best they could until the capitulation of September 2, 1945 allowed them to surrender.

On February 17, 1944 Spruance arrived at Truk with nine carriers, six battleships, ten cruisers, and 28 destroyers. In the next two days, Mitscher's carrier-based planes made 1,250 sorties and sank three destroyers, seven fleet auxiliary vessels, six tankers, and 17 cargo vessels, whilst more than 250 Japanese planes were either shot down or destroyed on the ground. The light cruiser *Agano* was also sunk by the submarine *Skate.* Meanwhile Spruance sailed round the atoll with his battleships and succeeded in sinking by gunfire the light cruiser *Katori* and

the destroyer *Maikaze,* which were trying to escape Mitscher's bombs and which went down heroically.

The cost to the Americans of this operation, called "Hailstone", was quite modest: 35 planes shot down and the fleet carrier *Intrepid* damaged by a torpedo.

This surprise defeat resulted in a Radio Tokyo communiqué. Softpedalling its usual bombastic tone, it stated bluntly:

"A powerful American task force suddenly advanced to our Caroline Islands Wednesday morning and repeatedly attacked our important strategic base, Truk, with a great number of ship-based planes. The enemy is constantly repeating powerfully persistent raids with several hundred fighters and bombers, attacking us intermittently. The war situation has increased with unprecedented seriousness–nay, furiousness. The tempo of enemy operations indicates that the attacking force is already pressing upon our mainland."

Tojo used the pretext of the surprise at Truk to sack Admiral Osami Nagano, the Navy Chief-of-Staff, and to replace him with Admiral Shimada, a man completely devoted to Tojo but not necessarily endeared thereby to his junior colleagues. As for Nimitz, he applied to Truk and Ponape the procedure which had been so successful at Jaluit, Wotje, and other atolls in the Marshall Islands: isolate them and leave them to rot.

General Tojo's "Fortress Asia", facing

the American forces in the Central and South-West Pacific, had an Eastern and a Southern Front which joined at the Vogelkop ("bird's head"), the name given by the Dutch to the western part of New Guinea. With limited means, MacArthur was going to destroy this hinge, making use of his air superiority and the freedom of movement this gave him, a freedom which he could also deny his enemy.

He began by a full-scale attack on Rabaul. Since January 1, 1944, he had had a bridgehead and an airfield on Cape Gloucester at the southern extremity of New Britain. From February 29 to March 16, three well-organised amphibious operations gave his 1st Marine Division (Major-General William Rupertus) and the dismounted 1st Cavalry Division (Major-General William C. Chase) Los Negros island in the Admiralty group and Emirau Island to the east. The Japanese 8th and 17th Armies were thus cut off, the former (General Imamura) defending Rabaul

An American patrol in the jungle of New Britain Island.

and Kavieng, the latter facing the U.S. XIII Corps (Major-General Oscar Griswold) in the Bougainville jungle. In particular, this success was to allow MacArthur to tackle and resolve the problem of New Guinea without having to worry about his rear.

Events had reached this stage when, together with Nimitz, MacArthur received a new directive, dated March 12, from the Joint Chiefs-of-Staff. This ordered:

1. Cancellation of the Kavieng operation.
2. Early completion of the occupation of the Admiralties and development of air and naval bases there.
3. Occupation of Hollandia by General MacArthur's forces on 15 April; Nimitz to furnish fast carrier and other fleet cover and support.
4. Neutralisation, not capture, of Truk and other Caroline islands by Nimitz.
5. Occupation of Saipan, Tinian, and Guam, starting 15 June, and the Palaus, starting 15 September, by Nimitz, with the object of controlling the eastern approaches to the Philippines and Formosa, and establishing fleet and air bases.
6. Occupation of Mindanao by MacArthur supported by the Pacific Fleet, starting 15 November, with object of establishing air bases from which Japanese forces in the Philippines could be reduced and contained "preparatory to a further advance to Formosa, either directly or via Luzon," and mounting air strikes against enemy bases in the Netherlands East Indies.

It was 500 miles from the Allies' positions in New Guinea to their objectives in Hollandia. This was why MacArthur decided to secure an intermediary bridgehead at Aitape, so that he could bring in his fighters. Meanwhile Major-General G. C. Kenney's 5th Air Force eliminated enemy aircraft from this sector, destroying 500 of them.

Whilst the Allied forces in the South-West Pacific were preparing for this new leap forward, those in the Central Pacific did not remain idle. On March 22, Task Force 58, with three carrier task groups, six fast battleships, 13 cruisers, and 26 destroyers, left Majuro lagoon and in the last days of the month launched a series of devastating raids against the Japanese bases on the Palau Islands and on Yap, an island north-east of this group. This attack led Koga to send the Japanese fleet to find a safer refuge in the neighbourhood of Tawitawi, an island not far from the north tip of Borneo.

This brought it close to the Tarakan oil wells, which with certain restrictions, could provide fuel for its bunkers. Koga personally took off for Davao, but his plane was lost in mysterious circumstances. Imperial H.Q. nominated Admiral Soemu Toyoda to succeed him.

The Hollandia operation was carried out by Australian forces under General Sir Thomas Blamey, the American 6th Army under Lieutenant-General Walter Krueger, the U.S. 7th Fleet (Vice-Admiral Thomas C. Kinkaid) with four cruisers, including two Australian, and eight escort carriers, and finally the 5th Air Force. The landing proper, under Rear-Admiral Daniel E. Barbey, brought in 84,000 men and 114 capital and other ships. The 5th Fleet, which had just forced Koga to withdraw from the Palau Islands, where he might have caught MacArthur in flank, put out to sea again on April 13 to take part in the operation. On the way back it raided the enemy installations on Truk, which drew from Rear-Admiral Hara the following reflections which betrayed his disillusion:

"The seasons do not change. I try to look like a proud rear admiral, but it is hard with a potato hook in my hands. It rains every day, the flowers bloom every day, the enemy bombs us every day–so why remember?"

This impressive success cost Spruance 26 planes, although 28 of their 43 crew were rescued, 22 of these by the submarine *Tang* (Commander Richard H. O'Kane) which had daringly ventured into the lagoon.

Although he had superior strength, Mac-Arthur put on a cunning diversionary operation to make the Japanese believe they were going to be attacked frontally in the area of Wewak. Lieutenant-General Hatazo Adachi, C.-in-C. Japanese 18th Army in New Guinea, fell into the trap. April 22, 1944 was thus a day of triumph for the U.S. I Corps (Lieutenant-General Robert L. Eichelberger) which landed, without much difficulty, its 24th Division (Major-General F. A. Irving) at Tanahmerah Bay and its 41st (Major-General H. H. Fuller) at Hollandia and Aitape. When he had got over his surprise, Adachi tried to turn his forces round and re-establish his communications. During July the Aitape sector was the scene of furious fighting, throughout which Adachi urged on the Japanese 18th Army in terms of mingled despair and determination:

"I cannot find any means or method which will solve this situation strategically or tactically. Therefore, I intend to overcome this by relying on our Japanese *Bushido*. I am determined to destroy the enemy in Aitape by attacking him ruthlessly with the concentration of our entire force in that area. This will be our final opportunity to employ our entire strength to annihilate the enemy. Make the supreme sacrifice, display the spirit of the Imperial Army."

This appeal was understood and followed, but the time and trouble it cost Adachi to turn round gave the Allies an advantage which they did not let slip, especially as they were also able to decode the Japanese radio messages. And so, during the night of July 11-12, the 18th Army's counter-attack found the Allies alert and reinforced by Major-Generals Charles P. Hall's XI Corps and William H. Gill's 32nd Division. The Japanese were held.

MacArthur was already hopping from one island to the next along the coast of New Guinea. On May 17, his 41st Division landed at Wakde, 125 miles west of Hollandia. On the 27th, a further hop of 200 miles brought him to Biak, where the Japanese put up fierce resistance. Virtually ignoring this as a local incident, he pushed on to the island of Numfoor on July 2 and on the 30th he reached the beak of the Vogelkop. This was at Sansapor, over 600 miles from Hollandia. By now some 120,000 Japanese were cut off, trapped in the "green hell" of the jungle in one of the worst climates in the world, and defenceless against malaria. It is understandable that, in face of this great success, MacArthur telegraphed to Eichelberger:

"The succession of surprises effected and the small losses suffered, the great extent of territory conquered and the casualties inflicted on the enemy, together with the large Japanese forces which

have been isolated, all combine to make your operations of the past one and a half months models of strategical and tactical manoeuvres."

In fact, according to a table drawn up by General Willoughby, chief of Intelligence, Allied Forces in the South-West Pacific, in dead alone the losses on both sides were:

Battle areas	American	Japanese	Ratio
Arawe-Gloucester	472	4,914	1:10
Saidor	55	1,275	1:23
Admiralty Islands	155	4,143	1:27
Hollandia	87	4,441	1:51
Aitape	440	8,370	1:19
Wakde	646	3,899	1:6
Biak	524	5,093	1:10
Numfoor	63	2,328	1:37
Sansapor	2	374	1:187

It should also be remembered that the death-rate in American hospitals was three per cent, whereas it was very much higher amongst the Japanese because of the appallingly unsanitary conditions under which they had to fight. Mac-Arthur received Marshall's congratulations with justifiable satisfaction, but was even more pleased when the Pentagon announced that he was to get another corps, of five divisions, an extra air force, and 60 extra ships. What he had called the "stony-broke" war was a thing of the past.

The attack on Biak made the first dent in the Japanese defensive perimeter as described by the Imperial H.Q. directive of September 1943. So Admiral Toyoda, who like the Americans had just formed a 1st Mobile Fleet (C.-in-C. Vice-Admiral Jisaburo Ozawa), resolved to attack MacArthur's flank. He despatched to the Moluccas an Attack Division (Vice-Admiral Matome Ugaki) consisting mainly of the giant battleships *Yamato* and *Musashi,* but on June 11, when it had scarcely reached its departure-point, it was suddenly ordered to abandon the operation and to rejoin Ozawa east of the Philippines. The reason was the air attacks on Saipan, Tinian, and Guam in the Marianas.

The double offensive which had paid off for Nimitz at Tarawa was now working for MacArthur. Mitscher's bombers had an easy job of it over their objectives because the Biak affair had drawn off many fighters from the defence of the Marianas. Washington's own misgivings were thus allayed by events.

As the Joint Chiefs-of-Staff directive of March 12 pointed out, the capture of the three islands mentioned above gave them a base for an attack on Mindanao in the Philippines. At Saipan, Army Air Force engineers would lay down the runways needed for the B-29 Superfortresses of the 20th Air Force to take off on their missions of destruction over the great

industrial centres of the Japanese mainland. Operation "Forager", started on July 6, involved 535 warships and 127,571 men of the Marine Corps and the Army. Task Force 58 was followed by the Joint Expeditionary Force, Task Force 51, whose job it was to put ashore two corps of four divisions and one brigade:

1. V Amphibious Corps (Lieutenant-General Holland M. Smith: 2nd and 4th Marine Divisions);
2. III Amphibious Corps (Major-General Roy S. Geiger: 3rd Infantry Division and 1st Provisional Marine Brigade); and
3. floating reserve: 27th Division (Major-General Ralph Smith).

Admiral Spruance was C.-in-C., and Vice-Admiral Turner commanded the sea, air, and land forces involved in the landing. Both had recently been promoted.

This powerful combination of forces spelled the end of Japanese strategy as it had been conceived since the Washington Naval Conference of 1922. Then, when they had conceded a numerical superiority to the U.S. of five to three in battleships, the Japanese could still persuade themselves that their security was not at risk. In their opinion the bulk of the enemy's forces would be trapped and destroyed piecemeal in ambushes laid for them in the Marshall and Caroline Islands. The balance of strength would thus be in their favour in the Marianas. This turned out to be incorrect. In fact, far from losing strength as he advanced, Spruance was much stronger in Operation "Forager" than he had been in "Galvanic". This is shown by the number of fast carriers available to the 5th Fleet: 11 at the Gilberts, 12 at the Marshalls, and 15 at the Marianas.

The same was true for other types of ship. When the clash came, the opposing forces had the following:

	Spruance	Ozawa
Carriers	15	9
Battleships	7	5
Cruisers	21	13
Destroyers	69	28
Totals	112	55

American superiority in naval aircraft was over two to one. Spruance had 891, his adversary 430. The Japanese pilots, after their idleness at anchor in Tawitawi, had lost what little efficiency they had ever possessed.

Ozawa, in whom the historian Samuel Eliot Morison recognised, "a scientific brain and a flair for trying new expedients, as well as a seaman's innate sense of what can be accomplished with ships", overlooked all these weaknesses in the hope of overcoming them by close collaboration with land-based aircraft from the Marianas and the organisation of a shuttle-service between his own and the "unsinkable carriers" of Guam and Rota. But this plan was thwarted by Spruance.

Moreover, Japanese strategy could no longer choose between offensive and defensive operations for, unless the 1st Mobile Fleet were engaged, they would lose the Marianas, and the Philippines soon afterwards. In which case, Admiral Toyoda declared later:

"Even though the fleet should be left, the shipping lane to the south would be completely cut off so that the fleet, if it should come back to Japanese waters, could not obtain its fuel supply. If it should remain in southern waters, it could not receive supplies of ammunition and arms. There would be no sense in saving the fleet at the expense of the loss of the Philippines."

This was why, when he heard about the bombing of the Marianas, Toyoda ordered Ozawa to put in action the plan for a counter-offensive which had been drawn up for this purpose. During the evening of June 15, Ozawa sailed into the Philippine Sea through the San Bernardino Strait and 24 hours later joined up with Ugaki's Attack Division. At 0008 hours on the 18th, he sent the following message to the Mobile Fleet:

"I humbly transmit to you the message I have just received from the Emperor via the Chief-of-Staff, Naval Section, Imperial G.H.Q.: 'This operation has immense bearing on the fate of the Empire. It is hoped that the forces will exert their utmost and achieve as magnificent

A Japanese destroyer keels over following an American attack. Survivors cling desperately to the sides of the sinking ship.

results as in the Battle of Tsushima.' "

There was, however, nothing in common between the American 5th Fleet and the Russian 2nd Pacific Squadron destroyed by Admiral Togo on May 27 and 28, 1905.

On June 14, Turner's old battleships and aircraft-carriers took over the bombardment of Saipan from Task Force 58. The following night frogmen cleared the obstacles to a landing on the southwest tip of the island. At 0850 hours on June 15, the forward units of the 2nd and 4th Marine Divisions (Major-Generals T. E. Watson and Harry Schmidt) landed on a 7,000-yard front. In the evening of the same day, V Amphibious Corps had 20,000 men on Saipan (including 2,000 killed and wounded) and was half way to its day's objective, having met stiff resistance from the 32,000 Japanese under Lieutenant-General Yoshitsugu Saito. The following day, after receiving news of Ozawa's progress, Spruance postponed the Guam operation and sent the 27th Division to reinforce V Amphibious Corps.

Patrolling off Tawitawi and at the exit of the San Bernardino Strait, Vice-Admiral Lockwood's submarines had signalled the approach of the Japanese Mobile Fleet and, with some uncertainty, its composition. In view of the coming battle, Spruance called back his forces which had just been bombing the Bonin and Volcano Islands north of the Marianas, and redeployed his units. On the flanks of his four carrier task groups, still under Vice-Admiral Mitscher, he

drew up a Battle Line under Vice-Admiral W. A. Lee: his seven fast battleships, four cruisers, and 13 destroyers. At 1415 hours on June 17 he defined his intentions to his immediate subordinates:

"Our air will first knock out enemy carriers, then will attack enemy battleships and cruisers to slow down or disable them. Battle line will destroy enemy fleet either by fleet action if the enemy elects to fight or by sinking slowed or crippled ships if enemy retreats. Action against the enemy must be pushed vigorously by all hands to ensure complete destruction of his fleet."

Spruance's intentions were thus purely offensive. He could not, however, go outside the parameters of his mission, which was to take, occupy, and defend Saipan, Tinian, and Guam. By giving chase to the enemy he would have left V Amphibious Corps' bridgehead unprotected and risked exposing it to attack from any Japanese force moving in from north or south. He therefore decided to sit back and wait a while.

At dawn on June 19, the Japanese Mobile Fleet consisted of two detachments: a Van Force (Vice-Admiral Takeo Kurita) with three divisions, two of battleships and one of heavy cruisers, each protecting a light carrier, (their role being to act as decoy for Spruance's carrier-borne aircraft), and 120 miles behind it a Main Body (Ozawa) composed of Forces "A" and "B", with six carriers, five of them fleet carriers. Their task was to destroy Spruance's carriers by surprise once their aircraft were engaged against Kurita's forces. The Japanese

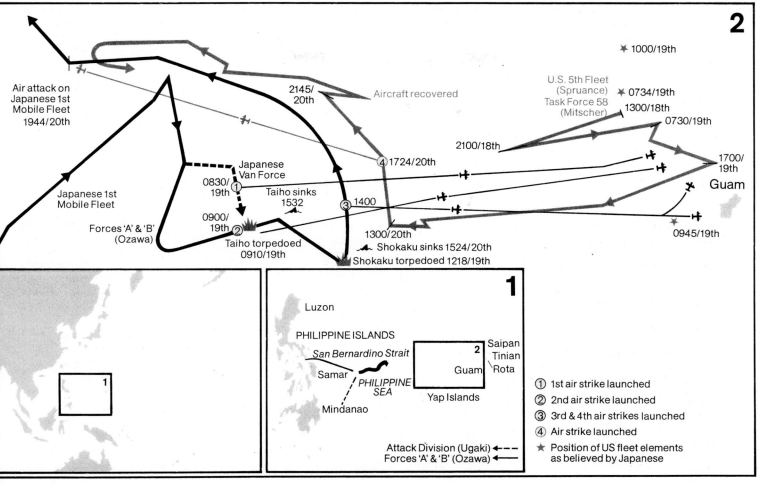

2

1000/19th

U.S. 5th Fleet
(Spruance)
Task Force 58
(Mitscher)

0734/19th

1300/18th

0730/19th

Air attack on
Japanese 1st
Mobile Fleet
1944/20th

2145/
20th

Aircraft recovered

2100/18th

④1724/20th

1700/
19th

Guam

Japanese
Van Force

0830/
19th ①

Taiho sinks
1532

③ 1400

Japanese 1st
Mobile Fleet

0900/
19th ②

Forces 'A' & 'B'
(Ozawa)

Taiho torpedoed
0910/19th

1300/20th

Shokaku sinks 1524/20th

Shokaku torpedoed 1218/19th

0945/19th

1

Luzon

PHILIPPINE ISLANDS

San Bernardino Strait

Samar

PHILIPPINE
SEA

Mindanao

Saipan
Tinian
Rota

2

Guam

Yap Islands

① 1st air strike launched
② 2nd air strike launched
③ 3rd & 4th air strikes launched
④ Air strike launched
★ Position of US fleet elements
as believed by Japanese

Attack Division (Ugaki) ◄---
Forces 'A' & 'B' (Ozawa) ◄─

sailed against the wind: their planes were thus able to take off straight towards the enemy, with the return flight shorter than the outward one.

The Japanese plan was a failure, however, for once again American Intelligence had warned Spruance; so he was ready when between daybreak and 1445 hours, Ozawa made four raids on the 5th Fleet. These were all disastrous because of American superiority in training and in the quality of their aircraft. 373 of the 473 Japanese planes available (including float-planes) took off and met 450 U.S. fighters, which massacred them. Those which escaped got caught in the massive A.A. fire of the Task Groups and the Battle Line. Those of the fourth wave which attempted to land at the airfield on Guam were destroyed in the air or so badly damaged on landing (the runways being pitted with bomb craters) that none of them ever took off again. Only 130 Japanese planes returned to their ships. There was no compensation for the Japanese as the U.S. forces lost only 18 fighters and 12 bombers and suffered only slight damage to the carrier *Bunker Hill* and the battleship *South Dakota*. The 5th Fleet lost altogether 58 men killed, including 27 pilots. Worse still for Ozawa, at 0910 hours the submarine *Albacore* (Commander J. W. Blanchard) put a torpedo into the fleet carrier *Taiho* (29,300 tons), Vice-Admiral Ozawa's flagship. Then at 1220 hours the submarine *Cavalla* (Lieutenant-

Commander H. J. Kossler) scored three hits on the carrier *Shokaku*; she sank towards 1730 in the afternoon with 22 of her planes, which had just returned, on board. Both the *Shokaku* and the *Taiho* were lost because of explosions of the fumes from the fuel taken on at Tarakan. Damage to the *Taiho* was negligible, but a damage-control officer unfortunately gave the order to ventilate the ship and the petroleum fumes swept through from stem to stern. This led to a colossal explosion, as a result of which the ship sank immediately.

Ozawa transferred his flag to the heavy cruiser *Haguro* and, misinformed about Japanese losses and misled by exaggerated reports by his own pilots of U.S. casualties, pressed on with his attack regardless. There is no doubt that the remainder of the Japanese fleet would have been wiped out in the course of June 20 if Spruance's aerial reconnaissance had spotted it in time, but it failed to do so, despite the beautiful weather. It was 1600 hours before a plane sighted the Japanese "250 miles" (it was in fact over 300) north-north-west of Task Force 58. Despite the distance and the lateness of the hour, Spruance turned his carriers into the wind and sent up 85 fighters, 77 dive-bombers, and 54 torpedo-bombers inside ten minutes.

The sun was sinking below the horizon when the Americans saw the fighter screen protecting the Mobile Fleet. Each

The battle of the Philippine Sea marked the end of the Japanese Navy's air arm.

Japanese ship then took a separate zig-zag course and opened up with all its guns. Forty Japanese planes were shot down for a loss to the Americans of 20, but only a small carrier, the *Hiyo*, was sunk. Meanwhile Mitscher was sailing full steam ahead to save his planes as much milage as possible. To get them back on board at 2000 hours, Task Force 58 turned up-wind and, in spite of the submarine danger, turned on all their landing lights. A few hours later, on board the cruiser *Montpelier*, Leading Seaman James J. Fahey noted in his invaluable diary:

"It was a great decision to make and everyone thought the world of Admiral Marc Mitscher for doing this. This would make it easier for our pilots to land, and if they did hit the water they could be saved. The big carriers were all lighted so the pilots could see where to land, a lot of our destroyers were left behind to pick the men out of the water. I saw one pilot on the wing of his plane waving his shirt. There were so many lights it must have been hard to land on the carriers. A Jap plane also tried to land on one of our carriers. Our planes continued to land as we continued on our way after the Jap fleet. It was quite a sight to see all the ships lit up, flares and rafts in the water and some planes crashing into the water, and pilots and crews also in the water.

You could see the planes circle and then land on the carriers. A great job was done by everyone to save our pilots' lives. The Japs would never do anything like this."

Even so, out of 176 planes which got back to Task Force 58, 80 ran out of fuel and fell into the sea or crash-landed. Thanks to Mitscher's initiative, 101 crew were picked up. Another 59 were saved on the following day, making the losses for the 20th 49. Ozawa was informed that only 35 out of his 473 planes were left, and so he broke off contact.

The Philippine Sea was thus the grave-yard of the Japanese naval air arm. The Japanese carriers, bereft of planes and pilots, were like rifles without cartridges. At the cost of 130 of the 956 planes his task force had at dawn on June 19, and of 138 sailors and airmen killed or missing, Spruance had thus scored a victory the consequences of which were to last until the Japanese capitulation of September 2, 1945.

The fact remains that a number of Spruance's subordinate officers and fellow-commanders, who did not know of the loss of the *Taiho*, however, expressed their disappointment that the Mobile Fleet had not been destroyed, a result of what they considered excessive caution on Spruance's part. Nimitz and King backed him up, however. Perhaps by so doing they were merely vindicating themselves in that this incomplete victory could have been the result of their somewhat restrictive instruction to take, occupy, and defend Saipan, Tinian, and Guam. Be that as it may, some months later Admiral W. F. Halsey found that the order sending him to Leyte contained the following paragraph:

"In case opportunity for destruction of major portion of the enemy fleet offers or can be created, such destruction becomes the primary task."

A short while after the Anglo-American landings in Normandy, and coinciding with the rout of the German armies in Belorussia, the loss of Saipan fell like a thunderbolt on Japanese public opinion. Tojo in vain tried to win back the sympathy of the navy by dissociating himself from Admiral Shimada, who was unanimously disliked throughout the fleet. The crisis of confidence spread to the Council of Peers, or *genros*, which considered that, by combining the offices of Prime Minister, Minister of War, Minister of Munitions, Chief-of-Staff, and C.-in-C. of the Army Air Force, General Tojo bore total responsibility for this disaster, which was clearly only a forerunner of others. Unable to ride out the storm of protest which had its echoes

A P-47 Thunderbolt lands after a flight from Saipan (left, above). American artillerymen on Tinian with a field howitzer (left, below). A Marine shakes sand from his boot while sitting on a 16-inch shell (right).

even amongst his cabinet colleagues, he tendered his resignation to the Emperor. Against his expectations, it was accepted.

On July 18, 1944, Hirohito appointed General Kuniaki Koiso as Tojo's successor. The new Prime Minister had been Governor of Korea, had left the Army in 1938, and had the reputation of being a moderate. The War Ministry went to Field-Marshal Sugiyama, the Navy to Admiral Yonai. Shigemitsu, who had taken part in the conspiracy within the Tojo cabinet, remained Foreign Minister.

The Emperor ended his audience with the new Prime Minister with the following words: "You will need to collaborate to put an end to the war in Asia and I recommend you not to upset Russia."

In guarded terms the Emperor was therefore ordering Koiso and Yonai to attempt a negotiated settlement with the United States and Great Britain. The new Navy Minister saw the situation in the same light. When he had asked Admiral Toyoda: "Can we hold out until the end of the year?" the reply was: "It will in all probability be very difficult."

When we realise that the Japanese language is full of circumlocutions and delicate shades of meaning we see what that meant. The army chiefs had still to be reckoned with, however, and they refused to admit that any negotiated settlement could be compatible with the Emperor's honour, of which they considered themselves the absolute and final judges, regardless of their devotion to his person. "Divine Presence" was one of the Emperor's attributes, but for the military man this was only on condition that he took no part in major policy decisions. Even if the army leaders had been more foreseeing than this, General Koiso would still have found it just as difficult to overcome this obstacle. Potter

and Nimitz note this clearly:

"On the Allied side, the goal of unconditional surrender set by Roosevelt and Churchill at Casablanca forbade the proffering of terms which might have served as bases for negotiation."

And so from Saipan the road led inevitably to Hiroshima and Nagasaki.

The reduction of the Marshalls had been quick and efficient, and had profited by lessons learned at Tarawa: more amphtracks, and better air and gunfire preparation were needed. Seemingly, little fault could be found with the operation, but earlier, before "Flintlock", as it was called, was even launched, Lieutenant-General Robert C. Richardson, Commanding General, U.S. Army Forces, Pacific Ocean Areas, had asked that Holland M. Smith be relieved and his V 'Phib Corps headquarters be replaced with an Army corps headquarters. Nimitz had forwarded the recommendation to the J.C.S., who had turned it down, but that would not be the end of the matter.

On March 12, 1944, the J.C.S. directed Nimitz to move on into the Marianas with a target date of June 15. These were the islands Magellan had called Los Ladrones, "the Thieves". Except for Guam, a United States' possession since the Spanish-American War, the islands had been mandated to the Japanese after World War I. The United States had dutifully (or carelessly) failed to fortify Guam and after a token struggle it had fallen to the Japanese on December 10, 1941.

Other than Guam, Saipan, 14 miles by six, was the largest and most important of the islands. It had a civilian population of Japanese and natives called Chamorros, most of whom made their livelihood in the cane fields or sugar mills. Saipan was the headquarters of the Japanese Central Pacific Area Fleet under Vice-Admiral Chuichi Nagumo, the same

A marine of the 2nd Marine Division prepares to hurl a phosphorus grenade into a Japanese-held cave on Saipan.

admiral who had led the raid against Pearl Harbor but had lost at Midway. Also at Saipan were the headquarters of the 31st Army, under Lieutenant-General Hideyoshi Obata. The admiral and the general did not get along. Responsibility for the defence of the Marianas was divided. Nagumo did not think the Americans would attack the Marianas until November.

The codename for the invasion of the Marianas was Operation "Forager". While halfway around the world the British and Americans got ready for the invasion of Normandy, a vast armada was assembled in the Marshalls—Spruance's 5th Fleet with over 800 ships and more than 162,000 men. Joint Expeditionary Force would be under Kelly Turner; Expeditionary Troops under Holland Smith. The titles were new but the jobs would be the same. Northern Troops and Landing Force was to land on Saipan on June 15. Southern Troops and Landing Force was to land on Guam on June 18. A few days later there was to be a third landing, on Tinian, just to the south of Saipan.

V Amphibious Corps formed the headquarters for Northern Troops and Landing Force (N.L.T.F.) under the personal and continued command of Holland Smith, newly promoted to Lieutenant-General. N.L.T.F. had the 2nd Marine Division, commanded now by Major-General Thomas ("Terrible Tommy") E. Watson, and the 4th Marine Division under Major-General Harry ("the Dutchman") Schmidt. Ralph Smith's 27th Infantry Division was in floating reserve and the 77th Infantry Division was to be held in Hawaii in strategic reserve.

American Intelligence thought there were about 20,000 defenders on Saipan. Actually there were 25,469 soldiers and 6,160 sailors. The island had been divided into four defence sectors. The northern sector had two battalions of the 135th Infantry Regiment. The navy sector had the 5th Special Base Force, 55th Guard Force, the Yokusuka 1st Special Naval Landing Force, and a battalion of the 136th Infantry Regiment, and the large southern sector had the 47th Independent Mixed Brigade and the 9th Tank Regiment. General Obata was away on an inspection trip to the Palaus and tactical command had devolved on Lieutenant-General Yoshitsugu Saito, commanding general of the incomplete 43rd Division.

Saipan is rugged, mountainous, and ringed with coral reefs. On board the *Rocky Mount,* an amphibious command ship whose facilities he was sharing with Kelly Turner, Holland Smith said: "We are through with the flat atolls now. We learned how to pulverize atolls, but now we are up against mountains and caves where the Japs can dig in. A week from today there will be a lot of dead Marines."

Air bombardment began on June 11, naval gunfire on June 13. The landing was to be on the southern end of the west coast with 2nd Division on the left and 4th Division on the right; the two divisions would be separated by Afetna Point. The four Marine regiments in the assault were, from left to right, the 6th, 8th, 23rd, and 25th. They landed in 700 amphtracks behind a wave of new armoured amphibians, mounting 75-mm howitzers. The Americans came under heavy fire as they crossed the reef, and suffered some 2,000 casualties on this first day. One battalion lost four commanding officers before sunset. In the 4th Division's zone was the sugar mill town of Charan Kanoa, and to the left front of the 2nd Division was the island's key terrain, Mount Tapotchau. During that first night Saito tried to drive a wedge between the two Marine divisions, but this proved a costly mistake.

On shore at Saipan, during the 16th, the Americans pushed forward to con-solidate the beach-head and, as night fell, the 165th Infantry began coming ashore. That night the Japanese 9th Tank Regiment struck the first sizeable tank attack of the Pacific war. The 1st Battalion, 6th Marines, bore the brunt and the Japanese lost 31 light and medium tanks.

The attack went ahead slowly on the 17th. Swampy Lake Susupe, which separated the two divisions, was troublesome. On the 18th, the 4th Division with all three infantry regiments abreast pushed across to Magicienne Bay on Saipan's east coast. On their right flank the 165th Infantry had seized Aslito airfield and to the 165th's right the 105th Infantry had reached the cliffs on the southern tip of the island. By July 19 the Japanese defenders in the south had been compressed into a pocket at Nafutan Point.

General Holland Smith, having bisected the island, planned now to face his three divisions around into line and attack to the north. The 27th Division was ordered to leave one battalion behind to clean out the Japanese on Nafutan Point and to move in between the 2nd and 4th Marine Divisions. On June 23 the attack jumped off, but the 27th Division was slow in getting started and the line soon sagged in the middle. Holland Smith lost patience with Ralph Smith, and after confering with Spruance and Turner, relieved him, asking Major-General Sanderford Jarman, an Army general standing by to become island commander, to take command of the division temporarily.

Next day, June 25, a Marine battalion reached the top of Mount Tapotchau and -except for the troublesome pocket at Nafutan Point-the Japanese had nothing left but the northern end of the island. On the night of June 26 the defenders of Nafutan Point expended themselves in a wild, futile *banzai* attack. On July 1 the final phase of the battle began. As the island narrowed, the 4th and 27th Divisions continued in the assault and the 2nd Division passed into reserve.

On July 6 General Saito issued his final attack order. "Whether we attack or whether we stay where we are, there is only death." Each Japanese soldier was ordered to exact seven enemy lives in exchange for his one. After delivering the order the general had a farewell meal of *sake* and canned crabmeat. Next morning some 2,500 Japanese launched a last *banzai* against the 27th Division. Later that day Saito cut his stomach ceremonially with his *samurai* sword and his adjutant then shot him in the head. About this same time Admiral Nagumo shot himself.

Half the civilian population and the remnant of defenders had crowded onto Marpi Point, the northern tip of the island. Urged on by the Japanese soldiers, men and women hurled their children over the 220-foot cliff and then jumped themselves. The soldiers followed them or else blew themselves up with hand grenades.

Of the 29,000 defenders, less than a thousand had been taken prisoner. American losses in dead and wounded were 16,525, of whom 12,934 were Marines.

The landing on Guam came next. Originally set for June 18, W-day had been re-scheduled for July 21. III Amphibious Corps (a redesignation of I Marine Amphibious Corps, which had conducted the Bougainville operation), under Major-General Roy S. Geiger, a Marine aviation pioneer, had come up from Guadalcanal to provide the command for the Southern Troops and Landing Force. Geiger would have the 3rd Marine Division and the 1st Provisional Marine Brigade in the assault, and the 77th Infantry Division in reserve. Peanut-shaped Guam is 28 miles long and four to eight miles wide. Less cultivated than Saipan, the northern half was then covered with dense brush and undergrowth, the southern half, more mountainous, was mostly jungle. General Obata, in the Palaus when the American attack against Saipan began, had hurried back but had been able to get no further than Guam. He left the immediate direction of the island's defences to Lieutenant-General Takeshi Takeshina. Takeshina, nominally in command of the 29th Division, had only the 38th Infantry Regiment from that division on the island. His other major formations were the 48th Independent Mixed Brigade and the 10th Independent Mixed Regiment. Altogether there were about 13,000 Army troops. In addition there were some 5,500 Navy men under the command of Captain Yutaka Sugimoto.

Agana, capital of Guam, is on the west side of the island at the pinched-in waist. South of it is Apra Harbour, formed by Cabras Island on the north and Orote Peninsula on the south. Behind Apra Harbour is Mount Tenjo, 1,100 feet high and the loftiest elevation on the island. Orote was the site of an airfield and the old Marine barracks. South of Orote is the small town of Agat. The naval defenders were mostly concentrated on Orote and around the rim of Apra Harbour. Two battalions of the 38th Regiment were south of Orote in a good line of entrenchments. Behind them in the hills was the 10th Regiment. Takeshina himself was north of Apra with the rest of the 38th and the 48th Independent Mixed Brigade.

The most obvious landing site was Tumon Bay, north of Agana. The 3rd Marine Division under Major-General Allen H. Turnage would avoid that and come in over a crescent beach south of Agana between Asan and Adelup Points. The 1st Provisional Marine Brigade, made up for the occasion of two veteran regiments, the 4th and 22nd Marines, and under Brigade-General Lemuel C. Shepherd, Jr., would land south of Agat. H-hour for both landings was 0830 on July 21. The naval gunfire shelling began on July 2. Rear-Admiral Richard L. ("Close-in") Conolly was in charge and it was the most deliberate and plentiful preparation of the war up to that time.

The fighting was bitter but the situation was never as touch-and-go as it had been at Saipan. The two battalions of the 38th were virtually destroyed at Agat by the 1st Brigade, which went on to engage the naval defenders on Orote. Major-General Andrew D. Bruce's 77th Division landed behind the brigade and went after the 10th Regiment in the hills. Patrol contact was made between the 1st Brigade and the 3rd Division on July 25.

That night Takeshina made his major counter-attack against the 3rd Marine Division. He found a gap between the 21st and 9th Marines and some of the attackers got as far as the division command post and hospital. But by dawn the momentum was gone and ten battalions had been virtually used up. Takeshina had fought and lost his battle and after that it was really all mop-up. On the 28th, Mount Tenjo was taken. That same day Takeshina was killed by machine gun fire from a Marine tank and General Obata assumed tactical command.

By the end of July the two beach-heads had merged and the two divisions were in position for a shoulder-to-shoulder sweep northwards, 77th Division on the right, 3rd Division on the left, 1st Brigade in corps reserve. They jumped off at 0630 on July 31 against only light to moderate resistance. On August 7, as the island widened out, the 1st Brigade went into line on the left of the 3rd Division. By August 10, the Japanese had been backed to the rims of the northern cliffs overlooking the sea.

On that day, General Obata sent his last message to the Imperial General Headquarters: "The holding of Guam has become hopeless. I will engage the enemy in the last battle . . . tomorrow, the 11th . . ." In front of him was the 1st Battalion, 306th Infantry. Sometime during the next morning's fighting, General Obata took his own life.

Japanese losses on Guam were counted by the Marines at 17,300 killed and 485 prisoners taken. Survivors would continue to be killed for months–even years–to come, and this would run up the count. The last known survivor surrendered in 1972. American casualties were 1,919 killed, 7,122 wounded, and 70 missing. Of these, U.S. Army losses were 405 killed, 1,744 wounded, and 51 missing.

Meanwhile, the landing on Tinian had been made. This smaller island, covering 50 square miles and about 12 miles from north to south, is mostly a low, fairly level plateau densely planted to sugar cane. The engineers said that it offered room for six 8,500-foot B-29 runways. Only 2½ miles south of Saipan, it was within easy artillery range of the bigger island and, by July 15, V 'Phib Corps and 13 battalions of Marine and Army artillery in position to bear on it. Intelligence on what was waiting at Tinian was good. The battle plan for its defence had been captured during the fight for Saipan and there was also a co-operative Japanese major who had been taken prisoner.

Vice-Admiral Kakuji Lakuda, commander of the 1st Air Fleet, was the senior officer on the island, but he seems to have left its defence to Colonel Kaishi Ogata, commander of the 50th Infantry Regiment. Also present was the 1st Battalion, 135th Infantry Regiment, and some other Army remnants.

The bombardment of Guam.

Men of the 3rd Marine Division move into Guam on July 31, 1944.

Naval elements were under Captain Goichi Oya and consisted principally of the 56th Naval Guard Force. In all, there were 4,700 Army and 4,110 Navy defenders. There was the usual numerous but mixed bag of guns, ranging here in calibre from 25-mm to 140-mm, with a bonus of three British 6-inch naval guns, Model 1905.

For the Tinian operation, V 'Phib Corps would use the 2nd and 4th Marine Divisions with the Army's 27th Division in reserve. Infantry strength in the Marine divisions was down to 65 per cent as a result of the Saipan operation, otherwise their combat readiness was superb. Harry Schmidt, who had commanded the 4th Division at Saipan, had moved up to command of V Corps; Holland Smith had relinquished that post to be Commanding General, Fleet Marine Force, Pacific.

There was a good beach on the southwest coast near Tinian Town but it was too obvious an objective and reconnaissance showed it to be strongly defended. There were also two other beaches on the west coast near the northern tip of the island, so small as to be hardly taken seriously by the defenders. The northernmost was barely 60 yards wide; the other had a usable width of about 75 yards. The problem was how to thread a corps through such a pair of needles' eyes.

The plan was for the 4th Division to make the initial landing while the 2nd Division made a demonstration off Tinian Town. The new commander of the 4th Division was Major-General Clifton B. Cates, a World War I hero and a regimental

commander at Guadalcanal. J-day was July 24, 1944. The 24th Marines came across the northern beach, designated White 1, in column of battalions, landing just before 0800. The 25th Marines landed on White 2, managing to squeeze in two battalions abreast. Opposition was "light" on White 1, "moderate" on White 2, where a block-house with about 50 Japanese had to be reduced. The 23rd Marines, the 4th Division's remaining infantry regiment, landed in reserve about 1100 on White 2. By nightfall there was a beach-head 4,000 yards wide by 2,000 yards deep.

Naval gunfire had been plentiful, delivered by three battleships, five cruisers, and a gaggle of destroyers. Air support came from Army and Marine squadrons already in place on Saipan, as well as from three attack carriers and five escort carriers. Off Tinian Town the battleship *Colorado* had taken some bad hits from the British 6-inch guns; two 5-inch gun mounts were knocked out and there were 150 casualties. Her escort, the destroyer *Norman Scott,* was hit seven times and had 22 killed and 47 wounded. But *Colorado* had kept firing with her 16-inch guns and with the help of the cruiser *Cleveland* had knocked out the Japanese guns.

Colonel Ogata had planned a night counter-attack, a convergence on the beach-head with his Army troops moving north and Oya's Navy men moving west. It was supposed to be spearheaded by a company of tanks, but these had been caught during the afternoon as they moved into their attack position and only six had survived. At 0200, the 56th Naval Guard Force struck the 24th Marines, who were very solidly in position on good

ground on the left flank of the perimeter. At almost the same time the 1st Battalion, 135th Infantry, hit the 25th Marines in the centre of the line. An hour later, Ogata's tank-led attack with the 1st Battalion, 50th Infantry, found the juncture between the 23rd and 25th Regiments. One company got through as far back as the Marine 75-mm pack howitzers. The artillerymen depressed their muzzles and blasted the attackers into oblivion at point-blank range. Nowhere was the attack successful and when morning came the Marines counted 1,241 Japanese bodies across their front.

The 4th Division began the day's advance at 0930, clearing the beach-head to allow Tommy Watson's 2nd Division room to land. The 2nd Division was given the eastern half of the island. They took Ushi airfield near the northern tip, then swung around and formed on the 4th Division's left flank for a systematic, shoulder-to-shoulder sweep, marching southwards at the rate of 3,000 to 4,000 yards a day. On J + 7 (July 31) the 4th Division occupied Tinian Town. There was a *banzai* attack next morning, accompanied by a rumour of Ogata's death.

The fate of Ogata, or for that matter, of Kakuda and Oya, was never substantiated, but later in the same day, August 1, General Schmidt announced that "all organised resistance had ceased". By August 12 a total of 13,262 civilians had been rounded up and put safely into stockades. Combatant prisoners taken numbered 235. The death count of the Japanese defenders was put at 6,050. The Marines had lost 290 killed, 1,515 wounded, and 24 missing.

CHAPTER 54
Planning the Pacific counteroffensive

The return of General Douglas MacArthur to the Philippines was assured. As his aircraft climbed above Oahu in the afternoon sunlight he turned to an aide and said, "We've sold it!"

He had sold his plan for an invasion of the Philippines to President Roosevelt and Admiral Nimitz. On board the *Baltimore* and at a private house near Pearl Harbor they had spent the afternoon of July 26, 1944 and the morning of the following day in discussion. Finally they agreed that both sound strategy and national honour required the liberation of the Philippines.

It was further agreed that "the Philippines should be recovered with ground and air power then available in the Western Pacific" as they were not going to wait until the defeat of Germany.

Nimitz was to add that "from hindsight I think that decision was correct". But at the time there were two differing strategic concepts of the war in the Pacific.

In the autumn of 1943, MacArthur submitted his views for the future to the Joint Chiefs-of-Staff. After neutralising the Japanese air base in Rabaul by capturing the neighbouring base of Kavieng, and establishing himself further up the New Guinea coast at Hollandia and Aitape, he wished to strike north at Mindanao in the southern Philippines, and thence if possible at Luzon. These operations depended on a clear superiority of air and sea power over the Japanese in the area. They would probably require the presence of the main American fleet, as well as the other naval forces in the south Pacific.

With these forces MacArthur felt that he could be in Mindanao in December 1944, and Luzon the following spring. With his existing forces he was committed to a subsidiary rôle.

But in addition to these strategic considerations there was an emotional tie with the Philippines for MacArthur. As military adviser to the Philippine Army he had created and trained it on the model of the Swiss Army.

When the Japanese landed 200,000 men in December 1941, MacArthur led a mixed American and Filipino army of about half that number. Fighting a defensive battle, he retreated to the Bataan peninsula and the island of Corregidor.

In the spring of 1942 Roosevelt ordered MacArthur to Canberra as C.-in-C. of the newly-formed S.W. Pacific Area. He was reluctant to go, but obeyed the order, and when he arrived in Australia promised "I came through and I shall return." He had thought that the Allies could mount an attack to relieve the Bataan garrison before it was overwhelmed by the Japanese, but now he felt that this promise was true for the whole of the Philippines.

General MacArthur held an unusual position in the American military hierarchy. Unlike other senior commanders, he had not for some time had any direct connection with the War Department, yet he was considerably senior to any other serving officer, having retired as a Chief-of-Staff of the U.S. Army in 1935, when Marshall held the rank of Colonel. His background and his own self-confidence did not incline him to act as a subordinate in the manner of the other commanders.

A pronounced consciousness of his position, and the political importance which it fostered, gave to his relations with Washington something of the flavour of an independent power. But in service circles Admiral Leahy commented that "the mention of the name of MacArthur seemed to generate more heat than light".

He had not been to America since 1935, did not meet any of the American chiefs-of-staff until December 1943, had not received a direct communication from the President since assuming command of the South-West Pacific Area, and at the end of 1943 had never met Admiral Nimitz, his colleague in the Central Pacific.

Added to this difference of personalities there was the natural rivalry of the Army and Navy which was brought out by the two proposed plans.

Admiral King, supported by Admiral Nimitz, based his planning on the experience of the fighting in New Guinea and Guadalcanal (see Chapter 48). He considered it "essential to avoid as long as possible fighting the Japanese army in any land area where they could delay . . . operations". American strength lay at sea and in the air, and not in slow and expensive fighting in jungle and urban areas.

The Navy submitted that the most fruitful line of advance therefore lay through the Carolines and the Marianas, with Formosa as the eventual goal. Given the necessary priority, it was confident that it could capture the eastern Carolines by the end of July 1944, and Guam and the Marianas in September or October. By the end of the year, it could begin to bomb Japan from the latter base.

The Joint Chiefs-of-Staff were in favour of the plan, for as King had put it, it would "put the cork in the bottle" of the enemy communications when the Americans captured Formosa. From bases in China, Formosa, and the Bonin islands they could strangle the Japanese mainland islands by submarine and air attack on the traffic through the South China Sea. MacArthur would liberate Mindanao and set up bases for the Far Eastern Air Forces to pound down Japanese air power on Luzon, after which he would help the Pacific Fleet to capture Formosa.

The Navy felt that this plan would bring about the defeat of Japan more quickly than the rather more systematic approach advocated by MacArthur. By-passing the Philippines would be no real hardship for its inhabitants, and might even liberate them more quickly than by landing on the islands themselves.

It was as protagonists for these two conflicting doctrines that MacArthur and Nimitz met with President Roosevelt at Oahu.

The shipyards of Beaumont, Texas, were the scene of feverish contruction activity in preparation for the Philippine invasion.

Admiral Leahy, who was one of those present at the meetings, remembers: "It was both pleasant and very informative to have these two men who had been pictured as antagonists calmly present their differing views to the Commander-in-Chief." Rear-Admiral Wilson Brown stated that in no conference attended by him did the speakers stick so closely to the subject or make such clear, concise, and candid expressions of opinion.

Undoubtedly the conference was also a triumph for Roosevelt who "was at his best as he tactfully steered the discussion from one point to another and narrowed down the area of disagreement between MacArthur and Nimitz". At the meetings the speakers were dealing with facts, and not second-hand reports handled by politicians.

When MacArthur took his leave on July 27, he assured the President that he need have no concern about differences between himself and Nimitz. "We see eye to eye, Mr. President, we understand each other perfectly," he said.

There could be no firm decision on strategy: that was up to the Joint Chiefs-of-Staff, but the two sides had reached agreement. Leahy was later to assert that "the agreement... and the President's familiarity with the situation at this conference were to be of great value in preventing an unnecessary invasion of Japan which the planning staffs of the Joint Chiefs and the War Department were advocating, regardless of the loss of life that would result from an attack on Japan's ground forces in their own country."

Despite this top-level agreement, the J.C.S. continued to discuss the Pacific strategy. It was almost a year later, on September 1, 1944, that Rear-Admiral Forrest Sherman, Admiral Nimitz's chief planner, confronted them. He said that it was high time a decision was reached, and that even a bad one would be better than none. Central Pacific armed forces had no directive for anything beyond the Palaus objective, which was due in two weeks. Admiral King still opposed Luzon, which he said would slow up the war for mere sentimental reasons (earlier he had dismissed MacArthur's plans as "desires and visions").

The plans, however, had won a powerful ally in General Marshall, who appreciated the argument about national honour, and also that Luzon would be easier to capture than Formosa. MacArthur had warned the J.C.S. that if they left the 16 million population of the Philippines to "wither on the vine" until the end of the war with Japan, they would not only inflict unpredictable hardships on the loyal Filipinos, but also cause all Asia to lose faith in American honour.

The J.C.S. planners worked out a timetable to be presented to the "Octagon" Combined Chiefs-of-Staff conference at Quebec on September 11, 1944:
1. September 15, South-West Pacific Forces occupy Morotai; Central Pacific forces occupy Peleliu October 5; occupy

Yap, with Ulithi to follow.
2. October 15, South-West Pacific Forces occupy Salebaboe Island; November 15, land at Sarangani Bay, Mindanao; December 20, at Leyte.
3. South-West Pacific and Central Pacific forces then combine to occupy either (1) Luzon, to secure Manila by February 20, or (2) Formosa and Amoy on the China coast by March 1, 1945.

But as with many of the best plans, this timetable was scrambled within a week.

Task Force 38, under Admiral Halsey, left Eniwetok on August 28, 1944, to bomb Yap, the Palaus, and Mindanao, and make a one-group diversionary strike on the Bonin Islands. The aim was to destroy Japanese air forces which might challenge the forthcoming landings on Morotai and Peleliu, and to deceive the enemy as to the next target. The Palaus were bombed on September 6-8, Mindanao airstrips near Sarangani Bay on September 9-10. These attacks were unopposed, and this caused Halsey to cancel later strikes for Mindanao and move to the Visayas on the 12th. The task force moved in close and flew 2,400 sorties in two days; about 200 enemy planes were shot down or destroyed on the ground. Several ships were sunk and many installations destroyed.

It seemed to Halsey and his staff that the Japanese air forces were practically finished, and at noon on September 13, he sent a very important signal to Nimitz. He recommended that the Palau, Yap, Morotai, and Mindanao landings be cancelled as unnecessary, and that Task Force 38 and the men earmarked for these operations be diverted to MacArthur for an immediate seizure of Leyte. This signal was passed on to King and Mac-Arthur.

With a force of fast carriers available MacArthur no longer needed to develop airfields in the southern Philippines before invading Leyte or Luzon; the Navy could furnish the air support the Army needed until it had captured or developed airfields on the target island.

If the 30,000 troops who were to land on Mindanao on November 15, and XXIV Corps (intended for Yap) could be diverted to Leyte, MacArthur would have an effective invasion force.

In MacArthur's name General Sutherland informed the J.C.S. and Nimitz on September 14 that if Halsey's recommendations were adopted, MacArthur would invade Leyte on October 20, that is two months ahead of the target date. Nimitz agreed, but said that the Palaus operation should not be cancelled because it would be needed as an anchorage and air base.

After their earlier performance, the J.C.S. acted with commendable alacrity. The Combined Chiefs-of-Staff conference, with Roosevelt, Churchill, and Mackenzie King, was still in session at Quebec when the new proposals came through. Breaking off from a dinner, the J.C.S. held a brief consultation. "Having the utmost confidence in General MacArthur, Admiral Nimitz and Admiral Halsey,"

wrote General Marshall, "It was not a difficult decision to make. Within 90 minutes after the signal had been received in Quebec, General MacArthur and Admiral Nimitz had received their instructions to execute the Leyte operation."

The target date was fixed for October 20, and this avoided the three intermediate landings at Yap, the Talauds, and Mindanao. MacArthur's acknowledgment reached Marshall as he was leaving the dinner to return to his rooms.

The instructions were formalised soon after in the following message:
"1. Admiral Wilkinson's YAP ATTACK FORCE, the XXIV Army Corps, then loaded or at sea, will be assigned to General MacArthur to land LEYTE 20 October.
"2. All shipping used in the Palaus operation, after unloading, to be sent to Southwest Pacific ports to help VII 'Phib lift General Krueger's Sixth Army to LEYTE.
"3. ALL FIRE SUPPORT SHIPS and ESCORT CARRIERS used in the Palaus operation to be assigned temporarily to Admiral Kinkaid, Commander Seventh Fleet, to help cover LEYTE.
"4. ULITHI to be seized promptly, as an advanced fleet base".

There followed a series of planning conferences by the commanders of the forces involved. The operation would employ all the American military forces not engaged in Europe or on garrison duties in places like the Aleutian and Marshall Islands. Though no Australian troops were to be used, ships of the Royal Australian Navy would participate, and one ship of the Royal Navy, the fast minelayer *Ariadne*.

While the ships were assembled, and planning continued at all levels, the J.C.S. discussed the next move after Leyte. Was it to be Luzon, or Formosa?

After pressure against the Formosa operation by General Millard Harmon, commanding the Army Air Forces in the Central Pacific, and by General Simon Bolivar Buckner, commanding the 10th Army, it was shelved in favour of Luzon.

It was a logical and strategically sound move, for if Leyte could be captured in reasonable time, III and VII Amphibious Forces would be capable of putting in a second major landing before the end of 1944. Formosa would require an assault force of at least nine divisions, which would not be available until about the middle of 1945.

Japanese air strength was still too great to allow the invasion of Okinawa, so after clearing Luzon, the Americans could take Iwo Jima, as a rung in the "ladder up the Bonins", and Okinawa, as a base for air attacks and the final invasions of the Japanese home islands.

On October 3, 1944 the Joint Chiefs-of-Staff issued a directive to Nimitz and MacArthur, which seemed to be the final tribute to the general's skills as a salesman.

"General MacArthur will liberate

Luzon, starting 20 December, and establish bases there to support later operations. Admiral Nimitz will provide fleet cover and support, occupy one or more positions in the Bonin-Volcano Island group 20 January 1945, and invade the Ryukyus, target date 1 March 1945.''

Yet the liberation of the Philippines had been decided by many events beyond his control. Landings on the China coast in support of the Formosa operation were ruled out because of the strength of the Japanese in both areas. Chinese Nationalist forces would be of little help, partly because of their lack of equipment

The greatest Allied commander and one of the strongest personalities of the war: General Douglas MacArthur.

and training, but also because of the enmity between Stilwell and Chiang Kai-shek.

The naval forces assigned to him from Halsey's Task Force 38, had been released through a misconception. Halsey believed that Japanese air-power in the Palaus, Mindanao, and Visayas was finished; in fact the Imperial General Headquarters had ordered that it be held back in readiness for the major landings which were expected in that area.

Yet despite this, the landings on Leyte and Luzon vindicated MacArthur's promise to return, and set the American forces in the Pacific on a return journey which would end less than 11 months after ''Octagon'', with the surrender of Japan.

Two amphibious operations brought the converging forces of MacArthur and Nimitz to within striking range of Leyte.

On September 15, 1944, the 31st Division under MacArthur began landing on Morotai island. He planned to expand its partially-completed airfield to cover operations to the south of the Philippine islands.

There was no opposition, but the airfield was unusable; another (ready for fighter operations on October 4 and bombers on the 15th) was quickly built.

On September 15 Halsey assaulted the Palau Islands. Fringed by coral reefs, this island group is 470 miles east of Mindanao. Halsey planned to use it as a seaplane base and anchorage for the attack on the Philippines.

The landing on Peleliu was strongly

opposed. On the first day the 1st Marine Division had secured a beach-head; on the second it had occupied, but not secured, the airfield. The tough, well-sited bunkers which covered the airfield were eventually cleared, and by October 1 the field was taking fighters and a week later medium bombers. The Japanese, however, hung on in the island for another six weeks.

On September 17, the 81st Division landed on Angaur island, six miles south of Peleliu, and by noon had practically secured it. By the 21st an airstrip had been built and was taking Liberators. On the 23rd the 81st was landed on Ulithi atoll, which proved to be abandoned. It was quickly developed and became the main fleet base in October.

MacArthur, by way of the south-west, and Nimitz, through the central Pacific, had now reached their forming-up points for Leyte.

U.S. Marines struggle through the mud of Bougainville (right). A Japanese soldier commits Hara-Kiri rather than face the dishonour of capture (below).

CHAPTER 55
Anzio and the drive to Rome

Before the spring of 1944, Allied public opinion did not attempt to conceal its disappointment, not to say impatience, at the results of Anglo-American strategy in the Mediterranean. As can well be imagined, political and military leaders in London and Washington were hardly able to pacify these frustrations by making public the vast organisation, training, and preparation then going on towards an operation which was to bear its first fruits at dawn on June 6. Certainly after five months of marking time the Allies scored a decisive victory over their enemy in Italy, but only less than 30 days before the Normandy landings and thus a little late in the day. The normal course of development of Allied strategy was hindered by a chain of unfortunate circumstances which, it must be said, had nothing to do with politics.

On January 16, 1944 the American 5th Army, still under the command of Lieutenant-General Mark Clark, renewed its attack on the Cassino redoubt, which was defended by XIV Panzer Corps from the 10th Army (General von Vietinghoff-Scheel). The main objective of this undertaking in such difficult terrain was to force Kesselring to move up the reinforcements at present around Rome to strengthen his front. When this had been achieved, the American VI Corps (Major-General John P. Lucas), which was to effect a surprise landing on the beaches at Anzio and Nettuno, would find the way open to drive inland and attack the enemy's communications. This was the fundamental idea of Operation "Shingle", a pet scheme of Churchill, who had succeeded in winning over both Roosevelt and Stalin. He had even agreed to sacrifice to it the amphibious forces collected together for a landing on Rhodes. Did Churchill see further than his Allies? It seems likely that had the German 10th Army been annihilated during the first two weeks of February, nothing would have prevented Churchill from renewing his demands on his Allies and perhaps demanding an exploitation of this victory in the direction of Ljubljana and the abandonment of a landing in Provence, as planned at Teheran.

But everything was to go against him. First of all, General Clark considerably toned down the instructions given to him on January 12 by Sir Harold Alexander, commanding the 15th Army Group. Alexander saw the mission of the American VI Corps as follows: "to cut the enemy's main communications in the Colli Laziali (Alban Hills) area southeast of Rome, and threaten the rear of the XIV German Corps". Clark's directive of the same date to General Lucas merely required him "to seize and secure a beachhead in the vicinity of Anzio" and thence "to advance on the Colli Laziali".

This threefold manoeuvre (seize, secure, and advance) clearly did not reflect Alexander's original intention, but Alexander did not order Clark to change his directive so as to bring it into line with his own. As we shall see him giving in to his subordinate again on the following May 26, we can take it that it was not merely an oversight. We must believe that in acting as he did, General Clark was still under the strain of the Salerno landings, though he says nothing of this in his memoirs. John Lucas, entrusted with carrying out Operation "Shingle", noted in his diary: "It will be worse than the Dardanelles". His friend George S. Patton, spitting fire and smelling a fight in the offing, had said to him:

"'John, there is no one in the Army I would hate to see killed as much as you, but you can't get out of this alive. Of course, you might be badly wounded. No one ever blames a *wounded* general!' He advised Lucas to read the Bible when the going got tough, and then turned to one of the VI Corps commander's aides and said, 'Look here; if things get too bad, shoot the old man in the backside; but don't you dare kill the man!'"

About a week before D-day, an ill-fated landing exercise hastily carried out in the Gulf of Salerno only served to confirm Major-General Lucas's pessimistic forecast.

The 5th Army plan to take the Cassino defile placed the main burden on the American II Corps (Major-General Geoffrey Keyes). Forcing the Rapido at San Angelo, five miles south of Cassino, it would drive up the Liri valley and its tanks would exploit the success towards Frosinone then Anzio. This action was to be supported on the right by the French Expeditionary Corps (General Juin) and on the left by the British X Corps (Lieutenant-General Sir Richard McCreery).

"It was a somewhat simple concept," wrote Marshal Juin, "revealing a bold temperament which everyone recognised in the 5th Army commander, but at the same time it was at fault in that it ignored certain strategic principles and betrayed a false notion of distances and especially of the terrain in this peninsula of Italy where mountains–and what mountains! –dominate the landscape."

Sure enough the British X Corps, though it established a bridgehead on the right bank of the Garigliano (resulting from the confluence of the Liri and the Rapido), came to grief on the slopes of Monte Majo. The American 36th Division (Major-General F. L. Walker) of II Corps was even less fortunate, losing the strip of land it had won two days before on the right bank of the Rapido with casualties of 143 dead, 663 wounded, and 875 missing. On the right the 3rd Algerian Division (General de Monsabert) and the 2nd Moroccan Division (General Dody), attacking in line abreast, captured the heights of Monna Casale and Costa San Pietro (4,920 ft). But the French Expeditionary Corps did not have the reserves to exploit this success in the direction of Atina, from where it might have been possible to get down into the Liri valley behind the defence line along the Rapido.

General Clark had six divisions (54 battalions) and his opponent, General von Senger und Etterlin (XIV Panzer Corps), had four with only six battalions apiece. This indicates how the terrain favoured the defenders, who were also valiant, well-trained, and better led. They were, however, stretched to the limit and Vietinghoff had to ask Kesselring for reinforcements. Kesselring took it upon himself to send him the 29th and the 90th *Panzergrenadier* Divisions from Rome, where they had been stationed in reserve.

"Considering what happened," General Westphal, at the time chief-of-staff of Army Group "C", wrote in 1953, "it was a mistake. The attack and the landing at the mouth of the Garigliano were only a diversion intended to pin down our forces and to get us to drain our resources away from Rome as far as possible. The Allied commander's aim was fully achieved." Three years later Kesselring answered this charge, though without naming Westphal, to some point:

"I was well aware of the enemy's possible moves. One of these possibilities always stood out more clearly than the others. The attack by the American II Corps and the French Expeditionary Corps on positions north of Monte Cassino was clearly linked to the fighting on the Garigliano and increased its chances of success.

"Another possibility, that is the landing, was still only a faint one. We did not know yet when or where this would be. If I had refused the request of the 10th Army's commander, his right flank could have been dented and there seemed to be no way of knowing how it could have been restored." The German field-marshal seems to have been right in his judgement because on the eve of the event Admiral Canaris, head of the *Abwehr,* had told him that in his opinion no Allied landing was to be expected in Italy in the near future.

No other landing in Europe or the Pacific was initially as successful, and at such little cost, as that at Anzio-Nettuno in Operation "Shingle". By midnight on January 22, that is after 22 hours of operations, Rear-Admirals Frank J. Lowry of the U.S. Navy and Thomas H. Troubridge of the Royal Navy had landed 36,034 men, 3,069 vehicles, and 90 per cent of the assault equipment of the U.S. VI Corps. This comprised the British 1st Division (Major-General W. Penney), the American 3rd Division (Major-General L. K. Truscott), a regiment and a battalion of paratroops, three battalions of Rangers, and a brigade of Commandos. Losses

Landing supplies in the harbour at Anzio.

amounted to 13 killed, 44 missing, and 97 wounded. The supporting naval forces, four light cruisers and 24 destroyers, had neutralised the fire of the shore batteries and two German battalions had been overrun on the beaches. "And that was all," wrote General Westphal as he reckoned up his weak forces. "There was nothing else in the area we could have thrown against the enemy on that same day. The road to Rome (37 miles) was now open. No-one could have prevented a force which drove on hard from entering the Eternal City. For two days after the landing we were in a breath-taking situation. Our counter-measures could only take effect after 48 hours."

The General Staff of Army Group "C" had made several studies of a possible Allied landing of some strategic importance. For each hypothesis envisaged (Istria, Ravenna, Civitavecchia, Leghorn, Viareggio), the formations which would fight it had been detailed off, the routes they would have to take marked out, and their tasks laid down. Each hypothetical situation had been given a key-

word. Kesselring only had to signal "*Fall Richard*" for the following to converge on the Anzio bridgehead:

1. the "Hermann Göring" Panzer Division from the area of Frosinone and the 4th Parachute Division from Terni, both in I Parachute Corps (General Schlemm)
2. from the Sangro front LXXVI Panzer Corps (General Herr: 26th Panzer and 3rd *Panzergrenadier* Divisions); from the Garigliano front the 29th *Panzergrenadier* Division, newly arrived in the sector; and
3. from northern Italy the staff of the 14th Army and the 65th and 362nd Divisions which had crossed the Apennines as quickly as the frost and snow would allow them.

But O.K.W. intervened and ordered Field-Marshal von Rundstedt to hand over to Kesselring the 715th Division, then stationed in the Marseilles area, and Colonel-General Löhr, commanding in the Balkans, to send him his 114th *Jäger* Division.

On January 23, when Colonel-General von Mackensen arrived to take charge of operations against the Allied forces, all that lay between Anzio and Rome was a de-

tachment of the "Hermann Göring" Panzer Division and a hotchpotch of artillery ranging from the odd 8.8-cm A.A. to Italian, French, and Yugoslav field guns. Despite the talents of Kesselring as an improviser and the capabilities of his general staff, a week was to pass before the German 14th Army could offer any consistent opposition to the Allied offensive.

On the Allied side, however, Major-General John P. Lucas thought only of consolidating his bridgehead and getting ashore the balance of his corps, the 45th Division (Major-General W. Eagles) and the 1st Armoured Division (Major-General E. N. Harmon). It will be recognised that in so doing he was only carrying out the task allotted to the 5th Army. On January 28 his 1st Armoured Division had indeed captured Aprilia, over ten miles north of Anzio, but on his right the American 3rd Division had been driven back opposite Cisterna. On the same day Mackensen had three divisions in the line and enough units to make up a fourth; by the last day of the month he was to have eight.

Was a great strategic opportunity lost between dawn on January 22 and twilight on the 28th? In London Churchill was champing with impatience and wrote to Sir Harold Alexander: "I expected to see a wild cat roaring into the mountains – and what do I find? A whale wallowing on the beaches!"

Returning to the subject in his memoirs, Churchill wrote: "The spectacle of 18,000 vehicles accumulated ashore by the fourteenth day for only 70,000 men, or less than four men to a vehicle, including drivers and attendants . . . was astonishing."

Churchill might perhaps be accused of yielding too easily to the spite he felt at the setbacks of Operation "Shingle", for which he had pleaded so eagerly to Stalin and Roosevelt. These were, however, not the feelings of the official historian of the U.S. Navy who wrote ten years after the event:

"It was the only amphibious operation in that theater where the Army was unable promptly to exploit a successful landing, or where the enemy contained Allied forces on a beachhead for a prolonged period. Indeed, in the entire war there is none to compare with it; even the Okinawa campaign in the Pacific was shorter."

We would go along with this statement, implying as it does that the blame lay here, were it not for General Truscott's opinion, which is entirely opposed to Morison's quoted above. Truscott lived through every detail of the Anzio landings as commander of the 3rd Division, then as second-in-command to General Lucas, whom he eventually replaced. He was recognised by his fellow-officers as a first-class leader, resolute, aggressive, and very competent. His evidence is therefore to be reckoned with:

"I suppose that armchair strategists will always labour under the delusion that there was a 'fleeting opportunity' at Anzio during which some Napoleonic figure would have charged over the Colli Laziali (Alban Hills), played havoc with the German line of communications, and galloped on into Rome. Any such concept betrays lack of comprehension of the military problem involved. It was necessary to occupy the Corps Beachhead Line to prevent the enemy from interfering with the beaches, otherwise enemy artillery and armoured detachments operating against the flanks could have cut us off from the beach and prevented the unloading of troops, supplies, and equipment. As it was, the Corps Beachhead Line was barely distant enough to prevent direct artillery fire on the beaches.

"On January 24th (i.e. on D+2) my division, with three Ranger battalions and the 504th Parachute Regiment attached, was extended on the Corps Beachhead Line, over a front of twenty miles . . . Two brigade groups of the British 1st Division held a front of more than seven miles."

In his opinion again the Allied high command overestimated the psychological effect on the enemy's morale of the simple news of an Anglo-American landing behind the 10th Army. This is shown by the text of a leaflet dropped to German troops, pointing out the apparently impossible strategic situation in which they were now caught, pinned down at Cassino and outflanked at Anzio, and urging them to surrender.

But far from allowing himself to be intimidated, Kesselring assembled his forces with a promptness underestimated by Alexander and Clark. Another reason why he was able to race them to it was because the latter were somewhat short of *matériel* for amphibious operations. The figures speak for themselves: on June 6, 1944 for a first wave of 12 divisions Eisenhower had 3,065 landing craft, whereas Anzio had 237 for four divisions.

Under these conditions, even if Lucas had had the temperament of a Patton, one could hardly have expected him to throw his forces into an attack on the Colli Laziali, over 20 miles from Anzio, with the two divisions of his first echelon and not worry also about his flanks and communications. Finally, Lucas did not have this cavalier temperament, and the day after the landings he noted in his diary: "The tension in a battle like this is terrible. Who the hell would be a general?"

The chances lost here, however, were to give rise during the months of February and March to two of the most furious battles of the war. They both ended in defeat for the attacker. On February 29 Mackensen had to abandon his attempt to crush the Anzio beach-head and Clark reported that his repeated attempts to force the Cassino defile had failed.

The battle for the beach-head arose from Hitler's initiative. On January 28 he sent Kesselring the following directive, which is worth quoting in full, so well does it reveal the Führer's state of mind on the day after the disasters suffered by Army Group "South" on the Dniepr at Kanev, and at a time when everyone was expecting an Anglo-American attack across the Channel.

"In a few days from now," he wrote, "the 'Battle for Rome' will start: this will decide the defence of Central Italy and the fate of the 10th Army. But it has an even greater significance, for the Nettuno landing is the first step of the invasion of Europe planned for 1944.

"The enemy's aim is to pin down and to wear out major German forces as far as possible from the English base in which the main body of the invasion force is being held in a constant state of readiness, and to gain experience for their future operations.

"The significance of the battle to be fought by the 14th Army must be made clear to each one of its soldiers.

"It will not be enough to give clear and correct tactical orders. The army, the air force, and the navy must be imbued with a fanatical determination to come out victorious from this battle and to hang on until the last enemy soldier has been exterminated or driven back into the sea. The men will fight with a solemn hatred against an enemy who is waging a relentless war of extermination against the German people, an enemy to whom everything seems a legitimate means to this end, an enemy who, in the absence of any high ethical intention, is plotting the destruction of Germany and, along with her, that of European civilisation. The battle must be hard and without pity, and not only against the enemy but also against any leader of men who, in this decisive hour, shows any sign of weakness.

"As in Sicily, on the Rapido, and at Ortona, the enemy must be shown that the fighting strength of the German Army is still intact and that the great invasion of 1944 will be an invasion which will drown in the blood of the Anglo-Saxon soldiers."

That is why the German 14th Army, whilst it drove off the repeated attempts of the U.S. VI Corps to break out from Aprilia and to cut off the Rome–Gaeta railway at Campoleone, actively prepared to go over to the counter-attack as ordered. On February 10 a counter-attack led by the 3rd *Panzergrenadier* Division (Lieutenant-General Graeser) re-took the station at Carroceto. That day the German communiqué announced 4,000 prisoners taken since January 22, whereas the Allies' figure was only 2,800. Rightly alarmed by these setbacks, General Clark sent the British 56th Division (Major-General Templer) into the bridgehead; also, at Alexander's suggestion, he appointed Truscott second-in-command of VI Corps. Meanwhile Colonel-General von Mackensen had been called to O.K.W. to put his plan for a counter-offensive before the Führer. The latter offered no objection when Mackensen explained his idea of driving his attack along the Albano – Anzio line, with diversionary attacks on either side. Hitler did not stop there, however, but took it upon himself to interfere in every detail of the plan, from which he expected wonders. Mackensen thus saw the front on which he was to attack, the troops he was to use, and even the deployment these forces were to adopt, all altered by Hitler.

The operation was entrusted to LXXVI Panzer Corps. It was to attack on a front of less than four miles with two divisions up and the 26th *Panzergrenadier* Division (Lieutenant-General von Lüttwitz) and the 20th *Panzergrenadier* Division (Lieutenant-General Fries) in army reserve. So, Hitler ordered, the infantry could be given supporting fire which would pulverise the enemy's defence. Mackensen tried in vain to point out that such a massive concentration would present a sitting target to the Anglo-American air forces and that *Luftflotte* II, under the command of Field-Marshal von Richthofen, did not have the means to fight them off. It was no good. Hitler also refused to listen to the argument that it was useless lining up the guns wheel to wheel with insufficient ammunition for them to fire at the required rate.

Alexander with General Clark and Lieutenant-General McCreery at Anzio.

The attack started on February 16 as ordered by Hitler. There was a preliminary softening up by 300 guns, but the 114th and 715th Divisions, which were to advance side by side, were to be denied the support of a creeping barrage. The spongy ground of the Pontine marshes prevented the tanks and the assault guns, which were to support the waves of infantry, from getting off the roads. The 14th Army's offensive might have had the intermittent support of 20 to 30 Luftwaffe fighter-bombers, but the German troops on the ground had to withstand the assault of no less than 1,100 tons of bombs. The Anglo-American tactical air forces boxed in the battlefield and considerably hindered the movement of supplies up towards the 14th Army's front line units.

By nightfall LXXVI Panzer Corps had advanced some three to four miles into the Allied lines and was about seven to eight miles from its objective of Anzio-Nettuno. Its guns had fired 6,500 shells, but had received ten times as many. For three days Mackensen attempted to regain the upper hand, but in vain: Truscott, who had just relieved Lucas, was too vigilant for him. On February 29, I Parachute Corps took up the attack again in the Cisterna area, but this came to a halt a few hundred yards from its point of departure. The battle around the bridgehead died down and General Clark reinforced the position with the British 5th and the American 34th Divisions. The beaches and the Allies' rear positions continued to be harassed by German heavy artillery with its observation posts up in the Colli Laziali. A huge 11-inch railway gun in particular played havoc among the defenders. The air force was unable to silence it since, as soon as it had fired, "Leopold", as its crew, or "Anzio Annie", as the Allies called it, withdrew into a tunnel near Castel Gandolfo.

At sea, Operation "Shingle" cost Admiral Sir Andrew Cunningham, C.-in-C. Mediterranean, the light cruisers *Spartan* and *Penelope* and three destroyers, all of the Royal Navy. Amongst the weapons used by the Germans were glide bombs and human torpedoes, the latter making their first appearance with the Kriegsmarine.

On the Cassino front General Clark strove to take up the offensive again the day after the Anzio landing. The intention was that the American II Corps, now only one division strong (the 34th, commanded by Major-General Ryder) should cross the Rapido north of Cassino whilst the French Expeditionary Corps, after taking Monte Belvedere, would move down the Liri valley, sweeping past the back of Monte Cassino. This turning movement, to be carried out as it were within rifle range, did not appeal to General Juin, who thought it would have been better to hinge the manoeuvre on Atina. Out of loyalty to General Clark, however, he did not press the point.

After rapidly regrouping at an altitude of 325 feet in the area of San Elia, the 3rd Algerian Division set off to attack its objectives: Belvedere (2,370 feet) and Colle Abate (2,930 feet).

In view of the nature of the terrain, the operation seemed to face insurmountable difficulties. Marshal Juin acknowledges this in his memoirs. Describing an occasion when he was visited by General Giraud he wrote: "The last time I had seen him was during the most critical moment of my Belvedere operation. I took him up to General Monsabert's front line H.Q., from which it was possible to watch the whole action of the Tunisian 4th *Tirailleur* Regiment. He expressed surprise that I had taken upon myself such a

hazardous affair and could not refrain from reproaching me, adding: 'I thought I was the only hot-headed fool in our army, but I see today that it's catching'."

The defile was defended by the 44th Division, a famous unit which had been re-formed after Stalingrad and which, recruited in Austria, had taken the name, famous in Prince Eugene's army, of *"Hoch und Deutschmeister"*. The opposing forces were men of equal courage and tenacity. In the afternoon of January 25 the Tunisian 4th *Tirailleur* Regiment (Colonel Roux) raised the tricolour on the two heights it had scaled under withering cross-fire, but one of its battalions was virtually wiped out on the Colle Abate, whilst the other two drove off one counter-attack after another to stay on Belvedere, but only at a heavy price.

René Chambe has left this account of the dramatic combat: "Night passes. This is one of the most critical of all. From right to left the Gandoët, Bacqué, and Péponnet battalions are clinging to the sides of Hills 862, 771, and 700. The enemy is counter-attacking furiously everywhere. He is driven off by bayonet and grenade. But none of these three peaks is retaken. And ammunition runs out again; the parsimoniously distributed mouthfuls of food which make up our rations are far away. Hunger comes again and with hunger thirst, the terrible thirst which gnaws at your stomach and drills into your brain. As for sleep, that real sleep which restores, we haven't had any for a long time. Men are falling asleep now under shelling, in the midst of mines and bullets. They're killed almost before they know it. Only wounds wake them up. Some answer back, aiming their rifles and throwing their grenades in a state of half-consciousness." When it was relieved, the Tunisian 4th *Tirailleur* Regiment had lost its colonel, 39 officers, and 1,562 N.C.O.s and men: it was reduced to a third of its strength.

The Germans on their side had lost 1,200 prisoners, and to strengthen the 44th Division, which threatened at any moment to give way under the furious hammer-blows of the 3rd Algerian Division's attack, 10th Army had to send in one regiment of the 90th *Panzergrenadier* Division and another of the 71st Division, both from XIV Panzer Corps. So the French Expeditionary Corps managed to draw onto itself two-thirds of the 44 battalions then fighting opposite the American 5th Army.

The value of this force was well appreciated by General Clark. On the day after the furious fighting on Belvedere he wrote to Juin to express his admiration for the "splendid way" in which the corps had accomplished its mission, adding:

"By a carefully prepared and co-ordinated plan of operations you have launched and sustained a series of attacks which have had remarkable success in attaining their main objective, that is: to pin down by hard fighting the maximum possible number of enemy troops and thus prevent them from intervening against our landing and the establishment of our bridgehead at Anzio. By doing this you have thrown back the enemy along the whole length of your front and inflicted severe losses on troops which were already weary."

Some days later General Alexander associated himself with this praise, and these were no empty words. In his book on the Cassino battle, in which he took part the following February and March as paratroop battalion commander in the famous 1st Parachute Division, Rudolf Böhmler makes the same observation:

"The greatest surprise, however, was the fighting spirit shown by the French Expeditionary Corps. The 1940 campaign had cast a sombre shadow over the French Army, and no one believed that it would ever recover from the devastating defeat that had been inflicted on it. But now General Juin's divisions were proving to be the most dangerous customers. Nor was this attributable solely to the Algerians' and Moroccans' experience in mountain warfare. Three factors combined to mould these troops into a dangerously efficient fighting force: the mountain warfare experience of the French colonial troops, the ultra-modern American equipment with which they had been equipped, and the fact that they were led by French officers who were masters of the profession of arms. With these three basic elements Juin had moulded a formidable entity. In the battles that followed, the Corps proved equal to every demand made of it, and Field-Marshal Kesselring himself assured the author that he was always uneasy about any sector of the front on which the French popped up.

"Had Clark given more heed to Juin's views in the Cassino battles and accepted his plan of thrusting via Atina into the Liri valley, the three savage battles of Cassino would probably never have been fought and the venerable House of St. Benedict would have been left unscathed."

With two divisions so hard pressed there was no question of Juin's being able to exploit his costly victory at Belvedere, which now left him in front of the rest of the Allied line. Some time afterwards he was reinforced by General Utili's motorised group, the first Italian formation to move up to the front again (having had its first taste of fighting in December). It operated on the right of the French Expeditionary Corps in the snowy massif of the Abruzzi and acquitted itself well.

In the American II Corps area, the 34th Division did not succeed in breaking out of the bridgehead it had won on the right bank of the Rapido.

Not wishing to leave things in this state of half-failure, General Alexander put at the disposal of the 5th Army the New Zealand Corps (Lieutenant-General Freyberg), consisting of the 2nd New Zealand, the 4th Indian, and the British 78th Divisions.

But before launching his attack, General

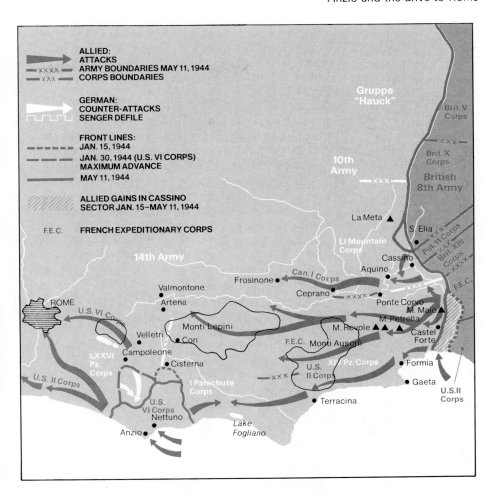

Freyberg demanded the destruction of the historic Monte Cassino abbey which overlooked the Liri valley from a height of 1,700 feet. General Clark showed some scepticism when informed by his subordinates that the Germans were using the monastery as an artillery observation post and had heavy weapons stored inside it. He thus wholeheartedly opposed this act of vandalism and it is a fact, proved over and over again, that on the evening before February 15 the only soldiers anywhere near the monastery were three military policemen stationed there to keep the troops out.

Freyberg appealed to Alexander, who finally agreed with him, perhaps on the evidence of a misinterpreted radio message. A German voice had been heard asking:

"Wo ist der Abt? Ist er noch im Kloster?" (Where is the 'Abt'? Is it still in the monastery?)

'Abt' is the German military abbreviation for 'abteilung', meaning a section. But unfortunately 'Abt' also means 'Abbot', and since 'Abt' is masculine and 'abteilung' feminine, the conversation referred to the Abbot.

Sir Henry Maitland Wilson, C.-in-C. Mediterranean, made available the necessary air formations. In the morning of February 15, therefore, 142 four-engined and 87 two-engined American bombers flew over Monte Cassino in three waves, dropping 453 tons of high explosive and incendiary bombs, and reduced the monas-

Allied attacks and German counterattacks at Anzio and the break-through at Cassino during the early months of 1944.

tery of Saint Benedict to a complete and absolute ruin.

"The monks had no idea that the rumble of heavy bombers which they could hear approaching from the north concerned them in any way. Prayers were just being said in the bishop's small room. The monks were praying to the Mother of God to protect them, and when they reached the words *'pro nobis Christum exora'*, a terrific explosion shattered the peace. The first bombs were bursting. It was nine forty-five."

This bombardment, of which he disapproved, aroused two different impressions in General Clark. In his book *Calculated Risk* he says:

"... and when the clock got around to nine-thirty, I immediately heard the first hum of engines coming up from the south. I tried to judge their progress by the steadily increasing volume of sound, a mental chore that was interrupted by a sudden roaring explosion. Sixteen bombs had been released by mistake from the American planes; several of them hit near my command post, sending fragments flying all over the place, but fortunately injuring no one, except the feelings of my police dog, Mike, who at that time was the proud mother of six week-old pups.

"Then the four groups of stately Flying

General Clark awards battle streamers to a Nisei unit.

Fortresses passed directly overhead and a few moments later released their bombs on Monastery Hill. I had seen the famous old Abbey, with its priceless and irreplaceable works of art, only from a distance, but with the thundering salvoes that tore apart the hillside that morning, I knew there was no possibility that I ever would see it at any closer range."

After the massive Allied air attack of February 15, Monte Cassino lay in ruins. But following this bombardment the German defenders moved into the ruins of the monastery and drove off with heavy losses the 4th Indian Division (Major-General Tuker) coming up to assault the peak. The 2nd New Zealand Division (Major-General Kippenberger) suffered the same fate before Cassino.

The second battle for the Liri valley was a definite success for the defenders, XIV Panzer Corps. The third brought General von Senger und Etterlin the high honour of Oak Leaves to his Iron Cross.

Clark and Freyberg, in spite of Juin's further representations in favour of the Atina manoeuvre, stuck to the narrower pincer, which had just failed, combined with carpet bombing, which was of more use to the defenders than the Allies.

On March 15 775 bombers and fighter-bombers, including 260 B-17 Flying

Fortresses, dropped 1,250 tons of bombs on the little town of Cassino and its immediate surroundings. It was then shelled for two hours from 1230 hours by 746 guns. But when the Ghurkas and the New Zealanders moved in to attack they found to their cost that, as Böhmler says:

"The U.S. Air Force had presented the Germans with a first-class obstacle: the towering piles of rubble, the torn and debris-strewn streets, the innumerable deep bomb craters made it quite impossible for the New Zealand 4th Armoured Brigade to penetrate into the town and support the infantry. Its tanks had to halt on the edge and leave the infantry to its own devices as soon as the latter penetrated the zone of ruin and rubble. The most strenuous efforts to clear a way for the tanks with bulldozers made painfully slow progress."

The attackers, whether stumbling over the rubble in the little town of Cassino or trying to scale the heights of the monastery above it, were up against the 1st Parachute Division, an élite German unit with a fine commander, Lieutenant-General Richard Heidrich, and commanding positions. The area was sown with mines, on one of which Major-General Kippenberger, commanding the 2nd New Zealand Division, had both his feet blown off. The defenders, though cruelly decimated, were ably supported by concentrated fire from a regiment of *Nebelwerfers*.

The fighting in the streets of Cassino resembled that in Stalingrad in its ferocity. On the slopes up to the monastery Ghurkas and paratroops fought for a few yards of ground as in the trench warfare of World War I.

On March 23 Freyberg called off his attack, which had already cost him over 2,000 men and had reached none of its objectives.

From January 16 to March 31 the American 5th Army alone suffered casualties amounting to 52,130 killed, wounded and missing (American 22,219, British 22,092, French 7,421, and Italian 398).

This would appear to justify Clausewitz's principle, quoted shortly before by Manstein to Hitler, that defence is the "most powerful form of warfare".

Faced with the setbacks of Anzio and Cassino, Sir Harold Alexander now had to remedy the situation. He did so by bringing the British V Corps directly under his command and allotting to it the Adriatic sector. The British 8th Army, under the command of General Sir Oliver Leese since December 23, was given the sector between the Abruzzi peaks and the Liri valley. The American 5th Army, though still responsible for the Anzio front, was thus restricted to the area between the Liri and the Tyrrhenian Sea. It also had to hand the British X Corps, on the Garigliano, over to the 8th Army.

The decision of the Combined Chiefs-of-Staff Committee not to go on with Operation "Anvil" as the prelude to a landing in Normandy was communicated to General Maitland Wilson on February 26. He was thus able to divert to the 15th Army Group units and *matériel* previously reserved for this operation. On May 11 Alexander had under his command nine corps, of 26 divisions and about ten independent brigades.

His aim was the destruction of the German 10th Army by a double pincer movement: the first would open up the Liri valley to the Allies and the second would begin, once they had passed Frosinone, by VI Corps breaking out of the Anzio beach-head and advancing to meet them.

In the French Expeditionary Corps, which had taken over from the British X Corps in the Garigliano bridgehead, General Juin was not satisfied with the objective assigned to him, Monte Majo. It was the same kind of narrow turning movement "within rifle range" that had led to the Belvedere butchery and the setbacks at Cassino. So on April 4 he set out his ideas on the manoeuvre in a memorandum to General Clark. In his opinion, instead of turning right as soon as Monte Majo had been captured, "they should infiltrate under cover of surprise into the massif dominated by the Petrella and seize the key points . . . and, from there, by an out-flanking movement, open the way to frontal advances mounted concurrently to secure Highway 7 and the road from Esperia up to and including the road running parallel to the front of Arce.

"The aim being to bring to bear on the Arce sector a force of considerable size so as to be able to break out in strength behind the enemy's rear and advance towards Rome."

After a little hesitation Clark was won over to his subordinate's plan. This had the great advantage of including in the French Expeditionary Corps' out-flanking movement the Hitler Line or "Senger defile", which blocked off the Liri valley at Pontecorvo. On the other hand there was a formidable obstacle in the Monti Aurunci, which reached over 5,000 feet at Monte Petrella. It might be assumed that the enemy had not occupied the heights in strength, and that surprise could be achieved by using the natural features as Guderian had done in the Ardennes in May 1940 and List in the Strumitsa gap on April 6, 1941.

However, everything depended on the speed with which an early success could be exploited. As usual, Kesselring would not take long to muster his forces, but General Juin was relying on the legs of his Moroccan mountain troops and of his 4,000 mules.

Though Clark agreed to the French plan, he could not get Sir Oliver Leese to accept its corollary, the Atina plan, and though he used a corps against Cassino where Freyberg had sent in one

division, the pincer was still too short and there were heavy losses.

Kesselring had 23 divisions, but most of them were worn out and short of ammunition, whereas the Allies had an abundance of everything. Here again the Germans were waging "a poor man's war" as General Westphal put it.

Another serious disadvantage for Kesselring was his enemy's overwhelming superiority in the air and at sea. This was so important that it caused him to worry not only about a landing at Civitavecchia or at Leghorn but also about whether Allied air power would cut off XIV Panzer Corps' communications at Frosinone. The uncertainty of his situation compelled Kesselring to write in his memoirs about his main reason for concern at this time: "The great dangerous unknown quantity which lasted until D-day plus 4 was the following: where would the French Expeditionary Corps be engaged, what would be its main line of advance and its composition?"

And so the 10th Army and subordinate staffs were ordered to signal back with maximum urgency to Army Group as

soon as the French had been identified on the front. The Expeditionary Corps had camouflaged itself so well when it moved into position in the foothills of the Monti Aurunci that Kesselring only realised it was there when the Monte Majo action was over. A clever decoy movement by Alexander made him think that the frontal attack would be combined with a landing in the area of Civitavecchia and would start on May 14, and so two German divisions were held north of Rome, and arrived too late for the battle of the Gustav Line.

At zero on D-day the German 10th Army was deployed as follows:

1. from the Tyrrhenian Sea to the Liri: XIV Panzer Corps (94th and 71st Infantry Divisions);
2. from the Liri to the Meta (7,400 feet): LI Mountain Corps (*Gruppe* "Baade", 1st Parachute, 44th Infantry, and 5th *Gebirgsjäger* Divisions);
3. from the Meta to the Adriatic: *Gruppe* "Hauck" (305th and 334th Infantry Divisions, 114th *Jäger* Division); and
4. in army reserve: 15th *Panzergrenadier*

An American machine gun post.

Division behind LI Mountain Corps.

The first encounter was thus to be between the 12 Allied divisions (two Polish, four British, four French, and two American) and six German. The inferiority was not only numerical: at the moment when the attack started both General von Senger und Etterlin, commander of XIV Panzer Corps and Colonel-General von Vietinghoff were on leave, and, in spite of Kesselring's order, 94th Division (Lieutenant-General Steinmetz) had no men on the Petrella massif.

At 2300 hours on May 11, 600 Allied batteries (2,400 guns ranging from 25-pounders to 9.4-inch) opened up simultaneously on a front of some 25 miles. At midnight the Allied infantry moved forward. When dawn broke both General Leese and General Clark had to admit that in spite of the surprise effect the night attack had not brought the expected success. The Polish II Corps (General Wladislas Anders: 3rd "Kressowa" and 5th "Carpathian" Divisions) had failed on the slopes of Monte Cassino and, for all the fighting spirit shown by these men, refugees from Russian jails, their losses were very heavy. In the Liri valley the British XIII Corps (Lieutenant-General Kirkman) had got two of its divisions across the Rapido, but without really denting the resistance put up by LI Mountain Corps (General Feuerstein) and here again 1st Parachute Division was particularly successful.

Though the French Expeditionary Corps had been strengthened by the 4th Moroccan Mountain Division (General Sévez) and the 1st Motorised Infantry Division (General Brosset) its task was not made any easier by the fact that the enemy opposite (71st Division: Lieutenant-General Raapke) was ready and expecting to be attacked. During this night operation, which they were ordered to carry out so as to facilitate the British XIII Corps' crossing of the Rapido, the French stumbled on to minefields and were attacked by flame-throwers. By the end of the day on the 12th it was feared that the French attack might have run out of steam and that Kesselring would have time to occupy the whole of the Petrella massif. Without losing a minute, General Juin reshaped his artillery attack so as to concentrate everything on the Monte Majo bastion. This bold stroke broke the resistance of the German 71st Division and in the afternoon of May 13 the Moroccan 2nd Division raised an immense tricolour on the top of the 3,000-foot hill. On its right the 1st Moroccan Motorised Infantry Division had cleared out the bend in the Garigliano. On its left the 3rd Algerian Division had captured Castelforte and was moving forward towards Ausonia.

Further over to the left the American II Corps was well on its way to Formia. On that day, as Marshal Juin wrote, "having toured the fronts in the lower areas from end to end of the bridgehead where the actions were developed, I was able to see with what ardour and enthusiasm the troops drove forward to their objectives. It is true that the commanders were there in the breach in person: Brosset, driving his own jeep, was giving orders through a loud-hailer and Montsabert was conducting his battle by means of a portable radio which never left his side. There were also other reasons for this feverish excitement. Towards mid-day a message was heard in clear from the enemy ordering his troops to withdraw and the prisoners were flowing in."

Without losing a moment General Juin threw his Mountain Corps into the breach. This now included the 4th Moroccan Mountain Division and General Guillaume's Moroccan *Tabors*. Leaving the beaten tracks, with their machine guns and mortars on their backs, they scaled the steep slopes of Monte Petrella like mountain goats, reaching the top on May 15. Without waiting to get their breath back they then hurled themselves at the Revole massif (4,150 feet). Meanwhile, passing behind the Mountain Corps, the 3rd Algerian Division took Ausonia and reached Esperia, thus extending the action of the 1st Moroccan Motorised Infantry Division which had captured San Giorgio on the right bank of the Liri.

What would have happened if at the same time the British 8th Army, in a sweep as wide as General Juin had wanted, had outflanked the Pontecorvo position? In all evidence XIV Panzer Corps would have faced total disaster, a disaster which would then have overtaken the 10th Army. It was only on May 17 that the Polish II Corps, now attacking again, found the monastery on Monte Cassino deserted. It was again only on May 19 that the British 78th Division (XIII Corps) attacked the "Senger defile" in the Aquino area, but unsuccessfully. This lack of liaison between the French and the British naturally held up the French Expeditionary Corps' exploitation towards Pico and the Monti Ausoni.

But Kesselring, throwing in everything he could lay hands on, sent units of the 90th *Panzergrenadier,* the 305th, and the 26th Panzer Divisions to stop them. He also sent the 29th *Panzergrenadier* Division against the American II Corps, which had advanced through Formia and Itri and by May 22 was threatening Terracina. This was trying to pay Paul by robbing Peter, that is to say Colonel-General von Mackensen. Reinforced to the equivalent of eight divisions by the transfer of the American 36th Division to the Anzio bridgehead, the American VI Corps had no particular difficulty in breaking the resistance of the German 14th Army during the day of May 23. Forty-eight hours later II and VI Corps met on the shores of Lake Fogliano. On the same May 23 the French Expeditionary Corps was spreading out over the Monti Ausoni whilst the Canadian I Corps (Lieutenant-General E. L. M. Burns: 1st Infantry and 5th Armoured Divisions), which had just relieved the British XIII Corps, was forcing its way through the Pontecorvo defile.

Kesselring tried once more to protect Rome by establishing a new position on the line Colli Laziali–Monti Lepini to secure Vietinghoff's right, and to achieve this he withdrew from the Leghorn area his last reserve motorised division, the "Hermann Göring" Panzer Division, and sent it immediately to Valmontone. The bombing by the Anglo-American air force, which on one single day (May 26) destroyed 665 vehicles of the 14th Army alone, considerably held up these troop movements. Now Valmontone was, in accordance with General Alexander's instructions, precisely the objective of the American VI Corps. If Truscott, now in Cisterna, therefore advanced with the main body of his forces along the Corti–Artena axis, he had every chance of cutting off the 10th Army's move to cover Rome. The latter's rearguard was still at Ceprano, some 40 miles or more from Valmontone, and the Germans would thus be driven back against the Abruzzi mountains, which were virtually impassable, and entirely cut off.

But, for reasons which Alexander said were inexplicable, Clark ordered VI Corps to attack with its 34th, 45th Infantry, and 1st Armoured Divisions north west to the line Velletri–Colli Laziali, sending only a slightly reinforced 3rd Division along the Valmontone axis (northwards). This decision, taken in the afternoon of May 25, brought only a slight reaction from Alexander, who remarked to General Gruenther, the American 5th Army chief-of-staff, when the latter brought him the news: "I am sure that the army commander will continue to push toward Valmontone, won't he?"

"Rome the great prize" was the title General Mark Clark gave to the 15th chapter of his memoirs. We are thus forced to conclude that this able but impetuous man had lost sight of the fact that a commander's supreme reward is to receive in his tent those who have been sent on behalf of the enemy commander to sue for conditions of surrender. But Alexander was also taken in by the Roman mirage at this time: did he not forbid the French Expeditionary Corps, then coming down from the Monti Lepini, to use the Frosinone–Rome highway, which he intended to restrict to the British 8th Army?

Oddly enough, back in London, Churchill tried to put Alexander on his guard against the attractions of this prestige objective. On May 28 he wrote to him: "at this distance it seems much more important to cut their line of retreat than anything else. I am sure you will have carefully considered moving more armour by the Appian Way up to the northernmost spearhead directed against the Valmontone-Frosinone road.

A cop is much more important than Rome which would anyhow come as its consequence. The cop is the one thing that matters." Two days later he came back to the point: "But I should feel myself wanting in comradeship if I did not let you know that the glory of this battle, already great, will be measured, not by the capture of Rome or the juncture with the bridgehead, but by the number of German divisions cut off. I am sure you will have revolved all this in your mind, and perhaps you have already acted in this way. Nevertheless I feel I ought to tell you that it is the cop that counts."

These were words of wisdom indeed, but in Italy the die was cast in the shape of the objective given to the American VI Corps. On May 31 its 36th Division found a gap in the German 14th Army defences, turned the Velletri position and scaled the Colli Laziali. Furious at this setback, Kesselring recalled Mackensen and replaced him by General Lemelsen. He now had to order the evacuation of Rome, which he proclaimed an "open city". On June 4 the American 88th Division (Major-General J. E. Sloan) was the first unit to enter the Eternal City.

General Clark tells a story worthy of inclusion in any history of the campaign. Writing of his first visit to Rome he says:

"Many Romans seemed to be on the verge of hysteria in their enthusiasm for the American troops. The Americans were enthusiastic too, and kept looking for ancient landmarks that they had read about in their history books. It was on that day that a doughboy made the classic remark of the Italian campaign when he took a long look at the ruins of the old Colosseum, whistled softly, and said, 'Geez, I didn't know our bombers had done *that* much damage in Rome!'"

On May 11 Kesselring had 23 divisions. These had been reduced to remnants. The 44th, 71st, 94th, 362nd, and 715th had been virtually wiped out. His Panzer and *Panzergrenadier* divisions had lost most of their equipment. Amongst the reinforcements which Hitler had sent through the Brenner there were badly trained divisions such as the 162nd, recruited from Turkman contingents, the Luftwaffe 20th Infantry Division, and the 16th *Panzergrenadier* Division of the *Waffen* S.S. These went to pieces at the first onslaught.

During the same period the Americans lost 18,000 killed, missing, and wounded, the British 10,500, the French 7,260, the Canadians 3,742, and the Poles 3,700. Some 25,000 Allied prisoners were taken.

These losses were not enough to hold up the 15th Army Group's advance. Also, in North Africa the 9th Colonial Infantry Division and the 1st and 5th French Armoured Divisions were now ready for combat. It is clear that a bold action along the Rome–Terni–Ancona axis could have brought to an end all enemy resistance south of the Apennines.

On June 7, three days after the fall of Rome, Alexander reported that not even the Alps could daunt his army. He struck a chord in Churchill's mind for the Prime Minister now saw a chance of reaching Yugoslavia or even Vienna (across the so-called Ljubljana gap) before the Russians, whose political ambitions he was beginning to fear. Additionally Churchill had always favoured an invasion of German-occupied Europe from the south, through the Mediterranean.

However, not even the British Chiefs-of-Staff believed that an advance to the Alps and beyond that year was practical, while President Roosevelt and the American Chiefs-of-Staff remained adamant that Operation "Dragoon", (formerly "Anvil"), the landing in the south of France, must, as formally agreed, now take precedence over any other operations in the Mediterranean theatre now that "Overlord" was so close, and all efforts had to be concentrated.

Marshall, it would appear, was merely obeying the dictates of high strategy. It was clear to him, in effect, that an Anglo-American drive towards Vienna, and out of line with the main thrust, would contribute less to the success of Operation "Overlord" than would a landing in Provence, which would open up the ports of Marseilles and Toulon to Allied men and *matériel*, whilst a strong Franco-American force, operating first up the Rhône, then the Saône, would give a right wing to Eisenhower when he broke out into Champagne. To him this reasoning respected the principle of the convergence of effort, so dear to American military doctrine. It can easily be seen how Marshall froze at Churchill's passionate arguments.

In any case, it is highly doubtful on military grounds whether an advance

to the Alps or into Yugoslavia in 1944 was practicable, even if Alexanders' armies had not been weakened for the sake of "Dragoon". The German commanders had proved themselves masters of defensive warfare in mountain regions, and they were to continue giving the Allies immense problems even when operating with minimal resources and under pressure from all sides.

Although Roosevelt could not accept his colleague's views, he was nevertheless unable to bring nearer by even a single day because of questions of transport, men, and *matériel*, the start of Operation "Anvil" scheduled for August 15. Between June 11 and July 22, three American and five French divisions successively dropped out and became inactive, though the 9th Colonial Division did take Elba between July 17 and 19 in Operation "Brassard", led by General de Lattre de Tassigny. This Allied inactivity allowed Kesselring, who lost no chances, to re-establish himself in the Apennines and especially to give Field-Marshal von Rundstedt his 3rd and 15th *Panzergrenadier* Divisions, whilst the "Hermann Göring" Panzer Division was sent off to the Eastern Front.

As for the case for getting to the Danube basin before the Russians, Marshall was not qualified to follow the Prime Minister in this field, which was reserved for politicians. It will be noticed that less than a year later General Eisenhower adopted the same attitude when, having reached the Elbe, he showed little further interest in Berlin which, from the strictly military point of view, was no longer of any importance.

The Italian Co-Belligerent Forces, newly supplied with British equipment, parade near the Coliseum in June 1944.

CHAPTER 56
German defences in the West

Though so much time has elapsed since they occurred, there is no difficulty in reconstructing the logical succession of events which in less than 11 months – from June 1944 – would take the Western Allies from the Normandy beaches to the heart of the Third Reich.

On March 20, 1944, Adolf Hitler delivered an appreciation of the situation to the commanders-in-chief of his land, sea, and air forces in the Western theatre of operations. By and large, he was less pessimistic with regard to the immediate future than most of his generals, and the arguments he advanced were not without relevance. As he considered the threat assembling on the other side of the Channel, he no doubt remembered his own hesitation in autumn 1940 and the arguments he had put to Mussolini and Count Ciano in January 1941 to excuse his procrastination over "Seelöwe":

"We are," he had told them, "in the position of a man with only one cartridge in his rifle. If he misses the target, the situation becomes critical. If the landing fails, we cannot begin again because we would have lost too much *matériel* and the enemy could bring the bulk of his forces into whichever zone he wanted. But so long as the attack has not come, he must always take into account that it may."

And so, according to Rommel, he declared to his generals, whom he summoned that day to the Berghof:

"It is evident that an Anglo-American landing in the West will and must come. How and where it will come no one knows. Equally, no kind of speculation on the subject is possible ... The enemy's entire landing operation must under no circumstances be allowed to last longer than a matter of hours or, at the most, days, with the Dieppe attempt as a model. Once the landing has been defeated it will under no circumstances be repeated by the enemy. Quite apart from the heavy casualties he would suffer, months would be needed to prepare for a renewed attempt. Nor is this the only factor which would deter the Anglo-Americans from trying again. There would also be the crushing blow to their morale which a miscarried invasion would inflict. It would, for one thing, prevent the re-election of Roosevelt in America and with luck he would finish up somewhere in jail. In England, too, war-weariness would assert itself even more greatly than hitherto and Churchill, in view of his age and his illness, and with his influence now on the wane, would no longer be in a position to carry through a new landing operation. We could counter the numerical strength of the enemy – about 50 to 60 divisions – within a very short time, by forces of equal strength. The destruction of the enemy's landing attempt means more than a purely local decision on the Western front. It is the sole decisive factor in the whole conduct of the war and hence in its final result."

And so Hitler made the final issue of the conflict depend on the check that his enemies would receive during the first hours of the landing on the coasts of France. Hitler's vision was clear. There can be no doubt that a defeat of the nature of the one suffered by the 2nd Canadian Division at Dieppe, but five times as great, would have struck a terrible blow at the morale of the British and Americans. Nor can there be any doubt that long months, perhaps even a year, would have passed before the Allies could launch another attack.

By that time, O.K.H. would have received the necessary means from the West to stabilise the situation between the Black Sea and the Gulf of Finland, while the Luftwaffe and the Kriegsmarine would have once more challenged the British and Americans by bringing new arms of terrifying efficiency into use.

1. V-1 and V-2
It is, in fact, well known that the strides forward taken by German science in the field of jet propulsion could have taken a heavy toll of the British and American bomber squadrons if they had been applied with priority to fighter interception. In addition to (and in spite of) the delays caused by the bombing of Peenemünde on the night of the August 17–18, 1943, the Wehrmacht was still getting ready for its new attack on London with the help of its V-1 flying bomb and V-2 rocket. The former, flying at a maximum speed of 410 mph, was still within the capacity of fighter defence and anti-aircraft fire, but not so the V-2. This was a real missile in the sense in which we now use the word. It plunged on to its target at a speed close to 2,350 mph and was un-

stoppable. These missiles, carrying nearly a ton of explosive, had a range of between 190 and 250 miles. The V-1 was technically simple and could be mass-produced, unlike the V-2 which was more complex and suffered considerable teething troubles.

2. The 'Schnorkel'
At the time when Hitler was expressing the opinions just quoted, U-boats fitted with the *Schnorkel* (or more properly *Schnorchel*) device were first appearing in the Atlantic. This device had been invented in the Netherlands, and consisted of a retractable pipe through which, so long as it stayed at a depth of 20 to 25 feet under water, a U-boat could run its diesels and vent its exhaust. The U-boats could also recharge their batteries without surfacing for weeks on end.

It has been calculated that from summer 1944 the *Schnorkel* had become so common that the success rate of Allied destroyers in their battle against the submarines had fallen by half. But there is a bad side to everything and, some 15 years ago, Admiral Barjot wrote in this connection:

"On the other hand, the *Schnorkel* slowed down their strategic speed. From a surface speed of 17 knots (20 mph) the *Schnorkel*-equipped submarines found their rate reduced to six knots (6 or 7 mph). The unavoidable delays in reaching their targets were doubled or even tripled."

The consequences he drew can be illustrated by the following: of the 120 operational boats, 39 were in port and 81 at sea. Of the last, 64 were in transit and only 17 actually in their operational sectors.

"So," Barjot concludes, "in April 1942,

An MG-34 team in training on the Channel beaches.

though the number of operational submarines was similar, only 23 per cent of them were in transit, whereas after the *Schnorkel* had been fitted, half of the U-boats were in transit."

Therefore at best the *Schnorkel* was only a palliative for the problems faced by Dönitz, and there was even another disadvantage: it appeared on the screens of the new British and American radar sets operating on centrimetric wavelengths.

3. The Type XXI . . .

On the other hand, if the Type XXI and XXVI U-boats had come into service earlier, they might have been able to change the course of the submarine war.

The Type XXI U-boat, beautifully designed, was driven under water by two electric engines with a total of 500 horsepower. These enabled it to travel for an hour and a half at the up till then unheard of speed of 18 knots (21 mph) or for ten hours at a speed of between 12 and 14 knots (14 or 16 mph). It could, therefore, hunt convoys while submerged and then easily avoid the attack of the convoy escort. Furthermore, it was remarkably silent and could dive to a depth of more than 675 feet, an advantage not to be scorned in view of the limitations of the listening devices used by its enemies.

Dönitz intended to use prefabricated methods of production and thus hoped to see the new U-boats come off the slipways at a rate of 33 per month from autumn 1944 onwards. The parts would be assembled in three yards, in concrete shelters. But he had failed to take into account the destruction of the German railway system under the hammer blows of British and American strategic bombing, and so the pieces which had been prefabricated in the heart of the country reached the assembly shops at very irregular intervals.

And, in fact, of this class of ship, only *U-2511* (Lieutenant-Commander A. Schnee) actually went to sea on service. This was on April 30, 1945.

4. . . . and XXVI U-boats

The Type XXVI U-boat was driven, both on the surface and underwater, by a Walter turbine which used hydrogen peroxide and could reach, even while submerged, speeds of 24 knots (28 mph), that is four times the best performance claimed for its British or American rivals.

But neither type was operational by the time Germany capitulated. The fact is, however, that after the war, the Type XXVI U-boat was copied by all the navies of the world, and has sailed in particular under the Soviet flag, which calls to mind, inevitably, that imitation is the sincerest form of flattery.

Evidently then, the Führer had quite a number of good cards up his sleeve, but only – as he himself admitted – provided that his Western enemies could be wiped out on the beaches on the very day they landed, for the Wehrmacht could no longer fight a long holding battle between the rivers Orne and Vire. The situation

German coastal artillery, part of the Atlantic Wall.

demanded unquestionably that victory in the West should be swift, so that the victors could be sent with the minimum delay to the Eastern Front.

But the least that can be said is that in the west, considered so decisive by Hitler, the German high command was as badly organised as it could possibly be, perhaps by virtue of the principle "divide and rule".

On the other side of the English Channel, General Eisenhower had absolute control not only over the land forces in his theatre of operations, but also over the naval forces under Admiral Sir Bertram Ramsay and over the Tactical Air Forces commanded by Air Chief Marshal Sir Trafford Leigh-Mallory. He also retained overall command of Lieutenant-General Carl A. Spaatz's Strategic Air Force. The situation was quite different at Saint-Germain-en-Laye, headquarters of the Commander-in-Chief West or O.B.W. *(Oberbefehlshaber West)* and at

la Roche-Guyon, headquarters of Army Group "B".

The O.B.W., Field-Marshal von Rundstet, was not entitled to give orders to Admiral Krancke, who commanded German naval forces in the West, to Field-Marshal Sperrle, head of *Luftflotte* III, or General Pickert, who commanded III Anti-Aircraft Corps. Krancke came directly under the command of Grand-Admiral Dönitz, and the two others were responsible to *Reichsmarschall* Göring. Of course Krancke had only a small number of light ships and Sperrle found his forces reduced by June 6 to 419 aircraft, of which just 200 were operational. Nevertheless, considering that the aim was to destroy the enemy on the beaches, the lack of co-ordination between the three arms was to have catastrophic consequences for Germany.

In regard to the Navy it should be said that though Rommel, commanding Army Group "B", had a judiciously chosen naval attaché on his staff in the person of Vice-Admiral Ruge, he still could not manage to make Krancke lay down a sufficiently thick minefield in the estuary of the Seine. Yet the Germans possessed a mine triggered by the pressure wave of a ship passing over it, and this could have proved a devastating weapon.

In addition to these already considerable failings, naval gunners and army men could not reach agreement on the question of coastal batteries, their location, and the fire control methods to be used. The ex-Commander-in-Chief in Norway, Colonel-General von Falkenhorst, later expressed his thoughts in terms which were rather critical of his naval colleagues, when he wrote:

"When I look back, I can see that responsibilities were badly apportioned, and that this brought several mistakes in its train. The results were severe overwork, difficulties, and conflict. Army artillery officers had received a totally different training from the naval gunners, a training which had developed under very different sets of circumstances. Moreover, the ideas of the older senior officers—the generals and the admirals—on the problems often differed greatly. The locations of covered or uncovered batteries, camouflage, the setting of obstacles, etc, were in general fields which were entirely new to the naval gunners, since these problems never arose on board their ships, and, consequently, did not appear in their training schedules. They used naval guns as they had been installed by the engineers and could not or would not change anything at all. The result of this was that, all along the coast, batteries were set in the open, near the beaches, so that they were at the mercy of the direct fire of every enemy landing ship but could not effectively contribute to the defence of the coast. There followed several most unhappy conflicts between generals and admirals."

Falkenhorst, who had installed 34 coastal defence batteries covering the approaches to Bergen, would seem competent to level these criticisms. Some of these guns, between Narvik and Harstad, were of 16-inch calibre. It is nonetheless true that the naval gunners also had some right on their side, because the army gunners thought they could hit moving targets like ships by using indirect fire methods.

The deployment of anti-aircraft forces also created new tension between the arms. This time the disagreement arose between the commanders of the land and air forces, under whose joint command the anti-aircraft defences came. Rommel knew, better than anyone else, how efficient the 8.8-cm anti-aircraft gun could be when used as an anti-tank gun, and he would have liked to place a large number of such batteries between the Orne and the Vire. But Göring was obstinately opposed to any such redeployment and Rommel had to resign himself to not having his own way.

This tension lasted after the Allied landing, and brought these bitter words from Colonel-General Sepp Dietrich of the *Waffen*-S.S., commander of the 5th *Panzerarmee*:

"I constantly ordered these guns to stay forward and act in an anti-tank rôle against Allied armour. My orders were just as often countermanded by Pickert, who moved them back into the rear areas to protect administrative sites. I asked time and time again that these guns be put under my command, but I was always told by the High Command that it was impossible."

On the other hand, Major-General Plocher, chief-of-staff of *Luftflotte* III at the time, has taken up the cudgels for Pickert:

"We had insisted on these guns being controlled by Luftwaffe officers because the army did not know how to handle such equipment. There was always a great deal of argument about who was to deploy the 88's but Field-Marshal von Rundstedt finally allowed us to chose our own localities." He adds, with a sting in the tail: "This was necessary in order to prevent the army from squandering both men and equipment. We used to say that the German infantryman would always fight until the last anti-aircraft man."

The least that can be said of these incoherent remarks is that, though Rommel and Rundstedt had received orders to wipe out the Allied landings in the shortest time possible, they were refused part of the means necessary to carry out their orders.

On D-Day, Rundstedt, as Commander-in-Chief in the West, had the following under his command: two army groups ("B" and "G"), comprising four armies (7th, 15th, 1st, and 19th). These in turn had 15 corps between them, totalling 40 infantry, four parachute, four Luftwaffe field, nine Panzer, and one *Panzergrenadier* divisions.

However, for all this it is by no means true that Rundstedt exercised over this force the authority normally given to a commander-in-chief. In the first place, the Luftwaffe units (one corps, eight divisions) were only under his tactical command; the same was true of his four *Waffen*-S.S. divisions and the I S.S. Panzer Corps. He had no authority over these units in the questions of training, promotions, the appointment of commanders or in the field of discipline. That is what Hitler cruelly reminded Rommel, who had requested that action be taken against the 2nd "Das Reich" Panzer Division of the *Waffen*-S.S., after the appalling massacre at Oradour-sur-Glâne.

Even more, O.B.W. had had it made quite clear that it could not, without the Führer's permission, move two of its best armoured divisions, the 12th "Hitlerjugend" *Waffen*-S.S. Panzer Division, stationed near Lisieux, and the 130th Panzer-"Lehr" Division, formed the previous winter from Panzer instructors and now stationed around Châteaudun. Moreover, O.K.W. did not cease interfering in Rundstedt's sphere of command, as the latter explained bitterly to the British officers who questioned him after his capture:

"I did not have my way. As Commander-in-Chief in the West my only authority was to change the guards in front of my gate."

As will be seen later, everything confirms the truth of this account. Therefore it appears that Hitler did not appreciate the complete incompatibility between despotic, arrogant, and meddling authority, and the need to make rapid decisions, the vital importance of which he soon came to recognise.

A major part of the success of the landings can be explained by the inefficiency of the German Intelligence services. Here the Nazis Kaltenbrunner and Schellenberg, who had ousted the professionals Canaris and Oster, could neither get a clear idea of the British and American plans nor escape being deceived by the Allies' diversionary manoeuvres. Therefore hypotheses were the order of the day at O.K.W. as well as Saint-Germain-en-Laye, headquarters of Western Command (O.B.W.) and la Roche-Guyon, headquarters of Army Group "B".

Hitler had given a long analysis on the situation on March 20. Though he recognised that there was no way of being sure in which area the Allies would land, over the whole coastline from Norway to Greece, he nevertheless made his point:

"At no place along our long front is a landing impossible, except perhaps where the coast is broken by cliffs. The most suitable and hence the most threatened areas are the two west coast peninsulas, Cherbourg and Brest, which are very tempting and offer the best possibilities for the formation of a bridgehead, which would then be enlarged systematically by the use of air forces and heavy weapons of all kinds."

This hypothesis was perfectly logical and the order of battle of the German 7th Army (Colonel-General Dollmann), was correctly arranged to face this possibility. Of its 14 divisions, 12 were deployed between the Rivers Vire and Loire.

Rundstedt did not share Hitler's opinion, and considered that there were a great many more advantages from the Allied point of view in crossing the Channel for a landing in the Pas-de-Calais. Later, in 1945, he supported his views by using these arguments, according to Milton Shulman:

"In the first place an attack from Dover against Calais would be using the shortest sea route to the Continent. Secondly, the V-1 and V-2 sites were located in this area. Thirdly this was the shortest route to the Ruhr and the heart of industrial Germany, and once a successful landing had been made it would take only four days to reach the Rhine. Fourthly, such an operation would sever the forces in Northern France from those along the Mediterranean coast. Against the Pas-de-Calais being chosen was the fact that this area had the strongest coastal defences, and was the only part of the

Atlantic Wall that even remotely lived up to its reputation. I always used to tell my staff that if I was Montgomery I would attack the Pas-de-Calais."

But this would have meant coming up against the strongest part of the Atlantic Wall, whose concrete-housed batteries on either side of Cape Gris-Nez kept the English coast between Ramsgate and Dungeness under the fire of their 14 11-, 12-, 15-, and 16-inch guns; also Colonel-General von Salmuth's 15th Army was well deployed in the area, with 18 divisions between Antwerp and Cabourg. These troops were of good quality, and so it would seem that at O.K.W. Field-Marshal Keitel and Generals Jodl and Warlimont expected a landing between the mouths of the Rivers Somme and Seine, outside the range of the heavy artillery mentioned above but still within the 15th Army's sector.

Rommel commanded Army Group "B", which included the 7th and 15th Armies and LXXXVIII Corps, with three divisions for the defence of Holland. His main worry was the weakness of the defences on the beaches of the bay of the Seine, where three divisions were thinly stretched between Cabourg (exclusive) and the port of Cherbourg. More important, this weakness was not compensated for by the density or heavy calibre of the coastal artillery. Actually, on the 125-mile front between Le Havre and Cape Barfleur, the Swedish coastal artillery expert Colonel Stjernfelt has identified only 18 batteries, 12 of which could not reach the Calvados beaches or did not fire at all on D-Day.

Another concern of Rommel's was what form he should give to this defensive battle for which he was responsible and which might begin any day. But on this question, his point of view was almost exactly the same as the Führer's, detailed above.

In his opinion, a sea-borne landing differs from a ground attack essentially in that the latter has its maximum force on the first day of the offensive. It then decreases in momentum because of the losses that are suffered and logistic difficulties. This allows the defending army to put off its counter-attack. On the other hand, the enemy who comes from the sea will be weak at the moment of landing, but will become steadily stronger within his bridgehead, so that any delay at all in the counter-attack will reduce in like proportion its chance of success.

The Panzers were indubitably the best means of counter-attack, and so the sensible thing was to deploy them in such a manner that they could be hurled against the enemy wherever he might appear (Low Countries, Pas-de-Calais, Normandy, or Brittany) on the actual day of the landing. This is what Rommel explained in a letter to Jodl on April 23, 1944:

"If, in spite of the enemy's air superiority, we succeed in getting a large part of our mobile force into action in the

threatened coast defence sectors in the first few hours, I am convinced that the enemy attack on the coast will collapse completely on its first day."

But he added: "My only real anxiety concerns the mobile forces. Contrary to what was decided at the conference on the 21st March, they have so far not been placed under my command. Some of them are dispersed over a large area inland, which means they will arrive too late to play any part in the battle for the coast. With the heavy enemy air superiority we can expect, any large-scale movement of motorised forces to the coast will be exposed to air attacks of tremendous weight and long duration. But without rapid assistance from the armoured divisions and mobile units, our coast divisions will be hard put to it to counter attacks coming simultaneously from the sea and from airborne troops inland. Their land front is too thinly held for that. The dispositions of both combat and reserve forces should be such as to ensure that the minimum possible movement will be required to counter an attack at any of most likely points . . . and to ensure that the greater part of the enemy troops, sea and airborne, will be destroyed by our fire during their approach."

This led him to conclude: "The most decisive battle of the war, and the fate of the German people itself, is at stake. Failing a tight command in one single hand of all the forces available for defence, failing the early engagement of all our mobile forces in the battle for the coast, victory will be in grave doubt. If I am to wait until the enemy landing has actually taken place, before I can demand, through normal channels, the command and dispatch of the mobile forces, delays will be inevitable. This will mean that

German A.A. gunners in training. The employment of A.A. guns and their crews caused considerable rancour in O.B.W., as the Army wanted them as anti-tank weapons.

they will probably arrive too late to intervene successfully in the battle for the coast and prevent the enemy landing. A second Nettuno, a highly undesirable situation for us, could result . . ."

And, in fact, after the conference of March 20, Rommel had received from the Führer the right to have *Panzergruppe "West"* put immediately under his direct command. This force, under General Geyr von Schweppenburg, constituted Rundstedt's armoured reserve and, on D-Day, consisted of:

1. I *Waffen* S.S. Panzer Corps;
2. 1st *"Leibstandarte Adolf Hitler"* S.S. Panzer Division (at Beverloo, 45 miles east of Antwerp);
3. 2nd Panzer Division (at Amiens);
4. 116th Panzer Division (in the Gisors–Beauvais region);
5. 12th *"Hitlerjugend"* S.S. Panzer Division (in the Evreux–Lisieux region);
6. 130th Panzer-*"Lehr"* Division (near Châteaudun); and
7. 21st Panzer Division (at Saint-Pierre-sur-Dives, 20 miles south-east of Caen).

But no order had come from O.K.W. to give executive force to Hitler's concession. And so Schweppenburg refused the rôle which Rommel allotted to him. His view was that the Western Front's armoured reserve should be concentrated in a central position downstream from Paris, so that it could intervene with all its strength in that sector where it looked as if the enemy was about to make his main push, after all tricks and feinting movements had been discounted. From this point of view, the way that Army Group "B" at la Roche-Guyon wanted to distribute the Panzers seemed to fit the verdict that Frederick the Great had proclaimed against all systems of wide-stretched defence: *"Wer alles defendieren will, defendiert gar nichts"* (He who tries to defend everything, defends nothing).

Rundstedt, and also Colonel-General Guderian, agreed with this point of view, which could clearly be defended on the principles of war. But were they applicable in those circumstances? Rommel denied that they were and cited as an example, as has been seen, his North African experience. His opponents had not had this experience as they had all come from the Eastern Front, where the enemy's tactical air force was only just beginning to show its power to paralyse ground movement. Events showed that his reasoning was without doubt the more pertinent. However that may be and in spite of his attempt on April 23, Rommel received no satisfaction on this vital point. Better–or worse still–depending on one's point of view, the Führer was equally negative when Rommel suggested that he should advance the Panzer-*"Lehr"* Division to between the Orne and the Vire, deploy the *"Hitler-jugend"* Division in the region of Saint-Lô, and reinforce this sector, which seemed dangerously weak to Rommel, by a brigade of *Nebelwerfers* (976 15-, 21-, and 30-cm barrels) and a large number of heavy (8.8-cm) anti-aircraft batteries. Faced with silence from Hitler, Rommel left la Roche-Guyon at dawn on June 4 for Berchtesgaden, not without having consulted his barometer and obtained Rundstedt's leave.

In spite of the documents published since 1945, Hitler's attitude when faced with the problems of the German high command remains incomprehensible, for it abounds in contradictions. The facts speak for themselves.

Though he did not believe the forecasts of his subordinates at O.K.W. and of Rundstedt, all of whom envisaged the British and the Americans approaching the French coast between Le Havre and the Pas-de-Calais, he accepted their forecast the day after the Allies landed in the bay of the Seine and stuck to it obstinately until a decisive hole was punched in the German line on the left bank of the Vire by the 1st American Army. In fact he was convinced, up to July 24, that the only purpose of the Battle of Normandy was to trick him into lowering his guard in the Pas-de-Calais. Here he too was deceived by the Allied cover plan, which continued to give the impression that there were powerful forces in south-east England about to attack directly across the Channel in the Pas-de-Calais.

Furthermore, though his hypothesis of March 20, concerning the first objec-

A German soldier on guard by a 16-inch coastal gun.

tives of the Allied attack, only partially coincided with Rommel's views, in other respects there was perfect agreement between the two men concerning the way to repel it: an immediate counter-attack on the beaches so as to avoid a long battle of attrition, like the one the armies had fought at Anzio–Nettuno.

But here there came a further contradiction. If, for perfectly valid reasons, the Führer rejected the plans of deployment put forward by Geyr von Schweppenburg, he nevertheless refused Rommel

the means to fight the battle according to the plans on which he had been in entire agreement with him. Though it is a risky business to try to rewrite history, it will be noted that if Hitler had drawn all the conclusions from the principles he had enunciated, and had agreed with the suggestions of his distinguished general, the following would have happened:

1. Rommel would have been at his headquarters at la Roche-Guyon on June 6, and would have been alerted by British and American parachute drops,

slightly after 0130 hours, while in the event he only knew of them five hours later while still at his private house in Herrlingen near Ulm.

2. The counter-attack launched in the afternoon of June 6 by just the 21st Panzer Division in only the British sector, could have been executed by the Panzer-*"Lehr"* Division and the 12th *"Hitlerjugend"* S.S. Panzer Division. From the positions which Rommel wanted them to occupy, they could have simultaneously attacked the bridgeheads that the Americans were establishing. By reinforcing these two with 400 or 450 tanks and assault guns, the first would almost certainly have wiped out "Omaha" Beach before nightfall and the second was well-placed to attack the poorly placed parachute units around Saint Mère-Eglise.

True enough, if this had in fact happened, the Panzer-*"Lehr"* would have found itself under the fire of the Allied naval forces, and the precedents of Gela and Salerno showed how redoubtable and efficient their heavy shells were against tanks. This argument had been used by Geyr von Schweppenburg during the stormy arguments he had had with Rommel about the distribution of armoured divisions. But though this was a real danger, does it follow that they should have abstained from any attack at all on D-Day and that they should not have taken advantage of the fleeting moment when the enemy had not yet consolidated his bridgeheads?

CHAPTER 57
The Allies prepare for D-Day

Let us cross the Channel and watch the preparations for "Overlord" from London. S.H.A.E.F. (Supreme Headquarters Allied Expeditionary Forces) had been set up under the initiative and the control of the Combined Chiefs-of-Staff Committee. In fact, it did not function with absolute smoothness but it should be noted that, with a few exceptions, the disagreements were not manifest during the preparation period. And up to mid-July 1944, Generals Eisenhower and Montgomery did really work shoulder to shoulder, though the functions that Montgomery took on himself did lead to some misunderstanding and were not understood in the same way by both men.

Writing to General Marshall on this matter on December 23, 1943, Eisenhower expressed his views as follows:

"In the early stages of OVERLORD I see no necessity for British and American Army Group Commanders. In fact, any such setup would be destructive of the essential co-ordination between Ground and Air Forces."

Consequently, he entrusted Montgomery with the command of British and American land forces taking part in the landing itself and in later operations designed to consolidate and then extend the bridgeheads. Therefore Montgomery would have the responsibility of preparing and leading to its conclusion the offensive which would seal the fate of the German armies engaged in Normandy.

But later, when the Allies were out of Normandy, the victory would be exploited and this would take the Grand Alliance right to the very heart of Germany. This would be preceded by the establishment of two army groups, one Anglo-Canadian and the other American.

Montgomery would assume command of the first and Bradley was called upon to lead the second. Eisenhower would once more take over the command of land operations and remain C.-in-C.

Nothing, in the documents we have, indicates that Eisenhower left Montgomery under any misconception about his intention of taking over the reins from him again, but everything goes to suggest that, in his heart of hearts, Montgomery had flattered himself that his superior would change his mind in view of the successes that he (Montgomery) would win for him, and that, until the final victory, Eisenhower would leave him as commander of land forces which he had entrusted to him for the first stages of "Overlord". But even if Eisenhower had resigned himself to playing the rôle of a figurehead, his powerful American subordinates would not have put up with it, nor would his superior General George C. Marshall, and much less still American public opinion, which was influenced by a swarm of war correspondents accredited to S.H.A.E.F. The least that can be said about them is that

they were not very responsive to their British ally's point of view or methods.

But furthermore, and perhaps this is the most important point, it must be noted that, rightly or wrongly, General Eisenhower's talents did not greatly impress Montgomery. The latter had a real superiority complex in matters of strategy towards his chief. But Montgomery was not the only general in the British hierarchy who felt like this in regard to the American supreme commander. On May 15, 1944, leaving a conference during which Eisenhower, together with his subordinates, had explained his operational plans in the presence of George VI, the Prime Minister, and Field-Marshal Smuts, Brooke noted in his diary:

"The main impression I gathered was that Eisenhower was no real director of thought, plans, energy or direction. Just a co-ordinator, a good mixer, a champion of inter-Allied co-operation, and in those respects few can hold the candle to him. But is that enough? Or can we not find all qualities of a commander in one man? May be I am getting too hard to please, but I doubt it."

Re-reading his notes two years later, Lord Alanbrooke changes this portrait only in tone. This is how he depicts him:

"A past-master in the handling of allies, entirely impartial and consequently trusted by all. A charming personality and good co-ordinator. But no real commander . . . Ike might have been a showman calling on various actors to perform their various turns, but he was not the commander of the show who controlled and directed all the actors."

Unlike Brooke, Montgomery, MacArthur, and Patton, Eisenhower had not taken part in World War I and the highest command he had ever had in the interwar years had been that of an infantry battalion. So, though he was completely at home with all aspects of staff work, he did not possess the tactical imagination which characterised to a rare degree men such as Bradley and Montgomery. Certainly, though, he had a remarkable aptitude for assimilating the ideas of others and fitting them into the more general picture of his own sphere of responsibility.

In addition, there is much to admire in the calm authority, the tact, and the psychological deftness of a man who could get on with a subordinate as difficult as Montgomery, who, when asked, "But don't you ever obey orders?" could reply: "If I don't like them I'll go as far as I can in disobedience and try to bluff my way through. But, of course, if I can't get what I want, then I must submit in the end."

Likewise, Eisenhower managed to soften the verbal brutality of the brilliant but at times unbearable George S. Patton, at the same time as he promoted above his

head the "serious, zealous and very cultivated" Omar N. Bradley, who had been Patton's subordinate in Sicily, without the least tension between these two soldiers of such great difference in temperament and method. The respect he had for them did not, nevertheless, prevent him from turning a deaf ear when some depreciatory remark about their British allies passed their lips.

It has been said that Eisenhower did not impose his will. It would be more accurate to say that he did not impose himself often, but that he did so whenever the situation demanded his personal intervention, and then always very decisively. Two examples will suffice to justify this point of view.

One week before the launching of "Overlord", Air Chief-Marshal Leigh-Mallory, commanding the tactical air forces, came for the last time to protest that a useless massacre awaited the American 82nd and 101st Airborne Divisions if the command insisted on landing them in the Cotentin peninsula. According to him, losses of glider-borne troops would amount to 70 per cent and half the paratroops would be killed or wounded in the drop. As Eisenhower himself later recorded: "I instructed the air commander to put his recommendations in a letter and informed him he would have my answer within a few hours."

After the few hours had passed, Eisenhower telephoned Leigh-Mallory. As the "Utah" Beach landing could not be abandoned, he was sticking to his decision, but he did not omit to tell Leigh-Mallory that his orders would be confirmed in writing. As it turned out, Leigh-Mallory's fears were to prove unfounded by events. On December 19, 1944, with the Panzers advancing on Bastogne in the Ardennes, Eisenhower demonstrated the same characteristic *sang-froid* of a great leader. He had gone to Verdun, where he was awaited by Generals Bradley, Devers, and Patton. He said boldly as he opened the sitting: "The present situation is to be regarded as one of opportunity for us and not of disaster. There will be only cheerful faces at this conference table."

What is more, as his deputy he kept Air Chief-Marshal Sir Arthur Tedder, who had been attached in this capacity since the end of January 1943. Here he could count on a first class ally, particularly qualified to get him the unreserved support of the British strategic air forces. He also brought to S.H.A.E.F. his incomparable chief-of-staff, Lieutenant-General Bedell Smith who, according to Lord Alanbrooke, served him in the most fortunate and efficient manner possible.

On January 2, 1944 Eisenhower returned to the U.S. capital, where he had been summoned by General Marshall, and then went to the bedside of President Roosevelt, who was incapacitated for a few days. He would willingly have foregone having to go so far out of his way on his journey from Tunis to London, for time was pressing and what he knew of the plan drawn up by Lieutenant-General Sir F. E. Morgan and the C.O.S.S.A.C. group (Chief-of-Staff Allied Supreme Commander) was only partly to his liking.

"I was doubtful about the adequacy of the tactical plan because it contemplated an amphibious attack on a relatively narrow, three-division front with a total of only five divisions afloat at the instant of assault . . . In addition to being disturbed by the constricted nature of the proposed manoeuvre, I was also concerned because the outline I had seen failed to provide effectively for the quick capture of Cherbourg. I was convinced that the plan, unless it had been changed since I had seen it, did not emphasize sufficiently the early need for major ports and for rapid build-up."

Therefore, even before he flew off to the United States, he instructed Montgomery to get together with Bedell Smith and begin an analysis and, if necessary, a revision of the C.O.S.S.A.C. plan and to report to him on the results of this on his return to London in mid-January.

As soon as his eye fell on the documents submitted to him, Montgomery made up his mind. The plan was "impracticable". This abrupt opinion was based on the following considerations:

"The initial landing is on too narrow a front and is confined to too small an area.

"By D + 12 a total of 16 divisions have been landed on the same beaches as were used for the initial landings. This would lead to the most appalling confusion on the beaches, and the smooth development of the land battle would be made extremely difficult—if not impossible.

"Further divisions come pouring in, all over the same beaches. By D 24 a total of 24 divisions have been landed, all over the same beaches; control of the beaches would be very difficult; the confusion, instead of getting better, would get worse."

It will be noted that the objections which Montgomery raised about the C.O.S.S.A.C. plan, which he submitted confidentially to Churchill, convalescing in Marrakesh at the time, were based on considerations different from Eisenhower's. Nevertheless, they reinforced his determination to throw the whole project back into the melting-pot when he returned to London on January 14.

Here, as Montgomery was responsible for the landings and their initial advance, he was not content with the severe analysis just quoted from, but proposed another plan. Considering only the land forces, Montgomery's memorandum concluded on the following points:

"(a) The initial landings must be made on the widest possible front.

(b) Corps must be able to develop operations from their own beaches, and other corps must NOT land *through* those beaches.

(c) British and American areas of landing must be kept separate. The provisions of (a) above must apply in each case.

(d) After the initial landings, the operation must be developed in such a way that a good port is secured quickly for the British and for American forces. Each should have its own port or group of ports."

Having laid down these principles, which were eminently sensible, Montgomery proceeded to deduce from them a plan of operations, one of whose many merits was the inclusion of a properly co-ordinated plan for co-operation by the tactical and strategic air forces available:

"The type of plan required is on the following lines:

(a) One British army to land on a front of two, or possibly three, corps. One American army similarly.

(b) Follow-up divisions to come in to the corps already on shore.

(c) The available assault craft to be used for the landing troops. Successive flights to follow rapidly in any type of unarmoured craft, and to be poured in.

(d) The air battle must be won before the operation is launched. We must then aim at success in the land battle by the speed and violence of our operations."

General Eisenhower is to be praised for siding with his subordinate. And so the plan which was put into effect on June 6, 1944, was a very much amended form of the C.O.S.S.A.C. project:

1. The narrow front which had aroused criticism was widened to take in Saint Martin-de-Varreville ("Utah" Beach) on the right, and Lion-sur-Mer ("Sword" Beach), on the left.

2. The taking of a bridgehead on the eastern side of the Contentin peninsula allowed the Allies to deal with the problem of Cherbourg at their ease and not to have to worry later about the serious obstacle presented by the River Vire.

3. Plan C.O.S.S.A.C. allowed for the initial landing of three divisions supported by a "floating reserve" against the 716th and 352nd Infantry Divisions of the German LXXXIV Corps. On the day that "Overlord" began, there were eight Allied divisions facing four German divisions. Moreover, in the "Utah" sector, the 91st and 709th Divisions would only be engaged in part. In addition, the second stage of the landing had been increased to include seven divisions.

From all this, should it be concluded that Sir Frederick Morgan and the staff of C.O.S.S.A.C. had not looked far enough ahead and had come up with a plan which was too narrow and unambitious? If this is the conclusion, it can only be reached if one does not know that they were caught in an impossible situation because of Operation "Anvil", which, according to the decision of the Combined British and American Chiefs-of-Staff, confirmed by the Teheran Conference, was to precede "Overlord" and retain considerable quantities of landing equipment in the

A mobile, swastika-bedecked target for anti-tank gunners on practice shoots.

Western Mediterranean.

That is why on February 21, Montgomery wrote to Eisenhower: "I recommend very strongly that we now throw the whole weight of our opinion into the scales against ANVIL."

For strictly strategic reasons, Eisenhower refused to accept this point of view, for the mission which had been entrusted to him had read:

"You will enter the Continent of Europe and, in conjunction with the other Allied Nations, undertake operations aimed at the heart of Germany and the destruction of her Armed Forces."

This instruction seemed to Eisenhower to demand an advance up the valleys of the Rhône and the Saône, linking up somewhere in France with the right wing of the armies which had crossed the Channel. Nevertheless, he gave in to the argument that the success of "Overlord" could only be assured by the postponement of "Anvil" until after July 15.

However, the alterations which came with the re-shaping of the C.O.S.S.A.C. plan forced the initial landing date to be put back from early May to early June. The actual date was subject to these considerations:

1. The parachute drop at night on both flanks of the attacking front required a date as close as possible to the full moon.

2. As three airborne divisions would be in action from midnight onwards, they had to be supported as soon as possible. Between dawn and the landing, a small interval of time would, nevertheless, be left free for the air forces and warships to neutralise and saturate the enemy's coastal defences.

3. Rommel's energetic multiplication of the quantity of mined obstructions on the beaches made it essential that

Allied troops should reach them while the tide was still low enough not to have covered them, in order that the sappers in the first wave might have the utmost opportunity of dealing with the danger.

All these elements taken together timed the mighty enterprise within the dates of June 5 and June 7. It is worth noting in this connection that the Germans were taken unawares, for at every level of the Wehrmacht's hierarchy (Army Group "B", O.B.W., and O.K.W.), all were agreed that the invasion would be launched on the morning tide.

Eisenhower could not conceive of any later date for the landing which would not bring the whole Allied cause into serious danger. From the reports of his Intelligence network and from photographic reconnaissance, it appeared that there was a great increase in the number of launching ramps under construction in the Pas-de-Calais and the Cotentin peninsula, and that, within a few weeks,

The S.H.A.E.F. team – Bradley, Ramsay, Tedder, "Ike", Montgomery, Leigh-Mallory, Bedell Smith.

England would come under a new type of Blitz. Moreover the information he received from the U.S.A. concerning the advanced stage of development reached by bacteriological and atomic weapons encouraged him to make haste, because there was, of course, no guarantee that German science was not working in the same direction.

In his memoirs, which appeared in 1958, Lord Montgomery explains his plan of attack:

"It is important to understand that, once we had secured a good footing in Normandy, my plan was to *threaten* to break out on the eastern flank, that is in the Caen sector. By pursuing this threat relentlessly I intended to draw the main enemy reserves, particularly his armoured divisions, into that sector and to keep them there–using the British and Canadian forces under Dempsey for this purpose. Having got the main enemy strength committed on the *eastern* flank, my plan was to make the break-out on the *western* flank–using for this task the American forces under General Bradley. This break-out attack was to be launched

southwards, and then to proceed eastwards in a wide sweep up to the Seine about Paris. I hoped that this gigantic wheel would pivot on Falaise. It aimed to cut off all the enemy forces south of the Seine, the bridges over the river having been destroyed by our air forces."

Some critics have said that as Montgomery was writing after the war, he was constructing long-term aims of which he was not thinking at the time, so that he could say that Rommel had been forced to dance to his tune in France as well as in North Africa.

Martin Blumenson, one of the contributors to the monumental *U.S. Army in World War II*, put the question in this way in 1963:

"Did Montgomery, from the beginning of the invasion, plan to attract and contain the bulk of the German power to facilitate an American advance on the right? Or did he develop the plan later as a rationalisation for his failure to advance through Caen? Was he more concerned with conserving the limited British manpower and was his containment of the enemy therefore a brilliant expedient that emerged from the tactical situation

in June? The questions were interesting but irrelevant, for the Germans had massed their power opposite the British without regard for General Montgomery's original intentions."

Questions like these are not idle, for other great captains, notably Napoleon and the older Moltke, have posed for posterity by remodelling their victories in order to attribute their successes to long and brilliant preparation, when really they were due to their facility for improvisation, and, in a situation which upset their careful calculations, to their aptitude for taking maximum advantage of the smallest favourable circumstances. In this argument, we do not hesitate to come down on the side of Lord Montgomery, and this can be proved with the aid of three texts contemporary with the events. They come from Sir Arthur Bryant's *Triumph in the West* which clothes, as it were, Brooke's daily notes:

1. On June 15, 1944 Montgomery wrote to Brooke: "When 2nd Panzer Division suddenly appeared in the Villers-Bocage–Caumont area, it plugged the hole through which I had broken. I think it had been meant for offensive action against I Corps in the Caen area. So long as Rommel uses his strategic reserves to plug holes, that is good."

2. On June 18, Brooke noted, from a message sent by Montgomery to his army commanders: "Once we can capture Caen and Cherbourg and all face in the same direction we have a mighty chance–to make the German Army come to our

threat and defeat it between the Seine and the Loire."

3. On June 27 Montgomery wrote to Brooke: "My general broad plan is maturing . . . All the decent enemy stuff, and his Pz. and Pz. S.S. divisions are coming in on the Second Army front–according to plan. That had made it much easier for the First U.S. Army to do its task."

The case seems proved.

The British and American strategic and tactical air forces were a vital element in the success of Operation "Overlord", after five months of intensive training.

For this purpose, General Eisenhower had managed to have all strategic bomber formations, based in Great Britain and southern Italy, placed at his disposal. Under the immediate command of Lieutenant-General Carl A. Spaatz, they comprised:

1. R.A.F. Bomber Command (Air Chief Marshal A. T. Harris);
2. The American 8th Air Force (Lieutenant-General James H. Doolittle) in Britain; and
3. The American 15th Air Force (Lieutenant-General Nathan F. Twining) in Italy.

In addition, through Air Chief Marshal Leigh-Mallory, he was able to use the American 9th Air Force (Major-General Hoyt S. Vandenberg), and the British 2nd Tactical Air Force (Air Marshal Sir Arthur Coningham).

For this air assault, American industry smashed all previous records. Between

"Somewhere in England"–an American artillery unit moves toward Southampton.

1942 and 1943, its annual production had gone up from 48,000 to 86,000 machines of all types, until it reached a daily average of 350 in February 1944, i.e. close to one aeroplane every four minutes.

For its part, the R.A.F. had received 28,000 aircraft in 1943, of which 4,614 were four-engined bombers, 3,113 two-engined bombers, and 10,727 fighters and fighter-bombers. But by then British industry was working to its limit.

As regards the bombing of Germany, the division of labour between the British and the Americans worked according to a system established in 1943. Nevertheless, though Air Chief Marshal Harris stuck obstinately to his theory that the Third Reich could be forced into defeat merely by the effects of mass area bombing, General H. H. Arnold, commanding the U.S. Army Air Force, saw another objective for the daytime raids of his Flying Fortresses and Liberators, escorted further and further into the heart of Germany by ever-increasing numbers of long-range fighters.

The idea was to force Göring's fighters to stretch themselves to the limit to defend the Reich's centres of industrial production and to destroy them there. Thus total mastery of the air would be gained, and this would guarantee success for the troops who were preparing to cross the Channel and invade the continent.

CHAPTER 58
The bomber offensive on Germany

By 1943 ruins were piling up from one end of the Third Reich to the other, the effect of night raids by R.A.F. Bomber Command and day raids by the American 8th Air Force, joined by the 15th Air Force from October 9 from their air base at Foggia, hastily brought back into action after its capture by the British 8th Army on September 27. These round-the-clock attacks were the result of a plan adopted at Casablanca late in January 1943 at a meeting of the British and American Combined Chiefs-of-Staff Committee. A list of proposed objectives was drawn up in order of priority:

> "(a) German submarine construction yards.
> (b) The German aircraft industry.
> (c) Transportation.
> (d) Oil plants.
> (e) Other targets in enemy war industry."

However, this order did not reflect the realities of strategic bombing. In fact the agreed directive specified the general objective of the strategic air offensive as the destruction of the German industrial system and the undermining of German home morale.

After the complete failure of a series of American bombing raids on German submarine construction yards, followed by a similar British lack of success, it became clear that bombing techniques would need drastic improvement, or, at least, that less demanding targets should be selected. Fortunately for the Allies, by the end of 1943 the U-boat menace was no longer pressing. It should be recalled that in order to keep up his U-boat campaign against all opposition Dönitz was at this time claiming that to abandon it would subject Germany's cities to even greater ordeals as enemy bombing raids grew in ferocity. In this he was not mistaken.

It had not been easy for the British and the Americans to come to an agreement over the best use of the U.S. 8th Air Force. The first unit of this force had arrived in Great Britain on July 1, 1942 when the Flying Fortress "Jarring Jenny" had touched down at Prestwick airport in Scotland.

It was the opinion of Air Chief Marshal Sir Charles Portal, Chief of the Air Staff, that the squadrons of Flying Fortresses should take part in the night bombing raids of Bomber Command, whose C.-in-C. naturally welcomed the idea of having eventually twice or three times as many planes at his disposal. Both men thought that day bombing against A.A. and Göring's fighters would suffer unbearable losses for a very mediocre profit. But in Washington, General H. H. Arnold, U.S.A.A.F. Chief-of-Staff, and at H.Q. 8th Air Force, Lieutenant-General Ira C. Eaker both disagreed with British optimism about night operations. If the Anglo-

American strategic force was to carry out its mission successfully it would, in their opinion, have to attack by day and nothing would make them change their minds. But if, under certain conditions, which were not all fulfilled late in 1942, the Flying Fortresses and the Liberators were to take on the considerable risks of day bombing, this was not to be so for the R.A.F., whatever the courage or the state of training of its crews.

And so that task was divided round the clock equally between the British and the Americans, the former taking off at nightfall and the latter by day, each sticking to his task with ruthless obstinacy and without complaining of his losses. This was the system adopted after heated discussions. For Generals Arnold and Eaker there was the additional advantage (though perhaps not admitted) that the Americans would still retain their autonomy though working under a joint command. This division of labour meant that the two air forces came to use totally different methods of action.

By day the 8th Air Force performed what it called precision bombing. Well-defined objectives were thus allotted: a particular factory, construction-yard, assembly-shop in Germany or in an occupied country, in the latter of which only where civilian casualties could be spared as far as was compatible with the successful completion of the mission. The American crews nevertheless greatly exaggerated the degree of precision they could obtain with their Norden bomb-sights.

As it operated by night, Bomber Command could not expect results like these, and so performed area bombing, applying to Germany what nuclear arms specialists today have come to call "anti-city" strategy. In addition to H.E. bombs, they used a great variety of incendiary devices, some packed with jellied products of horrifying efficiency. Air Chief-Marshal Sir Arthur Harris, A.O.C. Bomber Command, did not limit his task to the simple destruction of the Third Reich's war potential, but aimed also at destroying the morale of the German people. In this he was free to act. Returning to the matter after the event, he wrote that the Casablanca Conference released him from his last moral scruples. His hands from that time forward were free as far as the bombing war was concerned.

After this account of the basic methods used by the Anglo-American forces in their air offensive against Germany we must now consider briefly the material means which they used with varying success.

From January 1 to December 31, 1943, in spite of the loss during the year of 1,261 four-engined planes and most of their crews, the growing strength of the 8th Air Force is shown in the figures of the

following table:

| | Groups | |
	B-17 Flying Fortresses	B-24 Liberators
January 1	5	2
April 1	5	2
July 1	11	–
October 1	17	4
December 1	19	7

This shows that the number of four-engined bombers at the disposal of Major-General James H. Doolittle, who succeeded Eaker as 8th Air Force commander at the end of the year, increased over three and a half times in 12 months. The number of sorties made by these planes rose at an even faster, one could say spectacular, rate:

January	279
April	379
July	2,334
October	2,159
December	5,618

Compared with the Consolidated B-24 Liberator, the American crews operating over Germany preferred the Boeing B-17 Flying Fortress, of which over 12,000 were finally made by a consortium of the original builders with Douglas and Lockheed-Vega. Weighing 24 tons loaded, this four-engined plane could reach a top speed of 325 mph and had a range of 2,000 miles. The B-17E had eleven .3- and .5-inch machine guns which the Americans believed gave it all-round fire-power. This optimism was proved false by experience. For example, on August 17, 1943 the 8th Air Force lost 60 out of the 376 Flying Fortresses sent on raids on the Schweinfurt ball-bearing factory and the Messerschmitt assembly plant at Regensburg. On October 14 a new attack on the first of these objectives cost another 60 planes out of the 291 which had taken off, and altogether the loss of aircraft on these raids over the month was running at the intolerably high level of 9.1 per cent. Under these conditions it can be imagined that questions were raised as to whether or not the methods advocated by General Arnold were failing for, if it was relatively easy to replace the planes, it was not the same thing for the crews and, after the second attack on Schweinfurt some loss of morale was noticeable among their ranks. This can be illustrated by one anecdote quoted by Werner Girbig in his *1000 Tage über Deutschland*. There was a manufacturer's advertisement in a magazine which, occupying a complete page, showed an Army Air Force machine gunner, his eye staring fiercely through the back-sight of his .5-inch gun, which he was aiming at a swarm of Focke-Wulf 190's. The caption read: "Who's afraid of the Big Bad Wolf?"

"An 8th Air Force pilot tore the page out, pinned it up on the blackboard in the Orderly Room and stuck on it a long strip of paper on which he wrote in red ink

'WE ARE'. Every officer, including the Station Commander, added his signature. Then the whole lot was sent back, without comment, to the manufacturer."

By the autumn of 1943, the Luftwaffe had won a major victory: deep penetration raids had to be abandoned. The result was the 8th Air Force's losses fell by more than half: in November they were 3.9 per cent, in December 3.4 per cent.

The R.A.F.'s night offensive was based on three types of four-engined plane:
1. the Avro Lancaster: 28 tons, 287 mph, 1,660 mile range, and eight .303-inch machine guns;
2. the Handley-Page Halifax: 27 tons, 282 mph, 1,030 mile range, and nine .303-inch machine guns; and
3. the Short Stirling: 26.5 tons, 260 mph, 1,930 mile range, and eight .303-inch machine guns.

With the help of Canadian industry 16,000 bombers of these three types were built. Nearly half of them were Lancasters. As will be seen, their armament was insufficient to allow them to carry out daylight raids. They took off at dusk and the device for guiding bombers known as "Gee" then, after March 5, 1943, the "Oboe" blind bombing device, gave them their position at all times and then enabled them to locate their targets with considerable accuracy.

The objective was also indicated by pathfinders using coloured flares. As soon as they came into service they were, of course, fitted with the new "H₂S" radar. It was not enough to see clearly: the enemy also had to be blinded, that is his radar had to be jammed. From late July 1943 the British used a device called "Window". This consisted of thousands and thousands of strips of metallic paper which confused the echoes of the Germans' *Würzburg* apparatus for directing A.A. and fighters. Even better, the British succeeded in breaking in on the enemy radio-traffic between ground control and the fighters up in the air, sending his planes off in the wrong direction by mimicking exactly the ground-controller's voice. In the night of October 22-23, during an attack on Kassel, the authentic German controller, infuriated by the interference, let out an oath and the Luftwaffe pilots heard the "phantom voice" exclaim: "That cretin of an Englishman's starting to swear!" Whereupon the German, beside himself with rage, shouted into the microphone: "It's not the Englishman who's swearing, it's me!"

For evident reasons, on their day raids, the Americans rarely sent in more than 200 planes on the same objective. By night the British attacked the towns of the Reich with three and sometimes five times as many and made the raids as brief as possible so as to saturate the active and the passive defence, particularly the latter which, within two hours after the raids had begun, was faced with hundreds of fires concealing delayed-action bombs. Sometimes in these two

A Handley-Page Halifax four-engined bomber.

hours 1,500 and even 2,000 tons of bombs were dropped.

And so by September 1, according to the figures given by Georg W. Feuchter in his excellent book *Der Luftkrieg*, Bomber Command had attacked the following German cities with the amounts of bombs shown over the previous eight months:

	tons		tons
Hamburg	11,000	Berlin	6,000
Essen	8,000	Dusseldorf	5,000
Duisburg	6,000	Nuremberg	5,000

The massive attacks on the capital of the Third Reich began again on November 18 and between that date and January 1, 1944 no less than 14,000 tons of bombs transformed it into an immense heap of rubble. It was during this period that the archives of the French G.H.Q., discovered in the station at La Charité-sur-Loire on June 19, 1940 by the 9th Panzer Division and then preserved in an annexe of the German Foreign Office, were lost.

In the last week of July, 1943, Hamburg and its port were reduced to ruins by the concerted efforts of Bomber Command and the 8th Air Force, a combined operation unique of its kind. The operation was called "Gomorrah" and started on the evening of July 24 with an enormous release of "Window". To follow the effect of this decoy device, let us go with Cajus Bekker to Stade on the lower Elbe and into the command post where Lieutenant-General Schwabedissen was about to send up the fighters of his 2nd

Fliegerdivision:

"But on this July 24 the inconceivable took place. It was shortly before midnight when the first reports reached Stade, and the projections on the screen showed the enemy bomber formations flying eastwards over the North Sea, parallel to the coast. The Bf 110's of NJG [*Nachtjagdgeschwader*] 3 were duly ordered off from their bases at Stade, Vechta, Wittmundhaven, Wunstorf, Lüneburg and Kastrup, and took up their positions over the sea under "*Himmelbett*" control. Meanwhile it was confirmed that the initial Pathfinders were being followed by a bomber stream of several hundred aircraft, all keeping to the north of the Elbe estuary. What was their objective? Would they turn south to Kiel or Lübeck, or proceed over the Baltic for some target as yet unknown? All now depended on closely following their course without being deceived by any feint attack.

"Suddenly the Stade operations room throbbed with disquietude. For minutes the illuminations on the screen representing the enemy had stuck in the same positions. The signals officer switched in to the direct lines to the radar stations and asked what was the matter. He received the same answer from all of them: 'Apparatus put out of action by jamming.'

"The whole thing was a mystery. Then came reports from the 'Freya' stations, operating on the long 240-cm wave, that they too were jammed. They at least could just distinguish the bomber formation's echo from the artificial ones. But the screens of the 'Würzburgs', operating on 53-cm, became an indecipherable jumble of echo points resembling giant insects, from which nothing could be recognised at all.

"It was a portentous situation, for the control of the night fighters entirely depended on exact information as to position and altitude being given by the 'Würzburgs'. Without it the controllers were powerless and the fighters could only fumble in the dark.

"2nd *Fliegerdivision* had to turn for help to the general air-raid warning system–to the corps of observers watching and listening throughout the land. These could only report what they saw. At Dithmarschen, not far from Meldorf, they saw yellow lights cascading from the sky; more and more of them all in the same area. Presumably they marked a turning point. The bomber stream had veered to the south-east, as fresh reports confirmed. In close order the enemy was heading parallel with the Elbe–direct to Hamburg."

Similarly handicapped, the 54 batteries of heavy (8.8-cm) A.A. and the 26 batteries of light A.A. defending the great city of Hamburg could only fire in barrage. They thus claimed only 12 victims out of the 374 Lancasters, 246 Halifaxes, 125 Stirlings, and 73 Wellingtons which had taken off that evening, 721 of which reached their objective. On the following morning 235 Flying Fortresses took over from their R.A.F. comrades and on the 26th started their attacks again, concentrating their efforts on the shipyards and port installations. During the night of the 27th-28th Air Chief Marshal Harris sent up 722 four-engined bombers against Hamburg and 48 hours later another 699. As weather conditions had deteriorated, only 340 reached their objective during the night of August 2-3. During these six attacks nearly 3,000 British and American planes dropped 9,000 tons of bombs. In the resulting holocaust half the city was devoured by flames which ravaged 277,330 dwellings. Civilian victims totalled some 43,000 men, women, and children. All this was achieved at the cost of 89 British bombers shot down by fighters and A.A. These losses were light, of course, but this was not always to be the case for Bomber Command. In fact, between March 1 and July 1, 1943 the night attacks on the industrial complex of the Ruhr, when 18,506 sorties were made, cost 872 four-engined bombers and 5,600 crew. Replacements at the right time were not always easy, in spite of the efforts of the Dominions and the Allied powers.

For its day operations over the Reich, which consisted of harassment or diversionary raids, the R.A.F. used principally the de Havilland Mosquito. Constructed

almost entirely of wood, in which the firm had considerable experience, it was nevertheless one of the most successful of all the weapons which left British workshops. It weighed nine tons on take-off and its two motors delivered 2,500 hp, giving it a top speed of 400 mph, thus putting it virtually out of reach of enemy fighters. The Mosquitoes took part in 1,000 raids in 1943, attacking 40 German towns, including Berlin 27 times.

When Hitler heard from Colonel Christian, his Luftwaffe A.D.C., about the first attack on Hamburg, he poured recrimination on the Luftwaffe for its shortcomings. From the shorthand transcript of this interminable indictment we quote only one passage, significant however in the way it reveals the way of thinking and reasoning of the master of the Third Reich: "That they should attack our aerodromes, I care little; but when they demolish the cities of the Ruhr! And they [the British] are very easily upset: a few bombs filled with the new explosives soon put the wind up them. 'The Germans have got a new weapon!' I don't know why we're beating about the bush here in Germany. The only way to stop this is to impress those on the other side; otherwise people will go mad here. In time things will come to such a pass that they will lose all confidence in the Luftwaffe. Anyway that

confidence is partly gone already. Then you can't come and say 'We've laid mines in the enemy's waters!' For whether he comes over Hamburg with 400 to 500 planes, or only 200 to 300 it's all the same. But look at us dithering about! The only way we can make any impression is ourselves to bomb the towns on the other side methodically. But when I hear people say: 'We didn't find our objective,' and then the next time: 'We haven't got enough planes!' well, we have enough to do other things than what we are doing. On another occasion someone said: 'It wouldn't have the effect we want anyway,' and then he added: 'We must sow mines,' and another time: 'The A.A. was very heavy' and the next day: 'The A.A. fire was no good!' Most of what I hear all the time means: 'We can't find our objective'. Not to find London, that's shameful! And then I have to hear some idiot tell me: 'Yes, *mein Führer,* when the British planes come over Dortmund with their ray-guided bomb-aimers they can drop their bombs precisely on blocks of buildings 500 yards wide and 250 yards long.' Fool! But we can't even find London which is 35 miles across and less than 100 miles from the coast! That's what I told those gentlemen. I'm not saying this for your benefit Christian. You can't do anything about it. You're an A.D.C. I'm saying it for the benefit of others."

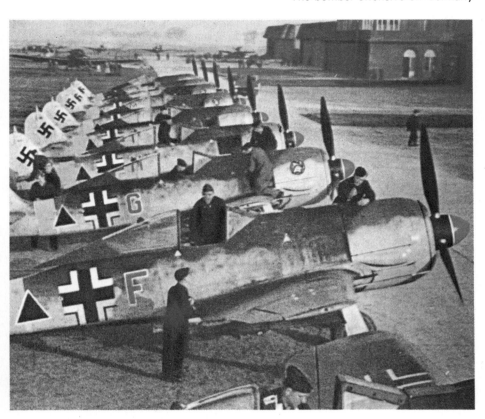

Flying Fortresses of the 8th Air
Force in training over southern England
(left). The heavily armed Fortress
(or B-17) was the mainstay of the
American day offensive over Germany.
Focke-Wulf 190's line up (above).
With later models of the Messerschmitt
Bf 109, this superb fighter formed the
backbone of the Luftwaffe's day
fighter force.
The de Havilland Mosquito (below).
This plane of laminated wood
construction, was one of the most
versatile to see service during the
war, acting as bomber, night fighter,
and reconnaissance plane.

As we can see, Hitler accused the Luftwaffe of "beating about the bush" when he had asked for reprisals against English cities. Shortly before this he had said to Christian: "You can only break terror with terror. We must get to counter-attack; everything else is folly."

But how could the *Reichsmarschall* counter-attack with the means then at his disposal? The fear of a raid on London by 50 two-engined bombers was not likely to put Harris off sending 700 or 800 four-engined bombers over Berlin the next night. Hitler's grievance was thus imaginary. But for all that, the high-ranking officers of the Luftwaffe were not without blame, though Hitler in his diatribe did not touch on the real reason: the failure to take advantage of the brilliant team of scientists and technologists then working in Germany on jet and rocket propulsion.

The aircraft manufacturer Ernst Heinkel had prospected in both these directions as early as 1935 with the collaboration of the young Wernher von Braun in the field of the rocket and of the engineer Pabst von Ohain in that of the turbojet. The rocket-powered Heinkel 176, using a liquid propellant, was the first to be ready and it was demonstrated to Hitler, who was accompanied by Generals Göring, Milch, Jeschonnek, and Udet of the Luftwaffe, on July 3, 1939 by test pilot Erich Warsitz. On the following August 27, three years ahead of the British Frank Whittle's plane of the same type, the Heinkel 178, the first jet aeroplane in the world, took off from a landing strip near Berlin. On October 27, 1939, in the absence of Göring, who could not be bothered to attend, it was seen by Secretary of State Milch and General Udet, who were not impressed.

The idea was taken up again by Messerschmitt and on July 26, 1943 Major-General Adolf Galland, who in the previous year at the age of 30 had been appointed head of the German Fighter Command,

The marshalling yard of Orleans was one target for massive bombing behind the German lines.

was invited by the makers to fly the twin-engined jet propelled Me 262. "It's like being driven by an angel," he said when questioned on his impressions after the test flight, and in his memoirs he added: "On landing I was more enthusiastic than I had ever been before. Feelings and impressions were, however; no criterion; it was the performance and characteristics that mattered. This was not a step forward, this was a leap!"

In fact the Messerschmitt Me 262 could do 540 mph in level flight, twice the speed, that is, of the British and American four-engined bombers. It could climb at record speed, had a range of 50-70 minutes' flying time, and used low-grade fuel.

Was Germany going to have another chance, then, after the inconceivable indifference shown by Göring, Milch, Jeschonnek, and Udet towards Heinkel's revolutionary plane? Evidently not, for at the first demonstration of Messerschmitt's pure-bred interceptor Hitler demanded that it be changed into a fighter-bomber. And in what terms! "For years," he said in front of Göring, Galland, and Messerschmitt, "I have demanded from the Luftwaffe a Speed Bomber which can reach its target in spite of enemy defence. In this aircraft you present me as a fighter plane I see the *Blitz* Bomber, with which I will repel the Invasion in its first and weakest phase. Regardless of the enemy's air umbrella, it will strike the recently landed mass of material and troops, creating panic, death and destruction. *At last this is the Blitz Bomber!* Of course none of you thought of that.'"

This meant a whole series of modifications to the prototype, listed by Bekker thus:

"Bombs would make the take-off weight too heavy for the slender legs. Undercarriage and tyres had to be reinforced. For bombing missions the range was inadequate, so auxiliary tanks had to be built in. That displaced the centre of gravity, upsetting the plane's stability. No approved method of bomb-suspension, nor even a bomb-sight, existed for such a plane, and the normal fighter reflector-

sight bombs could only be aimed in a shallow angle of dive. For regular dive-bombing the machine was too fast safely to hold on target. An order from Führer H.Q. expressly forbade such dives–or indeed any speed exceeding 470 m.p.h."

And so, instead of taking part in the defence of the skies over Germany from 1943-1944, the redoubtable Messerschmitt Me 262 failed to turn up over the beaches assigned to it by Hitler. It was first seen over the Albert Canal when it was reported in Allied communiqués at the beginning of September 1944. Yet in spite of this disastrous delay it came into use eight months before its R.A.F. counterpart, the Gloster Meteor, the first Allied plane of this type.

"Break terror by terror." When Hitler had said this on July 25, 1943 he was thinking not merely of the counter-attacks which he was demanding from the Luftwaffe, but especially of the retaliatory weapons which were then being perfected at the Peenemünde testing station on the shores of the Baltic under the command of General Walter Dornberger. Since January 1943 the Allies' secret services had been on the alert for a new enemy weapon which French resistance agents were calling the "self-propelled shell". In his memoirs Churchill reports certain boasts which Hitler made about this weapon to reassure his entourage:

"By the end of 1943 London would be levelled to the ground and Britain forced to capitulate. October 20 was fixed as zero day for rocket attacks to begin. It is said that Hitler personally ordered the construction of 30,000 rockets for that day. This, if true, shows the absurd ideas on which he lived. The German Minister of Munitions, Dr. Speer, said that each V2 required about as many man-hours to make as six fighters. Hitler's demand was therefore for the equivalent of 180,000 fighters to be made in four months. This was ridiculous; but the production of both weapons was given first priority and 1,500 skilled workers were transferred from anti-aircraft and artillery production to the task."

As the threat grew more real, the Prime Minister charged his son-in-law Duncan Sandys with the task of centralising all work connected with rockets, their characteristics, their manufacture, and their installation, as well as the best methods of fighting them. On June 11 Duncan Sandys wrote to Churchill:

"The latest air reconnaissance photographs provide evidence that the Germans are pressing on as quickly as possible with the development of the long-range rocket at the experimental establishment at Peenemünde, and that frequent firings are taking place. There are also signs that the light anti-aircraft defences at Peenemünde are being strengthened.

"In these circumstances it is desirable that the projected bombing attack upon this establishment should be proceeded with as soon as possible."

A direct hit on the viaduct at Poix (left). A train can be seen steaming onto the viaduct at the bottom of the picture, but subsequent air reconnaissance did not reveal whether it stopped in time. Above: B-24 Liberators unload.

The raid recommended in these terms was carried out during the night of August 16-17 by 597 four-engined bombers of Bomber Command which were ordered to drop 1,500 tons of high explosive and incendiaries from the then unusual height of just over 8,000 feet. On take-off the pilots were warned that in case of failure they would begin again without regard to the losses sustained or about to be sustained. The operation was carried out with magnificent dash and spirit and without excessive losses, a diversionary raid on Berlin having drawn off most of the German fighters. At the time the Anglo-American propaganda no doubt exaggerated the results of the raids, yet the operation did appreciably slow down the German V-1 and V-2 programme which, according to Hitler, was going to bring Britain to face the alternative of annihilation or capitulation before the end of the year. It was in fact on the eighth day of Operation "Overlord", that is only on June 13, 1944, that the first V-1 flying bomb took off for London.

Altogether, 135,000 tons of bombs were dropped on Germany between January 1 and December 31, 1943. With what result? As we have seen, following the proclamation of full mobilisation as a consequence of Stalingrad, German war production shattered all records in every variety of weapon. And, in spite of fearful suffering, the morale of the German people was not badly affected by this pitiless offensive.

This is not to say that, accurate though these statements are, the Anglo-American offensive was a failure. On this point Georg Feuchter, in his *Der Luftkrieg*, makes two valuable observations.

The first concerns the ever-increasing ratio of A.A. weapons being made within the German armament industry. This eventually reached first 20 per cent and then 30 per cent of all artillery and brought with it a corresponding inflation in guncrews. In 1942 these amounted to 439,000 men, in 1943 there were 600,000, and there were nearly 900,000 in 1944. The increase was achieved at the expense of the Eastern Front where there were virtually none left. The second observation is equally, if not more, important. The German war industry owed its survival to a system of extreme decentralisation. The maintenance of its production depended in the last resort on keeping open the railways, the rivers, and the roads. On the day when the Anglo-Americans shifted the centre of gravity of their operations to the communications within the Third Reich, Dr. Speer's already over-stretched network began rapidly to disintegrate and, once started, this became irreversible. The two Western Allies no longer lacked the means. At the end of the year Lieutenant-General Ira C. Eaker, from whom his colleague James H. Doo-

little had taken over in Great Britain, assumed command of the 15th Air Force, a large new American strategic bombing formation.

In the space available it is not possible to present a complete picture of the operations carried out by the British and American strategic air forces against the German industrial machine. The following is a summing-up of these operations and an analysis of the results achieved by June 1944.

On January 11, some 720 four-engined bombers of the 8th Air Force, forming a column of more than 200 miles long, shared between them the targets of Halberstadt, Braunschweig, Magdeburg, and Aschersleben. During the battles in the Westphalian sky, no less than 59 American bombers were shot down. It would still have been a great success if 152 German aircraft had shared the same fate, as was announced by General Doolittle's headquarters. However, it was learnt after the war that the Luftwaffe's losses that day were no more than 40 aircraft.

United States airmen refer to the week of February 20 to February 26 as the "Big Week". For seven days the 8th and 15th Air Forces, relieved at night by R.A.F. Bomber Command, concentrated on the German aircraft industry. In a report to Stimson on February 27, 1945, General Arnold declared:

"The week of February 20-26, 1944 may well be classed by future historians as marking a decisive battle of history, one as decisive and of greater world importance than Gettysburg."

After calm appraisal, though, the historian cannot ratify this opinion, which puts the "Big Week" on the same level as July 3 and 4, 1863, days that saw Robert E. Lee and the cause of the Confederacy falling back finally before the superiority of the Union. Flying 3,000 sorties, the Americans suffered the loss of 244 bombers and 33 fighters while the R.A.F. lost 157 four-engined aircraft. The communiqué from London which announced, when the operations had finished, that 692 enemy aircraft had been shot down or destroyed on the ground, was very much mistaken in its figures. Nevertheless, thanks to the new Mustang long-range fighter escorts, American bomber losses were only 3.5 per cent of aircraft despatched, while the rate of German fighter losses began to rise steeply. The heart of the Luftwaffe was being gradually torn out—inside the Reich itself.

However, in spite of the carpet of bombs which fell on the factories of Braunschweig, Aschersleben, Bernburg, Leipzig, Augsburg, Regensburg, Stuttgart, Fürth, Gotha, Schweinfurt, Tutow, and Posen, German industry continued to build aircraft, by an elaborate process of decentralising production away from major cities. By August 1, 1944, the average monthly figure for the first seven months of the year had reached 3,650, of which 2,500 were day fighters, 250 night

Armourers load bombs into a drab-camouflaged American B-17F Flying Fortress.

Aviation fuel (in thousands of tons)

	Pro-grammed	Produced	Con-sumed
January	165	159	122
February	165	164	135
March	169	181	156
April	172	175	164
May	184	156	195
June	198	52	182
July	207	35	136
August	213	17	115
September	221	10	60
October	228	20	53
November	230	49	53
December	223	26	44

Similar conclusions could be reached from the figures for ordinary petrol and diesel fuel. It is calculated that a Panzer division, according to its 1944 establishment, consumed in battle some 55,000 gallons of fuel a day. Towards the end of summer 1944, the aircraft and tanks of the Third Reich were running on almost empty fuel tanks.

Sir Trafford Leigh-Mallory's air forces had the mission of preparing for the landings and creating conditions which would permit the British and American armies fighting in Normandy to win the great air and ground battle over the Reich which, it was expected, would lead to final victory.

Even so, all General Eisenhower's energy and power of argument was required to get the green light from Churchill for the bombing planned, for the Prime Minister hated the idea of bombing the peoples whom Operation "Overlord" was to free from the German yoke.

While attacks on the V-1 launching sites and on German industry continued, the bulk of the Allied effort, including Bomber Command whose aircraft could now bomb more accurately, and with heavier loads than American bombers, was to be devoted to destroying enemy communications in France. On 17 April 1944, the objectives were defined as follows.

1. To halt the movement of reserves
The systematic attack on communications was aimed at preventing O.K.W. and Army Group "B" reserves from reaching the battlefields. But at the same time it was at all costs essential to avoid revealing, by the choice of targets, the primary objectives of Operation "Overlord".

Bearing in mind these two contradictory requirements, which had to be satisfied at the same time, the Allied squadrons began by dropping two curtains of bombs, one along the Seine between Rouen and Paris and the other following the line of the Albert Canal from Antwerp to Liège, finishing at Namur. Within these lines, about 20 principal railway junctions were completely wiped out. As the Allies did not wish to inflict this treatment on

---

fighters, and 250 bombers. All the same, Göring had to defend the vital targets, and to do this he was forced to make painful decisions and to take aircraft away from the fighter squadrons behind the Atlantic Wall. Here it is true to say that the American attack on the German aircraft industry helped the Allied landings in France.

For 36 days and 55 nights, from January 1 to June 5, 1944, the great cities of the Reich suffered 102 serious attacks which devastated Berlin (17 raids), Braunschweig (13 raids), Frankfurt (eight raids), Hanover (five raids), Magdeburg, Leipzig, Duisburg, and many others. In January, the 15th Air Force bombed Klagenfurt; on March 17, Vienna was raided for the first time. May 18 saw the port of Gdynia and the East Prussian city of Marienburg under attack. As can be seen, it was the whole of Germany which was now within range of British and American bombing aircraft.

Though General Spaatz's success in the battle against Germany's aircraft industry had only been partial, he unquestionably won a great victory in the attack he launched at the beginning of April 1944 against the Reich's sources of liquid, natural, and synthetic fuel.

On August 1, 1943, 179 B-24 Liberators of the American 9th Air Force had taken off from Benghazi and bombed the oil-wells and installations at Ploieşti. But the success of the raid had not been equal to its boldness, for the Americans had lost 53 aircraft, eight of which were interned in Turkey. On April 4, 1944, the 15th Air Force, based around Foggia, made a fresh start with 230 four-engined bombers and produced far better results. The bombers extended their raids to refineries in Bucharest, Giurgiu, Budapest, and Vienna, to the Danube ports and the convoys of barges going up the river, and this managed to reduce the amount of oil that Germany was drawing from Rumania by 80 per cent. From 200,000

tons in February 1944, the amount had fallen to 40,000 in June.

But the most important aspect was the plan approved on April 19 by General Eisenhower, by which the 8th Air Force and Bomber Command began a systematic attack on the German synthetic fuel industry. On May 12, 935 American bombers dropped a hail of high-explosive and incendiary bombs on plant at Leuna, Böhlen, Zeitz, Lützkendorf, and Brüx. On May 28 and May 29, the well-defended American four-engined bombers returned to the targets and completely laid waste the great coal hydrogenation plants of Politz in Pomerania. In their struggle against German war sinews, the 8th Army Air Force had found the right target. This was seen clearly by General Spaatz, though perhaps not by others, when on June 8 he sent a directive to the 8th and 15th Air Forces ordering them to concentrate on Germany's fuel production centres. Bomber command now joined the offensive, with devastating effect.

In a memorandum to the Führer on June 30, Speer, the German Minister of War Production, wrote:

"If we cannot manage to protect our hydrogenation factories and our refineries by all possible means, it will be impossible to get them back into working order from the state they are in now. If that happens, then by September we shall no longer be capable of covering the Wehrmacht's most urgent needs. In other words, from then on there will be a gap which will be impossible to fill and which will bring in its train inevitable tragic consequences."

Albert Speer, whose organisational gifts are recognised by all, did not exaggerate matters in Hitler's style. This is clearly evident from the following table, the figures for which are taken from the book which Wolfgang Birkenfeld wrote in 1964 on the history of the manufacture of synthetic fuel during the Third Reich.

A smashed German supply-train in France. One of the principal objectives of Allied bombing was to prevent German reserves from reaching the front lines. Another objective was to disrupt the enemy's communications.

below Paris. On the same day the Loire bridges downstream from Blois had met the same fate.

This campaign against the railway communications of Western Europe met with absolute success, particularly because from May 1 onward the British and American tactical air forces harried locomotives, both on the track and in the repair sheds. So intense and accurate was this offensive that by June 6, railway traffic had fallen to half its January 1943 level in the rest of France and to only 13 per cent in the area north of the Loire. Catastrophic consequences for German strategy followed. Here the example often given is that of the *Waffen*-S.S. II Panzer Corps, which had been lent to Model to re-establish the line in Eastern Galicia. When the invasion was reported, the corps was entrained at L'vov and took five days to reach Nancy. After here, the railways were in such a state that the corps had to be detrained and sent to the Normandy front by road. At a time when every hour was vital, this brought it into battle four days later than calculated.

Another result of the bombing had not been foreseen by S.H.A.E.F. Because of the destruction and the absolute priority given to military transport, iron ore ceased to flow into the Saar factories, while the coal stocks at the pit-heads mounted up.

3. To destroy coastal radar and guns
Another success for British and American air forces was the action they took against the radar network set up by the Germans between Cape Gris-Nez and Cape Barfleur. Also the attack on the coastal batteries placed or in course of emplacement between Le Havre and Cherbourg brought about the destruction of a certain number of large-calibre guns or caused the Germans to move them back inland, with the result that they took no part in repelling the landings. In any case, there had been so much delay in building the concrete shelters intended to house them that they were not usable.

Sperrle's air force in France had been defeated in the air or wiped out on the ground and was almost destroyed. And so, as they instructed raw recruits moving up to the front, the old soldiers of the Wehrmacht would say: "If you see a white plane, it's an American; if it's black, it's the R.A.F. If you don't see any planes, it's the Luftwaffe."

Not only did the Allies possess a vast numerical superiority in fighter aircraft, they were also able to field a number of superb aircraft, foremost of these being the P-51 **Mustang**. In addition to a remarkable top speed of 437 mph, the other great virtue of the Mustang was its range –up to 3,000 miles with drop tanks– making it invaluable as a bomber escort.

Paris, they restricted themselves to destroying the marshalling yards of its outer suburban area: Trappes, Juvisy, and Villeneuve Saint Georges. In this way the Allies counted on preventing the German 15th Army from intervening on the left bank of the Seine and at the same time convincing German high command that the probable landing-zone was the Pas-de-Calais.

2. To cut lines of communication
Even so, Rundstedt had to be prevented from reinforcing the Normandy battlefields with the eight divisions he had in Brittany, or from Army Group "G" (Colonel-General Blaskowitz), which had 15, including three Panzer, divisions between Nantes and Hendaye and

between Perpignan and Menton. This was the reason for the hail of bombs which fell at intervals on Rennes, Nantes, Le Mans, Angers, and the most important towns of the Loire valley, while the bombing of Lyons, Saint Etienne, Avignon, Marseilles, and Toulon made Hitler think an attack on the Côte d'Azur was being prepared. Finally, in Lorraine, Alsace, and Champagne, the lines along which O.K.W. might route its reserves to reinforce the Western Front were also cut.

On May 4, the bridge at Gaillon collapsed under the very eyes of Rommel, who had just completed an inspection at Riva Bella. Mantes bridge had also been destroyed on the same day, leaving no other passable bridges over the Seine

CHAPTER 59
D-Day

Cornelius Ryan, in his book *The Longest Day*, emphasises the importance of the H-hour decision when he described the historic scene:

"Eisenhower now polled his commanders one by one. General Smith thought that the attack should go in on the sixth – it was a gamble, but one that should be taken. Tedder and Leigh-Mallory were both fearful that even the predicted cloud cover would prove too much for the air forces to operate effectively . . . Montgomery stuck to the decision that he had made the night before when the June 5 D-Day had been postponed. 'I would say Go,' he said.

"It was now up to Ike. The moment had come when only he could make the decision. There was a long silence as Eisenhower weighed all the possibilities. General Smith, watching, was struck by the 'isolation and loneliness' of the Supreme Commander as he sat, hands clasped before him, looking down at the table. The minutes ticked by; some say two minutes passed, others as many as five. Then Eisenhower, his face strained, looked up and announced his decision. Slowly he said, 'I am quite positive we must give the order . . . I don't like it, but there it is . . . I don't see how we can do anything else,' Eisenhower stood up. He looked tired, but some of the tension had left his face."

When one reviews the first 24 hours of Operation "Overlord", the rôle of the Resistance must first be mentioned. It was in fact vital. This opinion is based on the evidence of the Allied and German combatants, and the works on the Resistance by Colonel Rémy, Pierre Nord, and George Martelli should also be carefully considered. No military operation was ever based on such comprehensive Intelligence as "Overlord". Evidence for this is offered by the remarks of the operations officer of the 12th *"Hitlerjugend"* S.S. Panzer Division when he examined a map which had been found on June 8 in the wreck of a Canadian tank. "We were astounded at the accuracy with which all the German fortifications were marked in; even the weapons, right down to the light machine guns and mortars, were listed. And we were disgusted that our own Intelligence had not been able to stop this sort of spying. We found out, later on, that a Frenchman had been arrested who admitted that he had spied for years in the Orne sector, appearing every day in his greengrocer's van on the coastal road. We could clearly see on this map the result of his activities, and that of other spies also."

These were the results obtained by the networks organised by Colonel Rémy from 1942 onwards. Admittedly there were some slight errors and omissions in their summaries: these were inevitable. The English would probably not have embarked on the dangerous airborne attack on the Merville battery if they had known that instead of the 4-inch guns it was thought to have had, it had four 3-inch guns which were not powerful enough to affect the landing of the British 3rd Division at Riva-Bella. Similarly, the Rangers would not have scaled Pointe de Hoe had they known that its casemates were without the six long range guns they were reported to have.

General Bradley moreover did not know that Rommel had advanced five battalions from the 352nd Division to support the regiment on the left wing of the 716th Division. The two carrier-pigeons bringing news of this considerable reinforcement of the enemy's defences had been shot down in flight. However, the Allies' otherwise excellent information concerning the German army's plans was gained at the expense of considerable personal sacrifice and much loss of life.

It is well known that weather conditions played an important part in the way that the Germans were taken by surprise at dawn on June 6. They had a paralysing effect. Rommel's opinion, that the landing would only take place when dawn and high tide coincided, was also mistaken. His naval commander, Vice-Admiral Ruge, noted in his diary on June 4: "Rain and a very strong west wind". Moreover, before leaving la Roche-Guyon via Herrlingen for Berchtesgaden, Rommel noted in the Army Group "B" diary at 0600 hours on the same day that "he had no doubts about leaving as the tides would be very unfavourable for a landing in his absence, and air reconnaissance gave no reason to think that a landing could possibly be imminent." At the same time, on the other side of the Channel, Eisenhower had just postponed "Overlord". On the next day, owing to the temporary spell of good weather forecast by Group-Captain Stagg, Eisenhower decided to cross on June 6, while the German weathermen at O.B.W. still maintained that a landing was out of the question.

Up to now the weather conditions had favoured the Allies. After midnight on June 5, the weather turned against them; although the wind had fallen a little, as Group-Captain Stagg had predicted, it was blowing strongly enough to scatter widely the paratroopers of the 82nd and 101st American Airborne Divisions, who had dropped over the Cotentin peninsula, and the British 6th Airborne Division which had dropped between the Orne and the Dives.

A few hours later, the bomber attack failed for the same reason to neutralise the "Omaha" Beach defences. In the same sector, disaster met the amphibious tank formation which was to support the left wing of the American 1st Division: of the 32 tanks which were launched into the water 6,000 yards from the shore, 27 sank like stones with most of their crews; the canvas flotation skirt supported by a tubular framework gave the tanks only about 3 feet free-board – but the sea was running with a swell of more than 3 feet. The Americans who landed between Vierville and Saint Laurent were therefore put to a gruelling test.

One other apparently accidental factor this time favoured the attackers. On the evening of June 5 Lieutenant-Colonel Hellmuth Meyer, chief Intelligence officer of the German 15th Army, interrupted Colonel-General von Salmuth's game of bridge and told him that the B.B.C. had just broadcast a special message for the French resistance networks:

"Blessent mon coeur
D'une langueur
Monotone"

(a quotation from Verlaine's poem *Chanson d'automne*).

The *Abwehr* had found out, though it is not yet known how, that the code message meant that the landing would take place within 48 hours after midnight of the day of the message.

When he received this news, the commander of the 15th Army not only alerted his staff without delay, but also transmitted this vital information to his superiors at Army Group "B", O.B.W., and O.K.W. At la Roche-Guyon Lieutenant-General Speidel, who was deputising in Rommel's absence, did not think of urging the 7th Army at Le Mans to prepare for action, and at St. Germain-en-Laye no one checked that he had done so.

In his book, *Invasion – They're Coming*, Paul Carell comments:

"Here is the well-nigh incredible story of why, nevertheless, they were caught unawares." Can we do better than the author of *Invasion – They're Coming*? Field-Marshal von Rundstedt can be exonerated, since he had just signed an Intelligence report for the German High Command. The following excerpts are taken from Cornelius Ryan's book:

"The systematic and distinct increase of air attacks indicates that the enemy has reached a high degree of readiness. The probable invasion front remains the sector from the Scheldt (in Holland) to Normandy . . . and it is not impossible that the north front of Brittany might be included . . . it is still not clear where the enemy will invade within this total area. Concentrated air attacks on the coast defences between Dunkirk and Dieppe may mean that the main Allied invasion effort will be made there . . . (but) imminence of invasion is not recognisable."

After accepting the report's rather vague conclusions (it was called *The Allies' Probable Intentions)*, Rundstedt, it can be assumed, considered that the 15th Army's alert position, with its right on the Escaut and its left at Cabourg, was ready for any emergency.

One may also assume that Speidel, the

chief-of-staff of Army Group "B", was still influenced by Rommel, who had said definitely the day before that the Allies could not possibly make the big attempt in his absence. Moreover, there is no doubt that too frequent alerts would have harmed the troops' morale and prejudiced their training, as well as interrupting the fortification work in which they were engaged.

Admittedly, if the 7th Army and LXXXIV Corps had been alerted at about 2300 hours on July 5, the *coup* attempted by a glider detachment of the British 6th Airborne Division and the U.S. 82nd Airborne Division's attack on Sainte Mère-Eglise would almost certainly have failed.

Admiral Sir Bertram Ramsay, the commander of the naval Operation "Fortune" supporting "Overlord", is said to have likened the invasion army to a shell fired by the navy, but Montgomery asserted that only air supremacy would ensure naval supremacy.

On June 6, 1944, the Anglo-American forces conformed to the two conditions laid down by the two British war leaders. In the air General Eisenhower, faced with 419 Luftwaffe planes, had more than 10,500 fighting planes at his disposal:

3,467 four-engined bombers
1,645 twin-engined bombers
5,409 fighter bombers and interceptor fighters

Therefore he was in a position to use 2,355 transport planes and 867 gliders carrying about 27,000 troops and their *matériel* including light tanks, with no risk of attack by German fighters, though there

was still the threat of anti-aircraft defences.

At sea, the embarkation fleet from British ports consisted of 4,126 transport vessels, including converted liners acting as floating headquarters to the major units being landed, and the LCT(R) support craft firing salvoes of 792 5-inch rockets which saturated an area of 750 by 160 yards. This fleet included 1,173 large and small ships transporting armoured vehicles, which shows how important it was for the infantry attacking the Atlantic Wall to have support from tanks and their guns. The fleet for the initial assault consisted (it is reliably reported) of 1,213 ships of all sizes flying seven different flags; three-quarters of them flew the Royal Navy's White Ensign. They included:

7 battleships (3 American)
2 monitors
23 cruisers (3 American, 2 French, 1 Polish)
80 destroyers (34 American, 2 Polish, 2 Norwegian)
25 torpedo-boats (1 French, 2 Polish, 1 Norwegian)
63 corvettes (3 French, 2 Norwegian, 2 Greek)
2 Dutch gunboats
98 minesweepers (9 American)

Of this fleet, all the warships, monitors and gunboats, 18 cruisers and about 50 destroyers had been assigned fire targets of the German batteries between Villerville (opposite Le Havre) and the Barfleur cape: these batteries were therefore engaged by 52 12-inch, 14-inch, and 15-inch guns and more than 500 medium

calibre guns whose fire was all the more effective as it was controlled from the air by Spitfire fighters especially detailed for this purpose.

This huge fleet of 5,339 ships was in the Channel on Sunday June 4 when it received the signal that the assault was deferred from the following day to June 6; a part of the fleet spent the day cruising in the area. But the bad weather which caused the postponement also kept the Luftwaffe patrols grounded; otherwise they would have spotted and reported this unusual concentration of ships. On the evening of June 5 the fleet assembled south of the Isle of Wight and made for its objectives in ten columns.

Admiral Lemonnier, who was on the bridge of the *Montcalm*, described the night crossing: "Spotted the buoy at the entrance to the channel which we must follow for four hours behind a flotilla of minesweepers.

"Now we are only doing 6 knots. The sweepers aren't moving. Possibly they've found some mines and the rough sea is hampering them in their work.

"We have to stop continually. We can only move forward in fits, as we have to take care to stay in our narrow channel. This isn't the time to be put stupidly out of action by a mine.

"We feel as though we are in one of those endless rows of cars blocked outside a big city on a Sunday evening, moving forward by pressing the accelera-

Men of the 3rd Canadian Division, carrying their own transport, disembark at Courselles on "Juno" beach.

German prisoners in a P.O.W. cage await transport to England.

tor slightly, then putting the brake on, touching the rear light of the car ahead – with one difference, that here there is not the slightest light to mark the stern of the ship ahead. Luckily there is just enough light to make out the outlines of the *Georges Leygues* and to keep a look-out."

Admiral Ramsay had divided his forces into two:

1. Under the American Rear-Admiral A. G. Kirk, the Western Naval Task Force was to land and support the American V and VII Corps on the "Utah" and "Omaha" Beaches on both sides of the Vire estuary. All ships flying the Stars and Stripes, including the *Nevada,* a survivor from Pearl Harbor, had appropriately been assigned to him.
2. Under Rear-Admiral Sir Philip Vian, the Eastern Naval Task Force was to perform identical services for the British I and XXX Corps which were to come ashore between Ver-Plage and Ouistreham on the beaches called (from west to east), "Gold", "Juno", and "Sword".

When reviewing the Allied air and naval forces, the power and quality of the support they gave the land forces in the hard fighting against the defenders of the Atlantic Wall must be emphasised. For example, two of the three Czechoslovak 8-inch guns comprising the Saint Marcouf battery had been destroyed; similarly the four 6-inch guns of the Longues battery, near Port-en-Bessin, were silenced by the fire of the cruisers *Ajax, Montcalm,* and *Georges Leygues.* In addition, Allied aircraft over the battle sector had been increased and they responded rapidly, accurately and efficiently to all requests from the ground forces. From dawn to dusk they had made over 4,600 sorties, while only about 50 planes reminded both sides of the Luftwaffe's existence.

The Germans guarding the coast on the night of June 5-6 were frequently caught off their guard, and several comic incidents were reported. Paul Carell gives an example:

"Hoffman stepped outside the bunker. He gave a start. Six giant birds were making straight for his battle head-quarters. They were clearly visible, for the moon had just broken through the clouds. 'They're bailing out.' For an instant Hoffman thought the aircraft had been damaged and its crew was going to jump. But then he understood. This was an airborne landing by para-troops. The white mushrooms were float-ing down–straight at his bunker.

"'Alarm! Enemy parachutists!' The men at 3rd Battalion head-quarters had never pulled on their trousers so fast before.

"Besides reports of parachute landings, radar stations began to signal huge concentrations of aircraft.

"But both in Paris and in Rastenburg the news was received sceptically. 'What, in this weather?' Even the chief-of-staff C.-in-C. West scoffed: 'Maybe a flock of seagulls?'"

At the end of the first day, Eisenhower and Montgomery were in a position to make the following estimate of their gains and losses:

On the whole, the landing had been successful, but the Americans and the British had nowhere gained their pre-scribed objectives for the evening of D-Day. North of the Vire the American 82nd and 101st Airborne Divisions, under Major-Generals M. B. Ridgway and M. D. Taylor respectively, which were due to protect VII Corps' right (Lieutenant-General J. L. Collins) and give it access to the right bank of the Merderet, had scattered in small pockets in the night; in addition they lost many men and much *matériel* in the shallow floods and mine-fields laid by the Germans. In short, of the 17,262 fighting men of the two divi-sions who jumped or landed on "the

longest day", 2,499, or nearly 15 per cent, were missing.

Nevertheless a regiment from the 82nd Airborne Division had occupied the small town of Sainte Mère-Eglise (because of the panic flight of a service unit of German A.A. defences), maintained its ground, and in the evening had made contact with the American 4th Division which had landed on "Utah" Beach. This unit under Major-General Barton had had a relatively easy task, as the air and naval bombardment on the support points of the German 709th Division (Lieutenant-General von Schlieben) barring its way had been completely and devastatingly effective.

"In Ste. Mère-Eglise, as the stunned townspeople watched from behind their shuttered windows, paratroops of the 82nd's 505th Regiment slipped cautiously through the empty streets. The church bell was silent now. On the steeple Private John Steele's empty parachute hung limp . . .

"Passing round the back of the church, P. F. C. William Tucker reached the square and set up his machine-gun behind a tree. Then as he looked out on the moonlit square he saw a parachute and, lying next to him, a dead German. On the far side were the crumpled, sprawled shapes of other bodies. As Tucker sat there in the semi-darkness trying to figure out what happened, he began to feel that he was not alone–that somebody was standing behind him. Grabbing the cum-bersome machine-gun, he whirled around. His eyes came level with a pair of boots slowly swaying back and forth. Tucker hastily stepped back. A dead paratrooper was hanging in the tree looking down at him.

"Then (Lt.-Colonel) Krause pulled an American flag from his pocket. It was old and worn–the same flag that the 505th had raised over Naples . . . He walked to the townhall, and on the flagpole by the side of the door, ran up the colours. There was no ceremony. In the square of the dead paratroopers the fighting was over. The Stars and Stripes flew over the first town to be liberated by the Americans in France."

Paul Carell, who conducted a careful survey among the German survivors of this campaign, describes the destruction of the defence-works W.5 surrounding the beach near the small village of la Madeleine.

"All the fortifications they had laboriously dug and built through the weeks had been churned up like a children's sand-pit. The 75-millimetre anti-tank gun was a heap of twisted metal. The 88-millimetre gun had taken some bad knocks. Two ammunition bunkers had blown up. The machine-gun nests had been buried by avalanches of sand.

"Immediately the infernal concert started – rockets. They were firing only at the two corner bunkers with their 50-millimetre armoured carrier-cannon. The rockets slammed against the bunkers. They smacked through the apertures. The left bunker blew up at once, evidently a direct hit, through the aperture, among the stored shells. The bunker on the right was enveloped in smoke and flames. When the attack was over both bunkers and guns were only rubble and scrap metal. The crews had been killed or severely wounded."

A plane appeared and disappeared. "But evidently it delivered its message. The heavy naval bombardment began. Continuous, uninterrupted hell. Blow upon blow the huge shells crashed into the strongpoint. Trenches were levelled. Barbed wire was torn to shreds. Minefields were blown up. Bunkers were drowned in the loose sand of the dunes. The stone building with the telephone exchange crumbled. The fire-control posts of the flame-throwers received a direct hit."

It is not therefore surprising that the losses of the American 4th Division amounted only to 197 killed, wounded, and missing on June 6. At midnight the whole division had landed (with the exception of one battery), a total of 21,328 men, 1,742 vehicles, and 1,950 tons of *matériel*, munitions, and fuel.

When it landed at "Omaha", the American 1st Division (Major-General C. R. Huebner) had been given the main road N. 13, which runs from Caen to Cherbourg, as its objective for the day. This required an advance of three miles from the Vierville beach. It was also to extend its right as far as Isigny and its left as far as the western approach to Bayeux, where it was to make contact with the inner flank of the British 2nd Army. For this purpose Major-General L. T. Gerow, commander of V Corps, had reinforced his corps with a combined regiment drawn from the 29th Division. At nightfall the 1st Division had not got beyond the small villages of Saint Laurent and Colleville.

In addition the air bombardment had missed its target, the majority of the D.D. tanks had sunk before they reached

the beaches, and the 1st Division had come up against the newly arrived, elite 352nd Division. Although U.S. Command knew of this development they had failed to inform their combat troops. At about 1000 hours General Bradley, the commander of the American 1st Army, had sent ashore his chief-of-staff and received a discouraging report from him:

"The 1st Division lay pinned down behind the sea wall while the enemy swept the beaches with small-arms fire. Artillery chased the landing craft where they milled offshore. Much of the difficulty had been caused by the underwater obstructions. Not only had the demolition teams suffered paralysing casualties, but much of their equipment had been swept away. Only six paths had been blown in that barricade before the tide halted their operations. Unable to break through the obstacles that blocked their assigned beaches, craft turned toward Easy Red where the gaps had been blown. Then as successive waves ran in toward the cluttered beach-head they soon found themselves snarled in a jam offshore."

Admiral Kirk, however, had no intention of letting his colleagues on land bleed to death; he bunched together his destroyers on the coast, and they fired at the maximum rate on all the German fire-points that showed themselves. At the same time, the German 352nd Division battery positions began running out of shells, and as the Allies' cruisers and their tactical air forces attacked all the crossroads, the Germans were not able to supply their artillery with fresh ammunition. At about 1300 hours, the crisis was over and the infantrymen, after the sappers had blown up the anti-tank dike surrounding the beach, infiltrated the German position through the narrow gullies running up the cliff.

During the night of June 6-7, the remainder of the 29th Division (Major-General C. H. Gerhardt) was landed. But V Corps' losses had been heavy: 3,881 killed, wounded, and missing.

The British 2nd Army (General Miles C. Dempsey) had been assigned Bayeux, Caen, and Troarn (9 miles east of Caen) as its D-Day objectives. It was also ordered to extend its reconnaissance to Villers-Bocage and Evrecy, that is along approximately 18 miles of the Calvados coast. This ambitious programme was not fulfilled.

The British 6th Airborne Division (Major-General Richard N. Gale) was to protect the flanks of the operation. It was ordered:

1. To capture intact the bridges across the Orne and its canal between Bénouville and Ranville;
2. To destroy the Merville battery;
3. To destroy the Dives bridges between Troarn and the coast.

Although the wind prevented the paratroopers from landing accurately on their targets, the division completed these three missions brilliantly. At 0030 hours

the British sappers and infantry had jumped from five gliders and captured the Bénouville bridges, clearing them of mines. At about 0400 hours Lieutenant-Colonel Otway had only collected 150 paratroopers from his battalion which was practically without *matériel*, and the gliders which were due to land on the superstructure of the defence works had failed to appear. Nevertheless, he had captured the Merville battery in a fierce fight in which he lost 70 dead and wounded, whilst the garrison of 130 men was left with only 22 survivors. The Dives mission was also completely successful. "All around the battery", according to Georges Blond, "the grass was strewn with corpses, British and German mixed together. Several attackers who had already gone into the defence works ran back:

"'The guns aren't 6-inch, sir, they're 3-inch.'

"'Fine,' said Otway, 'Blow them up.'

"The British had lost 5 officers and 65 N.C.O.'s and men, killed and wounded in the attack. It was now nearly dawn. Otway saw one of his officers apparently searching for something in his battle-dress blouse:

"'What are you doing?'

A victim of the overwhelming Allied fire power.

" 'I'm sending a message to England, sir.'

"The communications officer pulled a pigeon with closed wings from his breast, turning its little head from side to side. It had taken part in the attack too. When it was released, it rose unhesitatingly into the whitening sky."

At dawn, Rear-Admiral Vian's naval forces opened fire on the German defences, and up to nightfall discharged 500 15-inch shells, 3,500 6-inch shells, and 1,380 small calibre missiles. They made wide breaches in the Atlantic Wall. Two further circumstances favoured the British landing. First, the amphibious tanks were lowered into the water much closer to the shore than at "Omaha", and were sometimes landed directly on the beaches. Secondly, large numbers of the special vehicles designed by Major-General Sir Percy Hobart, commander of the 79th Armoured Division, were used in the first waves of the infantry attack.

In addition to the Crabs, or flail tanks, which cleared the ground of the mines obstructing their tracks and had been used since El Alamein, the British 2nd Army also brought its Crocodiles and its A.V.R.E.s into the line: the Crocodiles were flame-thrower tanks which cast a 360-foot jet of burning oil beyond the range of the enemy's rocket-launchers; these tanks had trailers filled with about 400 gallons of fuel and could sustain prolonged actions; the A.V.R.E.s were mortar tanks carrying a 9-inch mortar on a Churchill tank chassis, and intended for work against armoured strongpoints.

On the other hand, against the British I and XXX Corps (commanded respectively by Lieutenant-Generals J. T. Crocker and G. T. Bucknall) the German 716th Division (Lieutenant-General W. Richter) only had four battalions and their quality was inferior to that of the Allies.

In these conditions, the 50th Division (Major-General D. A. H. Graham), the advance-guard of XXX Corps, proceeded from "Gold" Beach without much difficulty. By the end of the day it had some armour at the approaches of Bayeux and had moved forward about six miles.

In I Corps, the 3rd Canadian Division (Major-General R. F. L. Keller) had a more difficult landing because the Calvados reefs presented a natural obstacle; nevertheless it had advanced eight miles from Bernières ("Juno" Beach) and was near its objective, the Carpiquet airfield. On the other hand the armoured column which it had launched towards Evrecy was driven back with losses above Bretteville-l'Orgueilleuse. The result was that between its left at Saint Aubin-sur-Mer and the right of the 50th Division, towards Arromanches, the Atlantic Wall had been breached over a front of 12 miles.

Landing at "Sword" Beach in the Riva-Bella area, the British 3rd Division (Major-General G. T. Rennie) had managed to join with the 6th Airborne Division over the Bénouville bridge. In the evening it had advanced to Biéville three miles north of Caen and repelled a counter-attack from the 21st Panzer Division. With its right close up against Lion-sur-Mer it was four or five miles from the Canadian 3rd Division.

The British 2nd Army had a total of less than 3,000 killed, wounded, and missing on D-Day.

Allied naval and air losses were insignificant: 114 planes, mainly brought down by A.A. fire; some landing craft and two destroyers–one of these, the Corry (U.S. Navy) blew up on a mine in the "Utah" Beach waters; the other, the Norwegian Svenner, succumbed to an attack on the Eastern Naval Task Force by

three German destroyers from Le Havre commanded by Lieutenant-Commander Hoffmann.

At 0111 hours (German time) General Erich Marcks, commander of LXXXIV Corps, was at his H.Q. in Saint Lô celebrating his 53rd birthday when he heard from the 716th Division that the paratroopers were coming down between the Orne and the Dives and that the bridges of these two rivers were apparently their objectives. Twenty minutes later the 709th Division signalled the landing of American paratroopers on both sides of the Merderet in the Sainte Mère-Eglise area. Quite correctly, Marcks decided that this was the invasion. He therefore alerted the troops on the coast and informed the 7th Army H.Q. at Le Mans.

The 7th Army quickly transmitted the information to la Roche-Guyon and Saint Germain. Although he hesitated when he received LXXXIV Corps' appreciation, supported by the 7th Army, Rundstedt alerted the Panzer-"Lehr" Division and the 12th "Hitlerjugend" Panzer Division and contacted O.K.W., but Hitler forbade him to move them till further orders, which would be given him as soon as the situation was clear.

There was no further news till 0630 hours, when information was received that the Calvados coast defences were being subjected to intensive naval bombardment. At that time, however, the Führer, who had gone to bed as usual two hours earlier, was fast asleep, thanks to Dr. Morell's pills, and no one dared to have him woken. When they finally plucked up the courage, Hitler's reaction was fairly dramatic:

"He was in a dressing-gown when he came out of his bedroom. He listened calmly to the report of his aides and then sent for O.K.W.'s chief, Field-Marshal

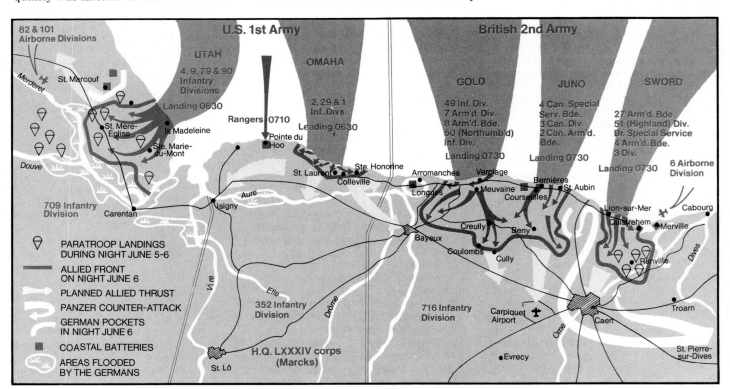

PARATROOP LANDINGS DURING NIGHT JUNE 5-6

ALLIED FRONT ON NIGHT JUNE 6

PLANNED ALLIED THRUST

PANZER COUNTER-ATTACK

GERMAN POCKETS IN NIGHT JUNE 6

COASTAL BATTERIES

AREAS FLOODED BY THE GERMANS

Wilhelm Keitel, and Jodl. By the time they arrived Hitler was dressed and waiting—and excited.

"The conference that followed was, as Pultkamer recalls, 'extremely agitated'. Information was scanty, but on the basis of what was known Hitler was convinced that this was not the main invasion, and he kept repeating that over and over again. The conference lasted only a few minutes and ended abruptly, as Jodl was later to remember, when Hitler suddenly thundered at him and Keitel, 'Well, is it or isn't it the invasion?'"

Therefore it was only at 1432 that Army Group "B" received the authority, which it had sought for 12 hours, to order the 12th S.S. Panzer Division to support the 7th Army, and at 1507 hours to move the *Waffen*-S.S. I Panzer Corps and the Panzer-*"Lehr"* Division.

But after so much delay, Colonel-General Dollmann now showed excessive haste. Lieutenant-General Bayerlein, commander of the Panzer-*"Lehr"* Division, after leaving his unit to obtain instructions from 7th Army H.Q., was ordered to move towards Caen at 1700 hours. Without success the former chief-of-staff of the *Afrika Korps* (who had had much experience of British air tactics) attempted to persuade Dollmann how foolish it was to set out on the French roads before nightfall. Nevertheless Dollmann kept to his decision, thinking he would thus be able to bring the Panzer-*"Lehr"* Division into action south of Caen at dawn on the following day, June 7. But the first bombs began falling before Bayerlein and his staff had passed Beaumont-sur-Sarthe, south of Alençon.

"For once we were lucky. But the columns were getting farther and farther apart all the time. Since the Army had ordered a radio silence we had to maintain contact by dispatch riders. As if radio silence could have stopped the fighter-bombers and reconnaissance planes from spotting us! All it did was prevent the divisional staff from forming a picture of the state of the advance—if it was moving smoothly or whether there were hold-ups and losses. I was for ever sending off officers or else seeking out units myself.

"We were moving along all five routes of advance. Naturally our move had been spotted by enemy air-reconnaissance. And before long the bombers were hovering above the roads, smashing crossroads, villages, and towns along our line of advance, and pouncing on the long columns of vehicles. At 2300 we drove through Sées. The place was lit up by flares hanging above it like candles on a Christmas-tree, and heavy bombs were crashing down on the houses which were already burning. But we managed to get through."

In the Saint Pierre-sur-Dives region, the 21st Panzer Division (Major-General Feuchtinger) was in a rather different situation: it was Army Group "B" 's reserve, but its commander was authorised to put his infantry into action to support the 716th Division if there was a landing; however, he was not allowed to engage his armour. In accordance with these orders Feuchtinger launched one of his grenadier regiments on the right bank of the Orne to engage the British paratroopers and as he received no orders from la Roche-Guyon, he sent his armoured regiment to follow them. At 0700 hours, he was informed that he was subordinate to the 7th Army; two hours later that he would now take his orders from LXXXIV Corps.

But now General Marcks was becoming more aware of the danger from the sea; for this reason, at 1000 hours, he ordered his new subordinate to abandon the action his armoured regiment was about to take against the enemy paratroopers, and to send it over the Orne to give support to the 716th Division units barring the approach to Caen from the British. This move was completed at 1430 hours and the Germans counter-attacked at 1700 hours. At nightfall the 21st Panzer Division had managed to reach Luc-sur-Mer with its infantry, but its armoured regiment had been engaged by the British 3rd Division and had suffered heavy losses. Moreover it had nearly run out of petrol. Therefore Feuchtinger, who had 146 tanks and 51 assault guns when the engagement commenced, retreated on orders, abandoning the wrecks of 40 vehicles.

At 1300 hours, a report from LXXXIV Corps to the 7th Army gave an accurate description of the fluctuations of this merciless struggle: "In the Caen area, in the British sector, the enemy is successful. East of the American sector, the landing is more or less repulsed at Vierville. Our counter-attack is in progress in the Sainte Mère-Eglise district; the 8th Regiment of the American 4th Division (Colonel van Fleet) is pinned down there. Where is our air support? Enemy aircraft prevent us from moving or supplying our troops by day."

At midnight, an entry in the 7th Army's signals diary showed the worsening situation in the afternoon in the Caen sector:

"2400 hours. 716 Infantry Division is still defending itself at strongpoints. Communications between division, regimental and battalion headquarters, however, no longer exist, so that nothing is known as to the number of strong-points still holding out or of those liquidated . . . The Chief-of-Staff of Seventh Army gives the order that the counter attack of June 7 must reach the coast without fail, since the strong-point defenders expect it of us."

The Battle of Normandy had started unpromisingly for the Wehrmacht. Nevertheless the Allies took a little more than six weeks to break out of the Avranches bottleneck, although according to plans they should have done so on D+20, June 27; they required another three weeks to complete the defeat of Army Group "B". This delay was due to two different factors:

1. The Normandy *bocage* (mixed woodland and pastureland), where the defenders were undoubtedly favoured by their natural surroundings. The countryside between Troarn and Bayeux, the British 2nd Army sector, was certainly suitable for use by armoured formations, but it assisted the German tanks and anti-tank devices even more; the range of their guns was greater than the Allies'. Moreover in the Norman *bocage* between Bayeux and the western Cotentin coast, the U.S. 1st Army sector, there were fields surrounded by tall, thick hedges with sunken roads between them, very suitable for ambushes, whether by the *Chouans* at the time of the French Revolution, or by the German grenadiers, who spotted enemy tanks and discharged the almost invariably lethal shots from *Panzerfaust* or *Panzerschreck* launchers at very short range. The attackers' task was also complicated by the rivers Vire, Taute, Douve, and Merderet, marshy tracts, and the 7th Army's flooding operations. General Bradley wrote: "Not even in Tunisia had we found more exasperating defensive terrain. Collins called it no less formidable than the jungles of Guadalcanal."

2. The inferior quality of their armour compared with the Germans' was another very serious handicap for the Allies. The journalist Alan Moorehead, who was a war correspondent at Montgomery's G.H.Q., stated quite frankly after the end of the war: "Our tanks were Shermans, Churchills and Cromwells. None of them was the equal of the German Mark V (the Panther), or the Mark VI (the Tiger) . . .

"The Germans had much thicker armour than we had. Their tanks were effective at a thousand yards or more: ours at ranges around five hundred yards . . . Our tanks were unequal to the job because they were not good enough. There may be various ways of dodging this plain truth, but anyone who wishes to do so will find himself arguing with the crews of more than three British armoured divisions which fought in France."

Admittedly Moorehead was a journalist, but General Bradley is recognised as one of the best brains in the American army. "Originally", he wrote, "the Sherman had come equipped with a 75-mm gun, an almost totally ineffective weapon against the heavy frontal plate of these German tanks. Only by swarming around the panzers to hit them on the flank, could our Shermans knock the enemy out. But too often the American tankers complained it cost them a tank or two, with crews, to get the enemy's panzers and only by expending more tanks than we cared to lose. Ordance thereafter replaced the antedated 75 with a new 76-mm high-velocity gun. But even this new weapon often scuffed rather than penetrated the enemy's armour.

"Eisenhower was angry when he heard of these limitations of the new 76."

We shall not repeat him, as we know that the Pzkw V Panther had an armour

British forces come ashore,
moving forward to join
the fighting further inland.

thickness of 4½ inches and the Pzkw VI Tiger 5½ inches. The British got their best results when the re-armed their Shermans with the 17-pounder anti-tank guns which they had had since 1943. Firing an armour-piercing shell at an initial velocity of about 2,900 feet per second, it was certainly superior to the American version, but nevertheless it was markedly inferior to the Panther's 7.5-cm, which fired at 3,068 feet per second, and even more to the 8.8-cm of the Tiger II or the *Königstiger* with shells of 20- and 22-lb with a higher velocity, which at 500 yards could penetrate 112 and 182-mm of armour respectively. Even worse, the British and the Americans found that their Shermans were inclined to catch fire suddenly like bowls of flaming punch.

However, the Panzers' undeniable technical superiority was of little help to Rommel, as he was unable to supply them with the required fuel or to defend them against the continuous attacks of the Allied tactical air force, of which they were rightly a priority target.

The word *Jabo* (*Jagdbomber*: fighter-bomber) recurs in all the accounts left by the German combatants after the Normandy battle. In their attacks against enemy armour, the Allies preferred rockets, which were more accurate than bombs and more effective than the 20-mm or 40-mm shell. The R.A.F.'s Hawker Typhoon fighter carried eight 60-pounder rockets, whilst the Republic P-47 Thunderbolt had ten 5-inch anti-tank rockets.

In this ground-air battle, the rôle of the Allied engineers has perhaps not been

sufficiently appreciated. They quickly cleared the rubble left in the Normandy towns and villages by the bombardments and restored communications as the troops moved forward. They also had better equipment, notably in machines of American manufacture, and in the Bailey bridge, which had prefabricated components and could be assembled in a great variety of combinations. By May 8 1945, 7,500 Bailey bridges had been built in the Western and Italian war theatres; they certainly contributed not only to the defeat of the Third Reich, but also to the reconstruction of this part of the continent.

On June 7 and 8 successively the 12th *"Hitlerjugend"* S.S. Panzer Division and the Panzer-*"Lehr"* Division failed to drive the British back to the Channel. On June 7 the first of these major units (which under Major-General Witt included 177 tanks and 28 assault guns) should have counter-attacked in the direction of the Douvres operational base (six miles north of Caen) with the 21st Panzer Division, which was immediately to its left. It managed to maul a Canadian armoured brigade in the Carpiquet region but when it reached its goal it was halted by massive artillery fire and turned to the left.

The following day the Panzer-*"Lehr"* Division came into the line on the left of the 12th S.S. Panzer Division, but between Sées and Tilly-sur-Seulles it had lost five tanks, 84 all-purpose transport vehicles, 90 cars and lorries, and 40 petrol tankers; these considerable losses caused no less concern to Lieutenant-General Bayerlein than the 12th S.S. Panzer Division's had to his colleague Witt. Moreover Vice-Admiral Ruge noted in his personal diary at the la Roche-Guyon H.Q., to which Rommel had returned late in the

afternoon on June 6: "The enemy's air superiority is having the effect the Field-Marshal had foreseen: our movements are extremely slow, supplies don't get through, any deployment is becoming impossible, the artillery can't move to its firing positions any more. Precisely the same thing is happening on land here as happened at sea in the Tunisian campaign."

On June 8, when the U.S. 1st Army and the British 2nd Army joined up at Bayeux, Rundstedt put Rommel in charge of *Panzergruppe* "West", which became responsible for the conduct of operations in the sector between the mouth of the Dives and the Tilly-sur-Seulles area, while the 7th Army from now on faced the Americans alone. General Geyr von Schweppenburg, when he assumed this heavy task, was assigned the mission of retaking Bayeux and he proposed that he should break through to the Channel with his three Panzer divisions. But as soon as he set up his headquarters in the Thury–Harcourt region, he was seriously wounded in an air attack which killed many of his staff. Sepp Dietrich took over and ordered his troops to stay on the defensive while they waited for better days.

In fact on June 12, with the intervention of the 2nd Panzer Division (Lieutenant-General von Lüttwitz) which had been brought up from the Amiens region, Dietrich managed to halt an attempt by the British XXX Corps which had launched the 7th Armoured Division (Major-General G. W. Erskine) against its left wing and its rear. The celebrated Desert Rats got the worst of this chance encounter, which was fought for Villers-Bocage, not for lack of energy and courage but because they were let down by their *matériel*. Chester Wilmot proves this in his description of the episode:

"The troops had dismounted to stretch their legs while the tanks reconnoitred the way ahead, when the crack of a gun split the crisp morning air and the leading half-track burst into flames. Out of the woods to the north lumbered a Tiger tank, which drove on to the road and proceeded right down the line of half-tracks 'brewing up' one vehicle after another. Behind these there was some incidental armour–a dozen tanks belonging to Regimental H.Q., the artillery observers and a reconnaissance troop. The Tiger destroyed them in quick succession, scorning the fire of one Cromwell, which saw its 75-mm shells bounce off the sides of the German tank even at the range of a few yards! Within a matter of minutes the road was an inferno with 25 armoured vehicles blazing–all the victims of this one lone Tiger."

While we do not want to undervalue Captain Wittmann's exploit (he was the tank's commander) we must point out that the Cromwell was very inadequately armed with a 75-mm gun and also had totally inadequate armour protection; for this reason the Desert Rats' morale suffered seriously for several weeks.

The British 2nd Army's defeat was fully compensated for on the same day by the fall of Carentan, whose defenders succumbed to the concentric thrust of the American 29th Division and 101st Airborne Division. The 17th S.S. *Panzergrenadier* Division *"Götz von Berlichingen"* (Lieutenant-General Ostermann) was alerted on June 7 at its stations at Thouars but arrived too late to prevent General Bradley's V and VII Corps from joining up. When it crossed the Loire it received the same treatment from the fighter-bombers as the Panzer-*"Lehr"* Division. The Anglo-Americans now had a continuous front between the Dives and Saint Marcouf. During the first days of battle the Germans had already lost 10,000 prisoners and 150 tanks. Even more important, Montgomery and Eisenhower were as aware as Rommel and Rundstedt that, contrary to expectations, the defenders were not getting reinforcements as quickly as the attackers at this stage.

From June 7 to 12 the British and Americans put in their floating reserves, which had sailed on the same day as the first echelon; these consisted of five infantry and three airborne divisions. The American V Corps was joined by the 9th and 20th Divisions; the British XXX Corps by the 7th Armoured and the 49th Divisions; and the British I Corps by the 51st Highland Division, giving 15 divisions (eight American) out of a total of 37 stationed in the U.K.: 362,547 men, 54,186 vehicles, and about 102,000 tons of supplies landed in a week.

According to S.H.A.E.F.'s estimates, Montgomery was faced by 21 divisions on June 12. In fact, the defence was reinforced at the following rate:

June 6 21st Panzer Division
June 7 12th Panzer Division
June 8 Panzer-*"Lehr"* Division
June 9 353rd Panzer Division
June 11 17th S.S. *Panzergrenadier* Division
June 12 2nd Panzer and 3rd Parachute Divisions

Including the five divisions guarding the area between Cabourg and Mont Saint Michel on D-Day, *Panzergruppe* "West" and the German 7th Army had 12 divisions (including five armoured divisions) in the line; however, the 716th Division was only a cypher and the 352nd and 709th Divisions had been badly mauled. The Panzers went into the attack at random, always behind schedule, and under strength.

The air offensive against the French and Belgian railway networks broadly paid the dividends expected of it. This action continued, but from the night of June 5-6 it was made doubly successful by the intervention of the Resistance against the German communications in accordance with the "Green Plan" compiled by French Railways, while the "Tortoise Plan" drawn up by the French Post Office was carried out just as successfully against the occupying forces' telephone communications.

Pierre de Préval has listed 278 acts of sabotage carried out by the French Resistance from June 6 to September 15, 1944 in the department of Meurthe-et-Moselle, and the position was similar in the other departments. On the route from Montauban to the Normandy front, the *Waffen*-S.S. 2nd Panzer Division *"Das Reich"* (Lieutenant-General Lammerding) was harried by the Corrèze *maquis;* the terrible reprisals taken on the inhabitants of Tulle and Oradour by this division to avenge these ambushes remain unforgotten.

From now on the delay in building up the German defence on the invasion front is perfectly understandable, as the combined action of the Anglo-American forces and the French Resistance networks was effectively assisted by Hitler's personal interference in war operations.

We have mentioned that when he was expecting the landing, the Führer had an intuition that Normandy might well be the invasion's objective. But he revised his view as soon as Eisenhower had launched Operation "Overlord". Plainly, he thought, he was faced with a diversionary manoeuvre aimed at making him lower his guard in the Pas-de-Calais. If he were to fall into the trap laid for him, the final thrust would be aimed at him in the sector he had unwisely uncovered ... but he was not so stupid! Nevertheless on June 8 Major Hayn, LXXXIV Corps' chief Intelligence officer, was brought a copy of U.S. VII Corps' battle orders which had been discovered on board a barge that had grounded near Isigny after its crew had been killed. This document, which was quite unnecessarily verbose, not only revealed General Collins's intentions, but also listed V Corps' and the British XXX Corps' objectives. The Americans' mission was to reach the Cotentin western coast as soon as possible, and then to change direction to the north and capture Cherbourg. Without delay this battle order was passed through the correct channels; 7th Army, Army Group "B", Supreme Command West, and O.K.W. Hitler, however, obstinately stuck to his opinion that this was a deceptive manoeuvre, and in support of his view he quoted the *Abwehr*'s summaries stating that just before the landing there were 60 or even 67 British and American divisions stationed in Britain. He never asked himself whether the real deception lay in simulating the existence of 30 divisions concentrated in Kent and ready to cross the English Channel at its narrowest point. At the front, on the other hand, where the Germans saw most of the Allied units they had previously met in Africa and Sicily (U.S. 1st and 9th Divisions, British 7th Armoured Division and 50th and 51st Divisions), they dismissed the idea of a second landing in the north of France. But nothing was done and Rommel was forbidden to use the 18 divisions of the 15th Army which, with the exception of the 346th and 711th

Divisions, which were engaged on the right bank of the Orne, remained in reserve until after the breakthrough.

After a week's fighting, Rommel transmitted his appreciation and his intentions to Keitel: "The Army Group is endeavouring to replace the Panzer formations by infantry formations as soon as possible, and re-form mobile reserves with them. The Army Group intends to switch its *Schwerpunkt* in the next few days to the area Carentan–Montebourg to annihilate the enemy there and avert the danger to Cherbourg. Only when this has been done can the enemy between the Orne and the Vire be attacked."

The following conclusions can be drawn from this telephone message:

1. Rommel stated he was compelled to give up his first plan to push the enemy back into the sea immediately. Hitler therefore was not able to recover on the Western Front the forces which he hoped to collect to support the Eastern Front.
2. In order to release his armoured formations from the front, he would have had to have the same number of infantry formations at his disposal at the appropriate time. For this purpose the veto imposed on him by Hitler on taking troops from the 15th Army did not simplify matters.
3. Even if he had obtained these infantry formations, what he stated in any case shows that Montgomery's idea of free manoeuvre, which he put into practice in Normandy, was soundly and judiciously conceived.
4. Without these formations he could not displace Army Group "B"'s point of main effort from the Caen–Tilly-sur-Seulles area to the Carentan–Montebourg area, and therefore the "strong point" of Cherbourg was from now on virtually written off.

Georges Blond has written: "On Monday June 12 shortly after midday a D.U.K.W. landed at Courseulles and drove over the sand. A group of officers who had been looking at the D.U.K.W. through their field glasses for a few moments came forward quickly. A corpulent gentleman was sitting behind the driver, wearing a blue cap and smoking a cigar. As soon as the vehicle had stopped he asked the officers in a loud voice: 'How do I get down?' Just then a soldier hurried up carrying a small ladder. Churchill walked down it with all possible dignity. He shook hands with Montgomery who was standing in front of him in a leather jacket and a black beret, and then with the other officers, Field-Marshal Smuts, Field-Marshal Alan Brooke, and Rear-Admiral Sir Philip Vian, commander of the British Eastern Naval Task Force.

"He then went to his waiting jeep. The jeep started off."

On the following morning, June 13, the first V-1 rockets were fired in the direction of London.

CHAPTER 60

The battle for Normandy

Back on the defensive as the result of the failure of his counter-attacks, Rommel now had no illusions about the fate awaiting his forces, and on June 11 he spoke quite openly about it to Vice-Admiral Ruge, in whom, quite justifiably, he had full confidence. In his view, the best thing that Germany could do, given her situation, was to end the war now, before the territorial bargaining counters she still held were prised from her grasp. But Hitler did not see things that way, and in any case, none of Germany's enemies was willing to enter into any negotiations.

Rommel's pessimism in no way tempted him to give up at the military level. He was quite certain that the interests of his country demanded that he hang on and defend the front with which he had been entrusted with all the resolution at his command. His sympathy with the anti-Hitler conspiracy in no way changed his views. As he saw it, the death of Hitler might lead to a general peace conference, and the German representatives at any such discussions should not be left empty-handed. So Rommel's conclusion was that he had to continue fighting, whatever happened in German politics.

This explains the ferocity with which, for two months, the Normandy battles were fought, for Field-Marshal von Kluge, who had succeeded Rundstedt on July 3, and Rommel a fortnight later, seems, quite unexpectedly, to have had the same reasoning as his predecessor.

According to the plan worked out by General Montgomery, the port of Cherbourg was the first objective of the American 1st Army, and especially of VII Corps, which, with the landing of the 90th and 91st Divisions, and the 2nd Armoured Division, had gradually been brought up to six divisions. On the German side, LXXXIV Panzer Corps had been taken over by General von Choltitz, following the death of General Marcks, killed by a fighter-bomber on leaving his command post at Saint Lô. "May I respectfully request you not to take too many risks. A change of command now would be most unfortunate." This remonstrance on the part of his chief-of-staff, just as Marcks was getting into his car to visit the front, brought forth the following reply: "You and your existence! *We* can die honourably, like soldiers; but our poor Fatherland..." A few seconds later he was dead, struck by a shell which cut through the femoral artery of the one leg left to him since the retreat in Russia in the winter of 1941-42.

To defend the Cotentin area, Choltitz had five divisions (the 77th, 91st, 243rd, 353rd, and 709th); however, in their ranks was a certain number of Soviet volunteers, recruited mainly in the Ukraine, in the Crimea, and in the valleys of the Caucasus,

from a dozen different nationalities, and this incredible hotch-potch had scarcely made them better fighting units. As Lieutenant-General von Schlieben, commander of the 709th Division, who was fully aware of this, said: "How do you expect Russians, in German uniform, to fight well against Americans, in France?" His own division was made up of rather elderly troops (30- to 35-year-olds), and some of the artillerymen of the coastal batteries were over 40.

The first part of General Bradley's plan to capture his objective was to advance to the west coast of the Cotentin, and then turn north, making his columns converge on Cherbourg. The 90th Division, however, in its first engagement, got into such trouble in crossing the Douve that at one time the Allied command thought seriously of breaking it up, and distributing it amongst the other divisions. Finally, General Bradley merely replaced its commander with Major-General Landrum, who, however, was quite incapable of infusing any life into it, so badly had its morale been affected by its baptism of fire.

In happy contrast, on June 14 the American 9th Division, which had already distinguished itself in Tunisia, crushed enemy resistance, which had been favoured by the marshy terrain. Commanded by a resolute and skilful soldier, Major-General Manton Eddy, it advanced quickly along a line Pont l'Abbé–Saint Sauveur-le-Vicomte–Barneville, reaching the western coast of the Cotentin at dawn on June 15, and thus isolating to the north the 77th, 243rd, and 709th Divisions –or what was left of them. Then Lieutenant-General Collins's VII Corps, covered in the south by his two airborne divisions and his 91st Division, launched an assault on Cherbourg. On the right was the 4th Division, commanded by Major-General Barton, and on the left, the 79th Division (Major-General Ira Wyche), which had just landed, and the 9th Division. The latter had less than a day to wheel from west to north, with all its supplies and arms–a difficult military exercise which General Eddy accomplished brilliantly.

"Within 22 hours", wrote General Bradley, "he was expected to turn a force of 20,000 troops a full 90 degrees toward Cherbourg, evacuate his sick and wounded, lay wire, reconnoitre the ground, establish his boundaries, issue orders, relocate his ammunition and supply dumps, and then jump off in a fresh attack on a front nine miles wide. Eddy never even raised his eyebrows and when H-hour struck, he jumped off on time."

It is true that the German LXXXIV Corps had been very badly mauled, and that under the incessant attacks of the Anglo-American air force, Generals Hellmich and Stegmann, commanding the 77th and 243rd Divisions respectively,

had been killed. However, the speed with which the 9th Division switched fronts enabled the remnants of the 77th Division, now under the command of Colonel Bacherer, to slip through the American forward posts and regain the German lines, having captured on the way 250 prisoners, 11 jeeps, and thousands of yards of telephone cable.

Meanwhile, on either side of Carentan, the American XIX Corps had entered the line, between the left wing of VII Corps and the right wing of V Corps. On the whole, General Bradley could consider himself satisfied with the situation, until, on June 19, a storm destroyed the artificial port being set up on "Omaha" Beach, and hundreds of landing craft and thousands of tons of supplies were lost; this, in turn, created a very difficult weapons shortage for the 1st Army, and delayed the entry into the line of General Middleton's VIII Corps.

In spite of these difficulties, VII Corps succeeded in overcoming the resistance that Schlieben, with forces much too slender for the wide front he was holding, tried to put up, on Hitler's own orders, at Cherbourg. However, he refused to reply to General Collins's first call to surrender, couched in the following terms: "You and your troops have resisted stubbornly and gallantly, but you are in a hopeless situation. The moment has come for you to capitulate. Send your reply by radio, on a frequency of 1520 kilocycles, and show a white flag or fire white signal flares from the naval hospital or the Pasteur clinic. After that, send a staff officer under a flag of truce to the farmhouse on the road to Fort-du-Roule, to accept the terms of surrender."

Fort Roule, the key to this great port, had indeed just fallen to the Americans, and Fort Octeville, where Schlieben and Rear-Admiral Hennecke had taken refuge, was being subjected to such an intense bombardment that clouds of poisonous fumes were seeping into the galleries where more than 300 wounded lay sheltering. This being so, Schlieben sent his negotiators to General Eddy on June 26, at 1400 hours, specifying that only Fort Octeville was to be discussed.

The time thus gained by the Germans enabled their pioneers to carry out the destruction of the port installations, and mine the ruins of the town, making the clearing up of the roads a longer and more costly process. In actual fact, only a month was needed before the Americans were able to bring in their first ships to Cherbourg; a few weeks later, an immense drum, 36 feet in diameter, was towed into Cherbourg harbour; around it were strung the last few yards of "Pluto" (Pipe Line Under The Ocean), the latest development by the Allied technicians, who had been responsible for the artificial port of Arromanches, which had resisted

The "battle of the hedgerows" – American troops dash for cover across a lane behind the hulk of a knocked-out Panther tank.

the storm of June 19 better than "Omaha". Starting at Sandown, on the Isle of Wight, Pluto's four tubes, each three inches in diameter and about 170 miles long, enabled 250,000 gallons of petrol a day to be pumped to the Allied armies.

The last strongholds of the town did not fall until July 3. On June 27, receiving the surrender of Major Küppers, Osteck fortress commander, General Barton, commanding the 4th Division, showed Küppers his map of the situation; later Küppers told Paul Carell:

"The entire network of the German positions was shown on the map with absolute accuracy, and in far greater detail than our own maps. On the back were listed precise data about the types of weapons and ammunition at each emplacement and bunker, as well as the names of all strongpoint commanders, and of the battalion and regimental commanders to whom they were responsible. The adjoining sheet covered the former defence sector 'East' in the Saint-Pierre-Eglise area outside the Cherbourg fortified zone . . . All command-posts showed the names of their principal officers. True, the entry for 11th Battery, 1709th Artillery Regiment still listed its commander Lieutenant Ralf Neste, who had lost his life in an accident with a

Panzerfaust on May 5, 1944 – but that seemed to be the only mistake.

"Their success had been tremendous. The full story of this gigantic espionage and Intelligence operation still remains to be written. It is the story of the Alliance of Animals, that most important secret Intelligence organization of the Allies in France; the story of 'Panther', the French Colonel Alamichel who set up the organisation; the story of Colonel Fay, who was known as 'Lion', and of Marie-Madeleine Merrie, that young, pretty, and courageous French woman who oddly enough bore the code-name of *Hérisson* ('Hedgehog').

"The chief of the Alliance had three headquarters in Paris for the staff of officers and for his British chief radio-operator, 'Magpie'. One of these headquarters was the contact point for couriers, the second was an alternative headquarters for emergencies, and the third, in the Rue Charles Laffitte, was headed by 'Odette', the famous Odette. At these headquarters all information converged. Here it was sorted according to Army, Navy, Air Force, political or economic."

But Bradley had no intention of resting on his laurels. He quickly brought his VII Corps into the line, in between the left wing of VIII Corps and the right wing of XIX Corps, such was his impatience to begin phase two of the Normandy campaign, which meant break-

ing up the German front between Saint Lô and Coutances, and then exploiting this breakthrough in the direction of Avranches. The operation had to be carried out quickly, so as to prevent the enemy digging in and returning to the techniques of trench warfare which had caused such bloody losses in 1914-18.

On June 24, Bradley's 1st Army consisted of VIII, VII, XIX and V Corps (nine infantry divisions, two armoured divisions, and the 82nd and 101st Airborne Divisions, although these latter were badly in need of a rest). His resources were thus greater than those of the enemy's 7th Army, but the Germans were tough, well commanded, and in good heart, as is shown by this letter, written by a German sergeant who had been taken prisoner: "The R.A.F. rules the skies. I have not yet seen a single plane with a 'swastika', and despite the material superiority of the enemy we Germans hold firm. The front at Caen holds. Every soldier on this front is hoping for a miracle and waits for the secret weapons which have been discussed so much."

In particular, between the sea and the Vire, in the sector where the American VII and VIII Corps were in action, the nature of the terrain favoured the defence, since both towards Coutances and Saint Lô marshy land alternated with woodland. If the tanks took to the main roads, they fell victims to the redoubtable German 8.8-cm, which pounded them whilst remaining safely out of range; if they took to the little-used country roads, they got in everybody's way and at the same time exposed themselves to the risk of being shot at by a *Panzerschreck* or a *Panzerfaust* fired through a neighbouring hedge. Furthermore, the wet weather of the second half of June and the whole of July reduced to a minimum those air force sorties which could have helped the American 1st Army; even in fine weather the rolling green woodlands of the region would have made air support difficult; bad weather made air sorties, if not impossible, at least very dangerous, not least for the troops they were intended to support.

These different factors explain the slowness of the American advance across the swollen rivers and the flooded meadows of this neck of the Cotentin which extends between the Channel and the estuary of the River Vire. VIII Corps only took la Haye-du-Puits at the cost of exhausting combat; whilst VII Corps, despite the nickname "Lightning Joe" which they had bestowed on their dynamic General Collins, only became masters of what was left of the ruins of Saint Lô on July 20, 44 days later than laid down in the plan drawn up the April before . . . And not without quite considerable losses.

General Bradley, referring to this fierce resistance which halted his advance and cost so many lives, has given the following description of the ordeals his men had to undergo as they fought through Normandy, Lorraine, the Ardennes, the Siegfried Line, and then into the very heart of Germany:

"The rifleman trudges into battle knowing that statistics are stacked against his

*Some G.I.'s take a break,
amidst the wreckage of war.*

survival. He fights without promise of either reward or relief. Behind every river, there's another hill–and behind that hill, another river. After weeks or months in the line only a wound can offer him the comfort of safety, shelter, and a bed. Those who are left to fight, fight on, evading death but knowing that with each day of evasion they have exhausted one more chance for survival. Sooner or later, unless victory comes, the chase must end on the litter or in the grave."

And indeed, between June 22, the seventeenth day of the invasion, and July 19, American losses had leapt from 18,374 (including 3,012 dead), to 62,000, more precisely 10,641 dead and 51,387 wounded, two-thirds of whom, if not more, were as usual the long-suffering infantrymen.

These mounting losses and the very slow progress being made by the American 1st Army provoked a fair amount of criticism from the host of correspondents accredited to S.H.A.E.F., especially as from June 22 the Russian summer offensive, with its almost daily victories, allowed unflattering comparisons to be made on Eisenhower and Bradley: compared with Vitebsk, Orcha, Mogilev, Bobruysk, and Minsk, la Haye-du-Puits, Pont-Hébert, Tribehou, and even Saint Lô were but puny things. Some even went so far as to say that the "halting" of operations on the Western Front was part of some concerted plan, drawn up at the highest level, and intended to bleed the long-suffering Russians white with a view to the future.

The unsavoury gossip about Bradley was nothing to the criticisms made of Montgomery regarding the mediocre victories which the British 2nd Army could claim at that time. It had in fact to attack three

times, and it was not until July 9, 1944 that it was able to announce the capture of Caen, its D-Day objective.

Of course, Montgomery could hardly reveal to the journalists whom he gathered round him for periodical press conferences that he had no intention of opening up the route to Paris. Still less could he tell them that his plan aimed first and foremost at forcing Rommel to concentrate his Panzers against the British 2nd Army, and wearing them down on this front by a series of purely local actions. Having said this, however, it may be said that in this battle of equipment, Montgomery the master-tactician did not sufficiently bear in mind the enormous technical superiority that German armour enjoyed over the British and American tanks. If we look again at accounts of the furious battles fought out in the Caen sector in June and July, 1944, all we seem to read about is Sherman tanks burning like torches, Cromwell tanks riddled like sieves, and Churchill tanks, whose armour was considered sufficiently thick, never surviving a direct hit. Here, for example, is part of Major-General Roberts's description of Operation "Goodwood" on July 19 and 20.

"But 3 R.T.R. were through. They had started with 52 tanks, been given 11 replacements, making 63 tanks in all. With Bras now in their hands, they had nine tanks left. Major Close's A Squadron had lost 17 tanks in two days, seven being completely destroyed, the others recoverable; all Troop officers had been killed or wounded, and only one troop Sergeant was left. The Fife and Forfar had fared rather worse."

In the circumstances it is not surprising that the famous units that had formed part of the 8th Army in North Africa (the 50th and 51st Infantry Divisions, and the 7th

Armoured Division) did not have the success expected of them in this new theatre of operations. Writing of these veterans of Bir Hakeim, Tobruk, and El Alamein, Belfield and Essame remind us of the old saying current in the British Army–"An old soldier is a cautious soldier, that is why he is an old soldier." Quite probably. But perhaps the hiding the Desert Rats received at Villers-Bocage on July 12, when they first came into contact with the 2nd Panzer Division, was such as to make even the most reckless prudent.

As for the 12 British divisions which came under fire for the very first time in Normandy, however realistic their training may have been, however keen they may have been to fight, the real thing was very different, and the conditions they were called upon to face in real combat sometimes took away some of their aggressiveness.

It is also possible to criticise the British High Command for the tendency in its instructions to try to foresee everything, even the unforeseeable. Having seen orders issued by the main American commanders, we know that they subscribed to the same theory as the Germans, that the order should contain all that the lesser commander needs to know to carry out his task but nothing more; whereas British orders tended to go into further detail, limiting the initiative of the tactical commanders, because of theoretical situations that did not always arise. For in war, it is said, it is the unexpected that happens.

In this list of Montgomery's resources, an honourable mention must be made of the artillery, for which Rommel's grenadiers had a special dislike, for it fired quickly and accurately. In particular, the 25-pounder "gun-howitzer" fired so rapidly that the Germans thought it must have been fitted with a system of automatic loading. And this fact goes a long way to explain the form which the fighting took in the Caen sector, for if the British tanks failed in all their attempts at breakthrough whenever they came up against the German Panthers, Tigers, and the 8.8-cm anti-tank guns of *Panzergruppe* "West", the German counter-attacks collapsed under the murderous fire of the British artillery concentrations whenever they went beyond purely local engagements. All the more so since at that distance from the coast the big guns of the Royal Navy were able to take a hand. So it was that on June 16 in the region of Thury-Harcourt, about 20 miles from Riva-Bella, a 16-inch shell from the *Rodney* or the *Nelson* killed Lieutenant-General Witt, commanding the 12th S.S. Panzer Division "*Hitlerjugend*".

The failure of British XXX Armoured Corps and the 7th Armoured Division to turn the front of *Panzergruppe* "West" at Villers-Bocage seems to have caused Montgomery to shift the centre of gravity of his attack to the countryside around Caen, where his armour would find a more suitable terrain.

Operation "Epsom", begun on June 25, brought into action VIII Corps, just landed in Normandy and commanded by Sir Richard O'Connor, released from captivity by the signing of the Italian armistice. Covered on his right by XXX Corps' 49th Division, O'Connor was to cross the Caen–Bayeux road to the west of the Carpiquet aerodrome, push on past the Fossé de l' Odon, then switching the direction of his attack from south to south-west, he would finally reach Bretteville-sur-Laize, ten miles south of Caen, near the Caen–Falaise road. This would give the British 2nd Army not only the capital of Normandy, but also the Carpiquet air base, upon which Air-Marshals Coningham and Leigh-Mallory had long been casting envious eyes.

VIII Corps had 60,000 men, 600 tanks, and 700 guns. The 15th and 43rd Divisions, each reinforced by a brigade of Churchill tanks, provided O'Connor with his shock troops, whilst the 11th Armoured Division would then exploit the situation. For all three divisions it was their first taste of combat.

Whilst the left wing of XXX Corps attacked the Panzer-"*Lehr*" Division, VIII Corps' attack brought it into contact with the 12th S.S. Panzer Division "*Hitlerjugend*", commanded, since the death of General Witt, by General Kurt Meyer, a leader of extreme resolution, of rapid

Heavily-laden British Shermans. Although armed with an improved gun, they were no match for the Panzers.

and correct decisions, whom his men had nicknamed "Panzer-Meyer". By nightfall, at the price of fierce combat and despite incessant counter-attacks, the British infantry was able to bed down near the Caen–Villers-Bocage road, three miles from their starting point. On June 27, the 15th Division managed to capture a sound bridge over the Odon, and the 11th Armoured Division advanced and began the switching movement mentioned earlier: the first objective was Hill 112, the summit of the ridge which separates the Odon and Orne Valleys.

The VIII Corps, however, was now behind schedule, and some very troublesome bottlenecks were building up at its rear. These difficulties enabled Sepp Dietrich, commanding I S.S. Panzer Corps, to avoid the worst by bringing in General Paul Hausser's II S.S. Panzer Corps, which had just come back from the Galician front. He even tried to take the 11th Armoured Division in a pincer movement between the 9th S.S. Panzer Division "Hohenstaufen" and the 10th S.S. Panzer Division "Frundsberg" and only failed because O'Connor evacuated his troops from a salient that had become too exposed.

On the other hand the *Panzergruppe* "West" failed in its efforts to turn this defensive success into a general offensive, for II S.S. Panzer Corps was literally pinned down by artillery fire and tactical air bombardment whenever it made the slightest move. In this connection General Harzer, Chief Operations Staff Officer of the 9th S.S. *Panzergrenadier* Division said later: "Now, if the Luftwaffe had been able to deal with the Allied navies and also stop the accurate bombing of certain targets, I think that the British-Canadian landings would once again have 'fallen in the ditch', as they say. As it was, our counter-offensive broke down under air attack and artillery fire, particularly the heavy guns of the battleships. They were devastating. When one of these shells dropped near a Panther, the 56-ton *(sic)* tank was blown over on its side, just from the blast. It was these broadsides from the warships, more than the defensive fighting of the enemy's troops, which halted our division's Panzer Regiment." At all events, after this sharp lesson, the Germans gave up any further idea of throwing the enemy back into the sea. Instead, they had been forced to feed into a defensive battle the reserves they needed for a major counter-strike.

Montgomery, in his June 30 directive to Generals Bradley and Dempsey, declared himself to be quite satisfied with the results obtained, although Operation "Epsom" had only dented the enemy line.

"All this is good . . . by forcing the enemy to place the bulk of his strength in front of the Second Army, we have made easier the acquisition of territory on the western flank.

"Our policy has been so successful that the Second Army is now opposed by a formidable array of German Panzer Divisions – eight definitely identified, and possibly more to come . . .

"To hold the maximum number of enemy divisions on our eastern flank between Caen and Villers Bocage, and to swing the western or right flank of the Army Group southwards and eastwards in a wide sweep so as to threaten the line of withdrawal of such enemy divisions to the south of Paris."

The carrying out of this plan meant continuing to place the main weight of this battle of attrition on the shoulders of General Dempsey, for the slightest slackening of pressure would mean that Rommel would be able to reorganise and re-form.

On July 9, Caen and Carpiquet aerodrome fell to Lieutenant-General J. T. Crocker's British I Corps. The old Norman town, already badly bombed by the R.A.F. on the night of June 5-6, was now reduced to rubble by the dropping of 2,500 tons of bombs. The only part more or less spared was the area around the majestic Abbaye-aux-Hommes, which was protected by the Geneva Convention and was a refuge for many thousands of homeless. Although this pitiless bombing

forced the *"Hitlerjugend"* Division to retreat, it also created such ruin, and slowed down the advance of the Canadian 3rd Division so much, that when it arrived at the river Orne the bridges were blown.

Because of a delay by the U.S. 1st Army in preparing Operation "Cobra", the break-out on the Allied right which was to crush German resistance, Montgomery asked Dempsey for one more effort to engage and tie down the Panzers on his front, and, if possible, to advance the armoured units of his 2nd Army into the region around Falaise. To this end, Operation "Goodwood" had moved the centre of gravity of the attack back to the right bank of the Orne, where the British 1st and 8th Armies were massed, whilst the Canadian II Corps, two divisions strong, was concentrated within the ruins of Caen. To it fell the task of capturing the suburbs of the town to the south of the river, and of developing an attack towards Falaise. The enemy's front, tied down in the centre, would be by-passed and rolled back from left to

An American section prepares to break cover from a ditch which had become an impromptu trench a few moments before.

right by the three armoured divisions (the 7th and 11th, and the Guards Armoured Divisions), breaking out from the narrow bridgehead between the Orne and the Dives, which General Gale's parachute troops had captured on the night of June 5-6. VIII Corps possessed 1,100 tanks, 720 guns and a stockpile of 250,000 shells. But above all, the Allied air forces would support and prepare the attack on a scale hitherto undreamed of: 1,600 four-engined planes, and 600 two-engined planes and fighter-bombers would drop more than 7,000 tons of explosives on enemy positions, and then support VIII Corps' armour as it advanced.

However, the Germans had seen through the Allies' intentions, and had organised themselves to a depth of ten miles; it is true that they only had in the line one division, the 16th Luftwaffe Field Division, and what was left of the

21st Panzer Division, but they still possessed considerable fire-power, in the shape of 272 6-tube rocket launchers and a hundred or so 8.8-cm anti-aircraft guns operating as anti-tank guns.

On July 18, at 0530 hours, the thunder of 720 guns signalled the beginning of Operation "Goodwood". Then, as one member of VIII Corps put it, the aircraft "came lounging across the sky, scattered, leisurely, indifferent. The first ones crossed our lines, and the earth began to shake to a continuous rumble which lasted for three-quarters of an hour; and at no time during that period were fewer than fifty 'planes visible. The din was tremendous. We could see the bombs leaving the 'planes and drifting down almost gently, like milt from a salmon, and as they disappeared behind the trees the rumble rose a little and then sunk to its old level again. The Jocks were all standing grinning at the sky. After weeks of skulking in trenches, here was action; action on a bigger scale than any of them had dreamed was possible."

At 0745 hours the 11th Armoured Division, preceded by a continuous barrage of an intensity never before experienced, began to advance, and quickly got through the first position, defended by troops still groggy from the pounding inflicted by Bomber Command. But towards mid-day the attack came up against the railway line running from Caen to Paris, where it stopped.

This was due, first, to the fact that the British artillery, which had stayed on the left bank of the Orne, no longer had the enemy within range; and second, that on the bridges which the Guards and the 7th Armoured Division had to take to get across to the right bank and link up with the 11th Division, there were tremendous bottlenecks. Above all, however, was the fact that 8.8-cm guns and *Nebelwerfers* were firing from the many villages on the outskirts of the town. At nightfall the 1st S.S. Panzer Division *"Leibstandarte"*, which formed Sepp Dietrich's reserve, surprised the 11th Armoured Division, just when it was about to bed down, and according to its commander, Major-General Wisch, destroyed about 40 of its tanks.

On July 19, with the rain taking a hand, the terrain got into such a state owing to the bombing the day before, that operations had to stop. South and south-west of Caen, the British and Canadians had advanced about five miles into the enemy's defensive positions, but had not succeeded in overrunning them. All in all it was rather a meagre success, especially as it had been paid for at the enormous price of 413 tanks, but there was a certain strategic compensation, as the 116th Panzer Division of the German 15th Army, stationed up till then near Amiens, was ordered to move towards Caen; even worse, Kluge, Rundstedt's successor at the head of Army Group 'B', afraid of a British breakthrough in the direction of Falaise, thought it advisable to move his 2nd Panzer Division from Saint Lô to Caen, less than a week before the beginning of Operation "Cobra".

By this same day of July 19, the losses of the British 2nd Army since June 6 had amounted to 34,700 officers and men, of whom 6,010 were killed, and 28,690 were missing. They were therefore far less severe than those suffered during the same period by the American 1st Army (62,028 men). Of course, on D-Day the American 1st Division, on "Omaha" Beach, and the 82nd and 101st Airborne Divisions, around Sainte Mère-Eglise, had had a harder time of it. But in the Normandy woodlands the infantry-based American attacks had also been more expensive, in terms of men, than the British tank-based attacks in the Caen area—which seemed to prove once more Guderian's theory that tanks are a weapon that saves lives.

Basing his calculations on the figures supplied by Brigadier Williams, head of his Intelligence staff, Montgomery saw a situation arising in which, in spite of the apparent failures of the British 2nd Army, he would in a few days be able to send in the American 1st Army. Between June 6 and July 25, German strength had shifted away from the American front to that of their Allies, the British. Thus by July 15, there were over three times as many German tanks facing the British as were deployed on Bradley's front.

Although, of course, Montgomery's superiors, General Eisenhower and the Combined Chiefs-of-Staff Committee, as well as his most important subordinates, were aware of the strategic objective hidden by his apparently slow manoeuvres, S.H.A.E.F. was beginning to show some signs of impatience. Writing ten years after the event, Montgomery thought he saw personal reasons, unconnected with the military situation, behind many of the criticisms made of his methods within the Allied High Command.

"One of the reasons for this in my belief was that the original COSSAC plan had been, in fact, to break out from the Caen–Falaise area, on our eastern flank. I had refused to accept this plan and had changed it. General Morgan who had made the COSSAC plan was now at Supreme Headquarters as Deputy Chief of Staff. He considered Eisenhower was a god; since I had discarded many of his plans, he placed me at the other end of the celestial ladder. So here were the seeds of discord. Morgan and those around him (the displaced strategists) lost no opportunity of trying to persuade Eisenhower that I was defensively minded and that we were unlikely to break out anywhere!"

As far as Sir Frederick Morgan is concerned, Montgomery may have been right, but he is surely on more dangerous ground when he goes on to assert that Air-Marshal Coningham, commander of the Tactical Air Force, associated himself with these criticisms for similar reasons. Coningham, he wrote, "was particularly interested in getting his airfields south-west of Caen. They were mentioned in the plan and to him they were all-important. I don't blame him. But they were not all-important to me. If we won the battle of Normandy, everything else would follow, airfields and all. I wasn't fighting to capture airfields; I was fighting to defeat Rommel in Normandy. This Coningham could scarcely appreciate: and for two reasons. First, we were not seeing each other daily as in the desert days, for at this stage I was working direct to Leigh-Mallory. Secondly, Coningham wanted the airfields in order to defeat Rommel, whereas I wanted to defeat Rommel in order, only incidentally, to capture the airfields."

And events were to show that in order to defeat Army Group "B", it was unnecessary to be in possession of the airfields that Coningham would have liked. It is still true, however, that by remaining in the Caen area, instead of wearing the enemy down in the Falaise area, 15 miles further south, as the original project had planned, the British 2nd Army asked its air force for a great deal of support, and yet placed it in a difficult position.

In the Normandy beach-head airfields were scarce, and their runways were so short that for the pilots getting fighter-bombers loaded with a ton of bombs or rockets into the air was a real problem. And landing posed similar problems; as Belfield and Essame have noted, "anyone who flew over the bridgehead in Normandy must have retained vivid memories of fighter aircraft, twin engined Dakotas (used as ambulances) and the small Austers all milling about in a horribly confined airspace. The perpetual risk of collisions greatly increased the strain on the pilots who had to fly from the bridgehead".

It may be that the commander of the 2nd Tactical Air Force did not like being treated as a subordinate by the man with whom he had been on equal terms in North Africa, but his criticisms did not all spring from personal ill-feeling. And it should be noted that at S.H.A.E.F. Air-Marshals Leigh-Mallory and Tedder both approved Coningham's attitude.

As for Eisenhower, it may fairly be said that his memoirs are marked with a calm philosophy that he was far from feeling when Operation "Goodwood" was breaking down on the Bourguébus ridge. For after all, according to the plan worked out by Montgomery, Bradley's enveloping movement ought to have begun on D-Day plus seventeen, June 23, when the Allies would be firmly established on a front extending from Granville to Caen, passing through Vire, Argentan, and Falaise. "This meant", he wrote, "that Falaise would be in our possession before the great wheel began. The line that we actually held when the breakout began on D plus 50 was approximately that planned for D plus 5.

Tank-hunting near St. Lô: bazooka-equipped American troops accompany an M-10 tank destroyer down a dusty road, keeping a careful watch.

"This was a far different story, but one which had to be accepted. Battle is not a one-sided affair. It is a case of action and reciprocal action repeated over and over again as contestants seek to gain position and other advantage by which they may inflict the greatest possible damage upon their respective opponents."

Be that as it may, in his opinion Montgomery needed a touch not of the brake, but of the accelerator, and Eisenhower's repeated efforts to get Montgomery to show more aggression could not have failed to annoy his troublesome subordinate.

In this argument, which went as far as Winston Churchill, Montgomery had a faithful defender in Brooke, who did all he could to prevent this potential conflict from becoming too bitter. At the time Montgomery was also on the best of terms with Bradley, who wrote that "Montgomery exercised his Allied authority

with wisdom, forbearance, and restraint. While coordinating our movements with those of Dempsey's Monty carefully avoided getting mixed up in U.S. command decisions, but instead granted us the latitude to operate as freely and as independently as we chose. At no time did he probe into First Army with the indulgent manner he sometimes displayed among those subordinates who were also his countrymen. I could not have wanted a more tolerant or judicious commander. Not once did he confront us with an arbitrary directive and not once did he reject any plan that we had devised."

There is no doubt therefore that Bradley, who enjoyed Eisenhower's full confidence, tried to influence him the same way as Brooke. The differences over strategy that arose between Bradley and Montgomery from the autumn of 1944, and the coolness that affected their relations afterwards, right up to the end of the war, are very well known, which makes Bradley's comments on Montgomery's handling of this initial phase of the Battle of Normandy all the more valuable. "Whilst Collins was hoisting

the flag of VII Corps above Cherbourg, Montgomery was losing his reputation in the long and arduous siege of the old university town of Caen. For three weeks he had been engaging his troops against those armoured divisions that he had deliberately lured towards Caen, in accordance with our diversionary strategy. The town was an important communications centre which he would eventually need, but for the moment the taking of the town was an end in itself, for his task, first and foremost, was to commit German troops against the British front, so that we could capture Cherbourg that much easier, and prepare a further attack.

"In this diversionary mission Monty was more than successful, for the harder he hammered toward Caen, the more German troops he drew into that sector. Too many correspondents, however, had overrated the importance of Caen itself, and when Monty failed to take it, they blamed him for the delay. But had we attempted to exonerate Montgomery by explaining how successfully he had hoodwinked the German by diverting him toward Caen from Cotentin, we would have also given our strategy away. We desperately wanted the Germans to believe this attack on Caen was the main Allied effort." It seems pretty clear that Montgomery was right. During World War I, Joffre had been severely criticised for his phrase "I'm nibbling away at them". Thirty years later, it must be admitted that Montgomery, though paying a heavy price, "nibbled" his opponent's armoured units, which were technically superior and on the whole very well trained, to excellent effect.

Caen may thus be compared with Verdun, in World War I, where Colonel-General Falkenhayn intended to bleed the French Army white. But where the head of the Kaiser's General Staff failed against Joffre, Montgomery succeeded against Rommel, and with the American 1st Army and Patton behind Bradley, he had at his disposal a force ready to exploit the situation such as Falkenhayn never had.

At all events, the accredited pressmen at S.H.A.E.F. did not spare Montgomery, and above him Eisenhower, whom they criticised for tolerating the inefficiency of his second-in-command. It was even insinuated in the American press that with typical British cunning, Montgomery was trying to save his troops at the expense of the Americans, and that, most careful of English lives, he preferred to expend American soldiers, without the naïve Eisenhower realising what was happening.

However far-fetched such quarrels may seem, they continued long after the war, but under a different guise. For after the brilliant success of Operation "Cobra", which took Bradley almost in one fell swoop from Avranches, in Normandy, to Commercy and Maastricht on the Meuse, it would have been both indecent and ridiculous to accuse Montgomery of having kept the best things for the Anglo-Canadian troops, and given the Americans nothing but the scraps. Critics now tried to show that his attempts to tie down the enemy's mobile reserves with General Dempsey's troops failed. Thus, in 1946, Ralph Ingersoll, a war correspondent with Bradley's forces, portrayed the "Master" as being impatient to fight it out with Rommel: "The blow . . . could be struck with British forces under a British headquarters, for British credit and prestige". This would have confirmed Montgomery's domination of the American armies. "The result of Montgomery's decision was the battle of Caen–which was really two battles, two successive all-out attacks, continuing after Caen itself had fallen. Beginning in mid-June and ending nearly a month later, it was a defeat from which British arms on the continent never recovered. It was the first and last all-British battle fought in Europe. As he had feared, Montgomery was never again able to fight alone but thereafter had always to borrow troops and supplies to gain the superiority without which he would not even plan an attack."

What does this mean? That the 2nd British Army's attacks did not reach their geographical objectives is beyond question, but when one realises the tactical and material advantages gained over the enemy, it is impossible to join with Ingersoll and talk of "defeat". This can be seen in the cries of alarm, and later of despair, which German O.B. West sent to O.K.W. Of course, Ingersoll wrote his book in 1946, and was not in a position to appreciate all this.

Colonel-General Count von Schlieffen, the old Chief-of-Staff of the Imperial German Army, used to say to his students at the Military Academy, that when analysing a campaign, due allowance was never given to the way in which the vanquished positively helped the victor. It will therefore be instructive to see how Rommel, Rundstedt, and Hitler smoothed the path of Montgomery and Eisenhower.

In all this Rundstedt played a very secondary rôle. The great strategist whose Army Group "A" had conquered Poland, and who had played such a big part in the defeat of France, no longer dominated, nor did he seem to want to do so; Lieutenant-General Speidel, Chief-of-Staff of Army Group "B", paints him as having adopted an attitude of "sarcastic resignation", considering the "representations" and "despatches full of gravity" sent to Hitler as being the height of wisdom. He did, however, loyally support Rommel in his discussions with Hitler–nothing more, nothing less.

Responsibility for the German defeat in the West therefore has to be shared between Rommel and Hitler. On D-Day, both wondered if this attack was not rather a diversion, covering a second landing aimed at the Pas-de-Calais. And due to the successful Allied deception measures, Hitler remained fixed to this idea until the end of July, whilst Rommel abandoned it when the American VII Corps' orders fell into his hands. The results of such blindness were catastrophic. To stop the Allies on the front they had reached by June 12, it would have been necessary to disengage the armoured units that Rommel had thrown in against Montgomery in the Caen sector, but this would only have been possible by drawing upon the 15th Army, stationed between the Seine and the Escaut, and the best placed to intervene. But Hitler expressly forbade Army Group "B" to do this. The Germans were therefore obliged, after scouring Brittany, to seek reinforcements at the very opposite end of France, and on June 12, the 276th Division received orders to leave Bayonne and get to the front: "The broken railways, the destroyed bridges and the French Maquis so delayed them that the last elements of the division finally arrived at Hottot in Normandy on July 4. In other words, to make a journey of some 400 miles, which could normally be completed by rail in seventy-two hours, required no less than twenty-two days. The main body of the division had to march

at least one-third of the distance on foot, averaging approximately twenty miles each night."

Similar misfortunes befell the 272nd Division, drawn from Perpignan, and the 274th Division, hastily organised in the Narbonne area; whilst, in order to reach the Caen sector, the 16th L.F.D., on watch over the coast at IJmuiden, had first to follow the Rhine as far as Koblenz. All this makes it easy to understand why Army Group "B" was confined to a series of piecemeal tactical operations, devoid of any overall strategy.

At Rundstedt's urgent request, Hitler agreed to meet him and Rommel together at the command post he had installed in 1940, at Margival, near Soissons, when Operation "Seelöwe" had been planned to conquer Great Britain. According to Lieutenant-General Speidel's account: "Hitler had arrived with Colonel-General Jodl and staff on the morning of June 17. He had travelled in an armoured car from Metz, where he had flown from Berchtesgaden. He looked pale and worn for lack of sleep. His fingers played nervously with his spectacles and the pencils before him. Hunched on a stool, with his marshals standing before him, his former magnetism seemed to have vanished.

"After a few cold words of greeting, Hitler, in a high, bitter voice, railed on about the success of the Allied landing, and tried to blame the local commanders. He ordered that Cherbourg be held at all costs."

Rommel, who also spoke for Rundstedt, defended his officers from these attacks. When they began to discuss future action, the gulf between the two commanders and their garrulous leader became even more pronounced.

In Hitler's view, the use of flying bombs would soon bring the Third Reich victory, provided that they were concentrated against London; whereas, logically, it was suggested that he ought to use them against the embarkation ports which were sending over reinforcements to Normandy. Hitler did not deny the shortcomings of the Luftwaffe, but asserted that within a short time the coming into service of jet fighters would wrest from the Allies their present supremacy, and thus allow the Wehrmacht's land forces to

A German dummy tank.

resume the initiative. But without Hitler's earlier intervention, the jets would have already entered service . . .

Above all, however, was the fact that Rommel, backed by Rundstedt, categorically rejected the possibility of a second Allied landing north of the Seine, and demanded complete freedom of action, for it was now to be expected that the enemy would "break out of the Caen and Bayeux areas, and also from the Cotentin, towards the south, aiming for Paris, with a secondary attack upon Avranches to isolate Brittany". To cancel out this threat, they would have to bring into action the infantry divisions stationed in the Orne sector, then carry out "a limited withdrawal to be made southwards, with the object of launching an armoured thrust into the flank of the enemy and fighting the battle outside the range of the enemy's naval artillery . . . "

Hitler vetoed this plan absolutely: it was to be total resistance, no retreat, as at the time of the Battle of Moscow. Events have shown that this policy condemned the German forces in Normandy to disaster. But whether Rommel's plan would have been possible, given the enormous Allied superiority and the dilapidated state of his troops, is doubtful, to say the least.

As was to be expected, the fall of Cherbourg and the Cotentin operations in-

Was this the attack that wounded Rommel? These "stills" from a camera-gun show a strafing attack near Livarot.

creased even further the tension between those at the front and Hitler.

Furious at the way things were going, the Führer, despite Rommel's and Rundstedt's objections, ordered Colonel-General Dollman to be the subject of a judicial enquiry. On hearing this news, Dollman suffered a heart attack at Le Mans on June 29, and was replaced at the head of the 7th Army by General Hausser, who handed over command of II *Waffen*-S.S. Panzer Corps to his colleague Bittrich. On the same day *Panzergruppe* "West" was re-christened the 5th *Panzerarmee,* but General Geyr von Schweppenburg, only just recovered from the wounds he had sustained on June 12, having resumed command, had been dismissed and replaced by General Eberbach, because he had had the temerity to point out the strategic patching-up of the Supreme Command.

The same day also, Rommel and Rundstedt were called to the Berghof by Hitler, who, however, refused to speak to them in private, and added nothing new to the rantings with which he had assailed their ears at Margival, about the decisive effect which the new weapons would have upon the course of the war. As for the two marshals, they emphasised the urgent necessity of ending the war on the west, so as to enable the Reich to fight on in the east. On seeing the indignant way in which their suggestion was greeted, they both thought they were going to be sacked on the spot. In fact the Führer's wrath fell only on Rundstedt, and even then it was somewhat mitigated by the award of the Oak Leaves to his Knight's

Cross. He was replaced by Kluge, who had now recovered from the winter car accident which had obliged him to give up his command on the Eastern Front. At the Berghof, the new Supreme Commander in the West was duly spoken to by Hitler, Keitel, and Jodl, who impressed upon him the necessity of making his subordinate, Rommel, see reason. Hence the violent incident which took place at la Roche-Guyon, when the hero of Tobruk was told in no uncertain terms by his new chief that "he would now have to get accustomed to carrying out orders".

Rommel reacted to these remarks with a written protest on July 3, to which he added a long aide-mémoire in justification, whose reasoning, both honest and full of good sense, led Kluge, an intelligent man, completely to revise his opinion.

In any case, the developing situation in Normandy allowed no other conclusion than Rommel's. The 5th *Panzerarmee* and the 7th Army were still containing the Allied advance, but with more and more difficulty. Despite their losses, Allied numbers and supplies were increasing daily, whereas the German forces' losses could not be made up. Between June 6 and July 15 it had only received 6,000 men to replace 97,000 killed, missing, and wounded, amongst whom there were 2,360 officers, including 28 generals and 354 lieutenant-generals. And its supply position had become so precarious because of enemy bombing that the most drastic economies were imposed.

Such were the facts that Rommel, with the approval of Kluge, pointed out in his last report to Hitler on July 15 1944 – a sad catalogue leading to the following conclusions:

"It must therefore be expected that within the next two to three weeks, the enemy will break through our weakened front, and advance in depth through France, an action which will have the gravest consequences.

"Everywhere our troops are fighting heroically, but this unequal struggle is inevitably drawing to a close. I am forced to ask you to draw the necessary conclusions from this situation, without delay. As leader of your Western forces, I felt it my duty to explain it to you as clearly as possible."

What would have happened if Rommel had not been badly wounded on the Livarot–Vimoutiers road, the very day after dispatching this strong message? Hitler would almost certainly have refused, told him that he must not surrender, and would probably even have dismissed him. In that event, would Rommel have sent officers to parley with Montgomery? He would have been able to count on all his general staff, and certain field-commanders, such as Lüttwitz and Schwerin, at the head of the 2nd and 116th Panzer Divisions respectively. But would he have taken this enormous step after the shattering news came through of the bomb attempt on Hitler's life and the collapse of the "July Plot"?

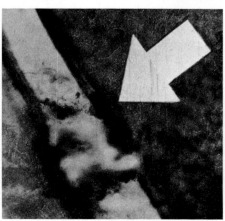

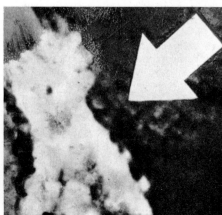

CHAPTER 61
Breakout from Normandy

It is now time to return to the battle itself, for on July 25 General Bradley began Operation "Cobra".

On that day the German forces defending Normandy consisted of:

1. from the coastal battery at Merville to the area of Caumont-l'Eventé: 5th *Panzerarmee* (General Eberbach) comprising LXXXVI Corps, I and II *Waffen-S.S.* Panzer Corps, LXXIV Corps, with between them 11 divisions, including two Panzer and two *Panzergrenadier* with about 645 tanks. facing British and Canadian forces); and

2. from Caumont-l'Eventé to the western coast of the Cotentin peninsula: 7th Army (General Hausser) astride the Vire with three corps of 13 divisions: on the right bank of the river XLVII Panzer Corps and II Parachute Corps with between them six infantry divisions and on the left bank LXXXIV Corps with one *Panzergrenadier* and two Panzer divisions with about 190 tanks. (facing Americans).

But, we would repeat, there are divisions and divisions. Let us take the case of LXXXIV Corps, which was going to bear the brunt of the attack. Its 91st, 243rd, and 352nd Divisions had only 2,500 rifles between them, after the fierce fighting in the *bocage*, and its three armoured divisions ("Lehr" and 2nd S.S. "Das Reich" Panzer, and 17th "Götz von Berlichingen" *Panzergrenadier*) were down to something like half their establishment. The German front twisted and turned along the stretch Bradley was to attack, and the German 7th Army was very weak because Montgomery had drawn the weight of the German forces towards Caen. Bradley brought up no less than 12 divisions, including four armoured:

1. on the left the American VII Corps (Major-General J. L. Collins), with its left flank along the Vire, was given the job of making the breakthrough. The 30th, 4th, and 9th Divisions were engaged in first echelon along a four mile front. The breach came in the Marigny area and the 1st Infantry and the 2nd and 3rd Armoured Divisions poured through south and south-west, not, however, going beyond Coutances on their right, so as to leave the way open for VIII Corps; and

2. VIII Corps (Major-General T. H. Middleton) had the 8th, 79th, 83rd, and 90th Infantry and the 4th and 6th Armoured Divisions and, by a frontal attack, seized Coutances and pressed on to Avranches. When it reached Pontaubault on the Brittany border, it was to come under General George S. Patton's 3rd Army, which was to exploit this success towards the Loire and the Seine.

The attack of July 25 had the benefit of exceptionally powerful air preparation, the details of which were drawn up by General Bradley and Air Chief-Marshal Leigh-Mallory. On July 24 4,000 tons of bombs fell on LXXXIV Corps' positions. During the morning of the following day no fewer than 1,880 four-engined and twin-engined bombers, and 550 fighter-bombers dropped 4,150 tons of bombs opposite the American VII Corps front to a depth of a mile and a half and on the bridges upstream of the Vire from Saint Lô. By special orders from Bradley, who did not want the terrain to be pitted with deep craters, only light bombs and napalm were used.

In spite of precautions, bombing errors caused casualties to the tune of 111 dead and 490 wounded in VII Corps. Amongst the dead was Lieutenant-General McNair, C.-in-C. of the "shadow" army group ostensibly stationed in south-east England to deceive the enemy into expecting a landing across the Straits of Dover. These were tragic losses: on the enemy side the bombing cut a swathe of death through the defences. "Nothing could withstand it," wrote the German historian Paul Carell. "Trenches, gun-emplacements: ploughed up. Petrol-, ammunition- and supply-dumps: set on fire." The Panzer-"Lehr" Division, in particular, down to 5,000 men, was heavily knocked about: "at least half its personnel was put out of action: killed, wounded, buried alive or driven out of their minds. All the tanks and guns in the forward positions were wiped out. Every road in the area was made useless."

Neither Colonel-General Hausser nor Field-Marshal von Kluge expected an attack of such violence from the American 1st Army between the Vire and the Channel. General von Choltitz, commanding LXXXIV Corps, who had seen it coming and whose warning had not been heeded by his superiors, now had to rely on his own resources to plug the gap created by the annihilation of the Panzer-"Lehr" Division. On July 26 Collins was able to pass his 2nd and 3rd Armoured Divisions (respectively Major Generals Edward H. Brooks and Leroy H. Watson) through his infantry lines. By evening the 3rd had passed through Marigny and was on its way to Coutances and the 2nd was patrolling through Saint Gilles and Canisy, some seven to eight miles from its point of departure.

The 2nd and 116th Panzer Divisions were hastily withdrawn from the 5th *Panzerarmee* in the Caen area but did not get to the breach until July 29, by which time it was widening every hour. There was therefore no alternative for LXXXIV Corps but to retreat, and do so quickly, as its left flank had been pierced in the area of Périers by the American VIII Corps. The direction this retreat was to take gave rise to a conflict between the LXXXIV Corps and 7th Army commanders. The latter, anxious to retain some coherence in his dispositions, wan-

ted Choltitz to withdraw south-eastwards, whereupon the latter protested vehemently that if he were to do this he would be opening the way for the enemy to get into Brittany. This is what happened, in fact; Kluge wrongly attributed the blame to Choltitz and replaced him by Lieutenant-General Elfeldt. Choltitz had no difficulty in clearing himself and was rewarded with the command of *Gross Paris*.

On July 28 the U.S. 4th Armoured Division (Major-General John S. Wood) took Coutances and that same night got across the Sienne at Cérences. Twenty-four hours later 6th Armoured Division (Major-General Robert W. Grow), moving on the right flank of the 4th, crossed the See and took Avranches. Facing them there was absolute confusion: continually compelled to move their headquarters by the advancing Americans, the German leaders lost all contact with their men, units got mixed up together and many of them, overtaken by Allied tanks, became moving pockets. At 0100 hours on July 31 Lieutenant-General Speidel telephoned Kluge: "The left flank has collapsed."

A few minutes later the C.-in-C. West was again called: this time by General Farmbacher, commanding XXV Corps, to say that, responsible now for organising the defence of Brittany, he found that the Kriegsmarine and the Luftwaffe, sheltering respectively behind Dönitz and Göring, were being removed from his authority. At 1045 hours the wretched Field-Marshal got in touch with O.K.W. and gave General Warlimont, Chief of Operations, a realistic picture of the situation:

"C.-in-C. West . . . informs that enemy is in Avranches and possibly also in Villedieu . . . These key positions for future operations must be held at all costs . . . All available strength from Saint Malo has been brought up. Spare naval and air force units, absolutely necessary for decisive struggle which will determine future of bridgehead, . . . impossible to get. General Warlimont agrees to put matter before the Führer.

"C.-in-C. West describes the situation with impressive eloquence. It might even be asked if the enemy can in fact be stopped at this point. His air superiority is terrifying and stifles our every move. On the other hand all his movements are prepared and protected by air strength. Our losses of men and *matériel* are extraordinary. Morale of troops has suffered greatly from the enemy's constant withering fire, especially as all infantry units are now only hastily-assembled groups and can no longer offer solid and co-ordinated resistance. Behind the front lines the terrorists [resistance] feel the end is at hand and are becoming ever

Americans pause during their swift advance towards Saint Gilles, which fell to the 2nd Armoured Division following the opening of Operation "Cobra".

bolder. This, and the destruction of many communication installations, makes an ordered command very difficult."

Kluge therefore demanded reinforcements, and urgently, reminding O.K.W. of the example of the taxis of the Marne.

Faced with the development of Operation "Cobra", Hitler at O.K.W. finally gave up the obsession with a second landing north of the Somme which had dominated all his strategy since dawn on June 6.

Responding to Kluge's call for help, Hitler ordered Salmuth to withdraw LXXXI Corps and 85th and 89th Divisions from the 15th Army and send them at once to 5th *Panzerarmee*. Meanwhile Army Group "G", responsible for the defence of "Fortress Europe" between the Loire estuary and the Franco-Italian frontier, was ordered to send its LVIII Panzer Corps, 708th Infantry, and 9th Panzer Divisions to the 7th Army. The 9th Panzer was stationed in the Avignon area and the army group's commander, Colonel-General Blaskowitz, would have liked to see it replaced by the 11th Panzer, stationed in Montauban, as an Allied landing in Provence was expected. The Führer, as was to be expected, failed to see that this was common sense.

Hitler's decisions, however, came too late. On July 31, General Patton, who now controlled VIII Corps (and was soon to become commander of a new 3rd Army) was given the welcome information from the corps H.Q. that the 4th Armoured Division had reached its objective at Sélune and that the bridge at Pontaubault was still in good order. He made up his mind at once: "All through military history", he cried, "wars have been lost because rivers weren't crossed." He sent off the 6th Armoured and 79th Infantry Divisions (Major-General Ira T. Wyche) towards Brest and the 4th Armoured and 8th Infantry (Major-General Donald Stroh) towards Rennes. The breach was complete, the German 7th Army was beaten and LXXXIV Corps, from which most of the 20,000 prisoners taken by the Americans since July 25 had come, was virtually wiped out. On August 1, General Bradley, now commanding 21 divisions, including six armoured, took over the American 12th Army Group in accordance with decisions taken in London on the eve of "Overlord". He handed over his 1st Army to General Courtney H. Hodges, having no qualms about the ability of his successor:

"A quiet and methodical commander, he knew his profession well and was recognised in the army as one of our most able trainers of troops. Whereas Patton could seldom be bothered with details, Hodges studied his problems with infinite care and was thus better qualified to execute the more intricate operations. A steady, undramatic, and dependable man with great tenacity and persistence, Hodges became the almost anonymous inside man who smashed the German Seventh Army while Patton skirted the end."

The 1st Army at this time included V, VII, and XIX Corps. It had transferred VIII Corps to the 3rd Army, fighting alongside it, and Bradley had also moved over to 3rd Army XII, XV, and XX Corps (respectively Major-Generals R. Cook, Wade H. Haislip, and Walton H. Walker). The new C.-in-C. 12th Army Group, promoted over the head of the impetuous Patton, six years his senior, did not much relish the idea of having to send him directives but acknowledged that "George" was a great-hearted and highly intelligent soldier who, in spite of his celebrated outbursts of temper, served him with "unbounded loyalty and eagerness".

The same occasion brought the formation of the British 21st Army Group, under General Montgomery, with the British 2nd Army, still under Sir Miles Dempsey, and the Canadian 1st Army (Lieutenant-General H. D. G. Crerar). On August 15, 21st Army Group was to have five corps of 16 divisions, including six armoured, and several brigades. This reorganisation of the land forces ought to have brought General Eisenhower to their head as previously agreed. Thinking that his presence was more necessary in England, he postponed taking over command until September 1. Montgomery therefore, continued to act as Eisenhower's representative, sending orders to Bradley under his authority, whilst at the same time retaining the command of his own army group.

In the afternoon of July 30 Colonel-General Jodl, having informed Hitler of his concern at the capture of Avranches, noted in his diary: "The Führer reacted favourably to the idea of an order for eventual withdrawal in France. This confirms that he thinks such an order is necessary at the present time.

"1615 hours: called Blumentritt (chief-of-staff to C.-in-C. West). Advised him in guarded terms to be ready for such an order, adding that certain actions had to be taken straight away within G.H.Q. and that he should put a small working party on to it from the general staff."

The matter of withdrawal seemed virtually settled and Lieutenant-General Warlimont was designated as liaison officer with C.-in-C. West. But on the following morning, when the O.K.W. delegate was leaving, the Führer said: "Tell Field-Marshal von Kluge that his job is to look forwards to the enemy, not backwards!"

Warlimont was thus in an embarrassing situation, caught between the "yes" of July 31 and the "no" of August 1. On August 3, the expected order from O.K.W. reached Kluge in the morning, but instead of confirming the withdrawal intimated by Jodl, it ordered a counter-attack. By driving towards Avranches Hitler hoped the 7th Army would trap those American forces which had ventured into Brittany.

Allied troops wait while their artillery "softens up" a German-held village during the drive from Normandy. Note the confusion of vehicles.

And, doing half Kluge's job for him, O.K.W. issued an order giving details for the operation. According to General Blumentritt:

"O.K.W. settled the precise divisions which were to be used and which were therefore to be taken out of the line as soon as possible. The exact limits of the sector in which the attack was to take place were laid down, as well as the routes to be taken and even the villages the troops were to pass through. These plans were all made in Berlin on large-scale maps and the opinions of the commanding generals in France were neither asked for nor encouraged."

The plan was to assemble an armoured mass on the left flank of the 7th Army under General von Funck, C.-in-C. XLVII Panzer Corps, attack towards Avranches through Mortain, and cut the communications of the American 3rd Army. But Hitler would not stop there. Funck was then to press on to Saint Lô and over-whelm the American 1st Army by an out-flanking attack. This would give Germany an eleventh-hour game and match in the West.

Kluge was dumbfounded when he read Hitler's directive. He wrote to Hitler on August 18, before he took poison, to say that, except for the one single division, the 2nd Panzer, "the armoured units, after all the fighting they had done, were so weakened that they were incapable of any shock tactics . . . Your order was based on a completely erroneous supposition. When I first learned of it I immediately

had the impression that I was being asked to do something which would go down in history as a grandiose and supremely daring operation but which, un-fortunately, it was virtually impossible to carry out so that, logically, the blame would fall on the military commander responsible . . .

"On the basis of these facts I am still convinced that there was no possible chance of success. On the contrary: the attacks laid down for me could only make the situation of the Army Group decidedly worse. And that is what happened."

Kluge was in no position to claim free-dom of action in face of this order, as stupid as it was absolute. He was aware that Hitler knew of the part he had played in the July 20 plot and that the slightest disobedience would cost him his life. The discussion therefore centred less on the principles involved than on the date of the operation, which was to be called *"Lüttich"* (Liège). Hitler wanted to hold back until as many American divisions as possible had been drawn into the net; Kluge urged the threat to the left flank and even to the rear of the 7th Army and asked for a start on August 7, to which Hitler agreed.

At dawn on D-day, helped by fog, XLVII Corps (116th and 2nd Panzer Divisions, 1st *"Leibstandarte"* and 2nd *"Das Reich"* S.S. Panzer Divisions) attacked between the See and the Sélune towards Avranches. Mortain fell fairly easily. But neither the American 30th Division (Major-General

Leland S. Hobbs), though it had one battalion surrounded, nor the American VII Corps (Major-General J. L. Collins) were thrown off their stride, and towards mid-day *"Das Reich"* was stopped less than two miles from Saint Hilaire-du-Harcouët, over 14 miles from its objective of Pontaubault.

The fog had lifted by now, and the Panzers were caught by British Typhoon fighter-bombers, whose armour-piercing rockets again proved their deadly efficiency. The previous day General Bülowius thought he could guarantee the C.-in-C. 7th Army that 300 Luftwaffe fighters would be continuously sweeping the skies above the battlefield. These had been intercepted by Anglo-American fighters as soon as they took off from the Paris area.

Faced with this lack of success, Kluge gave it as his opinion that the German forces should hold on to what they had got, or even let go. The answer was an order to throw in II S.S. Panzer Corps (General Bittrich: 9th *"Hohenstaufen"* and 10th *"Frundsberg"* Panzer Divisions), to be withdrawn from the already depleted 5th *Panzerarmee*. Once more C.-in-C. West had to give in, in spite of vehement protests from General Eberbach, who was expecting a strong Anglo-Canadian attack southwards along the Caen–Falaise axis.

A British column pushes south from Caen.

In spite of appearances, the first engagements of the American 3rd Army in Brittany betrayed a certain lack of initiative. This is not attributable in any way to lack of enthusiasm on Patton's part, but seems rather to have sprung from the inadequacy of his means of communication, which prevented his driving spirit from reaching down to his men. At the speed with which the armoured formations advanced, the supply of telephone cable within VIII Corps turned out to be insufficient, with a consequential overloading of the radio network and the use of squadrons of message-carrying jeeps to make up for it.

There were also interferences in the chain of command. The 4th Armoured Division received the order from VIII Corps, confirmed by General Bradley, not to go beyond Dinan until Saint Malo was cleared, whereas Patton had ordered it to drive on towards Brest (150 miles west of Rennes) with no intermediate objective. This left a gap in the enemy lines once Rennes had been passed, which 6th Armoured Division exploited along the axis Chartres–Paris, turning then towards Chateaubriant instead of Lorient. It was recalled to its original objective and found, when it got to Lorient, the German 265th Division in a defensive position around this large base. The 4th Armoured Division did manage to destroy the 266th Division, which had tried to take refuge inside Brest, but the German 2nd Parachute Division got there first and its commander, Lieutenant-General Ramcke, was not the sort of man to be impressed by cavalier raids, even ones made in considerable force.

The responsibility for this Allied mix-up must belong to the Anglo-American high command, which had given two objectives to the forces breaking out of the Avranches bottleneck: the Breton ports and the rear areas of Army Group "B". This was how Eisenhower saw it when on August 5 he ordered only the minimum indispensable forces to be engaged in Brittany.

This directive from Eisenhower gave Patton the chance to streak out through the enormous gap (65 miles) between Rennes and Nantes, which he did with XV Corps on the left, XX Corps in the centre, and XII Corps on the right with its right flank along the Loire. By August 7, XV Corps was in Laval and Château-Gontier whilst XII Corps liberated Nantes and Angers, ignoring enemy resistance in Saint Nazaire.

Thus Operation *"Lüttich"* did not deflect Montgomery and Bradley from their initial plan. On D-day the German XLVII Corps lost some 50 tanks out of the 120 with which it had started out at dawn. The American VII Corps, strengthened to five divisions, including one armoured, immediately went over to the counter-attack. This was the last chance for Army Group "B" to break out of the ring now beginning to take shape as Patton pushed ahead towards Le Mans. But Hitler obstinately refused to consider any withdrawal.

Montgomery now had a chance to start a pincer movement which was to bring about the defeat of Army Group "B" between the Orne and the Dives on August 18 and the disgrace and suicide of the wretched Kluge. At 2330 hours on August 7 the Canadian 1st Army attacked south of Caen with its II Corps of four divisions, including two armoured. It was the beginning of Operation "Totalize", which was to capture Falaise.

At zero hour four mechanised columns, consisting of one armoured brigade on each flank and two motorised infantry brigades in the centre, crossed the first German line. When they had covered between two and three miles in the dark, the Canadian and Scottish infantry, from the 2nd Canadian and 51st (Highland) Divisions, left their vehicles to attack the strongpoints of the German line, illuminated for them by green tracer shells. At dawn it was clear that the H.Q. of I S.S. Panzer Corps had been overrun, the 89th Division, recently arrived on the scene, had collapsed, and the 272nd looked like giving way.

Once more the famous Panzer-Meyer (Brigadier Kurt Meyer) and his 12th *"Hitlerjugend"* Panzer Division saved the situation with the help of 80 assault guns and the 8.8-cm guns sent to them as reinforcement. These young veterans, who had been in the line since June 8, were pitted against the Canadian 4th Armoured Division (Major-General G. Kitching) and the Polish 1st Armoured Division (Major-General S. Maczek), both of which were in action for the first time. The military cemeteries in the area bear witness to the valiant fighting of the Allied forces, but they did not succeed in breaking though and "Totalize" ground to a halt some ten miles short of Falaise on August 9.

On the same day the American XV Corps, having captured Le Mans, turned north. On its left the French 2nd Armoured Division (General Leclerc) was moving down to Alençon with the 79th Division in its wake. On the right the American 5th Armoured Division (Major-General Lundsford E. Oliver) was on the road to Argentan, followed by the 90th Division which, newly commanded by Major-General Raymond S. MacLain, was to recover from the unfortunate reputation it had acquired in the *bocage*. Conscious of the threat to his rear areas, Kluge attempted to ward it off by improvising a *Panzergruppe* "Eberbach" consisting of LXXXI Corps (General Kuntzen), 708th Division (Lieutenant-General Wilck), and 9th Panzer Division (Lieutenant-General Jolasse) brought up from the south.

The French 2nd Armoured Division, vigorously led by General Leclerc, ran into the 9th Panzer Division on August 11, just as the Germans were moving into their positions. As night fell the French took the bridges at Alençon whilst they were still intact. On their right, the American 5th Armoured Division had crossed the Sarthe and captured Sées, having overcome the feeble resistance of the German 708th Division. On the following day Leclerc had to fight it out with the 2nd *"Das Reich"* S.S. Panzer Division's forward units and the 116th Panzer Division, both of which Kluge had thrown into XV Corps' sector without any further regard for O.K.W.'s orders. The French nevertheless pushed their left flank as far as Carrouges and their right to the outskirts of Argentan.

At dawn on August 13 the American XV Corps was within 16 miles of Falaise, whilst the German 7th Army, caught up in the Condé-sur-Noireau–Tinchebray–Domfront area, had between 34 and 37 miles to go under enemy-controlled skies before it broke out of the pocket. In the afternoon, however, Haislip was ordered by Patton to stop and even to pull back the units "in the neighbourhood of Falaise or north of Argentan".

Why Bradley, via Patton, should have forbidden XV Corps to close the ring round Army Group "B" in the Falaise area has often been discussed, and the reasons given by the two generals in their memoirs do not carry conviction. No more do the arguments of General Eisenhower, who takes up Bradley's argument in his *Crusade in Europe*, saying:

"Mix-ups on the front occurred, and there was no way to halt them except by stopping troops in place, even at the cost of allowing some Germans to escape. In the aggregate considerable numbers of Germans succeeded in getting away. Their escape, however, meant an almost complete abandonment of their heavy equipment and was accomplished only by terrific sacrifices.

"I was in Bradley's headquarters when messages began to arrive from commanders of the advancing American columns, complaining that the limits placed upon them by their orders were allowing Germans to escape. I completely supported Bradley in his decision that it was necessary to obey the orders, prescribing the boundary between the army groups, exactly as written; otherwise a calamitous battle between friends could have resulted."

Certainly by exploiting his success on August 12 north of Argentan Haislip had overstepped the boundary between 12th and 21st Army Groups and risked running into the bombing destined for the Germans opposite the Canadian 1st Army. Was this boundary so vague, though, that the Anglo-American strategic air force, which was admittedly sometimes not very accurate, could not have been given clear orders? And the juncture between the Polish 1st Armoured Division and the American 90th did in fact take place without incident in the area of Chambois-sur-Dives on August 19.

This is why one is inclined to believe, like Jacques Mordal, that Eisenhower and Bradley, under the influence of Montgomery, were unwilling to content themselves with a "little" pincer around Falaise, as they were sure that they could bring about a much bigger one on the left bank of the Seine. They ignored the proverb of the bird in hand and when they said "stop" to Haislip they were intending to give him a new and bigger task.

From August 15, Army Group "B" was on the retreat. Kluge did not wait for O.K.W. to confirm, but went ahead, setting in motion an operation involving two armies, seven corps, and no fewer than 23 divisions of all types. On August 17 General Dietrich, who had succeeded Eberbach as C.-in-C. 5th *Panzerarmee*, got I S.S. Panzer Corps out of the net and re-assembled the bits at Vimoutiers. But the Canadians took Falaise and the Polish 1st Armoured Division, advancing up the right bank of the Dives, established contact with the American V Corps (1st Army) which at that moment formed the southern arm of the pincer.

On August 20, according to Martin Blumenson, the author of the volume devoted to this episode in the official history of the U.S. Army, there occurred in 90th Division the "artillery-man's dream":

"Five battalions pulverized columns driving towards the Dives. American soldiers cheered when German horses, carts, trucks, volkswagens, tanks, vehicles, and weapons went flying into

The Allied breakout reached Brittany and the Loire, but German counter-attacks created the Falaise pocket.

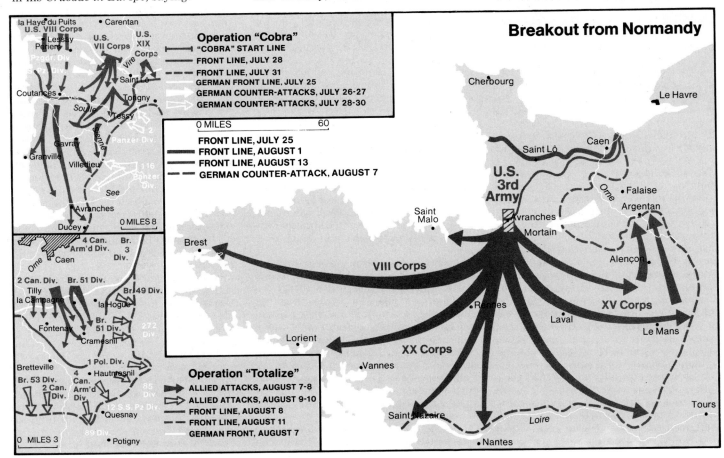

A burnt-out German column in Normandy testifies to Allied air power.

the air, disintegrating in flashes of fire and puffs of smoke."

Nevertheless I S.S. Panzer Corps, which had got out of this attack, collected together some 20,000 Germans from all units and, refusing to be dismayed, managed to find a crack in the Allied lines, through which they got 25 tanks and 60 guns. Included in these forces was General Hausser, C.-in-C. 7th Army, who was seriously wounded in the face. On the following day, however, all firing ceased in the Argentan–Nécy–Brieux–Chambois area. Here the Allies took 50,000 prisoners; there were 10,000 dead. The unhappy decision of August 13 thus left the Germans now with only 40,000 men. Fifteen divisions of Army Group "B" were wiped out in the course of this pitiless battle. According to Blumenson, one American officer, a veteran of the 1918 battles in the area of Soissons, Saint

Mihiel, and the Argonne in 1918 and the terrible bombing of London in 1940, said:

"None of these compared in the effect upon the imagination with what I saw yesterday south west of Trun . . . The grass and trees were vividly green as in all Normandy and a surprising number of houses (were) . . . untouched. That rather peaceful setting framed a picture of destruction so great that it cannot be described. It was as if an avenging angel had swept the area bent on destroying all things German.

"I stood on a lane, surrounded by 20 or 30 dead horses or parts of horses, most of them still hitched to their wagons and carts . . . As far as my eye could reach (about 200 yards) on every line of sight there were . . . vehicles, wagons, tanks, guns, prime movers, sedans, rolling kitchens, etc., in various stages of destruction.

"I stepped over hundreds of rifles in the mud and saw hundreds more stacked along sheds . . . I walked through a mile or more of lanes where the vehicles had been caught closely packed . . . I saw probably 300 field pieces and tanks, mounting large caliber guns, that were apparently undamaged.

"I saw no foxholes or any other type of shelter or field fortifications. The Germans were trying to run and had no place to run. They were probably too tired even to surrender.

"I left this area rather regretting I'd seen it . . . Under such conditions there are no supermen – all men become rabbits looking for a hole."

Most of the German *matériel* was lost. The French 2nd Armoured Division alone took 100 guns and 700 vehicles and the 90th Division 380 armoured vehicles, 700 guns, and more than 5,000 lorries.

This was the situation which Field-Marshal Model inherited when he took over from Kluge at his H.Q. at Saint Germain-en-Laye on August 17. Two days previously a fortuitous incident had, if not provoked, at least hastened, the disgrace of Kluge. Whilst he was up at the front an aircraft bomb had demolished the radio truck which gave him permanent contact with O.K.W., and the ensuing prolonged silence caused Hitler to conclude that C.-in-C. West had finally betrayed him and gone to see Montgomery about surrender terms.

When he said goodbye to his successor, Kluge assured him that he would speak to Hitler with all the clarity which the situation demanded. But in the car taking him back to Germany he rightly persuaded himself that the dictator would give him, not an audience at O.K.W., but a criminal trial and an ignominious death. Potassium cyanide removed him from the Führer's vengeance, but before he committed suicide on August 18, 1944 he sent a letter to Hitler, the conclusion of which is worth recalling:

"I do not know if Field-Marshal Model, who has proved himself in all respects,

will be capable of mastering the situation. I hope so with all my heart. If that is not to be the case and if the new weapons – especially air weapons, which you are so eagerly awaiting, are not to bring you success, then *mein Führer,* make up your mind to finish the war. The German people have endured such unspeakable sufferings that the time has come to put an end to their terrors. There must be ways to arrive at this conclusion and, above all, to prevent the Reich from being condemned to the hell of Bolshevism . . . *Mein Führer,* I have always admired your greatness and your iron will to assert your authority and uphold National Socialism. If your destiny overcomes your will and your genius, it will be because Providence has willed it so. You have fought a good and honourable fight. History will bear witness to this. If it ever becomes necessary, show yourself great enough to put an end to a struggle which has become hopeless."

We know what became of this advice from a man about to die: if it had been accepted Germany would have been spared, not the rigours of occupation (this had been decided at Teheran), but at least the appalling horrors of invasion.

On the same August 15 when Army Group "B" was trying to escape from the Normandy net, the landing of an Allied force in Provence compelled O.K.W. for the first time to impose on the C.-in-C. West a withdrawal of considerable strategic importance. Right up to the last minute Churchill had tried to urge his American allies to abandon this operation, which was called first "Anvil" then "Dragoon", in favour of his projected offensive towards Vienna and the Danube across the Apennines, the Giulian Alps, and the Ljubljana gap.

In a letter dated August 6 to his friend Harry Hopkins, Churchill expressed his conviction that as the ports of Brest, Lorient, Saint Nazaire, and Nantes might fall into Allied hands "at any time", there was no logistic value left in Toulon or Marseilles. On the other hand, why not take the bull by the horns ? "Dragoon", he wrote, would have to be carried out against an enemy who "at the outset [would] be much stronger than we are, and where our advance runs cross-grained to the country, which abounds in most formidable rocky positions, ridges, and gullies."

"But", he noted in particular, "after taking the two fortresses of Toulon and Marseilles we have before us the lengthy advance up the Rhône valley before we even get to Lyons. None of this operation can influence Eisenhower's battle for probably ninety days after the landings."

On the next day he went to Portsmouth and saw Eisenhower about it, speaking his mind more openly than he had done to Hopkins, and not concealing his interest in a campaign in the Balkans, a subject which he had not broached in his letter.

Eisenhower soon realised that the Prime Minister, in his opposition to "Dragoon", was putting forward reasons of strategy so as not to have to declare the political reasons which had made him take up this attitude.

As a good American soldier General Eisenhower reckoned that he should not interfere in matters which were the responsibility of the White House and the State Department. He was to react the same way over Berlin later. He makes this perfectly clear in his memoirs when he says:

"Although I never heard him say so, I felt that the Prime Minister's real concern was possibly of a political rather than a military nature. He may have thought that a post-war situation which would see the western Allies posted in great strength in the Balkans would be far more effective in producing a stable post-hostilities world than if the Russian armies should be the ones to occupy that

region. I told him that if this were his reason for advocating the campaign into the Balkans he should go instantly to the President and lay the facts, as well as his own conclusions on the table. I well understood that strategy can be affected by political considerations, and if the President and the Prime Minister should decide that it was worth while to prolong the war, thereby increasing its cost in men and money, in order to secure the political objectives they deemed necessary, then I would instantly and loyally adjust my plans accordingly. But I did insist that as long as he argued the matter on military grounds alone I could not concede validity to his arguments."

And he was clearly right. The supreme commander may lay down strategic objectives, but it is the political leaders who set the aims of warfare. Moreover Churchill was too late. The drive for Vienna may have been conceivable on June 5 so long as everything was done

Great dumps of ruined matériel, such as this one at Rouen, and scenes of wholesale destruction greeted the Allied forces when they reached the Seine.

to annihilate Kesselring south of the line Rimini–La Spezia, but it was not now, on August 7, by which time the enemy, whose losses in retreat had not been overwhelming, was re-establishing his line along the ridges of the Apennines. At best the Allies would have been caught in late autumn on the narrow hemmed-in roads in the area of Klagenfurt or Ljubljana and have had to fight for peaks between 3,000 and 4,000 feet high. The mountainous terrain and the weather, to say nothing of enemy action, would have severely restricted all movement. As Michael Howard explained in *The Mediterranean Strategy in the Second World War*: "a pursuit to Vienna through terrain where even comparatively small units could have imposed repeated delays would have been a very difficult matter indeed."

501

CHAPTER 62
The liberation of France

Operation "Dragoon", supervised by General Maitland Wilson, C.-in-C. Mediterranean, was to be the landing between Saint Raphael and le Lavandou of the American 7th Army under Lieutenant-General A. M. Patch, who the previous year had been so successful in cleaning up Guadalcanal. The landing operation was to be carried out by the American VI Corps with its 3rd, 36th, and 45th Divisions, well experienced in amphibious operations. It was to be supported by an Anglo-American parachute division under Major-General Robert T. Frederick landing in the area of le Muy with the object of opening up the Argens valley. A position nearer Toulon was not chosen because of the danger of the two twin turrets at Cap Cépet whose guns could hurl a 119-pound shell a distance of nearly 22 miles.

A thousand ships were required: warships, troop transports, and supply vessels. These included five battleships, nine escort carriers (216 aircraft), 24 cruisers, 122 destroyers and escort vessels, and 466 landing craft, all from five navies: American, British, Australian, French, and Greek. The fleet, named the Western Task Force, was commanded by Vice-Admiral H. Kent Hewitt. On board his flagship was James Forrestal, the new U.S. Navy Secretary.

Air support came from the U.S. 12th Air Force, under Brigadier-General Gordon P. Saville, with 2,100 aircraft. Its heavy bombers operated from the area of Rome, its medium bombers, fighter-bombers, and fighters from 14 airstrips which had been built in the Bastia area. Any objectives out of range of the latter would be dealt with by carrier-based aircraft under Rear-Admiral T. H. Troubridge, R.N. On August 13 and 14, the four-engined bombers prepared the way for the landings by attacking gun-emplacements, communication centres, bridges, and viaducts. These attacks were spread over an area from Port-Vendres to Genoa to deceive the enemy.

The defence of the 400 miles of coastline between Menton and Cerbère was the responsibility of the German 19th Army. On D-day it had six divisions, deployed with three on each side of the Rhône. Between June 6 and August 4 it had had to give up its 217th, 272nd, and 277th Divisions, receiving in exchange only the 198th and the remnants of the 716th, which had been thrashed at Caen. Colonel-General Blaskowitz, C.-in-C. Army Group "G", wrote to C.-in-C. West on that day:

"The Army Group does not in the least deny the necessity of weakening the 19th Army to this extent, having regard to the situation of Army Group "B". It nevertheless feels obliged to point out that the consequences of these losses of men and *matériel* will be such that the Army's defences will be so diminished

that it cannot guarantee to hold the coastline."

On August 10, however, the 19th Army had to lose its 338th Division. 11th Panzer Division was ordered to Avignon from Montauban by Hitler, but not until August 13, so that by the following day the whole of this division was still over on the right bank of the Rhône. This was the situation facing General Wiese, C.-in-C. 19th Army.

The German naval forces in the south of France consisted of only a limited number of small units and a few U-boats. The American air forces increased their attacks on Toulon, however, and four U-boats were sunk on August 6. The Luftwaffe had only 70 fighters and 130 bombers, a total of only one-tenth of the Allied aircraft used in Operation "Dragoon".

On the single day of August 15, Allied aircraft flew 4,250 sorties and only 60 German planes managed to get off the ground. Admiral Hewitt's fleet fired 50,000 shells, including 3,000 12-inch or heavier, either during the preparations or at the request of the troops landing. The American VI Corps' attack, supported by the "Sudre" Combat Command of the French 1st Armoured Division, was against the German 148th Division (Lieutenant-General Otto Fretter-Pico) on the right and the 242nd Division (Lieutenant-General Bässler) on the left, the latter being responsible for the defence of Toulon. Both German units were part of LXII Corps (General Neuling) but corps H.Q. at Draguignan was cut off from its troops by the landing of the "Frederick" Division, supported by the Var *maquis*. The only Allied unit to run into difficulties was the U.S. 36th Division (Major-General John E. Dahlquist) in the area of Agay. Everywhere else the operation went like clockwork. By evening the Allies had landed 60,000 men, 6,000 vehicles, and 50,000 tons of *matériel*, all at the cost of 320 killed who, for the most part, had stumbled onto mines.

Amongst the day's exploits those of Colonel Bouvet's commando are worth recording. It landed in the middle of the night between Cavalaire and Cavalière and captured the fortifications on Cap Nègre. By the evening of the 15th it had advanced over nine miles and taken 1,000 prisoners.

Twenty-four hours later the 7th Army beach-head extended from Anthéor on the right through Draguignan, where General Neuling and his staff were taken prisoner, to le Luc on the road to Aix and over 24 miles from Fréjus, then back to the Mediterranean between Cavalière and le Lavandou. On the beaches Patch's second echelon arrived ahead of time and landed with the 1st Moroccan (General Brosset), the 3rd Algerian (General de Monsabert), and the 9th Colonial (General

Magnan) Divisions, the remainder of the French 1st Armoured Division (General Touzet du Vigier) and General Guillaume's Moroccan *goumiers*, North African mountain troops.

On the following day this vanguard of the French 1st Army went into battle under General de Lattre de Tassigny. In the exercise of his command de Lattre seemed to be everywhere and to appear as if by miracle in places where his decision was needed. He cared deeply for the fate of his men and was often rude to staff and services on their behalf if the occasion warranted it.

Two men from very different backgrounds have borne witness to his character. On September 30, 1935, as he left manoeuvres at Mailly, Captain Hans Speidel, assistant military attaché at the German Embassy in Paris, made the following comment on the officer commanding the 151st Regiment: "De Lattre makes an exceptional impression: he is a man of great vitality and fine intelligence and his bearing and discernment are quite out of the ordinary. His fellow-officers predict a great future for him in the French Army." This judgement by Rommel's future chief-of-staff is echoed by General de Gaulle in his memoirs:

"De Lattre was emotional, flexible, far-sighted and a man of wide interests, influencing the minds around him by the ardour of his personality, heading towards his goal by sudden and unexpected leaps, although often well thought out ones.

"De Lattre, on each occasion, courted opportunity above all. Until he found it he endured the ordeal of his tentative efforts, devoured by an impatience that often provoked scenes among his contacts. Suddenly seeing where, when and how the issue could be determined, he then set about the task of building it up and exploiting it. All the resources of a rich personality and extraordinary energy were put to work, demanding a limitless effort of those he engaged in it, but certain that he was preparing them for success."

It is no disrespect to this strategist and leader of men to say that the weapon Weygand and Giraud had forged for him, and which General Juin had tempered in the recent Italian campaign, had a keen edge. The Frenchmen from North Africa were enthusiastic at the idea that they were going to liberate their brothers in the home country, and were encouraged by the presence amongst them of 18,000 escapees from the unhappy armistice army. Considering the 9th Colonial Division's attack on the German positions in the area of Villars-les-Blamont on November 14 and 22, when the division's artillery crushed the 198th Division in the area of le Puix-Suarce, we can say with some justice that the 1st Army, by its bravery and its accomplishments, was the equal of any other Allied force.

A better judge was Major-General von Mellenthin, then chief-of-staff of Army Group "G". In *Panzer Battles* he writes: "The French tanks, reflecting the temperament of their army commander, General de Lattre de Tassigny, attacked with extraordinary spirit and *élan*." A worthy tribute from an enemy who knew what he was talking about, to General du Vigier and his colleague Vernejoul, commander of the French 5th Armoured Division. The French opened their score with the capture of Salernes, Brignoles, and Cuers, the latter some nine miles north-east of Toulon.

The American VI Corps, acting on local information, sent a motorised column along the axis Digne–Sisteron with orders to intercept the German 19th Army at Montélimar. Close on its heels was the 36th Division. The 45th Division (Major-General William W. Eagles) had taken the road to Aix-en-Provence.

In view of the reports he had received, and realising that there was no longer any hope of throwing the enemy back into the sea, on August 16 Hitler ordered Colonel-General Blaskowitz to begin at once the evacuation of south and south-west France. Army Group "G" would link up in the region of Sens with Model's left as the latter fell back to the Seine, whilst the 19th Army would proceed up the Rhône valley and hold as long as possible the line Côte d'Or–Lyon–Aix-les-Bains so as to keep Switzerland encircled. The 242nd Division at Toulon and the 244th at Marseilles (Major-General Schaeffer) would defend the ports to the last and raze their installations to the ground. The 148th Division, fighting in the Estérel massif, and the 157th in the Dauphiné, would come under Field-Marshal Kesselring's command and hold the French side of the Alps.

General von der Chevallerie, C.-in-C. of the German 1st Army, had transferred his H.Q. from Bordeaux to Fontainebleau on August 10 and so the conduct of the German retreat in the south-west fell to General Sachs, commander of LXIV Corps (158th and 159th Divisions). He left strong garrisons in the "fortresses" of la Pointe-de-Grave, Royan, and la Rochelle. General Wiese's task was to co-ordinate the movements of the Luftwaffe IV Corps (General Petersen: 189th, 198th, and 716th Divisions) and LXXXV Corps (338th Division). The 11th Panzer Division, under a particularly distinguished commander, Lieutenant-General Gustav von Wietersheim, was ordered to cover the retreat.

On August 20, as a consequence of this order to Army Group "G" and the increasingly serious situation of Army Group "B", whose left flank was being rolled up by Patton and the American 3rd Army, the Führer issued a new directive. This has been summarised by Professor Percy Ernst Schramm, then editor and now publisher of the O.K.W. war diaries for 1944 and 1945:

"C.-in-C. West was ordered to hold the bridgehead west of Paris and prevent the enemy drive towards Dijon. First of all what remained of the 5th *Panzerarmee* and the 7th Army had to be withdrawn behind the River Touques and reorganised so that their armoured formations could be brought back into the left flank. If it turned out to be impossible to hold out in front of the Seine, the Paris bridgehead had to be held and also the line Seine–Yonne–Burgundy Canal–Dijon–Dôle–Swiss frontier. The withdrawal of the 7th Army behind the Seine was to be prepared at once. The 5th *Panzerarmee* would protect its crossing over to the right bank so as to prevent the enemy engaged in the Seine valley from driving north and then eastwards after crossing the river."

Downstream from Paris the 1st Army, now under Army Group "B", would block off the narrow valleys on either side of Montargis to allow the occupation of the Burgundy Canal and the area north-west of Dijon.

This directive calls for two remarks. Firstly, it took no account of the 230,000 men from the army (86,337), navy and air

force trapped in the "fortresses" in the West.

Amongst these, Saint Malo had fallen on August 17 after epic resistance. It took the 8-inch and 240-mm howitzers of the U.S. artillery, the 15-inch guns of the battleship *Warspite,* and the use of napalm to force Colonel von Aulock to hoist the white flag on the little island of Cézembre, the last centre of resistance, on September 2. The Brest garrison was attacked by the U.S. 2nd, 8th, and 29th Divisions and defended with equal tenacity by Lieutenant-General Ramcke and the 2nd Parachute Division. On September 17 fighting ceased in this unhappy town, which had been very heavily shelled. A further 48 hours were to elapse before Ramcke gave up the struggle in the Crozon peninsula.

Neither of the "fortresses" of Lorient or Saint Nazaire on opposite banks of the Loire was attacked; nor were the Channel Islands, where the 319th Division (Lieutenant-General von Schmettow) had some 30,000 men. The latter

"Dragoon" pushed northwards to link up with the advance from Normandy.

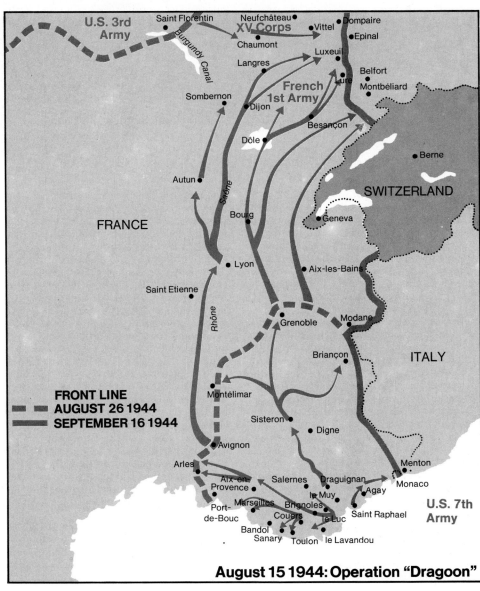

**FRONT LINE
AUGUST 26 1944
SEPTEMBER 16 1944**

August 15 1944: Operation "Dragoon"

503

were sufficiently aware of the futility of their mission to call themselves the "Guernsey P.O.W.s" or the "non-stop card-players". But on the other hand, the shortage of useable ports was to prove a considerable handicap to the Allied supply network, and hence to the whole advance to Germany.

Our second remark is that this directive certainly came too late. It might have been possible to carry it out on August 1, when the vanguard of the 4th Panzer Division was forcing a crossing of the Sélune at Pontaubault. But it was no longer possible on the 20th, when Patton was driving his XII and XX Corps towards Sens and Montereau and ordering XV Corps to cross the Seine at Mantes without a moment's delay.

Hitler's directive, overtaken by events, was also at fault because it was issued without regard to the means left at Field-Marshal Model's disposal. In effect, according to H. M. Cole of the historical service of the U.S. Army, who bases his figures on minute research of German military archives, on August 31 the 60-odd divisions of the Wehrmacht and the *Waffen*-S.S. then engaged on the Western Front had lost 293,802 officers, N.C.O.s, and men killed, wounded, and missing

since June 6. This was an average of about 5,000 men per division, a loss which must have sapped the strength of every formation. In July the Inspector General of the *Panzerwaffe* recorded the destruction of 282 Pzkw IV, 375 Panther, and 140 Tiger tanks; in August these figures were respectively 279, 358, and 97, giving an overall total of 1,529 in 62 days of fighting. It was the same for the rest of the equipment: by August 25, 1,500 guns, (field, A.A., and anti-tank) and 500 assault guns had been destroyed. The Führer's order to the C.-in-C. West might have been impossible to carry out, but there was also little chance of the latter's beaten armies establishing themselves in the position just reconnoitred by General Kitzinger of the Luftwaffe behind the Seine and the Burgundy Canal. This line ran along the Somme, the Crozat Canal, the Aisne at Soissons, the Marne from Epernay to Chaumont, the Langres plateau, and ended up at the Swiss frontier in the region of Pontarlier.

On August 24 Hitler dictated to Seyss-Inquart, the Nazi High Commissioner in Holland, *Gauleiters* Simon, Bürkel, and Wagner (his representatives in Luxembourg, Lorraine, and Alsace), and the

Men of the F.F.I. (Forces Françaises de l'Intérieur) *shift a wrecked enemy vehicle while Sherman tanks roll past.*

military authorities concerned an order to develop a "German position in the West" for which they would have recourse to a mass levy.

There would be a continuous anti-tank obstacle, behind which the land would be laid waste and positions in depth organised. It would straddle the Scheldt estuary, use the line of the Albert Canal, cover Aix-la-Chapelle and Trier, the fortified complex of Thionville–Metz, turn up the Moselle as far as Saint Maurice and finally block the gap at Belfort.

Did Hitler realise that, from Model's reports, his directive of August 20 was out of date by the 24th? The fact remains that twice in four days he had recognised that he was beaten in the West.

On August 16, the very day when the American XX Corps reached Chartres, the Paris police went on strike. This was the start of the uprising in the city. S.H.A.E.F.'s plan was not to mount a frontal attack on an urban area of this importance, but to outflank it on both sides so that it would fall of its own accord, thus sparing the city the fighting and all the destruction this would entail. According to calculations made in London, this operation was to take place between 120 and 150 days after D-Day. On August 16 at Chartres General Patton was about 20 days ahead of schedule.

"What to do about Paris?" Eisenhower asked himself. A critical problem indeed, as he has pointed out in his memoirs, since the liberation of Paris would bring the need for supplying food to the capital at a rate calculated by S.H.A.E.F. experts at 4,000 tons a day. This figure caused the C.-in-C. 12th Army Group to say "no":

"However, in spite of this danger of famine in Paris, I was determined that we would not be dissuaded from our plan to by-pass the city. If we could rush on to the Siegfried Line with tonnage that might otherwise be diverted to Paris, the city would be compensated for its additional week of occupation with an earlier end to the war. But we had not reckoned with the impatience of those Parisians who had waited four years for the armies that now approached their gates. My plan to pinch out Paris was exploded on an airstrip near Laval the morning of August 23."

General de Gaulle, in his rôle of head of the provisional government, had also addressed himself to the Allied C.-in-C. On August 21, newly arrived at Rennes from Algiers, he had said:

"Information reaching me from Paris leads me to believe that as the police and the German armed forces have almost disappeared from the city, and as there is an extreme shortage of food, serious trouble may be expected within a very short time. I think it is vital to occupy Paris as soon as possible with French and Allied troops, even if some fighting results and there is some damage in the city.

"If a disorderly situation arises now in Paris, it will be difficult later on to get control of the city without serious incidents and this could even affect later operations.

"I am sending you General Koenig, who has been nominated Military Governor of Paris and C.-in-C. of the Paris Region, to study the occupation question with you in case, as I request of you, you decide to proceed without delay."

In his war memoirs de Gaulle tells us why he intervened. It was a matter of preventing the formation, under cover of an uprising, of a predominantly Communist government. If this were to happen, he said, "on my arrival I should find this 'popular' government functioning: it would crown me with a laurel wreath, invite me to take my place within its organisation, and then pull all the strings. For those in control the rest would then be alternate boldness and prudence, the spread of state interference everywhere under cover of purges, suppression of public opinion by control of information and a militia, the progressive elimination of their earlier associates until the dictatorship of the proletariat was established."

Eisenhower agreed to the request, and Leclerc's division was sent off to Paris. This was what they had been waiting for, stamping with impatience until they were given free rein, ever since they had been transferred from North Africa to Great Britain. Meanwhile this French 2nd Armoured Division had been moved from the U.S. 3rd to the U.S. 1st Army and put under V Corps. The least that can be said about this new arrangement is that Generals Gerow and Leclerc just were not on the same wavelength.

On the German side the principal actors in the drama where General Dietrich von Choltitz, the Swedish Consul-General Raoul Nordling, and the leaders of the Paris insurrection.

Choltitz's behaviour is to be explained thus: since the previous autumn, when he had commanded XLVIII Panzer Corps on the Dniepr, he had maintained, in the presence of his chief-of-staff, Major-General von Mellenthin, that the tide of the Soviet advance would sooner or later burst over the dykes the Germans were erecting to hold it, and flood out all over Germany. Events since 1943 had only served to confirm his pessimism. When he left the O.K.W. meeting on August 7 after being invested by Hitler with the command of *Gross Paris* he had the impression that he had been dealing with a madman:

"Finally Hitler came to July 20 and I witnessed the explosion of a man filled to bursting with hatred. He yelled at me that he was glad to have bagged the whole opposition at one go and that he would crush it. He was in a state of feverish excitement. Saliva was literally running from his mouth. He was trembling all over and the desk on which he was leaning shook with him. He was bathed in perspiration and became more agitated still as he shouted that his generals would be 'strung up'. I was convinced there and then: the man opposite me was mad!"

If the means at Choltitz's disposal were enough to contain an uprising within the capital, the situation became completely different on August 21 as soon as O.K.W. ordered that the "Paris bridgehead" was to be held against the Americans. Hitler himself wrote to Choltitz to underline the "supreme importance of the defence of Paris from the military and political points of view" and declare that "its fall would cause the breakdown of the whole coastal front north of the Seine and compel us to abandon bases used by our V-weapons against England". And Choltitz could also be reminded that "in the course of history the loss of Paris has also meant the loss of France". This did not, however, alter in any way the situation of the 22,000 men from two or three different divisions with whom he was being asked to hold a bridgehead from the Seine at Poissy to the Marne at Creteil (about 32 miles). The end of the order: "The Seine bridges will be prepared for destruction. Paris must only fall into enemy hands as a heap of rubble", re-

vealed more a state of terrorism than sound strategic thinking. As an experienced soldier Choltitz was well aware that neither the heap of rubble nor the destruction of the bridges (if they were all blown) would slow down the Allied advance. There would have to be more than 60 demolition charges laid, two or three at least would fail to go off and all the experience of the Blitzkrieg had shown that destroyed bridges are no good unless protected by covering fire. For all these reasons the C.-in-C. *Gross Paris* lent a willing ear to Raoul Nordling, not however forgetting that in Germany the freedom and perhaps the lives of his wife and children might depend on the way his behaviour was judged by the Führer. In this double life he was compelled to live he was ably seconded by Lieutenant-General Speidel, chief-of-staff of Army Group "B", though they both had to converse in guarded terms because their telephones were liable to be tapped.

On August 23 the French 2nd Armoured Division bore down on Paris, the "Langlade" and "Dio" Combat Commands along the axis Sées–Rambouillet–Pont de Sèvres, and the "Billotte" Combat Command via Alençon–Chartres–Arpajon–Porte d'Italie, causing an overlap along the sector given by U.S. V Corps to its 4th Division and a new disagreement between Generals Gerow and Leclerc. During the advance German 8.8-cm guns in ambush along the roads caused the loss of 317 men and 41 tanks and self-propelled guns. In the night of August 24-25 Captain Dronne and the tanks *Romilly, Champaubert,* and *Montmirail* passed through the Porte de Gentilly and reached the square in front of the Hôtel de Ville.

On the following day, with the aid of the *Forces Françaises de l'Intérieur* under Colonel Rol-Tanguy, the 2nd Armoured Division liberated Paris, and Choltitz, who had not left his headquarters in the Hôtel Meurice, surrendered.

As soon as he heard that Paris had fallen, Hitler flew into a rage and ordered it to be wiped out. With this end in view he had the great siege mortar *Karl* readied. This huge weapon had a calibre of 60 cms (23.6 inches), fired 2.2-ton shells, and had not been in action since Sevastopol'. The V-weapons and all available aircraft were now also to be brought into action.

Speidel forbade the transmission of this order. It had not the least strategic value and it would have caused thousands of civilian victims, and the destruction of buildings of inestimable artistic value. Speidel was later arrested on suspicion of being implicated in the July 20 plot and was lucky to escape the horrible torture which befell Witzleben and Hoeppner. If any conclusion is to be drawn from this episode it must come in the form of a question: what stage would the intellectual and moral reconstruction of Western Europe have reached today if Generals von Choltitz and Speidel had

Sheltering behind an American tank, civilians shoot at a building still held by German troops in Paris.

not, at the risk of their lives, thwarted the bloodthirsty plans of Adolf Hitler?

In Provence, General de Lattre de Tassigny had meanwhile managed to wriggle out of the plan by which he was intended to concentrate all his efforts on Toulon, and only move on to Marseilles when the large military port had been mopped up. This plan was calculated to lead to the hoisting of the tricoleur on Notre Dame de la Garde on D-day plus 45, that is on September 28, if all went well.

On August 18 two solutions seemed possible to this ardent, yet calculating leader, as he says in his memoirs: "Given our recent successes, ought I to stick to the original plan? Or should I try to extend its scope? These were the alternatives that faced me on that day. It was very difficult, for the consequences of an error of judgement could only be very serious. If I opted for prudence, I could attack in strength, but all the benefits of surprise, and the chaos this would have caused in the enemy's ranks, would be lost. The Germans would have time to redeploy, move up reserves, and make full use of the enormous capabilities of the Toulon defence system. Thus caution would mean a siege, with all its consequent delays and suffering.

"If, on the other hand, I opted for boldness, I could expect to profit from the confusion caused by the strength of Truscott's attack, but my men would have to attack with one man against two, in the open and against reinforced concrete and protected gun emplacements. Boldness could break the French Army before it was even brought together.

"These were dramatic moments for the soul of a commander, but they could not be prolonged. After all, if the surprise attack failed, I could halt it and allow another commander to try again with more reinforcements. The risk was small compared with the enormous gains that might result from a swift success."

De Lattre went for boldness and got the approval of General Patch, who overcame the misgivings of his staff. The French commander was, we would suggest, bolstering up a right decision with wrong premises, because on the same day, far from thinking of reinforcing the defence of Marseilles and Toulon, his adversary, acting under a directive from O.K.W., was actually putting into effect an order for withdrawal which was to take his 19th Army back to the area Lyons–Aix-les-Bains. De Lattre did not know, and could not have known, that Wiese was getting ready to retreat. The risk he mentioned was a real one to him and had to be faced.

This points to the difference between the military historian and the war-time commander: the one draws upon documents calmly collated in the peace of a library; the other makes his decisions from information which is never complete and "works on human skin", as Catherine the Great remarked forcibly to the intellectual Diderot, who carried no responsibility.

Now left to its fate, 242nd Division defended Toulon to the last ounce of its strength. On August 21 the 1st Free French Division had got as far as Hyères, in spite of stiff resistance, and Colonel Bouvet's commandos, working under the 9th Colonial Division, had scaled the walls of Fort Coudon on ropes and hunted down the 120 men of the garrison in the galleries: "At 1530 hours," General de Lattre reported, "when the Kriegsmarine decided to give in, it had only six unwounded men. But at the moment of surrender, their commander signalled: 'Fire on us.' Violent shelling then began on the fort and lasted for several minutes. Germans and Frenchmen alike were hit, and amongst the latter was Lieutenant Girardon, one of the heroes of the assault."

The same thing happened the next day in the ammunition magazine at Toulon, where the galleries had to be taken one by one by Lieutenant-Colonel Gambiez's battalion of shock troops, supported by two tank-destroyers firing point-blank and a battalion of artillery, which reduced the works above the ground.

"Only the dead stopped fighting," de Lattre wrote when describing this action. At nightfall, when the flame-throwers had overcome the last of the resistance, he went on, "the inside of the fortress is nothing more than a huge open charnel-house over which hangs a frightful stench of death. It is being devoured by flames which cause boxes of ammunition to explode at every moment. There are 250 corpses strewn on the ground and only 180 men have been taken prisoner. Of these 60 are seriously wounded. This macabre spectacle suddenly reminded me of the most tragic sights at Douaumont and Thiaumont in 1916. It is a fine thing that our lads, many of whom are in battle for the first time, have equalled the exploits of the hardened *poilus* of Verdun. Their enemy was in no way inferior to the one their fathers faced. One of the defenders was asked to give the reason for this heroic and desperate resistance. 'We defended ourselves, that's all. I am an officer, a lieutenant. It's war for me as well as for you, gentlemen,' he replied."

The victorious advance of the 9th Colonial Division through the defences of Toulon relieved the 3rd Algerian Division of its first mission, during which it had reached Sanary and Bandol, thus ensuring the investment of the western side of the fortress.

Reinforced in due time by General Guillaume's *goums*, General de Monsabert rapidly turned towards Marseilles, where the firemen, the sailors, and the F.F.I. had taken up arms on August 21. The French forces took the mountain route and outflanked 244th Division's defence points along the main axes. On the 23rd General de Monsabert presented himself at 15th Military District H.Q. He sent for Lieutenant-General Schäffer, who then refused to surrender.

The liberation of Toulon was completed on August 27 by the capitulation of Rear-Admiral Ruhfus, who had found a last refuge from the shells of the navy and the bombs of the air force in the Saint Mandrier peninsula. The assault on Toulon had cost the French 2,700 men killed and wounded, but they had taken over 17,000 prisoners and several hundred guns. The Cape Cépet battery, which had been such a thorn in the flesh of the attackers, was pounded by 1,400 shells of 12-inch calibre or higher and 809 1,000- and 2,000-lb bombs. There were four direct hits on its turrets. One jammed, the other had one gun put out of action. The only gun undamaged fired 250 shells, but without appreciable effect.

On August 23 de Lattre sent the 1st Armoured Division into Marseilles, and together with the 3rd Algerian Division and the Moroccan *goums* it overcame the resistance within the city. As in Toulon, the Germans defended themselves bitterly, using rocket launchers, mines, and flame-throwers. The loss successively of Notre Dame de la Garde and Fort Saint Nicolas, however, ended Schäffer's resistance and in the evening of the 27th he wrote to Monsabert:

"Prolonged resistance seems pointless in view of your superior strength. I ask you to cease firing from 2100 to 0800 hours so that surrender terms may be finalised for mid-day on the 28th and that I may have a decision from you which will allow me either to surrender with honour or to fight to the finish."

Neither General de Monsabert nor his commander were men to overlook the valour of the 244th Division. And so the armistice was signed on August 28 shortly before 0800 hours.

The Allies were now a month ahead of schedule. The fury of their attacks had cost them 4,000 killed and wounded, but they had wiped out two enemy divisions and captured 37,000 prisoners.

Before ceasing all resistance the Germans blew up the port installations in Marseilles and Toulon. Until these were restored, the Provence beaches had landed 380,000 men, 69,312 vehicles, 306,000 tons of supplies and *matériel,* and 17,848 tons of fuel. By May 8, 1945, 905,512 men and 4,123,794 tons of *matériel* had passed through the hastily-reconstructed ports of Marseilles, Toulon, and Port de Bouc. These figures are taken from Morison, who claims, and we would agree with him, that for this alone Operation "Dragoon" was justified.

In late August 1944 the Franco-American victory in Provence thus usefully complemented the Anglo-American victory in Normandy. All those who followed the progress of the war on wall maps and every day moved the little blue flags representing the Allied forces further north, north-east, and east, must have thought that on the Western Front the Germans were on the point of final collapse and the Third Reich on the eve of invasion. On August 26, the 21st Army Group had the left of its Canadian 1st Army in the area of Honfleur and linked up with the British 2nd Army around Louviers; the right of the British 2nd Army was in Vernon, where it had a bridgehead on the north bank of the Seine. Between Mantes and Saint Nazaire, the American 12th Army Group formed an immense hairpin including the Seine crossings at Mantes, Paris, Melun, and Troyes, then through Saint Florentin and Joigny, back to the Loire at Gien. In the south, whilst the 7th Army Group (U.S. 7th and French 1st Armies) was mopping up in Toulon and Marseilles, the American VI Corps had liberated Grenoble and was trying to cut off the retreat of the German 19th Army in the area of Montélimar.

By September 10 the Germans had only three fortresses in the north of France: Boulogne, Calais, and Dunkirk. Montgomery, newly appointed a Field-Marshal, occupied Bruges, Ghent, and Antwerp whilst his 2nd Army, down river from Hasselt, was on the north bank of the Albert Canal. The American 12th Army Group was in Liège, Bastogne, and Luxembourg, and on the outskirts of Thionville, Metz, and Nancy. Until its XV Corps came back into the line, the 3rd Army had its right flank exposed in the area of Neufchâteau, but by September 11 it was in contact at Sambernon with the French II Corps, which formed the left wing of the Franco-American 7th Army Group. The right flank of this army group was in Pont-de-Roide near the Swiss border. Finally, between Mont Blanc and the Mediterranean Kesselring still held on to Modane and Briançon for a few days, but Savoy, the Dauphiné, Provence, and the Alpes Maritimes were virtually free.

This exceptionally rapid progress and the capture of 402,000 prisoners reported in the Allied communiqué of September 15 caused wild optimism at S.H.A.E.F. and at the headquarters of the 21st and 12th Army Groups. Between June 6 and September 11, Allied losses in killed and wounded were no greater than 40,000 and 20,000 respectively. Eisenhower now had 49 divisions in the field.

It is not surprising that the editor of the information bulletin at S.H.A.E.F. should blow the victory trumpet and write:

"Two and a half months of bitter

A tank rumbles across a newly completed pontoon bridge over the Seine at Vulaines-sur-Seine.

fighting, culminating for the Germans in a bloodbath big enough even for their extravagant tastes, have brought the end of the war in Europe within sight, almost within reach. The strength of the German Armies in the West has been shattered, Paris belongs to France again, and the Allied armies are streaming towards the frontiers of the Reich." A few days later he concluded:

"The only way the enemy can prevent our advance into Germany will be by reinforcing his retreating forces by divisions from Germany and other fronts and manning the more important sectors of the Siegfried Line with these forces. It is doubtful whether he can do this in time and in sufficient strength."

Montgomery agreed with this forecast and desired S.H.A.E.F. to come to a quick decision about the form and directions to be given to the pursuit. Indeed, on August 17 he had put to General Bradley an outline plan of operations which was, in essence:

1. After crossing the Seine, the 12th and 21st Army Groups would form a "solid mass of some forty divisions" which would move north of the Ardennes and put a pincer round the Ruhr, the 12th to the south and the 21st to the north.

2. South of the Ardennes a "strong American force" would be "positioned in the general area Orléans–Troyes– Châlons–Reims–Laon with its right flank thrown back along the R. Loire to Nantes".

3. The American 7th Army Group would be directed from Lyons to Nancy and the Saar. But, Montgomery remarked: "We ourselves must not reach out with our right to join it and thus unbalance our strategy." He concluded: "The basic object of the movement would be to establish a powerful air force in Belgium to secure bridgeheads over the Rhine before the winter began and to seize the Ruhr quickly."

According to Montgomery, Bradley agreed with the plan, whereas in his memoirs the former C.-in-C. 12th Army Group makes no mention of it. It is common knowledge, however, that Eisenhower was unwilling to ratify the suggestions of Montgomery, though the latter returned to the question on August 22 through Major-General Sir de Guingand, his chief-of-staff and, on the following day, in person during talks which took place between the two leaders alone at Condé-sur-Noireau. But, on the point of taking over the conduct of land operations himself, General Eisenhower rejected the idea with his customary affability. In fact, though Montgomery did not expressly say so, the formation of a "solid mass of some forty divisions" to operate north of the Ardennes would have meant the inclusion of the whole American 1st Army. In a note which he sent to his chief-of-staff on August 22, moreover, he implicitly excluded Bradley from any part in the race for the Ruhr, even attempting to dissuade Eisenhower

from his intention of effectively controlling land operations. This can be read between the lines of paragraphs 3, 4, and 5 of Montgomery's note which de Guingand handed to Eisenhower:

"3. Single control and direction of the land operations is vital for success. This is a WHOLE TIME JOB for one man.

4. The great victory in N.W. France has been won by personal command. Only in this way will future victories be won. If staff control of operations is allowed to creep in, then quick success becomes endangered.

5. To change the system of command now, after having won a great victory, would be to prolong the war."

Eisenhower was in no way inclined to support a plan contrary to the agreement of the preceding winter. But neither did he intend to accept the plan which reduced Bradley and his 12th Army Group to some ten divisions, invited to mark time on the outskirts of the Argonne–for that is what the "strong American force" would have amounted to. Even if he had fallen in with Montgomery's ideas, he would probably have been caught between the discontent of Patton, Hodges, and Bradley and the repudiation of his action by Washington.

By preferring to the concentrated effort proposed by Montgomery a wide-front pursuit aimed at both the Ruhr and the Saar, did Eisenhower nullify the Anglo-American victory in Normandy? Montgomery's memoirs, finished in September 1958, do suggest this. Certainly the Allied advance began to slow down: by December 15 Hodges was bogged down before the Roer and Patton was only just approaching the Saar.

Yet it was not inevitable that the "concentrated effort" would have brought the Allies out-and-out victory before the first snows fell. If Patton had been halted on the Troyes – Châlons – Rheims front, Model and Rundstedt would not have lost the forces he trapped and decimated between the Marne and the Moselle, with a loss to the Germans of 22,600 prisoners, 474 tanks, and 482 guns. Also, if the inner flanks of Patton and Patch had not linked up, it would not have been possible to trap the 19,600 Germans whose capture Major-General Elster reported to U.S. 81st Division H.Q. at Beaugency on September 8.

When Montgomery's memoirs appeared, Eisenhower was President of the United States and thus not in a position to answer them. Even after he had left the White House he still remained silent. He would appear to have stuck throughout to his original opinion as expressed in 1949 in *Crusade in Europe* when, denying that the Allies could have overrun the enemy, he concluded: "General Montgomery was acquainted only with the situation in his own sector. He understood that to support his proposal would have meant stopping dead for weeks all units except the Twenty-first Army Group. But he did not understand the impossible situation that would

have developed along the rest of our great front when he, having outrun the possibility of maintenance, was forced to stop and withdraw."

A very pertinent remark, we would suggest, as on the right bank of the Rhine, somewhere between Wesel and Munster, it is difficult to imagine what chances of success the 21st Army Group would have had if the 12th had been stuck back at Châlons-sur-Marne through lack of fuel and ammunition. Instead of a "reverse Schlieffen plan" such as Montgomery had envisaged, we might have seen Rundstedt manoeuvring between Montgomery and Bradley as Hindenburg had done 30 years before between Rennenkampf and Samsonov at Tannenberg. In all probability, Montgomery's plan would have proved a catastrophe.

In any case, logistics provided an inevitable and crippling brake on the conduct of Allied operations. It must be remembered that Patch in front of Belfort, Patton at Nancy, Hodges at Aix-la-Chapelle, Dempsey on the Albert Canal, and Crerar between Boulogne and Zeebrugge were all being supplied via the beaches of Provence and Normandy. But when the German engineers withdrew, they had carried out 4,000 demolitions over and above the damage caused by Allied bombing in the first six months of the year. The French national railway network was in ribbons and its rolling stock reduced to practically nothing after German requisitioning and Allied air attacks. It is not, therefore, surprising that supplies had not been able to keep up with the advancing troops, in spite of the so-called "Red Ball Highways", major one-way roads along which the heavy lorries rolled for 20 hours a day.

Certain mishaps also occurred in Allied strategy. The American 7th Army failed in its attempt to cut the retreat of the German 19th Army. The Germans did, it is true, leave 5,000 prisoners, including Lieutenant-General Richter, commander of the 198th Division, at Montélimar, and had only 64 guns left out of the 1,480 of the preceding August 15. But, General de Lattre tells us, Wiese "knew his job" and, moreover, the French and the Americans were always running out of petrol.

On the left the French II Corps (General de Monsabert: 1st Free French Infantry and 1st Armoured Divisions), which crossed the Rhône at Avignon on August 29, liberated Lyons on September 2 and won a brilliant victory over a detachment of the German 1st Army in the area of Autun on September 9. This gave it Dijon 48 hours later. In the centre the U.S. VI Corps, operating along the axis Bourg en Bresse–Besançon, was held up at Luxeuil and Lure. Finally, on the right was a French group, consisting mainly of the 3rd Algerian Division, the 9th Colonial having had to be stopped when it reached the Swiss frontier between Geneva and Pont-de-Roide. On September 6 General de Lattre formed this group into the French I Corps and put it under the command of General Béthouart.

The following day it was held up for lack of ammunition. It held on to its position on top of le Lomont, where the old fort had been captured by the F.F.I at the end of July and from which the Germans had been unable to dislodge them. This was an exploit which, de Lattre says, "gives us an incomparable observation post over the plain of Montbéliard and the 'watchdog' of the Belfort gap. The 3rd Algerian Division is in sight of the promised land, but it is out of breath after its terrific run and can't get in."

We now go over to the American 12th Army Group. The chapter of Patton's war memoirs dealing with this part of the campaign is entitled *Touring with an Army in France*. He could also have adapted the message Colonel-General von Kleist is supposed to have sent to Field-Marshal List in the race for the Caucasus in July 1942: "In front of us, no enemy; behind us, no supplies." On August 25, Patton had been ordered to reach in one bound the line Vitry-le-François–Châlons–Rheims; he was then to move off from there, on the orders of army group, to take the Rhine bridges between Mannheim and Koblenz.

Patton still had under his command U.S. VIII Corps, then occupied in taking Brest. His other units were two corps and six divisions: at Troyes was XII Corps under Major-General Manton S. Eddy, who had just relieved General Cook, evacuated after a heart attack; in the bridgehead at Montereau XX Corps was eager and ready for the chase.

On August 28, XII Corps crossed the Marne at Châlons where 80th Infantry and 4th Armoured Divisions filled up with petrol thanks to a captured German dump of 88,000 gallons. On the following day XX Corps passed through Epernay and Château-Thierry, then occupied Rheims without any difficulty.

In spite of the threat of petrol supplies running out, Patton had got Bradley's agreement that he should push on from the Marne to the Meuse, and Eddy captured the river crossings at Vaucouleurs, Commercy, and Saint Mihiel on the last day of the month. On his left, Major-General W. H. Walker, after an advance of some 75 miles, occupied Verdun and crossed the river, the bridges being still intact thanks to the F.F.I. But, writes Martin Blumenson, "in possession of Meuse River bridge-heads between Verdun and Commercy, Patton was in position to attack toward the Moselle between Metz and Nancy, and from there the Rhine River was barely a hundred miles away. This was his intention, but by then his supply lines were drawn to the breaking point. Soldiers in the forward echelons needed shoes, heavy underwear, and socks, and these items could not move fast enough to reach the advancing spearheads. The mechanical beasts of burden needed spare parts and maintenance. Still the most critical shortage was gasoline . . . By then the army was virtually bone dry. Individual tanks were dropping out of combat formations

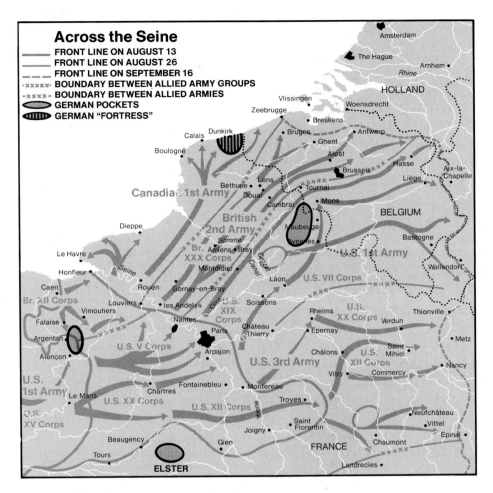

Across the Seine
— FRONT LINE ON AUGUST 13
— FRONT LINE ON AUGUST 26
--- FRONT LINE ON SEPTEMBER 16
·×××· BOUNDARY BETWEEN ALLIED ARMY GROUPS
·×××· BOUNDARY BETWEEN ALLIED ARMIES
⬭ GERMAN POCKETS
⬮ GERMAN "FORTRESS"

for lack of gasoline. The chance of speedy resumption of the pursuit east of the Meuse, a hope that depended on motorised columns, appeared nil."

Patton tried to get Eisenhower to change his point of view, urging that the way to the Rhine between Mannheim and Koblenz was virtually wide open to his tanks, the Siegfried Line not being strongly held. His eloquence failed to move Eisenhower.

By September 15 the enemy was considerably reinforced and, though Patton had liberated Nancy, he had lost any hope he might have had of taking the *Westwall* in his stride or of capturing Metz and Thionville on the way. XV Corps, given to him somewhat late in the day, was engaged on his right in the area Chaumont–Neufchâteau. This gave rise to a battle on September 13 between Vittel and Epinal during which the "Langlade" Combat Command of the French 2nd Armoured Division, sharing equally the honours with the 406th Group, U.S. 9th Air Force from Rennes (365 miles away), severely trounced the newly-formed 112th Panzer Brigade, destroying 34 Panther and 26 Pzkw IV tanks out of the 96 it had set out with.

As we have seen, the U.S. 1st Army, with its right in Melun and its left in Mantes, though not entirely under the command of the Anglo-Canadian 21st Army Group, was given the rôle of supporting, along the axis through Aachen and Cologne, Montgomery's drive towards the

After the slogging match in Normandy, the Allied crossing of the Seine seemed to move forward at break-neck speed.

north of the Ruhr. and so, in the matter of fuel and transport, General Hodges was relatively well supplied.

On the right, U.S. VII Corps with its 3rd Armoured Division (Major-General Maurice Rose) in the lead, broke out of the Melun bridgehead, passed through Laon on August 30, and crossed the Franco-Belgian frontier from Avesnes and Maubeuge, getting into Mons at dusk on September 2.

On the left of the U.S. 1st Army, XIX Corps advanced at the same speed along the axis Mantes–Montdidier–Cambrai–Tournai. 25,000 Germans from 20 different divisions were trapped between the two advancing American columns between Mons and Cambrai and surrendered to VII Corps by order of General Straube, commanding LXXIV Corps.

From Mons and Tournai VII and XIX Corps then changed direction from north to north-east, the former towards Liège, which it reached on September 8, the latter towards the Albert Canal, where it made contact with the 21st Army Group. V Corps, having left Paris, had only got as far as Landrecies. General Bradley, hoping to get Patton out of his supply difficulties, moved it over behind VII Corps and sent it through the Ardennes. On September 9 his 5th Armoured Division (Major-General Lumsford E. Oliver) liberated

Two U.S. soldiers (top) camouflage their machine gun nest. Eisenhower confers with Major-General E. H. Brooks (above).

Luxembourg and, better still, as part of the same advance, crossed the Sûre at Wallendorf (seven miles east of Diekirch) thus making a breach in the Siegfried Line.

At Koblenz, where on September 5 Field-Marshal von Rundstedt had just relieved Model as C.-in-C. West, this news, according to his chief-of-staff Lieutenant-General Westphal, not one inclined to panic, "burst like a bombshell".

"All available forces, all that could be pulled out from other sectors," he added, "were thrown into the breach. Overcoming the most serious hesitations, we went so far as to denude the Trier sector completely. After a week of pitched battles, the enemy went back over the west bank of the Sûre. A gigantic catastrophe was thus averted. If the enemy command had thrown in greater strength at this point, not only the defensive organisation we were trying to build in the Eifel, but the whole Western Front, which had no reserves worthy of the name, would have crumbled."

This shows that the Koblenz H.Q. had simply no idea of the logistic crisis already affecting the U.S. 7th and 3rd Armies and now extending to the 1st. Nor did

they know that Bradley had no reserves with which to exploit Oliver's success. It is true that, according to Westphal, C.-in-C. West's Intelligence services thought that Eisenhower had 60 divisions, whereas the figure was actually 50.

As his notes of August 17 and 23 show, Montgomery claimed for his reinforced 21st Army Group the distinction of inflicting the final blow on the enemy by a "concentrated push" north of the Ruhr. Yet he had only 18 divisions and six or seven independent brigades, and the Canadian 1st Army had been given (by him) a job which was to divert it from his ultimate objective. Using six divisions and two brigades, it liberated the ports of Le Havre, Dieppe, Boulogne, Calais, and Dunkirk, captured the V-rocket launching-sites and mopped up the Cape Gris-Nez shore batteries, which used to harass the English coast between North Foreland and Dungeness.

Thus only the British 2nd Army was left to continue the thrust northwards, but by August 30 it had only two of its three corps across the Seine. These had altogether five divisions, including three armoured, two brigades of tanks, and General Piron's Belgian motorised brigade. This was a long way from the "concentrated push" (40 divisions) mentioned the previous week.

Montgomery, usually so cautious towards overweening displays of ill-considered optimism, seems to have yielded to the feeling of euphoria evident at all levels of the Allied high command. And yet the "great encirclement" west of the Seine, for which Patton had been halted in front of Falaise, had not come up to expectations. And, though now reduced to three corps and six divisions, the German 15th Army in the Pas-de-Calais was still a considerable fighting force. On August 23 its new C.-in-C. was Zangen, who took over from Salmuth. Sir Brian Horrocks, C.-in-C. British XXX Corps (11th Armoured, Guards Armoured, and 50th Infantry Divisions and 2nd Armoured Brigade), left the Vernon bridgehead with 600 tanks and made such good progress that 36 hours later his 11th Armoured Division took Amiens by surprise during the night of August 30-31, capturing General Eberbach, who had replaced the wounded Hausser as C.-in-C. 7th Army. The F.F.I. had seized the bridges in the town and the 11th Armoured was thus able to push on to the area of Lens, which it reached on September 11.

On Horrocks's right the Guards, who had crossed the Somme at Bray, were at Douai by nightfall on the same day. On September 3 they were off again and by 1400 hours, having done over 70 miles, got into the outer suburbs of Brussels, accompanied by the Piron brigade, amidst great popular rejoicing. That same evening General Horrocks, who set up his H.Q. in Laeken Park, invited Queen Elisabeth of the Belgians to dinner in his tent.

At the same time 11th Armoured Division had reached Alost and been given the

task of seizing the port of Antwerp to prevent the destruction of its installations. In this it was admirably seconded by the Belgian resistance so that on September 4 its quays (34 miles of them!), docks, and locks, its equipment and the tunnel under the Scheldt all fell intact into Allied hands. In 1960, however, General Horrocks said he thought that the order given to 11th Armoured to go straight for the Antwerp Dock area was a "serious error".

"My excuse is that my eyes were fixed entirely on the Rhine, and everywhere else seemed of subsidiary importance. It never entered my head that the Scheldt would be mined, and that we should not be able to use Antwerp port until the channel had been swept and the Germans cleared from the coastline on either side. Nor did I realise that the Germans would be able to evacuate a large number of the troops trapped in the coastal areas across the mouth of the Scheldt estuary."

He also wrote that it would have been much wiser to have ordered his division to by-pass Antwerp and go on across the Albert Canal in one solid mass, then make for the Woensdrecht isthmus (15 miles north-east of Antwerp) which has the only metalled road linking the Zeeland archipelago to the mainland. This would have cut off the Germans left behind in the Scheldt estuary and freed the port within a few days.

Horrocks must have had in mind the memoirs of Field-Marshal Montgomery, published two years earlier, which maintained that the "free use of the port of Antwerp" was not the only way of bringing the war to a speedy end; it was necessary at the same time to strike a "violent decisive blow" against Germany. It is significant that Horrocks does not dwell on his former commander's opinion. Colonel Stacey, the official historian of the Canadian Army, concluded, as did Horrocks, but in stronger and more vivid terms: it was "a considerable Allied misfortune". It would seem that the blame for this mishap must lie largely with Montgomery, for Eisenhower had been urging the importance of opening the port of Antwerp since the third week of August. Indeed, his reason for refusing a thrust north of the Ruhr was the need to open Antwerp first.

On Horrocks's left Lieutenant-General Ritchie's XII Corps (7th Armoured and 53rd Infantry Divisions, with 4th Armoured Brigade) avenged its commander's defeats in Libya. Though it had a harder task, as it was manoeuvring in the rear of the German 15th Army, it drove forwards along the axis les Andelys–Gournay–Saint Pol–Béthune and freed Ghent on September 5. In the Bruges area it made contact with the Canadian 1st Army busy mopping up the Channel ports.

As we can see, General Dempsey had driven forward at top speed and the British 2nd Army had equalled the best records of the American 3rd, though to get the fuel for XXX and XII Corps, VIII Corps had had to be immobilised.

CHAPTER 63

The Russian advance into Poland

In 1944 the Soviet summer offensive was to move forward successively over all sectors of the front from the Arctic tundra to the mouth of the Dniestr on the Black Sea. It can thus be compared in extent to Hitler's Operation "Barbarossa" begun three years before. Now the situation was reversed.

In addition to the will to destroy the armed forces of Germany and her satellites, the U.S.S.R. also had territorial and political ambitions: to impose a dictated peace on Finland; to bring Estonia, Latvia, and Lithuania back under Soviet rule; to install a puppet government in Poland; and to prepare to take over Rumania, Bulgaria, Hungary, and Yugoslavia.

Stalin, the head of the Soviet Government and Secretary General of the Soviet Communist Party, was not only taking as axiomatic Clausewitz's view of war as subordinate to politics; but he was also going further, along the principles laid down by Lenin: "War is essentially a political fact . . . war is one part of a whole: that whole is politics", and by Frunze, the Soviet military theorist: "Questions of military strategy and political and economic strategy are closely inter-related and form a coherent whole."

This is clearly opposed to the American military doctrine which Eisenhower obeyed in early April 1945 when he stopped his 12th Army Group on the Elbe at Magdeburg, since Berlin no longer had any importance militarily. There have, it is true, been many cases in which military operations have been gravely compromised by political interference.

In view of the failing strength of the Wehrmacht, Stalin could well afford to plan boldly, using the Red Army's material superiority in pursuit of long-term goals. Early in the summer of 1944 *Stavka* had 500 infantry and 40 artillery divisions, and 300 armoured or mechanised brigades with over 9,000 tanks, supported by 16,600 fighters, fighter-bombers, and twin-engined bombers, whilst behind the front the effort put into training, organisation, and industrial production in 1943 was kept up at the same rate in 1944. It should also be emphasised that the Red Army's conduct of operations was now more relaxed. A judicious series of promotions had brought to the top of the major units many exceptionally able commanders. Stalin and *Stavka* allowed them an easier rein than in the past, whereas their enemy was being deprived of all initiative by the despot of Berchtesgaden.

The first blows of the Soviet summer offensive fell on Finland. As we have seen, thanks to the Swedish Government's action as an intermediary, negotiations were on the point of being concluded between Helsinki and Moscow in the late winter, and the Finns were no longer insisting on the return to the *status quo* of March 1940. The talks fell through, however, because Moscow demanded from this small unhappy country an indemnity of 600 million dollars' worth of raw materials and goods, spread over the next five years.

When spring came, the situation of Finland and her valiant army could hardly give rise to optimism. The defeat of Field-Marshal von Küchler and the German Army Group "North", driven from the banks of the Neva to those of the Narva, deprived Marshal Mannerheim of any hope of German help in the event of a Soviet offensive.

Mannerheim had therefore divided the bulk of his forces in two: in the isthmus between the Gulf of Finland and Lake Ladoga he had put six divisions, including his 1st Armoured Division, and two brigades, all under III and IV Corps; on the front of the river Svir', which runs from Lake Onega to Lake Ladoga, he had nine divisions and three brigades. This was a lot, to be sure but, Mannerheim wrote:

"A reduction of the troops in East Karelia would, however, constitute a surrender of this strategically valuable area and be a good bargaining-point for the attainment of peace. The disposition of the troops was also based on the not unreasonable hope that the fortifications of the Isthmus would compensate for the weakness of man-power."

The Finnish III and IV Corps could in fact count on three successive lines of fortifications, the first two from 44 to 50 miles long and the third 75 miles. This was small stuff against the powerful forces massed by the Russians, especially in artillery, for the Leningrad Front, still under the command of General L. A. Govorov. Finnish Intelligence sources revealed that the Russians put some 20 infantry divisions on the Finnish front, together with four armoured brigades, five or six tank regiments, and four regiments of assault guns, that is some 450 armoured vehicles in all, and about 1,000 aircraft. For their part the official Soviet sources give no figures, so that we are inclined to believe the Finns. Silence implies consent.

On June 9 the Leningrad Front went over to the attack, with an artillery barrage of up to 250 guns per mile. Lieutenant-General D. N. Gussev and his 21st Army had been given the main task and this developed over a ten-mile front along the coastal sector, which allowed the Red Navy's Baltic Fleet to take part under the command of Admiral V. F. Tributs.

Mannerheim wrote: "June 10th may with reason be described as the black day of our war history. The infantry assault, carried out by three divisions of the Guards against a single Finnish regiment, broke the defence and forced the front in the coastal sector back about six miles. Furious fighting raged at a number of holding lines, but the on-storming massed armour broke their resistance.

"Because of the enemy's rapid advance, the 10th Division fighting on the coast sector lost most of its artillery. On June 11th, its cut-up units were withdrawn behind the V.T. (Vammelsuu-Taipale) position to be brought up to strength."

But hardly had the defenders of the isthmus taken up their positions than they were driven back by an attack which broke through north of the Leningrad–Viipuri (Vyborg) railway. The 1st Armoured Division counter-attacked, but to no avail. Faced with this rapidly deteriorating situation, Mannerheim left the defence of the isthmus to General Oesch and ordered the evacuation of Karelia. This enabled him to pull out four divisions. Before there could be any redeployment in force in the threatened sector, the Russian 21st Army made a fresh breakthrough and seized Viipuri on June 20.

What would have happened to the defence if the armies of the Karelian Front (General K. A. Meretskov) had come into battle on the same day as the Leningrad Front and had trapped the Finnish V and VI Corps between Lakes Ladoga and Onega? For unknown reasons the Russians only started their attack five or six days after Mannerheim had ordered the defenders to break off contact.

The Russian offensive in eastern Karelia took the form of a pincer movement. One army crossed the Svir' and pushed northwards to meet the other which, having forced the Masselskaya defile, exploited this success southwards. But the pincers closed on a vacuum and at the beginning of July the Finns, though reduced to four divisions, had nevertheless succeeded in re-establishing their positions on a pre-arranged line from Lake Ladoga on their right to Lake Loymola on their left, some 45 miles from the present Soviet-Finnish frontier.

Between Lake Ladoga and the Gulf of Finland, Govorov had a few more successes, in particular establishing a bridgehead on the north bank of the Vuoksa, along which ran the third defensive position between Viipuri and Taipale. But finally everything quietened down and about July 15 General Oesch was able to state that the enemy forces opposite him were considerably thinner on the ground.

It would certainly be absurd to deny that the Red Army had won. The Finns had been driven back to their last line of defence and had lost the Karelia area, which they had intended to use as a counter in the forthcoming peace negotiations. The Soviet Union had also got the use of the Leningrad–Murmansk railway and canal which the Finns had begun in 1941.

In spite of the defeat, however, the fighting spirit of the Finish Army lived on. It counter-attacked incessantly and in the whole campaign very few Finns were taken prisoners. On balance Moscow seems to have realised that to wipe out the Finnish Army would have cost more than the literal submission of Helsinki to the March 1940 conditions was worth.

As we can see, Mannerheim had played the cards of dissuasion well. But, like his government, he agreed that the time had come for Finland to get out of the war. During the battle, instead of the six divisions for which he had asked O.K.H., he had got only one, the 129th, and a brigade of 80 assault guns. All the assurances, intermingled with threats, proffered by Ribbentrop to President Ryti could not make up the difference. The day after Viipuri fell, and with it Finland's hopes, the Wehrmacht was suffering in Russia one of the heaviest defeats in the history of the German Army, including the tremendous setbacks at Jena and Stalingrad.

On June 28, when he rejoined the German 20th Army fighting north of the Arctic Circle, Colonel-General Rendulic wrote of the impression Mannerheim made on him at their first meeting: "In spite of the prudence which he continually showed in official declarations, his words had an unmistakably pessimistic ring." This goes to show that the 76-year old Marshal saw further than Rendulic.

Russian T-34 tanks move forward, with infantrymen (wearing forage caps instead of helmets) in close support.

On June 22, 1944, as if to celebrate the third anniversary of the German aggression, Stalin opened his last great summer offensive, between the Polotsk area and the north bank of the Pripet. This brought into action Bagramyan's 1st Baltic Front, Chernyakhovsky's 3rd Belorussian Front, Zakharov's 2nd Belorussian Front, and Rokossovsky's 1st Belorussian Front.

According to the *Great Patriotic War,* which we quote in Alexander Werth's version, the following were engaged in this offensive, including reserves: 166 infantry divisions, 31,000 guns and mortars, 5,200 tanks and self-propelled guns, and 6,000 aircraft. The Red Army had never before achieved such a concentration of force or had such huge quantities of supporting *matériel,* which included 25,000 two-ton lorries.

Michel Garder gives a lively account of the atmosphere of the Soviet summer offensive in his book *A War Unlike The Others.* He says:

"The patient work of the Red Army's general staff, which had prepared in great detail the grand plan of *Stavka,* resulted in this fantastic cavalcade. This was the true revenge for the summer of 1941! In the burning-hot July sky the Red Air Force was unopposed. White with dust the T-34's drove on westwards, breaking through the hedges, crushing down thickets, spitting out flame . . . with clusters of infantry clinging on to their rear platforms, adventure-bound. Swarms of men on motor-cycles . . . shouting cavalry . . . infantry in lorries . . . rocket-artillery cluttering up the road . . . the tracks . . . the paths . . . mowing down everything in their way.

"This was a long way from the stereotyped image of 'dejected troops herded to slaughter by Jewish political commissars'."

Marshal Vasilevsky had been sent to Bagramyan and Chernyakhovsky as *Stavka's* representative to co-ordinate their operations. Zhukov performed the same function with Zakharov and Rokossovsky.

The objective of the Soviet offensive was the destruction of Army Group "Centre", then commanded by Field-Marshal Busch, who in the early days of 1944 had taken over from Kluge at the latter's H.Q. at Minsk. Busch had four armies deployed from north to south as follows:

1. 3rd *Panzerarmee* (Colonel-General Reinhardt)
2. 4th Army (General von Tippelskirch)
3. 9th Army (General Jordan)
4. 2nd Army (Colonel-General Weiss)

By the end of the winter the withdrawals forced upon Army Groups "North" and "South" by the Soviet winter offensives had left Army Group "Centre" in a salient: the fortified area of Vitebsk on the Dvina was two-thirds encircled, whereas south of the Pripet Marshes Rokossovsky had got as far as the approaches to Kovel'. To counteract the threat to Field-Marshal Model's left at the end of March, Busch had been asked to send him eight divisions, including two Panzer.

When the Soviet summer offensive started, Army Group "Centre" was thus reduced to 37 divisions. On June 22 the 2nd Army was not attacked, and so the initial clash in the battle for Belorussia was between 166 Soviet and 28 German divisions, on a front extending over 435 miles. The Russian divisions each had 10,000 men. Those of Generals Jordan, Tippelskirch, and Reinhardt were very much understrength, as can be seen in the account given by Major-General Heidkämper, chief-of-staff of the 3rd *Panzerarmee.* He showed that the Vitebsk salient was being held by LIII Corps along a front of 55 miles with the 206th, 4th and 6th Luftwaffe, and 246th Divisions, with 8,123 men (about 150 men per mile). Reserves consisted of a battalion of heavy artillery, two heavy anti-tank companies, and one Luftwaffe special service battalion.

Colonel-General Reinhardt's VI and IX Corps were no better off, nor were the 4th and 9th Armies. German dispositions between the Pripet and the Dvina were thus as thin as a spider's web.

The mobile reserves which were to slow down then stop the onslaught of 4,500 Soviet tanks consisted of only the 20th Panzer and the 18th, 25th, and 60th *Panzergrenadier* Divisions with 400 tracked vehicles between them. For good measure add the same number of assault guns, and it will be seen that in armour the Germans were outnumbered by 5.6 to 1.

It was the same in the air: *Luftflotte* VI could get only an insignificant number of planes off the ground.

The situation of Army Group "Centre" was such that if the enemy unleashed against it an attack of any strength it could not expect to hold it. Again Hitler was to intervene and make Stalin's task easier. Firstly he laid down, in an order dated March 8, 1944, the building on the Eastern Front of a number of "fortified areas" to take over the rôles of the former fortresses. "Their task," his *Führerbefehl* of that day ordered, "is to prevent the enemy from seizing centres of decisive strategic importance. They are to allow themselves to be encircled so as to engage as many of the enemy as possible. They are to create opportunities for fruitful counter-attacks."

Controlled by an army group or army, the strongpoint garrison had instructions to hold out to the last man and no one except the Führer, acting on information from the army group commander, had the right to order withdrawal.

In the Army Group "Centre" sector nine towns were to be made fortified areas. These included Bobruysk on the Berezina, Mogilev and Orsha on the Dniepr, and Vitebsk on the Dvina. The troops manning these new areas were to be taken from the armies in the field, which their commanders regarded as a heresy.

Reinhardt made repeated objections to Hitler's orders, transmitted to him through Field-Marshal Busch, to shut away LIII Corps (General Gollwitzer) and three divisions in the so-called "fortified area" of Vitebsk. In the event of an attack in this sector the absence of these units would open up a breach which could not possibly be stopped, and enemy armour would thus pour through. Reinhardt even went to Minsk to state his case and was told sharply on April 21:

"Vitebsk's value is as a fortified area and the Führer will not change this point of view at any price. His opinion is that Vitebsk can engage between 30 and 40 enemy divisions which would otherwise be free to attack west and south west," then: "It is also a matter of prestige. Vitebsk is the only place on the Eastern Front whose loss would resound throughout the world."

Reinhardt was dismissed in these terms; neither Tippelskirch nor Jordan were any better received by Busch. Jordan, who on the following May 20 proposed to Hitler that if it were to appear likely that the Soviets would launch an offensive in Belorussia, the Germans should withdraw to the Dniepr and the Berezina, thus shortening their line from 435 to 280 miles, was summarily dismissed with "Another of those generals perpetually looking backwards".

It is true that the Führer did not consider that Army Group "Centre" would be the immediate objective of the offensive which, he admitted, the enemy would launch as soon as the ground was sufficiently hard again. In all evidence it was Army Groups "North Ukraine" and "South Ukraine" which were threatened, as Stalin clearly had his eyes fixed on the

Rumanian capital and the Ploieşti oilfields, then the Balkan peninsula and the Turkish narrows, the age-old goal of Imperial Russia, not to mention Budapest and the rich Hungarian plains.

From early June onwards reports from the front, based on direct information, on aerial reconnaissance by the Luftwaffe, on the interception and analysis of radio messages, and on the interrogation of prisoners and deserters, all seemed to indicate the progressive build-up of a powerful assault force between the Pripet and the Dvina. In particular the Red Air Force was growing steadily in numbers every day. When Major-General Gehlen, head of Section East of O.K.H. Intelligence, told Hitler about all this, the Führer retorted that it was merely a clumsy decoy movement. Stalin wanted the Germans to bring over from Moldavia to Belorussia the forces they were holding opposite the true centre of gravity of Russian strategy, but Hitler was not going to fall into that trap.

This opinion was so fixed in his mind that during the night of June 24-25 he obstinately refused to yield to the despair of his closest collaborators, who entreated him to agree to the measures which had become necessary consequent upon the collapse of the 3rd *Panzerarmee* in the Vitebsk sector, whilst at the confluence of the Dniepr and the Berezina the 9th Army had reached the limits of endurance under ever increasing attacks. There was an eye-witness to these events.

Colonel-General Dr. Lothar Rendulic was at the Berghof that evening, having been summoned there urgently to be given command of the German 20th Army (Lappland) after the accidental death of

Colonel-General Dietl. In his memoirs Rendulic says:

"Hitler thought that the main Soviet effort was developing in the south and considered that these Russian attacks east of Warsaw were mere demonstrations. It was a notable miscalculation, as events were to show. He forbade any reserves to be taken from the south and moved to Warsaw. I can say here that when I came out of the conference I asked Colonel-General Jodl how he could let this appreciation of the situation go unchallenged. He replied: 'We fought the Führer for two whole days, then when he ran out of arguments he said: "Leave me. I am relying on my intuition." What can you do in a situation like that?'"

During the night of June 19-20 the 240,000 partisans who controlled the forests in Belorussia cut the lines of communication of Army Group "Centre" in more than 10,000 places as far west as Minsk. At dawn on the 22nd the forces of the 1st Baltic and the 3rd Belorussian Fronts went over to the attack on both sides of Vitebsk. The 1st Belorussian Front went into action on the following day. Generals Bagramyan and Chernyakhovsky had been given as their first objective the capture of Vitebsk by a pincer movement, which would give their comrade Rokossovsky the time to pierce the German 9th Army's positions in the area of Bobruysk. When both these results had been achieved the two Belorussian Fronts would let loose their armoured formations, which would converge in the direc-

A Soviet ground crew work on a Lavochkin fighter on a forward airfield in central Russia in 1944.

513

tion of Minsk. A second pincer would thus be formed and this would crush Army Group "Centre". Bagramyan and Chernyakhovsky took just 48 hours to overpower the resistance of the 3rd *Panzerarmee* north-west and south-east of Vitebsk. During this brief spell the German commander also used up his meagre reserves as well as the 14th Division, sent to him by Busch as a reinforcement. Busch could ill afford the loss. In particular the German right wing, which consisted of VI Corps (General Pfeiffer, killed in this action), collapsed completely under the impact of the Soviet 5th Army and four armoured brigades, whose attack was preceded and supported by V Artillery Corps (520 heavy guns) and tactical air formations acting with a strength, a spirit, and an accuracy hitherto unknown on the Eastern Front.

At 1520 hours on June 24 Zeitzler called Reinhardt from the Berghof to ask if he considered the mission assigned to him at the fortified area of Vitebsk to be vital. The army commander, according to his chief-of-staff, replied candidly that "LIII Corps was surrounded, though still only weakly; that this was the moment to order him to try to break out; that every quarter of an hour the Russian ring to the west of Vitebsk was thickening."

When Zeitzler remarked that the Führer feared heavy losses in supplies of all kinds if the fortified area were to be abandoned hastily, Reinhardt burst out: "If the ring closes we shall lose not only supplies and ammunition, but the whole of LIII Corps with its five divisions." As usual nothing came of these remonstrations, for at 1528 hours Zeitzler came back from seeing Hitler and informed Reinhardt: "The Führer has decided that Vitebsk will be held." According to Major-General Heidkämper, Reinhardt stood "petrified" at the news.

At 1830 hours, however, the incompetent despot agreed to some relaxation of this grotesque order and signalled 3rd *Panzerarmee:* "LIII Corps will leave one division to garrison Vitebsk and break out westwards to rejoin our lines. Report name of commander of this division. Swear him in by radio as new commander of 'Vitebsk fortified area'. Make him confirm his oath."

This order was no less absurd than the one which went before it. The 206th Division (Lieutenant-General Hitter) was nominated. To this unit alone was entrusted the defence of positions prepared for four divisions. And it was too late. LIII Corps was intercepted and crushed during its retreat and when its commander, General Gollwitzer, surrendered to the Russians on June 27 he had only 200 of his men with him and of these 180 were wounded. The worst had happened: the destruction of Vitebsk opened a breach in the German line more than 28 miles wide. Reinhardt was now reduced to three worn-out divisions and 70 guns. Nothing and nobody could now stop the thrustful Chernyakhovsky from driving on along

the Lepel'–Minsk axis with the 5th Guards Army under Marshal of Armoured Forces Pavel A. Rotmistrov.

Further south on the Belorussian front, the same causes could only produce the same effects and General Jordan, C.-in-C. 9th Army, was no luckier than Reinhardt; XXXV Corps, defending the fortified area of Bobruysk with four divisions, suffered the same fate as LIII Corps. When he opened his offensive on June 24, General Rokossovsky had taken good care not to launch his 1st Belorussian Front forces against the German fortified areas, but to push them into gaps north and south of the River Berezina. Three days of hard fighting brought him victory. South of Bobruysk he overcame XLI Panzer Corps (Lieutenant-General Hoffmeister) and cut off the retreating XXXV Corps (Lieutenant-General von Lützow), leaving it trapped in the fortified area.

On June 29 16,000 Germans emerged from the pocket and gave themselves up, leaving behind them the bodies of 18,000 of their comrades. By now the mounted, motorised, mechanised, and armoured forces of General Pliev, one of the most brilliant cavalry commanders of the war, had reached Ossipovichi, some eight miles south-east of Minsk, and were rumbling forward to meet the 5th Guards Tank Army, which had passed Lepel' and was now in Borisov.

The situation of the German 4th Army, now at grips with greatly superior forces on the 2nd Belorussian Front, was scarcely any better. Faced with disasters on his right and left, General von Tippelskirch, now in command *vice* Colonel-General Heinrici, had to use all his initiative to get his army out of its positions along the river Proina and back to the Dniepr. The fortified areas of Mogilev and Orsha on the Dniepr, however, were soon overcome by Zakharov and Chernyakhovsky, and became the graveyards respectively of the 6th (Lieutenant-General Henie) and the 12th (Lieutenant-General Wagner) Divisions.

Tippelskirch thus had to continue his retreat westwards across rough forest land infested with marches and, particularly, thick with partisans. It is no wonder that, as planned by *Stavka,* Rotmistrov and Pliev got to Minsk before him on July 3, joining forces behind his back and condemning his XII and XXVII Corps and XXXIX Panzer Corps (respectively under Generals Vincenz Müller, Voelkers, Martinek) to the sad fate of "moving pockets".

It was June 28 before Hitler finally admitted that the Belorussian offensive was something more than a diversion. On that day he sacked General Busch, who had obeyed his directives unquestioningly, and replaced him by Field-Marshal Model, who strove to limit the extent of the disaster. Army Group "North", though now uncovered on its right flank by the defeat of the 3rd *Panzerarmee,* was required to give up three divisions. Ten more, including four Panzer, were taken from Army Group "North

Ukraine". These units were sent to the Belorussian front in the hope of an attack on the flank of Rokossovsky, who was now exploiting his victory along the line Minsk – Baranovichi – Brest-Litovsk. The breach now open between the Pripet and the Dvina was some 185 miles wide and, according to the O.K.H., this was swallowing up 126 infantry divisions and no fewer than 62 armoured or mechanised brigades with at least 2,500 tanks. On July 8 the last "moving pocket" surrendered behind the Russian lines with 17,000 men, having run out of ammunition. Out of 37 divisions in Army Group "Centre" on the previous June 22, 28 had been badly mauled, if not actually cut to pieces, and an enormous mass of *matériel,* including 215 tanks and more than 1,300 guns, had been captured.

According to statistics from Moscow, which appear reliable, the Germans lost between these two dates some 285,000 dead and prisoners, including 19 corps and divisional commanders. The Belorussian disaster was thus worse than Stalingrad and all the more so since, when Paulus resigned himself to the inevitable, the "Second Front" was still only a distant threat to the Third Reich.

Stalin celebrated in true Roman style by marching seemingly endless columns of 57,600 prisoners-of-war through the streets of Moscow with their generals at the head. Alexander Werth, the *Sunday Times* correspondent, was there and he described the behaviour of the Russian crowd as the men passed by:

"Youngsters booed and whistled, and even threw things at the Germans, only to be immediately restrained by the adults; men looked on grimly and in silence; but many women, especially elderly women, were full of commiseration (some even had tears in their eyes) as they looked at these bedraggled 'Fritzes'. I remember one old woman murmuring 'just like our poor boys . . . tozhe pognali ne voinu (also driven into war)'."

Stalin gave Bagramyan, Chernyakhovsky, Zakharov, and Rokossovsky the job of exploiting as deeply and as fast as possible the victory at Minsk, the extent of which, thanks to Hitler, seems to have exceeded even *Stavka's* highest hopes.

Under the terms of the new directives, the forces of the 1st Baltic Front were given as their objective the Gulf of Riga, whilst the three Belorussian Fronts would move first on to the line Kaunas–Grodno–Brest-Litovsk, then force their way across the Niemen and the Bug, as they had done over the Dniepr and the Berezina. Colonel-General Chernyakhovsky would then take on the defences of eastern Prussia, whilst Zakharov and Rokossovsky (the latter just having been promoted Marshal of the U.S.S.R.) would invade Poland.

For three weeks the victors of Minsk covered their ten to fifteen miles a day,

Russia's summer offensive in 1944 which took her to the borders of Prussia.

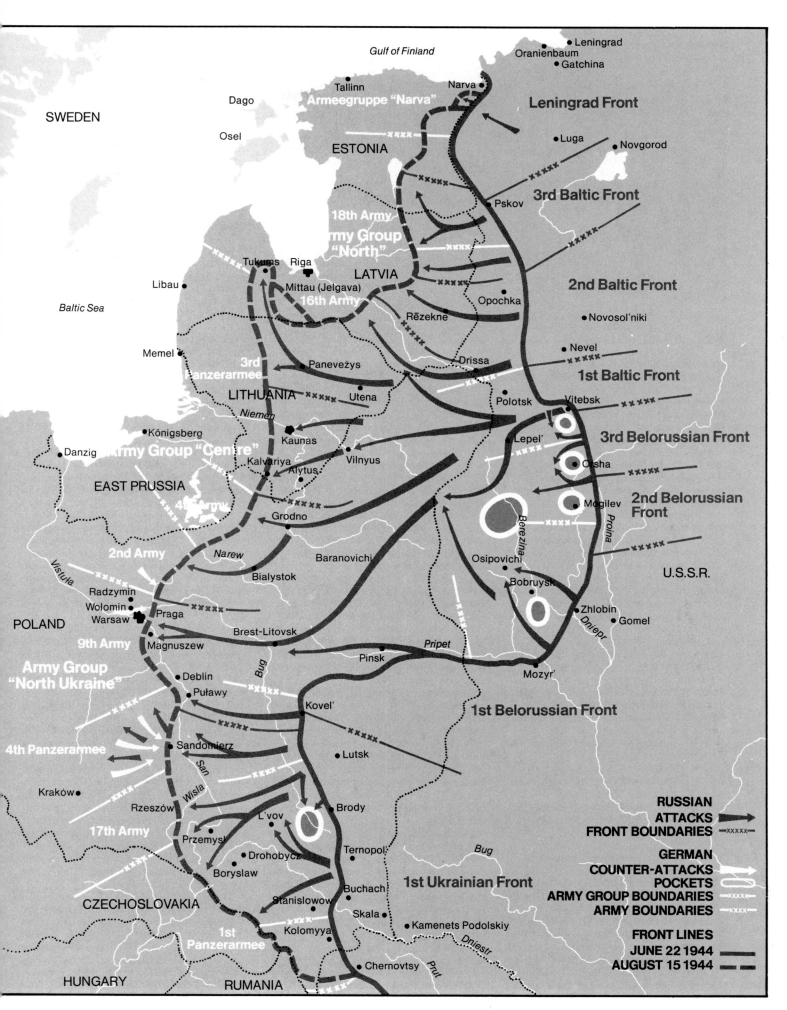

SWEDEN

Gulf of Finland

● Leningrad
Oranienbaum ●
● Gatchina

Tallinn ●
Narva ●

Dago

Armeegruppe "Narva"

Leningrad Front

Osel

ESTONIA

● Luga

● Novgorod

3rd Baltic Front

Pskov ●

18th Army

Army Group "North"

2nd Baltic Front

Libau ●

Tukums ● ● Riga

Mittau (Jelgava)

16th Army

Opochka ●

Baltic Sea

LATVIA

Rēzekne ●

● Novosol'niki

Memel ●

3rd Panzerarmee

Panevežys ●

Drissa ●

● Nevel

1st Baltic Front

LITHUANIA

Utena ●

Polotsk ●

Vitebsk ●

Niemen

● Lepel'

3rd Belorussian Front

Königsberg ●

Kaunas ●

● Orsha

Danzig ●

Army Group "Centre"

Kalvariya

Alytus ●

Vilnyus ●

● Mogilev

2nd Belorussian Front

EAST PRUSSIA

4th Army

Berezina

Proina

Grodno ●

Osipovichi ●

Narew

2nd Army

Baranovichi ●

● Bobruysk

U.S.S.R.

Vistula

Radzymin ●

Bialystok ●

● Zhlobin

Wolomin ●

Praga ●

● Gomel

POLAND

Warsaw ●

Brest-Litovsk ●

Dniepr

9th Army

Magnuszew ●

Pripet

Pinsk ●

Mozyr' ●

Army Group "North Ukraine"

Deblin ●

Bug

Puławy ●

Kovel' ●

1st Belorussian Front

4th Panzerarmee

Sandomierz ●

San

Lutsk ●

Kraków ●

Wisła

Brody ●

Rzeszów ●

L'vov ●

17th Army

Przemyśl ●

Ternopol' ●

Bug

1st Ukrainian Front

Drohobycz ●

Boryslaw ●

Buchach ●

CZECHOSLOVAKIA

Stanislowow ●

Skala ●

● Kamenets Podolskiy

Kolomyya ●

Dniestr

1st Panzerarmee

Prut

HUNGARY

RUMANIA

Chernovtsy ●

RUSSIAN ATTACKS
FRONT BOUNDARIES –xxxxx–

GERMAN COUNTER-ATTACKS
POCKETS
ARMY GROUP BOUNDARIES xxxxx
ARMY BOUNDARIES xxxx

FRONT LINES
JUNE 22 1944
AUGUST 15 1944

515

Russian soldiers load a 45-mm anti-tank gun during a German counter-attack.

by-passing without much difficulty at first the units which Field-Marshal Model, like General Weygand after June 11, 1940, threw in piecemeal to stop the gaps. Model, the new C.-in-C. Army Group "Centre", now had the job of holding back the enemy long enough for O.K.H. to regroup its forces and to reform the indispensable continuous front. He was more highly regarded by Hitler than his unfortunate predecessor, and was thus able to obtain in time permission to evacuate a whole series of so-called "fortified areas" which otherwise would have become so many death-traps for the army's divisions. This meant, of course, considerable sacrifices of territory:

July 13: Chernyakhovsky takes Vilnyus;
July 14: Rokossovsky envelops Pinsk, on the Pripet;
July 15: Chernyakhovsky forces the Niemen at Alytus, while Zakharov takes Grodno;
July 18: Rokossovsky crosses the Russo-Polish frontier fixed at Teheran;
July 23: Rokossovsky's advance guard enters Lublin;
July 27: Zakharov breaks through the defences of Białystok;
July 28: Rokossovsky takes Brest-Litovsk;
July 31: Rokossovsky enters Praga, across the Vistula from Warsaw;
August 1: Chernyakhovsky reaches Kalvariya, 15 miles from the Prussian frontier; and
August 2: Chernyakhovsky takes Kaunas.

On Chernyakhovsky's right, General Bagramyan and the armies of the 1st Baltic Front poured through the breaches in the inner flanks of Army Groups "North" and "Centre" caused by the Vitebsk catastrophe. Whilst the means were lacking to stop the enemy's advance towards Riga, was it advisable to keep the German 16th and 18th Armies on the Polotsk–Pskov–Lake Peipus line, which they had been holding since their painful retreat of the preceding winter? Colonel-General Lindemann, C.-in-C. Army Group "North", concluded that it was not and advised the withdrawal of his forces on the left bank of the Dvina. He was also being asked to transfer certain of his units to Army Group "Centre", which strengthened his point of view.

But to abandon Estonia might risk the "defection" of Finland, as O.K.W. put it. And so on July 2 Hitler relieved Lindemann of his command and handed it over to General Friessner, who in February 1944 had distinguished himself as commander of *Armeegruppe* "Narva". This change of personnel did nothing to improve the strategic situation.

On July 11 Bagramyan crossed the Dvina at Drissa and further to the left his advance guard reached Utena in Lithuania. On the following day the 2nd Baltic Front (General A. I. Eremenko) came into the battle and, breaking out from the area of Novosol'niki, drove deep into the positions of the German 16th Army (General Loch).

Caught up in front by Eremenko and behind by Bagramyan, the latter threatening his communications, Friessner, who had had to give up 12 divisions to Model, could only come to the same conclusions on July 12 as his predecessor had done. But, faced with the same refusal from Hitler to meet the situation with common sense, he did not hesitate, at the end of his letter dated that day, to stake his command:

"If, *mein Führer*," he wrote, "you are not prepared to accept my idea and give me the liberty of action necessary to carry out the measures proposed above, I shall be compelled to ask you to relieve me of the responsibilities I have assumed so far." Summoned by return of post to Rastenburg, Friessner upheld his view in the presence of the Führer, who reproached him for having used threats and for having shown an unmilitary attitude throughout. Reminding Hitler that he was responsible for some 700,000

men, and that he was fighting at the relative strength of one to eight, according to the account he has left of this interview he went so far as to say:

"I am not trying to hang on to my job. You can relieve me of it. You can even have me shot if you want to. But to ask me, *in full knowledge of the facts and against the dictates of my conscience,* to lead the men entrusted to me *to certain destruction*–that you can never do."

Hitler, with tears in his eyes, is thereupon supposed to have seized General Friessner's hand and promised him every support. But the facts are that each one stuck to his own position. And so Colonel-General Schörner, C.-in-C. Army Group "South Ukraine", was ordered on July 23 to change places immediately with Friessner, C.-in-C. Army Group "North", who was himself promoted to Colonel-General.

Amongst the general officers of the Wehrmacht, Schörner was one of the few who was unswerving in his loyalty to the Führer. However great his National Socialist zeal, however, it was not in his power to satisfy Hitler, for the 3rd Baltic Front (General Maslennikov) now went over to the offensive and extended the battle further northwards. This was followed on July 25 by an attack by the Leningrad Front (Marshal of the U.S.S.R. L. A. Govorov). In all a dozen armies totalling at least 80 divisions took part in this concentric offensive.

Whilst Govorov was breaking through the Narva defile and Maslennikov, after liberating Pskov on July 21, was also driving on into Estonia, on July 26 Eremenko, anchoring his left flank on the Dvina, captured the towns of Rēzekne (Rositten) and Dvinsk (Daugav'pils) in Latvia. Bagramyan, who was using what Hitler called the "hole in the Wehrmacht", or the still gaping breach between the right and left of Army Groups "North" and "Centre", changed direction from west to north west and, driving through Panevežys, Jelgava (Mittau), and Tukums, reached the Gulf of Riga to the west of the great Latvian port in the evening of August 1. As Generals Lindemann and Friessner had never ceased to predict, Army Group "North", with some 30 divisions, was cut off in Estonia and northern Latvia. More fortunate than Paulus at Stalingrad, however, Schörner could confidently rely on the Baltic for supplies and evacuation, since the Gulf of Finland was blocked right across so that Soviet submarines could not operate in the open sea. In the Gulf of Riga his right flank was efficiently supported by the guns of the German fleet – by the very warships which Hitler had wanted to scrap in 1943.

On the German side of the immense front line stretching from the Baltic to the Carpathians, the second fortnight in July brought defeat to Army Group "North Ukraine". This added further disaster to the crushing of Army Group "Centre", the last consequences of which were still far from being played out. The tension was such that, taking also into account the American breakthrough in Normandy, it might have been thought that the last hour had struck for the Wehrmacht and for Greater Germany's Third Reich. This was how Marshal Rokossovsky saw events when he stated to a correspondent of the British *Exchange Telegraph* on July 26:

"It is no longer important to capture such and such a position. The essential thing is to give the enemy no respite. The Germans are running to their deaths ... Their troops have lost all contact with their command."

On the following day a spokesman of *Stavka* spoke in the same terms at a press conference: "The Führer's G.H.Q. will no more be able to hold the line of the Vistula than it did those of the Bug and the San. The German Army is irremediably beaten and breaking up."

Also on July 13 Marshal Konev and the forces of the 1st Ukrainian Front had come into the battle, extending the action of the three Belorussian Fronts from the area of Kovel' to the left bank of the Dniestr. According to the Soviet military historian Boris S. Telpukhovsky, whose account we have no reason to doubt, Konev had been given by *Stavka* all the necessary men and *matériel* to secure an easy victory over Army Group "North Ukraine", which was still, together with Army Group "Centre", under the command of Model. For this assault Konev had 16,213 guns and rocket-launchers, 1,573 tanks, 463 assault guns, 3,240 aircraft, and no fewer than seven armies, including the 1st and 3rd Guards Tank Armies and the 4th Tank Army, commanded respectively by Generals M. E. Katukov, P. S. Rybalko, and D. D. Lelyushenko, all three very experienced tank commanders.

On the German side, Army Group "North Ukraine" had had to give up to Army Group "Centre" four Panzer and three infantry divisions since June 22 and was reduced to 43 divisions (of which five were Panzer and one *Panzergrenadier*) and two mountain brigades. Assuming that between April and June the German armoured divisions had been brought up to their normal strength of 160 fighting and command tanks which, knowing the aberrations of Adolf Hitler, seems highly unlikely, the Russians outnumbered them by two to one. In the air Russian superiority was of the order of five to one. Hence the disaster which befell 8th Panzer Division on July 14. Disregarding orders, it took the main road to Brody to speed up its counter-attack. Major-General von Mellenthin writes:

"Eight Panzer was caught on the move by Russian aircraft and suffered devastating losses. Long columns of tanks and lorries went up in flames, and all hope of counterattack disappeared."

Marshal Konev had forces so powerful and so numerous at his command that he could give his offensive two centres of gravity. On the right, in the area southwest of Lutsk, a first group containing notably the 1st Guards Tank Army, was to break up the 4th *Panzerarmee* (General Harpe) then exploit its victory in a general south-west direction. On the left a second group, containing the 3rd Guards Tank Army and the 4th Tank Army, had concentrated in the area of Ternopol': attacking due west it was to engage the 1st *Panzerarmee* (Colonel-General Raus) and form a pincer with the first group.

By evening on D-day the German defences in the two sectors were already seriously damaged. On the following day Colonel-General Raus put the 1st and 8th Panzer Divisions under XLVIII Panzer Corps for an eventual counter-attack, but this failed as a result of the circumstances described above by Mellenthin. Twenty-four hours later not only had the Russians broken through at the points previously designated by Konev, but the pincers had closed on General Hauffe's XIII Corps between L'vov and Brody.

And so a new "moving pocket" was formed, from which several thousand men managed to escape during a night-attack of hand-to-hand fighting. On July 23, however, General Hauffe had been taken prisoner together with 17,000 men of his corps and the victors counted 30,000 German corpses on the battlefield.

In the German sectors facing Rokossovsky and Konev, it was Model's intention to re-establish his line along the Bug. This evidently over-optimistic plan came to nothing in view of the weakness of Army Group "Centre" and the recent defeat of Army Group "North Ukraine". Worse still, the breach between the right flank of the 4th *Panzerarmee* and the left flank of the 1st was now wide open and there was the great danger that the latter's communications with Kraków would be cut and that the army would be driven back against the Carpathians. Hence, in full agreement with Colonel-General Guderian, who had succeeded Zeitzler as Chief-of-Staff at O.K.H. after the attempt on Hitler's life on July 20, Model drew back to the line of the Vistula and its extension the San above Deblin.

Even if the Germans, after their defeats of June 22 and July 13, had managed to establish a front line behind these ditches, this last-minute attempt could not have saved the Polish oilwells at Drogobycz and Boryslaw which became a heavy and irreparable loss to the military economy of the Third Reich. The situation between the Narew and the Carpathians was now deteriorating so rapidly that O.K.H. had to draw on the strength of Army Group "South Ukraine" and send four Panzer and seven infantry divisions from Moldavia to Galicia.

Before these reinforcements could be put to use, Marshals Rokossovsky and Konev had reached the Vistula and the San at Blitzkrieg speed, mopping up German columns retreating on foot or in horse-drawn vehicles. Between July 28 and 31, tanks of the 1st Belorussian Front covered the 120 miles between Brest-Litovsk and the suburbs of Warsaw. They also crossed the Vistula at Magnuszew and Pulawy, upstream from the capital. Rokossovsky's optimistic view of events quoted above seems to have been justified. The 1st Ukrainian Front had similar quick successes, covering 125 miles on a front some 250 miles wide on July 27. On that same day its formations on the right got beyond Przemysl on the west bank of the San and cleaned up

A Russian junior lieutenant checks his map with his sergeant.

L'vov on the way, whilst on the left, having crossed the Dniestr, it captured Stanislawow and threw back to the Carpathians the Hungarian 1st and 2nd Armies, which had formed the right flank of Army Group "North Ukraine" since the end of the winter. The situation now looked very dangerous.

A few days later Konev got a bridge-head over 30 miles deep over the Vistula in the area of Sandomierz, drove on beyond the San as far as Rzeszów, more than 90 miles beyond L'vov, and on August 7 occupied the oil wells at Drogobycz and Boryslaw.

A Moscow communiqué dated July 25 put the German losses since the start of the summer offensive at some 60 divisions, or 380,000 killed and more than 150,000 prisoners. The figures seem acceptable. On the other hand, the figure of 2,700 tanks destroyed or captured, as the complement of 17 fully-equipped Panzer divisions, seems unlikely.

From the Dvina at Vitebsk to the Niemen at Kaunas is 250 miles as the crow flies and from the Dniepr at Orsha to the Vistula at Warsaw 400; the bridgehead at Sandomierz reached by Konev's advance guard was over 180 miles from the area of Lutsk. The whole of this rapid advance, carried out on the old cavalry principle of "to the last breath of the last horse and the last horseman" had there-fore reached its strategic limit.

Between the Carpathians and the Narew, O.K.H.'s reinforcements, though desperate and improvised, were beginning to take effect. The 17th Army (General Schulz) filled the gap between the 1st and 4th *Panzerarmee* and the 9th Army (General von Vormann) occupied the left flank of the 4th *Panzerarmee* between the Sandomierz bridgehead and a point downstream of Warsaw. There also came into the battle from the interior or from Moldavia a good half-dozen armoured divisions, including the "Hermann Gör-ing", the S.S. 3rd *"Totenkopf"* and 5th *"Wiking"* Panzer, and the excellent *"Grossdeutschland" Panzergrenadier.* Volume IV of the *Great Patriotic War* gives a good account of this change in the situation of the two sides:

"At the end of July . . . the tempo of the offensive had greatly slowed down. The German High Command had by this time thrown very strong reserves against the main sectors of our advance. German resistance was strong and stubborn. It should also be considered that our rifle divisions and tank corps had suffered heavy losses in previous battles; that the artillery and the supply bases were lagging behind, and that the troops were short of both petrol and munitions.

"Infantry and tanks were not receiving nearly enough artillery support. During the delays in re-basing our air force on new airfields, this was much less active than before. At the beginning of the Belorussian Campaign, we had complete control of the air. At the beginning of August our superiority was temporarily

lost. In the 1st Belorussian sector between August 1 and 13 our planes carried out 3,170 sorties and the enemy planes 3,316."

Doubtless, and for reasons which we shall see shortly, these statements by the Soviet writers are not completely impartial. Nevertheless by August 16, soon after Model had been given the job of repairing the situation, the position on the Eastern Front can be said to have stabilised temporarily between Kal-variya and the Carpathians. In particular the 4th *Panzerarmee* and the 9th Army had managed to reduce the bridgeheads at Sandomierz (Baranow), Pulawy, and Magnuszew, but not to eliminate them completely. On the right bank of the Vistula the Soviet 2nd Tank Army suffered a defeat at Wolomin and Radzymin, a few miles from Warsaw, which cost 3,000 killed and 6,000 prisoners together with a considerable amount of *matériel.*

This short pause gives us an opportunity to put forward some conclusions on these six weeks of operations on the Eastern Front:

1. Warsaw may be 400 miles from Orsha, but it is only 350 from Berlin. So a repetition of the German mistakes which led to this victory by the Red Army would land the Russians in the heart of the Third Reich.

2. Between June 1 and August 30, 1944, Germany's land forces lost on the Eastern Front alone 916,860 in killed, wounded, and prisoners. The human resources of the Third Reich were therefore rapidly running out and would not be made up by the expedient of "people's grenadier" *(Volksgrena-dier)* divisions.

3. French émigrés returning to their country after the fall of Napoleon were said to have learned nothing and forgotten nothing. Hitler's example shows that one can do worse: he learned nothing and forgot everything. The failure of the attempt on his life on July 20 would therefore allow him to indulge his despotism and incom-petence to the full.

4. The fourth and last conclusion comes in the form of a question. The *Great Patriotic War* says that the forces of the 1st Belorussian Front arrived exhausted on the banks of the Vistula, which explains the halt in their advance: but could not *Stavka* have made up its strength with units and *matériel* already earmarked for cam-paigns in Rumania and Hungary so as to maintain the drive westwards?

As we are aware that a theatre of opera-tions can only absorb as many men and as much *matériel* as can be supplied by its means of communication, we leave the last question unanswered.

We are thus brought to the controversy which arose between the West and the Soviets over the behaviour of Stalin, *Stavka,* and the Red Army towards the Warsaw rising started at 1700 hours on August 1 by General Bor-Komorowski, C.-in-C. of the Polish Home Army. We cannot imitate Telpukhovsky, who main-

tains a prudent silence on this subject but nevertheless devotes a page and a half of his extensive work to the liberation of the little Polish village of Guerasimowichy on July 26, 1944. In his memoirs, Winston Churchill, reporting the return to Praga of Rokossovsky about September 15, made no bones about the reasons for the tragic episode as he saw them:

"The Russians occupied the Praga suburb, but went no further. They wished to have the non-Communist Poles des-troyed to the full, but also to keep alive the idea that they were going to their rescue.

"Such was their liberation of Poland, where they now rule. But this cannot be the end of the story."

Churchill was doubtless writing under the influence of the exchange of telegraph messages he had had with Stalin on the subject of Warsaw, and was remembering the help he had wanted to give by air to the stricken city and its heroic defenders. He did not know then as well as we do now about the operations in the suburbs of the Polish capital between August 1 and 4. Michel Garder, writing in 1961 after carefully researching Soviet material published after 1953, agrees in broad essentials with Churchill. "With Rokos-sovsky within 32 miles of Warsaw," he writes, "it seemed to General Bor-Komorowski that the arrival of the Russian troops could only be a matter of a few days. It was the duty of the Poles to welcome the Soviets as allies and not as 'liberator-occupiers'. This was just what Stalin did not want.

"In the eyes of the Kremlin, the Polish Home Army was merely a tool of the 'reactionary Polish clique' in London whose leaders, in addition to their 'en-slavement to capitalism' and their 'bourgeois chauvinism' had had the effrontery to state that the Katyn massacres were the work of the N.K.V.D.

"Having suddenly run out of steam, the irresistible 1st Belorussian Front offensive had found itself facing the German bridgehead in front of Warsaw. To get so far had, it is true, cost Rokossov-sky's armies a great effort. Their lines of communication were stretched. They needed a few days' respite and probably considerable reinforcements in men and *matériel* to bring them back up to strength. But nothing, other than political con-siderations by the Kremlin, could justify the semi-inertia of the Soviet troops in September when they reached the suburbs of Praga."

Werth is less certain than Churchill or Garder. He seems to give credence to the pessimistic figures for the 1st Belo-russian Front on August 1 quoted above from the *Great Patriotic War.* On the other hand, he does not omit the passage which refers to the defeat of the Soviet 2nd Tank Army before Praga, where it was attacked on its left flank by five German divisions, including four Pan-zer. It is interesting to see that he was personally involved on one occasion. Received in Lublin by Rokossovsky he recorded the following on the spot:

"'I can't go into any details. But I'll tell you just this. After several weeks' heavy fighting in Belorussia and eastern Poland we finally reached the outskirts of Praga about the 1st of August. The Germans, at this point, threw in four armoured divisions, and we were driven back.'

'How far back?'

'I can't tell you exactly, but let's say nearly 100 kilometres (sixty-five miles).'

'Are you still retreating?'

'No—we are now advancing–but slowly.'

'Did you think on August 1 (as was suggested by the *Pravda* correspondent that day) that you could take Warsaw within a very few days?'

'If the Germans had not thrown in all that armour, we could have taken Warsaw, though not in a frontal attack; but it was never more than a 50-50 chance. A German counter-attack at Praga was not to be excluded, though we now know that before these armoured divisions arrived, the Germans inside Warsaw were in a panic, and were packing up in a great hurry.'

'Wasn't the Warsaw Rising justified in the circumstances?'

'No it was a bad mistake. The insurgents started it off their own bat, without consulting us.'

'There was a broadcast from Moscow calling on them to rise.'

'That was routine stuff *(sic).* There were similar calls to rise from *Swit* radio [Home Army], and also from the Polish service of the BBC–so I'm told, though I didn't hear it myself. Let's be serious. An armed insurrection in a place like Warsaw could only have succeeded if it had been carefully co-ordinated with the Red Army. The question of timing was of the utmost importance. The Warsaw insurgents were badly armed, and the rising would have made sense only if we were already on the point of *entering Warsaw. That point had not been reached at any stage,* and I'll admit that some Soviet correspondents were much too optimistic on the 1st of August. We were pushed back. We couldn't have got Warsaw before the middle of August, even in the best of circumstances. But circumstances were not good, but bad. Such things do happen in war. It happened at Kharkov in March 1943 and at Zhitomir last winter.'

'What prospect is there of your getting back to Praga within the next few weeks?'

'I can't go into that. All I can say is that we shall try to capture both Praga and Warsaw, but it won't be easy.'

'But you have bridgeheads south of Warsaw.'

'Yes, but the Germans are doing their damnedest to reduce them. We're having much difficulty in holding them, and we are losing a lot of men. Mind you, we have fought non-stop for over two months now.'"

A veteran of the Red Army's campaigns.

A section of Russian soldiers move through Praga, a suburb of Warsaw.

Whilst accepting the good faith and accuracy of Werth's report, it would seem that it should be interpreted as follows: Rokossovsky and, behind him, the Soviet high command, had well and truly got over their elation of July 26, and at a distance now of 30 days were claiming never to have felt it. However, at 2015 hours on July 15 Radio Moscow broadcast a stirring appeal to the population of Warsaw and a few hours later the Union of Polish Patriots station, which followed the Soviet line, took up the call:

"The Polish Army now entering Polish territory had been trained in the U.S.S.R. It unites with the People's Army to form the body of the Polish Armed Forces, the backbone of our nation in her struggle for independence. The sons of Warsaw will rally to its ranks tomorrow. Together with the allied army they will drive out the enemy to the west, expel Hitler's vermin from Poland and deal a mortal blow to the remains of Prussian imperialism. For Warsaw which did not yield, but fought on, the hour has struck."

And, as it was to be expected that the enemy, now cornered, would retreat into the capital, the appeal for an uprising continued: "This is why . . . by energetic hand-to-hand fighting in the streets of Warsaw, in the houses, the factories, the warehouses, not only shall we hasten the coming of our final liberation, but we shall safeguard our national heritage and the lives of our brothers."

On August 5 Churchill sent Stalin a request to intervene on behalf of the insurrectionists, but he was answered by scepticism: Stalin doubted, if not the reality, at least the importance of the uprising.

On August 16, when Churchill repeated his demands, Stalin expressed his conviction that "the Warsaw operation is a horrible and senseless venture which is costing the lives of a great many of the population. This would not have arisen if the Soviet Command had been informed beforehand and if the Poles had kept in constant touch with us."

However, it was not Mikołajczyk's Polish Government-in-Exile which had broken off relations with the Kremlin. Must one therefore assume that Stalin supposed that the Home Army would be deaf to the call to arms given on July 29? Surely not. Be that as it may, this led Stalin to the following conclusion: "From the situation thus created, the Soviet Command deduces that it must dissociate itself from the Warsaw adventure, as it has no responsibility, either direct or indirect, in the operation."

Stalin was not content, however, merely with dissociating himself from the insurrectionists (whom he called on August 22 a "handful of criminals who, in order to seize power, have unleashed the Warsaw venture") but also obstinately refused to allow Anglo-American aircraft to land on Soviet territory in order to refuel from their operations over Warsaw. He knew that this would severely restrict the Allies, who were attempting to fly in supplies to the defenders of the unhappy city.

Would Stalin eventually have given in to Churchill if Roosevelt had thrown in the weight of his authority? We do not know. What we do know, however, is that on August 26, taking into account the "general perspectives of the war", the American President refused to join forces with the British Prime Minister in a new approach to Stalin. He was doubtless influenced by Hopkins and Morgen-thau. On September 2, James V. Forrestal, who had succeeded Frank Knox (who died on April 28, 1944) as Secretary of the Navy, noted in his diary:

"I find that whenever any American suggests that we act in accordance with the needs of our own security he is apt to be called a god-damned fascist or imperialist, while if Uncle Joe suggests that he needs the Baltic Provinces, half Poland, all Bessarabia and access to the Mediterranean, all hands agree that he is a fine frank, candid and generally delightful fellow who is very easy to deal with because he is so explicit in what he wants."

The rest is history. The defenders of Warsaw met their fate with the most sublime heroism. Having driven the Russians back over 30 miles from the right bank of the Vistula, the Germans calmly set about the reconquest of the Polish capital with large numbers of Tiger tanks, assault guns, and little Goliath tanks, a kind of remote-controlled bomb on tracks. The heaviest weapons the defenders had were of 20-mm calibre.

They fought from barricade to barricade, from house to house, from storey to storey and even in the sewers. The area occupied by the defenders gradually shrank, so that the meagre supplies dropped by Anglo-American aircraft fell increasingly into enemy hands. The repression of the uprising was entrusted to Himmler. He appointed *Waffen*-S.S. General von dem Bach-Zalewski and gave him, amongst others, S.S. police units, a brigade of Russian ex-prisoners, and a brigade of ex-convicts, all of whom had committed such excesses that Guderian had persuaded Hitler to remove them from the front.

In the second fortnight of September the Russians reoccupied Praga but remained virtually passive opposite the capital. Under these conditions Bor-Komorowski, who had had 22,000 killed, missing, or seriously wounded out of his 40,000 fighters, resigned himself to surrender on October 2, obtaining from von dem Bach-Zalewski an assurance that his men would without exception be treated under the Geneva Convention of August 27, 1929 governing prisoners-of-war.

From this brief summary of the essential facts it is possible to conclude:

1. The Warsaw "venture", which aroused the ire and indignation of Stalin, was sparked off by a radio broadcast from Moscow, but without criminal intent.
2. Since the Russians played down as much as possible the defeat of Rokossovsky at Praga, the will to let the Polish Home Army be massacred was imputed to an inertia which arose to a great extent from impotence.
3. Under these conditions it cannot be proved that Anglo-American aircraft taking off from Foggia could have saved the Home Army if Stalin had allowed them to land on Soviet territory.

CHAPTER 64
The battle of Leyte Gulf

On the U.S. side, although everyone stuck to the item of the March 12 directive which laid down that the major objective of the coming offensive was to be Mindanao, opinion varied as to the direction the offensive was to take after this objective had been secured.

In the Pentagon Admiral King, supported, albeit with slight differences of opinion, by Nimitz, reckoned that there would be no harm in neglecting the rest of the Philippines and taking a leap forward to Formosa and Amoy on the south coast of China. This would cut communications between the Japanese homeland and its sources of raw materials and fuel, and would thus force a capitulation. But in his command post at Hollandia, General MacArthur was sickened by the idea of leaving Luzon and more than seven million Filipinos exposed to the rigours of a Japanese military occupation any longer. When he left Corregidor in March 1942, he had given his solemn promise to the Filipinos that he would return, and he did not intend that anyone should make him break his word. Roosevelt summoned MacArthur to Pearl Harbor and there MacArthur laid before him arguments not only of sentiment and prestige but also of sound military strategy:

"I argued against the naval concept of frontal assault against the strongly held island positions of Iwo Jima or Okinawa. In my argument, I stressed that our losses would be far too heavy to justify the benefits to be gained by seizing these outposts. They were not essential to the enemy's defeat, and by cutting them off from supplies, they could be easily reduced and their effectiveness completely neutralized with negligible loss to ourselves. They were not in themselves possessed of sufficient resources to act as main bases in our advance.

"In addition, I felt that Formosa, with a hostile population, might prove doubt-

American landing-craft in action.

ful to serve as a base of attack against Japan itself."

This was how MacArthur, according to his memoirs, spoke to Roosevelt, who had Admiral Leahy with him. And, as it later turned out, MacArthur was to a certain extent right. He captured Luzon, at the cost of some 8,300 dead, between January 9 and June 25, 1945. The seven and a half square miles of the little island of Iwo Jima cost Nimitz 7,000 more, and Okinawa was captured by the U.S. 10th Army with the loss of 8,000 dead. As was his wont, the President took no part in this strategic debate, and Leahy and Nimitz were not insensitive to MacArthur's argument. The "Octagon" Conference, which opened at Quebec on September 11, 1944, envisaged, after preliminary operations and the capture of Mindanao, that there would be a landing at Leyte in the central Philippines on December 20, after which the two Allied forces in the Pacific would unite to occupy "either (1) Luzon to secure Manila by 2nd February, or (2) Formosa and Amoy on the China coast by 1st May 1945."

By now Nimitz's fleet was so large that it was decided to appoint two flag officers under him to command alternately. While one was at sea, the other would be at Pearl Harbor planning the next major operation. When commanded by Admiral Spruance it would be known as the 5th Fleet; while under Halsey, the 3rd Fleet. Sub-units would similarly exchange commanders and designations.

In August 1944 Spruance was relieved by Halsey, and Vice-Admiral Theodore Wilkinson relieved Richard Turner in command of the 5th (now the 3rd) Amphibious Force. However, Mitscher remained in command of the Fast Carrier Force of 17 fast carriers, six new battleships, 13 cruisers, 58 destroyers, and 1,100 fighters, and dive- and torpedo-bombers, now task force 38 instead of 58.

On August 28, Halsey set out from Eniwetok to bombard Yap Island, the Palau Islands, and Mindanao, paving the way for the landings Nimitz and MacArthur were preparing at Peleliu and Morotai. The results exceeded all expectations: in 2,400 sorties Mitscher's squadrons shot down 200 enemy aircraft at a cost of only eight of their own and dealt a very hard blow to the Japanese bases in this sector.

Interpreting the weakness shown by the enemy somewhat optimistically, the impetuous Halsey submitted the following suggestion to Nimitz on September 13: cut out the intermediate objectives and make straight for Leyte. MacArthur seized upon this idea, remarking that this would save two months on the schedule and, as Nimitz agreed, the Chiefs-of-Staff, still in session at Quebec, took only an hour and a half to concur, such was the confidence of General Marshall and Admiral King in their subordinates. Yap and Mindanao were thus set aside and a landing on Leyte was fixed for October 20. On October 3, Allied commanders in the Central and South-West Pacific received the following directive for the next stage in the operations:

"General MacArthur will liberate Luzon, starting 20 December, and establish bases there to support later operations. Admiral Nimitz will provide fleet cover and support, occupy one or more positions in the Bonin-Volcano Island group 20 January 1945, and invade the Ryukyus, target date March 1945."

Formosa and Amoy were thus to be taken off the Pentagon's calendar of events. MacArthur and Nimitz, the one leaving from Australia and the other from Hawaii, were to meet in Leyte Gulf. Their commands remained contiguous, and the only transfer of units was that of 3rd Amphibious Force and XXIV Corps (Major-General J. R. Hodge) from Nimitz to MacArthur.

Whilst waiting for the start of this new offensive operation, to be called "King II", MacArthur seized the island of Morotai north of Halmahera. His losses were insignificant as the Japanese were not expecting to be attacked. Yet its fall meant that the Moluccas were now useless to them.

Meanwhile, Halsey's 3rd Fleet attacked Peleliu in strength. The island was defended by the excellent Japanese 14th Division, whose commander (Lieutenant-General Inouye) had intelligently applied the new instructions from Tokyo. Instead of the usual cordon of men defending the beach, he had deployed his forces in depth, taking advantage of the caves to provide cover from aerial and naval bombardment. And so, although the first wave of the U.S. 1st Marine Division (Major-General W. H. Rupertus) landed on September 15, it was not until November 25 that the last enemy surrendered,

A Japanese destroyer is smashed in two close to Leyte.

and meanwhile the Americans had had to bring in their 85th Division (Major-General P. J. Mueller) as reinforcement. The U.S. forces suffered considerable losses: 2,000 killed and over 8,500 wounded, or approximately the same as the garrison which they completely wiped out. On the other hand, in the same group of the Palau Islands, 3rd Amphibious Force occupied the large atoll of Ulithi without loss, giving the U.S. 3rd Fleet a very safe, well-sited base 1,000 miles from Manila and 1,400 from Okinawa. This action ended on September 23.

So, ten months after the assault on Tarawa, Nimitz had reached a point 4,250 miles from Pearl Harbor.

Between October 10 and 15, and using the method which had been so successful against the Gilberts, the Marshalls, and the Marianas, Task Force 38 ensured the success of Operation "King II" by plastering the bases on the Ryūkyū Islands, Formosa, and Luzon, from which the Japanese might have attacked the Leyte

landings. A thousand Japanese planes took off, but Mitscher scored a clear victory, knocking out over 500 of them at a cost of 110 of his own. It is true that two cruisers were torpedoed during this action, which took Task Force 38 to within 60 miles of Formosa, but the U.S. Navy's rescue services were so efficient that the damaged ships were able to be towed to Ulithi. The Japanese airmen greatly exaggerated this little success, which was no compensation for the loss of their planes and some 40 merchant ships. They claimed to have sunk 11 aircraft-carriers, two battleships, and four cruisers and to have damaged or set on fire 28 other vessels. It would appear that the threat to the Japanese Empire had miraculously melted away.

This was what Tokyo was beginning to believe when, at dawn on October 17, a huge U.S. armada sailed into Leyte Gulf. It was the 7th Fleet under Vice-Admiral Thomas C. Kinkaid, 700 ships strong, which was also carrying 174,000 men of the U.S. 6th Army. On the same day, detachments seized the island commanding the entrance to Leyte Gulf

then, for two whole days, the guns of the old battleships, cruisers, and destroyers of 3rd and 7th Amphibious Forces, or Task Forces 79 and 78, (Admirals T. S. Wilkinson and D. E. Barbey) roared out and the aircraft of 18 escort carriers joined in.

The defence of the Philippines had been entrusted to the victor of Singapore, General Tomoyoki Yamashita, under Field-Marshal Count Hisaichi Terauchi, C.-in-C. Southern Army. Yamashita's 14th Area Army had seven divisions, with a total of 265,000 men, but on Leyte there was only one division, the 16th (Lieutenant-General Makino). However, the Japanese High Command had now decided to fight for Leyte rather than concentrate for the defence of Luzon, although the American attack had pre-empted their planned reinforcement of the island.

The landing achieved local tactical surprise. In the evening of October 20 the U.S. 6th Army (General Krueger) had established a front of over 17 miles. On the right, X Corps (Major-General F. C. Sibert: 1st Cavalry and 24th Divisions) had occupied Tacloban and its aerodrome; on the left, XXIV Corps (Major-General J. R. Hodge: 96th and 7th Divisions) had got as far as Dulag, where 100,000 tons of *matériel* and stores had been landed on the beach. The cruiser *Honolulu* had been hit by an aerial torpedo, but this was the only noteworthy incident of the day. General MacArthur landed with the third wave: his promise to return had at last been kept.

MacArthur, certainly the most forceful and determined man in the American high command, had been planning this moment ever since he had left the starving American garrison on the Bataan peninsula in March 1942. His implacable will and dynamic personality had ensured that the Philippines would have priority. But one major obstacle stood before his return to Manila: the Japanese fleet.

In expectation of the U.S. offensive, Admiral Toyoda, C.-in-C. Combined Fleet, had drawn up Plan *"SHO GO"* (Operation "Victory"), one variant of which was to cover the event which actually took place. And so at 0809 hours on October 17, he had merely to signal *"SHO GO 1"* from the Tokyo area for his subordinates to set the plan in motion. This alert order found the Japanese fleet disposed as follows:

1. in Japan, under Vice-Admiral Ozawa, a carrier force (of which only four carriers were operational through lack of trained aircrew), the battleship-carriers *Ise* and *Hyuga*, three light cruisers, and eight destroyers;

2. in the Ryukyus, under Vice-Admiral K. Shima, a force of two heavy cruisers, one light cruiser, and nine destroyers; and

3. in Lingga roads, off a group of islands half way between Singapore and Sumatra, Vice-Admiral Kurita's force of seven battleships, 11 heavy cruisers, two light cruisers, and 19 destroyers.

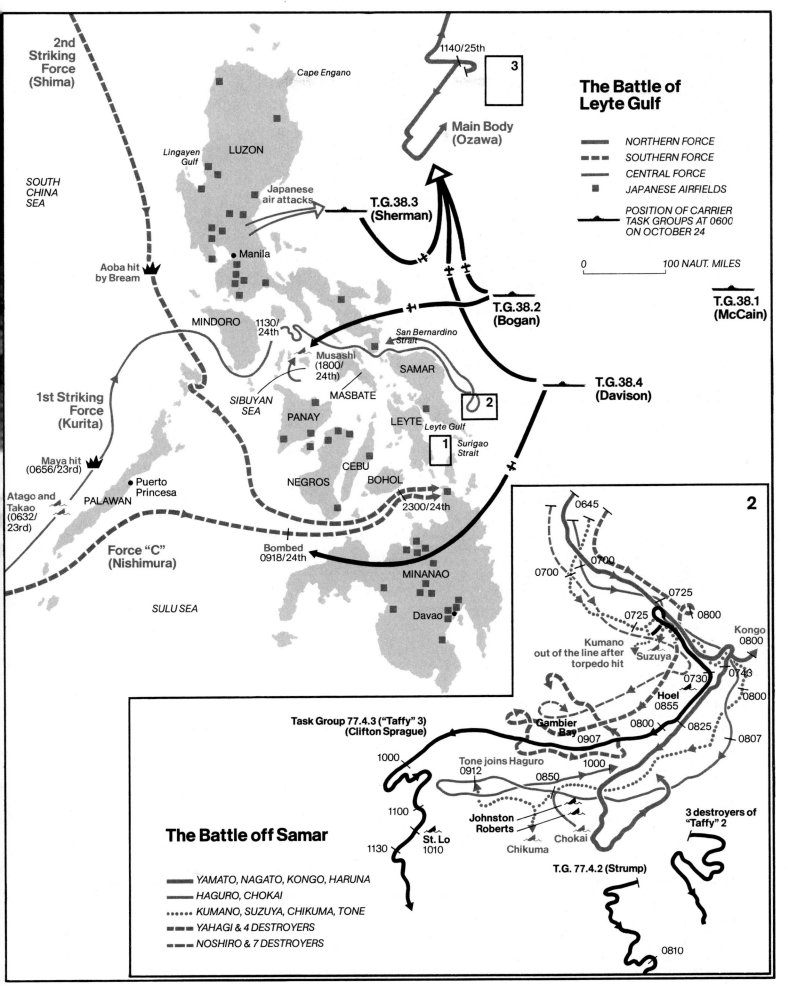

2nd Striking Force (Shima)

Cape Engano

SOUTH CHINA SEA

1140/25th

3

Main Body (Ozawa)

LUZON

Lingayen Gulf

The Battle of Leyte Gulf

— — NORTHERN FORCE

- - - SOUTHERN FORCE

···· CENTRAL FORCE

■ JAPANESE AIRFIELDS

⚓ POSITION OF CARRIER TASK GROUPS AT 0600 ON OCTOBER 24

0   100 NAUT. MILES

Japanese air attacks

T.G.38.3 (Sherman)

Manila

Aoba hit by Bream

MINDORO

1130/24th

San Bernardino Strait

T.G.38.2 (Bogan)

T.G.38.1 (McCain)

Musashi (1800/24th)

SAMAR

MASBATE

SIBUYAN SEA

1st Striking Force (Kurita)

PANAY

T.G.38.4 (Davison)

2

LEYTE

Leyte Gulf

1

Surigao Strait

Maya hit (0656/23rd)

CEBU

Puerto Princesa

BOHOL

2300/24th

Atago and Takao (0632/23rd)

PALAWAN

NEGROS

Force "C" (Nishimura)

Bombed 0918/24th

MINANAO

SULU SEA

Davao

The Battle off Samar

0645

0700

0700

0725

0725

0800

Kongo 0800

Kumano out of the line after torpedo hit

Suzuya

0730

0743

Hoel 0855

0800

0800

Gambier Bay

0825

0907

0807

Task Group 77.4.3 ("Taffy" 3) (Clifton Sprague)

1000

Tone joins Haguro 0912

0850

1000

3 destroyers of "Taffy" 2

1100

Johnston Roberts

Chokai

1130

St. Lo 1010

Chikuma

T.G. 77.4.2 (Strump)

0810

—— *YAMATO, NAGATO, KONGO, HARUNA*

—— *HAGURO, CHOKAI*

···· *KUMANO, SUZUYA, CHIKUMA, TONE*

- - - *YAHAGI & 4 DESTROYERS*

— — *NOSHIRO & 7 DESTROYERS*

523

The plan was as follows:
The carrier force with its 116 aircraft, including 80 fighters, would act as bait, advancing without too much precaution into the Philippine Sea east of Luzon; it would thus draw out Mitscher's carrier force towards the north and, by sacrificing itself, would enable Kurita and Shima to destroy the U.S. landing forces and their escort ships of the 7th Fleet.

Kurita would form two sub-forces:
1. Force "A", under Kurita himself, and composed of five battleships, 12 cruisers, and 15 destroyers, would advance through the San Bernardino Strait between Samar and Luzon to meet Force "C" in Leyte Gulf, and
2. Force "C", of two battleships, one cruiser, and four destroyers under Vice-Admiral S. Nishimura would sail through the Surigao Strait between Leyte and Mindanao.

Shima finally received the order to follow Nishimura and, when the time came, to co-operate with him. After the destruction of the U.S. transports and the 7th Fleet in Leyte Gulf, MacArthur would have to surrender to Yamashita, who was already counting on greeting him with the trenchant words he had used to Percival at Singapore: "All I want to know is: Do you surrender unconditionally or not?"

Cunning though the plan was, it nevertheless meant 68 Japanese ships against 275 American, and a one to four inferiority in aircraft for the Japanese. Even including the planes they had in the Philippines, the Japanese were a long way from matching Halsey's and Kinkaid's 1,500. Also, it would take greater co-ordination than could be expected between Kurita and Nishimura to close their pincer in Leyte Gulf. Again, and this was the most important point, "SHO GO" envisaged nothing beyond October 25 and ignored what the 3rd Fleet was likely to do after Ozawa's diversion had fizzled out and Halsey set off full-steam ahead southwards with his 17 carriers and six fast battleships. If he did nothing, Toyoda would be left in Japan with Ozawa and no fuel oil, and Kurita would be left at Lingga with no ammunition or spare parts. Like Hitler on the Western Front, he was thus forced to go over to the offensive. He gave his order at 1100 hours on October 18.

On October 22, having refuelled at Brunei, Kurita separated from Nishimura. At dawn on the 23rd he was heading north-east of the island of Palawan, a stepping-stone between Borneo and Mindanao, when he was attacked by the submarines *Dace* and *Darter* (Commanders Claggett and McClintock). *Dace* scored a bulls-eye on the heavy cruiser *Maya*, which blew up. *Darter* scored a double, damaging the *Takao* so badly that she had to be sent back under escort, and sinking Kurita's flagship, the heavy cruiser *Atago*. The admiral was saved but he lost part of his signals and coding staff, which was to hamper his control of operations.

Despite the loss of these three cruisers, Kurita was off Mindoro 24 hours later, and at the same time Nishimura was between Mindanao and Negros Islands. Shima, coming down from the north, was following Nishimura at a great distance and remained out of contact with him for fear of interception by U.S. tracking devices.

Ozawa finally set out from Kure on October 20 and progressed without incident along the path of sacrifice. In the evening of the 23rd the carrier *Zuikaku*, his flagship, sent out a long message designed to draw to herself the attentions of the enemy.

As expected, the *Darter* sent out a signal to report contact. This reached Halsey at 0620 hours on the 23rd. Nishimura and Shima were spotted in the early morning of the 24th. When he got McClintock's message from the *Darter*, the C.-in-C. of the 3rd Fleet, now reduced to Task Force 38, closed in to within 150 miles of the Philippines with his total force except for Vice-Admiral J. S. McCain's Task Group 38.1, which was re-forming at Ulithi. So Halsey had Rear-Admiral F. C. Sherman's Task Group 38.3 off Luzon, Rear-Admiral G. F. Bogan's Task Group 38.2 off San Bernardino Strait, and Rear-Admiral R. E. Davison's Task Group 38.4 off Leyte. This gave Mitscher a total of 835 aircraft.

From the information given by tactical reconnaissance in the early morning of the 24th, Admiral Halsey deduced that he could leave all enemy forces observed in the south-east to be dealt with by Kinkaid and that he himself should concentrate his attention on the larger enemy force apparently intending to pass through the San Bernardino Strait. As one can never be too strong in attack, he ordered Vice-Admiral McCain to join him. Between 1026 and 1350 hours, Task Force 38 flew 259 sorties against Kurita's force, concentrating most of its attacks on the giant (64,200-ton) battleship *Musashi*. In spite of protective A.A. fire from nearly 130 guns, the *Musashi* was hit by 19 torpedoes and 17 bombs and went down during the evening with half her crew. The heavy cruiser *Myoko* had to be sent back to Brunei; three other cruisers suffered minor damage. These attacks forced the Japanese admiral to turn about and caused him to be late on the schedule agreed with Nishimura. No Japanese planes were used in this first engagement. Admiral Fukudome, C.-in-C. of the 2nd Air Fleet in the Philippines, considered that his pilots were incapable of measuring up to the U.S. airmen and sent them instead against 3rd Fleet. At the cost of heavy losses one of them scored a direct hit on the light carrier *Princeton*. Explosions and fires rent the unhappy vessel and caused heavy losses amongst the ships which went to her rescue. So Rear-Admiral Sherman ordered her to be finished off with a torpedo. Once again the quality of the veteran American forces proved superior to the empty fanaticism of the Japanese Navy.

Halsey now assumed that Kurita's force no longer offered a threat. He therefore took his entire fleet north to attack Ozawa's carriers, so completely taking the Japanese bait. His reaction has since been the subject of lively discussion in the U.S. Navy and Army. The day after his victory he explained his decision as follows:

"As it seemed childish to me to guard statically San Bernardino Strait, I concentrated TF 38 during the night and steamed north to attack the Northern Force at dawn. I believed that the Center Force had been so heavily damaged in the Sibuyan Sea that it could no longer be considered a serious menace to Seventh Fleet."

As we can see, Halsey greatly exaggerated the effects of his aircraft on Kurita's force, but he could not know that the hangars of the four enemy carriers, of whose approach he had just been informed, were half empty. He had to ask himself if his reconnaissance had given him the full tally of this new force. Moreover, by sailing northwards, Halsey was conscious of obeying the instructions of Nimitz who, as we have seen, required him to consider as his main mission the destruction of an important part of the Japanese fleet if the opportunity arose. This reveals the serious snags in the organisation of command as conceived by the Pentagon, for if the 3rd Fleet had been under MacArthur, there is no doubt that he would have forbidden it to leave the San Bernardino Strait uncovered.

Though he was told just before nightfall that Kurita had turned eastwards again, Halsey refused to part with his battleships, not wishing to leave them without air protection and wanting to give his carriers the cover of their guns. Mitscher, Bogan, and Vice-Admiral W. A. Lee, the last of whom commanded Task Force 34, all disapproved of their commander's initiative, but Halsey was in no mood to extemporise and they gave in.

In Leyte Gulf, Vice-Admiral Kinkaid was hourly following the movements of Nishimura and Shima. He spent the afternoon setting a series of ambushes for them in Surigao Strait. He had six old battleships, eight cruisers, and 28 destroyers, whereas his adversary had only 19 warships altogether.

As Vice-Admiral Kinkaid sailed up the Surigao Strait between 2300 hours on October 24 and 0300 hours on the 25th, Nishimura was attacked by 30 P.T. boats, which fired torpedoes; all of them missed. A few minutes later his force, steaming in line ahead, was caught in a crossfire from the destroyers of the Eastern and Western Attack Groups under Captain Coward and Commander Phillips. The battleship *Fuso* was hit, and 30 minutes later broke in two; three destroyers were wrecked. Though hit, Nishimura's flagship, the battleship *Yamashiro*, maintained her course and, followed by the cruiser *Mogami*, sailed into Leyte Gulf. At 0353 hours Rear-Admiral G. L. Weyler's six

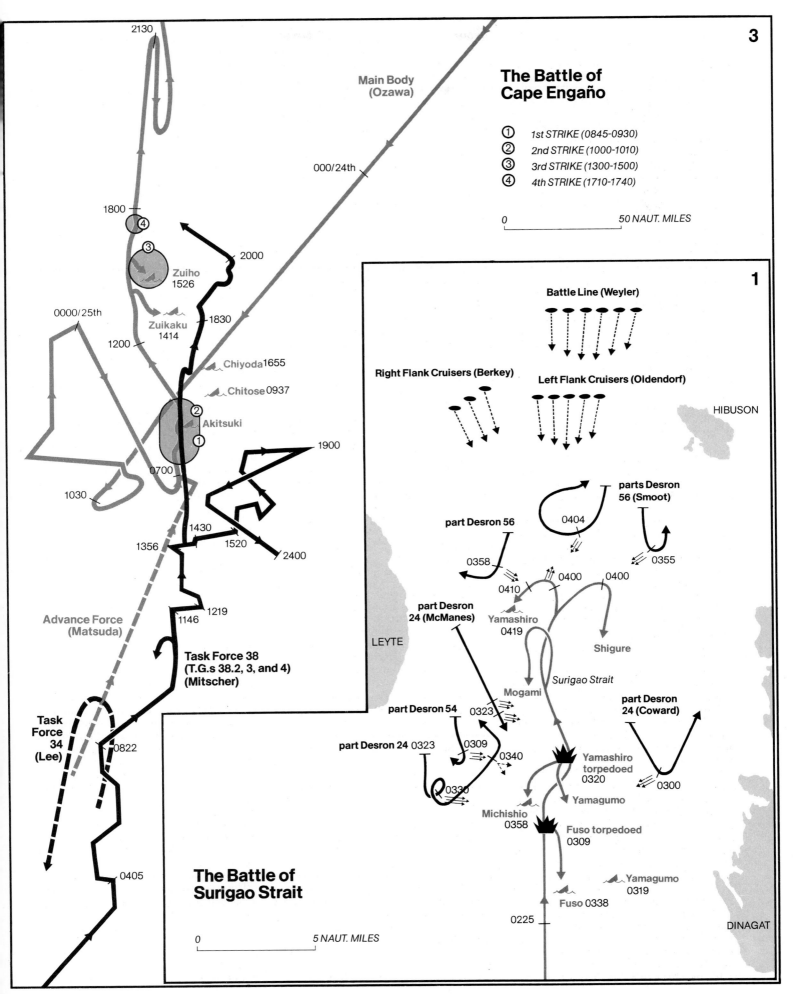

3

The Battle of Cape Engaño

Main Body (Ozawa)

① 1st STRIKE (0845–0930)
② 2nd STRIKE (1000–1010)
③ 3rd STRIKE (1300–1500)
④ 4th STRIKE (1710–1740)

0   50 NAUT. MILES

2130

1800 — ④

③ Zuiho 1526

0000/25th

Zuikaku 1414

1200

1830

2000

000/24th

Chiyoda 1655

Chitose 0937

② Akitsuki ①

1900

0700

1030

1430

1356   1520

2400

1219

1146

Advance Force (Matsuda)

Task Force 38 (T.G.s 38.2, 3, and 4) (Mitscher)

Task Force 34 (Lee)

0822

0405

1

Battle Line (Weyler)

Right Flank Cruisers (Berkey)   **Left Flank Cruisers (Oldendorf)**

HIBUSON

parts Desron 56 (Smoot)

part Desron 56

0404

0358

0355

0410

0400

0400

part Desron 24 (McManes)

Yamashiro 0419

Shigure

LEYTE

Mogami

Surigao Strait

part Desron 24 (Coward)

part Desron 54

0323

part Desron 24 0323

0309

0340

0300

0330

Yamashiro torpedoed 0320

Yamagumo

Michishio 0358

Fuso torpedoed 0309

Yamagumo 0319

Fuso 0338

0225

DINAGAT

The Battle of Surigao Strait

0   5 NAUT. MILES

battleships "crossed the T" and opened fire on the Japanese, loosing off 285 14- and 16-inch shells. *Mogami* succeeded in turning about, but *Yamashiro* capsized and sank at 0419 hours, taking down with her her obstinate admiral and almost all her crew. At this moment Shima appeared, having followed Nishimura some 30 miles behind. It did not take him long to sum up the situation, and at 0425 hours he decided on a "temporary withdrawal". In doing so he came under attack from the P.T. boats then, when dawn came, from the 7th Fleet's aircraft. All told, out of 19 Japanese ships which ventured into this trap, only two survived, including the old destroyer *Shigure* which had so often flirted with death in the Solomon Islands. Rear-Admiral J. B. Oldendorf lost 39 men killed and 114 wounded.

On board their floating H.Q., the amphibious force flagship *Wasatch*, Kinkaid and his staff hardly had time to congratulate themselves on their night victory at Surigao before the astounding news reached them that off Samar Island Task Group 77.4, consisting of 16 escort carriers and 20 destroyers under Rear-Admiral Thomas L. Sprague, was engaging a heavy Japanese force.

When asked by Kinkaid at 0412 hours "Is Task Force 34 guarding San Bernardino Strait?" Halsey had replied: "Negative. TF 34 is with carrier groups now engaging enemy carrier force."

Kinkaid had misinterpreted ambiguous instructions from Halsey which said that Task Force 34 "will be formed" to block the San Bernadino Strait—a statement of future intention, not of fact. Kinkaid was now exposed to attack by vastly more powerful forces.

Kurita's force, much less heavily damaged than Halsey had supposed, had returned to the attack at the steady speed of 20 knots. Nishimura's catastrophe had in no way put Kurita off his intention of making for Leyte Gulf and destroying everything he found there.

At 0658 hours on October 25, the first shells fell on the American ships nearest the Japanese, Task Group 77.4.3 (Rear-Admiral Clifton A. F. Sprague).

If victory had depended on *matériel* superiority, the Americans would have suffered total defeat. No U.S. ship had a gun over 5-inch in calibre and the escort carriers' top speed was 20 knots. Kurita, on the other hand, had the 33 14-, 16-, and 18-inch guns of his four battleships, the 8- and 6.1-inch guns of his eight cruisers, and the torpedoes of his 15 destroyers. And the slowest of his ships could do five knots more than the fastest of the Americans'. But his first order was "General chase". This was a blunder, as it prevented any concerted action.

The Americans, in spite of what could only seem a desperate situation from the point of view of *matériel,* conducted themselves with gallantry and a spirit of both sacrifice and initiative. Whilst the escort carriers commanded by Admiral Sprague

protected themselves behind a smoke screen or took refuge in the rainstorms, the U.S. destroyers fired off their torpedoes and then opened up with their guns. In the air, Task Group 77.4's planes flew back empty over their targets in increasing numbers, after dropping their last bombs, to draw the Japanese fire.

This confusion allowed the Japanese no time to take advantage of their enormous numerical and *matériel* superiority. The carrier *Gambier Bay* was sunk by the 8-inch shells of the cruiser *Chikuma* which, together with her sister-ship *Chokai*, was then sunk by Commander R. L. Fowler's torpedo-bombers. The destroyer *Johnston* torpedoed the *Kumano* then, though hit by three 14-inch shells, went on fighting until the last of her guns was destroyed. The *Hoel* and the escort destroyer *Samuel B. Roberts* met with an equally heroic end. These sacrifices were not in vain, as the heavy cruiser *Suzuya* was sunk in its turn. So E. B. Potter and Admiral Nimitz are right when they say of the battle off Samar:

"The history of the United States Navy records no more glorious two hours of resolution, sacrifice, and success."

Rear-Admiral C. A. Sprague writes:

"At 0925 my mind was occupied with dodging torpedoes when near the bridge I heard one of the signalmen yell, 'God-dammit, boys, they're getting away!' I could not believe my eyes, but it looked as if the whole Japanese Fleet was indeed retiring. However, it took a whole series of reports from circling planes to convince me. And still I could not get the fact to soak into my battle-numbed brain. At best, I had expected to be swimming by this time."

All Kurita had to do at that moment was to draw in his forces so as to start again in better conditions, but on reflection he decided to pull out and before nightfall he had returned to the San Bernardino Strait. From the somewhat confused explanations of his decision he has given since the war, it turns out that he thought he was up against Task Force 38, and that he reckoned he had carried out his mission when his ships reported the destruction of three or four light carriers and several cruisers. The least that can be said is that he missed the chance of a great victory for which he would most likely have had to pay within the following 48 hours with an equally crushing defeat.

Kurita's withdrawal did not put an end to the troubles of Task Group 77.4. Some hours later Vice-Admiral T. Ohnishi sent out his new weapon, the *kamikazes*. One of them sank the escort carrier *Saint Lo*, and five others caused losses and damage to five more. By the end of the day the battle off Samar had cost Thomas Kinkaid five ships, 23 planes, 1,130 men killed and 913 wounded.

At midnight on October 25, Admiral Ozawa had only 29 fighters and bombers left, whereas Halsey was bearing down on him with ten fast carriers, whose planes were to carry out 527 sorties in

six waves from dawn to dusk. The first wave took off at 0540 hours. It caught the Japanese forces sailing north toward Halsey off Cape Engaño, sank the light carrier *Chitose* and left the fleet carrier *Zuikaku* so badly damaged that Ozawa had to transfer his flag to a cruiser. The second wave set fire to the light carrier *Chiyoda*, which was then left limping behind. Towards mid-day Mitscher sent up his third wave of 200 planes. This settled its account with the *Zuikaku*, the last survivor of the six carriers which had bombed Pearl Harbor. She succumbed under the blows of three torpedoes at 1414 hours. About an hour later, the fourth wave sank the light carrier *Zuiho*.

This success was only partial, however, as Halsey could not turn a deaf ear to Kinkaid's S.O.S., which came first in code then in clear. At 0848 he ordered McCain's task group to hasten to the rescue then, shortly before 1100 hours, on an order from Nimitz, he sent Task Force 34 and Bogan's task group southwards. The Japanese withdrawal was greatly helped by these detachments, though Rear-Admiral Du Bose's cruisers did finish off the *Chiyoda* with gunfire and sink two of Ozawa's destroyers. The latter also lost the light cruiser *Tama*, shattered by a clutch of torpedoes from the submarine *Jalloa*.

Leyte Gulf, the greatest naval battle in history, had involved 244 ships totalling 2,014,890 tons. By comparison, Jutland brought together under Scheer and Jellicoe some 254 ships totalling 1,616,836 tons. Thirty-two ships were lost:

	Japanese	U.S.
Battleships	3	0
Aircraft-carriers	4	1
Escort carriers	0	2
Cruisers	10	0
Destroyers	9	3
Totals	26	6
Tonnage	306,000	37,000

These figures reveal the crushing defeat inflicted on the Japanese Navy, although Ozawa had carried out his decoy mission brilliantly, albeit at great sacrifice.

When questioned after the capitulation by an American commission of enquiry about the consequences of this battle, Admiral Yonai, Navy Minister in General Koiso's cabinet, replied:

"Our defeat at Leyte was tantamount to the loss of the Philippines. When you took the Philippines, that was the end of our resources."

Indeed Yamashita was virtually cut off in the archipelago and, what is more, could only move his troops from one island to another with the greatest of difficulty, whereas his adversary had complete liberty of movement.

The stage was now set for the sweeping American advance through the Philippines, MacArthur's great triumph.

A Kamikaze plane scores a direct hit on the escort carrier, Saint Lo *(above). Hellcats take off during the battle off Samar (below).*

CHAPTER 65

The return to the Philippines

The first Americans to return to the Philippines were a small Ranger task force with their destroyer transports and escort.

The Dinagat Attack Group, under Rear-Admiral Arthur D. Struble, transported the 500 men of Company D, 6th Ranger Battalion, U.S. Army, commanded by Lieutenant-Colonel H. A. Mucci. In the darkness of October 17 and 18, 1944 they were to demolish the Japanese radio location equipment on four islands at the two entrances to Leyte Gulf. If these electronic feelers were not ripped out, it was feared that they would signal the arrival of the invasion fleet on the 20th.

The main landings were planned for mid-day to allow a daylight run into the gulf, in which floating mines and obstacles had been reported. Throughout the morning the warships moved into position, and the transports halted about eight miles off the beach. The landing craft were hoisted out, and began circling round their larger parent ships. The noise and apparent confusion of a major amphibious operation had begun to build up.

From 0700, fire support units had been in action in the pre-landing shoot. First to arrive were the battleships *Mississippi, Maryland,* and *West Virginia.* At 0900 they were relieved by the Close Covering Group, after they had sent 30 shells per main battery gun rumbling over the fleet into the jungle coast line.

Throughout these manoeuvres, fighters, torpedo-bombers, and reconnaissance aircraft from the 3rd and 7th Fleets made attacks on the airfields in northern Mindanao, Cebu, Negros, Panay, and Leyte, and conducted sweeps over the surrounding areas.

Rear-Admiral D. E. Barbey, whose air plan was administered by Captain White-head, had ordered a break in the bombing and strafing of the beach 45 minutes before H-hour. This was a departure from the standard operating procedure of that time. The gap was covered by high-angled naval gunfire and rocket barrages from 0915 to 1000.

By 0930 the bombardment was reaching its cacophonous climax and the landing craft and formed up for the 5,000 yard dash for the beach. At 0943 the signal flag was run up on the control vessel *PC-623,* and preceded by 11 L.C.I. rocket craft, the boats went in.

In a couple of minutes the L.C.I.s had fired 10,000 4.5-inch rockets in a close pattern over the northern and southern landing areas.

Behind the L.C.I.s came the first wave of amphtrack tanks, followed by L.V.T.s and then the amphtrack personnel carriers.

By the time the fourth wave had hit "Red" Beach in the northern landing area, the enemy had begun to hit back with mortars sited in the neighbouring hills. With the correct range and deflec-

tion they dropped bombs on the L.C.V.(P.)s from the *Elmore* and sank a boat from *Aquarius,* killing three men and injuring 15.

On the southern beaches a 75-mm battery near Catmon Hill took on the destroyer *Bennion,* straddling her repeatedly and wounding five men with a near miss. Artillery and mortar fire fell on "Blue" Beach as the 96th Division was landing.

MacArthur had 200,000 men of General Walter Krueger's 6th Army, Lieutenant-General C. Kenney's 2,500 combat aircraft, and the 7th Fleet–often called "MacArthur's Navy" which had an additional 500 aircraft. The 3rd Fleet had 1,000 aircraft as well as nearly 100 of the most modern warships in the world.

He would need these resources because the Leyte invasion would be conducted out of range of land-based aircraft. However, MacArthur did not exercise direct command over Halsey and the 3rd Fleet, who were under Nimitz and so could be ordered away to attack the Japanese fleet if it approached.

The 7th Fleet had some small escort carriers, but they would be inadequate to defend the fleet and transports, and cover the beach-head if major units of the Japanese Navy or Air Forces succeeded in evading the 3rd Fleet.

Consequently it was essential that Kenney's Far East Air Forces should start operating from local airstrips as soon as the invasion forces had captured them.

With this in mind the invasion beaches chosen were close to, or opposite, the coastal airstrips near Tacloban and Dulag.

As soon as he heard of the landings, Suzuki (35th Army) instructed the 16th Division to keep control of the airfields at all costs, and ordered Leyte to be reinforced by four battalions. On the October 22 Yamashita told him that he was to fight a decisive battle on Leyte and that he would be getting two divisions and an independent mixed brigade from Luzon. With further reinforcements from Davao and Cebu, Suzuki had the equivalent of four strong divisions on the island.

If the decisive naval and air battles were successful, the Japanese land forces could be sent against the estimated two divisions which the Americans had put ashore. The 16th Division was ordered to hold a line Burauen–Dagami, whilst the bulk of the Japanese forces concentrated in the Carigara plain.

These deployments assisted the Americans, who advanced rapidly against light opposition, and by November 2 the 6th Army had reached a line Carigara–Jaro – Dagami – Abuyog. They had an advanced detachment at Baybay and had captured all five airstrips.

Before examining the American plans for the break-out from their beach-head, let us recall an incident which took place on the first day.

General George MacArthur had last visited Leyte Gulf in 1903 as a 2nd Lieutenant of Army Engineers. Forty-one years later he boarded a landing craft with President Osmeña, Resident Commissioner Romulo, Chief-of-Staff Sutherland, and Air Commander Kenney.

After the craft had grounded, MacArthur waded through the knee-deep surf, inspected the beach, and walked inland about 200 yards to examine the effects of the bombardment.

It may not have looked like the return of a conquering hero, but MacArthur made up for this in his broadcast on the "Voice of Freedom" network.

Standing on the beach in front of the microphone, his hands shook and his voice betrayed his deep emotion:

"People of the Philippines, I have returned. By the grace of Almighty God our forces stand again on Philippine soil."

He urged the population to rally to him, and also introduced the new president Sergio Osmeña. A passionate yet restrained speech, it was an outlet for powerful emotions held in check and only betrayed earlier when, with a smile, he had remarked "Well, believe it or not, we're here."

After the war General Yamashita said that he had imagined that the film of MacArthur's return had been mocked up in New Guinea. Had he known that the general was at the front he would have launched the whole strength of the Japanese forces in a suicide raid on MacArthur's headquarters to avenge the death of Admiral Yamamoto.

Meanwhile unloading was proceeding at a ·fast and sometimes chaotic rate. L.S.T.s originally intended for "Red" Beach were diverted to Tacloban airstrip, and here the rapidly-growing supply dump began to restrict the work of the airfield engineers. On October 24, Kenney made the drastic threat that everything not removed from the airstrip by dawn on the 25th would be bulldozed into the sea.

The airstrips proved to be almost unusable, despite the hard work and constant attention of the Army Engineers and Filipino labourers. The Dulag strip was still soft, with many rough spots, on October 25, but served as an emergency landing ground during the Leyte sea battle. Tacloban was a little better, despite the fact that the water table was only 18 inches below the surface. One engineer reported that "an airstrip there could at best be a thin slice of coral or metal laid upon a jelly mold".

Krueger visited this airstrip and told the engineers that unless they started

U.S. troops walk through the surf at Leyte on October 24, 1944.

laying gravel, they would be digging fox-holes for their lives in 24 hours. The work was done, and again this strip saved about 100 pilots, though the surface was so bad that about a quarter of the aircraft were destroyed when they crash-landed or nosed over on soft spots.

Three of the fast carrier groups remained in the area to provide air cover and attack the Japanese airfields which were beginning to receive reinforcements from Formosa.

Japanese troop reinforcements began to arrive via Ormoc, but the shipping and naval escorts suffered heavy losses. Four battalions from Davao and Cebu arrived between the 26th and 28th. The main body of the 1st Division and some 2,000 men of the 26th Division from Luzon were landed between November 1 and 2. The convoy carrying the remainder of the 1st Division and some 10,000 of the 26th Division left Manila on November 8th. It came under low level attack by the 5th U.S.A.A.F. and sustained considerable superficial damage. The men were landed without their equipment. A day later the empty convoy was caught again by the 5th U.S.A.A.F. and all but one ship were sunk. A day later, aircraft from Halsey's carriers attacked a convoy carrying the remainder of the 26th Division, and for the loss of nine aircraft, sank all the transports and four of the escorting destroyers.

Between October 22 and December 11, the Japanese succeeded in reinforcing the original garrison of 15,000 men with some 45,000 men and 10,000 tons of stores. Their operations cost them one light cruiser, eight destroyers, six escort craft, and 17 transports–shipping they could ill afford to lose. Despite this, the 35th Army was outnumbered by the 6th Army, whose strength stood at 183,000 by December 2.

By November 1, Suzuki realised that he was up against two American corps, each of two divisions, and that he lacked the strength to carry out his original plan. He ordered the 1st Division and the truncated 26th, when they arrived at Carigara and Jaro respectively, to hold the U.S. X Corps in the north. The remaining reinforcements were sent to assist the 16th Division under attack by the U.S. XXIV Corps in the south. In the ensuing heavy fighting the Americans were halted near Limon and to the west of Jaro.

At a conference with Terauchi, on November 9 and 10, Yamashita urged that the reinforcement of Leyte was weakening the defences of Luzon, and proving too costly in transports and naval vessels. Terauchi agreed that there was little hope of holding the island and that supply operations should cease.

Despite this, Yamashita ordered the 35th Army to use the 26th Division on the Burauen front with a view to launching an attack with the 16th Division to recapture some of the airfields. Suzuki, who had hoped to concentrate his forces in the north, was now forced to send the 26th Division along the Albuera–Burauen track and the 102nd Division to the Mount Pina area to protect the right of the 1st Division, holding out at Limon.

The 4th Air Army proposed an airborne counter-attack with the 40 aircraft and 250 paratroops of the 2nd Raiding Group, which had flown in from Japan. Yamashita decided that a joint air and ground attack should be launched near the end of the month, preceded by an air attack between the 23rd and 27th.

In a spectacular, but fumbled, attack on November 27, three transport aircraft carrying demolition troops were sent to crash-land on the strips at Dulag and Tacloban.

One aircraft crashed on Buri airstrip killing all its occupants, the second hit the beach and most of the men escaped, and the third landed in the surf near the H.Q. of the U.S. 728th Amphibious Bat-talion, between Rizal and Tarragona. A brisk hand-to-hand fight ensued, in which some Japanese were killed and others escaped to the jungle.

A second and more serious attempt was made on the Buri strip on the night of December 5-6. About 150 infantrymen had worked down through the mountains and attacked American troops bivouack-ing near the strip. The Japanese were driven off at dawn.

Through a piece of bad co-ordination, the paratroop attack came 20 hours later. Between 39 and 40 aircraft, carry-ing about 15 to 20 men apiece, roared over Tacloban and Dulag. At the former they were destroyed or driven off by the A.A. fire, while the Dulag section crash-landed killing crew and paratroopers.

However, a drop from 35 different aircraft on the Burauen strips met with greater success. The Japanese set fire to stores, fuel, ammunition, and some small liaison aircraft. For two days and nights ground crews and other air force personnel stalked one another and the Japanese, before the paratroopers were eliminated.

Ironically, the weather had proved more effective than these airborne sorties, for the U.S.A.A.F. had abandoned the Burauen strips, which had become water-logged, leaving only rear echelon units behind.

With his X Corps held up near Limon, and XXIV Corps delayed in its advance north from Baybay, Krueger decided to make a fresh landing south of Ormoc, to drive a wedge between the two wings of his opponents.

On the morning of the 7th, the U.S. 77th Division landed four miles south of Ormoc and met no resistance. The convoy and escorts, however, came under attack after the landing and during the return, and lost two destroyers sunk and two damaged to *kamikaze* attacks.

Suzuki was forced to switch his 16th and 26th Divisions from the front to oppose this landing. On December 10, however, the 77th beat him in the race for Ormoc.

With the main Japanese base in American hands, Yamashita told Suzuki that he was on his own. Japanese resistance began to crumble fast. On December 20, X Corps and the 77th Division met at Cananga, and part of this force turned west. On Christmas Day, with the help of a force moved by sea from Ormoc, it captured Palompon, the only port of any significance left to the Japanese.

Though organised resistance ceased, there were still groups of Japanese obeying Yamashita's order to live off the country and keep up the struggle with the Americans. As the official naval history comments "Japanese unorganised resistance can be very tough." Following his instructions to keep up the struggle, Yamashita added a message explaining that the high command had decided to concentrate on the defence of Luzon, and that he was shedding "tears of remorse" for the tens of thousands of his countrymen who must fight to the death on Leyte.

Mopping up continued until March 17, 1945. There was still over a full division of Japanese troops on the island. Some used the rugged and badly-mapped terrain for guerrilla tactics, whilst small units tried to escape to Cebu across the 25 miles of the Camotes Sea.

By March 1945, despite sweeps by the U.S. 77th Division, there were still several thousand Japanese at large. On March 17, two ships appeared off the coast and embarked Suzuki and part of his staff. For a month they sailed in search of a Japanese-held port until on April 16 they were caught by U.S. aircraft off Negros, and General Suzuki was killed.

Small groups of Japanese continued to be hunted and killed by Filipino guerrillas until the end of the war.

The Leyte campaign was a costly operation. The U.S. Navy and Marine Corps lost several hundred men on and around the island, in addition to the heavy losses sustained in the battle off Samar.

The Army, not including the A.A.F., had 15,584 battle casualties, of which the 3,508 killed were about equally distributed between X and XXIV Corps. In January their full strength stood at 257,766 officers and men.

Understandably, estimates of Japanese casualties vary greatly. The 6th and 8th Armies reported 80,557 confirmed dead, almost one-third of which had occurred during the mopping up operations. The American forces took only 828 Japanese prisoners.

Despite the fact that Luzon, the "capital island" of the Philippines, was the largest Japanese-held island between New Guinea and Tokyo, the American planners had by no means been unanimous in the opinion that it should be recaptured. Admirals King and Nimitz had argued that it would be better, once a foothold had been established in the Philippines with the capture of Leyte and Mindanao, to by-pass Luzon and go straight for Formosa. General MacArthur was the passionate champion of the liberation of all the Philippine islands before making the next advance towards Japan. When it was decided to invade Leyte in October 1944 – two months ahead of the original schedule – MacArthur announced that he would be ready to invade Luzon by the end of December, giving the 20th as a provisional date. This was so much in advance of the earliest possible date by which an invasion force could be deployed for an assault on Formosa that it was decided – a fortnight before the troops went in on Leyte – to invade Luzon.

MacArthur was forced to postpone the date for the Luzon landing by the slow progress of the battle for Leyte. Here the American forces were bedevilled by sluicing autumnal rains, which converted the island battlefield into a quagmire. By the end of November the Luzon attack had been put back to the second week of January: the 9th. In addition, it was decided to capture the island of Mindoro as a curtain-raiser to the main landing on Luzon. This would mean that the Luzon force would not have to rely on the flooded airfields on Leyte – apart from the fleet aircraft-carriers – to provide air cover for the landings. Mindoro, right on Luzon's doorstep, would provide excellent "front-line" airstrips for round-the-clock operations; and its capture was entrusted to a specially-formed unit known as the Western Visayan Task Force. Consisting of two reinforced regiments under the command of Brigadier-General William C. Dunckel, it was to attack on December 15, while the struggle for Leyte was still moving to its close.

During the three-day voyage from Leyte to Mindoro the ships of the Task Force had to endure heavy *kamikaze* attacks; the flagship *Nashville* was badly damaged by a *kamikaze*, and Dunckel himself was wounded (though he was able to stay in command). But the Mindoro landing went in according to plan on the morning of the 15th. It was unopposed; Dunckel's men pegged out a large beach-head with no difficulty and work on the airstrips began at once, while the interior was still being mopped up. By December 23 two new airstrips were already in use on Mindoro and the build-up of aircraft for the Luzon attack could begin. To use MacArthur's own words, "Mindoro was the gate": the turn of Luzon had come.

On paper, the Japanese force which would defend Luzon looked a formidable one: over 250,000 men of the 14th Area Army, commanded by General Tomoyuki Yamashita. But in fact Yamashita's prospects were not bright, and he knew it very well. Most of his units were under-strength and short of supplies. The virtual elimination of the Japanese Combined Fleet at Leyte Gulf meant that he would be getting no more supplies by sea. And the air battles during the prolonged fight for Leyte had whittled down the number of operational aircraft on Luzon to around 150. These would have no chance of halting the American invasion force as it approached Luzon, let alone of commanding the skies over the land battlefield. Yamashita knew that his troops would not be able to stop the invaders getting ashore, and that he did not have sufficient men to defend the whole of Luzon.

In total contrast was the strength of the American forces. They were organised in the fashion which had launched the attack on Leyte. The land fighting was entrusted to General Walter Krueger's 6th Army – over 200,000 men, exclusive of reinforcements – which would be conveyed to its destination and shielded on landing by Vice-Admiral Thomas C. Kinkaid's 7th Fleet. The 7th Fleet – over 850 vessels strong – included the battle fleet, under Vice-Admiral Jessie B. Oldendorf, which had smashed Nishimura's battle squadron in the Surigao Strait during the battle of Leyte Gulf, and which was now to spearhead the invasion of Luzon by bombarding the landing beaches. Admiral William F. Halsey's 3rd Fleet would provide strategic air cover by launching carrier strikes on northern Luzon and Formosa, and land-based air cover would be the contribution of General George F. Kenney's Far East Air Forces, which would begin the battle from their bases on Leyte and Mindoro.

It was obvious to both sides where the invasion must be directed: across the superb beaches of Lingayen Gulf, which was where the Japanese had landed their main forces in December 1941. Lingayen Gulf leads directly into the central plain of Luzon, to Manila and the magnificent anchorage of Manila Bay.

Yamashita was not going to attempt to meet the invaders on the beaches, nor offer them a set-piece battle once ashore. He grouped his forces in three major concentrations which, he hoped, would confine the Americans to the central plain. Yamashita's strategy, in short, was very like Rommel's attempts to "rope off" the Allies in the Normandy *bocage* after D-Day. But – as events in Normandy had already proved conclusively – the most dogged defence was not likely to hold out for long against an invader with control of the air and uninterrupted supplies and reinforcements from the sea.

On January 2, 1945, the first ships of Oldendorf's bombardment force headed out of Leyte Gulf, their destination Lingayen. A punishing ordeal lay ahead of them, for they became the prime targets for Luzon-based *kamikaze* attacks which began on the 4th, while Oldendorf's force was still threading its way through the Sulu Sea. On that day a twin-engined *kamikaze* crashed into the escort carrier *Ommaney Bay,* damaging her so badly that she was beyond salvation and had to be sunk. On the 5th the American force was well within reach of the Japanese airfields on Luzon – under 150 miles – and the *kamikaze* attacks rose in pitch. In the afternoon, while the Americans were passing the mouth of Manila Bay, 16 *kamikazes* broke through the American air screen and attacked, inflicting damage on nearly a dozen American and Australian ships, including two escort carriers, two heavy cruisers, and two destroyers. Nor were the Japanese attacks confined to aircraft alone; two Japanese destroyers appeared, but were seen off in short order. Air strikes from the escort carriers sank one, *Momi,* and damaged the other.

On January 6 Oldendorf's ships entered Lingayen Gulf and began to move into position for the bombardment—and the *kamikaze* attacks reached their climax. The weather was working for the Japanese. A low, dense overcast blanketed the airfields on northern Luzon, preventing Halsey's pilots from masking them with continuous patrols. Bad weather meant nothing to the Japanese pilots—except that their chances of immolating themselves on their targets were enhanced. By nightfall on the 7th two American battleships—*New Mexico* and *California*—three cruisers, three destroyers, and several other vessels had been more or less badly damaged, and three of them, fast minesweepers (*Palmer, Long,* and *Hovey*), sunk. But this was the last great effort of the *kamikazes* of Luzon. On the 7th, Halsey's planes battered the Luzon

A column of American amphibian tanks pauses along the road to Luzon.

airfields so heavily that the last operational Japanese aircraft were withdrawn from the Philippines.

Oldendorf's ships had played an invaluable rôle in soaking up the punishment which might otherwise have savaged the troop transports and landing-craft bringing the invasion force. Now they went ahead with their bombardment programme, which raged for the next three days. Early on the morning of January 9 the troop convoys moved into Lingayen Gulf. At 0700 hours the final stage of the pre-landing barrage was opened and at 0900 the first wave of landing-craft headed in to the beaches. Shortly after 0930 the spearhead troops were ashore—but there were no Japanese troops to meet them. Yamashita had pulled back all his forces not only from the beaches but from the immediate hinterland, with the result that by nightfall on the 9th Krueger's army had established for itself a beach-head 17 miles wide, which reached four miles inland at its deepest extremities. And, true to form, MacArthur himself had landed in triumph, duly captured for posterity by the camera.

The 6th Army punch was a two-corps affair. On the right flank was Major-General Oscar W. Griswold with XIV Corps, consisting of the 37th and 40th Infantry Divisions. Griswold's corps had the task of breaking through to Manila and liberating the capital, a task obvious-

ly dear to MacArthur's heart. But before this could be done the left flank of the lodgment area had to be made secure from any heavy counter-attacks from the north, and this was the job of Major-General Innis P. Swift's I Corps (the 6th and 43rd Infantry Divisions). Until Swift had made the left flank secure, Krueger was going to take his time about pushing on to Manila—and he was wise to do so. For Swift's corps was faced by the "*Shobu*" Group, the largest of Yamashita's three concentrations, 152,000-men strong and well dug in along a chain of strongpoints 25 miles long, from Lingayen Gulf to the Cabaruan Hills. Foul weather on the 10th, ramming home the vulnerability of the landing beaches by causing considerable disruption, made it clear that Swift's task was of vital importance. But his progress against the tough Japanese defences remained slow, much to MacArthur's chagrin. Not until the end of the month did I Corps, reinforced with the 25th and 32nd Divisions, push the Japanese back into the mountains after a tank battle at San Manuel on the 28th. They reached the approaches to Yamashita's H.Q. at Baguio and drove east through San Jose to reach the eastern shore of Luzon, pushing a corridor across the island. This now cut off Yamashita from his troops in the island's centre and south.

Griswold and XIV Corps met with scanty opposition as they began their advance to the south. By the 16th they

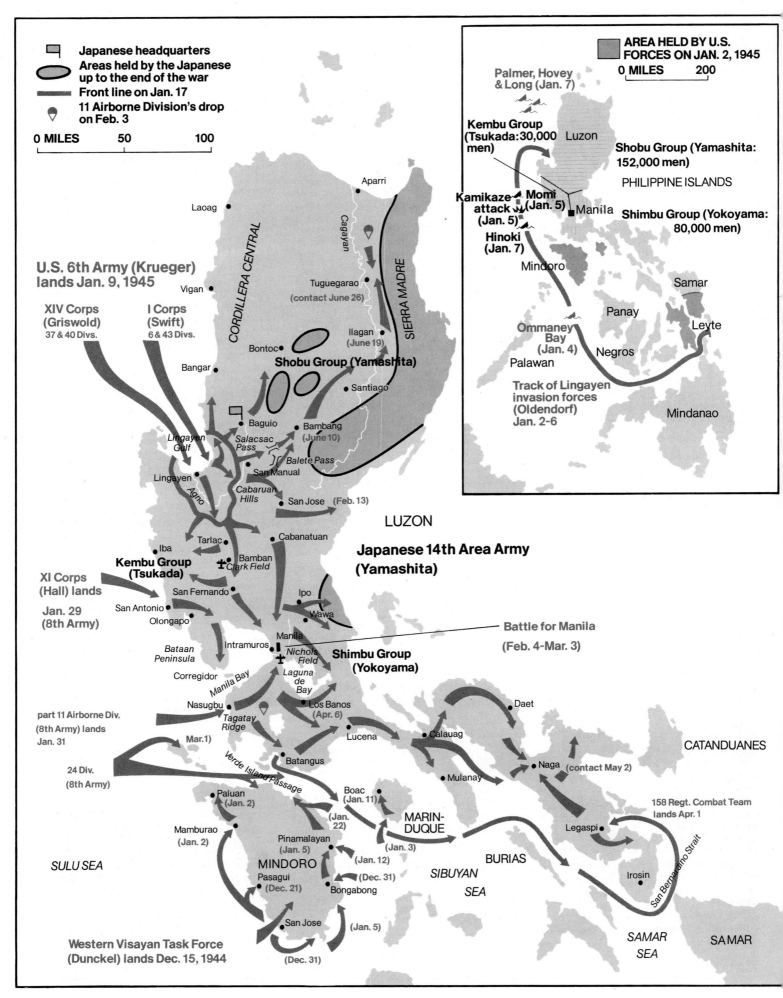

Japanese headquarters

Areas held by the Japanese up to the end of the war

Front line on Jan. 17

11 Airborne Division's drop on Feb. 3

0 MILES 50 100

AREA HELD BY U.S. FORCES ON JAN. 2, 1945

0 MILES 200

Palmer, Hovey & Long (Jan. 7)

Kembu Group (Tsukada: 30,000 men)

Luzon

Shobu Group (Yamashita: 152,000 men)

PHILIPPINE ISLANDS

Kamikaze attack (Jan. 5)

Momi (Jan. 5)

Manila

Shimbu Group (Yokoyama: 80,000 men)

Hinoki (Jan. 7)

Mindoro

Samar

Panay

Ommaney Bay (Jan. 4)

Palawan

Negros

Leyte

Track of Lingayen invasion forces (Oldendorf) Jan. 2-6

Mindanao

Aparri

Laoag

Cagayan

U.S. 6th Army (Krueger) lands Jan. 9, 1945

Vigan

CORDILLERA CENTRAL

SIERRA MADRE

Tuguegarao (contact June 26)

XIV Corps (Griswold) 37 & 40 Divs.

I Corps (Swift) 6 & 43 Divs.

Ilagan (June 19)

Bontoc

Bangar

Shobu Group (Yamashita)

Santiago

Baguio

Bambang (June 10)

Lingayen Gulf

Salacsac Pass

Balete Pass

San Manual

Cabaruan Hills

Lingayen

Agno

San Jose (Feb. 13)

Tarlac

Iba

Cabanatuan

LUZON

Kembu Group (Tsukada)

Bamban

Clark Field

Japanese 14th Area Army (Yamashita)

XI Corps (Hall) lands

Jan. 29 (8th Army)

San Fernando

San Antonio

Ipo

Olongapo

Wawa

Bataan Peninsula

Manila

Nichols Field

Battle for Manila (Feb. 4-Mar. 3)

Intramuros

Corregidor

Laguna de Bay

Shimbu Group (Yokoyama)

Manila Bay

Nasugbu

Los Banos (Apr. 6)

Daet

part 11 Airborne Div. (8th Army) lands Jan. 31

Tagatay Ridge

Lucena

Calauag

CATANDUANES

Mar. 1)

24 Div. (8th Army)

Verde Island Passage

Batangus

Mulanay

Naga (contact May 2)

Boac (Jan. 11)

158 Regt. Combat Team lands Apr. 1

Paluan (Jan. 2)

(Jan. 22)

MARIN-DUQUE

Legaspi

Mamburao (Jan. 2)

Pinamalayan (Jan. 5)

(Jan. 3)

BURIAS

SULU SEA

(Jan. 12)

SIBUYAN SEA

Irosin

Pasagui (Dec. 21)

(Dec. 31)

MINDORO

Bongabong

SAMAR SEA

SAMAR

San Jose

(Jan. 5)

Western Visayan Task Force (Dunckel) lands Dec. 15, 1944

(Dec. 31)

San Bernardino Strait

were across the Agno river, still with little or no opposition—but Krueger was yet unwilling to push too far ahead in the south until he was convinced that the northern flank was secure. But on January 17 MacArthur intervened, stressing the need for an immediate drive on Manila. There were plenty of good reasons. The Americans needed the port; they needed the airfield complex at Clark Field for Kenney's planes; and they were anxious to liberate the inmates of military and civilian prison camps before the Japanese had time to harm them further. But now Griswold's corps in its turn came up against the second of Yamashita's defensive concentrations.

This was the "Kembu" Group, 30,000 men under Major-General Rikichi Tsukada, stationed in the mountains west of the central plain of Luzon to defend the Clark Field sector. Griswold's corps first encountered heavy opposition from the "Kembu" Group at the town of Bamban on January 23. It took over a week of extremely heavy fighting before XIV Corps forced the Japanese back from Clark Field. By January 31 the "Kembu" Group had lost over 2,500 men and had been forced to retreat into the mountains; the Clark Field complex was in American hands and Griswold was able to resume his drive on Manila.

In the last days of January, two more American units landed on Luzon. The first was XI Corps, commanded by Major-General Charles P. Hall, consisting of the 38th Infantry Division and a regiment of the 24th Division. It landed on the west coast of the island to the north of the Bataan Peninsula, and its mission was to capture the Olongapo naval base and drive across the root of the Bataan Peninsula to Manila Bay. Unlike MacArthur in 1942, Yamashita refused to run the risk of getting any of his troops trapped on Bataan, but Hall's corps had two weeks of tough fighting before it reached Manila Bay. The second landing went in south of the bay at Nasugbu, 50 miles south-west of Manila. It was made by the bulk of the 11th Airborne Division; the plan was to tie down Japanese troops in southern Luzon and open up a second approach route to the capital. On February 3 the rest of the division dropped inland, on Tagaytay Ridge; the division concentrated and moved north-east towards Manila, but was fought to a standstill as it approached the outskirts.

It was clear that if Manila was to be taken it would have to be from the north. Once again the impetus came from MacArthur. "Go to Manila!" he urged on January 30. "Go around the Nips, bounce off the Nips, but go to Manila!" His exhortations went right down the line of Griswold's corps to the two divisions which would do the job: the 37th Infantry and the newly-arrived 1st Cavalry.

Their main concern and objective was the big civilian internment camp at Santo

The U.S. Army landings and operations on Luzon in 1944–45.

Tomas, which was liberated on February 3 by a "flying column" of tanks from the 1st Cavalry. The prisoners in Santo Tomas were in an unenviable position, hearing the sounds of a tough battle outside the walls and fearing the worst until an unmistakable American bellow of "Where the hell's the front gate?" was followed by 1st Cavalry tanks smashing through the entrance. Hard on the heels of 1st Cavalry came the 37th Infantry, which pushed through to Old Bilibid Prison and liberated 1,300 civilian internees and P.O.W.s. The northern suburbs of Manila were in American hands. But the battle for the city was only beginning.

In 1942 MacArthur had declared Manila an open city rather than turn it into a battlefield, and Yamashita had no intention of fighting for the city in 1945. But there were 17,000 fighting men in Manila over whom he had no control— they were not Army troops. They were naval forces under the command of Rear-Admiral Sanji Iwabachi, who was determined to hold Manila to the last. He split his men into separate battle groups, gave each of them a section of the city to defend, and prepared for an all-out battle. A unique episode was about to be added to the history of the Pacific war: its only urban battle.

The Americans took some time to realise what lay before them, but a week of vicious fighting and rapidly-mounting casualties forced them to accept that there could be no question of taking Manila without cracking the Japanese out of their positions at the expense of the city's buildings. By the 12th, XIV Corps had forced the Japanese in front of them back into Intramuros, the old walled inner city of Manila. South of the city the paratroopers of the 11th Airborne Division had run up against tough defensive positions built by the Japanese sailors on Nichols Field. Here, too, an inch-by-inch struggle developed, with the paratroopers getting artillery support from the guns of XIV Corps to the north. It was an unrelieved killing-match, eliciting a grim signal from one of 11th Airborne's company commanders: "Tell Halsey to stop looking for the Jap Fleet; it's dying on Nichols Field."

Even after the 11th Airborne joined hands with 1st Cavalry on February 12, the battle for Manila was far from over. Iwabachi's sailors held on grimly both in Intramuros and the rest of the city and over a fortnight of murderous fighting lay ahead. It was given a fresh element of horror by the fact that the Japanese refused to evacuate non-combatants, and it went on until the very last flickers of Japanese resistance were stamped out on March 3. MacArthur's obsession with the recapture of Manila had exacted a terrible price. The Filipino capital lay in ruins. Civilian casualties have been set as high as 100,000. American losses topped 1,000 killed and 5,500 wounded. As for the Japanese defenders of Manila, they had upheld the fighting traditions of the Imperial Japanese Navy by dying virtually to a man.

While the slaughter in Manila was still running its course, the clearing of the island forts in Manila Bay had begun. First came the overrunning of the Bataan Peninsula by XI Corps, begun on the 14th and aided by a landing at Mariveles, at the tip of the peninsula, on the following day. It only took a week to flush the scanty Japanese forces out of their positions on Bataan; compared with the carnage in Manila it was an easy task.

Corregidor, the strongest fortress in Manila Bay, was a different story. In May 1942 the American garrison had capitulated within 48 hours of the first Japanese landings on the island. In 1945 it took over ten days of bitter fighting before the Americans got the island back. Their assault went in on February 16, a combined parachute drop and amphibious landing which rapidly gained control of the surface defences. But the Japanese still had to be flushed from their positions underground, and the island was not declared secure until the 28th. MacArthur himself visited Corregidor on March 2. Ready as always with a memorable *bon mot*, he announced: "I see that the old flagpole still stands. Have your troops hoist the colours to its peak and let no enemy ever haul them down."

The three smaller forts in the Bay remained. On Caballo and El Fraile, horrible measures were taken to break the resistance of the Japanese when they refused to surrender. Diesel oil was pumped into their positions and ignited with phosphorus shells and fused T.N.T. Caballo was cleared on April 13, El Fraile on the 18th. The Japanese evacuated the third island, Canabao, and the Americans encountered no resistance when they landed there on April 16.

Three months after the first American landings in Lingayen Gulf the Japanese had been forced out of central Luzon, the capital had been liberated, and Manila Bay was clear to Allied shipping. But still the battle for Luzon was far from over. Yamashita still had 172,000 Japanese troops under arms. They held the north and south-east of the island; Manila itself was still within range of Japanese guns, and the dams and reservoirs containing the bulk of the capital's water supplies were still in Japanese hands.

Moreover, the Japanese still controlled the most direct sea route through the central Philippines, forcing any Allied shipping heading west for Manila to take an expensive 500-mile detour. Until these problems had been solved and Yamashita's forces had been ground down to total impotence, there could be no question of taking the next step towards Tokyo. The last stage of the battle for Luzon began.

The most urgent problem facing the 6th Army was the big Japanese concentration east of Manila. This was the "Shimbu" Group, under the command of Lieutenant-General Shizuo Yokoyama: 80,000-odd troops, based on the 8th and 105th Divisions. The bulk of the "Shimbu" Group,

30,000 strong, was dug in along the southern end of the Sierra Madre range along the line Ipo Dam–Wawa Dam–Antipolo, extending south to the great lake of Laguna de Bay. Griswold and XIV Corps launched the first determined narrow-front attack against this strong position on March 8, following two days of intense softening-up by Kenney's bombers. By the 12th, the 1st Cavalry Division had battered its way through the maze of fiercely-defended Japanese cave defences and was relieved on the 13th by the 43rd Division, which kept up the pressure and, in conjunction with 6th Division, punched deep into the centre of the "Shimbu" Group's line. On the 14th, General Hall's XI Corps relieved Griswold on this front and continued the offensive. By the end of March, the 43rd Division had struggled through to the east side of Laguna de Bay and had completely unhinged Yokoyama's left.

Further to the north, however, the 6th Division failed in its drive to capture Wawa and Ipo Dams. It took the whole of April, in the face of indomitable Japanese resistance, for the 6th Division to struggle forward into position for a final assault. By this time the successes in the south enabled the 43rd Division to be switched north to add more weight to the next attack.

This was heralded by three days of saturation bombing which dumped 250,000 gallons of napalm on the Japanese positions. The attack proper was launched on the night of May 6 by the 43rd Division.

In this battle the American forces were aided to the north by 3,000 Filipino guerrillas, who kept Yokoyama's left flank fully engaged. At last, on May 17, joint American and Filipino attacks seized Ipo Dam intact. Further south, the 6th Division was relieved by the 38th Division, which ground away at the exhausted Japanese. Finally American persistance told, and the "Shimbu" Group's survivors began to melt away. Wawa Dam fell–also intact –on May 28, by which time the "Shimbu" Group had been destroyed.

By this time, too, the lesser problem of the "Kembu" Group, west of Clark Field, had also been solved. While the bulk of Griswold's corps prepared for the final advance on Manila at the end of January, the 40th Division had been left to mask the "Kembu" force of 25,000 in the heights to which it had retreated after the loss of Clark Field. Here, too, the Japanese made the fullest use of their advantage in terrain and it took over two months of concentrated pressure by three American divisions–first the 40th, then the 43rd, and finally the 38th–before Tsukada accepted the inevitable. On April 6 he ordered his surviving forces to go over to independent guerrilla warfare.

Two more Japanese concentrations south of Manila were also successfully broken up in these gruelling weeks. These were the "Fuji" Force commanded by Colonel Fujishige–an Army/Navy agglomeration of about 13,000 men, originally part of "Shimbu" Group–and 3,000 Army

American soldiers move through the suburbs of Manila in February 1945.

and Navy troops down on the Bicol Peninsula, the south-eastern "tail" of Luzon. Again, it was a story of repeated battles throughout February and March, with Filipino guerrillas working in co-ordination with the regular American forces. By the end of April "Fuji" Force had gone the same way as the "Kembu" Group, while an amphibious landing at Legaspi on the Bicol Peninsula by the 158th Regimental Combat Team had battered west and joined up with 1st Cavalry Division. Southern Luzon was free.

But the greatest obstacle of all remained: Yamashita and the 110,000 troops of the "Shobu" Group in the north. While the battles in the centre and south of Luzon continued, it was impossible for Krueger to send more than three divisions against Yamashita: the 33rd, 32nd, and 25th. Aided by the 37th Division, the 33rd pushed forward to take Baguio, Yamashita's former H.Q., on April 26; but it took the whole of May and June for Swift's I Corps to break across the Balete Pass, take Bambang, and push on into the Cagayan valley. Airborne forces were dropped at the northern end of the Cagayan valley towards the end of June; they drove south and joined up with 37th Division at Tuguegarao on June 26.

By the end of June Yamashita had 65,000 men still under arms. They had been forced back into the mountains to

A flame-thrower hits a Japanese strong-point during street-fighting, a grim task against the Japanese.

the south of Bontoc and although it was now quite impossible for them to make any effective challenge to the American hold on Luzon, they nevertheless held out until the end of the war and kept four divisions tied down in consequence. Of all the Japanese forces told to hold the Philippines for the Emperor, Yamashita's men were the ones who came closest to fulfilling their mission.

Thus by the end of June 1945 the battle of Luzon was over. It had been a unique struggle, the most "European" battle of the entire Pacific war. Fought out on an island the size of Britain, it had seen tank battles, amphibious landings, paratroop drops and guerrilla warfare, with a bloody street battle as well. Japanese losses were immense, totalling around 190,000. American losses were 8,000 killed and 30,000 wounded. Further hard fighting lay ahead before the Pacific war would be brought to its close. But there would never be another conflict like the fight for Luzon.

MacArthur had never been ordered to liberate the entire Philippine archipelago. In fact, the British had been told by General Marshall that once the vital objectives had been secured in the Philippines, the liberation of the smaller islands would be left to the Filipinos themselves, with no major American forces taking part. But MacArthur had other ideas; and as long as it was clear that there were no other major objectives for the considerable American land, sea, and air forces in the Philippine area, he was

allowed to have his way.

The clearing of the central and southern Philippines was entrusted to the U.S. 8th Army, under Lieutenant-General Robert L. Eichelberger, whose first task was to clear the short-cut sea route through the Visayan Passages. This began with a landing on the north-west coast of Samar on February 19 to clear the San Bernardino Strait and it continued through the month of March, with the occupation of small islands such as Burias, Siniara, Romblon, and Tablas. The last in the sequence was Masbate, and on April 5 Eichelberger reported to MacArthur that the Visayan Passages had been cleared.

In the meantime, the liberation of the key islands in the central and southern Philippines had already begun.

Eichelberger's opponent in the area was the commander of the Japanese 35th Army: Lieutenant-General Sosaku Suzuki. His forces numbered 100,000, dotted over scores of islands, unable to concentrate or assist each other, but prepared to put up as tenacious a fight as their colleagues on Luzon. And fight they did. By the middle of April Eichelberger's forces had made a grand total of 38 amphibious landings in the central and southern Philippines. None was on the same scale as Leyte or Luzon–but each met with resistance that was no less determined.

Palawan was the first major target: 270 miles long, the westernmost outrider of the Philippine archipelago. The American 186th Regimental Combat Team from the

41st Division landed on Palawan on February 28, but it took it over a week to break the resistance of the 1,750 Army and Navy troops on the island. On March 20 an airstrip at Puerto Princesa began to function.

Ten days before this, however, the rest of the 41st Division had descended on the westernmost tip of Mindanao, second largest and most southerly of the Philippine group. The long, thin Zamboanga Peninsula was their objective, but again it took over two weeks of fighting before their foothold was secure. In the meantime, 41st Division units had been detached to clean out the Sulu Archipelago, the string of diminutive islands stretched between Mindanao and Borneo. This started easily–Basilan, nearest island in the Sulu group to Zamboanga, was unoccupied–but Jolo, in the centre of the chain, was another matter. It was held by 4,000 Japanese troops who fought hard for three weeks after the landing went in on April 9. Even after the main resistance was broken mopping-up continued in the interior of Jolo until July.

Next came the turn of the southern Visayas, four medium-sized islands on roughly the same latitude: from east to west, Bohol, Cebu, Negros, and Panay. Eichelberger divided this group into two, aided by the mountain spine of Negros which partitions the island into Negros Occidental and Negros Oriental. Panay and western Negros were given to the 40th Division; eastern Negros, Cebu, and Bohol to the Americal Division, originally raised in New Caledonia from non-divisional units in the Pacific theatre, and veterans of Guadalcanal, Bougainville, and Leyte.

The 40th Division landed on Panay on March 18 and wasted no time in completing its assignment. It was considerably helped by strong guerrilla forces; they took Panay's largest port, Iloilo, on the 20th, crossed straight to the island of Guimaras, and landed on the western coast of Negros on March 29. Surprise had been their biggest ally to date, but awaiting them was the biggest Japanese force in the Visayas: 13,500 Army and air force troops commanded by Lieutenant-General Takeshi Kono. A prolonged battle lasted through April and May before Kono made the inevitable decision to take to the mountains. Over 6,000 of his men were still alive when the war ended.

By far the biggest fight in the Visayas fell to the Americal Division, which landed near Cebu City on March 26. There it found formidable defences, including mined beaches—an obstacle which 8th

American Sherman medium tanks ford a river near Luzon in the Philippines.

Army forces had not had to tackle before. A fortnight's hard fighting was needed to prise the Japanese out of their defences and start the mopping-up—but, once again, the Japanese were still holding out in June. In the meantime, American troops had subdued Bohol in a mere two weeks after their landing on April 11, and had crossed to eastern Negros, where they joined 40th Division in hunting down the last 1,300 Japanese troops still on the run.

After the clearing of the Visayas and the Sulu Archipelago, only Mindanao remained: Mindanao, second largest island in the Philippines, and the island which MacArthur had originally planned to liberate first. It was a formidable obstacle. Suzuki had placed over half the 35th Army on Mindanao, intending to make the island the last bastion of Japanese resistance in the Philippines. He did not live to fight this last-ditch battle himself, as he was killed by American aircraft in April. His successor was Lieutenant-General Gyosaku Morozumi, who took over the 43,000 men of the garrison.

Despite the imposing size of their forces on Mindanao, the Japanese only controlled about five per cent of the island. The remainder was under the virtual control of the best equipped, organised, and led guerrilla forces in the Philippines, under the command of Colonel Wendell W. Fertig. The fact remained, however,

that the Japanese held all the populated areas of Mindanao—hence MacArthur's determination to oust them.

The battle for Mindanao began on April 17, 1945, when General Sibert's X Corps landed at Illana Bay. Driving rapidly inland, Sibert's forces covered 115 miles in 15 days and pounced on Davao, depriving the Japanese of their last major town in the Philippines. Davao fell on May 3, but over a month of hard fighting in the hills of the interior lay ahead. Subsequent landings on the north coast of Mindanao, at Macalajar Bay and Butuan Bay, sent further American columns inland to split up the Japanese mass, which was not disrupted and forced into the jungle until the last week of June.

There remained some 2,000 Japanese in the extreme south of the island, who had been cut off there ever since Sibert's pounce on Davao in April-May. These fugitives were the objective of the last seaborne landing of the long struggle for the Philippines which had begun in Leyte Gulf in October 1944. On July 12 a battalion of the 24th Division went ashore to work with the local Filipino guerrillas in rounding up the Japanese. And they landed in Sarangani Bay, the southernmost inlet on Mindanao's coast. Once MacArthur had planned to launch the reconquest of the Philippines at this point. Instead it was the scene of the very last action in the campaign.

CHAPTER 66

Clearing the Baltic and Balkan states

The dramatic circumstances in which Field-Marshal Model just managed to hold the Soviet push between the Niemen and the Carpathians have already been noted. On August 16 he was recalled to replace Kluge as C.-in-C. West, and handed over command of Army Group "Centre" to Colonel-General Reinhardt, while Army Group "North Ukraine" passed from his hands into those of Colonel-General Harpe, under the title of Army Group "A".

Until the end of December, Marshal Rokossovsky and General Zakharov, commanders respectively of the 1st and 2nd Belorussian Fronts, restricted themselves to operations with limited objectives. Halfway through September Rokossovsky, with 70 divisions, had taken his revenge for the check he had received six weeks previously on the approach to Warsaw. He had fallen back to Wołomin and reoccupied Praga, on the outskirts of the Polish capital. The German defenders were at the end of their tether. Further north, Rokossovsky had pushed as far as Modlin at the confluence of the Bug and the Vistula.

On his right, Zakharov, at the head of 71 infantry divisions and five tank corps, had penetrated the corridor between the Bug and the Narew. On the right bank of the latter he had taken a wide bridgehead around Pułtusk from the German 2nd Army (Colonel-General Weiss). And so, between the 2nd and 3rd Belorussian Fronts–the latter still under the command of Colonel-General Chernyakhovsky–the outline of the pincer movement which would lead to the encirclement and then the conquest of East Prussia was forming.

Meanwhile, behind the Polish front, a series of events of great importance for the future was taking place. First of all, east of the Curzon Line the Russians established–or purely and simply restored–their own authority. Moreover, a "Polish Committee of National Liberation" was set up in Lublin under the Communist E. B. Osóbka-Morawski, who was so totally submissive to the Kremlin that he made no protest when the Russians systematically organised a persecution of the Polish Home Army fighters on Polish soil.

At Tukums, as has been described, the 1st Baltic Front (General Bagramyan) had cut the last land contact between Army Group "North" (Colonel-General Schörner) and the other armies of the Reich. But Bagramyan was himself attacked on August 16 and his flank turned by the 3rd *Panzerarmee,* now under Colonel-General Raus after Reinhardt's promotion. It had been reinforced to the strength of two Panzer corps, with five Panzer divisions and the "Grossdeutschland" Panzergrenadier Division.

It launched its attack from the region north of Taurage and met few difficulties other than the natural ones of terrain. By August 20, it had covered 125 miles and had established a solid link with the right wing of the 16th Army near Tukums.

This new Russian success led to a clash between Hitler and the new Chief-of-Staff of O.K.H., Colonel-General Guderian. Guderian tried in vain to impress upon the Führer that he should use this temporary respite to evacuate Estonia and the eastern part of Lithuania as quickly as possible, though maintaining a bridgehead around Riga. In this way, more solidity would be given to Army Group "North", which would then have some chance of success in checking the Russians. The Führer cut him short sharply. To abandon Tallinn and Paldiski, he said, would automatically provoke the "defection" of Finland.

Was he unaware that this was as good as complete already? In any event he was informed of the Finno-Soviet armistice on September 3, 1944, and this cut away the ground from his argument. Nevertheless, he refused to send new orders to Colonel-General Schörner. This time he lyingly claimed the support of Grand-Admiral Dönitz when he spoke to Guderian. But by now Army Group "North" had only 32 divisions to put into the field against 130 Russian ones of the Leningrad and three Baltic Fronts.

Overwhelming *Armeegruppe* "Narva" by September 24, Marshal Govorov's Leningrad Front had occupied Estonia almost completely. Then his 8th Army (General Paern), using American landing-craft, began, first with Moon and Dagö, to take the islands in the Gulf of Riga defended by the 23rd and 218th Divisions. With the aid of a naval force under Vice-Admiral Thiele, including the pocket-battleships *Lützow* and *Scheer* and the cruisers that Hitler had wanted to send to the scrapyard, these two divisions managed to hold out on the Sworbe peninsula against six Soviet divisions until November 23 and then cross over to Kurland without too many losses. This was the first example on the Eastern Front of those amphibious retreats which the Kriegsmarine would effect, saving the Army serious losses of men and equipment.

On October 13, the advance parties of General A. I. Eremenko's 3rd Baltic Front had entered Riga. The day after Colonel-General Raus's success, Guderian had obtained Hitler's approval for a directive requiring Army Group "North" to transfer the 3rd *Panzerarmee* from the south to halt the Russian drive on Memel. But Schörner did nothing about it, for he did not believe that Memel was in danger.

While Guderian vainly pleaded with Schörner, the *Stavka* had discovered that the road to Memel was very weakly held by the Germans. And so, on September 24, General Bagramyan received the order to transfer the centre of gravity of the 1st Baltic Front without delay from the Mitau area to the Siauliai region, exactly where Guderian wanted to place the 3rd *Panzerarmee,* and to break the German line at that point.

The attack began on October 5. On the first day 14 divisions and four armoured corps (more than 500 tanks) breached Schörner's defensive screen. Covering a distance of 90 miles in five days, Bagramyan reached the Baltic at Palanga, 15 miles north of Memel. For the second time, Army Group "North" which, on October 10, had 26 divisions, including two Panzer, found itself cut off. It is true that it received supplies by sea and that the Kurland pocket, along the Tukums–Auce–Weinoden–south of Liepāja line, was about half the size of Belgium. In spite of this, once Bagramyan had made his drive, there was no way of maintaining the German 18th Army around Riga.

In contrast, Colonel-General Chernyakhovsky received a bloody check on his first attempt to invade East Prussia. And yet the 3rd Belorussian Front put about 40 divisions into the line, strongly backed by armour and aircraft, over a front of 90 miles, while the German 4th Army could muster only 15 on a front of 220 miles between the Niemen and the Narew at Nowogród.

But the defence was commanded by a resolute leader, General F. Hossbach, and had the advantages of permanent fortifications. Moreover, the Soviet attack did not enjoy the benefit of surprise. At the beginning (October 16-19) the 11th Guards Army, which formed Chernyakhovsky's spearhead, managed to break General Matzky's XXVI Corps and advance 30 miles over the same east-west line that had been followed by the Russian forces under General Rennenkampf in August 1914. Meanwhile, further to the south, the 31st Army took Gołdap.

Withdrawing five or six divisions from his less threatened sectors, Hossbach managed to seal the breaches. Later, with the aid of armoured formations placed at his disposal by O.K.H. he was able to counter-attack. On October 21 and 22, trying to force a passage over the River Angerapp, the 11th Guards Army was assailed from the north and south and thrown back in disorder onto the right bank of the Rominte. Chernyakhovsky left behind him 1,000-odd tanks and more than 300 guns. He also left clear traces of atrocities of all kinds committed by his troops against the inhabitants of some 300 villages. As may well be imagined, Goebbels made great play with these atrocities. The result of his propaganda was that, three months later, five or six million Germans fled before the Soviet invasion, in temperatures of 20 degrees below zero.

Among the causes of the check of the Russian 3rd Belorussian Front on the Kaunas–Königsberg line should be mentioned the inability of the 2nd Belorussian Front to move out of its bridgeheads on the Narew and thus catch Hossbach in a pincer movement. This would have imitated the manoeuvre attempted by Samsonov as he marched to meet Rennenkampf in August 1914. Should the dismissal of General Zakharov be considered as a punishment for this lack of success? Whether or not this was the reason, at the turn of the year, General Zakharov was called upon to hand over his command to Marshal Rokossovsky.

In Helsinki, on August 1, acting out a previously-prepared drama, President Ryti resigned as head of state and the Finnish parliament appointed Marshal Mannerheim as his successor. This 75-year-old soldier would have to pilot the nation out of the war. For this purpose, he held a trump card in the performance

Finnish Infantry. Although famed for their fighting spirit they were unable to stem the Russian tide.

of the Finnish Army during the recent battle of Karelia. So much heroism, spirit, and tenacity could effectively have shown the Kremlin that Finland's unconditional surrender could only be bought at a price much greater than any benefit that might be obtained from it. But before negotiating with Moscow, Finland could not wait for the Red Army to settle itself solidly in Tallinn and Paltiski, which would allow it to launch an amphibious operation across the Gulf of Finland and to use its crushing superiority in men and *matériel* to the best advantage.

In his task Mannerheim had to take into account the German 20th Army. This possessed three corps (ten mountain divisions) and faced Russia between the Arctic Circle and the Rybachiy peninsula on the frozen Arctic Ocean. This force, including the naval gunners in the many coastal batteries and the air force, totalled 204,000 men under the command of Colonel-General Dr. Rendulic.

O.K.W. had envisaged the possibility of a Finnish defection since the spring. It had prepared two operations to counteract its effects. Operation *"Birke"* (Birch tree) provided for the 20th Army to retreat on the Finno-Norwegian frontier, while Operation *"Tanne"* (Pine tree) would require the army and the navy to prepare to occupy the Åland Islands, in the south of

the Gulf of Bothnia, and the island of Sur Sari or Hogland in the Gulf of Finland.

Meanwhile on June 26, with the Soviet offensive at full force in the Karelian Isthmus, Ribbentrop had agreed to supply arms to the Finns only if they bound themselves unconditionally to the Third Reich. Trapped, President Ryti, with the verbal approval of his ministers, had agreed to this in writing. Therefore his resignation could imply a tacit rejection of the signature as being put on the agreement entirely on his own responsibility. Such a subterfuge was absolutely justified in view of Germany's blackmail.

That was how Blücher, Germany's minister in Helsinki, and General Erfurth, O.K.W.'s liaison officer attached to Marshal Mannerheim, interpreted the crisis of August 1 and the solution adopted. Rendulic, for his part, pointed out that the Finnish Minister of War, General Walden, had made no reference to Finno-German military partnership during that interview. And so the staff of the 20th Army began to prepare Operation *"Birke"* with all speed.

To clarify the situation, Hitler sent the O.K.W. chief-of-staff to see the new President of the Finnish Republic. Keitel was received by Mannerheim on August 17 and had the arrogance or the tactlessness to tell the latter that the people of the Greater Reich would maintain their

war effort for another ten years if it were necessary. This swagger was received coldly and politely with the answer that "it was probably true for a nation of 90 million people".

As may be well imagined, Mannerheim did not express his thoughts too openly. All the same, he did not conceal the fact that Ryti's resignation had come because "in view of circumstances beyond his control, the ex-President had not been able to maintain his freedom of action", and that Mannerheim himself had agreed to combine in his person the supreme military and civil power in order that "in their precarious situation the Finnish people could rely on having the freedom to act within their own interests".

Though he put a brave face on this, Keitel did not fail for a moment to realise the meaning and the importance of these prudent statements. Mannerheim was going to begin to "guide" Finland out of the war.

And, in fact, on August 25, the Soviet minister in Stockholm, Mme. Kollontai, was surprised by a message from the Finnish Government, asking her what the Soviet conditions would be for re-opening the peace talks which had been broken off on April 18 at Finland's request. The Soviet reply arrived at Helsinki in record time and included only two conditions:

1. Immediate breaking-off of diplomatic relations between the Republic of Finland and the Third Reich.
2. Evacuation in two weeks, the absolutely final date fixed for September 14, of all Wehrmacht forces stationed in Finnish territory, after which the Helsinki Government agreed to intern any men left behind.

Great Britain associated herself with these conditions and the United States, who had not declared war on Finland, made it known that they approved. On September 2, after a session behind locked doors, the Finnish parliament authorised the government to begin discussions on the basis of the above conditions.

In consequence there was a cease-fire between the Russians and the Finns at 0700 hours on September 5.

As Minister Blücher was receiving his passports on September 2, Mannerheim had a handwritten letter given to General Erfurth to be passed on to the Führer.

It was, Mannerheim wrote, first of all the general development of the war which "more and more prevents Germany from providing us, in the precarious situations which will doubtless arise and at the right time and in sufficient quantity, the aid of which we shall have urgent need and which Germany, as I sincerely believe, would be willing to grant us".

Moreover, if the worst occurred, the risks run by both countries, as Mannerheim told Keitel, were far from equal. Here, he added, "I must point out that even if fate did not favour German arms, Germany could continue to exist. Nobody could say the same for Finland."

And, at the same time as he heaped praises on the behaviour of "our German brothers-in-arms" towards the Finnish population, he declared that he cherished the hope that "even if you disapprove of my letter you will want, as do I and all Finns, to control the present situation and avoid any worsening of it".

However, the implementation of the second condition imposed by Moscow on Helsinki would set the Finns and Germans against each other – and for good reason, for it could not be done in the time allowed. Both Marshal Mannerheim and Colonel-General Rendulic agree on this in their memoirs.

Though XIX Mountain Corps (General Ferdinand Jodl), whose left faced the Rybachiy peninsula, could get over the Norwegian frontier in a few days' march, this did not apply to the right wing of the 20th Army, consisting of XXXVI Mountain Corps (General Vogel); in action halfway between the White Sea and the Russo-Finnish frontier in the south, in a fortnight he would have to cross a good 625 miles before he left Finnish territory. That is why, from September 3, Mannerheim began to study the means at his disposal to keep his word regarding the internment of his ex-comrades in arms.

Hitler was the first to make a move. Though he ordered Rendulic to carry on with Operation "Birke" and abandoned the idea of a landing on the Aland Islands for fear of possible Swedish reaction, he nevertheless maintained his decision to put Sur Sari under firm Wehrmacht control, in spite of the objections of Vice-Admiral Buchardi, commander of the Kriegsmarine in that part of the Baltic.

The expedition was launched in the night of September 14-15 and resulted in total defeat for the Germans. Colonel Mietinnen, under whose command the island's garrison had been placed, conducted a spirited defence and then counter-attacked with such energy that the following evening the Germans had lost 330 killed and wounded, and surrendered a good 1,000 of their men.

Awaiting the armistice decision, Finnish troops rest in a northern town late in the summer of 1944.

The news of this unpardonable act of aggression and its defeat was welcomed in official circles in Helsinki with certain relief. From now on there was no need to bother about an ally of that sort.

In any case, even if Hitler had restrained himself from committing this act of brutal stupidity, events would not have taken a very different course. A few days later, it would have been known in Helsinki that Rendulic had received orders to stay in Finnish Lappland so as to keep the base at Petsamo and the precious nickel mines of Kolosjoki for the Third Reich.

Mannerheim now transferred his III Corps into the region of Oulu on the Gulf of Bothnia. This corps was commanded by General Siilasvuo, who had distinguished himself during the campaign of the winter of 1939-40. But the Germans did not permit a breakthrough, although their new enemies tried to cut them off by an unexpected landing at Kemi, close to the Finno-Swedish frontier.

On October 15, the Germans evacuated the little town of Rovaniemi after having reduced it to ashes. Then they slipped into Norwegian territory along the route they had prepared between Rovaniemi and Pörsangerfjord. It was difficult to pursue the retreating Germans because they methodically destroyed all bridges, and also because of the season and the fact that the Finnish Army was due to complete its demobilisation by December 5, 1944.

On October 4, O.K.W. ordered Colonel-General Rendulic to abandon Petsamo and to fall back on Lyngenfjord. His preparations for the retreat were almost complete when, on October 7, XIX Corps was attacked in great strength and most energetically by the Karelian Front troops under General K. A. Meretskov. The 20th Army met this Soviet offensive with delaying tactics, using the many rivers in the region. On October 9, XIX

Corps was on the point of being surrounded but the danger was averted by the fast 400 mile transfer of the 163rd Division, which hurled itself into Salmijärvi, and then by the rest of XXXVI Mountain Corps.

Petsamo was occupied on October 15 by the Russians, who then pushed on as far as Kirkenes, on Norwegian soil. This battle, fought above the Arctic Circle, earned Meretskov the title of Marshal of the Soviet Union. In spite of this, it is strange that Soviet accounts, normally so rich in detail, make no mention of trophies or prisoners when they speak of this battle.

The Lyngenfjord base included the fjord of that name, half-way between the North Cape and Tromsö, and also the salient of Finnish territory which protrudes into the region. This meant the sacrifice of the Norwegian province of Finnmark, whose population was evacuated while the Germans burnt Lyngenfjord and Hammerfest. After its retreat, the 20th Army was dissolved. Three of its divisions were given to O.B.W., and a fourth was put at the disposal of O.K.W. Colonel-General Rendulic received the command of the "Norway" Army.

On September 19, 1944, the new Finnish minister, Enckell, was in Moscow to sign an "armistice treaty" which can be taken as a real preliminary and whose clauses regarding territory and payments were reproduced in the definitive peace treaty.

In addition to the loss of territory which Finland had had to suffer by the treaty of March 7, 1940, she now had to witness the amputation of the Petsamo region, thus losing her access to the Atlantic as well as the advantages she gained through the export of nickel from Kolosjoki.

In exchange for the lease of the Hangö peninsula, which the first Treaty of Moscow had granted Russia for 50 years, in the second treaty the Soviet Union obtained the same rights over the Porkala promontory on the Gulf of Finland, less than 25 miles from Helsinki.

Out of a population of four million, the valiant little nation had lost 55,000 dead and 47,500 wounded.

On August 20, 1944, the troops of the 2nd Ukrainian Front attacked Iaşi, capital of Moldavia. On Christmas Eve, acting in concert with the 3rd Ukrainian Front, it laid siege to Budapest, while the Soviet Union took complete control over Bulgaria. It exercised no less strong an influence over those provinces of Yugoslavia liberated by Marshal Tito, as well as over the ex-kingdom of Albania.

Not only had the "New Order" instituted by Hitler and Mussolini been upset, but also the old European balance, established in these parts in the 19th Century. On June 22, 1944, Army Group "South Ukraine", which had responsibility for the 400-mile front running between the mouth of the Danube and the Carpathian range, included 23 Rumanian and 33 German divisions, nine of which were

Panzer or *Panzergrenadier*. But the defeat in Belorussia, the rout in the western Ukraine, and the invasion of Poland had forced O.K.H. to remove six Panzer and seven infantry divisions from this army group. They had only been partially replaced by units of lesser worth. With everything included, when Colonel-General Hans Friessner succeeded Schörner at the head of Army Group "South Ukraine" at the beginning of August, he took over 52 divisions, 24 of which were German. What made the circumstances more serious was that he had only four Panzer divisions.

It had become evident that the Russians had two formidable bridgeheads on the Dniestr, at Tiraspol and Grigoriopol, and that between the Dniestr and the Prut the position of the front favoured one of those pincer movements so liked by the Russians. So Marshal Antonescu, the Rumanian *Conducator,* summoned to O.K.W. on August 5, offered as his advice that Army Group "South Ukraine" should be pulled back along a line running from the northern arm of the Danube, through Galati to the right bank of the Siretul and then the Carpathians. This line had been surveyed and partially fortified by the Belgian General Brialmont at a time when fear of the Russians had caused Rumania to flirt with the Triple Alliance. Strategically sound, this solution nevertheless required the evacuation of the southern districts of Bessarabia and Moldavia, a serious sacrifice for Rumania that Antonescu nevertheless made.

The day after the last interview between the Führer and Antonescu, the latter summoned Colonel-General Guderian to go over the political and military scene with him. Guderian wrote:

"He soon came to talk about the assassination attempt of July 20, without hiding his horror at it. 'Believe me,' he said, 'I could trust any of my generals with my life. In Rumania, it would be inconceivable for any officer to take part in a *coup d'état!'* There and then, I was not in a position to answer his grave reproaches. A fortnight later, Antonescu would find himself in a very different situation, and so should we."

It seems, therefore, that the Rumanian dictator had not the slightest idea of the plot led by King Michael I and the leaders of the main political parties, who were preparing to seize power from his hands. As was seen earlier, following the battle of Stalingrad, Rumanian diplomats had attempted to re-establish contact with Great Britain and the United States. In 1944, Alexander Creziano, the Rumanian minister in Ankara, contacted the representatives of the two Western powers while the embassies in Madrid and Stockholm went forward with other soundings. Finally, with the consent of the King, the leader of the National Peasants' Party, Julius Maniu, who was the principal conspirator, sent two

emissaries to Cairo in the persons of Constantin Visoïano and Prince Stirbey. But neither Washington nor London was disposed to reply to these overtures before Bucharest had reached agreement with Moscow on the conditions for a cease-fire.

Now, on April 2, Antonescu's adversaries noted a statement by Molotov that they interpreted as an encouraging overture.

"The Soviet Union," proclaimed Stalin's Foreign Minister, "in no way seeks to acquire any part of Rumanian territory or to change the present social order. Russian troops have entered Rumania solely as a result of military necessity."

Certainly, when Molotov spoke of "Rumanian territory", he excluded the provinces of Bessarabia and Bukovina, which the ultimatum of June 26, 1940 had placed under Soviet control. All the same, Julius Maniu informed the Allies that he was ready to enter discussions on this basis and to consent to substantial reparations being paid to Moscow. It is also true that Rumania had been assured that, as soon as she left the German camp, she would be able to get back the part of Transylvania that the Vienna agreement of August 30, 1940 had transferred to Hungary.

The Rumanian dictator was more or less aware of these dealings, but did not forbid them absolutely. He merely refused to agree to them, considering that his honour bound him to the Wehrmacht. Moreover, he did not feel personally threatened, ignoring the fact that it was not to him but to the sovereign that the officer corps had sworn loyalty.

The Rumanian situation caused great puzzlement in Hitler's circle for the reports being received were in disagreement with each other.

On August 3, Friessner had sounded the alarm and indicated how little confidence he felt in his Rumanian subordinates, particularly the senior officers. Hence his conclusion:

"If these symptoms of insecurity among the Rumanian troops go on being noted for long, it will be necessary to order an immediate retreat on the front behind the Prut on the Galati–Focşani–Carpathians line."

But General Hansen, who had been the "German General in Rumania" since October 1940, held a diametrically opposed opinion. The representative of the Third Reich in Bucharest, Ambassador von Killinger, telegraphed Ribbentrop on August 10: "Situation absolutely stable. King Michael guarantees the alliance with Germany."

Certainly this diplomat was not very highly thought of by Ribbentrop, but Marshal Antonescu had the entire confidence of Hitler. That is why, in view of Hitler's optimism, nothing was prepared by the Germans to ease the consequences of a "defection".

The German armies' retreat in the Balkans which avoided destruction in 1944.

CZECHOSLOVAKIA

Brno

Army Group "South"
8th Army

Košice

4th Ukrainian Front

U.S.S.R.

Danube

Vienna

AUSTRIA

6th Army

Graz

Uzhgorod

Mukachevo

Miskolc

Komárom

Eger

Hatvan

Nyiregyháza

Debrecen

2nd Ukrainian Front

3rd Ukrainian Front

Dniestr

Tiraspol

Győr

Budapest

Lake Velencei

Székesfehérvár

Lake Balaton

Karcag

Mezőtúr

HUNGARY

Szolnok

Kecskemét

Csongrád

Szeged

Oradea

Salonta

Rumanian 4th Army

8th Army (Wöhler)

Iasi

Prut

Siretul

Husi

Leovo

6th Army

Dunaföldvár

2nd Panzerarmee

Kaposvár

Barcs

Pécs

Mohács

Baja

Cluj

Alba Iulia

Galati

Rumanian 3rd Army (Dumitrescu)

Army Group "South Ukraine"

Zagrab

Drava

RUMANIA

Sibiu

Brasov

Army Group "E"

Sava

YUGOSLAVIA

Belgrade

Turnu Severin

IRON GATES

Bucharest

Constanta

Fiume

Zara

Spalato

Sarajevo

Visegrad

Užice

Kraljevo

Danube

Giurgiu

Silistra

Ruse

Varna

Novi Pazar

Niš

XXII Mountain Corps

Mitrovica

Bulgarian 5th Army

Pleven

Burgas

XXI Mountain Corps

Ragusa

Cattaro

Scutari

Skopje

Sofia

Plovdiv

BULGARIA

Istanbul

ALBANIA

Durazzo

Tiranë

Vardar

XIC Corps

Salonika

ITALY

Valona

LXVIII Corps

Metsovon

Yannina

GREECE

TURKEY

Kos

Milos

Tilos

Rhodes

Megara

Athens

Patrai

Corinth

Crete

FRONT LINE ON AUGUST 20 1944

FRONT LINE ON OCTOBER 6

FRONT LINE ON OCTOBER 25

FRONT LINE ON NOVEMBER 25

FRONT LINE ON DECEMBER 31

2nd UKRAINIAN FRONT ATTACKS

3rd UKRAINIAN FRONT ATTACKS

4th UKRAINIAN FRONT ATTACKS

FRONT BOUNDARIES

GERMAN COUNTER-ATTACKS AND RETREATS

ISLANDS HELD BY THE GERMANS UNTIL THE END OF THE WAR

ARMY GROUP BOUNDARIES

ARMY BOUNDARIES

AXIS POCKETS

AREAS HELD BY YUGOSLAV PARTISANS IN JANUARY 1945

On the vital day, that is at dawn on August 20, Army Group "South Ukraine" was divided into two sections:
1. From the Black Sea to Korneshty, *Armeegruppe* "Dumitrescu" included the Rumanian 3rd Army (General Dumitrescu) and the German 6th Army (General Fretter-Pico).
2. From Korneshty to the Yablonitse pass (contact on the right with Army Group "North Ukraine") *Armeegruppe* "Wöhler" put the German 8th Army (General Wöhler) and the Rumanian 4th Army (General Steflea) into the field.

So, of 250 miles of front, 100 were defended by Rumanian troops but, for reasons of security, "integration" as it is now called, of the Axis forces had gone as far as army level and, in some places, down to corps level. The system, which in his jargon Hitler had curiously named "whalebone stays", was at its height here. It was – ignoring for the moment the plans

of King Michael and the suspicions of Colonel-General Friessner – to ignore the wisdom of the old saying that a chain is only as strong as its weakest link.

As usual, the Soviet sources say nothing of the numbers of men which the *Stavka* put at the disposal of Generals Malinovsky and Tolbukhin; the Germans, for their part, calculate them as 90 or 94 infantry divisions and seven tank corps. In armoured strength alone, this gave the attackers an advantage of at least five to one. In his centre of gravity, which pivoted on Iaşi, Malinovsky had massed 125 guns and mortars per mile. Tolbukhin's advance from the Tiraspol bridgehead was, in addition, aided by 7,800 guns. Soviet aircraft dominated the skies and, during the preparation of the attack, the Red Air Force co-operated with the artillery in attacking enemy positions, then transferred its effort to attack the Germans' reserve armour.

Cheerful Russians are greeted by Rumanian musicians as they enter Rumania.

By the evening of August 20, both Malinovsky and Tolbukhin had already gained victory. In the German 8th Army, IV Corps (General Mieth) resisted fiercely in the outskirts of Iaşi, but the Rumanian IV Corps on its left foundered in spite of the help of the 76th Division. *Armeegruppe* "Dumitrescu" had been attacked at the link-point between the German 6th Army and the Rumanian 3rd Army, and the rupture was even more decisive after the collapse of the two Rumanian divisions which completed General Brandenberger's XXIX Corps. And while the Russians followed up their advantage, Friessner had already used up his armoured reserves (13th Panzer Division, 10th *Panzergrenadier* Division, and Rumanian 1st Armoured Division).

In this situation, there was nothing Friessner could do but take the responsibility himself of ordering his army group to retreat without waiting for Hitler's authorisation. He did so that same evening. But, as he himself remarked:

"In spite of the preparations we had made in more leisurely moments, we were naturally unable to disengage ourselves from the enemy methodically. The way the situation was developing, any movement of ours could only be carried out under the enemy's control and only step by step. This was not now a retreat, it was a fighting withdrawal."

The *Führerbefehl* reached Friessner on August 22. The following day King Michael summoned Antonescu and his Minister of Foreign Affairs to the palace and ordered them to conclude an immediate armistice with the Allies. The Marshal's reply was vague, and the King immediately had them both arrested. Then, at 2200 hours, Radio Bucharest broadcast the cease-fire order to all Rumanian forces. When the commander of Army Group "South Ukraine" heard the news, he rang up Generals Dumitrescu and Steflea. Both men refused to disobey the oath of loyalty they had sworn to their sovereign. At the same time, Ambassador von Killinger and General Hansen were confined to the German legation.

Hitler was totally surprised by this turn of events and, without even warning Friessner of his intentions, ordered Luftwaffe formations based on Ploieşti to bomb Bucharest, concentrating particularly on the Royal Palace and the Prime Minister's residence. This was a particularly stupid thing to do and the new Prime Minister, General Sanatescu, took advantage of it to declare war on the Third Reich on August 25. As a result, Rumanian troops occupied the Danube, Prut, and Siretul crossings, opening them to the Russians.

This was followed by a complete disaster for the German 6th Army. Cut off from the Danube by Tolbukhin's armour, which had pushed through as far as the Prut at Leovo, it could not cross the river higher up because that would have thrown it into the arms of Malinovsky, whose 6th Guards Tank Army (Colonel-General Chistyakov) had pushed on swiftly from Iaşi towards Huşi. Fourteen German divisions were annihilated in the pincers thus formed, and only two divisional commanders escaped death or capture. All four corps commanders were taken prisoner. In the German 8th Army, IV Corps, which had retreated along the right bank of the Prut, was trapped by the Russian 2nd Ukrainian Front, and the remains of its 79th and 376th Divisions were forced to lay down their arms with their commanders, Lieutenant-Generals Weinknecht and Schwarz. General Mieth did not suffer the same humiliation, having succumbed in the meantime to a heart attack. To sum up, of 24 German divisions which he had under his command on August 20, Colonel-General Friessner had lost 16 in the space of a fortnight. The Soviet communiqué of September 5 claimed 105,000 German dead and 106,000 prisoners.

Seeing their country subjected to the Communist yoke and enslaved to the U.S.S.R., certain emigré Rumanians see the events of August 23 as the cause of their country's unfortunate fate. In this they do not appear to be correct. In the first place the destruction caused by the war on land stopped at the left bank of the Danube and the Siretul and the cease-fire saved the lives of hundreds of thousands of young Rumanians, for the battle for Moldavia and Bessarabia was already irrevocably lost, and in the worst conditions.

It is also evident that neither King Michael nor those who had advised him could imagine that they would be purely and simply abandoned to the Communist subversion ordered from a distance by Moscow. Having re-established the liberal constitution of 1921, restored political rights, and freed political prisoners, they counted on being granted the benefits of the Atlantic Charter of August 14, 1941 and the principles it had proclaimed in the face of Hitler.

But the fatal process was already under way. The Rumanian emissaries who had arrived in Cairo were sent to Moscow. The British and Americans agreed to appear in the background in the armistice agreement, which was signed on September 12 between King Michael's plenipotentiaries and Marshal Malinovsky, who spoke for the governments of the U.S.S.R., Great Britain, and the U.S.A., but was the only one to sign. What was more serious was that, while Ambassador Bogomolov sat as an equal partner in the organisation charged with carrying out the Italian armistice, the Allied commission set up by Article 18 of that agreement, with the same rôle, had its activity strictly limited; it read:

"The Allied Commission will follow the instructions of the Soviet High Command (Allied) acting in the name of the Allied Powers."

On the military side, it is also worth noting that the armistice of September 12 obliged Rumania to declare war on Germany and Hungary and pursue it with a minimum of 12 divisions, placed under the "Soviet High Command (Allied)". But already, on September 6, the Bucharest Government had declared war against Hungary.

And so it was as on a peace-time route march that Marshal Malinovsky sent 25 divisions of his front from Wallachia to Transylvania, while his left marched towards Turnu Severin on the frontier with Yugoslavia. By September 1, Tolbukhin had reached Giurgiu on the Danube.

The Rumanian cease-fire raised the question of Bulgaria. The situation in Sofia was as follows. On December 12, 1941 King Boris had declared war against the United States and Great Britain but, for historical reasons, had been careful not to engage in hostilities against the Soviet Union. On his mysterious death, which occurred on August 28, 1943 after a visit to Hitler, a Regency Council, composed of his brother Prince Cyril, Professor Filov, and General Michov, assumed power in the name of King Simon II, who was only a child.

It was thus logical that the Regents should send a delegation to Cairo to enquire about the armistice conditions that London and Washington might be willing to grant them. At the same time they formed a democratic-style government and denounced the Anti-Comintern Pact, which Bulgaria had joined on November 25, 1941.

These peaceful overtures were received by Stalin, on September 5, by a declaration of war. The Bulgarian Government thought it could counter this by declaring war against Germany on September 8. For the Kremlin the important point was to bring the negotiations to Moscow and exclude the British and the Americans. The signing of the armistice took place in Moscow on October 28 and General Maitland Wilson, commander-in-chief of the Allied forces in the Mediterranean, was reduced to the rôle of a mere spectator. Meanwhile, forces of the 3rd Ukrainian Front had penetrated Bulgaria at Silistra and Ruse, amid popular acclaim. Several days later the Gheorghiev government, preponderantly Communist, was formed. Soon the reign of terror began in Bulgaria. Dismissed, imprisoned, dragged before a carefully selected court, all three Regents fell before a firing squad on February 2, 1945. They were naked, as a diplomat at the time posted to Sofia recounted later, because the authorities wanted to preserve their clothes.

Following the declaration of war on September 8, Bulgaria sent its 5th Army against Germany. It was commanded by General Stanchev and had ten divisions equipped by the Wehrmacht, including one armoured division which had just received 88 Pzkw IV tanks and 50 assault guns. Acting as Marshal Tolbukhin's left wing, it was given the task of cutting the Germans' line of retreat as they pulled back from the Balkans. It was only partially successful in this, as we shall see in the following pages.

On August 23, the German forces occupying Albania, mainland Greece, and the Aegean Islands came under Colonel-General Löhr, commanding Army Group "E" with headquarters at Salonika. These forces were subdivided into four corps (Tiranë, Yanina, Athens, and Salonika) totalling ten divisions (seven of which were on the mainland) and six fortress brigades: in all, about 300,000 men, to whom must be added 33,000 sailors (most of whom were attached to the coastal artillery) and 12,000 airmen and anti-aircraft gunners.

Men and women of the Greek Communist resistance group E.L.A.S. dressed and armed with uniforms and weapons from both the Allied and Axis armies.

The day following the Rumanian cease-fire, Löhr was confronted by an order from O.K.W. ordering him to begin evacuation of the Aegean and Ionian islands and mainland Greece, south of a line running from Corfu to Métsovon and Mt. Olympus. But a few days later Sofia's declaration of war on Berlin forced Hitler to annul this order and to instruct Army Group "E" to retreat to a line running along the line Scutari–Skopje–Bulgarian/Yugoslav frontier of 1939–Iron Gate Pass on the Danube. On the other side of the river he would be in contact with the 2nd *Panzerarmee* (General de Angelis). The latter would relieve Field-Marshal von Weichs's Army Group "F". In this way a continuous front between the Carpathians and the Adriatic would be formed to bar the enemy from the Danube plain.

Time was pressing, and it was not possible to recover all the 60,000 men who garrisoned the Aegean. Using the very few transport aircraft available and a large number of powered *caiques,* two-thirds of the men were brought back to mainland Greece. The remainder continued to hold Rhodes, Léros, Kos, and Tílos under the command of Major-General Wagner, as well as Crete and the island of Mílos under General Benthak. They remained there until after the end of the war on May 9, 1945.

The evacuation of the Peloponnese gave rise to some clashes between the 41st Division (Lieutenant-General Hauser) and the royalist guerrillas of Napoleon Zervas, opportunely reinforced by the British 2nd Airborne Brigade, which liberated Patras on October 4. All the same, the Germans reached Corinth, then Athens which General Felmy, commanding LXVIII Corps, handed over to the control of its mayor that same day. In Epiros, the troops of XXII Mountain Corps (General Lanz) fought bitter battles with partisans. But, all in all, the evacuation of Greece took place with very few losses and serious delays to the retreating Germans.

Mention should be made here that in 1947, the Greek Government revealed to the United Nations the text of an agreement made between a representative of the 11th Luftwaffe Division and a delegate of the "E.L.A.S." partisans, according to whose terms the men of the "Peoples' Army" agreed not to hinder the German retreat on the condition that they were given a certain quantity of heavy arms and other military equipment for their forthcoming war with the loyalists.

It was in Yugoslavia that things became difficult for Army Group "E". On October 14, the Bulgarian 5th Army took Niš, on the most practical route for the Germans to reach the Danube. In addition, on October 1, Tolbukhin had crossed the Danube near Turnu Severin and then forced his way over the Morava against the resistance of XXXIV Corps' (General F. W. Müller) two divisions. Then the Russians marched on Belgrade. On October 20, working with Marshal Tito's troops, they overcame the final resistance in the streets of the Yugoslav capital, undertaken by *Armeegruppe* "Felber" (Army Group "F").

The fall of Niš had forced Löhr to think of a way to escape the noose and he decided to follow a route through Skopje, Mitrovica, Novi Pazar, and Višegrad. The Belgrade road would have enabled Tolbukhin to cut Army Group "E"'s last line of retreat if his enemy had not opportunely guarded his flanks around Kraljevo and Užice. In short, Colonel-General Löhr established his headquarters at Sarajevo on November 15, having managed to bring his four corps through without being encircled. Marshal Tito's Yugoslav partisans had failed in their attempts to hinder the retreat of Army Group "E" for long enough to allow Tolbukhin to develop his manoeuvre. All the same the partisans sowed hostility behind the Germans' backs in Bosnia and Hercegovina and increased their activities in Croatia and Slovenia. On the Adriatic Coast they liberated Cattaro (Kotor), Ragusa (Dubrovnik), and Spalato (Split) and, on November 8, occupied the Italian town of Zara (Zadar), which would be "slavicised" by means which Hitler would not have disdained.

As has been mentioned, on October 4 a British airborne force had helped to liberate Patras. A few days later, other parachute forces dropped on the aerodromes at Elevsís and Mégara. On October 14, a mixed Greek and British squadron under Rear-Admiral Troubridge dropped anchor in the Piraeus and disembarked most of the British III Corps under the command of Lieutenant-General R. M. Scobie.

This operation, code-named "Manna", had two aims. Following the terms of the armistice, the Bulgarian Government had agreed to return to the borders of April 6, 1941. But although Tito and Gheorghiev reached immediate understanding, the Bulgarian leader cherished the hope of being able to keep the Greek provinces of Western Thrace and Eastern Macedonia within Communist Bulgaria. These provinces had been granted to King Boris by Hitler. Here he knew he could count on the aid of E.L.A.S. (Greek Peoples' Liberation Army).

Furthermore, General Scobie was ordered to prevent, by force if need be, the Peoples' Liberation Army from overturning the established system in Greece by absolutely unconstitutional means. The personality of the prime minister, George Papandreou, gave this régime a liberal, democratic, and social hue to which it was difficult to object. But the danger of subversion was growing day by day and, summoned by a Liberation Committee of Communist inspiration (E.A.M.), units of E.L.A.S. converged on Athens, passing the retreating Germans without clashing.

In spite of the reservations of the White House and the State Department, and the furious onslaughts of the Labour M.P.s Emmanuel Shinwell and Aneurin Bevan, the cold disapproval of *The Times* and the *Manchester Guardian,* everybody knows that Churchill did not hesitate to oppose force with force without heed for his own person. Nevertheless, it was the beginning of a civil war. It would be waged savagely until the day in June 1948 when the quarrel broke between Tito and Moscow. Deprived of the important aid that Tito provided, the insurrection wavered and then collapsed under the blows struck at it in the following year by Marshal Papagos.

Marshal Malinovsky was last seen crossing the Wallachian Carpathians and establishing his front along the Braşov–Sibiu–Alba Iulia line. Doubtless his intention was to push straight on north and to strike the German 8th Army in the rear. This German army had established itself along the Moldavian Carpathians. But Colonel-General Friessner foresaw Malinovsky's plan, and counter-attacked from near Cluj (known then as Koloszvar) in a southerly direction, with the Hungarian 2nd Army (General Veress) and III Panzer Corps (General Breith), which had just been attached to his command. He was able to pull his 8th Army out of the Szecklers salient. In spite of this, a breach was opened between the right of the Army Group "South" (ex-"South Ukraine") and the left of Army Group "F". This breach was weakly held by the Hungarian IV and VII Corps. The 6th Guards Army plunged into it and though Friessner had received five divisions as reinforcements, two from Field-Marshal von Weichs and three from O.K.H., he could not stop Malinovsky establishing himself along a line from Oradea (Nagyvárad) through Arad to Timişoara. And so, on Rumanian soil, was fought the prologue to the battle of Hungary.

The fact that, in this duel between the 2nd Ukrainian Front and the German Army Group "South", Malinovsky needed four attempts and the aid of Tolbukhin to overcome the Axis forces, when the superiority of forces was entirely to his advantage, speaks highly for the tactical ability of the German command and the standard of training of its officers and men. At the beginning of October, with his right to the south of Timişoara and his left on the Carpathians, Colonel-General Friessner could present a line between plains and mountains composed of the following:

1. Hungarian 3rd Army (General Heszlenyi);
2. German 6th Army (General Fretter-Pico); and
3. *Armeegruppe* "Wöhler", with the Hungarian 2nd Army and the German 8th Army.

In all there were nine corps and 26 divisions or their equivalent. True, they were at half their establishment strength. But IV Panzer Corps and the 24th Panzer Division would join the force shortly.

One important point was that in this force there were 14 Hungarian divisions, whose combat performance caused the commander of Army Group "South" some anxiety.

On October 6, the 2nd Ukrainian Front went over to the offensive towards the north-west and the west, and attacked Salonta and south of Arad with the 6th Guards Tank Army and the 53rd and 46th Armies, whose seven tank and mechanised corps gave considerable impetus to the attack. Under the impact, the Hungarian 3rd Army broke, confirming the most pessimistic estimates of Colonel-General Friessner. Even before night had fallen, the Russians were fanning out over the Hungarian plain, some towards Debrecen, some towards Szolnok or Szeged across the Tisza.

Yet the Soviet tanks hurled themselves ahead to exploit their success at a speed that the infantry could not match. Furthermore, the mostly treeless Hungarian plain allowed the Panzers, as in North Africa, to adopt "warship" tactics and seek out the flanks and rear of enemy columns which kept to the roads. On the outskirts of Debrecen on October 10 the 6th Guards Tank Army was trapped in such a manoeuvre by III Panzer Corps while, on its left, the Soviet 27th Army was itself violently halted in front of Mezotúr and Karcag.

In spite of these obstacles, Malinovsky took Debrecen on October 20 and thus, on the 22nd, the armoured group under General Pliev managed to thrust 47 miles into the Tokay vineyards on the left bank of the Tisza. He profited little by it, for he was caught in a pincer from the east and the west near Myregihaza.

On October 30, an O.K.W. communiqué claimed that Malinovsky had lost close on 12,000 killed and 6,662 prisoners, and suffered the destruction or capture of about 1,000 tanks and more than 900 guns. But the losses of the German 6th Army, the temporary victors, were not small. Its six Panzer divisions now had no more than 67 tanks and 57 assault guns.

It was by paying this price that Friessner had checked Malinovsky for the second time in his attempt to cut off the retreat of the German 8th Army and to drive it into a corner in the Carpathians. Now it could align itself on the west bank of the Tisza, with the 6th Army. Following hard behind it, Colonel-General Petrov's 4th Ukrainian Front penetrated the ancient Czech province of Ruthenia. On October 26, it occupied Mukachevo and the day after, Uzhgorod.

In spite of the occupation of Hungary, Admiral Horthy had managed to maintain his secret contacts with the British and Americans. As the situation grew worse he was obliged to give way to the demands of London and Washington, who directed him towards the Soviet Union. And so, at the end of September, Lieutenant-Marshal Farago, once a military attaché in Moscow, slipped away from the watching eye of the Gestapo and arrived in the Russian capital. He was, Horthy tells us, authorised to conclude an armistice, if possible under the following conditions:

"Immediate cessation of hostilities. The British and Americans to share in the occupation of Hungary. Unhindered retreat of German troops."

And so, on October 11, a preliminary armistice agreement received the signature of both parties. Did Stalin mean to press matters so as to place a *fait accompli* before the Western powers while Washington, through Churchill and Eden (then on a visit to Moscow), protested against being left out of the negotiations?

This is the version that Horthy gives in his memoirs. Eden's contain no suggestion of any such procedure. And Churchill, on October 12, 1944, telegraphed to his colleagues:

Churchill and Eden (centre) during their short visit to Athens in February 14, 1945 following the Communist defeat.

"As it is the Soviet armies which are obtaining control of Hungary, it would be natural that a major share of influence should rest with them, subject of course to an agreement with Great Britain and probably the United States, who, though not actually operating in Hungary, must view it as a Central European and not a Balkan State."

From this it is clear that Great Britain, and more so the United States, took little interest in the negotiations in course between Budapest and Moscow.

Meanwhile Admiral Horthy reached full agreement with the Prime Minister, Lakatos, and, at one in the afternoon of October 15, proclaimed an armistice in a broadcast over Budapest radio.

This broadcast was a complete condemnation of Hitler and his policies, and concluded:

"Today for everyone who can see plainly, Germany has lost the war. All governments responsible for the fate of their countries must draw their conclusions from this fact, for, as was said once by the great German statesman Bismarck: 'No nation is forced by its obligations to sacrifice itself on the altar of an alliance.'"

But the secret of the Hungarian-Soviet negotiations had leaked out and Hitler could count on the complicity of the Hungarian Nazis. Everything was ready for a strike. Led by the Ministers Rahn and Weesenmayer, the Waffen-S.S. General von dem Bach-Zalewski, and Colonel Skorzeny, it took place with lightning speed. Admiral Horthy was kidnapped in his mansion in Buda and taken under escort to the castle of Weilheim, close to Munich.

Major Szálasi, leader of the "Arrow Cross", was summoned to replace him, but in spite of his fanaticism and his ferocity, it was beyond his powers to breathe new life into the Hungarian Army. General Vörös, the chief-of-staff, surrendered at Malinovsky's headquarters. So did General Miklos, commander of the 1st Army and Louis Veress, the latter in the motor car which Guderian had just given him. The coup could do nothing to halt the slide of German fortunes in the East, and was a forlorn gesture in the face of the mounting Soviet pressure.

The fall of Szeged around October 10 had forced Friessner to organise a defence line between the Tisza at Csongrád and the Danube at Baja, where he was in contact with Army Group "F". This sector was evidently the weakest, and thus it was here that Malinovsky transferred his 6th Guards Tank Army. On October 29, the 6th reopened the offensive. Its attack was directed on the Hungarian 3rd Army, which broke like a reed and opened the road to Budapest to three Soviet tank corps. In one single movement, they reached Kecskemét, only 40 miles from the capital.

But Friessner and Fretter-Pico did not lose a moment in preparing their defence. In the Budapest bridgeheads III Panzer Corps repelled the attackers and, at the same time, the "Feldherrnhalle" Panzergrenadier Division (Colonel Pape) with the four Panzer divisions of LVII Panzer Corps (General Kirchner) caught the enemy columns in the flank as they moved out of Cegléd. The Russians were better organised than before, and held their ground everywhere except between Debrecen and Nyiregyháza. Moreover, the defection of the Hungarian troops in the centre and on the left of the German 6th Army allowed them to obtain several bridgeheads on the west bank of the Tisza. Even so, Malinovsky had to regroup his forces for the drive which, he hoped, would finish the business.

The Germans were nearing the end of their tether. There were very few infantry battalions which could muster 200 men. The Panzer divisions, so essential for counter-attack, were no longer more than a shadow of what they had been. The consequences of an insufficient inspection and test programme at the end of the factory assembly-lines were mechanical defects which became more and more frequent in the new machines reaching the front. So the number of tanks available to each division daily was no more than five or six.

Even though it is true that the losses of the 2nd Ukrainian Front since October 6 had not been light, it still maintained an enormous numerical and *matériel* advantage over its adversary.

Faced with this situation, Hitler agreed to send three new Panzer divisions into Hungary. These were the 3rd, 6th, and 8th Panzer Divisions. He also sent three battalions of Panther tanks. But while waiting for these reinforcements to be put into line, Army Group "South" had to fall back from the Tisza above Tokay and dig in on the heights of the Mátra mountains, overlooking Hatvan, Eger, and Miskolc. It had to limit its counter-attacks to local actions only, as a result of the previously mentioned exhaustion of its men and equipment. And so the curtain fell on the third act of this tragedy, the overall direction of which was assumed by Marshal Timoshenko in the name of the *Stavka*.

Soviet troops run forward past a burning assault gun.

The curtain rose again on November 27 with the appearance on the stage of the forces of the 3rd Ukrainian Front, available now that Belgrade had surrendered. On that day, Marshal Tolbukhin unexpectedly forced the Danube at Mohacs. This was 125 miles up river from Belgrade past the confluence of the Drava and the Danube. Brushing aside the weak defences of the 2nd *Panzerarmee,* his 57th Army swept along a line from Pécs to Kaposvár and, by December 5, called a halt after an advance of 75 miles between the south-west tip of Lake Balaton and the River Drava at Barcs.

On December 3, on Tolbukhin's right, the 3rd Guards Army arrived at Dunaföldvár, 60 miles north of Mohacs. As a result, in order to avoid its right being rolled up, the German 6th Army could only pull back along a line Lake Balaton–Lake Velencei–Budapest.

Tolbukhin's advance northward allowed his partner Malinovsky to re-arrange his deployment yet again. At the foot of the Mátra mountains, he built up a strategic battering-ram, with the Pliev Group and the 6th Guards Tank Army. Near Hatvan on December 7, the exhausted German 6th Army broke under the force of the attack launched by the Russians and, several days later, Pliev reached the elbow formed by the Danube above the Hungarian capital and could now bring the strings of barges which supplied it under the fire of his artillery. Furthermore, between the Danube and the Mátra mountains, on December 14, Soviet armour captured Ypolisag. And so the Russians had almost completely out-flanked the right of the 8th Army, and were once more threatening to hem it in against the Carpathians.

However the 8th Panzer Division, newly arrived, was immediately put under the command of LVII Panzer Corps, and this formation kept disaster at bay. Friessner would have liked to reinforce Kirchner with the 3rd and the 6th Panzer Divisions, which had just been stationed on the isthmus which separates Lakes Balaton and Velencei. If they hurried, he maintained, there was a great opportunity to crush the 6th Guards Tank Army, which was in a salient around Ypolisag. When Hitler received this proposal, he ordered Friessner to attack from the isthmus between the two lakes and to throw Tolbukhin back to the Danube. To which the commander of Army Group "South" retorted that the state of the ground between Lake Balaton and the Danube, after long weeks of sleet and rain, was absolutely impassable.

Guderian forced a very poor compromise in this dispute on December 18: the *Führerbefehl* would be carried out when frost had hardened the ground. Meanwhile, the 3rd and 6th Panzer Divisions would cross the Danube at Komarom, carry out Friessner's proposed counter-attack, but leave their tank battalions behind. In vain did Friessner

protest that this plan would deprive them of their entire striking power. He was told that he should either obey or resign. This is the version that Friessner gives of this episode, and Guderian's silence on it seems to indicate that he agrees.

Forty-eight hours later, Tolbukhin was attacking the sector between the Danube and Lake Balaton defended by III Panzer and LXXII Corps (General August Schmidt) of the 6th Army. In front of him roved a first echelon of about ten divisions which, very cleverly, moved along the roads impassable to tanks because of the soft terrain. Between the river and Lake Velencei, the 217th *Volksgrenadier* Division was crushed on the first day. Between Lake Velencei and Lake Balaton, the 153rd Infantry Division and the 1st and 23rd Panzer Divisions defended the little mediaeval town of Székesfehérvár to the end, without the tanks held in reserve by Guderian's express order being of any help to them. By December 24, all was over and the Kremlin communiqué claimed that the Germans had lost 12,000 dead, 5,468 prisoners, 311 tanks, and 248 guns destroyed or captured.

On the same day Tolbukhin launched his armoured formations through this gap, now over 40 miles wide. On December 27, after an excursion of 55 miles through the rearguard of the Army Group "South", they occupied Esztergom on the right bank of the Danube and, from the other side of the river, recognised the 6th Guards Tank Army that LVII Panzer Corps had been quite unable to dislodge.

On December 1, the Führer had proclaimed that the Hungarian capital was a "fortress". This took it out of the authority of Army Group "South". The garrison consisted of the S.S. IX Mountain Corps (General Pfeffer-Wildenbruch). When Friessner realised that the 3rd Ukrainian Front was attacking, he wan-

Russians man a 45-mm anti-tank gun during the fierce fighting in Budapest.

ted to take it in flank by a counter-attack with this corps, but the manoeuvre would involve the evacuation of Budapest. So, on the night of December 22/23, Friessner was relieved and ordered to hand over to General Wöhler. Fretter-Pico shared his disgrace.

Two S.S. cavalry divisions, the 13th Panzer Division, and the *"Feldherrn-halle" Panzergrenadier* Division were thus caught in the trap. Having got them cut off, Hitler now had to get them out, so without consulting O.K.H., he robbed Army Group "Centre", which was responsible for the defence of East Prussia. He took IV S.S. Panzer Corps (General Gille: 3rd *"Totenkopf"* Panzer Division and 5th *"Wiking"* Panzer Division) and sent them over the Carpathians. This order was made on Christmas Day, and, though Guderian tried to have the units recalled, he wrote:

"All my protests were useless. Hitler thought it was more important to free the city of Budapest than to defend Eastern Germany."

The day before, while Guderian tried to draw Hitler's attention to the increasing number of signs pointing to a coming Soviet offensive between the Carpathians and the Niemen, the Führer had riposted:

"Now, my dear General, I do not believe in this Russian attack. It is all a gigantic bluff. The figures produced by your 'Foreign Armies: East' section are far too exaggerated. You worry too much. I am firmly convinced that nothing will happen in the East."

Obsession with the Soviet threat could deceive Major-General Gehlen, head of "Foreign Armies: East" of O.K.H.; it could even impress Colonel-General Guderian. But it had no effect on the far-sightedness and *sang froid* of the Führer!

CHAPTER 67

Arnhem and the Allied autumn campaign

General Bradley has described his stupefaction on learning of Operation "Market Garden" which Montgomery had got Eisenhower to approve and with which Bradley did not agree:

"Had the pious teetotaling Montgomery wobbled into S.H.A.E.F. with a hangover, I could not have been more astonished than I was by the daring adventure he proposed. For in contrast to the conservative tactics Montgomery ordinarily chose, the Arnhem attack was to be made over a 60-mile carpet of airborne troops. Although I never reconciled myself to the venture, I nevertheless freely concede that Monty's plan for Arnhem was one of the most imaginative of the war."

In effect the "carpet" over which XXX Corps was to advance towards the northern outskirts of Arnhem was 60 miles long and criss-crossed six times by canals and watercourses. Eisenhower had put at Montgomery's disposal the 1st Airborne Army. Commanded by U.S. Lieutenant-General L. H. Brereton, it engaged its I Airborne Corps (Lieutenant-General F. A. M. Browning) as follows:

1. U.S. 101st Airborne Division (Major-General Maxwell D. Taylor) would take Eindhoven by surprise and seize the bridges on the Wilhelmina Canal, the Dommel, and the Willems Canal;
2. U.S. 82nd Airborne Division (Major-General James M. Gavin) would take the Grave bridge over the Maas and the Nijmegen bridge over the Waal (the southern arm of the Rhine); and
3. British 1st Airborne Division (Major-General R. E. Urquhart) would take the bridges over the Neder Rijn (the northern arm of the Rhine) at Arnhem. It would then establish a bridgehead around the town and be reinforced by the Polish 1st Parachute Brigade, then by the British 52nd (Airportable) Division.

It was along the corridor opened up by these forces that the three divisions of the British XXX Corps (the Guards Armoured, the 43rd, and the 50th Divisions) under Horrocks were to advance towards Arnhem and, breaking out of the bridgehead, drive on at full speed to the Zuiderzee, a final run of about 37 miles.

All things considered, it does seem that Operation "Market Garden" relied heavily on what Frederick the Great called "Her Sacred Majesty Chance" and the expectation that she would favour Generals Browning and Horrocks for several days and under all circumstances. Even had she favoured them throughout, however, it is unlikely that XXX Corps could have made the run to Berlin all alone, as Eisenhower had no strategic reserves or logistic resources to exploit fully any initial success of this risky enterprise.

Yet XXX Corps' advance had to take place up a single road flanked by low-lying country, covered with a network of drainage ditches. This was to provide ideal terrain for the Germans to slow down or even halt the advance with a tenacious anti-tank defence, while launching flank attacks against XXX Corps' own communications. And this, in fact was what was to happen.

Although Montgomery knew from intelligence reports that two Panzer divisions were re-fitting north of Arnhem, he believed them incapable of effective action and Horrocks, the commander of XXX Corps, was not even informed that these German forces lay so near the battle area.

Operation "Market Garden" would clearly involve a great deal of risk; and it seemed a highly dangerous operation to informed critics such as Bradley, who wrote later:

". . . as soon as I learned of Monty's plan, I telephoned Ike and objected strenuously to it. For in abandoning the joint offensive, Monty would slip off on a tangent and leave us holding the bag. But Ike silenced my objections; he thought the plan a fair gamble. It might enable us to outflank the Siegfried Line, perhaps even snatch a Rhine bridgehead."

Events were to prove Bradley all too right.

On Sunday September 17, 1944, zero hour struck at 1430. Under the near or distant cover of 1,200 fighters the first elements of Lieutenant-General Browning's three airborne divisions, which had been packed into 2,800 aircraft and 1,600 gliders, jumped or landed as close as possible to their objectives without undue losses.

For the 101st Airborne Division all went well, except for the Son bridge over the Wilhelmina Canal which it could not save from destruction. The 82nd managed to surprise the Grave bridge, but in the evening, when the Germans had got over the shock, it failed in its first attempt on Nijmegen. By this time General Student had got the plans for "Market Garden" which had been found on board an American glider shot down behind the German lines. Because of heavy A.A. fire round Arnhem it had been decided that the first echelon of the British 1st Airborne Division would drop in heath-land seven miles from the Neder Rijn bridges. Moreover there were not enough aircraft to carry the whole division in one lift, so that three successive drops were necessary.

H.Q. Army Group "B" was at Oosterbeek, and here Field-Marshal Model watched the landing and nearly got put in the bag together with his general staff. He jumped into a car, alerted General Bittrich, commanding II S.S. Panzer Corps, and counter-attacked with the 9th "Hohenstaufen" Panzer Division through Arnhem and the 10th "Frundsberg" along the left bank of the Neder Rijn.

The British no longer had surprise in their favour, and were losing the initiative; now problems mounted as for technical and topographical reasons, their radio communications broke down. The divisional commander, Urquart decided to go up to the front himself, and within minutes he had lost all means of co-ordinating the movements of his division. Towards 2000 hours Lieutenant-Colonel Frost's battalion, whose commander had led the raid on Bruneval in 1941, had reached a point opposite the road bridge at Arnhem, but was almost surrounded.

Supported on the left by XII Corps and on the right by VIII Corps (Lieutenant-General Evelyn H. Baring), XXX Corps got off to a good start. Admirably supported, as its commander said, by No. 83 Group, Tactical Air Force (Air Vice-Marshal H. Broadhurst), it reached Valkenswaard at the end of the day. A day later its Guards Armoured Division was at Son, where the bridge over the canal was repaired by dawn on the 19th. There was good contact with the 82nd Airborne Division, which had resumed its attack on Nijmegen, but without much success.

By now it had begun to rain. "Market Garden", in fact, enjoyed only one day of blue skies out of ten. Were the weather forecasts ignored? There were consequential delays in the reinforcement of the airborne divisions and a notable drop in efficiency of the ground support. XXX Corps had only one axis along which to advance its 23,000 vehicles. During the 19th, Horrocks was able to get his tanks from Son to Nijmegen (36 miles), but it was not until the evening of the following day that the British and the Americans, fighting side by side, succeeded in crossing the Waal and seizing the road and rail bridges which Model had ordered to be left intact for a counter-attack.

When he had been given his orders in Monty's caravan the day before "Market Garden" was launched, Browning had asked how long he would be required to hold the bridge at Arnhem.

"Two days" said Monty briskly. "They'll be up with you by then."

"We can hold it for four" Browning replied. "But I think we might be going a bridge too far."

The operation was now in its fifth day, and during the night of September 19-20 Urquhart had had to resign himself to abandoning Frost to his fate and to pulling his unit into the district of Oosterbeek with its back to the Neder Rijn. The bad weather continued, air supplies were reduced to practically nothing, and what was dropped fell equally amongst the Germans and the Allies. In the evening of the 21st, Lieutenant-Colonel Frost was seriously wounded and his battalion, now reduced to about 100 men, was captured by the Germans. On the 21st and 22nd the Polish 1st Parachute Brigade

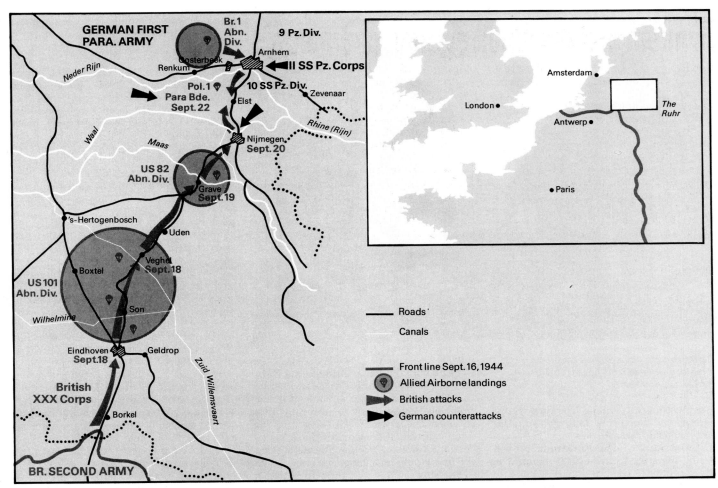

Operation "Market Garden" was an imaginative plan which went wrong because of unexpected logistic problems.

(Major-General Sosabowski) landed almost opposite Oosterbeek, whilst the Guards (Major-General Allan Adair) and the 43rd Division (Major-General Ivor Thomas) were caught in flank by the 10th *Frundsberg* S.S. Panzer Division as they tried to cover the ten miles between the Waal and the Neder Rijn. XXX Corps' forward positions, now sticking out like a finger in the German lines, risked being cut off at any moment from either east or west.

The survivors of the British 1st Airborne Division now received the order to pull back to the left bank of the Neder Rijn. 2,163 of them got across during the night of September 25-26 out of a total of 8,905 officers, N.C.O.s, and men and the 1,100 glider-pilots who had held off the attacks of II S.S. Panzer Corps for the last ten days. The Poles left behind 1,000 of their men and the U.S. 82nd and 101st Airborne Divisions lost respectively 1,669 and 2,074 killed, wounded, and missing. Between September 17 and 30, then, about one-third of the 34,876 men who fought between Eindhoven and Arnhem were lost. The people of Arnhem showed admirable devotion and courage in hiding 250 British paratroopers and helping them to escape: among the lucky ones were Brigadiers J. W. Hackett and G. W. Lathbury.

In a letter dated September 28 and written in his own hand, Field-Marshal Montgomery expressed the admiration he felt at the bearing of Major-General Urquhart's division. Recalling the centuries-old roll-call of famous deeds by British arms, he wrote to him:

"There can be few episodes more glorious than the epic of Arnhem, and those that follow after will find it hard to live up to the high standards that you have set.

"So long as we have in the armies of the British Empire officers and men who will do as you have done, then we can indeed look forward with complete confidence to the future. In years to come it will be a great thing for a man to be able to say 'I fought at Arnhem!'"

History will bear out this judgement. It is not certain, however, that it will also ratify Montgomery's conclusions on the glorious and tragic episode. In his opinion, if the success of the undertaking was not as great as had been expected, this was because the supply services, contrary to Eisenhower's orders, refused to cut down on rations for the American 3rd Army. General Bradley thought otherwise and wrote to the C.-in-C. on September 21: ". . . all plans for the future operations always lead back to the fact that in order to supply an operation of any size beyond the Rhine, the port of Antwerp is essential."

On September 4 the Scheldt estuary could have been cleared within a few days, and the rapidity of this success would have been a real shot in the arm to the Allied supply problem. Instead, the operation started on September 29 by the 21st Army Group dragged on for a whole month. By November 3 it was all over, but the Germans had profited from the delay by mining the canal, and clearing operations took another three weeks of dangerous and intensive work. Antwerp's major port facilities thus went unused from September 4 to November 23, whilst less than 90 miles away to the south-west the U.S. 1st Army was reduced to cutting down on petrol and ammunition. There were, of course, the "Red Ball Highways". The American historian Robert W. Merrian, writing of these roads, organised from August 25 onwards by Lieutenant-General J. C. H. Lee, says of the service:

"The Red Ball supply high road grew and grew, like Topsy, until it stretched over 700 well-marked miles, thoroughly equipped with fast wreckage and servicing stations manned twenty-four hours a day. The Red Ball began operating on August 25 with 5,400 vehicles, hauled a daily average of about 5,000 tons of supplies for the eighty-one days of its operation. On its peak day of operation, over 12,000 tons of supplies were hauled to the front, more than enough for twelve fighting divisions. Operating on a circle route, it was a vast one-way traffic circle, along which raced the life blood of the advancing troops. The driving was hard, the roads

*Allied troops move slowly through
a factory in Oosterbeek, searching
for German snipers.*

merciless on the vehicles, the turnover of equipment staggering, but the supplies were pushed through."

If Operation "Market Garden" proved Allied logistics to have been at fault, it also prejudiced the build-up of a 100-mile salient which was necessary to support Bradley's offensive towards Bonn and Cologne. As Bradley had feared, the British 2nd Army's northwards push ended up between Maastricht, Nijmegen, and Breda. When Antwerp finally got priority Bradley had had to lend two divisions temporarily to 21st Army Group to help in its capture.

Meanwhile the Canadian 1st Army had seized Le Havre (September 12), Boulogne (September 22), and Calais (October 1), capturing more than 28,000 prisoners. The combined effects of Allied bombardment and German destruction meant that it took longer than expected to get the ports working again. Le Havre in particular had had nearly 10,000 tons of bombs dropped on it and by late October was down to 15 per cent of its capacity. The day after the capture of Boulogne, however, the Allies were able to lay between this port and Dungeness a second 16-tube pipeline, which greatly alleviated the Allied petrol problem.

On the eve of the German offensive in the Ardennes it was possible to discern on the Allied side a certain degree of frustration similar to that prevailing in Britain and America immediately before the breakthrough at Avranches.

On September 15, victory seemed to be close at hand. Three months later, General Eisenhower could indeed claim to have liberated Mulhouse, Belfort, Strasbourg, and Metz, to have taken Aix-la-Chapelle (Aachen), cleared Antwerp and the Scheldt estuary, and taken more than

150,000 prisoners. Nevertheless, on December 15 the Rhine bridges and Ruhr basin were, if anything, further away from the Allied armies than at the end of the summer. It was clear to everyone that between the present positions and the final objective, there would be more major battles; however, no one suspected that the first would be a defensive one.

The slowing down of the Allied thrust can be explained by a combination of factors: bad logistics, the terrain, the degrees of determination shown and decisions made by commanders on both sides of a front line that ran from the Swiss frontier to the North Sea. As far as the weather was concerned, persistent rain fell throughout the latter part of the summer and the autumn of 1944, so much so that during the Ardennes offensive Patton required his chaplain to write a prayer for fine weather. The unseasonable climate and the shorter days resulted in a disastrous drop in the number of sorties effected by the tactical air forces in support of the infantry. The figures below relating to the American 3rd Army are typical of the whole front:

August 12,292 missions (396 per day)
September 7,791 missions (260 per day)
October 4,790 missions (154 per day)
November 3,509 missions (117 per day)
December
(1–22) 2,563 missions (116 per day)

Knowing the use made of their "flying artillery" by the Allies in the battle of Normandy, it is not surprising that such a reduction told heavily on the Allied advance. Furthermore, the terrain was now one of forest and mountain, country well-suited to a defensive strategy, in the sense that lines of attack were pressed into comparatively few axes that were easy to block. The Vosges, Hunsrück, and Eifel were such regions, and, in addition, their vast forests made aerial reconnaissance virtually impossible and reduced considerably the feasibility of air support. On

the plains of Lorraine, the defence made good use of flooded rivers as natural obstacles, as well as of the system of fortifications round Metz and Thionville. The Roer and the *Westwall* system fulfilled the same rôle in the Aix-la-Chapelle (Aachen) sector.

The British and Canadians soon found themselves obliged to mount amphibious operations.

As regards strategic factors behind the hold-up, it should be remarked that in Washington, General Marshall had been somewhat over-stringent in calculating the numbers to allocate to American ground forces, and that Eisenhower now found himself short of divisions, although it had seemed improbable that after two months of movement and retreat the enemy would manage to establish himself on a continuous front of some 500 miles, and thwart some 60 Allied divisions in their hopes of achieving a decisive breakthrough. In these circumstances, the Pentagon was obliged to turn various anti-aircraft units into infantry units, but the inactivity of the Luftwaffe caused no problem here.

Even so, at the time of transferring S.H.A.E.F. from Granville to Versailles, Eisenhower would have been somewhat embarrassed if a miracle had brought him the 30 additional divisions he needed to return to the attack. As it was, the logistic problem of keeping 60 divisions in the field was a major problem.

Clearance of the approaches to Antwerp enabled the Allies to end the vicious circle, although it took Field-Marshal Montgomery one more month to achieve this; and during the delay two divergent operations, in flagrant disregard of the "concerted thrust" which Montgomery had urged, took place. While the British 2nd Army, its right flank at Grave on the Maas, its left at Eindhoven, mounted an attack north-west towards Tilburg and Breda, the American 1st and 9th Armies were trying to breach the *Westwall* in the Aix-la-Chapelle (Aachen) sector, with the aim of reaching the Rhine below Cologne.

Obviously, Eisenhower's task was not an easy one. To appease Patton, he organised an American 9th Army on September 5 under the command of Lieutenant-General William H. Simpson, with the immediate objective of taking Brest. Once this fortress had fallen, the 9th Army was shifted to the Ardennes front, then on October 23, to the left of the 1st Army, with which it participated in the November offensive on the *Westwall*. Coming under General Bradley's command, it provided the link with the British and Canadian 21st Army Group.

On September 15, at Vittel, Lieutenant-General Jacob L. Devers assumed command of a new Allied 6th Army Group, directly subordinate to S.H.A.E.F. and responsible for the conduct of operations between Epinal and the Swiss frontier. In the course of these changes, Army Detachment "B" was designated as French 1st Army on September 19. Then, to give Generals Patch and de Lattre homogeneous sectors, the French II and American VI Corps were interchanged. On September 29 General Patton was ordered to hand his XV Corps over to the American 7th Army.

Such was the disposition of the Allied armies in preparation for the autumn campaign.

On September 4, when Hitler relieved Field-Marshal von Rundstedt as Commander-in-Chief in the West, a document prepared at O.K.W. gave the following situation for the German Army on the Western Front.

	Infantry divisions	Panzer divisions
Completely fit	13	3 (+ 2 brigades)
Partially fit	12	2 (+ 2 brigades)
Totally unfit	14	7
Dissolved	7	–
In process of reorganisation	9	2

Hence Rundstedt was faced with the task of giving battle with 30 divisions (five of them Panzer), these to be joined by 11 divisions being reorganised, thus enabling those qualified as "totally unfit" to be pulled back. Furthermore, Hitler intended to despatch 28 further divisions to the West, these being 28 of the 43 "people's grenadier divisions" (Volks-grenadierdivisionen), which Himmler, as commander of the reserves, was hastily preparing for the line. Their standard of training was very poor, their complement was on the small side (10,000 to 12,000), and their equipment was inferior.

In addition, three more Panzer brigades were assigned to Rundstedt, each of them comprising a battalion of 68 Panthers. At the same time, ten assault gun brigades, several Nebelwerfer brigades, and ten battalions of anti-tank vehicles, some of them equipped with the new and devastating "Jagdpanther", were sent to him. By sacrificing the fully traversing turret, this vehicle combined in its 46 tons the speed of a Panther with the fire-power of a "Königstiger", with an 8.8-cm, 71-calibre gun.

In fact, there was no shortage of new matériel in the arsenals of the Third Reich. While it was perfectly true that, at the front, Army Group "B" could only muster 100 operational tanks, factory production during the summer, in spite of air raids, totalled 1,500. At Dompaire, on September 16, it was established that some of the tanks belonging to the 112th Panzer Brigade, demolished by the French 2nd Armoured Division, bore the manufacturing date of August 15. At Friesen on November 23, Jagd-panthers which were roughly handled by the French 5th Armoured Division during General de Lattre's offensive in upper Alsace, had left Nuremberg only 12 days previously.

"I must hold on for six weeks," Rundstedt wrote on September 7, 1944 in his first report to O.K.W. But if fortune

denied General Weygand the 11-day respite he sought on June 4, 1940, a pause in the fighting of 65 days was granted to Rundstedt, General Bradley being unable to unleash his armies in the drive for the Saar and the Ruhr until November 8.

On October 1 or thereabouts, O.B.W. was responsible for 41 infantry divisions and ten Panzer or Panzergrenadier divisions. On November 26, according to O.K.W. records, these figures were 49 and 14 respectively. Even granted that most of these units were below strength, the effort implicit here in relation to the tricky situation of September 6 was remarkable.

After Arnhem, Rundstedt had two army groups under his command:

1. Army Group "B", in position between the estuary of the Scheldt to a point south of Trier (Treves), still under the command of Field-Marshal Model, Rundstedt's predecessor as Commander-in-Chief in the West.

   Under Model's command were the 15th Army (General von Zangen), whose task was to prevent the enemy obtaining access to the Scheldt estuary; the 1st Parachute Army (Colonel-General Student), at the head of the Arnhem salient between the Tilburg and Venlo areas; and the 7th Army, blocking the way to Cologne, Koblenz and Trier, with, at its head, General Brandenberger, who had succeeded General Eberbach when the latter was taken prisoner at Amiens.

2. The area from south of Trier to the Swiss frontier was the responsibility of Army Group "G". On Hitler's orders, Colonel-General Blaskowitz had handed over command on September 22 to General Balck, whose record on the Russian front was a distinguished one. Army Group "G" consisted of the 1st Army, command of which had been assumed by General Schmidt von Kno-belsdorff, who had made a name for himself at the head of XLVIII Panzer Corps, on September 6, with the task of blocking the route to Saarbrücken from a point north of Thionville to the Château Salins region; the 5th Pan-zerarmee (General von Manteuffel re-placing the wounded General Hausser), blocking the way to Strasbourg from positions in front of the Vosges between Château Salins and Saint Dié; and the 19th Army (General Wiese) holding a position on the upper Moselle and defending the Belfort gap on the Doubs above Montbéliard.

But the idea of a large-scale and decisive counter-offensive was already in the Füh-rer's mind. As early as September 1, realising the Allies' logistic problems, he urged O.B.W. to hurl the 5th Panzerarmee from the Nancy–Neufchâteau area on Rheims with a view to cutting the Ameri-can 3rd Army's lines of communication. The scheme was a hopeless one and its failure brought about Blaskowitz's disgrace.

On September 19, Hitler's strategic

reflections bore fruit again. He summoned General Balck, commander designate of Army Group "G", and Major-General von Mellenthin, his chief-of-staff, and, in Mellenthin's words, gave them the following appreciation of the situation: "According to the Führer, the British and American advance would come to a standstill on a line running from the mouths of the Scheldt, along the Westwall as far as Metz and from there along the Vosges. Supply problems would force the enemy to halt, and Hitler declared that he would make use of this pause to launch a counter-offensive in Belgium. He spoke of mid-November as the proper moment for such an operation."

The longer nights and late autumn mists would provide cover from Allied air reconnaissance and allow the plans to be prepared and carried out, and Hitler had taken the steps of ordering the formation of a 6th Panzerarmee, under the command of Colonel-General Sepp Dietrich of the Waffen-S.S., and of fetching the May 1940 "Fall Gelb" dossier from the archives.

On September 22, while the Battle of Arnhem was at its height, Eisenhower telegraphed Montgomery as follows: "I insist upon the importance of Antwerp. As I have told you I am prepared to give you everything for the capture of the approaches to Antwerp, including all the air forces and anything else you can support. Warm regard. Ike." The note of urgency detectable here would seem to suggest that Montgomery was so taken up with the vision of a lightning break-through towards Westphalia that he had come to give secondary consideration to Eisenhower's orders for the capture of Antwerp. However, failure at Arnhem made Montgomery more prepared to listen to Eisenhower, who this time offered him not only the air strength promised on September 22 but also the American 7th Armoured and 104th Divisions to strengthen the right flank of the 21st Army Group, and free British and Canadian troops for the clearing of the Scheldt. However, not until October 16, did Montgomery give clear and over-riding priority to this operation. But as September was drawing to a close, the German 15th Army, consisting of three corps (seven divisions), had had time to take up strong defensive positions and, even more important, recover morale, which had been badly shaken over the previous weeks. In the main, it responded to General von Zangen's appeal contained in an order of the day on October 7, where Antwerp was referred to as ". . . after Hamburg, the biggest port in Europe.

"When they have taken the Scheldt fortifications, the British will then be able to unload enormous quantities of matériel in a large and perfectly pro-tected harbour. With this matériel they could deal a deadly blow to the northern German plains and to Berlin before the onset of winter . . . The German people are watching us. At this moment the

French infantrymen, with tank support, advance through a forest in Alsace in the autumn of 1944.

Scheldt fortifications play a crucial part in our future. Every day in which we can deny access to the port of Antwerp to the enemy and his resources could be vital."

The fighting that followed was thus very bitter. With General Crerar ill, Lieutenant-General Simonds led the Canadian 1st Army's attack. In the first phase, the British I Corps (Lieutenant-General Crocker) moved northwards from Antwerp, and on October 10 closed the Woensdrecht isthmus giving access to the island of Zuid-Beveland, but only with heavy losses. Meanwhile, the Canadian II Corps (Major-General Foulkes) set about cleaning up the bridgehead, where the Germans had been able to hold on, with the help of flooding, between Knocke and a point opposite Terneuzen. This took three weeks (October 6-26), even though two and subsequently three divisions were ranged against the single 64th Division. According to Major Shulman of Canadian Army Intelligence, the German division put up "an admirable piece of defensive fighting.

"Utilising their experience to the full, they took advantage of the flooded terrain in which they fought and forced the Canadians to rely on the narrow roads and dykes for their forward movement. The morale of the defenders heightened with each day they continued to resist, and General Eberding succeeded in instilling in his troops that will to fight

which had been lacking in the Channel ports." Breskens, opposite Flushing (Vlissingen) fell on October 22, and on November 1 Eberding was taken prisoner.

On October 22, the left flank of the British 2nd Army (XII Corps) attacked from east to west towards 's-Hertogenbosch and Tilburg on a line converging with that taken by the Canadian right flank's thrust towards Breda. A second pincer movement from Woensdrecht and Terneuzen gave Zuid-Beveland to General Simonds on October 31. There remained Walcheren.

The centre of the island is below sea level and the breaching of the sea-dykes (effected with 1,263 tons of bombs) gave it the look of a saucer filled with water, with the defending troops clinging to the rim. These were men of the 70th Division (Lieutenant-General Daser), nicknamed the "White Bread Division", since it comprised men on a special diet for medical reasons. On November 1, with covering fire provided by the battleship *Warspite* and the monitors *Erebus* and *Roberts,* a brigade of Royal Marines landed at Westkapelle, while the British 52nd Division (Major-General E. Hakewill Smith) crossed the Scheldt between Breskens and Flushing. On November 3, resistance on the island was broken. Mopping up operations were completed on November 9, with the capture of Daser. In the meantime, Zangen, assisted by dreadful weather, had succeeded in putting the width of the lower Maas between his troops and the Canadian 1st Army.

It cost the Allies 12,873 casualties

altogether to clear Antwerp, many of whom were Canadians, while 41,043 German prisoners were taken. From November 3 on, mine-sweepers worked to clear the channel, and on the 28th the first convoy berthed in the great port, though on the previous day V-2's had claimed their first military and civil victims there.

But by then, two months had elapsed since the opportunity to take Antwerp on September 4 had occurred, and one is inclined to endorse Jacques Mordal's conclusion on the subject: "Allowing for 40,000 tons a day, the two months lost represented *matériel* amounting to 2,400,000 tons which, if supplied at the time required, would certainly have cost the Allies fewer disappointments in October. And possibly some might have been spared altogether if the people at S.H.A.E.F. had paid more heed to Admiral Ramsay, when he declared that he could think of nothing more vital than Operation 'Infatuate', the capture of Antwerp."

Bradley's 12th Army Group was restricted operationally in October and November as a result of the continued serious shortage of fuel and munitions.

As we have seen, on the express instructions of Eisenhower, the American 3rd Army was especially hard hit in this respect. And the 1st Army, to which General Bradley, acting on instructions, had given priority treatment, faced the *Westwall* and found itself attacking the Germans at their strongest points, since Hitler, Rundstedt, and Model were quite prepared to pay any price to block the principal route through to the Ruhr.

So it was that the October battle for the *Westwall* took on the aspect of an "updated version of the Battle of the Somme" as foreseen by General Gamelin at the time of Munich. The attack was launched on October 8 on a five-mile front. Entrusted to the American XIX Corps (Major-General Corlett: 30th Infantry and 2nd Armoured Divisions), the attack was opened and supported by 372 105- to 240-mm guns and 396 twin-engined bombers and fighter-bombers, while 1,250 four-engined bombers operating on the edge of the sector pounded rail junctions and marshalling yards at Kassel, Hamm, and Cologne.

The attack proceeded slowly across the Wurm which, in the vicinity of Maastricht, constitutes the Dutch-German frontier. In five days, Corlett advanced five miles against the German defences. However, this somewhat moderate success enabled General Hodges, commander of the 1st Army, to push his VII Corps (Major-General J. L. Collins) south-east, and by reaching Stolberg on October 10, he managed to complete the encirclement of Aachen, which had begun during the month of September. The town, with its 4,000 defenders, was reduced by the 1st Division after a week's street fighting. It was the first German city the Allies took.

On the same date, the American 1st Army announced that it had taken 10,000 prisoners since D-Day. During the same

*Mounted in a Sherman chassis,
an American 155-mm "Long Tom"
gun in action, near the Moselle.*

period, it had fired more than 300,000 105- and 155-mm shells, but the munitions crisis now forced it to call a halt.

The 3rd Army, reduced to XII and XX Corps, was marking time in front of Metz. On the right, XII Corps advanced from the area of Grand Couronné to the Seille above and below Nomény; on the left, XX Corps had reached the Moselle between Metz and Thionville, but in the centre its repeated attempts to take *"Kronprinz"* fort, commanding the Nancy–Metz road at Ars-sur-Moselle, failed in spite of the use of napalm, flame-throwers, and machine guns. Detachments of the 5th Division which had found their way into its galleries were finally thrown back with heavy losses.

On October 18, Eisenhower held a conference in Montgomery's headquarters in Brussels. The object of this meeting was to settle the strategic decisions which had to be taken before winter. No one favoured a defensive strategy, but there was disagreement between Montgomery, who still urged a single thrust aimed at the Ruhr, and Bradley, who wanted a simultaneous thrust whereby the 3rd Army would be hurled at Mannheim and Frankfurt and the 9th at Cologne. In support of his thesis, Bradley put forward the arguments which he sums up as follows and which convinced Eisenhower:

"My reasoning on the *double* thrust was quite simple. Were Eisenhower to concentrate his November offensive north of the Ardennes, the enemy could also concentrate his defences there the better to meet that single attack. On the other hand, if we were to split our effort into a double thrust with one pincer toward Frankfurt, we might both confound the enemy and make better use of the superior mobility of our Armies. Patton had the most at stake for if Montgomery's views were to prevail, Third Army would be consigned to the defensive south of the Ardennes and there perhaps wait out the war behind the Moselle River. Could not those divisions be better employed against the Saar, I asked S.H.A.E.F.?"

The northern attack got under way on November 16, and met only qualified success, although Generals Hodges (1st Army) and Simpson (9th Army) had engaged 14, and subsequently 17 divisions, including four armoured. On October 20, however, the 5th *Panzerarmee* took up position between Brandenberger's right and Student's left. Consequently the defence gave ground, but held seven miles further back.

On December 10, a S.H.A.E.F. communiqué announced that between Düren and Linnich all resistance on the left bank of the Roer had stopped: this put the Americans within 25 miles of Cologne, but the communiqué failed to mention that the crossing of the Roer depended on a condition that had not been fulfilled. The American V Corps, attacking upstream, had not, in spite of repeated efforts, suceeded in taking the Roer and Erft dams. And, according to calculations made at General Bradley's headquarters, if the Germans were to breach these dams, an expanse of water, approxi-

mately 1½ miles wide with a maximum depth of more than 25 feet, would form for a few days near Düren, effectively halting the Allied advance.

Whilst Bradley's offensive in the north was at a standstill again, south of the Ardennes, Patton was preparing to force the *Westwall* in the region of Saarlouis, and had already chosen the date December 19 to do so. The transfer of the 5th *Panzerarmee* had left the defence of Lorraine to the German 1st Army alone. In spite of the addition of LXXXIX Corps (General Hoehn), this was reduced to nine divisions (each numbering on average fewer than 10,000 men) spread across a 125-mile front. Facing it, the American 3rd Army, reinforced to three corps (nine divisions, three of them armoured), numbered 250,000 men. Furthermore, Patton had the advantage of surprise, because, on November 8, the rain was so heavy that any important action seemed unlikely.

Sure enough, that evening, XII Corps (General M. S. Eddy: 26th, 35th, and 80th Infantry, 4th and 6th Armoured Divisions) threw aside the three feeble divisions which LXXXIX and XIII S.S. Corps (the latter under General Priess) put in its path and captured Moyenvic and Nomény. Eddy rapidly exploited this success: to the right along the line Château Salins – Morhange – Rohrbach (4th Armoured Division, 35th Infantry Division); to the left by Han-sur-Nied –

A last view of the vaunted Westwall *for a group of German prisoners en route to a P.O.W. camp.*

Faulquemont–Saint Avold (6th Armoured Division, 80th Infantry Division) in spite of counter-attacks by the 17th S.S. *Panzergrenadier* Division *"Götz von Berlichingen"*, then by the 21st Panzer Division. Within XX Corps, the 5th Infantry Division set about outflanking Metz to the south and east of the fortress. The 95th Infantry Division (Major-General Twaddle) crossed the Moselle above Thionville during the night of November 8-9, then turning south met up with the 5th Infantry Division on November 19 on the Metz-Saarlouis road. This was the division's first experience under fire. Meanwhile, the 90th Infantry Division, which had forced a crossing of the Moselle below Thionville and which was followed by the 10th Armoured Division (Major-General W. H. H. Morriss), reached the Franco-German frontier on November 20.

The mopping up of Metz was entrusted to III Corps under Major-General J. Millikin. The fortress works mounted only 30 guns, and the 462nd *Volksgrenadier* Division which constituted its garrison numbered barely 7,000 men. On November 25, fighting in the centre of the town ceased and the Americans found Lieutenant-General Kittel, the fortress commander, severely wounded in hospital. The western fortifications fell one after the other. The "Jeanne d'Arc" Fort, which covered the district round Gravelotte, was the last to capitulate (December 13).

LXXXII Corps (General Sinnhuber) had no better success than XC and XIII S.S. Corps. Furthermore, the reserves which Army Group "G" and O.K.W. made available to give support to the 1st Army were in too poor shape to remedy the situation. So it was that Major-General Walker and his XX Corps were able to bite into the *Westwall*. On December 3, the 95th Infantry Division managed to secure by surprise the bridge over the Saar between Saarlouis and Fraulautern, on the right bank of the river, then secure the right bank area after reducing 50 pill-boxes. On December 18, the 5th Infantry Division joined it in this bridgehead, while slightly downstream the 90th Infantry Division, overcoming two concrete positions, secured a second bridgehead occupying half of Dillingen.

Patton's optimism with regard to the offensive he was preparing for December 19, with the help of 3,000 planes from the Tactical Air Force, appeared to be well grounded. Events would prove otherwise. Even so, between November 7 and December 21, at the cost of 4,530 dead, 21,300 wounded, and 3,725 missing, his army in Patton's own reckoning accounted for 21,300 Germans killed and 37,000 taken prisoner. At O.K.W. Hitler reacted to the 1st Army's defeat by dismissing General Schmidt von Knobelsdorff. On December 4 he was ordered to hand over his command to General Obstfelder.

If for the 12th Army Group victory on the Saar was to some extent compensation for failure on the Roer, the 6th Army Group won so convincing a victory in the Saverne gap and to the south of the Vosges that for a time it seemed likely it would reach positions along the left bank of the Rhine between Lauterbourg and Huningue. Fortunately for the Germans this did not occur, and the opportunity did not come about again.

It has been mentioned above that the American 7th Army had earlier been reinforced by XV Corps (79th Infantry Division and French 2nd Armoured Division). During October it also received the 44th, 100th, and 103rd Infantry Divisions, then after its breakthrough into lower Alsace, the 14th Armoured Division. And the French 1st Army, still responsible for the Mont Blanc–Barcelonnette sector, in addition to keeping its 2nd Moroccan Division (General Carpentier), received the 5th Armoured Division (General de Vernejoul), transferred from North Africa. At the end of November, the 4th Moroccan Mountain Division was relieved of its duties on the French-Italian border by the newly-constituted 27th (Alpine) Division and was transferred to the French 1st Army.

When he established his H.Q. at Vittel, General Devers had seven divisions under his command between Epinal and the Swiss frontier. At the start of the new offensive, his army group numbered 14 divisions, three of them armoured.

Outlining his new mission to General Balck on September 19, Hitler had conveyed to him the paramount necessity, for political reasons, of holding Alsace and Lorraine at all costs. The transfer of the 5th *Panzerarmee* to the Roer sector was not compensated for, however, by new reinforcements, and the German 1st Army had to extend its left flank to block the way to Strasbourg between Château Salins and Raon-l'Etape. Meanwhile the 19th Army had taken up defensive positions on a line linking Saint Dié, Gérardmer, and the western spurs of the Vosges, and ending to the west of Montbéliard in front of the Belfort gap.

The first plan conceived by General de Lattre de Tassigny, whose left flank reached Rupt-sur-Moselle at the end of September, was to force a way across the Vosges by the Col de la Schlucht. He was forced to change his mind, however, and accept Guebwiller as the initial objective for II Corps, which in a later phase of the battle thrust forward vigorously to reach the Rhine at Chalampé, thus pinning the left flank of the German 19th Army back on the Swiss frontier. With this aim, he reinforced General de Monsabert with three further divisions and the support of two others. Nevertheless the plan came to nothing, for two reasons. Firstly, while the French II Corps was struggling to reach the crest of the Vosges, the American 7th Army found itself drawn off in the divergent direction of the Saverne gap, and de Lattre was most reluctantly forced to use some of the troops he wanted to throw into attack for purposes of consolidation. Patch and Devers above him had simply acted in conformity with the instructions they received from S.H.A.E.F., namely to provide cover for the 12th Army Group (3rd Army) in its advance north-eastwards.

Secondly, the very heavy rains of autumn 1944 slowed down infantry, and blinded artillery and aircraft, with the added effect that as winter closed in and the men of II Corps scaled the long slopes of the Vosges, cases of frostbite grew numerous. The leather ankle-boot with its rubber sole was not the most successful article of American equipment.

On October 17, after a fortnight's sustained drive which took the 3rd Algerian Division up the Moselotte as far as Cornimont, General de Lattre decided to change his plans and make a surprise attack on the Belfort gap. But it was important nevertheless that II Corps should not lessen its pressure and allow the enemy to redeploy his forces. The offensive forged ahead, and on November 5 the 3rd Algerian Division (General Guillaume) reached the outskirts of the Col d'Oderen, more than 3,000 feet high; the opposing enemy forces here included as many as 15 infantry battalions as well as the 169th Division, which had been refitted after its return from Finland.

Such deployment of force was combined with a piece of trickery, whose aim (in de Lattre's own words) was "to give the enemy the impression of total security in Vosges sector. Counterfeit troop movements and the setting up of fictitious H.Q.s were made conspicuous in the area of Remiremont. At Plombières a detachment of the 5th Armoured Division set up roadsigns, signposted routes and made full use of radio. All this activity drew the attention of enemy spies and if by chance it escaped them the Intelligence agents were there to open their eyes to what was going on." All these indications were corroborated, in General Wiese's mind, by bogus orders and letters, bearing General de Lattre's personal signature, which reached him from reliable sources. The supreme instance of planned deception being "General Directive No. 4", in which the French 1st Army commander announced his intention of simulating troop concentrations in the region of the Doubs to encourage the enemy to withdraw troops from the Vosges.

At any event the Swiss 2nd Division, in the Porrentruy area, using sound detection apparatus, was able to follow the progressive deployment of powerful artillery on the slopes of the Lomont, for all the discretion the French used in their registration shoots. It is not known whether these indications escaped the notice of the Germans.

De Lattre decided on his plan on October 24: I Corps (General Béthouart) was given the objective of capturing the roads eastwards out of the Belfort gap and simultaneously storming the fortress

town. In the event of success, II Corps would join battle, its objective being the Rhine between Huningue and Neuf-Brisach and the line linking Neuf-Brisach–Colmar–Ribeauville. General Devers, whose intention was to push his 7th Army onwards from Saverne to Strasbourg, fully approved the plan drawn up by his immediate subordinate, and allocated him a battalion each of 203-mm guns and 240-mm howitzers, in addition to other weapons.

General Béthouart's first line troops consisted of the 9th Colonial Division (General Magnan) which, reinforced by a Combat Command of the 1st Armoured Division, was to attack between the Swiss frontier and the Doubs (it should be remarked that his Senegalese troops were relieved by Zouaves and Moroccan light infantry, and F.F.I. [French Resistance forces] recruited in the area); also, of the 2nd Moroccan Division, which was given Montbéliard, Héricourt, and Belfort as objectives. The main action would devolve on this latter division, so it was given two Combat Commands, from the 5th Armoured Division.

On the enemy side, LXIV Corps (General Schalk) was deployed on a 30-mile front. On the left was the 338th Division with its back to the Swiss frontier; on the right the 159th, barring the Belfort direction. These were divisions of poor-quality infantry, mainly composed from heterogeneous elements and of differing morale (there was even one deaf battalion).

They were covered by deep, dense anti-tank minefields whose clearance proved to be particularly hazardous, as they were protected by a fearsome array of anti-personnel devices and explosive traps. Requisitioned workers from occupied France–from the Delle district of Belfort–completed the main construction of a 12-mile anti-tank ditch; this would have constituted a formidable obstacle to the French 1st Army if General de Lattre had deferred the date of his offensive, giving the enemy time to mine it and man its defensive positions.

The attack got under way on November 14 in conditions of sleet, and serious losses were sustained in the minefields. I Corps got a foothold in the enemy positions, but was unable to break through. Two factors favoured the French, however: Lieutenant-General Oschmann, commanding the 338th Division, was killed by a patrol from the 2nd Moroccan Division near the Besançon–Montbéliard road, and his aide-de-camp's briefcase yielded a plan of the division's positions, in addition to copies of several orders. Also, it would appear that for 48 hours, General Wiese's H.Q. minimised the gravity of the French offensive.

At all events, on November 16, the 19th Army received order from Army Group "G" to fall back on to the Belfort–Delle positions. But its LXIV Corps was so enfeebled that its rearguard was overtaken and mauled by the enemy. The main action took place the following day.

On the evening of November 17, the 4th Combat Command (Colonel Schlesser), having adroitly managed to conceal its movement forward from the enemy, took the bridges over the Luzine at Montbéliard by surprise and opened the way for the 2nd Moroccan Division. Near the Swiss frontier, the 9th Division broke through the scanty line of the German 338th Division, enabling Béthouart to unleash the 1st Armoured Division (General du Vigier).

Leaping at the chance, de Lattre the same evening issued a "general order to exploit the situation in full": he issued simultaneous orders to I Corps to head for the Rhine (1st Armoured Division), to reduce the fortress of Belfort (2nd Moroccan Division), and to reincorporate the 5th Armoured Division with a view to attacking Cernay (at a later stage it was his intention to direct it on Colmar and Neuf-Brisach, while the 1st Armoured Division moved towards Sélestat and Strasbourg); at the same time, II Corps would thrust its right forward via Giromagny on Colmar and its left would storm the Col de Bussang and the Col de la Schlucht.

On November 18, the 2nd Moroccan Division, co-operating with the 1st Free French Division (General Brosset) made contact with the defences of Belfort. The 1st Armoured Division, for its part, almost up against the Swiss frontier, crossed the anti-tank ditch mentioned above with barely any loss of momentum and found the bridge over the Allaine at Delle, still intact thanks to the F.F.I. It then took the little town and later that evening destroyed an anti-aircraft unit. The 1st Armoured Division covered more than 18 miles in the course of the day.

A Sherman tank covers a column of American infantry moving up a country lane towards Metz.

The following day the same division covered more than 25 miles. The 3rd Combat Command (Colonel Caldairou) led the column. During its race to the Rhine it encountered only scant resistance and at 1700 hours, after crossing the Ill, it passed through Jettingen, only eight miles from its objective. "Then", wrote de Lattre, "the advance became a charge. At full speed, a detachment commanded by Lieutenant de Loisy, including a group of Sherman tanks and a section of the 1st Zouaves dashed eastwards, Helfranzkirch, Kappeln, Bartenheim . . . Occasional burst of machine gun fire at isolated enemy. Barely four miles more. Rosenau: 15 bewildered prisoners. A quarter of a mile to go. A screen of trees . . . The Rhine! . . . What a moment to be alive! 1830 hours on November 19, 1944, what humiliations avenged! First of all the Allied armies, the French 1st Army reached the banks of the Rhine."

True, to the south of Belfort, the enemy, though thrown back sharply on one flank near Morvillars, was offering stubborn resistance to attacks from the 9th Colonial Division. At the same time the roads between Montbéliard and Morvillars, and Montbéliard and Fesche-l'Eglise was so crowded with vehicles that it proved impossible to clear it for the 5th Armoured Division in time for its new assignment (given in the orders of November 17). Nevertheless, on the 20th, the 3rd Combat Command of the 1st Armoured Division took Mulhouse, and just missed capturing General Wiese; in its wake, Colonel Gruss, at the head of the 1st Combat Command, struck at Altkirch from Seppois-le-Haut. Finally, on the same day, the fortress town of Belfort was completely invested.

At Army Group "G" H.Q., General Balck was in a quandary. On the one hand,

Hitler had given him orders to counter-attack the French 1st Army, cutting off those of its elements that had reached the Rhine; on the other, the American 7th Army offensive in the Saverne sector was likely at any moment to lead to sever the line of his 1st and 19th Armies. Hence on November 20 he suggested to Rundstedt that Schmidt von Knobelsdorf be buttressed with reinforcements intended for the counter-attack, allowing that Wiese could be withdrawn north of Mulhouse. But, characteristically, Hitler was intractable and Balck had no alternative but to set about making the–in his view unworkable–plan work.

The 198th Division was withdrawn from the Saint Dié–Gérardmer sector, brought back over the Schlucht to Dannemarie, from where it launched a counter-attack on November 21 towards the Swiss frontier. At its point of departure, it was reinforced with the 106th Panzer Brigade, equipped with *Jagdpanthers* and Pzkw IV's. On its left it had the support of the 30th S.S. Division, composed of Russian renegades. Torrential rain prevented the French seeing the troop movements behind the enemy lines, as the 198th Division took up position. Furthermore, for the reasons already given, General de Lattre had not been reinforced by the 5th Armoured Division in the time required by his order of November 17. So it was that Schiel broke the weak link in the French lines south of Dannemarie and cut the road, between Delle and Seppois, which constituted the 1st Armoured Division's supply line.

However, on November 22, the 198th Division was itself outflanked by the 5th Armoured Division and the 9th Colonial Division and subjected to a tremendous artillery battering. Forty-eight hours later, General Béthouart, at the cost of furious effort and appreciable losses, cut

American and French troops push into the outskirts of Belfort, sheltering behind a camouflaged Sherman tank.

it in two along the line of the Delle–Seppois road, and the 1st Armoured Division's communications were restored. The greater part of the 308th and 326th Grenadier Regiments fought their last battle with their backs to the Swiss frontier. The ordeal was over by the end of the afternoon of November 24. The German square made an heroic last stand.

The issue here was still undecided when on November 22 de Lattre unleashed II Corps in a manoeuvre that elevated the whole battle from the tactical to the strategic level. On the same day the 2nd Moroccan Division won a fierce struggle to capture the fort and village of Giromagny, and on November 25 the fortress of Belfort was wholly in its possession. This made it possible to surround the German 19th Army by a pincer movement, with II Corps from Belfort moving to join I Corps attacking from a line between Mulhouse and Altkirch, westwards and south-westwards. But in the meantime de Lattre had to release his excellent 1st Free French Division, which had received orders to go and clear the Gironde sector of enemy forces. In addition, de Lattre again found himself short of munitions. Hence it cost considerable effort for General de Monsabert to force a way through and, on November 28, to link up with his comrade Béthouart.

The liquidation of the pocket so formed round the 159th, 198th, and 338th Divisions brought the number of prisoners taken by the French in this action to more than 17,000. More than 10,000 German dead, 120 guns, and 60 tanks, some of them *Jagdpanthers,* littered the battlefield. The French 1st Army losses were

1,440 killed and missing, 4,500 wounded, and 1,694 evacuated with severe frostbite. Among the dead was the intrepid General Brosset, killed in a jeep accident on November 20. General Garbay succeeded him in command of the 1st Free French Division.

So it was that at the beginning of December, for lack of two or three additional divisions, the 1st Army halted its thrust forward on a line linking the Huningue Canal, a point north of Mulhouse, Thann, Saint Amarin, and the Col de la Schlucht.

On the 6th Army Group's left, the American 7th Army, still under General Patch, after an equally promising start experienced similar frustration for similar reasons.

General Devers had given it the job of liberating the plain of Alsace between, and including, Strasbourg and Wissembourg, and of throwing the enemy back across the Rhine. Already, on October 31, the French 2nd Armoured Division had taken the initiative of forcing the Meurthe and pushing beyond Baccarat, so that by D-day, November 13, the American XIII Corps, which had been responsible for the main action, held a line in front of Badonviller, Blâmont, and Réchicourt. Opposing it, the 708th and 553rd Divisions, on the left flank of the German 1st Army, stood across the Saverne gap. General Haislip, commanding XV Corps, had the 79th and 44th Infantry Divisions up, with the French 2nd Armoured Division to exploit the breakthrough, which came on November 16.

To this effect, General Leclerc had been preparing his plan on a huge relief map. On November 10 he summoned Colonel de Langlade, commanding one of his three Combat Commands, and told him: "You must move down into Alsace at top speed... and surprise the Boches beyond possibility of recovery . . . You won't go via Sarrebourg and Saverne, it'll be Dio's job to try that way. All the main roads will be riddled with obstructions . . . you'd be stuck somewhere in the middle... You will see to it to find a way through here . . ."

Thereupon, with a pointer he indicated a network of minor roads starting out from Cirey, twisting and turning in all directions, crossing the White Sarre and the Red Sarre before reaching the Rethel crossroads, six miles south-east of Sarrebourg, deep in the southern spurs of the Vosges.

And Leclerc went on: "Once at Rethel, we'll see, but you'll have to do all you can to take the road following the Dabo; it's the shortest way to drop down onto Wasselonne or Marmoutier in the plain of Alsace. The enemy will be expecting you along the Saverne roads, he won't think of your taking the Dabo, it simply wouldn't occur to him that an armoured division could come through on these mountain tracks . . . All right?"

General de Langlade, as he now is, confesses he felt somewhat aghast at the itinerary he had been given, wondering how his 32-ton Shermans would manage the steep gradients, the curves, and the hairpin bends; he was thinking too that such terrain would be ideal for enemy ambushes and that in any event the torrential and persistent rain of the previous days might have made the route all but impassable.

But Leclerc went on: "Yes, I know, such an itinerary must seem to you madness . . . But it's the right one and will bring you success. Anyway, I'm not asking you to follow every detail of my plan and please don't discuss it. If I've entrusted you with this cavalry mission which seems so fraught with danger, it's precisely because so far you have always carried out my orders swiftly and to the letter. All I ask is for you to go ahead and this time surpass yourself . . ."

Once at Cirey-sur-Vezouse, Leclerc split his force into two parts. On the right, Combat Command "L", incorporating Lieutenant-Colonel de Guillebon's Combat Command "W", set off on the itinerary assigned to it on November 19, with the order: "Go hell for leather!" Matching the deed to the letter, Major Massu, sticking to the Dabo, came out into the plain of Alsace in torrential rain at 0930 on November 21, closely followed by Combat Command "W", which at the end of the day reached and liberated Marmoutier, on the Saverne–Strasbourg road.

On the left, overtaking the 44th Division, Combat Command "D" (Colonel Dio) had the mission of pushing on towards Sarrebourg, Phalsbourg, and Saverne, to the north of the *Route Nationale* 4: so doing it crossed the Marne–Rhine Canal at Xouaxange by a bridge that was still standing, thanks to the local lock-keeper who kept giving *vin gris* to the sappers whose job it was to destroy it. Major Quiliquini was stopped at Phalsbourg, but his frontal assault on the 553rd Division enabled Colonel Rouvillois to outflank the enemy, finding a way round by la Petite Pierre; on the way, he had a go at the 316th Division, and during the evening of November 21 he too had reached the plain of Alsace north-east of Saverne.

The next day, early in the afternoon, Combat Command "L" stormed Saverne from the rear, and Massu, who led the attack, achieved such an element of surprise that, among the 800 prisoners the little town's capture yielded, figured Lieutenant-General Bruhn, commanding the 553rd Division. A few hours later, coming at the strong but west-facing defences of Phalsbourg from the east, Minjonnet's right-hand column from Combat Command "L" re-established communication between the 2nd Armoured Division and XV Corps along the Saverne–Sarrebourg road.

"Thus", writes General de Langlade, "one November evening, Saverne was

captured; the Saverne gap, blocked at Phalsbourg by solidly entrenched enemy forces, fell into our hands; liaison between American units (44th Division) and Dio's Combat Command 'D' was all but complete again. The way to Strasbourg was open."

The manoeuvre to take Strasbourg began on November 23 at 0645 hours and involved four routes; two were taken by Colonel de Guillebon and two by Colonel de Langlade. Kehl was the final objective. Three hours later, three of the four French columns came upon the outlying forts, interconnected by an anti-tank ditch. The fourth (Rouvillois's subsidiary group) which had taken the itinerary Hochfelden–Brumath–Schiltigheim, surprised the defence by emerging from this unexpected direction, and at 1010 hours sent the agreed coded message: *"Tissu est dans iode"* (fabric in iodine, or Rouvillois in Strasbourg). It was soon followed by the remainder of Combat Command "L" and all of "W", but was unable to prevent the destruction of the Kehl bridge. Amidst the confusion, superbly stage-managed on the telephone system by 2nd Lieutenant Braun, Colonel de Langlade's Intelligence officer, issuing bogus orders to the enemy staffs, resistance was throttled in the course of the afternoon and at 1800 hours, the French flag was seen flying at the top of the cathedral spire, telling Strasbourg and the world that General Leclerc had kept the promise he had made at Kufra Oasis on March 1, 1941, when the least partisan observers had considered Hitler's victory assured.

In the afternoon of November 25th, Lieutenant-General Vaterrodt, commanding the garrison, and his second-in-command, Major-General Uttersprungen, who had sought refuge in Fort Ney, surrendered to a detachment of the 2nd Armoured Division. So ended General Leclerc's amazing exploit.

Eighty-two days' misery: that, in General de Langlade's words, was to be the lot of the 2nd Armoured Division on the morrow of its brilliant victory. Without necessarily disagreeing with this opinion, it should, however, be observed that the same run of bad luck afflicted the American 7th Army, indeed the whole of the 6th Army Group.

After cutting through the solid front formed by the enemy 1st and 19th Armies, General Patch threw his VI and XV Corps forward towards the German frontier in accordance with his orders to provide support for the 3rd Army in its attack on the *Westwall*. On his right, VI Corps, now commanded by Major-General Edward H. Brooks, following General Truscott's appointment as commander of the American 5th Army in Italy, got its 79th Division to Lauterbourg on December 6, while the 45th was attacking the Siegfried Line parallel to Bergzabern, both of them biting deep into the German defensive system. On his left, XV Corps was hammering away at the fortifications in the area of Bitche, the only section of the Maginot Line to play a rôle in 1944. It had reduced them when the Ardennes offensive forced it to let go its hold.

At Strasbourg, the American 3rd Division (VI Corps) had relieved the French 2nd Armoured Division which, in company with the American 36th and 103rd Divisions, tried to prevent the enemy establishing new positions round Colmar. Here General Patch was endeavouring to do two things at the same time: effect a break-through in the *Westwall* between the Rhine and the Saar, and clear the enemy from the left bank of the Rhine above Strasbourg. This double assignment was given him by General Devers who, in calling for two divergent operations, was doing no more than conform to instructions from S.H.A.E.F. where the enemy's capacity for resistance was not fully realised.

However, on December 2 H.Q. 6th Army Group took the American 7th Army off the Colmar assignment and gave it to the French 1st Army, at the same time allocating the 36th Division and the 2nd Armoured Division. This was indeed a logical decision, but one that resolved nothing, since the switch produced no reinforcements. And de Lattre, as we know, had been reluctantly obliged to part with his 1st Free French Division and was further expecting, according to orders received from Paris, to lose his 1st Armoured Division, which was to be sent to Royan.

Then again, at Vittel, General Devers's Intelligence staff took an optimistic view: the stiffening of enemy resistance in Alsace was recognised, but attributed to O.K.W.'s concern not to pull its troops back from the left bank of the Rhine until it had had ample time to provide for the defence of the right bank of the river.

In fact, this view was quite mistaken. On the contrary, in the middle of all this, Hitler dismissed General Balck and put General Wiese and his 19th Army under a new command known as *"Oberrhein"*, which he entrusted to *Reichsführer*-S.S. Heinrich Himmler; and far from proceeding to evacuate the Colmar bridgehead he set about reconstituting its defence, which he did with great success.

Carrying out the orders that had come from the 6th Army Group, General de Lattre incorporated the two divisions he had been allotted as well as the 3rd Algerian Division, the Moroccan troops, and the 4th Combat Command (5th Armoured Division) in II Corps and ordered it to attack the north-west front of the pocket, from a line linking the Col du Bonhomme, Ribeauville, Sélestat, and Rhinau. At the same time, I Corps had orders to attack from a line between Mulhouse and Thann, both corps being given Neuf-Brisach as their objective. We drew attention earlier to the reasons for the reverse suffered by Béthouart around December 10. And Monsabert, for all his dash, had troops that were too

few and too battle-weary to bring him greater success. The energy he displayed enabled him to batter the enemy front but not break it, as his orders required; in arctic conditions, he managed to capture Orbey and Kayserberg, taking 5,568 prisoners, but his own losses were heavy and on December 19 he was ordered to take up a defensive position on the line he had reached.

In this battle, the French 1st Army, as General de Lattre de Tassigny remarks, was at a disadvantage in that the Wehrmacht's Panthers and *Jagdpanthers* outclassed the Shermans and Allied tank destroyers with disastrous consequences. In addition to this, morale on the German side had been greatly strengthened.

The diminished success of the Colmar offensive caused some friction between de Lattre and Devers, the first asking the second for two further divisions and the second replying that the other Allied armies were managing well enough without receiving reinforcements. It would seem that in drawing this comparison, General Devers quite failed to appreciate the factor of air cover, which operated very much to the advantage of Simpson, Hodges, Patton, and even Patch, while his French subordinate was cruelly deprived. Apart from that, neither Devers nor General Eisenhower even had the two divisions requested by de Lattre available to give him. The supply of reinforcements from across the Atlantic

An American M-10 tank destroyer in action in the streets of Aachen.

had been speeded up, but in early December 1944 S.H.A.E.F. had only 66 divisions immediately available, so that its main reserves were barely sufficient.

And this leads us to draw the following conclusion on the whole episode. In every army in the world, before the appearance of atomic weapons, it was an article of faith that the commander-in-chief's power of decision depended on the number of men at his disposal. Thus, on the eve of the German counter-attack of March 21, 1918, behind the 119 divisions at the front, Haig and Pétain had 62 in reserve. In the present instance, this was far from the case. So Eisenhower should not be blamed, as so often he is, for not exercising greater authority over his immediate subordinates, since he lacked the means that would have enabled him to enforce his decisions.

This situation led to defeat at Arnhem, qualified success or failure on the Roer. As for the victories won on fronts which Montgomery would have preferred to leave inactive, they were not exploited for want of the ten or so divisions that would have allowed Patton, Patch, and de Lattre to attack the *Westwall* between the Moselle and the Rhine, before Hitler moved in the Ardennes.

CHAPTER 68
The battle of 'the Bulge'

It is now well known that the "Battle of the Bulge", the offensive often known as Rundstedt's, was in reality forced upon him, and that the rôle played by O.B. West in the attack begun on December 16 was limited to that of passing on to Army Group "B" the instructions of Hitler, Keitel, and Jodl at O.K.W.

It was quite clear to Rundstedt, Model, and even to Sepp Dietrich, that the objectives assigned to Operation "Herbstnebel" ("Autumn Fog") were far too ambitious for the Wehrmacht's limited capabilities, and they tried to convince the Führer of this. On the other hand they agreed with him–and history bears out their judgement–that if the Third Reich was not to be annihilated in less than six months, they would have to go over to the offensive, the Western Front being the only theatre where this might be possible. Italy was not vital to the Western Allies, even if the terrain and the season had made such an operation there successful; and in the East, it was generally agreed that they would not be able to force a decisive result. According to Major-General Gehlen's calculations, Stalin had something like 520 infantry divisions and more than 300 armoured and mechanised brigades at his command, and so could lose up to 30 divisions, or retreat up to 150 miles, without suffering a decisive defeat. In any case, what could be the advantage to the Germans of advancing once more to the Dniepr or the Dvina, if in the meantime the Western Allies broke through the *Westwall* and occupied the Ruhr and Saar basins?

The German chiefs thus agreed unanimously on a counter-offensive in the West, being fully aware of the logistical difficulties and man-power shortage by which Eisenhower was being plagued. However, there was deep disagreement between the Führer and his front-line generals on how far to carry the offensive. Hitler maintained that they ought to go all out, and inflict on Eisenhower a defeat as crushing as that suffered by Gamelin when the Panzer divisions had pushed through to the Somme estuary in 1940. And the fact that the Ardennes mountains were so lightly held seemed to provide him with an opportunity identical to the one he had exploited in May 1940– we now know that he did in fact send to Liegnitz for the documents pertaining to "Fall Gelb". The plan was being prepared at H.Q. in absolute secrecy–and neither Rundstedt nor Model knew of it. Three armies were to take part: the newly formed 6th S.S. *Panzerarmee,* commanded by Colonel-General Dietrich; the 5th *Panzerarmee* under General Hasso von Manteuffel, which was withdrawn from the front at Aachen (neither Model nor Rundstedt was informed of the rôle it was going to play); and the 7th Army,

under General Brandenberger, which was then in the Eifel sector.

According to O.K.W.'s plan, the 5th and 6th *Panzerarmee* were to get to the Meuse in 48 hours; after this Sepp Dietrich, crossing the river north of Liège, would aim for Antwerp, via Saint Truiden and Aarschot, whilst Manteuffel, crossing the river on both sides of Namur, would aim for Brussels. The 7th Army would pivot round at Echternach and thus cover the operation against any Allied counter-attack coming from the south. With Manteuffel and Dietrich intercepting their communications at Namur and Antwerp, the whole of the Allied 21st Army Group, and most of the 12th Army Group, would be attacked on two fronts and annihilated, with the destruction of 37 of the 64 divisions that Eisenhower deployed at that time.

On October 24, Lieutenant-Generals Krebs and Westphal, chiefs-of-staff of Army Group "B" and of O.B. West respectively, had an interview with the Führer, who informed them of the plan which he had conceived, and whose execution was provisionally fixed for November 25. Both at Koblenz and at Field-Marshal Model's H.Q., the *Führerbefehl* had been severely criticised by those who would have to carry it out, as– and Krebs and Westphal had already hinted as much on a previous visit to O.K.W.–the plan bore no relationship to the resources being made available to them. Since, however, they were both in favour of a strategic counter-attack, on November 3 they submitted a counter-proposition to Hitler, better suited to the capabilities of Army Group "B", and called the "little solution" (*kleine Lösung*).

Instead of embarking on the very risky task of recapturing Antwerp, they suggested that it would be better to take advantage of the salient that the American 1st and 9th Armies had created in the *Westwall,* east and north-east of Aachen, and then envelop it in a pincer movement, enabling Dietrich to break out of the Roermond region and Manteuffel out of the Eifel region. If such an attack were completely successful, 20 Allied divisions would be destroyed and Model could then perhaps exploit Bradley's defeat and strike out for Antwerp.

As can be seen, Model, who had conceived this plan, and Rundstedt, who had forwarded it to O.K.W. with his approval, looked upon the operation as a mere sortie, just as the commander of a besieged 18th Century fortress would suddenly make a night attack on the besieging forces, forcing them to start their siege preparations anew. But such an operation gained only a few weeks' respite and, sooner or later, unless help was forthcoming from elsewhere, surrender would be inevitable. Understandably then, Hitler angrily rejected such a solution, for

what he needed was not a short respite, but a decisive military victory in the West. So, as early as November 1, he had written at the head of his orders to O.B. West, that "the intention, the organisation, and the objective of this offensive are irrevocable". On receiving the counter-proposition of Model and Rundstedt, he got Jodl to reply within 24 hours that "the Führer has decided that the operation is irrevocably decided, down to its last details".

However, none of the H.Q. staff had solved any of the difficulties which the men in field command of the operation had felt obliged to point out. As Rundstedt explained on October 25, 1945, whilst being interrogated by Major Shulman of Canadian 1st Army Intelligence:

"When I was first told about the proposed offensive in the Ardennes, I protested against it as vigorously as I could. The forces at our disposal were much, much too weak for such far-reaching objectives. It was only up to one to obey. It was a nonsensical operation, and the most stupid part of it was the setting of Antwerp as the target. If we reached the Meuse we should have got down on our knees and thanked God– let alone try to reach Antwerp."

Hitler paid no more heed to Sepp Dietrich than he had to Model and Rundstedt, his only concession being to put back the date of the offensive from November 25, first to December 10, then to December 16. He also agreed to Manteuffel's suggestion to replace the three-hour artillery barrage that he had ordered by an artillery attack of only 45 minutes.

The operation forced O.K.W. to redeploy its western forces. To free Model of any worries concerning his right wing, an Army Group "H" was organised, responsible for operations between the North Sea and Roermond, and commanded by Colonel-General Student, who relinquished his 1st Parachute Army to General Schlemm.

The 15th Army relieved the 5th *Panzerarmee* on the Roer being relieved in turn between the North Sea and Nijmegen by a 25th Army under the command of General Christiansen.

According to General von Manteuffel, at 0530 hours on December 16, 21 German divisions of all types launched their attack on the American line between Monschau and Echternach, on a 90-mile front. From north to south, the forces involved were:

1. 6th S.S. *Panzerarmee:* LXVII Corps (General Hitzfeld), with the 272nd and 326th *Volksgrenadier* Divisions; I S.S. Panzer Corps (General Priess), with the 277th and 12th *Volksgrenadier,* 3rd Parachute, and 1st and 12th S.S. Panzer Divisions; and II S.S. Panzer Corps (General Bittrich), with the 2nd and 9th S.S. Panzer Divisions.

2. 5th *Panzerarmee*: LXVI Corps (General Lucht), with the 18th and 62nd *Volksgrenadier* Divisions; LVIII Panzer Corps (General Krüger), with the 116th Panzer and 560th *Volksgrenadier* Divisions; and XLVII Panzer Corps (General von Lüttwitz), with the 2nd Panzer, Panzer-*"Lehr"*, and 26th *Volksgrenadier* Divisions.

3. 7th Army: LXXXV Corps (General Kniess), with the 5th Parachute and 352nd *Volksgrenadier* Divisions; and LXXX Corps (General Beyer), with the 276th and 212nd *Volksgrenadier* Divisions.

It should be noted that although the four *Waffen*-S.S. Panzer divisions had been brought up to full strength, with a total of 640 Panther and Pzkw IV tanks available to Dietrich, Manteuffel's three Panzer divisions had only been restored to about two-thirds of their full strength, about 320 tanks in all. And in fact, if they had been at full strength, the fuel problem would have been even more acute than it was. According to the plan, the Panzers should have attacked with sufficient petrol for five refuellings, which would have given them a range of up to 170 miles; on the day of the attack, they had

A massive Tiger II advances through the Ardennes.

only enough for two refills, as for camouflage reasons Hitler had forbidden the creation of fuel dumps close to the line. More important, he had made no allowances either for the difficult terrain or for the very bad weather. On December 28, describing the failure of the Ardennes offensive to his generals, Hitler described as follows the misfortunes that befell the 12th *"Hitlerjugend"* Panzer Division on the roads of the Ardennes:

"Only the first wave of the 12th S.S. Panzer Division's tanks were in action, whilst behind them there was an enormous convoy jammed solid, so that they could go neither forward nor back. Finally, not even the petrol could get through. Everything was stationary, and the tanks' engines were merely idling. To avoid frost damage, etc., the engines had to be run all night, which also had the advantage of keeping the men warm. This created enormous petrol requirements. The roads were bad. They could only use first gear . . . there was no end to it."

Among the special forces used during this operation, mention should be made of the so-called 150th Panzer Brigade, made up of about 2,000 men conversant with American army slang, using jeeps and even old Sherman tanks rescued from the battlefield. The brigade had a double

purpose: firstly, small patrols were to infiltrate the enemy lines and cause panic by spreading alarmist rumours and sabotaging telephone communications and signposts; then, when the breakthrough was being exploited, small motorised columns would be sent out to capture the Meuse bridges and hold them until the rest of the armour arrived.

This "Trojan horse" invented by Hitler was placed under the command of Otto Skorzeny, who had been promoted to colonel after capturing Admiral Horthy. The stratagem, which was quite contrary to the Geneva Convention, had some initial success because of its surprise element, but the counter-measures immediately devised by the Americans were most effective. Germans captured in American uniforms were immediately tried and shot, although some of them had only taken part in the operation when threatened with a German firing-squad.

The paratroops who spread confusion deep behind the American front line, even as far as France, never numbered more than 1,200, discounting the dummies used, and were commanded by Lieutenant-Colonel Heydte; but the pilots of the Junkers Ju 52's from which they were to jump were so badly trained that three-quarters of them jumped behind the German lines. The Allies thought they

had been entrusted with the task of killing Eisenhower, but post-war research has revealed how groundless these suppositions were, although they did interfere with the normal functions of the Allied high command.

Behind the first wave of troops, there were eight reserve divisions, seven of which were subject to O.K.W. orders. Model thus found himself with very little chance of exploiting any slight advantages he might gain without referring to Hitler. In addition there were two newly formed Panzer brigades, but that was all.

Theoretically, the attack was to be supported by 3,000 bombers and fighter-bombers, but on the first day a mere 325 planes took off, of which 80 were jets. Hitler could not bring himself to expose German towns to Allied air attacks by depriving them of fighter cover.

On December 10, O.K.W. left Berlin for Ziegenberg near Giessen, where, in preparation for the 1940 Blitzkrieg against France, a command post—never used— had been set up. It was here that two days later, having first made them hand in their pistols and brief-cases, Hitler harangued the commanders of the units engaged in this action. "There were about 30 generals including divisional commanders," writes Jacques Nobécourt. "They had been brought from Koblenz during the night by bus, twisting, turning, and going back on its tracks to deceive them regarding the route being followed. All along the wall of the lecture hall stood S.S. men keeping an eagle eye on all present."

"No one in the audience dared move, or even take out a handkerchief," wrote Bayerlein, commander of the Panzer-"Lehr", who thought Hitler looked ill and depressed.

"For two solid hours Hitler spoke, using no notes." Although we do not have the authentic verbatim account of his speech, the French version presented by Raymond Henry takes up 11 pages of his book. In it, Hitler once more reminded his listeners of the steadfastness of Frederick the Great refusing to surrender in 1761, in spite of the heavy pressure exerted on him by his brother, his ministers, and his generals; and Hitler spoke of the weakness of the coalition opposing Germany:

"On the one hand the ultra-capitalist states, on the other ultra-marxist states; on the one hand a great empire, the British Empire, slowly dying; on the other a colony just waiting to take over. Countries whose aims are becoming more and more different day by day. And if you watch closely, you can see differences arising hour by hour. A few well-struck blows and this artificial common front could come crashing down at any moment."

When Hitler had finished, Rundstedt assured him of the devoted loyalty of all his generals.

Amongst the Allies, the battle of the Ardennes was and has been the subject of considerable argument. It allowed Montgomery once more to lay claim to the

Jochen Peiper, commander of the celebrated Kampfgruppe "Peiper".

title of head of Allied land forces, and even today the discussion rages between supporters of the American supreme commander and of his brilliant but independent second-in-command; just as for 20 years after the disappointing Battle of Jutland, there were divisions between supporters of Admiral Beatty, and those of Admiral Jellicoe. In his *Memoirs,* published in 1958, Montgomery expresses himself with his usual freedom, whereas Eisenhower, both during his tenure of the White House and during his later retirement, maintained a discreet silence.

We are here simply concerned with two questions: the first concerns the Allied forces holding the Ardennes, the second concerns the surprise offensive of December 16, 1944.

It must first be noted that with his right wing north of Trier and his left in the Losheim gap, south of Monschau, Major-General Middleton, commanding the American VIII Corps, held an 80-mile front with only four divisions. The 4th and 28th Divisions had been badly mauled in the unsuccessful attack on the Roer dams; the 9th Armoured Division (Major-General John W. Leonard) had never been under fire, nor had the 106th Division (Major-General Alan W. Jones) which had only taken over the Schnee Eifel sector of the front on December 11, after trailing all through France and southern Belgium in freezing rain and open lorries.

But did the Americans have any choice? In his *A Soldier's Story,* General Bradley explains the situation in a perfectly convincing way: to give Middleton more troops would have meant taking troops away from the two groups due to attack, to the north and south, in November. Even as it was, Hodges and Simpson had only 14 divisions between them for their 60-mile front north of the Ardennes, whilst to the south, Patton had only nine divisions, stretched over a 90-mile

front. The Americans were so short of troops that the offensive was put back a week so that they could get back from Montgomery just one division they had lent him to mop up the Scheldt estuary. And to concentrate the 3rd Army's attack on a narrow front, the Americans had to transfer part of Patton's sector to Devers's 6th Army Group. If they had wanted to reduce the risks of a German attack against Middleton's thinly held Ardennes positions, the Americans could have cancelled Patton's offensive, as Montgomery had suggested, and even dug in along the front for the winter. Both these alternatives were, to Bradley, out of the question. Middleton's forces would be stretched as thinly as possible, risking the chance of an enemy attack, and the Americans would throw all available divisions into the November offensive. Thus troops were taken away from the Ardennes to reinforce the winter offensive. It was a calculated risk which Bradley had decided to take, and one to which he stuck both during and after the event. Bradley's decision had not been taken lightly. As one of the most successful commanders of the war, he always had a clear understanding of the issues involved in such troop deployments.

Eisenhower, whilst claiming his due share of responsibility, justifies Bradley:

"The responsibility for maintaining only four divisions on the Ardennes front and for running the risk of a large German penetration in that area was mine. At any moment from November 1 onward I could have passed to the defensive along the whole front and made our lines absolutely secure from attack while we awaited reinforcements. My basic decision was to continue the offensive to the extreme limit of our ability, and it was this decision that was responsible for the startling successes of the first week of the German December attack."

It seems quite clear, after this, that the calculated risk about which Eisenhower and Bradley talk was not something dreamed up after the event to excuse the weaknesses of their actions.

It must be admitted, however, that Eisenhower and Bradley calculated things very tightly, as neither imagined for one minute that Hitler would fix Antwerp as the objective for his Panzers. And, of course, their reasoning followed the same lines as that of Model, Rundstedt, and Manteuffel, who all declared that the plan was impracticable and would have the most catastrophic consequences.

When he became aware of enemy troop concentrations, Colonel Dickson, head of General Hodges's Intelligence staff, said on December 10 that the defence of the Reich was based on the following strategy: the halting of the Allied offensive, followed by a counter-attack, with all forces concentrated between the Roer and the Erft.

In other words, Dickson assumed that if there was a counter-attack, it would follow the lines of the "little solution" that Rundstedt and Model had unsuccessfully suggested to Hitler, since more ambitious plans were far beyond the Wehrmacht's capabilities.

The Allies were thus quite aware that German troops had been brought into position in readiness for a counter-attack, but they thought that these concentrations would form a flank attack on Hodges's troops preparing to attack Cologne, and that it would be combined with the breaching of the Roer dams. Later, Dickson's assumption was taken as being the correct one, and it was only on the day before the attack took place that Allied Intelligence found out that rubber boats and other craft had been assembled on the German side of the River Our.

Oddly enough, Colonel Koch, head of the American 3rd Army's Intelligence staff, was more worried than Dickson about the American situation; he even managed to get General Patton to share his apprehension, since on December 12 the latter ordered his chief-of-staff to work out "a study of what the Third Army would do if called upon to counter-attack such a break-through". And on the night of December 15-16, when he knew that the enemy was observing radio silence, he said "I want you, gentlemen, to start making plans for pulling the Third Army out of its eastward attack, change the direction ninety degrees, moving to Luxemburg and attacking north."

With all the information before us, Bradley was probably right when he said that although the Allies may have been wrong about the enemy's intentions, their estimate of his capabilities at that time was on the whole correct. For–and events were to bear this out in the following weeks–against forces as large as the Allies', Rundstedt did not have the re-

sources necessary to ensure the success of an offensive strategy.

Thus, because they had failed to reckon with Adolf Hitler's megalomania, the Allied chiefs were caught badly napping on December 16–not least Field-Marshal Montgomery, who on the very morning of the German offensive had summed up the enemy's possibilities of action in the following words:

"The enemy is at present fighting a defensive campaign on all fronts, his situation is such that he cannot stage major offensive operations. Furthermore, at all costs he has to prevent the war from entering on a mobile phase; he has not the transport or the petrol that would be necessary for mobile operations, nor could his tanks compete with ours in the mobile battle."

On the first day of the offensive, the 6th S.S. *Panzerarmee* attacked with its infantry divisions, keeping its Panzers in reserve to exploit the initial success. On the right it came up against the American 2nd and 99th Divisions, of V Corps, still commanded by Major-General Leonard Gerow; the 2nd Division was an experienced, battle-hardened unit which overcame its surprise very quickly, whereas the 99th Division, which had never before seen major action, had more difficulty in recovering its composure. In the end, V Corps managed to hold on to the Elsenborn ridge in spite of all enemy attacks. But Dietrich easily broke through the Losheim gap, lightly held by the 14th Armoured Division, which opened up the road to Stavelot, and in addition enabled him to turn the left flank of the 106th Division.

On the very same day this division was pierced on its left by the 5th *Panzerarmee*'s attack, which also threw back the 28th Division towards Clervaux (Clerf). The two regiments of the 106th Division holding the Schnee Eifel plateau were in imminent danger of being surrounded.

The 7th Army, reduced to four divisions, had to be satisfied with pivoting around Echternach, instead of including Luxembourg in its plan of attack, as originally planned. Although it had to yield some ground, the American 4th Division, which made up Middleton's right flank, was less severely tested than the 28th.

When the first news of the German attack reached S.H.A.E.F., Bradley was in Versailles, conferring with General Bedell Smith, Eisenhower's chief-of-staff. A few hours later, a further report indicated that the American 1st Army had identified eight German divisions.

Eisenhower and Bradley immediately realised the implications of this offensive, but the reserves available to them on December 16 were even less than those available to General Gamelin on May 13, 1940. They were in fact limited to XVIII Airborne Corps (Major-General Ridgeway), two of whose divisions, the 82nd and the 101st, were being reformed near

Rheims, after two months' action in the Nijmegen salient. This corps was immediately alerted, and the 9th and 3rd Armies received orders to make their 7th and 10th Armoured Divisions respectively available to the 1st Army.

In a few days' time Eisenhower would also be able to call upon the 2nd Armoured Division, which had just landed in France, as well as the 87th Division and the 17th Airborne Division, which were still in England, but about to embark for France. Even then it would take time for them to come into the line. In addition, although the successes of Skorzeny's commandos and von der Heydte's paratroopers were very slight, rumour greatly magnified them. Above all, the bad weather of that week reduced Allied air strikes almost to nothing. "Low cloud" and "thick fog" were phrases that the weather forecasters repeated with monotonous regularity throughout the week December 16-23.

Weather has often played a crucial role in warfare, never more so than in that fateful week.

In the public mind the Ardennes campaign is summed up in the one word: Bastogne, and rightly so, since Brigadier-General A. C. McAuliffe and his 101st Airborne Division fought heroically around the little town, although the behaviour under fire of the 7th Armoured Division and its commander, Brigadier-General Robert Hasbrook, was also worthy of the highest praise. Between December 18 and 22, the defensive position of Saint Vith compelled the 5th *Panzerarmee* to disperse its energies, and the town was only evacuated after an express order.

It is true that on December 19, in the Schnee Eifel plateau region, two regiments of the 106th Division were trapped, and 6,000 men had to surrender, but everywhere else the Americans stood up gallantly under all the attacks. As Jacques Mordal very rightly says:

"The great merit of the American troops was that despite the surprise and initial disorder, a few commanders and a few handfuls of troops were found who saved the situation by holding on grimly to certain vital positions; and it may be said that rarely has the fate of so many divisions depended on a few isolated engagements. A mere handful of artillerymen firing their few guns saved Bütgenbach on December 16, and prevented the complete isolation of the 2nd and 99th Divisions. A battalion of sappers was to save Malmédy; and a company of the 51st Engineer Combat Battalion stopped the advance of the leading elements of *Kampfgruppe* 'Peiper'. They blew up the Trois-Ponts bridge across the Salm, and forced Peiper to go back via Amblève, and find a further bridge at Werbomont, where the pioneers of the 291st Battalion fought heroically to prevent his crossing; for the second time the German troops saw a bridge being blown up in front of them, and they also suffered severe losses

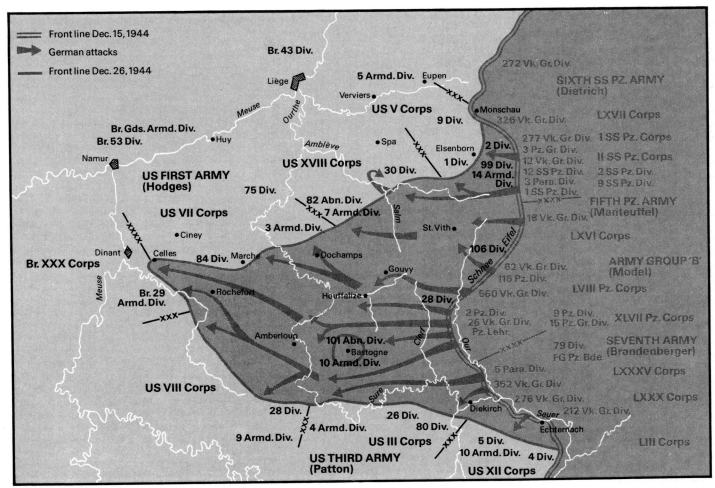

Front line Dec. 15, 1944
German attacks
Front line Dec. 26, 1944

Br. 43 Div.

Liège

272 Vk. Gr. Div.

SIXTH SS PZ. ARMY
(Dietrich)

5 Armd. Div. Eupen

LXVII Corps

Verviers

Monschau

US V Corps

326 Vk. Gr. Div.

Meuse

Ourthe

9 Div.

Ambléve

Spa

Br. Gds. Armd. Div.
Br. 53 Div.

Huy

Elsenborn

2 Div.

277 Vk. Gr. Div. 1 SS Pz. Corps
3 Pz. Gr. Div.
12 Vk. Gr. Div. II SS Pz. Corps

Namur

US FIRST ARMY
(Hodges)

US XVIII Corps

30 Div.

1 Div.

99 Div.

14 Armd.
Div.

12 SS Pz. Div. 2 SS Pz. Div.
3 Para. Div. 9 SS Pz. Div.
1 SS Pz. Div.

75 Div.

FIFTH PZ. ARMY
(Manteuffel)

US VII Corps

82 Abn. Div.
7 Armd. Div.

18 Vk. Gr. Div.

Salm

Ciney

3 Armd. Div.

St. Vith

LXVI Corps

Dinant

Celles

84 Div.

Marche

Dochamps

106 Div.

ARMY GROUP 'B'
(Model)

Br. XXX Corps

Schnee Eifel

62 Vk. Gr. Div.
116 Pz. Div.

Meuse

Br. 29
Armd. Div.

Rochefort

Houffalize

Gouvy

28 Div.

560 Vk. Gr. Div.

LVIII Pz. Corps

Amberloup

101 Abn. Div.

Clerf

2 Pz. Div.
26 Vk. Gr. Div.
Pz. Lehr.

9 Pz. Div.
15 Pz. Gr. Div.

XLVII Pz. Corps

Bastogne

Our

79 Div.
FG Pz. Bde.

SEVENTH ARMY
(Brandenberger)

10 Armd. Div.

5 Para. Div.

LXXXV Corps

US VIII Corps

352 Vk. Gr. Div.

Sure

276 Vk. Gr. Div.

LXXX Corps

28 Div.

26 Div.

Diekirch

Sauer 212 Vk. Gr. Div.

4 Armd. Div.

80 Div.

Echternach

9 Armd. Div.

US III Corps

5 Div.

LIII Corps

US THIRD ARMY
(Patton)

10 Armd. Div.

4 Div.

US XII Corps

"The Bulge" was the scene of some of the fiercest fighting in the war, especially around the town of Bastogne.

from air attacks launched in spite of the bad weather.

"Stavelot, lost on December 17, was recaptured two days later. The battle went on in the sunken valley of the Amblève, where after five days of hard combat, Peiper, out of fuel, was forced to leave behind all his equipment and withdraw the few hundred men remaining on foot, in the snow, and following impossible tracks."

On the German side, Dietrich made the big mistake of stubbornly trying to take the Elsenborn ridge, whose defences had been greatly strengthened by the transfer to General Gerow of that first-class fighting unit, the American 1st Division; thus the 12th "Hitlerjugend" S.S. Panzer Division was halted around Bütgenbach. As for the celebrated "Leibstandarte", it became separated from its advanced elements, which had pushed forward into the Amblève valley, on Colonel Peiper's orders. In short, four days after the initial attack, the 6th *Panzerarmee* was still far from the Meuse bridges—which it should have reached within 72 hours of the start of the operation.

On Dietrich's left, Manteuffel had shown more tactical flair, being further helped by the fact that General Hodges was

finding it more difficult to reinforce his VIII Corps in Luxembourg than between Elsenborn and Trois-Ponts; Clervaux and Wiltz fell easily, thus opening up the way to Bastogne. Faced with this most un-expected development—for after all, it had been thought that Dietrich's forces would have the starring rôle in this offensive—Model and Rundstedt recom-mended the immediate transfer of II S.S. Panzer Corps from the 5th to the 6th *Panzerarmee*, following the principle that successful operations ought to be exploited in preference to the less successful.

But Hitler refused categorically to allow this transfer; no doubt because he dreaded admitting, even implicitly, the failure of Dietrich and the *Waffen*-S.S., and did not want to place one of the Nazi Party's armed units under the command of the Wehrmacht generals for whom for a long time he had felt nothing but mistrust, and even hate.

Had Eisenhower known that his adver-sary was making this tactical mistake, he would probably have refrained from taking some of the measures which mar-ked his intervention on December 19. But with all his reports from the front indicat-ing that Bastogne and the 101st Airborne Division were practically surrounded, he decided that the time had come to throw all his authority into the struggle. So, at 1100 hours on December 19, he con-vened a meeting with Bradley and Devers, together with Patton.

According to his memoirs, Eisenhower opened the meeting by declaring that "the present situation is to be regarded as one of opportunity for us and not disaster. There will be only cheerful faces at this conference table."

And in fact these confident phrases represented exactly the calm coolness that Eisenhower really felt on that im-portant day. Thus the American historian Ladislas Farago, in his biography of General Patton, which he bases upon numerous unpublished documents and eye-witness accounts, has written:

"The historic Verdun conference of 19th December 1944 was, I submit, one of the high points of Dwight D. Eisen-hower's generalship in the war. He was variously described as having been pale and nervous, showing not only signs of the strain but also an intimate kind of concern, as if he worried about his personal future in the aftermath of this crisis. Actually, Ike was in top form, concise and lucid, holding the conference with iron hands to its key issue—the Allied counter-attack. It was obvious to all that he knew what he wanted and was the full master of the situation. He had in full measure that special inner strength which always filled him when he was called upon to make *absolute* decisions."

The main decision taken was to move the six divisions of General Patton's III and XII Corps from the Saar front to the Echternach–Diekirch–Bastogne front, at the same time subordinating VIII Corps to the 3rd Army. This meant that the right flank of General Devers's army group would be extended from Bitche to Saarbrücken. Such a manoeuvre had already been discussed at 3rd Army H.Q., so that a single telephone call made from Verdun by its commander was enough to get it started. According to Farago, this order, which meant the moving of 133,178 vehicles over a total of some 1,500,000 miles, was carried out in five days. During this time, the 3rd Army's rear echelons transported 62,000 tons of supplies, the Intelligence staff distributed thousands of maps of the new sector, and the communications section put down 40,000 yards of telephone cable. And all this was achieved in snow and on roads covered with black ice. This proves that Patton may have been a swashbuckler (that very day he said to Bradley: "'Brad, this time the Kraut's stuck his head in the meatgrinder.' With a turn of his fist he added, 'And this time I've got hold of the handle.'"), but he was also a thinker, and an organiser of the highest class.

On December 20, Eisenhower placed Montgomery in charge of the northern

Armed with a long-barrelled 7.5-cm weapon, the Sturmgeschütz III was a highly effective assault gun.

flank of the German penetration (with the U.S. 1st and 9th armies under his command), and gave Bradley the southern flank. As he reported to the Combined Chiefs-of-Staff: with the enemy thrusting towards Namur, "our front is divided into two main parts on each of which we must act aggressively and with our full capabilities."

During the morning of December 19, the 101st Division entered Bastogne, joining up with those elements of the 9th and 10th Armoured Divisions defending the town. The next day, XLVII Panzer Corps, following its instructions, bypassed the town to north and south, leaving the 26th *Volksgrenadier* Division the job of laying siege to it. When the commander of this formation, Lieutenant-General Heinz Kokott, called upon General McAuliffe to surrender, he received the rudest of replies: "Nuts". The garrison's high morale was kept up, firstly, by the wholehearted support of the town population under their mayor, Monsieur Jacmin, and secondly by the sound of III Corps' guns announcing the beginning of the counter-attack in the south.

On the northern half of the bulge, an attack by the 30th Division, called by the Germans "Roosevelt's S.S.", enabled Hodges to close up the Amblève valley sector by lengthening the position held

by V Corps. However, by sending in II S.S. Panzer Corps to the left of I S.S. Panzer Corps, Dietrich succeeded in re-vitalising the offensive, forcing Has-brook to evacuate Saint Vith on December 21. The intervention, firstly of XVIII Airborne Corps (although reduced to the 82nd Airborne Division), and secondly, of General Collins's VII Corps, comprising the 75th, 83rd, and 84th Divisions, and the 3rd Armoured Division, enabled a continuous front to be re-established on a line Manhay – Grandmenil – Hotton – Marche.

In carrying out his tasks as commander of the 21st Army Group, Montgomery had a few difficulties with his American subordinates. His main aim was to prevent the Germans from crossing the Meuse, and provided this was done he was not very worried by the loss of a small Ardennes village here or there. He conducted the campaign according to the methods of 1918: plug the gap then, when quite ready, counter-attack. Hodges, Collins, and Ridgeway, on the other hand, hated giving up ground, and wanted to make the enemy feel the weight of their strength. To guard against every eventuality, the meticulous Montgomery established General Horrocks's British XXX Corps, comprising the 43rd, 51st, and 53rd Divisions, and the Guards Armoured

Division half-way between Namur and Brussels, thereby greatly facilitating the American 1st Army's movements, which up to December 24, had involved 248,000 men and 48,000 vehicles.

By December 22, at Koblenz, Rundstedt had decided upon immediate withdrawal from the engagement, already running into trouble. Of course, Hitler, at Ziegenberg, refused to ratify this suggestion; he thought that if they threw in the O.K.W. reserves, especially the 9th Panzer and 3rd and 15th *Panzergrenadier* Divisions, they would be able to resume the offensive, or at least capture Bastogne, the main thorn in their side.

On December 23, an anti-cyclone brought with it a week of brilliant sunshine over the whole of the Ardennes front. The Allied air forces were immediately unleashed, flying 2,000 missions on the first day, and 15,000 in the next three days. On Christmas Eve, at a cost of 39 planes lost, 2,000 American bombers, escorted by 900 fighters, attacked the airfields near Frankfurt and the communications networks of Kaiserslautern, Bad Munster, Koblenz, Neuwied, and Euskirchen. At the same time, other air attacks were successfully launched on the enemy's rear and on certain battlefield objectives. Last, but not least, 961 Dakotas and 61 gliders were able to drop 850 tons of supplies and ammunition to beleaguered Bastogne.

On the darker side, the small town of Malmédy, already in American hands, was twice bombed in error. Whilst the 6th *Panzerarmee* was now exhausted, the 5th managed to advance yet again some 25 miles on a line Saint Hubert–Rochefort–Dinant, moving north-west.

This movement laid bare Patton's left flank, and Eisenhower transferred to the 3rd Army the 87th Division, the 11th Armoured Division, and the 17th Airborne Division. Thus, by December 24, 32 Allied divisions were in action or in reserve on the Ardennes front, against the 29 German divisions calculated by S.H.A.E.F. to be involved.

Faced with this further deterioration of the situation, Rundstedt renewed his plea that the offensive be abandoned. He was very strongly supported this time by General Guderian, who knew that in the East, Soviet forces were massing on the Vistula bridge-heads. Once again the Führer refused categorically, in spite of the arguments of his H.Q., only too aware of the disasters that his obstinacy would inevitably bring. In the meantime Lieutenant-General von Lauchert's 2nd Panzer Division had reached Ciney, Beauraing, and Celles, in contact with the British 29th Armoured Brigade, and only six miles from the Meuse at Dinant. On Christmas Day, it suffered a flank attack at the hands of the American 2nd Armoured Division (Major-General Harmon), which had just been transferred to VII Corps. The effect was one of

A Sherman tank fitted with a 17-pounder gun, far superior to the more usual 75- and 76-mm guns.

total surprise, and the disaster was no less complete. By the end of the day, Lauchert's losses were as follows: 1,050 prisoners, 2,500 killed, 81 tanks (out of a total of 88), seven assault guns, all his artillery (74 pieces), and 405 vehicles. That day the American 2nd Armoured Division certainly lived up to its nickname of "Hell on Wheels". Confronted with this crushing blow, Manteuffel could only withdraw his XLVII Panzer Corps to Rochefort.

Patton's 3rd Army had a little more difficulty in relieving Bastogne, as the German 5th Parachute Division under Lieutenant-General Hellmann, on the right of the German 7th Army, put up a very spirited resistance. It was not until December 26 that the American 4th Armoured Division under Major-General Gaffey managed to link up with the beleaguered garrison, and even then it was only by means of a narrow corridor a few hundred yards wide.

Faced with these defeats, Hitler disengaged. But was he deceiving himself, or trying to deceive others? On December 28, haranguing his generals who were about to take part in Operation *"Nordwind"*, against the American 7th Army, he pretended to be satisfied with the results of *"Herbstnebel"*:

"There is no doubt that our short offensive has had the initial result of greatly easing the situation along the whole front, although unfortunately it has not had quite the great success we expected. The enemy has been forced to abandon all idea of attack; he has been compelled to regroup his forces completely, and put back into action troops completely worn out by previous engagements. His strategic intentions have been completely thwarted. The psychological factor is against him, for public opinion is bitterly critical. He now has to assert that an end to the fighting cannot be envisaged before August, perhaps before

the end of the year. We have therefore a complete reversal of the situation, which was certainly not considered possible a fortnight ago."

What does all this mean? Probably that Hitler would have been far better advised to have taken his head out of the "meatgrinder", when the results were in his favour. However, instead of rapidly withdrawing his 5th and 6th *Panzer-armee* behind the *Westwall,* he insisted on their trying to hold the Ardennes salient in impossible conditions, so turning his half-success of December 16 into a clear failure. That this is so is clear from the losses of the two sides: in manpower the Americans had suffered 76,890 casualties to the Germans' 81,834; in tanks 733 to 324; and aircraft 592 to 320. Whereas the Americans could replace their *matériel* losses with little difficulty, the Germans could not.

When one realises that German possibilities of rebuilding the Wehrmacht's strength were slowly diminishing, and that on January 12, 1945 Stalin unleashed his fifth and last winter offensive, there is no doubt that these figures confirm the German defeat, not only in the Ardennes, but on the whole of the Western Front.

To the despair of Guderian the abandonment of Operation *"Herbstnebel"* did not mean a reinforcement of the Eastern Front forces, for Hitler saw *"Herbstnebel"* as only the first of a set of offensives in the West. The next, aimed at the recovery of Alsace and Lorraine, was propounded by Hitler to his generals on December 18. "Our first objective", he said, "must be to clean up the situation in the West by offensive action."

In this mood of total fantasy, Germany's Supreme Commander brought in the New Year, 1945.

CHAPTER 69

Advance to the Rhine

Before he could accept the German surrender, the offer of which was to be brought to him at Rheims by a delegation headed by Colonel-General Jodl, General Eisenhower still had to repel two attacks, one directed against his own authority, and the other against the 6th Army Group in lower Alsace.

On December 28, 1944, Eisenhower went to Hasselt, where Montgomery had set up his headquarters. He wanted to go over the plans for future operations with him, to begin as soon as the Ardennes pocket had been nipped off. Eisenhower and Montgomery had no difficulty in reaching agreement on the objective to be set for the offensive they were about to launch. Both favoured the Ruhr. But Montgomery thought that the "major crisis" that had just been resolved authorised him to adopt the claim he had pressed at the beginning of the preceding August. He wanted control of operations, and he thought himself the more qualified to bear the responsibility since Eisenhower had put the American 1st and 9th Armies under his command. Hence his letter to "Ike", dated December 29. Point 6 of this read:

"I suggest that your directive should finish with this sentence:

"'12 and 21 Army Groups will develop operations in accordance with the above instructions.

"'From now onwards full operational direction, control, and co-ordination of these operations is vested in the C.-in-C. 21 Army Group, subject to such instructions as may be issued by the Supreme Commander from time to time.'"

In writing this, Montgomery was disregarding the prudent advice contained in Brooke's letter of December 24 to him:

"I would like to give you a word of warning. Events and enemy action have forced on Eisenhower the setting up of a more satisfactory system of command. I feel it is most important that you should not even in the slightest degree appear to rub this undoubted fact in to anyone at S.H.A.E.F. or elsewhere."

Eisenhower rejected his subordinate's suggestion by return of post. But, even had he not done this on his own initiative, he would have been ordered to do so by General Marshall, who cabled him from Washington on December 30:

"They may or may not have brought to your attention articles in certain London papers proposing a British deputy commander for all your ground forces and implying that you have undertaken too much of a task yourself. My feeling is this: under no circumstances make any concessions of any kind whatsoever. I am not assuming that you had in mind such a concession I just wish you to be certain of our attitude. You are doing a grand job, and go on and give them hell."

The matter would have stopped there if, on January 5, 1945, Montgomery had not given a press conference on the Battle of the Ardennes, which drove the American generals to the limit of exasperation. The text of the conference was published by General Bradley and it can be said that although Montgomery polished his own image and took some pleasure in exaggerating the part played by British forces in the Ardennes, he did not criticise his allies or their leaders in any way. But the journalists accredited to S.H.A.E.F. and army group seized on his speech and commented bitterly on it, some standing up for Montgomery, others for Eisenhower.

The crisis reached flashpoint when Bradley informed his old friend Eisenhower that he would ask to be recalled to the United States rather than serve under Montgomery's command. In view of the rumours spread by Goebbels's propaganda services, Churchill thought he ought to step in, which he did in the House of Commons on January 18. His excellent speech made special mention of the all-important part that the U.S. Army had played in the battle and placated everyone.

Besides this, another move of the Prime Minister's contributed to relieving the tension between S.H.A.E.F. and the 21st Army Group. As operations in Italy had slowed down considerably, it was suggested that Alexander was being wasted there. So Eisenhower's deputy, Tedder, was to be recalled to ordinary R.A.F. service, his place being taken by Alexander. Though this compromise did not win Eisenhower's approval, it also came up against Montgomery's decided opposition. If he could not control operations himself, he did not want to see anybody else get the job. From this point of view, he thought that nothing should be changed in the pattern of command.

Nevertheless, Montgomery's importunity had brought him within an ace of losing his own job. Only an emollient letter of apology personally from him to Eisenhower prevented a final showdown which Montgomery would have lost.

During the night of December 31/January 1, Himmler, as commander of Army Group "Oberrhein", unleashed Operation "Nordwind", giving his troops as objective the Saverne gap. In this way the American 7th Army would be cut in two and its fighting troops in the Bitche–Lauterbourg–Strasbourg salient annihilated. After the fast advance that Patton had been ordered to make on December 19, General Patch had had to extend his left flank as far as Saint Avold and, in the threatened sector, could only field VI Corps against eight German divisions, including the 21st Panzer and the 17th *"Götz von Berlichingen"* S.S. *Panzergrenadier* Divisions.

When he had redeployed as ordered (which stretched the seven divisions of the 7th Army over a front of 90 miles), the commander of the 6th Army Group, General Devers, had naturally been concerned about what to do in the event of a German offensive. In agreement with S.H.A.E.F., he had provided in such an event for his forces to fall back on the eastern slopes of the Vosges and the Belfort gap. This implied abandoning the plain of Alsace. In the afternoon of January 1, after a telephone call from Eisenhower, he issued the order to begin the movements planned for this eventuality.

As Chief-of-Staff to the French Ministry of National Defence, General Juin had been advised since December 28 of the intentions of the 6th Army Group, confirmed by S.H.A.E.F. He had immediately informed General de Gaulle. The latter, seeing the possibility approach, wrote to General Eisenhower on January 1:

"For its part, the French Government cannot allow Strasbourg to fall into enemy hands again without doing everything in its power to defend it."

At the same time, he gave General de Lattre the following order:

"In the event of Allied forces falling back from their present positions to the north of the French 1st Army, I instruct you to act on your own and take over the defence of Strasbourg."

These letters had gone when General de Gaulle was advised of the order to withdraw that had been circulated by General Devers. On receiving the news, he cabled President Roosevelt and the Prime Minister to make clear that he was opposed to evacuating Strasbourg and he instructed General Juin to express the same opinion at S.H.A.E.F.

The interview between Juin and General Bedell Smith, who met him the next day at S.H.A.E.F., was stormy, as was to be expected from two such plain-spoken men. There were even threats about what would happen if the French 1st Army removed itself from the authority of General Devers. All the same, noted Juin:

"Bedell Smith, who had blanched, nevertheless seemed to want to help and assured me before I left that he would try once more to convince his superior and I secured an interview for General de Gaulle with General Eisenhower the next day."

On receiving the report prepared for him by Juin, de Gaulle once more appealed against the S.H.A.E.F. decision which, he had just learned, affected not only Strasbourg but the entire plain of Alsace. In particular, he wrote to Eisenhower on January 3:

"In any case, I must confirm that the French Government cannot accept that Alsace and a part of Lorraine should be intentionally evacuated without fighting, so to speak, especially since the French Army occupies most of the area. To agree to such an evacuation and in such conditions would be an error from the point of view of the general conduct of the war, which stems not only from the military command, but also from the Allied governments. It would also be a serious error from the French national point of view, to which the government is answerable.

"Therefore I have once more to instruct General de Lattre to use the French forces he has to defend the positions he now occupies and also to defend Strasbourg, even if the American forces on his left withdraw.

"From my point of view, I am extremely sorry that this disagreement has occurred at a serious moment and I should like to hope that we can resolve our differences."

In *Crusade in Europe,* General Eisenhower mentions this incident and writes that:

"At first glance de Gaulle's argument seemed to be based upon political considerations founded more on emotion than on logic and consideration."

This represents the typical reasoning of the American strategist of the time, according to whom a military leader should not consider any objective but the destruction of the enemy's organised forces, without regard for political, geographical, sentimental, or prestige aims. In short, his thought regarding Strasbourg was the same as it had been before Paris the previous summer, and as it would be before Berlin three months later. Nevertheless, against this same point of view, he had to think of the consequences that a Franco-American crisis could have on Allied relations.

Churchill had been alerted by de Gaulle and, accompanied by Brooke, travelled to Paris. According to Brooke, they found Eisenhower "most depressed looking" when they walked down the steps from the plane, and it is certain that, at the lunch that followed, the Prime Minister was preaching to one already half-converted. A few hours later, Generals de Gaulle and Juin met Eisenhower, in the presence of Bedell Smith, Churchill, and Brooke, who noted that very evening:

"De Gaulle painted a gloomy picture of the massacres that would ensue if the Germans returned to portions of Alsace-Lorraine. However, Ike had already decided to alter his dispositions so as to leave the divisions practically where they were and not to withdraw the two divisions that were to have been moved up into Patton's reserve."

Juin confirms this: "When General de Gaulle and I arrived at Eisenhower's headquarters at Versailles . . . Churchill was already there. As soon as we came in he informed us that it was all settled and that Strasbourg would not be abandoned. There was not even any discussion, and the only thing that was decided was that I should go with General Bedell Smith the next day to Vittel to inform General Devers, commanding the 6th Army Group."

Moreover, the tension between Eisen-

G.I.s catch up with the news from home while waiting for the German "Nordwind" offensive to break over them.

hower and de Gaulle eased so much as soon as this incident was settled that Eisenhower could not restrain himself from confiding to de Gaulle the difficulties he was having in his personal dealings with Montgomery.

Both on his own initiative and in virtue of the orders he received from Paris, General de Lattre was absolutely determined to hold Strasbourg. And so, on the night of January 2-3, he promptly sent in the solid 3rd Algerian Division, under the command of General du Vigier, recently appointed governor of the city. But, in spite of this, de Lattre intended to remain as long as he could under the control of General Devers and not make difficulties for inter-Allied strategy. That is why, at 2200 hours on January 3, he was very happy to receive the signal announcing that the 6th Army Group had received new orders.

As a result, the American VI Corps, between the Rhine and the Sarre, received orders to continue its retreat only as far as the Moder. But, on January 5, while VI Corps was digging in at this position and the 3rd Algerian Division completed its positions in Strasbourg, the 553rd *Volksgrenadier* Division crossed the Rhine at Gambsheim, between Strasbourg and the confluence of the Moder and Rhine. The next day, it was the turn of the German 19th Army to go over to the offensive, from the Colmar bridgehead. Pressing between the Ill and the Rhône-Rhine Canal, the *"Feldherrnhalle"* Panzer Brigade and the 198th Division managed to get as far as the Erstein heights, less than 13 miles from Strasbourg and

20 from the Gambsheim bridgehead that the 553rd Division had extended as far as the village of Killstett.

Around Strasbourg, attack and counter-attack followed ceaselessly. The Germans had forced the Moder a little above Haguenau and for a short time managed to establish a link with their 553rd Division. However, on January 26, they had definitely lost it again and the battlefield fell silent. O.B. West was very unhappy with the tactics Himmler had used in this offensive, for, instead of wearing down the enemy, he had wasted 11 divisions, four of them of the *Waffen*-S.S., frittering them away in piecemeal actions, ignoring the fact that the barrier of the Rhine prevented him from co-ordinating their movements. All the same, it was General Wiese who paid for the failure of *"Nordwind"*. He received the order to hand over command of the 19th Army to his comrade Rasp. As for Himmler, his flattering promotion to the command of Army Group "Vistula" led, on January 28, to the appointment of Colonel-General Hausser, still recuperating from the wounds he had received during the bloody fighting in the Falaise pocket, to command of Army Group *"Oberrhein"*.

In spite of Operation *"Nordwind"*, on January 15 de Lattre signed his "Personal and Secret Instruction Number 7":

"Leave the Germans no chance of escape. Free Colmar undamaged. The task consists of strangling the pocket

An M3 half-track of the French 1st Army moves into Colmar on February 2, 1945. The American and French offensive pushed the Germans out of the pocket.

alongside the Rhine where it receives its supplies, that is around Brisach.

"Two convergent wedges will be driven in this direction. The first will go northward and will be made by Béthouart's I Corps, which will throw the enemy off balance and suck in his reserves. Then, two days later, II Corps will go into action. This staggering is required by the time it will take to get the expected reserves into place. Its effect will be to increase the surprise of the enemy. Between the two offensive blocs, in the high Vosges, the front will remain inactive at the beginning. It will begin to move when our net along the Rhine is so tightly stretched that the fish is ready to be pulled in."

At this time, Devers and Eisenhower were so concerned about cutting off the Colmar pocket quickly that they did not hesitate to provide substantial reinforcements for the French 1st Army: the U.S. 3rd Division remained under its command, and it also received, though with certain limitations, the 28th Division and the 12th Armoured Division (Major-Generals Norman D. Cota and Roderik R. Allen), as well as the French 2nd Armoured Division under Leclerc, transferred from the Strasbourg area specifically for this purpose.

So, by January 20, 1945, the forces available to de Lattre amounted to 12 divisions, four of which were armoured. However, it should be pointed out that the 3rd Algerian Division was still engaged in and around Killstett and did not take part in the battle of Colmar and that, in the high Vosges, the newly-created 10th Division (General Billotte) was restricted to the modest rôle described above.

Facing these forces along the 100-mile long Alsace bridgehead, the German 19th Army deployed its LXIV and LXIII Corps north and south under the command, respectively, of General Thumm and Lieutenant-General Abraham. The two corps had seven infantry or mountain divisions and the 106th *"Feldherrnhalle"* Panzer Brigade. But these forces were threadbare. Including the reinforcements attached to them, the best-equipped (the 198th Division: Colonel Barde) had exactly 6,891 men in the line, and the 716th *Volksgrenadier* Division (Colonel Hafner) had only 4,546. Furthermore, although de Lattre complained about not receiving all the supplies he thought he needed, by the eighth day of battle General Rasp was reduced to ordering strict economy to his gunners: 12 15-cm and 15 10.5-cm shells per day per gun, compared with 90 155-mm and 120 105-mm shells in the French 1st Army.

Three circumstances, however, compensated a little for the numerical and *matériel* inferiority of the defenders:

1. the terrain, which was no more than "a network of streams and rivers" according to de Lattre. Within it are many woods and even more villages, among which should be mentioned the manufacturing and industrial towns of the Mulhouse region;
2. the weather. On the first day, I Corps attacked LXIII Corps in the face of a snowstorm blowing from the northeast. At night, the temperature fell to 20 and even 25 degrees Centigrade below zero. Finally, just when German resistance was softening, an unexpected rise in the temperature swelled the rivers and made the roads into sloughs of mud; and
3. though far less numerous, the Panther tanks and *"Jagdpanther"* and *"Nashorn"* tank destroyers, with

their very high velocity 8.8-cm guns, were far superior to the French 1st Army's Sherman tanks and M10 tank destroyers. This superiority was emphasised by the German vehicles' wide tracks, which allowed them to manoeuvre on the snow in weather conditions with which their opponents were not able to cope.

At 0700 hours on January 20, H-hour sounded for the reinforced I Corps. Its task was to break the enemy line between Thann and the Forest of Nünenbruck, to capture Cernay, and then to push on without stopping towards Ensisheim and Réguisheim on the Ill. For this purpose, over a 14-mile front, Béthouart had the 9th Colonial Division (General Morlière) around Mulhouse, the 2nd Moroccan Division (General Carpentier) in the centre, and the 4th Moroccan Mountain Division (General de Hesdin) around Thann. In spite of the support of the tanks of the 1st Armoured Division (General Sudre), the attempt to break the enemy lines towards Cernay was not very successful, both because of the tough resistance met, aided by well-sited minefields, and because of the snowstorms which made artillery observation impossible.

On the other hand, the secondary attack, which had been entrusted to the 9th Colonial Division, took the villages of Burtzwiller, Illzach, Kingersheim, Pfastadt, and Lutterbach, a remarkable success due to the dash with which General Salan had led the infantry of this division.

On the following day, LXIII Corps counter-attacked and, on January 22, with the storm blowing worse than ever, General Béthouart expressed the opinion that they should wait for it to blow itself out. But any let-up on the part of I Corps would have prejudiced the attack of II Corps, which was just finishing its preparations. So Béthouart was ordered to press on with his attack, and a fierce, bitter struggle was waged close to Wittelsheim, in the Forest of Nünenbruck, and for the factory towns with their potassium deposits. These towns had to be cleared one by one.

On January 23, II Corps, still under the command of General G. de Monsabert, forced a second wedge into the German line. This was achieved with more ease than the first, even though General Rasp had got wind of the French plans.

On the right, the American 3rd Division had taken Ostheim. On the left, the 1st Free French Division had fought bitterly to capture the village of Illhausern and had formed a bridgehead on the right bank of the Ill, thus preparing to outflank Colmar to the north. But LXIV Corps stiffened its resistance and counter-attacked, preventing Monsabert from any swift exploitation of his success towards Neuf-Brisach. LXIII Corps was likewise preventing Béthouart from moving on. Hidden in the woods, or even inside houses, the Panzers exacted a heavy toll from the men of the 2nd and 5th Armoured

Divisions, supporting the infantry. However, on January 27, the U.S. 3rd Division reached the Colmar Canal, while General Garbay's 1st Free French Division, reinforced by Colonel Faure's paratroops, took the villages of Jebsheim and Grussenheim. Seeing how serious the situation had become, O.K.W. authorised Rasp to pull the 198th Division back over the Rhine, i.e. to give up all the ground won between Rhinau and Erstein by the attack of January 7.

Wishing to press on and complete the attack, General Devers, at the request of the commander of the French 1st Army, put XXI Corps (Major-General Frank W. Milburn) under his command, as well as the U.S. 75th Division (Major-General Porter). Milburn, who from this time on commanded all the American forces involved in the offensive, and the French 5th Armoured Division, was ordered to position his forces between Monsabert's II Corps and Billotte's 10th Division, and then push on towards Neuf-Brisach and also south towards Ensisheim to meet Béthouart. The offensive began again. In the evening of January 30, after a terrifying artillery bombardment of 16,438 105-mm and 155-mm shells, the United States 3rd Division (Major-General O'Daniel) succeeded in crossing the Colmar Canal, and this allowed the United States 28th Division to advance as far as the suburbs of Colmar. The division did not enter Colmar itself, for at the gates of the city, which had been left intact, General Norman D. Cota was courteous enough to give that honour to his comrade-in-arms Schlesser, commanding the 4th Combat Command (5th Armoured Division).

The United States 12th Armoured Division sped south to exploit its victory, with the intention of linking up with I Corps, which had taken Ensisheim, Soultz, and Guebwiller on February 4 and then pushed its 1st Armoured Division and 4th Moroccan Mountain Division forward.

The next day, French and American forces linked up at Rouffach and Sainte Croix-en-Plaine. Twenty-four hours later, in the light of searchlights shining towards the night sky, General O'Daniel's infantry "scaled" the ramparts of Neuf-Brisach in the best mediaeval style. Lastly, at 0800 hours on February 9, a deafening explosion told the men of the French 1st and 2nd Armoured Divisions, who were mopping-up the Forest of la Hardt, together with the 2nd Moroccan Division, that the Germans had just blown the Chalampé bridge, on the Mulhouse–Freiburg road, behind them as they pulled back over the Rhine.

And so, at dawn on the 20th day, the battle of Colmar reached its end. General Rasp left 22,010 prisoners, 80 guns, and 70 tanks in the hands of the enemy, but he had succeeded in bringing back over the Rhine some 50,000 men, 7,000 motor vehicles, 1,500 guns, and 60 armoured vehicles, which underlines his personal qualities of leadership.

As for Allied losses, the figures provided by General de Lattre will allow the reader to appreciate the cost of a modern battle. Of a total of 420,000 Allied troops involved (295,000 French, 125,000 American), casualties were as follows:

	French	*American*
Killed	1,595	542
Wounded	8,583	2,670
Sick	3,887	3,228
Totals	14,065	6,440

Considering just the French, de Lattre's figures also show that the infantry had taken the lion's share. On January 20, it had put 60,000 men into the line, that is about a fifth of the men in the 1st Army. On February 9, it could own to three-quarters of the losses, with 1,138 killed and 6,513 wounded. Add to these figures the 354 killed and 1,151 wounded which the battle cost the armoured units, and it becomes clear that the other arms lost only 1,022 killed and wounded. Finally, due credit must be given to the magnificent effort of the medical services under Surgeon-General Guirriec. In spite of the appalling weather they had only 142 deaths, that is 0.9 per cent of the cases received.

As a conclusion to the story of this battle, some tribute should be paid to the men who fought in it. In the *Revue militaire suisse*, Major-General Montfort has written:

"The French, under superb leadership and enjoying powerful *matériel* advantages, made a magnificent effort, fully worthy of their predecessors in World War I.

"The Germans, under extraordinarily difficult conditions and three differing requirements (operational, *matériel,* and morale), defended themselves with great ability and fought . . . with courage worthy of praise."

It should be noted that there had been much inter-Allied squabbling about the length of time that the battle for Colmar was taking: the Allied high command wanted this irritating pocket cleared out of the way as quickly as possible, so that all available Allied forces might be readied for the last devastating blow against Germany that would win the war in the West. The irritation caused by the Colmar delay was perhaps exacerbated by another clash between Eisenhower and Montgomery. But what increased the trouble even more was the fact that Brooke backed Montgomery with all the weight of his authority. Once more S.H.A.E.F. and the 21st Army Group were divided on the alternatives of the "concentrated push" or the "wide front".

Eisenhower rejected Montgomery's intention of supervising Bradley's operations, but nevertheless, on December 31, 1944, informed Montgomery of his plan of operations:

"Basic plan–to destroy enemy forces west of Rhine, north of the Moselle, and to prepare for crossing the Rhine in force with the *main effort north of the Ruhr.*"

Once the Ardennes salient had been pinched out (Point *a*), Eisenhower envisaged the following general offensive:

"*b.* Thereafter First and Third Armies to drive to north-east on general line Prum-Bonn, eventually to Rhine.

"*c.* When *a* is accomplished, 21st Army Group, with Ninth U.S. Army under operational command, to resume preparations for 'Veritable'."

In practical terms, this plan required Montgomery to force the Reichswald forest position, which bars the corridor between the Maas and the Rhine on the Dutch-German frontier, to secure the left bank of the Rhine between Emmerich and Düsseldorf, and to prepare to force a passage of the river north of its junction with the Ruhr. This sketch of a plan pleased Montgomery, who wrote:

"It did all I wanted except in the realm of operational control, and because of Marshall's telegram that subject was closed. It put the weight in the north and gave the Ninth American Army to 21 Army Group. It gave me power of decision in the event of disagreement with Bradley on the boundary between 12 and 21 Army Groups. In fact, I had been given very nearly all that I had been asking for since

American infantry move up through a snowstorm, typical of the weather that helped the Germans considerably.

August. Better late than never. I obviously could not ask for more.''

Nevertheless, when one considers the allotment of forces and in particular the fixing of objectives, there is no avoiding the fact that the two sides did not speak a common language any more.

Actually, Montgomery estimated that if ''Veritable'' was to be successful, American reinforcements should consist

Canadian troops on winter patrol near the Rhine.

of five corps, (16 divisions), of which four corps (13 divisions) should be placed under the command of the American 9th Army, and the rest under the British 2nd Army. In these estimates, he seems to have been completely unaware of the principles established by his superior at the beginning of his outline dated December 31: ''to destroy enemy forces west of Rhine''. According to Eisenhower's clearly-expressed opinion, this required a second push from around Prüm towards the Rhine at Bonn, which

would reduce the United States forces which could be detached for ''Veritable'' to only three corps and 12 divisions.

Montgomery was obliged to give in, but he resumed the argument on January 20 when he heard the news that Bradley, far from limiting himself to reducing the Ardennes salient, intended to follow up his attack for another fortnight. Montgomery wrote to Brooke:

''Both Ike and Bradley are emphatic that we should not—not—cross the Rhine in strength anywhere until we are lined

up along its entire length from Nijmegen to Switzerland."

Two days later, in a second letter which, like the first, he has not quoted in his memoirs, he harped on the same question: "My latest information is that S.H.A.E.F. are very worried about situation in South about Colmar and Strasbourg . . ."

As the commander-in-chief seemed ready to reinforce this sector, it followed that "Veritable" would be postponed indefinitely. This led him to conclude bitterly:

"I fear that the old snags of indecision and vacillation and refusal to consider the military problem fairly and squarely are coming to the front again . . . The real trouble is that there is no control and the three Army Groups are each intent on their own affairs. Patton to-day issued a stirring order to Third Army, saying the next step would be Cologne . . . one has to preserve a sense of humour these days, otherwise one would go mad."

Brooke was appreciative of this argument and "cordially, but very gravely", as General Eisenhower writes, expressed the view to him that putting his plan into effect would have the result of producing an "organised dispersion" of Allied forces. Eisenhower opposed this view, and events proved him right. First of all, the Germans had to be deprived of the advantage of permanent fortifications which allowed them to economise their means and then build up massive forces in the sector where the main attack would be launched:

"If, however, we should first, in a series of concentrated and powerful attacks, destroy the German forces west of the Rhine, the effect would be to give us all along the great front a defensive line of equal strength to the enemy's. We calculated that with the western bank of the Rhine in our possession we could hurl some seventy-five reinforced divisions against the German in great converging attacks. If we allowed the enemy south of the Ruhr to remain in the Siegfried, we would be limited to a single offensive by some thirty-five divisions.

"A second advantage of our plan would be the deflection of the enemy forces later to be met at the crossings of the Rhine obstacle. Moreover, the effect of the converging attack is multiplied when it is accompanied by such air power as we had in Europe in the early months of 1945. Through its use we could prevent the enemy from switching forces back and forth at will against either of the attacking columns and we could likewise employ our entire air power at any moment to further the advance in any area desired."

But although Eisenhower had refuted Brooke's point, he was unable to convert the latter to his way of thinking. That is why he travelled to Marseilles on January 25 to explain to Marshall, who was on his way to Yalta via Malta, his plan of operations and the objections it was coming up against among the British. He had no

difficulty in obtaining Marshall's complete agreement, and the latter said to him at the end of the interview:

"I can, of course, uphold your position merely on the principle that these decisions fall within your sphere of responsibility. But your plan is so sound that I think it better for you to send General Smith to Malta so that he may explain these matters in detail. Their logic will be convincing."

This was done and, after some explanations by Bedell Smith and some amendments on the part of the Combined Chiefs-of-Staff Committee, Eisenhower's plan, comprising of a double push towards the Rhine and a double encirclement of the Ruhr, was adopted and Montgomery would spare nothing to make it a success.

On January 16, the American 3rd and 1st Armies crushed the tip of the Ardennes salient and linked up in the ruins of Houffalize. The following day, as agreed, the 1st Army was returned to the command of Bradley, to his great satisfaction. But he was far less pleased with the task now given him, that of engaging the Germans in the wooded and hilly region of Schleiden and Schmidt, which had cost him so dear the previous autumn, and of capturing the hydro-electric system of the Roer, the Erft, and the Olef. On February 8, V Corps (under Major-General L. T. Gerow), of the 1st Army had reached its objective. That was that. At dawn, on the next day, the Germans blew up the reservoir gates and from mid-day onwards the water was rising at a rate of nearly two and a half feet an hour in front of the 9th Army.

Meanwhile, the left of this army, still under the command of Lieutenant-General William H. Simpson, and the right of the British 2nd Army, under General Miles C. Dempsey, were taking out the salient which the enemy was holding between the Maas and the Roer, now an enclave between the Allied flanks. The little Dutch village of Roermond was still held by the German 15th Army, which formed the right of Army Group "B". On January 28, this rectifying operation, a prelude to the pincer attack called "Veritable/Grenade", was brought to a successful conclusion.

In this duel between Field-Marshal von Rundstedt and General Eisenhower, the former had at his disposal at the beginning of February (after he had lost the 6th *Panzerarmee*, taken away to help the Hungarian front), 73 divisions, including eight Panzer or *Panzergrenadier*. But the infantry divisions had fallen to an average of about 7,000 men each. As for the armoured formations, whatever may have been the excellent quality of their *matériel*, they suffered a continual shortage of petrol because of the Allied air offensive against the German synthetic petrol plants. In other words, as had started to become evident in the battle of Colmar, the crisis in munitions was getting ever more desperate at the front. The land forces of the Third Reich, more-

over, could not rely on any support from the Luftwaffe, whose jet fighters were fully engaged attempting to defend what was left of Germany's cities against the redoubled attacks of the British and American Strategic Air Forces.

The last straw was that Rundstedt, in his office at Koblenz, was faced by a hopeless situation, and had been stripped of all initiative in the direction of operations. On January 21, he received the following incredible *Führerbefehl*, with orders to distribute it down to divisional level:

"Commanders-in-chief, army, corps, and divisional commanders are personally responsible to me for reporting in good time:

"(a) Every decision to execute an operational movement.

"(b) Every offensive plan from divisional level upwards that does not fit exactly with the directives of the higher command.

"(c) Every attack in a quiet sector intended to draw the enemy's attention to that sector, with the exception of normal shock troop actions.

"(d) Every plan for withdrawal or retreat.

"(e) Every intention of surrendering a position, a strongpoint, or a fortress.

"Commanders must make sure that I have time to intervene as I see fit, and that my orders can reach the front line troops in good time."

And the *Führer* further announced that any commander or staff officer who by "deliberate intent, carelessness, or oversight" hindered the execution of this order, would be punished with "draconian severity".

From the Swiss frontier to the North Sea, Eisenhower had 70 divisions under his command on January 1, 1945:

	Infantry	Armoured	Airborne	Total
U.S.	31	11	3	45
British	7	4	1	12
Canadian	2	1	–	3
French	6	3	–	9
Polish	–	1	–	1
Totals	46	20	4	70

By May 8 this number would have been increased by another 15 American divisions (including four armoured), six French divisions, and two Canadian divisions (including one armoured).

Deducting six divisions fighting in the Alps or besieging German fortresses, this would give S.H.A.E.F. 87 divisions at the end of the war.

Despite the losses they had to bear, the Allied divisions at this time were far less restricted than their German counterparts. The supply crisis, so acute in September, was now no more than an unpleasant memory. Petrol was in good supply and there was no shortage of shells at the front. The proximity fuses with which they were fitted allowed the gunners to fire shells which burst in the air, wreaking havoc among

A smoke-screen attempts to hide the Tirpitz *from a Lancaster bomber.*

exposed troops. With reference to armour, the introduction into the United States Army of the heavy (41-ton) M26 General Pershing tank was significant. It was well-armoured, and had a 90-mm gun and good cross-country performance, the result of its Christie-type suspension and wide tracks. The Americans had rediscovered this suspension after seeing the results it gave in the service of the Germans, who had borrowed the idea from the Russians. The latter had acquired a licence to build the Christie suspension from the United States, after 1919, when the American military authorities had refused, in spite of the urging of the young Major George S. Patton, to take any firm interest in Christie and his designs.

Thus the Allies' land forces were far more numerous than the Germans'. They also enjoyed powerful air support from a force which was both numerous and well-trained. Here General Devers had the Franco-American 1st Tactical Air Force (Major-General R. M. Webster), in which the French I Air Corps (Brigadier-General P. Gerardot) was itself attached to the French 1st Army. The United States 9th Air Force (Lieutenant-General Hoyt S. Vandenberg,) came under the overall command of General Bradley, and the British 2nd Tactical Air Force (Air-Marshal Sir Arthur Coningham) efficiently seconded Field-Marshal Montgomery's operations. On the German side there was nothing which could resist this formidable mass of flying artillery.

On November 12, 1944, 28 R.A.F. Lancasters attacked the great battleship *Tirpitz* in Tromsö with 12,000-lb "Tallboy" bombs and sank her at her anchorage.

What was now left of the surface forces of the Kriegsmarine was being expended in the Baltic in attempts to help the army. As for the U-boats, which had lost 242 of their number during 1944, their successes in the North Atlantic between June 6, 1944 and May 8, 1945, were limited to the sinking of 31 merchant ships, displacing altogether only 178,000 tons. This was virtually nothing at all.

At 0500 hours on February 8, 1,400 guns of the Canadian 1st Army blasted the German 84th Division, which had dug itself in along a seven-mile front between the Maas and the Waal close to the Dutch-German frontier. At 1030 hours, the British XXX Corps, which Montgomery had put under the command of General Crerar, moved in to the attack with five divisions (the British 51st, 53rd, and 15th and the Canadian 2nd and 3rd) in the first wave and the 43rd Division and the Guards Armoured Division in reserve. In all, according to the commander of the corps, Lieutenant-General Horrocks, there were 200,000 men and 35,000 vehicles.

The German position was heavily mined, and included a flooded area on the right and the thick Reichswald forest on the left. Moreover, the day before the attack, a thaw had softened the ground. Neither Hitler, at O.K.W., nor Colonel-General Blaskowitz, commanding Army Group "H", had been willing to accept the idea that Montgomery would choose such a sector in which to attack. Yet General Schlemm, commanding the 1st Parachute Army, had warned them of this possibility. At the end of the day the 84th Division had lost 1,300 prisoners and was close to breaking-point.

Meanwhile the American 9th Army had been ordered to unleash Operation "Grenade" on February 10. This would

cross the Roer and advance to the Rhine at Düsseldorf. Now came the flooding caused by the destruction of the Eifel dams, which held up the American 9th Army completely for 12 days and slowed down the British XXX Corps. The latter's units were also hopelessly mixed up. These delays allowed Schlemm to send his 7th and 6th Parachute, 15th *Panzergrenadier*, and then 116th Panzer Divisions to the rescue one after the other. And as Colonel C. P. Stacey, the official Canadian Army historian, notes, the Germans, at the edge of the abyss, had lost none of their morale:

"In this, the twilight of their gods, the defenders of the Reich displayed the recklessness of fanaticism and the courage of despair. In the contests west of the Rhine, in particular, they fought with special ferocity and resolution, rendering the battles in the Reichswald and Hochwald forests grimly memorable in the annals of this war."

On February 13, the Canadian 1st Army had mopped up the Reichswald and the little town of Kleve, and had reached Gennep, where it was reinforced across the Maas by the British 52nd Division and 11th Armoured Division. Schlemm threw two divisions of infantry into the battle as well as the famous Panzer-*"Lehr"* Division, and so the intervention of Lieutenant-General G. G. Simonds's Canadian II Corps at the side of the British XXX Corps did not have the decisive effect that Crerar expected. The 11th day of the offensive saw the attackers marking time on the Goch–Kalkar line about 15 miles from their jumping-off point.

But, just like the British 2nd Army in Normandy, the Canadian 1st Army had attracted the larger part of the enemy's forces, while the flood water in the Roer valley was going down. The weather also turned finer, and Montgomery fixed February 23 for the launching of Operation "Grenade". In his order of the day to the men of the 21st Army Group, Montgomery assured them that this was to be the beginning of the last round against Germany. The Third Reich was ready for the knock-out blow, which would be delivered from several directions.

Then, as an opening move, the Anglo-American Strategic Air Force launched 10,000 bombers and fighter escorts and made the heaviest attack of the war on the Third Reich's communications network.

More than 200 targets featured on the programme of this attack, which went under the name of Operation "Clarion". Some of these objectives were bombed from only 4,500 feet because enemy anti-aircraft action was almost totally ineffective since Hitler had stripped it to supply the Eastern Front. The results of this bombing on February 22 were still noticeable when Colonel-General Jodl came to bring General Eisenhower the surrender of the Third Reich.

The following day, at 0245 hours, the artillery of the United States 9th Army opened fire on German positions on the

Roer. The 15th Army (General von Zangen) which defended them, formed the right of Army Group "B" (Field-Marshal Model). Though it defended itself well, his 353rd Division was still thrown out of the ruins of Julich by the American XIX Corps (Major-General Raymond S. Maclain). Meanwhile, in the Linnich sector, XIII Corps (Major-General Alvan C. Gillem) had established a bridgehead a mile and a half deep. VII Corps (Lieutenant-General John L. Collins) of the American 1st Army, had also taken part in the attack and, by the end of the day, had mopped up Duren.

Hitler, Rundstedt, and Model used every last resource to tackle this new crisis looming on the horizon. Schlemm was stripped of the reinforcements which had just been despatched to him, and to these were added the 9th and 11th Panzer Divisions and the 3rd *Panzergrenadier* Division. These forces were instructed to hit the enemy's north-easterly push in its flank.

All the same, by February 27, the Allied breakthrough was complete near Erkelenz, and two days later, XIII Corps swept through the conurbation of Rheydt–Mönchengladbach. At the same time, to the right of the 9th Army, XVI Corps (Major-General J. B. Anderson) hurtled towards Roermond and Venlo behind the 1st Parachute Army, while on the right, XIX Corps was approaching Neuss opposite Düsseldorf.

In these circumstances Schlemm was ordered to retreat to the right bank of the Rhine, and he must be given all credit for carrying out this delicate and dangerous mission with remarkable skill. Rearguard skirmishes at Rheinberg, Sonsbeck, and Xanten gave him the time to get the bulk of his forces across and to complete the planned demolitions without fault. On March 6, the United States 9th Army and the Canadian 1st Army linked up opposite Wesel.

This joint Operation "Veritable/Grenade" cost the 18 German divisions engaged 53,000 prisoners. But Crerar alone had suffered 15,634 dead, wounded, and missing, of which 5,304 were Canadian troops.

On that same day, March 6, the leading division of the American VII Corps entered Cologne. Now the Allies were lining the Rhine between Cologne and Nijmegen, more than 100 miles downstream, where the river, if the stream slows down, widens to reach a breadth as great as 250 or 300 yards, and all the bridges had been destroyed. Forcing the Rhine north of the Ruhr, according to Montgomery's formula, would result in a delay of two weeks and necessitate considerable reinforcements for the 21st Army Group. And here can be seen Eisenhower's farsightedness in keeping to his plan of operations of December 31, 1944: to defeat the enemy west of the Rhine. For, if he had kept Bradley marking time then, Hitler could have detached the forces necessary to check Montgomery on the Rhine below Cologne.

This did not happen, for, on March 6, Army Group "B" was fighting the American 1st Army on its right and the 3rd on its centre. Its 5th *Panzerarmee* (Colonel-General Harpe) was now well and truly outflanked and overrun on both wings. According to the original plan, the American 1st Army was to provide the left flank of Operation "Grenade". With this in view, General Bradley had increased its size to three corps (14 divisions). But it was not foreseen that the 3rd Army would take part in the attack and it was only by a rather surreptitious move that, during the second week of January, Patton had pushed his forces as far as the Moselle in Luxembourg, the Sûre, and the Our near the *Westwall,* covering himself at S.H.A.E.F. by claiming that his moves were "offensive defence", when his aggression had no other aim but that of reaching the Rhine at Koblenz.

The defeat of the German 15th Army opened a breach in Field-Marshal Model's line which General Hodges and his 1st Army did not delay in exploiting. Having occupied Cologne, VII Corps set off for Bonn on March 7. III Corps (Major-General J. Millikin), which was advancing on the right of VII Corps, had orders to take the crossings over the Ahr. This task was entrusted to the 9th Armoured Division (Major-General John W. Leonard).

Towards the end of the morning of March 7, Brigadier-General William M. Hoge, leading Combat Command "B" of the 9th Armoured Division, was informed that the Ludendorff Bridge near Remagen was still intact. He decided not to follow his orders (which had specified Sinzig as his target) to the letter and resolved there and then to chance his luck and seize the bridge. A little before 1600 hours, 2nd Lieutenant Karl Timmermann ventured on to the bridge, followed by the Burrows section. Seeing them, the German guard tried to set off the demolition charges, but in vain. Under American fire, Sergeant Faust, another hero of this episode, then lit the fuse. But the effect of the explosion was insignificant, and, a few minutes later, Sergeant Alex Drabik was the first American fighting man to step on the right bank of the Rhine. Behind him, Lieutenant Hugh B. Mott, a combat engineer, and three sappers tore the charges from the girders and threw the explosives into the river.

"The enemy had reached Kreuzberg and as far as a bridge near Remagen which, it appears, was encumbered with fugitives. They crossed the bridge and succeeded in forming a bridgehead on the eastern bank of the river. Counterattack early this morning. The 11th Panzer Division will be brought from Bonn. But petrol is in short supply."

The O.K.W. war diary records this national catastrophe in these unemotional words. Therefore it gives no account of Hitler's rage, which was terrible. Major Scheler and three others were declared responsible, on Hitler's orders, for the

success of the Allied surprise attack, court-martialled, and shot.

Twenty-four hours after this surprise, there were already 8,000 Americans in the bridgehead. By March 17, four divisions (9th, 78th, 99th, and 9th Armoured) were dug in. On the same day the bridge collapsed. Hitler had concentrated the fire of a battery of 17-cm guns on it, as well as ordering aircraft and V-2 attacks, and even attempts by Kriegsmarine human torpedoes and frogmen. But, protected by booms and nets, 1st Army engineers had already built another bridge and both banks of the Rhine were bristling with anti-aircraft guns.

Having transferred III Corps (three divisions) to the 1st Army, Patton remained in command of VIII, XII, and XX Corps, which had 12 divisions, three of which were armoured. The crossing of the Our and the Sûre, on the Saint Vith–Echternach line, was no little matter because the rivers were in flood. The forcing of *Westwall* was also very tough. In XII Corps there was one division which had

The Allied advance to the Rhine and the establishment of the first bridgeheads.

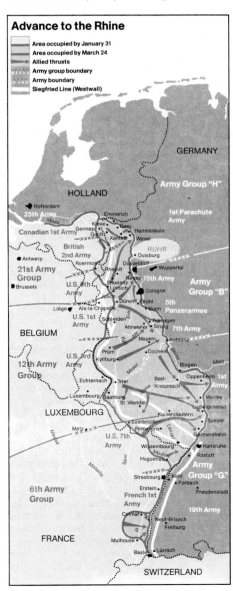

573

to reduce 120 concrete casemates. This it did with self-propelled 155-mm guns, pounding the embrasures from a range of only 300 yards.

In spite of everything, by the end of February VIII and XII Corps were on the Kyll, having advanced about 20 miles into German territory. XX Corps had taken Saarburg and advanced as far as the apex of the triangle formed by the Mosel and the Saar at their confluence a little above Trier. Up till then the German 7th Army (General Brandenberger), which faced Patton, had defended itself tenaciously, but this very tenacity explains why, on March 1, having exhausted its supplies, it literally collapsed. On that day, wrote Patton:

"At 14.15, Walker [commander of XX Corps] called up to say the 10th Armoured Division was in Trier and had captured a bridge over the Moselle intact. The capture of this bridge was due to the heroic act of Lieutenant Colonel J. J. Richardson, deceased. He was riding in the leading vehicle of his battalion of armoured infantry when he saw the wires leading to the demolition charges at the far end of the bridge. Jumping out of the vehicle, he raced across the bridge under heavy fire and cut the wires. The acid test of battle brings out the pure metal."

On March 3, the forcing of the Kyll at Kyllburg by the 5th Division, under Major-General S. LeRoy Irwin, enabled Major-General Manton Eddy, commanding XII Corps, to detach his 4th Division. Under the command of Major-General Hugh J. Gaffey, this division made a raid of mad audacity, covering 26 miles on March 4 alone and reaching Daun in the evening. Two days later, it reached the Rhine above Koblenz. On its left, the 11th Armoured Division (Major-General Holmes E. Dager), advancing ahead of VII Corps, established first contact with the American 1st Army on March 11, near Brohl.

On March 8, the O.K.W. war diary noted that LIII Corps had been steamrollered and that any co-ordinated conduct of operations was henceforth impossible. The truth of this is illustrated by the capture of General von Rothkirch und Panthen, in command of LIII Corps. Bradley recounts the story thus:

"So rapid was the dissolution that even the senior German commanders lost touch with their crumbling front. One day a German corps commander drove into a field of listless soldiers and asked why they were not fighting the Allies. Not until an American MP clasped him on the shoulder and invited him to join the throng, did the general learn that he had stumbled into a PW concentration."

Altogether, the second phase of the battle for the Rhineland, called Operation "Lumberjack", had brought the 12th Army Group 51,000 prisoners. It had also given it the priceless bridgehead at Remagen, which the German 15th Army was unable to destroy, since the four Panzer divisions which Model had given the energetic Lieutenant-General Bayer-

lein for this purpose did not total more than 5,000 men, 60 tanks, and 30 guns. On the other side of the battlefield, the Americans spread out in all directions. So great and thorough was their push that, on March 22, they were on the right bank of the Rhine in a bridgehead 25 miles long and ten miles deep.

As explained earlier, because of the forces and *matériel* requested by Montgomery in order to lead his army group across the Rhine to the north of the Ruhr, Eisenhower had at first limited his operation to the left bank of the Mosel. However, Hitler's obstinate decision to keep his Army Group "G" inside the salient limited by Haguenau, Saarbrücken, Cochem (north of the Mosel), and Koblenz, would convince him that the best thing to do was to strike a third blow at the enemy on the west of the Rhine, which meant that the 3rd Army and the 6th Army Group would be able to take part.

Colonel-General Hausser, commanding Army Group "G", had just been given the 7th Army, recently taken over by General Obstfelder, and which was at present heavily engaged against Patton.

Hausser still had the 1st Army (General Foertsch), which was occupying the Moder front and the Siegfried Line or *Westwall* as far as the approaches to Forbach. The 19th Army, having evacuated the Colmar pocket, now came directly under the command of O.K.W. But at this time all these units totalled only 13 divisions, most of them badly worn, though some of them still gave a good account of themselves, for example the 2nd Mountain Division (Lieutenant-General Degen), and the 6th S.S. Mountain Division (Lieutenant-General Brenner).

Under these conditions, Hausser and his army commanders were of the opinion that they ought to put the Rhine, between the junctures of the Mosel and the Lauter, behind them as soon as possible and be ready to abandon the Siegfried Line after having destroyed all its installations. But Hitler reacted indignantly to this suggestion of destroying a masterpiece of German military engineering to which he had contributed so much.

The Führer was mistaken about the value of this construction, however. Patton, who visited one of the fortresses taken by the 76th Division, points out its weak point with his usual perspicacity:

"It consisted of a three storey submerged barracks with toilets, shower baths, a hospital, laundry, kitchen, store rooms and every conceivable convenience plus an enormous telephone installation. Electricity and heat were produced by a pair of identical diesel engines with generators. Yet the whole offensive capacity of this installation consisted of two machine guns and a 60-mm mortar operating from steel cupolas which worked up and down by means of hydraulic lifts. The 60-mm mortar was peculiar in that it was operated by remote control. As in all cases, this particular

pill box was taken by a dynamite charge against the back door. We found marks on the cupolas, which were ten inches thick, where our 90-mm shells fired at a range of two hundred yards, had simply bounced."

But neither Hitler nor his subordinates imagined that Patton would need only four or five days to shift the centre of gravity of his 3rd Army from Brohl and Koblenz on the Rhine to Mayen on the Nette and Cochem on the Mosel. On the left, VIII Corps, now reduced to two divisions, would keep watch on Koblenz. In the centre, XII Corps, increased to six divisions (5th, 76th, 89th, and 90th Infantry, and 4th and 11th Armoured), was given Bingen on the Rhine and Bad-Kreuznach on the Nahe as its first targets. On the right, XX Corps with four divisions (26th, 80th, and 94th Infantry and 10th Armoured) had orders to press on to Kaiserslautern behind the backs of the defenders of the *Westwall*, which would be attacked frontally by the American 7th Army. The latter, commanded by Lieutenant-General Alexander M. Patch, had 12 divisions, including the 3rd Algerian Division. As can be seen, the third act of the Battle of the Rhine, named "Undertone" was about to match 22 more or less intact Allied divisions against 13 worn-out German ones. Actually, since the end of January, the 7th Army had been waiting poised between Haguenau and Forbach.

As for the 3rd Army, its losses, between January 29 and March 12, amounted to only 21,581 officers, N.C.O.s, and men, of which 3,650 had been killed and 1,374 were missing, which gives a daily divisional average of eight killed or missing and 32 wounded. These figures would suggest that despite his nickname of "Blood and Guts", Patton was not at all prodigal with the lives of his men.

On the evening of March 14, XII Corps had already got most of its 5th and 90th Divisions over on the right bank of the Mosel at Treis, eight miles below Cochem. Eddy then wasted no time in unleashing his 4th and 11th Armoured Divisions.

To his right, XX Corps was attacking towards Saint Wendel, in the rear of the *Westwall*. At last, at dawn on March 15, H-hour came for the 7th Army. Its VI Corps (3rd Algerian, 36th, 42nd, and 103rd Divisions and 14th Armoured Division), went into the attack on the Moder front. Its 15th Division attacked the *Westwall*, its left towards Saarlautern, the French Sarrelouis, in contact with XX Corps.

By March 16, the 4th Armoured Division had advanced 32 miles in 48 hours. As it crossed the Nahe, near Bad-Kreuznach, it clashed violently with the 2nd Panzer Division (Major-General von Lauchert). But Patton was aware of the audacity of Gaffey, his ex-chief-of-staff, and had not let him fight it out alone. Opportunely reinforced, the 4th Armoured Division defeated the desperate counter-attack and moved forward again. By March 19, it had arrived seven miles west of Worms and 12 miles south-west of Mainz. On the same day, XX Corps, to which the 7th Army had given the 12th Armoured Division, under Major-General R. R. Allen, pushed its armoured spearheads as far as 15 miles from Kaiserslautern. Since the crossing of the Mosel, the 3rd Army had lost, including accidents, only 800 men, while it had taken 12,000 prisoners.

Forty-eight hours later, in XII Corps, the 90th Division, which had lost two commanders in Normandy, was busy mopping up Mainz, the 4th Armoured Division was occupying Worms, and the 11th was pushing on to the south of the city.

In XX Corps, Major-General Walton H. Walker had thrown his 12th Armoured Division into Ludwigshafen and was pushing his 10th towards Landau. Just as the difficult terrain of the Eifel had been no impediment, that of the Hunsruck, which is just as bad, had not been able to hold back the *élan* of the 3rd Army, supported flexibly and efficiently by Major-General Otto P. Weyland's XIX Tactical Air Command of the 9th Air Force.

Facing the German 1st Army, the American 7th Army had had a considerably more difficult task. There is some evidence of this in a note made by Pierre Lyautey who, as liaison officer, was with the 3rd Algerian Division (General Guillaume), when it attacked across the Moder.

"March 15: Artillery preparation. The planned 2,000 shells light up the scene. Attack by the 4th Tunisians. Skirmishes. The leading company runs, at seven in the morning, from ruin to ruin, lonely wall to lonely wall, reaches the railway, dives into the underground passage and jumps up into the mangled and dismantled gasworks. Violent reaction from German artillery, mortar, and machine guns. Impossible to move out. The whole sector is alive with fire. The company shelters in the gas-works. First one tank explodes, then another. Beyond the church, the scene is one of a major offensive: stretcher-bearers, stretchers, limping men walking around with white cards, a smell of blood, stifling heat. The last cows of Oberhoffen-Bénarès are in their death agony among the rubble."

It took four days for Major-General Edward H. Brooks, commanding VI Corps, to take back from the Germans the ground lost in lower Alsace as a result of Operation *"Nordwind"*. Then he closed in on the *Westwall* between the Rhine and the Vosges.

Both General de Gaulle and General de Lattre had no intention, however, of allowing the French Army to be restricted to a purely defensive function on the left bank of the Rhine. They wanted to see it play a part in the invasion of the Third

Reich. While awaiting a definite decision from S.H.A.E.F., General de Gaulle writes, "General Devers, a good ally and a good friend, sympathised with de Lattre's wishes".

That is why, on March 18, General de Monsabert received command of a task force comprising the 3rd Algerian Division and two-thirds of the 5th Armoured Division; aiming for Speyer, it would give the French 1st Army a front over the Rhine in Germany.

The three infantry divisions of the United States VI Corps took three days and lost 2,200 men to overcome that part of the *Westwall* allotted to them as objective, but using its infantry and engineers in turn, Brooks finally pierced the defences between Wissembourg and Pirmasens. As for Monsabert, he had difficulty in front of the Bienwald. Nevertheless, his tanks were around Maximiliansau opposite Karlsruhe by the evening of March 24.

Patch had taken Landau the day before, so the Battle of the Palatinate, the third act of the Battle of the Rhine, was drawing to its end.

The battle had been conducted to Eisenhower's complete satisfaction. Between February 8 and March 24, the enemy had lost 280,000 prisoners, the remains of five German armies which had crossed back over the Rhine between the German-Dutch and Franco-German frontiers. Army Group "B" had suffered most. Patton alone could claim 140,112 prisoners, against the 53,000 taken by the 21st Army Group in Operation "Veritable/Grenade". Therefore Eisenhower had proved his superiority not only over Hitler's arms but also over Montgomery's arguments.

Furthermore, on the night of March 22/23, Patton also succeeded in crossing the Rhine as Bradley had recommended, profiting from the Germans' disorder.

Men and vehicles of the American 1st Army pour across the intact Ludendorff railway bridge at Remagen.

The banks there being suitable, Patton chose the stretch near Oppenheim, which was occupied by the 5th Division (Major-General S. LeRoy Irwin), half-way between Worms and Mainz.

At 2230 hours, 200 Piper L-4 Grasshoppers began to shuttle from one bank to the other. These small observation and artillery-spotting aircraft carried an armed infantryman instead of an observer. Once the first bridgehead had thus been formed, the 12 L.C.V.P.s (Landing Craft Vehicle/Personnel) of the "naval detachment" which Patton had trained to a high pitch of efficiency on the Moselle at Toul, entered the river while his bridging crews, from which he had refused to be separated (lest he not get them back) when he had driven hard from the Sarre to the Ardennes, began to work at once under the command of Brigadier-General Conklin, the 3rd Army's chief engineer.

At dawn on March 23, the 5th Division had already placed six infantry battalions, about 4,000 or 5,000 men, on the right bank of the Rhine, at the cost of only eight killed and 20 wounded. The Germans were so surprised that when Patton made his report to Bradley, he asked him not to publicise the news, so as to keep the Germans in the dark while they expected him at the approaches to Mainz. As an all-American soldier, he was happy to have stolen a march over "Monty" by forcing the Rhine before him and without making any demands on anybody.

As a result, 48 hours later, five divisions of the 3rd Army had crossed the Rhine at Oppenheim, stretched along the valley of the Main: XII Corps towards Aschaffenburg, and XX Corps towards Hanau.

CHAPTER 70
The Russians invade East Prussia

January 12, 1945 saw the Red Army pour out in a great torrent over the bridge-heads it had won the previous summer on the left bank of the Vistula. Two days later it was assaulting the German positions on the Narew and the defences of Eastern Prussia which, three months earlier, had defied the efforts of Zakharov and Chernyakhovsky. Two months later Konev crossed the Oder both above and below Breslau (Wrocław), Zhukov reached it between Frankfurt and Küstrin (Kostrzyn), Rokossovsky was at its mouth and Vasilevsky was about to take the fortress of Königsberg.

To the Wehrmacht, the Third Reich, and Hitler, defeated also on the Western Front, this was the death blow. It was to mean the end of nine centuries of conquest, occupation, and civilisation by the Germans of the whole area between the Oder-Neisse line and the eastern frontiers of Germany as drawn up at Versailles. By May 8, 1945 nearly eight million inhabitants of East Prussia, Pomerania, and the borderland between Brandenburg and Silesia had fled their homes before the invading Soviets. Over three and a half million more Germans were to be driven out of these same areas between 1945 and 1950. The defeat of Germany's military might was thus to bring about the greatest movement of peoples since the collapse of the Roman Empire and the invasions by the Germans, Iranians, and Huns in the 5th Century A.D.

We turn now to the forces with which Germany fought the Red Army in the last stage of their merciless duel.

At the turn of the year O.K.W. had 288 divisions, including 45 Panzer and *Panzergrenadier*. This number does not, however, include the divisions in course of formation under *Reichsführer* Heinrich Himmler, C.-in-C. of the *Ersatzheer* since the attempt on Hitler's life of July 20, 1944. In any case, this grandiose total is misleading, as all formations were understrength and short of equipment.

124 of these divisions were under O.K.W.:

O.B. West (France) under
  Rundstedt: 74
O.B. *Süd* (Italy) under Kesselring: 24
O.B. *Süd-Ost* (Bosnia and Croatia)
  under Weichs: 9
Crete, Rhodes, and dependencies: 2
20th Mountain Army (Norway)
  under Rendulic: 15

Take away from this total the *Süd-Ost* forces fighting the Yugoslav Liberation Army and the six divisions of Colonel-General Rendulic keeping the Russians out of Narvik in the area of Lyngenfjord, and we see that the Western fronts between them were engaging 109 German divisions, or some 40 per cent of Germany's military strength at the end of 1944.

This gave O.K.H. 164 divisions with

which to fight the Red Army on a front running from the Drava at Barcs on its right to the Gulf of Riga in the area of Tukums on its left. Army Group "South" in Hungary (General Wöhler) had 38 divisions, including 15 Panzer or *Panzergrenadier*. In the Kurland bridgehead Colonel-General Schörner had 27 divisions, including three Panzer. This left 99 divisions for Army Groups "A" and "Centre" to hold the front between the southern slopes of the Carpathians and Memel on the Baltic.

When Major-General Gehlen reported his conclusion that a powerful enemy offensive was imminent against Army Groups "A" and "Centre", Guderian expressed his dissatisfaction with the deployment of the German forces. He wanted Kurland to be evacuated and no more reinforcements to be sent to the Hungarian theatre of operations. In his opinion, the essential thing was to protect Germany from the invasion now threatening her and, to this end, to keep the enemy out of the approaches to upper Silesia, to Breslau, Berlin, Danzig, and Königsberg.

He put this to Hitler and his O.K.W. colleagues at Ziegenberg on December 24. But, as we have pointed out before, Gehlen's report left the Führer incredulous. Worse still, when Guderian had got back to Zossen, south of Berlin, where O.K.H. had moved after the evacuation of Rastenburg, he was informed that during his return journey he had been deprived of IV S.S. Panzer Corps, which was now to go to the Hungarian front. The corps was in Army Group "Centre" reserve behind the Narew, and this group's mobile reserves between the Carpathians and the Baltic were thus reduced at a stroke from 14 to 12 divisions, or, if they were all up to strength, by 1,350 armoured vehicles.

In spite of this snub, Guderian went back to Ziegenberg on January 1, 1945 in the hope of getting O.K.W. to see things his way. In his view, the centre of gravity of German strategy had to be brought back to the Eastern Front. But when Himmler was about to unleash the *"Nordwind"* offensive which was to follow *"Herbstnebel"*, with Saverne as its objective, Jodl was as unenthusiastic about Guderian's ideas as Hitler had been. "We have no right," he pointed out to him, "to give up the initiative we have just regained; we can always give ground in the East, but never in the West."

Shown the door for the second time, Guderian nevertheless made a third attempt to see Hitler to remind him of his responsibilities towards the Eastern Front. As the days passed without any decision being made, the Russians completed their preparations and, according to Gehlen's reckoning, their "steamroller", now building up its pressure, had

at least: 231 infantry divisions, 22 tank corps, 29 independent tank brigades, and three cavalry corps, supported by air forces that the Luftwaffe could not hope to match.

After taking the advice of Colonel-Generals Harpe and Reinhardt, commanders of Army Groups "A" and "Centre", against which the threat was mounting, Guderian drew up the following programme and presented it to Hitler on January 9:

1. Evacuation of the Kurland bridgehead.
2. Transfer to the East of a number of armoured units then fighting on the Western Front.
3. Abandonment of the line of the Narew and withdrawal of Army Group "Centre" to the East Prussian frontier, which was shorter and better protected.
4. Evacuation of the Army Group "A" salient between the bridge at Baranów and Magnuszew through which, according to Gehlen, 91 Soviet infantry divisions, one cavalry corps, 13 tank corps, and nine tank brigades were ready to break out.

In presenting these proposals, Guderian might have had in mind Jodl's opinion that some ground could still be sacrificed in the East. But he had hardly put before Hitler the comparative table of opposing forces which accompanied the plan, than the Führer broke out into a spate of abuse and sarcasm. A violent scene then took place which Guderian has described as follows:

"Gehlen had very carefully prepared the documentation on the enemy situation, with maps and diagrams which gave a clear idea of the respective strengths. Hitler flew into a rage when I showed them to him, called them 'absolutely stupid' and demanded that I send their author immediately to a lunatic asylum. I too became angry then. 'This is General Gehlen's work,' I said to Hitler. 'He is one of my best staff officers. I wouldn't have submitted it to you if I hadn't first agreed it myself. If you demand that General Gehlen be put into an asylum, then send me to one too!' I curtly refused to carry out Hitler's order to relieve Gehlen of his post. The storm then calmed down. But no good came of it from a military point of view. Harpe's and Reinhardt's proposals were turned down to the accompaniment of the expected odious remarks about generals for whom 'manoeuvre' only meant 'withdraw to the next rearward position'. This was all very unpleasant."

As in Hitler's eyes the Soviet threat was insignificant, not to say non-existent, the measures to meet it proposed by Guderian were therefore completely meaningless. A strictly logical conclusion, such as madmen are liable to arrive at after starting from radically wrong premises, led Hitler to give Guderian this meagre food for thought for his return journey to Zossen: "The Eastern Front must fend for itself and make do with what it has got." Could it be that Guderian was right when he said that Hitler the Austrian and Jodl the Bavarian were indifferent to the threat to Prussia? That might be somewhat far-fetched, but one might equally well suppose that Guderian the Prussian was ready to accept defeat in the West if the 6th *Panzerarmee*'s reinforcements were to be taken out of the Ardennes and given to him to block the Soviet advance towards Berlin. The least we can say is that events confirmed this latter assumption.

In any event it is clear that, reasoning *a priori* as was his custom and despite always being contradicted by events, Hitler took it that Stalin's intention was to deploy his main effort in the Danube basin towards Vienna, the second capital of the Reich, then Munich. On the other hand, after allowing IX S.S. Mountain Corps to become encircled in the so-called fortress of Budapest, it now seemed to Hitler that he should extricate it again as a matter of urgency.

So if the Eastern Front was required to go it alone, the Führer did not give any priority to dealing with Soviet advances towards Königsberg and Berlin or providing any of the resources necessary to stop them.

On January 12, 1945 German forces were deployed between the Carpathians and the Baltic as follows:
1. Army Group "A" (Colonel-General J. Harpe), with the 1st *Panzerarmee* (Colonel-General G. Heinrici), 17th Army (General F. Schulz), 4th *Panzerarmee* (General F. Gräser), and 9th Army (General S. von Lüttwitz).
2. Army Group "Centre" (Colonel-General G. Reinhardt), with the 2nd Army (Colonel-General W. Weiss), 4th Army (General F. Hossbach), and 3rd *Panzerarmee* (Colonel-General E. Raus).

1. Enormous manpower
On January 1, 1945 *Stavka*'s strength, according to Field-Marshal von Manstein, was as follows: 527 infantry and 43 artillery divisions, and 302 tank and mechanised brigades, totalling 5,300,000 men, to the Germans' 164 divisions (1,800,000 men) on the Eastern Front.
2. The JS-3 tank
In the last six-month period, Soviet armoured strength had increased from 9,000 to about 13,400 vehicles, in spite of battle losses. This was all the more remarkable in that the Russians had changed over from the heavy KV-85 to the Stalin tank. This weighed 45 tons and its 122-mm gun was the most powerful tank gun of the war. It had a 600-hp diesel engine, a range of 120 miles, and a top speed of 25 mph. The Soviets also continued to build self-propelled guns, and in particular their SU-85, 100, and 152

A Russian SU-100 assault gun in Prussia.

vehicles were to take a heavy toll of German fortifications.
3. Zhukov's and Konev's enormous resources
If we refer to Alexander Werth's version of *The Great Patriotic War*, Volume 5, we see that *Stavka* allotted to Marshals Zhukov and Konev, commanders of the 1st Belorussian and 1st Ukrainian Fronts respectively, the following forces:
1. 160 infantry divisions;
2. 32,143 guns and mortars;
3. 6,460 tanks and self-propelled guns; and
4. 4,772 aircraft.
The air forces were divided into two air armies, one to each front. The 16th Air Army (General S. I. Rudenko) was under Marshal Zhukov and the 2nd (General S. A. Krasovsky) under Marshal Konev. *Stavka* had thus done things well and the 1st Belorussian and 1st Ukrainian Fronts had a superiority over the German Army Group "A", according to Werth, of:
   (a) 5.5 to 1 in men;
   (b) 7.8 to 1 in guns and mortars;
   (c) 5.7 to 1 in armoured vehicles; and
   (d) 17.7 to 1 in aircraft.
If we realise that the superiority of the 2nd and 3rd Belorussian Fronts (respectively under Marshal Rokossovsky and General Chernyakhovsky) must have been similar, it will be realised that, rather than trying to create a bogey with which to frighten Hitler, Gehlen was on the contrary somewhat modest in his calculations.

The start of the Soviet fourth winter offensive had been fixed for January 20. In fact, it started on the 12th on the 1st Ukrainian Front as the result of an urgent approach to Stalin by Churchill. When he got back from S.H.A.E.F. on January 6, a visit to which we shall refer again, the British Prime Minister sent a very detailed telegram to the Kremlin in these terms:

"The battle in the West is very heavy and, at any time, large decisions may be called for from the Supreme Command. You know yourself from your own ex-perience how very anxious the position is when a very broad front has to be defended after temporary loss of the initiative. It is General Eisenhower's great desire and need to know in outline what you plan to do, as this obviously affects all his and our major decisions. Our Envoy, Air Chief Marshal Tedder, was last night reported weather-bound in Cairo. His journey has been much delayed through no fault of yours. In case he has not reached you yet, I shall be grateful if you can tell me whether we can count on a major Russian offensive on the Vistula front, or elsewhere, during January, with any other points you may care to mention. I shall not pass this most secret information to anyone except Field Marshal Brooke and General Eisenhower, and only under conditions of the utmost secrecy. I regard the matter as urgent."

Approached in these terms, Stalin did not have to be asked twice. Before 24 hours had passed, he replied to Churchill in exceptionally warm terms. Only the weather conditions, he said, preventing the Red Army from taking advantage of its superior strength in artillery and aircraft, were holding back the start of the offensive:

"Still, in view of our Allies' position on the Western Front, GHQ of the Supreme Command have decided to complete pre-parations at a rapid rate and, regardless of weather, to launch large-scale offensive operations along the entire Central Front not later than the second half of January. Rest assured we shall do all in our power to support the valiant forces of our Allies."

In his memoirs Churchill thought: "It was a fine deed of the Russians and their chief to hasten their vast offensive, no doubt at a heavy cost in life."

We would agree with him, though not with Boris Telpukhovsky of the Moscow Academy of Sciences, who in 1959 was inspired to write as follows about this episode in Allied relations:

"In December 1944 on the Western Front the Hitler troops launched an offensive in the Ardennes. With the relatively weak forces at their disposal they were able to make a break-through, which put the Anglo-American command in a difficult position: it even began to look as though there would be a second Dunkirk. As a result on January 6 Churchill approached Stalin with a request for help for the troops fighting in the West."

After quoting from the two telegrams given above, he concludes: "Faithful to undertakings given to his Allies and unlike the ruling Anglo-Americans, who knowingly and willingly delayed the opening of the Second Front, the Soviet Government brought forward the starting date of their offensive from January 20 to 12."

In the face of these statements by the Soviet historian, it must be pointed out that ten days before January 6, Hitler had personally acknowledged in the presence of his generals at Ziegenberg that Operation "Herbstnebel" had failed. Twelve days previously Patton had freed Bastogne and it was even longer since the ghost of a new Dunkirk had been laid once and for all. It should also be remembered that the sending of Air Chief-Marshal Tedder, Eisenhower's second-in-command at S.H.A.E.F., to Moscow was decided before the start of the German offensive in the Ardennes and that his presence there was aimed at co-ordinating the final operations of the Allies in the West with those of the Soviets coming from the East, and to arrange their link-up in the heart of Germany. This was Eisenhower's version as given in his memoirs. Not only does this version seem more acceptable but it is confirmed by President Roosevelt's message to Stalin dated December 24:

"In order that all of us may have information essential to our coordination of effort, I wish to direct General Eisenhower to send a fully qualified officer of his staff to Moscow to discuss with you Eisenhower's situation on the Western Front and its relation to the Eastern Front. We will maintain complete secrecy.

"It is my hope that you will see this officer from General Eisenhower's staff and arrange to exchange with him information that will be of mutual benefit. The situation in Belgium is not bad but we have arrived at the time to talk of the next phase . . . An early reply to this proposal is requested in view of the emergency."

On that same day Churchill, who "did not consider the situation in the West bad", pointed out to his Soviet opposite number that Eisenhower could not "solve his problem" without prior information, albeit not detailed, of Stavka's plans. As we see, this telegram of Churchill's dated January 6 did not look like an S.O.S.

From January 12 to 15, the Soviet offensive extended from the Baranów bridgehead on the Vistula to Tilsit on the Niemen, finally covering a front of 750 miles. On D-day the Baranów bridgehead was 37 miles deep and held by XLVIII Panzer Corps, part of the 4th Panzer-

armee. It had three weak infantry divisions (the 68th, 168th, and 304th) strung out along a front twice as long as it would normally cover. Each division was down to six battalions, having each had to give up one to form a corps reserve. Corps reserve had in addition 30 tank destroyers and one company of 14 self-propelled 8.8-cm guns.

Some 12 miles from the front, in the area of Kielce–Pińczów, was the O.K.H. reserve: XXIV Panzer Corps (General Nehring: 16th and 17th Panzer Divisions). Harpe had opposed, to the best of his ability, the positioning of this unit so near to the front line, but Hitler had stuck to his decision, refusing to believe that the Soviet tanks could cover 12 miles in a day, such an idea smacking of defeatism in his opinion. And so Harpe and Gräser (4th Panzerarmee) must not be allowed to use up this precious reserve too soon. Like Rommel during "Overlord" they were expressly forbidden to engage it without a formal order from the Führer. Now Hitler was at Ziegenberg near Giessen and, as usual, unobtainable before 1100 hours.

Marshal Konev had ten armies, including three tank, plus three independent tank corps and three or four divisions of artillery. He had formed a first echelon of 34 infantry divisions and 1,000 tanks which he pushed into the bridgehead, giving him at the centre of gravity of the attack a superiority of 11 to 1 in infantry, 7 to 1 in tanks, and 20 to 1 in guns and mortars.

At 0300 hours on January 12, the Russians started their preparatory fire on the German positions: this stopped an hour later, and the Russians then made a decoy attack which drew the fire of XLVIII Panzer Corps and revealed the position of the German batteries. The Russians, with 320 guns per mile, then crushed the German guns with a concentration of unprecedented violence. Zero hour for the infantry and tanks was 1030 hours: two waves of tanks followed by three waves of infantry set out to mop up the pockets of resistance left behind by the T-34's and the JS's. They were supported by self-propelled guns firing over open sights.

By early afternoon the tanks had overrun the German gun positions and destroyed the few left after the morning shelling. By nightfall they had covered between nine and 15 miles; they carried on in spite of the darkness.

In less than 24 hours the 4th Panzer-armee had suffered a strategic as well as a tactical defeat, as Konev threw into the breach his 3rd Guards Tank Army (Colonel-General Rybalko) and 4th Guards Tank Army (Colonel-General Lelyushenko), with the task of cutting off the Germans retreating from Radom and Kielce when they had crossed the Pilica. He sent his 5th Guards Army (General A. S. Zhadov) towards Czestochowa and set Kraków and the upper Silesia industrial basin as the objectives of the armies of his left.

On January 14, it was the turn of Zhukov and his 1st Belorussian Front to come into the battle. The Soviet 33rd and 69th Armies (respectively under Generals V. D. Zvetayev and V. J. Kolpakchy) ran into two German divisions as they broke out of the Pulawy bridgehead. The 5th Shock Army (General N. E. Berzarin) and the 8th Guards Army (General V. I. Chuikov) found themselves facing three as they in their turn advanced from the Magnuszew bridgehead. Thus, by evening on D-day the German 9th Army was broken up for good, cut to pieces even. This allowed the Russians to loose the 1st and 2nd Guards Tank Armies (Colonel-General M. E. Katukov and Colonel-General S. I. Bogdanov), sending the former off along the axis Kutno–Poznań and the latter along the axis Gostynin–Inowrocław–Hohensalza.

On January 13 and 14, the 2nd and 3rd Belorussian Fronts, supported by the 4th and 1st Air Armies (Generals K. A. Vershinin and T. T. Khriukin), attacked the German Army Group "Centre". In this duel between Marshal Rokossovsky and General Chernyakhovsky and Colonel-General Reinhardt, the Russians used 100 divisions, giving them a superiority of three to one. Even so, the battle raged for two days, in stark contrast to what had happened on the Vistula. General A. V. Gorbatov, commander of the Soviet 3rd Army, who had the job of driving the Germans out of their positions in the Pultusk area on the Narew, has left an account of the bitterness of the fighting: on the opening day, in spite of an "initial barrage of unprecedented violence" he had only advanced "three to seven kilometres in the main direction, two to three the secondary direction and one to one and a half during the night's fighting". On January 14 in particular, Gorbatov had to face furious counter-attacks by the "Grossdeutschland" Panzer Corps which he describes as follows:

"A struggle of unparalleled violence and ferocity developed on the second day: this too was foggy. The enemy threw in all his reserves plus his 'Grossdeutschland' Panzer Division (sic). The latter had been on the southern frontier of East Prussia in the area of Willenberg, and our Intelligence service had failed to pick them up. Taking advantage of the fog, within 24 hours it had concentrated in the area of the break-through with the task of re-establishing the situation in our army sector, then in that of the nearest formation on our left. We had decided to attack again at 0900 hours, but the enemy prevented us. At 0820 he laid down an artillery barrage with 23 batteries of guns and 17 batteries of mortars, some six-tube Nebelwerfers and some heavy howitzers. At 0830 he then counter-attacked the troops which had got through into his defences. In two hours seven counter-attacks were driven off. At mid-day the German Panzer division came into action. By evening we had had 37 counter-attacks. Fighting died down only at nightfall."

On the other leg of the right-angle formed by Army Group "Centre", Chernyakhovsky's efforts were concentrated on the Schlossberg–Ebenrode front. He broke into the 3rd *Panzerarmee*'s positions but, against Germans now fighting on their own soil, was unable to achieve anything like the successes won by Zhukov and Konev in Poland, where they were now exploiting their early victories.

On January 16, Hitler finally abandoned what Guderian called his "little Vosges war" and returned to his office in the Chancellery. Here he made two decisions which brought a show-down with the O.K.H. Chief-of-Staff. First of all he stuck to his order to transfer the *"Grossdeutschland"* Panzer Corps from Army Group "Centre" to Army Group "A" and send it over to Kielce, where it was to attack the flank of the Russian tank forces advancing on Poznań. Guderian repeated the arguments he had put forward the previous evening on the phone, but in vain.

"They would not arrive in time to stop the Russians and they would be withdrawn from the defences of East Prussia at a time when the Russian offensive was reaching its peak. The loss of this formation would give rise to the same catastrophe in East Prussia as we had had on the Vistula. Whilst we were struggling for a final outcome, the divisions up to full fighting strength would still be on the trains: the *'Grossdeutschland' Panzergrenadier* and the Luftwaffe 'Hermann Göring' Panzer Division of the *'Grossdeutschland'* Panzer Corps, under General von Saucken, the staunchest of commanders."

It was no good, as usual, and events bore out the gloomiest of forecasts: not only did the German 2nd Army cave in and Rokossovsky set off for Elbing as ordered, but the *"Grossdeutschland"* Panzer Corps arrived at Łódź under a hail of Soviet shelling and only saved its neck by a prompt retreat. Reduced to a moving pocket, together with XXIV Panzer Corps, it nevertheless managed to filter back through the Soviet columns and to cross over to the left bank of the Oder.

Hitler may have satisfied Guderian's demand by announcing that he would go over to the defensive on the Western Front, but he aroused his indignation by ordering to Hungary the best of the formations salvaged in this manner, in particular the 6th S.S. *Panzerarmee*. In Guderian's opinion, the Hungarian railways could not cope with the traffic and it would take weeks before Army Group "South" could go over to the counterattack as Hitler had ordered, whereas Sepp Dietrich's Panzers could concentrate on the Oder in ten days. Beaten on the military question, the Führer counterattacked on the grounds of the economy, maintaining "that Hungarian petroleum deposits and the nearby refineries are

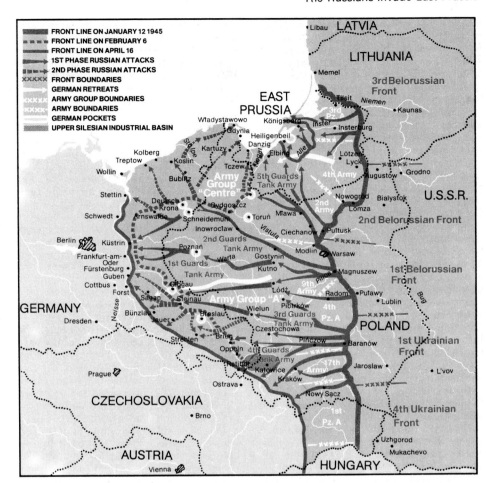

The drive from the Vistula to the Oder.

indispensable after the bombing of the German coal hydrogenation plants, and have become decisively important for the conduct of the war. No more fuel means your tanks can't run or your planes take off. You must see that. But that's the way it is: my generals understand nothing of the economy of war!"

Hitler's reasoning was clearly not devoid of foundation as petroleum, until uranium came along, was the life-blood of war. But his chief-of-staff's calculations turned out to be correct, since the 6th *Panzerarmee* had to wait until March 6 before it could launch its offensive on the Hungarian front. Even so, its intervention north of the Carpathians was hardly likely to have prevented Zhukov from reaching the Oder between Küstrin and Frankfurt. Diverting it to the south made the Soviet invasion easier.

The catastrophe in Poland demanded a scapegoat. Hitler chose one in the person of Colonel-General Harpe, C.-in-C. Army Group "A", forgetting that he had himself ordered the imprudent stationing of XXIV Panzer Corps in O.K.H. reserve very close to Harpe's lines. This was the root of the trouble, as Hitler realised, but only after dismissing Harpe's warnings.

Harpe was replaced by Colonel-General Schörner, and Rendulic, Schörner's colleague, received command of Army Group "North", which had just driven off strong Soviet attacks in the Kurland bridgehead.

Scarcely had Rendulic left Oslo, received the Swords to his Knight's Cross from Hitler, and unpacked his bags in his new command post than on January 26 he received the order to go to East Prussia and take over immediately the command of Army Group "Centre". Unfortunately for this group, in spite of the valour of its new commander, nothing could be done to stave off the impending disaster.

It cannot, of course, be argued that Reinhardt could have forced Rokossovsky and Chernyakhovsky to give up their offensive if he had had the use of the *"Grossdeutschland"* Panzer Corps. There is no doubt, however, that by depriving him of this formation, Hitler virtually condemned Army Group "Centre" to inescapable defeat, a defeat which reached the proportions of a strategic catastrophe, involving the total destruction of 28 German divisions.

In planning the offensive, *Stavka* had given the 3rd Belorussian Front the task of destroying the enemy forces in Tilsit and Insterburg, then of making for Königsberg. The 2nd Belorussian Front was to overcome the enemy resistance in the Przasnysz–Mława area and then advance along the axis Deutsch-Eylau–Marienburg–Elbing. This would prevent the Germans driven out by Chernyakhovsky from crossing the Vistula, and they would then fall into the hands of Rokossovsky. Apart from slight variations this was the manoeuvre attempted by Rennenkampf and Samsonov in August 1914 against East Prussia, which ended up in their defeat at Tannenberg and the Masurian Lakes. Here, however, all resemblance between the two campaigns ceases. Chernyakhovsky and Rokossovsky were younger and more energetic than their predecessors in the Tsar's army. Trammelled by the despotic authority of the Führer, Reinhardt on his side had none of that perfect freedom of action which von Hindenburg enjoyed under the Kaiser and Moltke.

In spite of the German 2nd Army's resistance, the 2nd Belorussian Front's attack began again on January 16, favoured by a bright spell which allowed efficient support by General Vershinin's planes. Two days later the Russian forward troops were engaged some 21 miles from their point of departure, in the area of Przasnysz and Ciéchanow. Forty-eight hours later Rokossovsky took Mława and Dzialdowo (Soldau), reached the East Prussian frontier, which he then crossed, and launched his 5th Tank Army towards its objective at Elbing. From then on things moved quickly, and Hitler only just had time to blow up the monument to the German victory at Tannenberg and to have the mortal remains of Field-Marshal von Hindenburg and his wife exhumed and evacuated.

On the same day the 3rd Belorussian Front had overcome the 3rd *Panzerarmee,* which finally succumbed on January 19. By the 21st, the Russians had taken the fortified position along the Inster, with the little town of Insterburg, and Tilsit, where Lieutenant-General Rein's 69th Division had held out, almost to the last grenadier, Rein himself sharing the fate of his men. A few days later Chernyakhovsky had his right at Labiau, at the edge of the frozen lagoon of the Kurisches Haff, his centre at Wehlau, on the west bank of the Alle less than 31 miles from Königsberg, and his left from Goldap to Lyck in the Masurian Lakes area.

On January 17, when it became clear that Rokossovsky's battering-ram would destroy his 2nd Army, Reinhardt had asked permission to pull back the 4th Army from its 140-mile wide front (Nowogród–Augustów–Goldap) to a line Ortelsburg–Lötzen – Masurian Lakes canal. This would save three divisions, which would make up for the loss of the "Grossdeutschland" Panzer Corps and stave off a break-through. Quoting his "five years experience of warfare", Hitler refused this sensible request; Reinhardt could not bring himself to remind Hitler of the sinister experience of Vitebsk.

Three days later, when the German 2nd Army positions had been breached and Chernyakhovsky had been successful at Tilsit on the Inster, Lieutenant-General Heidkämper, chief-of-staff of Army Group "Centre", noted in his diary: "To keep the 4th Army in its present exposed position now appears grotesque. At 2030 hours the C.-in-C. (Reinhardt) again puts before the Führer the reasons for its immediate withdrawal. 'Mein Führer', he began, 'in

my anxiety for the safety of East Prussia, I venture again to turn to you. According to my appreciation of the situation, we shall tomorrow face an attack on the whole of East Prussia. Examination of a captured map reveals that the 5th Guards Tank Army, with four tank corps, is to make for Danzig. The strength of our 2nd Army is so depleted that we cannot withstand this attack. The second strategic danger is in the 3rd *Panzerarmee,* which the enemy has broken into. If the Guards Tank Army is able to force its way through we shall be caught in the rear: here we have no resources at all.'"

There followed long exchanges between Reinhardt and Hitler. The latter, never short of arguments, advised Reinhardt to use the *Volkssturm* militia against the Soviet tanks and told him that the 4th Panzer Division had been withdrawn from Kurland, loaded on five liners, and was expected to reach him very soon. This would be followed very shortly by 20 infantry battalions from Denmark. It was for these reasons that he opposed Reinhardt's request, and when at mid-day on January 21 he finally agreed, the fate of Army Group "Centre" had been sealed.

By remaining in its allotted positions on January 17, 4th Army suffered the inevitable encirclement, with 350,000 men trapped around the strongpoint of Lötzen, where supplies were reckoned to be enough for one division for 70 days. The commander, General Hossbach, realising the impossibility of his position, tried to fight his way out, down towards the Vistula. He was thus knowingly disobeying O.K.H.'s orders, but he had the approval of Colonel-General Reinhardt, who saw in this a chance of saving the 3rd *Panzerarmee* as well.

Holding off Chernyakhovsky on the line Sensburg – Rastenburg – Friedland – left bank of the Pregel, Hossbach, after 125 miles of forced marches in five days through snowstorms, nevertheless failed to get to Elbing before the Soviet 5th Guards Tank Army. The latter had reached the shore of the Frisches Haff near the little town of Tolkemit on January 27 and had cut the last link between East Prussia and the rest of the Reich. Further south, XXVI and VI Corps (Generals Matzky and Grossmann) had attacked the previous night and got as far as Preussisch-Holland, 12 miles south of Elbing.

On the one hand Rokossovsky was thus able to avoid the opposition intended for him and consequently to reinforce his strength. On the other the secret evacuation of East Prussia by Hossbach, with the connivance of Reinhardt, was denounced to Hitler by Erich Koch, the *Gauleiter* of the province. The Führer dreaded the setting up in Königsberg of a government of "Free Germany" once the Russians were in the town. It was here that Frederick I, the Elector of Brandenburg, had been crowned in 1701. It therefore had to be held at any price, even at the cost of 28 divisions.

And so Reinhardt was relieved by

Rendulic on January 27. Three days later Hossbach was ordered to hand over command of the 4th Army to General Friedrich-Wilhelm Müller. Stalin had, of course, no intention of setting up a Free German Government (even one devoted to him and presided over by General von Seydlitz-Kurzbach) in Königsberg, which had been allotted to the Soviet Union by the Teheran Conference, and which he was going to rename Kaliningrad. Was this just mistrust on Stalin's part, or did he think it best to leave things as they were?

Whilst the ring was closing round the 3rd *Panzerarmee* and the 4th Army, and what was left of the 2nd Army was powerless to prevent the forces of the 2nd Belorussian Front from crossing the lower Vistula, Colonel-General Schörner's savage energy was unable to hold back the onrush of Marshals Zhukov and Konev, though their losses, the strain on their equipment, and the stretching of their lines of communication eventually slowed the Russians down to advances of less than half a mile in places.

On January 15, between the Baranów bridgehead and the Carpathians, the 4th Ukrainian Front came into action with 18 infantry divisions and two tank corps. At Jaslo it easily broke through the thinly-held line of the 1st *Panzerarmee* and set off for Kraków without hindrance.

On January 16, Guderian noted, the Russian advance "gathered extraordinary speed". In effect, on the 1st Belorussian Front the 4th Tank Army, having passed through Jedrzejów the night before, reached Czestochowa on the 17th in two stages, covering a total distance of 70 miles. On its right the 3rd Guards Tank Army reached Radomsko from Kielce (50 miles). It was therefore to be concluded that all organised resistance had ceased in front of Lelyushenko's and Rybalko's forces.

This explains how Konev was able to take Kraków by an outflanking movement, so that on January 19 the Poles found it left virtually intact. The same procedure, in an operation which he shared equally with Petrov's 4th Ukrainian Front, gave him the industrial labyrinth of upper Silesia with its factories only slightly damaged. And, a more difficult task, he had managed to prevent the Germans from sabotaging them.

On the 1st Belorussian Front the advance proceeded at an equally fast pace. On January 16 Zhukov's right having seized Modlin, where the Bug joins the Vistula, the Warsaw garrison of four incomplete battalions and a few artillery batteries sought and obtained O.K.H.'s approval to abandon the ruins of the city and escape encirclement. This common-sense decision put Hitler in a state of indescribable fury. In spite of Guderian's vehement protests, he arrested three officers of the operations staff and had Guderian himself undergo a wearisome interrogation by Kaltenbrunner.

By January 19, the 1st and 2nd Guards Tank Armies had reached their first objectives. Konev advanced from Gostynin to Inowrocław then to Bydgoszcz (Bromberg). On January 23, having covered 90 miles in four days, he occupied the latter without resistance. On the left, Colonel-General Bogdanov took a week to cover the 110 miles from Kutno to Poznań. The old fortress of Poznań, dating back to the Prussian era, had been hastily re-armed and put under the command of Major-General Mattern. The 2nd Guards Tank Army had better things to do, and so by-passed it and drove on: next stop Frankfurt on the Oder.

On the same day, the left of the 1st Belorussian Front took Lódz, and south of it advanced to make contact with the 1st Ukrainian Front. Remnants of retreating German units of Army Group "A" mingled with the advancing Russians. "The enemy," Guderian said, "had virtually nothing in front of him. Only the moving pockets of XXIV and the 'Grossdeutschland' Panzer Corps moved on westwards, fighting all the time, imperturbable, picking up a host of smaller units as they went along. Generals Nehring and von Saucken carried out a military exploit during these days every bit worthy to be recounted by a new Xenophon."

Marshals Zhukov and Konev now had no difficulty in overcoming the resistance put up by Colonel-General Schörner to slow their advance. On January 18, the 72nd Division was wiped out near Piotrków, then the 10th Panzer, 78th, and 291st Divisions succumbed trying to block the way into Silesia to the Soviet tanks. They were no more of an obstacle than the Oder would be. By the end of January the forward troops of the 1st Ukrainian Front had reached the Oder above Oppeln (Opole) and on either side of Breslau (Wrocław) had established two vast bridgeheads at Brieg (Brzeg) and Steinau (Scinawa) on the right bank. This marked the beginning of the encirclement of the Silesian capital.

Further down the Oder, Generals Nehring and von Saucken had managed to escape from the pursuing 1st Belorussian Front and had crossed back over the river at Glogau (Glogów). Zhukov's two Guards Tank Armies covered a good 60 miles along the Poznań–Berlin axis, where two weak divisions, without artillery, had been sent to prop up what was left of the German 9th Army. Without halting at the small garrison of Schneidemühl (Piła), which they by-passed, they reached the Oder at Küstrin in the early days of February. This brought them opposite Frankfurt, around which bridgeheads on the left bank were soon established. And so Zhukov's forward troops were now only 50 miles as the crow flies from the New Chancellery bunker.

On the 30th day of the offensive, Moscow published the first figures from Konev's and Zhukov's victories: 70 German divisions destroyed or cut to pieces; 295,000

Russian cavalry ride past a burning village in central Poland in 1945.

men killed and 86,000 taken prisoner; 15,000 guns and mortars, 34,000 vehicles, and 2,955 tanks destroyed or captured. If it is realised that the mobile reserves behind Army Group "A" consisted of five Panzer and two *Panzergrenadier* divisions, the last figure seems to bear no relation to reality. As for the ratio of killed to prisoners, as Alexander Werth has pointed out, it belies the statements of the Soviet propagandist Ilya Ehrenburg, who described to his readers "Germans running away like rabbits". And Werth also recalls the confidential statement of an officer from the front who said to him "In some places their resistance reminds me of Sebastopol: those German soldiers can be quite heroic at times."

At the same time, Zhukov was in front of Küstrin and 335 miles from his point of departure, whilst Konev in Silesia was 300 miles from his. Logistic considerations now became of prime importance to the two marshals' tank armies, especially as they had greatly outdistanced the infantry following them on foot. And so February, March, and early April were devoted to small-scale operations only, though these were important as they led to the mopping up of East Prussia and the deployment of the Red Army on what is now called the Oder-Neisse line, ready for the final offensive.

Marshal Rokossovsky's break-through towards Elbing and the crushing defeat of the German 2nd Army (which was driven back to Danzig) left the left wing of Army Group "A" uncovered, and west of a line running north-south through Toruń the whole of Pomerania lay open to the Soviet invader. In mid-January there was little more than a handful of troops, mostly infantry, to defend it.

To close this enormous breach, Guderian got Hitler to approve the formation of an Army Group "Vistula", but the two men were violently opposed on the question of who was to command it. The reshuffling of commands in the Danube

theatre meant that the general staff of Army Group "F" were out of jobs, as also was Field-Marshal von Weichs, whom Guderian described as "a man who is as intelligent as he is brave and upright and one certainly cut out to master such a difficult situation, insofar as it can be mastered." But Weich's profound religious feelings disqualified him in Hitler's eyes. So, despite Guderian's violent protests, this delicate command was given to *Reichsführer*-S.S. Heinrich Himmler. Himmler had no religious feelings, to be sure, but during Operation *"Nordwind"* in lower Alsace he had shown both ineptitude and hesitation in command. What was worse, Hitler refused Guderian's proposal that the staff of Army Group "F" should come under his control. Himmler was thus able to recruit his own from amongst his cronies, and as chief-of-staff he chose Lieutenant-General Lammerding of the *Waffen*-S.S., whose name will for ever be linked with Oradour-sur-Glane.

On January 25, Army Group "North" was renamed "Kurland", "Centre" was renamed "North", and "A" became "Centre". The general staff of the 3rd *Panzerarmee* were withdrawn from East Prussia and put under Army Group "Vistula". By emptying the depôts, schools, and training centres and sending part of Berlin's A.A. defences down to the Oder, O.K.H. was able for the last time to reconstitute some kind of coherent force with which to face the Russians.

In early February it had five army groups with a total of 135 divisions deployed as follows:

	Infantry divisions	Panzer and Panzer-grenadier divisions	Totals
"Kurland"	20	2	22
"North"	19	5	24
"Vistula"	25	8	33
"Centre"	20	8	28
"South"	19	9	28
Totals	103	32	135

In less than a month, in spite of the reinforcements we have mentioned, the number of German divisions facing the Red Army had dropped from 164 to 135. Most of these were below strength and some were down to the equivalent of an infantry regiment. Under these circumstances, Guderian understandably thought that Ribbentrop should be informed of the situation. He suggested that the two of them should approach Hitler to recommend that Germany lay down her arms in the West. Ribbentrop was unwilling, so Guderian attempted to win Hitler over to a manoeuvre which, for some weeks at least, would avert the threat to Berlin.

"I resolved," he said, "to demonstrate once more to Hitler that the Hungarian offensive had to be abandoned. Instead we would attack the Russian salient on the Oder between Frankfurt and Küstrin by going for its flanks, which were not very strong, in the south on the line Glogau–Guben and in the north of the line Pyritz–Arnswalde. I thus hoped to strengthen the defence of the capital and the interior of the Reich and gain time to conclude armistice talks with the Western powers."

But this proposal, which presupposed the evacuation also of Kurland, Norway, and Italy, merely provoked Hitler to an attack of maniacal fury.

As the 6th *Panzerarmee* finally set off for Hungary, Guderian's proposed pincer round the tank armies of the 1st Belorussian Front became impossible through lack of resources. He therefore fell back on a flank attack which was to bring into operation Army Group "Vistula". Breaking out south-east from Arnswalde, it would beat the enemy forces north of the Warta, which would protect Pomerania and force Zhukov to give up his positions before Frankfurt and Küstrin. Speed was essential, but Himmler and his staff took a week to get ready. Konev's vigorous attacks in Silesia, moreover, obliged O.K.H. to reinforce Army Group "Centre" at the expense of Army Group "Vistula".

On February 13, the 3rd *Panzerarmee* finally mounted a counter-attack, starting from Arnswalde, and scored some initial success. But it was soon compelled to go over to the defensive, as *Stavka* turned on to it Rokossovsky's centre and left as well as Zhukov's two tank armies. With his left at Könitz and his right on the Oder at Schwedt, Colonel-General Raus was defending a front of 160 miles with only eight divisions. It is therefore not surprising that this was quickly broken by the two Soviet marshals' offensive on February 24. They had nine tank corps and no fewer than 47 infantry divisions.

Driving on through Schlochau and Büblitz, the 2nd Belorussian Front's tanks reached the Baltic north of Köslin on February 28, cutting the German 2nd Army's last land communications with the rest of the Reich. This army now had its back to the sea, its right on the Stolpe

and its left on the Nogat. A few days later Zhukov broke through to Dramburg and drove on to Treptow, in spite of the intervention one after the other of four Panzer or *Panzergrenadier* divisions. During this fighting General Krappe's X S.S. Panzer Corps was wiped out and Raus was just able to save some 50,000 men of his army who, on March 11, were sheltering on Wolin Island. Eight days later a special Kremlin communiqué announced the capture of the port of Kolberg (now Kołobrzeg) where the 163rd and the 402nd Divisions were cut to pieces almost to the last man.

Konev's job in Silesia was to align his front with Zhukov's, according to Russian official histories today. But was it to be only this? Judging by the means employed, it seems unlikely.

On February 4, Konev launched a first attack when he broke out of the bridgehead at Brieg and advanced nearly 13 miles along the left bank of the Oder. South-east of Breslau, the Russians advanced as far as Ohlan, some 13 miles from the Silesian capital, and south down to Strehlen. A special Moscow communiqué claimed that this action brought in 4,200 prisoners.

A week later the 3rd Guards Tank and the 4th Tank Armies broke out from the Steinau bridgehead and advanced at Blitzkrieg speed over the plain of Silesia. On February 13, Colonel-General Lelyushenko was attacking Glogau, 25 miles north-west of Steinau. On his left, supported by a division of artillery and followed by Colonel-General K. A. Koroteev's 52nd Army, Rokossovsky had forced a crossing of the Bober at Bunzlau the night before. On February 15, after a 60-mile dash north-west, the Soviet tanks reached Guben, Sommerfeld, Sorau, and Sagan, which they lost and regained in circumstances still unknown.

So Konev's aim was not merely to align his front with Zhukov's but to cross the Neisse, roll up the front along the Oder down-river from Fürstenberg, and advance towards Berlin through Cottbus. Halted on the Neisse, either by *Stavka* or by enemy opposition, however, he closed the ring round Breslau. At the beginning of March, he was facing Schörner on the line Bunzlau – Jauer – Schweidnitz – Neisse – Ratibor, at the foot of the mountains separating Silesia from Bohemia and Moldavia.

Mopping up East Prussia fell to the 3rd Belorussian Front, reinforced up to 100 divisions against the 24, including five Panzer, of Army Group "North", at the beginning of February. At the same date the Russians were in the outskirts of Königsberg; from here the front moved along the course of the river Alle between Friedland and Guttstadt, then turned north-west to reach the coast near Frauenberg. This left the Germans trapped in a rectangle about the size of Brighton – Guildford – Winchester – Portsmouth. Colonel-General Rendulic did not limit himself merely to defensive

German corpses in the city of Brieg after its capture in April 1945.

operations. On February 19 he counter-attacked in a pincer manoeuvre and re-established communication, though precariously, between Königsberg and Pillau, the latter a Baltic port giving him a supply and evacuation link with the rest of the Reich less exposed than Königsberg.

Chernyakhovsky's idea had been to cut East Prussia in two from south-west to north-east, but on February 18 he was killed in front of Mehlsack by a shell splinter as he was on his way to the H.Q. of General Gorbatov, commander of the 3rd Army. Twice decorated a Hero of the Soviet Union, he was the youngest and one of the most gifted of the great Russian war leaders. In his honour the small Prussian town of Insterburg was renamed Chernyakhovsk.

Stalin nominated Marshal A. M. Vasilevsky to succeed him, while Vasilevsky's job as Chief-of-Staff of the Red Army was taken over by General A. I. Antonov.

The offensive proceeded along the same axis, in spite of obstinate German resistance, which General Gorbatov emphasises in his memoirs. The invaders' superior strength soon began to tell, however. On March 14, the Russian 3rd Army concentrated on a narrow front twice as much infantry and five times as much artillery as the Germans, gained over three miles in three days and got to within eight miles of the sea, which it finally reached on March 25. "What a sight on the coast!" Gorbatov writes. "Several square miles of lorries and vans loaded with *matériel*, food, and domestic equipment. Between the vehicles lay corpses of German soldiers. Some 300 horses were attached in pairs to a chain and many of these were dead too."

And so the German 4th Army was cut in two and trapped in two pockets. Meanwhile, on March 12, Hitler had replaced Rendulic as C.-in-C. Army Group "Kurland" and Colonel-General Weiss, C.-in-C. 2nd Army, was given the sad honour of presiding over the death-throes of Army Group "North". On March 30, the pocket which had formed round the little towns of Braunsberg and Heiligenbeil surrendered, yielding (if we are to believe a Soviet communiqué of the period) 80,000 dead and 50,000 prisoners. In the night of April 9-10 General Lasch, commander of the Königsberg fortress, decided to send envoys to Marshal Vasilevsky. The town had been under heavy and incessant air bombardment for some ten days, whilst the attackers, having taken the fortifications, infiltrated the streets amidst the burning buildings. No German authors we have consulted blame the commander for surrendering, though 92,000 men were taken prisoner and 2,232 guns were lost. Lasch was condemned to death in his absence, however, and his family imprisoned.

On April 15, the Russians invaded the Samland peninsula, from which they had been driven out two months previously. Ten days later, the last remnants of the German 4th Army, now under the command of General von Saucken, evacuated the port of Pillau, which had served as a transit station for 141,000 military wounded and 451,000 civilian refugees since January 15.

Along the lower Vistula, Rokossovsky had the right of the 2nd Belorussian Front, and in particular the Polish 2nd Army (General Swierczewski) facing the six corps and 17 divisions, all very dilapidated, which the reorganisation of command in late June had put into the incapable hands of the sinister Heinrich Himmler.

By February 18, on the right bank of the Vistula, the Russians had reached Graudenz (Grudziadz) but it took them until March 5 to overcome the last resistance of this small town. On February 21 they took Dirschau (Tczew) on the left bank 21 miles from Danzig. On March 9, the Soviet forces which had reached the Baltic north of Köslin crossed the Stolpe and drove on towards Kartuzy, turning the right flank of the German 2nd Army, which had come under the command of General von Saucken after the transfer of Colonel-General Rendulic.

The struggle was now concentrated around Danzig and Gdynia, which the Germans had renamed Gotenhafen. In this hopeless battle the defenders brought in the pocket-battleship *Lützow* and the cruisers *Prinz Eugen* and *Leipzig,* which several times knocked out Soviet tanks with their gunfire, though their ammunition was gradually more and more severely rationed. On March 23, the

Polish 2nd Army took Sopot, half-way between Danzig and Gdynia, and by the 30th it was all over. The German 2nd Army held out obstinately until May 9 in the Hela peninsula, in the Vistula estuary, and in the narrow strip of land enclosing the Frisches Haff, so that between January 15 and April 30 no fewer than 300,000 military personnel and 962,000 civilians had been embarked for Germany.

The strongpoint of Poznań gave in on February 24 after a resistance to which the Red Army paid considerable tribute. Then it was the turn of Schneidemühl and Deutsche Krone in Pomerania.

On the Oder, the fortress of Glogau, first attacked on February 13, held out until April 2. By the latter date, apart from the coastal strips held by Saucken and the Kurland bridgehead which continued to defy the Soviet assaults, the only point still holding out east of the Oder-Neisse line was Breslau. Its garrison, commanded by Lieutenant-General Niehoff, was now closely hemmed in by the 6th Army of the 1st Ukrainian Front under the command of General V. A. Gluzdovsky.

This military tragedy was echoed by a national tragedy: the exodus of nearly eight million Germans who had taken refuge on the other side of the Oder-Neisse line at the time of the capitulation of May 8, 1945. But not all those who fled before the Soviet invasion managed to find shelter. The journalist Bernard George reckons that 1,600,000 people, mostly old men, women, and children, died of exhaustion, cold, and brutal treatment from a soldiery drunk for revenge. And so in five months, this catastrophe cost Germany more civilians than France lost soldiers in the whole of the 52 months of World War I. Much of the responsibility for this affair must naturally be laid on Hitler (and his collaborators in the government and the party) and on the party authorities in Germany's eastern provinces: *Gauleiters* Erich Koch in Eastern Prussia, Forster in Danzig and Western Prussia (the former Polish corridor), and Arthur Greiser in the Warthegau, the new German name for the provinces of Poznań, Lódź (Litzmannstadt), and Czestochowa, annexed to the Third Reich in October 1939.

Hitler had obstinately refused to consider the possibility of a Russian invasion and went into fits of furious temper when anyone dared broach the subject in his presence. All preparations, even all estimates for the evacuation of the civilian population in the threatened provinces appeared to the *Gauleiters* of Königsberg, Danzig, and Poznań a scandalous demonstration of defeatism and an intolerable attack on the dogma of the Führer's infallibility. And so in many areas the exodus was improvised actually under enemy shelling. In June 1940, when the French refugees poured out along the roads there were vehicles and petrol supplies and the weather was good. In January and February 1945, the Germans

had only their animals and carts, it was snowing hard, and the temperature was 20 to 25 degrees below zero Centigrade.

In his war memoirs, Colonel-General Rendulic, who saw these pitiful convoys pass by, remarked how they were often led by French prisoners, the only able-bodied men left in the villages of East Prussia, whom the refugees praised unstintingly for their devotion. On many occasions, and this was borne out by other witnesses, they protected the women and girls from the violence of their Allies.

Much has been written in Germany about the atrocities committed by the Soviet invaders. The evidence has been doubted by some, but a Red Army officer said to Werth:

"In Poland a few regrettable things happened from time to time, but, on the whole, a fairly strict discipline was maintained as regards 'rape'. The most common offence in Poland was 'dai chasy' –'give me your wrist-watch'. There was an awful lot of petty thieving and robbery. Our fellows were just crazy about wrist-watches–there's no getting away from it. But the looting and raping in a big way did not start until our soldiers got to Germany. Our fellows were so sex-starved that they often raped old women of sixty, or seventy or even eighty–much to these grandmother's surprise, if not downright delight. But I admit it was a nasty business, and the record of the Kazakhs and other Asiatic troops was particularly bad."

It is hardly surprising that the Soviet soldiers, after the devastation of their villages, and after just seeing the abominations of the extermination camps of Maidenek, Treblinka, and Oswiecim (or Auschwitz) should exact revenge on the German people. On the other hand, the American, British, and French troops who discovered Ravensbrück, Bergen-Belsen, Buchenwald, and Dachau seem to have reacted differently. It would appear that neither the military nor the political authorities, normally so strict in matters of discipline, took the trouble at the time to stem this tide of bestiality. Very much to the contrary, journalists and intellectuals such as the well-known Ilya Ehrenburg incited the Red Army in the press and on the radio to dishonour their victory. And this homicidal propaganda cannot but have had the approval of the Kremlin. On April 14, as Alexander Werth reported, there was a sudden change of tone: Ehrenburg was brutally disowned in an official-looking article in *Pravda* by Comrade G. F. Alexandrov, then the licensed ideologist of the Central Committee of the Communist Party of the U.S.S.R. His "clumsy error" was not to have noticed that Stalin had just proclaimed: "Hitlers come and go, but the German people go on for ever."

It seems that the Kremlin feared that the horrors caused by the invasion might prevent the free flowering of communism in Central Europe. That was right, but it was too late.

CHAPTER 71
The conferences at Quebec, Moscow and Yalta

On Tuesday September 6, 1944, Churchill and his three chiefs-of-staff left the Clyde on board the liner *Queen Mary* for Halifax, Nova Scotia. Here a special train took them to Quebec late in the morning of September 11. President Roosevelt and his military colleagues were waiting for the British party. To Winston Churchill's great disappointment Harry Hopkins had excused himself: apart from the health reasons which explained his absence (and these were real enough), he was also suffering the consequences of his loss of favour at the White House at this time.

During this Anglo-American conference, which had been named "Octagon", the discussion concerned mainly the form of participation to be taken by the British forces in the fight against Japan, after the Third Reich had been driven to unconditional surrender. Planning included operations in Burma, a possible air and naval offensive from Australia against Singapore, and putting a Royal Navy formation under the command of the American Pacific Fleet, which had just won a victory at the Marianas Islands and was about to win another at Leyte.

In the European theatre, it was decided not to withdraw a single division from the Allied forces in the Mediterranean until the result of the attack the 15th Army Group was preparing to launch across the Apennines was known; its objective was the Adige line, just short of the Piave.

Churchill, now fearful of a Russian take-over of central Europe, expressed hope at Quebec that Alexander's forces in Italy might in fact be able to reach Vienna before the Red Army.

An agreement was also made between the British and the Americans to mark off their future occupation zones in Germany. After some argument about the allocation of the Westphalian industrial basin, it was decided, according to Admiral Leahy, President Roosevelt's Chief-of-Staff, to divide the zones as follows:

"(a) The British forces, under a British commander, will occupy Germany west of the Rhine and east of the Rhine north of a line from Coblenz following the northern border of Hessen and Nassau to the border of the area allocated to the Soviet Government.

(b) The forces of the United States, under a United States commander, will occupy Germany east of the Rhine, south of the line from Coblenz following the northern border of Hessen–Nassau and west of the area allocated to the Soviet Government.

(c) Control of the ports of Bremen and Bremerhaven and the necessary staging areas in that immediate vicinity will be vested in the commander of the American zone.

(d) American area to have, in addition, access through the western and north-western seaports and passage through the British controlled area.

(e) Accurate delineation of the above outlined British and American areas of control can be made at a later date."

Reading this text one notices that:
1. at this time no French occupation zone was provided for;
2. Bremen and Bremerhaven were included in the American occupation zone because President Roosevelt wanted to make sure that his troops would be supplied without using French territory; and
3. Berlin was not mentioned and there was no reference to the facilities which the two Western powers would require from their Soviet ally if they were to have free access to the German capital at all times.

Robert Murphy, the American diplomat who had just taken up his duties as adviser to General Eisenhower on German affairs, frequently mentioned and deplored this last point. He states in his memoirs that "no provision had been made for the Anglo-American powers to reach that city", and notes that his colleague James Riddleberger, the State Department's delegate to the European Consultative Council in London, who was equally aware of this omission, had suggested that "the occupation zones should converge upon Berlin like slices of pie, thus providing each zone with its own frontage in the capital city". Murphy also asked Riddleberger whom he had approached with his plan. The latter had told Ambassador Winant, who had been opposed to any modification of the original plan and accused Riddleberger of not having confidence in Soviet Russia. Riddleberger replied that on this he was exactly right. Winant told Murphy that the right of access to Berlin was implicit in the Western Allies' presence there.

In addition, according to Murphy, the "daydreams" of Winant, the U.S. Ambassador in London, and therefore the American representative for Russo-American affairs at the European Consultative Council, relied too much on Roosevelt's usual formula: "I can handle Stalin."

During the "Octagon" Conference the notorious Morgenthau Plan (named after its author, the Secretary of the Treasury), which dealt with the treatment of Germany after its defeat, was endorsed by the British and American Governments.

Since the beginning of August, Eisenhower had been requesting instructions on the attitude to be adopted after the German defeat, and the War Department sent him a note on the subject, asking him to make his observations. However, a member of Eisenhower's staff committed

the double indiscretion of getting hold of a copy of this memorandum and sending it to Henry Morgenthau. Morgenthau had wormed his way into the President's favour to such an extent that he was the only member of his cabinet to call him by his first name.

After the cabinet session of August 26, 1944, James V. Forrestal, the Secretary of the Navy, noted in his valuable diary:

"The Secretary of the Treasury (Henry Morgenthau, Jr.) came in with the President with whom he had had lunch. The President said that he had been talking with the Secretary of the Treasury on the general question of the control of Germany after the end of the war. He said that he had just heard about a paper prepared by the Army and that he was not at all satisfied with the severity of the measures proposed. He said that the Germans should have simply a subsistence level of food–as he put it, soup kitchens would be ample to sustain life–that otherwise they should be stripped clean and should not have a level of subsistence above the lowest level of the people they had conquered.

"The Secretary of War (Henry L. Stimson) demurred from this view, but the President continued in the expression of this attitude and finally said he would name a committee composing State, War, and Treasury which would consider the problem of how to handle Germany along the lines that he had outlined, that this committee would consult the Navy whenever naval questions were involved."

According to the plan, Germany would not only have her factories, in particular her steel plants, dismantled, but all her raw material resources also cut off, because she would be permanently forbidden to mine coal and iron ore. Her mines were to be flooded and the German people would have to subsist on crops and cattle-breeding as in the early times of the Holy Roman Empire. Secretary of State Cordell Hull and Secretary of War Henry L. Stimson were firm in their objections, but Roosevelt remained obstinate and, leaving his diplomatic chief in Washington, took Morgenthau with him to the Quebec Conference. It is interesting to note the reception given by Churchill to this inhuman and preposterous project.

In the volume of his memoirs entitled *Triumph and Tragedy,* which he wrote in 1953, Churchill tells us:

"At first I violently opposed this idea. But the President, with Mr. Morgenthau–for whom we had much to ask–was so insistent that in the end we agreed to consider it."

This is both true and false. There is no doubt that he recoiled when he learned of the Morgenthau plan, as Lord Moran heard him say on September 13 at the dinner of the Citadel Night, when the

Henry Morgenthau. Jr.

subject came up:

"I'm all for disarming Germany, but we ought not to prevent her living decently. There are bonds between the working classes of all countries, and the English people will not stand for the policy you are advocating." And he is said to have muttered: "You cannot indict a whole nation."

On the other hand, when Roosevelt and Morgenthau insisted, Churchill, in spite of what he said, not only promised them that he would examine the plan for reducing Germany to a pastoral existence, but after it had been examined by Professor Lindemann (later Lord Cherwell), put his signature to it on September 15. According to Lord Moran, Cherwell as Churchill's scientific adviser had persuaded the Prime Minister, explaining what he had not noticed at first sight, that "the plan will save Britain from bankruptcy by eliminating a dangerous competitor".

It is tempting to dismiss the versions of Churchill and his doctor out of hand, as they are contradictory. However, the evidence given by Anthony Eden, now Lord Avon, supports Lord Moran's version point by point; he writes:

"On the morning of September 15th I joined the Prime Minister and the President, who were by now in agreement in their approval of the plan. Cherwell had supported Morgenthau and their joint advocacy had prevailed. Large areas of the Ruhr and the Saar were to be stripped

of their manufacturing industries and turned into agricultural lands. It was as if one were to take the Black Country and turn it into Devonshire. I did not like the plan, nor was I convinced that it was to our national advantage.

"I said so, and also suggested that Mr. Cordell Hull's opinion should be sought for. This was the only occasion I can remember when the Prime Minister showed impatience with my views before foreign representatives. He resented my criticism of something which he and the President had approved, not I am sure on his account, but on the President's."

Meanwhile, Cordell Hull, on whose territory Morgenthau was trespassing, and Stimson, who refused to admit defeat, were left behind in Washington. However, they did not relax their opposition to the Morgenthau plan and on September 18, the deputy Secretary of War, John McCloy, also condemned it to Forrestal:

"In general the programme according to Mr. McCloy, called for the conscious destruction of the economy in Germany and the encouragement of a state of impoverishment and disorder. He said he felt the Army's role in any programme would be most difficult because the Army, by training and instinct, would naturally turn to the re-creation of order as soon as possible, whereas under this programme they apparently were to encourage the opposite."

McCloy was not exaggerating in interpreting the feeling of the U.S. high command as he did. Already in August, when Morgenthau had visited S.H.A.E.F.,

Eisenhower had told him that "it would be madness" to deprive the Germans of their natural resources and he rejected all arguments to the contrary. In *Crusade in Europe* Eisenhower bluntly describes his attitude:

"I emphatically repudiated one suggestion I had heard that the Ruhr mines should be flooded. This seemed silly and criminal to me . . . These views were presented to everyone who queried me on the subject, both then and later. They were eventually placed before the President and the Secretary of State when they came to Potsdam in July 1945."

Harry Hopkins himself joined this protest; Roosevelt and Morgenthau therefore had to shelve indefinitely the plan so accurately described by General Eisenhower. Moreover in London, the Treasury informed the Prime Minister that if German productivity were completely destroyed, she would no longer be able to pay for her imports, and England would therefore lose an important market as soon as peace came. The argument with which Morgenthau had won over Lord Cherwell was therefore entirely refuted. In these circumstances, Churchill made no bones about going back on his agreement, and was quite ready, when he wrote the penultimate volume of his war memoirs, to forget that he had given it, even in writing: he had in fact contributed to drawing up the resolution that had been formulated. The Morgenthau plan was a dead letter.

Given Churchill's distrust of Stalin, why did he go to Moscow in October 1944?

According to Churchill's own account, the Soviet penetration into south-east Europe compelled him to make this journey. With Rumania's about-face, followed by the Bulgarian armistice, the launching of the Soviet autumn offensive, and "in spite of the Warsaw tragedy . . . I felt the need of another personal meeting with Stalin . . . As the victory of the Grand Alliance became only a matter of time it was natural that Russian ambitions should grow. Communism raised its head behind the thundering Russian battle-front. Russia was the Deliverer, and Communism the gospel she brought."

At this juncture, neither Bulgaria's nor Rumania's fates were of the slightest concern to Great Britain; on the other hand Churchill was very worried about what would happen to Poland and Greece. Great Britain considered herself responsible for the restoration of their governments-in-exile, if this was what their peoples really wished. And it was essential that they should be able to express themselves freely. In fact, this was far from certain since Stalin had set up a Polish government subservient to him in Lublin, and George Papandreou's Greek Government seemed to be dependent on the Communist resistance group.

On the other hand, work was not proceeding well at Dumbarton Oaks, where an inter-Allied conference was meeting for the purpose of laying the foundations of a future United Nations Organisation.

Eden and Averell Harriman at the Moscow Conference in October 1944.

The Russians clashed with the British and Americans both on the composition of the General Assembly and on the balloting method for the Security Council. Moscow was now determined that the rule of Great Power unanimity should prevail. Once again, according to Churchill in 1953, he felt he should strike while the iron was hot:

"I felt sure we could only reach good decisions with Russia while we had the comradeship of a common foe as a bond. Hitler and Hitlerism were doomed; but after Hitler what?"

Therefore Churchill took the initiative in a telegram on September 27, and proposed a visit to the Kremlin. Stalin, in his reply of September 30, welcomed the idea "warmly". Roosevelt excused himself from accompanying Churchill to Moscow as the presidential elections were imminent, and his absence from the U.S.A. at this time might well have prejudiced the result to his disadvantage. However, his ambassador in the U.S.S.R., Averell Harriman, was to replace him, taking part in the conversations as an observer, and as Roosevelt's message of October 4 stated:

"While naturally Averell will not be in a position to commit the United States – I could not permit anyone to commit me in advance – he will be able to keep me informed, and I have told him to return and report to me as soon as the conference is over."

And as he feared that his British partner might indulge in some passing whim, Roosevelt sent word to Stalin on the same day:

"I am sure you understand that in this global war there is literally no question, military or political, in which the United States is not interested. I am firmly convinced that the three of us, and only the three of us, can find the solution of the questions still unresolved. In this sense, while appreciating Mr. Churchill's desire for the meeting, I prefer to regard your

forthcoming talks with the Prime Minister as preliminary to a meeting of the three of us which can take place any time after the elections here as far as I am concerned."

Churchill does not mention it in his memoirs, but he took great offence at the President's precaution, according to Lord Moran, who in his capacity as Churchill's doctor saw him every day. But what was more serious, according to Moran, by the end of September "the advance of the Red Army has taken possession of [Churchill's] mind. Once they got into a country, it would not be easy to get them out. Our army in Italy was too weak to keep them in check. He might get his way with Stalin by other means.

"All might be well if he could win Stalin's friendship. After all it was stupid of the President to suppose that he was the only person who could manage Stalin. Winston told me that he had found he could talk to Stalin as one human being to another. Stalin, he was sure, would be sensible. He went on to speak of this proffer of friendship to Stalin as if it were an ingenious idea that had just occurred to him, and while he spoke his eyes popped and his words tumbled over each other in his excitement. He could think of nothing else. It had ceased to be a means to an end; it had become an end in itself. He sat up in bed.

"'If we three come together,' he said, 'everything is possible – absolutely anything.'"

As can be seen, there is a strong difference between Churchill's attitude in his memoirs and his reactions at the time as his doctor saw them; in 1953, when the cold war was at its height and he had just been re-elected, Churchill could not admit to his readers that he had deluded himself into thinking he could win Stalin over.

Accompanied by Anthony Eden, General Sir Hastings Ismay, his chief-of-staff, and Field-Marshal Sir Alan Brooke, the C.I.G.S., the Prime Minister travelled via Naples, Cairo, and Simferopol' and arrived in Moscow on the evening of October 9. At 2200 hours, he and Eden were conducted to Stalin's office. Stalin, accompanied by Molotov, was waiting for him. And in the absence of Averell Harriman, the four men lost no time in making a preliminary survey of the world situation.

Doubtless Harriman would not have objected to their decision to invite the Polish government to send a delegation to Moscow. But perhaps he would have thought that Churchill was unduly compromising the future as well as the U.S.A. if he had heard him tell Stalin:

"Let us settle about our affairs in the Balkans. Your armies are in Roumania and Bulgaria. We have interests, missions, and agents there. Don't let us get at cross-purposes in small ways. So far as Britain and Russia are concerned, how would it do for you to have ninety

per cent predominance in Roumania, for us to have ninety per cent of the say in Greece, and go fifty-fifty about Yugoslavia?"

And even more so if he had seen Churchill make in writing a proposal which had never been agreed by London and Washington. Churchill in fact, whilst his words were being translated, scribbled on a half sheet of paper:

"Rumania				
Russia	..	..	..	90%
The others	..	..	10%
Greece				
Great Britain	..	..	90%
(in accord with U.S.A.)			
Russia	..	..	..	10%
Yugoslavia	..	..	50-50%
Hungary	..	..	50-50%
Bulgaria				
Russia	..	..	..	75%
The others	..	..	25%"

Stalin ticked the paper passed to him by Churchill, who wrote: "It was all settled in no more time than it takes to set down."

In exchange for a half-sheet of paper the Western Powers, on Churchill's initiative, had abdicated all influence in Bucharest and Sofia, and implicitly left the Rumanians and Bulgarians to face the Soviet giant alone. Yet such a division of spheres of influence was merely realistic, in view of the Red Army's advances, as the case of Poland was to show.

In addition, it was later observed that this arrangement on October 9 did not remove the threat of Communist subversion from Greece, in spite of the percentage of that unhappy country conceded to Great Britain by the Kremlin. The 50 per cent influence allotted to Britain in Yugoslavia dropped to zero even before hostilities ended in Europe, and Tito tore up the agreement he had concluded in the previous year with Dr. Subašić, Prime Minister of the Yugoslav government-in-exile. Obviously, in October 1944, Churchill and Eden no longer had any illusions about the future direction of Marshal Tito's policy, in spite of the Anglo-American arms deliveries which had saved him from defeat and death. Moreover, in this division of spheres of influence, it was clear that Churchill had completely forgotten Albania, on which Greece had some claims.

But before 24 hours had passed, Molotov tried to obtain from Eden some modifications of the percentages agreed on the day before. He received a curt refusal, but a note of Eden's shows that his own report of the incident was coolly received by the Prime Minister, who was wrapped up in his own illusions:

"W. rather upset by my report. I think he thought I had dispelled good atmosphere he had created night before. But I explained this was the real battle and I could not and would not give way."

His firmness was rewarded, as Molotov undertook to call on the Bulgarians to evacuate immediately the Greek and Yugoslav provinces which they had occupied by German agreement in April and May 1941. As regards Yugoslavia, Eden wrote:

"We also spoke of Yugoslavia, when Stalin said that Tito thought the Croats and Slovenes would refuse to join in any government under King Peter. He himself had the impression that the King was ineffective. I replied that I was sure the King had courage and I thought that he had intelligence. Mr. Churchill interjected that the King was very young.

"'How old is he?' asked Stalin. 'Twenty-one,' I answered. 'Twenty-one!' exclaimed Stalin with a burst of pride, 'Peter the Great was ruler of Russia at seventeen.' For that moment, at least, Stalin was more nationalist than communist, the same mood as had seen the disappearance for the time being of the portraits of Marx and Engels from the Kremlin rooms and their replacement by Kutuzov and Suvorov."

On October 13, the Polish delegation of the government-in-exile, consisting of its Prime Minister, Stanislas Mikolajczyk, Professor Grabski, and Foreign Minister Tadeusz Romer started discussions with Stalin, Molotov, Churchill, Eden, and Harriman, who had been instructed to keep strictly to his rôle as observer. They intended to reach an agreement on two questions: firstly, the eastern frontiers of Poland; and secondly, the formation of a unified Polish government, including the London government's representatives and members of the Lublin "National Committee". Although they expected to make some territorial sacrifices to the

Yugoslav leader Josip Broz ("Tito").

Soviet Union, Mikolajczyk and his colleagues were aghast when they discovered that the Teheran agreement (which had been concluded behind their backs by the "Big Three") had prescribed the Curzon Line as their country's frontier; thus 48 per cent of Polish territory would be surrendered to the U.S.S.R. without the population involved being consulted about the transfer.

The Polish prime minister's protests against the acquiescence which was being demanded of him left Stalin cold and uncompromising.

After this session, the British and Poles met. Churchill lost his temper and started threatening the unfortunate Mikolajczyk:

"I pressed Mikolajczyk hard to consider two things, namely, *de facto* acceptance of the Curzon Line, with interchange of population, and a friendly discussion with the Lublin Polish Committee so that a united Poland might be established."

This is the version of the meeting in Churchill's memoirs, but it seems to be a typically British understatement. In fact, on the next day the Prime Minister confided to Moran: "I was pretty rough with Mikolajczyk . . . He was obstinate and I lost my temper." A few hours later Churchill returned to the subject: "I shook my fist at him and lost my temper."

It is hard to accept Mikolajczyk's account of the conversation; his memoirs were published in New York and Toronto and were not challenged by Churchill. The striking thing about Churchill's diatribes, as recounted by Mikolajczyk, is not so much their violence ("You're not a government! You're an unreasonable people who want to shipwreck Europe. I'll leave you to stew in your own juice. You have no sense of responsibility when you want to abandon the people in your care, and you've no idea of their sufferings. You've no thought for anything but your own wretched, mean, and egotistical interests.") and their threats ("We shall not part as friends. I shall tell the world how unreasonable you've shown yourselves to be . . . We'll take a stand and break away from you if you continue to prevaricate. I'll consider opening relations with the other Poles. The Lublin government can work perfectly. They'll be the government for sure.") as his confidence that if the Polish Government gave in to the Big Three, all would be for the best in the best of all possible Europes. Churchill continued:

"Our relations with Russia are better than they've ever been. I expect them to remain so . . . we do not intend to jeopardise the peace of Europe . . . Your discussions are nothing more than criminal attempts to undermine goodwill between the Allies with your *Liberum veto*. It is a criminal act of your doing!"

Assuming this determinedly optimistic point of view, Churchill described to Mikolajczyk the advantage which would compensate Poland for the sacrifices he was calling upon her to make:

"But think what you will get in exchange. You will have a country. I will see that a British ambassador is sent to you. And there will also be an ambassador from the United States, the greatest military power in the world . . .

"If you accept the Curzon line, the United States will devote themselves most actively to the reconstruction of Poland and will doubtless give you large loans, perhaps even without your having to ask for them. We will help you too, but we will be poor after this war. You are *obliged* to accept the decision of the great powers."

Mikolajczyk, in spite of Churchill's tone of voice, was not completely insensitive to this argument. He proposed a compromise, in which he was prepared to recognise the Curzon Line as Poland's eastern frontier, provided that the Drohobycz and Boryslaw oil wells, as well as the great historically and traditionally Polish cities of L'vov and Vilnyus on the east of the line, remained Polish. But Stalin refused to countenance any such concessions.

In doing this, Stalin was risking nothing; on the one hand his armies had crossed the Curzon Line on the entire front between the Niemen and the Carpathians; on the other hand, the Lublin Committee delegates, Osóbka-Morawski and Bierut, stated in the presence of Churchill, Eden, and Harriman:

"'We are here to demand on behalf of Poland that Lvov shall belong to Russia. That is the will of the Polish people.'

"When this had been translated from Polish into English and Russian I looked at Stalin and saw an understanding twinkle in his expressive eyes, as much as to say, 'What about that for our Soviet teaching!'"

In their memoirs Churchill and Eden made no attempt to conceal their disgust when they heard these servile commonplaces. Nevertheless Mikolajczyk received the peremptory advice to accept these foreign agents in his government. Otherwise it would be the end of Poland.

As Roosevelt had wished, the problems relating to the articles of the future international organisation were not mentioned during the conference. The agenda was devoted to presenting, discussing, and putting final touches to the plans for the last phase of the war in Europe and for the participation of the Red Army in the war against Japan.

With his usual clarity, Brooke set out the situation on the Western Front and in Italy, and explained General Eisenhower's intentions. The deputy chief-of-staff of the Red Army, General Antonov, then spoke, and Brooke noted in his diary that he was extremely pleased with the ensuing discussion.

On October 15, the war against Japan was discussed, with particular reference to the Red Army and the possibility of moving supplies via the trans-Siberian railway for an offensive in

Manchuria with 60 divisions and appropriate air forces. Stalin took over from his military colleague and explained the difficulties of the project. According to Brooke:

"He displayed an astounding knowledge of technical railway details, had read past history of fighting in that theatre and from this knowledge drew very sound deductions. I was more than ever impressed by his military ability."

Complete military agreement was reached almost at once. With regard to a future peace settlement, Churchill and Stalin agreed that Germany might be divided after the war, and that a southern state, consisting of Baden, Württemberg, Bavaria, and Austria, would be formed. To give more stability to this Danubian confederation, Churchill wanted Hungary to join it, but Stalin who had designs on Hungary, refused.

The only success claimed by the British Government was the *de jure* recognition by London, Washington, and Moscow of General de Gaulle's provisional government as the government of France.

Much has been written, at any rate in the West, about the "Argonaut" Conference, during which Roosevelt, Churchill, Stalin, and their chief political and military colleagues met at Yalta in the Crimea. In 1955, the State Department published a wide collection of diplomatic documents relating to the Big Three's meeting, the discussions they had together, and the resolutions and agreements they signed. Thus we can compare these authentic records with the statements of those taking part in the conference.

During the period between Churchill's Moscow journey and the Yalta conference, a number of occurrences which influenced the course of negotiations should be mentioned.

On November 7, 1944, the American people re-elected Roosevelt to a fourth term as President, admittedly by about 3,000,000 fewer votes than in 1940. Obviously, in making his choice, the American voter was relying on the adage that one should not change horses in mid-course. Nevertheless, the victor of this exhausting campaign had neglected his brief and, in addition, he was in a very poor state of health.

"The President looked old and thin and drawn; he had a cape or shawl over his shoulders and appeared shrunken; he sat looking straight ahead with his mouth open, as if he were not taking things in." This was Moran's description of him on February 3, and the next day he wrote:

"It was not only his physical deterioration that had caught their attention. He intervened very little in the discussions, sitting with his mouth open. If he has sometimes been short of facts about the subject under discussion his shrewdness has covered this up. Now, they say, the shrewdness has gone, and there is nothing left." Again, Moran noted on the 7th:

"To a doctor's eye, the President

appears a very sick man. He has all the symptoms of hardening of the arteries of the brain in an advanced stage, so that I give him only a few months to live."

For personal reasons Roosevelt, before starting on his electoral campaign, had dropped his previous Vice-President, Henry A. Wallace, in favour of Harry S. Truman, the senator from Missouri. This was a stroke of luck for the Americans. Truman, a man of strong character, was, however, quite unprepared for his task when on April 12, 1945 he was suddenly called upon to take over.

Moreover the Secretary of State, Cordell Hull, had now reached retirement age. Roosevelt appointed Edward R. Stettinius in his place. Stettinius was a conscientious civil servant who knew his job thoroughly, but he was called upon to take over his duties under a President in very poor health, to say the least, and was faced by an opposite number as redoubtable and experienced in international affairs as Molotov.

Mikolajczyk, when he returned to London, found that the majority of his government disapproved of the concessions he had felt compelled to make to the U.S.S.R. He therefore accepted the consequences, and resigned. He was succeeded by Tomasz Arciszewski, a militant social-democrat. But although he was more to the left than his predecessor, the new head of the exile government failed to move the Kremlin.

When he resigned on November 24, 1944, Mikolajczyk handed over two documents concerning the policy of the U.S.A. and Great Britain towards the future Polish state. In a letter after he had been re-elected, President Roosevelt defined the American attitude clearly and positively:

"The Government of the United States is, most determinedly, in favour of a strong Polish state, free, independent, and conscious of the rights of the Polish people, to run its internal politics as it sees fit, without any outside interference."

Certainly the U.S.A. could not depart from their traditional policy and guarantee the frontiers of the future Polish state, but they were ready to play a very large part in its economic reconstruction.

Moreover, on the previous November 2, on Churchill's instructions, Sir Alexander Cadogan, Permanent Under-Secretary of State at the Foreign Office, wrote to Romer, the Polish Foreign Minister, a letter of which the following is an extract:

"Finally you ask if His Majesty's Government will guarantee the independence and integrity of the new Polish state. On this point the reply of His Majesty's Government is that they are ready to give this guarantee conjointly with the Soviet Government. If the Government of the United States also believed that it could associate itself in this guarantee, that would be so much the better, but His Majesty's Government does not make this a condition of the guarantee, which it is ready to give con-

jointly with that of the Soviet Government."

It is evident that Great Britain's attitude in this declaration fell considerably short of the U.S.A.'s, as she made her guarantee of Polish independence subject to an agreement with the Soviet Union. What would happen if Stalin refused this guarantee?

On December 18, a statement by Secretary of State Stettinius, recalling the terms of Roosevelt's letter to Mikolajczyk, was brought to Stalin's notice. On December 27, Stalin in his reply to Roosevelt maintained that this statement had been overtaken by events; then after a long diatribe against Arciszewski and his colleagues, he added in so many words:

"I must say frankly that in the event of the Polish Committee of National Liberation becoming a Provisional Polish Government, the Soviet Government will, in view of the foregoing, have no serious reasons for postponing its recognition."

Then, in spite of a letter from Roosevelt, who said he was "disturbed and deeply disappointed" by this declaration and by the hasty Moscow decision, he proceeded to recognise the Lublin Committee on January 5, 1945; he gave Roosevelt the following explanation:

"Of course I quite understand your proposal for postponing recognition of the Provisional Government of Poland by the Soviet Union for a month. But one circumstance makes me powerless to comply with your wish. The point is that on December 27 the Presidium of the Supreme Soviet of the U.S.S.R., replying to the corresponding question by the Poles, declared that it would recognise the Provisional Government of Poland the moment it was set up. This circumstance makes me powerless to comply with your wish."

But he omitted to say that he had dictated this request for recognition to the "Polish Committee of National Liberation."

It was in this sort of atmosphere that the Yalta Conference opened. Certainly Roosevelt had no intention of recognising the puppet government which Stalin controlled, and Churchill even less so. But in the meantime events had moved on. In fact just when the three delegations were holding their first session, Zhukov's advance guard reached the bend of the Oder whilst Konev's was about to take Breslau. Except for the Polish corridor, all Polish territory was in the hands of the Russians, who were everywhere setting up the Lublin Committee's representatives and hunting down the partisans who had been fighting the Germans for five years under the command of the Polish government-in-exile.

On February 2, Roosevelt, who had arrived on the cruiser *Quincy,* and Churchill, who had flown in, met at Valletta in Malta. They joined the Combined Chiefs-of-Staff Committee, which had been in session for three days and

The failing President Roosevelt (right) and his successor, Truman (above).

was completing plans for the great operation to take the British and the Americans into the centre of Germany. Then the two delegations flew to the Crimea and on the evening of February 3 moved into the buildings reserved for them: the Americans into the former imperial palace of Livadia; the British five miles away in the Vorontzov villa. Stalin and his colleagues were to stay at the Yusupov Palace halfway between them, an arrangement obviously calculated to prevent any Anglo-American private conversations and to make *tête-à-tête* talks with Roosevelt easier.

The first such meeting took place in the afternoon of February 4, and the President was moved to get Stalin to repeat his Teheran toast (that 50,000 German officers should be shot) because Roosevelt maintained the devastation caused by the Wehrmacht in the Crimea gave him a desire for revenge.

A few hours later the conference opened in the Livadia Palace, and Stalin im-mediately proposed that there should be no rotation of chairmanship, but that Roosevelt should chair the proceedings for the whole meeting.

Arthur Conte, in his *Yalta ou le partage du monde,* has noted that this was a skilful Soviet manoeuvre, as it was not intended merely as a practical working arrangement: "This also showed a remarkable appreciation of Roosevelt's psychology, by strengthening him in the awareness of his superiority. He was also dissociating himself from British imperialism. It in fact separated the British and the Americans by conferring the chairmanship on the American; Roosevelt thus had power to arbitrate, a conciliatory rôle which would naturally lead him to show increased understanding of the Russian position. Stalin immediately gave himself a big advantage while appearing to give it to Roosevelt."

Eden also noted that the American president was "vague and loose and ineffective", letting the discussion drift on, without being able to pin Stalin and Churchill down to firm and precise terms. The various questions on the agenda were discussed unmethodically, by fits and starts, and Harry Hopkins several times had to bring the discussion back to the subject by passing notes to Roosevelt. But the bias of these notes can easily be guessed, as in spite of the troublesome state of his health, the so-called *éminence grise* of the White House was still strongly pro-Soviet.

Secretary of State Stettinius was too new in his job to know how to assert himself usefully in the discussion. As for the fourth member of the American delegation, the diplomat Alger Hiss, whose particular responsibility was questions relating to the future United Nations Organisation, he was later condemned to five years' imprisonment on January 22, 1950 by a New York court for perjury about his Communist associations.

Another circumstance played against the two Western powers; this was the ten day period allowed by the American constitution to the President to approve or veto bills adopted by the Congress. As he could not do this by cable or radio, it was essential for him not to prolong his stay in the Crimea beyond a week. Stalin, however, was in no hurry and was ready to sell Roosevelt time.

Since he had seen Stalin at work, Anthony Eden refers to his diplomatic

Churchill, Roosevelt and Stalin with their foreign secretaries at Yalta.

talents in a way that reminds one of Field-Marshal Sir Alan Brooke's references to his strategic abilities:

"Marshal Stalin as a negotiator was the toughest proposition of all. Indeed, after something like thirty years' experience of international conferences of one kind and another, if I had to pick a team for going into a conference room, Stalin would be my first choice. Of course the man was ruthless and of course he knew his purpose. He never wasted a word. He never stormed, he was seldom even irritated. Hooded, calm, never raising his voice, he avoided the repeated negatives of Molotov which were so exasperating to listen to. By more subtle methods he got what he wanted without having seemed so obdurate."

Nevertheless, Eden also acknowledged that Molotov was a first-rate assistant to Stalin. One may well suppose that when responsibilities were assigned, the orders given to Molotov were to adopt such a harsh tone that when Stalin took over negotiations in the style so vividly described by Eden, the British and American representatives (in particular Roosevelt, Stettinius, and James) could tell one another gratefully: "After the rain comes the sun."

Under these circumstances it is not hard to see that the British delegation had no easy task, faced with the vacillations of American policy and Stalin's firm resolve to make the maximum possible advances in all parts of the world. Thus the British did not receive the immediate support of their natural allies when they proposed the immediate and simultaneous evacua-

tion of Persia by the British and Soviet forces that had occupied the country since August 1941. Similarly, the Soviet Union succeeded in imposing its attitude about a revision, once peace came, of the Montreux Convention. This had, since July 20, 1936, laid down the law concerning the control of the Turkish narrows.

Therefore Churchill left the Crimea full of forebodings, quite the reverse of his happy mood of the previous October 9, when he landed at Moscow airport. But to the last day of his life he did his best to deny any responsibility for the inexorable process which led to the enslavement of 120 million Europeans behind the Iron Curtain. According to Churchill, everything was decided at Yalta during the conference when he was, if one can put it like that, "sandwiched" between Stalin and Roosevelt. In this way he was able to divest himself of his responsibility in this most unjust settlement of World War II, making Roosevelt shoulder it all. But in view of the documents just quoted, it is impossible to confirm this black and white judgement, and Alfred Fabre-Luce's judgement in *L'Histoire démaquillée,* "Churchill changed tack too late", seems more correct. All the same, he changed tack a year before Truman.

We may now quote the resolutions adopted by Churchill, Roosevelt, and Stalin and drawn up by Eden, Stettinius, and Molotov. We shall limit our comments to the resolutions on Poland, Germany, and the Far East.

(a) The reorganisation of Poland
Stalin conceded to the Allies that the

Soviet-Polish frontier could in places run three and even five miles to the east of the Curzon Line, which he claimed had been originated by Clemenceau, although neither the British nor the Americans pointed out this obvious historical error. The Oder and the Neisse were to constitute the western frontier of the new Poland. But although, at Teheran, they had agreed on the eastern Neisse (which runs through the town of Neisse), as is clear from a question from Churchill concerning the allocation of the upper Silesian industrial basin, Stalin and Molotov claimed they had been referring to the western Neisse, which meets the Oder near the town of Guben.

Churchill pointed out in vain that this additional modification of the German-Polish frontier would entail the further expulsion of eight million Germans. Stalin replied that the matter was now settled, as the province's inhabitants had fled from the Soviet advance, which was only half true, and they then went on to consider the agenda.

As regards Poland's political reorganisation, we must refer to Point 7 of the protocol recorded on February 11 by the foreign ministers of the Big Three. Taking into consideration the Red Army's complete "liberation" of Poland, it stated:

"The provisional government actually operating in Poland must in the future be reorganised on a larger democratic base, to include the popular leaders actually in Poland and those abroad. This new government is to be called the Polish Government of National Unity.

"Mr. Molotov, Mr. Harriman, and Sir A. Clark Kerr are authorised to form a commission to consult initially the members of the Provisional Polish Government, as well as other Polish leaders (both in Poland and abroad), with a view to the reorganisation of the actual government along the lines set out below. The Polish Government of National Unity must set about organising free and open elections as soon as possible, on the basis of a universal franchise and a secret ballot. All democratic and anti-Nazi parties will have the right to take part and put up candidates."

It can be seen that there is a great difference between this tripartite declaration and Stalin's statement to Roosevelt on May 4, 1943: "As regards the Hitlerites' rumours on the possibility that a new Polish government will be formed in the U.S.S.R., it is scarcely necessary to give the lie to these ravings."

The two Western powers did not expressly recognise the government formed from the Lublin Committee, but they took note of its existence, and the men who were to give it the character of national unity provided for by the protocol gathered round it and not round the legal government in London. No one stated how many of these men were to come from London and how many from Lublin; but this question was to be examined by a commission and Molotov, who was to be at its centre, would have much greater authority than the British and American Ambassadors in Moscow. Yalta, therefore, consummated Churchill's failure to preserve Polish independence and democracy and Stalin's success in making Poland a Communist satellite.

(b) Germany's fate

In order to snatch these concessions from his allies, in exchange for a more vague promise of "free and open elections on the basis of a universal franchise and a secret ballot", Stalin put forward the argument that in the event of a German revival the Soviet Union's security demanded the existence of an independent and friendly Poland. In this respect, it is odd to note that neither Churchill nor Roosevelt thought of pointing out to Stalin that the arrangements they had just decided on for the treatment of Germany eliminated any danger of aggression on her part for centuries to come.

Apart from the Oder-Neisse frontier which was to be imposed on Germany, Point 3 of the Yalta protocol is absolutely clear in this respect. Churchill and Eden with some difficulty secured France's right to take part in the occupation of Germany and to send delegates to sit on the Allied Control Commission charged with administering the defeated power. In spite of the treaty he had just signed with General de Gaulle, Stalin at first refused this in terms that were most offensive to France.

As for Roosevelt, he wavered between these two opposing points of view and finally sided with Churchill; but it was agreed that the French occupation zone would be cut out of the British and American zones. It was at this point in the discussions that Roosevelt, in reply to one of Stalin's questions, made a blunder by telling him that he could not possibly obtain authorisation from Congress to maintain American troops in Europe for more than two years after the end of the war. Stalin, it can readily be imagined, found this statement most helpful to his cause.

It was agreed between Roosevelt and Stalin that Germany should pay 20,000 million dollars in reparations; half of this sum would go to the Soviet Union, which would be paid in kind in the form of a transfer of industrial equipment, annual goods deliveries, and the use of German manpower. The final settlement of reparations owed by Germany, and their distribution among the nations that suffered as a result of her aggression, would be determined by a commission in Moscow. Great Britain had reserved her position on the question of the figure of 20,000 million dollars agreed by the Soviets and the Americans.

The principle of dividing Germany up was recorded in the protocol of February 11, and was not clarified during the Yalta discussions; the commission set up under Eden's chairmanship to examine the problem received no directives from the Big Three. It has been assumed from this silence that it was Stalin's intention to transform the Soviet occupation zone into a Communist state which would be Moscow's satellite. Undoubtedly there is much evidence for this assumption.

Meanwhile the Conference finally agreed on the borders of the Allied occupation zones in Germany, so concluding negotiations that had been in progress since the beginning of 1943.

(c) The Far East

As Russia's relations with Japan were governed by the non-aggression pact signed in Moscow on April 13, 1941, the question of Russia taking part in the war being waged by the Anglo-Americans against the Japanese was settled by a special protocol which was kept secret.

As a reward for its intervention, the U.S.S.R. was to recover the rights it had lost by the Treaty of Portsmouth (U.S.A.) in 1905 which had crowned the Emperor Meiji's victory over Tsar Nicholas II. As a consequence, it was to regain possession of the southern part of Sakhalin island, the Manchuria railway, the port of Dairen (Lü-ta) which was to be internationalised, and its lease of Port Arthur. In addition, the Russians would receive the Kurile islands, which they had surrendered to Japan in 1875 in exchange for the southern part of Sakhalin island.

It is clear that the agreement of February 11, 1945 took little account of the interests of the fourth great power, Chiang Kai-shek's China. Admittedly it was agreed that the eastern China and southern Manchuria railways would be run jointly by a Soviet-Chinese company and that China would retain "full and complete sovereignty" in Manchuria. Nevertheless the power mainly involved in this arrangement had taken no part in the negotiations, and had not even been consulted. On this matter, the agreement merely stated:

"It is agreed that the arrangements for Outer Mongolia, as well as for the ports and railways mentioned will require the assent of Generalissimo Chiang Kai-shek. The President will take the necessary measures to obtain this assent, acting on the advice of Marshal Stalin."

But the agreement did not state what would happen if the Chunking government refused its agreement. Moreover, the British and American negotiations about this arrangement lost sight of the fact that as in 1898, the Russian reoccupation of Port Arthur and Dairen in the Kuantung peninsula automatically raised the question of Korea. However, Korea does not appear in the text.

President Roosevelt relied on his own intuition, and did not heed the warnings of Ambassador William Bullitt: "Bill, I am not challenging your facts; they are correct. I am not challenging the logic of your argument. But I have the feeling that Stalin isn't that kind of man. Harry [Hopkins] says he isn't and that all he wants is his country's security. And I think that if I give him all I can give him, and ask for nothing in return, *noblesse oblige,* he won't try to annex anything and he will agree to work with me for a world of democracy and peace."

CHAPTER 72
Victory in Italy

Originally known as the Apennine Position, the Gothic Line ran across the mountains, coast to coast, for 200 miles, from near La Spezia on the Gulf of Genoa to Pesaro on the Adriatic. It was longer than the line through Cassino, and the mountain barrier reached across the peninsula to within a short distance of Route 16, which followed the coast-line through the narrow plain to Rimini. Orders for the line to be reconnoitred and fortified had in fact been given by Jodl almost a month before the evacuation of Sicily, but more recently the work had been interrupted by the pressing demands for *matériel* and labour for building the defences of the Gustav and Hitler Lines.

At the time of the capture of Rome, Alexander estimated that Kesselring would have only the equivalent of ten divisions to man the Apennine positions, but Hitler's immediate reaction to the threat of an Allied advance into northern Italy had completely changed the situation. Kesselring was now able to gain much-needed time for the Organisation Todt to complete most of the defences that had been so carefully planned.

At the very height of the fighting in Normandy, Hitler dispatched no fewer than seven divisions, withdrawn from Denmark, Holland, Hungary, and even the Russian front, to reinforce Army Group "C" in Italy. Finally O.K.W. sent a battalion of Tiger tanks from France and the whole of three divisions, forming in Germany, to fill up the ranks of the infantry divisions that had been virtually annihilated in the Liri valley.

Although Alexander had been warned as early as May 22, 1944, that he must be prepared to provide seven divisions for a landing in the south of France, it was not until July 5, when the battle for Arezzo was in the balance and the Polish II Corps was still short of Ancona, that he was told that his pleas to be allowed to keep his force intact, for a thrust into northern Italy and beyond, had finally been turned down.

The task that Alexander was now given was:

1. to cross the Apennines to the line of the River Po; and
2. to cross the river and seize the line Venice – Padua – Verona – Brescia.

After this he would receive further instructions.

In spite of the loss of so many divisions, including the French Expeditionary Corps with all its mountain troops, the Allied offensive must continue.

The long summer days were running out and the chance of any large scale penetration into the Po valley before winter set in now appeared most unlikely. But in Normandy the Battle of Caen was about to start – it was imperative that the pressure by the Allies in Italy should be maintained, even increased.

So long as there had been hopes of a rapid advance, the bridges over the Po had been spared by the Allied bombers. On July 12 the Tactical Air Force went to work and in three days cut all 23 of the rail and road bridges over the river. The battle for the Gothic Line had begun.

In the mountains the German engineers had already constructed a series of strong-points astride the routes leading to the Po valley at Borgo a Mozzano, Porretta, the Vernio pass north of Prato, and the Futa and Il Giogo passes north of Florence. From here the line ran south-east, again with every route blocked, from Casaglia to below Bagno and the Mandrioli pass, before turning eastwards to drop down to the valley of the Foglia and Pesaro on the Adriatic. Here, in the narrow coastal plain, was Route 16, the only road that the Allies could take which did not entail a climb across the great mountain barrier. This corridor, however, between the foot-hills and the sea, was cut across by numerous rivers; and the succession of ridges, which similarly were at right angles to the line of advance, was admirably suited for defence. Moreover, the rivers were liable to sudden flooding and rain quickly turned the heavy soil into a sea of mud. The fortifications in this sector had been skilfully prepared, with anti-tank ditches, extensive minefields, and the usual deep bunkers. In June and July, while Kesselring's rearguards were slowly falling back through Tuscany, Todt engineers, with thousands of conscripted Italian labourers, were frantically engaged in constructing a ten mile deep belt of obstacles along the whole line, and in the mountains a series of positions to link up with the main strongholds, so as to form a continuous front. A report on the defences that had been completed when the battle started listed 2,376 machine gun nests, 479 anti-tank gun, mortar, and assault gun positions, 120,000 yards of wire entanglement, and many miles of anti-tank ditches. Only four out of the 30 7.5-cm Panther gun turrets ordered by O.K.W., however, were in position.

The balance of forces in the opening stages of the forthcoming battle pitted 26 German divisions, including six Panzer and *Panzergrenadier* divisions, and some six Italian divisions, against 20 Allied divisions, which included four armoured divisions. For the Germans the battle would be fought solely on the ground, as the Luftwaffe in Italy was reduced to 170 aircraft, the majority of which were obsolete. The Allies, with some 75 complete squadrons in the Tactical Air Force alone, enjoyed complete air superiority. This advantage, however, would soon be reduced as the weather deteriorated. Meanwhile Kesselring could neither "see over the hill", nor strike out at his enemy's rear communica-

tions. In spite of this and a weakness in both artillery and armour, he viewed his task of beating off the coming offensive with growing confidence, especially after an inspection of the defences on his eastern flank.

Throughout the whole campaign the Germans had overestimated the Allied capability to carry out amphibious operations against their rear and Kesselring, sensitive to the preparations for "Dragoon" (as "Anvil" was now named), feared a landing on the Ligurian coast or even in the Gulf of Venice. Consequently he allocated no fewer than six divisions to coastal defence. A further weakening of his forces resulted from the active resistance, backed by the Communists, of Italian workers in the industrial areas to Mussolini's puppet government. In effect civil war had broken out, and in spite of the arrival of two German-trained Italian divisions the partisans were also beginning to show their true strength in attacks on military depots and lines of communication. Thus there remained only 19 divisions to hold the Gothic Line itself. On the right was the 14th Army, with XIV Panzer Corps allocated to the long mountain stretch from the coast to Empoli, and I Parachute Corps to hold the shorter and more critical central section facing Florence, both with three divisions. In reserve were the inexperienced 20th Luftwaffe Field Division and the 29th *Panzergrenadier* Division, north of Florence. East of Pontassieve was the 10th Army, with LI Mountain Corps (five divisions) holding the spine of the Apennine range as far as Sansepolcro and LXXVI Panzer Corps in the foothills and coastal plain, again with five divisions, of which two were echeloned back watching the coast. The newly arrived 98th Division was in army reserve around Bologna. This again emphasised Kesselring's preoccupation with the central section of the mountain barrier, which was only 50 miles deep at this point, in spite of his prediction that the attack would be made on the Adriatic flank. Meanwhile the front line remained on the line of the Arno.

Alexander's initial plan was to press an early attack, with both armies side by side, into the mountains on the axis Florence–Bologna. Indeed the cover plan, with fake wireless traffic and soldiers arriving in the Adriatic sector wearing Canadian I Corps flashes, had already started. But this was before Clark's 5th Army was reduced to a single corps and the total strength of both armies to 20 divisions. Moreover there was no chance of any reinforcements other than the U.S. 92nd (Negro) Division in September and a Brazilian division by the end of October. So there could be no diversionary operations and no reserve to maintain the impetus of the advance.

In spite of this, General Harding, Alexander's chief-of-staff, recommended the plan should stand. Lieutenant-General Sir Oliver Leese, the 8th Army commander, whose troops would have to bear the brunt of the fighting, felt there was a far better chance of breaking through on the Adriatic sector, where his superiority in tanks and guns could be employed to greater effect.

Furthermore General Clark would have greater freedom to make his own dispositions. This plan suited one of Alexander's favourite strategies, the "two-handed punch", in that by striking at both Ravenna and Bologna the enemy's reserves would be split. At a secret meeting in Orvieto on August 4, 1944, between the two commanders, with only Harding present, the matter was decided by Alexander in favour of Leese's alternative proposal. As practically the whole of the 8th Army had to be moved across the mountains to the east coast, D-day was put back to August 25. The cover plan was put into reverse, with 5th Army being told to make "ostentatious preparations" for an attack against the centre of the mountain positions. In the greatest secrecy the regrouping of both armies was started immediately.

The transfer to north of Ancona of the bulk of the 8th Army—two complete corps headquarters, some eight divisions, and a mass of corps troops, with over 80,000 vehicles—was achieved in 15 days. This was a remarkable feat as there were only two roads over the mountains, and both had been systematically demolished by the Germans during their retreat. In many places the roads had to be entirely rebuilt and no fewer than 40 Bailey bridges were constructed by the Royal Engineers before the roads could be reopened. Even so the roads were largely one-way, and the movement tables were further complicated by the need to operate the tank transporters on a continuous shuttle service as a result of the short time available for the concentration of the tank brigades.

Meanwhile the British XIII Corps, of three divisions under Lieutenant-General Sidney Kirkman, joined the U.S. 5th Army, so as to be ready alongside U.S. II Corps to deliver the second blow of "the two-handed punch" towards Bologna. The remaining two U.S. divisions, joined by the 6th South African Armoured Division and a mixed force of American and British anti-aircraft and other support units, hastily trained as infantry, formed Major-General Crittenberger's U.S. IV Corps. This had the task of holding the remainder of the 5th Army front. On the inner flank, acting as a link between the two armies, was X Corps, with the 10th Indian Division, a tank brigade, and several "dismounted" armoured car regiments. Every other available man of the 8th Army was committed to the main assault on the right flank.

Leese's plan was to break into the Gothic Line defences on a narrow front, with the Polish II Corps directed on

Pesaro (before going into reserve), and the Canadians making straight for Rimini. The main attack would be through the hills further inland towards Route 9 by Lieutenant-General Sir Charles Keightley's V Corps, with the British 4th, 46th, and 56th, and 1st Armoured Divisions, and 4th Indian Division. The latter was briefed for the pursuit, and would attack alongside the Canadian 5th Armoured Division as soon as the breakthrough was achieved.

Initially all went well. When the Allied advance started the Germans were engaged in carrying out a series of reliefs in the coastal area, which involved the pulling back of a division from forward positions on the Metauro. Kesselring indeed assumed that the attack on August 25 was no more than a follow-up of this withdrawal. Vietinghoff himself was on leave and only got back late on August 28. The next day the Allied infantry reached the Foglia and Kesselring, who had been taken completely by surprise, at last ordered up reinforcements. But it was too late to stop the penetration of the carefully prepared Gothic Line positions. On August 31 the 46th Division held the formidable bastion of Montegridolfo and the following night Gurkhas of the 4th Indian Division, using only grenades and kukris, captured the strong-

*Canadian Sherman tanks cross a
Bailey bridge over the river Arno
at Pontassieve.*

ly fortified town of Tavoleto. In the plain, the Canadians had suffered heavily crossing the river but by dawn on September 3 had a bridgehead across the Conca alongside Route 16. Meanwhile both the 26th Panzer and 98th Divisions had reached the battle area and already suffered heavily.

The way to a breakthrough by V Corps lay in the capture of two hill features, the Coriano and Gemmano Ridges, situated just where the plain begins to widen out. These afforded the Germans excellent observation and fine positions. The task of breaking through was given to the 46th and 56th Divisions. Meanwhile, the British 1st Armoured Division, with some 300 tanks, had already started (on August 31) to move forward in accordance with the original plan. The approach march over narrow and often precipitous tracks, which got progressively worse, proved a nightmare. On one stage "along razor-edged mountain ridges" to reach the Foglia, which was crossed on September 3, drivers of the heavier vehicles had to reverse to get round every corner and some spent 50 hours at the wheel. The tank route proved even more hazardous, and 20 tanks were lost before reaching

the assembly area. The driving conditions were extremely exhausting and as the column ground its way forward in low gear many tanks ran out of petrol, while those at the rear of the column were engulfed in dense clouds of choking white dust.

At this critical moment the German 162nd Division and Kesselring's last mobile reserve, the experienced 29th *Panzergrenadier* Division (from Bologna) began to arrive. The renewed attacks by V Corps were broken up and held. Into the confused and unresolved struggle the armoured divisions were ordered forward late on September 4. There had been no breakthrough; the fleeting opportunity, if it had ever existed, had passed. The advance of the armoured brigades was met with a storm of shot and shell and an unbroken defence which now included tanks and self-propelled guns. In their advance towards Coriano, the British armoured brigades lost 65 tanks and many more were still struggling to cross the start line as dusk came.

That night rain began to fall and more German reinforcements (from the 356th Division) reached the front. By September

6 the tracks had turned to mud and air strikes could no longer be guaranteed. Alexander now ordered a regrouping for a set-piece attack (on September 12) to clear the two vital ridges. Now was the time for Clark to launch his attack into the mountains.

Since early August Kesselring's front line troops had been kept short of supplies through the interdiction programme of the Allied air forces. With the Brenner pass frequently blocked, north Italy was virtually isolated from the rest of Europe. There was no direct railway traffic across the Po east of Piacenza and south of the river the railway lines down as far as the Arno had been cut in nearly 100 places. But in spite of every difficulty, sufficient supplies were kept moving forward. Each night, pontoon bridges were built across the Po and then broken up and hidden by day; and ferries were operating at over 50 points on the river.

The Desert Air Force, which had supported the 8th Army so magnificently at a time when almost all the American air effort had been diverted to the "Dragoon" landing, now switched its whole effort to helping Clark's offensive to get

An M24 Chaffee light tank of the U.S. 81st Reconnaissance Squadron of the 1st Armoured Division in Vergato.

under way. Clark's attack came as no surprise to General Joachim Lemelsen, whose 14th Army had already been milked of three divisions to reinforce Colonel-General Heinrich von Vietinghoff's 10th Army. The latter was now seriously short of infantry, and had been ordered to fall back to the prepared defences in the mountains. Even after the transfer to his command of the 334th Division from the adjacent LI Mountain Corps, Lemelsen had no reserve and with all his force in the line, each division was on at least a ten mile front. From his post on the "touch-line", as it were, in the quiet and inaccessible Ligurian coastal sector, General von Senger und Etterlin correctly forecast the outcome of this impasse. He later wrote:

"The incessant prodding against [the left wing of] our front across the Futa pass was like jabbing a thick cloth with a sharp spear. The cloth would give way like elastic, but under excessive strain it would be penetrated by the spear."

The 5th Army attack was made by two corps and on a narrow front east of the Il Giogo pass, at the junction of the two German armies, and initially fell on two thinly stretched divisions. Holding the Il Giogo pass was the 4th Parachute Division, which had been made up with very young soldiers with barely three months' training. The pass itself was nothing but a way over a ridge only about 2,900 feet high, but overlooked by some of the highest peaks in the whole mountain range.

Clark used Lieutenant-General Geoffrey Keyes's II Corps of four divisions (U.S. 34th, 85th, 88th, and 91st) as his spearhead against the Il Giogo defences. On the tail of the German withdrawal he launched his offensive on September 13. Once again, Kesselring misread the situation. In spite of the efforts of two U.S. divisions, a considerable artillery concentration, and 2,000 sorties by medium and fighter-bombers, the 4th Parachute Division more than held its ground for the first four days. Meanwhile Kirkman's XIII Corps was attacking on the right flank of the Americans along the parallel routes towards Faenza and Forlì. By September 14 the 8th Indian Division was over the watershed and the following day the British 1st Division took Monte Prefetto and, turning to help its neighbours, attacked the German parachute troops on Monte Pratone. As the pressure mounted on the 4th Parachute Division, the leading American infantry began to make ground, and between September 16 and 18 Monti Altuzzo and Monticelli and the nearby strongholds and peaks were captured.

II Corps now held a seven-mile stretch of the Gothic Line defences either side of the Il Giogo pass. At last Kesselring awoke to the danger of a breakthrough to Imola and from either flank rushed in an extra division to hold Firenzuola and the road down the Santerno valley. This was indeed a critical sector for the Germans, for it was one of the few areas on the northern slopes of the mountains where any quantity of artillery and transport could be deployed once over the watershed.

By September 27 Clark's infantry had fought its way forward to within ten miles of Route 9 at Imola, before being halted by fierce and co-ordinated counter-attacks by no less than four German divisions. In attempting to recapture Monte Battaglia, Kesselring threw in units from many divisions, including some pulled out from the Adriatic front, against the U.S. 88th Division. The battle lasted for over a week before the exhausted German infantry was ordered to dig in. But with mounting casualties and deteriorating weather, Clark also called a halt and turned his attention to Route 65, which would lead him to Bologna.

On the 8th Army front the Canadians and V Corps resumed the offensive on the night of September 12 and drove the Germans off the Coriano and Gemmano ridges, but it took the Canadians three whole days of bitter and costly fighting to clear San Fortunato. On September 20, Rimini fell to the 3rd Greek Mountain Brigade, who fought well in this its first engagement, and the following day Allied patrols were across the Marecchia. Now, as Freyberg's 2nd New Zealand Division passed through on Route 16, the rivers were filling and near spate and the heavy soil of the Romagna was beginning to grip both men and vehicles as they struggled forward. The Romagna is an immense flat expanse of alluvial soil carried down by a dozen or so rivers and innumerable smaller watercourses that discharge into the Adriatic. Reclaimed and cultivated over centuries, it is still essentially a swamp, criss-crossed by ditches and with the watercourses channelled between floodbanks that rise in places 40 feet above the plain. Moreover, the numerous stone-built farmhouses and hamlets, vineyards, and long rows of fruit trees afforded the defence ready-made strongpoints and cover. Inauspicious terrain indeed, with all the odds against a rapid advance. By the 29th only the leading elements of the New Zealand and 56th Divisions had reached the banks of the River Fiumicino and the Germans were still entrenched in the foot-hills south of Route 9. Torrential rain, however, brought all forward movement to a halt, sweeping away bridges and making fords impassable. But in the mountains X Corps still fought on and by October 8 was within ten miles of Cesena.

General Leese, who had been given command of the Allied Land Forces in South-East Asia, had now been succeeded by General Sir Richard McCreery. The new army commander, deciding to avoid the low ground, launched in succession the 10th Indian Division and the Poles through the mountains. And by October 21 Cesena had been taken and bridgeheads seized over the Savio. After resisting for four days the Germans voluntarily withdrew to the line of the Ronco.

Striking now towards Bologna, Clark's II Corps met growing resistance. Initially it had benefited from heavy air support, including strategic bombers, and the efforts of the 8th Army to break out along Route 9. It had been opposed by less than two divisions. By the time it reached the Livergano escarpment, however, it was faced by no less than five divisions (including the 16th S.S. Panzer Division), and elements from three other divisions. This was the work of von Senger, who was temporarily in command of the 10th Army owing to the illness of Lemelsen. Helped by a spell of fine weather, which gave the Allied air forces the chance to intervene, II Corps drove the Germans off the escarpment on October 14. But von Senger was bringing in more and more troops and had the defences of Bologna properly co-ordinated and well covered by artillery. Although the 88th Division captured Monte Grande on October 20, with the assistance of fighter-bombers and the expenditure of 8,600 rounds of gun ammunition, the Americans were beaten back from the little village of Vedriano on three successive nights by fierce counter-attacks.

Since September 10, in just over six weeks II Corps had lost 15,716 men, and over 5,000 of these casualties had been in the 88th Division. On October 25, Clark gave the order to dig in. He himself chose to share some of the discomforts of his men and proposed to sit the winter out in his caravan near the Futa pass, one of the highest parts of the Apennines.

On the other flank, the 8th Army's operations were similarly halted; the weather had broken completely and both

A mine clearing team from the U.S. 85th Division at work on a road near Bologna.

sides were exhausted. Alexander wrote that "the rain, which was at that time spoiling Fifth Army's attack on Bologna, now reached a high pitch of intensity. On 26th October all bridges over the Savio, in our immediate rear, were swept away and our small bridge heads over the Ronco were eliminated and destroyed."

Since August the Germans had lost 8,000 prisoners, and LXXVII Panzer Corps alone had suffered over 14,500 battle casualties. Over a third of Kesselring's 92 infantry battalions were down to 200 men each and only ten mustered over 400. In the 8th Army, battle casualties since July totalled 19,975, and every infantry battalion had to be reorganized. Tank casualties were well over 400 and the 1st Armoured Division had to be disbanded.

In north-west Europe all chances of a decisive victory over Nazi Germany in 1944 ended with the reverse at Arnhem and the delay in opening the port of Antwerp. A winter campaign was now inevitable. In Italy, Kesselring's Operation *"Herbstnebel"* (Autumn Fog), to shorten his line by withdrawing to the Alps, was peremptorily turned down by Hitler. Alexander's long-term proposal for an enveloping attack by landing in Yugoslavia could make no immediate contribution to Eisenhower's present predicament and indeed proved to be a pipe dream that for political reasons alone would never have been authorised. So it was the mixture as before, with Hitler still obsessed with the Balkans, Kesselring over-sensitive of his coastal flank on the Adriatic, but ordered to fight where he stood, and Alexander with dwindling resources committed to a continuation of the battle of attrition against the grain of the country and in the most adverse climatic conditions. Furthermore, the bad weather was seriously limiting the use of Allied air power, at a time when the Allies were facing a world-wide shortage of certain types of artillery ammunition as a result of the extraordinarily sanguine and premature decision to set back production.

The fighting continued until early January, with the Allies aiming to reach Ravenna and break the line of the Santerno before reviewing the thrust to Bologna. In the north "Ponterforce", consisting of Canadian and British armoured units and named after its commander, co-operating with "Popski's Private Army" of desert fame, reached the banks of the Fiumi Uniti and Ravenna itself fell to I Canadian Corps. Soon the Canadians reached the southern tip of Lake Comacchio, but it was only after a fierce and costly battle that they were able to force the Germans back behind the line of the Senio. Astride Route 9, attacking westwards, V Corps captured Faenza, and in the foothills south of the road the Poles fought forward to the upper reaches of the Senio. At this point the 5th Army was stood-to at 48 hours'

American motor transport in typical Italian terrain.

notice on December 22 to resume the attack.

But the weather again broke and by a quirk of fate Mussolini, despised by friend and foe alike, and seeking a "spectacular" success for his newly formed divisions, made a last throw in a losing game. These two divisions, the "Monte Rosa" and the "Italia" Bersaglieri Divisions, led by the German 148th Division, now launched a counter-attack on the extreme left flank of the 5th Army. This advance towards the vital port of Leghorn came on the very day that virtually the whole of the 5th Army was concentrated and poised ready to attack Bologna. Only the 92nd (Negro) Division, posted around Bagni di Lucca, was in position to meet the attack down the wild and romantic valley of the Serchio. The arrival of 8th Indian Division on December 25 was only just in time to stop a complete breakthrough, as the leading German units overran the two main defence lines before being held and driven back by the Indians. Meanwhile this threat to the main supply base had caused two more of the 5th Army's divisions to be switched from the main battle area, and with heavy snow falling in the mountains, Alexander gave the order for both armies to pass to the defensive.

During the winter months there were changes in command on both sides. On the death of Sir John Dill, head of the British mission to Washington, Maitland Wilson was sent in his place and Alexander became Supreme Allied Commander Mediterranean, with promotion to Field-Marshal, backdated to the capture of Rome. Clark now commanded the 15th Army Group, and Truscott was recalled from France to take over the 5th Army. On the German side Lemelsen

still commanded the 14th Army and General Traugott Herr, whose corps had held the early attacks on the Adriatic flank, the 10th Army in what was to prove the critical eastern sector. Kesselring left in the middle of March to become O.B. West and Vietinghoff, hurriedly recalled from the Baltic, took his place with unequivocal orders from Hitler to hold every yard of ground. This further example of the Führer's inept "rigid defence" doctrine proved disastrous, as Vietinghoff entered the ring for the final round of the campaign like a boxer with his bootlaces tied together!

In conditions of heavy snow and frost, the struggle on both sides was now against the forces of nature, and the Allied supply routes could only be kept open by the daily and unremitting efforts of thousands of civilians and all but those units in the most forward positions. While the Germans hoarded their meagre supplies of petrol and both sides built up stocks of ammunition, the Allied units at last began to receive some of the specialised equipment they had for so long been denied; "Kangaroos", the Sherman tanks converted to carry infantry; D.D.s, the amphibious tanks that had swum ashore onto the Normandy beaches; and "Fantails", tracked landing vehicles for shallow waters, of which 400 were promised for use on Lake Comacchio and the nearby flooded areas. At the same time the armoured regiments were re-equipped with up-gunned Sherman and Churchill tanks, Tank-dozers, and "Crocodile" flame-throwing tanks, many of which were fitted with "Platypus" tracks to compete with the soft ground of the

Romagna. Throughout the remaining winter months the "teeth" arms were busy training with new assault equipment, such as bridge-laying tanks and flame throwers. The experience of the British 78th Division, back after refitting in the Middle East, is a typical example of the hard work put into preparing for the spring offensive.

"Training began almost at once—exercises for testing communications, in river crossings, in street fighting and, above all in co-operation with armour. 2 Armoured Brigade . . . was affiliated to the Division for these exercises . . . it was the first time in Italy that 78 Division had lived, trained, and held the line with the armour with which it was later to carry out full-scale operations: this was the genesis of the splendid team work between tanks and infantry soon to be shown in the final battle."

Before handing over, Kesselring kept his troops hard at work building defences on every river-line right back to the Reno and indeed on the line of the Po itself. Although milked of forces for the other fronts, his two armies still contained some of the very best German divisions. These were now well up to strength and fully rested, as for instance the two divisions of I Parachute Corps, commanded by the redoubtable General Richard Heidrich, which between them mustered 30,000 men. The active front, however, much of which was on difficult ground not of his own choosing, was 130 miles long, and his supply lines were constantly being attacked from the air and by partisans. To cover his front he allocated 19 German divisions (including the 26th Panzer, and 29th and 90th *Panzergrenadier*). Five more German infantry divisions, plus four Italian divisions and a Cossack division, were held back to watch the frontiers and, in particular, to guard against a landing in the Gulf of Venice. Here, had he but known, sand-bars precluded large-scale amphibious operations.

The relative strength of the 15th Army Group was now lower than ever before. Three divisions had been rushed to intervene in the civil war in Greece and I Canadian Corps had left for Holland in February. There remained only 17 divisions, including the newly arrived American 10th Mountain Division. But Alexander held an ace—overwhelming strength in the air. With the combined bomber offensive drawing to a close, more and more heavy bomber squadrons were released to support the coming offensive and by April were pounding away at the German supply routes. By D-day every railway line north of the Po had been cut in many places. Nor had the two tactical air forces been idle. On February 6, 364 sorties were flown against the Brenner pass and targets in the Venetian plain, while in March the German supply dumps, so carefully built-up during the winter, were systematically attacked. Above the battlefield, in clearing skies, the Allies' planes roamed at will and

when the offensive opened, a total of 4,000 aircraft was available to intervene directly in the land battle.

Alexander's plan was again for a double-fisted attack, but with a bold and carefully set up change of direction by the 8th Army at the very moment when the 5th Army was to deliver the second blow. Once again the Germans were to be misled into expecting a major landing (south of Venice) and realism was brought to this cover plan by the joint Commando/56th Division operations to clear the "spit" and "wedge", on the near shore, and the islands of Lake Comacchio, which in fact were vital to the real flanking thrust inland. Meanwhile the whole of the 8th Army, except for a skeleton force in the mountains, was secretly concentrated to the north of Route 9. On 9 April, V Corps (8th Indian and 2nd New Zealand Divisions) and the Polish II Corps would open the offensive across the River Senio astride Lugo, with the object of seizing bridgeheads over the Santerno and exploiting beyond. At this point the 5th Army would attack towards Bologna, while the 56th Division would cross Lake Comacchio in "Fantails" and the 78th Division would debouch from the Santerno bridgeheads and strike northwards to Bastia. This change of axis by the 8th Army aimed at breaking the "hinge" of the whole German position at Argenta and cutting their lines of withdrawal eastwards.

Shortly after mid-day on April 9, the Allied air forces went to work with their medium bombers and close support squadrons attacking command posts, gun positions, and strongpoints on the Senio and beyond, while in an hour and a half the heavy bombers, using a line of smoke shells in the sky as a bomb line, saturated the German defences on the immediate front of the two assault corps with 125,000 fragmentation bombs. This deluge of bombs was immediately followed by four hours of concentrated gun and mortar fire, alternating with low-level fighter-bomber attacks. At 1900 hours as the last shells burst on the forward defences, the fighter-bombers swept over in a dummy attack to keep the enemy's heads down until the infantry crossed the river. Within minutes the first flame-throwers were in action and "the whole front seemed to burst into lanes of fire". Overnight there was bitter fighting before the western flood banks were breached and bridges laid for the armour and anti-tank guns to cross. The next day over 1,600 Allied heavy bombers renewed their attack, and on the third day of the offensive the New Zealanders were across the Santerno at Massa Lombarda. The German 98th and 362nd Divisions had lost over 2,000 prisoners and their forward battalions had been virtually destroyed.

Meanwhile the battle for the Argenta Gap had started. The 78th Division, having crossed the Santerno, was advancing rapidly, led by a special striking force (the Irish Brigade and 2nd Armoured Brigade) of all arms, part of which was

entirely mounted on tracked vehicles, and which became known as the "Kangaroo Army". The approaches to Bastia, however, were covered by thousands of mines and the Germans fought to the last round, while in crossing Lake Comacchio, the 58th Division suffered heavy casualties. But slowly the pincer attacks closed on Argenta itself and McCreery's reserve divisions began to move up.

Now was the time for Truscott to launch his two corps, but poor flying conditions delayed the attack until April 14. Over the next four days the Allied air forces flew over 4,000 sorties in support and in the first 30 minutes of the attack on Monte Sole and the nearby Monte Rumici, 75,000 shells fell on the German mountain strongpoints. In three days' fighting the U.S. II Corps was held down and advanced less than two miles. West of Route 64, however, the 10th Mountain Division captured Montepastore and for two days the U.S. 1st Armoured Division and the 90th *Panzergrenadier* Division, Vietinghoff's last reserve, fought it out in the valley of the Samoggia. Suddenly the end was within sight. Around Argenta the 29th *Panzergrenadier* Division and the remnants of a number of other divisions kept up a bitter struggle to prevent a breakthrough by the 6th Armoured Division, but by April 20 V Corps' leading columns were within 15 miles of Ferrara, advancing on a broad front. Along Route 9 the New Zealanders and Poles had fought three German divisions to a standstill and at dawn on April 21 a Polish brigade entered Bologna unopposed. The previous day a company of the U.S. 86th Mountain Infantry was across Route 9, west of the city, and now Truscott's II Corps, with the 6th South African Armoured Division, swept past on Route 64. On April 23 the leading tanks made contact with a squadron of 16th/5th Lancers, 15 miles west of Ferrara.

On April 20, Vietinghoff, in defiance of Hitler's demands, ordered a withdrawal to the Po, but the fate of his armies was already sealed. What was left of his shattered units was trapped against the Po, where every bridge was down or blocked by packed columns of burning vehicles. Von Senger was amongst those who succeeded in crossing. "At dawn on the 23rd we found a ferry at Bergantino; of the thirty-six Po ferries in the zone of Fourteenth Army, only four were still serviceable. Because of the incessant fighter-bomber attacks it was useless to cross in daylight.

When the Allied armoured columns crossed 36 hours later, they left behind them "a scene of extraordinary desolation and fearful carnage. There was no longer any coherent resistance, and along the river lay the ruins of a German army." In the first 14 days of the offensive the German casualties were around 67,000, of whom 35,000 had been taken prisoner. Allied casualties were a little over 16,500. On May 2 the remaining German and Italian troops of Army Group "C", nearly a million men, surrendered.

CHAPTER 73
The Allies invade Germany

On March 8, 1945, Field-Marshal Kesselring was ordered to leave the Italian theatre of operations immediately and go to an audience with the *Führer*. The following afternoon, Hitler told him that as a result of the unfortunate situation at Remagen, he had decided to make him Commander-in-Chief in the West. In his account of the meeting, Kesselring writes:

"Without attaching any blame to Rundstedt, Hitler justified his action with the argument that a younger and more flexible leader, with greater experience of fighting the Western powers, and still possessing the troops' full confidence, could perhaps make himself master of the situation in the West. He was aware of the inherent difficulties of assuming command at such a juncture, but there was no alternative but for me to make this sacrifice in spite of the poor state of my health. He had full confidence in me and expected me to do all that was humanly possible."

Such was the conclusion of the general review of the situation that Hitler had spent several hours discussing with Kesselring, first alone, later in the company of Keitel and Jodl. On the whole, Hitler was optimistic about the future. One might have suspected him of trying to mislead Kesselring as to the true situation were it not for his own unique

A railway station in Berlin after an Allied air raid.

capacity for self-deception. In any event, he appeared satisfied with the course of events on the Eastern Front.

Hitler certainly thought that a collapse in the East would be the end of the war, but he had provided for this eventuality and added, according to Kesselring's notes taken immediately after the audience: "our main military effort is directed to the East. He [Hitler] envisages the decisive battle there, with complete confidence. And he expects the enemy's main attack to be launched at Berlin".

For this reason the 9th Army, which was charged with the defence of the city, had been given priority consideration. Under the command of General T. Busse, it had:

1. adequate infantry strength, together with Panzer and anti-tank forces;
2. standard artillery strength and more than adequate anti-aircraft defences, deployed in considerable depth under the best artillery commanders available;
3. excellent positions, with the best of defences, especially water barriers, on both sides of the main battle line; and
4. in its rear the strongest position of all, Berlin, with its fortified perimeter and whole defensive organisation.

So there were grounds for assurance that the Berlin front would not be broken; similarly with Army Group "Centre", on the borders of Silesia and Czechoslovakia, which had gained notable successes. Its commander, Schörner, assured Hitler that "with reinforcements and sufficient supplies, he would repel all enemy attacks launched at him".

As regards the situation on the Western Front, the heavy losses sustained by the British, Americans, and French over months of heavy fighting were a factor that should be taken into account. Furthermore, in Hitler's opinion, "the Allies could not dismiss the natural obstacles covering the German Army's positions. The Allied bridgehead at Remagen was the danger point and it was urgent it should be mopped up; but there too Hitler was confident."

In these conditions, Kesselring's task was to hold on long enough for the Eastern Front armies to be brought up to strength, so that O.K.W. could then despatch the necessary reinforcements to the armies in the West. Within a short while, the deficiencies of the Luftwaffe, held to blame for the failures of recent months, would be forgotten and Grand-Admiral Dönitz's new submarines would have turned the tables in the Battle of the Atlantic, bringing much needed relief to the defence of the Third Reich.

Thus armed with encouragement, Kesselring received his chief-of-staff's report in the night of March 9-10 at the H.Q. at Ziegenberg just vacated by Rundstedt.

General Westphal had been his chief-of-staff during his time as supreme commander in Italy, and Kesselring had complete confidence in him.

The new commander must have been considerably shocked by the un-embroidered account of the situation that he received. With 55 battle-worn divisions giving him, on average, a coverage of 63 fighting men for each mile of the front, it was his task to hold 85 full strength Allied divisions, which also enjoyed all the benefits of undisputed air superiority.

On March 11, at the H.Q. of LIII Corps, Kesselring met Field-Marshal Model and General von Zangen, commanding the 15th Army, which had been given the job of wiping out the Remagen bridgehead. All were agreed that this objective could not be attained unless there was considerable speeding up in the supply of substantial reinforcements, and above all of ammunition, and this filled Kesselring with apprehension. The morale of Army Group "H" gave him some comfort, however, especially since the enemy attack across the lower Rhine was taking time in getting under way. On the other hand, the position of Army Group "G", without any mobile reserves worthy of the name, seemed fraught with risk.

Hence Kesselring was not so much caught unawares as off guard by Operation "Undertone", the American offensive south of the Moselle, which he learnt had been launched when he returned from this rapid tour of inspection. The cadence given the attack by Patton, Walker, Eddy, and their excellent divisional commanders was a disagreeable revelation to the Germans; Kesselring wrote:

"What clearly emerged was the rapid succession of operations (showing that the Allies had abandoned their Italian campaign strategy) as well as the competency of command and the almost reckless engagement of armoured units in terrain that was quite unsuited for the use of heavy tanks. On the basis of my experience in Italy in similar terrain, I was not expecting the American armoured forces to achieve rapid success, in spite of the fact that the reduced strength of tired German troops gave undoubted advantage to the enemy operation."

In the face of this violent American thrust, O.B. West appealed to O.K.W. for authorisation to withdraw the German 1st and 7th Armies to the right bank of the Rhine; typically, Hitler procrastinated until it was too late to accept this eminently reasonable course. And the only reinforcement destined for the Western Front was a single division, which was not even combat-worthy as it had spent some considerable time in Denmark on garrison duties. To cap this, Kessel-

The last months of the war in Europe as the Allied trap closes on Germany.

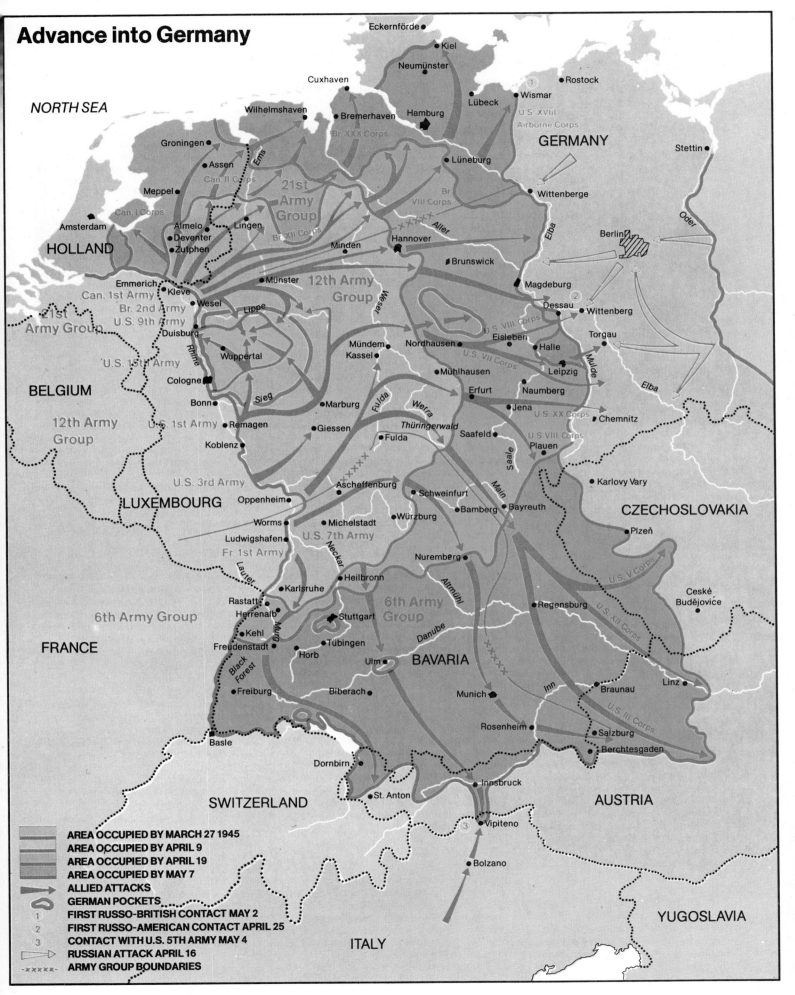

Advance into Germany

NORTH SEA

GERMANY

HOLLAND

BELGIUM

LUXEMBOURG

FRANCE

SWITZERLAND

ITALY

CZECHOSLOVAKIA

AUSTRIA

YUGOSLAVIA

BAVARIA

Eckernförde
Kiel
Neumünster
Rostock
Wismar
Lübeck
Hamburg
U.S. XVIII Airborne Corps
Stettin
Cuxhaven
Bremerhaven
Wilhelmshaven
Groningen
Assen
Lüneburg
Wittenberge
Meppel
Elba
Berlin
Almelo
Deventer
Zutphen
Lingen
Minden
Hannover
Br VIII Corps
Oder
Amsterdam
Emmerich
Kleve
Wesel
Münster
Brunswick
Magdeburg
Dessau
Wittenberg
Can. 1st Army
Br. 2nd Army
U.S. 9th Army
Lippe
Weser
Nordhausen
Eisleben
Torgau
Duisburg
Mündem
Kassel
Halle
U.S. 15th Army
Wuppertal
Mühlhausen
Leipzig
Mulde
Cologne
Sieg
Erfurt
Naumberg
Elba
Bonn
Marburg
Fulda
Werra
Jena
U.S. XX Corps
Remagen
Giessen
Thüringerwald
Saalfeld
Chemnitz
Koblenz
Fulda
Plauen
Karlovy Vary
U.S. 3rd Army
Ascheffenburg
Schweinfurt
Oppenheim
Bamberg
Bayreuth
Worms
Michelstadt
Würzburg
Plzeň
Ludwigshafen
Neckar
Nuremberg
Regensburg
České Budějovice
Lauter
Heilbronn
Karlsruhe
Altmühl
U.S. V Corps
Rastatt
Stuttgart
U.S. XII Corps
Herrenalb
Tübingen
Danube
Kehl
Horb
Ulm
Freudenstadt
Munich
Linz
Braunau
Black Forest
Biberach
Inn
U.S. III Corps
Freiburg
Rosenheim
Salzburg
Berchtesgaden
Basle
Dornbirn
Innsbruck
St. Anton
Vipiteno
Bolzano

21st Army Group
12th Army Group
6th Army Group

AREA OCCUPIED BY MARCH 27 1945
AREA OCCUPIED BY APRIL 9
AREA OCCUPIED BY APRIL 19
AREA OCCUPIED BY MAY 7
ALLIED ATTACKS
GERMAN POCKETS
1 FIRST RUSSO-BRITISH CONTACT MAY 2
2 FIRST RUSSO-AMERICAN CONTACT APRIL 25
3 CONTACT WITH U.S. 5TH ARMY MAY 4
RUSSIAN ATTACK APRIL 16
-xxxx- ARMY GROUP BOUNDARIES

599

A battery of 40-mm Bofors anti-aircraft guns fire across the Rhine in March 1945.

ring was informed of the surprise attack at Oppenheim, while the 1st Parachute Army brought news that north of the Ruhr, smokescreens maintained over several hours showed that Montgomery was putting the final touches to his careful preparations.

It was in these circumstances that Kesselring was contacted by *Obergruppenführer* Karl Wolff of the *Waffen*-S.S., whom he had known in the capacity of "Plenipotentiary for the Wehrmacht in the rear of the Italian Front". For the past few weeks, this officer had been engaged, via Major Waibel of Swiss Army Intelligence, in negotiation with Allen Dulles, head of the American Secret Services in Berne, about terms for the capitulation of the German forces fighting in Italy. On March 23, Kesselring, who knew what Wolff was up to, saw him in his office in Ziegenberg, where Wolff suggested directly that the German armies in the West should be associated with this bid for surrender.

Kesselring refused, in spite of the succession of telephone calls informing him of the rapid progress made by the Americans, who had broken out of the Oppenheim bridgehead. According to Wolff's report to Dulles, Kesselring's opposition was based on both moral and practical arguments:

"He was defending soil and he was bound to continue even if he died himself in the fighting. He said he personally owed everything to the Führer, his rank, his appointment, his decorations. To this he added that he hardly knew the generals commanding the corps and divisions under him. Moreover, he had a couple of well-armed S.S. divisions behind him

which he was certain would take action against him if he undertook anything against the Führer's orders."

Nevertheless Kesselring had no objection to a German capitulation in Italy, and the *Obergruppenführer* was quite free to convey to the former's successor, Colonel-General von Vietinghoff, that O.B. West entirely approved the project.

Whatever one may think of the ethical considerations behind Kesselring's refusal, he understandably felt no scruples in giving his support to Albert Speer, Reich Minister for Armaments and War Production, who was doing all he could to sabotage the execution of the "scorched earth" order promulgated by Hitler on March 19, 1945.

In setting out its motives, the monstrous *Führerbefehl* used the following line of argument:

"The fight for the existence of our people obliges us to make total use, even within the Reich, of whatever means may weaken the fighting power of the enemy and prevent him from pursuing his advance. Any means capable, directly or indirectly, of inflicting lasting damage on the offensive strength of the enemy must be resorted to. It is erroneous to think that by leaving them intact or with only superficial damage, we may more profitably resume exploitation of our communication and transport systems and our industrial or productive installations when we reconquer our invaded territory. When the enemy comes to retreat, he will have no consideration for the population, and will leave only scorched earth behind him.

"For this reason I command:

1. that within the Reich the com-

munications and military transport systems, and the industrial and productive installations, which the enemy may use immediately or within a limited period for the prosecution of the war, be destroyed."

Article 2 of the same decree divided powers for this purpose between the military chiefs and the civil administrators; and Article 3, ordering the immediate transmission of the order to army commanders, declared invalid any directive which sought to nullify it.

So Hitler joined Morgenthau, whereas even Churchill and Roosevelt had rejected the inhuman and demented notion of "pastoralising" the German people. Albert Speer, however, devoted his entire energies to opposing the implementation of this insane order: verbally on March 18; and in writing in two letters, the second of which, dated March 29, is preserved among the appendices that Percy Ernst Schramm adds as a supplement to his masterly edition of the O.K.W. war diary. Speer wrote:

"From what you have told me this evening [March 18] the following emerges clearly and unequivocally, unless I have misunderstood you: if we are to lose the war, the German people are to be lost as well. This destiny is unavoidable. This being so, it is not necessary to secure the basic conditions to enable our people to ensure their own survival even in the most primitive form. Rather, on the contrary, we should ourselves destroy them. For they will have proved themselves the weaker, and the future will belong exclusively to the people of the east, who will have shown themselves the stronger. Furthermore, only the unworthy will survive since the best and bravest will have fallen." Here revealed was the ugly bedrock of Hitler's totally nihilistic nature.

Speer did not limit his opposition merely to pious utterances. He put the enormous weight of influence he had as dictator of industrial production to the task of avoiding implementation of the "scorched earth" order.

In this covert activity he received positive support from Kesselring; as a result, in its retreat from the Rhine to the Elbe and beyond, the German Army restricted itself to forms of destruction which are common in such cases to all the armies in the world. Two circumstances favoured Speer in carrying out his policy: the headlong nature of the Allied advance after March 31 and, in the German camp, the explosives crisis, further exacerbated by the disorganisation of transport.

At the end of 1966, on his release from Spandau prison, to which he had been sent by the Nuremberg trial, Albert Speer was greeted by manifestations of sympathy. This was interpreted by some as the sign they had been seeking since 1945 of a recrudescence of Nazism in the Federal Republic. Such an interpretation seems quite unwarranted. Rather, it would seem that Speer's sympathisers wanted to show public recognition of the man who, in spite of Hitler and at the risk of his life, had chosen to safeguard the means of survival and recovery so that one day another Germany might live.

On March 23, at 1530 hours, under a clear sky and with a favourable weather forecast, Montgomery launched Operation "Plunder/Varsity" and addressed the American, British, and Canadian troops under his command with an order of the day which concluded with these words:
"6. 21 ARMY GROUP WILL NOW CROSS THE RHINE

The enemy possibly thinks he is safe behind this great river obstacle. We all agree that it is a great obstacle; but we will show the enemy that he is far from safe behind it. This great Allied fighting machine, composed of integrated land and air forces, will deal with the problem in no uncertain manner.

7. And having crossed the Rhine, we will crack about in the plains of Northern Germany, chasing the enemy from pillar to post. The swifter and the more energetic our action, the sooner the war will be over, and that is what we all desire; to get on with the job and finish off the German war as soon as possible.

8. Over the Rhine, then, let us go. And good hunting to you all on the other side.

9. May 'The Lord mighty in battle' give us the victory in this our latest undertaking, as He has done in all

our battles since we landed in Normandy on D-Day."

The Rhine, which in 21st Army Group's sector is about 400 yards wide and has a current of about six feet per second, was the "great obstacle" of which Montgomery spoke. But the means given him to cross it were also great.

Under his command he had two armies, eight corps, and 27 divisions (17 infantry, eight armoured, and two airborne; or, in national terms, 13 American, 12 British, and two Canadian). To these should be added the equivalent of three divisions represented by five armoured brigades, a British commando brigade, and the Canadian 9th Infantry Brigade.

The British 2nd Army's attack, supplemented by the Canadian II Corps, was prepared for and supported by 1,300 pieces of artillery, with 600 guns fulfilling the same function for XVI Corps, which was to open the right bank of the Rhine for the American 9th Army. Such concentration of firepower necessitated the transport and dumping of 60,000 tons of ammunition. Massive area bombing by the Allied air forces extended the artillery action to German rail and road communications, thus isolating the battlefield. Between March 20 and 22, R.A.F. Bomber Command and the U.S. 8th and 9th Air Forces made 16,000 sorties over the area in question and dropped 49,500 tons of bombs (including 22,000-lb "Grand Slams"). Special attacks were launched on airfields where the Luftwaffe's new jet aircraft were stationed.

To build bridges across the Rhine, 30,000 tons of engineering equipment and 59,000 engineers had to be transported to the area. But before the construction required by Operation "Plunder" could be used, divisions in the first line of attack had to be conveyed from one bank to the other by other means. This task was carried out by a detachment of the Royal Navy, which left Antwerp to reach its departure point by a series of Belgian, Dutch, and German canals. With Vice-Admiral Sir Harold M. Burrough in overall command, it comprised 45 landing craft (L.C.M.), plus a formation of the 12-ton amphibious tanks known by the British as Buffaloes and as Alligators by the Americans. Preparations on this scale were obviously observable by the enemy, but the final deployment of the Allied forces was concealed by the smokescreen which hid the left bank of the Rhine over a distance of 75 miles between dawn on March 21 and 1700 hours on March 23.

As is apparent, Montgomery had once more showed his immense capacity for organisation. In the course of the battle which followed, he would confirm his reputation as an exceptional tactician, by winning back for himself the advantage of surprise which he had lost as a result of such tremendous concentration of forces. And, it should be noted, there are few men who, like him, combine such attention to detail in preparation with such vigour of execution.

On the right bank of the Rhine, the 1st Parachute Army was deployed with its right slightly upstream of Emmerich and its left in the region of Duisburg. It was thus defending a front of 45 miles with seven divisions, which were battleweary, but nevertheless an adequate concentration for defence, bearing in mind the natural obstacle of the broad river, had the divisions been at full complement. During the relative lull following March 11, they had dug themselves in well and the rapid construction of their defensive positions was entirely satisfactory to Kesselring. General Schlemm had played a considerable rôle here; Major Milton Shulman, of the Canadian 1st Army, had the opportunity of interrogating him later, and writes:

"His record, coupled with an orderly mind and a keen grasp of tactical problems, placed him amongst the more able generals still available in the Wehrmacht."

Schlemm's only mobile reserves were the 116th Panzer and 15th *Panzergrenadier* Divisions, of XLVII Panzer Corps, which he had put in reserve behind his centre. At a higher command level, in Army Group "H", Colonel-General Blaskowitz was similarly short of men, and the meagre reserves found by Kesselring were spent in containing the twin thrust of the American 1st Army bursting out of the Remagen bridgehead, and the 3rd Army exploiting at record speed the bridgeheads it had won at Hanau and Aschaffenburg on the Main.

O.K.W. and O.B. West confidently expected an airborne landing. Accordingly, an entire anti-aircraft corps was put at the disposal of Blaskowitz, who deployed batteries all over the area between Munster and the right bank of the Rhine. But apparently to little effect: as on previous occasions the German soldier had to put up with implacable and practically unchallenged machine gun and cannon fire and bombing from Allied aircraft without seeing any fighters of his own in the sky.

At 1700 hours on March 23, the smoke-screen vanished and the entire artillery of the British 2nd Army and the American 9th Army opened fire on the enemy positions, maintaining their barrage of shells of all calibres until 0945 hours the following morning. This was, however, interspersed with pauses at times varying from sector to sector to allow the divisions launching the attack to feel out the enemy strength.

The main action devolved upon the British 2nd Army, in position north of the Lippe. On its left, XXX Corps had during the night got four battalions of the 51st Division (Major-General Thomas Rennie) across the Rhine; on its right, XII Corps had established its 15th Division (Major-General Colin Muir Barber) on the right bank of the river, opposite Xanten, while the 1st Commando Brigade went into action against the 180th Division in the ruins of Wesel. Further south, the American 9th Army, whose task was to cover the flank of the British attack, engaged its XVI Corps, whose 30th and 79th Divisions crossed the Rhine to either side of Rheinberg. According to Montgomery, German resistance was only sporadic, and certainly the two American divisions mentioned above suffered only 31 killed in the enterprise.

The offensive undertaken by the 21st Army Group was no surprise for Blaskowitz, who had even correctly estimated its main point of impact and line of advance. Accordingly–and with a degree of haste for which Kesselring reproached him–he judged it opportune to throw in his armoured reserves. The dawn saw furious counter-attacks which drew the following observation from Sir Brian Horrocks, then in command of XXX Corps:

"Reports were coming in of Germans surrendering in large numbers to the British and American forces on our flanks but there was no sign of any collapse on our front. In fact the 51st Highland Division reported that the enemy was fighting harder than at any time since Normandy. It says a lot for the morale of those German parachute and panzer troops that with chaos, dis-

An American soldier in a captured tank factory in southern Germany.

organisation and disillusionment all around them they should still be resisting so stubbornly."

In the course of the fighting between XXX Corps and the 15th *Panzergrenadier* Division, which brought into the line the paratroops from the German 6th and 7th Parachute Divisions, Major-General Rennie was killed, evidence enough of the enemy's determination.

However, at 1000 hours the "event", in the Napoleonic sense of the word, took place. In the German camp, remembering the precedent of Arnhem, the Allies' airborne troops were expected to attack at the time that Montgomery's infantry was attempting to cross the Rhine, and to drop to the rear of the battlefield to effect a vertical encirclement of the 1st Parachute Army. But their attack came three hours after it had been anticipated, and the drop took place in the region of Hamminkeln, barely five miles from the right bank of the river. Under the command of Lieutenant-General Matthew B. Ridgway, XVIII Airborne Corps comprised the British 6th Airborne (Major-General E. Bols) and the American 17th Airborne (Major-General William E. Miley) Divisions, their transport being undertaken by 1,572 planes and 1,326 gliders, under close escort from 889 fighters. The 6th Airborne Division took off from 11 airfields in the south-east of England, the

American 17th from 17 that had just been built in the area bounded by Rheims, Orléans, Evreux, and Amiens. The effect of surprise was so great and the German *flak* so well neutralised by Allied artillery pounding from the left bank that losses on landing amounted to no more than 46 transport planes and three per cent of the glider force employed in this operation, known as "Varsity".

The British and Americans fell on the enemy battery positions and reduced a good many of them to silence, then thrust on across the Diersforterwald to meet XII Corps, whose advance was strongly supported by 580 heavy guns of the 2nd Army, responding to calls for fire cover with most admirable speed and precision of fire.

At the end of the day, XVIII Airborne Corps made contact with the British XII Corps. Furthermore, thanks to units flown in by glider, XVIII Airborne Corps had taken intact a number of bridges over the IJssel which, flowing as it does parallel to the Rhine between Wesel and Emmerich, could have constituted an obstacle to the rapid exploitation of the day's successes. Moreover, the 84th Division was taken in rear and as good as annihilated, with the loss of most of the 3,789 prisoners counted by General Ridgway's Intelligence services.

As night fell, in the zone between Dinslaken and Rees, where resistance from German parachute troops had lost none of its spirit, the 21st Army Group had taken a bridgehead 30 miles wide on the right bank of the Rhine, running, in the British XII Corps' (Lieutenant-General Sir Neil Methuen Ritchie) sector to a depth of nearly eight miles; the Allied bridge builders were free to get to work without any threat of retaliation on the part of enemy artillery. Montgomery could feel all the more satisfaction with the way things had gone on March 24 as he had committed only four of his eight corps.

From an observation post situated a mile or so south of Xanten, which commanded a good view over the vast Westphalian plain, Churchill, together with Brooke and Eisenhower, saw the British and American XVIII Airborne Corps' transport planes cross overhead and return, but missed the drop itself because of the mist. As the success of the operation became apparent, General Eisenhower reports that Field-Marshal Brooke turned to him and said:

"Thank God, Ike, you stuck by your plan. You were completely right, and I am sorry if my fear of dispersed effort added to your burdens. The German is now licked. It is merely a question of when he chooses to quit. Thank God, you stuck by your guns."

Coming across this passage in *Crusade in Europe*, Lord Alanbrooke refers to an entry in his diary made at the close of that same March 24, claiming that Eisenhower's remarks resulted from a mis-

understanding, and that he had not in fact "seen the light" that day near Xanten. He wrote in 1949:

"To the best of my memory I congratulated him heartily on his success and said that, as matters had turned out, his policy was now the correct one; that, with the German in his defeated condition, no dangers now existed in a dispersal of effort."

Thus Brooke corrects the remark attributed to him (on this occasion) by Eisenhower. Obviously there is a difference between the two versions. Nevertheless, it does not necessarily follow that Eisenhower was mistaken in defending his strategic plans, unless it can be shown that the German armies would have fallen into the state of ruin and confusion noted by Brooke that March 25 evening had not Operations "Lumberjack" and "Undertone" taken place.

Kesselring settles that question with greater authority than we can possibly lay claim to when he writes:

"Just as Remagen became the tomb of Army Group 'B', the Oppenheim bridgehead seemed destined to become that of Army Group 'G'. There too, the initial pocket became a deep chasm, and devoured all the strength of the other parts of the front, that somehow or other had been rendered mobile, as well as all the units brought up from the rear to fill the gaps."

On March 25 and 28, two further events of comparable scale and importance took place on the 12th Army Group's front: firstly, the collapse of the German 15th Army, whose task it was to contain the enemy within the Remagen bridgehead; and secondly, adding its effect to the clean breakthrough by the American 1st Army, the crossing of the Main at the Aschaffenburg and Hanau bridges by the American 3rd Army. This manoeuvre followed from a carefully prepared plan

of General Bradley's after the launching of Operation "Lumberjack", which was given its final touches following the surprise assault on Remagen. He describes it as follows in *A Soldier's Story:*

"Now that Hodges had established the Remagen bridgehead to the south of Bonn, he was to trace that original pattern. First he would speed his tanks down the autobahn where it ran through Limburg on the road to Frankfurt. At Limburg he was to turn east up the Lahn Valley to Giessen. There he would join Patton's pincer coming up from the Main.

"The First and Third Armies would then advance abreast of one another in a parallel column with Hodges on the inside, Patton on his flank, up the broad Wetteran corridor toward a union with Simpson. Then while Hodges and Simpson locked themselves around the Ruhr preparatory to cleaning it out, Patton would face his Army to the east and be prepared to advance toward the oncoming Russians."

So it was, but according to Kesselring, the execution of Bradley's plan was considerably eased by Model's preconceived ideas of the enemy's intentions. The commander of Army Group "B" was obsessed with his right flank, fearing an attack down the eastern bank of the Rhine aimed at an assault on the Ruhr industrial complex from the south; and he was deaf to all telephone calls from his superior, remonstrating with him for leaving his centre thinly protected.

On March 25, the American 1st Army proved Kesselring's case by smashing LXXIV Corps in the region of Breitscheid. Hodges immediately unleashed his 3rd, 7th, and 9th Armoured Divisions, which reached Giessen and Marburg on the 28th, 53 and 66 miles respectively from the Rhine at Neuwied. On the same day, in the 3rd Army, VIII Corps completed the

A convoy of American trucks with a jeep escort in southern Germany.

mopping up of Frankfurt and made contact with Hodges's right in the region of Wiesbaden, thus trapping the enemy elements left on the right bank of the Rhine between the Lahn and the Main. But most strikingly, Patton's 4th, 6th, and 11th Armoured Divisions, in formation ahead of XII and XX Corps, had moved from the Main valley into that of the Fulda, making in the direction of Kassel. Thus Hodges, whose task was to reach the eastern outlets of the Ruhr basin, found himself provided with cover, just as Bradley intended, against a counter-attack striking from the Harz mountains.

On the day after the surprise breakthrough at Oppenheim, Kesselring, according to his own account, had wondered "whether it was not best to accept the army groups' proposals and withdraw the entire front from the Rhine. I finally refrained from doing so, because the only result would have been to retreat in disorder. Our troops were heavily laden, barely mobile, in large part battle-weary, and encumbered by units in the rear which were still in a state of disorder. The enemy had all-round superiority, especially in mobility and in the air. If nothing occurred to check or slow his advance, our retreating columns would be overtaken and smashed. This type of combat would have become an end in itself—no longer a means employed to an end—the end being to gain time. Every day on the Rhine, on the contrary, was a day gained, signifying a strengthening of the front, even if it were only to enable points in the rear to be mopped up or stray troops to be rounded up."

Quite clearly, at the point reached in the German camp on March 28, Kesselring's conclusions were still more justified. This was all the more true as the sappers of the 21st Army Group had by March 26 opened seven 40-ton bridges to traffic, and the American 9th Army and British 2nd Army came down both banks of the Lippe to overwhelm the 1st Parachute Army. Two days later, on the left bank of this river, Lieutenant-General Simpson had his 8th Armoured Division (Major-General J. M. Devine) in the region of Haltern, more than 25 miles east of the Rhine. At the same time, Sir Miles Dempsey pushed the Guards Armoured Division (Major-General Allan Adair) down the Münster road, while his XXX and Canadian II Corps, on a line linking Borken – Bocholt – Isselburg – Emmerich,

Ulm Cathedral rises above the rubble of the city.

reached the Dutch frontier. The 1st Parachute Army was helplessly cut off, and its LXIII Corps and XLVII Panzer Corps (five divisions) were thrown back onto Army Group "B". And Montgomery poured his armoured units resolutely into the breach.

On April 2, 1945, as the day closed, the inevitable happened. The American 3rd Armoured Division, driving ahead of VII Corps (1st Army), met up at Lippstadt with the 8th Armoured Division coming from Haltern. In the course of this fighting, Major-General Rose, commanding the 3rd Armoured Division in its finest foray, was killed. Now Army Group "B" was encircled, with the exception of LXVII Corps, which had been attached to Army Group "B" following the breakthrough at Breitscheid.

Including the ruins of the 1st Parachute Army mentioned above, there were the 5th *Panzerarmee* and the 15th Army, of seven corps or 19 divisions (three of them Panzer, and the 3rd *Panzergrenadier* Division) caught in a trap that Hitler was quick to qualify as "the fortified region of the Ruhr". To reduce it, General Bradley formed a new 15th Army, under the command of Lieutenant-General Leonard T. Gerow, with a strength of five corps, including the newly-formed XXII and XXIII Corps, in all 18 divisions taken from the 1st and 9th Armies.

The encirclement of the Ruhr meant not only the rapid destruction of Army Group "B", but more importantly, the end of all organised resistance on the part of the Wehrmacht between Würzburg on the Main and Minden on the Weser. Between the inside of the wings of Army Groups "G" and "H", a breach of more than 180 miles was opened. It was too late for the unfortunate Kesselring to cherish the notion of repositioning his armies on a line along the courses of the Weser, Werra, Main, Altmuhl, and Lech, as favoured by 18th Century strategists.

To stop this breach, O.K.W. still had, in the Harz mountains, the 11th Army, comprising five divisions under the command of General Wenck, and a 12th Army being formed on the right bank of the Elbe. But clearly the way to Berlin lay open to the 12th Army Group and on April 4 S.H.A.E.F. transferred to it the American 9th Army, to the great satisfaction of General Simpson, its commander, and even more so of General Bradley, who saw the forces under his command now rise to four armies (11 corps of 48 divisions, 14 of them armoured, with some 3,600 tanks). But Eisenhower had no intention of giving Bradley the German capital as an objective. The question had already been considered by him among other options open to him after the encirclement of the Ruhr, and he had decided against going for Berlin for strategic and logistic reasons – in particular the lengthening of his lines of communication that this would entail, and the obstacle of the Elbe, something short of 200 miles from the Rhine and 125

from Berlin.

As a result of this decision, Eisenhower set himself the following objectives:
1. to make contact without delay with the Soviet forces moving west, and thus make it impossible for the enemy to try to regroup;
2. to hurl the 21st Army Group to the north-east, its right wing keeping its objective steadily fixed on Lübeck, to cut off the Wehrmacht forces occupying Norway and Denmark; and
3. as for the 12th and 6th Army Groups, Eisenhower writes:

"Equally important was the desirability of penetrating and destroying the so-called 'National Redoubt'. For many weeks we had been receiving reports that the Nazi intention, in extremity, was to withdraw the cream of the S.S., Gestapo, and other organisations fanatically devoted to Hitler, into the mountains of southern Bavaria, western Austria, and northern Italy. There they expected to block the tortuous mountain passes and to hold out indefinitely against the Allies. Such a stronghold could always be reduced by eventual starvation if in no other way. But if the German was permitted to establish the redoubt he might possibly force us to engage in a long-drawn-out guerrilla type of warfare, or a costly siege. Thus he could keep alive his desperate hope that through disagreement among the Allies he might yet be able to secure terms more favourable than those of unconditional surrender. The evidence was clear that the Nazi intended to make the attempt and I decided to give him no opportunity to carry it out."

So, with the Elbe reached in the vicinity of Magdeburg, it was understood that Bradley would make his main line of advance along a line Erfurt–Leipzig–Dresden, with a secondary thrust on Regensburg and Linz. Contact would be made with the Russians in Saxony, and at the same time a march would be stolen on Army Group "G" in its task of occupying the redoubt. However logical this line of argument was from a strategic point of view, it rested on a hypothesis which was shown to be false after Germany's capitulation: the "national redoubt" concept was no more than a figment of the imagination of those who fed it to S.H.A.E.F.'s Intelligence services.

In any event, on March 24, in accordance with a decision taken at the Yalta Conference, Eisenhower communicated his plan, summarised above, to Stalin who approved it most warmly. In the terms of a telegram cited in Churchill's memoirs but absent from *Crusade in Europe*, Stalin assured Eisenhower that his plan "entirely coincides with the plan of the Soviet High Command . . . Berlin has lost its former strategic importance. The Soviet High Command therefore plans to allot secondary forces in the direction of Berlin." Knowing as we do that at the very moment these lines were dictated,

Stalin was concentrating five tank armies and 25,000 guns (expending 25,600 tons of shell) on an allegedly secondary objective, one sees what was in the wind.

The plan detailed by S.H.A.E.F. found its strongest opponent in Churchill. Embodying as he did the ancient traditions which had inspired British diplomacy since the reign of Henry VIII, he held as a maxim that "as a war waged by a coalition draws to its end political aspects have a mounting importance."

So it seemed obvious to him that since the military collapse of the Third Reich was a matter of only a few weeks, the time had come for the two great Anglo-Saxon powers quietly to dismiss purely strategic considerations and consider political issues while there was still time. And in this field he was forced to admit that Stalin and Molotov viewed the Yalta agreement about Poland as being worth no more than the paper it was written on, and were set in their determination to allow no régime in Warsaw that was not subservient to Moscow.

Likewise, on March 2, Vishinsky, Soviet Deputy Minister of Foreign Affairs, in the course of a scene of abominable violence, had imposed a government chosen by the Kremlin on King Michael of Rumania. The ten per cent minority voice that Churchill had reserved in that country had fallen to all but nothing, and things were worse still in Bulgaria.

Hence Churchill thought that future operations conducted by S.H.A.E.F. should take account of political as well as military considerations, and these he enumerated and summarised as follows:

"*First,* that Soviet Russia had become a mortal danger to the free world.
Secondly, that a new front must be immediately created against her onward sweep.
Thirdly, that this front in Europe should be as far east as possible.
Fourthly, that Berlin was the prime and true objective of the Anglo-American armies.
Fifthly, that the liberation of Czechoslovakia and the entry into Prague of American troops was of high consequence.
Sixthly, that Vienna, and indeed Austria, must be regulated by the Western Powers, at least upon an equality with the Russian Soviets.
Seventhly, that Marshal Tito's aggressive pretensions against Italy must be curbed.
Finally, and above all, that a settlement must be reached on all major issues between the West and the East *before the armies of democracy melted,* or the Western Allies yielded any part of the German territories they had conquered, or, as it could soon be written, liberated from totalitarian tyranny."

Eisenhower's plan therefore displeased him all the more because in communicating his intentions to Stalin, the Supreme Allied Commander appeared to have exceeded the commonly accepted limits of competence of a military chief; a somewhat dubious argument since Stalin had

concentrated in himself the functions of head of government and generalissimo of the Soviet armed forces, in which capacity the communication had been addressed to him. With the approval of the British Chief-of-Staffs Committee and of Montgomery, the Prime Minister endeavoured to persuade Eisenhower to go back on his decision, and on April 1 an appeal was made to President Roosevelt, Field-Marshal Brooke making a similar appeal to General Marshall.

Eisenhower then cabled Marshall:

"I am the first to admit that a war is waged in pursuance of political aims, and if the Combined Chiefs-of-Staff should decide that the Allied effort to take Berlin outweighs purely military considerations in this theatre, I should cheerfully readjust my plans and my thinking so as to carry out such an operation."

In fact, however, the future zonal boundaries had already been formally agreed between Russia, Britain and America, and there was little political point in occupying territory which would have to be evacuated.

In his appeal to the American President, Churchill based his case for the occupation of Berlin on the following hypothesis:

"The Russian armies will no doubt overrun all Austria and enter Vienna. If they also take Berlin will not their impression that they have been the overwhelming contributor to our common victory be unduly imprinted in their minds, and may this not lead them into a mood which will raise grave and formidable difficulties in the future?"

On the next day Eisenhower received a telegram from the American Joint Chiefs-of-Staff, telling him that despite the objections of the British chiefs, they supported him entirely, and that, in particular, the communication of his future plans to Stalin seemed to them "to be a necessity dictated by operations". Marshall concluded with the following point to his allies:

"To deliberately turn away from the exploitation of the enemy's weakness does not appear sound. The single objective should be quick and complete victory. While recognising there are factors not of direct concern to S.C.A.E.F., the U.S. chiefs consider his strategic concept is sound and should receive full support. He should continue to communicate freely with the Commander-in-Chief of the Soviet Army."

One of General Bradley's tasks was to reduce the "fortified area of the Ruhr" where, on Hitler's orders, Field-Marshal Model had shut himself in. Given the job of carrying out the operation, the American 15th Army attacked south across the Ruhr and west across the Sieg.

By April 12, Lieutenant-General Gerow had occupied the entire coal basin in which, despite the *Führerbefehl* of March 19, the Germans had done nothing to add to the destruction wrought by British and American bombing. Two days later,

the pocket had been cut in two from north to south. In these conditions, Colonel-General Harpe, commanding the 5th *Panzerarmee*, recognising the fact that his chief had disappeared, ordered Army Group "B" to cease fighting. Capitulation delivered 325,000 prisoners (including 29 generals) into Allied hands. A vain search was instituted for Field-Marshal Walther Model, and it was learnt only four months later that he had committed suicide on April 21, lest he be handed over to the Russians after his surrender, and had been buried in a forest near Wuppertal.

Without waiting for the outcome here, the American 9th, 1st, and 3rd Armies exploited their advance to the full. Resistance grew weaker every day, and the average daily haul of prisoners rose from 10,600 between February 22 and March 31 to 29,000 for the week April 2 to 9, and reached 50,000 in the middle of the month. Evidently, the *Landser* (German "Tommy") was at the end of his tether, in spite of the growing wave of drumhead courts martial and summary executions. In the heart of the Reich, the multiplication of divisions went on almost to the final day, but whether they belonged to the Wehrmacht or to the *Waffen*-S.S., these new divisions, *Volksgrenadier* for the most part, revealed the paucity of their training as soon as they came under fire.

The *Volkssturm*, which was intended to fill the gaps in defence, was a pitiful ragbag of middle-aged men and adolescents, armed and equipped with any weapon that came to hand. Witness the battalion leader, taken prisoner by the Canadian Army, who confided to Major Shulman:

"'I had 400 men in my battalion,' he said, 'and we were ordered to go into the line in our civilian clothes. I told the local Party Leader that I could not accept the responsibility of leading men into battle without uniforms. Just before commitment the unit was given 180 Danish rifles, but there was no ammunition. We also had four machine-guns and 100 anti-tank bazookas (Panzerfaust). None of the men had received any training in firing a machine-gun, and they were all afraid of handling the anti-tank weapon. Although my men were quite ready to help their country, they refused to go into battle without uniforms and without training. What can a Volkssturm man do with a rifle without ammunition! The men went home. That was the only thing they could do.'"

In these conditions, allowing for sporadic but short-lived retaliation here and there from a few units that still retained some semblance of order and strength, the advance of the 12th Army Group across Germany gathered speed and took on more and more the character of a route march, facilitated by the *Autobahn* system, which in by-passing the towns removed inevitable bottlenecks. As a result, American losses dropped to insignificant figures. In the 3rd Army, according to Patton's record, for three corps of 12, then 14, divisions, between March 22 and May 8, 1945, they amounted to 2,160 killed, 8,143 wounded, and 644 missing, under 11,000 in all, compared with nearly 15,000 evacuated because of sickness and accidental injury.

On the left of the 12th Army Group, the American 9th Army, straddling the *Autobahn* from Cologne to Frankfurt-am-Oder to the south of Berlin, thrust towards Hannover, which it took on April 10, and three days later reached Wol-

The heavy cruiser Admiral Hipper, *captured by the British at Kiel.*

mirstedt on the left bank of the Elbe, 85 miles further east. With the capture of Barby, slightly upstream of Magdeburg, it established a first bridgehead on the right bank of the river, thus putting its 83rd Division (Major-General R. C. Macon) some 75 miles from the New Chancellery. But then it turned instead towards Dessau and made contact there with the 6th Armoured Division (Major-General G. W. Read), which was moving ahead of the 1st Army.

The 1st Army had crossed the Weser at Münden and driven across Thuringia on a line linking Göttingen, Nordhausen,

and Eisleben, covering nearly 80 miles between April 8 and 12. As has been mentioned above, it was its left flank that made contact with the 9th Army's right. This pincer movement cut off the retreat of the German 11th Army, which had stayed in the Harz mountains as ordered. To clear a way through for withdrawal, O.K.W. sent the *"Clausewitz"* Panzer Division to the rescue. It attacked at the junction between the 21st and 12th Army Groups and inflicted some damage on the 9th Army. But having got 35 to 40 miles from its point of departure, in the region of Braunschweig, it too was

enveloped and annihilated. The same fate struck the 11th Army, falling almost to a man into Allied hands.

In the centre of the 1st Army, VIII Corps, after reaching the Elbe, managed to establish a bridgehead at Wittenberg, while to its right, VII Corps took Halle and Leipzig on April 14. The capture of Leipzig was a combined effort with the 9th Armoured Division, from the 3rd Army. In accordance with his instructions, General Hodges waited for some days on the Mulde, and it was only on April 26 at Torgau that he met up with Colonel-General Zhadov, commanding

the Soviet 5th Guards Army. In the course of this rapid advance the 1st Army came across 300 tons of *Wilhelmstrasse* archives deposited in various places in the Harz. At Nordhausen, it occupied the vast underground factories where most of the V-1 and V-2 missiles were manufactured.

On March 30 the impetuous Patton was on the Werra and the Fulda. On April 12, the 3rd Army, changing its direction from north-east to east, crossed the Saale at Naumburg, Jena, and Saalfeld, having broken the last serious resistance offered by the enemy at Mühlhausen in Thuringia. And on April 7 the 3rd Army took the 400,000th prisoner since its campaign opened. On the 21st following, XX Corps reached Saxony and the vicinity of Chemnitz, VIII Corps reached a point beyond Plauen, while XII Corps, changing course from east to south-east, had got well beyond Bayreuth in Bavaria. This was the last exploit by Manton S. Eddy who suffered a heart attack and had to hand over his corps to Major-General Stafford LeRoy Irwin. If the 1st Army had captured the *Wilhelmstrasse* archives, the 3rd discovered the last reserves of the *Reichsbank,* composed of gold bars worth 500,000,000 francs, small quantities of French, Belgian, and Norwegian currency and 3,000,000,000 marks in notes.

An ultimate regrouping by Bradley switched VIII Corps from Patton's command to Hodges's, and the progressive collapse of Army Group "B" permitted III and V Corps to be switched to the 3rd Army. Thus strengthened, it was given the assignment of supporting the activities of the 7th Army in Bavaria and upper Austria; specifically, to prevent the enemy establishing himself in the "national redoubt" zone, which General Strong, head of S.H.A.E.F. Intelligence, in a memorandum dated March 11, depicted as follows:

"Here, defended both by nature and by the most efficient secret weapons yet invented, the powers that have hitherto guided Germany will survive to reorganise her resurrection; here armaments will be manufactured in bombproof factories, food and equipment will be stored in vast underground caverns and a specially selected corps of young men will be trained in guerrilla warfare, so that a whole underground army can be fitted and directed to liberate Germany from the occupying forces."

Patton advanced with all speed, and on the day of the surrender he had pushed his XII Corps to a point ten miles below Linz on the Austrian Danube, and his III Corps, whose command had been taken over by Major-General James A. Van Fleet, as far as Rosenheim at the foot of the Bavarian Alps. On May 2, his 13th Armoured Division (Major-General Millikin) crossed the Inn at Braunau, birthplace of Adolf Hitler, who had just committed suicide in his bunker in the Berlin Chancellery.

Patton would have liked to complete his triumph by maintaining the drive of V (Major-General Clarence R. Huebner) and XII Corps as far as Prague. But on May 6, Eisenhower sent him categorical instructions via Bradley not to go beyond the Ceské Budejovice – Plzen – Karlovy Vary line in Czechoslovakia which he had reached. By this action, the Supreme Allied Commander, who had consulted Marshal Antonov, Stalin's Chief-of-Staff, on the matter, yielded to the objections such an operation raised in the Soviet camp. In any event, the American 3rd Army met the spearhead of the 3rd Ukrainian Front, which had come up the Danube from Vienna, at Linz.

Montgomery's main task now was to push through to Lübeck and cut off the German forces occupying Norway and Denmark. He put the more energy and dispatch into the task knowing that its accomplishment would bring supplementary benefits:

"With the Rhine behind us we drove hard for the Baltic. My object was to get there in time to be able to offer a firm front to the Russian endeavours to get up into Denmark, and thus control the entrance to the Baltic."

For this purpose, he disposed of the British 2nd Army and the Canadian 1st Army, comprising five corps of 16 divisions (six of them armoured). Before him in Holland he found the German 25th Army, of which General von Blumentritt had just assumed command, and the debris of the 1st Parachute Army. This debilitated force had been put under the overall command of Field-Marshal Busch, who had been placed at the head of a Northern Defence Zone, to include the Netherlands, north-west Germany, Denmark, and Norway. Weakness in numbers and *matériel* was, however, to some extent offset by the fact that tracts of bog and the otherwise marshy nature of the ground kept the tanks to the main roads.

Having captured Münster, the key to Westphalia, General Dempsey, commanding the British 2nd Army, pushed forward his XXX Corps in the direction of Bremen, XII Corps towards Hamburg, and VIII Corps towards Lübeck.

On the right, VIII Corps (Lieutenant-General Sir Evelyn H. Barker) was momentarily delayed by the *"Clausewitz"* Panzer Division's counter-attack which, as has been mentioned above, was aimed at the point of contact of the 21st and 12th Army Groups. Nonetheless, VIII Corps reached the Elbe opposite Lauenburg on April 19. Here, Montgomery, anxious to move with all possible speed, requested support from Eisenhower and was given the U.S. XVIII Airborne Corps (8th Division, 5th and 7th Armoured Divisions, and the U.S. 82nd Airborne and British 6th Airborne Divisions). On April 29-30, British and Americans under cover provided by the first R.A.F. jet fighters, Gloster Meteors, forced the Elbe. On May 2, 11th Armoured

Division (Major-General Roberts), which was the spearhead of the British VIII Corps, occupied Lübeck and the 6th Airborne Division entered Wismar, 28 miles further east, six hours ahead of Marshal Rokossovsky's leading patrols.

XII Corps (Lieutenant-General Ritchie) had to sustain one last challenge on April 6 when crossing the Aller, a tributary on the right bank of the Weser. Afterwards, it took advantage of the bridgehead won on the Elbe by VIII Corps and closed in on Hamburg. On May 2, Lieutenant-General Wolz surrendered the ruins of the great Hanseatic port. Two days later, the 7th Armoured Division (Major-General Lyne) captured intact a bridge over the Kiel Canal at Eckernförde. Ritchie, who was within 35 miles of the town of Flensburg, where Grand-Admiral Dönitz had recently taken over the responsibilities of head of state, had brilliantly avenged the defeat inflicted on him at Tobruk.

In their drive on Bremen, Sir Brian Horrocks and his XXX Corps were held up by a great deal of destruction, and met with altogether fiercer resistance. Before Lingen, what was left of the 7th Parachute Division carried through a hand-to-hand counter-attack with frenetic *"Heil Hitler"* battle cries.

The 2nd *Kriegsmarine* Division showed the same aggressive spirit in defence, and it needed a pincer movement staged by three divisions to bring about the fall of Bremen on April 26. A few hours before the cease-fire, the Guards Armoured Division occupied Cuxhaven at the mouth of the Elbe.

On April 1, General Crerar, commanding the Canadian 1st Army, recovered his II Corps, reinforced by the British 49th Division, thus bringing his divisions up to six. His mission was twofold: to drive between the Weser and the Zuiderzee with the British XXX Corps in the general direction of Wilhelmshaven and Emden; and to liberate the Dutch provinces still occupied by the enemy. The Canadian II Corps (Lieutenant-General Simonds), which had taken part in the crossing of the Rhine, fulfilled the first of these missions. On April 6, it liberated Zutphen and Almelo, and four days later Groningen and Leeuwarden. In this fine action, it was greatly helped by Dutch resistance while the French 2nd and 3rd Parachute Regiments dropped in the area of Assem and Meppel to open a way for it over the Orange Canal. On German territory, however, General Straube's II Parachute Corps put up a desperate fight, and Crerar had to call on Montgomery for help from the Polish 1st Armoured Division, the Canadian 5th Armoured Division, and the British 3rd Division. With this shot of new blood, the Canadian II Corps accelerated its advance and on May 5, 1945, General Maczek's Polish 1st Armoured Division was within nine miles of Wilhelmshaven, and the Canadian 5th Armoured Division near Emden.

The Canadian I Corps (Lieutenant-General C. Foulkes) took Arnhem by an outflanking movement and three days later reached the Zuiderzee at Harderwijk. The Germans responded to this attack by opening the sea-dykes, and Crerar, who was concerned to spare the Dutch countryside the ravages of flooding, agreed to a cease-fire with General von Blumentritt, stipulating in exchange that British and American aircraft be given free passage to provide the Dutch population with food and medical supplies. This dual operation cost the Canadian 1st Army 367 officers and 5,147 N.C.O.s and other ranks killed, wounded, and missing.

While Field-Marshal Busch had been entrusted with the command of a "Northern Defence Zone", Kesselring was called upon to lead a "Southern Defence Zone" which included the German forces fighting between the Main and the Swiss frontier. So during the final phase of the campaign he found himself facing General Devers, whose 6th Army Group numbered 20 divisions on March 30, 1945, and 22 (13 American and nine French) the following May 8.

The task of Lieutenant-General Patch and the American 7th Army was to cross the Rhine upstream of the 3rd Army, then having gained enough ground to the east, turn down towards Munich and make an assault on the "national redoubt", where, according to Eisenhower's Intelligence, Hitler would seek ultimate refuge. But there was no such mission in store for the French 1st Army which, in the initial plans, was ordered to send a corps over the Rhine, following the Americans, to operate in Württemberg, and later a division which would start off from Neuf-Brisach and occupy Baden-Baden.

Neither General de Gaulle nor General de Lattre accepted this view of their intended mission. On March 4, de Gaulle remarked to de Lattre on "reasons of national importance that required his army to advance beyond the Rhine"; and de Lattre expounded the plan he had conceived to this end, which involved moving round the Black Forest via Stuttgart.

While de Gaulle worked on Eisenhower, de Lattre convinced General Devers of his point of view. The operation as conceived by de Lattre required possession of a section of the left bank of the Rhine below Lauterbourg; this was provided by the dexterity with which General de Monsabert managed to extend his II Corps from Lauterbourg to Speyer in the course of Operation "Undertone".

On March 26, XV Corps of the American 7th Army managed without much trouble to cross the Rhine at Gernsheim below Worms. Patch exploited this success by taking Michelstadt then, turning south, he took Mannheim and Heidelberg on March 30. On April 5, having moved up

the Neckar as far as Heilbronn, he captured Würzburg in the Main valley. With his left as spearhead, he hurled his forces in the direction Schweinfurt–Bamberg–Nuremberg and on April 19, after some violent fighting, ended all resistance in Munich. With its right wing in contact with the French 1st Army in the Stuttgart area, and the left in touch with the American 3rd, the 7th Army moved in a south-easterly direction. On April 25, it crossed the Danube on an 80 mile front, capturing on the way what was left of XIII Corps with its commanding officer, Lieutenant-General Count d'Oriola.

From that moment German resistance in Bavaria collapsed. On May 2, the American XV Corps occupied Munich. Two days later, the French 2nd Armoured Division, once more free for assignment with the Royan pocket liquidated, scaled the slopes of the Obersalzberg and occupied the Berghof, from which *Reichsmarschall* Hermann Göring had just fled. On the same day, the American 3rd Division, which had sped through Innsbruck, crossed the Brenner Pass and met up with the 88th Division of the American 5th Army at Vipiteno. On May 5, General Schulz, last commander of Army Group "G", avoiding capture by the French, surrendered at General Jacob L. Devers's H.Q.

On March 29, General de Gaulle telegraphed de Lattre: "It is essential that you cross the Rhine even if the Americans are against you doing so and even if you cross in boats. It is a matter of the highest national interest. Karlsruhe and Stuttgart are expecting you even if they don't want you."

When he received this message, de Lattre was on his way back from General Devers's H.Q. with the task of sending one corps, of at least three divisions (one of them armoured), across the Rhine to take Karlsruhe, Pforzheim, and Stuttgart. De Lattre had done all in his power to wring this order out of the army group commander. Pierre Lyautey remarks, on seeing him in the H.Q. of the Algerian 3rd Division on March 17, that he was in the process of conceiving "a great German campaign", which would be "full of Napoleonic dash and fury".

In any event, the 1st Army had ceded most of its bridging equipment to the 7th Army to compensate it for similar equipment made over to the 21st Army Group; in addition, in the afternoon of March 30, the French II Corps had barely completed the relief of the American VI Corps at Germersheim and Speyer. Nevertheless, Monsabert, who was down to about 50 motorised and unmotorised boats, was ordered to take two divisions across that very night.

The venture succeeded in conditions of apparently impossible improvisation, and in spite of resistance from the 47th *Volksgrenadier* Division, on March 31. By nightfall, the 3rd Algerian Division (General Guillaume), opposite Speyer, and the 2nd Moroccan Division (General Carpentier), opposite Germersheim, already had five battalions in Baden-Baden. The next day, the two bridge-heads were connected and the French advanced as far as the Karlsruhe–Frankfurt *Autobahn,* over 12 miles from the right bank. As for the 5th Armoured Division (General de Vernejoul), it crossed the Rhine either by ferrying or with the co-operation of General Brooks, commanding the U.S. VI Corps, "the perfect companion in arms" in de Lattre's words, over the American bridge at Mannheim. Finally, on April 2, the 9th Colonial Division, now under the command of General Valluy, crossed the river in its turn at Leimersheim (six miles south of Germersheim). Two days later, the 1st Army had taken its first objective, Karlsruhe.

As the German 19th Army was resisting fiercely in the Neckar valley and in the hills above Rastatt, making a stand in a strongly fortified position which covered the Baden-Baden plain, de Lattre shifted the weight of his thrust to the centre. This gave him Pforzheim on April 8, and he then sent his 2nd Moroccan Division, 9th Colonial Division, and 5th Armoured Division deep into the relative wilderness of the Black Forest. On April 10, the fall of Herrenalbon and the crossing of the Murg allowed Valluy to by-pass Rastatt and open the Kehl bridge to General Béthouart's I Corps.

In the meantime, Monsabert had seized Freudenstadt, the key to the Black Forest, and Horb on the Neckar above Stuttgart, while the American VI Corps was moving up on the capital of Württemberg by way of Heilbronn. On April 20, pushing on from Tübingen, the 5th Armoured Division completed the encirclement of the city. All resistance ceased after 48 hours. The French took 28,000 prisoners, what was left of the four divisions of LXIV Corps (Lieutenant-General Grimeiss).

The Stuttgart manoeuvre was the third act of this military tragedy, although by April 22, the fourth act, which saw the entrance of I Corps (4th Moroccan Division, 9th Colonial Division, 14th Division, and 1st Armoured Division), was well under way. Béthouart moved on Horb by way of Kehl and Oberkirch, where he turned south up the Neckar, reaching the Swiss frontier in the vicinity of Schaffhausen on the day Stuttgart fell. This led to the cutting off of XVIII S.S. Corps (General Keppler), which comprised four army divisions. These 40,000 Germans attempted to cut their way through the lines of the 4th Moroccan Mountain Division but they were taken in the rear by the 9th Colonial Division and on April 25 all resistance ceased.

The manoeuvre employed here by the 9th Colonial Division was the result of a request made by the Swiss High Command–as is told in the *History of the French 1st Army*–who were understandably not very enthusiastic about disarming and interning thousands of allegedly fanatical Germans. Although his plans were slightly put out by this development, de Lattre agreed:

"It is an obligation of another kind to give consideration to the permanent interests of Franco-Swiss friendship, especially when Switzerland, while keeping to its age old principle of neutrality, has always been faithful to this cause.

The twin spires of Cologne Cathedral rise above the ruins.

609

German torpedoes, unused as a result of the increasingly powerful Allied air offensive.

"The problem confronted me while Valluy was still about to attack the Kaiserstuhl and Lehr's combat command (5th Armoured Division) was still some hours away from Schaffhausen. But my hesitation was only momentary. I had no illusions as to the risks I ran but my inclination was on the side of Franco-Swiss comradeship. This inspired me to issue General Order No. 11 in the night April 20-21, ordering I Corps to 'maintain the drive of the right flank along the Rhine towards Basle, then Waldshut, with simultaneous action from Schaffhausen towards Waldshut so as to link up with the forces coming from Basle', hence ensuring the complete encirclement of the Black Forest and at the same time denying the S.S. divisions any opportunity to force the Swiss-German frontier."

In addition, the alacrity with which General Valluy tackled this new mission without the slightest warning deserves mention, Waldshut being not far short of 90 miles from the Kaiserstuhl via Lorrach.

The fifth and final act of the Rhine–Danube campaign involved the pincer movement carried out by Monsabert and Béthouart on Ulm, the one with the 5th Armoured Division and 2nd Moroccan Division (General de Linarès) to the north of the Danube, the other thrusting his 1st Armoured Division (General Sudre) south of the river along the line of Donaueschingen and Biberach. On April 24 at noon, the *tricolour* flew above the town which on October 21, 1805, had seen Mack surrender his sword to Napoleon. With the capture of Ulm a new pocket was established, and this yielded 30,000 prisoners.

On April 29, General de Lattre reformed I Corps, putting the 2nd Moroccan Division, the 4th Moroccan Mountain Division, and the 1st and 5th Armoured Divisions under its command, and giving it the task of destroying the German 24th Army, recently formed under General Schmidt with the object of preventing the French from gaining access into the Tyrol and Vorarlberg.

On the next day the 4th Moroccan Mountain Division (General de Hesdin) and the 5th Armoured Division, of which General Schlesser had just assumed command, captured Bregenz in Austria.

Once over the frontier, the French could count on the Austrian resistance to provide guides and information, leading in numerous instances to preventing planned demolition being carried out by the Wehrmacht. At Dornbirn the tanks of the 5th Armoured Division were bombarded with bouquets of lilac; at Bludenz, which was liberated on May 4, General Schlesser was made an honorary citizen. Meanwhile, the 2nd Moroccan Division and the 1st Armoured Division were moving beyond Ulm up the valley of the Iller; from Oberstdorf General de Linarès's Moroccan troops scaled the snow-covered slopes of the Flexenpass (5,800 feet). Nightfall on May 6 found them at Saint Anton, on the road to the Arlberg, having made contact with the American 44th Division on their left.

On May 7, at 1340 hours, a cease-fire was declared in Austria, following Kesselring's capitulation to General Devers. During its five weeks' campaign, the French 1st Army had brought total destruction on eight German divisions and taken 180,000 prisoners. Among these was Field-Marshal Rommel's son, whom de Lattre, with other considerations than victory in mind, generously released.

CHAPTER 74
Victory in Europe

In the meantime the German resistance had collapsed before the Red Army. The ring was closing round the New Chancellery in Berlin, and Vienna, the second capital of the Nazi Greater Germany, had been under Tolbukhin's control since April 13.

Between the Drava and the Carpathians, General Wöhler, commanding Army Group "South", had tried to break the Budapest blockade during the first fortnight of January. Although he had been reinforced by IV S.S. Panzer Corps, which had been withdrawn from East Prussia just before the Soviet attack on the Vistula, he failed in this attempt. The German 6th Army, which had just been transferred to General Balck's command, nevertheless managed to regain possession of the important military position of Székesfehérvár, but the effort exhausted its strength.

This setback sealed the fate of IX S.S. Mountain Corps, which, under the command of General Pfeffer-Wildenbruch, made up the Hungarian capital's garrison. On February 13, Buda castle, the defenders' last stronghold, fell to Marshal Malinovsky's troops (2nd Ukrainian Front), whilst the 3rd Ukrainian Front under Marshal Tolbukhin cleared Pest. The Russians claimed the Germans had lost 41,000 killed and 110,000 prisoners. The figures are certainly exaggerated, but nevertheless the 13th Panzer Division, the "Feldherrnhalle" Panzergrenadier Division, and the 33rd Hungarian S.S. Cavalry Division had been wiped out.

On March 6, the 6th Panzerarmee (Colonel-General Sepp Dietrich) went over to the offensive from the bastion of Székesfehérvár. Dietrich had left the Ardennes front on about January 25; it had taken six weeks for him to travel and take up his position. He might, on the other hand have reached the Oder front between February 5 and 10 if the plan that Guderian had vainly recommended to the Führer had been followed. The Führer in fact expected a miracle from this new offensive, indeed even the recapture of the Ploiești oilfields.

The 3rd Ukrainian Front was to be smashed under the impact of a triple attack:

1. the left, the 6th Panzerarmee, consisting of eight Panzer (including the "Leibstandarte Adolf Hitler", "Das Reich", "Hohenstaufen", and "Hitlerjugend"), three infantry, and two cavalry divisions, was to deliver the main blow; it was to reach the Danube at Dunaföldvar and exploit its victory towards the south, with its left close to the Danube, its right on Lake Balaton;
2. between Lake Balaton and the Drava, the 2nd Panzerarmee (General de Angelis: six divisions) would immobilise Tolbukhin by attacking towards Kaposzvár; and

3. on the right, Army Group "E" (Colonel-General Löhr), in Yugoslavia, would send a corps of three divisions across the Drava, and from Mohacs move to the Danube.

The offensive of March 6 therefore committed 22 German divisions, including 19 from Army Group "South", out of the 39 that General Wöhler had under his command at the time. But this tremendous effort was of no avail. On the Drava and south of Lake Balaton, the German attack collapsed after 48 hours. The outlook for the 6th Panzerarmee seemed better on the day the engagement started, as the Panzers, massed on a narrow front, succeeded in breaking through, but the poorly-trained infantry proved incapable of exploiting this brief success. Tolbukhin, on the other hand, had organised his forces in depth and countered with his self-propelled guns. In fact, on March 12, Dietrich was halted about 19 miles from his starting point, but about 16 miles from his Danube objective.

On March 16, Marshals Malinovsky and Tolbukhin in their turn went over to the attack from the junction point of their two Fronts. Malinovsky planned to drive the German 6th Army back to the Danube between Esztergom and Komárom, whilst Tolbukhin, driving north-west of Lakes Velencei and Balaton, intended to

split at its base the salient made in the Soviet lines by the 6th Panzerarmee.

The 2nd Ukrainian Front's troops had the easier task and reached their first objective by March 21, cutting off four of the 6th Army's divisions.

Tolbukhin, on the other hand, met such firm resistance on March 16 and 17 from IV S.S. Panzer Corps, forming Balck's right, that the Stavka put the 6th Guards Tank Army at his disposal. However, because of Malinovsky's success, Wöhler took two Panzer divisions from the 6th Panzerarmee and set them against Malinovsky's forces. As the inequality between attack and defence became increasingly marked, Dietrich managed to evacuate the salient he had captured between March 6 and 12, and then on March 24 he brought his troops back through the bottleneck at Székesfehérvári but now they had neither supplies nor equipment.

On March 27, the 6th Guards Tank Army was at Veszprém and Devecser, 35 and 48 miles from its starting point. On March 29, Tolbukhin crossed the Rába at Sárvár, and Malinovsky crossed it at Györ, where it meets the Danube. The Hungarian front had therefore collapsed; this was not surprising as Wöhler, who had no reserves, had had 11 Panzer divisions more or less destroyed

The battle of Lake Balaton

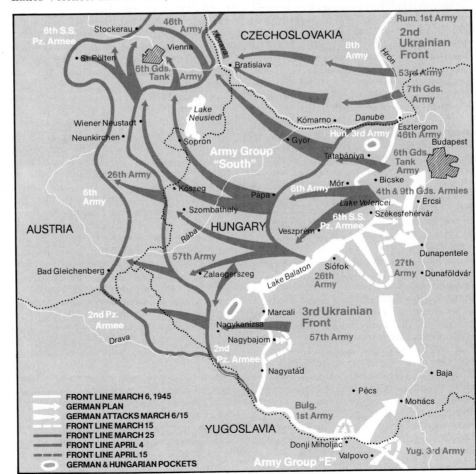

611

A mud-spattered Kubelwagen, *the versatile equivalent of the Allied jeep.*

between March 16 and 27.

On April 6 Hitler, consistent in his misjudgement, stripped Wöhler of command of Army Group "South" and gave it to Colonel-General Rendulic, whom he recalled from the Kurland pocket for the task.

But Malinovsky had already driven between Lake Neusiedl and the Danube on April 2, and had forced the Leitha at Bruck, whilst Tolbukhin, who had captured the large industrial centre of Wiener Neustadt, launched one column along the Semmering road towards Graz and another towards Mödling and Vienna. The day he took over his command, Rendulic was informed that the advance guard of the 3rd Ukrainian Front was already in Klosterneuburg north of Vienna, and that the 2nd Ukrainian Front was already approaching it from the south. A week later, a cease-fire was signed in the famous Prater Park, but in addition to the ordeal of a week's street fighting, the wretched Viennese still had to suffer much brutality and shameless looting from their "liberators".

Tolbukhin, who boasted of the capture of 130,000 prisoners, 1,350 tanks, and 2,250 guns, went up the right bank of the Danube, but his main forces did not go further than Amstetten, a small town 75 miles west of Vienna. On May 4, his patrols in the outskirts of Linz met a reconnaissance unit of the U.S. 3rd Army, and on the same day made contact with the advance guard of the British 8th Army on the Graz road. After helping to clear Vienna, Malinovsky sent his armies on the left across the Danube in the direction of Moravia. At Mikulov they crossed the pre-Munich (1938) Austro-Czechoslovak frontier. On the left bank of the Danube, the right wing of the 2nd Ukrainian Front, including the Rumanian

1st and 4th Armies (Generals Atanasiu and Dascalesco), liberated Slovakia and then, converging towards the north-west, occupied Brno on April 24 and were close to Olomouc when hostilities ceased. Slovakia's administration was handed over to the representatives of the Czechoslovak government-in-exile under Eduard Beneš as the occupation proceeded. On the other hand, Stalin seized Ruthenia in the lower Carpathian mountains; it had never even been a part of the Tsarist empire.

On March 10, 1945, Hitler told Kesselring that he viewed the offensive Stalin was preparing to launch against Berlin with complete confidence. Colonel-General Guderian viewed the matter differently; urging Himmler to take soundings in Stockholm for surrender, he repeated several times: "It's not 11.55 now – it's 12.05!" In view of the open pessimism of his O.K.H. Chief-of-Staff, Hitler dismissed him on March 28 on grounds of ill health and appointed Colonel-General H. Krebs, who had been the German military attaché in Moscow on June 22, 1941, as his successor.

Army Group "Vistula" was charged with the defence of Berlin; Heinrich Himmler had just been replaced by Colonel-General Gotthard Heinrici, who rightly enjoyed the complete confidence of his staff and his troops. Cornelius Ryan's judgement seems quite correct: "A thoughtful, precise strategist, a deceptively mild-mannered commander, Heinrici was nevertheless a tough general of the old aristocratic school who had long ago learned to hold the line with the minimum of men and at the lowest possible cost."

Heinrici was in contact with Army Group "Centre" a little below Guben on the Neisse, and was in control of the Oder front between Fürstenberg and Stettin, but the 1st Belorussian Front on both sides of Küstrin already had a wide bridgehead on the left bank of the river.

The German 9th Army, under General

Busse, had the special mission of barring the invader's path to Berlin. It was accordingly deployed between Guben and the Hohenzollern Canal connecting the Oder and the Havel:

1. V S.S. Mountain Corps (337th, 32nd "Freiwilligen" S.S. Grenadier, and 236th Divisions) under General Jeckeln;
2. Frankfurt garrison of one division;
3. XI S.S. Panzer Corps ("Müncheberg" Panzer, 712th, 169th, and 9th Parachute Divisions) under General M. Kleinheisterkamp;
4. XCI Corps (309th "Berlin", 303rd "Döberitz", 606th, and 5th *Jäger* Division) under General Berlin.

This gave a total of 12 divisions on an 80 mile front. Busse, on the other hand, had kept the *"Kurmark"* Panzer Division in reserve on the Frankfurt axis and the 25th Panzer Division on the Küstrin axis.

The 3rd *Panzerarmee* was deployed between the Hohenzollern and Stettin canal; on a 95-mile front it had about ten divisions incorporated in XLVI Panzer Corps, XXXII Corps, and the 3rd Marine Division.

Heinrici kept his 18th *Panzergrenadier*, 11th *"Nordland"* S.S. *Freiwilligen Panzergrenadier,* and 23rd *"Nederland"* S.S. *Freiwilligen Panzergrenadier* Divisions, composed of Norwegian, Danish, Dutch, and Belgian volunteers.

Finally, O.K.H. kept control of XXXIX Panzer Corps, but as Hitler's intuition told him that the Russians' main attack would be directed not against Berlin, but along the Görlitz–Dresden–Prague axis, he handed over this corps to Field-Marshal Schörner and put LVI Panzer Corps, which was considerably weaker, in the rear of Army Group "Vistula".

On April 12, Franklin Roosevelt's sudden death seemed to Hitler like a long awaited and providential miracle, comparable in every respect to the divine intervention which had eliminated the Tsarina Elizabeth and saved Frederick II, who had been on the point of taking poison at the worst moment of the Seven Years' War. Hitler thought he would not only defeat the Russians at the gates of Berlin, but that the English, American, and Soviet forces would become inextricably confused in Mecklenburg and Saxony, German guns would fire themselves, and he would remain master of the situation.

The Russians, according to the message sent to Eisenhower by Stalin, were using only "secondary forces" against Berlin in this last battle of the war on the Eastern Front. These "secondary forces" totalled at least three army groups or fronts, consisting of 20 armies, 41,000 mortars and guns, 6,300 tanks, and 8,400 planes in the attack, which started at 0400 hours on April 16. On the 1st Belorussian Front, which broadly speaking was facing the German 9th Army, Marshal Zhukov had ten armies: 3rd and 5th Shock Armies, 8th Guards Army (General V. I. Chuikov), 1st and 2nd Guards Tank Armies (Generals M. E. Katukov and S. I. Bogdanov), the 1st Polish Army (General S. G. Poplavsky), and the 61st, 47th, 8th, and 33rd Armies. He also had eight artillery divisions and General S. I. Rudenko's 16th Air Army. His task was to encircle and take Berlin.

On Zhukov's left, Marshal I. S. Konev's 1st Ukrainian Front contained seven armies: 3rd and 5th Guards Armies (Generals V. N. Gordov and A. S. Zhadov), 3rd and 4th Guards Tank Armies (Colonel-General P. S. Rybalko and General D. D. Lelyushenko) 2nd Polish Army (General K. Swierczewski), and 13th and 52nd Armies. He also had seven artillery divisions and Colonel-General K. A. Vershinin's 4th Air Army. After forcing the Neisse, Konev was to exploit his victory along the Bautzen–Dresden axis, but in case Zhukov's thrust slowed down, he was to be prepared to converge his mobile troops on Berlin and take part in the encirclement and assault on the city.

To the right of Zhukov, the 2nd Belorussian Front (Marshal K. K. Rokossovsky) had five armies (2nd Shock, and 19th, 65th, 70th, and 49th) with four tank or

Marshal Konev, commander of the 1st Ukrainian front.

mechanised corps, and Colonel-General S. A. Krasovsky's 2nd Air Army. On April 20, Rokossovsky was to attack on the Schwedt–Neustrelitz axis, drive the 3rd *Panzerarmee* to the Baltic, and link up with Field-Marshal Montgomery's forces. Although Telpukhovsky as usual does not state the number of Soviet divisions taking part in this campaign, they may be assessed at 140 divisions or their equivalent. The Germans had 37 weakened divisions to take the first blow, including the 4th *Panzerarmee,* which faced the 1st Ukrainian Front on the Neisse. Another difficulty was caused by the fact that the defence was extremely short of fuel and munitions, and the German troops were seriously undertrained. Moreover, as Telpukhovsky points out, Soviet planes had complete air supremacy. Busse, for instance, only had 300 fighters, all desperately short of fuel, to oppose Zhukov's 16th Air Army.

As Zhukov and Konev started the attack, the German troops were handed out Adolf Hitler's last order of the day, which included the following passages:

"For the last time, the deadly Jewish-Bolshevik enemy has started a mass attack. He is trying to reduce Germany to rubble and to exterminate our people. Soldiers of the East! You are already fully aware now of the fate that threatens German women and children. Whilst men, children, and old people will be murdered, women and girls will be reduced to the rôle of barrack-room whores. The rest will be marched off to Siberia."

But the Führer had provided the means to put a stop to this terrible assault; everything was ready for meeting it, and the outcome now depended on the tenacity of the German soldiers. He therefore wrote: "If every soldier does his duty on the Eastern Front in the days and weeks to come, Asia's last attack will be broken, as surely as the Western enemy's invasion will in spite of everything finally fail.

"Berlin will remain German. Vienna will become German again and Europe will never be Russian!"

At the same time the Soviet leaders told their front-line troops: "The time has come to free our fathers, mothers, brothers, sisters, wives, and children still languishing under the Fascist yoke in Germany. The time has come to draw up the balance sheet of the abominable crimes perpetrated on our soil by the Hitlerite cannibals and to punish those responsible for these atrocities. The time has come to inflict the final defeat on the enemy and to draw this war to a victorious conclusion."

Over the 30 miles of the Küstrin bridgehead, the attack started at 0400 hours, lit up by 143 searchlights. Five armies, including the 1st Guards Tank Army, took part in it, but this concentration did not favour the attack, which had only advanced between two and five miles by the end of the day. In the Frankfurt sector, Zhukov's successes were even more modest, and his crude frontal attacks were blocked by the German defences in depth. Nevertheless, on the first day, O.K.W. had to hand over LVI Panzer Corps (General Weidling) to Busse, who put it between XI S.S. and LI Corps.

On the Neisse, between Forst and Muskau, the troops of the 1st Ukrainian Front had had a better day. At 0655 hours the engineers had already thrown a bridge across this 130-foot wide obstacle so that at nightfall Konev had a bridgehead which was eight miles deep in places on a 16-mile front. The 4th *Panzerarmee* (General F.-H. Gräser) was more than half shattered, which appeared to confirm the soundness of Hitler's instinct in showing him that the enemy's main effort would bear on Dresden rather than Berlin; this was his last victory over his Intelligence service.

For three whole days attacks and counter-attacks followed each other on the Oder's left bank to a depth of nine miles. German supplies brought up towards the line were stopped by the ceaseless attacks of countless Soviet fighter-bombers. But Zhukov had suffered heavy losses and Hitler was confident that at a daily rate of loss of 250 T-34's and JS-3's, the enemy offensive would finally become exhausted. But again Busse, to stop the gaps which

*Russian T34/85 medium
tanks pass through a
congested Austrian village*

were opening every day along his front, was in the position of a player forced to throw down his last chips onto the table: LVI Panzer Corps, 25th and 18th *Panzergrenadier, "Nordland"* and *"Nederland"* Panzer Divisions; and the defeat of the 4th *Panzerarmee*, which became more and more complete, threatened his communications.

April 19 was the decisive day on the Oder front: on that day the German 9th Army disintegrated. LI Corps, which was thrown back against Eberswalde, lost all contact with LVI Panzer Corps, which was itself cut off from XI S.S. Corps; through this last breach Zhukov managed to reach Strausberg, which was about 22 miles from the New Chancellery bunker.

On the same day Konev, on the 1st Ukrainian Front, was already exploiting the situation; he crossed the Spree at Spremberg and penetrated Saxon territory at Bautzen and Hoyerswerda. The *Stavka*, which was not satisfied with Zhukov's manner of conducting his battle, urged Konev to carry out the alternative plan previously discussed.

For the last time, Hitler's dispositions favoured the enemy. Certainly neither Heinrici nor Busse opposed LI Corps' attachment to the 3rd *Panzerarmee*, but the order given to LVI Panzer Corps to reinforce the Berlin garrison without allowing the 9th Army to pull back from the Oder appeared madness to them: outflanked on its right by Konev's impetuous thrust, it was also exposed on its left. But, as always, the Führer remained deaf to these sensible objections, and Busse received the imperious order to counter-attack the 1st Ukrainian Front's columns from the north whilst Gräser attacked them from the south.

The result was that on April 22, the 1st Guards Tank Army (1st Belorussian Front), leaving the Berlin region to its north-west, identified at Königs Wuster-hausen the advance guard of the 3rd Guards Tank Army (1st Ukrainian Front) which, executing Stalin's latest instruction, had veered from the west to the north from Finsterwalde. The circle had therefore closed around the German 9th Army. That evening, Lelyushenko's armoured forces pushed forward to Jüterborg, cutting the Berlin–Dresden road, whilst Zhukov, advancing through Bernau, Wandlitz, Oranienburg, and Birkenwerder (which had fallen to Lieutenant-General F. I. Perkhorovich's 47th Army and Colonel-General N. E. Berzarin's 5th Shock Army) cut the Berlin–Stettin and Berlin–Stralsund roads. The encirclement of the capital, therefore, was completed two days later when the 8th Guards and 4th Guards Tank Armies linked up in Ketzin.

Hitler refused to abandon the city and insisted on taking personal charge of its defence. He had a little more than 90,000 men at his disposal, including the youths and 50-year-old men of the *Volkssturm*, as well as the remainder of LVI Panzer Corps. But in spite of this he did not regard the battle as lost. Whilst he galvanised the resistance, Field-Marshal Keitel and Colonel-General Jodl, who had both left Berlin on his instructions, would mount the counter-attacks which would complete the enemy's defeat. The 11th Army (General F. Steiner) would emerge from the Oranienburg–Eberswalde front and crush Zhukov against the north front of the capital whilst Konev, on the south front, would meet the same fate from General W. Wenck and his 12th Army. Meanwhile, the Brandenburg *Gauleiter,* Joseph Goebbels, launched into inflammatory speeches and blood-thirsty orders:

"Your Gauleiter is with you," he shouted through the microphone, "he swears that he will of course remain in your midst with his colleagues. His wife and children are also here. He who once conquered this city with 200 men will henceforth organise the defence of the capital by all possible means." And these were the means: "Any man found not doing his duty," he decreed, "will be hanged on a lamp post after a summary judgement. Moreover, placards will be attached to the corpses stating: 'I have been hanged here because I am too cowardly to defend the capital of the Reich'–'I have been hanged because I did not believe in the Führer'–'I am a deserter and for this reason I shall not see this turning-point of destiny'." etc.

The 11th Army's counter-attack never materialised, mainly because of the offensive launched on April 20 against the 3rd *Panzerarmee* by Rokossovsky across the lower Oder. Elsewhere, as Zhukov spread out towards the west, Steiner was compelled to thin out his forces even more, some of which were entirely worn out and the rest badly undertrained. Finally on April 26, the troops of the 2nd Belorussian Front, after making a breach below Schwedt, moved towards Prenzlau. Heinrici withdrew two or three divisions from the 11th Army to stop them. As he was unable to have him shot for insubordination, Keitel could only relieve him of his command. In the present position, he would have found no one to pronounce a death sentence and have it carried out.

Meanwhile, Hitler had addressed the following order of the day to the 12th Army on April 23: "Soldiers of the Wenck Army! An immensely important order requires you to withdraw from the combat zone against our enemies in the West and march East. Your mission is simple. Berlin must remain German. You must at all costs reach your planned objectives, for other operations are also in hand, designed to deal a decisive blow against the Bolsheviks in the struggle for the capital of the Reich and so to reverse the position in Germany. Berlin will

never capitulate to Bolshevism. The defenders of the Reich's capital have regained their courage on hearing of your rapid approach; they are fighting bravely and stubbornly, and are firmly convinced that they will soon hear your guns roaring. The Führer calls you! You are getting ready for the attack as before in the time of your victories. Berlin is waiting for you!"

The German 12th Army gave way to the Western Allies on the Elbe between Wittenberge and Wittenberg and carried out the regrouping and change of front prescribed. With a strength of two Panzer corps and a handful of incomplete and hastily trained divisions it moved on Berlin. During this forward movement, which brought it to Belzig, 30 miles from the bunker where Hitler was raging and fuming, it picked up the Potsdam garrison and the remnants of the 9th Army (estimated at 40,000 men), who had with great difficulty made their way from Lübben to Zossen, leaving more than 200,000 dead, wounded, and prisoners and almost all its *matériel* behind it. On April 29, however, Wenck was compelled to note that this last sudden effort

had finished the 12th Army, and that it could no longer hold its positions.

In Berlin, the armies of the 1st Belorussian Front started to round on the last centres of resistance on the same day. A tremendous artillery force, under Marshal Voronov, supported the infantry's attacks. It had 25,000 guns and delivered, according to some reports, 25,600 tons of shells against the besieged city, that is, in less than a week, more than half the 45,517 tons of bombs which British and American planes had dropped on the German capital since August 25, 1940.

When he heard of Steiner's inability to counter-attack, Hitler flew into an uncontrollable fury; and Wenck's defeat left him with no alternative but captivity or death. In the meantime he had dismissed Hermann Göring and Heinrich Himmler from the Party, depriving them of all their offices, the former for attempting to assume power after the blockade of Berlin, the latter for trying to negotiate a cease-fire with the Western powers

Five Russian armies were employed in the spring campaign to crush these defenders of the capital of the Reich.

*The surrender at Rheims on May 7, 1945:
Bedell Smith signs for Eisenhower.*

through Count Folke Bernadotte. On
the evening of April 28, he married Eva
Braun, whose brother-in-law he had just
had shot for abandoning his post, made his
will on the next day with Joseph Goebbels,
Martin Bormann, and Generals Burgdorf
and Krebs as witnesses, and committed
suicide a little before 1600 hours on
April 30, probably by firing his revolver
at his right temple.

Much has been written about Hitler's
"disappearance" and the various places of
refuge that he reached outside Germany.
But in fact Marshal Sokolovsky, the
former chief-of-staff of the 1st Belorussian
Front who was interviewed by Cornelius
Ryan in Moscow on April 17, 1963, admitted
to him that the Führer's body had been
unmistakably identified by his dentist's
assistants early in May 1945. Nevertheless on May 26 Stalin, who must have
known this fact, assured Harry Hopkins
that in his opinion Hitler was not dead
and that he was hiding somewhere.
When Hopkins put forward the suggestion
that Hitler had escaped to a U-Boat
Stalin added, according to the account
of this meeting, that "this was done with
the connivance of Switzerland."

On May 2, 1945, after Generals Krebs
and Burgdorf had also committed suicide,
General H. Weidling surrendered to
Chuikov, the heroic defender of Stalingrad, all that remained of the Berlin
garrison, about 70,000 totally exhausted
men.

Zhukov's crushing victory should not,
however, appear to overshadow the
equally significant successes obtained by
Konev over Schörner, whom Hitler had
at the eleventh hour promoted to Field-
Marshal. Having routed the 4th *Panzerarmee*, Konev went on to occupy the ruins
of Dresden after a last engagement at
Kamenz. Two days later, his 5th Guards
Army (General Zhadov) established its
first contact with the American 1st
Army, whilst Marshal Rybalko and
General Lelyushenko's forces made off
towards Prague, whose population rose
up against their German "protectors"
on May 4. Army Group "Centre", which
had about 50 divisions, was now cut off
from its communications.

Grand-Admiral Dönitz, who had been
invested by Hitler's last will with supreme
power over what remained of Germany,
now had to put an end to this war in conditions which Kaiser Wilhelm II,
unbalanced as he was and a mediocre

politician and strategist, had managed to
spare his empire and his subjects in
November 1918. In his attempt to finish
off the war, the new head of state tried
to save the largest possible number of
German troops from Soviet captivity,
and was quite ready to let the British and
Americans take them prisoner.

On May 3, General E. Kinzel, Field-
Marshal Busch's chief-of-staff, and
Admiral H.-G. von Friedeburg, new head
of the Kriegsmarine, presented themselves on Lüneburg Heath to Field-
Marshal Montgomery and offered him
the surrender of the German forces in
the north of Germany, including those
retreating from Marshal Rokossovsky.

They were dismissed, and on May 4,
at 1820 hours, they had to accede to the
conditions stipulated in Eisenhower's
name by Montgomery. The instrument
they signed now only related to the land
and sea forces opposed to the 21st Army
Group in the Netherlands, in north-west
Germany, in the Friesian Islands, in
Heligoland, and in Schleswig-Holstein.
In spite of this fair dealing, the Russians
occupied the Danish island of Bornholm.

General Eisenhower kept to the same
principle in the surrender document
which put an end to the European war

at 0241 hours on May 7, 1941. This merciless war had lasted a little over 68 months.

When he received the German delegation in the Rheims school which housed S.H.A.E.F., Lieutenant-General Walter Bedell Smith, Eisenhower's chief-of-staff, read out the document decided by the Allies. It ordered the simultaneous cessation of hostilities on all fronts on May 8 at 2301 hours, confirmed the total defeat of the armed forces of the Third Reich, and settled the procedure for their surrender according to the principles governing the surrender on Lüneburg Heath. Colonel-General Jodl, General Admiral Friedeburg, and Major Oxenius of the Luftwaffe signed the surrender document in Germany's name. After Bedell Smith, Lieutenant-General Sir Frederick Morgan signed for Great Britain, General Sévez for France, and Major-General Susloparov for the U.S.S.R. Finally Lieutenant-General Carl A. Spaatz, Vice-Admiral Sir Harold M. Burrough, and Air Marshal Sir J. M. Robb signed for the U.S. Air Force, the Royal Navy, and the R.A.F. respectively.

The following day, Air Chief Marshal Sir Arthur Tedder, as Eisenhower's deputy, flew to Berlin accompanied by General Spaatz for the final act of the Wehrmacht's and the Third Reich's unconditional surrender. The ceremony took place at the 1st Belorussian Front's H.Q. Field-Marshal Keitel, Admiral Friedeburg, and Colonel-General Stumpff, who signed for the Luftwaffe, appeared before Marshal Zhukov, General de Lattre de Tassigny, and the two previously mentioned officers at 0028 hours. On May 8 the European part of World War II ended.

The surrender of the German forces, with the exception of Army Group "Centre", took place at the time specified. Wireless communication was irregular between Flensburg, the seat of Dönitz's government, and Josefov in Bohemia, where Schörner had set up his last H.Q. In any event, this last corner of German resistance had given up the struggle by May 10.

In the period between the various stages of surrender, though it was brief, hundreds of thousands of Wehrmacht soldiers, even on the other side of the Elbe, managed to get past Montgomery's and Bradley's advance guards and surrender to the Western Allies. The Kriegsmarine also made full use of its last hours of freedom and as far as it could evacuated its Baltic positions.

Watched by Admiral von Friedburg, Jodl signs the surrender for the Wehrmacht.

Finally Colonel-General C. Hilpert, commander of Army Group "Kurland" since his colleague Rendulic's sudden transfer to Austria, handed over to the Russians a little less than 200,000 men, what was left of his two armies (five corps or 16 divisions). Similarly General Noak surrendered XX Corps (7th, 32nd, and 239th Divisions) which still held the Hela peninsula and the mouth of the Vistula. The German 20th Army, occupying Norway with five corps of 14 divisions (400,000 men and 100,000 Soviet prisoners) surrendered at Oslo to Lieutenant-General Sir Alfred Thorne. The 319th Division abandoned its pointless occupation in the Channel Islands, as did the garrisons at Dunkirk, Lorient, and Saint Nazaire; finally the surrender at Rheims saved la Rochelle from the tragic fate that had befallen Royan.

On the following June 4, at Berlin, Marshal Zhukov, Field-Marshal Montgomery, and Generals Eisenhower and de Lattre de Tassigny approved four agreements governing Germany's disarmament, occupation, and administration, and decreeing that the principal

Nazi war leaders should appear before an international court of military justice. It should be noted with reference to these agreements that as they were not in a position to prejudge the territorial decisions of the future peace conference, the four contracting parties defined Germany as the Reich within its frontiers of December 1937.

During the last weeks of their furious pursuit, Montgomery had advanced from Wismar on the Baltic to the Elbe just below Wittenberge, and General Bradley had reached the right bank of the Elbe as far as Torgau and to the south beyond Chemnitz (now Karl Marx Stadt). Both had gone beyond the limits set out in the Yalta agreements about the British, American, and Soviet occupation zones. Montgomery had gone about 45 miles ahead, Bradley about 125 miles. In fact, in the interests of their common victory, and without arousing the Kremlin's protests, the British and the Americans had exercised their "right of pursuit" beyond the demarcation line. Nevertheless on the day after the Rheims and Berlin surrenders, Stalin insisted on the precise implementation of all the promises given.

But had he kept his own promises about the constitution of a Polish government in which the various democratic factions of the nation would be represented? In London it was well known that the

Soviet secret services were systematically destroying all elements opposed to the setting up of a communist régime in Poland loyal to Moscow, and that in the Kremlin the commission established by the Yalta agreements to carry out the reorganisation of the government was paralysed by Molotov's obstruction.

In these circumstances, Churchill offered the opinion that the British and American armies should continue to occupy the positions they had reached in Germany up to the time when the coming conference of the Big Three in Berlin had clarified the situation. He also thought that this conference, which was first arranged for July 15, should be held earlier. For this reason he wrote to President Truman on June 4:

"I am sure you understand the reason why I am anxious for an earlier date, say 3rd or 4th (of July). I view with profound misgivings the retreat of the American Army to our line of occupation in the central sector, thus bringing Soviet power into the heart of Western Europe and the descent of the iron curtain between us and everything to the eastward. I hoped that this retreat, if it has to be made, would be accompanied by the settlement of many great things which would be the true foundation of world peace. Nothing really important has been settled yet, and you and I will have to bear great responsibility for the future. I still hope

Victorious Soviet troops ride by, under the gaze of curious German civilians.

therefore that the date will be advanced."

On June 9, arguing that the Soviet occupation authorities' behaviour in Austria and the increasing number of irregularities against the missions of the Western powers justified his position, he returned to the charge:

"Would it not be better to refuse to withdraw on the main European front until a settlement has been reached about Austria? Surely at the very least the whole agreement about zones should be carried out at the same time?"

Harry Truman turned a deaf ear to these arguments and Churchill was informed that the American troops' retreat to the demarcation line would begin on June 21 and that the military chiefs would settle questions about the quadripartite occupation of Berlin and free access to the capital by air, rail, and road between them. This was done and on July 15, when the Potsdam conference began, the Red Army had set up its advanced positions 30 miles from the centre of Hamburg, within artillery range of Kassel, and less than 80 miles from Mainz on the Rhine.

It was a "fateful decision", Churchill wrote.

CHAPTER 75
The Arakan offensives

By May 1942, the Japanese had reached the limits they had set themselves in South-East Asia. They had driven the British from Burma and now prepared to go over to the defensive. The British forces under General Wavell, the Commander-in-Chief in India, took this opportunity to attack, and a series of campaigns began which were to continue until the final Japanese surrender. This fighting in Burma often seemed isolated from the rest of the war, for it had its own momentum, set by the monsoon rains and enormous supply problems.

It was on September 17, 1942, that Wavell despatched from India an operation instruction to the G.O.C.-in-C. Eastern Army, Lieutenant-General N. M. S. Irwin, which gave the objects for the army in the 1942–1943 dry season (October–May): first to develop communications for the purpose of reconquering Burma and opening the Burma Road; and second to bring the Japanese to battle in order to use up their strength, especially in the air.

Wavell gave four objectives as his immediate intention in order to attain these ends:
1. to capture Akyab and reoccupy the upper Arakan;
2. to strengthen British positions in the Chin hills;
3. to occupy Kalewa and Sittaung on the Chindwin; and thence to raid Japanese lines of communication (Wavell had already given Brigadier Orde Wingate orders to raise and train a Long Range Penetration Brigade for this purpose); and
4. to make necessary administrative arrangements to allow for a rapid advance into upper or lower Burma should opportunity offer.

We are here immediately concerned with the first objective, the British attempt to capture Akyab in the dry season 1942–43. Throughout this narrative it is important to remember that the Japanese forces in the Arakan were seasoned victorious soldiers, whereas their British and Indian opponents were raw, inexperienced troops, often new recruits. The Japanese 213th Regiment in the Arakan, under the command of Colonel K. Miyawaki and consisting of two battalions (II/213th and III(213th), had moved into Akyab during the summer of 1942 after chasing the British/Indian forces from Yenangyaung, Myingan, Monywa, Shwegyin, and finally Kalewa, which it had captured on May 11. The 33rd Division, of which it formed a part, had advanced from Siam for the initial invasion of Burma, but the 213th Regiment had been left in Siam and had not rejoined its division until after the fall of Rangoon. It was, therefore, the freshest regiment and had had the fewest casualties in the conquest of Burma and was full of fight.

As the British/Indian 14th Division started its southward advance from Chittagong to Cox's Bazar and beyond, Miyawaki in mid-October sent his II/213th battalion up the Mayu river by launch to occupy the line Buthidaung–"Tunnels" Road–Maungdaw, where first contact was made with the 1/15th Punjab battalion on October 23. The "Tunnels" Road was the only all-weather road in the area in 1942.

On September 21 Lieutenant-General Irwin had ordered the 14th Indian Division, commanded by Major-General W. L. Lloyd, to move towards Akyab to forestall the Japanese arrival on the Buthidaung-Maungdaw line.

Earlier in the year the 14th Division had been earmarked for operations in Burma, but the fall of Rangoon had prevented its arrival. After the British defeat in Burma a special committee had reported that one of the reasons for this defeat was the over-modernisation of Indian divisions. Certain divisions were, therefore, reorganised to become "light divisions" with their transport mainly on a jeep and animal basis. The 14th Division, which had recently been responsible for the defence of Bengal, Bihar, and Orissa, was not so reorganised.

This division consisted of four brigades (47th, 55th, 88th, and 123rd), with two British and ten Indian battalions plus one British field regiment and one Indian mountain regiment of artillery. The Indian battalions came mainly from the dry areas of the Punjab, Baluchistan, and Rajputana and were unused to the hot, steamy, malarial swamps of the Arakan. Later another brigade joined the division. For this rôle the 14th Division was supported by a special reconnaissance force ("V" Force) hidden, with its wireless sets, in the hills, and No. 2000 Flotilla, a scratch collection of steamboats, launches, and sampans, to help the units across and down the rivers and to supply them.

The Arakan, on Burma's north-west coast, is a country of steep, densely-forested hill ranges up to 2,000 feet high, running parallel from north to south, separated by narrow cultivated valleys filled with rice fields, mangroves, and tidal creeks. The coastal strip from Maungdaw to the tip of the Mayu peninsula, Foul Point, opposite Akyab Island, is 45 miles long and ten miles wide in the north but tapers down to a few hundred yards wide at Foul Point.

To the east winds the Mayu river (called the Kalapanzin in its upper reaches), flanked by swamps of elephant grass and bamboo, and divided by knife-edged limestone ridges, 150 feet high.

East of the Mayu valley rises the great jumbled mass of the Arakan Tracts, reaching as far as the Kaladan river valley, and 2,500 feet high. Further east again are the Arakan Yomas.

As it advanced, the 14th Division's line of communication from railhead was by sea from Chittagong to Cox's Bazar, motor transport to Tumbru, sampans on the Naf river to Bawli Bazar, and pack transport onwards.

In spite of reinforcements of motor launches, landing craft, and three paddle-steamers given to him, Major-General Lloyd by November 17 could still guarantee the maintenance of only four battalions to attack the Japanese. Being able to apply superior strength was always a problem for the British in the Arakan.

The Japanese, although outnumbered, were much better trained in watermanship and were thus able to take full advantage of all types of river transport, especially as Akyab Island was at the hub of the river system running north. Thus their water communication could easily be switched from one valley to another, whereas the British lines of approach were divided by virtually inaccessible ridges.

In December 1942, the Japanese air situation in the south-west Pacific had become so grave that two Japanese air brigades were despatched from Burma, leaving the 5th Air Division with only about 50 fighters and 90 medium bombers available for the whole of the Burma front–growing Allied strength.

No. 224 Group, R.A.F., consisting of six Hawker Hurricane squadrons, two light bomber squadrons of Bristol Blenheims and Bisleys, and one Beaufighter squadron (totalling about 120 aircraft), was ordered to support the 14th Division's advance. But at that time these squadrons had not been trained in close air support, the Hurricanes were not fitted with bomb racks, and there were no ground controllers with the brigades, so the group's efforts were initially of little value to the infantry (especially in comparison with later operations). Thus the group's aircraft were used chiefly for interdiction along the sparse Japanese supply routes, including the sea-lanes to Akyab. In fact, during the first year the R.A.F. had very little effect on the ground campaign apart from moral support by the sound of the engines. Except at high altitude the Hurricane was no match for the Mitsubishi A6M Zero, and the R.A.F. had no long-range fighters available to sustain an offensive against the Japanese air bases. In spite of this the R.A.F. did slowly begin to win air superiority, which made efficient close air support, as well as vital air supply, possible later.

All these administrative and training shortcomings of the British forces must be remembered, as otherwise it is difficult to understand how Colonel Miyawaki, with a maximum of only two battalions on the mainland, could hold up 12 battalions of infantry supported by six batteries of artillery for a period of 13 weeks from

Japanese propaganda, playing on the nationalist aspirations of India.

first contact on October 23 to January 22 1943, when the first detachments of the 55th Division started to arrive in the Akyab area. The difficulty Lloyd had was to apply his strength.

Irwin's original plan was for a seaborne landing on Akyab accompanied by a land advance down the Mayu peninsula to Foul Point. But by the end of October Wavell came to the conclusion that a direct seaborne attack in which transport and warships would be exposed to heavy air attack for a minimum of three days was no longer practicable.

Irwin therefore decided to use the 6th Infantry Brigade Group from the British 2nd Division to land on Akyab Island with the help of five motor launches, 72 landing craft, and three paddle-steamers, which Admiral Sir James Somerville had placed at his disposal, as soon as Lloyd had advanced to Foul Point. The speed of the overland advance was therefore vital.

However, Irwin postponed Lloyd's advance to the attack in order to give him time to improve his communications, so that he could bring an extra brigade to bear. This delayed Lloyd by three weeks so that just when he was about to attack, Miyawaki withdrew his II/213th battalion facing Lloyd to a general line Gwedauk–Kondon, thus drawing Lloyd further away from his base.

Lloyd finally made contact again on December 22, when he attacked on either side of the Mayu range and also detached one battalion to the Kaladan river. The Japanese repulsed all attacks but the wide front forced Miyiwaki to commit his only other battalion, the III/213th, on December 29. Further British attacks were repulsed. The confident Japanese,

having now got a measure of their enemy, started to harass Lloyd's two forward brigades by small patrol attacks at night and sudden bombardments from mortars, which startled these inexperienced troops and led them to believe that there were many more Japanese opposing them than just two battalions. Miyawaki, however, during this period took the risk of leaving the defence of Akyab Island to his anti-aircraft gunners, supported by administrative personnel.

During a visit with Wavell to the Donbaik front on December 10, Irwin criticised Lloyd for dispersing his force so widely that he had insufficient strength on the coast. He ordered Lloyd to concentrate and break through at Donbaik.

However, two more attacks by the 14th Division on their two objectives, Rathedaung and Donbaik, during the first two weeks in January, again failed. Repeated attacks by fresh troops on January 18 and 19 also failed with comparatively heavy losses.

But early in January, Lieutenant-General Shojiro Iida, commanding the 15th Army, realising the importance of, and threat to, Akyab ordered Lieutenant-General Takishi Koga to move his 55th Division to hold Akyab. The 55th Division was a battle-trained formation which had fought in China and then advanced from Siam to Burma in 1942. During the previous year, it had fought through from Moulmein in the south via Pegu, Toungoo, and Mandalay to Bhamo and the Chinese frontier.

Koga ordered a rapid overland advance via Pakokku to the Kaladan valley on the one hand, whilst at the same time opening up an administrative sea route from Toungup to Akyab. He ordered Miyawaki's 213th Regiment to hold the Rathedaung–Laungchaung–Donbaik line at all

costs. On January 22 No. 224 Group R.A.F. attacked the Japanese columns on the Pakokku trail.

Irwin reinforced Lloyd with two fresh brigades, artillery, and eight Valentine tanks. On February 1, after a heavy but badly co-ordinated R.A.F. bombardment, these fresh troops with the Valentines attacked the Japanese dug-in position at Donbaik, but after repeated assaults and heavy casualties over two days, were thrown back. Two days later similar frontal attacks on Rathedaung also failed.

The Japanese had won the race to Akyab, for by the end of February Koga had assembled the whole of the 55th Division, less one battalion, in that area.

Iida expected Koga to consolidate, but the latter saw the six British/Indian brigades under Lloyd split up the rivers and ranges into three quite separate identities, with his own forces holding a central position at the confluence of the Arakan rivers. Koga realised that it was an excellent opportunity to counter-attack these tired brigades and destroy them piecemeal.

Koga laid a three-phase plan. First, the enemy forces in the Kaladan valley were to be overwhelmed by the "Miyawaki" Column (one infantry battalion and one mountain artillery battalion). Then the brigade east of the Mayu river was to be encircled by the "Tanahashi" Column (two infantry battalions and one mountain regiment) operating from Rathedaung and supported by a flank advance by Miyawaki from the Kaladan. Finally, the combined forces of this right hook, resupplied by launches moving up the Mayu, would cross the river and the Mayu range to seize Indin. This would cut off the British/Indian brigades threatening the Donbaik–Laungchaung line. Koga left one battalion to hold Akyab and three battalions ("Uno" Column) to hold the Mayu peninsula.

Meanwhile, Lloyd was reorganising for another attack on Donbaik, but Irwin, aware of supply difficulties and danger from the east flank, ordered him to withdraw, intending to replace his division with the 26th. However, Wavell, egged on by Churchill, felt that it was essential for the morale of the whole Indian Army to score some sort of victory, rather than ignominiously retreat after suffering, by European standards, quite minor casualties. On February 26 Wavell directed Irwin to order Lloyd to attack Donbaik again with two brigades and to destroy "the numerically insignificant opposition". Irwin delayed the attack and also the withdrawal. At this time Irwin sent Slim, then commanding XV Corps in India, to visit the front and report on the situation. He later told Irwin that Lloyd's command was now far too large for a single divisional headquarters, and that Lloyd's tactics were too obviously frontal (a reflection on Irwin's own instructions). But Irwin did not place Slim in command of operations, nor heed his advice.

On February 21 the first phase of Koga's plan started.

By March 7 the "Miyawaki" Column had cleared the Kaladan valley as far as Kyauktaw, and "Tanahashi" Column had captured Rathedaung. The British/Indian 6th Brigade, with six battalions, obeyed Wavell's orders and carried out a deliberate attack on March 18 on the "Uno" Column dug in at Donbaik, but fell back after receiving only 300 casualties out of the 6,000-strong attacking force. With the "Miyawaki" and "Tanahashi" Columns now poised on the east bank of the Mayu river, and the "Uno" Column as the anvil, having withstood the British attack at Donbaik, Koga launched the third phase of his attack, starting on the night March 24–25. He called for and was given all available air support from the 5th Air Division.

Tanahashi sent one battalion northwest, which cut the coastal road at Gyindaw, whilst he, with the remaining two battalions of his force, advanced on Indin. In spite of a strenuous counter-attack and exhortations from their commanders, the brigades of the 14th Division on the coastal plain were unable to stop Tanahashi, who occupied Indin on April 6, thus cutting off 11 British/Indian battalions and attached troops south of that point. After an attack by a third brigade from the north had failed to remove this block, the 6th Brigade managed to escape with its transport along the beach at low tide, but the 47th Brigade had to leave all its transport and guns and retreat in small dispersal groups through the jungle.

Lieutenant-General Koga had completed his three-phase encirclement of the British/Indian brigades in one calendar month, exactly according to plan, and had inflicted severe casualties on a much larger force. With seven battalions and one pack regiment of artillery he had temporarily destroyed the 47th Brigade and defeated the 4th, 6th, and 71st Brigades with their three regiments of artillery (totalling seven British and ten Indian battalions).

With the arrival of his fresh II/214th battalion, which completed the strength of his division, Koga, who saw his enemy reeling, asked Iida if he could continue to attack until the monsoon. Iida, who trusted Koga, gave him *carte blanche.*

Meanwhile, Lloyd had been replaced by Major-General C. E. N. Lomax and his 26th Division headquarters. Lieutenant-General Slim, commander of XV Indian Corps, whose duties during the past seven months had been to suppress the vicious insurgency campaign in Bengal led by the Indian Congress Party, which had stated categorically that they would prefer Japanese to British rule, was placed in overall command of the Arakan front on April 5. Slim had been in active command of the British/Indian forces in their 1,000-mile retreat from Burma the previous year and, as was his wont, had learnt much from his victorious, pugnacious enemy, who was trained to expect to fight against all odds. Slim found a most un-

satisfactory state of affairs. Most of the units now under command of the 26th Division had had their morale lowered by abortive attacks on Rathedaung and Donbaik, and then had been eased out of their own defensive positions by the Japanese capacity for manoeuvres, flank attacks, and ability to bring all their weapons and troops, however inferior in numbers, to bear at a decisive point. All units, especially the Indian ones, were frustrated and bewildered and, as the British official history states, "the morale of the troops was generally poor and in some units very low". Time and time again numerically superior Allied forces were beaten by the better trained and led Japanese Army.

Slim ordered Lomax to hold the Maungdaw–"Tunnels"–Buthidaung line. He reinforced Lomax's four brigades (4th, 6th, 55th, and 71st) with the 36th Brigade, bringing the force to a total of 19 battalions including seven British, 11 Indian, and one Gurkha.

Meanwhile, General Koga had eight battalions available for attack. He left one battalion to contain the British

forces on the coastal strip, and one battalion with a mountain artillery regiment ("Miyawaki" Column) to hold his enemy east of the Mayu river. He divided his remaining six battalions, each supported by pack artillery, into "Uno" and "Tanahashi" Columns, and gave them the task of seizing Buthidaung and the Tunnels line and then wheeling left to capture Maungdaw. At this juncture the "Miyawaki" Column, east of the Mayu, would advance due north and capture Taung Bazar. The Japanese started their advance on April 23.

The "Uno" Column met with stubborn resistance at Kanthe, so the "Tanahashi" Column by-passed Kanthe by advancing along the razor-backed Mayu range and seized Point 551 overlooking the Tunnels area of the Maungdaw–Buthidaung Road. Lomax cleverly formed an open box to trap the advancing Japanese between his 4th and 6th Brigades to the west, 55th Brigade to the east, and 71st Brigade to the north, forming the lid. The Japanese, however, launched their northward drive

The disastrous first Arakan campaign between December 1942 and March 1943

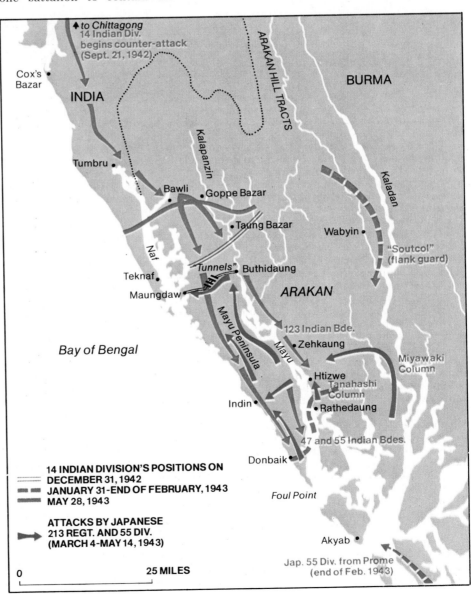

Troops of the Indian National Army.

in earnest on May 2 and, by May 3, the sides of the box had crumbled and the lid had opened "without adequate reason". The plan was a good one, but the training and morale of the British/Indian troops inevitably led to its failure.

As Buthidaung and the Tunnels area fell to the Japanese, Slim, realising how badly his superior forces had once again been defeated in the jungle, wanted to retreat 60 miles back to Cox's Bazar with the intention of luring the Japanese forces into open country where his troops could oppose them on ground more suitable to their training and armament, and at the same time stretch and expose the enemy's communications.

Irwin, however, thwarted this plan and ordered Slim to hold the line Bawli Bazar – Goppe Bazar – Taung Bazar, only 20 miles north of the line Maungdaw – Buthidaung, and gave Lomax a sixth brigade, with orders to prepare a counter-attack to retake Maungdaw by surprise. British operations in the Arakan ended in May 1943 with their forces back on their start-line and the stubborn and mistaken Irwin, who had wished to sack Slim, being sacked himself.

By May 11 General Koga had again won a striking victory over superior forces. The partial failure of the British demolition plan, and the disappearance in panic of all the civilian labour on which the British/Indian forces relied overmuch,

resulted in very large quantities of booty falling into his hands. In view of the depth of the British retreat and the arrival of the monsoon, Koga decided to take up a defensive position on the general line Buthidaung – Maungdaw with five battalions and a regiment of artillery and withdraw the remainder of his division to Akyab for rest and recuperation. In 16 weeks he had caused his enemy to suffer over 5,000 battle casualties.

The news of the British failure in the Arakan, resulting in the loss of Buthidaung and Maungdaw, reached Washington just when the "Trident" Conference, which had been called to decide on future Allied policy in South-East Asia, was taking place. General Wavell, the Indian Army commander, and the commanders in the Arakan all came under most severe criticism. Churchill ordered that new commanders must be found and battalions whose morale had broken should be severely disciplined. If, he said, Indian Army troops were incapable of fighting in the jungle, commando formations should be formed as a prototype and an example to show them how to fight. Answers from India were that the Indian Army had been grossly over-expanded since Pearl Harbor and the best Indian units were in the Middle East, leaving a "second class army" to oppose the Japanese. Jungle fighting required, above all, good infantry but the infantry had also been milked of its best and most intelligent men to form technical corps like the expanded Indian

artillery, previously manned wholly by the British. Indian troops had had their loyalty undermined by subversion from the newly formed Indian Independence League with its Indian National Army fighting alongside the Japanese. British officers drafted into the Indian Army had not had time to learn the language and get to know their men. Reinforcements to replace battle and malarial casualties had arrived piecemeal and many of them half-trained. Some units had been left in the front line for many months without relief. Congress-sponsored riots in August and September 1942, accompanied by maldistribution of food as a result of their depredations and destruction of communications, resulted in widespread famine in which 4 million had died, and this led to a disaffection amongst reinforcements moving though these areas to the battle line, so that they spread subversion amongst the forward troops.

The only optimistic sign for the British seemed to lie in the first Chindit operation, under Lieutenant-Colonel Orde Wingate. Wingate had come to Burma in February 1942, on Wavell's request, and had outlined a scheme for "Long Range Penetration Groups" to operate behind Japanese lines, and to be supplied from the air. The 77th Indian Brigade was designated for this task, and after a period of intensive training, crossed the Chindwin river on February 14, 1943 in two groups. By mid-March, these had crossed the Irrawady, 100 miles further east, but they then met stiff Japanese opposition, and were forced to withdraw. Their losses were heavy – about one third of those involved – and the practical results of their ambushes and attacks on communications were slight. But the very fact that the Chindits had operated for so long behind Japanese lines was a great boost to British and Indian morale.

Meanwhile, high command was restructured. Wavell was promoted Viceroy of India to look after the civil side and to see that the population would support its armed forces. General Sir Claude Auchinleck was recalled from the Middle East to be C.-in-C. India and to make the Indian sub-continent into an efficient administrative and training base from which the fighting forces could draw their strength. He eventually created a self-confident new model Indian Army which became one of the best in the world by 1945.

Lord Louis Mountbatten, who had previously been head of Combined Operations in Britain, was now appointed Allied Supreme Commander, South-East Asia Command with his headquarters in Ceylon. Under him was a new 11th Army Group (General Sir George Giffard), and under Giffard a new 14th Army (Lt.-General Slim) responsible for operations in Burma. Additionally XV Corps, under Lieutenant-General A.F.P. Christison, operating in the Arakan, came under Slim's command.

Brigades were to be formed of one British, one Indian, and one Gurkha battalion. Much more reliance was to be placed on the redoubtable Gurkhas, who had been represented by only one battalion in the Arakan débâcle.

After the first Chindit operation had proved the reliability of air supply, this form of support would be developed and taught to all units so that they need never retreat or disintegrate if the Japanese got behind them.

The R.A.F. was persuaded to co-operate more fully in developing more reliable and accurate close air support for the army involving more intimate mutual signal arrangements and co-operation so that aircraft could take the place of artillery where necessary in the deep jungle.

All ranks were given more jungle, river, and night training so that they could feel that these features were on their side and not against them.

Rations and methods of cooking in the forward areas were improved so that detachments could fend for themselves for many weeks, and special rations were issued during training to build up men before operations so that they were capable of enduring long periods of duress.

Malaria, which was causing a hundred times more casualties than bullets or shells, was tackled by mepacrine, strict anti-malarial measures, and forward malarial treatment centres so that men needing treatment were not evacuated to base areas but remained in the line as a reserve to protect communications. This reform was one of the most effective means of ensuring that battalions in the line maintained their strength.

An illustration of the disproportionate losses from diseases is the British XXXIII Corps' casualty figures for June to November 1944, which were typical of all formations in this theatre:
Battle casualties   3,289
Sickness   47,089 (including 20,430 malaria cases).

These remedial actions have been emphasised because they were to turn the scales in the Arakan in 1944 when the Japanese for a third time launched their short range penetration forces with again, it must be added, numerically very much inferior forces. Also it must be remembered that if the Japanese had had air superiority and as good air support, air supply, and intercommunication as the British were to enjoy the outcome might have been very different.

XV Corps in November 1943 consisted of the 5th and 7th Indian Divisions with 81st West African Division (less one brigade) in the Kaladan. No. 224 Group, with headquarters at Chittagong, consisted of 14 fighter and fighter-bomber squadrons made up of Hurricanes, Spitfires, Beaufighters, and Vengeances, totalling 200 aircraft. At call were the U.S.A.A.F. and R.A.F. Strategic Air Force and Brigadier-General W. D. Old's U.S.A.A.F. and R.A.F. Troop Carrier Command. During this phase of the Arakan fighting, XV Corps was reinforced by No. 3 Special Service Brigade (two, later four, commandos), 25th and 26th Indian, and British 36th Divisions,

making a total of 6½ divisions.

A large engineer contingent was employed in improving communications and building airfields, whilst flotillas of small boats from the Royal Navy, the Royal Engineers, and the Service Corps supplemented the supply lines.

Opposing this formidable force was the Japanese 55th Division (Lieutenant-General T. Hanaya) and a depleted 5th Air Division (maximum 80 aircraft) which was responsible for the defence of all Burma. The 54th Division was moving to protect the coast-line south of Akyab but took no part in the Arakan operation. Hanaya's fragile communications were by track across the Arakan Yomas to Pakokku on the Irrawaddy and from Prome by track to Taungup and thence by launch to Akyab.

During the post-monsoon months of 1943 Christison had advanced his forces methodically down the Mayu peninsula so that by mid-January 1944 he was poised to attack the heavily-fortified Japanese Maungdaw-Buthidaung line.

Meanwhile the Japanese high command, realising from the exploits of the Chindits in the previous year that neither the jungles nor the hills of Burma were impassable to determined troops, and seeing the British forces in Assam hanging down on a 300-mile-long stalk from the main stem on the Brahmaputra like a bunch of grapes ripe for plucking, had decided that the best means for the defence of Burma was attack. Their main plan for 1944 was to attack west over the Chindwin hills, to cut the lines of communication of IV Corps at Imphal and destroy the Allied forces in that area. As a diversion to draw away as many divisions as possible over the other side of the Arakan Yomas they would first use penetration tactics to attack and destroy the Allied forces in the Arakan. This was named the "HA-GO" offensive and was planned to start on February 3.

By that date the 5th Division, supported by tanks, was attacking the Japanese in the Tunnels area with three brigades up; the 7th Division in the Mayu valley was attacking Buthidaung, and the 81st West African Division was far away on the Kaladan river, where it achieved very little effect on the campaign apart from being a drain on the Allied air supply resources. Also behind these forward divisions were the 26th and 36th Divisions.

Hanaya divided his division into four. Two battalions would hold Akyab. One battalion could guard the coast of the Mayu peninsula. Two battalions ("Doi" Column) could hold the redoubts between the Mayu river and the sea which was being attacked by the six brigades (with tanks) of the 5th and 7th Divisions. He entrusted his reconnaissance regiment to screen off the West Africans in the Kaladan valley. This left Hanaya five battalions and an engineer regiment (about 5,000 strong) for his penetration force under Major-General T. Sakurai. The

rôle of the "Sakurai" Column was to pass straight through the 7th Indian Division on the night of February 3–4, seize Taung Bazar, turn left, cross the Mayu river, and cut the communications of both the 5th and 7th Divisions. Meanwhile, the "Doi" Column, manning the redoubts, would attack from the south.

All at first went well for the "Sakurai" Column. Sixteen abreast they strode along the flat paddy fields, through the heart of the 7th Division at midnight and occupied Taung Bazar 12 miles away by morning. Within an hour one battalion had crossed the Mayu river in captured boats. By noon on February 5 the whole force was behind the 5th Division and one detachment had seized Briasco Bridge on the coast road whilst the remainder overran the 5th Division's headquarters and started attacking the Administrative Area, at Sinzweya.

Here Slim's new training instructions and orders started to take effect. The Administrative Area, the capture of which the Japanese depended on for their supplies, closed up like a box. All brigades stood firm. Air supply was made available to the two forward divisions. They fought on, improvising where necessary. Giffard ordered the 36th Division to move south from Chittagong. Hanaya reinforced "Doi" Column and urged it to attack north all the harder to help Sakurai. The 7th Division cut Sakurai's tenuous lines of communication running through the area. Sakurai's code book with wireless frequencies was captured and with it his signals communication list of call signs with the result that his powers of command and control of the battles started to fail. The Administrative Box held out, all

An Allied sniper patrol moves up through the jungle.

General William Slim. His careful planning was the cornerstone of British success in Burma.

"*HA-GO*" offensive was carried out by about eight battalions totalling not more than 8,000 troops. Twenty-seven Indian, 18 British, seven West African, and five Gurkha battalions, accompanied by a total of 26 regiments of artillery, were brought against them. It was no fault of the Japanese soldiers that, owing to Allied technical superiority, many of these battalions and regiments could be and were quickly switched by air to the Imphal front to restore the situation there.

Meanwhile, during the "*HA-GO*" offensive, the Japanese 28th Army had relieved Hanaya of responsibility for the Kaladan front and had on February 18 formed the "Koba" Force, under Colonel T. Koba, which consisted of a regimental head-quarters, the 55th Reconnaissance Regiment, plus the equivalent of three infantry battalions, to face Major-General C. G. Woolner's 81st West African Division. Woolner underestimated the Japanese strength. Koba, by manoeuvre, ambush, and outflanking movement, but never by frontal attack, drove the West Africans 40 miles back from Kyauktaw and started to ooze them out of the Kaladan valley.

The attack on Imphal had now started, and Giffard wanted to transfer the 5th and 7th Divisions by air to that front as soon as possible. He allowed Christison time for the 7th Division to capture Buthidaung and 5th Division Razabil, before they were relieved by the 26th Indian and British 36th Divisions on March 22. The 25th Indian Division was also moved forward and relieved the 36th Division, which was to come under General Stilwell's command in north Burma to relieve the Chindits. Hanaya ordered all his forward units to attack and harass the British forces from all directions and to give an impression of strength during the next four weeks, so as to hold the British in the area before he withdrew to monsoon positions. By using false identity badges and other deception methods, he made British Intelligence believe that the 54th Division had moved into the area. Koga, in the Kaladan, followed suit so successfully that the West Africans were thrown right out of the Kaladan valley and ceased to be a threat to the Japanese flank. Christison's forces, however, obtained possession of Maungdaw and the much fought over Point 551, which he thought would be a good starting line for the post-monsoon offensive.

But Giffard realised that the Arakan was a bad area in which to fight the Japanese. Having inflicted over 3,500 casualties on the British in the "*HA-GO*" offensive, the Japanese had caused a further 3,360 casualties in the period before the monsoon, and this excludes casualties from sickness, which were always high. So Giffard, on July 14, 1944, recommended that any idea of an offensive in Arakan in the dry season of 1944-45 should be abandoned. Yet the Arakan had, in its own way, been the scene of a true British victory—for the myth of Japanese invincibility had now been destroyed.

ranks of whatever arm taking part in its defence.

Christison at one point wavered, believing his 7th Division overrun, and ordered the 5th Division to move back across the Mayu range. But the more experienced Slim countermanded this order and exhorted the 26th and 36th Divisions to hasten forward to destroy the Japanese penetration forces. As long as the "Admin. Box" at Sinzweya held out, the Japanese could get no supplies and their offensive was doomed. It held from February 6 to 24, when the Ngakyedauk Pass was reopened.

The Japanese put their whole air strength into the battle and flew 350 bomber sorties. But the R.A.F. counter-attacked and, although losing some transport aircraft shot down, Troop Carrier Command succeeded in delivering 2,710 tons of supplies to the Sinzweya box and the two forward divisions.

On February 24, with the approval of his army headquarters, Hanaya abandoned the "*HA-GO*" offensive. This was the end. The Japanese withdrew uneventfully. XV Corps had suffered 3,506 casualties but had held its ground, thus giving a tremendous fillip to morale throughout the army in India, an event of which the political, psychological, and propaganda sections made the maximum use.

But the Japanese in the Arakan had achieved the object given to them. One Japanese division had thrown two divisions into temporary disarray, and tied down a total 6½ divisions. The actual

CHAPTER 76

The Imphal and Kohima battles

The so-called "March on Delhi", the Japanese offensive against the British IV Corps on the Tiddim-Imphal-Kohima front which started rolling when Lieutenant-General G. Yanagida's 33rd Division crossed the Chindwin in force on the night of March 7-8, was the brainchild of Lieutenant-General Renya Mutaguchi, aged 55.

To the Japanese it was known as the "U-GO" offensive and its limited objectives was to forestall a British offensive by attacking and destroying the British base at Imphal, thus strengthening the Japanese defence of Burma.

A subsidiary objective was, with the use of the Indian National Army division raised and commanded by the plausible and resourceful Subhas Chandra Bhose, to "exercise political control over India". This was to be achieved by encouraging and supporting dissident anti-British elements, who had in the previous year created a most serious situation in Bengal and Bihar by their widespread sabotage of bridges, communications, and airfields. As it happened Chandra Bhose stayed comfortably in Rangoon and the I.N.A. division, which had the strength of only a brigade (totalling about 7,000 men), had little effect on either the battle or the political situation.

The date of the "U-GO" offensive was timed to phase in with the successful outcome of Major-General T. Sakurai's "HA-GO" offensive in the Arakan. The latter's purpose was to draw off the Allied reserve divisions to the Arakan prior to Mutaguchi's attack on Imphal. This task Sakurai's 55th Division had successfully achieved for, by the end of February 1944, six divisions (5th, 7th, 25th, 26th, 36th, and 81st West African), a parachute brigade, and a special service (commando) brigade, had been drawn into that theatre. This concentration, coupled with the extensive use of air supply, had certainly foiled Sakurai's raid after three weeks of hard fighting. But Mutaguchi should have crossed the Chindwin in mid-February as planned in order to take the maximum advantage of Sakurai's feint.

Unfortunately Lieutenant-General M. Yamauchi's 15th Division, which Mutaguchi intended to use for the direct assault on Imphal, had become stuck in Siam. It was not until February 11, after Mutaguchi himself had signalled Field-Marshal Count Terauchi, commander of the Southern Army at Singapore, that the 15th Division started to concentrate in Burma, arriving ill-equipped, ill-fed, and ill-tempered.

This division had been training in northern Siam and some of its units had been improving the Chiengmai–Toungoo road as an alternative route to the much bombed Burma–Siam railway. Assisted by ten motor transport companies, it had marched the 700-mile long road from Chiengmai to Shwebo via Kentung and Mandalay in order to toughen itself up and prepare itself for its task ahead.

D-day for the "U-GO" offensive was fixed for March 15, by which time the 15th Division must not only be re-equipped but have moved to its start line between Paungbyin and Sittaung on the Chindwin, as well as organising its communications forward from Indaw and Wuntho on the railway via Pinlebu.

The other two divisions in Mutaguchi's 15th Army were in a much better state. The 33rd Division had operated for many years in China and had taken part from the start in the conquest of Burma as well as combatting the first Chindit operation in 1943. This division, advancing initially along comparatively good roads, would carry with it all the armour and heavy artillery (4th Tank Regiment, 1st Anti-Tank Battalion, 3rd and 18th Heavy Field Artillery Regiments) that the Japanese could muster for this attack.

The 31st Division (Lieutenant-General K. Sato), whose task was the unenviable one of advancing from Homalin and Tamanthi on the upper reaches of the Chindwin river, and then over a series of parallel ridges (reaching a height of over 7,000 feet) to Jessami and Kohima, had previously operated only in China, although some of its units had been stationed on islands in the Pacific. It had arrived in Burma between June and September 1943 and had immediately been sent to the Chindwin front, where it had crossed swords with the battle-experienced 20th Indian Division (Major-General D.D. Gracey). The 31st Division had had, therefore, plenty of time to get inured to the conditions in that area. It would operate on a mule and horse transport basis, trusting on a tenuous 100-mile long line of communications from Mawlu and Indaw on the railway to Tamanthi and Homalin, supported by a three-week reserve of food, ammunition, and fodder built up on the line of the Chindwin.

Mutaguchi, "the victor of Singapore", had previously commanded the 18th Division in north Burma and had been most impressed by the activities of the Chindits and their leader, Brigadier Wingate, whom he held in high regard. Mutaguchi had, with some difficulty, sold his plan to knock out IV Corps by a three-pronged, three-divisional thrust against the 200-mile road leading down from the Brahmaputra valley parallel to the Chindwin. Prime Minister Tojo and Count Terauchi agreed to this gamble only because they needed some offensive success to offset the disasters which had been occurring in the Pacific. They then agreed only with the proviso that it should be combined with an attempt to start widespread insurrection in East India with the co-operation of Subhas Chandra Bhose's Indian National Army, on which they placed great hopes of success.

Lieutenant-General M. Kawabe, commanding the Burma Area Army, was sceptical of the whole plan and had orders to prevent Mutaguchi from over-reaching himself. Lieutenant-General Tazoe, commanding the 5th Air Division, had no faith in Mutaguchi's plan whatsoever. He was apprehensive of what the Allied airborne forces (the Chindits) would do, a force that his reconnaissance aircraft had shown were ready to be sent in again. He pointed out to Mutaguchi that he would be totally incapable of helping him with air supply once he had crossed the Chindwin.

Mutaguchi's plan was for the 33rd Division, with the bulk of his armour and artillery, to advance from its bridgehead at Kalewa and to attack and surround the 17th Indian Division (Major-General D.T. Cowan) at Tiddim and Tongzang. Leaving a small containing force, the 33rd Division would push forward with all speed northwards to the Imphal plain, where it would also cut the Bishenpur Track running west to Silchar. One regiment, under Major-General T. Yamamoto, would meanwhile advance north from Kalemyo up the Kabaw valley and open a road through to support the 15th Division, bringing most of the wheeled and track vehicles with it.

The 33rd Division would start its advance one week before D-day, when the 15th and 31st Divisions would cross the Chindwin.

The 15th Division's task was to cross the Chindwin near Thaungdut and advance on tracks via Ukhrul to cut the Dimapur road north of Imphal near Kanglatongbi. It would also detail one column to contain the 20th Division (Gracey) east of Palel. With the 33rd Division, its final objective was to overrun the rich Imphal plain, destroy IV Corps, and capture the airfields and a vast quantity of supplies.

The 31st Division had the more arduous task of advancing 70 to 100 miles along footpaths from the riverine villages of Tamanthi and Homalin, through the Naga Hills, and over a series of bare mountain ranges to capture Kohima, a small, obscure village and staging post on a 4,000-foot pass on the Dimapur–Imphal road. Whether it would exploit its success from there by attacking the undefended railhead at Dimapur depended on circumstances.

Mutaguchi hoped that the whole operation would be resolved within three weeks, by which time he also hoped to have road communications functioning from Kalewa via Palel to Imphal and north to Kohima.

The command set-up in Burma as far as 14th Army was concerned was rather top heavy. The Supreme Commander, Lord Louis Mountbatten, gave his orders to General Giffard, commanding 11th Army Group, who commanded only one army,

A rifleman and Bren gunner of the 1st Punjab Regiment in action.

Lieutenant-General Slim's 14th Army. 14th Army initially had under command XV Corps (Lieutenant-General A.F.P. Christison) in the Arakan, IV Corps (Lieutenant-General G.A.P. Scoones), the Northern Combat Area Command (Lieutenant-General J.W. Stilwell), and Special Force (Major-General O.C. Wingate). Later XXXIII Corps (Lieutenant-General M.G.N. Stopford) was formed in the Bramhaputra valley to counter the Japanese advance, and XV Corps came under the direct command of General Sir George Giffard's 11th Army Group.

Slim had not been deceived by the violence of Sakurai's Arakan attack and his countering the threat by flying-in overwhelming numbers, coupled with his strict orders that all units should stand firm if their communications were cut and await supply by air, had converted what might have been a disaster in the Arakan to a morale-raising victory.

Slim realised from Intelligence reports that IV Corps might suffer similar long-range penetration attacks, but he thought that these could not be in a strength greater than two regiments. He made his plans accordingly. On the night of March 5-6 he allowed the Chindit airborne operation to start its fly-in across the Chindwin to block the Japanese communications facing General Stilwell's forces (N.C.A.C.), in accordance with the orders of the Combined Chiefs-of-Staff.

IV Corps consisted of three divisions (17th, 20th, and 23rd) and the 254th Indian Tank Brigade (with Shermans and Grants). The 17th Division, after its retreat from Burma in 1942, had stayed for two years patrolling in the 7,000-foot Tiddim Hills, 100 miles south of Imphal. This light division consisted of two, mainly Gurkha, brigades on a mule/jeep transport basis.

The 20th Division was based on Palel and Tamu south-east of Imphal and patrolled towards the Chindwin.

The 23rd Division (Major-General O.L. Roberts) was in reserve at Imphal.

Lieutenant-General Scoones, who had commanded IV Corps since its formation, was a clever, quiet, forceful personality who achieved results through efficiency and attention to detail rather than by flamboyant leadership. With him his subordinates would know that everything would be in its place and up to strength.

Scoone's plan, which had been approved by Slim, was, on being attacked, to withdraw his two forward divisions back to the wide open Imphal plain, where he would be able to bring to bear his superiority in tanks heavy artillery, and close air support, which could outgun and destroy anything that the Japanese could bring over the hills and across the Chindwin against them. He would then have three divisions, with a promise of a fourth to be flown in, to combat the Japanese raid. The vital factor in his plan was when to give the order for the 17th Division to start its 100-mile retirement back from Tiddim to Imphal.

Slim planned to fly in the 5th Indian Division (Major-General H.R. Briggs) from the Arakan as soon as news of an attack in strength was confirmed. The 50th Parachute Brigade (Brigadier M.R.J. Hope-Thompson) was due to be flown into Imphal and directed towards Ukhrul. Scoones planned to fly out all unnecessary administrative personnel and the very large number of engineers and their civilian working force who were engaged on improving communications and airfields within the Imphal area. In fact over 40,000 "unwanted mouths" were flown out as the battle progressed.

IV Corps consisted eventually of the 5th, 17th, 20th, and 23rd Indian Divisions, the 50th Indian Parachute Brigade, and the 254th Indian Tank Brigade (Shermans and Grants), comprising 49 infantry battalions (nine British, 24 Indian, and 16 Gurkha), and 120 tanks. Besides this, IV Corps had the 8th Medium Regiment, Royal Artillery, with 5.5-inch guns, as well as the usual complement of divisional artillery and engineers. In all there were about 120,000 men, excluding constructional engineers and Royal Air Force.

The strength of the Japanese 15th Army which crossed the Chindwin was 84,280 Japanese and 7,000 Indians. A further 4,000 reinforcements arrived during operations. The Japanese divided each division into three columns of varying size and composition, according to their tasks, but the total number of units which can be compared with those of IV Corps were as follows: nine infantry regiments, totalling 26 battalions (one battalion of the 15th Division had been sent back to deal with the landing of the airborne forces, but was later returned to the 15th Division during its attack on Imphal); two heavy artillery regiments; and one tank regiment.

Besides these there were divisional artillery, with much of it on a light mountain pack basis, and three engineer regiments, which were often used as infantry.

The British XXXIII Corps at its maximum strength consisted of two divisions (British 2nd and 7th Indian, under Major-Generals J.M.L. Grover and F.W. Messervy respectively), the 149th Regiment, Royal Armoured Corps, the 23rd (L.R.P.) Brigade (Brigadier L.E.C.M. Perowne), the 3rd Special Service (Commando) Brigade (Brigadier W.I. Nonweiler), and the Lushai Brigade (Brigadier P.C. Marindin), totalling about 75,000 troops, including 34 infantry battalions (20 British, 11 Indian, and three Gurkha).

Yanagida started his advance to attack on the night of March 7-8. The 215th Regiment went up the high mountains to Fort White and crossed the Manipur river to get into a position west of the 17th Indian Division's position at Tiddim and Tongzang.

The 214th Regiment marched northwest and advanced directly on Tongzang. Both regiments formed blocks across the Tiddim–Imphal road. Cowan, commanding the 17th Indian Division, had not told his brigadiers that there were plans for withdrawal, so on March 13, when he got

Scoones's order to withdraw, his brigades had to have time to see that the orders reached every man. This meant a 24-hour delay. This particular division, consisting of a preponderance of Gurkhas, was well trained and had great confidence in itself and its quiet commander. Withdrawal continued according to plan and at each road-block the Gurkhas put into operation plans they had rehearsed and the Japanese blocks were removed without great difficulty, but with considerable loss to the Japanese.

However, Scoones was apprehensive of how successfully the 17th Division would be able to carry out this 100-mile long withdrawal on a road through high hills and where there were ambush positions every few hundred yards. So he committed some of his reserve division, the 23rd, which he had moved to Torbung. The 37th and 49th Brigades, with a squadron of tanks, were moved forward to Milestone 100.

Yanagida pressed on, but his troops were losing their momentum and after the fourth block across the road had been successfully removed by the British forces, Yanagida became depressed. On the night of March 23, after receiving many casualties, Yanagida sent a rather panicky signal to Mutaguchi implying that his position was hopeless. Yanagida had been appalled at the success of the Sherman and Grant medium tanks, against which neither his artillery nor his anti-tank guns seemed to have any affect.

After an exchange of furious signals Mutaguchi decided to remove Yanagida and sent for a successor. It must be emphasised that this took place at the beginning of the campaign and affected the command and consequently the morale of the division on which the success of the whole operation depended.

Major-General Yamamoto's column which, it will be remembered, had the preponderance of Japanese armour, advanced quickly and surely up the Kabaw valley until by March 11 it had reached a position at Maw on the right flank of Gracey's 20th Indian Division. Gracey had taken his brigade commanders into his confidence about what action the division would take when Scoones gave the order to withdraw. So his brigades knew exactly what to do when he ordered them to destroy unnecessary stores, disengage, move back, and reform on the Shenam Heights just east of Palel. This withdrawal took place in good order and without a hitch, but was followed up by Yamamoto. Heavy fighting soon took place on the Palel road at a point that became known as Nippon Hill.

Moving further north, Yamauchi's 15th Division crossed the Chindwin on the night of March 15-16 and moved quickly up the hills towards Ukhrul. According to plan he also sent a detachment to make contact with Yamamoto's column on the Palel Road. By March 21 Yamamoto was in contact with the 50th Parachute Brigade at Ukhrul, where it had taken over from the 23rd Division's 49th Brigade,

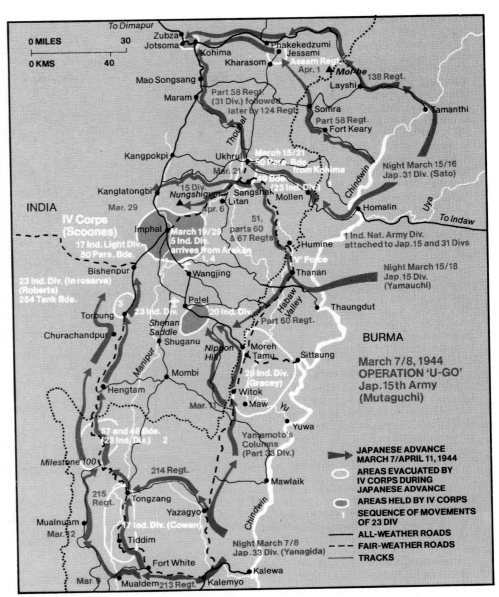

The Japanese 15th Army's advance.

which in turn had been moved to assist the 17th Division. All this time it must be remembered that Mutaguchi was in May-myo, 200 miles to the east, the pleasant hill station in which he had set up his headquarters. It was from this viewpoint that he sent signals exhorting his three divisional commanders to greater effort.

The 15th Division's orders were to by-pass Ukhrul and move towards the hills north of the Imphal plain to seize Kanglatongbi.

Further north still, Sato's 31st Division which, having been in the area for many months, had had time to reconnoitre the routes over the hills, and done remarkably well. Crossing the Chindwin between Homalin and Tamanthi on the night of March 15-16, his left-hand column reached Ukhrul, where it made contact with Yamauchi's forces. Whilst Yamauchi pushed on, Sato's left-hand column, under the command of Major-General Shigesburo Miyazaki, made contact with the Indian Parachute Brigade at Sangshak near Ukhrul. After pushing out the paratroops, Miyazaki advanced north-west and set up a road block at Maram on March 27, a few miles south of Kohima.

Meanwhile Sato's 58th and 124th Regiments advanced on Jessami. Jessami was weakly held by the Assam Regiment and was captured on April 1.

Kohima itself had originally been defended by Brigadier D.F.W. Warren's 161st Brigade of the 5th Division, which had been flown up from the Arakan to Dimapur. When Lieutenant-General Stopford took command of the area with his XXXIII Corps, he unfortunately withdrew Brigadier Warren from Kohima to protect Dimapur itself, where there were 60,000 unarmed rear echelon troops looking after the stores and administration. This move left Kohima virtually unprotected. Sato continued his advance and by April 15 Kohima itself was invested.

Meanwhile Giffard, commanding the 11th Army Group, had started to move the remainder of the 5th Indian Division from the Arakan into the Imphal plain, and had also given Slim orders that the 7th Indian Division should disengage in the Arakan and be available to be flown up to the Brahmaputra valley to join Stopford's XXXIII Corps. Two brigades of the 5th

Indian Division were quickly flown into Imphal between March 19 and 29, whilst all unnecessary troops were in turn flown out.

Scoones had mapped out a very sensible defence of the Imphal plain. He formed fortresses or "boxes" around each area where there were stores or airfields, and had detailed a commander with staff in charge of that area with a force to defend it. This worked well, but when pressure from the Japanese intensified he had to reduce the size of these areas and give up some of the stores, which then fell into Japanese hands. By this time he had four divisions and the parachute brigade with the formidable 254th Medium Tank Brigade to fight his battle. He also had 27 squadrons of fighters and fighter-bombers at short call to harass and destroy the Japanese, who were better targets now that they were emerging into the open plain. It must also be remembered that on the high ground the hills were bare and Sato's 31st Division suffered heavily from air attack when caught out in the open at Litan during its advance on Kohima.

In the Brahmaputra valley XXXIII Corps, whose nucleus was the 2nd British Division (which had originally been the theatre reserve and had been training for operations in Sumatra or Malaya), was now forming fast. The 2nd Division had too many vehicles for the type of country, but as it advanced it soon learnt how to fight with only one road as its main axis. Stopford, realising his mistake in withdrawing Warren's 161st Brigade, sent them back to the Kohima area, where a tiny garrison of the Royal West Kents and Assam Rifles was holding out gallantly.

It was now five weeks since Sato had crossed the Chindwin, and his supplies were beginning to dry up. As far as his division was concerned, a disaster had occurred when the Chindits had cut his communications back to the railway at Indaw and had blown bridges behind ten transport companies (300 trucks) which were unable to get back from Homalin.

Sato signalled Mutaguchi that he was running out of supplies and was having to eat his mules. He suggested that he should start retiring whilst he still had some pack animals left. Mutaguchi was appalled by this message and sent some extremely rude signals to the conscientious Sato.

Meanwhile, the Chindit 23rd (L.R.P.) Brigade had been put under Stopford's command. He gave it the task of making a wide sweep to the east to get behind the Japanese 31st Division and to advance all the way to Ukhrul. The eight columns of the brigade pushed on along the footpaths over the high ridge with their mule transport and with supply by air. Many small actions were fought and

Japanese Type 97 CHI-HA medium tanks move forward (top). A British Sherman tank of the 19th Lancers advances through the rough country around Kohima (below).

although it was not possible in this country with its many paths to "cut" communications, the force threatened Sato's communications to such an extent that he told Mutaguchi that he must withdraw.

Mutaguchi was going through a bad time. He had replaced Yanagida with Major-General N. Tanaka, who was a tough, resilient, earthy soldier who had fought in north China. Mutaguchi had no luck with the 15th Division either, as the divisional commander, Yamauchi, died of malaria. He was replaced by Lieutenant-General U. Shibata, a man, it was said, "with an ox-like presence".

Mutaguchi was issuing orders of the day appealing to all ranks, saying that the throne of the Emperor depended on them and so on. But this did not move the intelligent and worldly-wise Sato. Mutaguchi sent staff officers to see him, but Sato took no notice of them. On April 30 Sato signalled again, pointing out the hopelessness of his position. These signals continued until on June 1 Sato signalled "Propose retreating from Kohima with rearguard." Mutaguchi replied "Retreat and I will court-marshal you." Sato replied "Do as you please I will bring you down with me." This gives some idea of the division and state of mind of the Japanese force commanders, who were fighting against odds at Kohima and Imphal. Sato was quite adamant as he saw his men staggering back half naked, without ammunition and weapons, and relying on bamboo shoots and roots for their sustenance. He was determined that Mutaguchi should be brought back to Tokyo for court-marshal for basic neglect of administration.

Sato left Miyazaki with 750 of his best and fittest men to form a rearguard south of Kohima, which had now been cleared by the 2nd Division, and re-treated. The rest of his division, all supplies having been stopped by the Chindits, ceased to exist and melted away.

Around Imphal, however, very heavy fighting continued. With their two new divisional commanders, the 15th Division and 33rd Divisions were attacking Scoones from all directions, and it was only as a result of the skill and high morale of his divisions, coupled with the technical superiority of his tanks, the R.A.F., and the 8th Medium Artillery Regiment, that he could keep at bay the fanatical assaults of these Japanese.

From a distance, in London and Washington, it appeared that IV Corps was not making sufficient effort to fight its way out, and some criticism was received on this count, but IV Corps had also to expend and disperse men to protect air-fields and stores against suicide attacks and so was not quite free to launch the strong offensive towards Ukhrul which it had been ordered to make. Both the 20th and 23rd Divisions had been ordered to capture Ukhrul, but both had made little progress.

The 2nd Division continued its advance down the road and on June 22 contact was made between the two corps at Milestone 109, just north of the Imphal plain. Stopford had advanced 70 miles from Kohima but Scoones had fought less than ten miles uphill out of the plain. The monsoon was now in full spate, but Slim ordered the two corps to pursue. This was easier said than done. The Japanese 15th Division, suffering severely from disease and lack of supplies, as the Chindits had cut their communications east to the railway, was in a very bad way. But it managed to hold out at Ukhrul and had prevented the pincer movement which Slim had designed to cut it off.

The 33rd Division, with its new commander, was in better shape and was fighting well on the roads running south to Kalemyo and Kalewa.

The 19th Indian Division had joined the British 2nd Division in its advance south so that the Allied forces had managed to collect the equivalent of nine divisions with overwhelming air superiority against the Japanese three divisions and the I.N.A. brigade. As the monsoon wore on, the Japanese defeat became more complete as a result of disease and lack of supplies. The British have the reputation of not being good in pursuit, and there was undoubtedly a slackening in follow-up, but the British commanders felt that the monsoon was completing their victory. Chandra Bhose's I.N.A. melted away, whilst Sato returned accusing Mutaguchi of negligence and incompetance, stating that his division had received no ammunition or supplies for six weeks. Mutaguchi had on May 15 moved his headquarters to Tamu, and it was only then when he saw the condition of his men and experienced the absolute dominance of the air by the R.A.F. that he realised the extent to which he was being defeated. Of the 88,000 Japanese (including reinforcements) who had crossed the Irrawaddy, 53,505 became casualties, including 30,502 from disease.

British and Indian casualties during the battles of Imphal and Kohima were just under 16,700, of which approximately a quarter were incurred at Kohima. In spite of strict medical and anti-malarial precautions, sickness caused more than 12 times the number of battle casualties, although many of those who went sick could return to their units.

Victory at Kohima/Imphal would probably not have been possible without absolute air superiority, air supply, and close air support.

Deliveries to IV Corps on the Imphal plain between April 18 and June 30 totalled 18,824 tons of stores of all sorts and at least 12,561 personnel. On their return flights the transport aircraft (R.A.F. and U.S.A.A.F.) evacuated 13,000 casualties and 43,000 non-combatants. The total number of reinforcements carried is difficult to calculate, as space was always made available to take in extra men. But 1,540 sorties were flown to move the 5th Division, the 7th Division (33rd and 89th Brigades), and the 4th Brigade of the 2nd Division to the Central Front. The Lushai Brigade and the 23rd Brigade were wholly, and XXXIII Corps was partially, supplied by air during their advance.

Between March 10 and July 30, R.A.F. fighters of the 3rd T.A.F. flew 18,860 sorties and those of the U.S.A.A.F. 10,800 sorties, losing 130 R.A.F. and 40 U.S. A.A.F. aircraft. The majority of these 29,660 sorties flown was for close air support of troops on the ground. During the same period the J.A.A.F. flew 1,750 sorties.

Air power was also crucial in the second Chindit operation, which took place during March and April, 1944. Since May 1943, when the first operation ended, the strength of the Chindits had grown to six brigades, Wingate himself had been promoted to major-general, and a special unit of about 11 squadrons was attached to this force. Wingate intended his troops to establish a set of strongholds behind Japanese lines near Indaw on the Irrawady, as the spearhead of a British advance.

The operation began on March 5, when 62 gliders flew in the first wave of troops, but there were difficulties even on the initial landings, and the Japanese, although surprised, assembled enough men to put great pressure on the Chindits. On March 24, Wingate himself died in a plane crash. His scheme was by then, however, not the success he had hoped – partly because the supporting forces he had considered essential were not all made available. In India, it was felt that the Chindits were not having a decisive effect on Japanese reinforcements moving towards Imphal, and were themselves a drain on resources; and so these well-trained, redoubtable fighters were moved north, to help Stilwell.

After Imphal was relieved on June 22, Slim reformed his forces on that front. IV Corps, with the 17th and 20th Divisions who had been holding the line for two years, was withdrawn to India for a refit. The 50th Parachute Brigade was also withdrawn. Slim moved his own headquarters into Imphal and ordered Stopford's XXXIII Corps to continue the pursuit of the Japanese 33rd Division southwards. XXXIII Corps now consisted of the British 2nd, 5th and 20th Indian, and 11th East African Divisions. Movement through the mountains in the monsoon, coupled with extensive demolitions by the Japanese 33rd Division, slowed the British advance to a snail's pace, so that the Chindwin was not reached or crossed until early December, by which time Northern Combat Area Command's British 36th Division (Festing) had advanced down the railway from Mogaung to within 100 miles north of Mandalay. This "turned" the front of the Japanese facing XXXIII Corps so that the former swung back facing north, with their axis on Kalewa.

Under Slim's tenacious and intelligent leadership, the British had thrown back the Japanese 15th Army, and were now poised to reconquer all Burma.

CHAPTER 77
Victory in Burma

There has been a tendency amongst some historians of the Burma campaign to neglect the Allied fighting forces which operated on either side of their advance and give the impression that it was the 14th Army alone who confronted the Japanese armies when they advanced down from Imphal to Mandalay and Rangoon. This, of course, was not the case and it was the Northern Combat Area Command under Stilwell with his three and then five Chinese divisions, coupled with first the Chindit operations and then the operations of the British 36th Division which first penetrated the plains of north Burma and turned the flank of the Japanese 15th Army facing the 14th Army. The ill-equipped 12 Chinese divisions on the River Salween have been denigrated for their lack of initiative and attacking spirit. But it must be remembered that these particular Chinese divisions each amounted to only a weak British brigade in strength, and from their point of view they were hundreds of miles away in a remote corner of China, facing one of the swiftest and most incalculable rivers in the world, the Salween, while the best armies and technical weapons available were being used to combat the 25 Japanese divisions occupying eastern and central China. Whilst the operations described here were going on, the Japanese, incensed by American air attacks from China on shipping in the South China Sea and as far north as Japan itself, attacked and overran the Chinese provinces of Kwangsi and Hunan, an area about the size of France. It must also be remembered that the objective given to Mountbatten and Stilwell for 1944, to which Stilwell stuck, as he felt that they must govern all his actions, was the capture of Mogaung and Myitkyina and an area south sufficient to protect those two towns, so that a road and petrol pipeline could be opened to China and help keep her in the war. Stilwell had responsibilities to China as well as South-East Asia.

General Giffard had judged that the Arakan coastal terrain was an area in which it was uneconomic to operate and had, therefore, decided to stop any further attempt to advance there. But when Mountbatten, who was still without sufficient landing craft to capture Rangoon, was given permission to conquer Burma from the north, he found that he was faced with a big logistic problem. Once the 14th Army, with its 260,000 troops, crossed the Irrawaddy, their communications to a railhead and air bases in Assam lengthened to such an extent that they became uneconomic. It was, therefore, necessary to capture and develop airfields along the coast of Burma which could be supplied easily by sea, so that Slim's 14th Army could in turn be supplied from there by air. Thus plans were made to expand the port and airfields at Chittagong and to capture Akyab and Ramree Islands, where airfields could be developed.

The 14th Army had started to cross the Chindwin early in December 1944 and Major-General T. W. Rees's 19th Indian Division, which had never been in action before, quickly crossed the formidable Zibyu Taungdan Range and made contact at Wuntho on the railway with Festing's British 36th Division, which was on a two brigade animal transport/jeep basis.

Lieutenant-General Slim at first imagined that the Japanese would hold a line from Kalewa along the Zibyu Taungdan Range, which was immediately in front of his 14th Army. But Rees's rapid advance and link-up with Festing gave him information that the Japanese were not going to hold any area in force east of the Irrawaddy. Slim had made extensive plans for an operation which he had called "Capital", whose objective was to capture the area west of the Irrawaddy. As soon as he realised that the advance of Stilwell's forces had made the Japanese face two ways, Slim made a new plan.

This new plan was called "Extended Capital". It must be realised here that each successive plan had not only to be devised and approved by both the 11th Army Group and South-East Asia Command planners in Calcutta and Ceylon respectively, but also had to obtain the agreement of first the Chiefs-of-Staff in London and then the Combined Chiefs-of-Staff in Washington, with the hope that Chiang Kai-shek in Chungking would also agree. This complicated planning procedure, although it was necessary to ensure that men, stores, weapons, and equipment were made available and that there would be some co-ordination between the four Supreme Commanders, Mountbatten, Chiang Kai-shek, Mac-Arthur, and Nimitz, fighting the Japanese war, both tended to delay operations and often failed to catch up with events. So Slim carried on ahead of approval.

"Extended Capital", in brief, entailed a fairly direct advance by Lieutenant-General M. G. N. Stopford's XXXIII Corps from Kalewa via Yeu and Monywa onto Mandalay, but included a left-hook with Rees's 19th Division crossing the Irrawaddy and advancing down the left bank on to the town of Mandalay itself. In this way XXXIII Corps could keep in touch with Stilwell's N.C.A.C.

The second and most important part of "Extended Capital" was for IV Corps (Lieutenant-General F. W. Messervy) to move due south down the Gangaw valley towards Pauk and Pakokku below the confluence of the Chindwin and Irrawaddy, cross the Irrawaddy, and advance due east on to the rail, road, and air communications centre of Meiktila. This change of plan meant some swapping of divisions between XXXIII Corps and IV Corps, but this was quickly done on paper.

The 14th Army would now, during the fine weather, be debouching into the dry zone of Burma where the "going" was good for armour and the air forces had good visibility for ground attack on troops and their communications.

A 1,150-foot Bailey bridge was built over the Chindwin at Kalewa and XXXIII Corps, consisting of the British 2nd Division, the 20th Indian Division, the 254th Indian Tank Brigade, and the 268th Indian Infantry Brigade, advanced with deliberation towards Yeu and Shwebo in the north and Monywa and Myinmu in the south, with the 19th Division, also under command, crossing the Irrawaddy and causing the initial threat to Mandalay.

IV Corps under Messervy decided to make the 28th East African Brigade and the locally recruited "Lushai" Brigade be the vanguard of his corps down the Gangaw valley, with a cover plan that they were another Chindit-type penetration force moving around the Japanese flanks. Behind them would move the hard-hitting 7th and 17th Indian Divisions and the 255th Indian Tank Brigade.

By February 1, 1944, XXXIII Corps was on the right bank of the Irrawaddy. By February 13, IV Corps was reaching its jumping-off positions along the Irrawaddy, south of Myinmu. Meanwhile it would be opportune to review how the Japanese saw the situation and how the operations taking place on both flanks of the 14th Army affected their advance.

After the failure of the "HA-GO" offensive, some changes were made in the Japanese command. Lieutenant-General H. Kimura replaced M. Kawabe as commander of the Burma Area Army. Lieutenant-General S. Katamura took over command of the 15th Army from R. Mutaguchi, who was sent home in disgrace but, in spite of Sato's threat, not courtmartialled.

Kimura's orders were to cover the strategic areas of Burma as his main job, but, without prejudice to this task, to try to interrupt if possible Allied communications with China. He still had three armies under command and, with the arrival of the 49th Division from Korea, these numbered a total of ten divisions and two independent mixed brigades. But these figures give no indication of the real strength of his force. For instance, the four divisions making up the 15th Army, which had been largely destroyed in north Burma and Imphal, now numbered only 21,400 men. This total was split up between the 53rd Division from Mogaung (4,500), 31st Division (7,000), 33rd Division (5,400), and 15th Division (4,500). These numbers included artillery regiments with less than half their complement of guns, and other ancillary units.

Against this 15th Army strength of 21,000 men, plus a few local reinforcements and corps and army troops, Slim's 14th Army of six divisions, two independent brigades, plus the lines of communication troops east of the Chindwin and two tank brigades, totalled a ration strength of 260,000 men. With this overwhelming superiority, tactics were not so important for victory as the logistics of manoeuvring such a force into position when so far away from reliable bases.

On the Northern and Salween fronts, Stilwell's five Chinese divisions (kept efficiently up to strength), the British 36th Division, "Mars" Force, (successors to Merrill's Marauders) and the 12 Chinese divisions in Yunnan, were faced by Lieutenant-General M. Honda's 33rd Army, consisting of the 18th, 56th, and 49th Divisions, and the 24th Independent Mixed Brigade. All these formations, except the 49th Division, were also now very much diminished by earlier operations. The 49th Division was Burma Area Army's reserve, of which one regiment was sent to support the 15th Army on the Irrawaddy and the remaining two regiments were deployed behind the 33rd Army on the Burma Road near Maymyo.

The 2nd Division, which had been guarding the coast of south Burma, had been ordered to move to Indo-China where the Japanese had decided to take over complete control from the French colonial government.

Stilwell's forces at this time consisted of the Chinese New 1st Army (30th and 38th Division), the Chinese New 6th Army (14th, 22nd, and 50th Divisions), the British 36th Division, and the "Mars" Task Force (American 475th Infantry and 124th Cavalry Regiments, Chinese 1st Regiment, and American 612th Field Artillery Regiment (Pack)), totalling about 140,000 troops.

On the coast the Japanese 28th Army

still had the 54th and 55th Divisions (reinforced by the 72nd Independent Mixed Brigade), whose task was to prevent Christison's XV Corps from advancing over the An and Taungup passes to attack the Japanese communications in the Irrawaddy valley in the rear of the Japanese armies facing north. Opposing these two depleted Japanese divisions were the 25th and 26th Indian Divisions, the 81st and 82nd West African Divisions, and an aggressive and efficient 3rd Commando Brigade, comprising Nos. 1, 5, 42, and 44 Commandos. In all, the forces totalled some 120,000 men. Later an East African brigade was added.

The Allied administrative situation was that the 14th Army could still be supplied as far as the Irrawaddy as long as it was not more than the equivalent of seven divisions totalling 260,000 troops, but after that the numbers must be decreased to a strength of about five divisions. In the latter stages air supply must come from the coastal airfields and not from the Imphal and Agatarla fields. As it happened Akyab was occupied on January 2 and Ramree Island was fully occupied by February 22.

The Allies were again in a dominant position in the air at the beginning of January 1945. They had a first-line strength of 48 fighter and bomber squadrons. These consisted of 17 fighter, 12 fighter-bomber, three fighter-reconnaissance, ten heavy bomber, five medium bomber, and one light bomber squadrons. Together these totalled 4,464 R.A.F. and 186 U.S.A.A.F. aircraft.

Air Command had four troop carrier

squadrons and 16 transport squadrons, of which four were R.A.F. and 12 U.S.A.A.F. These were increased to 19 transport squadrons in March and 20 in May, totalling a maximum of 500 transport aircraft. Yet this air transport strength was still insufficient to meet all demands, and the Arakan advance had later to be halted because of the amount of aircraft which had to be diverted to the voracious 14th Army to keep it moving.

Against this air strength the Japanese had a maximum of 66 aircraft, of which only 50 were serviceable by April 1. The Japanese were still using the same type of aircraft as in 1942-3, and their performance could not compare with the modern British and American aircraft of this period.

General Stilwell had agreed to serve under the 11th Army Group, but only with the stipulation that when he captured Kamaing he should come under direct command of the Supreme Commander himself. The result was that Mountbatten had now to deal with two army commanders. In order to regulate this position satisfactorily, Mountbatten asked the Chiefs-of-Staff to appoint a Commander-in-Chief Land Forces South-East Asia who had had experience of having satisfactorily commanded American forces in the field. So, in November 1944, the 11th Army Group was abolished and a new headquarters Allied Land Forces South-East Asia (A.L.F.S.E.A.) was formed to command

The advance to Mandalay and the crossing of the Irrawaddy in 1945.

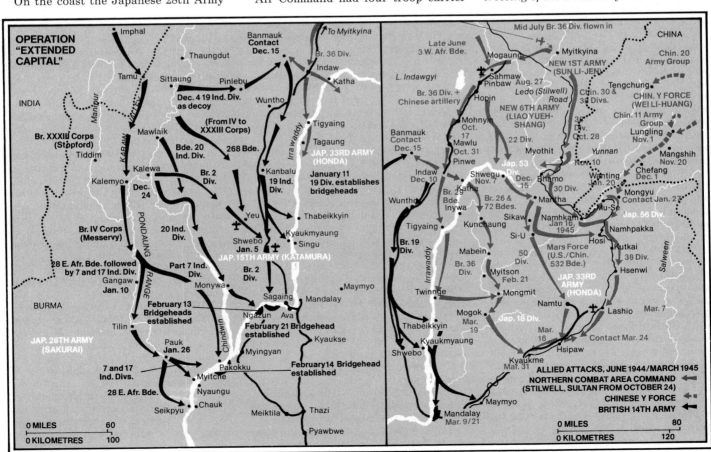

all land operations against the Japanese in Burma. This meant the departure of General Giffard. Lieutenant-General Sir Oliver Leese. who had commanded 8th Army in Italy. was appointed Commander A.L.F.S.E.A.

Shortly afterwards, Christison's XV Corps, which was mainly concerned in combined operations with the navy along the coast, was taken out of Slim's hands and came directly under the command of Leese, who had had much more experience of seaborne operations. At the same time Slim was relieved of the responsibility of his communications back to India so that he could get on with his tactical land battle without having to worry about administrative problems. It was felt that Slim could best serve the Allies by his undoubted great powers of command and example in the field.

Slim's plan was to destroy the Japanese 15th Army between the hammer of Stopford's XXXIII Corps advancing on Mandalay and the armoured anvil of Messervy's IV Corps capturing Meiktila.

This plan depended on the speed and secrecy of Messervy's 150-mile advance west of the Irrawaddy, whilst Stopford held the attention of XV Corps near Mandalay. Ree's 19th Division, to the north of Mandalay, was still the main attraction for the Japanese. Stopford's 20th Division started to cross the Irrawaddy at Myinmu on February 12 at a point about 30 miles downstream from Mandalay. This immediately attracted the Japanese, who counter-attacked the bridgehead for the next two weeks.

Stopford's British 2nd Division had to wait for the boats and pontoon rafts used by the 20th Division before they could start to cross on February 21 at Ngazun at a point 15 miles from Mandalay. Unfortunately, many of the boats and pontoons had been inadvertently damaged by the 20th Division and the 2nd Division had a difficult crossing. However, these assault crossings achieved the desired strategic effect of attracting the full attention of the tiny Japanese 15th Army, so that when Messervy's 7th Division crossed 90 miles further south on February 13, there was little or no opposition. By the end of February Slim's 14th Army had crossed the 1,000-yard wide swift-flowing Irrawaddy in four places with his northern bridgeheads attracting a violent reaction from the Japanese.

Messervy built up his bridgehead at Nyangu before he made his dash to Meiktila. By February 20 Messervy had got his 17th Division and 255th Tank Brigade across the Irrawaddy into his bridgehead at Nyangu, and was ready to start. Meiktila was 80 miles away across sandy scrub country, broken up by dry river beds. On February 21 Messervy's tanks began to roll. At the same time Major-General G. C. Evan's 7th Division, which had carried out the crossing, was ordered to capture the oil town of Chauk and lead on to Myingyan to the north east. Major-General D. T. Cowan's 17th Division, with its tank brigade, reached the

outskirts of Meiktila by the end of February and on March 1, Cowan attacked.

Meiktila fell the following day and its airfield on the eastern edge of the town, which was vital for re-supply and the reinforcement of the defence, was captured on March 3. Cowan did not settle down but immediately sent out fighting patrols of tanks and infantry to seek out and find the enemy.

At this vital juncture Slim flew in with Messervy to visit Cowan and was present to observe a quite severe Japanese counter-attack, in which the British tanks caused many casualties and dispersed the attackers. Two men in the army commander's party were wounded by Japanese artillery fire but Slim, Messervy, and Cowan stood unmoved on the hilltop like Old Testament prophets whilst their men below gained victory.

After a new brigade was flown in Cowan withstood a series of local Japanese counter-attacks. Meanwhile to the north, Stopford, having seen his bridgeheads were secure, made plans for a deliberate advance to capture Mandalay. His plan was that the 19th Division would attack from the north. The 2nd Division would advance through the old capital of Ava along the Irrawaddy from the west and the 20th Division would sweep round the south to attack Mandalay from the south and the south-east. The 19th Division soon penetrated the town but was held up by defences on Mandalay Hill and the battlements of Fort Dufferin. The 2nd Division was delayed amongst the pagodas of Ava, but the 20th Division made good progress around the south where the opposition was negligible.

As soon as Slim realised that Mandalay was not held in strength, he ordered the 20th Division to send a column south towards Meiktila, leaving the British 2nd Division to surround it from the south.

What was left of the 15th Army in Mandalay was destroyed by heavy bomber attacks. Mandalay became a bomb trap. Meiktila had fallen on March 1 and Mandalay fell on March 20.

At this time the Japanese Intelligence had become completely confused and they did not seem to know what was hitting them and from where; a tribute to Slim's offensive plan of attack. The battles for Meiktila and Mandalay were the death knell of the already depleted 15th Army.

In mid-January the Yunnan Armies at last began to advance across the Salween. Namkham and Wamting were soon captured. By January 18 the American "Mars" Force was overlooking the Mandalay-Lashio road at Hsenwi and was carrying out guerrilla raids along it. On January 21 the Ledo Road to China via Bhamo, Namkham, Muse, and Wamting was opened, followed by the first convoy to China, which arrived at Kunming on February 4.

This date, February 4, 1945, can be said, therefore, to be the date of the completion of the "Quadrant" plan. However, Chiang Kai-shek made this the occasion to start to withdraw his Yunnan armies back into

China for the very sensible reason that he wanted now to retake the huge areas of China which the Japanese had recently overrun. This was naturally supported by the Americans, who required these areas for air bases to support their advance towards the invasion of Japan. But some of the more parochial commanders in A.L.F.S.E.A. tended to denigrate the Chinese for marching away from the "battlefields in Burma", perhaps forgetting that the Chinese had been fighting since 1937.

However, Stilwell's forces were still active. By March 1 the Chinese 30th Division had occupied Hsenwi and the British 36th Division was crossing the Shweli at Myitson and Mongmit against the now 3,000-strong 18th Division. The British received 360 casualties during this crossing.

On March 6 the Chinese 38th Division occupied Lashio and by March 24 the Burma Road from Mandalay to Lashio was in Allied hands. The British 36th Division, having captured the ruby mine town of Mogok on March 19, moved to Mandalay when the Northern Combat Area Command ceased to exist.

The American "Mars" Force, the worthy successors of Merrill's Marauders, was moved to China to be dispersed into training cadres to rebuild the Chinese Army along the same lines as Stilwell's Chinese New Armies.

Thus ended the American army involvement in the war in Burma. It can be said with truth that the few representatives of the American army, Merrill's Marauders and "Mars" Force, gave a very good impression by their fighting capabilities and thrustful initiative to their Allies fighting in Burma.

Parts of the Japanese 33rd Army had been moved from the Lashio Road at the end of the Meiktila battle in a vain attempt to save the town. But even with this last-minute reinforcement, the British forces outnumbered their enemy by about ten to one on the ground and about twenty to one in tanks.

IV Corps casualties from the crossing of the Irrawaddy to the end of March were 835 killed, 3,174 wounded, and 90 missing. The high proportion of wounded was because in the Indian Army, anyone who incurred a wound obtained a pension, and so the smallest wounds were noted, whereas in the British units there was no point in worrying about or recording minor wounds. During these battles IV Corps had 26 tanks destroyed and 44 damaged.

XXXIII Corps, in its capture of Mandalay, lost 1,472 killed and 4,933 wounded, with 120 missing. It had one more division than IV Corps and was in action for six weeks before IV Corps had crossed the Irrawaddy, so that the proportion of casualties is comparable.

No. 221 Group (Air Vice-Marshal S. F. Vincent) was in support throughout and flew 4,360 sorties, of which 2,085 were attacks on Japanese positions or their communications, during which 1,560 tons of bombs were dropped.

The 14th Army was now all set for its dash to capture Rangoon and obtain a port before the monsoon, the opposition to its advance being negligible.

The build-up of Allied naval forces resulted in the command of the Indian Ocean and the Bay of Bengal being regained by the Allies by the beginning of 1945. This made possible not only the more rapid reinforcement of India because troopships were able to sail independently without escort, but amphibious operations could now be undertaken along the coast of Burma without fear of heavy losses to submarines, and without the need for powerful naval covering forces.

Lieutenant-General Sir Philip Christison was given two tasks to carry out. When the 14th Army crossed the Irrawaddy in February 1945 their supply lines to Assam had become uneconomic. It was therefore necessary to capture airfields along the coast of Arakan, from which the 14th Army could be re-supplied during its advance to Meiktila and south to Rangoon. Without these airfields and the necessary sea ports to land stores, the 14th Army could not advance south. Fortunately the Japanese, as a result of the pressure of the 81st West African Division east of them, had evacuated Akyab on December 31 so that Christison's XV Corps landed unopposed on January 2. He immediately arranged to re-open the port of Akyab for supplies.

The total strength of the British portion of A.L.F.S.E.A. (that is not including the Americans and Chinese) was, by the beginning of 1945, 971,828 men, including 127,139 British troops, 581,548 Indians, 44,988 East Africans, 59,878 West Africans, and 158,275 civilian labourers. Of these, 260,000 were in the 14th Army, including its line of communications troops.

It was calculated, therefore, that in order to supply the 14th Army as well as XV Corps, whose secondary rôle was to try to contain all Japanese forces (including the 54th Division and remnants of the 55th Division) in the area and to try to prevent their being re-deployed in the Irrawaddy valley, it was necessary to open two new ports. The first was at Akyab, and the second at Kyaukpyu on Ramree Island. From these two ports and from Chittagong the divisions of the 14th Army in central Burma, and the formations of XV Corps operating on the Arakan coast could be maintained if the ports could be built up to a capacity sufficient to handle the necessary sea lift tonnage required.

It was calculated that the port of Akyab would have to maintain 46,000 men, as well as the construction stores required for two all-weather airfields and the tonnage necessary to build up a 20,000-ton reserve for the 14th Army. This would require a maximum sea lift of 850 tons a

Crossing the Irrawady river (above).
Men of the 11th East Africa Division
near Kalewa (below)

Equipped with a tommy gun, one of "Merrill's Marauders".

day in February and March 1945, dropping down to 600 tons in May when the unnecessary formations of XV Corps, having achieved their object, were sent back to India.

In the same manner it was calculated that the port of Kyaukpyu must maintain 36,000 men from February to May and handle stores sufficient to construct two all-weather airfields and build up a stockpile of 22,000 tons for the 14th Army. The daily sealift required would be 450 tons in February, rising to 650 tons from March to May.

Lieutenant-General M. Kawabe had ordered the 28th Army (Lieutenant-General S. Sakurai) to send its 2nd Division, with a large part of the army's motor transport, to the 33rd Army, which as facing the 14th Army, and to hold with his remaining two divisions (54th and 55th) the Irrawaddy delta and the Arakan

coast up to 35 miles north of Kyaukpyu. Later the 2nd Division was to move to Indo-China.

Sakurai was told to hold the offshore islands of Cheduba and Ramree for as long as possible. The removal of the Japanese 2nd Division (on its way to Indo-China), which had previously been responsible for the delta and the remainder of the Burmese coastline further south, meant that Sakurai had to withdraw his 55th Division to protect that area, leaving the 54th Division to face Christison's XV Corps.

Lieutenant-General S. Miyazaki's 54th Division had received orders in December 1944 to protect the rear of the 15th Army in the Irrawaddy valley from any risks of XV Corps cutting their communications between Meiktila and Rangoon. It will be remembered that Miyazaki had carried out the rear guard action of 33rd Division during its wholesale retreat from Kohima brilliantly.

To carry out his orders, Miyazaki had to hold the An and Taungup passes at all coasts. As the 81st and then the 82nd West African Division advanced slowly down the Kaladan, Miyazaki decided that he would use a covering force to delay these two divisions for as long as possible whilst basing his main defence in the north at Kangaw, 40 miles east of Akyab. His other strongpoint would be at Taungup itself. Ten miles west of Kangaw lay the Myebon peninsula.

Before Akyab had fallen Christison had already made plans to land on the Myebon peninsula.

XV Corps consisted of the 25th and 26th Indian Divisions, the 81st and 82nd West African Divisions, and the 3rd Commando Brigade (which was to be increased to four Royal Marine and Army Commandos). Christison now had plenty of landing craft, reinforced with locally constructed craft. Now that the Royal Navy had regained command of the Bay of Bengal and Akyab had fallen, it was possible for XV Corps to advance south. The Myebon peninsula and Ramree Island were held by Japanese outposts covering

the main defences on the mainland.

On January 14, the joint force commanders (Rear-Admiral B. C. S. Martin [Flag Officer Force "W"], Lieutenant-General Christison, and Air Vice-Marshal The Earl of Bandon) decided that the 26th Division would assault Ramree on January 21 and the 25th Division (Major-General C. E. N. Lomax) and 3rd Commando Brigade (Brigadier C. R. Hardy) would occupy the Myebon peninsula and strike east towards Kangaw to cut the Japanese 54th Division's communications to the north.

The 3rd Commando Brigade would spearhead the attack on Myebon with the 74th Brigade passing through.

A reconnaissance of the beaches at Myebon by a special boating party found that a line of coconut stakes had been driven in just below the low-water mark about 300 yards offshore. So before the attack, a Combined Operation Piloted Party (part of the special Small Operations Group) went ashore and attached to these stakes explosives timed to go off at zero hour. The anti-boat stakes were thus blown, tearing a gap 25 yards wide for No. 42 (Royal Marine) Commando to land under cover of a smokescreen laid from the air on the morning of January 12.

The Commandos suffered a few casualties from mines on the beach, but quickly formed a beach-head. The landing was supported by the cruiser *Phoebe*, the destroyer *Napier*, the sloops *Narbada* and *Jumna*, and four minesweepers. Forty-nine landing craft of all types (including three L.C.I., five L.C.T., 12 L.C.M., and 18 L.C.A.) landed the commandos.

The Royal Marines found that the beach was too muddy for tanks, vehicles, and stores to land so the Royal Engineers reconnoitred and constructed a new route, using explosives to smooth out a nearby rocky outcrop on which tanks and vehicles could land.

Shortly afterwards No. 5 Commando landed and passed through No. 42 Commando to widen the beach-head.

Nos. 1 and 44 (Royal Marine) Commandos also inadvertently landed on the same beach and pushed ahead. By this time the tanks belonging to the 19th Lancers were ashore.

The Royal Marines of No. 42 Commando occupied Myebon village on the 13th and the village of Kantha was also captured. At this stage the 74th Brigade (Brigadier J. E. Hirst) took up the advance and overcame the remaining opposition and the Commando Brigade was withdrawn to prepare for the Kangaw operation. By the 17th the whole of the Myebon peninsula was captured.

The 82nd West African Division had relieved 81st Division, which was still in the Kaladan valley. The 82nd Division was now commanded by Major-General H. C. Stockwell, who had previously commanded one of the aggressive British 36th Division's two brigades. Advancing

A Priest 105-mm self-propelled howitzer is manned in a hurry.

south, Stockwell occupied the ancient capital of Arakan, Myohaung, on January 25 and applied pressure on the Japanese facing him. Christison was anxious to cripple the 54th Division by cutting its communications at Kangaw.

The joint force commanders rather over-insured in the force that they used to overcome opposition on Ramree and Cheduba Islands. But at this time of the war it was common policy for the Allies to deploy as much *matériel* strength as possible to save Allied lives if that *matériel* strength could be easily brought to bear without too much delay.

The naval component of this combined operation included the battleship *Queen Elizabeth*, the cruiser *Phoebe*, the destroyers *Rapid* and *Napier*, the Royal Naval sloop *Flamingo*, and the R.I.N. sloop *Kistna*. No. 224 Group supported the attack with its Thunderbolts and Mitchells. Prior to the attack 85 Liberators of the Strategic Air Command bombarded the beaches and its surrounds.

After the naval and air bombardment, the 71st Brigade (Brigadier R. C. Cottrell-Hill), with a squadron of tanks, a regiment of field artillery, and two companies of the Frontier Force machine gun battalion, landed unopposed at 0942 on January 21 west of the town of Kyaukpyu. The leading motor launch and landing craft both struck mines and were blown up, causing some confusion, but the remainder of the landing proceeded without opposition or further delay.

Next day the 4th Brigade (Brigadier J. F. R. Forman) took over the beachhead and the 71st Brigade moved south.

On January 26 the Royal Marine Commandos landed unopposed on the neighbouring Cheduba Island.

By January 31 Lomax had landed the remainder of his 25th Division on Ramree Island. The opposition from the Japanese outposts increased and the Indian brigades, with tanks, slowly and methodically cleared the island until Ramree town itself was occupied on June 9. On this day, under cover of an attack by the remains of the Japanese 5th Air Division, a Japanese destroyer (accompanied by 20 launches) rushed to the rescue of the Japanese and took off over 500 men. By January 17 resistance on the island ended.

The 22nd East African Brigade, which had come under Christison's command, arrived to garrison Ramree and Cheduba Islands so that the 26th Division would be available to land at Toungup.

The fight at Kangaw turned out to be one of the bloodiest and most savage of the Burma campaign. But this fight succeeded in crippling a major part of Miyazaki's 54th Division, which was one of the few divisions in Burma at this time which had not suffered a defeat, was not too depleted, and was still full of fight.

Major-General G. N. Wood's plan for the capture of Kangaw was for the 3rd Commando Brigade (Nos. 1, 5, 42, and 44 Commandos) to seize a bridgehead on the east bank of the Diangbon Chaung two miles south-west of Kangaw. Then his

Men of a Chinese mortar regiment prepare for action.

51st Brigade would pass through the bridgehead and join forces with the 74th Brigade, which was advancing from Kantha across the Min Chaung from the Myebon peninsula. The Japanese would find themselves hemmed in between the two Indian brigades and the West African 82nd Division advancing from the north. Hardy, commanding the 3rd Commando Brigade, wished to go by the indirect route, which he had reconnoitred, and advance up the Diangbon Chaung from the south and not via the Myebon peninsula, although this meant a trip of 27 miles by boat. On January 21, 50 vessels (including the R.I.N. sloop *Narbada*, a minesweeper, a Landing Craft Tank (carrying a bulldozer and R.E. equipment), four L.C.I.s, 22 L.C.A.s, and some "Z" craft carrying artillery, anchored off the southern entrance of the Diangbon Chaung. The "Z" craft were large but manoeuvrable lighters whose decks had been strengthened with steel so that a troop of 25-pounders could fire from them.

The Diangbon Chaung, as Hardy predicted, had not been mined and the Japanese did not see the approach of the attack. The Royal Navy and R.I.N. bombarded the beaches, supported by the medium bombers of No. 224 Group, which also laid a smokescreen. Surprise was complete and No. 1 Commando pushed on to Hill 170 which was to be the scene of heavy fighting. By nightfall No. 5 Commando had landed, with the next day Nos. 44 (R.M.) and 42 (R.M.) Commandos.

The Japanese on the spot counterattacked fiercely and efforts to infiltrate the village of Kangaw were rebuffed. The Japanese heavily bombarded the beaches with field artillery on the 24th and 25th,

but on the 26th the 51st Brigade (Brigadier R. A. Hutton) landed with a troop of medium tanks followed by the 53rd Brigade (Brigadier B. C. H. Gerty).

As soon as he heard of the landing, General Miyazaki ordered Major-General T. Koba, commanding the "Matsu" Detachment, to repel the invaders and keep open the road. Koba, as a colonel, had commanded the two battalion column which had so successfully driven the 81st West African Division out of the Kaladan in March 1944. The "Matsu" Detachment consisted of the 54th Infantry Group, comprising three infantry battalions and an artillery battalion. Koba arrived on January 31 and immediately launched a heavy attack on Hill 170, which was held by Nos. 1 and 42 Royal Marine Commandos, commanded by Colonel Peter Young, Hardy's second in command.

The Commandos, supported by three tanks, repulsed Koga's most determined assaults. Attack and counter-attack waged around Hill 170 for 36 hours. The "Matsu" Detachment finally launched a pole-charge tank hunting party of engineers. They destroyed two tanks and damaged the third with a loss of 70 of their own men killed. By this time the 74th Brigade was moving in from the north-west: but not before the Commandos had killed over 300 Japanese at a loss to themselves of 66 killed, 15 missing, and 259 wounded. Lieutenant Knowland, of No. 1 Commando, won a posthumous Victoria Cross for his part in the fighting.

As soon as Miyazaki heard that Ramree Island had been occupied he feared that the 26th Division might land in his rear, so he ordered the "Matsu" Detachment to break off the engagement and withdraw to the An Pass, which was vital to the 54th Division's communications. By February 18, the 25th Indian Division had relieved the Commando brigade.

Miyazaki had received heavy casualties but had skillfully avoided the destruction of his force.

It will be remembered that during February IV Corps and XXXIII Corps had crossed the Irrawaddy and by March 1 Meiktila had fallen. Also at this time the Chinese were asking for an air lift of their forces in Burma to take part in the offensive to regain the two provinces that they had lost a few months previously. Transport aircraft, therefore, were at a premium and S.E.A.C. decided that air supply to XV Corps must cease.

Lieutenant-General Sir Oliver Leese (C.-in-C. A.L.F.S.E.A.) therefore decided to withdraw the 25th and 26th Divisions to India. The 26th Division was withdrawn to prepare for a landing at Rangoon. The Commandos had already been withdrawn to train for a landing on the coast of Malaya.

It is an opportune time to consider the effects of the Arakan campaign. Strangely enough, both sides achieved their main objects. The Japanese, with their depleted forces, prevented XV Corps from breaking into the Irrawaddy valley although this was never XV Corps' intention. On the other hand XV Corps captured Akyab without a shot being fired and Ramree Island with trifling loss, although again the Japanese never had any intention of defending them strongly. Without doubt Miyazaki had done very well against the equivalent of five divisions (25th and 26th Indian, 81st and 82nd West African, and 22nd East African Brigade and 3rd Commando Brigade), supported by overwhelming numbers of aircraft and naval ships. As so often occurred in this campaign, XV Corps' main enemy was geography and the problem of how to apply their superior forces effectively against a skilful enemy in difficult terrain. However, it is now known that Christison had a greater success than he first realised. Only four battalions of both the Japanese 54th and 55th Divisions arrived in time to assist the 33rd Army in its operations against 14th Army. The result was that the 14th Army had nothing but the remains of divisions which had already been virtually destroyed to oppose it in its advance south.

During these operations XV Corps lost 5,089 casualties, of which 1,138 were killed. No. 224 Group (The Earl of Bandon) lost 78 aircraft, but claimed 63 Japanese aircraft destroyed. Fortunately there had never been any serious opposition to the seaborne landings, but during them the Royal Navy fired 23,000 rounds varying from 4-inch to 15-inch calibre. The Navy had landed in all 54,000 men, 800 animals, 11,000 vehicles, and 14,000 tons of stores.

The final seaborne operation of the Burma war was the assault on Rangoon, which started with an airborne attack on Elephant Point, which covered the entrance of the main navigable arm of the Irrawaddy river leading from the sea to Rangoon itself. The amphibious operation for the capture of Rangoon was launched on April 27, while the 14th Army was held up at Prome and the Pegu river.

Two naval forces set sail to give long range protection to the large convoy during its voyage to the mouth of the Rangoon river and to intercept any fleeing Japanese.

The first, under Vice-Admiral Walker, was directed against the Andaman and Nicobar Islands, covering Rangoon from the west. It consisted of the battleships *Queen Elizabeth* and *Richelieu*, the cruisers *Cumberland*, *Suffolk*, *Ceylon*, and *Tromp*, the escort carriers *Empress* and *Shah*, six destroyers, and two resupply oil tankers. On the morning of April 30, Walker bombarded targets in the Nicobars and in the evening put in airstrikes and naval bombardments on to airfields, docks, and shipping at Port Blair in the Andamans. Before leaving the area on May 7, Walker also attacked Victoria Point and Mergui near to the Malay border and returned for a second strike at Port Blair and the Nicobars.

The second naval force consisted of three destroyers under Commodore A. L. Poland. On the night of April 29-30 Poland intercepted a convoy of small ships carrying about 1,000 men and stores from Rangoon to Moulmein. He sank ten craft and picked up some survivors.

At 0230 hours on May 1 a visual control post was dropped as a marker for a parachute landing. Thirty-eight Dakotas dropped a composite battalion of the 50th Gurkha Parachute Brigade at 0545 hours. There were five minor casualties. A further 32 casualties were caused amongst the Gurkhas when some Liberators, aiming at another target, dropped a stick of bombs on the paratroopers. The Gurkhas overcame a small force of 37 Japanese holding Elephant Point itself. The way was then clear for landing craft carrying the assault troops to advance up the river as soon as any mines had been swept.

Aircraft flying over Rangoon saw the words "Japs gone" and "Extract Digit" painted on the roof of Rangoon Jail. Wing-Commander A. E. Saunders (commanding No. 110 Squadron R.A.F.), seeing this well known R.A.F. slang and seeing no signs of the enemy, landed at Mingaladon Airfield, but unfortunately damaged his Mosquito in the craters on the runway. Saunders, having contacted the British prisoners-of-war in Rangoon Jail and hearing that the Japanese had evacuated Rangoon on April 29, went down to the docks and sailed down the Rangoon River in a motor launch to report that the Japanese had gone. Meanwhile, the brigades of the 26th Division moved up the Rangoon river in landing craft and soon occupied Rangoon. It was a tragedy that Colonel Dick Ward, who had been Commander Royal Engineers of the 17th Indian Division from its retreat from Moulmein in 1942 to India and had fought throughout the campaign, was killed when the landing craft in which he was travelling in the van to occupy Rangoon on May 2, 1945 struck a mine.

The battles for Mandalay and Meiktila were over. The Japanese 15th Army which had attacked Kohima/Imphal, and the 33rd Army had both suffered a major defeat. The 33rd Army had been severely mauled by the Chinese and Stilwell's N.C.A.C. (including the British 36th Division). During their counter-attack to recapture Meiktila, their losses were again heavy. The 18th Division also had suffered 1,773 casualties, which was about one-third of its strength and lost about half of their 45 guns. The 49th Division, which (being fairly new in Burma) started with a total strength of 10,000, suffered 6,500 casualties and lost all but three of its 48 guns. Casualties amongst the other divisions were of a similar order. As the official British history states of this period, the Burma Area Army had virtually ceased to exist as a fighting force. Already, by August 1944, the Southern Army had been told that it could expect no further reinforcements in men or *matériel* from Japan, and the divisions were now living on their own fat.

The 28th Army, which was mainly concerned with defending the coast of Burma, had a small force (72nd Independent Mixed Brigade) in the Mount Popa-Chauk-Yenangyaung area but, as related, only four battalions of the 54th and 55th Divisions facing XV Corps were ever deployed in Central Burma to oppose the 14th Army.

General Leese had ordered Slim to reduce the strength of his army to four and two-thirds divisions, which was the maximum number which could be supplied by air during his drive south. XXXIII Corps (Stopford) was to advance down the Irrawaddy valley from Yenanyaung, via Magwe and Allanmyo to the railhead at Prome and on towards Rangoon if it had not already been captured. IV Corps (Messervy) was to use the main road route to Rangoon via Pyabwe, Pyinmana, Toungoo, and Pegu. Each corps would consist of two motorised infantry divisions and one armoured brigade.

The plan was that each corps would move in bounds one division at a time passing through the other, from airfield to airfield, supplied by air-landed stores at each point. Travelling with the divisions would be a large number of airfield construction engineers. As the left flank of Messervy's IV Corps would be in the air, Mountbatten decided to organise the loyal Karens in the hills flanking his advance into levies to protect his eastern flank. Over 3,000 of these fine guerrilla fighters were recruited, and Messervy had then no reason to worry about any unexpected attack from that direction.

Each corps had a distance of 350 miles to go to its objective. XXXIII Corps consisted of the 7th and 20th Indian Divisions and the 268th Indian Infantry Brigade, plus the 254th Indian Tank Brigade. IV Corps consisted of the 5th and 17th

Indian Divisions and the 255th Indian Tank Brigade. Each corps had its own artillery component which included two medium regiments with XXXIII Corps and one medium regiment with IV Corps. There was a special headquarters Royal Engineer Regiment to control the forward airfield engineers and bridging companies.

A brigade from the 19th Indian Division accompanied IV Corps and garrisoned its communications as it advanced.

Stopford was held up at Pyabwe by the fine defence of the remnants of the famous 18th Division (now only 2,000 strong) which had captured Singapore, had been one of the first divisions to conquer Burma, and had fought for so long on the northern front against Stilwell.

Otherwise there were no hitches except those caused by geography and the weather. Messervy reached Pyinmana on April 19, Toungoo on the 22nd, and Pegu, within 50 miles of Rangoon, on May 1. At Pegu a Japanese improvised brigade, made up of training unit personnel and numbering 1,700 men, delayed his advance. Unseasonable heavy rain on May 2 stopped IV Corps' advance abruptly. However, the engineers managed to clear 500 mines and to throw a bridge across the Pegu river and at 0930 hours on May 4, IV Corps continued its advance. On May 6 the 1/7th Gurkhas, crossing a blown-up bridge at Hlegu, met a column of the Lincolnshire Regiment from the 26th Division, which had advanced northwards from Rangoon.

Meanwhile XXXIII Corps advanced down the Irrawaddy valley. Stopford captured Chauk on April 18 and Magwe and Yenangyaung on April 21, overcoming resistance from the 72nd Independent Mixed Brigade and some battalions from the 28th Army. Allanmyo on the Irrawaddy was captured on April 28 and Stopford entered Prome on May 3. A patrol from XV Corps, advancing from Taungup, contacted him shortly afterwards so that by that date all three corps of Leese's forces were in touch. The Burma victory was now complete.

On June 1, 1945, a 12th Army was formed under command of General Stopford to control operations in Burma, including the maintenance of internal security and the re-establishment of civil government. The 12th Army consisted of IV Corps in the Sittaung valley and the 7th and 20th Indian Divisions and the 268th Brigade in the Irrawaddy valley.

IV Corps consisted of the 5th, 17th, and 19th Indian Divisions, and the 255th Tank Brigade. So with the 7th and 20th Indian Divisions and 268th Brigade, Stopford had five divisions and two brigades under command, with the 26th Division awaiting transport for India. His air support was provided by No. 221 Group R.A.F., but now that the monsoon had broken and flying conditions and visibility was bad, the R.A.F. was not in a position to give good close support to the troops on the ground. Slim, now promoted General, replaced Leese as Commander, Allied Land Forces, South-East Asia,

and on August 16 he took up his post in Kandy, Ceylon.

Stopford's main problem was the Japanese 28th Army which still totalled nearly 30,000 troops, including a multitude of small administrative units.

Sakurai, the army commander, had managed to get the remains of his 54th and 55th Divisions back from the coast and delta over the Irrawaddy and into the Pegu Yomas, a series of jungle-covered hills lying between the Irrawaddy valley on the one hand and the Sittang valley on the other, north of Rangoon. Sakurai's object was to break out and join the remains of the Burma Area Army, which was now regrouping east of the wide flowing and flooded Sittang River. At this time the Sittang was flooded as far north as Shwegyin, a distance of nearly 50 miles upstream from the Gulf of Martaban. Sakurai decided therefore to advance on a wide 100-mile front between Toungoo and Nyaunglebin, just west of Shwegyin.

It would be tedious here to attempt to describe the numerous small operations which occurred as Sakurai's 28th Army attempted to cross the road in dispersal groups during May and August, all the

The 14th Army's drive to Rangoon in April and May 1945.

while being hunted by Stopford's Indian battalions, tanks, and armoured cars. These operations were carried out mainly by junior officers and it was very important to them.

However, a brief resumé of the casualties incurred at that time will indicate the intensity of the fighting and the miserable defeat of the remnants of a once fine army.

On June 28, 1945 the strength of the 28th Army was stated to be 27,764. Three months later, on September 22, the 28th Army's reported strength to the Burma Area Army was as follows: present on duty 7,949; in hospital 1,919; and missing 3,822, some of whom were expected to return.

IV Corps' losses over much the same period were 435 killed, 1,452 wounded, and 42 missing.

Thus in effect ended the war in Burma, where an army of ten Japanese divisions, two Independent Mixed Brigades, and about two Indian National Army divisions was not only defeated, but to all intents and purposes, wiped out as a fighting force.

CHAPTER 78
Iwo Jima and Okinawa

On October 3, 1944, the Joint Chiefs-of-Staff had decided to stretch Japanese resources to their limits by attacking Luzon, Iwo Jima and Okinawa. In January 1945, the invasion of Luzon had begun, and then it was the turn of the other chosen targets. The campaigns on Iwo Jima and Okinawa were among the bitterest of the war, with close-quarters fighting of shocking ferocity.

As a piece of real estate, Iwo Jima has little to offer anyone: it is an island 4⅔ miles long and 2½ miles wide at its southern end, dominated by the 550-foot high Mount Suribachi, an extinct volcano. There are some sulphur deposits, a plain of black volcanic sand, and in the north a plateau of ridges and gorges between 340 and 368 feet high. In 1944 there were five villages on the island, in the centre and to the north of the plateau.

The importance of the island to both the Japanese and the Americans lay in the two airfields that had been built, and the third under construction, by the Japanese. From these bases Japanese aircraft could intercept the B-29's bombing Japan, and operate against the bomber bases in the Marianas. The island, if

U.S. Marines raise the Stars and Stripes on the top of Iwo Jima's Mount Suribachi on February 23, 1945.

captured, would provide the U.S. with a fighter base and emergency landing strips for crippled bombers.

The island's commander, Lieutenant-General Tadamichi Kuribayashi, was fully aware of the island's importance, and set out a series of "Courageous Battle Vows" for the defenders. One of these was "Above all, we shall dedicate ourselves and our entire strength to the defence of the islands."

Kuribayashi's men worked hard, and by the summer of 1944 had driven tunnels through the plateau, laid minefields, and built gun and machine gun emplacements. U.S. reconnaissance aircraft and submarines located 642 blockhouses before the landings.

Never loath to expend vast amounts of material in an effort to spare the lives of their men, the Americans began early with the bombardment of Iwo Jima. On June 15, 1944, carrier planes struck at the island. The attacks continued during the rest of the year, reaching a climax with continuous strikes for 74 days by Saipan-based bombers. The final three-day naval bombardment was carried out by six battleships and their support elements.

The leading wave of L.V.T.s hit the beach at 0902 hours on February 19, 1945 to the north-east of Mt. Suribachi and began immediately to claw its way up the black sand.

The assault troops were men of the 4th Marine (Major-General Clifton B. Cates) and 5th Marine (Major-General Keller E. Rockey) Divisions, both part of Major-General Harry Schmidt's V 'Phib. Corps. The 3rd Marine Division (Major-General Graves B. Erskine) was in corps reserve. In overall command was Lieutenant-General Holland M. Smith.

The troops had practised landings on a similar stretch of beach, and had "stormed" a hill resembling Mount Suribachi. Reconnaissance had also given them some idea of the strength of the defences and the initial bombardment had blown away some of the camouflage and exposed further emplacements. But what they did not know was that their adversaries had built what was probably the most complex defence system in the Pacific. Although only eight square miles in area, Iwo had 800 pillboxes and three miles of tunnels (Kuribayashi had planned 18). Guns were carefully sited to cover the beaches and a series of inland defence lines. The formation entrusted with the defence, the 109th Division, had 13,586 men by February 1, and there were also some 7,347 Navy troops on the island. There were 361 guns of over 75-mm calibre (with 100,000 rounds of ammunition), 300 A.A. guns (150,000 rounds), 20,000 light guns and machine guns (22 million rounds), 130 howitzers (11,700 rounds), 12 heavy mortars (800 rounds), 70 rocket launchers (3,500 rounds), 40 47-mm anti-

tank guns (600 rounds), 20 37-mm anti-tank guns (500 rounds), and 22 tanks.

Kuribayashi had elected to fight a static battle inshore from the beaches, but the Navy had insisted that possible landing beaches should be covered by bunkers. The Japanese tanks were no match for the American Shermans, and so were positioned hull down in the gullies that scored the island. The gun sites were dug so that the weapon slits were just visible at ground level, and the positions were linked with tunnels.

The naval bombardment had driven the Japanese into their bunkers, and when the Marines landed, optimists suggested that it might be an easy operation. Indeed, it is hard to imagine that any of the defenders could have survived the bombardment, whose finale had included 1,950 rounds of 16-inch shell, 1,500 of 14-inch, 400 of 12-inch, 1,700 of 8-inch, 2,000 of 6-inch, and 31,000 of 5-inch. It was the heaviest pre-landing bombardment of the war. In addition to shellfire, the Navy had also used aircraft to drop bombs and napalm, and fire a multitude of rockets. But although some of their weapons were destroyed, "the Japanese garrison cozily sat it out in their deep underground shelters".

The first wave of Marines had crossed just 200 yards of the beach when they were caught in a savage cross-fire from hidden machine guns. Simultaneously, mortars firing from pits only a few feet wide began to drop bombs on the men and vessels along the shore. The U.S. Marine Corps had embarked on the most costly operation of its history.

Despite the fire from these positions that needed explosives, flame-throwers or tanks to overcome, elements of the 5th Marine Division managed to drive across the island on the morning of D-day. When the advance halted for the night at 1800 the Americans were far short of their objectives, but had managed to isolate Mount Suribachi.

Such was the strength of the Japanese positions, however, that it was not until D 3 that the extinct volcano was firmly surrounded. The following morning, the 28th Marines (with the 2nd and 3rd Battalions forward and the 1st in reserve) gained 200 yards of the mountain's lower slopes. The next day an air strike by 40 planes preceded an attack that reached the foot of the mountain. On the 23rd a patrol of the 2nd Battalion's Company F reported that the Japanese had gone to ground. A larger patrol reached the rim of the crater and was involved in a brisk fire fight.

This patrol, under Lieutenant Harold G. Shrier, hoisted a small (54 × 28 inch) Stars and Stripes flag. Shortly afterwards a larger flag was obtained from an L.S.T., and Schrier decided that this should be raised instead of the first flag. This was photographed by Joe Rosenthal, an Associated Press photographer. The picture of the six men struggling to drive the pole into the volcanic soil has become a classic of the last war.

On March 1, the 28th Marines were moved to the northern sector, to join battalions of the 23rd, 24th, and 25th Marines (4th Division) and the 26th and 27th Marines (5th Division), which had been entrusted with the task of clearing Airfield No. 1 and driving northwards.

It was a battle in which daily gains were measured in hundreds of yards. On February 21 the 21st Marines (3rd Division) were ordered ashore to help.

On the morning of the 24th, after a 76-minute naval bombardment, an air strike, and fire from Marine artillery, the tanks of the 4th and 5th Divisions moved off. One thrust was directed along the western side, and the other along the eastern side, of the airfield. Mines and anti-tank guns stopped the first, but the second pushed on and began to take Japanese emplacements under close range fire. The 5th Division had gained some 500 yards by the end of the day.

On the same day, the 3rd Marine Division landed, and was allotted the task of driving along the centre of Iwo's northern plateau. Once this was taken, the Marines would be able to push down the spurs leading to the sea. The plateau was an extraordinary feature, eroded into fantastic shapes by wind, rain, and volcanic activity.

The division launched its attack at 0930 on the 25th. It was a slow and costly operation, as the attack met the main Japanese line of defences. Three days of attacks, in which the Marines brought up flame-throwing tanks to incinerate the Japanese in their shell-proof bunkers, finally broke through the line. On the 28th the Marines secured the ruins of Motoyama village and the hills overlooking Airfield No. 3. The Americans now held all three airfields, the objectives of the landings, but the fighting was by no means over.

On the last day of the month, the Marines attacked the two small features of Hills 382 and 362A. Their size was misleading, for each contained a warren of tunnels and bunkers. The crest of Hill 382 had been hollowed out and turned into a huge bunker housing anti-tank guns and other artillery. Tanks were sited in the gullies. To the south of the hill there was a massive rock which became known as Turkey Knob, with a natural bowl christened the Amphitheater. The fighting for both features became so intense that they became known as the Meatgrinder. A series of savage local battles was fought on March 1. And although Hill 382 fell that day, it was not until the 10th that the Japanese defending Turkey Knob and the Amphitheater were destroyed.

The attack on the Hill 362A complex on March 2 was a marked departure from normal Marine practice—they attacked at night. Although movement through the rugged terrain was slow and tiring, the tactics surprised the enemy. After a fierce fight on the 8th, the Marines were in possession of the whole area.

Despite the loss of these key points, the

Japanese continued to fight with their customary aggressiveness. On the 8th they launched an attack on the junction between the 23rd and 24th Marines. Caught in the open without artillery support, the attack failed with 650 dead. With this defeat the Japanese defence began to crumble, and the battle moved into the mopping up stage. Individual strongpoints were in no mood to surrender, however, and as they had ample stocks of food, water, and ammunition, they could hold out for some time. Indeed, on March 15, many of the last defenders attempted to infiltrate the American lines.

The last pocket to be destroyed was that at Kitano Point, which was declared officially secure on March 25. But that night over 200 Japanese emerged from the flame-blackened and shell-scarred rocks. Led in person by Kuribayashi, some say, they tore into the bivouac area occupied by the sleeping men of the 5th Pioneer Battalion. A defensive line was set up by the Army's VII Fighter Command and the Marines' 8th Field Depot and by dawn at least 223 Japanese, including their leader, lay dead.

The conquest of Iwo Jima had cost the Marines 5,931 dead and 17,372 wounded. But by the end of the war the island's airfields had saved the lives of 24,761 American pilots and aircrew. Of the 21,000 Japanese defending the island, only 216 were taken prisoner. If this was the cost of taking an island of only eight square miles and which had been Japanese only since 1891, what would be the cost of the conquest of Japan?

Operation "Iceberg" was the name of the plan; the island of Okinawa was the target. The American aim was to achieve the penultimate victory of the Pacific war: the seizure of a firm base on the very doorstep of Japan as a prelude to the final conquest of the Japanese home islands. And the ensuing battle was fought on a scale as yet unknown in the course of the Pacific war: a bloody, protracted fight to the finish which forced the Americans to exert every ounce of their strength. After all the agonising first-hand experience gained in the long road from Guadalcanal to Iwo Jima, Okinawa proved yet again that the Japanese will to resist defied all possible estimates when tested on the battlefield.

In view of the vital nature of the target—a major bastion of Japan's inner island defences—it was essential that as much Intelligence as possible should be amassed. Aerial photography was an obvious source, but the difficulties were considerable. Okinawa was 1,200 miles from the nearest American air bases when it was selected as the objective of "Iceberg". B-29's flying at their high altitude only obtained small-scale photographs; carrier aircraft could only be assigned to Okinawa for photographic reconnaissance when the programme of carrier operations permitted. Other problems included the prevalence of local cloud cover and the large size of Okinawa itself: 60 miles long and from 2 to 18 miles wide, making it extremely difficult to obtain a mosaic of photographs covering the whole island. However, reconnaissance did collect sufficient information to suggest that the main strength of the Japanese defences would be encountered in the southern half of the island around Naha and Yontan–the best two out of the four operational airfields on Okinawa. The final estimate of the strength of the garrison was 65,000 men.

What the cameras failed to reveal was that Lieutenant-General Mitsuru Ushijima's 32nd Army was in fact over 100,000 strong. Regular troops (infantrymen, gunners, and special services) totalled 77,199, and there were 20,000 auxiliary troops known as *Boeitai*. These were drafted into the Japanese Army to serve in labour and supply duties, relieving the fighting troops of ammunition worries, and thus playing an important part in the battle. In addition to the *Boeitai* there was a large contingent of Okinawan conscripts assimilated by the regular units on the island. Precise figures for these conscripts are not available but have been set as

A Marine machine gun crew gives covering fire during the fighting on Okinawa.

high as one-third of the total garrison strength.

Japanese hopes for the defence of Okinawa were strikingly similar to those for the defence of Luzon. The high command ordered that the island must be held. Wildly exaggerated estimates were pinned on the hitting power of the air and sea *kamikaze* forces. It was expected that *kamikaze* attacks on the American invasion fleet and the initial beach-head would cut off the first troops ashore from their supports, making it possible for the Japanese garrison to sally out against the stranded American troops and fling them back into the sea. Like Yamashita on Luzon, however, Ushijima knew how heavily the odds were stacked against him. He had no illusions about what was coming and accepted that he would be unable to stop the Americans from getting ashore and establishing a beach-head too strong to be destroyed.

Ushijima therefore planned to hold the strategically vital southern half of the island with the bulk of the 32nd Army, digging it in and forcing the Americans to batter away at its positions at as high a cost as the Japanese troops could exact. Naha and Shuri were the central nodes of the defence. No landing north of Chaton on the west coast or Taguchi on the east coast (just south of Kadena air-

field) would be opposed. The Americans might get ashore. They might overrun the spindly northern region of the island. But until they had destroyed every last stronghold held by the units of the 32nd Army in the south they could not force a decisive victory–let alone claim the conquest of Okinawa and move on to more deadly operations against the Japanese homeland.

The American forces earmarked for the conquest of Okinawa constituted an awesome armada of battle-wise fighting units. Responsibility for taking the troops to their target and shielding and supporting them once they came ashore rested with Admiral Raymond A. Spruance's 5th Fleet. Its Joint Expeditionary Force, commanded by Admiral Richmond K. Turner, was designated Task Force 51. This, the invasion fleet proper, comprised half a million servicemen, over 300 warships, and over 1,139 auxiliary vessels and landing craft. It was shielded by Vice-Admiral Marc A. Mitscher's Task Force 58, which would also carry out the initial bombardment and neutralisation of the Japanese defences. Task Force 58 consisted of four fast carrier groups, together with the British carrier force commanded by Vice-Admiral Sir Bernard Rawlings, designated Task Force 57 although it was only the equivalent of a single American carrier group.

The land forces consisted of the newly-formed 10th Army under General Simon B. Buckner. Okinawa would be the first battle for 10th Army but not for its component units, as the following breakdown shows:

1. XIV Corps (Major-General John B. Hodge)
7th Infantry Division–Attu, Kwajalein, Leyte
96th Infantry Division–Leyte
2. III Amphibious (Marine) Corps (Major-General Roy S. Geiger)
1st Marine Division–Guadalcanal, New Britain, Peleliu
6th Marine Division–regiments from Marshalls, Guam, Saipan
3. Reserve
27th Infantry Division–Gilberts, Marshalls, Saipan
77th Infantry Division–Guam, Leyte
2nd Marine Division–Guadalcanal, Tarawa, Saipan, Tinian.

Thus the seven divisions which would land on Okinawa were made up of officers and men steeped in the overall experiences and lessons of the Pacific war since August 1942. They totalled about 154,000 men–116,000 of them belonging to the five divisions which would make the initial landings along the eight-mile sweep of the Hagushi beaches on the west coast between Sunabe and Zampa Point. D-day for Okinawa was set for the morning of April 1, 1945. It was to be preceded by the capture of the Kerama Retto, a group of small islands 20 miles west of southern Okinawa, which would then be used as an advanced base. Diversionary landings would be made on the far side of Okinawa from the Hagushi beaches; if necessary

Marines assemble on the beach at Geruna, on March 25, 1945.

these landings could be reinforced to confront the Japanese with a double beach-head.

Mitscher's big carriers began the first phase of the softening-up process on March 18, launching heavy strikes against Japanese airfields on Kyūshū. On the 19th the Americans switched to the naval bases at Kobe, Kure, and Hiroshima and to Japanese shipping in the Inland Sea. *Kamikazes* and bombers hit back fiercely, damaging *Yorktown, Wasp,* and *Enterprise* and setting *Franklin* ablaze. Task Force 58 began to withdraw on the afternoon of the 19th, and during the next 48 hours was harried by repeated Japanese air attacks. These, however, were fought off by the American fighter pilots, who ran up impressive scores. The tally of Japanese aircraft destroyed between March 18 and 22 was 528, and 16 surface ships were damaged during the same period, including the super-battleship *Yamato.* Mitscher's force had amply ful-

filled its rôle. When the main landings went in on Okinawa, the Japanese were unable to throw in a serious air counter-attack for a week.

Next on the schedule was the seizure of the islands of the Kerama Retto group, a task entrusted to the 77th Division under Major-General Andrew D. Bruce. This was a campaign within a campaign, a faithful miniature of the "island-hopping" programme as a whole. A pre-liminary reconnaissance and bombard-ment preceded the actual assault, which was launched on the islands of Aka, Geruma, Hokaji, and Zanami on March 26. Initial progress was so rapid that Bruce decided to take Yakabi Island as well, and it fell with minimal resistance on the first day. The Japanese reacted in familiar fashion on Aka and Zanami, pulling back into the interior after conceding the fight for the beaches. The same thing happened the following day when Tokashiki was attacked, together with Amuro and Kuba. The Keramas were declared secure on the 29th, but the Japanese on Aka and Toka-shiki insisted on refusing to surrender until the official capitulation of Japan.

The occupation of the Keramas was rounded out with the emplacement of two batteries of 155-mm guns on the coral islands of Keise Shima, a mere 11 miles off the Haguchi beaches. These guns would add to the fire-power of the pre-invasion bombardment, and their emplacement on Keise Shima was a repetition of a trick used with great success during the battle for Kwajalein.

While the Keramas were still being cleared, the intricate work of preliminary bombardment and minesweeping in the approaches to Okinawa had already been started by Vice-Admiral William H. Blandy's Task Force 52. The first offshore shelling began on March 25, but the job of clearing the dense minefield which the Japanese had laid off the Hagushi beaches was not completed until the evening of the 29th. Blandy himself called it "pro-bably the largest assault sweep operation ever executed". In the week before the assault the American warships pounded the Japanese defences with over 13,000 shells of calibres ranging from 6-inch to 16-inch, while the carrier planes flew 3,095 sorties, covering targets requested

641

by 10th Army. In the last three days, as the offshore obstacles were cleared, the warships steadily shortened the range and intensified their fire. With the method born of experience and the most detailed planning, an intricate naval ballet manoeuvred 1,300 ships into position for the assault on the morning of April 1.

"Land the landing force"

Admiral Turner's order was signalled to the invasion fleet at 0406 hours on the 1st–four and a half hours before the moment scheduled for hitting the beaches with the first wave. As the long ranks of landing-craft jockeyed into position for the approach, the terrain behind the beaches shuddered and smoked like a volcano under the shellfire of the bombardment force. The boats moved off at 0800 in perfect conditions and the run-in proceeded as easily as a peace-time manoeuvre. As the bombardment lifted and the gunfire shifted inland the first boats began to ground, almost exactly on schedule, just after 0830. To the troops the actual landing came as an almost ludicrous anti-climax. "Where are the Japs?" was the question every man was asking as the cautious advance into the interior began. Meanwhile the landings continued without a hitch. By the evening of April 1 over 60,000 troops had landed on Okinawa and had pegged out a beach-head over eight miles wide and over two miles deep in places.

"An enemy landing attempt on the eastern coast of Okinawa on Sunday morning was completely foiled, with heavy losses to the enemy." That was how the Japanese boasted of the feint attack made by 2nd Marine Division (Major-General Thomas E. Watson) on the far side of the island from the Hagushi beaches. The Marines had made it look like a genuine attempt, with eight waves of boats dressed in line and covered by bombardment. They moved in simultaneously with the approach to the Hagushi beaches, reversed course precisely at 0830, and headed back to their parent vessels. The same performance was made on the morning of the 2nd and the force was then withdrawn.

On the second and third days the Marines and infantry pushed right across the island and cut it in two, with 96th and 7th Divisions wheeling to the south on the right flank and feeling out the first serious Japanese resistance around Momabaru. By the evening of April 3 interrogated Japanese civilians and liberated P.O.W.s had informed the advancing troops that the main Japanese forces had pulled back to the south. The puzzle of the non-existent enemy had been solved: the battle for Okinawa had still to begin.

The push to the south was carried out by XXIV Corps: 96th and 7th Divisions, who began the cautious probing of Ushijima's defence outposts. For both divisions, April 5 marked the first day when genuine resistance at last was encountered. The advance continued during the next three days but by April 9 both

divisions had been fought to a halt and XXIV Corps had not attained its prescribed objective. On the 9th the 383rd Infantry fought its way on to Kakazu Ridge but were forced to withdraw after a bloody fight. A "powerhouse attack" on April 10 was also repulsed, and the Japanese were still very much in possession of their strongpoint at Kakazu on the 12th. The first round had undoubtedly gone to the Japanese in precisely the sort of battle that Ushijima had planned. American morale was also depressed by President Roosevelt's death, which the Japanese promptly exploited for propaganda. "We must express our deep regret over the death of President Roosevelt," ran one leaflet. "The 'American Tragedy' is now raised here at Okinawa with his death . . Not only the late President but anyone else would die in the excess of worry to hear such an annihilative damage. The dreadful loss that led your late leader to death will make you orphans on this island. The Japanese special assault corps will sink your vessels to the last destroyer. You will witness it realised in the near future."

In the overview the Japanese were whistling in the dark: they certainly had little to boast about as far as naval victories were concerned. On April 7 the "Special Sea Attack Force" had sortied on a one-way mission to Okinawa. It was a suicide run, aimed at sending the super-battleship *Yamato* into the midst of American invasion fleet and dealing out as much destruction as possible before meeting her inevitable end. But *Yamato* had been sunk by carrier planes before she had even sighted Okinawa. With the grip of the American navy unshaken, it was the Japanese who remained the "orphans of Okinawa", for all the local successes they might win. Much more important was the nature of the battle itself, with the Japanese having to accept the consequences of their defensive strategy. The cost of halting XXIV Corps by April 12 had been grievous: about 5,570 for the Japanese and 451 for the Americans. Despite this twelve-fold imbalance, 32nd Army now went over to the offensive to try to exploit the discomfiture of XXIV Corps by pushing it back to the north.

In two days of intense fighting the Japanese counter-attack, carried out by components of 62nd and 24th Divisions, was repelled at all points. It was a costly deviation from the basic strategy of staying in strongpoints and letting the Americans suffer the losses. By dawn on the 14th stalemate had settled once again over the front line.

Meanwhile Buckner had reversed the original plan of tackling southern Okinawa before clearing the north of the island, and had unleashed Geiger's Marines (6th Marine Division) on April 3. Driving north-eastwards along the narrow "neck" of Okinawa, the 6th Marines had reached the sea and cut off the Motobu Peninsula by April 8. But it took them another 12 days to clear the peninsula and they had to exert every effort to

crush the main Japanese position at Yae-Take with concentric attacks. Not until the 20th was Japanese resistance in the peninsula broken, and enough Japanese escaped to the hills to begin organised guerrilla warfare.

After changing his plan and clearing northern Okinawa, Buckner also decided to press ahead with the capture of Ie shima, the 5-mile-long oval island 3½ miles off the Motobu Peninsula. The Japanese had built three airstrips on Ie shima and that was Buckner's main objective: to seize the island and use it as a natural aircraft-carrier to intensify the air umbrella over the Okinawa battlefield. Ie shima was a formidable nut to crack. The 2,000 troops on the island had, by exploiting civilian labour, made it a miniature Iwo Jima as far as prepared defence positions were concerned. Major-General Andrew D. Bruce's 77th Division was earmarked for the capture of Ie shima, and the landings went in on April 16. Despite vigorous resistance, the 77th Division had overrun the western half of the island with its airstrips by the end of the 16th. But the Japanese still held out in Ie town. Five more gruelling days were needed before the island was declared secure, and even then the fighting continued until the 24th. The fight of Ie shima epitomised the bitterness of the Okinawa campaign; commenting on it, General Bruce said that "the last three days of this fighting were the bitterest I ever witnessed".

Back on the southern front, Buckner was preparing to succeed with stealth where open attacks had failed: a surprise attack on the Shuri defences, pushing deep into the Japanese lines and by-passing strongpoints such as the Kakazu Ridge. The attack was set for April 19 and was to be launched by a surprise penetration by General Hodge's 27th Division on the 18th. Hodge summed it all up when he said: "It is going to be really tough. There are 65,000 to 70,000 fighting Japs holed up in the south end of the island, and I see no way to get them out except blast them out yard by yard." The attack of April 19 was a complete failure and cost XXIV Corps 720 casualties. The Japanese fought like furies and held off all the American attempts to slip round their strongpoints. The zones of fire of their artillery and mortars had been carefully drawn and covered all sectors of the front. One regimental commander in the 96th Division commented bitterly after the battle: "You cannot bypass a Jap because a Jap does not know when he is bypassed."

Despite their failure in the attack of April 19 the Americans had no choice but to keep up the pressure on the Shuri defences. When the fighting died down with the coming of darkness on the 19th a gap of nearly a mile yawned between 27th and 96th Divisions and General Griner, commander of the 27th, knew that it must be plugged. But the attack of April 20 went the same way as that of the 19th. This time the problem was a Japan-

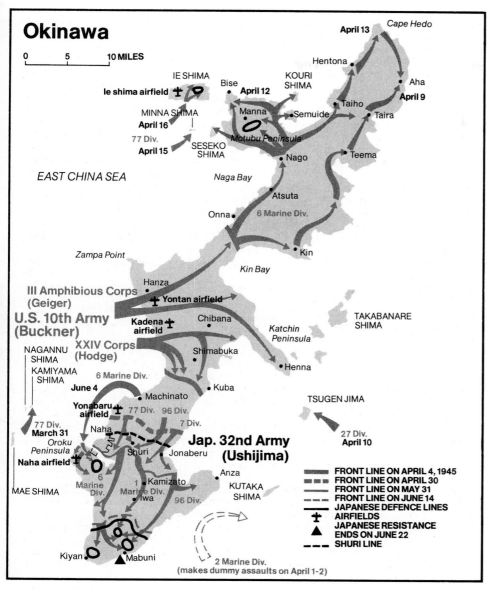

Okinawa

0   5   10 MILES

Cape Hedo
April 13

IE SHIMA
le shima airfield ✝ ⊕   Bise   Hentona
April 12
MINNA SHIMA   KOURI   Aha
April 16   SHIMA   **April 9**
77 Div.   Taiho   Taira
April 15   SESEKO   Manna   Semuide
SHIMA   *Motubu Peninsula*   Teema

EAST CHINA SEA   Nago

Naga Bay

Atsuta

Onna   **6 Marine Div.**

Zampa Point   Kin
Kin Bay

Hanza   TAKABANARE
III Amphibious Corps   ✝ Yontan airfield   SHIMA
(Geiger)
U.S. 10th Army   Kadena ✝   Chibana
(Buckner)   airfield   *Katchin*
NAGANNU   **XXIV Corps**   *Peninsula*
SHIMA   **(Hodge)**   Shimabuka
KAMIYAMA   6 Marine Div.   Henna
SHIMA
June 4   Machinato   Kuba   TSUGEN JIMA
Yonabaru ✝   77 Div.   96 Div.
airfield   7 Div.
77 Div.   Naha   **Jap. 32nd Army**   27 Div.
March 31   **(Ushijima)**   **April 10**
Oroku   Shuri   Jonaberu
Peninsula   **FRONT LINE ON APRIL 4, 1945**
Naha airfield ✝   Anza   **FRONT LINE ON APRIL 30**
6   1   Kamizato   KUTAKA   **FRONT LINE ON MAY 31**
MAE SHIMA   Marine   Marine Div.   SHIMA   **FRONT LINE ON JUNE 14**
Div.   Iwa   **JAPANESE DEFENCE LINES**
96 Div.   ✝ **AIRFIELDS**
▲ **JAPANESE RESISTANCE**
Kiyan   ▲ Mabuni   **ENDS ON JUNE 22**
SHURI LINE
2 Marine Div.
(makes dummy assaults on April 1-2)

The American landings and operations on Okinawa from April to June 1945.

ese strongpoint which squarely blocked the line of advance west of Gusukuma towards the Machinato airfield – a strongpoint which had got the very best out of the terrain, was heavily manned, and which had to be cleared out, not bypassed. The Americans called it "Item Pocket" and it took them another exhausting week before it fell. Impromptu names for the key landmarks – "Charlie Ridge", "Brewer's Hill", "Dead Horse Gulch" – became feared and hated names during the incessant fighting between April 20 and April 27, when the Pocket was eventually declared secure. Weeks later, however, Japanese were still emerging from the deep bolt-holes and caves which had given the position its strength.

In the meantime the 7th, 27th, and 96th Divisions battered away at the outer Shuri defences on the centre and left of the front. On the latter sector the Japanese had based their defence on "Skyline Ridge", blocking the approach to Unaha and Yonabaru airfield. In the centre, Kakazu Ridge was still in Japanese hands. While the fight for Item Pocket

raged on the right flank, the Americans struggled painfully forward until at last, by April 24, they had taken both Kakazu and Skyline Ridges. After three weeks' ordeal the outer shell of the Shuri defences had finally been cracked.

At the end of April, Buckner reshuffled his front-line divisions, many units of which were badly in need of a rest. The 27th Division was relieved by the 1st Marine Division on April 30, and the 6th Marine also earmarked for a shift south to the front. The fall of Item Pocket on April 27 was followed by an exact replica of the preceding seven days – and then, on May 4, the Japanese unleashed a counter-offensive aimed at smashing the centre of 10th Army and driving its fragments into the sea. It was an ambitious plan, envisaging amphibious landings deep in the rear of the American positions – but it suffered the same fate as the earlier Japanese attack. The amphibious operation was a total fiasco. Despite a temporary breakthrough in the centre and the recapture of Tanabaru Ridge, the Japanese 24th Division had shot its bolt by the 7th and Ushijima had no choice but to fall back on the defensive, having achieved little but to delay the American

advance for just under a week. (During the fighting for the Tanabaru Ridge the news of the German surrender reached Okinawa. "Well, now," said a colonel of the 17th Infantry Division, as he sniped at the Japanese with an M1 carbine, "if we just had the Japs off the escarpment we'd be all right, wouldn't we?")

Once Ushijima's counter-attack had been safely held, Buckner saw in it a chance for a breakthrough. The attack had drawn the last fresh Japanese reserves into the line, and a prompt resumption of the initiative could well prove decisive. The result was the renewal of the attack on May 10 and its culmination on the 21st with the clearing of a "funnel" on the left flank which enabled the 7th Division to edge forwards into the inner ring of the Shuri defences. In this phase the decisive actions were the clearing of the eastern sides of Conical and Sugar Hills, which bent back the extreme right wing of the Japanese line. Plotted on a map, it seemed that the way was open for the rolling-up of the front from the east – but the Japanese remained in firm control of their positions and no breakthrough came. And now, in the fourth week of May, the elements sided with the Japanese. The rain poured down and the battlefield of Okinawa dissolved in mud.

Transport was paralysed and it was impossible to move heavy equipment through the floods and quagmires – but there was no diminution of the pressure. With the Japanese centre north of Shuri still rock steady, Buckner ordered the flanking divisions to intensify operations and bend back the Japanese wings as far as possible. It was an exhausting and undramatic process. With every day's new advances the "bulge" being formed round Shuri seemed to herald the total envelopment of Ushijima's men – but still the Japanese refused to break and the casualties continued to soar. With the rain and the mud and the pattern of attrition in men's lives (one dead American for every ten dead Japanese by the end of May) the battle of Okinawa was taking on the nature of the most hideous trench-warfare pounding match of World War I – and with as few obvious results.

Yet now at last the persistence of the Americans was rewarded. Even before the ominous constriction of the flanks of the 32nd Army in the last weeks of May, General Ushijima had made the decision to yield the Shuri Line and withdraw to the south after a conference with his staff on May 21. The consensus of opinion had been that to hold on at Shuri would only mean that the 32nd Army would be destroyed earlier than necessary, without having inflicted sufficient losses on the Americans. The 32nd Army would make its last stand at the southern tip of Okinawa. Supplies and wounded began moving south on the night of May 22-23, heading for the positions previously constructed by the 24th Division.

With the rearguard holding on in front of Shuri, the Japanese pulled out with skill and discipline, and their move was largely

Marines watch a phosphorus barrage on Okinawa.

completed by the end of May. The Japanese move was helped by the sluicing rains and the lowering, overcast sky, which seriously impeded American aerial reconnaissance. From May 26, however, the long Japanese columns were kept under general surveillance from the air: and a 10th Army staff meeting on the evening of May 30 reached the conclusion that although the Japanese were still holding before Shuri, their line was little but a tough shell. It was widely believed that Ushijima had made his decision too late and that the campaign was all over bar the mopping-up. Once again it was a serious under-estimation of the actual situation. Shuri fell at long last on May 31, but Buckner's divisions did not, as expected, trap the 32nd Army in a pocket and wipe it out. Nor were they able to prevent it from pulling back and forming yet another solid front in the south. For this the Americans could certainly blame the adverse weather conditions: "We had awfully tough luck to get the bad weather at the identical time that things broke," lamented Buckner.

Thus the scene was set for the last round of the battle for Okinawa. The southern end of the island is best described as a downward-pointing arrowhead. The Shuri Line had crossed the shank of the arrowhead above the barbs; and now the 32nd Army had pulled right down into the very tip of the arrow. An amphibious operation coped with the western barb of the arrowhead, the Orotu Peninsula, trapping the remnants of Rear-Admiral Minoru Ota's naval troops and wiping them out by June 15 after a ten-day battle. Meanwhile the first attacks on the main Japanese position behind the Yaeju-Dake Ridge had begun.

It took five murderous days—June 12-17—to crack the Yaeju-Dake position: five days in which the fighting was as intense as ever. The Japanese still had to be blasted and burned from their foxholes, and a new American flame-throwing tactic was to bring up a 200-foot fuel supply hose from which to spray napalm on Japanese positions. By June 17 the survivors of the 32nd Army had been blasted out of their front-line position and compressed into an area eight miles square. After more than two and a half months of superb endurance, the men of

the 32nd Army had reached the end of their tether. Between the 18th and the 21st they were split into three independent pockets and it was obvious that the end was near. Buckner sent a personal appeal to Ushijima to see reason and save the lives of his last men. Ushijima received it with vast amusement. He radioed his last message to Tokyo on the evening of the 21st, and he and his chief-of-staff, General Isamu Ota, committed ritual *hara-kiri* the same night. The last organised resistance–on Hill 85, between Medeera and Makabe–was broken on the 21st. Although "Old Glory" was formally raised over Okinawa at the 10th Army headquarters on the morning of the 22nd, mopping-up operations lasted until the end of the month; and the Ryūkyūs campaign was officially declared ended on July 2.

The Allies had conquered Okinawa and were now only 350 miles from Kyūshū itself. The objective of "Iceberg" had been achieved, but at a terrifying cost. Total American battle casualties were 49,151. The Americans had lost 763 aircraft and 36 ships sunk; another 368 of their ships had been damaged. But the Japanese had lost 110,000 men, including conscripts and drafted civilians, and even this has to be an approximate figure. Only 7,400 Japanese prisoners were taken on Okinawa – most of them in the last days when the 32nd Army was disintegrating. Ten major *kamikaze* attacks had been thrown against Okinawa, using up some 1,465 aircraft; and the total number of suicide sorties was 1,900. The Japanese losses in aircraft were staggering: 7,800. The Imperial Navy lost 16 ships sunk and four damaged.

What did the Okinawa campaign prove? First and foremost, it gave a bitter foretaste of what the Allies could expect if they ever tried to land on Japanese soil. It was the bloodiest fight of the Pacific war. But above all it proved that nothing could stop the Allies in the Pacific from moving where they wanted, even if it did mean killing every Japanese in their way. And Ushijima himself paid tribute to this in his last message to Tokyo. "Our strategy, tactics, and techniques all were used to the utmost and we fought valiantly," he reported. "But it was as nothing before the material strength of the enemy."

After the Battle of Leyte Gulf in October 1944, the Japanese Combined Fleet could no longer be recognised as the proud and efficient fighting force which had gone to war in December 1941. It was a shrivelled husk, largely immobilised by lack of fuel. Never again after Leyte did the Combined Fleet concentrate its strength to fight the carrier task forces of the American and British Pacific fleets. But the surviving Japanese warships still had a part to play, and they remained high-priority targets for the Allies until the end of the war.

The Midway disaster of 1942 had caused the Japanese to adopt an accelerated and expanded carrier-building programme, but they never made good the losses of Coral Sea and Midway. The programme was a dual affair, including the construction of brand-new carriers from the keel up and the conversion of merchantmen and suitable warship hulls. Typical of the former category was the *Taiho*, lost in her first battle – the last big carrier clash of the Pacific war in the Philippine Sea (June 19, 1944) during the campaign in the Marianas. *Taiho* had actually been laid down before Pearl Harbor, but for months work on her had proceeded at a crawl. She displaced 29,300 tons, compared with the 25,675 tons of *Shokaku* and *Zuikaku*. She could achieve 33 knots and carried 74 aircraft (53 of them operational and 21 spare). But the details of her fate reveal the very great changes which had affected the Japanese carrier force between the days of Pearl Harbor and the last year of the war. The American submarine *Albacore* put a torpedo into *Taiho* on the morning of June 19. At first there seemed very little to worry about; two fuel tanks had been ruptured and the flight-deck elevator jammed shut, but *Taiho* could still maintain full speed. The immediate hazard was the spreading fumes from the liberated oil and aviation

spirit. The principal fuel of the vessel in 1944 was crude oil, as a result of overall shortages. The ship's ventilators were put on full blast in an attempt to dispel the fumes – a fatal decision. The fumes were spread throughout the vessel and continued to accumulate. The inevitable end came when a spark on the hangar deck detonated them. The effects were cataclysmic. A tremendous explosion shook *Taiho* from stem to stern, blowing out the hangar walls, ripping the flight deck, and perforating the ship's bottom. She sank within minutes, the victim of an elementary hazard of carrier life which had been obvious for years.

As for the second category of the "last generation" of Japanese carriers, a typical example may be cited with *Shinyo*. She started life as the German luxury liner *Scharnhorst*, which had been at Kobe since the outbreak of war in 1939. *Scharnhorst* was purchased by the Japanese Government in the months after Midway; she was renamed *Shinyo*, and her conversion was begun at the Kure Naval Yard in November 1942. Parts were cannibalised from the uncompleted skeleton of "Hull III", the fourth "Yamato" class super-battleship (significant of the belated swing away from Japan's pre-war obsession with the big battleship as the prime mover of sea power). *Scharnhorst's* original electric turbines were retained; they were in fact only the second set to be used by a ship of the Imperial Navy. In her new guise, *Shinyo* finally joined the fleet in mid-December 1943. She was not present at the Battle of the Philippine Sea but was given a further eight 50-mm A.A. guns after that action, giving her a total of 50. Completely unarmoured, *Shinyo* had a best speed of 22 knots. Her air group consisted of a maximum of 33 planes: 27 operational and six spare. And she fell victim to the far-ranging American submarine arm, being torpedoed by the *Spadefish* in the China Sea on November 17, 1944.

But the biggest conversion job in the Japanese carrier programme was that of the giant *Shinano*, originally the third (after *Yamato* and *Musashi*) of the super-battleships. *Shinano's* whole story was one of monstrous error and wasted effort – much like the giant Japanese "I-400" submarines. To start with, argument raged for weeks over what sort of aircraft-carrier she should be: an orthodox carrier or a giant floating depot-ship and mobile base, carrying no aircraft of her own but able to supply and equip – and provide an additional flight-deck for – an entire carrier fleet. The final result was a compromise. *Shinano* would be a carrier supply-ship, but she would also have a few fighters of her own for self-defence and a hangar for storing them. This caused immense difficulties, because *Shinano's* hull had been completed up to the main deck by the time of the decision to convert her. The work crawled along – as slowly, in fact, as did that on Germany's only aircraft-carrier, *Graf Zeppelin* – in

a dreary stop-go rhythm. When the builders were finally galvanised into an all-out effort, after the defeat in the Philippine Sea, it was too late. All the reserves of trained aircrew had been whittled away to the point of extinction. Nevertheless, the work on the useless giant moved to completion and *Shinano* was ready for service in November 1944.

She was the biggest aircraft-carrier in the world, and the best protected. Her armoured flight-deck stretched 840 feet by 131 feet. She could steam at 27 knots, she bristled with defensive armament, and she could carry 47 aircraft. At last, the backbone of Japan's new carrier fleet was finished – but the carrier fleet did not exist. There were carriers; there were aircraft; but there was little or no fuel for either, and certainly no trained aircrew. *Shinano* was, in fact, an awe-inspiring but thoroughly useless white elephant. And her end was little short of bathos. On November 28, 1944, she left Yokosuka for a brief shake-down cruise, escorted by three destroyers. She had not been at sea 24 hours, let alone moved out of sight of land, when she was caught by the American submarine *Archerfish,* and hit by a salvo of four torpedoes.

In the Battle of Leyte Gulf, *Shinano's* sister-ship *Musashi* had proved what tremendous punishment the class could take and still stay afloat. *Musashi* had been singled out as the main target for American air attacks as Kurita's battle fleet struggled through the Sibuyan Sea. Plastered by bombs and ripped by repeated torpedo hits, she had refused to sink, and her expert crew kept her afloat by skilful counter-flooding for hours until the end. *Shinano* was not vitally damaged at all by *Archerfish's* torpedoes and could still make 18 knots. But her inexperienced crew neglected practically every damage-control rule in the book. The waters rose and spread from compartment to compartment; she kept on her course at full speed; and her captain would certainly have been court-martialled for gross negligence if he had not gone down with *Shinano,* seven hours after the torpedoing, at 1017 on November 29.

Mobility and hitting-power are the prerequisites of a carrier force, and by 1945 the Japanese carrier force had no fuel and no aircrew. This in turn meant that the surviving units of the Imperial Navy were now finally denuded of their air umbrella and were, from a strategic point of view, little more than floating scrap-iron. The Americans went ahead with the last major offensives of the Pacific war – Luzon, Iwo Jima, and Okinawa – secure in the knowledge that the Japanese Navy would never pose a serious threat to them again.

To the Japanese high command it was unthinkable that the Emperor's last warships should be bombed to destruction in their home ports, or hunted down independently at sea. The *kamikaze* strategy was therefore applied to the Japanese Navy – but, as with the Army and Navy air forces, the problem remained one of *matériel,* not men. There were thousands of eager volunteers willing to show their veneration for their Emperor by immolating themselves on an enemy carrier and taking as many Americans with them as possible. The difficulty was in getting them there. The Navy, as we have seen, developed two main *kamikaze* weapons of its own: *kaiten* and explosive speedboats. However, the best suicide weapon remained the aircraft, plummeting down on its target from the skies.

The ambitious *"SHO"* plan which had thrown the massed strength of the Combined Fleet against the Americans at Leyte had been motivated by the *kamikaze* mentality: to do as much damage as possible with inferior resources. And the same held true of one of the most bizarre episodes in naval history: the suicide sortie of the *Yamato* during the opening phase of the long battle for Okinawa, in April 1945.

Japan's defensive strategy was based on the idea of "Dunkirking" the spearhead troops, once they had got ashore, and disrupting the Allied offensive plan by raising as much havoc as possible. And it was to this end that the "Special Sea Attack Force" was formed. It consisted of the *Yamato* and a light destroyer escort. Using literally the last dregs of the country's fuel oil stocks, the *Yamato* would make straight for the invasion beaches at Okinawa, deal out maximum destruction to the American invasion fleet, then beach herself and fight to the last shell available for her huge 18-inch guns.

Under the command of Vice-Admiral Seiichi Ito, the force sailed from Tokuyama in Japan's Inland Sea on the afternoon of April 6: *Yamato,* surrounded by a ring of eight destroyers and the light cruiser *Yahagi.* The Japanese squadron had barely cleared Japanese territorial waters before it was spotted by American submarines patrolling the Bungo Strait, between the islands of Shikoku and Kyūshū. Once out at sea, Ito altered course to the west, steering into the East China Sea preparatory to a last turn to the south for the final run down to Okinawa, and his ships were sighted at 0822 hours on the 7th by reconnaissance aircraft from Admiral Marc Mitscher's Task Force 58. A mighty strike of 380 dive-bombers and torpedo-bombers took off from Mitscher's carriers at 1000, when the Japanese force was some 250 miles away–just before *Yamato* and her frail ring of escorts swung to the south. Around noon the first contact was made and the final ordeal of the *Yamato* began.

The American pilots were impressed by the massive A.A. fire which came up at them: the Japanese had learned the lesson of air power well, and by the time of her last voyage *Yamato* bristled with no less than 146 25-mm A.A. guns. Most impressive of all, however, were the *San-Shiki* shells fired by her main armament, which may be best described as 18-inch shotgun shells. *Yamato's* main battery

was designed for use in the anti-aircraft rôle and the *San-Shiki* shells were crammed with incendiary bullets. The idea was that the shells would be fired into a group of enemy aircraft; the shells would then burst, like a shotgun fired into a flock of birds, mowing down the enemy planes. It was found, however, that the terrifying blast of *Yamato's* 18-inch guns when fired at maximum elevation only served to disrupt the main volume of A.A. fire. The *San-Shiki* shells proved to be a failure, like so many other impressive-sounding Japanese ideas.

The Japanese had the weather–squalls and low clouds–on their side, but little else. The Special Attack Force had no fighter cover whatever and the American bombers were able to make almost unimpeded practice as repeated waves swept in to the attack. The ring of Japanese destroyers soon broke up under the stress of constant manoeuvre to avoid torpedoes. Pounded to a wreck, *Yahagi* sank shortly after 1400 hours; and 25 minutes later came the turn of *Yamato.* She had taken a fearful beating; at least ten torpedoes had hit her, plus seven bombs. Her crew was unable to cope with the inrush of water, or keep her upright by counterflooding. *Yamato* finally capsized and sank at 1425. Admiral Ito and nearly all the ship's company of 2,400 men went down with her. Four of the escorting destroyers were sunk as well, and the battered survivors turned for home.

Such was the Battle of the East China Sea on April 7, 1945. It was the end of the Dreadnought age–the last time that a battleship was sunk by enemy action on the high seas. The wheel had indeed come full circle since Pearl Harbor in December 1941, when the superb Japanese carrier arm had proved the vulnerability of the battleship once and for all. *Yamato's* sacrifice was totally useless; she had never even sighted Okinawa, let alone taken any pressure off the gallant Japanese garrison there. On the Japanese side of the ledger there was only one completely insignificant flicker of success: a *kamikaze* hit on the American carrier *Hancock.*

Cowering in the Japanese home ports lay the remnants of the Imperial Navy. At Yokosuka there was the battleship *Nagato,* in her heyday the strongest battleship in the world with her 16-inch main armament. Her last action had been Leyte Gulf, where she had escaped the holocaust of the battleships. Now in the summer of 1945 she was inoperative, inglorious, with her funnel and foremast removed to assist camouflage. The rump of the battle fleet lay at Kure, Japan's great naval base. There were the *Ise* and *Hyuga,* absurdly converted to seaplane-carriers by the removal of their after turrets. With equal absurdity they had been classified the 4th Carrier Division of the 2nd Fleet in November 1944. In March 1945 they had finally been taken off the active list and now served as A.A. batteries. Also at Kure was the *Haruna,*

the last survivor of the *"Kongo"* class battle-cruisers built on the eve of World War I. With the *Kongos* Japanese designers had shown the world that they had seen through the inherent weaknesses of the battle-cruiser concept by specifying their order for fast battle-ships; and the *Kongos* had been extensively reconstructed between the wars. Another genuine museum-piece at Kure in 1945 was the old target-ship *Settsu,* whose construction had helped place Japan fourth after Britain, the United States, and Germany as a Dreadnought naval power.

Seven Japanese aircraft-carriers were also in home waters. First among them was the little *Hosho,* the first carrier in the world to be designed as such from the keel up, which had been launched after World War I. When she served as fleet carrier training ship, most of the Japanese Navy's crack aircrews learned their trade aboard her. She had survived Midway as Yamamoto's last serviceable carrier and was still in service in 1945. The other six carriers–*Ibuki, Amagi, Katsuragi, Kaiyo, Ryuho,* and *Junyo*–represented the losing struggle to restore carrier protection and hitting-power to the Combined Fleet. Apart from destroyers and submarines still in service, the only other major units of the Combined Fleet in Japanese ports in 1945 were six cruisers.

With American carrier planes now able to range at will over the Japanese homeland, it was only a matter of time before these sorry survivors were singled out for destruction. Admiral Halsey planned it personally: it was to be a formal revenge for Pearl Harbor, an all-American operation without the British Pacific Fleet. It took the form of a fearsome three-day blitz on the Japanese naval bases, concentrating on Kure. Between July 24 and 26, 1945, the American carrier forces struck round the clock. In those hectic days they sank the *Amagi, Ise* and *Hyuga, Haruna, Settsu,* and five cruisers, effectively destroying Japanese hopes of forming a possible suicide squadron from their last heavy warships. If any one date is required for the formal annihilation of the Japanese fleet, it may be set as July 24-26, 1945.

Although the British did not participate in the mass attacks on the Japanese naval bases, they were nevertheless active during this final phase. Ranging over the Inland Sea, British carrier planes sank two frigates and several other small fry, and also claimed a hit on an escort carrier. The biggest feather in the caps of the British, however, was earned thousands of miles away: in a dramatic and successful midget submarine attack on the port of Singapore.

At Singapore lay the Japanese heavy cruisers *Takao* and *Myoko,* both of them marked down for attack by the Submarine Flotilla of the British Pacific Fleet. Two XE-craft–improved versions of the midget submarine which had crippled the German battleship *Tirpitz*

A flame-throwing tank of the 32nd Regiment, 7th Division in action on top of Hill 95 on Okinawa.

in her Arctic lair in late 1943–were detailed for the job: *XE-1* (Lieutenant J. E. Smart) and *XE-3* (Lieutenant Ian Fraser). On July 30, 1945, the two midgets were on their way to the approaches to Singapore Roads, towed by their parent submarines: *Spark* (*XE-1*) and *Stygian* (*XE-3*).

In the history of submarine warfare this attack is particularly interesting because of the use of the echo depth-finder in navigating to the target. By 0600 hours on July 31–set as the day for the attack–*XE-3* was manoeuvring up the Johore Strait at 30 feet. The boom–hardly a formidable affair, with a permanent gate some 300 yards wide–was safely passed at 1030 and the target, *Takao*, was sighted at 1250. As *XE-3* closed in on her victim there was a disconcerting moment. As Fraser put it, "I was very upset to see a motor cutter filled with Japanese liberty men only about 30 yards from my periscope." *XE-3*, however, remained undetected as she crawled towards *Takao* across the uneven harbour bottom, fetching up against the hull of the Japanese cruiser with a loud clang at 1442 hours.

With great daring, Fraser decided to make his attack with *XE-3* wedged squarely beneath *Takao's* hull. The attack used two weapons: limpet mines, attached to the enemy hull by the XE-craft's diver, and fused explosive charges, released from the midget's hull from inside. Operating with great difficulty in the murky waters of the harbour, diver Leading-Seaman J. Magennis attached six limpets to *Takao's* bottom. It was a long and exhausting job, for he had to scrape off patches of weed and barnacles to get the limpets to stick. After placing the mines and returning inside *XE-3*, Magennis had to go back outside and release the starboard explosive charge, which refused to

detach itself. Tired though he was, Magennis had no hesitation in immediately volunteering for this strenuous and extremely dangerous job. As Fraser's report has it: "He went on oxygen again at 16.25 hrs. and made his exit to the casing with a large spanner in his hand. After seven minutes he managed, by much banging at the carrier and levering at the release pins, to get the carrier away."

With the explosives safely placed in position, Fraser turned to the task of wriggling *XE-3* clear of her victim and retreating to the open sea for the rendezvous with *Stygian*. Despite several harrowing moments the retreat passed off safely. The boom was passed at 1949 hours and at 2100 *XE-3* was able to surface and proceed down the Johore Strait. Rendezvous was safely made with *Stygian* at 2345 hours.

Smart, in *XE-1*, had had bad luck from the start of the approach. One mishap after another had combined to delay his attack so badly that he risked being caught inside the boom if he had pressed on to his own target. Smart therefore took the extremely brave decision to attack Fraser's target as well and take the risk of being blown up by the detonation of *XE-3's* limpets and charges. The possibility of this was heightened by the fact that the detachable charges were fitted with disturbance fuses, and *XE-1* would stand a likely chance of setting them off. But the calculated risk taken by Smart paid off; he dropped his charges and retreated safely. A final mishap was a 24-hour delay in the rendezvous with *Spark*. Fraser and Magennis received the Victoria Cross for their attack, Smart the Distinguished Service Order.

As for the unfortunate *Takao*, left with two sets of explosive charges and six limpet mines, the resultant explosion effectively destroyed her as a fighting ship by blowing the bottom out of her.

The postwar fate of the Japanese warships which survived Halsey's Blitz of July 1945 was inglorious. *Nagato*, last of

the battle fleet, was used as a target ship during the Bikini Atoll atom test in 1946, together with the cruiser *Sakawa*. The other cruisers and carriers were either used as targets, scrapped, or sunk at sea by the victors–the Americans in particular sank a hecatomb of surrendered Japanese submarines off Gato Island in April 1946.

The fate of the last vessels of the Imperial Japanese Navy was the grim end to a remarkable story. Japan's emergence as a modern power only dates from the last three decades of the 19th Century. By careful study of the best European models, she built a navy second to none in either *matériel* or fighting spirit in under 30 years. In that period Japanese naval designers not only participated in the birth of the Dreadnought era: they proved again and again that they could lead the world in laying down new concepts for the development of the fighting ship and the evolution of naval warfare.

What went wrong? It is now generally accepted that Japan's decision to go to war in December 1941 was a calculated risk, a gamble which came within an ace of success. But as far as the total defeat of her prime instrument of war in the Pacific–the Combined Fleet–is concerned, several serious errors stand out. The first is that in 1941 the Combined Fleet was a contradiction in terms. Its carrier force was superb but the battle fleet–the big gun–was still looked to as the weapon which would bring decisive victory. Submarine strategy was totally misguided on the Japanese side, whereas the Americans used their submarines correctly and reaped the rewards. Above all, however, the Japanese naval strategists had to cut their coat according to their cloth: the one thing they could not afford was a war of attrition, and this they got. The Guadalcanal campaign, for example, cost them the equivalent of an entire peace-time fleet–losses which could never be replaced. The very speed with which the Americans assumed the offensive in the Pacific, never to lose it, showed what a narrow margin the Japanese Navy had.

And the result was an unreal metamorphosis which led the Japanese into building huge white elephants like *Shinano* and the aircraft-carrying "I-4400" submarines. It saw the Combined Fleet change from an instrument of the offensive and of victory to a sacrificial victim whose purpose was only to stave off defeat. This process first became dominant at the time of the Marianas campaign in June 1944, and it was the *leitmotif* of the final destruction of the Combined Fleet. That there was great heroism among the men who took *Yamato* out on her last voyage cannot be doubted. But the former cold professionalism which had carried the Japanese Navy to its high tide of victory in the summer of 1942 was gone. In ships, in men, and in men's ideas, too much had been lost in the disastrous naval operations in the Solomon Islands, at Midway, and in the battle of Leyte Gulf.

CHAPTER 79

The bomber offensive on Japan

As late as March 6, 1945, Major-General Curtis E. LeMay, who had recently replaced Brigadier-General H. S. Hansell as commander of the 21st Bomber Command, remarked: "This outfit has been getting a lot of publicity without having really accomplished a hell of a lot in bombing results."

To date, the tactics employed had been high level precision attacks by B-29's. However ice, high winds, poor visibility, and air turbulence made navigation and accurate bombing very difficult and it had taken up to eight separate H.E. raids to have any appreciable effect on some targets.

Late in 1944 the B-29's had been moved from China and India to bases on Saipan, Guam, and Tinian in the Marianas. They made their first raid on Truk on October 28, and on November 24 they hit Tokyo.

Japanese fighter attacks from Iwo Jima were eliminated when the island was secured in March 1945, and its landing grounds subsequently saved the lives of 24,761 men in 2,251 emergency landings by crippled B-29's.

Since high altitude daylight raids were not giving good results, LeMay, who was by nature an experimenter, decided to test the effectiveness of incendiary bombs against these targets. The attack would be a massed assault against the industrial cities, delivered at low level, at night.

Two light test raids were made against Nagoya on January 3, and Kobe on February 4. The planners were pleased in the United States and a full-scale operation was suggested to evaluate the effectiveness of this type of attack. It was mounted on the nights of March 9–10, 1945, and the target was Tokyo.

LeMay staked his career on the operation, for many pessimists had predicted that at low level the B-29's would suffer very heavy losses. To increase the bomb-load, and prevent the aircraft from firing at one another in the dark, he had ordered that they should fly with unloaded guns. In place of the 8,000 rounds of machine gun ammunition normally carried, they added 3,200 pounds of bombs. In addition, the low-level approach would save the engines and further increase the bomb-load. On average each plane would carry six tons.

The lead squadron was loaded with 180 M47 70-pound napalm bombs which were to start fires to bring out the motorised fire-fighting equipment. The planes which followed would carry 24 500-pound clusters of M69's, a six-pound oil incendiary, very effective against lightly constructed buildings. These clusters were set to burst so that they would give a minimum density of 25 tons, or 8,333 M69's, per square mile.

The 334 B-29's, loaded with about 2,000 tons of bombs, came over the area in three wings at altitudes between 4,900 and 9,200 feet. The weather was better than usual with little cloud cover and a visibility of ten miles. As they unloaded their bombs, the crews saw the flames spread to form bigger fires.

The crews reported they could bomb visually and were meeting only light A.A. fire, with no fighter opposition. Later formations found the target obscured by smoke and had to range wide over the area in search of new targets. Turbulence from the fires made the bomb runs difficult as the aircraft rose in the intense heat waves. On the return flight, tail gunners could see a glow for 150 miles.

For the raiders it was an inexpensive attack; flak damaged 42 bombers, 14 were lost, and of these the crews of five were rescued. The loss ratio was 4.2 per cent, which compared well with the 3.5 per cent figure for all B-29 raids and the 5.7 for January.

For the inhabitants of Tokyo it was a horrifying and awesome experience. Police records show that 267,171 buildings were destroyed and 1,008,005 people made homeless. There were 83,793 dead and 40,918 wounded, and it was nearly a month before the last body was removed from the ruins.

Photographs revealed that 15.8 square miles of the city had been burnt out; this included 18 per cent of the industrial area and 63 per cent of the commercial centre and the heart of the congested residential area. The Intelligence officers of the 21st Bomber Command removed 21 numbered industrial plants from their target lists.

Less than 24 hours after this attack a force of 313 B-29's began taking off on the afternoon of March 11 with the target of Nagoya, Japan's third largest city and centre of her aircraft industry. One aircraft ditched on take off, and 19 others turned back with mechanical trouble. The 285 which reached the city unloaded 1,790 tons of incendiary bombs from between 5,100 and 8,500 feet. Despite the fact that the bomb-load was 125 tons heavier than that dropped on Tokyo, there was no general holocaust.

There were 394 separate fires, and post-strike photographs revealed that 2.05 square miles of the city had been destroyed. Though 18 numbered industrial targets (that is plants given a special designation in target folders) were damaged or destroyed, the aircraft plants were not knocked out.

Nagoya survived because it had an adequate water supply, well-spaced fire breaks, an efficient fire-fighting service which operated promptly and effectively, and that night there was no wind to fan the initial fires into bigger blazes.

For the raiders the attack was again an inexpensive operation – the only bomber lost was the one that ditched at take off. Twenty others were damaged, 18 by flak and two by fighters.

Osaka was the next target. The city produced about one-tenth of Japan's war-time total of ships, one-seventh of her electrical equipment, and one-third of her machinery and machine tools. Its army arsenal furnished 20 per cent of the army's ordnance requirements, and though it did not assemble aircraft, Osaka contained many sub-contractors producing engine parts. Besides having major road and rail links, it was a great commercial and administrative centre. In 1945 it had an estimated population of 2,142,480.

Like other major cities, it was congested and inflammable. It had never been hit before by any major strikes, and now stood ready for destruction by fire.

On March 13, after heroic efforts by the maintenance crews, 301 B-29's took off, each carrying six tons of bombs, and this time the low wing carried .50-inch ammunition for lower forward and aft turrets as well as for the tail guns. The target was obscured by clouds when the 274 bombers that reached Osaka began their run. Using radar they achieved a better concentration than the attack on Nagoya.

In three hours they dropped 1,732.6 tons of bombs and burned out 8.1 square miles of the city centre. As the flames increased, fire fighting and A.R.P. services collapsed, and 119 major factories were destroyed and 134,744 houses burned down, with 1,363 damaged. The Osaka fire department listed 3,988 dead, 678 missing, and 8,463 injured. It was the Tokyo fire-storm again, with men and women suffocating in makeshift shelters or roasted alive as they rushed through the flames.

Now it was the turn of Japan's sixth largest city. On March 16 the bombers came to Kobe. Like Osaka it was "practically a virgin target".

A port with a long irregular water front, it was easy to pick out on a radar scope. On either side of the harbour were important heavy industrial installations. It was Japan's most important overseas port and a focus for inland transportation.

The bomb-load for the attack was different this time because the earlier operations had used up nearly all the available stocks of M47's and M69's. The B-29's would be carrying M17A1's, 500-pound clusters of 4-pound magnesium thermite incendiaries. While these bombs would be effective against the dockland and industrial buildings, they would have less impact on the flimsy houses.

In two hours and eight minutes, 307 bombers unloaded 2,355 tons. Japanese fighters were up this time, but they did not interfere with the raid – though they made 93 attacks, none of the three B-29's lost was hit by fighters.

The post-attack photographs looked disappointing. Only 2.9 square miles (about a fifth of the city) had been destroyed. However, on the ground the Japanese could assess the cost in human and industrial losses more accurately. About 500 industrial buildings were destroyed and 162 damaged. Among those heavily damaged were the Kawasaki shipyards, where 2,000-ton submarines were built. The loss of 65,951 houses left 242,468 people homeless. Police records showed 2,669 dead or missing and 11,289 injured.

The March campaign was brought to a close with a return visit to Nagoya on the night of the 19th. The bomb loads carried by the different wings reflected the way the fire raids had used up the available stocks of incendiaries. Every third plane carried two 500-pound general purpose H.E. bombs to disorganise the fire-fighters. The 314th Wing carried M69's, the 313th M47's, and the 73rd a mixed load of M47's and M76's.

A total of 1,858 tons of bombs was dropped by the 290 aircraft which reached Nagoya, and because of smoke and searchlights, the bomb aimers had to use radar. This time they burned out three square miles and damaged the Nagoya arsenal, the marshalling yards, and the Aichi engine factory; but the Mitsubishi plants escaped with minor damage.

It had been a good month for the 21st Bomber Command. It had flown 1,595 sorties in 10 days (three-fourths as many as had been flown in all previous missions) and the 9,365 tons of bombs dropped were three times the weight expended before March 9.

Though there had been a great strain on both flight and maintenance crews, they had recovered quickly and morale was very high. Men and machines had shown that they could achieve spectacular results for a loss ratio of 0.9 per cent in crew, far lower than that for day-light missions. The lower altitudes allowed a higher bomb-load to be carried and caused less wear on the engines. In Washington and Guam the planners adjusted their target programme and prepared a three-phase list with 33 targets rated A, B, or C according to their relative industrial value. Some like Nagoya, Osaka, and Kobe had been hit before, but the planners felt that some of their urban areas still merited attention. The first phase emphasised the destruction of ground ordnance and aircraft plants, the second machine tools, electrical equipment, and ordnance and aircraft parts. Phase three would be implemented in the light of the results from the first 22 targets.

And what of Japan? The attacks had left behind 32 square miles of cinders and fire-blackened buildings in four major cities. Not only had strategic targets been destroyed, but factories producing goods for home consumption. Workers lost their homes, or accommodation in factory dormitories, and the evacuation which followed added to the labour problems already caused by the conscription of adult males. Early in 1944 some 600,000 houses were demolished to provide fire breaks, and since building materials were

Bombs tumble down from a B-29 Superfortress onto the already blazing waterfront of a Japanese port (top). Some of the victims of the horrific incendiary raids on Tokyo which helped bring Japan to her knees by crippling the Japanese war economy (above).

not provided, the destitute families had to find shelter with friends and relatives, or in public buildings. Natural disasters added to their misery, for 1945 was a year of excessive rainfall and floods. Local fires and earthquakes destroyed a further 500,000 houses. By July about a quarter of all the houses in Japan had been destroyed by all causes and some 22 million people, about three-tenths of the population, had been made homeless.

Operations in support of the landings at Okinawa diverted the bombers from major incendiary attacks for two months. The savage fighting for the island, and the suicidal attacks on shipping, convinced LeMay that he should try to bomb Japan into surrender, rather than see this slaughter repeated on a larger scale in the invasion of the main islands.

The new campaign was inaugurated with a day-light attack on Nagoya on May 14. A total of 472 bombers dropped 2,515 tons of M69's from between 12,000 and 20,500 feet. Though the raid burned only about 3.15 square miles, Mitsubishi's No. 10 engine works lost its Kelmut bearing plant and suffered other damage.

An attack on the docks and industrial areas to the south on the night of May 16 showed how effective low-level night attacks were in contrast to the day-light high-level operations. In the May 14 raid ten B-29's were lost, two to enemy action. The night attack had only three losses, all due to mechanical failure. As it was a low-level attack, the aircraft carried eight tons as against 5.3 on day-light raids, and so a total of 3,609 tons of mixed M47's and M50's were dropped. The raid burned 3.82 square miles and heavily damaged Mitsubishi's No. 5 aircraft works. Nagoya was finished as a target for area attacks.

Little purpose is served in detailing all the raids made between May and June. With variations such as day-light escorted operations, or mixed bomb-loads, they

Burnt-out Tokyo, with only the shells of concrete buildings left standing, a testimony to the effects of incendiary bombing.

brought fiery destruction to the major cities of Japan.

City	Total urban area (in square miles)	Destroyed (in square miles)
Tokyo	110.8	56.3
Nagoya	39.7	12.4
Kobe	15.7	8.8
Osaka	59.8	15.6
Yokohama	20.2	8.9
Kawasaki	11.0	3.6
Totals	257.2	105.6

The Japanese capital received a double knock-out blow on the nights of May 23 and 25. In previous raids 5,000 tons of bombs had destroyed 34.2 square miles, and 2,545 tons had been expended in precision attacks.

In the first raid, for the loss of 17 bombers, 520 B-29's dropped 3,646 tons of bombs and destroyed 5.3 square miles.

The second raid brought the bombers close to the Imperial Palace and "took out" parts of the financial, commercial, and governmental districts of the city. The bomb-load was lighter, but some 3,262 tons dropped by 502 aircraft yielded results which had not been anticipated: 16.8 square miles, the greatest area destroyed in a single raid, lay smoking beneath the reconnaissance aircraft when they visited the city.

With 50.8 per cent of the entire city reduced to ashes and rubble, Tokyo was removed from the list of incendiary targets.

In the campaign some 4,678 sorties were flown and 27,164 tons of bombs dropped. And for the loss of 70 aircraft and damage to 420, a further 48 square miles of target areas were burned out. But there still remained the smaller cities undamaged by fire, and now they experienced the terror by night.

Sixty attacks, following the same tactics employed against the main targets, were made between June 17 and August 14. As a rule a B-29 wing would take one city, and in this way four targets could be attacked on one night. The 21st Bomber Command flew 8,014 sorties and dropped 54,184 tons of incendiaries, and for the loss of 19 bombers destroyed 63.75 square miles, about half the total area of all the targets.

Such was their confidence, the Americans now dropped leaflets to warn the civilians in these cities before they struck. But while 12 cities would receive the leaflets, only four would be attacked. Despite this, the people poured into the country. Sensing the desperate mood of the nation, the Minister of Home Affairs, Motoki Abe, said later: "I believe that after the 23–24 May (*sic*) 1945 raids on Tokyo, civilian defence measures in that city, as well as other parts of Japan, were considered a futile effort." But Mamoru Shigemitsu, the Foreign Minister, asserted that though "day by day Japan turned into a furnace . . . the clarion call was accepted. If the Emperor ordained it, they would leap into the flames. That was the people of Japan."

CHAPTER 80
Russia invades Manchuria

At midnight on August 8, 1945, the Japanese Ambassador in Moscow, Naotake Sato, received the Soviet declaration of war. Ten minutes later, on the other side of the Soviet Union, 1,500,000 Russian troops were launched on the last great offensive of the war.

Together with 5,500 armoured vehicles and nearly 4,000 aircraft, these forces would give a spectacular demonstration of mobile war against the 1,040,000 men of the Kwantung Army in Manchuria.

Throughout the war neither the Russians nor the Japanese had made any offensive moves – indeed Japan had taken great care to honour the Neutrality Pact of April 1941. On the strength of reports from their spy in Toyko, Richard Sorge, the Russian high command began to transfer men from the Far East as the war with Germany grew more intense.

In June 1941 the Russians had about 30 reasonably well equipped divisions in the Far East. Japanese Intelligence estimated that during the crucial period between June and December 1941, the Russians transferred 15 infantry divisions, three cavalry divisions, 1,700 tanks, and 1,500 aircraft to the German front.

New units were mobilised to replace them, including nine infantry divisions and four brigades and an air army headquarters. By December 1941 the Japanese estimate, which was fairly accurate, was that Russian strength stood at about 800,000 men, 1,000 tanks, and 1,000 aircraft. In fact by the end of 1942, when the last major transfers ceased, the Soviet order of battle stood at 19 infantry divisions, ten infantry brigades, 750,000 men, 1,000 tanks, and 1,000 aircraft – although of course these units were neither at a state of full readiness, nor completely trained.

These unit strengths remained about the same until the end of 1944. Training conditions were as harsh as the climate, and the armies had a low priority for re-equipment. In 1942, however, the garrisons in northern Sakhalin and Kamchatka were increased after the Japanese had captured Attu and Kiska.

Just as the numbers and quality of the Russian troops stationed in the Far East reflected the fortunes of war in Europe, so too as the war swung against Japan, the Kwantung Army began to serve as a pool for reinforcements.

Japanese strength in Manchuria reached its peak in January 1942, when the army stood at 1.1 million men. During 1942 and 1943 they were still able to equal at least 70 per cent of Soviet strength in the Far East. During 1944 many troops, including almost all the élite units, were gradually withdrawn to Japan. By July they were at their weakest, with only seven divisions in Manchuria.

These forces were increased and by August 9, 1945 there were 24 divisions and 11 brigades in Manchuria, seven divisions in Korea, and one brigade on Sakhalin and in the Kuriles. Total strength, including Manchukuan and Inner Mongolian satellite forces, stood at just over one million men, of which 787,600 were in the Kwantung Army. The Japanese had 1,215 armoured vehicles, 1,800 aircraft, and 6,700 guns and mortars. However, this equipment was almost all obsolete, and the Kwantung Army was a shadow of the well trained veteran force which had existed early in 1942. All the first line equipment and trained troops had been posted to the Pacific, and the most seasoned unit had only been established in the spring of 1944.

The Kwantung Army was brought up to numerical strength about ten days before the Soviet attack, when in a hurried mobilisation eight of its 24 divisions and seven of the nine infantry brigades, that is over one-quarter of the total Japanese military manpower in Manchuria, were formed from all the remaining Japanese males in the area. Until then they had been exempt from military duty, being unfit or over-age. One of the two weak tank brigades was formed in July 1945.

Although the standard Japanese infantry division had about 23,000 men, the actual strengths of those in Manchuria ranged between 11,000 and 15,000. Even divisions transferred from China were not complete: many had only one of the nine artillery companies prescribed per division.

Weapons too were inadequate: there was no artillery heavier than 75-mm, no modern anti-tank guns, and the tanks were very light, thinly-armoured, and under-armed.

The 2nd Air Army had a front line strength of only 225 fighters, 40 bombers, 45 reconnaissance, and 20 *kamikaze* aircraft, with 640 training aircraft in reserve. Most of these aircraft, moreover, were obsolete.

There was a shortage of ammunition, and the number of medium and light machine guns with infantry units was less than half the authorised figure. The Japanese estimated that the average efficiency of each division was not greater than three-tenths of that of a pre-war first line division. The morale of both officers and men was low, particularly in the newly formed units.

By 1943 the Western Allies had contained the Germans and Japanese and forced them on to the defensive. The Soviet Union and the United States began to discuss the possibility of Soviet entry into the war in the Far East. Stalin agreed in principle, and plans were made to enlarge the denuded armies in the east.

Between the Teheran Conference and the end of the war in Europe in May 1945, the Soviet High Command, or *Stavka*, reorganised the two "fronts" in the area, the Transbaikal and the Far East.

They were re-equipped with new tanks and guns, and stocks of ammunition, fuel, and supplies were moved up in great secrecy.

From April to August the Russians moved 30 divisions, nine brigades, and other units from Europe. The Japanese estimated that the Russians had moved only 20 to 45 divisions and that the total strength of Soviet forces by the end of July 1945 was between 40 and 45 divisions. Japanese Intelligence expected the Russians to build up a force of 60 divisions before attacking, and so they concluded that the Russians would not be ready until early August.

Soviet forces were divided between three Fronts, comprising 11 combined-arms armies, one tank army, and three air armies, in all 80 divisions, four tank and mechanised corps, 40 independent tank and mechanised brigades, and six infantry brigades. The total strength of the army and air force was 1,577,725 men (of whom 1,058,982 were front line troops), 26,137 guns and mortars, 3,704 tanks, and 1,852 self-propelled guns (the Japanese estimated 4,500 tanks), with 5,368 aircraft – including naval – of which 4,807 were combat aircraft (the Japanese estimated 6,300).

The Russian superiority was qualitative as well as quantitative. They had sent four of their most experienced armies from the European theatre. The 5th and the 39th had been in action at Königsberg in East Prussia and had a reputation for dealing with fixed defences and fortifications. The other two armies, the 6th Guards Tank Army and the 53rd Army, came from the 2nd Ukrainian Front, and were capable "Blitzkrieg" campaigners.

With these veterans came experienced commanders. Head of the new *Stavka* for Soviet Forces in the Far East was Marshal Aleksandr M. Vasilevsky, recently Chief of the General Staff. Colonel-General S. P. Ivanov became chief-of-staff for the new command. Of the three fronts, Marshal Rodion Ya. Malinovsky commanded the Transbaikal Front, Marshal Kyril A. Meretskov the 1st Far Eastern Front and General of the Army Maxim A. Purkaev the 2nd Far Eastern Front. Purkaev had been the Far Eastern commander through much of the Russo-German war. The Pacific Fleet came under Admiral Ivan S. Yumashev.

This new leadership was necessary because most of the officers in the old Far East Army had only seen action in 1941 in disorganised rear-guard actions against the Germans. They were also inexperienced in the tactics of massed armoured penetration with air support.

Swift and ruthless as the Soviet attack might be, the preparations for the operation in Manchuria are no less impressive.

For three and a half months the trans-Siberian railway was used to its maximum capacity, as men from Europe made the long journey to their new assembly areas (anything from 4,000 to 7,000 miles). Nearly 750,000 men made the journey, and between May and July 136,000 truck loads of equipment were sent east. To save the railway, all motorised units of the Transbaikal Front moved independently from the Chita-Karymskaya sector to the concentration areas in eastern Mongolia, a distance of 625 to 750 miles, mostly over desert. Even the infantry of the 17th and 36th Armies marched the last 150 to 300 miles.

The 6th Guards Tank Army left its tanks and assault guns in Czechoslovakia for other units, and at Choibalsan in Mongolia collected over 600 new vehicles sent directly from the Ural armaments factories. An ingenious idea in principle, it caused some disruption because of the short time allocated to the tank crews to collect their vehicles from the depot.

As with most Soviet operations, ammunition had priority in the build-up of reserves. Tank munitions topped the list, with artillery and mortar ammunition second and infantry ammunition third. Food for 15 days was stocked, but the petrol, oil, and lubricants amassed proved to be inadequate when the operation got under way.

Water was a special problem, because troops of the Transbaikal Front would have to cross the Gobi Desert before they reached the Great Hsingan mountain range. Engineer battalions and other units dug some 635 wells in the concentration and staging areas. Vehicles were loaded with water, fuel, and spares for the journey across the desert. In view of the known prevalence of epidemic diseases in northern China, all Soviet troops were inoculated against plague and other ailments.

As its occupation of eastern Europe had demonstrated, the Soviet Union did not fight simply to defeat the enemy and end the war. At the Yalta Conference in February 1945, President Roosevelt and Marshal Stalin came to a private agreement. Stalin would declare war on Japan three months after the end of the war in Europe, subject to the successful conclusion of a treaty with China; Soviet troops would operate in Chinese territory, Japanese-occupied Manchuria, and Jehol. In return for this, Stalin demanded American recognition of Soviet territorial claims in the Pacific: Russia was to have the Kurile Islands, the southern part of Sakhalin Island, and the old Russian bases of Port Arthur and Dairen in south Manchuria. Stalin even persuaded Roosevelt to approach the Nationalist Chinese Government on his behalf to secure Chiang Kai-shek's acceptance.

When on July 21 President Truman remarked to Stalin at the Potsdam Conference that the Allies had a new weapon of special destructive force, the Soviet leader showed no real interest but said he hoped the Allies would make "good use of it against the Japanese".

Whether Stalin realised the impact that the first atomic bomb would have on

the Japanese is difficult to say. Vasilevsky confirmed, after the war, that September had been fixed for the start of the offensive. The general staff was troubled when it was told in May that August 8 would be D-day. Finally, in a telephone call from Potsdam, Stalin told Vasilevsky to push the date forward to August 1. The Marshal explained that the state of preparation did not permit this, and so the two leaders finally agreed on August 9.

The troops may have been in position by August 9, but Japanese Intelligence had not been completely wrong when it predicted a later date for the offensive. Soviet logistic support was severely strained by the operation, and many tanks were halted by lack of fuel, which had to be flown in in an extemporised re-supply operation.

It was probably Stalin's military and political intuition which made him realise that the war would soon be over, with or without an atomic bomb, and that if he wanted land in the east he would have to act fast. With this land he took nearly 600,000 Japanese prisoners-of-war, who were sent to the Soviet Union and Mongolia as forced labour. Between 1948 and 1950, 513,139 were repatriated.

Despite the steady reduction of Japan's empire by land and air, culminating in the destruction of Hiroshima and Nagasaki, Soviet historians claim that Japan surrendered because of Russia's entry into the war. Ignoring this assertion, let us examine the Red Army's contribution to the war in the Far East.

The plans were fairly simple, but some parts of the execution were complicated and bold. The two main thrusts would be made by the Transbaikal Front from the west, cutting through most of Manchuria to Ch'ang-ch'un and Mukden, and by the 1st Far Eastern Front from the east, breaking through the fortifications facing the Maritime Province and moving to Kirin and on to Ch'ang-ch'un. The 2nd Far Eastern Front in the north would breach the Amur and make a thrust up the Sungari towards Harbin.

The main weight of the Soviet forces was Malinovsky's Transbaikal Front, which was deployed mainly in Mongolia. Between May and July the Marshal, his staff, and the entire 6th Guards Tank and 53rd Armies had been transferred from Prague to the grim landscape of Siberia and Mongolia.

At the same time the 39th Army had been transferred from Insterburg. They joined the 36th and 17th Armies already garrisoned in Siberia.

The Transbaikal Front comprised these five armies, with the supporting 12th Air Army (1,334 aircraft) under Marshal of Aviation S. A. Khudyakov, and a joint Russian and Mongolian composite "Cavalry-Mechanised Group", which was about six divisions of mostly horsed cavalry. Nearly half the Soviet strength in the Far East was assigned to this front, which was defended by light Japanese forces.

The Russian plans were based on the assumption, which subsequently proved to be correct, that the Japanese would not expect an attack to come across hundreds of miles of the Gobi Desert in Inner Mongolia and over the Great Hsingan mountain range. Indeed the Japanese forces were concentrated for a counter-attack in the Manchurian plain, and only small garrisons had been placed in the towns around Hailar, near the Soviet border. It was not only the Japanese who thought that the plan was unlikely; long-serving officers from the Red Army in the East regarded a crossing of the Gobi in August as near suicidal. For their pessimism they were relegated to the posts of deputy commanders.

In the Maritime Province, the 1st Far Eastern Front faced an equally daunting barrier, for here the Japanese expected an offensive. They had begun building permanent fortifications over 20 years earlier. The defences were from eight to 15 miles deep and set in difficult country among mountains, extinct volcanoes, steep river valleys, and patches of thick woodland. In the centre the 35th Army would have to cross the marshy valley of the Ussuri river, while to the south the 25th Army would tackle the formidable fortifications on the Manchurian border with Korea, notably the fortress area of Dunnin.

Meretskov decided to allocate most of his supporting artillery and armour to the 5th Army, under Colonel-General N. I. Krylov. Supported by the 1st Army on its right, its 12 divisions would plough into the Japanese defensive system around Mutan-chiang, north-west of Vladivostok.

In conjunction with these land operations, the Pacific Fleet was instructed to disrupt Japanese maritime communications, prevent the use of the northern Korean ports, and assist the army in preventing any Japanese landings in the Soviet Union. Later it received the additional mission, which proved to be its most important, of mounting amphibious assaults on the Japanese ports in northern Korea, southern Sakhalin, and the northern Kurile Islands.

The fleet consisted of two "Kirov"-class cruisers, a destroyer leader with 10 destroyers, 19 destroyer escorts, 49 submarine chasers, 78 submarines, and 204 M.T.B.s. In addition there were 1,549 land-based aircraft of Fleet Aviation under Lieutenant-General Piotr N. Lemeshko.

Japanese forces consisted of one old light cruiser, one destroyer, 45 small patrol minesweepers, and 170 aircraft, most of which were to remain in the northern bases of the Japanese home islands.

But let us return to the Transbaikal Front where Soviet forces were building up stocks of ammunition, and sweltering in the August sun.

The 500 miles from Tamsag Bulag to the Kwantung Army headquarters at

Ch'ang-ch'un, and on to Mukden, would be travelled without a break. The first task of the 6th Guards Tank Army was to cross the Great Hsingan range and reach the line Lu-pei–Li-chuan in five days. Emphasis was placed on the need to cross the mountains before the Japanese had time to react and deploy their reserves, which were known to be some 200 to 250 miles from their western frontier.

The 6th Guards Tank Army, under Colonel-General A. G. Kravchenko, would have the 39th Army, under Lieutenant-General I. I. Lyudnikov, on its left flank, facing the fortifications at A-erh-shan; on the right the 17th Army, under Lieutenant-General A. I. Danilov, would face the desert and mountains around Linh-sia and Chihfeng. The 53rd Army, under Colonel-General I. M. Managarov, would be held in reserve. In the north the 36th Army, under Lieutenant-General A. A. Luchinsky, would make supporting attacks on Hailar and towards Tsitsihar, while in the south the Soviet-Mongolian Cavalry-Mechanised Group, under Colonel-General I. A. Pliev, would thrust towards Ch'eng-te and Kalgan (Chiang-chia-k'ou).

Some units like the 36th and 17th Armies were accustomed to the Far East, while the joint Cavalry-Mechanised Group had been locally raised. Other armies had a local Siberian motorised

The Russian land and sea operations during the invasion of Japanese-held Manchuria in August 1945.

infantry division attached, except for the 6th Guards Tank Army, which had two.

Since it would bear the full weight of the operation, the 6th Guards Tank Army was given more than the usual mechanised infantry complement. It had two reinforced mechanised infantry corps, one tank corps, two motorised infantry divisions, two assault gun brigades, and four independent tank brigades. Its total strength stood at 826 tanks and 193 assault guns; this included 615 late model T-34 tanks (the remainder were older T-26, BT-5, and BT-7 tanks), 188 armoured cars, 6,489 other vehicles, and 948 motorcycles. It was supported by 995 field guns and heavy mortars, 43 *Katyusha* rocket-launchers, and 165 anti-aircraft guns. In all, it comprised some 44 motorised rifle and 25 tank battalions.

Drawing on the experience of their own and German mechanised operations in Europe, the Russians arranged for motor-cycle and air reconnaissance to cover the flanks and point of their armies. Aircraft covered the area from 30 to 60 miles ahead, while motorcycles operated between 45 to 50 miles in advance. Each of these reinforced motorcycle battalions carried powerful radio transmitters. Flank reconnaissance covered points 15 miles out, an important provision since there would be gaps between the armies, and even within the 6th Guards Tank Army the two columns would be separated by nearly 50 miles.

Opposite this carefully-balanced force stood the Japanese 3rd Area Army under

General K. Ushiroku, consisting of the 30th and 44th Armies. Their task was to defend the Ch'ang-ch'un–Ssu-p'ing-chieh –Seoul, and the Mukden–Dairen railways with the industrial centres located along them. They had permission to retreat to the fortified lines in the T'ung-hua area.

The 44th Army, under Lieutenant-General Y. Hongo, with headquarters at Liaoyuan, had positioned its three divisions and one tank brigade to cover the Inner and Outer Mongolian borders from A-erh-shan in the north through Taonan to Tungliao in the south. The 30th Army, under Lieutenant-General S. Iida (who had commanded the Japanese army which invaded Burma in 1942) had its headquarters at Mei-hok'ou, with four divisions covering Ch'ang-ch'un and the fortified zone.

Ushiroku retained one division, three independent mixed brigades, and a tank brigade in reserve near Mukden, and another at Jehol in south-west Manchuria.

The 4th Army, under Lieutenant-General M. Uemura, with headquarters at Tsitsihar, was composed of three divisions and four independent mixed brigades. Their task was to cover northern Manchuria. One division and an independent mixed brigade held positions in the Hailar area, a division and two independent mixed brigades were in the Heiho–Sunwu area, and one division was at Tsitsihar with a mixed brigade at Harbin. The 119th Infantry Division, which was at Hailar, was one of the best units in the Kwantung Army, but even then it was only rated 70 per cent effective. In the same area the 80th Independent Mixed Brigade was rated as the weakest unit, at 15 per cent effectiveness.

Against this opposition the 6th Guards Tank Army had been set a break-neck timetable. Two days were allocated to crossing the desert, making an average of 65 miles a day. During this move it was expected to seize suitable sites for building airstrips. Three days were allowed for crossing the mountains, securing the ridge, and moving down to the Lu-pei–Li-chuan line, a distance of 50 miles a day; then within five days it was to take Mukden and Ch'ang-ch'un.

On August 8, there were no rolling barrages to announce the attack in the east by the 6th Guards Tank Army, just the roar of massed tank engines. There was no need for any preparatory fire, for the army met no opposition during the first four days.

The northern axis was led by VII Mechanised Corps, the southern by IX Mechanised Corps, with V Guards Tank Corps in the rear. The lack of opposition changed this formation, and in a spectacular advance which at times reached 25 mph, each of the two mechanised corps formed into six to eight parallel columns.

By the time they reached the Great Hsingan range on August 10, IX Mechanised Corps was low on fuel. V Guards Tank Corps moved up to make the crossing during the night.

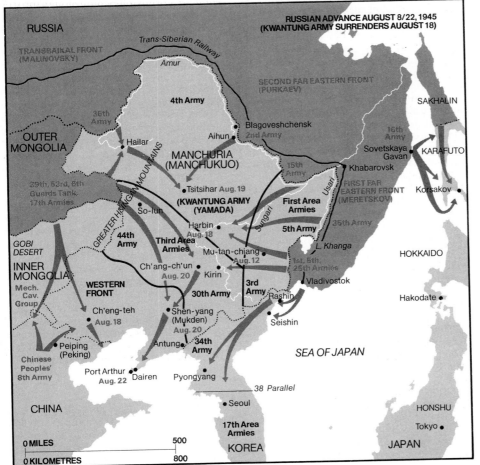

The mountain road was a nightmare, with 30-degree turns and many defiles, and at places it had to be shored up by engineers. V Guards Tank Corps made the 25-mile crossing in seven hours. VII Mechanised Corps moved more slowly and completed it by the evening of August 11.

Over the mountains, the corps adopted battle formation, and with no roads, petrol and oil consumption increased. Behind the tanks the tail units bogged down in their trucks on the battered mountain roads. On August 10 the first fuel supplies were brought in by air.

By the end of August 11 advanced units of V Guards Tank Corps had taken Lu-pei, and on the 12th, VII Mechanised Corps had taken Li-chuan. As yet they had made no real contact with the enemy. The first phase had been completed on time.

But now the incomplete logistic preparation caught up. For two days they waited: V Guards Tank Corps' fuel tanks were just over half empty, VII Mechanised Corps' were half empty, while IX Mechanised Corps' had no fuel at all left. Men as well as machines suffered; many had not had a hot meal for days.

Aircraft flew 2,072 tons of fuel and oil to the 6th Guards Tank Army and 384 tons to other units on the front during the operation. But the aircraft were not designed for heavy bulk cargoes and it needed 1,755 sorties to bring in the fuel.

In the north the 36th Army hit a fortified line near Man-chou-li, but this was soon overcome and the army advanced 25 miles in the first day. Hailar was by-passed and reduced slowly, falling on the 18th. It was a spectacular stand by the Japanese 80th Brigade which was attacked by the three rifle divisions and a tank brigade. The Japanese fought on, in ignorance of the capitulation on August 15.

The 39th Army also fought with units of the Japanese 107th Division, which had not heard of the surrender, and Wang-yeh-miao fell on the 21st. Though some 7,850 Japanese had surrendered by the 24th, some fought on until the end of August.

The 17th Army met no resistance crossing the Hsingan mountains and reached Dabanshan on August 15. Ironically the horsemen of the mixed Mongolian and Russian cavalry force did better than their mechanised comrades. By August 20 they had pushed over the border into China, leaving the tanks and armoured cars of the 17th Army stranded for lack of fuel.

On August 15 Marshal Malinovsky ordered the 6th Guards Tank Army and the 39th Army to give detachments of brigade strength the rôle that had previously been assigned to corps. These units were fully topped up with all the available fuel and ordered to press on with the advance. The rest of the corps would follow as fuel became available.

As it developed, smaller advanced reconnaissance units forged ahead and fulfilled the corps and army objectives. The Motorcycle Battalion of IX Mechanised Corps operated more than 100

miles ahead of the main force between August 14 and 17. V Guards Tank Corps' reconnaissance detachment took the bridge and airfield at T'ung-liao and VII Mechanised Corps' reconnaissance detachment took Taonan. Larger advanced units followed on August 16, but the main forces only arrived on the 18th.

Despite its surrender, the Kwantung Army continued to retreat and so Malinovsky ordered the 6th Guards Tank Army to take Ch'ang-ch'un and Mukden, and after leaving a reinforced brigade in each town, to proceed as quickly as possible to Port Arthur and other ports.

The 39th Army was ordered to liquidate the A-erh-shan pocket and move to Ch'ang-ch'un and Ssu-p'ing. The 36th Army was to mop up Hailar and move on to Tsitsihar, T'ai-lai, and An-kuang. The 53rd Army (Lieutenant-General I. M. Managarov) would fill the gap between the 6th Guards Tank Army and the 17th Army, and occupy K'ai-lu.

On August 18 a company-size force composed of engineers and some experienced airborne troops air-landed at Harbin. A day later 225 men landed at Mukden and 200 men at Ch'ang-ch'un; a landing was also made at Kirin. These operations were launched to prevent the escape to Japan of valuable prisoners and the destruction of equipment and stores.

On August 19, the 36th Army took

A Soviet T-34 tank crew bargain with a Chinese street trader in Dalny near Port Arthur in August 1945.

Tsitsihar. A day later advanced units of V Guards Tank Corps occupied Mukden, on the 21st VII Mechanised Corps took Ch'ang-ch'un. Air landings were made at Port Arthur and Dairen by 250 men on August 22. Tanks from V Guards Tank Corps were loaded on railway flat cars and sent from Mukden to Port Arthur, where they arrived on the 24th.

From August 24 to 29 the main force of the 6th Guards Tank Army concentrated in Mukden, Dairen, and Port Arthur. It had moved over 700 miles and been halted only by lack of fuel.

The 12th Air Army had flown 2,361 combat missions and 3,167 reconnaissance and supply missions. Bombers had dropped a modest 710.7 tons of explosive. Ground forces had fired 14,746 shells and 42,134 bullets, according to Soviet sources.

The Japanese had made little contact with them as a result of a breakdown in communications, and because they had deployed their forces well back from the frontier.

On the other side of Manchuria, the 1st Far Eastern Front went into action on August 8. Although it faced fixed defences, these were manned by the Japanese 1st

Russian marines cheer on the Golden Crag at Port Arthur on August 22, 1945, as an old score is settled with Japan.

Area Army (under General S. Kita), which included three divisions and one brigade formed from over-age reservists with less than one month's training. None of the divisions was fully equipped or had any combat experience, and the positions were short of artillery and ammunition. The anti-tank defences were also incomplete.

In a night attack, in driving rain, the Soviet 5th Army (Colonel-General N. I. Krylov) and the 1st Red Banner Army (Lieutenant-General A. P. Beloborodov) stormed the border fortifications. They were supported by 320 guns per mile of front, and each division was allocated a front of two miles. There was a brief but savage battle and by the end of the day the Russians had advanced about 7½ miles.

Hu-t'ou and Tung-ning fell within the first two days, and by August 11 Mu-leng and Hunchun had fallen. Some by-passed Japanese garrisons fought on until August 26. At Sui-fe-ho, fierce fighting lasted until August 10.

The key to the front was the town of Mu-tan-chiang, where the Japanese 5th Army (Lieutenant-General N. Shimizu) had concentrated. It was attacked from the air and LIX Rifle Corps and the 75th Tank Brigade of the 1st Army took Lin-k'ou and cut the town off from the north. While XXVI Rifle Corps and the 257th Tank Brigade tightened this grip from the north, the 5th Army ploughed ahead from the east. Fighting lasted from August 11 to 14, when XXVI Rifle Corps entered the town.

On the 15th the Japanese regained control of the town and their rear defence line, in a counter-attack that pushed XXVI Corps back six to eight miles to the northeast. It was only on the 16th that Soviet forces finally captured the town in the last major battle in the east.

When hostilities ceased, the 1st Area Army remained at about two-thirds of its effectiveness. Its 5th Army had sustained some heavy losses in the battle for Mu-tan-chiang, but the main forces were intact and falling back to the T'ung-hua redoubt according to plan.

In the Soviet 2nd Far Eastern Front, the smallest Russian forces faced the weakest enemy defences, for the Japanese had no plans to hold the salient of northeastern Manchuria.

The Russians achieved an uncontested crossing of the Amur on August 9 and a day later the bulk of the 15th Army (Lieutenant-General S. K. Mamonov) was shipped across. Men of the 361st Rifle Division moved over the Sungari

and hit Fu-chin, where they encountered the Japanese 134th Infantry Division.

It was a hard fight lasting several days, and General Purkaev assumed personal command despite the fact that he was also responsible for the crossing at Blago-veshchensk and the landings on Sakhalin Island. Only on August 14 was the Japanese 134th Division forced to withdraw.

The crossings at Blagoveshchensk were made on the night of August 9–10. Again the crossing was easy, but later the Russians hit fierce resistance at Aihun, where the Japanese 135th Brigade continued to fight until it learned of the capitulation on August 19.

The island of Sakhalin had been divided almost equally between the Japanese and the Russians since 1905. The original Soviet plans here had been to remain on the defensive, but following the initial successes in Manchuria, Marshal Vasilevsky decided to take the southern section in an amphibious and land attack.

There was a garrison of about 20,000 men in the south, but the Soviet forces outnumbered it in a ratio of 3.7 to 1 in infantry companies, 10 to 1 in artillery, and 4.3 to 1 in machine guns. The Russians had complete control of the air, and almost total control at sea.

Despite this, the Japanese put up a stiff resistance to the landings on August 11, made by the Soviet 79th Rifle Division. On August 14 they counter-attacked and cut off the 179th Regiment of the 79th Division.

Landings were made by marines at Maoka on August 19 in an attempt to outflank the Japanese defences, and on the 20th the defence began to crumble.

On the Kurile island chain there was almost parity in the strength of the opposing forces. Landings were made on Shumshu on August 18 but they were fiercely resisted by the Japanese. The capitulation came in time, however, to spare the Russians a real taste of what the Americans had experienced throughout the south Pacific.

In fact the Japanese capitulation came in time to spare all the Soviet forces in the Far East. Though the Transbaikal Front achieved a major victory, other fronts had encountered some characteristically fierce Japanese defensive fighting.

A measure of the cost of this fighting is reflected in the Russian ammunition expenditure (361,079 shells and 1,023,697 bullets) and their casualties, which are probably understated (8,219 killed and 22,264 wounded).

Estimates of Japanese losses vary; the Russians claim 83,737 killed and 594,000 prisoners, though unofficial and perhaps incomplete Japanese sources give 21,000 killed.

Weapons captured from the Japanese were made available to the Chinese Communist forces who used them in the Civil War, which ended in 1949. Not until then did peace come to China after nearly 50 years of war.

CHAPTER 81
Dropping the Atom Bomb

By the spring of 1945 the Imperial Household, nerve centre of Government, was struggling to bring the war to an end. Administered by the Army and Navy–the real rulers of Japan–the Imperial Household hoped that a negotiated peace would avoid Allied military occupation and preserve the centuries-old imperial system itself.

Japan was clearly defeated: following failure to secure Russia's good offices for negotiations, the last hope for a conditional peace, came the bitter proposal of the immovable Minister of War, General Korechika Anami, that Japan must fight to the end in defence of the home islands. Japan still had two million combat troops and 9,000 kamikaze aircraft. These forces could be expected to wreak tremendous casualties upon American invaders, who, in the end, would be compelled to negotiate a peace.

American assessments of the situation were not vastly different from those of General Anami. Japan was defeated, besieged from the sea, and was being pulverised by U.S. Navy carrier aircraft and by U.S. Army Air Forces B-29 bombers that were flying from bases in the Marianas. At a meeting in the White House on June 18, 1945, U.S. Army Chief-of-Staff General George C. Marshall urged that Japan must be invaded in order to end the war, and President Harry S Truman gave a go-ahead for planned landings on Kyushu on November 1, 1945 (Operation "Olympic"), and five months later against Honshu (Operation "Coronet"). While Marshall supported invasion, he was concerned about potential American casualties, estimating that 69,000 Americans would be killed or wounded in a 190,000-man operation against Kyushu. Japanese troops had amply demonstrated that they could and would fight desperately even when the outlook was hopeless.

However, the question must be asked: was an invasion of the Japanese home islands necessary even without using the atomic bomb? The American submarines had brought the Japanese economy to a standstill and the home islands alone would not produce enough food to feed the home population. Thus, it can be argued that actual invasion was now unnecessary. Yet this factor was not considered sufficient.

One hope for enforcing a Japanese surrender, short of invasion, which was discussed at the White House on June 18, 1945, was a prediction of the highly secret U.S. Army Manhattan Engineer District project that two atomic bombs would be available for operational employment by the end of July. The first of these revolutionary weapons would be the bomb called the "Little Boy", a gun-assembly weapon with an explosive Uranium-235 core–fissionable material that had been laboriously extracted at a giant Manhattan plant at Oak Ridge, Tennessee. Atomic scientists were confident that the gun principle would work, that an explosive charge would drive a plug of U-235 into the U-235 core, establishing a critical mass and an explosion of gigantic dimensions. The scientists were less confident that the other type of bomb could be made to function. This was the "Fat Man", and it was an implosion weapon which used plutonium (Pu-239) bred in nuclear reactors at Hanford, Washington. The implosion weapon principle would require testing in mid-July at a proving ground near Alamogordo, New Mexico: and, if the principle worked, a "Fat Man" would be available at the end of the month.

The United States Army Air Forces had already provided everything required to drop the atomic bombs when they were ready. The 509th Composite Group had been activated in December 1944 under the command of Colonel Paul W. Tibbets, Jr., and included the 393rd Bombardment Squadron with the most advanced model long-range B-29 bombers–the only American aircraft big enough to carry the first atomic weapons. The group had trained at Wendover, Utah, and in April-May 1945 had moved to North Field on Tinian Island in the Marianas. Both in training and in familiarisation flights to Japan, the 509th Group had been dropping orange-painted 10,000-pound T.N.T.-filled bombs (quite naturally called "Pumpkin bombs" because of their shape and colour), which were similar in ballistic characteristics to the "Fat Man". There was a derisive song being sung on Tinian to the effect that the 509th was going to win the war, but no one knew exactly how, since only Colonel Tibbets and a few others in the group shared the atomic secret. A target committee of Manhattan Project and Army Air Forces representatives had nominated the cities of Kokura, Hiroshima, Niigata, and Kyoto for the first atomic strikes, and afterward Nagasaki was substituted for Kyoto when Secretary of War Henry L. Stimson forbade an attack against Kyoto because of its cultural antiquities.

American military leaders understood Japan's reluctance to surrender her ancient Tenno or imperial system, and they also reasoned that the Emperor would be the only authority that could enforce a capitulation of Japan's military forces. The military leaders were therefore inclined to clarify the Allied unconditional surrender terms enough to permit Japan to retain her Emperor. This view was not accepted at the Allied heads of state "Terminal" conference in Potsdam. Instead, the Potsdam proclamation published on July 26 called for an unconditional surrender of all Japanese armed forces, or else acceptance of "prompt and utter destruction". In the assessment of historian Robert J. C. Butow, the absence of mention of the Emperor in the Potsdam proclamation was "an invaluable trump card" offered to the Japanese militarists, and on July 28 Prime Minister Kantaro Suzuki announced that his government would mokusatsu the proclamation–literally, "kill" it "with silence". Suzuki favoured peace and may well have used the wrong word, but the response unleashed violent reactions.

Events moved swiftly, and President Truman had learned of the world's first nuclear detonation at its occurrence at Alamogordo on July 16. The implosion principle–whereby a core of plutonium was wrapped with T.N.T. blocks which when detonated simultaneously squeezed the core into a critical mass–had worked, and the "Fat Man" was practicable. In Washington, General Carl A. Spaatz, on his way to take command of the United States Army Strategic Air Forces in the Pacific, was told of the atomic strike plans, and, after refusing to drop such bombs on oral directions, received written orders that the 509th Group would deliver its first "special bomb" as soon after about August 3 as weather would permit a visual attack against Hiroshima, Kokura, Niigata, or Nagasaki. The first bomb would be the reliable "Little Boy". The U.S. cruiser Indianapolis delivered most of the U-235 needed to arm it at Tinian on July 26 and headed on toward the Philippines. (Four days later it was sunk in mid-ocean by Japanese submarine torpedoes.) On August 2, the 20th Air Force mimeographed top secret operations orders for Special Bombing Mission No. 13; the primary target was Hiroshima, with Kokura the secondary and Nagasaki the tertiary. Since visual bombing was mandatory, an advance B-29 weather observer aircraft would scout and report on each target. The strike mission included an atomic laden B-29 and two observer B-29's.

Predictions of bad weather over southern Japan held off the attack until August 6, 1945, when at 0245 hours Colonel Tibbets lifted his B-29, named the "Enola Gay" after his mother, off the runway at North Field and was followed at two minute intervals by the observer planes. At take-off the "Enola Gay" grossed 65 tons in weight, eight tons over normal B-29 bombing weight, partly because of the fact that the "Little Boy" weighed 9,000 pounds. Since a crash of the plane while taking off might have blown one end off Tinian Island, Captain William S. ("Deac") Parsons, a U.S. Navy ordnance expert who accompanied Tibbets as weaponeer and bomb commander, armed the "Little Boy" during the flight toward Japan.

At 0715 hours on August 6, 1945, the weather scout B-29 over Hiroshima piloted by Major Claude Eatherly

The aircraft, the B-29 "Enola Gay"; the bomb, code-named "Little Boy", weighing only 9,000 lbs but with the power of 20,000 tons of T.N.T.; and the crew, with their pilot Colonel Tibbets second from the right.

signalled that the target was open, thus sealing the fate of the city. As the weather plane departed, the Hiroshima all-clear air defence signal was sounded at 0731. Until now the city had almost entirely escaped air attack, and few people took the appearance of a few high-flying planes seriously. Thus sightings at 0806 of two B-29's with a third in trail, all flying very high at an altitude of 31,600 feet, did not seem significant enough to call another defence alert. But those Japanese who watched the approaching planes (and who survived) noticed that the lead bombers suddenly separated in tight diving turns that carried them rapidly away from a point in space where something fell from the planes–the "Little Boy" from the "Enola Gay" and parachuted instruments from the observation plane. Exactly 17 seconds after 0815 hours an instant of pure, blinding, utterly intense bluish-white light cut across the sky, followed by searing heat, a thousand-fold crash of thunder, and finally an earth-shaking blast that sent a mushroom cloud of dust and debris boiling up to 50,000 feet. This was the moment that survivors at Hiroshima would remember as the *pikadon*–the *pika* or "flash" followed by the *don* or "thunder".

As a military objective, the city of Hiroshima was chiefly important as a port and the site of an army garrison. Located on seven finger-like deltaic islands where the mouth of the Ota river pushes out from the underside of Honshu into the Inland Sea, Hiroshima had been the point of embarkation for Japanese troops moving into China and to the South Seas. It was also the seat of the 2nd General Army, which was responsible for defence of the south-western section of the homeland. Volunteer and government-enforced evacuations had reduced the city's population from 380,000 in 1942 to about 255,200 in 1945, but it remained Japan's seventh largest city.

The "Little Boy" was aimed at a bridge in almost the centre of the built-up part of the city, and it detonated at an altitude of just below 2,000 feet, almost precisely on its mark, with a force later calculated to have been equivalent to 17,000 tons (or 17 kilotons) of T.N.T. By blast and by an ensuing firestorm, approximately 4.7 square miles around the ground zero (directly below the bomb burst) were completely destroyed. Approximately 60,000 out of 90,000 buildings within 9.5 square miles were destroyed or badly damaged. Very few people had taken shelter, and the full extent of personnel casualties at Hiroshima will never be known. The Japanese eventually inscri-

bed the names of 61,443 known dead on the cenotaph erected at ground zero. On the other hand, the United States Strategic Bombing Survey estimated that there were 139,402 casualties, including 71,379 known dead and missing (presumed to be dead) and 68,023 injured, of whom 19,691 were known to be seriously injured. The Bombing Survey estimated that over 20,000 of the killed and missing were school children. Ironically for a strategic bombing attack, most of Hiroshima's larger industrial factories were on the perimeter of the city, and these factories (and the workers who had already reported for duty) escaped destruction. The Bombing Survey concluded that only 26 per cent of Hiroshima's total production plant was destroyed in the atomic strike and that the plants could have been kept in operation if the war had continued.

Where the execution of the "Enola Gay" mission against Hiroshima was almost flawless and all crews returned immediately to Tinian, the 509th Composite Group's second mission, flown on August 9 with the more efficient "Fat Man" plutonium bomb, went much less smoothly. Again there were to be three planes in the striking force, an armed B-29 called "Bock's Car" piloted by Major Charles W. Sweeney and two observer aircraft. The city of Niigata was ruled out as too far distant for attack, leaving Kokura as the primary target and Nagasaki as the alternative. Kokura was important because it was the location of a vast army arsenal on the northern tip of Kyushu. Nagasaki had a fine harbour of some commercial importance and four large Mitsubishi war production industrial plants. Unlike Hiroshima's flat deltaic terrain, Nagasaki's topography was broken by hills and valleys, which promised to reduce destruction. Both Kokura and Nagasaki were to be scouted in advance by weather B-29's. Prediction of weather over Kyushu dictated that the strike mission had to be flown on August 9, and since a storm was building up *en route* to Japan the strike B-29 and the two observer planes to accompany it were scheduled to fly northward individually and rendezvous over Yakoshima Island off the south coast of Kyushu before proceeding to their target.

There was considerable apprehension on Tinian as Major Sweeney launched the "Bock's Car" from North Field at 0349 hours on August 9. Another U.S. Navy ordnance expert, Commander Frederick L. Ashworth, was aboard as bomb commander and weaponeer, but the 10,000-

pound "Fat Man" had to be armed before take-off, greatly increasing the hazard of an atomic accident. Major Sweeney also discovered that 600 gallons of gasoline could not be pumped from an auxiliary tank in his plane, and this substantially reduced his reserve fuel supply. Sweeney lost additional time and fuel circling Yakoshima Island awaiting one of the observer B-29's, and after 40 minutes he decided to go on without it. (This aircraft, which happened to carry the official British observers, scientist William Penney and Group-Captain Leonard Cheshire, would arrive at the target a few minutes after the blast.) Apparently during the delay, clouds closed over Kokura, and after three runs over the city had failed to permit visual observation of the aiming point (but used up about 45 minutes additional time), the "Bock's Car" strike plane was headed for Nagasaki. It too was hidden by clouds; and in the emergency, with fuel steadily dwindling, Commander Ashworth authorised a radar drop. At the last moment a hole in the clouds permitted the bomb to be visually aimed and dropped at 1101 hours, but the "Fat Man" nevertheless missed the assigned aiming point by about three miles, a distance which placed the bomb over Nagasaki's industrial section rather than in its built-up commercial area. After the drop, Major Sweeney headed to an emergency landing on Okinawa, where he landed with only a few gallons of fuel left.

Only vague references to an "incen-

The devastation at Hiroshima, where 60 per cent of the city was destroyed (above). The deadly mushroom cloud of the atom bomb at Nagasaki (opposite).

diary" attack at Hiroshima had appeared in Japanese newspapers, and the people at Nagasaki were little prepared for the atomic strike. The weather B-29 had touched off an air raid alert at 0748, but nothing had happened, and at 1101 only about 400 people were in the city's tunnel shelters, which could have accommodated a third of Nagasaki's 195,290 registered inhabitants. As at Hiroshima, the "Fat Man" at Nagasaki was detonated in the air and at an altitude of approximately 1,750 feet. Where the atomic scientists had estimated that the magnitude of the plutonium bomb blast would range from 700 to 5,000 tons of T.N.T., the implosion principle of the "Fat Man" was much more efficient than that of the gun-type weapon, and the force of the "Fat Man" was estimated at 20 kilotons. With the more powerful bomb, and surrounding hills concentrating the blast, the scale of destruction at Nagasaki was greater than at Hiroshima, but the area destroyed and personnel casualties were smaller because terrain afforded protection from radiant heat and ionizing radiations to about one-fourth of the population. The area of greatest destruction was oval-shaped inside the narrow Urakami valley, approximately 1.45 square miles in size, and intervening hills saved the central part of the city from destruction. (By comparison, in Hiroshima approximately 60 per cent of the population was within 1.2 miles of the centre of the explosion; and in Nagasaki only 30 per cent of the population was so situated.) Official Japanese casualty figures nevertheless include 23,753 killed, 1,927 missing, and 23,345 injured, and these statistics number only verified cases. The United States Strategic Bombing Survey believed that the casualties were actually in the order of 35,000 dead and somewhat more than that injured. There was no fire storm at Nagasaki and less public panic. Since several of the large factories were in the area of maximum destruction, damage to industry in the Nagasaki strike was quite heavy; excluding the dockyard area (outside the radius of the bomb's effect) 68.3 per cent of the industrial productive area of the city was destroyed.

After a detailed investigation of Japan's struggle to end the war, the United States Strategic Bombing Survey concluded that "certainly prior to 31 December 1945, and in all probability prior to 1 November 1945, Japan would have surrendered even if the atomic bombs had not been dropped, even if Russia had not entered the war, and even if no invasion had been planned or contemplated." On the other hand, the atomic attack doubtless hastened the Soviet Union's belated declaration of war upon Japan on August 8, and it certainly provided a powerful catalyst which enabled Japan's peace leaders to bring about a surrender over the continuing objections of War Minister Anami and the Army and Navy chiefs-of-staff. After Hiroshima the Japanese militarists attempted alternately to obscure the nature of the nuclear explosion and argued privately that the United States could not possibly possess enough radioactive material to permit a continuation of such attacks. The effect of these arguments failed with the Nagasaki strike, and in a hurriedly-called Imperial Conference on the night of August 9, 1945 Emperor Hirohito–the god figure who had never before been able to act without a consensus of his advisers–bluntly told the militarists that "to continue the war means nothing but the destruction of the whole nation" and that "the time has come when we must bear the unbearable". By the early morning hours of August 10, cables were on their way to Japan's diplomatic representatives in Berne and Stockholm announcing the nation's acceptance of the Potsdam ultimatum, with the sole proviso that the *Tenno* system would be preserved. This was to be the acceptable condition for the war's end when it came officially on September 2.

In plans for the atomic strikes, Manhattan Engineer District scientists were knowledgeable about the potential effects of radiation emitted from nuclear explosions, although the exact effect of nuclear radiation on human tissue was, and continues to be, incompletely explored. Nuclear radiation consists of alpha and beta particles and gamma rays, the latter being of great significance because of their long range and high penetrating character. It was expected that the air bursts called for over the Japanese cities would limit casualties for the most part to non-radioactive injuries; namely, those due to the force and the heat of the unprecedented explosions. But when the final results were known, it was apparent from the experience at Hiroshima and Nagasaki that even without the effects of blast and fire the number of deaths among people within a radius of one-half mile from ground zero would have been almost as great as the actual figures, and deaths among those within one mile would have been only slightly less than they were. The cause was radiation sickness, which the Japanese called *genshibaku-dansho,* or the "sickness of the original-child bomb", among the *hibak'sha,* the "people who received the bomb".

According to the Japanese, individuals very near to the centre of the atomic

explosions, but who escaped flash burns or secondary injuries, died rather quickly, the majority within a week, autopsies showing almost complete absence of white blood cells and deterioration of bone marrow. Most radiation cases, who were at greater distances, did not show severe symptoms for a week to a month after the bombs, when sudden high fevers marked the often-fatal onset of radiation sickness, again with dwindling white blood cell counts and disappearing bone marrow. The degree of the fever and the chance of survival bore a direct relation to the degree of exposure to radiation. Sperm counts done at Hiroshima revealed low counts or complete aspermia for as long as three months afterward among males who were within 5,000 feet of the centre of the explosion. Two months after the explosion, Hiroshima's total incidence of miscarriages, abortions, and premature births was 27 per cent as compared with a normal rate of six per cent.

At both Hiroshima and Nagasaki

British proclamations of Japanese defeat are displayed in Singapore.

immediate deaths from radiation peaked in three to four weeks and practically ceased after seven to eight weeks. Both Hiroshima and Nagasaki were rebuilt and regained prosperity, the prosperity ironically initially connected to defence production undertaken for the United States military forces during the Korean War. As for the *hibak'sha,* the atomic casualty lists were never closed, since persons originally exposed have continued to die, apparently—although not completely conclusively—before their time. Fifteen years after the *pikadon,* for example, Japanese physicians began to find abnormal incidence of thyroid cancer in people who were young children at the time of the bomb, and there has been an identified higher incidence of eye cataracts and leukaemia among the survivors of the A-bomb. The social trauma of keloid burn scars borne by many men and women immobilised these survivors in varying degrees. Many of these burn victims have expressed a belief that they have been discriminated against in gainful employment because of their disfigurements. Although children conceived

by irradiated parents have appeared quite normal, some scientists continue to fear that one or two more generations born of atomic survivors must mature before the possibility of genetic mutations resulting from one day's exposure to gamma rays can be measured.

In a retrospective look at the A-bomb strikes, Lieutenant-General Leslie R. Groves, war-time director of the U.S. Army Manhattan District, has summed up the American belief about the matter:

"The atomic bombings of Hiroshima and Nagasaki ended World War II. There can be no doubt of that. While they brought death and destruction on a horrifying scale, they averted even greater losses— American, English, and Japanese."

On the other side, the taped Japanese description of the bombing that may be heard in the Peace Memorial Museum in Hiroshima is more ambiguous, for here it is said: "When the Pacific War was finally about to end, at the stage where only a decisive battle on the mainland remained, the sudden disastrous event of Hiroshima was truly unfortunate to the people of Hiroshima, Japan and the whole world."

CHAPTER 82
The surrender of Japan

In May 1945, the Japanese Army high command was despondent. Germany had surrendered, and it was obvious that the British and Americans were planning to redeploy their military strength for a final assault on the Japanese homeland. Relations with the Soviet Union had grown steadily worse, and there were fears that the Soviets might break their non-aggression pact with Japan and join the Western Allies. The Americans had recently captured Okinawa, only 400 miles from Japan, making it even easier than before for the American bombers to wreak havoc on Japanese cities.

Haunted by the spectre of Allied invasion of the homeland, some members of the high command privately suggested that it was time to consider negotiations. The Navy had admitted in October 1944 that it no longer had enough strength to launch an offensive. In December of the same year, the Americans had completed the Leyte campaign in the Philippines – a campaign which the Japanese premier had said would be decisive. From a strategic standpoint, Japan had already lost the war. Should not the nation surrender now, while retaining some strength and bargaining power, rather than risk total destruction in the invasion?

These fears were not shared by the majority of the high command in May 1945. They agreed that diplomatic attempts to keep the Soviet Union out of the war should be stepped up, but they expressed confidence that any Anglo-American invasion of the Japanese homeland could be repulsed. The main strength of the Army remained intact, and Japan's air force had been dispersed to many airfields to preserve it from destruction by American bombers. Plans to repulse the invaders called for the entire air force to attack the American transports and task forces in waves of *kamikaze* assaults. Army operations would be concentrated on the elimination of the invaders at their debarkation sites. If these operations were not successful, Japanese volunteer reserves would continue operations further inland. Above all, Army leaders said, "what should be remembered in carrying out the general decisive battle is adherence to a vigorous spirit of attack" to "set the example for 100,000,000 compatriots". The high command felt that a single invasion could be defeated, although they held out no such hope of

A Japanese officer gives up his sword and salutes the flag during an official surrender ceremony.

victory if the Americans launched second or third assaults in quick succession.

Emperor Hirohito himself was soon convinced that it would be necessary to negotiate. His civilian advisers told him that the military situation was hopeless and the war must be ended immediately. Early in July 1945, therefore, while the high command was planning to repulse the invaders and fight to the last man, the diplomats appealed to the Soviet Union to act as mediator.

On July 17, Stalin met with Truman and Churchill at Potsdam. He informed the Western leaders that the Japanese had approached him about peace talks, but seemed unprepared to accept the Allies' demand for unconditional surrender. Truman and Churchill, along with Chiang Kai-shek, issued the Potsdam Proclamation on July 26, reiterating the demand that surrender be unconditional. Otherwise, the proclamation declared, Japan would face "prompt and utter destruction". It did not state that this destruction would be brought about by a new weapon – the atomic bomb.

The debate in top Japanese diplomatic and military circles now revolved around the meaning of the word "unconditional". Did this mean that the nation must surrender, as well as the armed forces? Did it mean that the Emperor would be deposed and the Imperial institution abolished? The Potsdam Proclamation had been silent on this point. Both the diplomats and the high command were determined to support the Emperor, and the generals knew that their men would never accept any agreement which abolished the Imperial institution. In the words of one high-ranking officer, "it would be useless for the people to survive the war if the structure of the State itself were to be destroyed. . . . even if the whole Japanese race were all but wiped out, its determination to preserve the national policy would be forever recorded in the annals of history, but a people who sacrificed their will upon the altar of physical existence could never rise again as a nation."

In the midst of this debate, on August 6, the first atomic bomb was dropped on

The surrender ceremony on board the Missouri *(opposite). A group of* Kempetei *lay down their swords (below).*

Hiroshima. Three days later the second atomic bomb devastated Nagasaki, and the Soviet Union finally declared war on Japan. A conference of the Emperor and his civilian and military advisers was hastily summoned, and met in an air-raid shelter in the grounds of the Imperial Palace in Tokyo shortly before midnight. In the light of the events of the past three days, even the military authorities agreed now that a surrender was unavoidable. Unlike Foreign Minister Togo, however, who advised surrender on the single condition that the Emperor's rights be preserved, the military leaders asked for three other reservations. First, they wanted to avoid an Allied military occupation of Japan. Second, they wanted to try war criminals themselves. Third, they wanted to disarm their own troops rather than surrender directly to the Allies. War Minister Anami explained that this last proviso could be taken to mean that the Japanese armed forces were not actually defeated, but had decided to stop fighting voluntarily in order to preserve the Japanese land and people from further destruction. When the two sides had expressed their views, the conference was found to be deadlocked. Then the unprecedented happened. The Emperor's advisers actually asked him for his own opinion. Instead of acting according to his advisers' instructions, the Emperor was being asked to advise them. He was to shed the rôle of observer and puppet and make his own decision. Hirohito had already made up his mind, and he soon made it clear that he believed the Foreign Minister's proposal – with only the Emperor's position safeguarded – was more likely to lead to a quick peace settlement and should therefore be accepted. The conference unanimously endorsed the Emperor's decision, and cables were sent within a few hours announcing the Japanese terms.

Later that same day, a reply was received from U.S. Secretary of State James Byrnes. This note explained that the Allies would not accept anything but an unconditional surrender, and that this meant that the Emperor would be subject to the Supreme Commander for the Allied powers. This statement produced another argument in the Japanese cabinet – what did "subject to" mean? At another meeting on the morning of August 14, it was pointed out that Byrnes' note indicated that the Imperial institution would not be abolished, and in any case the Japanese Emperors had often been "subject to" the power of the *shoguns*. Once again, Hirohito was asked for his own opinion, and once again he called for immediate acceptance of the Allied demand. The cabinet acceded to the Imperial will, and it was announced over the radio that Japan had surrendered.

That night, the Emperor recorded a message to be broadcast at noon on August 15, calling for all Japanese to accept the surrender. They were warned especially to "beware strictly of any

General Numata arrives to surrender the Japanese forces in South-East Asia.

outbursts of emotion" that might create needless complications. In other words, they were to ignore any violent "fight-to-the-finish" fanatics. But a small group of officers at the Army headquarters was determined not to surrender, and decided to attempt a *coup d'etat*. The Emperor was to be separated from his peace-seeking advisers and persuaded to change his mind and continue the war. On the night of August 14, the conspirators approached General Mori, the commander of the Imperial Guards, at the palace. They asked him to join with them in the *coup* to preserve the honour of the Japanese nation. Mori listened to their arguments, then said that he would go to pray at the Meiji Shrine to help him make up his mind. The conspirators were unwilling to allow any delay, and one of them shot Mori on the spot. Then, using the dead general's seal, they forged orders for the Imperial Guards and began tracking down the Emperor's advisers and the record which was to be broadcast the following day. The whole plot ended in failure when the Eastern Army District commander arrived at the palace, refused to join the rebels, and persuaded them to give up. The officer who had shot General Mori committed *hara-kiri* on the Imperial Plaza. When War Minister Anami heard of the attempted *coup* early in the morning of August 15, he also committed suicide.

In the next few days, several other suicides occurred, but most Japanese accepted the Imperial decision calmly. On August 30, the first American occupation forces (including a small British contingent) landed at Yokosuka. Three days later, at nine o'clock in the morning, Japan's new Foreign Minister, Mamoru Shigemitsu, boarded the *Missouri* in Tokyo Bay. On behalf of the Emperor and the Japanese Government, he signed the official surrender document. General Douglas MacArthur accepted the surrender, a scratchy record of *The Star-Spangled Banner* was played on the ship's speakers, and World War II was over.

Index

Page numbers in italic refer to captions

La Spezia 349
Lathbury, Brig.-Gen. G. W. 353, 549
Latona (minelayer) 225
Lattre de Tassigny, Gen. de 167
  autumn campaign (1944) 551, 554, 555, 556, 558
  France 89, 502, 503, 506, 507, 508, 509
  Strasbourg 566, 567, 568
Latvia 27, 113
Lauchert, Maj.-Gen. von 574
Laure, Gen. 87
Laurencie, Gen. de la 84
Laval, Pierre 99, 130, 134, 219
Lavarack, Maj.-Gen. J. D. 149
Lawrence, Col. T. E. 225
Leach, Capt. J. C. 209, 241
League of Nations 42
Leahy, Admiral William D. 196, 202, 521
  Cairo Conference 415
  on MacArthur 447, 448
  Quebec Conference 584
Leberecht Maass (destroyer) 123
Lebrun, Albert 64, 70, 88, 92, 94, 95, 97
Leclerc, Maj.-Gen. 221, 346, 347, 498, 499, 557, 568
Lee, Lt.-Gen. J. C. H. 549
Lee, Vice-Admiral W. A. 440, 524
Leeb, Col.-Gen. Wilhelm Ritter von
  "Bear" 90
  Eastern Front 164, 167, 173, 176, 179, 183, 188
  Poland 34
  "Tiger" 93
  Western Front 55, 162
Leese, Lt.-Gen. Sir Oliver
  Burma 632, 636
  Italy 456, 457, 458, 593, 595
  North Africa 289, 346, 351
Legentilhomme, Gen. 224
Legion (destroyer) 268
Le Havre 510, 550
Leigh-Mallory, Air Chief Marshal Sir
  Trafford 461, *468*
  Normandy 489, 491, 495
  "Overlord" 466, 469, 476, 478
Leipzig 607
Leipzig (light cruiser) 363, 583
Le Luc, Vice-Admiral 96, 101
Lelyushenko, Lt.-Gen. D. D. 186, 316, 428, 517, 578
LeMay, Maj.-Gen. Curtis E. 648, 650
Lemelsen, Lt.-Gen. Joachim
  Eastern Front 173, 374
  Italy 594, 595, 596
Lemeshko, Lt.-Gen. Piotr N. 652
Lemonnier, Admiral 359, 479
Lend-Lease Act 196, 197, 336, 365
  Britain 235
  China 216
  Russia 189, 196, 198, 253, 301, 376–7
Leningrad 176, 179, 315, 379
Leonard, Maj.-Gen. John W. 561, 573
Léopold III, King of Belgium 58, 59, 65, 66, 67, 68, 70, 72, 79, 83, 84
Leselidze, Lt.-Gen. K. N. 387
Levasseur, Lt. 367
Lexington (aircraft carrier) 211, 244, 245, 246, 396
Leyte 448, 530
Leyte Gulf, Battle of 521–7
L'Herminier, Lt.-Com. 349, 359
Libeccio (destroyer) 225
Libya 94, 125, 126
Lidice massacre 255, *255*
Lieb, Lt.-Gen. T. 425, 426
"Lightfoot", Operation 289, 290
Lille 84
Linares, Gen. de 610
Lindemann, Capt. 240
Lindemann, Col.-Gen. G. von 188, 379, 431, 516
Lindemann, Professor (Lord Cherwell) 585
Linlithgow, Lord 224
Lipski, Józef 18, 19, 31, 32
Liscome Bay (escort carrier) 393, 436
Liss, Maj.-Gen. Ulrich 36, 56

List, Field-Marshal Sigmund Wilhelm 162, *163*
  Greek offensive 134, 148, 150, 152, 154
  Poland 38
  Stalingrad 300, 302, 305, 306, 308
  Western offensive 55, 77, 89
Lithuania 27, 113
"Little Boy" bomb 656, 657
Littorio (battleship) 127, 132, 268, 276, 349
Litvinov, Maxim 25, 199
Lively (destroyer) 225
Liverpool (cruiser) 276
Ljungborg 47
Lloyd, Air Vice-Marshal H. P. 139
Lloyd, Maj.-Gen. W. L. 619, 620, 621
Lloyd George, David 105
Lobelia (corvette) 367
Loch, Gen. 431, 516
Lockwood, Vice-Admiral Charles A. 433, 440
Loerzer, Gen. 232
Löhr, Col.-Gen. Alexander 39, 152, 169, 303, 452
  Greece 543, 544
Lomax, Maj.-Gen. C. E. N. 621, 622, 634, 635
London, bombed 111, 112, *113*, 234, 460, 475
Long (minesweeper) 531
Long Island (escort carrier) 402
Longmore, Air Chief Marshal Sir Arthur 133, 137, 147, 148, 223
Lopatin, Gen. 187
Lorenzelli, Gen. Dante 342
Lorient 120
Lorraine 9
Lorraine (battleship) 106
Lossberg, Lt.-Col. von 112, 162
Low, Rear-Admiral Francis 368
Lowry, Rear-Admiral Frank J. 451
Lucas, Maj.-Gen. John P. 360, 361, 451, 452, 453
Luchinsky, Lt.-Gen. A. A. 653
Lucht, Gen. 560
"Lucy Ring" ("Red Trio") 172
"Lumberjack", Operation 574, 603
Lumsden, Lt.-Gen. Herbert 267, 273, 289, 290, 340
Lungershausen, Lt.-Gen. 290, 359
Lütjens, Admiral Günther 238–43 *passim*
"Lüttich" ("Liège"), Operation 497, 498
Lüttwitz, Lt.-Gen. S. von
  Battle of the Bulge 560
  East Prussia 577
  France 484, 494
  Italy 453
Lutz, Gen. 54
Lützow, Lt.-Gen. von 514
Lützow (pocket battleship) 46, 47, 114, 161, 262, 264, 362, 369, 537, 583
  See also Deutschland
Luzon 216, *216*, 447, 448, 521, 530–5, *533*
Lvov, Gen. 187
L'vov 175
Lyne, Maj.-Gen. 608
Lyngenfjord 540
Lyons 508
Lyster, Rear-Admiral 131
Lyttelton, Oliver 223, 224
Lyudnikov, Lt.-Gen. I. I. 309, 653

M

MacArthur, Gen. Douglas 208, 209, 211, 215, 216, 245, *449*, 663
  Battle of Philippine Sea 439
  Leyte Gulf 524
  New Guinea 406
  Pacific (1943) 391, 394, 395, *395*
  Philippines 447, 448, 449, 450, 521, 522
  Rabaul 432, 433, 434, 438
McAuliffe, Brig.-Gen. A. C. 562, 564
McCain, Vice-Admiral J. S. 524
McClintock, Com. 524
McCloy, John 585
McClusky, Lt.-Com. Clarence W. 250

McCreery, Lt.-Gen. Sir Richard L. 284, 360, 451, *454*, 597
Macedonia 138, 148
Macintyre, Capt. Donald 121, 236
Mack, Capt. P. J. 145
Mackay, Maj.-Gen. Sir Iven G. 134, 143, 148
Mackensen, Col.-Gen. August von
  Eastern Front 175, 304, 310, 314, 320
  Italy 452, 453, 454
Mackensen, Ambassador Hans Georg von 21, 31, 354
Mackesy, Maj.-Gen. P. J. 48, 50
Mackinnon, Lt. 255
MacLain, Maj.-Gen. Raymond S. 498, 573
McNair, Lt.-Gen. 295, 296, 495
MacNarney, Maj.-Gen. J. T. 277
Macon, Maj.-Gen. R. C. 606
Maczek, Maj.-Gen. S. 93, 498, 608
Madagascar 219
Maddox (destroyer) 354
Magennis, Leading-Seaman J. 647
Maginot Line 34, 55, 68, 87, 89, 99, 103
Magli, Gen. 359
Magnan, Gen. 502, 555
Magnien, Gen. 103
Maikaze (destroyer) 437
Makino, Lt.-Gen. 522
Malaya (battleship) 132, 139, 239, 276
Malenkov 175, 182
Maletti, Gen. 133
Malinovsky, Marshal Rodion Ya.
  Balkan states 542, 543, 545, 546, 547
  Kursk 385, 387, 388, 389
  Manchuria 651, 652
  Stalingrad campaign 305, 316, 320
  winter offensive, 3rd 424, 426, 429
Malta 91, 127, 139, 140, 144, 222, 225, 268–71, 274, 284–6
Maltby, Maj.-Gen. C. M. 210
Mamonov, Lt.-Gen. S. K. 655
Managarov, Lt.-Gen. I. M. 387, 653, 654
Manchester (cruiser) 285
Manchuria 651–5, *653*
Mandalay 629, 630, *631*, 632
Mandel, Georges 78, 94
Manila 531, 533
"Manna", Operation 544
Mannella, Gen. Pitassi 136
Mannerheim, Marshal Carl Gustav 41, 42, 43, 167, 183, 511, 512, 538, 539
Mannerini, Gen. 346
Manoilescu *129*
Manstein, Field-Marshal Erich von 159, *183*
  Poland 34, 40
  Russia
    "Barbarossa" 174, 176
    Kursk 373, 374, 375, 380, 382–90 *passim*
    Stalingrad 304, 305
    winter offensive, 1st 181, 187, 192
    winter offensive, 2nd 315–22 *passim*
    winter offensive, 3rd 422, 424, 426, 427, 428, 429, 431
  Western Front 55, 60, 63, *63*, 94, 112
Manteuffel, Gen. Hasso von 551, 559, 560
Maori (destroyer) 243
Marblehead (cruiser) 212
Marceglia 233
Marcks, Maj.-Gen. 162, 483, 486
Marcus Island 244
Mareth Line 34, 343, 344, 345
"Margarethe", Operation 431
Marianas 437, 439, 440, 443, 444
Mariassy 325
Marie-José, Princess of Piedmont 58
Marienburg 476
Marindin, Brig. P. C. 626
Marino 233
Mariscalco, Gen. 352
"Marita", Operation 134, 152, 165
"Market Garden", Operation 548, *549*
Marmoutier 557
Marras, Gen. Efisio 124
Marriot, Brig. J. C. O. 222, 228
Mars, Lt. Alastair 286
Marsa Brega 143
Marsa el Brega-Maràda 340

Acknowledgements:

Orbis Publishing Ltd. would like to thank the
following publishers and agents for permission
to quote from the undermentioned books:

A Full Life: Collins Publishers for *A Full
Life* by Lieutenant-General Sir Brian
Horrocks.
A Sailor's Odyssey: The Estate of Viscount
Cunningham and A. P. Watt & Son for *A
Sailor's Odyssey* by Admiral of the Fleet
Viscount Cunningham of Hyndhope.
A Soldier's Story: Holt, Rinehart and
Winston Inc. for *A Soldier's Story* by
General of the Army Omar Bradley, © 1951
by Holt, Rinehart and Winston, Inc.
Assignment to Catastrophe: Lady Spears
for *Assignment to Catastrophe* by Major-
General Sir Edward Spears, published by
William Heinemann.
**A Torch to the Enemy: A Fire Raid on
Tokyo:** Ballantine Books Inc., a Division of
Random House, for *A Torch to the Enemy*,
© 1960 by Martin Caidin.
Barbarossa: Alan Clark with the
permission of A. D. Peters Co. for
Barbarossa, © 1965 by Alan Clark.
Berlin Diary: Paul R. Reynolds for *Berlin
Diary*. © 1971 by William Shirer.
Calculated Risk: Harper & Row,
Publishers, Inc. for *Calculated Risk*, © 1955 by
General Mark Clark.
Ciano Diaries: The Chicago Daily News for
the *Ciano Diaries* by Count Galeazzo
Ciano, translated by Malcolm Muggeridge,
© 1947.
Crusade in Europe: Doubleday &
Company, Inc. for excerpts from *Crusade in
Europe* by General of the Army Dwight D.
Eisenhower, © 1948 by Doubleday &
Company, Inc.
Defeat in the West: Milton Shulman for
Defeat in the West by Milton Shulman,
published by Coronet Books.
Full Circle: Ballantine Books Inc., a
Division of Random House, Inc., for *Full
Circle* by Air Vice-Marshal J. E. Johnson,
© 1968.
Hitler's War Directives 1939–1945:
Sidgwick & Jackson Ltd. for *Hitler's War
Directives*, edited by Professor Hugh
Trevor-Roper.
I was There: Rear-Admiral William H.
Leahy, U.S.N. (Ret'd.) for passages from *I
Was There* by Admiral William D. Leahy,
published by Brandt and Brandt.
Krieg in Europa: Verlag Kiepenheuer und
Witsch for *Krieg in Europa* by General
Friedrich von Senger und Etterlin.

Main Fleet to Singapore: David Higham
Associates Ltd. for *Main Fleet to Singapore*
by Russell Grenfell.
Memoirs: Collins Publishers for *Memoirs*
by Field-Marshal Viscount Montgomery of
Alamein.
Memoirs of Marshal Mannerheim: E. P.
Dutton & Company, Inc., for the *Memoirs of
Marshal Mannerheim* by Marshal
Mannerheim, translated by Count Eric
Lewenhaupt, © 1954 E. P. Dutton &
Company, Inc.
Midway: The Battle that Doomed Japan:
The United States Naval Institute,
Annapolis, Maryland for *Midway: The
Battle that Doomed Japan* by Mitsuo
Fuchida and Masatake Okumiya,
© 1955 by The United States Naval
Institute.
73 North: Peter Janson-Smith for *73 North*
by Dudley Pope, published by Weidenfeld &
Nicolson.
Pacific War Diary 1942–1945: Houghton
Mifflin Company for *Pacific War Diary
1942–1945* by James Fahey, © 1963.
Panzer Leader: Michael Joseph for *Panzer
Leader* by General Heinz Guderian.
Reminiscences: Time Inc. for
Reminiscences by General of the Army
Douglas MacArthur.
Roosevelt and Hopkins: Harper & Row,
Publishers, Inc., for *Roosevelt and Hopkins*
by Robert E. Sherwood, © 1948 and 1950 by
Robert E. Sherwood.
Russia at War 1941–1945: E. P. Dutton &
Company, Inc. for *Russia at War 1941–1945*
by Alexander Werth, © by Alexander Werth.
Sixty Days that Shook the West: G. P.
Putnam's Sons for *Sixty Days that Shook the
West* by Jacques Benoist-Mechin, translated
by Peter Wiles.
Strange Alliance: Viking Press, Inc. for
Strange Alliance by General John R. Dean,
© 1946 and 1947.
The Battle of the Atlantic: B. T. Batsford
for *The Battle of the Atlantic* by Captain
Donald Macintyre.
The Battle of Cassino: Houghton Mifflin
Company for *The Battle of Cassino* by Fred
Majdalany.
The Battle of the Mediterranean: B. T.
Batsford for *The Battle of the Mediterranean*
by Captain Donald Macintyre.
The Battle for Normandy: B. T. Batsford
for *The Battle for Normandy* by E. Belfield
and General H. Essame.
The Bismarck Episode: Macmillan
Publishing Co., Inc. for *The Bismarck
Episode* by Russell Grenfell.

The Brutal Friendship: Harper & Row,
Inc. for *The Brutal Friendship* by F. W.
Deakin, © 1963.
The Coast Watchers: Angus and
Robertson (Publishers) Pty Ltd. for *The
Coast Watchers* by Eric Feldt.
The Eden Memoirs: reprinted by
permission of The New York Times
Company from *The Eden Memoirs* by the
Rt. Hon. the Earl of Avon, © 1960.
The First and the Last: Holt, Rinehart and
Winston, Inc. for *The First and the Last* by
General Adolf Galland, © 1955.
The Foxes of the Desert: E. P. Dutton &
Company, Inc. for *The Foxes of the Desert* by
Paul Carell, © 1960 in the English
translation by Mervyn Savill by E. P.
Dutton & Company, Inc.
**The Great Sea War: The Story of Naval
Action in World War II:** Prentice-Hall, Inc.
for *The Great Sea War: The Story of Naval
Action in World War II* by E. B. Potter and
Fleet Admiral Chester W. Nimitz (Editors),
© Prentice-Hall, Inc. of Englewood Cliffs,
N.J.
The Longest Day: Simon Schuster for *The
Longest Day* by Cornelius Ryan, © 1959.
The Luftwaffe War Diaries: Macdonald &
Co. Ltd. for *The Luftwaffe War Diaries* by
Cajus Bekker, © 1964 by Gerhard Stalling
Verlag and 1966 in translation by
Macdonald & Co. Ltd.
The Marines' War: William Morrow & Co.,
Inc. for *The Marines' War* by Fletcher Pratt,
© 1948.
**The Road to Stalingrad: Stalin's war
with Germany:** Harper and Rowe
Publishers Inc. for *The Road to Stalingrad:
Stalin's war with Germany* by Professor
John Erickson, © 1975.
The Rommel Papers: Harcourt Brace
Jovanovich, Inc. for excerpts from *The
Rommel Papers*, © 1953 by Captain Basil
Liddell Hart.
The Stilwell Papers: William Morrow &
Co., Inc. for *The Stilwell Papers* by General
Joseph Stilwell, © 1949.
The Turn of the Tide: Collins Publishers
for *The Turn of the Tide* by Sir Arthur
Bryant.
Top Secret: Ralph Ingersoll for *Top Secret*
by Ralph Ingersoll, published by Harcourt
Brace Jovanovich, © 1946.
Triumph in the West: Collins Publishers
for *Triumph in the West* by Sir Arthur
Bryant.
War As I Knew It: Houghton Mifflin
Company for *War As I Knew It* by General
George S. Patton, © 1947.

Picture Acknowledgements:

The publishers would like to thank the
following individuals and organisations:
Agence France-Presse; Aldo Fraccaroli;
Associated Press; Belga; Bibliothek für
Zeitgeschichte, Konrad Adenauer;
Bibliothèque Nationale; Blitz; British
Official Photos; Bundesarchiv, Koblenz;
Camera Press; Documentation Française;
Etablissement Cinématographique et
Photographique des Armées; FOT Library;
Fox Photos; Fujiphotos; A. Harlingue;
Harrisiadis; H. Le Masson; Holmès-Lebel;
H.M.S.O.; Imperial War Museum;
International News Photos; Keystone;
Library of Congress; Musée de la Guerre;
Novosti; Picture Press; Popperfoto; Punch;
R. Viollet; René Dazy; Robert Hunt Library;
Sikorski Institute; Staatsbibliothek, Berlin;
Süddeutscher Verlag; U.S.I.S.; U.S.
Airforce; U.S. Army; U.S. Navy; U.S.
Marine Corps; United Press; Ullstein;
Wiener Library.